M000275294

THE ROAD, THE RIDE, AND YOU

Harley-Davidson® *Ride Atlas of North America*™, 2nd Edition

RAND MCNALLY

CONTENTS

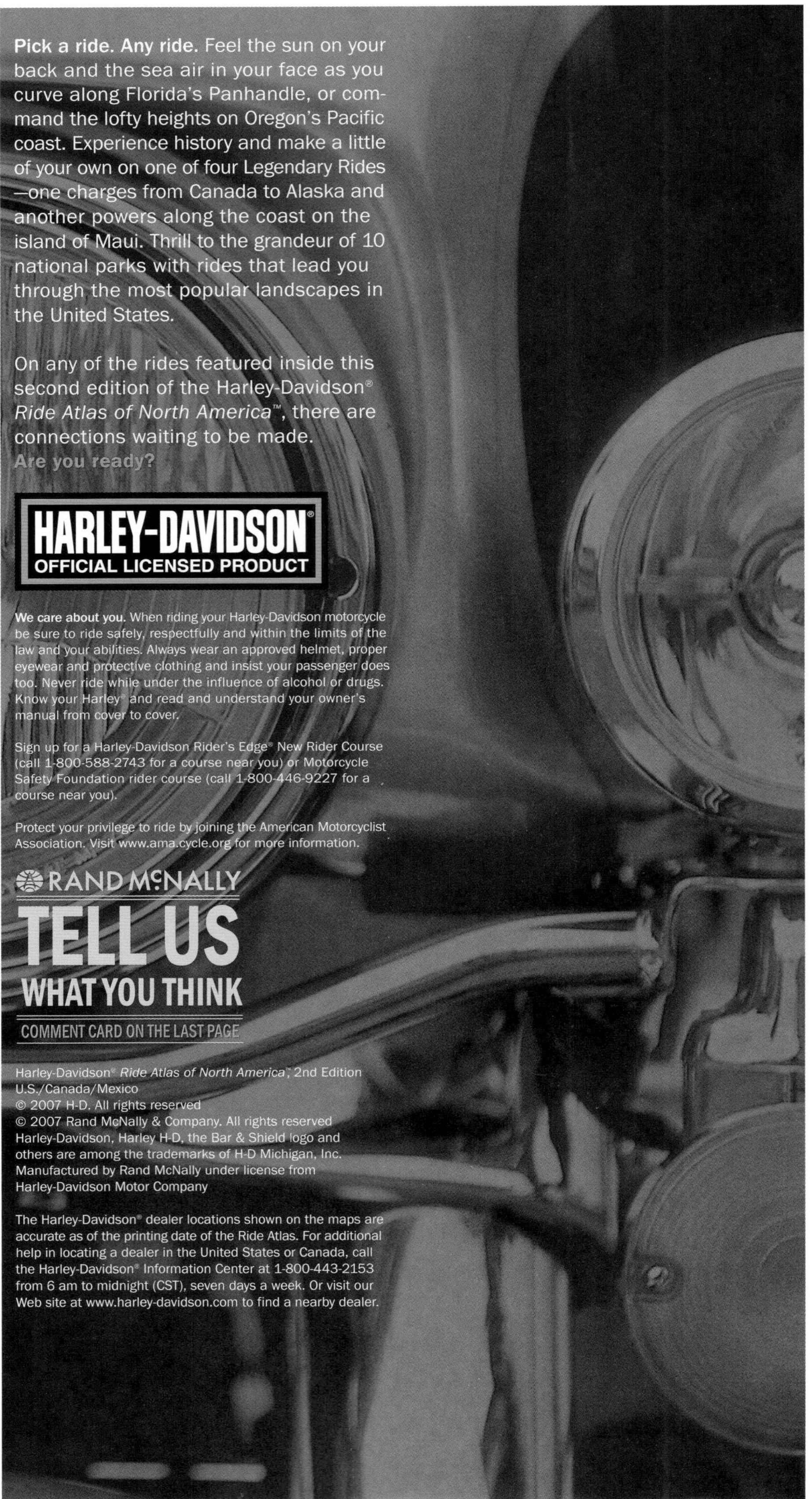
Pick a ride. Any ride. Feel the sun on your back and the sea air in your face as you curve along Florida's Panhandle, or command the lofty heights on Oregon's Pacific coast. Experience history and make a little of your own on one of four Legendary Rides —one charges from Canada to Alaska and another powers along the coast on the island of Maui. Thrill to the grandeur of 10 national parks with rides that lead you through the most popular landscapes in the United States.
On any of the rides featured inside this second edition of the Harley-Davidson® *Ride Atlas of North America*™, there are connections waiting to be made.
Are you ready?
HARLEY-DAVIDSON®
OFFICIAL LICENSED PRODUCT
We care about you. When riding your Harley-Davidson motorcycle be sure to ride safely, respectfully and within the limits of the law and your abilities. Always wear an approved helmet, proper eyewear and protective clothing and insist your passenger does too. Never ride while under the influence of alcohol or drugs. Know your Harley® and read and understand your owner's manual from cover to cover.
Sign up for a Harley-Davidson Rider's Edge® New Rider Course (call 1-800-588-2743 for a course near you) or Motorcycle Safety Foundation rider course (call 1-800-446-9227 for a course near you).
Protect your privilege to ride by joining the American Motorcyclist Association. Visit www.ama.cycle.org for more information.
RAND McNALLY
TELL US
WHAT YOU THINK
COMMENT CARD ON THE LAST PAGE
Harley-Davidson® *Ride Atlas of North America*™, 2nd Edition
U.S./Canada/Mexico
© 2007 H-D. All rights reserved
© 2007 Rand McNally & Company. All rights reserved
Harley-Davidson, Harley H-D, the Bar & Shield logo and others are among the trademarks of H-D Michigan, Inc.
Manufactured by Rand McNally under license from Harley-Davidson Motor Company
The Harley-Davidson® dealer locations shown on the maps are accurate as of the printing date of the Ride Atlas. For additional help in locating a dealer in the United States or Canada, call the Harley-Davidson® Information Center at 1-800-443-2153 from 6 am to midnight (CST), seven days a week. Or visit our Web site at www.harley-davidson.com to find a nearby dealer.

HOW TO USE THE RIDE ATLAS 2ND EDITION

Memorable rides and so much more—including information and the tools you'll need to navigate the second edition ride atlas developed exclusively for the rider R3

GUIDE TO RIDES AND RESOURCES

Alabama/Florida R6-R7
Alberta/British Columbia R8
Arizona R9
California R10
Colorado R11
Florida R12
Georgia/South Carolina R13
Indiana R14
Kansas R15
Maine R16-R17
Maryland/Delaware R18-R19
Michigan R20-R21
Missouri R22-R23
Nevada/California R24
Newfoundland and Labrador R25
New Mexico R26-R27
Nova Scotia R28-R29
Oregon R30-R31
South Dakota/Wyoming R32-R33
Utah R34
Vermont R35
Virginia R36
West Virginia R37
Wisconsin/Minnesota R38-R39
Wyoming/Colorado R40
Riding north & south of the border R41
Legendary Rides R42-R43
National park rides R44-R45
Harley-Davidson® Services R46
Harley-Davidson® Museum R47
State park camping R48
Ride log R49

MAPS AND INDEXES

Ride locator map R4-R5
Map legend 7
U.S. map 8-9
U.S. states and cities 10-235
Canada map 236-237
Canada provinces and cities 238-257
Mexico map 258-259
Puerto Rico map 259
Index to maps 260-275

Mileage Matters

Driving distances between hundreds of cities across North America 276-283

Miles and Minutes

Distances and driving times between hundreds of North American cities 284

HOW TO USE THE RIDE ATLAS

The sights, sounds, and seasons of the road . . . The Ride Atlas has just the right balance of information you need for a road trip without cluttering the page. Not only can you navigate the selected rides, you can create your own with the information included throughout this atlas.

1 MOTORCYCLE LAWS
An exclusive snapshot of state laws affecting motorcycle use including helmet law, riding two abreast, eye protection, and speed limits on each state map page and together on the gate fold.

2 STATE RESOURCE INFORMATION
Road conditions, construction updates, highway emergency numbers, tourism information, and state motor vehicle information are easily accessed with this handy reference.

3 HARLEY-DAVIDSON® DEALERSHIPS
The Harley-Davidson logo easily identifies the Harley-Davidson® dealers on the state maps. Check the map page listings for location including latitude and longitude.

4 FEATURED RIDE
On the map pages of the states/provinces featuring rides, look for this icon highlighted in yellow. Detailed information on each ride can be found within the "Guide to Rides and Resources" section.

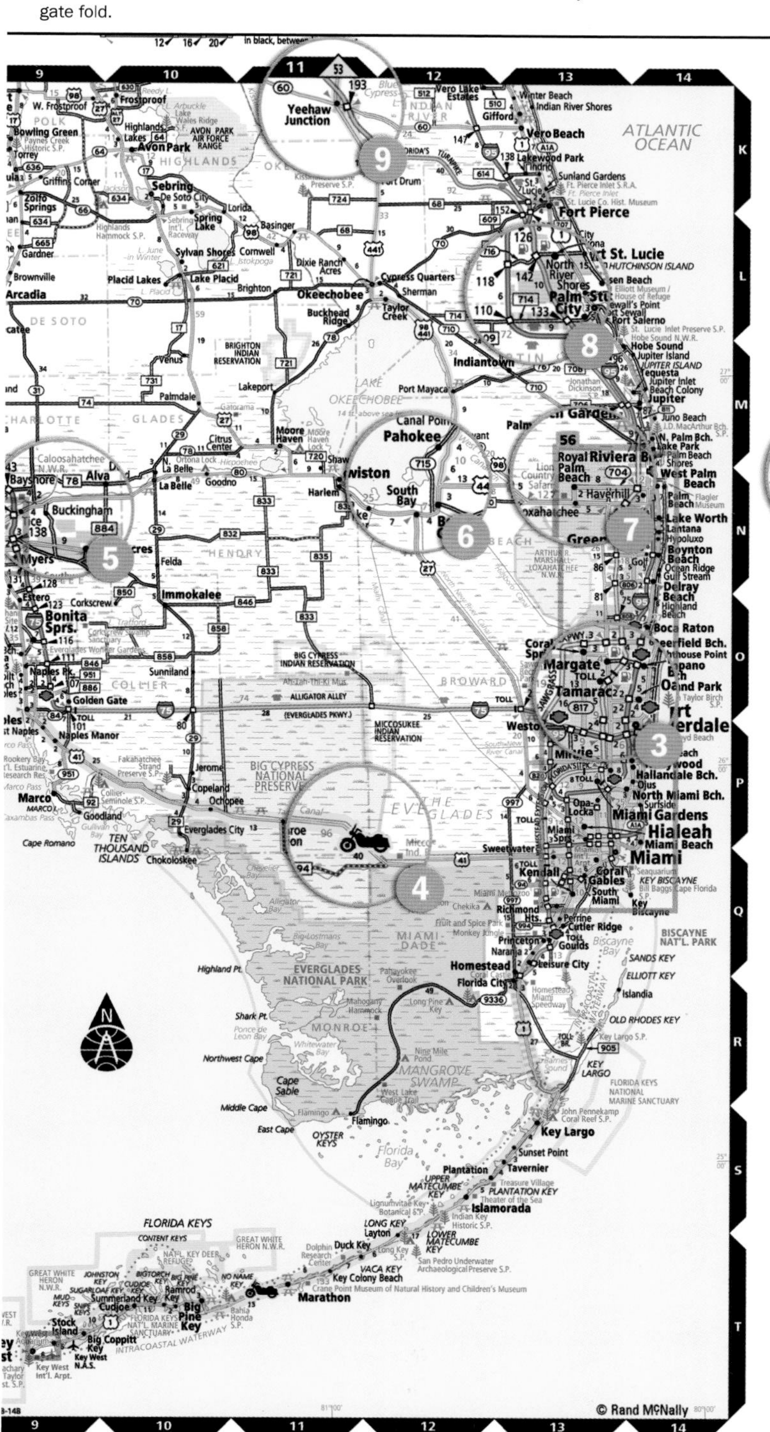

Yeehaw Junction
ATLANTIC OCEAN
Fort Pierce
Port St. Lucie
Okeechobee
LAKE OKEECHOBEE
Pahokee
Royal Palm Beach
West Palm Beach
Lake Worth
Boynton Beach
Delray Beach
Boca Raton
Immokalee
Bonita Sprs.
Naples
Margate
Tamarac
Hialeah
Miami Gardens
Miami
Miami Beach
Homestead
Florida City
EVERGLADES NATIONAL PARK
BIG CYPRESS NATIONAL PRESERVE
Key Largo
Islamorada
Marathon
Big Pine Key
Key West
FLORIDA KEYS
© Rand McNally
For Alabama ride, see page R6-7.
For Florida ride, see page R12.
FLORIDA MOTORCYCLE LAWS
Helmet use:
Not required over 21 with minimum of $10,000 medical insurance
Riding two abreast:
Yes. See state law for specifics
Eye protection: Required by law
Speed limit:
Primary roads: 70 mph Secondary roads: 65 mph
FLORIDA RESOURCES
Road conditions or construction: 511
www.fl511.com; www.511tampabay.com
Highway emergency numbers: *FHP
State motor vehicle information:
(850) 922-9000; www.hsmv.state.fl.us
HARLEY-DAVIDSON DEALERSHIPS
For the Miami, Tampa/St. Petersburg, and Ft. Myers areas, please see dealer listings on page 57.
Harley-Davidson of Ft. Walton Beach, S-4
788 N Beal Pkway. Ft. Walton Beach
(850) 862-4706
Lat N 30.446 Lon W 86.639
Orlando Harley-Davidson South Shop, P-3
5881 W Irlo Bronson Hwy. Kissimmee
(407) 944-3700
Lat N 28.333 Lon W 81.520
Orlando Harley-Davidson, P-2
1590 E Buena Vista Dr. Bldg One Lake Buena Vista
(407) 938-0522
Lat N 28.371 Lon W 81.513
Peterson's Harley-Davidson South, Q-13
19825 S Dixie Hwy. Miami
(305) 235-4023
Lat N 25.584 Lon W 80.365
Harley-Davidson of Naples, O-9
3645 Gateway Ln. Naples
(239) 594-5504
Lat N 26.212 Lon W 81.745
Orlando Harley-Davidson, M-3
3770 37th St. Orlando
(407) 423-0346
Lat N 28.505 Lon W 81.425
Orlando Harley-Davidson East, M-3
11898 Lake Underhill Rd. Orlando
(407) 447-7400
Lat N 28.547 Lon W 81.212
Orlando Harley Gear Store, M-3
8000 International Dr. at Sand Lake Rd. Orlando
(407) 351-3302
Lat N 28.461 Lon W 81.477
Orlando Harley-Davidson Airport Stores, M-3
9331-9347 Airport Blvd. Orlando
(407) 825-3470
Lat N 28.429 Lon W 81.302
Harley-Davidson of Pensacola, R-2
6385 Pensacola Blvd. (Hwy. 29) Pensacola
(850) 494-1224
Lat N 30.481 Lon W 87.255
Harley-Davidson of Port Charlotte, M-8
2224 El Jobean Rd. Port Charlotte
(941) 883-8000
Lat N 27.001 Lon W 82.181
Seminole Harley-Davidson, K-4
620 Hickman Circle Sanford
(407) 831-7888
Lat N 28.816 Lon W 80.213
Treasure Coast Harley-Davidson of Stuart, L-13
4967 SE Federal Hwy. Stuart
(772) 287-3871
Lat N 27.143 Lon W 80.213

5 ROAD HIERARCHY REVEALED
Follow back roads more easily with prominent secondary road coloration and designated symbols. These color-cased roads stand out on backgrounds and patterns, but take a step back when you need to read the names.

6 POINT-TO-POINT MILEAGES
Red numbers along the highways on maps represent mileage between red arrowheads.

The black numbers indicate mileage between intersections.

Only Rand McNally provides these mileages on maps. A handy mileage and driving times map is featured on page 284.

7 INSET MAP INDICATORS
Pale yellow boxes indicate that a larger scale inset map is provided. If the inset map appears on a different page, the page number is shown in a small box. 56

8 ROADS AND HIGHWAYS
Scenic routes are highlighted with yellow ribbons and construction zones are marked with orange-and-yellow stripes. For an explanation of other map symbols, see the symbols legend on each state map page or the legend on page 7.

9 CONTINUATION ARROWS
The page number of the continuing map appears in a small yellow triangle 53 at the map's edge.

RIDE LOCATOR MAP

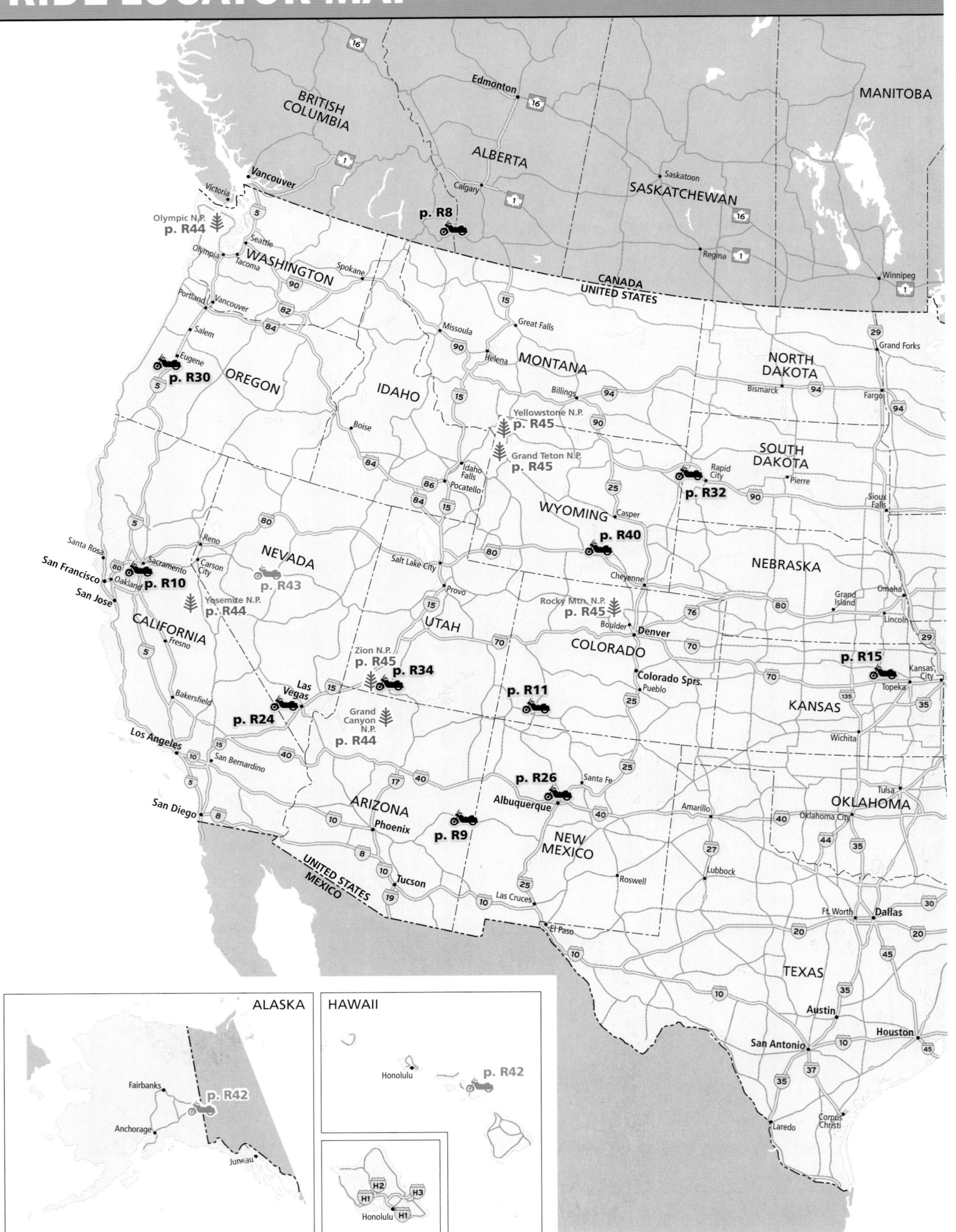
BRITISH COLUMBIA
ALBERTA
SASKATCHEWAN
MANITOBA
Edmonton
Calgary
Saskatoon
Regina
Winnipeg
Vancouver
Victoria
p. R8
CANADA
UNITED STATES
Olympic N.P.
p. R44
Seattle
Olympia
Tacoma
WASHINGTON
Spokane
Portland
Vancouver
Salem
Eugene
p. R30
OREGON
IDAHO
Boise
Missoula
Great Falls
Helena
MONTANA
Billings
NORTH DAKOTA
Bismarck
Grand Forks
Fargo
Yellowstone N.P.
p. R45
Grand Teton N.P.
p. R45
SOUTH DAKOTA
Rapid City
Pierre
p. R32
Sioux Falls
Idaho Falls
Pocatello
WYOMING
Casper
p. R40
Cheyenne
NEBRASKA
Omaha
Grand Island
Lincoln
Santa Rosa
San Francisco
Oakland
San Jose
Sacramento
p. R10
Reno
Carson City
NEVADA
p. R43
Yosemite N.P.
p. R44
Salt Lake City
Provo
UTAH
Rocky Mtn. N.P.
p. R45
Boulder
Denver
COLORADO
Colorado Sprs.
Pueblo
p. R11
CALIFORNIA
Fresno
Bakersfield
Las Vegas
p. R24
Zion N.P.
p. R45
p. R34
Grand Canyon N.P.
p. R44
p. R15
Kansas City
Topeka
KANSAS
Wichita
Los Angeles
San Bernardino
San Diego
ARIZONA
Phoenix
Tucson
p. R9
p. R26
Santa Fe
Albuquerque
NEW MEXICO
Roswell
Las Cruces
El Paso
Amarillo
Lubbock
OKLAHOMA
Oklahoma City
Tulsa
Ft. Worth
Dallas
TEXAS
Austin
Houston
San Antonio
Laredo
Corpus Christi
UNITED STATES
MEXICO
ALASKA
Fairbanks
Anchorage
Juneau
p. R42
HAWAII
Honolulu
p. R42

2007 selected rides

Legendary rides

Selected national park rides

p. R25
p. R28
p. R16
Acadia N.P. p. R45
p. R35
p. R20
p. R38
Cuyahoga Valley N.P. p. R45
p. R18
p. R14
p. R36
p. R37
p. R22
Great Smoky Mts. N.P. p. R44
p. R43
p. R13
p. R6
p. R12

ALABAMA TO FLORIDA

SEE ATLAS PAGES 12 AND 54.

ROUTE LENGTH – 244 miles or a leisurely two days

TOURING INFORMATION

The ride starts in Mobile and eases down the coast to US 98. The route hugs the coast of Florida's Panhandle, passing through coastal towns and past emerald green water and white sandy beaches with dunes crested by dense stands of sea oats.

TAKE A SIDE TRIP

Visit the Air Force Armament Museum, located seven miles north of Fort Walton on FL 85 at Eglin Air Force Base, the world's largest air base. The free museum traces military developments and showcases planes, including the SR-71 Blackbird spy plane.

VISITOR INFORMATION

www.touralabama.org | 800.252.2262
www.visitflorida.com | 888.735.2872

CAMPING INFORMATION

www.alapark.com | 800.252.7275
www.floridastateparks.org | 850.245.2157

Waterfront, Mobile, Alabama

Best season to ride:	Any time of year
Gasoline availability:	Plentiful
About the road:	A mostly four-lane, well-maintained road posted with 20 to 40 mph speed limits that are rigorously enforced
Insider tip:	The sun's ultraviolet rays are strong, especially when reflected off the water. Wear sunscreen and drink plenty of water. Watch for pedestrians.

From historic Pensacola to Apalachicola National Forest, the scenery is a joy to behold—lucid blue-green Gulf of Mexico waters and sugar-white sand that sparkles in the sun and squeaks under your feet. Don't resist the temptation to stop along the drive and wiggle your toes in the sand.

Anyone hankering for history will find Pensacola a favorite spot. Stop by Historic Pensacola Village with several small museums and homes where period-attired guides re-enact life in bygone times. The three-mile Pensacola Bay Bridge, which connects Pensacola and Gulf Breeze and spans Pensacola Bay, is such a thrill you might be tempted to turn around and ride it again.

The glorious stretch between Pensacola and Panama City is known as the Emerald Coast. One look and you'll know why. Recently named the best beach town in America, Grayton Beach is a favorite with artists who want to capture the beauty of trees sculpted by wind and salt water. Nearby Seaside, where the 1998 movie *The Truman Show* was filmed, is a planned community with pastel paint and tin roof construction.

Known as the Oyster Capital of the World, Apalachicola lies on the Panhandle's southern-most bulge. A historic working fishing village, Apalachicola has wide shady streets and century-old live oaks sheltering houses of the same vintage.

RIDE HIGHLIGHTS:

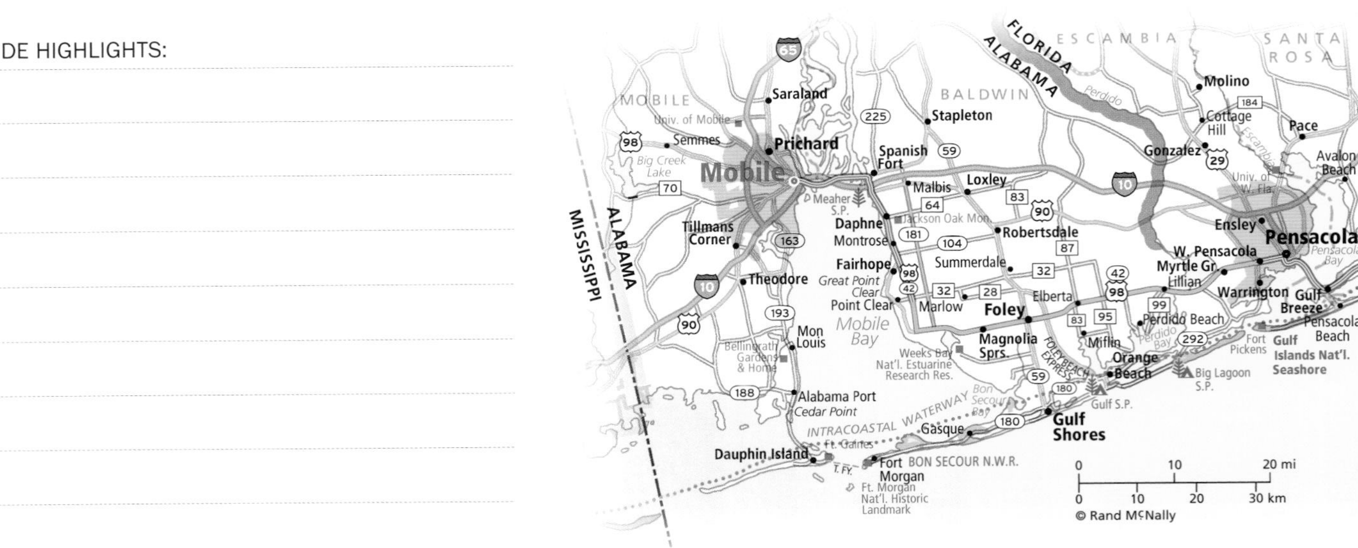
FLORIDA
ALABAMA
ESCAMBIA
SANTA ROSA
MOBILE
BALDWIN
MISSISSIPPI
ALABAMA
Saraland
Stapleton
Molino
Cottage Hill
Pace
Semmes
Prichard
Spanish Fort
Gonzalez
Avalon Beach
Mobile
Malbis
Loxley
Meaher S.P.
Daphne
Montrose
Robertsdale
Ensley
Pensacola
Tillmans Corner
W. Pensacola
Myrtle Gr.
Lillian
Fairhope
Summerdale
Theodore
Great Point Clear
Point Clear
Marlow
Foley
Elberta
Warrington
Gulf Breeze
Mobile Bay
Mon Louis
Magnolia Sprs.
Miflin
Perdido Beach
Pensacola Beach
Weeks Bay Nat'l. Estuarine Research Res.
Orange Beach
Fort Pickens
Gulf Islands Nat'l. Seashore
Big Lagoon S.P.
Alabama Port
Cedar Point
INTRACOASTAL WATERWAY
Gasque
Gulf Shores
Gulf S.P.
Dauphin Island
Fort Morgan
BON SECOUR N.W.R.
Ft. Morgan Nat'l. Historic Landmark
0 10 20 mi
0 10 20 30 km
© Rand McNally

View of coral reef, Florida

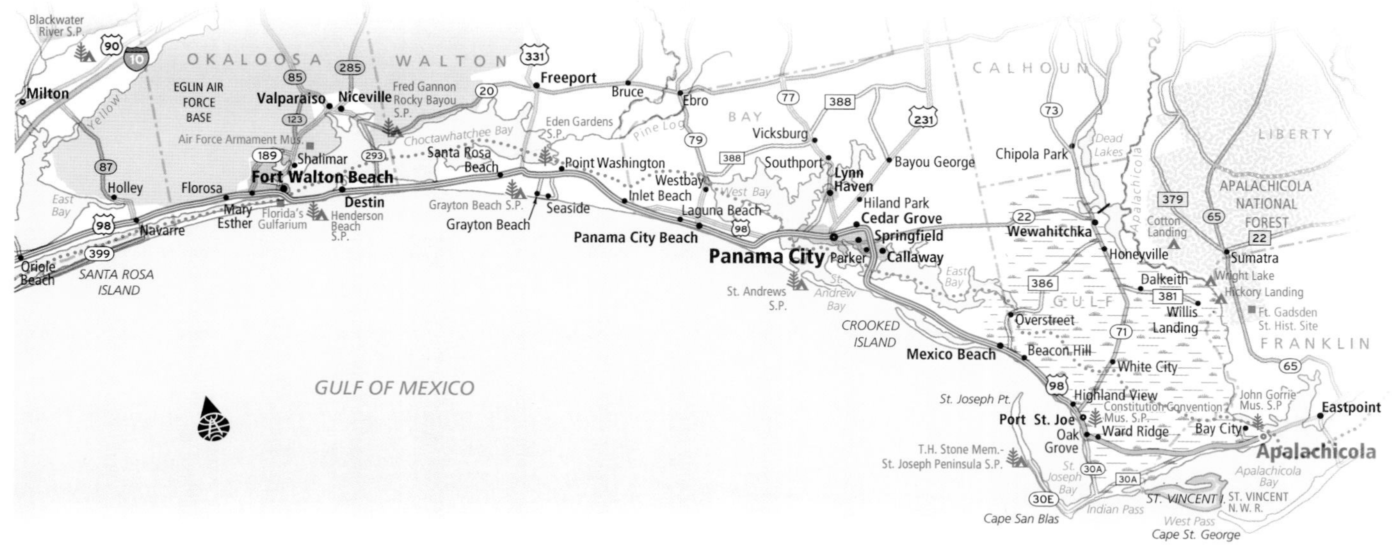
Blackwater River S.P.
Milton
OKALOOSA
WALTON
EGLIN AIR FORCE BASE
Air Force Armament Mus.
Valparaiso
Niceville
Fred Gannon Rocky Bayou S.P.
Freeport
Bruce
Ebro
Eden Gardens S.P.
Choctawhatchee Bay
Pine Log
Shalimar
Santa Rosa Beach
Point Washington
Holley
Florosa
Fort Walton Beach
Destin
Mary Esther
Florida's Gulfarium
Henderson Beach S.P.
Navarre
East Bay
Oriole Beach
SANTA ROSA ISLAND
Grayton Beach S.P.
Seaside
Grayton Beach
Westbay
West Bay
Inlet Beach
Laguna Beach
Panama City Beach
BAY
Vicksburg
Southport
Lynn Haven
Bayou George
Hiland Park
Cedar Grove
Springfield
Panama City
Parker
Callaway
St. Andrews S.P.
St. Andrew Bay
East Bay
CROOKED ISLAND
Mexico Beach
GULF OF MEXICO
CALHOUN
Chipola Park
Dead Lakes
Apalachicola
Wewahitchka
Honeyville
Dalkeith
GULF
Overstreet
Willis Landing
Beacon Hill
White City
Highland View
Constitution Convention Mus. S.P.
St. Joseph Pt.
Port St. Joe
Oak Grove
Ward Ridge
T.H. Stone Mem.- St. Joseph Peninsula S.P.
St. Joseph Bay
Cape San Blas
Indian Pass
ST. VINCENT
ST. VINCENT N. W. R.
West Pass
Cape St. George
LIBERTY
APALACHICOLA NATIONAL FOREST
Cotton Landing
Sumatra
Wright Lake
Hickory Landing
Ft. Gadsden St. Hist. Site
FRANKLIN
John Gorrie Mus. S.P.
Bay City
Eastpoint
Apalachicola
Apalachicola Bay
90
10
85
285
331
20
123
189
293
87
98
399
77
388
79
231
73
22
379
65
386
381
71
30A
30E

ALBERTA TO BRITISH COLUMBIA

SEE ATLAS PAGE 241.

TOURING INFORMATION
The route travels along the border of British Columbia and Alberta through quaint mining towns, mountain valleys, Kootenay National Park, and Banff National Park.

TAKE A SIDE TRIP
Within Banff National Park, Lake Louise is one of those must-see geo-destinations. At 5,680 feet, the turquoise lake glistens among snowcapped peaks. A flat trail flanks the water. Mountain hikes spiral up and peek out at lake views. Ride scenic, two-lane Bow Valley Parkway 36 miles to Lake Louise to spot wildlife and hike Johnston Canyon.

Mostly two-lane, the winding route travels through valleys, mountain passes, and dense conifer forests surrounding 19th-century boomtowns. Roadside provincial parks with lakes and natural hot springs offer settings for picnicking, camping, hiking, and fishing.

VISITOR INFORMATION
www.pc.gc.ca | 888.773.8888
www.kootenayrockies.com | 800.435.5622

CAMPING INFORMATION
www.pccamping.ca | 877.737.3783

RIDE HIGHLIGHTS:

ROUTE LENGTH – 252 miles or about 5 hours nonstop

Rockwall Pass, Kootenay National Park, Radium Hot Springs, British Columbia

Best season to ride:	May to October (snow still possible)
Gasoline availability:	Plentiful
About the road:	Winds through mountain passes, flattens in wide valley
Insider tip:	Bring rain gear; be aware of deer, elk, and bighorn sheep crossing.

From Crowsnest Pass, Alberta, through Sparwood, British Columbia, home of the world's largest dump truck, BC/AB 3 winds through Fernie, known for its Victorian architecture. In restored 1890s Fort Steele Heritage Town, actors dressed in period costumes bring pioneer boomtown days to life.

BC/AB 93/95 flattens through the Rocky Mountain Trench, where the powerful Columbia River flows and elk graze. Two to 10 miles wide and visible from outer space, the valley between the Rocky and Purcell mountain ranges cradles the Columbia River Wetlands, one of North America's largest continuous wetlands.

Soak in natural, steamy pools at Radium Hot Springs before entering Kootenay National Park via narrow Sinclair Canyon. Typical Kootenay scenery: soaring peaks, snow fields, and sheer rock faces. On this in-park route between Radium and Trans-Canada Highway 1, there's only one gas station open in summer. Must-stops are Hector Gorge Viewpoint, perched above the sparkling Vermillion River, and Marble Canyon, a slit in the bedrock plunging as far as 200 feet.

Crossing into Alberta, BC/AB 93 meets Trans-Canada Highway 1 going to the town of Banff. Note the land bridges arching over the highway. They allow wildlife to cross safely.

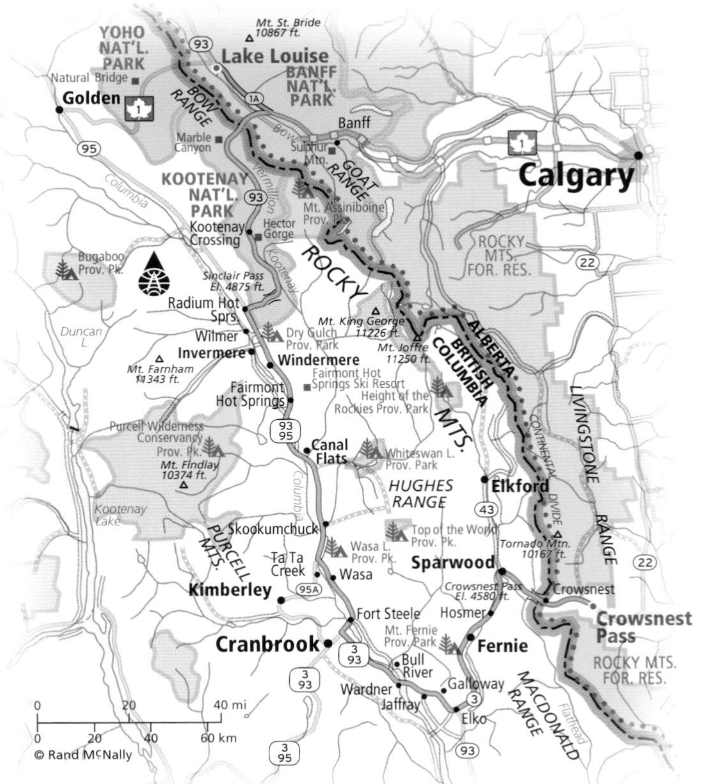
YOHO NAT'L. PARK
Mt. St. Bride 10867 ft.
Lake Louise
BANFF NAT'L. PARK
Natural Bridge
Golden
BOW RANGE
Banff
Marble Canyon
Sulphur Mtn.
GOAT RANGE
Calgary
KOOTENAY NAT'L. PARK
Mt. Assiniboine Prov. Pk.
Kootenay Crossing
Hector Gorge
ROCKY
ROCKY MTS. FOR. RES.
Bugaboo Prov. Pk.
Sinclair Pass El. 4875 ft.
Radium Hot Sprs.
Mt. King George 11226 ft.
Wilmer
Invermere
Dry Gulch Prov. Park
Windermere
Mt. Joffre 11250 ft.
ALBERTA
BRITISH COLUMBIA
Mt. Farnham 11343 ft.
Fairmont Hot Springs Ski Resort
Fairmont Hot Springs
Height of the Rockies Prov. Park
MTS.
LIVINGSTONE RANGE
CONTINENTAL DIVIDE
Purcell Wilderness Conservancy Prov. Pk.
Canal Flats
Whiteswan L. Prov. Park
Mt. Findlay 10374 ft.
HUGHES RANGE
Elkford
Kootenay Lake
Skookumchuck
Top of the World Prov. Pk.
PURCELL MTS.
Ta Ta Creek
Wasa L. Prov. Pk.
Wasa
Sparwood
Tornado Mtn. 10167 ft.
Kimberley
Crowsnest Pass El. 4580 ft.
Crowsnest
Fort Steele
Hosmer
Crowsnest Pass
Mt. Fernie Prov. Park
Fernie
Cranbrook
Bull River
ROCKY MTS. FOR. RES.
Wardner
Galloway
MACDONALD RANGE
Jaffray
Elko
0 20 40 mi
0 20 40 60 km
© Rand McNally

ARIZONA

SEE ATLAS PAGES 17 AND 19.

ROUTE LENGTH – 131 miles or about 3 hours nonstop

TOURING INFORMATION

The secluded Coronado Trail National Scenic Byway (US 191) precariously twists through eons-old volcanic fields, snow-capped mountains, lush forests, Sonoran desert, and copper mining country.

TAKE A SIDE TRIP

Two miles northwest of Springerville atop a mesa above the Little Colorado River rest the ruins of Casa Malpais, a sacred ceremonial complex built in the 1200s by Ancestral Puebloans. Underground caverns in the volcanic basalt rock once interred ancients. Casa Malpais access is available only through guided tours departing from the site's visitors' center in downtown Springerville three times a day.

More elk than automobiles follow the challenging Coronado Trail, a narrow, paved two-lane road. Snaking through the Apache-Sitgreaves National Forest on the Arizona-New Mexico border, the route offers eagle-eye views of mountains and desert. Constant switchbacks and steep elevations make this a gnarly adventure for even the most experienced riders.

In 1867, Mexican miners discovered gold and copper ore around Clifton. Phelps-Dodge Morenci Copper Mine, one of the world's largest open-pit mines, hosts guided tours of the production facilities.

VISITOR INFORMATION

www.arizonaguide.com | 866.298.3312

CAMPING INFORMATION

www.pr.state.az.us | 602.542.4174

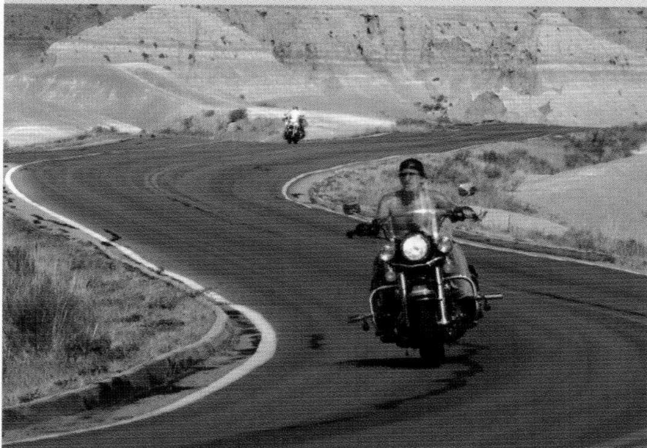

RIDE HIGHLIGHTS:

Morenci Copper Mine, Morenci

Best season to ride: Any season
Gasoline availability: Adequate; fill up at Springerville, Alpine, and Clifton
About the road: Narrow, no shoulders or guard rails; severe drop-offs
Insider tip: Killer curve near mile marker 217; drive 25 mph or less. Be alert for dramatic weather changes.

The rugged region's beauty is much the same as it was when 16th-century Spanish explorer Francisco Vasquez de Coronado searched the isolated forests for the legendary, solid gold Seven Cities of Cibola.

Start at Springerville, south of cattle country and sitting atop the nation's third-largest volcanic field. Head south on US 191, which snakes through Arizona's White Mountains and the two-million-acre Apache-Sitgreaves National Forest.

At 8,030 feet, Alpine is nestled in a grassy valley surrounded by aspen and conifer forests.

The switchback-riddled ride reaches 9,300 feet at Hannagan Meadow. Descending into Clifton, there are 70 miles of curving road with no services. Pull over at Blue Vista Overlook for stunning mountain views. The zig-zagged road tracing the Mogollon Rim plunges 6,000 feet into high desert with mesquite trees and saguaro cacti. End your ride at Three-Way, a tri-highway junction and the Clifton Ranger District information center.

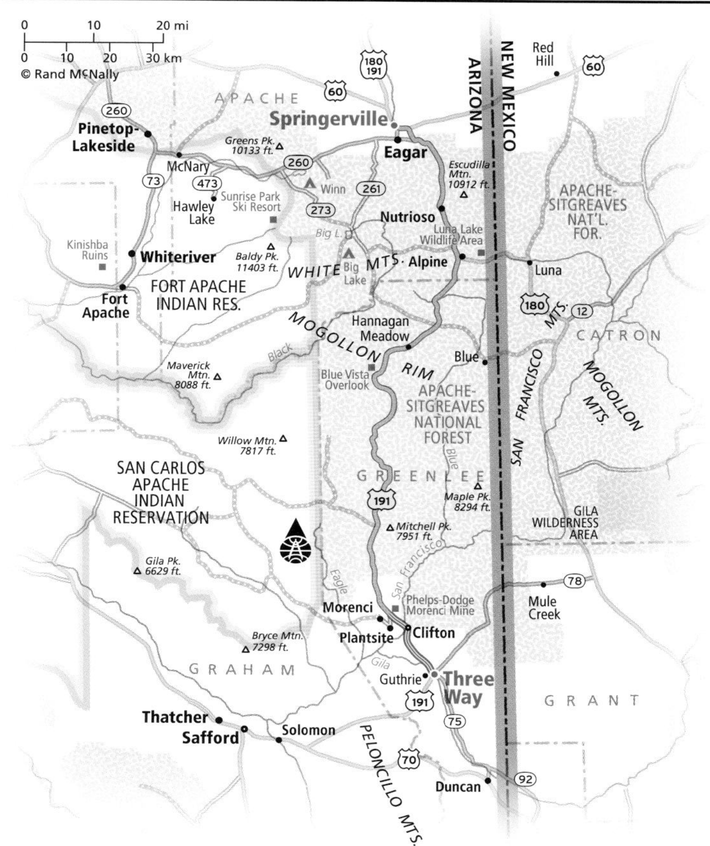
0 10 20 mi
0 10 20 30 km
© Rand McNally
APACHE
Springerville
Eagar
ARIZONA
NEW MEXICO
Red Hill
Pinetop-Lakeside
McNary
Greens Pk. 10133 ft.
Sunrise Park Ski Resort
Hawley Lake
Winn
Nutrioso
Escudilla Mtn. 10912 ft.
APACHE-SITGREAVES NAT'L. FOR.
Kinishba Ruins
Whiteriver
Baldy Pk. 11403 ft.
WHITE MTS.
Big Lake
Alpine
Luna Lake Wildlife Area
Luna
Fort Apache
FORT APACHE INDIAN RES.
MOGOLLON RIM
Hannagan Meadow
CATRON
Blue
Maverick Mtn. 8088 ft.
Blue Vista Overlook
APACHE-SITGREAVES NATIONAL FOREST
SAN FRANCISCO MTS.
MOGOLLON MTS.
Willow Mtn. 7817 ft.
SAN CARLOS APACHE INDIAN RESERVATION
GREENLEE
Maple Pk. 8294 ft.
Mitchell Pk. 7951 ft.
GILA WILDERNESS AREA
Gila Pk. 6629 ft.
Morenci
Phelps-Dodge Morenci Mine
Mule Creek
Plantsite
Clifton
Bryce Mtn. 7298 ft.
GRAHAM
Guthrie
Three Way
GRANT
Thatcher
Safford
Solomon
PELONCILLO MTS.
Duncan

CALIFORNIA

SEE ATLAS PAGE 25.

ROUTE LENGTH – 67 miles or about an hour & a half depending on stops

TOURING INFORMATION

Curvy, two-lane CA 160 meanders through the Sacramento San Joaquin Delta along the banks of the twisting Sacramento River, passing marinas, historic towns, fertile farmlands, and vineyards.

TAKE A SIDE TRIP

The city of Davis 15 miles west of Sacramento combines the best of a vibrant college town, lively artistic community, and laid-back California lifestyle. Art galleries, funky cafés, ethnic restaurants, and boutiques fill quaint, tree-lined streets. More than 100 miles of bicycle paths wind through Davis. The Design Museum, 100-acre arboretum, and Wednesday and Saturday farmers market entertain visitors.

Cruise the Sacramento Delta region for its peaceful scenery and good times. Houseboats laze in shady inlets surrounded by farmland. Tasting rooms of local vineyards, housed in landmark buildings, provide wine samples. Historic small towns host lively festivals celebrating the Delta's colorful past, agricultural bounty, and growing arts community.

VISTOR INFORMATION

www.yolocvb.org | 877.713.2847

CAMPING INFORMATION

www.parks.ca.gov | 800.444.7275

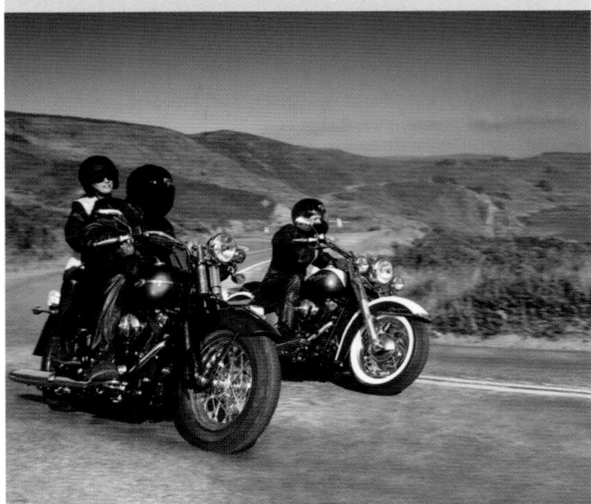

RIDE HIGHLIGHTS:

WELCOME

Sacramento River Delta, in Locke

Best season to ride:	March through October
Gasoline availability:	Plentiful
About the road:	Flanks the Sacramento River; cross bridges often to the west bank and cut through historic towns
Insider tip:	Bring sunscreen, an appetite, and no deadlines; watch for tractors, blue herons, and cranes.

From state capital Sacramento through the San Joaquin Valley, CA 160 leisurely curves southbound along the Sacramento River through the Delta. Fishermen cast for striped bass or sturgeon, and houseboats ply the Delta's calm waterways. Small town restaurants serve regional wines and hearty meals.

Chenin Blanc and Petite Sirah grapes grow in the Delta's fertile soil. For tastes, cross the Sacramento River at the Freeport Bridge to Clarksburg's Old Sugar Mill. A restored 1930s factory, it hosts free tastings of award-winning wines. Clarksburg's Dinky's Diner slings burgers, "burned weenies," and root beer floats from a marina-side trailer. South is Courtland, known for its July Pear Fair, and sleepy Locke, which is on the National Register of Historic Places. Built in 1915, Locke is the nation's only town constructed and settled by Chinese immigrants. They also helped build the Delta's levee and canal system.

In the roaring '20s, paddle wheel steamboats transported goods and passengers into Ryde. Next is Isleton, famous for its June Crawdad Festival. In Rio Vista, dine on a sizzling steak at Foster's Bighorn under the glassy-eyed gaze of more than 300 exotic animals brought down by bootlegging, big game hunter Bill Foster.

Ride 10 miles northwest of Concord to Benicia to see the "The Mothball Fleet," a ghostly collection of 77 World War II–era U.S. Navy war ships, barges, and tugs rusting in Suisun Bay. Pull over to view safely.

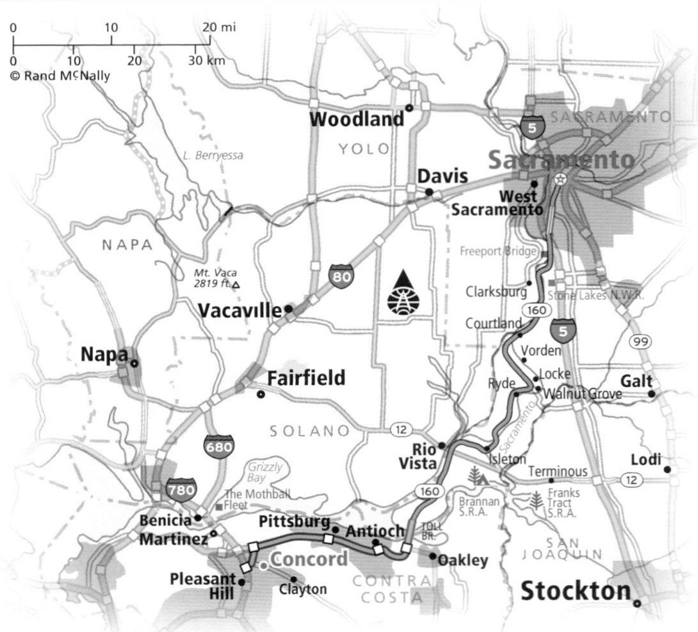
0
10
20 mi
0
10
20
30 km
© Rand McNally
Woodland
YOLO
Sacramento
SACRAMENTO
Davis
West Sacramento
L. Berryessa
NAPA
Mt. Vaca 2819 ft.
Freeport Bridge
Clarksburg
Stone Lakes N.W.R.
Vacaville
Courtland
Vorden
Napa
Fairfield
Ryde
Locke
Walnut Grove
Galt
SOLANO
Rio Vista
Isleton
Terminous
Lodi
Grizzly Bay
The Mothball Fleet
Brannan S.R.A.
Franks Tract S.R.A.
Benicia
Martinez
Pittsburg
Antioch
Concord
Oakley
SAN JOAQUIN
Pleasant Hill
Clayton
CONTRA COSTA
Stockton

COLORADO

SEE ATLAS PAGE 41.

ROUTE LENGTH – 283 miles or about 8 hours nonstop

TOURING INFORMATION
Several roads, including the Colorado Million Dollar Highway, create the San Juan Skyway, which winds through majestic mountain passes, canyons, mining towns, and Pueblo archaeological sites.

TAKE A SIDE TRIP
Turn off US 160 into Mesa Verde National Park, which preserves the mesa-top and cliff dwellings of the Ancestral Puebloans who lived here from AD 600 to 1300. A 15-mile ride into the park ends at the Far View Visitors' Center, where tickets for ranger-guided tours can be purchased to view Balcony House, Cliff Palace, and Long House. It's well worth a full day or more to explore the park's many archaeological sites and Chapin Mesa Archeological Museum.

The San Juan Skyway Scenic Byway's stunning mountain views are as priceless as the region's gold and silver mined in the late 19th century. A full day's ride, the loop links mining towns with fine shopping and dining set amidst soaring peaks, box canyons, and conifer and aspen forests.

VISITOR INFORMATION
www.colorado.com | 800.265.6723

CAMPING INFORMATION
www.fs.fed.us/r2/sanjuan | 970.247.4874

RIDE HIGHLIGHTS:

A mountain view from the San Juan Skyway

Best season to ride:	Mid-May through mid-October
Gasoline availability:	Adequate
About the road:	Winding, steep switchbacks, limited guard rails, and dirt shoulders
Insider tip:	Bring rain gear; layer clothing as temps drop at high altitudes.

The San Juan Skyway clings to the sides of snow-capped peaks rising from the dense Uncompahgre and San Juan National Forests. Three peaks reaching more than 14,000 feet can be seen to the east. The loop passes plunging waterfalls and encompasses lively mining towns rich with history and entertainment.

From Durango, the steep road climbs north through the 10,640-foot Coal Bank Pass, then over 10,899-foot Molas Pass to the 1874 mining town of Silverton, the destination of the Durango & Silverton Narrow Gauge Railroad. Handlebars Saloon slings tasty buffalo burgers. Ghost towns Howardsville, Eureka, and Animas Forks are within 14 miles.

The Colorado Million Dollar Highway twists between Silverton to Ouray through the 11,075-foot Red Mountain Pass, where many mines existed. Reduce speed there. The narrow road's tight switchbacks, tunnels, steep drop-offs, and few guard rails follow the original Ute Indian trail. Squeezed into a box canyon, quaint Ouray was founded in 1875 and looks like a Western movie set. Soak your saddle sores at the public pool, warmed by hot springs.

Telluride houses galleries, restaurants, and swank shops in Victorian buildings. A short tram ride up to the ski resort and Telluride Mountain Village promises gorgeous mountain views.

Three peaks soaring over 14,000 feet flank the 10,222-foot Lizard Head Pass connecting Telluride to Rico. The road then rolls through ranchlands surrounding Dolores. Anasazi Heritage Center showcases Ancestral Puebloan life. On the way to Durango is Mesa Verde, the only national park dedicated to the works of humankind.

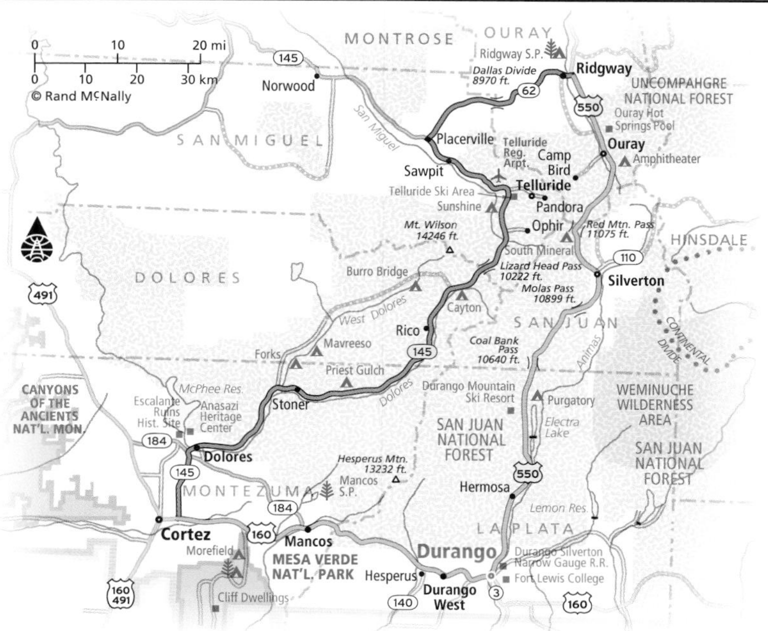
0 10 20 mi
0 10 20 30 km
© Rand McNally
MONTROSE
OURAY
Ridgway S.P.
Dallas Divide 8970 ft.
Ridgway
UNCOMPAHGRE NATIONAL FOREST
Ouray Hot Springs Pool
Ouray
Amphitheater
Norwood
SAN MIGUEL
Placerville
Telluride Reg. Arpt.
Camp Bird
Sawpit
Telluride Ski Area
Telluride
Sunshine
Pandora
Mt. Wilson 14246 ft.
Ophir
Red Mtn. Pass 11075 ft.
HINSDALE
South Mineral
Lizard Head Pass 10222 ft.
Molas Pass 10899 ft.
Silverton
DOLORES
Burro Bridge
West Dolores
Cayton
SAN JUAN
Rico
Mavreeso
Coal Bank Pass 10640 ft.
Forks
Priest Gulch
Durango Mountain Ski Resort
Purgatory
WEMINUCHE WILDERNESS AREA
CANYONS OF THE ANCIENTS NAT'L. MON.
McPhee Res.
Escalante Ruins Hist. Site
Anasazi Heritage Center
Stoner
SAN JUAN NATIONAL FOREST
Electra Lake
Dolores
SAN JUAN NATIONAL FOREST
Hesperus Mtn. 13232 ft.
Mancos S.P.
Hermosa
MONTEZUMA
Lemon Res.
LA PLATA
Cortez
Morefield
Mancos
MESA VERDE NAT'L. PARK
Durango
Durango Silverton Narrow Gauge R.R.
Fort Lewis College
Hesperus
Durango West
Cliff Dwellings
145
62
550
110
491
184
160
140
3

FLORIDA

SEE ATLAS PAGE 55.

ROUTE LENGTH – 235.4 miles or about 5 hours nonstop

TOURING INFORMATION
This ride begins in Naples on US 41 and sweeps southeast, skirting the northern Everglades, before eventually joining US 1 into the beautiful Florida Keys.

TAKE A SIDE TRIP
Ride into the heart of Everglades National Park to see 1.5 million acres of unspoiled wilderness. The scenic drive along FL 9336 from the Ernest Coe Visitor Center in Homestead to Flamingo passes numerous cypress groves and lakes, roadside parks, and turnouts. The boardwalk at Royal Palm virtually guarantees alligator sightings. Three visitor centers, in Everglades City, Homestead, and Flamingo, offer informational displays, films, and park brochures. Most are near food, lodging, and hiking and canoe trails. Expect palmetto bugs and mosquitoes from May to November.

The entire route is flat and, with the exception of Miami's busy suburbs, uncomplicated. As US 1 heads south, wildlife preserves and state parks dominate the landscape. The wind picks up, the weather warms, and the views are unforgettable.

VISITOR INFORMATION
www.visitflorida.com | 888.735.2872

CAMPING INFORMATION
www.floridastateparks.org | 850.245.2157

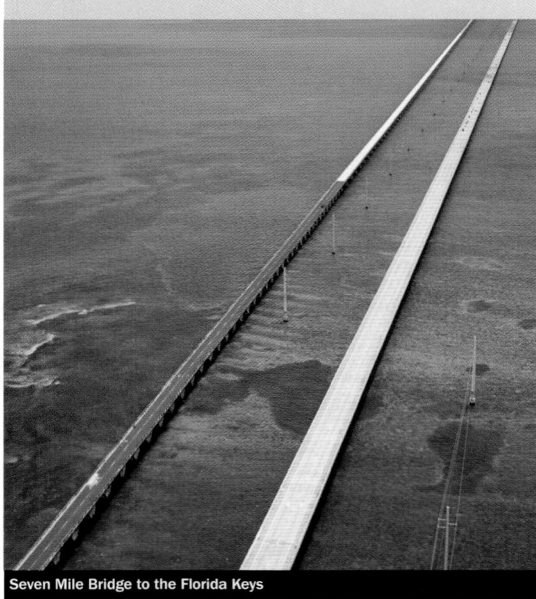
Seven Mile Bridge to the Florida Keys

RIDE HIGHLIGHTS:

Everglades National Park, near Homestead

Best season to ride:	All year
Gasoline availability:	Plan ahead
About the road:	Well maintained
Insider tip:	Be alert when riding at night in March and April for alligators crossing the road as this is mating season; also watch for Florida panthers

Soon after leaving Naples, commercial development yields to nature as US 41 approaches the Everglades. Sawgrass and cypress dominate beyond Carnestown. The Shark Valley Visitor Center features the half-mile Bobcat Boardwalk and Otter Hammock Trails, each traversing marshes and dense tropical hardwood forest.

As US 41 heads east, it crosses the slough before entering a landscape of residences and strip malls on FL 997. Be patient—your brief encounter with commuter traffic and suburbia is soon rewarded. Civilization gives way to mangroves and glimpses of water along US 1 before crossing Barnes Sound to Key Largo. On Largo do as South Floridians do and stop for a bite at Alabama Jacks, off FL 905.

The Keys are a biker's paradise. Stop at John Pennekamp Coral Reef State Park for snorkeling. Then dine at the Islamorada Fish Company, overlooking Florida Bay. West of Marathon, park in the lot just before the Seven Mile Bridge for great photo ops. Then ride through almost seven miles of endless sky and sea—watching for swirling winds that sometimes whip through the channel.

At Key West check into Key Lime Inn, a historic hotel that welcomes motorcyclists. Then tour the Old Town; take pictures at the buoy at the southernmost point in the continental U.S.; explore boutiques, art galleries, and cigar merchants on Duval Street. Head to Hogfish Bar & Grill on Stock Island for killer hogfish sandwiches and locals who love to talk motorcycles.

Naples
East Naples
Marco
Cape Romano
75
ALLIGATOR ALLEY
(EVERGLADES EXPWY.)
Collier-Seminole S.P.
29
MICCOSUKEE IND. RES.
THE EVERGLADES
Carnestown
Ochopee
41
Everglades City
TEN THOUSAND ISLANDS
EVERGLADES NATIONAL PARK
Ponce de Leon Bay
Whitewater Bay
Cape Sable
Flamingo
Shark Valley Visitor Cen.
Miccosukee Ind. Res.
Weston
Fort Lauderdale
Hollywood
Hallandale Bch.
Hialeah
Miami Beach
Miami
Seaquarium
Coral Gables
997
Homestead
Coe Visitor Cen.
Goulds
Coral Castle
BISCAYNE NAT'L. PARK
ELLIOTT KEY
Royal Palm
Florida City
1
9336
MANGROVE SWAMP
KEY LARGO
John Pennekamp Coral Reef S.P.
Key Largo
Florida Bay
Tavernier
Islamorada
Treasure Village
Theater of the Sea
Indian Key Historic S.P.
Long Key S.P.
INTRACOASTAL WATERWAY
BIG PINE KEY
MUD KEYS
Marathon
Seven Mile Bridge
Bahia Honda S.P.
Big Pine Key
Key West
Key West Aquarium
Key West N.A.S.
0 25 50 mi
0 25 50 75 km
© Rand McNally

GEORGIA TO SOUTH CAROLINA

SEE ATLAS PAGES 61, 186, AND 187.

ROUTE LENGTH – 203 miles or 5 to 6 hours

TOURING INFORMATION
This route follows US 17 the entire length of the South Carolina coast, from Savannah, Georgia, through Charleston, and up to Myrtle Beach, South Carolina.

TAKE A SIDE TRIP
Hilton Head Island is one of the United States' best-known vacation destinations. There are plenty of high-end resorts, shops, and golf courses worth visiting, but those who love quiet spaces won't be disappointed. Hiking is a popular pastime at the Audubon-Newhall and Sea Pines Forest Preserves on the island's south side; paddlers enjoy kayaking the island's salt marsh creeks from South Beach Marina Village.

After departing from Savannah, US 17 passes through Low Country marshes and the city of Charleston, then parallels the Intracoastal Waterway and the Atlantic coast to the white-sand beaches around Myrtle Beach.

VISITOR INFORMATION
www.discoversouthcarolina.com | 866.224.9339

CAMPING INFORMATION
southcarolinaparks.com | 866.345.7275

RIDE HIGHLIGHTS:

Live oaks, near Georgetown, South Carolina

Best season to ride:	Summer and autumn
Gasoline availability:	Adequate
About the road:	Follows the Atlantic Intracoastal Waterway; most of the road is good although there are older sections.
Insider tip:	Expect congestion in the cities at both ends of this ride; good ride to explore the shoreline and marshlands.

Grace and romance still live in the South. You'll see it along this ride, and nowhere more than in Savannah. Draped in Spanish moss, the Historic District is a great place for a stroll and a good meal. Try the Dockside Restaurant for its famous steampot, a stew of shellfish, sausage, and vegetables.

Cross into South Carolina and the heart of the Low Country, a swath of marshland bordered to the west by hills and to the east by the Atlantic Ocean. Gentle rises and broad curves carry riders past the rivers and inlets that feed the watery landscape. The scent of salt marsh fills the air.

The marshland continues to Charleston. Visit Charles Towne Landing, site of the first Carolina settlement in 1670. The state park features a 17th-century replica trading ship, interactive exhibits, and a natural habitat zoo. As you ride out of the city you'll join the Atlantic Intracoastal Waterway, a navigation route of canals, protected bays, and natural river channels stretching from Boston, Mass., to Key West, Fla. Along the way, expect stands of white and live oaks, pines, and frequent glimpses of the Atlantic.

Georgetown is the next stop. The town's 18th-century buildings comprise the historic downtown, but the city's intracoastal marinas are its modern hallmark. Visit the old docks, converted into a restaurant and shopping area called Harborwalk.

Georgetown marks the southernmost point of The Grand Strand, 60 miles of broad, white-sand beaches. For decades this region has attracted vacationers. End your Southern ride on Pawleys Island, known for its quiet beaches and hand-crafted hammocks, or Murrells Inlet, an old fishing village famous for seafood restaurants, or bustling Myrtle Beach, the hub of the Strand, with great beaches, shopping and nightlife.

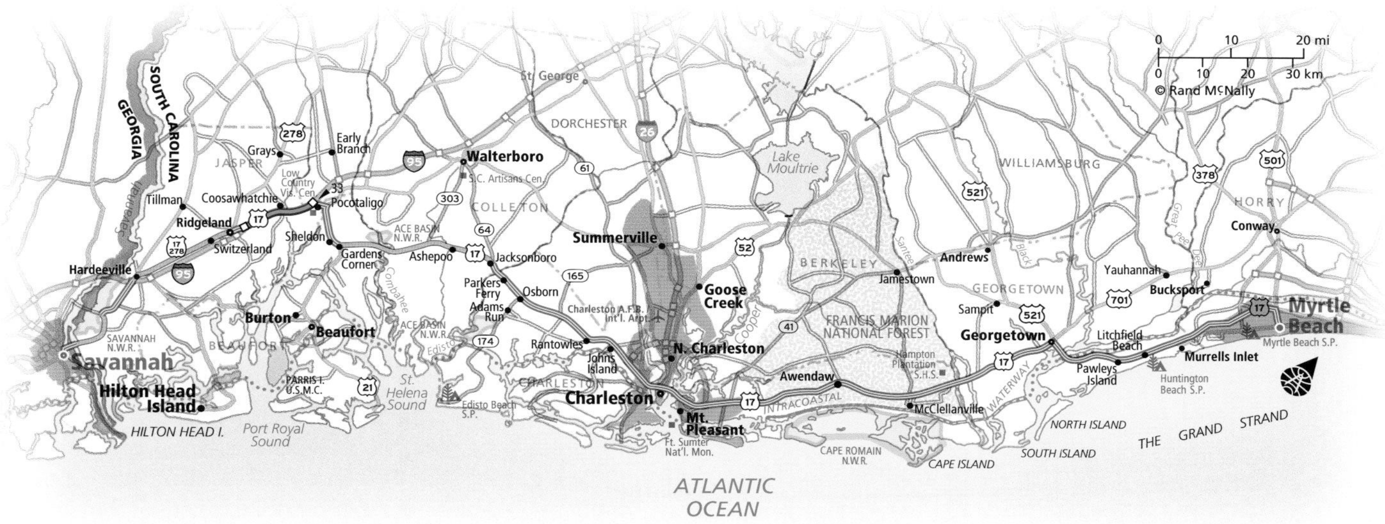

0 10 20 mi
0 10 20 30 km
© Rand McNally
GEORGIA
SOUTH CAROLINA
JASPER
Grays
Early Branch
Walterboro
S.C. Artisans Cen.
DORCHESTER
St. George
Lake Moultrie
WILLIAMSBURG
HORRY
Conway
Tillman
Coosawhatchie
Pocotaligo
COLLETON
Ridgeland
Switzerland
Sheldon
Gardens Corner
Ashepoo
Jacksonboro
Summerville
Andrews
Hardeeville
Parkers Ferry
Osborn
Adams Run
Goose Creek
BERKELEY
Jamestown
GEORGETOWN
Yauhannah
Bucksport
Myrtle Beach
Myrtle Beach S.P.
Burton
Beaufort
Charleston A.F.B. Int'l. Arpt.
FRANCIS MARION NATIONAL FOREST
Sampit
Georgetown
Litchfield Beach
Murrells Inlet
SAVANNAH N.W.R.
Savannah
Rantowles
Johns Island
N. Charleston
Hampton Plantation S.H.S.
Awendaw
Pawleys Island
Huntington Beach S.P.
Hilton Head Island
PARRIS I. U.S.M.C.
St. Helena Sound
Edisto Beach S.P.
Charleston
Mt. Pleasant
INTRACOASTAL
McClellanville
WATERWAY
HILTON HEAD I.
Port Royal Sound
Ft. Sumter Nat'l. Mon.
CAPE ROMAIN N.W.R.
CAPE ISLAND
NORTH ISLAND
SOUTH ISLAND
THE GRAND STRAND
ATLANTIC OCEAN

INDIANA

SEE ATLAS PAGES 76 AND 77.

ROUTE LENGTH – About 85 miles or a leisurely 3-hour ride

TOURING INFORMATION

The Hoosier Hills ride follows the contoured hills and scenic valleys around Brown County State Park, Hoosier National Forest, and Monroe Lake.

This run is considered one of the top motorcycle roads in Indiana. On any good-weather weekend, the roads are dotted with motorcyclists and organized rides. They are peaceful roads for the most part, but plan to share the scene with other travelers during peak seasons, especially autumn.

TAKE A SIDE TRIP

Ride to Story, Ind., along IN 135. A boomtown in the late 1800s, it now has a population of three. Plus a ghost. The old Story Inn is the heart of the community with unexpected gourmet fare, a summer courtyard bar with live music, and comfortable lodgings where the ghostly Blue Lady is said to make her presence known. Split rail fences, hitching posts, and a liars' bench on the weathered porch add to the old-time ambience.

IN 135 leads south into a secluded part of Brown County known locally as Stone Head. Watch for an unusual monument that serves as a marker by the side of the road—a white stone head atop a stone pillar.

VISITOR INFORMATION

www.visitindiana.com | 800.677.9800

CAMPING INFORMATION

www.in.gov/dnr/parklake | 866.622.6746

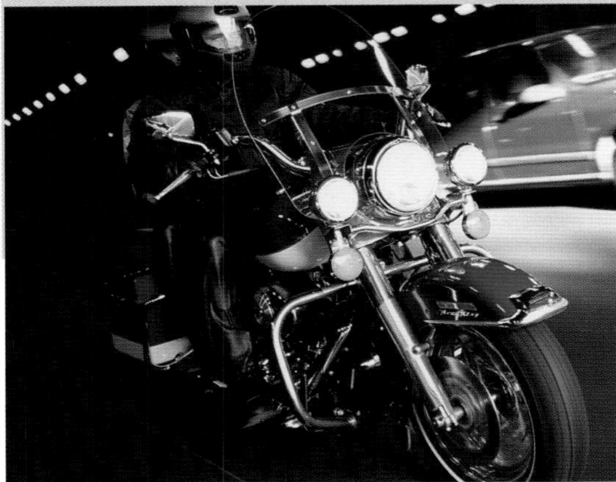

RIDE HIGHLIGHTS:

Ramp Creek Covered Bridge, Brown County

Best season to ride:	Late spring through late autumn
Gasoline availability:	Plentiful
About the road:	Varies from city traffic to small town roads to winding two-lane byways
Insider tip:	Watch for wildlife and bicycle riders, increased traffic on Indiana University football game days.

Nicknamed "The Little Smokies," the dramatic hills and valleys of this ride speak of bygone days when settlers worked the land and made by hand whatever they needed. The hills and serpentine roads make for a rugged roller coaster ride. Some of the descents are challenging with sweeping curves. The ascents are breathtaking.

Artists flock to this area for its inspirational scenery: rustic log cabins, covered bridges, fading barns, peaceful streams, small farming communities, forests that explode in autumn finery, charming hamlets, and scenic vistas. Morning mists rise from hills, and on cool days fingers of wood smoke spiral up from stone chimneys. Neither industry nor billboards mar the Brown County landscape. For a treat, ride the route in both directions to catch the varying wonders.

Stop in the village of Nashville, the art colony of the Midwest, with hundreds of specialty shops. The narrow streets are packed every weekend, especially during fall foliage season. Nashville has a Little Opry, winery, theater, and tasty fried biscuits served with apple butter.

Brown County is home to Indiana's largest state park, Brown County State Park, with 15,696 acres for horseback riding, hiking, bird watching, and mountain biking. With a lodge and dining room, the park is accessible at its northern entrance via Ramp Creek Covered Bridge, Indiana's only divided, two-lane covered bridge (see photo above).

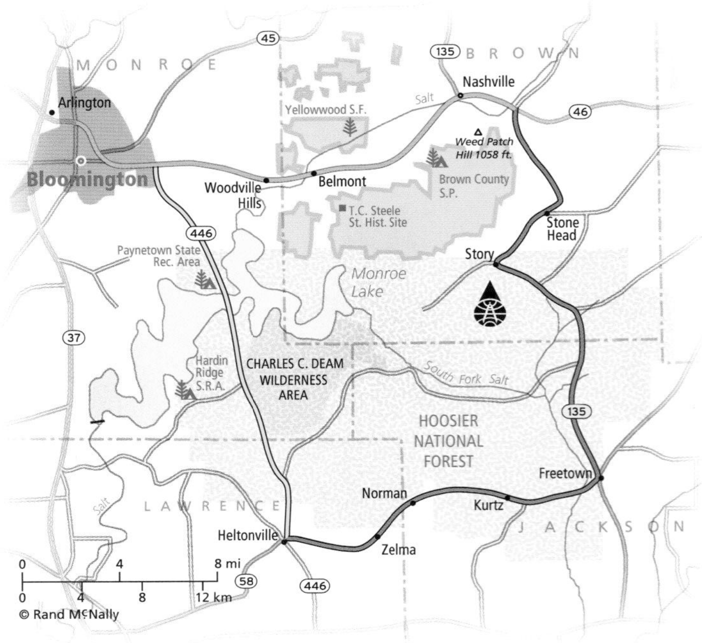
MONROE
BROWN
LAWRENCE
JACKSON
45
135
46
446
37
58
Arlington
Bloomington
Woodville Hills
Belmont
Yellowwood S.F.
Salt
Nashville
Weed Patch Hill 1058 ft.
Brown County S.P.
T.C. Steele St. Hist. Site
Stone Head
Story
Paynetown State Rec. Area
Monroe Lake
Hardin Ridge S.R.A.
CHARLES C. DEAM WILDERNESS AREA
South Fork Salt
HOOSIER NATIONAL FOREST
Freetown
Norman
Kurtz
Heltonville
Zelma
0 4 8 mi
0 4 8 12 km
© Rand McNally

KANSAS

SEE ATLAS PAGE 84.

ROUTE LENGTH – 107 Miles or about 3 hours nonstop

TOURING INFORMATION
KS 177 travels through the Flint Hills where the road dramatically rises and falls like an asphalt wave through endless tallgrass prairie.

TAKE A SIDE TRIP
The 10,894-acre Tallgrass Prairie National Preserve, run by the National Park Service and The Nature Conservancy, lies two miles north of Strong City. Tour Z Bar/Spring Hill Ranch's limestone barn and 1881 home. Exhibits explain the prairie ecosystem and history of Native American life. Hiking trails, the shortest leading to a one-room schoolhouse, meander through prairie where rattlesnakes, coyote, and deer live. Ranger-guided prairie bus tours operate late April through October.

Flint Hills Scenic Byway (KS 177) rolls through the largest remaining tract of tallgrass prairie in North America. Cattle outnumber people here where bison grazed and Osage and Kaw Indians hunted. Cowboy, Indian, and outlaw lore lives in roadside towns. See a rodeo and camp like a cowboy under the stars.

VISITOR INFORMATION
www.travelks.com | 800.252.6727

CAMPING INFORMATION
www.ksrvparks.com | 877.225.2782

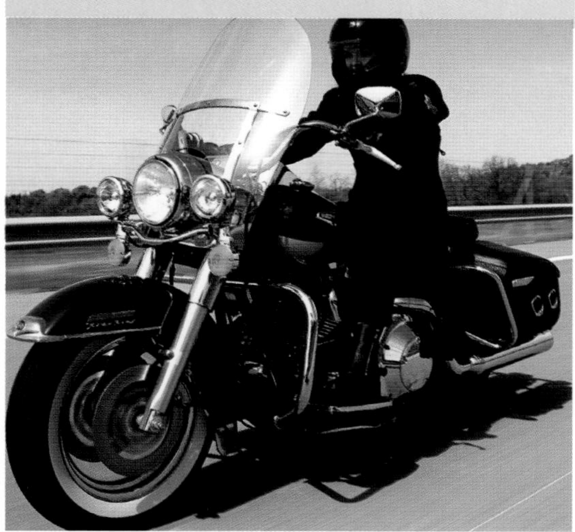

RIDE HIGHLIGHTS:

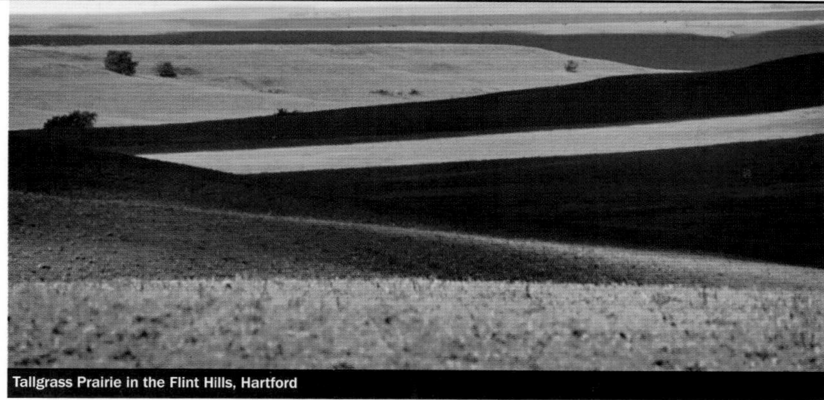

Tallgrass Prairie in the Flint Hills, Hartford

Best season to ride:	June
Gasoline availability:	Adequate
About the road:	Undulating, two-lane road with no shoulders; sides of road drop off
Insider tip:	Be alert for sudden, severe summer lightning and hail storms; bring rain gear.

America's romantic cowboy tune "Home on the Range," Kansas' state song, comes to life while riding KS 177 through the Flint Hills.

Manhattan, gateway to the prairie region, is home to Kansas State University, which co-owns the Konza Prairie Partnership with The Nature Conservancy. The free hiking trails offer impressive prairie views. In spring, cattle graze on tender green grass. By fall, tallgrasses reaching up to seven feet sweep the underbelly of vast blue sky.

Covered wagon trains traversing the prairie stopped in Council Grove, a staging area on the Santa Fe Trail, to stock up at the 1857 Last Chance Store, one of 13 registered historical sites in this preserved Wild West town. Desperadoes bunked in Early Day Jail while General Custer and Jesse James patronized Hays House, still serving tasty vittles. Council Grove honors its rich history with the annual Wah-Shun-Gah Days, a festival named for the last full-blooded chief of the Kaw Indians (June).

Strong City hosts the Flint Hills Rodeo, the oldest consecutively run, professional rodeo in Kansas, held the first weekend in June. While in Strong City, visit the town's limestone Chase County Courthouse. Built in 1873, it is the oldest operating courthouse west of the Mississippi.

The ride ends in El Dorado, called "Oil City" for its founding role in Kansas' discovery of "black gold." The Kansas Oil Museum is a 10-acre, reconstructed 1920s oil boom town of historic buildings and original, working drilling equipment. In early June, El Dorado Frontier Heritage Festival celebrates the region's cowboy heritage.

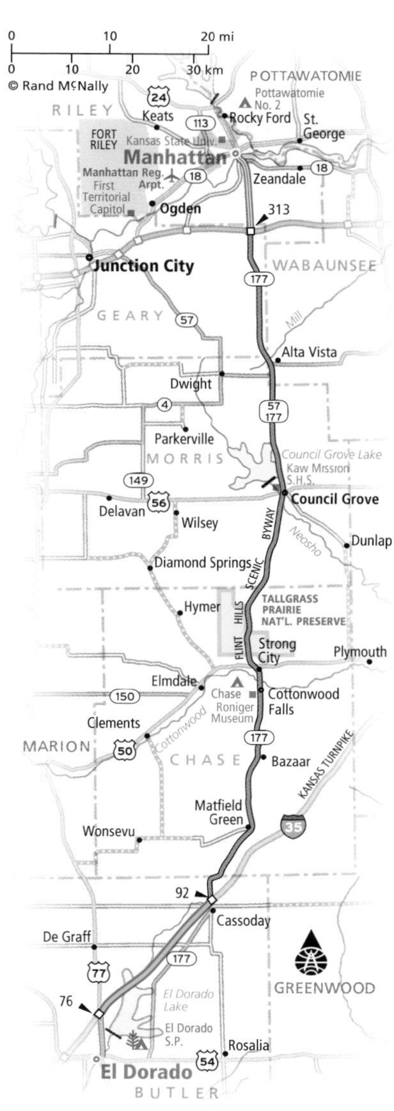
0 10 20 mi
0 10 20 30 km
© Rand McNally
POTTAWATOMIE
Pottawatomie No. 2
RILEY
Keats
24
113
Rocky Ford
St. George
FORT RILEY
Kansas State Univ.
Manhattan
Manhattan Reg. Arpt.
First Territorial Capitol
18
Zeandale
Ogden
313
Junction City
WABAUNSEE
177
GEARY
57
Mill
Alta Vista
Dwight
4
Parkerville
MORRIS
Council Grove Lake
Kaw Mission S.H.S.
149
Council Grove
56
Delavan
Wilsey
Neosho
Dunlap
Diamond Springs
FLINT HILLS SCENIC BYWAY
Hymer
TALLGRASS PRAIRIE NAT'L. PRESERVE
Strong City
Plymouth
Elmdale
Chase Roniger Museum
Cottonwood Falls
150
Clements
Cottonwood
MARION
50
CHASE
Bazaar
KANSAS TURNPIKE
Matfield Green
35
Wonsevu
92
Cassoday
De Graff
77
GREENWOOD
76
El Dorado Lake
El Dorado S.P.
Rosalia
54
El Dorado
BUTLER

MAINE

SEE ATLAS PAGE 92.

ROUTE LENGTH – About 165 miles or a leisurely day

TOURING INFORMATION
This road hugs the coast of Maine and follows US 1, also known as the Blue Star Memorial Highway, most of the way. US 1 used to be the main thoroughfare from Maine to Florida and was called the Main Street of America.

TAKE A SIDE TRIP
Be sure to visit Fort Knox. Fort Knox in Prospect, Maine, that is. It was built in the mid-1800s to protect the Penobscot River Valley from British naval attacks. The fort was named for Major General Henry Knox, America's first Secretary of War. America's other Fort Knox, the one located in Kentucky and famous for its gold bullion depository, also was named after him.

From Belfast, proceed north on US 1 through Searsport and Stockton Springs, and immediately before crossing the suspension bridge, take a left onto ME 174. Fort Knox is about a quarter mile on the right.

VISITOR INFORMATION
www.visitmaine.com | 888.624.6345

CAMPING INFORMATION
www.maine.gov/doc/parks | 207.287.3821

RIDE HIGHLIGHTS:

Mount Desert Island, near Bar Harbor

Best season to ride:	Late spring through autumn
Gasoline availability:	Plentiful
About the road:	Well-maintained two-lane road used by folks who want to enjoy the scenery from Portland to Acadia National Park
Insider tip:	Dress in layers and carry rain gear. Be prepared for changes in weather and occasional morning fog.

Start your motor running and head "down East"—Maine lingo for in the direction of the Canadian Maritimes. Picture-perfect images of coastal Maine are alive and vibrant on this ride: rocky coastlines, lighthouses on distant promontories, marinas packed with fishing boats, seaside villages, fresh lobster. Everywhere the ocean makes its presence known, whether by sight, sound, or smell.

The charming old port city of Portland crowns a hilly peninsula surrounded by rivers and harbors. Cobbled streets lined with shops and restaurants, vintage redbrick warehouses ringed by wharves, and grand sea captains' mansions are beautifully preserved.

Less than 20 miles north of Portland, Freeport is the home of upscale shopping and historic homes and churches. Stop by world-famous L.L. Bean, which is open 24 hours a day. Less than three miles outside of Freeport is a famed oddity, the Desert of Maine. Geologists believe that 11,000 years ago a melting glacier left behind this 40-acre sand dune.

Connected to the mainland by a causeway, Mount Desert Island and Acadia National Park offer 26 mountains, 22 lakes and ponds, 120 miles of hiking trails, beaches, and natural wonders galore. A 27-mile loop takes in the major attractions, including the pink granite summit of 1,528-foot Mt. Cadillac.

Facing Frenchman Bay, the island's biggest town of Bar Harbor has narrow streets filled with boutiques, restaurants, and resting places.

ADD ON: Portland Head Light

Start this ride on Broadway at "Bug" Light on Casco Bay, in South Portland. Head south on Madison Street, then east on Breakwater Drive, continuing onto Benjamin Pickett Street. After a left on Fort Road, you'll see Spring Point Light at the end of a breakwater, the Portland Harbor museum, and the clipper ship *Snow Squall*. Take Fort Road back south, turning left onto Preble Street, which becomes Shore Road.

The roadway straightens and glides past waterfront mansions in Cape Elizabeth.

At the sign for Fort Williams Park, turn left and anticipate the first glimpse of Portland Head Light, Maine's most celebrated lighthouse.

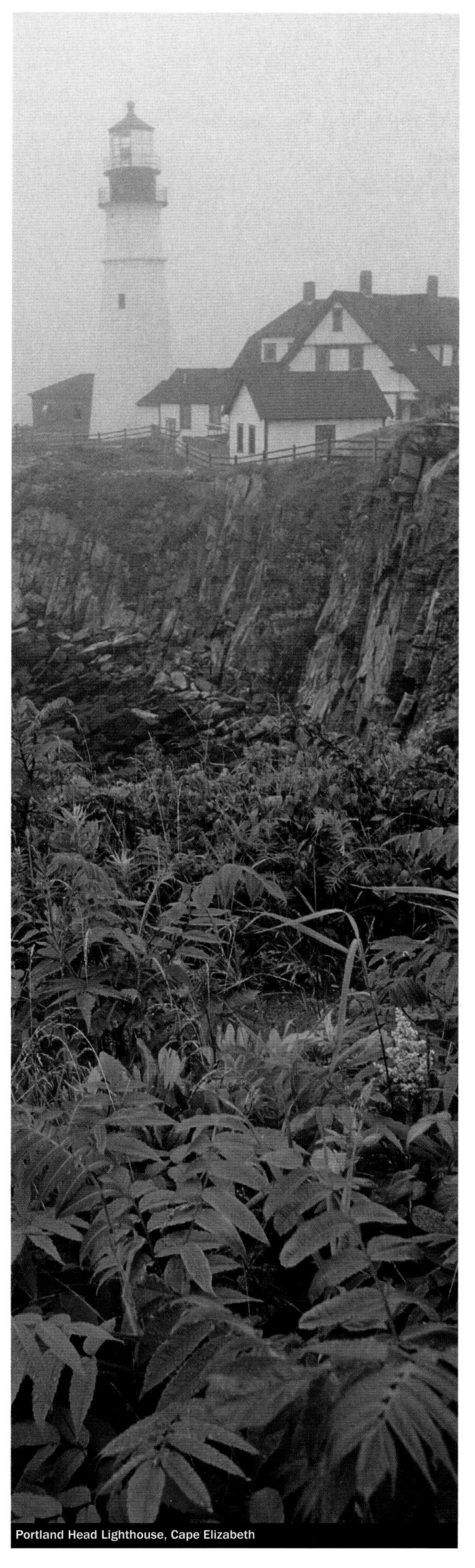

Portland Head Lighthouse, Cape Elizabeth

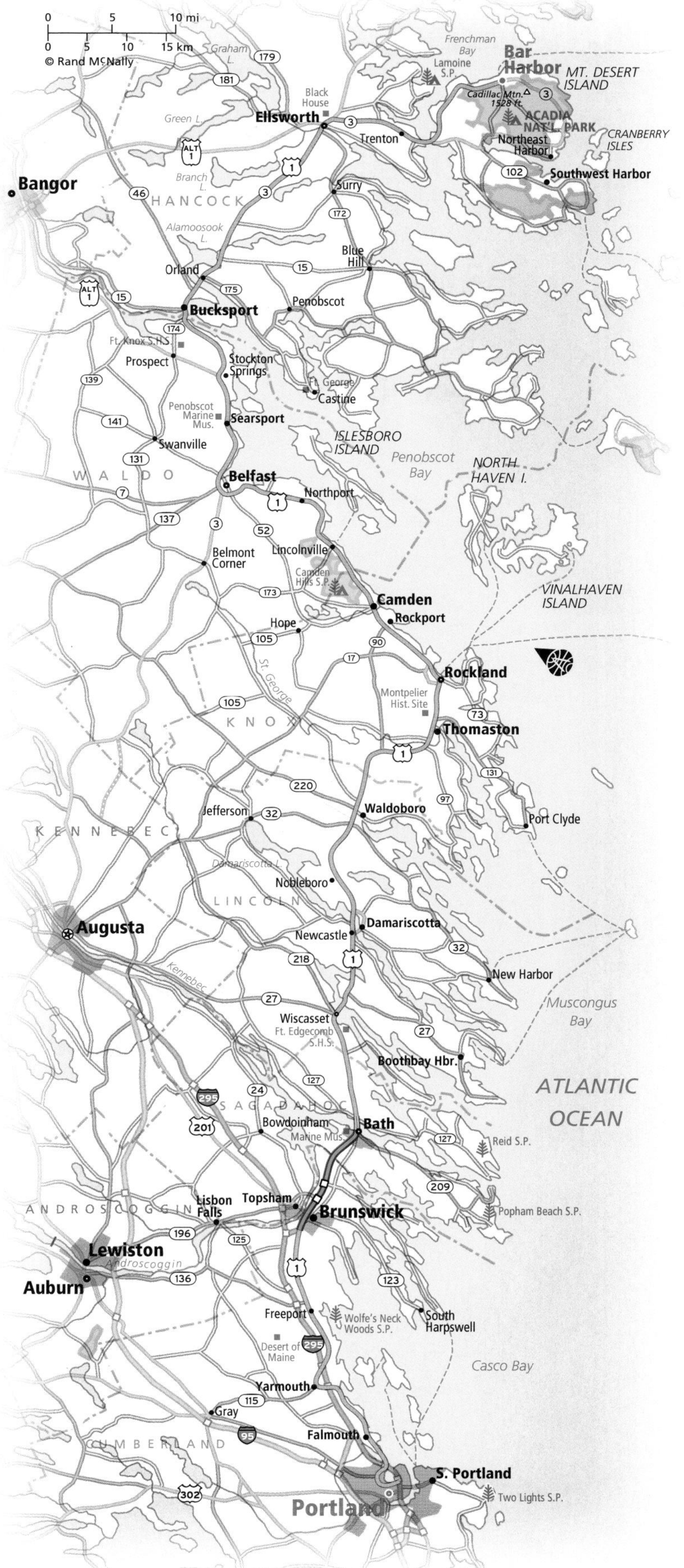

0 5 10 mi
0 5 10 15 km
© Rand McNally
Frenchman Bay
Lamoine S.P.
Bar Harbor
MT. DESERT ISLAND
Cadillac Mtn. 1528 ft.
ACADIA NAT'L. PARK
CRANBERRY ISLES
Northeast Harbor
Southwest Harbor
Graham L.
Black House
Ellsworth
Trenton
Green L.
Branch L.
Bangor
HANCOCK
Surry
Alamoosook L.
Blue Hill
Orland
Bucksport
Penobscot
Ft. Knox S.H.S.
Prospect
Stockton Springs
Ft. George
Castine
Penobscot Marine Mus.
Searsport
ISLESBORO ISLAND
Penobscot Bay
NORTH HAVEN I.
Swanville
WALDO
Belfast
Northport
Lincolnville
Camden Hills S.P.
Belmont Corner
Camden
Rockport
VINALHAVEN ISLAND
Hope
Rockland
St. George
Montpelier Hist. Site
KNOX
Thomaston
Waldoboro
Jefferson
Port Clyde
KENNEBEC
Damariscotta L.
Nobleboro
LINCOLN
Augusta
Newcastle
Damariscotta
Kennebec
New Harbor
Muscongus Bay
Wiscasset
Ft. Edgecomb S.H.S.
Boothbay Hbr.
ATLANTIC OCEAN
SAGADAHOC
Bowdoinham
Bath
Maine Mus.
Reid S.P.
ANDROSCOGGIN
Lisbon Falls
Topsham
Brunswick
Popham Beach S.P.
Lewiston
Androscoggin
Auburn
Freeport
Wolfe's Neck Woods S.P.
South Harpswell
Desert of Maine
Casco Bay
Yarmouth
Gray
Falmouth
CUMBERLAND
S. Portland
Two Lights S.P.
Portland

MARYLAND TO DELAWARE

SEE ATLAS PAGES 96, 97, 50, AND 51.

ROUTE LENGTH – 176 miles or about 4 hours depending on stops

TOURING INFORMATION

This ambling Maryland and Delaware route packs in Atlantic Coast beach towns, farmland, landmark architecture spanning 300 years, state capitals, and Colonial American historic sites.

TAKE A SIDE TRIP

Six miles north of Wilmington experience natural beauty, fine art, and history. These sites are within a 15-mile radius of one another. Brandywine River Museum displays artwork by Howard Pyle, N.C. Wyeth, and Maxfield Parrish. The 175-room, du Pont Family home Winterthur showcases American antiques including Chippendale-style furniture and silver tankards by Paul Revere. Near Longwood Gardens is the Hagley Museum complex preserving du Pont gunpowder mills. Nemours Mansion is the du Pont's 102-room château.

This leisurely, two-state route pleases American history buffs and beach lovers. Colonial American heritage comes to life in small towns' historic architecture and maritime museums. Atlantic Coast beach towns offer sandy solitude, water sports, estuaries, and nature preserves. Antique shop, then dine on the region's succulent crab, wines, and microbrews.

VISTOR INFORMATION

www.visitdelaware.com | 866.284.7483
www.mdisfun.org | 866.639.3526

CAMPING INFORMATION

www.destateparks.com | 877.987.2757
www.dnr.state.md.us | 888.432.2267

Spa Creek, Annapolis, Maryland

Best season to ride:	May through October
Gasoline availability:	Plentiful
About the road:	Two-lane roads skirting ocean shoreline and winding through historic countryside
Insider tip:	Make frequent stops to see historic sites; watch for crowds in June when NASCAR races run in Dover.

RIDE HIGHLIGHTS:

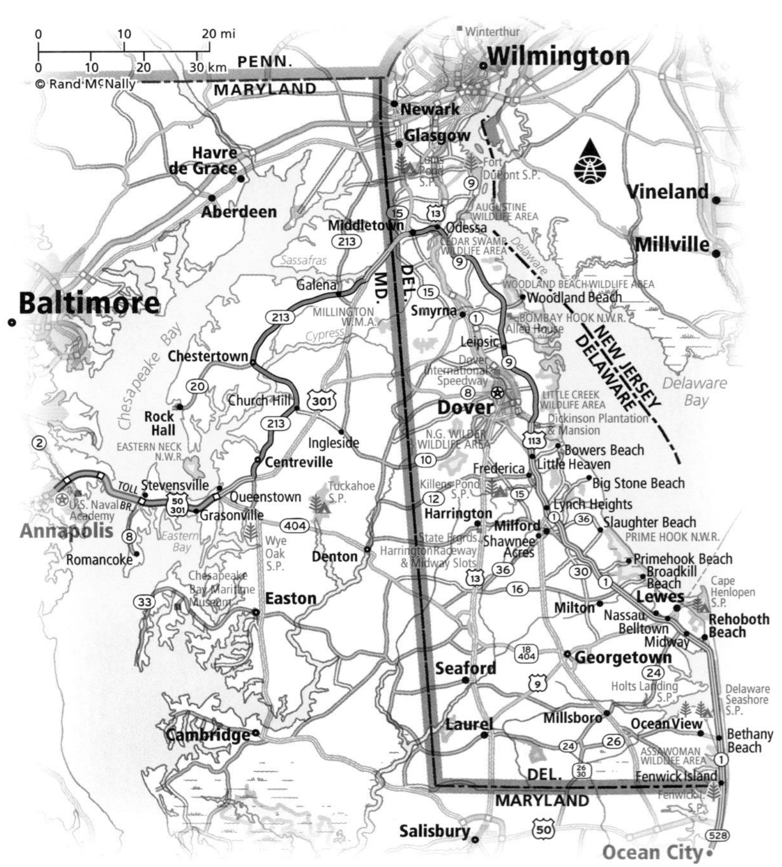
0 10 20 mi
0 10 20 30 km
© Rand McNally
PENN.
MARYLAND
Winterthur
Wilmington
Newark
Glasgow
Havre de Grace
Aberdeen
Vineland
Millville
Middletown
Odessa
Galena
Baltimore
Smyrna
Woodland Beach
Chestertown
Leipsic
Dover
Church Hill
Rock Hall
Ingleside
Centreville
Bowers Beach
Frederica
Little Heaven
Big Stone Beach
Stevensville
Queenstown
Grasonville
Harrington
Milford
Slaughter Beach
Annapolis
Romancoke
Denton
Primehook Beach
Broadkill Beach
Lewes
Easton
Milton
Rehoboth Beach
Georgetown
Seaford
Laurel
Millsboro
Ocean View
Bethany Beach
Cambridge
Fenwick Island
Salisbury
Ocean City
NEW JERSEY
DELAWARE
MD.
DEL.
Chesapeake Bay
Delaware Bay

Crab cake dinner, a Delmar favorite

From Ocean City, Md., head north, passing the 1859 Fenwick Island Lighthouse on the state line. DE 1 links coastal wildlife refuges like Prime Hook and Bombay Hook with Cape Henlopen. Henlopen's 80-foot sand dune is crowned by a WWII watchtower. Lewes Beach survived pirate raids and German U-boat surveillance. Today, ships offshore take visitors to whale watch and sport fish.

Inland, DE 9 North passes state capital Dover, where Delaware representatives were the first to ratify the U.S. Constitution in 1787. Dover International Speedway's NASCAR season revs up in June. The countryside's historic towns include Odessa, prized for its 30 landmark homes.

MD 213 rides through Eastern Shore farmlands and maritime towns settled along Chesapeake Bay tributaries. Chestertown's elegant brick homes look much the same as when George Washington and Thomas Jefferson traveled Kent County. Follow US 301 as it crosses Chesapeake Bay to Maryland's Western Shore and state capital Annapolis. Local bikers fill their tanks and tummies at "gourmet gas station" Kent Island Depot at the Stevensville exit. French family-owned, the station dishes delish eats.

Annapolis's architecture spans three centuries. Capital highlights include the City Dock where African slave Kunta Kinte, author Alex Haley's ancestor, arrived. Patriot sites include homes of Marylanders who signed the Declaration of Independence, early settlement London Town, St. John's College, and the wood-domed State House. At the U.S. Naval Academy, tour the museum and see John Paul Jones' crypt.

ADD ON: Assateague Island

Famous for its herds of wild ponies, Assateague Island stretches for 37 wind-raked miles between the Atlantic Ocean and Maryland's and Virginia's Eastern Shore. Native Americans first populated this 6,000-year old ever-shifting sand island. After European settlers wrested the land away from the Algonquins, they used it as a livestock grazing ground. Legend says the wild ponies swam onto the island from a sinking Spanish galleon, but they most likely were the property of English settlers.

Despite the island's popularity, it remains a valuable ecosystem preserving the habitats of many species. On your way over to the island, stop at the Barrier Island Visitor Center where you can walk through exhibits and see an audiovisual program about the island.

Exploring is encouraged, but the dunes are clearly marked as off limits. Dunes are extremely fragile, and even one person can unwittingly destroy years of natural work. As you ride or hike around the island, you'll not miss the famous ponies. Rangers strongly urge visitors not to go near the ponies or tempt them with food. They may appear friendly and tame, but they are still sometimes-dangerous wild animals.

Two campgrounds, one oceanside and one bayside, invite overnight stays. On your second day, you could consider riding south on the mainland to the Chincoteague National Wildlife Refuge on the other end of the island. There you'll get a chance to observe nature along several longer self-guided nature trails.

MICHIGAN

SEE ATLAS PAGES 102 AND 104.

ROUTE LENGTH – 248 miles or five hours or a leisurely 2-day trip

TOURING INFORMATION

This route follows Lake Michigan's shoreline, beginning as a divided highway in Muskegon before becoming a winding scenic route on its way north.

TAKE A SIDE TRIP

Cruise the Leelanau Peninsula, the pinkie of Michigan's mitten-shaped Lower Peninsula. MI 22 snakes around Leelanau, guiding riders past unforgettable Lake Michigan views, Sleeping Bear Dunes National Lakeshore, and steep hillsides of orchards, vineyards, and vibrant autumn foliage. The fishing village of Leland is worth a stop, as is the ghost town of Glen Haven. The eerily empty cannery town has a small maritime museum and a golden swimming beach.

US 31 north from Muskegon is a favorite with Michigan motorcyclists. The route hugs Lake Michigan's coast, passing unspoiled sand dunes, hardwood forests, orchards and small resort communities until finally reaching the stately Mackinac Bridge. The farther north you travel, the more the route meanders and slows.

VISITOR INFORMATION

www.michigan.org | 888.784.7328

CAMPING INFORMATION

www.midnrreservations.com | 800.447.2757

RIDE HIGHLIGHTS:

Sleeping Bear Sand Dunes, Sleeping Bear Dunes National Park, Empire

Best season to ride:	Summer and autumn
Gasoline availability:	Plentiful
About the road:	Good road conditions
Insider tip:	Watch for "Summer Celebration" festival crowds in Muskegon in late June

"Up North" begins just outside Muskegon. Small hills and gentle curves gradually become more pronounced as the road heads north. You'll leave the four-lane in Ludington, a town famous for its miles of public beaches. Hiking and swimming are popular from Stearns Beach downtown to Ludington State Park, known for its black-and-white-striped lighthouse.

Traffic gradually slows as US 31 winds toward Manistee through hills of hardwood forests and fruit orchards. Enjoy a picnic lunch at Orchard Beach State Park on a bluff overlooking the "Big Lake." To the north, Traverse City boasts Michigan's more famous wineries. Old Mission Peninsula has seven wineries (www.wineriesofoldmission.com) and Leelanau has 15 (www.lpwines.com).

On Leelanau, Shady Lane, Chateaux de Leelanau, and Willow Vineyards are north about eight miles on MI 22. Black Star Farms in Suttons Bay, also on MI 22, makes hard apple cider as well as wine. Black Star apple cider is made in a winemaker's style, which produces a sparkling cider with a true apple flavor.

As the route continues, it twists along the shore between Grand Traverse Bay to the west and several inland lakes (including Elk Lake, Torch Lake, and Lake Charlevoix) to the east. US 31 bridges Round Lake in Charlevoix on its way to Petoskey, where boats and whitecaps dot the deep blue of Little Traverse Bay. Relax in the turn-of-the-century Stafford's Bay View Inn or shop in Gaslight Village.

It's a straight shot north to Mackinaw City, home of Colonial Michilimackinac. The town is a reconstructed 18th-century fur trading village and military outpost once held by the French and the British. Just east of the fort is Old Mackinac Point Lighthouse. A climb up the four-story structure offers unsurpassed views of Michigan's favorite landmark: the Mackinac Bridge.

ADD ON: Stay awhile in Traverse City

Stretch your legs along the main streets in downtown Traverse City. The downtown area is filled with boutiques, coffee shops, and galleries. The tallest building is the 10-story Park Place Hotel. Spectacular views of the West Bay and the area's best sunset can be enjoyed at Beacon's, the hotel's rooftop lounge.

Or head out on a segment of the 18-mile Traverse Area Recreation Trail. The paved trail wends its way through the heart of downtown, along the river and lakefront. Maps are available at any of the three visitors and information centers.

For fine dining, try Stella's Trattoria, which occupies the lower level of Building 50 on the renovated campus of a former state mental institution now known as Grand Traverse Commons. The stark ambience is a perfect foil for the dramatic and delicious food presentations from the Italian kitchen.

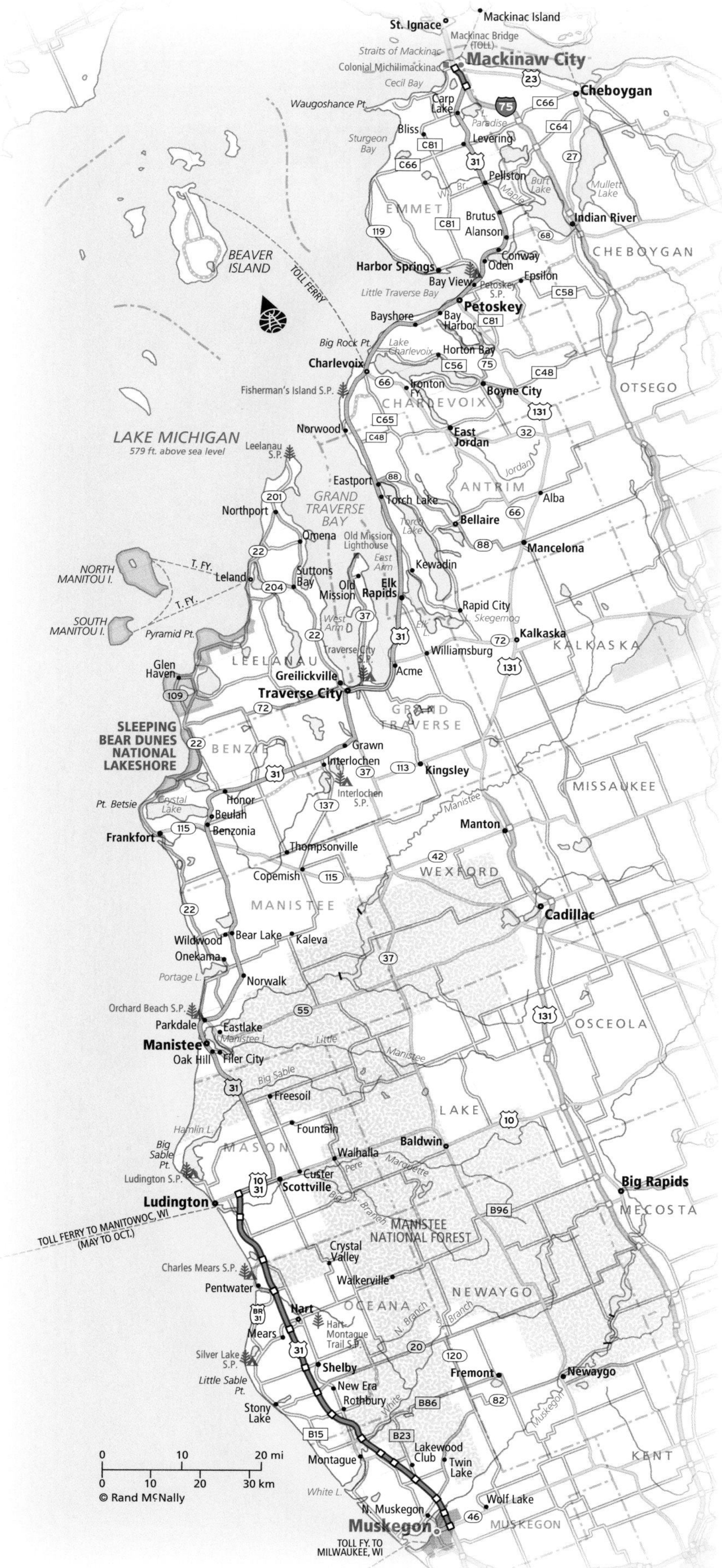

0 10 20 mi
0 10 20 30 km
© Rand McNally

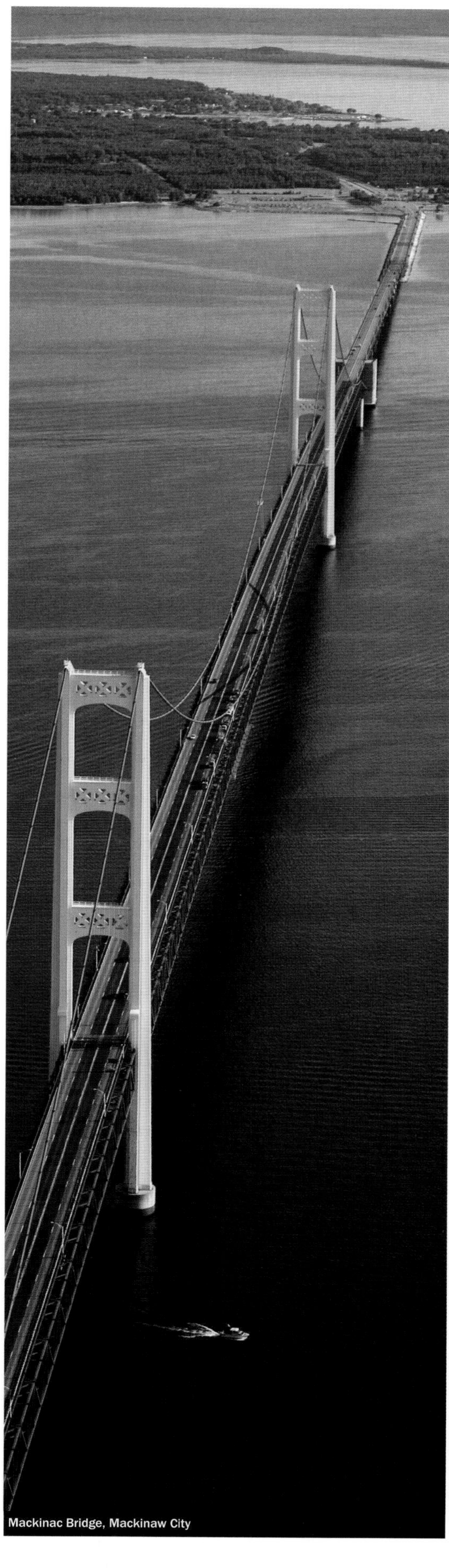

Mackinac Bridge, Mackinaw City

MISSOURI

SEE ATLAS PAGES 118 AND 119.

ROUTE LENGTH – 126 miles or 3 to 4 hours

TOURING INFORMATION
This route travels along MO 68 and MO 19 south through Missouri's Ozark Mountains from St. James to the Arkansas border.

TAKE A SIDE TRIP
Lake of the Ozarks State Park is located on the shores of one of Missouri's largest lakes. The park is most popular with water sports enthusiasts: boaters, fishers, canoeists, and swimmers. Ozark Caverns can be explored via a guided tour. Above ground, 12 hiking trails traverse the state park, meandering through oaks and hickories and ascending towering bluffs.

The ride leaves St. James and the wine region to wend through the rocky bluffs of the Ozarks. The route crosses two of the Ozark National Scenic Riverways, the Current and Jacks Fork Rivers. Be vigilant when riding at dawn or dusk; this region has a large deer population.

VISITOR INFORMATION
www.visitmo.com | 800.877.1234

CAMPING INFORMATION
www.mostateparks.com | 877.422.6766 (information)
877.422.6766 (reservations)

HaHa Tonka Springs, HaHa Tonka Springs State Park, Camdenton

Best season to ride:	Autumn
Gasoline availability:	Plentiful
About the road:	Well-maintained roads wind through national forests
Insider tip:	Great pull over spots; ride crosses three rivers.

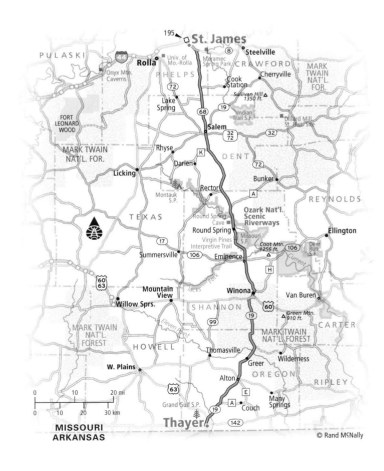

St. James
195
Steelville
PULASKI
Rolla
Univ. of Mo.-Rolla
Meramec Spring Park
CRAWFORD
Cherryville
MARK TWAIN NAT'L. FOR.
Onyx Mtn. Caverns
PHELPS
Cook Station
Sullivan Hill 1350 ft.
Lake Spring
Indian Trail S.F.
Dillard Mill St. Hist. Site
FORT LEONARD WOOD
Salem
MARK TWAIN NAT'L. FOR.
Rhyse
DENT
Darien
Licking
Bunker
Montauk S.P.
Rector
REYNOLDS
TEXAS
Ozark Nat'l. Scenic Riverways
Round Spring Cave
Round Spring
Virgin Pines Interpretive Trail
Missouri S.F.
Ellington
Coot Mtn. 1256 ft.
Deer Run S.F.
Summersville
Eminence
Current
Mountain View
Jacks Fork
Winona
Van Buren
Willow Sprs.
SHANNON
Green Mtn. 910 ft.
CARTER
MARK TWAIN NAT'L. FOREST
Eleven Point
MARK TWAIN NAT'L. FOREST
HOWELL
Thomasville
Wilderness
Greer
W. Plains
Alton
OREGON
RIPLEY
0 10 20 mi
0 10 20 30 km
Grand Gulf S.P.
Couch
Many Springs
Thayer
MISSOURI
ARKANSAS
© Rand McNally

RIDE HIGHLIGHTS:

BOA

Aquatic Trail, Lake of the Ozarks, Kaiser

Missouri's Ozark ride begins in St. James. Gently sloping, vineyard-covered hills characterize the surrounding landscape, which is home to five wineries. St. James Winery, the state's largest, offers tours and tastings of wine and juices.

A few miles south you approach the Mark Twain National Forest where the landscape becomes more rugged with towering bluffs, caves, and hardwood forests. Your motorcycle will rise and fall with the wilderness landscape along twisting, two-lane roads with an overhead canopy of oak, hickory, and pine. All around are the spring-fed rivers and rocky bluffs of America's most ancient mountains.

Tank up and eat in Salem before riding to the Ozark National Scenic Riverways. The park protects the crystal-clear Current and Jacks Fork Rivers. Round Spring Cave is a popular park feature; visitors can view underground formations via lantern tours. The half-mile Virgin Pines Interpretive Trail, two miles south of Round Spring on MO 19, offers a pleasant excuse to park your bike and stretch your legs.

In Greer this route traverses another Ozark river, the Eleven Point. Greer Spring feeds the river from an upper, cliff-side outlet and from a lower source that bubbles up from underground. The combined flows form an impressive waterfall before entering the Eleven Point. You can reach the springs via footpath from the access point on MO 19.

Missouri's Ozark ride ends in Thayer, home of Grand Gulf State Park, Missouri's "Little Grand Canyon." The gorge, nearly a mile long, is crisscrossed with trails. Follow the quarter-mile boardwalk or one of four viewing platforms for canyon views, or descend the stairway from the parking lot to the bottom.

NEVADA TO CALIFORNIA

SEE ATLAS PAGES 131 AND 34.

ROUTE LENGTH – 296 miles or about 6 hours

TOURING INFORMATION

This route makes a large loop from Las Vegas to Death Valley National Park and back following NV 160, CA/NV 372, CA/NV 190, CA/NV 374 and I-95.

TAKE A SIDE TRIP

Lake Mead is a welcome body of water in the middle of Nevada's desert. The lake, an impoundment of the Colorado River, draws boaters, fishers, and swimmers. Hoover Dam is likely the loveliest power generator in the world. The stunning desert surroundings provide another excuse to fill up your bike's gas tank. The Alan Bible Visitors Center is four miles east of Boulder City, at US 93 and Lakeshore Scenic Drive.

The large circuit departs Las Vegas and skims the southern edge of Red Rock Canyon en route to the other-worldly landscape of Death Valley. The route then heads north across the California border before returning to Las Vegas by way of the Nevada Test Site and Mt. Charleston.

VISITOR INFORMATION

www.travelnevada.com | 800.NEVADA.8

CAMPING INFORMATION

http://parks.nv.gov/ | 775.684.2770
(information only, no reservations required for camping in Nevada State Parks)

RIDE HIGHLIGHTS:

Ubehebe Crater, Death Valley National Park, Death Valley, California

Best season to ride:	October through June
Gasoline availability:	Plan ahead
About the road:	Interstate and two-lane road
Insider tip:	Air temperatures can each 115 degrees in the heat of summer.

Las Vegas' neon lights quickly dim once your bike hits CA/NV 160, the road that locals call the Blue Diamond Road.

After just 15 miles, Red Rock National Conservation Area's red sandstone and white limestone color the roadside rocks. The barren landscape continues to Pahrump.

Once across the California border, you enter Death Valley. The extreme environment is easily appreciated on a bike: sand dunes and salt flats; colorful canyons and snow-capped mountains; and, most of the year, intense heat. Pick up brochures at the Visitor Center at Furnace Creek so you don't miss the highlights of the area. Badwater, the lowest spot in the Western Hemisphere, is a brackish pond and salt flat ringed by an interpretive boardwalk. Devil's Golf Course's salt pinnacles poke upward through the earth. And the Borax Museum includes equipment and buildings once used by the Harmony Borax mine.

Stovepipe Wells Village, the first resort in Death Valley, has a motel, restaurant and grocery store for provisions before you return to Nevada. Four miles west of Beatty is Rhyolite, an old gold mining town that went bust in 1919.

You'll come across the barren landscape near Amargosa Valley, which houses the Nevada Test Site nuclear testing ground, before nearing Mt. Charleston, the highest point in southern Nevada. About 45 minutes from Las Vegas' center, the Mt. Charleston Wilderness Area offers a cool, scenic escape.

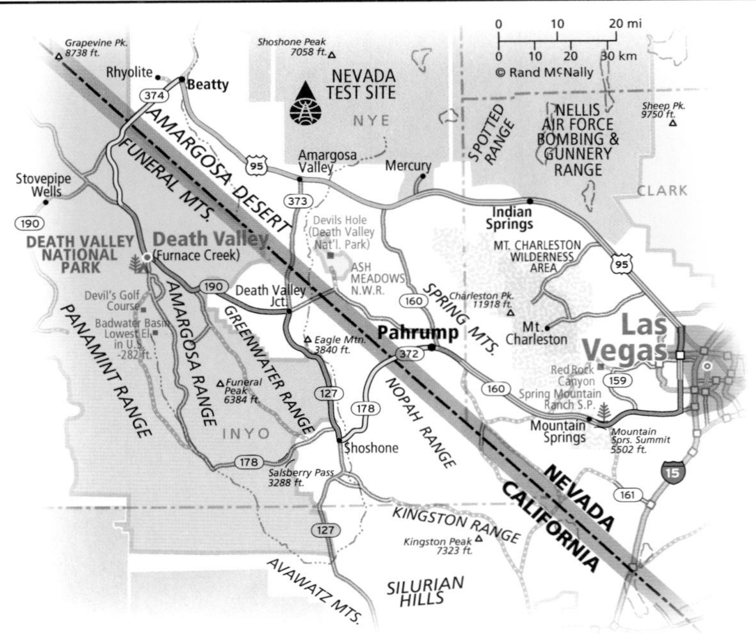
Grapevine Pk. 8738 ft.
Shoshone Peak 7058 ft.
Rhyolite
Beatty
374
NEVADA TEST SITE
NYE
AMARGOSA DESERT
FUNERAL MTS.
95
Amargosa Valley
Mercury
Stovepipe Wells
373
190
DEATH VALLEY NATIONAL PARK
Death Valley (Furnace Creek)
Devils Hole (Death Valley Nat'l. Park)
ASH MEADOWS N.W.R.
Death Valley Jct.
Devil's Golf Course
Badwater Basin Lowest El. in U.S. -282 ft.
PANAMINT RANGE
AMARGOSA RANGE
GREENWATER RANGE
Eagle Mtn. 3840 ft.
Funeral Peak 6384 ft.
127
178
INYO
Shoshone
Salsberry Pass 3288 ft.
NOPAH RANGE
KINGSTON RANGE
Kingston Peak 7323 ft.
AVAWATZ MTS.
SILURIAN HILLS
0 10 20 mi
0 10 20 30 km
© Rand McNally
SPOTTED RANGE
NELLIS AIR FORCE BOMBING & GUNNERY RANGE
Sheep Pk. 9750 ft.
CLARK
Indian Springs
MT. CHARLESTON WILDERNESS AREA
160
SPRING MTS.
Charleston Pk. 11918 ft.
Pahrump
372
Mt. Charleston
Las Vegas
Red Rock Canyon
159
Spring Mountain Ranch S.P.
Mountain Springs
Mountain Sprs. Summit 5502 ft.
15
161
NEVADA
CALIFORNIA

NEWFOUNDLAND AND LABRADOR

SEE ATLAS PAGE 256.

ROUTE LENGTH – 303 miles or about 6 hours depending on stops

TOURING INFORMATION
Trans-Canada Highway 1 joins Newfoundland and Labrador's Viking Trail (NL 430) passing the wild Western Region's plunging fjords, lone lighthouses, windswept barrens, and the Long Range Mountains.

TAKE A SIDE TRIP
NL 430 and NL 431 wind through Gros Morne National Park, inviting a thorough exploration of the UNESCO World Heritage Site that teems with wildlife and natural wonders. The Discovery Centre at Woody Point overlooks Bonne Bay, crowned by an 1897 lighthouse.

Because the Western Region's isolated beauty is a well-kept secret, the inspiring panoramic views and rolling road will be all yours. You'll be welcome at community festivals and lobster boils, and may be invited to a traditional kitchen party brimming with food, song, and laughter in a local's home.

VISITOR INFORMATION
www.pc.gc.ca | 888.773.8888
www.newfoundlandandlabradortourism.com
800.563.6353

CAMPING INFORMATION
www.pccamping.ca | 877.737.3783

RIDE HIGHLIGHTS:

Gros Morne National Park, Rocky Harbour, NL, Canada

Best season to ride:	June through mid-October
Gasoline availability:	Adequate
About the road:	Dramatic dips, drops, curves, some flats; windy, unpredictable weather
Insider tip:	Watch out for moose and logging trucks on the road.

Ascending north from Channel-Port aux Basques, Trans-Canada Highway 1 flanks the Long Range Mountains and passes hamlets established in the 1500s by Basque fishermen. Near Corner Brook, Atlantic salmon battle upstream at Big Falls on the Humber River in summer. At Deer Lake the scenic Viking Trail links Gros Morne National Park to historic Viking archaeological sites along the west coast.

Gros Morne National Park encompasses 697 square miles (1805 sq km) of raw natural beauty. Continue north of Cows Head where the terrain flattens out. To the west of NL 430 is the Gulf of St. Lawrence, where whales breach and occasional icebergs float. To the east lie vast stretches of barren land, bogs, and denuded trees.

Near Port Saunders, Port au Choix National Historic Site preserves 5,000-year-old archaeological findings of an Maritime Archaic Indian village. It's a short ride to Point Riche Lighthouse, perched above seething surf.

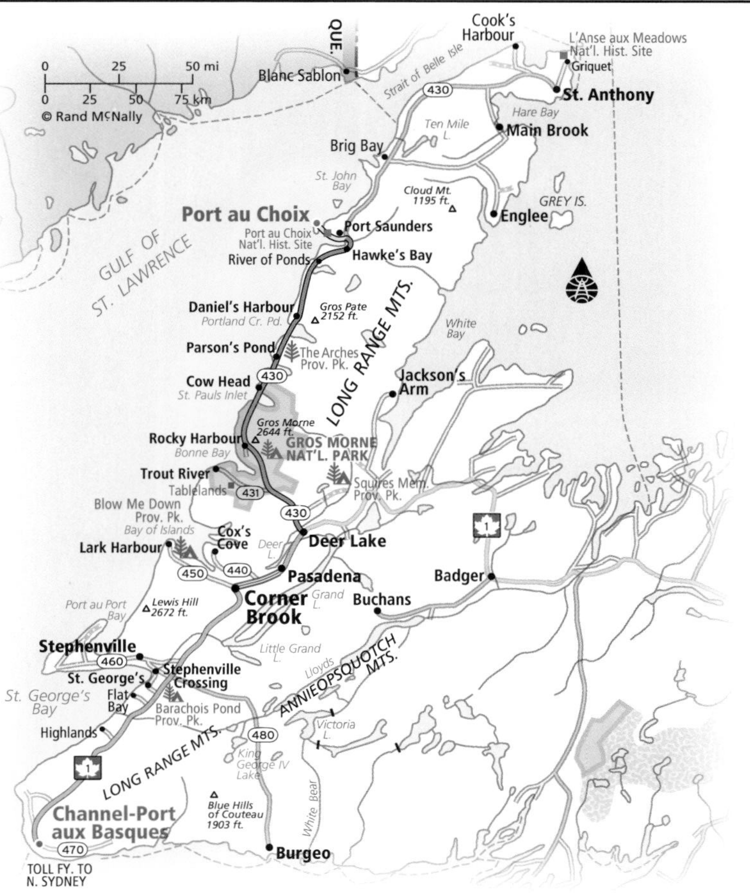
0 25 50 mi
0 25 50 75 km
© Rand McNally
QUE.
Blanc Sablon
Strait of Belle Isle
Cook's Harbour
L'Anse aux Meadows Nat'l. Hist. Site
Griquet
St. Anthony
Hare Bay
Main Brook
Ten Mile L.
Brig Bay
St. John Bay
Cloud Mt. 1195 ft.
GREY IS.
Englee
Port au Choix
Port au Choix Nat'l. Hist. Site
Port Saunders
River of Ponds
Hawke's Bay
GULF OF ST. LAWRENCE
Daniel's Harbour
Portland Cr. Pd.
Gros Pate 2152 ft.
LONG RANGE MTS.
White Bay
Parson's Pond
The Arches Prov. Pk.
Cow Head
St. Pauls Inlet
Jackson's Arm
Gros Morne 2644 ft.
Rocky Harbour
Bonne Bay
GROS MORNE NAT'L. PARK
Trout River
Tablelands
Squires Mem. Prov. Pk.
Blow Me Down Prov. Pk.
Bay of Islands
Cox's Cove
Deer L.
Deer Lake
Lark Harbour
Pasadena
Badger
Port au Port Bay
Lewis Hill 2672 ft.
Corner Brook
Grand L.
Buchans
Stephenville
Little Grand L.
St. George's
Stephenville Crossing
Lloyds
ANNIEOPSQUOTCH MTS.
St. George's Bay
Flat Bay
Barachois Pond Prov. Pk.
Highlands
Victoria L.
LONG RANGE MTS.
King George IV Lake
White Bear
Channel-Port aux Basques
Blue Hills of Couteau 1903 ft.
Burgeo
TOLL FY. TO N. SYDNEY
430
431
440
450
460
470
480
1

NEW MEXICO

SEE ATLAS PAGE 138.

ROUTE LENGTH – 366 miles or 7 hours or a leisurely 2-day trip

TOURING INFORMATION

Follow I-25 and US 285 north from Albuquerque to Espanola, then loop around the Carson National Forest on NM 68, US 64, and US 84 before making the final leg to Jemez Springs.

TAKE A SIDE TRIP

Explore the famed Turquoise Trail National Scenic Byway, NM 14 between Tijeras (east of Albuquerque) and Santa Fe. Visit Tijeras Pueblo, a 600-year-old archaeological site, before reaching the 14-mile Sandia Crest National Scenic Byway, which ascends 10,678-foot Sandia Crest. From the top unfold views of the surrounding landscape. The undulating route continues through desert on its way past several former mining towns: Golden, Madrid and Cerillos, now known for artists' galleries and quirky shops.

This route parallels the Rio Grande and Santa Fe Rivers from Albuquerque to Santa Fe and Taos. After crossing the San Juan mountain range, the tour circles a large portion of the Carson National Forest before heading west to the Jemez Mountains.

VISITOR INFORMATION

www.newmexico.org | 800.733.6396, ext. 0643

CAMPING INFORMATION

www.nmparks.com | 888.667.2757 (information)
877.664.7787 (reservations)

RIDE HIGHLIGHTS:

Red sky over New Mexico

Best season to ride:	All year
Gasoline availability:	Plentiful
About the road:	Well maintained
Insider tip:	Hot weather July to September

New Mexico, the "Land of Enchantment," surrounds riders with mountain vistas. Begin your ride on I-25 in Albuquerque. The four-lane highway quickly leaves suburbia for arid mountain landscapes of pinyon pine and juniper en route to New Mexico's capital, Santa Fe. The 400-year-old town, known for its original Plaza, boasts Southwestern art galleries, boutiques and restaurants.

US 285 and NM 68 follow the Rio Grande to Espanola and into apple country. Soon after, NM 68 rises and weaves between mountain peaks before reaching Taos, where scenes from *Easy Rider* were filmed. Outside of town, 500-year-old Taos Pueblo features adobe residences, handcrafted jewelry, and Native culture exhibits.

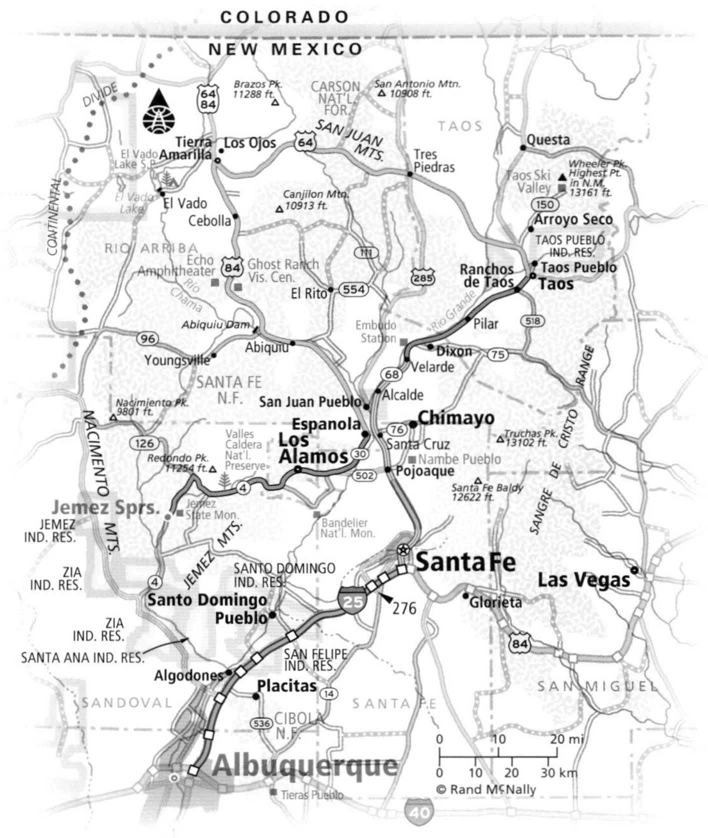
COLORADO
NEW MEXICO
Brazos Pk. 11288 ft.
CARSON NAT'L FOR.
San Antonio Mtn. 10908 ft.
SAN JUAN MTS.
TAOS
Questa
Tierra Amarilla
Los Ojos
Tres Piedras
Wheeler Pk. Highest Pt. in N.M. 13161 ft.
Taos Ski Valley
El Vado Lake S.P.
El Vado
Cebolla
Canjilon Mtn. 10913 ft.
Arroyo Seco
TAOS PUEBLO IND. RES.
Taos Pueblo
Taos
RIO ARRIBA
Echo Amphitheater
Ghost Ranch Vis. Cen.
Ranchos de Taos
El Rito
CONTINENTAL DIVIDE
Abiquiu Dam
Embudo Station
Pilar
Abiquiu
Youngsville
Dixon
Velarde
SANTA FE N.F.
Alcalde
Nacimiento Pk. 9801 ft.
San Juan Pueblo
Espanola
Chimayo
SANGRE DE CRISTO RANGE
Truchas Pk. 13102 ft.
Los Alamos
Santa Cruz
Valles Caldera Nat'l. Preserve
Nambe Pueblo
Redondo Pk. 11254 ft.
Pojoaque
Santa Fe Baldy 12622 ft.
NACIMIENTO MTS.
Jemez Sprs.
Jemez State Mon.
JEMEZ IND. RES.
Bandelier Nat'l. Mon.
Santa Fe
Las Vegas
JEMEZ MTS.
ZIA IND. RES.
SANTO DOMINGO IND. RES.
Santo Domingo Pueblo
276
Glorieta
ZIA IND. RES.
SANTA ANA IND. RES.
SAN FELIPE IND. RES.
Algodones
Placitas
SANDOVAL
SANTA FE
SAN MIGUEL
CIBOLA N.F.
Albuquerque
Tieras Pueblo
0 10 20 mi
0 10 20 30 km
© Rand McNally

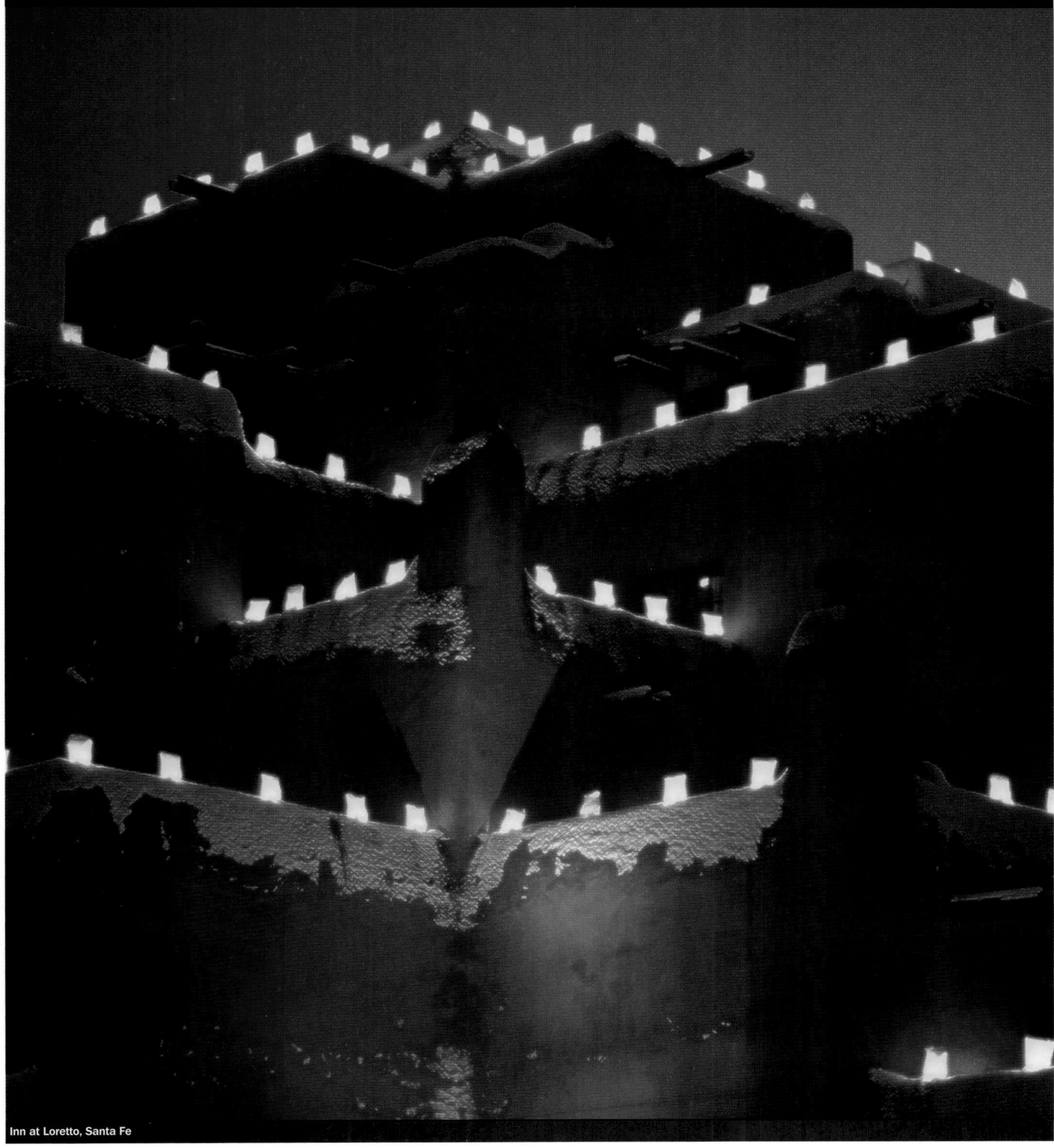

Inn at Loretto, Santa Fe

Cross the Rio Grande Gorge Bridge as you depart Taos on a gentle climb into cool mountain forests. Heron and El Vado Lakes in Los Ojos offer fishing, picnicking, and lakeside hiking. Tierra Wools creates and sells traditional wool products from locally raised sheep. US 84 continues through Georgia O'Keeffe country: desert documented by paintbrush. Just past Abiquiu, a detour along NM 554 climbs to El Rito, a high desert arts community bordering the Carson National Forest.

At Los Alamos, NM 4 winds westward past stark canyons and ponderosa forests. Visit Bandelier National Monument with Native American cliff dwellings, rugged mountain vistas, and hiking trails. Farther west is Valles Caldera National Preserve, a one million-year-old, 25-mile-wide volcanic crater.

As you continue, your route traverses the spine of the Jemez range to Jemez Springs. Local attractions include Jemez State Monument, with ruins of the 17th-century Church of San Jose, and the ever popular Soda Dam, a local swimming hole.

NOVA SCOTIA

SEE ATLAS PAGES 256 AND 257.

ROUTE LENGTH – 268 miles or a two-day trip

TOURING INFORMATION

The Ceilidh and Cabot Trails create the Cape Breton Loop. View windswept seascapes, observe wildlife, and dance jigs with friendly islanders. Tourist season is June through mid-October.

The ride is heart-pounding for its natural beauty as well as roller coaster ups and downs. Near Chéticamp, be alert for strong winds called "suêtes" that average 80 mph. The Breton Loop is not a day trip; plan at least a two-day ride.

TAKE A SIDE TRIP

The 20-mile ride north of Cape Breton Highlands National Park climbs to remote Meat Cove and Cape North, a massive headland plunging 1,465 feet into the ocean, where whales frolic offshore and eagles soar overhead. This is the tip of Nova Scotia and the northernmost point of the Cabot Trail, named after explorer John Cabot who landed here in 1497. Hike through towering maple forests and go whale watching with a local tour operator.

VISITOR INFORMATION

www.novascotia.com | 800.565.0000
www.cbisland.com

CAMPING INFORMATION

www.pccamping.ca | 877.737.3783

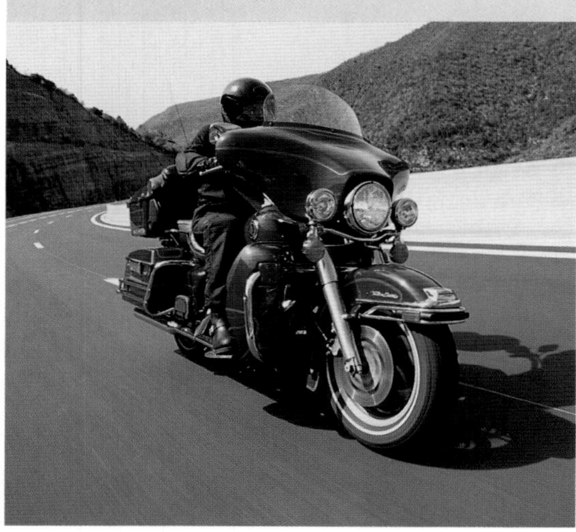

RIDE HIGHLIGHTS:

Beulach Ban Falls, Cape Breton Highlands National Park, near Ingonish Beach

Best season to ride:	September for fall color
Gasoline availability:	Plentiful
About the road:	Rolling, winding, and steep as a roller coaster in some parts
Insider tip:	Watch for wildlife in the highlands.

The Cape Breton Loop traces the perimeter of rugged Cape Breton Island's beaches, forest glens, and foreboding cliffs plunging into the sea. Rich maritime heritage thrives in fishing villages founded by Scottish, Irish, and Acadian French settlers.

The western coast's Ceilidh Trail promises sweeping seascapes and toe-tapping fiddle music. Join locals as they kick up their heels to robust Scottish reels at a ceilidh (pronounced kay-lee), a Celtic square dance. Judique and Mabou are ceilidh performance centers. Pull over at the famous Red Shoe Pub for daily ceilidhs. Glenora Inn & Distillery, North America's first single-malt-whisky distillery, offers tours, swig samples, and afternoon ceilidhs.

At Margaree, renowned for salmon fishing, the Ceilidh Trail joins Cabot Trail. The road winds through farmland entering the northern highlands where it fringes the dramatic cliffs at Chéticamp, the island's Acadian cultural center known for hooked rugs. Scan the sea for spouting whales migrating along the craggy coast battered by briny winds.

A stark northern wilderness, Cape Breton Highlands National Park stretches 365 square miles from the Gulf of St. Lawrence to the Atlantic. Mountains surround the park's plateau center of bogs, windswept barrens, and coniferous forest where eagles nest and moose graze.

On the eastern coast around Ingonish, jagged cliffs encircle natural bays bobbing with fishing boats. Don't miss a lobster supper at a local restaurant. Near Baddeck on the shores of Bras d'Or Lake is the Alexander Graham Bell National Historic Park and museum where the famed inventor's summer home still stands.

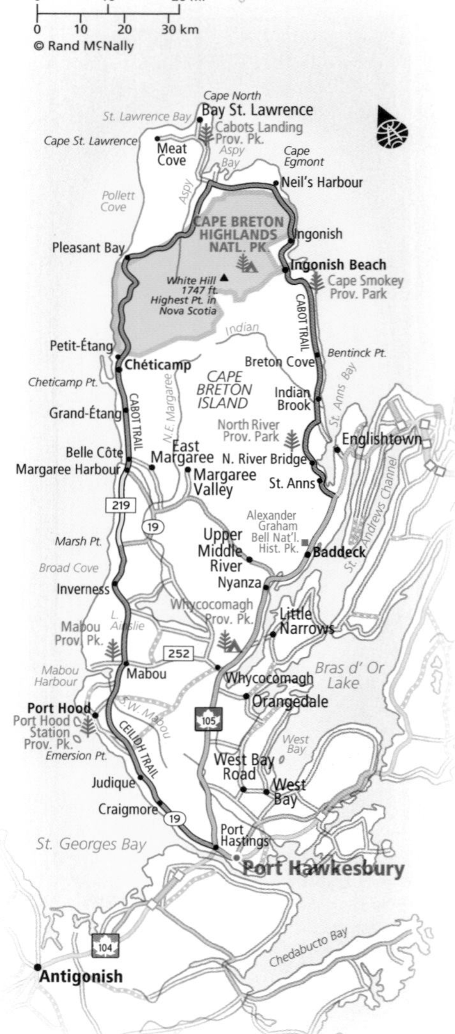
0 10 20 mi
0 10 20 30 km
© Rand McNally
Cape North
Bay St. Lawrence
St. Lawrence Bay
Cabots Landing Prov. Pk.
Cape St. Lawrence
Meat Cove
Aspy Bay
Cape Egmont
Neil's Harbour
Pollett Cove
Aspy
CAPE BRETON HIGHLANDS NATL. PK.
Ingonish
Pleasant Bay
Ingonish Beach
Cape Smokey Prov. Park
White Hill 1747 ft. Highest Pt. in Nova Scotia
CABOT TRAIL
Indian
Petit-Étang
Chéticamp
Bentinck Pt.
Breton Cove
Cheticamp Pt.
CAPE BRETON ISLAND
Indian Brook
St. Anns Bay
Grand-Étang
N.E. Margaree
North River Prov. Park
Englishtown
Belle Côte
East Margaree
N. River Bridge
Margaree Harbour
Margaree Valley
St. Anns
219
19
Alexander Graham Bell Nat'l. Hist. Pk.
Marsh Pt.
Upper Middle River
Baddeck
St. Andrews Channel
Broad Cove
Nyanza
Inverness
Whycocomagh Prov. Pk.
Little Narrows
Mabou Prov. Pk.
L. Ainslie
252
Mabou Harbour
Mabou
Whycocomagh
Bras d' Or Lake
Orangedale
Port Hood
Port Hood Station Prov. Pk.
S.W. Mabou
105
West Bay
Emersion Pt.
CEILIDH TRAIL
West Bay Road
Judique
West Bay
Craigmore
Port Hastings
St. Georges Bay
Port Hawkesbury
104
Chedabucto Bay
Antigonish

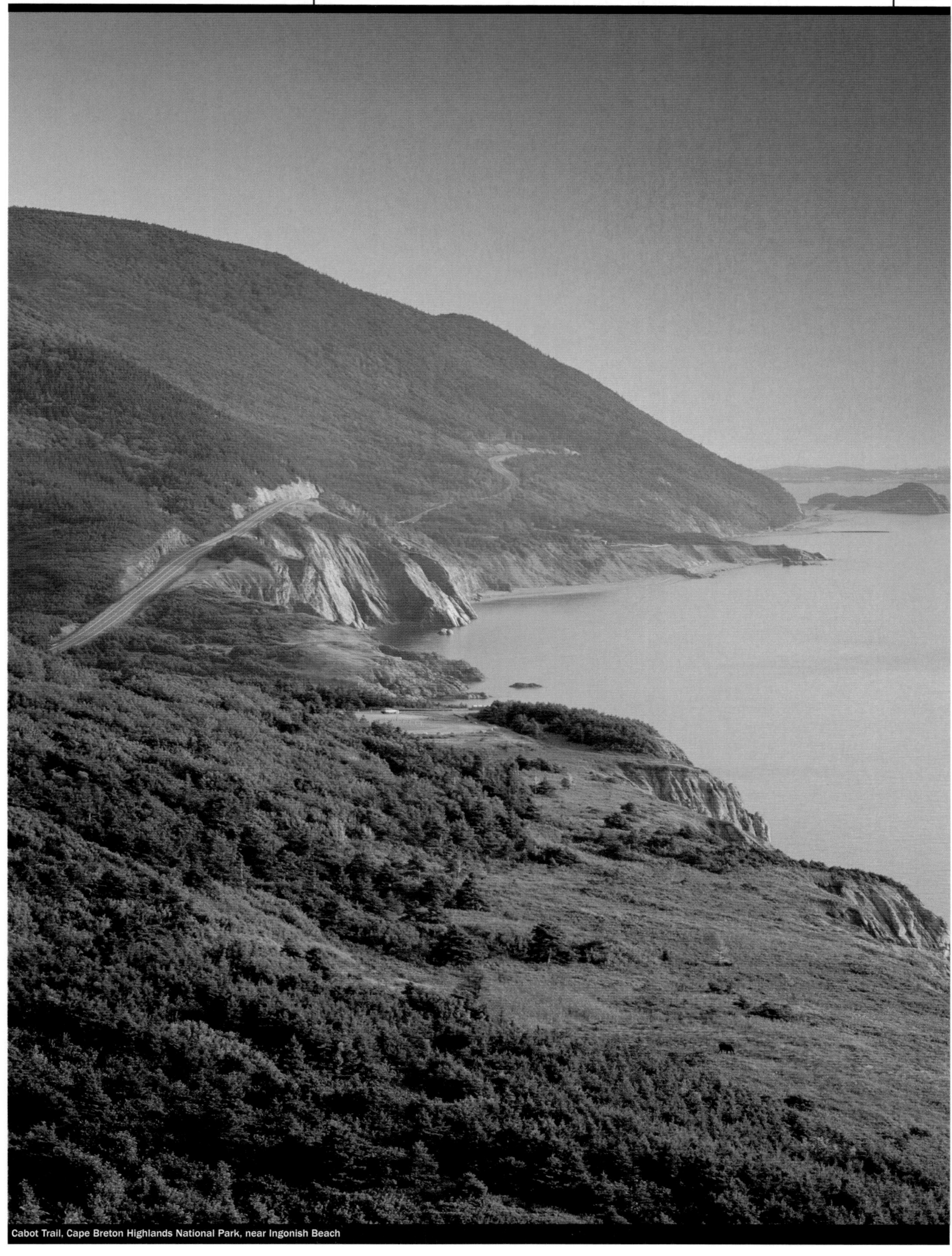

Cabot Trail, Cape Breton Highlands National Park, near Ingonish Beach

OREGON

SEE ATLAS PAGES 170 AND 171.

ROUTE LENGTH – 266 miles or a full day's ride

TOURING INFORMATION
OR 126 heads west from Eugene and intersects coastal US 101 at Florence. The ride then heads south to Coos Bay, and continues east and north via OR 42 and 99.

TAKE A SIDE TRIP
Head 11 miles north of Florence to Sea Lion Caves, one of the most popular stops on the Oregon coast. Descend a 2,000-foot embankment via stairs and elevator to see hundreds of Steller sea lions lounging on rocks and to hear their barks echo through one of the world's largest sea caves.

This coastal Oregon ride forms a loop beginning and ending in Eugene, traversing the wine region of the Willamette Valley, then passing through the Oregon Dunes National Recreation Area along the Pacific Coast Scenic Byway. Return to Eugene via the Coast Ranges and Umpqua Valley.

VISITOR INFORMATION
www.traveloregon.com | 800.547.7842

CAMPING INFORMATION
oregon.gov/OPRD | 800.551.6949 (park info) or
www.reserveamerica.com | 800.452.5687 (reservations)

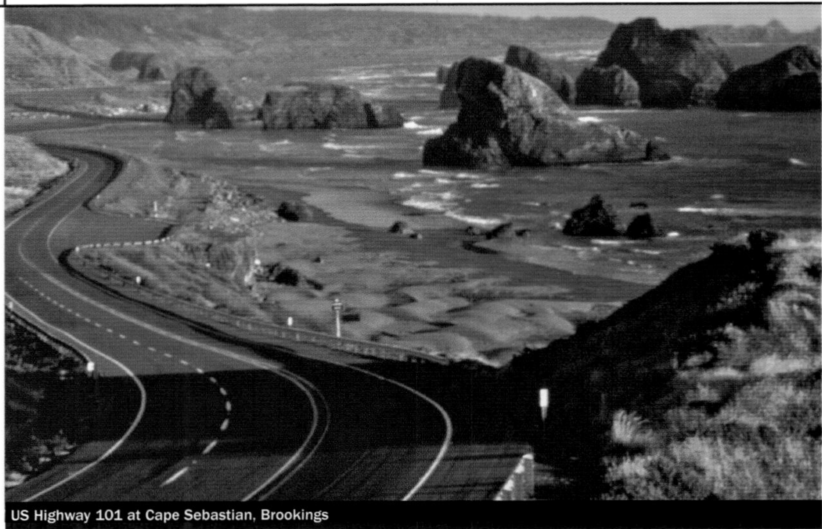

US Highway 101 at Cape Sebastian, Brookings

Best season to ride:	Summer and autumn
Gasoline availability:	Plentiful
About the road:	Well maintained
Insider tip:	Rain in spring and winter causes mud slides and flooding on US 101.

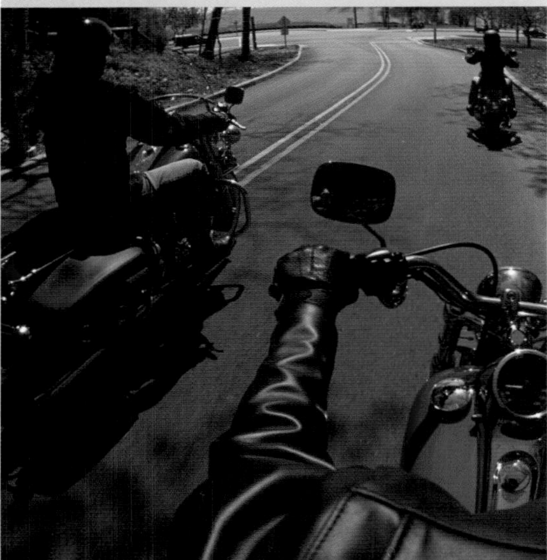

RIDE HIGHLIGHTS:

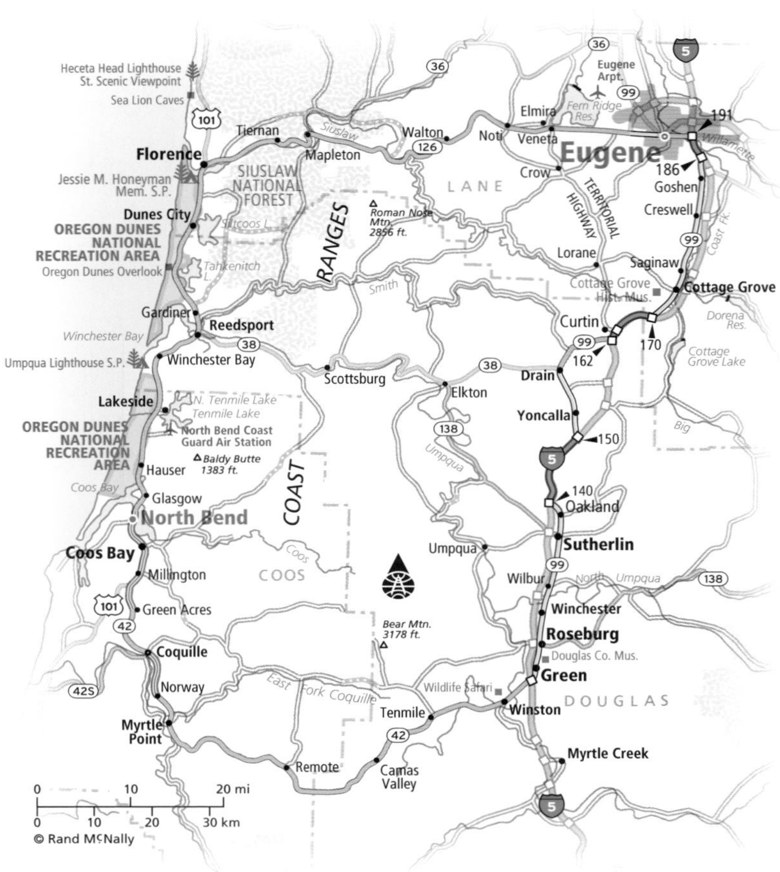

Heceta Head Lighthouse St. Scenic Viewpoint
Sea Lion Caves
101
Tiernan
Florence
Mapleton
Siuslaw
Walton
126
Noti
Elmira
Veneta
Fern Ridge Res.
Eugene Arpt.
36
99
5
191
Eugene
Willamette
Crow
186
Goshen
Creswell
Jessie M. Honeyman Mem. S.P.
SIUSLAW NATIONAL FOREST
LANE
TERRITORIAL HIGHWAY
Dunes City
Siltcoos L.
Roman Nose Mtn. 2856 ft.
RANGES
OREGON DUNES NATIONAL RECREATION AREA
Oregon Dunes Overlook
Tahkenitch L.
Smith
Lorane
Saginaw
Cottage Grove
Cottage Grove Hist. Mus.
Coast Fk.
Dorena Res.
Gardiner
Reedsport
Winchester Bay
38
Umpqua Lighthouse S.P.
Winchester Bay
Curtin
170
162
Cottage Grove Lake
Scottsburg
Elkton
Drain
Lakeside
N. Tenmile Lake
Tenmile Lake
North Bend Coast Guard Air Station
Baldy Butte 1383 ft.
138
Umpqua
Yoncalla
150
Big
OREGON DUNES NATIONAL RECREATION AREA
Hauser
Coos Bay
Glasgow
North Bend
COAST
140
Oakland
Sutherlin
Coos Bay
Millington
COOS
Coos
Umpqua
Wilbur
North Umpqua
Winchester
Green Acres
42
Bear Mtn. 3178 ft.
Roseburg
Douglas Co. Mus.
Coquille
Green
42S
Norway
East Fork Coquille
Wildlife Safari
Winston
DOUGLAS
Tenmile
Myrtle Point
Remote
Camas Valley
Myrtle Creek
0 10 20 mi
0 10 20 30 km
© Rand McNally

Oregon Dunes National Recreation Area, Reedsport

The rolling hills of Oregon's wine country, the snow-capped Cascades, and the breathtaking Oregon Dunes create a magnificent Pacific Northwest ride.

Begin the ride in Eugene, called "The Emerald City" for its rich forests. The town is surrounded by Douglas firs and intersected by the Willamette River. Eugene's suburban landscape soon yields to the rolling vineyards of Oregon's famed Willamette Valley region. Look for more than a dozen wineries along Territorial Highway.

Follow OR 126 to Florence, gateway to the Oregon Dunes National Recreation Area. Florence also is home to one of Oregon's loveliest and most famous lighthouses, Heceta Head. The 56-foot light stands watch north of town atop a 205-foot cliff.

The Pacific Coast Scenic Byway (US 101) leads through 47 miles of graceful sand dunes sculpted by pounding surf and constant winds. The Oregon Dunes Overlook at milepost 201 offers sweeping ocean views and a pleasant hike through Douglas fir and Sitka spruce to the beach. Adjacent to the Dunes, Jessie M. Honeyman Memorial State Park offers a place to camp, boat, canoe, and swim at inland lakes. Enjoy rhododendrons in spring, huckleberries and blackberries in fall. Tucked among the dunes, Winchester Bay and Lakeside provide places to tank up, eat dinner, or find lodging. The dunes end at Coos Bay, Oregon's deepest harbor and a major sport-fishing center.

From Coos Bay, follow OR 42 inland toward Myrtle Point, where a canopy of myrtlewood trees fills the air with a refreshing herbal scent as the route meanders through the Coast Range. The picturesque Umpqua River valley, another wine-producing region, is situated where the Coast and Cascade Ranges meet.

Before returning to Eugene, make time for Cottage Grove and its six covered bridges along a 30-mile loop. Pick up suggested routes from the Visitors Center on West Gibbs Avenue.

SOUTH DAKOTA TO WYOMING

SEE ATLAS PAGES 188 AND 235.

ROUTE LENGTH – About 150 miles or a leisurely day trip

TOURING INFORMATION

This circular ride starts in Deadwood, follows US 385 south to Hill City and on to Custer, on US 16 to Newcastle, Wyo., then US 85 to Four Corners, Wyo. Follow US 85 back into South Dakota to Lead and on to Deadwood.

This road is considered a traveling history book through some of the country's most legendary past. The road features curves, gentle climbs, steep passes, and a four-mile precipitous descent into shadowy Deadwood Gulch that is pure pleasure.

TAKE A SIDE TRIP

Mount Rushmore National Memorial is a symbol of America's democracy. The majestic 60-foot faces of four U.S. presidents gaze over the Black Hills—George Washington, Thomas Jefferson, Theodore Roosevelt, and Abraham Lincoln. For a closer look, walk the half-mile Presidential Trail that loops around the base of the mountain. Learn more at the Lincoln Borglum Museum.

VISITOR INFORMATION

www.travelsd.com | 800.732.5682

CAMPING INFORMATION

www.sdgfp.info/parks | 605.773.3391 (information) or 800.710.2267 (reservations)

Sturgis Rally and races, Sturgis

RIDE HIGHLIGHTS:

Black Hills, Custer

Best season to ride:	Late spring through autumn
Gasoline availability:	Adequate
About the road:	Primarily a well-traveled, two-lane road over hills and valleys
Insider tip:	For a special motorcycle experience, time your trip for the Sturgis Motorcycle Rally, held each year on the first week after the first full weekend in August.

The Dakota Indians called them "Paha Sapa"—the hills that are black—because a thick forest of pine and spruce trees covering the slopes makes them appear black from a distance. This ride will take you through the Black Hills of South Dakota. Buttes, canyons, upthrust granite, stone cliffs, waterfalls, and long stretches of dips and rises will be your riding companions.

Start off in Deadwood, a Gold Rush boomtown chock full of history. Wild Bill Hickok was shot dead in Deadwood while playing poker in a saloon. Wild Bill was holding aces and eights, which to this day is known as "dead man's hand." Hickok and Calamity Jane still rest in Deadwood's Mt. Moriah Cemetery (Boot Hill). Wild Bill might be pleased to know that Deadwood now has sprouted more than 80 casinos since gambling was legalized in 1989.

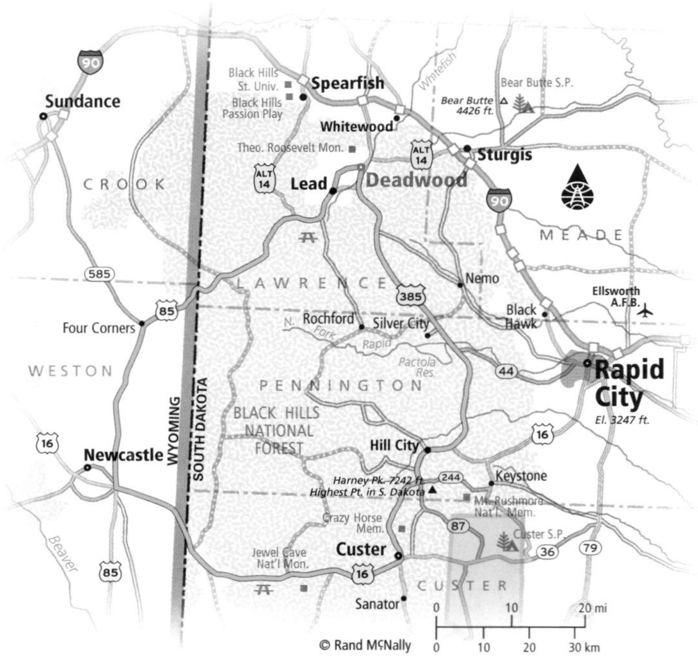

Sundance
Black Hills St. Univ.
Spearfish
Black Hills Passion Play
Whitewood
Bear Butte S.P.
Bear Butte 4426 ft.
Sturgis
Theo. Roosevelt Mon.
C R O O K
Lead
Deadwood
M E A D E
L A W R E N C E
Nemo
Ellsworth A.F.B.
Black Hawk
Four Corners
Rochford
Silver City
Pactola Res.
W E S T O N
Rapid City
El. 3247 ft.
P E N N I N G T O N
BLACK HILLS NATIONAL FOREST
WYOMING
SOUTH DAKOTA
Hill City
Newcastle
Harney Pk. 7242 ft. Highest Pt. in S. Dakota
Keystone
Mt. Rushmore Nat'l. Mem.
Crazy Horse Mem.
Custer S.P.
Jewel Cave Nat'l Mon.
Custer
C U S T E R
Sanator
0 10 20 mi
0 10 20 30 km
© Rand McNally

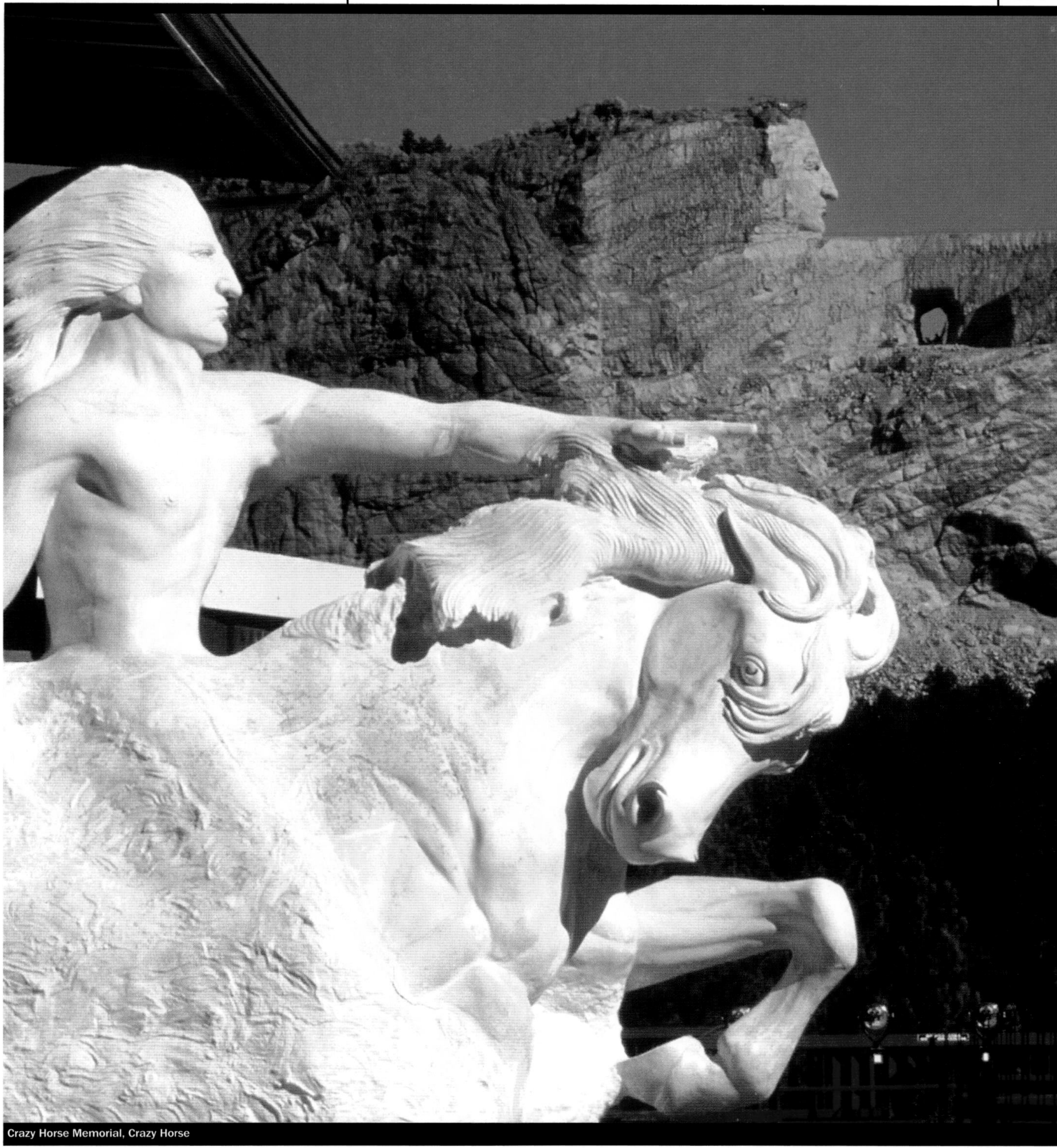

Crazy Horse Memorial, Crazy Horse

Back on the road, travel south through a long stretch of dips and rises offering views of pine-covered hills and exposed peaks that look like white-caps on a storm-tossed sea. Prehistoric creatures once roamed the land-scape of western South Dakota. Though they're long gone, they left behind a fascinating record of fossils and bone. The Black Hills Museum of Natural History in Hill City houses the 65-million-year-old *T. rex* Stan, as well as fossils of ancient sea animals, mammals, and meteorites.

About eight miles farther is the Crazy Horse Memorial, still being chiseled from the mountain. Continue south about six miles to the town of Custer, where George Custer's 1874 expedition found gold nearby and started a rush. The population quickly rose, then plunged as more gold was discovered in the northern Black Hills.

UTAH

SEE ATLAS PAGES 207 AND 209.

ROUTE LENGTH – About 380 miles or two-day drive

TOURING INFORMATION

This two-lane route follows some of Utah's famed state highways—9, 12, 24, and 95—along with US 89, for an unforgettable ride through the legendary West, from Virgin to Blanding. You can see why many of these roads have been identified as scenic byways.

This run is considered a Harley rider's dream—remarkable scenery, lots of exciting challenges, and a chance to see why the West is so well loved.

TAKE A SIDE TRIP

Take US 89 for 17 miles south from Mt. Carmel Junction to Kanab, located just north of the Arizona border. Nestled at the foot of the Vermilion Cliffs, Kanab is Utah's "Little Hollywood," where more than 200 movies and TV shows have been filmed, including *Gunsmoke* and *Planet of the Apes*.

VISITOR INFORMATION

www.travel.utah.gov | 800.200.1160

CAMPING INFORMATION

www.stateparks.utah.gov | 877.887.2757 (information)
800.322.3770 (reservations)

RIDE HIGHLIGHTS:

Orange Hoodoos by Scenic Byway 12, Bryce Canyon

Best season to ride:	Late spring to early fall
Gasoline availability:	Adequate but keep an eye on the fuel gauge and fill up when available.
About the road:	Spectacular twists and turns take you through long desert runs, colorful canyons, rugged and remote areas, steep mountains, lush vegetation, and pleasant small towns
Insider tip:	Traffic around the parks can be busy at peak times. Observe the 35 mph speed limit and do not stop on the road, except at designated pullouts. Be prepared for weather changes.

Saddle up and indulge your inner cowboy with this thrilling ride through the best of the West scenery: slot canyons, creeks, high deserts, rock formations, mountain peaks, and memorable sunsets. There's no question why these are national treasures.

At Springdale, you'll enter Zion National Park, where famed landmarks boast heavenly names—the Great White Throne, Angels Landing, Mountain of Mystery, and Heavenly Court of the Patriarchs. Anasazi and Paiute Indians probably used this canyon as a year-round refuge, as did some of the early white settlers. Among the first homesteaders was Isaac Behunin in 1861, who remarked, "A man can worship God among these great cathedrals, as well as in any manmade church—this is Zion."

Mosey into Hanksville, elevation 4,291 feet, population 196. Founded in 1882 by Ebenezer Hanks and other Mormon settlers along the Fremont River, the town soon became a regional supply depot for local miners, ranchers, and farmers. Hanksville is the last stop before Robbers Roost Canyon, where Butch Cassidy and the Wild Bunch hid out. Two miles north of Hanksville on UT 95, Hollow Mountain Gas & Grocery, a convenience store carved out of a mountain, sells gas, souvenirs, and snacks.

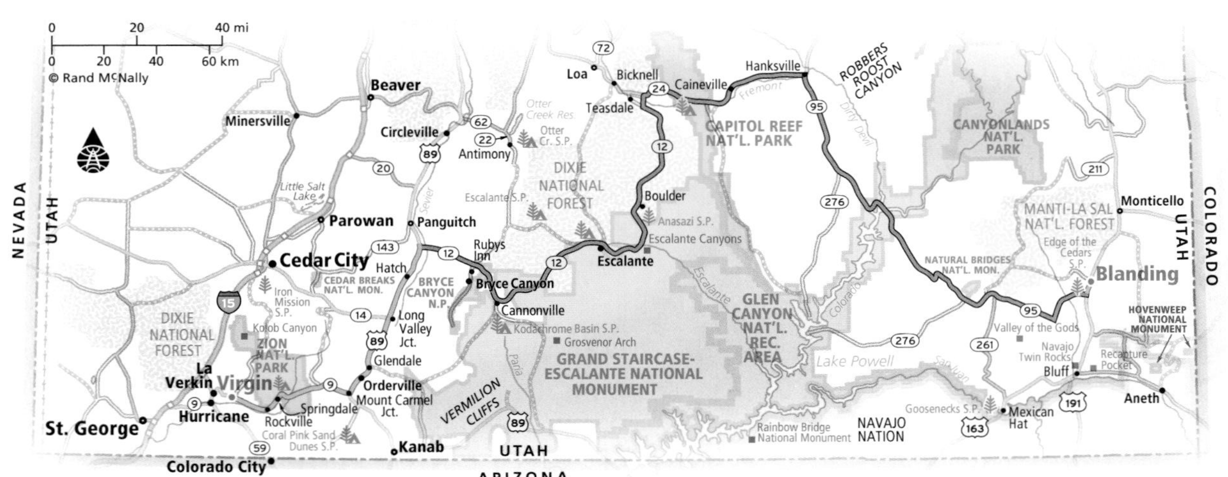
0 20 40 mi
0 20 40 60 km
© Rand McNally
NEVADA
UTAH
COLORADO
ARIZONA
Beaver
Minersville
Circleville
Antimony
Loa
Bicknell
Teasdale
Caineville
Hanksville
ROBBERS ROOST CANYON
CAPITOL REEF NAT'L. PARK
CANYONLANDS NAT'L. PARK
DIXIE NATIONAL FOREST
Boulder
Escalante
Parowan
Panguitch
Cedar City
Hatch
CEDAR BREAKS NAT'L. MON.
BRYCE CANYON N.P.
Bryce Canyon
Cannonville
Long Valley Jct.
Glendale
Orderville
Mount Carmel Jct.
La Verkin
Virgin
ZION NAT'L. PARK
Hurricane
Springdale
Rockville
St. George
Colorado City
Kanab
VERMILION CLIFFS
GRAND STAIRCASE-ESCALANTE NATIONAL MONUMENT
GLEN CANYON NAT'L. REC. AREA
Lake Powell
NAVAJO NATION
MANTI-LA SAL NAT'L. FOREST
Monticello
Blanding
NATURAL BRIDGES NAT'L. MON.
HOVENWEEP NATIONAL MONUMENT
Bluff
Mexican Hat
Aneth
UTAH

VERMONT

SEE ATLAS PAGES 210 AND 211.

ROUTE LENGTH – About 220 miles, a day or longer with stops

TOURING INFORMATION

VT 100, also known as the 43rd Infantry Division Memorial Highway or Grand Army of the Republic Highway, cleaves a path through the center of the Green Mountains and into the heart of Vermont.

This run is considered one of the longest and most scenic rides you're likely to find. From Stamford, VT 100 begins a northward path and bisects the state from the Massachusetts state line to just a bit short of the Canadian border. The two-lane road meanders through pastoral countryside with plenty of reasons to stop—such as the village of Weston (population 600), home to the Vermont Country Store, known as a "purveyor of the practical and hard to find."

TAKE A SIDE TRIP

Ride VT 108 from Stowe to Smugglers Notch, or as the locals call it, "Smuggs." Smugglers Notch Scenic Highway is a tight, twisty mountain pass with 1,000-foot cliffs and large boulders protruding into the narrow passageway.

With no smog and no pollution, the notch is home to many endangered species of plants found nowhere else in Vermont. It also features some of the state's most popular hiking trails, easily accessible from Smugglers Notch State Park.

VISITOR INFORMATION

www.travel-vermont.com | 800.837.6668

CAMPING INFORMATION

www.vtstateparks.com/htm/info.cfm
802.241.3655 (information)
888.409.7579 (reservations)

RIDE HIGHLIGHTS:

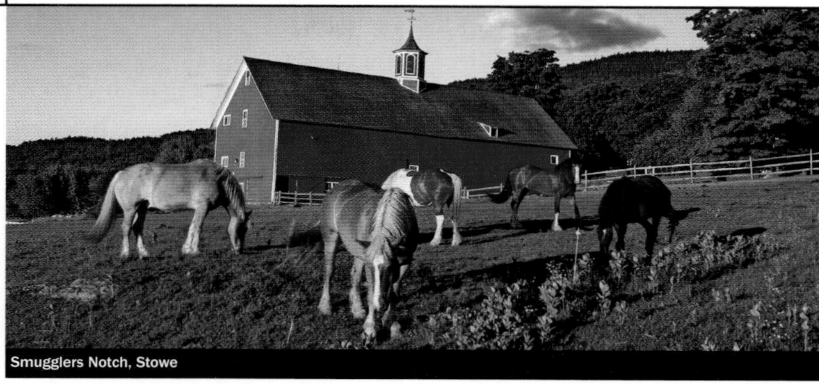

Smugglers Notch, Stowe

Best season to ride:	Fall color is splendid.
Gasoline availability:	Plentiful
About the road:	Both scenic and twisty, low traffic density, good road conditions
Insider tip:	A 40-50 mph speed limit is there for a reason and is enforced. Watch for wildlife.

For a ride that is both exhilarating and relaxing, this twisty, turning road has all the ingredients for motorcycle motoring memories. Long climbs up forested hills, rushing descents into scenic valleys, boulder-filled waterways, white steepled churches, family farms with weathered red barns, small towns with friendly folks, and only three stop lights on the whole route make this a joy. Be on the lookout for a church supper.

So many places deserve a stop that it's hard to pass them by. Near Stowe, in Waterbury, visit Ben & Jerry's Ice Cream Factory, the number one tourist attraction in the state. The factory offers a tour with samples, playground, souvenir shop, ice cream store, and a "graveyard" of retired flavors that seemed like a good idea but bombed with ice cream lovers.

Watch for Gold Brook Road as you enter Stowe. Emily's Bridge is a few miles up the road on the left. Built in 1844, Emily's Bridge has a serene beauty by day. At night the 50-foot-long covered bridge takes on a dramatically spooky appearance. Legend has it that the bridge has been haunted ever since Emily took her life there after losing her one true love. On windy nights it's said that you can hear her crying on the bridge.

With a population of only 4,400, Stowe has a surprising 70 shops, 50 restaurants, bungee trampolines, alpine slide, the Trapp Family Lodge (the singing family in *The Sound of Music*), and a gondola ride to the top of Vermont's tallest peak—4,393-foot Mt. Mansfield.

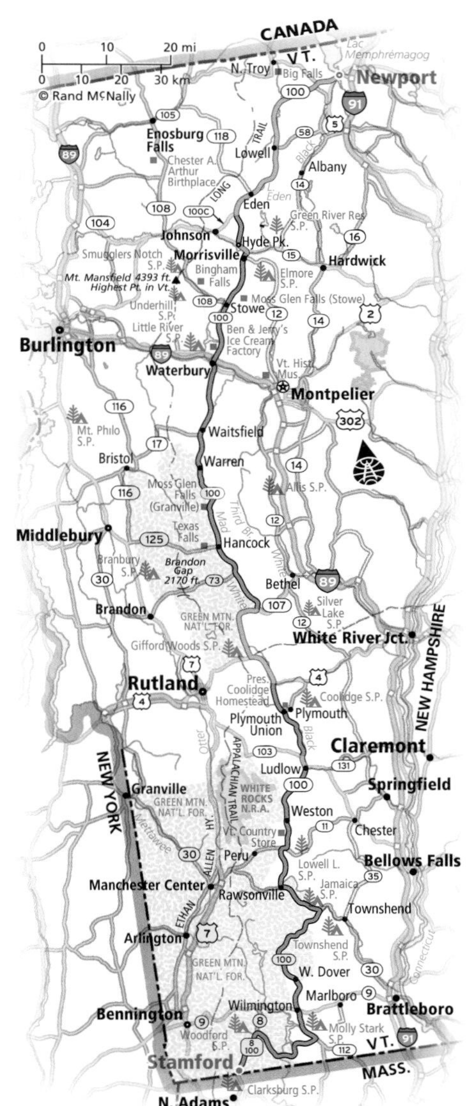
CANADA
VT.
0 10 20 mi
0 10 20 30 km
© Rand McNally
N. Troy
Newport
Enosburg Falls
Lowell
Albany
Eden
Johnson
Hyde Pk.
Morrisville
Hardwick
Smugglers Notch S.P.
Mt. Mansfield 4393 ft. Highest Pt. in Vt.
Stowe
Burlington
Waterbury
Montpelier
Waitsfield
Warren
Bristol
Middlebury
Hancock
Brandon Gap 2170 ft.
Bethel
Brandon
White River Jct.
NEW HAMPSHIRE
Rutland
Plymouth
Claremont
NEW YORK
Ludlow
Springfield
Granville
Weston
Chester
Bellows Falls
Manchester Center
Rawsonville
Townshend
Arlington
W. Dover
Marlboro
Brattleboro
Bennington
Wilmington
Stamford
MASS.
N. Adams

VIRGINIA

SEE ATLAS PAGES 212 AND 214.

ROUTE LENGTH – 106 miles or 4-5 hours

TOURING INFORMATION
Shenandoah's Skyline Drive (US 340) travels the heart of Shenandoah National Park at 35 mph. It has 75 scenic turn-outs. It's slow, but the view is worth the pace.

TAKE A SIDE TRIP
Take your time along the Blue Ridge Parkway, the southern extension of Skyline Drive that leads to the Great Smoky Mountains National Park. Drive the above route in reverse order, beginning in Front Royal. After a brief but steep ascent just south of Rockfish Gap, the Blue Ridge Parkway rises and falls gracefully over some of the most spectacular mountain scenery in the Mid-Atlantic states.

Skyline Drive follows the spine of the Blue Ridge Mountains. The route takes in views of the fertile Shenandoah Valley to the west and the Blue Ridge foothills to the east. Dickey Ridge Visitor Center (Mile 4.6) and Byrd Visitor Center (Mile 51) both offer informational displays and maps.

Skyline Drive bursts into color in the spring as it wends through Shenandoah National Park. In autumn, the woods glow red and yellow, the hues of the Blue Ridge Mountains in the distance. Around every bend, over every peak, there's another camera-ready view along this route.

VISITOR INFORMATION
www.visitshenandoah.com | 800.778.2851

CAMPING INFORMATION
www.nps.gov/shen/planyourvisit/campgrounds.htm
800.365.2267

RIDE HIGHLIGHTS:

Skyline Drive and the Shenandoah Valley from Stony Man Mountain, Luray

Best season to ride:	Spring and autumn.
Gasoline availability:	Plan ahead
About the road:	Winding with many pull offs
Insider tip:	$10 fee to enter the park, which is valid for one week; lots of automobile traffic. Watch for cars as well as deer, bear, wolves, and snakes.

Begin your northerly tour of US 340 in Rockfish Gap, the southern national park entrance. (The town's Information Center has local information and brochures.) You'll be tempted to stop at dozens of scenic turn-outs. Make time for Big Run Overlook (Mile 81), with a sweeping view of the Blue Ridge Mountains. Or park your bike and stretch your legs at Swift Run Gap (Mile 65.5), one of a dozen points where the Appalachian Trail crosses Skyline Drive. A more strenuous trail departs from Bearfence Mountain Parking. The one-mile circuit leads over a rock scramble to a rare 360-degree vista.

Near the midpoint of Skyline Drive are lodging choices for riders who want to prolong their stay: Lewis Mountain Cabins; Big Meadows Lodge, a restored 1939 inn; and Skyland Resort, set at Skyline Drive's highest point, with cabins, rooms, and access to riding stables.

As Skyline Drive continues north, it rises and twists past well-known rock formations, the Pinnacles and Stony Man Peak, as it rounds Hazel Mountain. Tunnel Parking Overlook (Mile 33) offers a preview of 600-foot-long Mary's Rock Tunnel before you experience it first-hand. Just north of here, Hogback Overlook (Mile 21) takes in views of the Shenandoah River snaking through the Shenandoah Valley.

Skyline Drive concludes in Front Royal, a canoeing and kayaking hub in this region. Outfitters are located in the Page Valley, just south of town on the South Fork of the Shenandoah River. Pick up directions and brochures at the Front Royal Visitor's Center.

0 5 10 mi
0 5 10 15 km
© Rand McNally
Middletown
66
Riverton
Front Royal
Happy Creek
55
Linden
Manassas Gap 950 ft.
81
Dickey Ridge Vis. Cen.
Chester Gap
Huntly
522
Elizabeth Furnace
Limeton
Browntown
Mt. Marshall 3368 ft.
Shenandoah R. "Andy Guest" S.P.
Bentonville
Hogback Overlook
RAPPAHANNOCK
Compton
678
Mathews Arm
211
340
Sperryville
Camp Roosevelt
522
Mary's Rock Tunnel
Hazel Mtn. 2880 ft.
231
675
Pinnacles 3350 ft.
Luray
Nethers
Stony Man 4011 ft.
Old Rag Mtn. 3268 ft.
Hamburg
Skyland
Etlan
211
PAGE
Ida
SKYLINE DR.
MADISON
Syria
New Market
Alma
Stanley
Hawksbill 4051 ft.
Big Meadows
Byrd Vis. Cen.
SHENANDOAH NAT'L. PARK
Graves Mill
Jollett
662
Bearfence Mtn. Parking
Lewis Mtn.
Shenandoah
Fletcher
Verbena
Furnace
Newtown
667
Elkton
ROCKINGHAM
Lydia
230
33
Stanardsville
Swift Run Gap 2365 ft.
Harrisonburg
High Top 3855 ft.
McGaheysville
Flat Top 3050 ft.
GREENE
810
Nortonsville
Big Run Overlook
Loft Mtn.
659
Port Republic
664
Browns Cove
Grottoes
256
Mountfair
Harriston
810
Doylesville
APPALACHIAN TRAIL
BLUE RIDGE MTS.
Charlottesville
81
AUGUSTA
ALBEMARLE
Crimora
Yancey Mills
Hermitage
Dooms
64
254
Waynesboro
Afton

WEST VIRGINIA

SEE ATLAS PAGE 226.

ROUTE LENGTH – 120 winding miles or one-day trip with plenty of stops

TOURING INFORMATION

The Midland Trail ride begins in the state capital of Charleston and follows US 60 through some of the most rugged terrain in West Virginia. The ride passes through both the Kanawha River Valley and the plateau high above.

TAKE A SIDE TRIP

Ride through parts of the New River Gorge National River area honoring one of the oldest rivers in the world and one of the few on Earth that flows north. The area is a mecca for rafting. Once a year, on the third Saturday of October, the New River Gorge Bridge is closed to vehicular traffic and open for pedestrians. Watch base jumpers and bungeed folks leap off the side of the longest arch bridge in North America.

A National Scenic Byway, the Midland Trail along US 60 was originally carved into the mountains by buffalo and Native Americans. Prior to 1988, the Midland Trail was heavily traveled, particularly by commercial vehicles. Traffic was significantly reduced in 1988 when the final touches of I-64 were completed. Now the trail is mostly for those who want to get away from interstates and enjoy an outstanding ride.

VISITOR INFORMATION

www.wvtourism.com | 800.225.5982

CAMPING INFORMATION

www.wvstateparks.com | 800.225.5982

New River Gorge Bridge, near Fayetteville

Best season to ride:	Late spring through late autumn
Gasoline availability:	Plentiful
About the road:	Generally good shape; road has segments where ride can get athletic with switchbacks and twisties.
Insider tip:	Watch for wildlife.

Travel the Midland Trail and enter a land of challenging white-water rafting, Civil War history, stunning scenery, and small towns full of country charm. The byway will carry you over hills and through valleys, and finally out into rolling farmland settled during the colonial era.

The Great Kanawha River provides a wonderful backdrop for travel as it hugs US 60 from its headwaters at Gauley Bridge to south of Charleston. Beginning just west of Kanawha Falls and continuing to Cathedral Falls near Gauley Bridge, there are more than a dozen seasonal waterfalls in fewer than five miles, all visible from the trail.

Hawks Nest State Park sprawls across the top of Gauley Mountain to the base of New River Gorge. Called the "Grand Canyon of the East," New River Gorge is best seen from Hawks Nest Park in Ansted. Take a short walk at Hawks Nest Roadside Park to the overlook or stop at the lodge and enjoy dinner while perched above the gorge.

East of Hico, the Midland Trail curves through top-notch scenery as it crosses the highest point on the trail—Big Sewell Mountain at 3,170 feet. At Gauley Mountain, the twisty turns near Chimney Corner are so sharp that travelers joke you can see your taillights in the rear view mirror as you round the bends.

Since the 18th century, the wealthy have flocked to White Sulphur Springs for the legendary curative powers of the area's springs. Visit The Greenbrier, a five-star resort and home of the nation's oldest golf course. To the east, mountains melt into Greenbrier Valley's rolling pastures, covered bridge, beautiful farms, and white steepled churches. The trip ends 72 miles from the Blue Ridge Parkway.

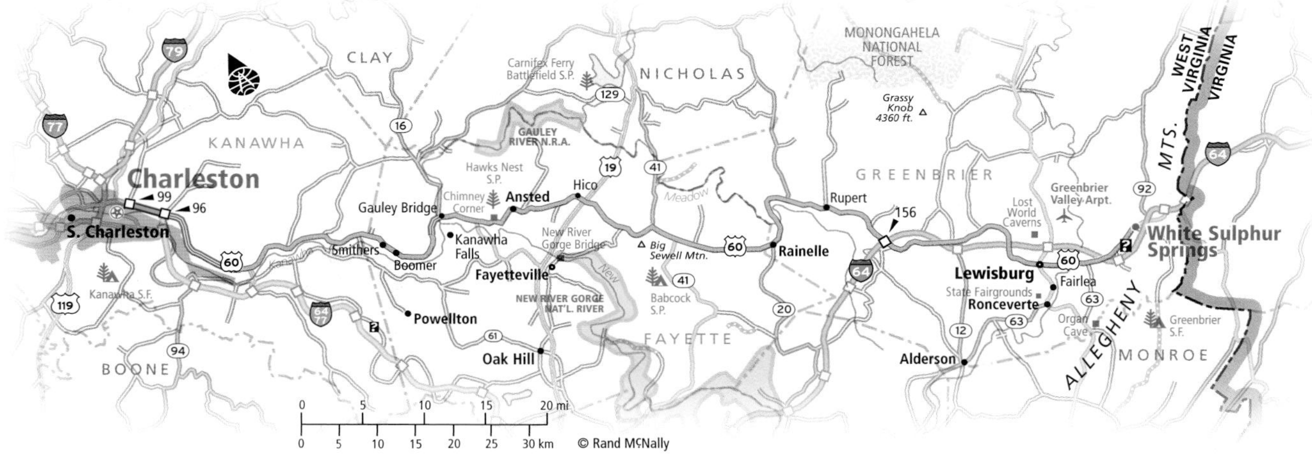
CLAY
KANAWHA
Charleston
S. Charleston
99
96
60
Kanawha S.F.
119
94
BOONE
79
77
16
Carnifex Ferry Battlefield S.P.
129
NICHOLAS
GAULEY RIVER N.R.A.
Hawks Nest S.P.
Gauley Bridge
Chimney Corner
Ansted
Hico
19
41
Meadow
Smithers
Boomer
Kanawha Falls
New River Gorge Bridge
Fayetteville
Powellton
61
Oak Hill
NEW RIVER GORGE NAT'L. RIVER
Big Sewell Mtn.
Babcock S.P.
FAYETTE
Rainelle
MONONGAHELA NATIONAL FOREST
Grassy Knob 4360 ft.
GREENBRIER
Rupert
156
64
20
Lost World Caverns
Greenbrier Valley Arpt.
92
Lewisburg
State Fairgrounds
Ronceverte
12
63
Alderson
Fairlea
Organ Cave
White Sulphur Springs
ALLEGHENY MTS.
Greenbrier S.F.
MONROE
WEST VIRGINIA
VIRGINIA
0 5 10 15 20 mi
0 5 10 15 20 25 30 km
© Rand McNally

WISCONSIN TO MINNESOTA

SEE ATLAS PAGES 228, 230, AND 111.

ROUTE LENGTH – About 200 miles or a leisurely day trip

TOURING INFORMATION
The route rambles south along Wisconsin's western border, following WI 35 along the Mississippi River. The symbol of a river pilot's wheel identifies the Great River Road on the road and on state map pages.

The Great River Road, which runs from Minnesota to Louisiana, is considered one of the most scenic drives in America. It's an excellent way to see the Mississippi River—known as the nation's first interstate—from the seat of your Harley. In Wisconsin, the road is nestled between the mighty river on one side and towering bluffs on the other, with short jaunts through rolling farmland and forested valleys.

TAKE A SIDE TRIP
Ride to Cashton, 30 miles east of La Crosse on WI 33, through farm country and over bluff tops. Warm and welcoming, Cashton is home to the largest Amish community in Wisconsin. See cheese being made at Old Country Cheese, visit Cashton Park, and shop at Cashton Mercantile, where products are locally handcrafted. Signs along the road direct riders to Amish homesteads selling quilts, furniture, and other handcrafted items.

VISITOR INFORMATION
www.travelwisconsin.com | 800.432.8747

CAMPING INFORMATION
www.dnr.state.wi.us/org/land/parks/ | 608.266.2181

RIDE HIGHLIGHTS:

Sunset on the Mississippi River, La Crosse

Best season to ride:	Late spring through late autumn
Gasoline availability:	Plentiful
About the road:	Primarily a well-traveled, two-lane road with peaks and valleys
Insider tip:	Be aware of slow-moving farm vehicles and heed deer-crossing signs.

A ride on Wisconsin's segment of the Great River Road—designated a National Scenic Byway—is a trip back in time along the magnificent Mississippi River. Explore museums, historic sites, river towns, and more than 30 historical markers that recount the early days along "Old Man River."

Mother Nature's handiwork abounds. For a view of the surrounding countryside, ascend Grandad Bluff, a 600-foot-high bluff and city park overlooking the city of La Crosse and the Mississippi River Valley. On a clear day, you can see three states—Wisconsin, Minnesota, and Iowa. In autumn, the bluffs are ablaze in gold and red.

The first weekend of May is a great time to ride, shop, and enjoy church lunches. A trail of colored ribbons identifies participants in the 100-Mile Garage Sale along WI 35 from Alma through Bay City across the Mississippi and south on US 61 from Red Wing through Winona, Minn. Bargain hunters can start anywhere along the route beginning about 7 a.m., with closing time around 5 p.m. for the three-day sale.

Built in 1848 by Swiss settlers, the city of Alma is two streets wide yet stretches along the Mississippi for seven miles. One of the best spots to watch barges, tows, and other boats as they move through a lock: Alma's Lock and Dam No. 4. Eagles are year-round residents.

Nelson is famous for its ice cream parlor and cheese factory, as well as for the Tiffany Wildlife Area, a 12,740-acre wildlife refuge that's a prime breeding and migratory bird habitat. Hang gliders launch from the 500-foot craggy promontories overlooking the town.

Recreational opportunities await around each bend and scenic pullovers are abundant. Allow time to park your bike and take a hike. The views are worth it.

ADD ON: Cross over to Minnesota

From La Crosse continue on the Great River Road into Minnesota to Winona, where the imprint of immigrant settlers is well documented. The Winona County Historical Society Museum has three levels of exhibits, including a full-size reconstructed Main Street from the early 20th century. The Watkins Heritage Museum and Store offers a brief look at the history of the home-remedy giant while the Polish Cultural Institute honors the contributions made by Polish laborers.

Continuing north, US 61 curves along flat lowland, then stretches east toward the river into Wabasha. The confluence of the Mississippi and Chippewa rivers is located at Wabasha, and the force from the two rivers is so great that the water never freezes. That's lucky for the bald eagles that are able to overwinter—luckier still for residents as eagle sightings are part of everyday life. The experts at the National Eagle Center report that eagles are partial to cottonwood trees when building a nest. Tree height and branch strength are important because eagles return to the same nest, repairing and enlarging it, year after year.

Visitors usually start their tour of the Center on the back porch for an opportunity to stand within reach of a bald eagle. There are three that live at the center. A deck extends over the Mississippi for viewing eagles in their natural environment—fishing, nesting, and on occasion, since eagles mate for life, celebrating the other's return with an aerial pas de deux.

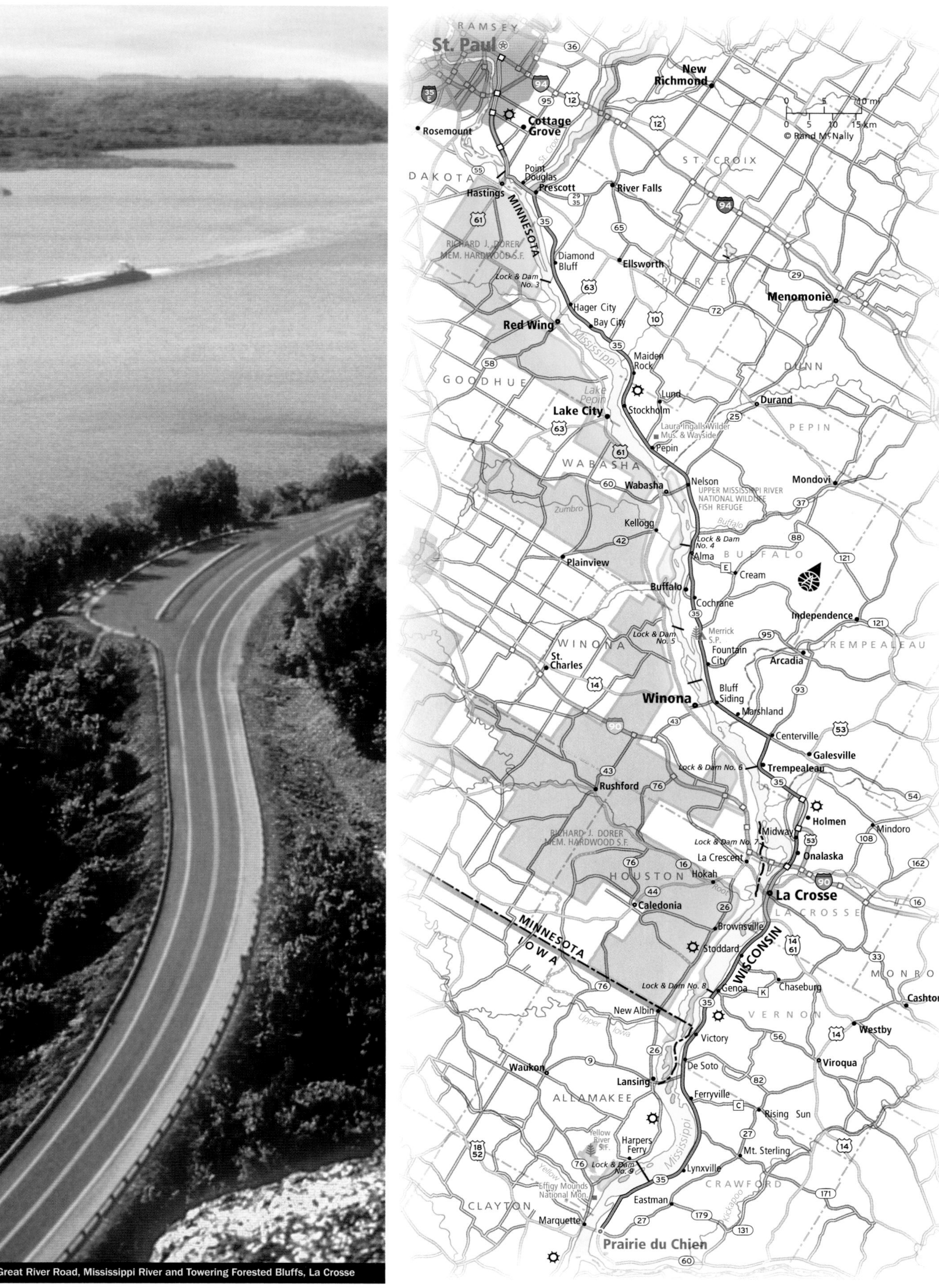

RAMSEY
St. Paul
New Richmond
0 5 10 mi
0 5 10 15 km
© Rand McNally
Cottage Grove
Rosemount
ST. CROIX
DAKOTA
Point Douglas
Prescott
Hastings
River Falls
MINNESOTA
RICHARD J. DORER MEM. HARDWOOD S.F.
Diamond Bluff
Ellsworth
PIERCE
Lock & Dam No. 3
Menomonie
Hager City
Bay City
Red Wing
Mississippi
Maiden Rock
DUNN
GOODHUE
Lake Pepin
Lund
Durand
Lake City
Stockholm
PEPIN
Laura Ingalls Wilder Mus. & Wayside
Pepin
WABASHA
Wabasha
Nelson
Mondovi
UPPER MISSISSIPPI RIVER NATIONAL WILDLIFE FISH REFUGE
Zumbro
Buffalo
Kellogg
Lock & Dam No. 4
Alma
BUFFALO
Plainview
Cream
Buffalo
Cochrane
Independence
Merrick S.P.
WINONA
Lock & Dam No. 5
Fountain City
TREMPEALEAU
Arcadia
St. Charles
Bluff Siding
Winona
Marshland
Centerville
Galesville
Lock & Dam No. 6
Trempealeau
Rushford
Holmen
Mindoro
RICHARD J. DORER MEM. HARDWOOD S.F.
Lock & Dam No. 7
Midway
Onalaska
La Crescent
HOUSTON
Hokah
Root
La Crosse
Caledonia
LA CROSSE
MINNESOTA
IOWA
Brownsville
Stoddard
WISCONSIN
MONROE
Lock & Dam No. 8
Genoa
Chaseburg
Cashton
New Albin
VERNON
Upper Iowa
Westby
Victory
Waukon
De Soto
Viroqua
Lansing
ALLAMAKEE
Ferryville
Rising Sun
Yellow River S.F.
Harpers Ferry
Mt. Sterling
Lock & Dam No. 9
Lynxville
Mississippi
Yellow
Effigy Mounds National Mon.
CRAWFORD
Kickapoo
CLAYTON
Eastman
Marquette
Prairie du Chien

Great River Road, Mississippi River and Towering Forested Bluffs, La Crosse

WYOMING TO COLORADO

SEE ATLAS PAGES 235 AND 42.

ROUTE LENGTH – About 200 miles or a leisurely day

TOURING INFORMATION
This ride follows US 287 from Walcott Wyo., to Fort Collins, Colo., with spectacular views of mountains, water, gorges, high plains, and trees. Much of the scenery looks the same as it did when early settlers passed through here.

TAKE A SIDE TRIP
Consider a ride to Saratoga, home of famed mineral hot springs and thermal waters, about 20 miles south of Walcott on WY 130. Free and open to the public, the Saratoga Hot Pool has water ranging from 102 to 128 degrees, along with changing facilities and restrooms. Located one mile north of Saratoga, Saratoga Lake is great for fishing, boating, and water sports.

VISITOR INFORMATION
www.wyomingtourism.org | 800.225.5996

CAMPING INFORMATION
wyoparks.state.wy.us | 877.996.7275

WYOMING

RIDE HIGHLIGHTS:

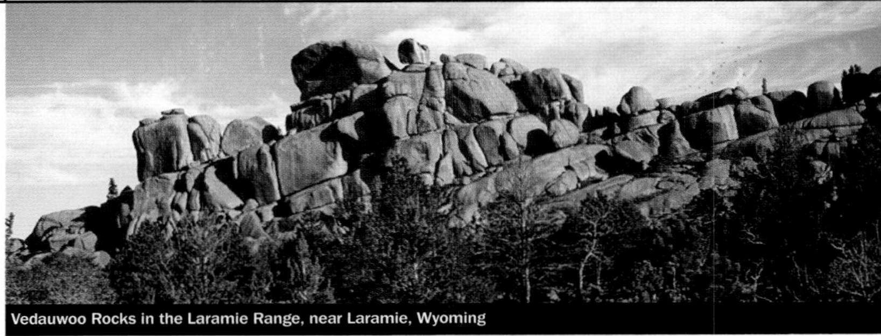

Vedauwoo Rocks in the Laramie Range, near Laramie, Wyoming

Best season to ride:	Summer
Gasoline availability:	Adequate
About the road:	Generally good shape, mostly two-lane road with 65 mph speed limit
Insider tip:	Don't attempt this ride in the late fall, winter, or early spring; be aware of the wind at any time of the year. There is no month of the year in which snow hasn't fallen in Laramie.

Follow the footsteps and wagon wheel ruts of the nation's pioneers, a testament to the skill of those early scouts and explorers who relied only on dead reckoning and the lay of the land to establish covered wagon routes. The Oregon Trail ran north of Medicine Bow, and the railroad line that took its place in the westward expansion runs right past the town's doorstep.

In Medicine Bow, stop by the historic Virginian Hotel, once the biggest hotel between Denver and Salt Lake City. Furnished in 1890s décor, the hotel derives its name from the classic novel by Owen Wister, *The Virginian*. You can eat in the dining room and rent a room—or just take a peek at those that aren't rented.

Laramie is situated on a high plain between two mountain ranges—the Laramie Range and the Medicine Bow Range (known locally as the Snowy Range). Because of the 7,200-ft. altitude, winters are long and summers are short and relatively cool. Starting with July festivities and running more than a week, Laramie's Jubilee Days celebrates with rodeos, music, and food. The Wyoming Territorial Prison in Laramie offers tours.

When you arrive in Fort Collins, celebrate the end of a glorious ride the same way many cowboys probably did—wet your whistle with a cool drink. Fort Collins is home to five award-winning craft breweries.

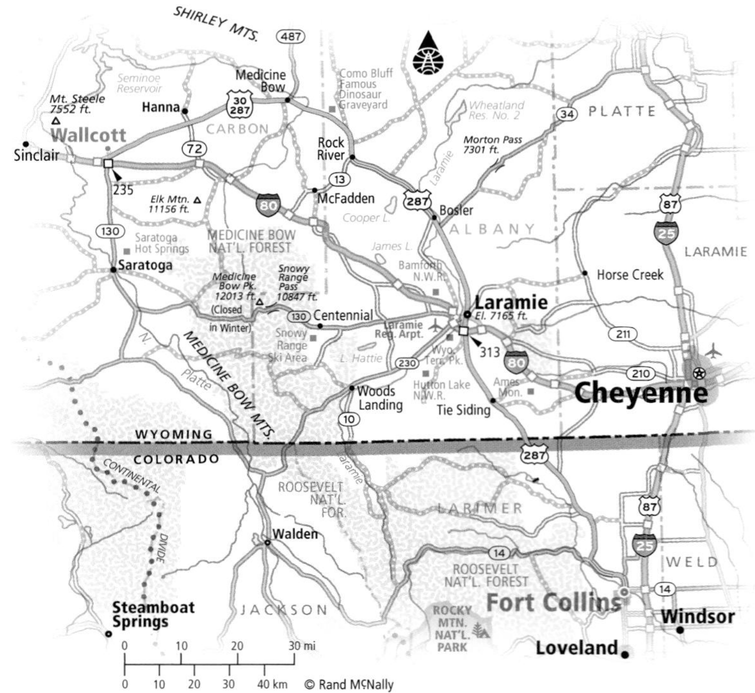
SHIRLEY MTS.
Medicine Bow
Como Bluff Famous Dinosaur Graveyard
Wheatland Res. No. 2
PLATTE
Mt. Steele 7552 ft.
Hanna
Wallcott
Sinclair
CARBON
Rock River
Morton Pass 7301 ft.
Elk Mtn. 11156 ft.
McFadden
Bosler
Cooper L.
ALBANY
Saratoga Hot Springs
MEDICINE BOW NAT'L. FOREST
Saratoga
Medicine Bow Pk. 12013 ft. (Closed in Winter)
Snowy Range Pass 10847 ft.
Centennial
Snowy Range Ski Area
Laramie
El. 7165 ft.
Laramie Reg. Arpt.
LARAMIE
Horse Creek
MEDICINE BOW MTS.
Woods Landing
Tie Siding
Cheyenne
WYOMING
COLORADO
CONTINENTAL DIVIDE
ROOSEVELT NAT'L. FOR.
LARIMER
Walden
WELD
ROOSEVELT NAT'L. FOREST
Steamboat Springs
JACKSON
ROCKY MTN. NAT'L. PARK
Fort Collins
Windsor
Loveland
0 10 20 30 mi
0 10 20 30 40 km
© Rand McNally

RIDING NORTH & SOUTH OF THE BORDER

Niagara Falls, Niagara, Ontario, Canada

With advance planning, crossing the border to Mexico or Canada can be easier than you think.

Citizenship Documents

A U.S. passport or proof of citizenship, such as an original or certified birth certificate and photo identification (such as a driver's license) is required for entry into Mexico or Canada. Naturalized U.S. citizens should carry citizenship papers; permanent residents of the United States must bring proof of residency and photo identification.

Re-entry to the U.S.

Proof of both citizenship and identity is required for entry into the United States. Be able to provide proof of U.S. citizenship via a U.S. passport, or a certified copy of your birth certificate, a Certificate of Naturalization, a Certificate of Citizenship, or a Report of Birth Abroad of a U.S. citizen. To prove your identity, present either a valid driver's license, or a government identification card that includes a photo or physical description.

By January 1, 2008, the Western Hemisphere Travel Initiative will require all U.S. citizens to carry a passport or other secure document in order to enter or re-enter the United States. This initiative will be rolled out in two phases:

- January 23, 2007: Requirement applied to all air and sea travel to or from Canada, Mexico, Central and South America, the Caribbean, and Bermuda.
- December 31, 2007: Requirement extended to all land border crossings.

In 2006, the government began producing a secure, alternative passport card for U.S. citizens in border communities who frequently cross to Mexico or Canada. The biometric card will meet the requirement for this initiative and help expedite travel through ports of entry.

Border Crossing Waits

Allow plenty of time. The average time for customs clearance is 30 minutes, but this varies greatly depending on traffic flow and security issues.

Traveling with Kids

For children under the age of 18, parents should be prepared to provide evidence, such as a birth certificate or adoption decree, to prove they are indeed the parents. Single or divorced parents and parents traveling without spouses should carry a letter of consent from the absent parent or guardian to bring a child across either border. Mexico requires the letter to be original and notarized. Divorced parents should also bring copies of their custody decree. Adults who are not the parents or guardians of the children they are traveling with must have written permission from the parents or guardians to supervise the children.

BORDER CROSSING INFORMATION

RIDING IN CANADA

Drivers need proof of ownership of the vehicle or documentation of its rental, a valid U.S. driver's license, and automobile insurance.

FAST PASS FOR FREQUENT TRAVELERS

For frequent travelers, the United States and Canada have instituted the NEXUS program, which allows pre-screened, low-risk travelers to be processed with little or no delay by U.S. and Canadian border officials. Approved applicants are issued photo identification and a proximity card, and they can quickly cross the border in a dedicated traffic lane without routine customs and immigration questioning (unless they are randomly selected).

For additional information on traveling in Canada, contact the Canadian Embassy in Washington, D.C.: (202) 682-1740; www.canadianembassy.org

DUTY-FREE DEFINED

Duty-free shops are shops where taxes on commercial goods are neither collected by a government, nor paid by an importer. For example, a Swiss watch purchased in a jewelry store in Mexico may cost you $250, a price that includes the duty and taxes that the importer paid to import it. The same watch purchased in a duty-free shop may only cost $175. That's because as long as the item stays in the duty-free shop, or exits the country with the purchaser, it has not been formally imported into the country. There has been no duty charged on it, and the duty-free shop owner has been able to pass on that savings. Its price is free of duty.

If you exceed your personal exemption, when you bring purchases home to the U.S from any shops, including those called duty-free, you will have to pay duty.
Source: *U.S. Customs and Border Protection*

FOOD POLICE

To protect community health and preserve domestic plant and animal life, many kinds of foods either are prohibited from entering the United States or require an import permit.

1. Every fruit or vegetable must be declared and presented for inspection, no matter how free of pests it appears to be. Failure to declare all food products can result in civil penalties.
2. Bakery goods and cured cheeses are generally admissible.
3. Permission to bring meats, livestock, poultry, and their by-products into the United States depends on the animal disease condition in the country of origin.
   - Fresh meat is generally prohibited from most countries.
   - Canned, cured, or dried meat is severely restricted from most countries.

Contact the U.S. Department of Agriculture, Animal Plant Health Inspection Services for more detailed information.
Source: *U.S. Customs and Border Protection*

RIDING IN MEXICO

According to U.S. Customs and Border Protection, visitors intending to drive in Mexico must obtain an automobile permit (valid for six months) from the Mexican Customs Office at the border. The permit must be held and then surrendered when leaving Mexico. A processing fee (about $27) is also mandatory, along with the posting of a bond to guarantee the departure of the car within the dates stated on the permit. To recover the bond, you must return to the same Mexican Customs office when you leave Mexico.

Carry proof of car ownership (the current registration card or a letter of authorization from the finance or leasing company). Auto insurance policies, other than Mexican, are not valid in Mexico. A short-term liability policy is obtainable at the border.

TOURIST CARDS

Tourist cards are valid up to six months, require a fee, and are required for all persons, regardless of age, to visit the interior of Mexico. Cards may be obtained from Mexican border authorities, Consuls of Mexico, or Federal Delegates in major cities. Cards are also distributed to passengers en route to Mexico by air.

For additional information on traveling in Mexico, contact the Mexican Embassy in Washington, D.C.: (202) 736-1000; www.embassyofmexico.org

LEGENDARY RIDES

A defiant road with a storied past and a demand for precision. That's what makes a great ride **LEGENDARY.**

ALCAN HIGHWAY – ALASKA

STATE MAP AND RIDE P. 14 | ROUTE LENGTH 1,364 miles or 7 days | GASOLINE AVAILABILITY Plan ahead

Fairbanks
ALASKA
Delta Junction
UNITED STATES
CANADA
YUKON TERRITORY
NORTHWEST TERRITORIES
Yellowknife
Beaver Creek
Haines Junction
Whitehorse
Teslin
Watson Lake
Fort Nelson
Juneau
BRITISH COLUMBIA
ALBERTA
Dawson Creek

This winding two-lane highway is an adventure for the most adventurous. The curvy, muddy mountain road twists through the wilderness as trekkers share the rough-country expanse with wild bear, moose, caribou, and wolf.

In the wake of the Japanese bombing of Pearl Harbor in 1941, the United States military immediately sought to strengthen the defense of Alaska and other states and territories it deemed vulnerable. The Alaska-Canadian Military Highway, later called Alcan, was born.

Alcan reaches a grade of 10 percent on Steamboat Mountain and an elevation of 4,250 feet at Summit Lake, and it boasts 25-percent grades and 90-degree turns. Among the best stretches of the 1,390-mile route is west of Whitehorse, Yukon, heading toward Kluane National Park. Riders navigate through glacier-covered mountains with Canada's highest peak, Mount Logan, looming in the background.

At the time of the Alcan's construction, a road already existed between Fairbanks, Alaska, and Delta Junction, Alaska, so officially the Alcan begins at Dawson Creek, British Columbia, and ends at Delta Junction. Richardson Highway continues on to Fairbanks. The Alcan Highway is open year-round. Watch for frost heaves, loose gravel, and frequent construction.

ROAD TO HĀNA – HAWAII

STATE MAP AND RIDE P. 63 | ROUTE LENGTH 51 miles or 7-8 hours | GASOLINE AVAILABILITY Plan ahead

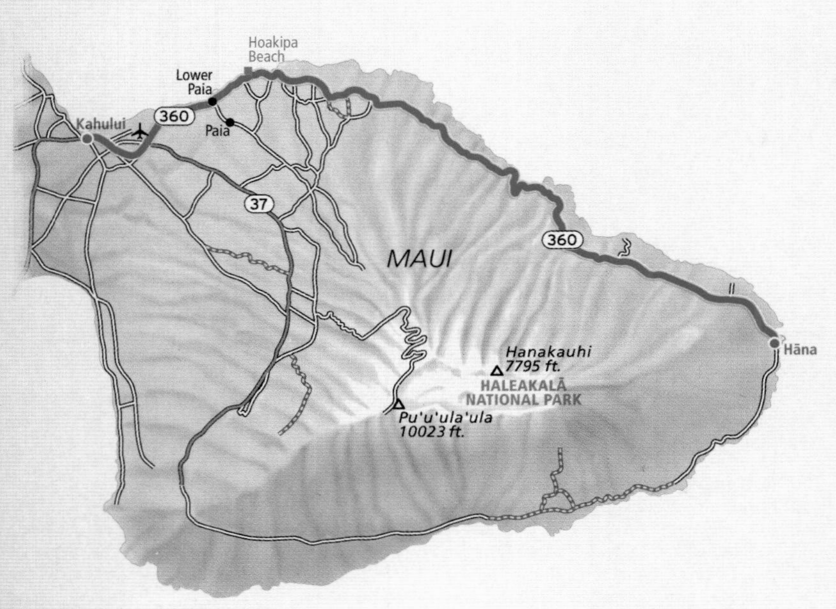
Hoakipa Beach
Lower Paia
Kahului
360
Paia
37
360
MAUI
Hanakauhi
7795 ft.
HALEAKALĀ NATIONAL PARK
Pu'u'ula'ula
10023 ft.
Hāna

The road has a reputation as one to be survived, as travelers navigate hairpin curves, hundreds of twists and turns, and more than 50 historic one-lane bridges.

A narrow two-lane stretch from Kahului to Hāna winds through a verdant forest broken by waterfalls and brief glimpses of the Pacific Ocean. Cloudbursts and overripe fallen fruit can slicken the roadway, and traffic can be dense in places. Lay off the horn—islanders consider it rude to honk.

When traveling east, gas up at the former plantation town of Paia because that is the last opportunity until Hāna. The sprinkling of homes in between are often called "rooster towns" because little else stirs within them. Though the views of the ocean are enticing, the tides can be dangerous. Take a dip instead in the many fresh waterfalls and water pools along the route, but avoid those on private land (trespassing laws are strictly enforced).

Travel one-way takes three hours, but for a more leisurely pace, secure advance reservations at one of the properties in Hāna and spend the night.

DRAGON'S TAIL – (US 129 DEAL'S GAP TENNESSEE)

STATE MAP AND RIDE P. 192 | **ROUTE LENGTH** 11 miles or one-half hour | **GASOLINE AVAILABILITY** Plan ahead

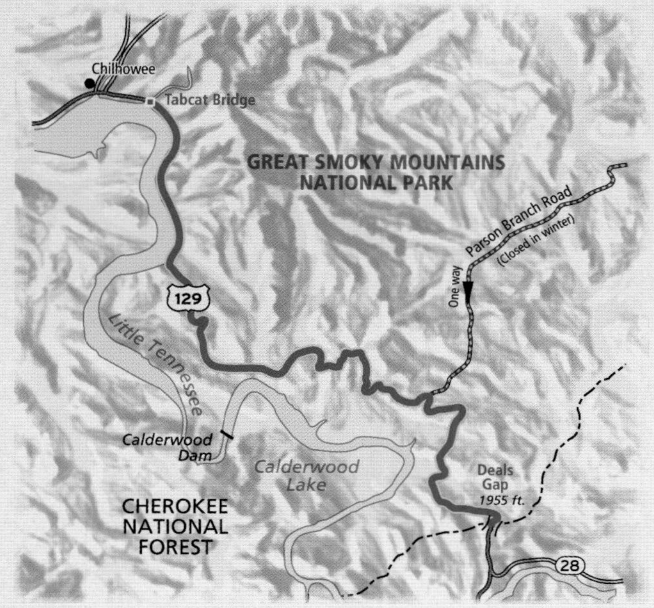
Chilhowee
Tabcat Bridge
GREAT SMOKY MOUNTAINS NATIONAL PARK
Parson Branch Road (Closed in winter)
One way
129
Little Tennessee
Calderwood Dam
Calderwood Lake
Deals Gap 1955 ft.
CHEROKEE NATIONAL FOREST
28

It is almost guaranteed that any road with named curves is bound to be exciting, and The Tail of the Dragon is no exception. This 11-mile stretch of US 129 has 318 curves with tight turns and blind spots, and motorists travel alongside wild boars and other wildlife that call this region home.

The Dragon's Tail begins at Deal's Gap, N.C., and immediately heads into Tennessee, between the Great Smoky Mountains to the northeast and the Appalachian Mountains to the southwest, paralleling the Little Tennessee River. There is more than a 1,000-foot change in elevation between Tabcat Bridge, Tenn., and Deal's Gap. Leave the sightseeing for another time or risk running off the road.

Some scenes from Robert Mitchum's 1958 moonshine flick *Thunder Road* and more recently, a scene from *The Fugitive* starring Harrison Ford, were filmed on this stretch of highway.

The Dragon's Tail has a rich history, first as a hunting trail used by American Indians, and later as haunted by Bushwackers during the Civil War. But until its discovery by outsiders in the 1990s, it was a low-traffic road used mostly by locals. Today, motorcyclists consider this among the best, and they regularly scrape their footpegs on their favorite turns.

US 50 – NEVADA

STATE MAP AND RIDE P. 130 | **ROUTE LENGTH** 285 miles or 7 hours nonstop | **GASOLINE AVAILABILITY** Plan ahead

This lonely road travels over nine mountain summits, and it passes through canyons and across vast stretches of desert basins. It offers a rare opportunity to get your bike up to cruising speed and for you to become one with the silence, sights, and smells of the open road.

The 285-mile stretch of US 50 between Ely and Fernley is known as the "Loneliest Road in America," but it is a welcome respite from the heavy traffic of I-80 to the north.

The highway's highest elevation is 7,588 feet at Robinson Summit; the lowest is 3,900 feet near Four Mile Flats, a salt flat about 20 miles southeast of Fallon. Sand dunes also lie to the east of Fallon before the highway crosses the Toiyabe, Toquima, and Monitor mountain ranges. A few casinos light up the night sky, but this region of Nevada is sleepy—pocked with ghost towns and old silver and copper mines. The Ruth Copper Pit near Ely is one of the world's largest, and Austin, once the second largest city in Nevada, has a rich mining history.

US 50 travels much the same general route as the early Pony Express riders who carried mail between St. Joseph, Mo., and Sacramento, Calif., in 1860. Historic markers for stagecoach stops and Pony Express stations dot the landscape.

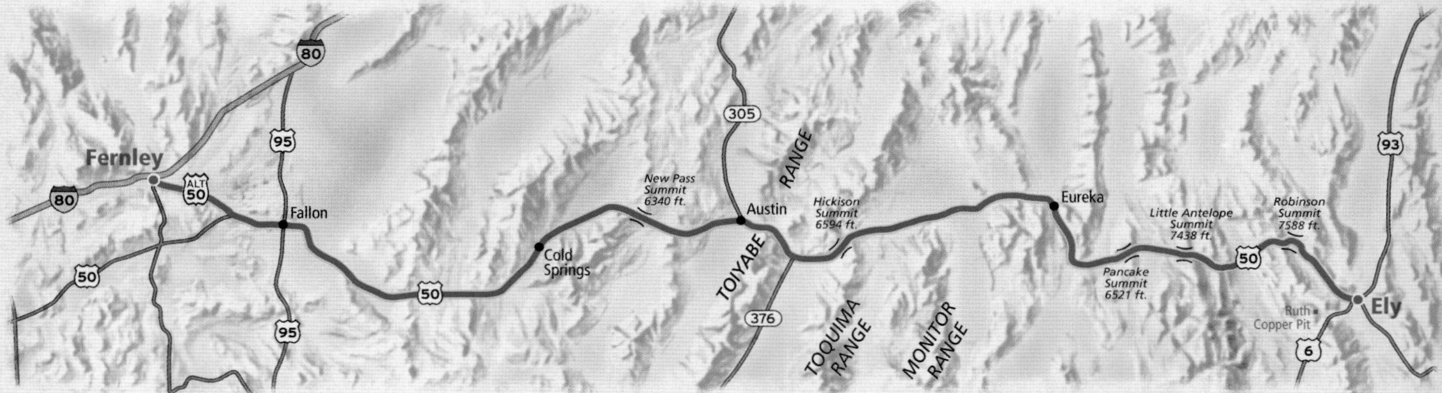
80
Fernley
ALT 50
95
Fallon
50
New Pass Summit 6340 ft.
Cold Springs
305
Austin
TOIYABE RANGE
376
Hickison Summit 6594 ft.
TOQUIMA RANGE
MONITOR RANGE
Eureka
Pancake Summit 6521 ft.
Little Antelope Summit 7438 ft.
Robinson Summit 7588 ft.
93
Ruth Copper Pit
Ely
6

RIDE 10 POPULAR NATIONAL PARKS

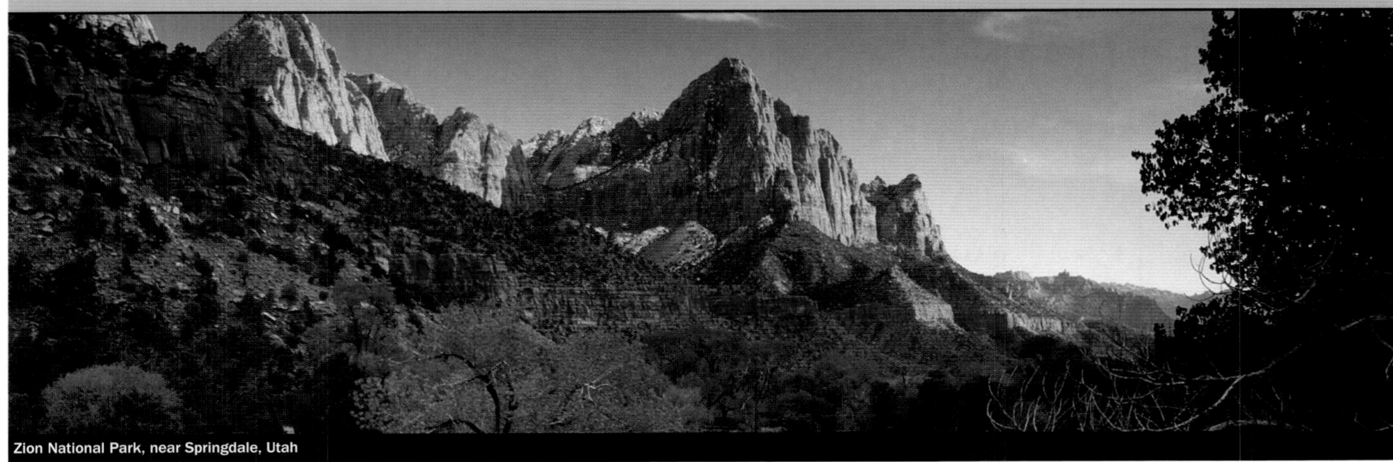
Zion National Park, near Springdale, Utah

1. Great Smoky Mountains National Park

Eastern Tennessee and western North Carolina
(P. 192, E-20)

Established: 1934
Visitors in 2005: 9,192,477
Website: www.nps.gov/grsm
Visitor Information: 865.436.1200

RIDE: Watch for black bears and other critters roadside as the main road (US 441) bisects the park, climbing through the Appalachians from Tennessee to North Carolina.

Stretching 800 square miles over ancient mountains, with the Appalachian Trail threading through the middle, Great Smoky Mountains National Park preserves one of the largest wilderness sanctuaries in the east. Mist-filled clouds produce the haze that resulted in the park's name.

Don't miss: The Roaring Fork Motor Nature Trail (closed in winter), which leads to Grotto Falls, the park's only waterfall that you can walk behind; Cades Cove, a valley with preserved log cabins, barns, and other structures built by mountain folk; Clingman's Dome, the park's highest point.

2. Grand Canyon National Park

Grand Canyon, Arizona
(P. 16, C-7)

Established: 1919
Visitors in 2005: 4,401,522
Website: www.nps.gov/grca
Visitor Information: 928.638.7888

RIDE: Arizona Highway 64 runs into the park at the edge of the Kaibab National Forest, with magnificent views of the canyon at Mather and Yavapai Points.

A geologic wonder, the Grand Canyon spans 277 miles, where the Colorado River and other water has eroded the Colorado Plateau as deep as 6,000 feet and up to 15 miles across at some points. The river still runs through the bottom of the canyon in this national park of 1.2 million acres.

Don't miss: Sunrise at Mather Point or anywhere along the South Rim Trail; mule rides down the Bright Angel Trail (reservations are taken up to 23 months in advance, so plan ahead); train ride into the heart of the park from nearby Williams, Arizona; hiking through forests of the North Rim trails; wild-life viewing in the mountain meadows.

3. Yosemite National Park

In the Sierra Nevada, California
(P. 27, NL-11)

Established: 1890
Visitors in 2005: 3,304,144
Website: www.nps.gov/yose
Visitor Information: 209.372.0200

RIDE: In summer, take the scenic Tioga Road, which bisects the park, to Tuolumne Meadows, crossing Yosemite Creek and passing by Porcupine Flat.

Championed by 19th-century environmentalist John Muir, Yosemite National Park epitomizes the splendor of the western Sierra Nevada range filled with granite cliffs, magnificent waterfalls, and ancient giant sequoias. Elevations range from 2,000 to more than 13,000 feet over its 761,000 acres.

Don't miss: Hiking on the John Muir Trail through Lyell Canyon; views from the bridge at the base of Lower Yosemite Fall; the stunning scene in summer and early fall from Glacier Point; the Mariposa Grove of giant sequoias.

4. Olympic National Park

Near Port Angeles, Washington
(P. 218, E-4)

Established: 1938
Visitors in 2005: 3,142,774
Website: www.nps.gov/olym
Visitor Information: 360.565.3130

RIDE: US Highway 101 from Sequim skirts the northern edge of the park, past falls and forest en route to the Pacific.

In northwest Washington, 60-plus miles of Pacific Ocean coastline, inland temperate rainforest, and glacier-capped mountains combine to offer incredible ecological diversity in nearly one million acres. Watch huge banana slugs slime over rainforest paths and hike or drive to high mountain vistas.

Don't miss: Wading in the Hole in the Wall tidal pools; nature walks through the Hoh Rain Forest; rafting on the Elwha River; gazing at the glaciers from Hurricane Ridge.

5. Yellowstone National Park

Northwestern Wyoming & parts of Montana and Idaho
(P. 234, B-5)

Established: 1872
Visitors in 2005: 2,835,649
Website: www.nps.gov/yell
Visitor Information: 307.344.7381

RIDE: Take the park loop (US 89) and pull over to watch bison, check out Yellowstone Lake, and smell and see the bubbling sulphurous thermal pools.

Dotted by more than 10,000 thermal features like mudpots, hot springs, and geysers (including Old Faithful), Yellowstone's landscape is at once eerie and serene. Wildlife to watch for includes wolves, grizzly bears, elk, bison, and osprey. Backcountry trails thread through the more than 2.2 million acres.

Don't miss: Old Faithful Geyser erupting every 80 minutes; massive white travertine terraces at Mammoth Hot Springs; colorful vistas at Grand Canyon of the Yellowstone; winter snowcoach tour of the park for wildlife viewing.

6. Rocky Mountain National Park

Near Estes Park and Grand Lake, Colorado
(P. 42, C-12)

Established: 1915
Visitors in 2005: 2,798,368
Website: www.nps.gov/romo
Visitor Information: 970.586.1206

RIDE: Trail Ridge Road (US 34) hugs the edge of Arapaho National Forest before climbing the lofty heights past several of the Rockies signature 10,000-plus-foot peaks.

Colorado is known for its 54 "Fourteeners," mountain peaks that rise 14,000 feet or higher. This park claims more than 60 peaks at more than 12,000 feet and the northernmost Fourteener, Longs Peak. Hike some of the 359 miles of trails, fly fish, or spot some of the amazing wildlife: Rocky Mountain bighorn sheep, mule deer, elk, moose, and eagles.

Don't miss: Longs Peak trail to Chasm Lake and the boulder field; snowshoeing in the Kawuneeche Valley; wildflower walks in the meadows in spring and summer; spectacular mountain vistas from Trail Ridge Road, the highest continuous paved road in the U.S.

7. Zion National Park

Near Springdale, Utah
(P. 207, M-6)

Established: 1919
Visitors in 2005: 2,586,665
Website: www.nps.gov/zion
Visitor Information: 435.772.3256

RIDE: Take the Zion Canyon Scenic Drive from the south entrance, winding up the switchbacks along the Zion-Mt. Carmel Highway. The mountain views are spectacular.

From the majestic 6,700-plus foot white peak of Great White Throne to the 21 switchbacks of Walter's Wiggles that climb up nearly 1,500 feet to Angel's Landing, this is a hiker's and rock climber's paradise. The 229 square miles of park preserve an amazing array of flora and fauna, including 290 species of birds.

Don't miss: The 10-mile scenic drive through tunnels and switchbacks on the Zion-Mt. Carmel highway; hiking in summer through the Narrows, a slot canyon that the icy-cold Virgin River flows through; narration from the witty, wise drivers of the park's shuttle bus system.

8. Cuyahoga Valley National Park

Between Cleveland and Akron, Ohio
(P. 160, NG-15)

Established: 2000
Visitors in 2005: 2,533,827
Website: www.nps.gov/cuva
Visitor Information: 216.524.1497

RIDE: Riverview Road runs right through the center of the park, providing easy access to the ski resort, Hunt Farm Visitor Information Center, and the park headquarters.

Encompassing a swath of 33,000 acres between Cleveland and Akron along the crooked path of the Cuyahoga River, the Cuyahoga Valley National Park has steep ravines and wooded uplands, historical tours and hiking along the Ohio & Erie Canal towpath, plus a winter sports center for sledding and tobogganing.

Don't miss: A scenic rail ride through the heart of the park on a circa-1940 rail coach of the Cuyahoga Valley Scenic Railroad; Brandywine Falls, a 67-foot high waterfall; hiking or biking the 20-mile Ohio & Erie Canal Towpath Trail; winter sledding on the Kendall Hills.

9. Grand Teton National Park

Northwestern Wyoming
(P. 234, C-5)

Established: 1929
Visitors in 2005: 2,463,442
Website: www.nps.gov/grte
Visitor Information: 307.739.3300

RIDE: Take US 89 through the flathead valley, pausing to look west at the Tetons and the Snake River flowing through the valley.

Sandwiched between the swanky town of Jackson Hole and Yellowstone National Park, Grand Teton holds its own. The Snake River cuts through the flatlands and meadows, with eight 12,000-plus foot peaks of the Tetons rising to the west. Hikers, rafters, and paddlers enjoy exploring the trails, lakes, and streams.

Don't miss: Rafting on the Snake River; searching for moose near Willow Flats; watching the sunset from Signal Mountain summit; snowshoeing with a park ranger in winter; wildflower walks in the valley in late spring.

10. Acadia National Park

Bar Harbor, Maine
(P. 92, F-7)

Established: 1919
Visitors in 2005: 2,051,484
Website: www.nps.gov/acad
Visitor Information: 207.288.3338

RIDE: Follow Maine Highway 3 as it loops around the northern section of Mount Desert Island, past Otter Cliffs and Thunder Hole and overlooking the Atlantic Ocean.

Originally Lafayette National Park, Acadia is the first national park established east of the Mississippi River. It perches on the Maine coast and was once a playground for the wealthy. Today, its 47,000 acres harbor tidepools, woods, and mountain peaks. Hikers like to climb Cadillac Mountain to watch the rays of the sun first touch the U.S.

Don't miss: Shore walk at Sand Beach; horsedrawn carriage rides at Wildwood Stable; biking along the 44 miles of carriage trails built by John D. Rockefeller; high cliffs and rocky coastline along the 27-mile Park Loop Road; fall foliage hikes in October.

HARLEY-DAVIDSON® SERVICES

HARLEY-DAVIDSON
RIDER'S EDGE
ACADEMY OF MOTORCYCLING

RIDER'S EDGE®

Learn to Ride

No matter what path takes you into the saddle of a Harley-Davidson® motorcycle, you should feel confident there. That's the mission of Rider's Edge®, the Harley-Davidson Academy of Motorcycling.

The New Rider Course uses the proven curriculum of the Motorcycle Safety Foundation's® Basic *RiderCourse*℠, with a twist provided by the enthusiasts at Harley-Davidson and Buell. It includes about 25 hours of instruction, both in the classroom, where you'll learn the basics of riding, and on a controlled practice range, where you'll hone the skills that will make you ready for the road. The Rider's Edge New Rider Course won't just teach you how to operate a motorcycle. It will show you a whole new world.

Learn to Ride Better

Whether you're a recent graduate of the Rider's Edge® New Rider Course or a seasoned road veteran, the Rider's Edge® Skilled Rider Course is the perfect place to brush up on your riding technique and to challenge your current skill level.

Hook up with a Rider's Edge course at a participating Harley-Davidson dealer or visit www.ridersedge.com.

LIFE STARTS AT THE EDGE.®

AUTHORIZED
HARLEY-DAVIDSON
RENTALS & TOURS

HARLEY-DAVIDSON® AUTHORIZED RENTALS

Whether vacationing or traveling on business, you can turn any trip into a thundering adventure with a Harley-Davidson Authorized Rental.

Harley-Davidson Authorized Rentals locations always offer the latest model Harley-Davidson motorcycles, strictly serviced and maintained to Motor Company standards.

Each Harley-Davidson Authorized Rentals experience includes the use of a Harley-Davidson country-approved helmet and raingear, short-term luggage storage, and 24-hour emergency roadside assistance.

Choose from over 260 worldwide locations—and discover our latest additions—at www.hdrentals.com.

THE GREAT AMERICAN FACTORY TOUR

MOTOR
HARLEY-DAVIDSON
CYCLES

FACTORY TOURS

Behind every great machine are people with a passion. Since 1903, Harley-Davidson has built the most coveted motorcycles on the planet. And now you can see first-hand how these machines come to life. Through exclusive exhibits and stops on the factory floor, Harley-Davidson Factory Tours give you a behind-the-scenes look at what it takes to create an American legend. They're guided and unlike anything you've ever experienced. Because you won't just watch motorcycles being built, you'll watch history being made.

For more information and specific site guidelines and safety requirements, call 1-877-883-1450 (toll free) or 414-343-7850 or visit www.harley-davidson.com/experience.

HARLEY-DAVIDSON® TRAVEL AND TOURS

Where are you headed? Need a little help getting there? Maybe you're looking for the best way to bring the bike with you. Or a place to stop for the night? Visiting harley-davidson.com/experience is a great place to start planning your next road trip. There you'll find information and services to make the most of the time on your bike. Whether you're looking for help in finding a hotel for your travel to a rally, information about renting a bike when you get where you're going, suggestions for guided or self-guided motorcycle tours, or even mapping out and sharing your favorite ride routes, Harley-Davidson Travel and Tours is here to help.

Before you swing a leg over and ride on, log on to www.harley-davidson.com/experience.

HARLEY-DAVIDSON
SHIPPING

MOTORCYCLE SHIPPING

Whether you are taking a riding vacation, attending a rally or relocating, Harley-Davidson Shipping has a range of transportation options designed to safely and affordably transport your Harley-Davidson® motorcycle. We can ship your motorcycle internationally or domestically taking care of all U.S. and foreign customs regulations and procedures as needed along the way. With competitive prices and a variety of transit schedules, we'll work to find a solution that fits your needs. Harley-Davidson Shipping welcomes all enthusiasts and offers discounted rates to full H.O.G. members as well as multi-bike shipment discounts.

For more information regarding rates, real time quotes, transit schedules, and other services visit www.harley-davidson.com/shipping or call 888-224-BIKE (2453).

HOG
HARLEY OWNERS GROUP

THE HARLEY OWNERS GROUP® - OR H.O.G.® - is the largest factory-sponsored motorcycle club in the world. Its stated mission is a simple one: "To Ride and Have Fun." With so many benefits, programs, and activities available, members can spend a lifetime fulfilling their motorcycling dreams. And with worldwide membership approaching 1,000,000, there is no shortage of fellow riders to share in your journey.

For more information, contact our United States office at 1-800-CLUBHOG (1-800-258-2464) or 414-343-4896 (outside U.S. and Canada) • www.hog.com
Contact our Canadian office at 800-668-4836 or 905-660-3500 (outside Canada and U.S.) • www.hog.com

HARLEY-DAVIDSON® MUSEUM

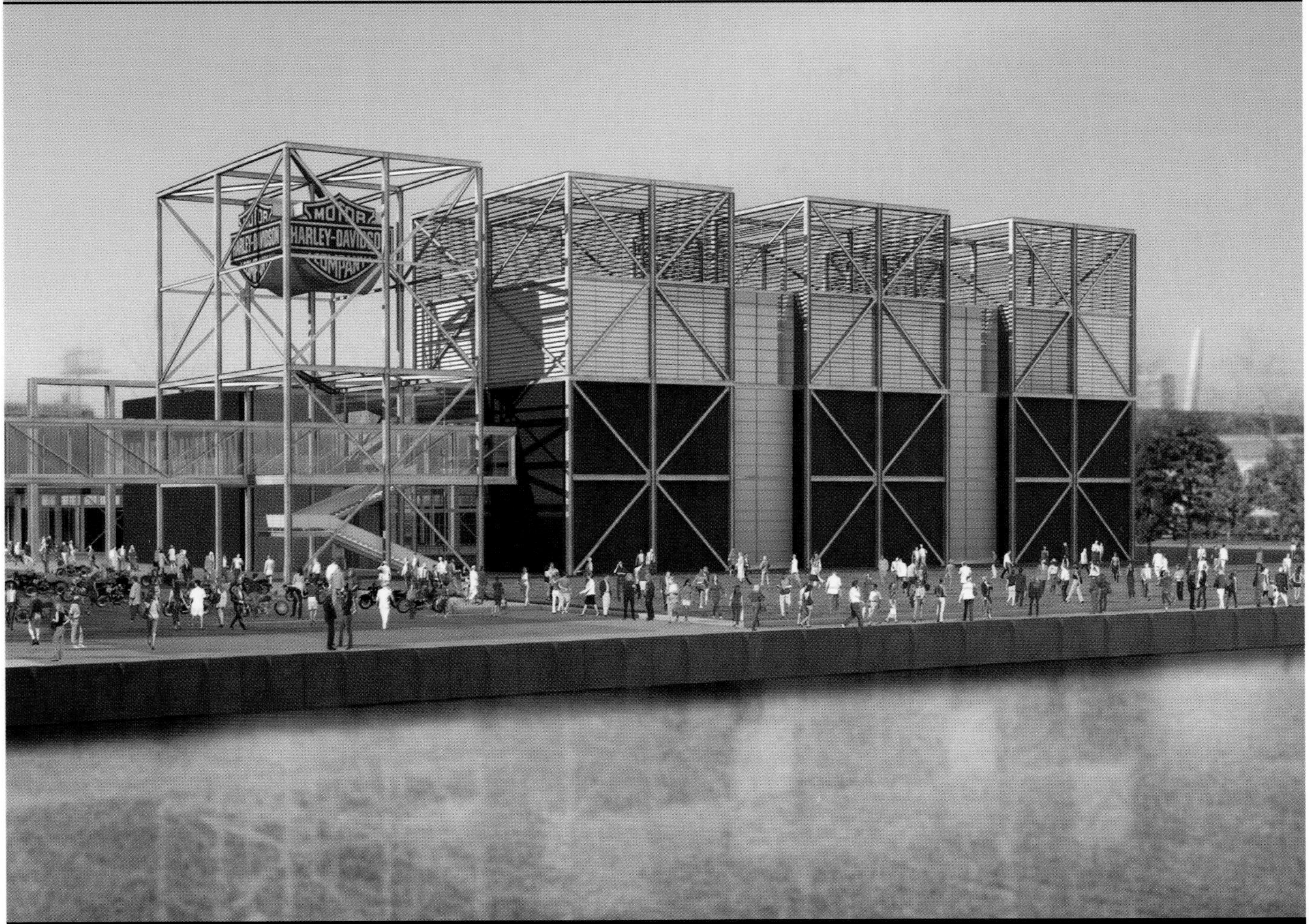

View to northwest from end of canal

HARLEY-
DAVIDSON
MUSEUM

MOTOR
HARLEY-DAVIDSON
COMPANY

Expected to open in 2008, Harley-Davidson Museum will be a showcase for the legendary motorcycles, passionate riders, and unforgettable stories that have made us famous around the world.

The Harley-Davidson Museum won't be a typical museum, and it's not just about motorcycles, it is about a great American success story. The Museum will feature over 400 motorcycles from the company collection including: the 1956 Model KH owned by Elvis Presley, the unique 40-feet long "King Kong" motorcycle customized over 40 years by a passionate rider, and the famous Serial Number One motorcycle built in 1903. There will be exhibits on Harley-Davidson in popular culture such as movies, music and fashion. In addition to exhibits, the Museum will feature a restaurant, café, retail shop, meeting space, special events facilities, and the company's archives. The Museum will be located in Milwaukee, Wisconsin at the corner of Sixth and Canal Streets near downtown.

Can't wait for the Museum to open? Visit the Harley-Davidson Museum webcam and watch construction progress at www.h-dmuseum.oxblue.com. The webcam displays new images several times an hour and images are archived so you can review the development leading up to the 2008 opening. Visit www.harley-davidson.com for additional Museum news, information and updates.

STATE PARK CAMPING

Fort Abraham Lincoln State Park, Mandan, North Dakota

Check out these numbers and websites for general information and camping availability in each state.

Alabama
800.252.7275 | www.alapark.com

Alaska
907.269.8400 | www.alaskastateparks.org

Arizona
602.542.4174 | www.pr.state.az.us/

Arkansas
888.287.2757 | www.arkansasstateparks.com

California
916.653.6995 | 800-777-0369
www.parks.ca.gov

Colorado
303-866-3437 | parks.state.co.us/

Connecticut
860.424.3200 | www.dep.state.ct.us/stateparks

Delaware
302.739.9220 | www.destateparks.com

Florida
850.245.2157 | www.floridastateparks.org

Georgia
404-656-3530 | www.gastateparks.org

Hawaii
808.587.0400
www.hawaii.gov/dlnr/dsp/hawaii.html

Idaho
208.334.4199 | www.idahoparks.org

Illinois
217.782.6302
www.dnr.state.il.us/lands/landmgt/parks

Indiana
317.232.4124 | www.in.gov/dnr/parklake

Iowa
515.281.5918 | www.exploreiowaparks.com

Kansas
620.672.5911 | www.kdwp.state.ks.us

Kentucky
800.255.7275 | www.parks.ky.gov

Louisiana
888.677.1400 | www.lastateparks.com

Maine
207.287.3821 | www.maine.gov/doc/parks

Maryland
800.830.3974 | www.dnr.state.md.us/publiclands

Massachusetts
617.626.1250 | www.massparks.org

Michigan
517.373.9900 | www.michigan.gov/dnr

Minnesota
888.646.6367 | www.dnr.state.mn.us

Mississippi
800.467.2757 | www.mdwfp.com/parks.asp

Missouri
800.334.6946 | www.mostateparks.com

Montana
406.444.3750 | www.fwp.state.mt.us

Nebraska
800.826.7275
www.ngpc.state.ne.us/parks/parks.asp

Nevada
775.687.4384 | parks.nv.gov

New Hampshire
603.271.3556 | www.nhstateparks.org

New Jersey
800.843.6420
www.state.nj.us/dep/parksandforests/parks/index.html

New Mexico
888.667.2757 | www.emnrd.state.nm.us/nmparks/

New York
518.474.0456 | nysparks.state.ny.us

North Carolina
919.733.7275
www.ils.unc.edu/parkproject/ncparks.html

North Dakota
701.328.5357 | www.parkrec.nd.gov

Ohio
866.644.6727 | www.dnr.state.oh.us/parks

Oklahoma
800.654.8240 | www.oklahomaparks.com

Oregon
800.551.6949 | www.oregonstateparks.org

Pennsylvania
888.727.3757
www.dcnr.state.pa.us/stateparks/index.asp

Rhode Island
401.222.2632 | www.riparks.com

South Carolina
803.734.1700 | www.southcarolinaparks.com

South Dakota
605.773.3391 | www.sdgfp.info/parks

Tennessee
888.867.2757
www.state.tn.us/environment/parks

Texas
800.792.1112 | www.tpwd.state.tx.us

Utah
801.538.7220 | www.stateparks.utah.gov

Vermont
802.241.3655
www.vtstateparks.com/htm/info.cfm

Virginia
800.933.7275 | www.dcr.state.va.us/parks

Washington
360.902.8844 | www.parks.wa.gov

West Virginia
800.225.5982 | www.wvstateparks.com

Wisconsin
608.266.2181 | www.wiparks.net

Wyoming
307.777.6303 | www.wyoparks.state.wy.us

RIDE LOG

Relive the road. Record your journey.

Sky Chief
GASOLINE

RAND McNALLY

RIDE LOG

9-4-09 to 9-8-09 -
Our first long trip in S.D. Went to the Black Hills. Stayed in Rapid City, Fri + Sat, Sun + Mon in Spearfish. Did all the loops for bikes in Black Hills and into Wy. Had a great time, perfect weather while there. Saw buffalo, deer, turkey, donkeys. Also saw a coal mine. traveled 1220 miles

RIDE LOG

Portland
Hood River
WEST
EAST
INTERSTATE
84
INTERSTATE
84
30

RIDE LOG

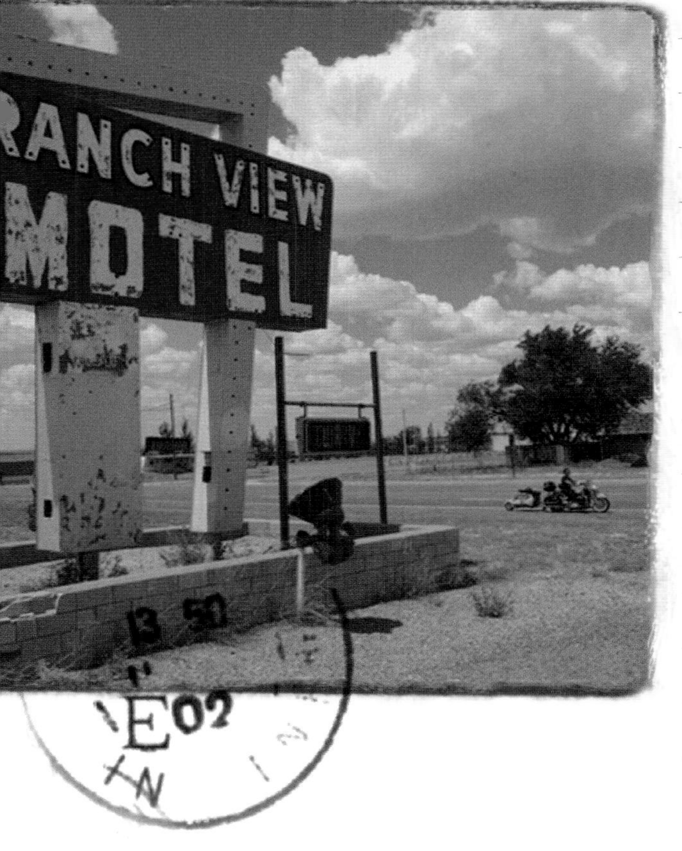
RANCH VIEW
MOTEL

RIDE LOG

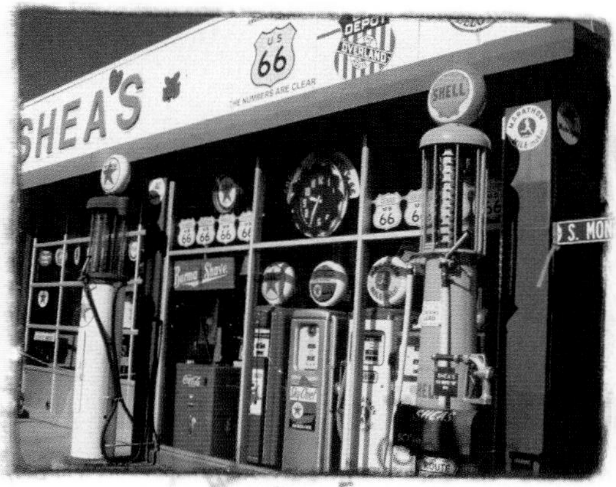

RIDE LOG

FOUR

RIDE LOG

RIDE LOG

RIDE LOG

MAP LEGEND

Roads and related symbols

- Free limited-access highway
- Toll limited-access highway
- New road (under construction as of press time)
- Other multilane highway
- Principal highway
- Other through highway
- Other road (conditions vary — local inquiry suggested)
- Unpaved road (conditions vary — local inquiry suggested)
- Ramp; one way route
- Ferry
- 96 BR 96 Interstate highway; Interstate highway business route
- 31 BR 31 U.S. highway; U.S. highway business route
- 15 Trans-Canada highway; Autoroute
- 1 Mexican or Central American highway
- 18 State or provincial highway
- 147 Secondary state, secondary provincial, or county highway
- NM County trunk highway
- Construction site or construction zone
- Featured ride
- Scenic route
- TOLL Service area; toll booth or fee booth
- Tunnel; mountain pass
- 2 8 10 Interchanges and exit numbers (For most states, the mileage between interchanges may be determined by subtracting one number from the other.)
- 9 4 3 2 Highway mileages (segments of one mile or less not shown): Cumulative miles (red): the distance between arrows Intermediate miles (black): the distance between intersections

Cities & towns

(size of type on map indicates relative population)

- National capital; state or provincial capital
- County seat or independent city
- City, town, or recognized place; neighborhood
- Urbanized area
- Separate cities within metropolitan area

Parks, recreation areas, & points of interest

- U.S. or Canadian national park
- U.S. or Canadian national monument, other National Park Service facility, state/provincial park or recreation area
- Park with camping facilities; park without camping facilities
- Campsite; wayside or roadside park
- National forest, national grassland, or city park
- Wilderness area; wildlife refuge
- Point of interest, historic site or monument
- Airport
- Building
- Foot trail
- Hospital or medical center
- Indian reservation
- Information center or Tourist Information Center (T.I.C.)
- Military or governmental installation
- Rest area with toilets; rest area without toilets
- Harley-Davidson Dealer

Physical Features

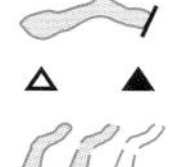

- Dam
- Mountain peak; highest point in state/province
- Lake; intermittent lake; dry lake
- River; intermittent river
- Desert
- Glacier
- Swamp or mangrove swamp

Other symbols

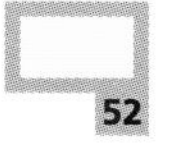

- Area shown in greater detail on inset map
- 52 Inset map page indicator (if not on same page)
- Great River Road
- Port of entry
- Intracoastal waterway
- Railroad
- COOK County or parish boundary and name
- State or provincial boundary
- National boundary
- Continental divide
- Time zone boundary
- 33° 00' 95°00' Latitude; longitude

Comparative distances

1 mile = 1.609 kilometers

1 kilometer = .621 miles

Population figures are from the latest available census or are Census Bureau or Rand McNally estimates.

For a complete list of abbreviations that appear on the maps, go to **www.randmcnally.com** and key in the Express Access Code **ABBR**.

PHOTO CREDITS

All Motorcycle photography - Harley-Davidson Motor Company; P. R6 *Mobile Bay Convention and Visitors Bureau*; P. R7 *Looe Key Reef* - The Florida Keys & Key West, Monroe County Tourist Development Council; P. R8 *Rockwall Pass in Kootenay National Park* - John E Marriott /Alamy; P. R9 *Morenci Copper Mine* - National Scenic Byways, www.byways.org; P. R10 *California Travel and Tourism Commission*; P. R11 *A farmer's Vista on the San Juan* Skyway - National Scenic Byways/Robert Reinhard P. R12 *Everglades* - Visit Florida; P. R13 *Road Running Through Tunnel of Spanish Moss Shrouded Live Oaks Near Georgetown South Carolina* - Daniel Dempster Photography/Alamy; P. R14 *Ramp Creek covered bridge built in 1838* - Mike Briner/Alamy; P. R15 *Tallgrass Prairie in the Flint Hills* - Mike Blair, Kansas Department of Wildlife and Parks; P. R16 *Mount Desert Island Maine* - Rubens Abboud/Alamy; P. R17 *Portland Head Lighthouse in Maine* - Bilderbuch/Design Pics/Corbis; P. R18 *Spa Creek, Annapolis* - Annapolis & Anne Arundel Country CVB; P. R19 *Steamed Crabs* - Annapolis & Anne Arundel Country CVB; P. R20 *Sleeping Bear Sand Dunes* - Robert de Jonge; P. R21 *Mackinac Bridge* - Brian Walters; P. R22 *HaHa Springs looking towards castle ruins* - Lake of the Ozarks CVB; P. R23 *Aquatic Trail* - Lake of the Ozarks CVB; P. R24 *Ubehebe Crater* - National Scenic Byways, www.byways.org; P. R25 *Gros Morne National Park* - Hemis/Alamy; P. 26 *Red Mountain Sky* - Jack Parsons; P. 27 *Inn at Loretto* - Jack Parsons; P. R28 *Beulach Ban Falls Cape Breton Highlands National Park* - Radius Images/ Alamy; P. R29 *Cabot Trail Cape Breton Nova Scotia* - Jon Arnold Images/Alamy; P. R30 *Highway 101 at Cape Sebastian* - Steve Terrill; P. R31 *Oregon Dunes National Recreational Area* - Robert L. Potts; P. R32 *Black Hills* - South Dakota Tourism; P. R32 *Sturgis Rally and Races* - South Dakota Tourism; P. R33 *Crazy Horse Memorial* - KORCZAK, Sc.; P. R34 *Orange Hoodoos by Scenic Byway 12 in Utah* - A. E. Crane; P. R35 *Smugglers Notch* - Dennis Curran; P. R36 *Skyline Drive and the Shenandoah Valley from Stony Man Mountain* - National Scenic Byways, www.byways.org; P.R37 *New River Gorge Bridge* - West Virginia Division of Tourism; P. R38 *Sunset on the Mississippi River La Crosse* – La Crosse, WI CVB; P. R39 *Great River Road, Mississippi River and Towering Forested Bluffs* - National Scenic Byways, www.byways.org; P. R40 *Vedauwoo Rocks in the Laramie Range* - Wyoming Travel & Tourism; P. R41 *Niagara Falls, Niagara, Ontario* - Joerg Metzner; P. R44 *Zion National Park, near Springdale, Utah* - National Parks Service; P. 48 *Fort Abraham Lincoln State Park* - Tom Bean

Library of Congress Catalog Number: 2007921096

For licensing and copyright permissions, contact us at licensing@randmcnally.com

If you have questions, concerns, or even a compliment, contact us by visiting our website at go.randmcnally.com/contact (800) 777- MAPS (-6277)
or e-mail us at: go.randmcnally.com/contact

or write to:
Rand McNally Consumer Affairs
P.O. Box 7600
Chicago, Illinois 60680-9915

Published in U.S.A.

Printed in China

1 2 3 4 LE 08 07

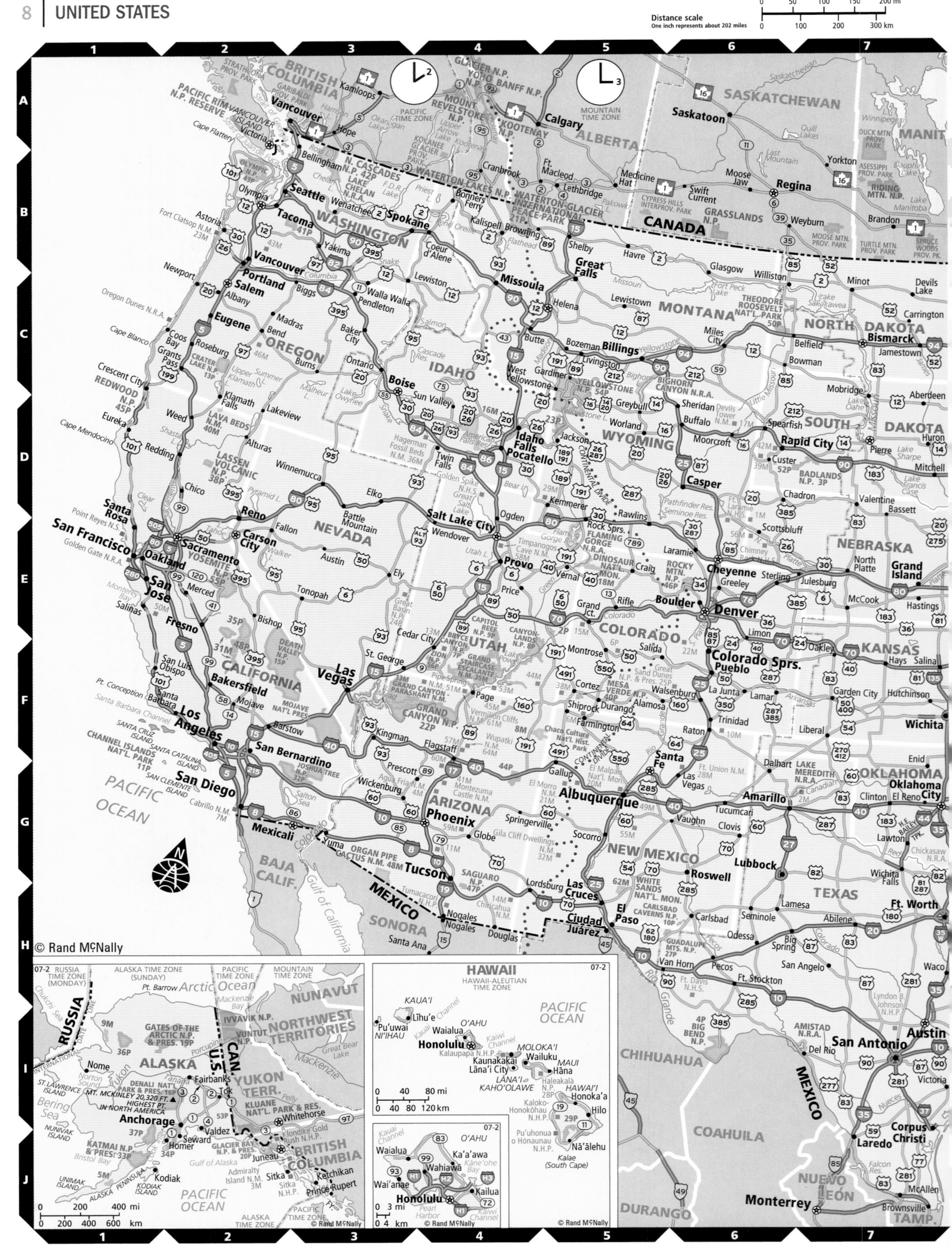

Distance scale
One inch represents about 202 miles
0 50 100 150 200 mi
0 100 200 300 km
PACIFIC TIME ZONE
MOUNTAIN TIME ZONE
BRITISH COLUMBIA
ALBERTA
SASKATCHEWAN
CANADA
WASHINGTON
OREGON
IDAHO
MONTANA
WYOMING
NORTH DAKOTA
SOUTH DAKOTA
NEBRASKA
NEVADA
UTAH
COLORADO
KANSAS
CALIFORNIA
ARIZONA
NEW MEXICO
OKLAHOMA
TEXAS
MEXICO
BAJA CALIF.
SONORA
CHIHUAHUA
COAHUILA
DURANGO
NUEVO LEÓN
PACIFIC OCEAN
Gulf of California
Vancouver
Victoria
Calgary
Saskatoon
Regina
Seattle
Tacoma
Olympia
Spokane
Portland
Salem
Eugene
Boise
Missoula
Helena
Great Falls
Billings
Bismarck
Pierre
Rapid City
Casper
Cheyenne
Salt Lake City
Provo
Reno
Carson City
Sacramento
San Francisco
Oakland
San Jose
Fresno
Bakersfield
Los Angeles
San Diego
Las Vegas
Phoenix
Tucson
Albuquerque
Santa Fe
Denver
Boulder
Colorado Sprs.
Pueblo
El Paso
Ciudad Juárez
Lubbock
Amarillo
Oklahoma City
Wichita
Ft. Worth
Austin
San Antonio
Corpus Christi
Laredo
Monterrey
Mexicali
Nogales
H © Rand McNally
ALASKA
RUSSIA
YUKON TERR.
NORTHWEST TERRITORIES
NUNAVUT
Anchorage
Fairbanks
Juneau
Whitehorse
HAWAII
HAWAII-ALEUTIAN TIME ZONE
Honolulu
Hilo

How to determine distance

Mileages in red between red arrowheads; in black, between intersections.

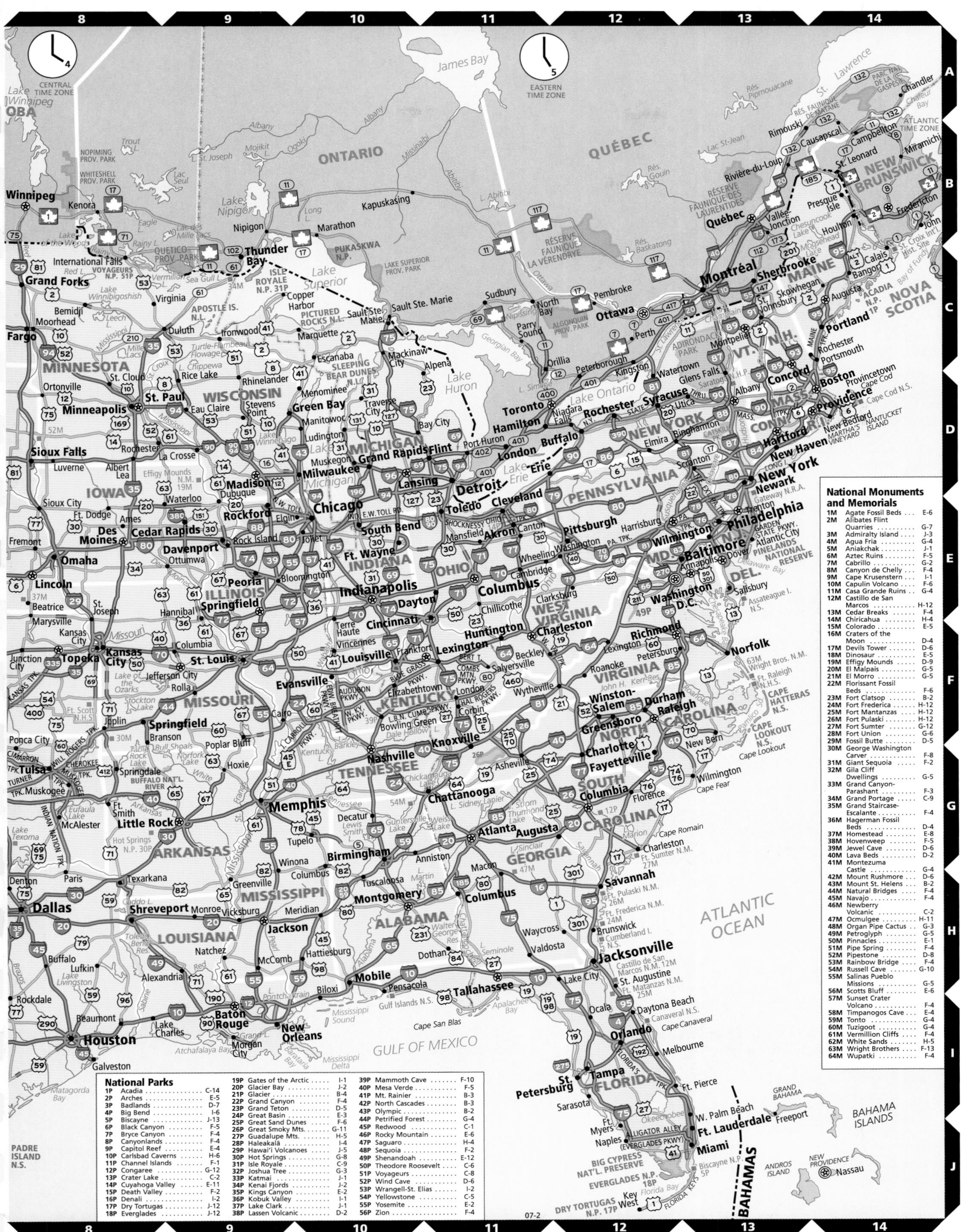
CENTRAL TIME ZONE
EASTERN TIME ZONE
ATLANTIC TIME ZONE
ONTARIO
QUÉBEC
NEW BRUNSWICK
NOVA SCOTIA
MAINE
VT.
N.H.
MASS.
CONN.
R.I.
NEW YORK
PENNSYLVANIA
N.J.
DEL.
MD.
WEST VIRGINIA
VIRGINIA
NORTH CAROLINA
SOUTH CAROLINA
GEORGIA
FLORIDA
ALABAMA
MISSISSIPPI
LOUISIANA
ARKANSAS
TENNESSEE
KENTUCKY
OHIO
INDIANA
ILLINOIS
MICHIGAN
WISCONSIN
MINNESOTA
IOWA
MISSOURI
James Bay
Lake Superior
Lake Michigan
Lake Huron
Lake Erie
Lake Ontario
ATLANTIC OCEAN
GULF OF MEXICO
BAHAMA ISLANDS
BAHAMAS
07-2

National Parks

1P	Acadia	C-14
2P	Arches	E-5
3P	Badlands	D-7
4P	Big Bend	I-6
5P	Biscayne	J-13
6P	Black Canyon	F-5
7P	Bryce Canyon	F-4
8P	Canyonlands	F-4
9P	Capitol Reef	E-4
10P	Carlsbad Caverns	H-6
11P	Channel Islands	F-1
12P	Congaree	G-12
13P	Crater Lake	C-2
14P	Cuyahoga Valley	E-11
15P	Death Valley	F-2
16P	Denali	I-2
17P	Dry Tortugas	J-12
18P	Everglades	J-12
19P	Gates of the Arctic	I-1
20P	Glacier Bay	J-2
21P	Glacier	B-4
22P	Grand Canyon	F-4
23P	Grand Teton	D-5
24P	Great Basin	E-3
25P	Great Sand Dunes	F-6
26P	Great Smoky Mts.	G-11
27P	Guadalupe Mts.	H-5
28P	Haleakalā	I-4
29P	Hawai'i Volcanoes	J-5
30P	Hot Springs	G-8
31P	Isle Royale	C-9
32P	Joshua Tree	G-3
33P	Katmai	J-1
34P	Kenai Fjords	J-2
35P	Kings Canyon	E-2
36P	Kobuk Valley	I-1
37P	Lake Clark	J-1
38P	Lassen Volcanic	D-2
39P	Mammoth Cave	F-10
40P	Mesa Verde	F-5
41P	Mt. Rainier	B-3
42P	North Cascades	B-3
43P	Olympic	B-2
44P	Petrified Forest	G-4
45P	Redwood	C-1
46P	Rocky Mountain	E-6
47P	Saguaro	H-4
48P	Sequoia	F-2
49P	Shenandoah	E-12
50P	Theodore Roosevelt	C-6
51P	Voyageurs	C-8
52P	Wind Cave	D-6
53P	Wrangell-St. Elias	I-2
54P	Yellowstone	C-5
55P	Yosemite	E-2
56P	Zion	F-4

National Monuments and Memorials

1M	Agate Fossil Beds	E-6
2M	Alibates Flint Quarries	G-7
3M	Admiralty Island	J-3
4M	Agua Fria	G-4
5M	Aniakchak	J-1
6M	Aztec Ruins	F-5
7M	Cabrillo	G-2
8M	Canyon de Chelly	F-4
9M	Cape Krusenstern	I-1
10M	Capulin Volcano	F-6
11M	Casa Grande Ruins	G-4
12M	Castillo de San Marcos	H-12
13M	Cedar Breaks	F-4
14M	Chiricahua	H-4
15M	Colorado	E-5
16M	Craters of the Moon	D-4
17M	Devils Tower	D-6
18M	Dinosaur	E-5
19M	Effigy Mounds	D-9
20M	El Malpais	G-5
21M	El Morro	G-5
22M	Florissant Fossil Beds	F-6
23M	Fort Clatsop	B-2
24M	Fort Frederica	H-12
25M	Fort Mantanzas	H-12
26M	Fort Pulaski	H-12
27M	Fort Sumter	G-12
28M	Fort Union	G-6
29M	Fossil Butte	D-5
30M	George Washington Carver	F-8
31M	Giant Sequoia	F-2
32M	Gila Cliff Dwellings	G-5
33M	Grand Canyon-Parashant	F-3
34M	Grand Portage	C-9
35M	Grand Staircase-Escalante	F-4
36M	Hagerman Fossil Beds	D-4
37M	Homestead	E-8
38M	Hovenweep	F-5
39M	Jewel Cave	D-6
40M	Lava Beds	D-2
41M	Montezuma Castle	G-4
42M	Mount Rushmore	D-6
43M	Mount St. Helens	B-2
44M	Natural Bridges	F-4
45M	Navajo	F-4
46M	Newberry Volcanic	C-2
47M	Ocmulgee	H-11
48M	Organ Pipe Cactus	G-3
49M	Petroglyph	G-5
50M	Pinnacles	E-1
51M	Pipe Spring	F-4
52M	Pipestone	D-8
53M	Rainbow Bridge	F-4
54M	Russell Cave	G-10
55M	Salinas Pueblo Missions	G-5
56M	Scotts Bluff	E-6
57M	Sunset Crater Volcano	F-4
58M	Timpanogos Cave	E-4
59M	Tonto	G-4
60M	Tuzigoot	G-4
61M	Vermillion Cliffs	F-4
62M	White Sands	H-5
63M	Wright Brothers	F-13
64M	Wupatki	F-4

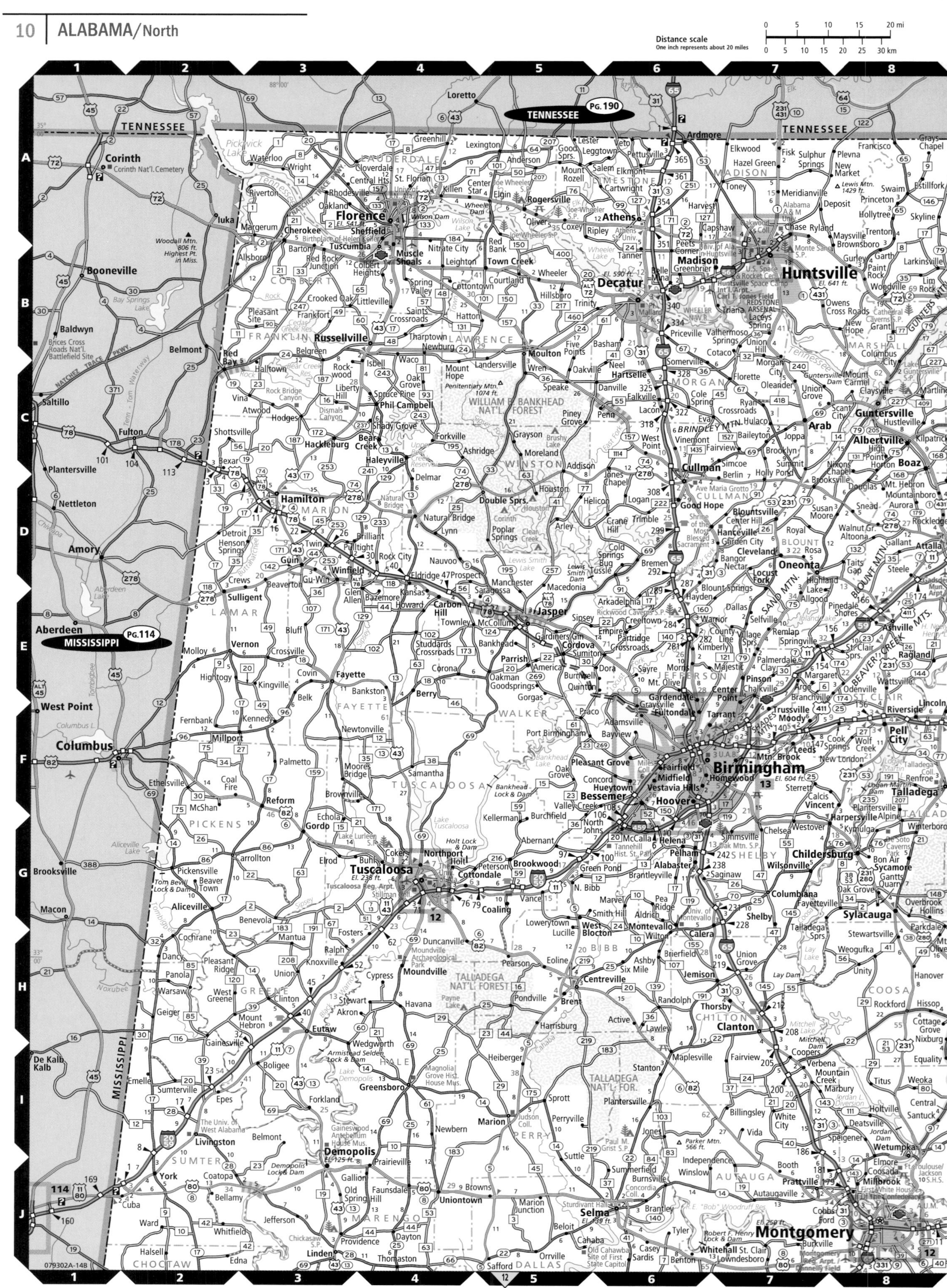

Distance scale
One inch represents about 20 miles
0 5 10 15 20 mi
0 5 10 15 20 25 30 km
TENNESSEE Pg. 190
MISSISSIPPI Pg. 114
TENNESSEE
MISSISSIPPI
Florence
Sheffield
Tuscumbia
Muscle Shoals
Athens
Decatur
Madison
Huntsville
Cullman
Jasper
Hamilton
Birmingham
Hoover
Bessemer
Tuscaloosa
Northport
Demopolis
Selma
Montgomery
Prattville
Columbus
Corinth
Amory
Aberdeen
Guntersville
Albertville
Gadsden
Talladega
Sylacauga
Clanton
Alabaster
Pelham
Childersburg
WILLIAM B. BANKHEAD NAT'L. FOREST
TALLADEGA NAT'L. FOREST
079302A-14B

How to determine distance

Mileages in red between red arrowheads; in black, between intersections.

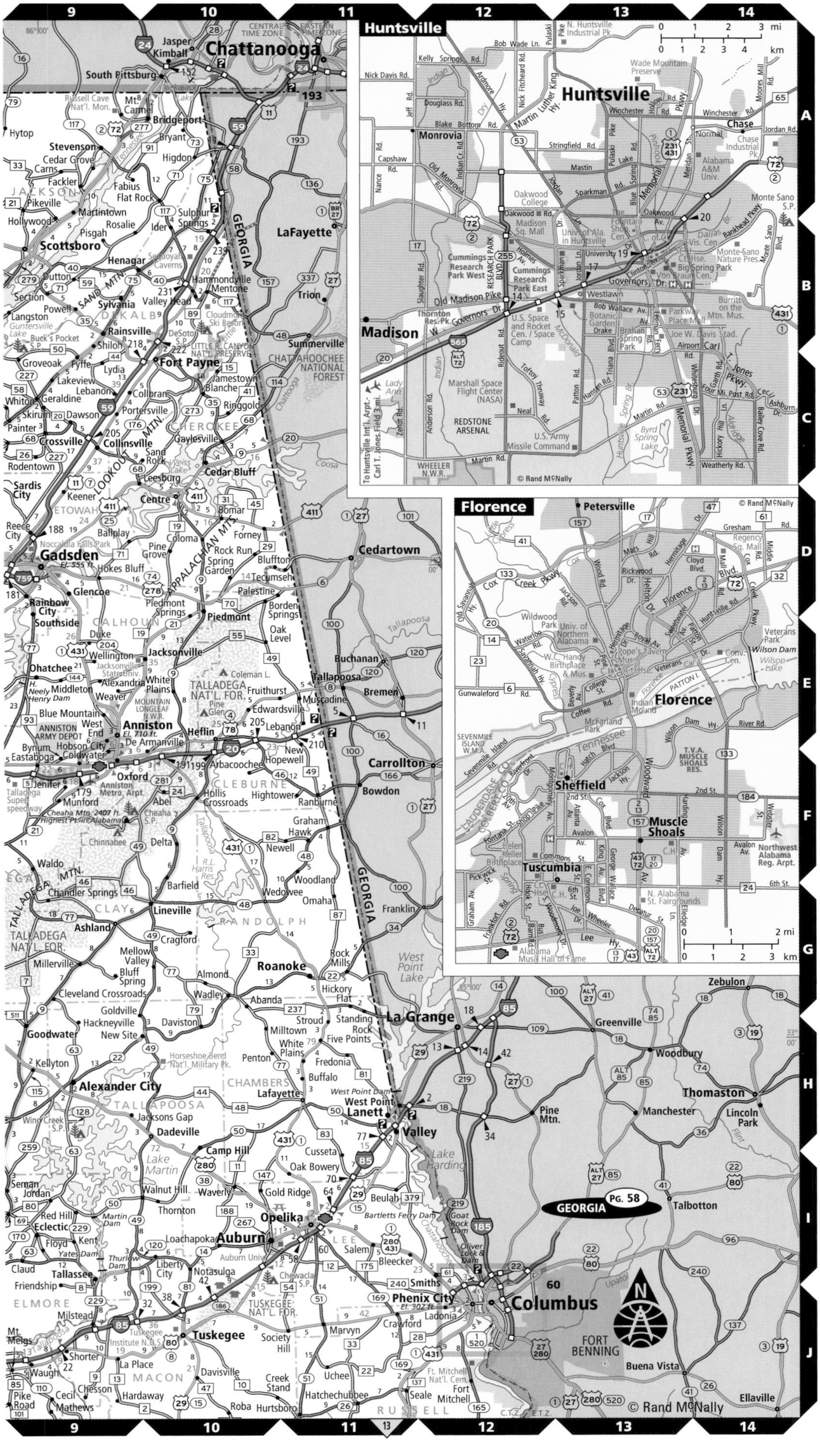

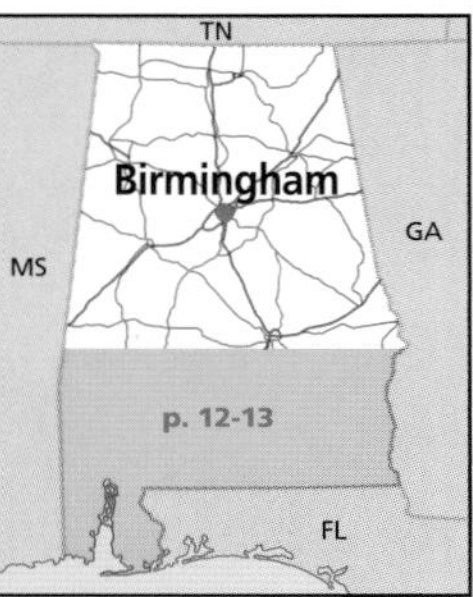
TN
Birmingham
MS
GA
p. 12-13
FL

SYMBOLS

Featured ride
Scenic route
Point of interest
Long-term construction
Harley-Davidson dealership

ALABAMA MOTORCYCLE LAWS

Helmet use:
Required

Riding two abreast:
Yes. See state law for specifics

Eye protection:
Not required

Speed limit
Primary roads: 70 mph
Secondary roads: 65 mph

ALABAMA RESOURCES

Road conditions or construction:
www.dot.state.al.us

Highway Emergency Numbers:
(334) 242-4378 or *HP

Tourism:
(800) 252-2262
www.800alabama.com
Tourism information and road construction updates also available at randmcnally.com

State motor vehicle information:
(334) 242-4371
www.dps.state.al.us

HARLEY-DAVIDSON DEALERSHIPS

Rocket Harley-Davidson Rocket Buell, B-6
15100 AL Hwy. 20 West **Madison**
(256) 340-7333; (888) 414-7316
Lat N 34.631 **Lon** W 86.876

Harley-Davidson of Montgomery, J-8
655 N. Eastern Blvd. **Montgomery**
(334) 277-2540
Lat N 32.402 **Lon** W 86.213

Big Swamp Harley-Davidson Shop, I-11
1201 Fox Run Pkwy. **Opelika**
(334) 364-0400
Lat N 32.656 **Lon** W 85.357

Mt. Cheaha Harley-Davidson, F-9
231 Davis Loop Rd. **Oxford**
(256) 832-8888
Lat N 33.595 **Lon** W 85.842

Heart of Dixie Harley-Davidson, G-6
333 Cahaba Valley Pkwy. **Pelham**
(205) 560-1234
Lat N 33.336 **Lon** W 86.784

Riders Harley-Davidson, F-7
4750 Norrell Dr. **Trussville**
(205) 655-1234
Lat N 33.641 **Lon** W 86.614

Foster Harley-Davidson, B-4
595 Hwy. 72 West **Tuscumbia**
(256) 383-5814
Lat N 34.714 **Lon** W 87.706

Distance scale
One inch represents about 20 miles
0 5 10 15 20 mi
0 5 10 15 20 25 30 km

1 2 3 4 5 6 7 8

K L M N O P Q R S T

PG. 114 MISS.

FLORIDA PG. 52

MISSISSIPPI

FLORIDA

GULF OF MEXICO

Mobile

Pensacola

Montgomery

Greenville

Monroeville

Brewton

Andalusia

Atmore

Jackson

Grove Hill

Camden

Evergreen

Foley

Gulf Shores

Pascagoula

Crestview

079302B-14B

Tuscaloosa

Northport

Tuscaloosa

0 1 2 mi
0 1 2 3 km

Montgomery

Montgomery

0 1 2 mi
0 1 2 3 km

Mobile

Chickasaw

Prichard

Mobile

Tillmans Corner

0 1 2 mi
0 1 2 3 km

How to determine distance

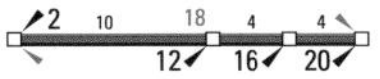

Mileages in red between red arrowheads; in black, between intersections.

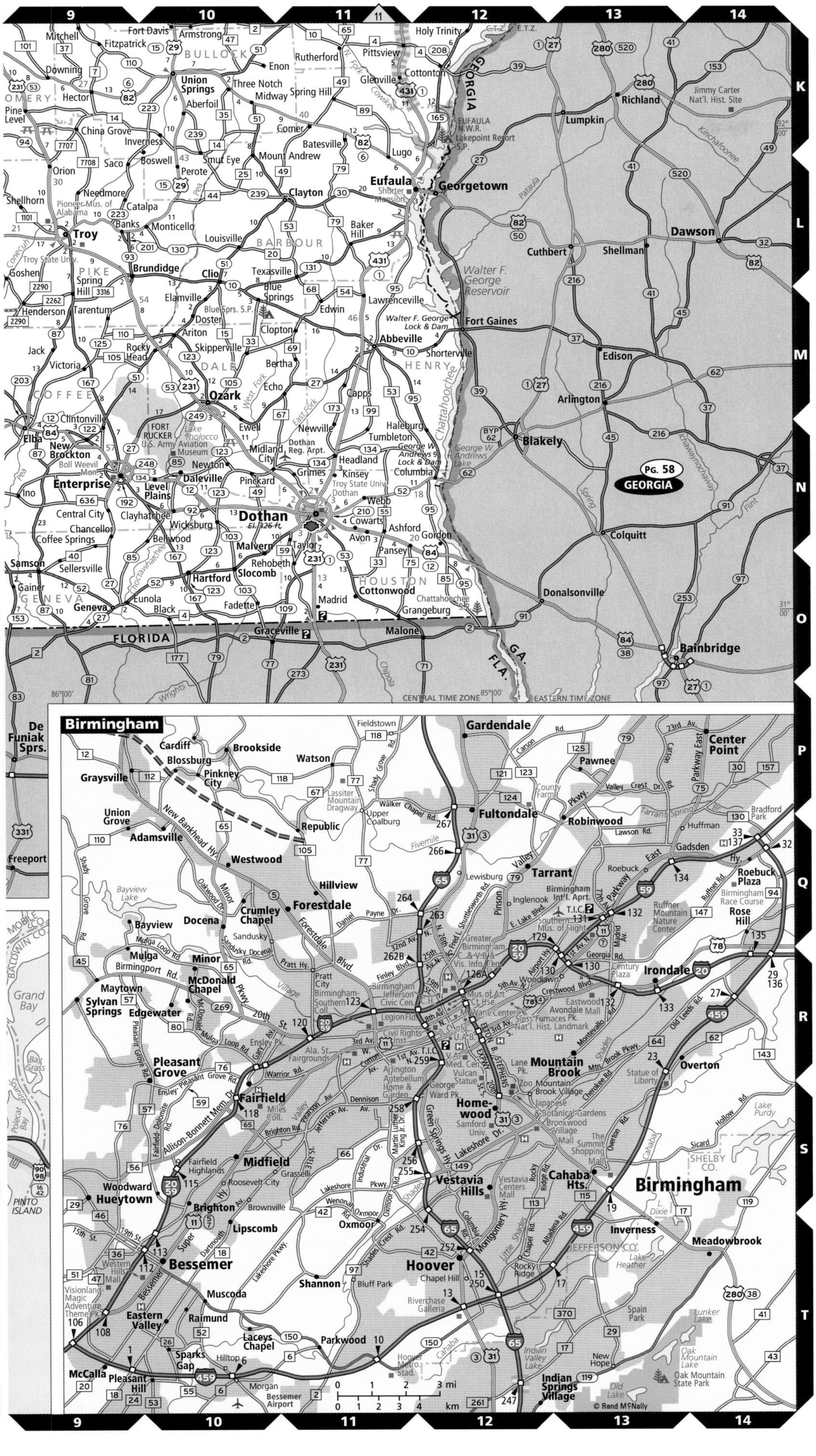

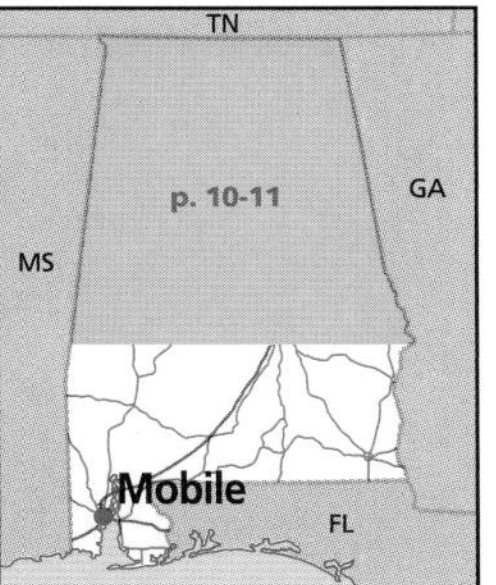
TN
p. 10-11
GA
MS
Mobile
FL

SYMBOLS

- Featured ride
- Scenic route
- Point of interest
- Long-term construction
- Harley-Davidson dealership

For Alabama/Florida ride, see page R6-7.

CITY-TO-CITY MILEAGE

	ATLANTA, GA	BIRMINGHAM	CHATTANOOGA, TN	DOTHAN	HUNTSVILLE	MOBILE	MONTGOMERY	TUSCALOOSA
Andalusia	249	181	319	75	277	125	89	194
Anniston	90	66	116	210	103	282	113	121
Atlanta, GA		148	115	202	193	329	160	203
Auburn	106	111	218	124	244	225	56	161
Birmingham	148		143	199	98	261	92	59
Chattanooga, TN	115	143		314	105	399	230	202
Decatur	227	80	130	277	26	339	170	135
Dothan	202	199	314		295	201	107	212
Eufaula	151	182	263	51	278	255	90	195
Florence	275	128	172	325	67	387	218	122
Gadsden	120	61	86	255	73	317	148	120
Huntsville	193	98	105	295		357	188	153
Jasper	188	41	183	238	90	300	131	56
Meridian, MS	290	146	289	253	240	134	152	93
Mobile	329	261	399	201	357		169	206
Montgomery	160	92	230	107	188	169		105
Pensacola, FL	319	251	389	156	347	55	159	261
Phenix City	105	141	217	97	276	257	88	193
Selma	210	94	232	151	190	193	50	75
Troy	193	142	280	57	238	173	50	155
Tuscaloosa	203	59	202	212	153	206	105	

HARLEY-DAVIDSON DEALERSHIPS

Eastern Shore Harley-Davidson Shop, P-3
7143 US Hwy. 90 **Daphne**
(251) 626-8050
Lat N 30.655 **Lon** W 87.901

Harley-Davidson of Dothan
Buell of Dothan, N-11
2418 Ross Clark Circle S.W. **Dothan**
(334) 792-0063
Lat N 31.198 **Lon** W 85.413

Mobile Bay Harley-Davidson, P-2
3260 Pleasant Valley Rd. **Mobile**
(251) 471-2174
Lat N 30.662 **Lon** W 88.124

PG. 58 GEORGIA

Birmingham

Distance scale
One inch represents about 141 miles
0 20 40 60 80 mi
0 40 80 120 km

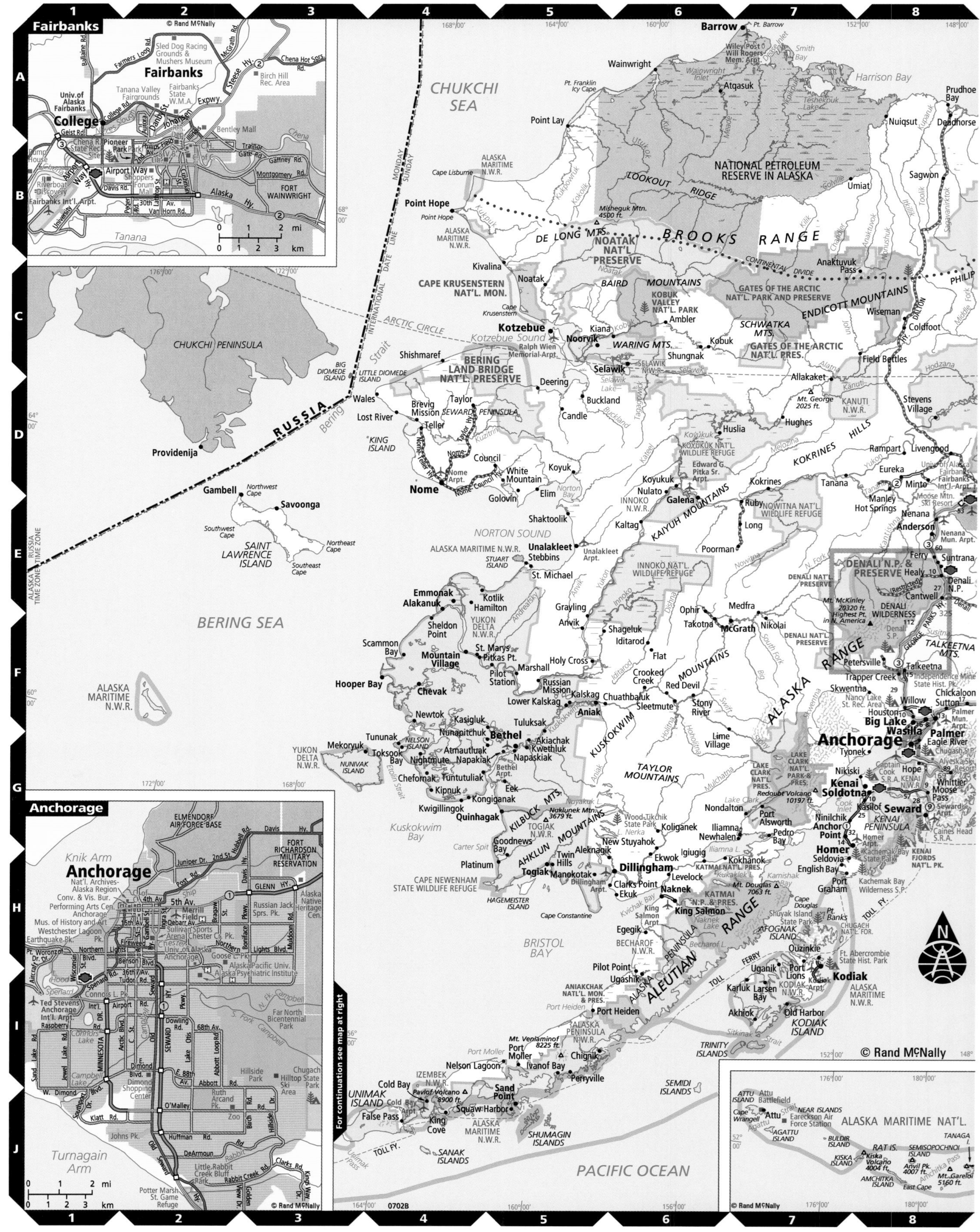

Fairbanks
© Rand McNally
Fairbanks
College
Univ. of Alaska Fairbanks
Sled Dog Racing Grounds & Mushers Museum
Tanana Valley Fairgrounds
Fairbanks State W.M.A.
Birch Hill Rec. Area
Chena Hot Sprs. Rd.
Farmers Loop Rd.
Steese Hy.
McGrath Rd.
Bentley Mall
Pioneer Park
Airport Way
Shoppers Forum Mall
Fort Wainwright
Alaska Hy.
Fairbanks Int'l. Arpt.
Riverboat Discovery
University Av.
Tanana
0 1 2 mi
0 1 2 3 km
CHUKCHI SEA
CHUKCHI PENINSULA
RUSSIA
Providenija
BIG DIOMEDE ISLAND
LITTLE DIOMEDE ISLAND
INTERNATIONAL DATE LINE
MONDAY SUNDAY
ARCTIC CIRCLE
RUSSIA TIME ZONE
ALASKA TIME ZONE
Gambell
Savoonga
Northwest Cape
Southwest Cape
Northeast Cape
Southeast Cape
SAINT LAWRENCE ISLAND
BERING SEA
ALASKA MARITIME N.W.R.
Barrow
Pt. Barrow
Wainwright
Wiley Post / Will Rogers Mem. Arpt.
Smith Bay
Atqasuk
Harrison Bay
Prudhoe Bay
Nuiqsut
Deadhorse
Pt. Franklin
Icy Cape
Point Lay
NATIONAL PETROLEUM RESERVE IN ALASKA
LOOKOUT RIDGE
Umiat
Sagwon
Cape Lisburne
ALASKA MARITIME N.W.R.
Point Hope
Misheguk Mtn. 4500 ft.
DE LONG MTS.
BROOKS RANGE
NOATAK NAT'L PRESERVE
CONTINENTAL DIVIDE
Anaktuvuk Pass
Kivalina
Noatak
BAIRD MOUNTAINS
KOBUK VALLEY NAT'L. PARK
GATES OF THE ARCTIC NAT'L. PARK AND PRESERVE
ENDICOTT MOUNTAINS
PHILIP
CAPE KRUSENSTERN NAT'L. MON.
Cape Krusenstern
Kotzebue
Kotzebue Sound
Ralph Wien Memorial Arpt.
Noorvik
Kiana
Ambler
Wiseman
Coldfoot
SCHWATKA MTS.
WARING MTS.
Shungnak
Kobuk
GATES OF THE ARCTIC NAT'L. PRES.
Shishmaref
BERING LAND BRIDGE NAT'L. PRESERVE
Selawik
SELAWIK N.W.R.
Field Bettles
Allakaket
Mt. George 2025 ft.
KANUTI N.W.R.
Stevens Village
Wales
Brevig Mission
Teller
Taylor
SEWARD PENINSULA
Deering
Buckland
Candle
Lost River
KING ISLAND
Huslia
Hughes
KOYUKUK NAT'L. WILDLIFE REFUGE
KOKRINES HILLS
Rampart
Livengood
Council
Nome
White Mountain
Koyuk
Elim
Golovin
Edward G. Pitka Sr. Arpt.
Koyukuk
Nulato
Galena
INNOKO N.W.R.
Kokrines
Tanana
Eureka
Minto
Manley Hot Springs
Ruby
NOWITNA NAT'L. WILDLIFE REFUGE
Nenana
Anderson
Long
Kaltag
KAIYUH MOUNTAINS
Shaktoolik
NORTON SOUND
Unalakleet
Stebbins
St. Michael
STUART ISLAND
Poorman
Ferry
Suntrana
Healy
DENALI N.P. & PRESERVE
DENALI NAT'L. PRESERVE
INNOKO NAT'L. WILDLIFE REFUGE
Emmonak
Alakanuk
Kotlik
Hamilton
Sheldon Point
YUKON DELTA N.W.R.
Grayling
Anvik
Ophir
Medfra
Takotna
McGrath
Nikolai
Mt. McKinley 20320 ft. Highest Pt. in N. America
DENALI WILDERNESS
Cantwell
Scammon Bay
Mountain Village
St. Marys
Pitkas Pt.
Pilot Station
Marshall
Holy Cross
Shageluk
Iditarod
Flat
ALASKA RANGE
TALKEETNA MTS.
Petersville
Talkeetna
Hooper Bay
Chevak
Russian Mission
Crooked Creek
Red Devil
Trapper Creek
Skwentna
Lower Kalskag
Kalskag
Aniak
Chuathbaluk
Sleetmute
Stony River
Willow
Houston
Big Lake
Wasilla
Palmer
Sutton
Chickaloon
Newtok
Kasigluk
Nunapitchuk
Tuluksak
Bethel
Akiachak
Kwethluk
Napaskiak
KUSKOKWIM MOUNTAINS
Lime Village
Anchorage
Tyonek
Eagle River
Tununak
Mekoryuk
NUNIVAK ISLAND
NELSON ISLAND
Toksook Bay
Nightmute
Atmautluak
Napakiak
Chefornak
Tuntutuliak
Eek
Kipnuk
Kongiganak
Kwigillingok
Quinhagak
TAYLOR MOUNTAINS
LAKE CLARK NAT'L. PARK & PRES.
Redoubt Volcano 10197 ft.
Nikiski
Kenai
Soldotna
Hope
Whittier
Moose Pass
Seward
Kasilof
KILBUCK MTS.
Nuklunek Mtn. 3679 ft.
TOGIAK N.W.R.
AHKLUN MOUNTAINS
Wood-Tikchik State Park
Koliganek
Nondalton
Port Alsworth
Iliamna
Newhalen
Pedro Bay
Ninilchik
Anchor Point
KENAI PENINSULA
Homer
Seldovia
English Bay
Port Graham
KENAI FJORDS NAT'L. PK.
Kuskokwim Bay
Goodnews Bay
Platinum
Togiak
Twin Hills
Aleknagik
New Stuyahok
Ekwok
Igiugig
Kokhanok
Dillingham
Manokotak
Clarks Point
Ekuk
Levelock
Naknek
King Salmon
KATMAI N.P. & PRES.
Mt. Douglas 7063 ft.
Cape Douglas
Shuyak Island State Park
AFOGNAK ISLAND
CHUGACH NAT'L. FOR.
Kachemak Bay Wilderness S.P.
CAPE NEWENHAM STATE WILDLIFE REFUGE
HAGEMEISTER ISLAND
Cape Constantine
Egegik
BECHAROF N.W.R.
BRISTOL BAY
ALEUTIAN RANGE
ALASKA PENINSULA
Pilot Point
Ugashik
Ouzinkie
Port Lions
Kodiak
Ft. Abercrombie State Hist. Park
Uganik
Karluk
Larsen Bay
Akhiok
Old Harbor
KODIAK ISLAND
ANIAKCHAK NATL. MON. & PRES.
Port Heiden
ALASKA PENINSULA N.W.R.
TRINITY ISLANDS
Sitkinak Strait
Mt. Veniaminof 8225 ft.
Port Moller
Chignik
Ivanof Bay
Perryville
Nelson Lagoon
IZEMBEK N.W.R.
Pavlof Volcano 8900 ft.
Cold Bay
Sand Point
Squaw Harbor
UNIMAK ISLAND
False Pass
King Cove
SHUMAGIN ISLANDS
SANAK ISLANDS
SEMIDI ISLANDS
PACIFIC OCEAN
© Rand McNally
ATTU ISLAND
Attu Battlefield
Attu
NEAR ISLANDS
Eareckson Air Force Station
AGATTU ISLAND
ALASKA MARITIME NAT'L.
BULDIR ISLAND
RAT IS.
KISKA ISLAND
Kiska Volcano 4004 ft.
SEMISOPOCHNOI ISLAND
Anvil Pk. 4007 ft.
AMCHITKA ISLAND
Mt. Gareloi 5160 ft.
TANAGA I.
Anchorage
ELMENDORF AIR FORCE BASE
FORT RICHARDSON MILITARY RESERVATION
Knik Arm
Nat'l. Archives-Alaska Region
Conv. & Vis. Bur.
Performing Arts Cen.
Anchorage Mus. of History and Art
Westchester Lagoon Pk.
Earthquake Pk.
Alaska Native Heritage Cen.
Russian Jack Sprs. Pk.
Merrill Field
Sullivan Sports Arena
Univ. of Alaska Anchorage
Alaska Pacific Univ.
Alaska Psychiatric Institute
Goose L. Pk.
Ted Stevens Anchorage Int'l. Arpt.
Far North Bicentennial Park
Hillside Park
Hilltop State Park Ski Area
Chugach State Park
Dimond Shopping Center
Ruth Arcand Pk.
Zoo
Johns Pk.
Little Rabbit Creek Bluff Pk.
Potter Marsh St. Game Refuge
Turnagain Arm
0 1 2 mi
0 1 2 3 km
© Rand McNally
For continuation see map at right
0702B

How to determine distance

Mileages in red between red arrowheads; in black, between intersections.

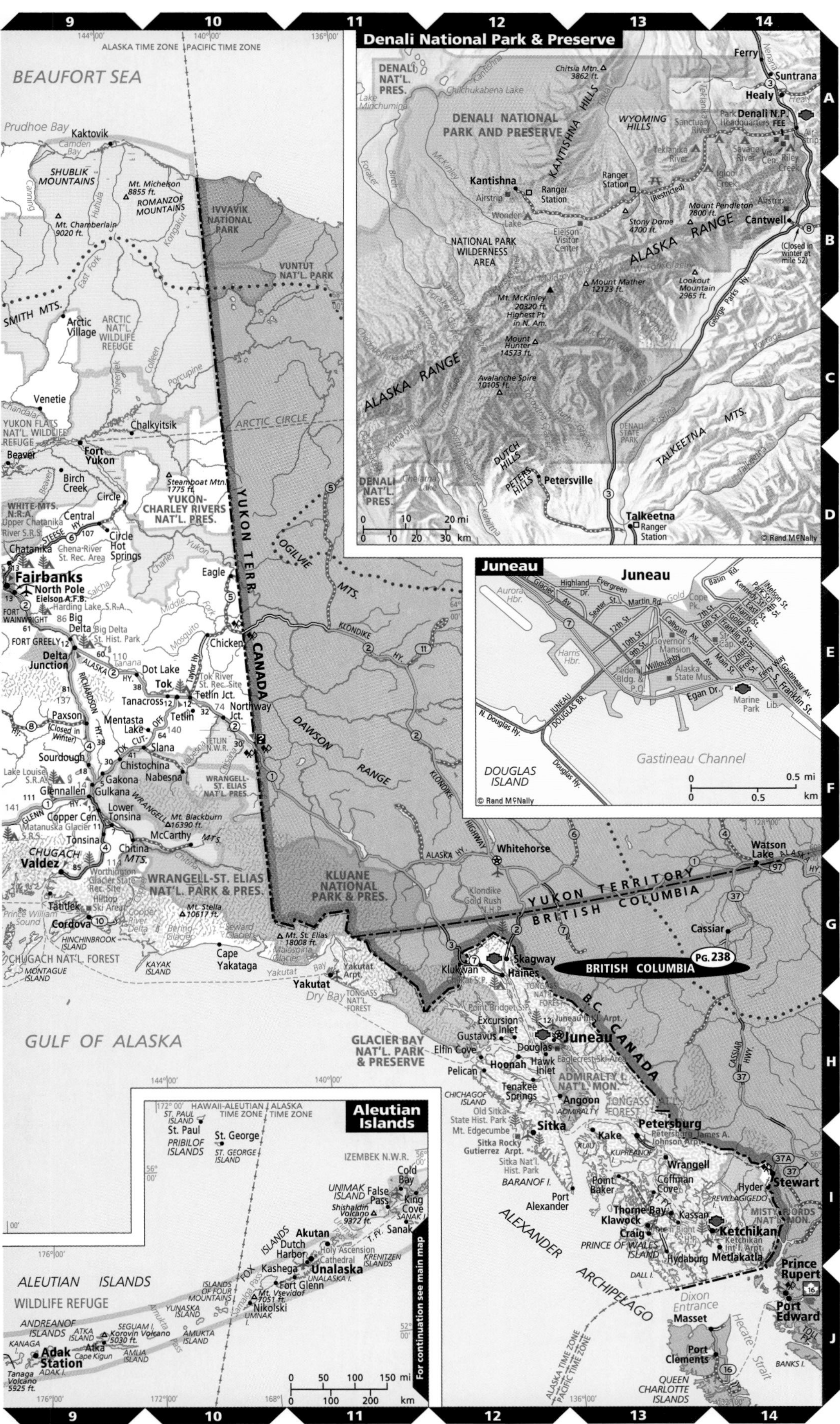

BEAUFORT SEA
GULF OF ALASKA
Denali National Park & Preserve
DENALI NATIONAL PARK AND PRESERVE
ALASKA RANGE
Juneau
Gastineau Channel
DOUGLAS ISLAND
Aleutian Islands
ALEUTIAN ISLANDS WILDLIFE REFUGE
For continuation see main map
BRITISH COLUMBIA PG. 238
YUKON TERRITORY
BRITISH COLUMBIA
YUKON TERR.
CANADA
Fairbanks
Juneau
Healy
Cantwell
Talkeetna
Petersville
Kantishna
Skagway
Haines
Sitka
Ketchikan
Valdez
Tok
Delta Junction
Whitehorse
Prince Rupert
ALEXANDER ARCHIPELAGO
© Rand McNally

SYMBOLS

Featured ride — Scenic route — Point of interest — Long-term construction — Harley-Davidson dealership

ALASKA MOTORCYCLE LAWS

Helmet use:
Required under age 18
Required for passengers

Riding two abreast:
Yes. See state law for specifics

Eye protection:
Required unless equipped with windscreen which is 15 inches or higher above handlebars

Speed limit:
Primary roads: 65 mph
Secondary roads: 55 mph

ALASKA RESOURCES

Road conditions or construction:
511
(866) 282-7577
(800) 478-7675 (in AK)
(907) 456-7623
(907) 269-0450
511.alaska.gov

Highway Emergency Numbers:
911

Tourism:
(907) 929-2200
www.travelalaska.com

State motor vehicle information:
(907) 269-5551
www.state.ak.us/dmv

HARLEY-DAVIDSON DEALERSHIPS

House of Harley-Davidson, G-8
4334 Spenard Rd. **Anchorage**
(907) 248-5300
Lat N 61.182 **Lon** W 149.934

Mt. McKinley Harley-Davidson, E-8
Mile 238.6 Parks Hwy. **Denali Nat'l Park**
(907) 683-4275
Lat N 63.624 **Lon** W 150.140

Harley-Davidson Farthest North Outpost, E-9
1450 Karen Way **Fairbanks**
(907) 456-3265
Lat N 64.835 **Lon** W 147.830

Taku Harley-Davidson Shop, H-12
263 Marine Way **Juneau**
(907) 586-4100
Lat N 58.298 **Lon** W 134.404

Inside Passage Harley-Davidson, I-14
34 Front St. Ste. 204 **Ketchikan**
(907) 225-4625
Lat N 55.343 **Lon** W 131.653

Chilkoot Pass Harley-Davidson, G-12
750 Broadway St. **Skagway**
(907) 983-3620
Lat N 59.460 **Lon** W 135.307

Kenai Peninsula Harley-Davidson Shop, G-8
41605 Sterling Hwy. **Soldotna**
(907) 260-6777
Lat N 60.498 **Lon** W 151.021

Denali Harley-Davidson Shop, F-8
1497 S Hyer Rd. **Wasilla**
(907) FREEDOM
Lat N 61.592 **Lon** W 149.458

Distance scale
One inch represents about 29 miles
0 10 20 30 mi
0 10 20 30 40 km

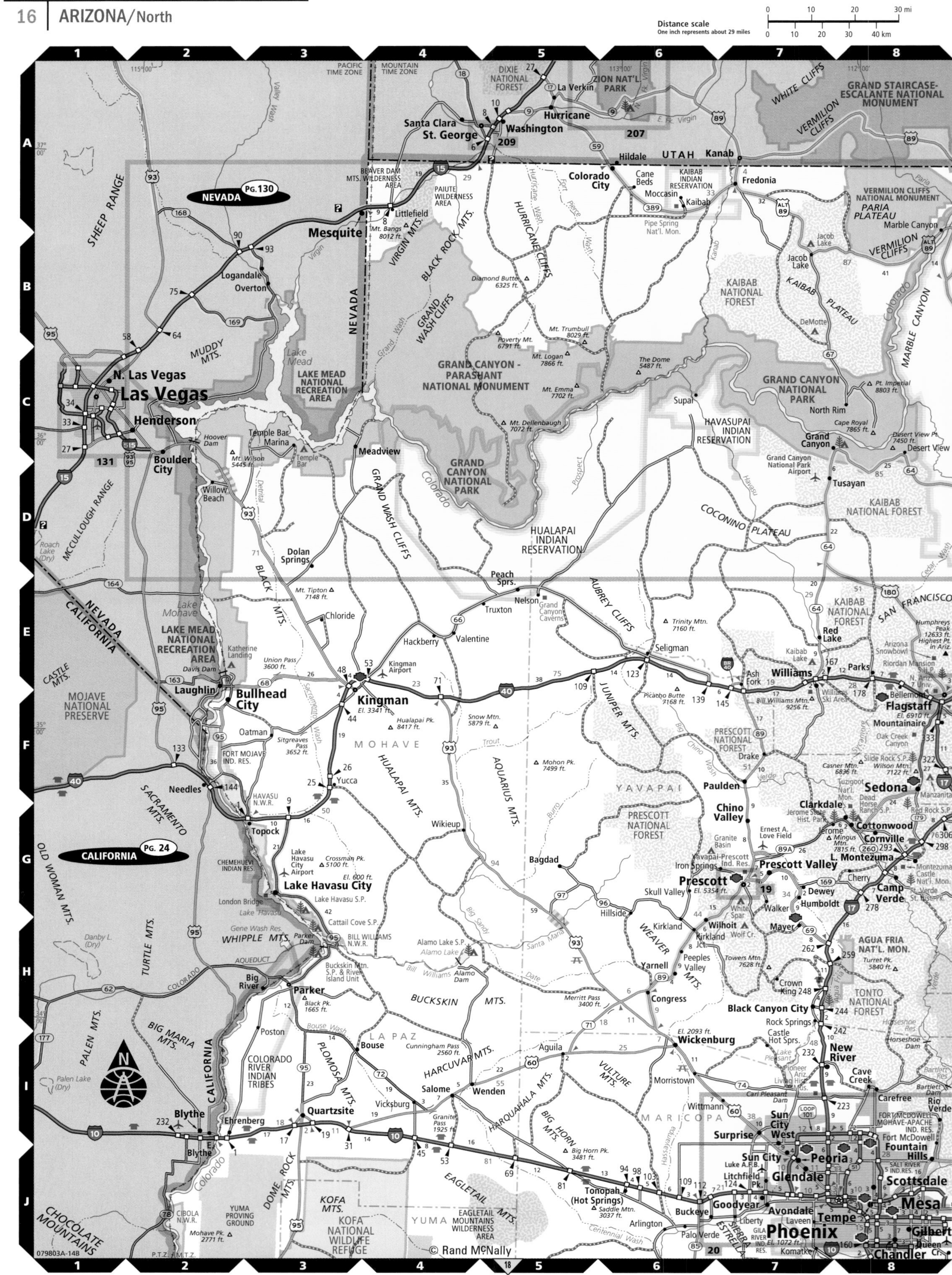

PACIFIC TIME ZONE
MOUNTAIN TIME ZONE
DIXIE NATIONAL FOREST
ZION NAT'L. PARK
La Verkin
Hurricane
Santa Clara
St. George
Washington
209
207
UTAH
Hildale
Kanab
Colorado City
Cane Beds
Moccasin
Kaibab
KAIBAB INDIAN RESERVATION
Fredonia
Pipe Spring Nat'l. Mon.
WHITE CLIFFS
VERMILION CLIFFS
GRAND STAIRCASE-ESCALANTE NATIONAL MONUMENT
VERMILION CLIFFS NATIONAL MONUMENT
PARIA PLATEAU
Marble Canyon
Jacob Lake
KAIBAB PLATEAU
KAIBAB NATIONAL FOREST
DeMotte
MARBLE CANYON
NEVADA PG.130
SHEEP RANGE
Mesquite
Littlefield
BEAVER DAM MTS. WILDERNESS AREA
PAIUTE WILDERNESS AREA
VIRGIN MTS.
BLACK ROCK MTS.
HURRICANE CLIFFS
GRAND WASH CLIFFS
Mt. Bangs 8012 ft.
Diamond Butte 6325 ft.
Logandale
Overton
MUDDY MTS.
NEVADA
Lake Mead
LAKE MEAD NATIONAL RECREATION AREA
Poverty Mt. 6791 ft.
Mt. Trumbull 8029 ft.
Mt. Logan 7866 ft.
Mt. Emma 7702 ft.
The Dome 5487 ft.
GRAND CANYON - PARASHANT NATIONAL MONUMENT
GRAND CANYON NATIONAL PARK
North Rim
Pt. Imperial 8803 ft.
Cape Royal 7865 ft.
N. Las Vegas
Las Vegas
Henderson
Boulder City
Hoover Dam
Temple Bar Marina
Mt. Wilson 5445 ft.
Meadview
Mt. Dellenbaugh 7072 ft.
Supai
HAVASUPAI INDIAN RESERVATION
Grand Canyon
Desert View Pt. 7450 ft.
Desert View
Grand Canyon National Park Airport
Tusayan
KAIBAB NATIONAL FOREST
Willow Beach
MCCULLOUGH RANGE
Roach Lake (Dry)
Colorado
GRAND WASH CLIFFS
HUALAPAI INDIAN RESERVATION
COCONINO PLATEAU
Dolan Springs
BLACK MTS.
Peach Sprs.
Nelson
Grand Canyon Caverns
AUBREY CLIFFS
Mt. Tipton 7148 ft.
Chloride
Truxton
NEVADA CALIFORNIA
Lake Mohave
LAKE MEAD NATIONAL RECREATION AREA
Katherine Landing
Davis Dam
Union Pass 3600 ft.
Hackberry
Valentine
Trinity Mtn. 7160 ft.
Seligman
SAN FRANCISCO
Humphreys Peak 12633 ft. Highest Pt. in Ariz.
Arizona Snowbowl
Red Lake
Kaibab Lake
Williams
Parks
Ash Fork
Riordan Mansion S.H.P.
CASTLE MTS.
MOJAVE NATIONAL PRESERVE
Laughlin
Bullhead City
Kingman
El. 3341 ft.
Kingman Airport
Hualapai Pk. 8417 ft.
Snow Mtn. 5879 ft.
JUNIPER MTS.
Picacho Butte 7168 ft.
Bill Williams Mtn. 9256 ft.
Williams Ski Area
Bellemont
Flagstaff
El. 6910 ft.
Mountainaire
Oak Creek Canyon
Oatman
Sitgreaves Pass 3652 ft.
FORT MOJAVE IND. RES.
MOHAVE
HUALAPAI MTS.
AQUARIUS MTS.
Mohon Pk. 7499 ft.
PRESCOTT NATIONAL FOREST
Drake
Slide Rock S.P.
Casner Mtn. 6836 ft.
Wilson Mtn. 7122 ft.
Sedona
Needles
Yucca
Paulden
YAVAPAI
Chino Valley
Tuzigoot Nat'l. Mon.
Clarkdale
Jerome State Hist. Park
Manzanita
SACRAMENTO MTS.
HAVASU N.W.R.
Topock
Wikieup
Jerome
Cottonwood
Cornville
Red Rock S.P.
CALIFORNIA PG. 24
OLD WOMAN MTS.
CHEMEHUEVI INDIAN RES.
Lake Havasu City Airport
Crossman Pk. 5100 ft.
El. 600 ft.
Lake Havasu City
Bagdad
PRESCOTT NATIONAL FOREST
Granite Basin
Ernest A. Love Field
Mingus Mtn. 7815 ft.
L. Montezuma
Montezuma Castle Nat'l. Mon.
Iron Springs
Yavapai-Prescott Ind. Res.
Prescott Valley
Prescott
El. 5354 ft.
Skull Valley
Dewey
Humboldt
Cherry
Camp Verde
London Bridge
Lake Havasu S.P.
Cattail Cove S.P.
Gene Wash Res.
WHIPPLE MTS.
Parker Dam
BILL WILLIAMS N.W.R.
Hillside
WEAVER MTS.
Kirkland
Kirkland Jct.
Wilhoit
Walker
Mayer
Wolf Cr.
AGUA FRIA NAT'L. MON.
Turret Pk. 5840 ft.
Danby L. (Dry)
TURTLE MTS.
AQUEDUCT
Alamo Lake S.P.
Alamo Lake
Alamo Dam
Santa Maria
Peeples Valley
Yarnell
Towers Mtn. 7628 ft.
Crown King
TONTO NATIONAL FOREST
Big River
Parker
Buckskin Mtn. S.P. & River Island Unit
Black Pk. 1665 ft.
BUCKSKIN MTS.
Merritt Pass 3400 ft.
Congress
Black Canyon City
Rock Springs
Castle Hot Sprs.
Horseshoe Res.
Horseshoe Dam
PALEN MTS.
BIG MARIA MTS.
CALIFORNIA
Poston
LA PAZ
Bouse
PLOMOSA MTS.
Cunningham Pass 2560 ft.
HARCUVAR MTS.
Aguila
VULTURE MTS.
El. 2093 ft.
Wickenburg
New River
Cave Creek
Palen Lake (Dry)
COLORADO RIVER INDIAN TRIBES
Salome
Wenden
HARQUAHALA MTS.
BIG HORN MTS.
Morristown
Lake Pleasant
Carl Pleasant Dam
Carefree
Rio Verde
Bartlett Dam
Blythe
Ehrenberg
Quartzsite
Vicksburg
Granite Pass 1925 ft.
Wittmann
MARICOPA
Sun City
Sun City West
Surprise
FORT MCDOWELL MOHAVE-APACHE IND. RES.
Fort McDowell
Fountain Hills
Big Horn Pk. 3481 ft.
Luke A.F.B.
Peoria
Glendale
Litchfield Pk.
SALT RIVER IND. RES.
Scottsdale
EAGLETAIL MTS.
Tonopah (Hot Springs)
Saddle Mtn. 3037 ft.
Buckeye
Goodyear
Avondale
Tempe
Mesa
Gilbert
CHOCOLATE MOUNTAINS
CIBOLA N.W.R.
YUMA PROVING GROUND
Mohave Pk. 2771 ft.
DOME ROCK MTS.
KOFA MTS.
KOFA NATIONAL WILDLIFE REFUGE
YUMA
EAGLETAIL MOUNTAINS WILDERNESS AREA
Arlington
Liberty
Laveen
Phoenix
Palo Verde
SIERRA ESTRELLA
GILA RIVER IND. RES.
El. 1072 ft.
Komatke
Chandler
Queen Cr.
© Rand McNally
079803A-14B

How to determine distance

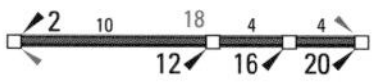

Mileages in red between red arrowheads; in black, between intersections.

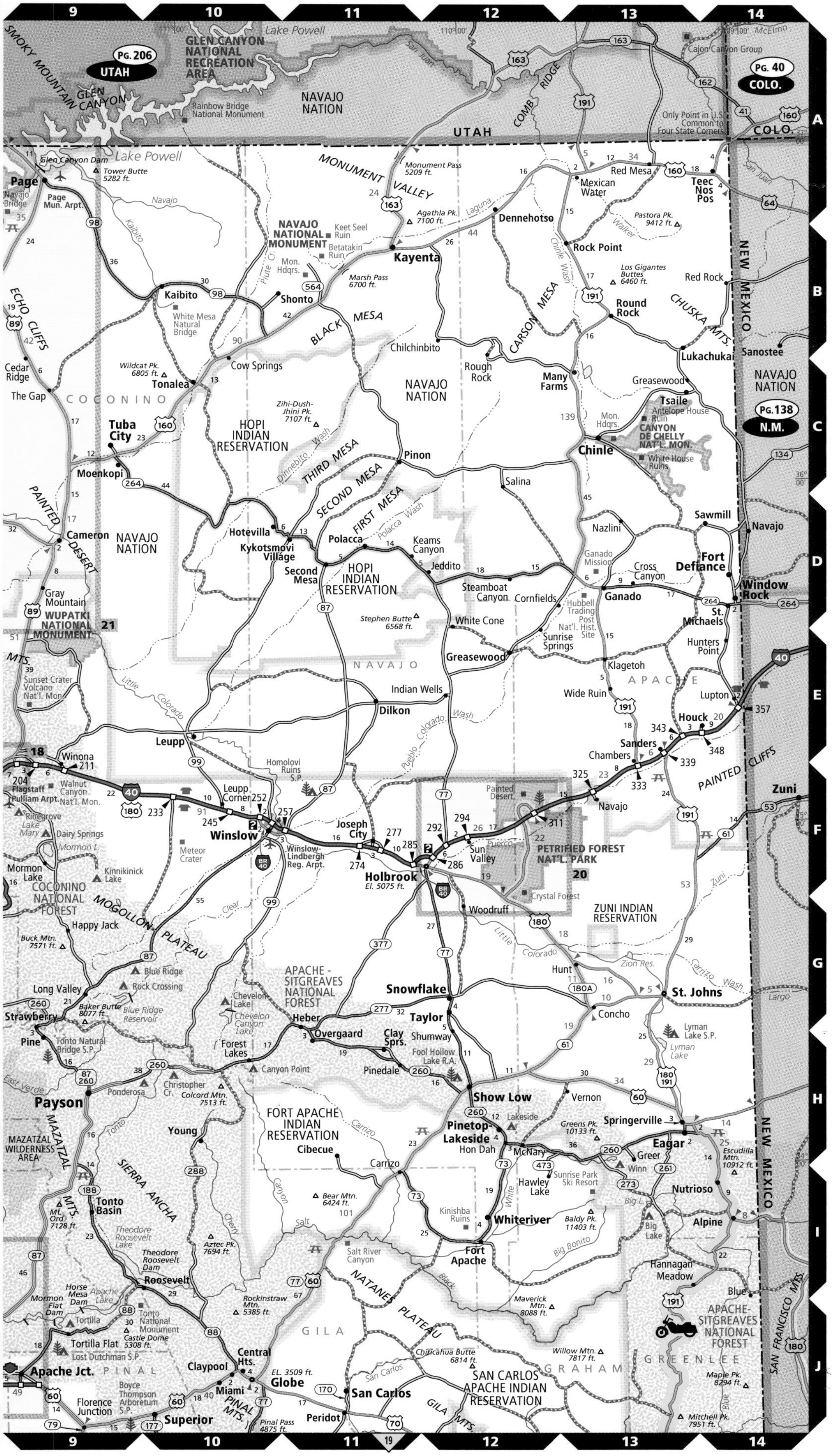

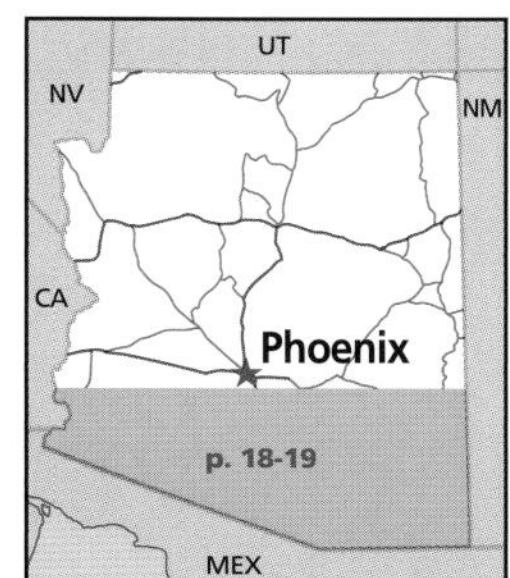
UT
NV
NM
CA
Phoenix
p. 18-19
MEX

SYMBOLS

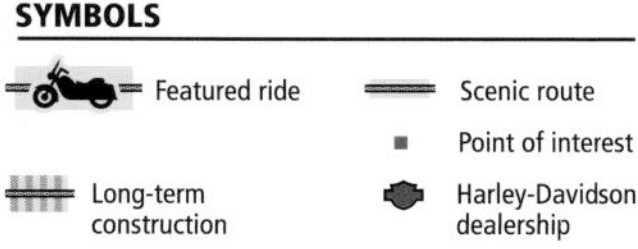
Featured ride
Scenic route
Point of interest
Long-term construction
Harley-Davidson dealership

For Arizona ride, see page R9.

ARIZONA MOTORCYCLE LAWS

Helmet use:
Required under age 18

Riding two abreast:
Yes. See state law for specifics

Eye protection:
Required unless equipped with windscreen

Speed limit:
Primary roads: 75 mph
Secondary roads: 55 mph

ARIZONA RESOURCES

Road conditions or construction:
511
(888) 411-7623
www.az511.com

Highway Emergency Numbers:
911

Tourism:
(866) 239-9712
www.arizonaguide.com

State motor vehicle information:
(602) 712-7090
www.dot.state.az.us/mvd

HARLEY-DAVIDSON DEALERSHIPS

For the Phoenix metro area, please see dealer listings on page 21.

- **Grand Canyon Harley-Davidson, F-8**
  I-40 Exit 185 **Bellemont**
  (928) 774-3896
  Lat N 35.174 **Lon** W 111.894
- **Mother Road Harley-Davidson, E-3**
  2501 Beverly Ave. **Kingman**
  (928) 757-1166
  Lat N 35.218 **Lon** W 114.020
- **Grand Canyon Harley-Davidson Shop, H-7**
  10434 S Hwy. 69 **Mayer**
  (928) 632-4009
  Lat N 34.392 **Lon** W 112.222
- **Grand Canyon Harley-Davidson, G-7**
  138 S Montezuma **Prescott**
  (928) 778-2241
  Lat N 34.541 **Lon** W 112.470
- **Grand Canyon Harley-Davidson, F-8**
  320 N Hwy. 89A **Sedona**
  (928) 774-3896
  Lat N 34.871 **Lon** W 111.759

Distance scale
One inch represents about 29 miles
0 10 20 30 mi
0 10 20 30 40 km

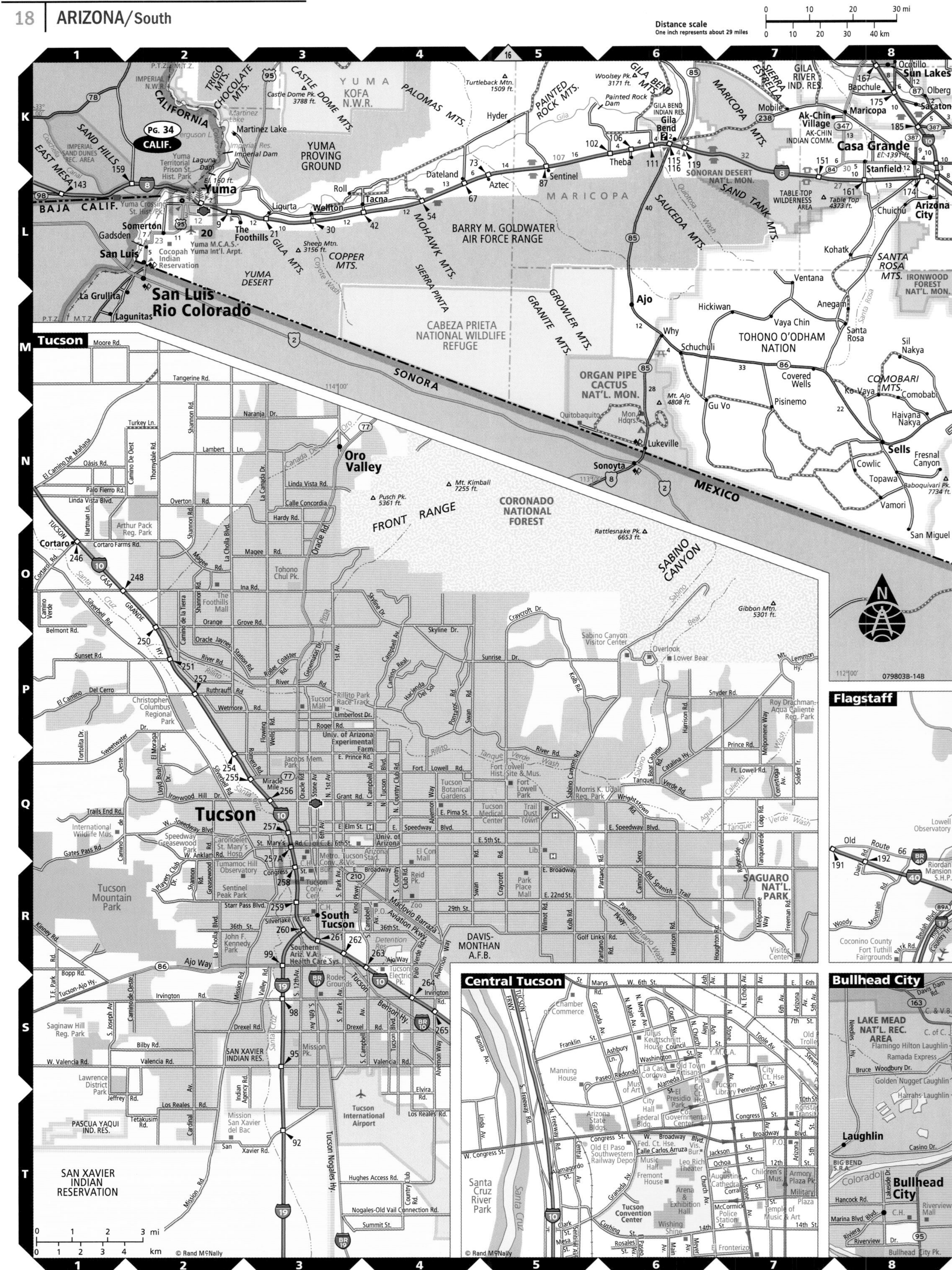

YUMA
KOFA N.W.R.
CASTLE DOME MTS.
Castle Dome Pk. 3788 ft.
PALOMAS MTS.
Turtleback Mtn. 1509 ft.
Hyder
PAINTED ROCK MTS.
Woolsey Pk. 3171 ft.
Painted Rock Dam
GILA BEND MTS.
GILA BEND INDIAN RES.
Gila Bend
MARICOPA MTS.
SIERRA ESTRELLA
GILA RIVER IND. RES.
Mobile
Ak-Chin Village
AK-CHIN INDIAN COMM.
Maricopa
Bapchule
Ocotillo
Sun Lakes
Olberg
Sacaton
Casa Grande
El. 1391 ft.
Stanfield
IMPERIAL N.W.R.
TRIGO MTS.
CHOCOLATE MTS.
CALIFORNIA
Martinez Lake
Imperial Dam
YUMA PROVING GROUND
PG. 34 CALIF.
SAND HILLS
IMPERIAL SAND DUNES REC. AREA
EAST MESA
Yuma Territorial Prison St. Hist. Park
Laguna Dam
El. 160 ft.
Yuma
Yuma Crossing St. Hist. Pk.
BAJA CALIF.
Roll
Dateland
Aztec
Sentinel
Theba
MARICOPA
SONORAN DESERT NAT'L. MON.
SAND TANK MTS.
TABLE TOP WILDERNESS AREA
Table Top 4373 ft.
Chuichu
Arizona City
Somerton
Gadsden
San Luis
Cocopah Indian Reservation
Yuma M.C.A.S.-Yuma Int'l. Arpt.
The Foothills
Ligurta
Wellton
Tacna
MOHAWK MTS.
BARRY M. GOLDWATER AIR FORCE RANGE
SAUCEDA MTS.
Kohatk
SANTA ROSA MTS.
IRONWOOD FOREST NAT'L. MON.
GILA MTS.
Sheep Mtn. 3156 ft.
COPPER MTS.
YUMA DESERT
SIERRA PINTA
GRANITE MTS.
GROWLER MTS.
Ajo
Ventana
Hickiwan
Anegam
Vaya Chin
La Grullita
San Luis Rio Colorado
Lagunitas
CABEZA PRIETA NATIONAL WILDLIFE REFUGE
Why
Schuchuli
TOHONO O'ODHAM NATION
Santa Rosa
Sil Nakya
SONORA
ORGAN PIPE CACTUS NAT'L. MON.
Mt. Ajo 4808 ft.
Covered Wells
Gu Vo
Pisinemo
COMOBARI MTS.
Comobabi
Ko Vaya
Haivana Nakya
Quitobaquito
Mon. Hdqrs.
Lukeville
Sonoyta
Sells
Fresnal Canyon
Cowlic
Topawa
Baboquivari Pk. 7734 ft.
Vamori
San Miguel
MEXICO
Tucson
Oro Valley
Mt. Kimball 7255 ft.
Pusch Pk. 5361 ft.
FRONT RANGE
CORONADO NATIONAL FOREST
Rattlesnake Pk. 6653 ft.
SABINO CANYON
Gibbon Mtn. 5301 ft.
Cortaro
Arthur Pack Reg. Park
Tohono Chul Pk.
The Foothills Mall
Sabino Canyon Visitor Center
Overlook
Lower Bear
Christopher Columbus Regional Park
Tucson Mall
Rillito Park Race Track
Univ. of Arizona Experimental Farm
Roy Drachman-Agua Caliente Reg. Park
Jacobs Mem. Park
Miracle Mile
Fort Lowell Hist. Site & Mus.
Tucson Botanical Gardens
Fort Lowell Park
Morris K. Udall Reg. Park
International Wildlife Mus.
Tucson Medical Center
Trail Dust Town
Speedway Greasewood Park
Carondelet St. Mary's Hosp.
Tumamoc Hill Observatory
Univ. of Arizona
Arizona Stad.
El Con Mall
Metro. Tucson Conv. & Vis. Bur.
Tucson Mountain Park
Sentinel Peak Park
Tucson Conv. Cen.
Reid Pk.
Park Place Mall
SAGUARO NAT'L. PARK
South Tucson
Zoo
DAVIS-MONTHAN A.F.B.
John F. Kennedy Park
Southern Ariz. V.A. Health Care Sys.
Detention Res.
Rodeo Grounds
Tucson Electric Pk.
Saginaw Hill Reg. Park
SAN XAVIER INDIAN RES.
Mission Pk.
Lawrence District Park
Mission San Xavier del Bac
Tucson International Airport
PASCUA YAQUI IND. RES.
SAN XAVIER INDIAN RESERVATION
Flagstaff
Lowell Observatory
Riordan Mansion S.H.P.
Coconino County Fort Tuthill Fairgrounds
Central Tucson
Chamber of Commerce
Julius Keuttschnitt House Council
Manning House
Old Town Artisans
La Casa Cordova
Mus. of Art
El Presidio Park
City Hall
Federal Bldg.
Co. Governmental Center
Tucson Library
City Ct. Hse.
Arizona State Bldgs.
Old El Paso Southwestern Railway Depot
Fed. Ct. Hse.
Music Hall
Leo Rich Theater
Fremont House
St. Augustine Cathedral
Children's Mus.
Armory Plaza Pk.
Military Plaza
Santa Cruz River Park
Tucson Convention Center
Arena & Exhibition Hall
McCormick Police Station
Temple of Music & Art
Wishing Shine
Bullhead City
LAKE MEAD NAT'L. REC. AREA
Flamingo Hilton Laughlin
Ramada Express
Golden Nugget Laughlin
Harrahs Laughlin
Laughlin
BIG BEND S.R.A.
Colorado
Riverview Mall
© Rand McNally
079803B-14B

How to determine distance

Mileages in red between red arrowheads; in black, between intersections.

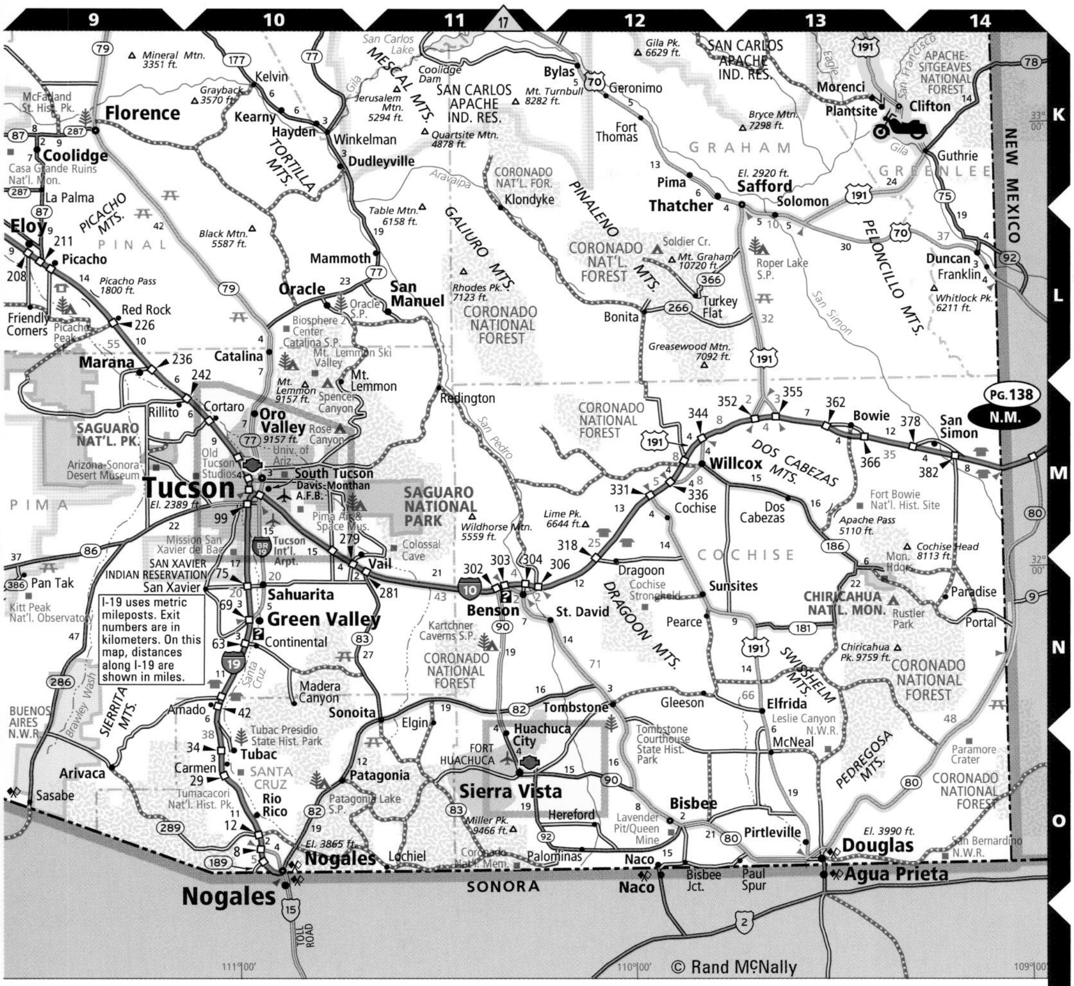

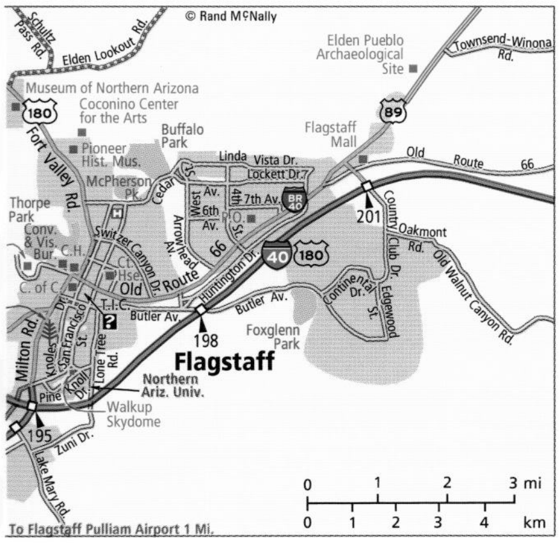

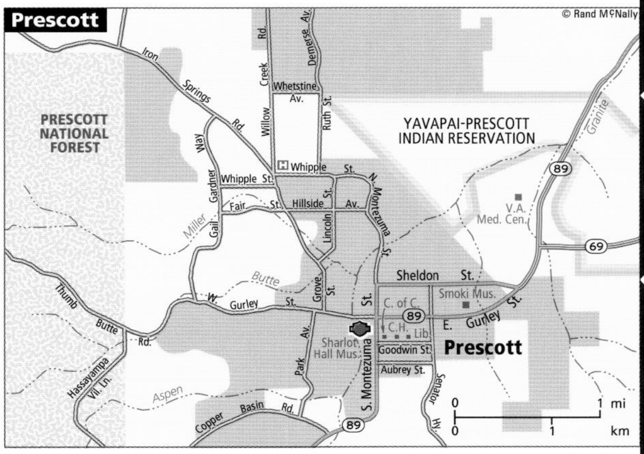

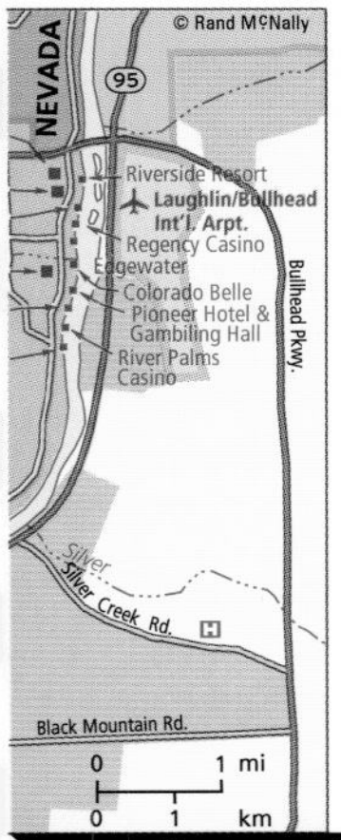

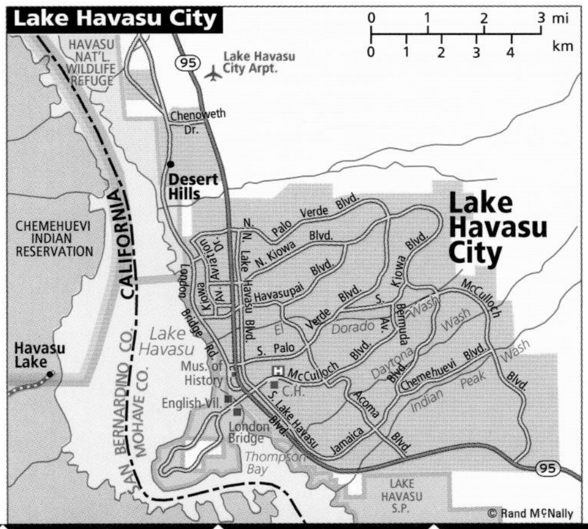

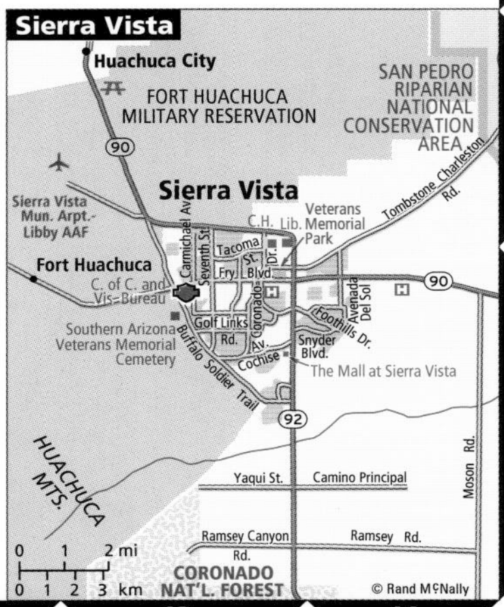

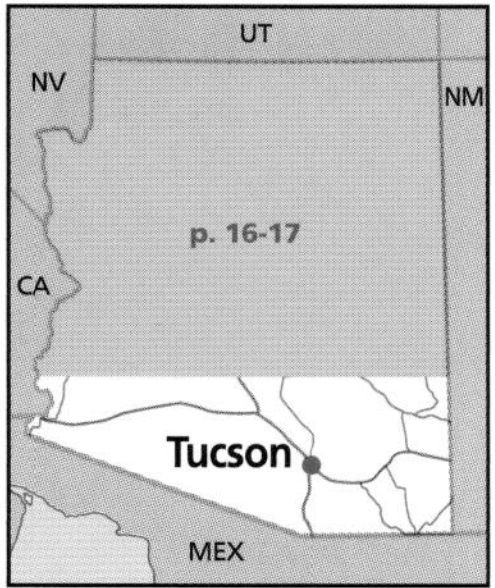
UT
NV
NM
CA
p. 16-17
Tucson
MEX

SYMBOLS

Featured ride — Scenic route — Point of interest — Long-term construction — Harley-Davidson dealership

For Arizona ride, see page R9.

CITY-TO-CITY MILEAGE

	CASA GRANDE	FLAGSTAFF	HOLBROOK	KINGMAN	PHOENIX	PRESCOTT	TUCSON	YUMA
Blythe, CA	197	282	374	157	146	155	263	103
Casa Grande		187	221	236	51	145	67	172
Eagar	221	179	87	323	225	272	241	397
Flagstaff	187		92	144	136	93	253	318
Gallup, NM	318	188	97	332	324	281	338	506
Grand Canyon	268	81	169	167	217	123	334	337
Holbrook	221	92		236	228	185	241	410
Kingman	236	144	236		185	146	302	215
Lake Havasu City	249	204	296	60	198	206	315	155
Las Vegas, NV	341	249	341	105	290	251	407	296
Lordsburg, NM	224	410	265	459	274	368	157	394
Nogales	131	317	305	366	181	275	64	301
Page	324	137	217	279	273	230	390	455
Phoenix	51	136	228	185		94	117	182
Prescott	145	93	185	146	94		211	214
Shiprock, NM	411	281	190	425	417	374	431	599
Tucson	67	253	241	302	117	211		237
Yuma	172	318	410	215	182	214	237	

HARLEY-DAVIDSON DEALERSHIPS

Sierra Vista Harley-Davidson Shop, O-11
176 W Fry Blvd. **Sierra Vista**
(520) 458-9500
Lat N 31.555 **Lon** W 110.301

Harley-Davidson of Tucson, M-10
250 E Grant Rd. **Tucson**
(520) 792-0111
Lat N 32.250 **Lon** W 110.968

Bobby's Territorial Harley-Davidson, L-2
2550 E Gila Ridge Rd. **Yuma**
(928) 782-1931
Lat N 32.688 **Lon** W 114.589

I-19 uses metric mileposts. Exit numbers are in kilometers. On this map, distances along I-19 are shown in miles.

Prescott

Lake Havasu City

Sierra Vista

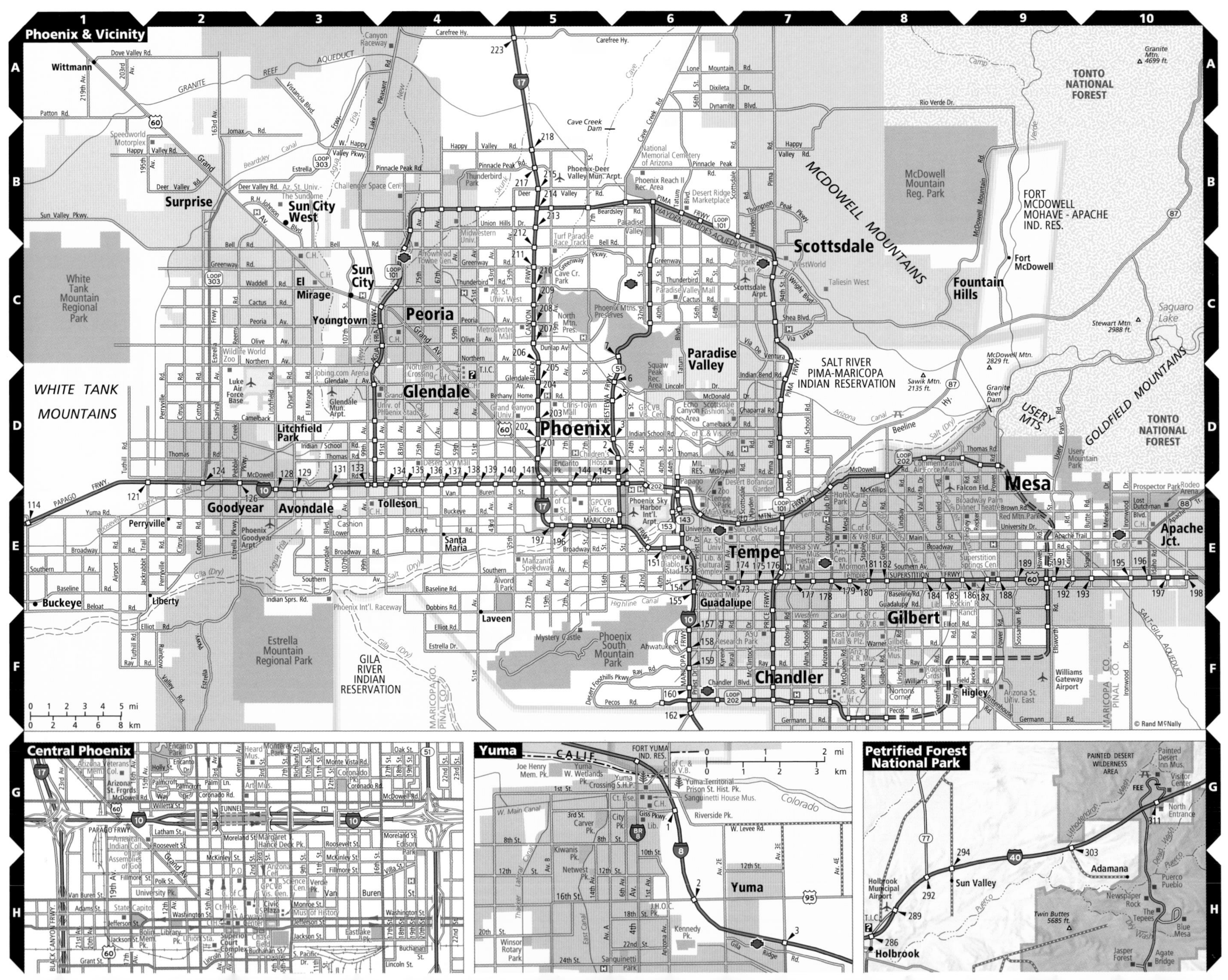
Phoenix & Vicinity
Central Phoenix
Yuma
Petrified Forest National Park
Phoenix
Scottsdale
Mesa
Tempe
Chandler
Gilbert
Glendale
Peoria
Paradise Valley
Fountain Hills
Apache Jct.
Sun City
Sun City West
Surprise
Goodyear
Avondale
Tolleson
Guadalupe
Higley
Buckeye
Laveen
MCDOWELL MOUNTAINS
WHITE TANK MOUNTAINS
GOLDFIELD MOUNTAINS
TONTO NATIONAL FOREST
SALT RIVER PIMA-MARICOPA INDIAN RESERVATION
GILA RIVER INDIAN RESERVATION
FORT MCDOWELL MOHAVE - APACHE IND. RES.
Estrella Mountain Regional Park
White Tank Mountain Regional Park
McDowell Mountain Reg. Park
Phoenix South Mountain Park
Holbrook
Adamana
Sun Valley
© Rand McNally

How to determine distance

Mileages in red between red arrowheads; in black, between intersections.

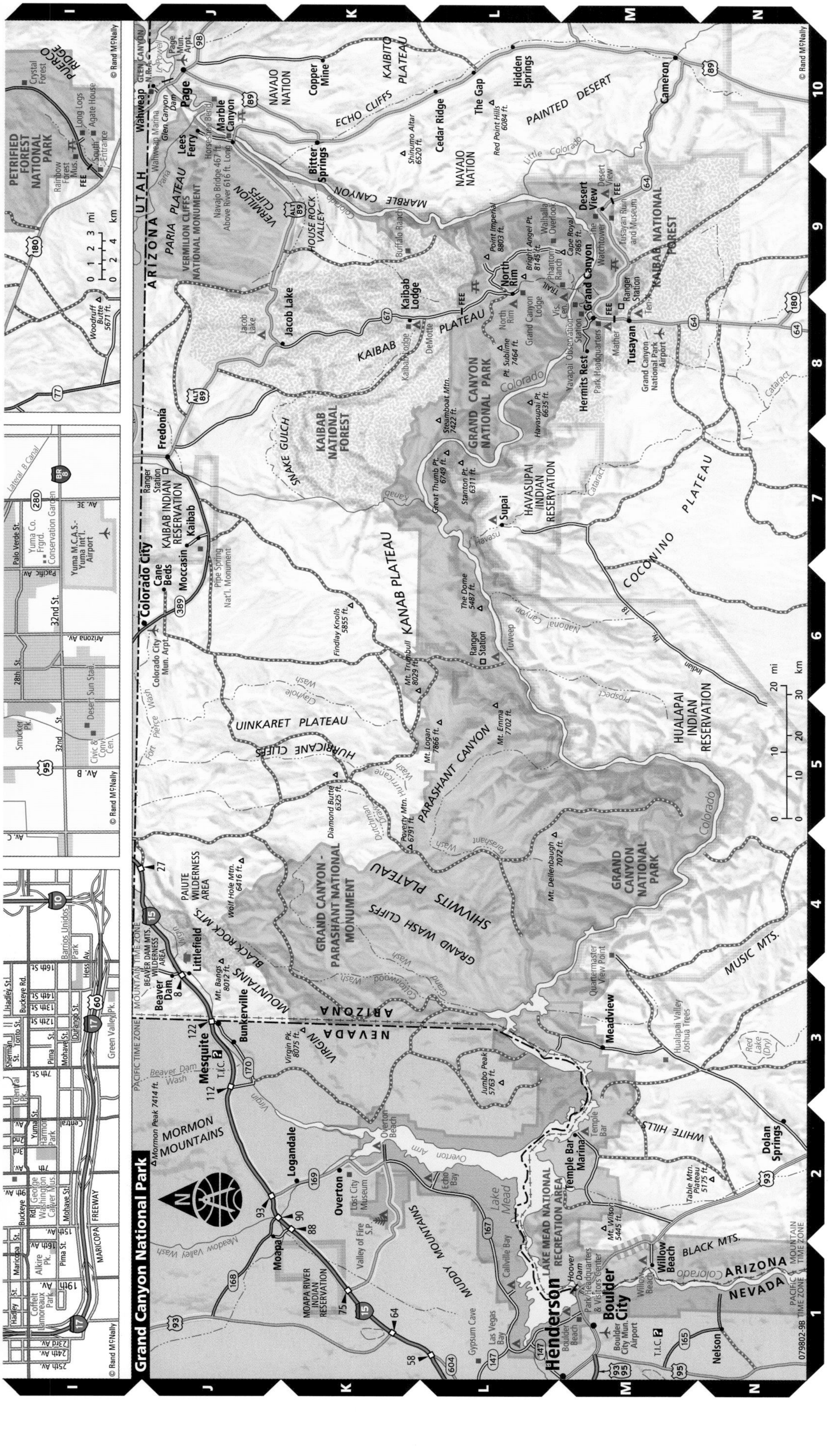

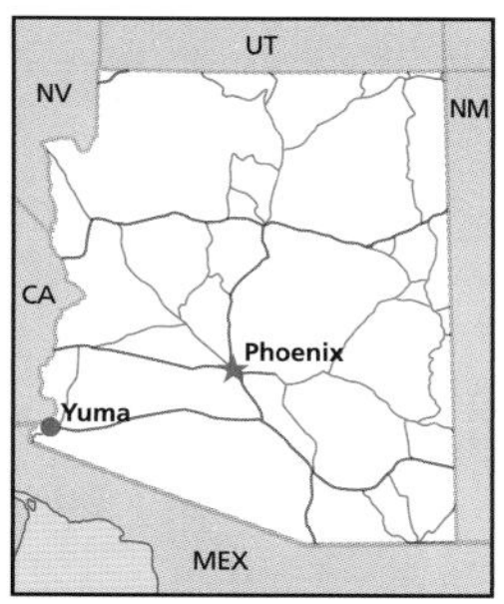
UT
NV
NM
CA
Phoenix
Yuma
MEX

SYMBOLS

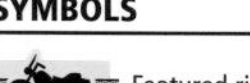
Featured ride

Scenic route

Point of interest

Long-term construction

Harley-Davidson dealership

ARIZONA MOTORCYCLE LAWS

Helmet use:
Required under age 18

Riding two abreast:
Yes. See state law for specifics

Eye protection:
Required unless equipped with windscreen

Speed limit:
Primary roads: 75 mph
Secondary roads: 55 mph

ARIZONA RESOURCES

Road conditions or construction:
511
(888) 411-7623
www.az511.com

Highway Emergency Numbers:
911

Tourism:
(866) 239-9712
www.arizonaguide.com

State motor vehicle information:
(602) 712-7090
www.dot.state.az.us/mvd

HARLEY-DAVIDSON DEALERSHIPS

Superstition Harley-Davidson, E-10
2910 W Apache Trail **Apache Junction**
(480) 346-0600
Lat N 33.415 **Lon** W 111.578

Harley-Davidson of Chandler, F-6
6895 W Chandler Blvd. **Chandler**
(480) 496-6800
Lat N 33.305 **Lon** W 111.961

Chester's Harley-Davidson, E-7
922 S Country Club Dr. **Mesa**
(480) 894-0404
Lat N 33.398 **Lon** W 111.840

Arrowhead Harley-Davidson, C-4
16130 N Arrowhead Fountain Center Dr. **Peoria**
(623) 247-5542
Lat N 33.634 **Lon** W 112.237

Buddy Stubbs Harley-Davidson, C-6
13850 N Cave Creek Rd. **Phoenix**
(602) 971-3400
Lat N 33.613 **Lon** W 112.035

Hacienda Harley-Davidson, C-7
15600 N Hayden Rd. **Scottsdale**
(480) 905-1903
Lat N 33.627 **Lon** W 111.896

Chester's Harley-Davidson, E-6
690 S Mill Ave. **Tempe**
(480) 355-6160
Lat N 33.423 **Lon** W 111.940

Grand Canyon National Park

Distance scale
One inch represents about 30 miles
0 5 10 15 20 25 mi
0 10 20 30 40 km

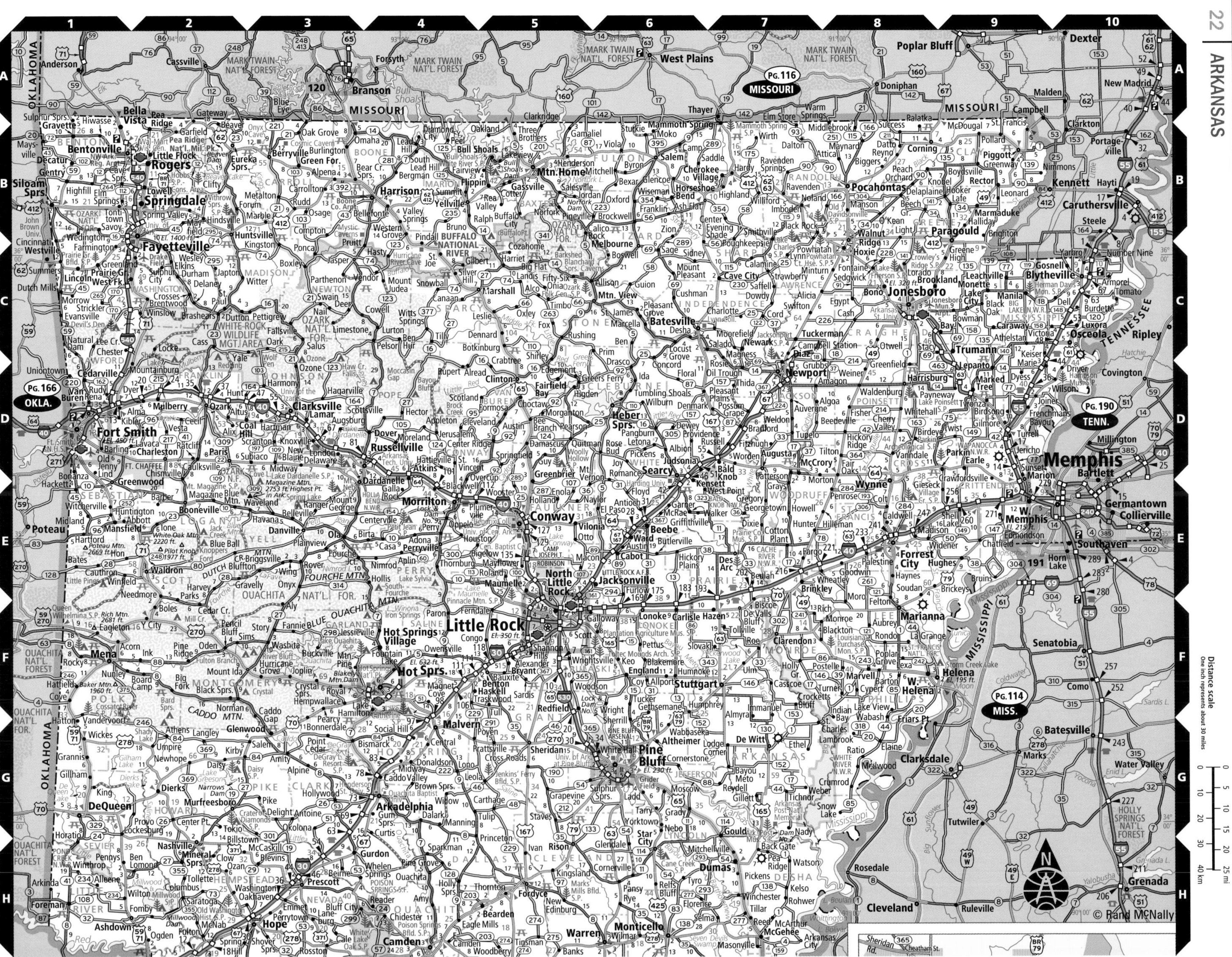
MISSOURI
OKLAHOMA
TENNESSEE
MISSISSIPPI
Little Rock
North Little Rock
Memphis
Fort Smith
Pine Bluff
Jonesboro
Fayetteville
Springdale
Rogers
Bentonville
Hot Sprs.
Conway
Searcy
Russellville
Arkadelphia
Blytheville
W. Memphis
Batesville
Harrison
Mtn. Home
Camden
Hope
Stuttgart
Helena
Pg. 116 MISSOURI
Pg. 190 TENN.
Pg. 114 MISS.
Pg. 166 OKLA.
© Rand McNally

How to determine distance

Mileages in red between red arrowheads; in black, between intersections.

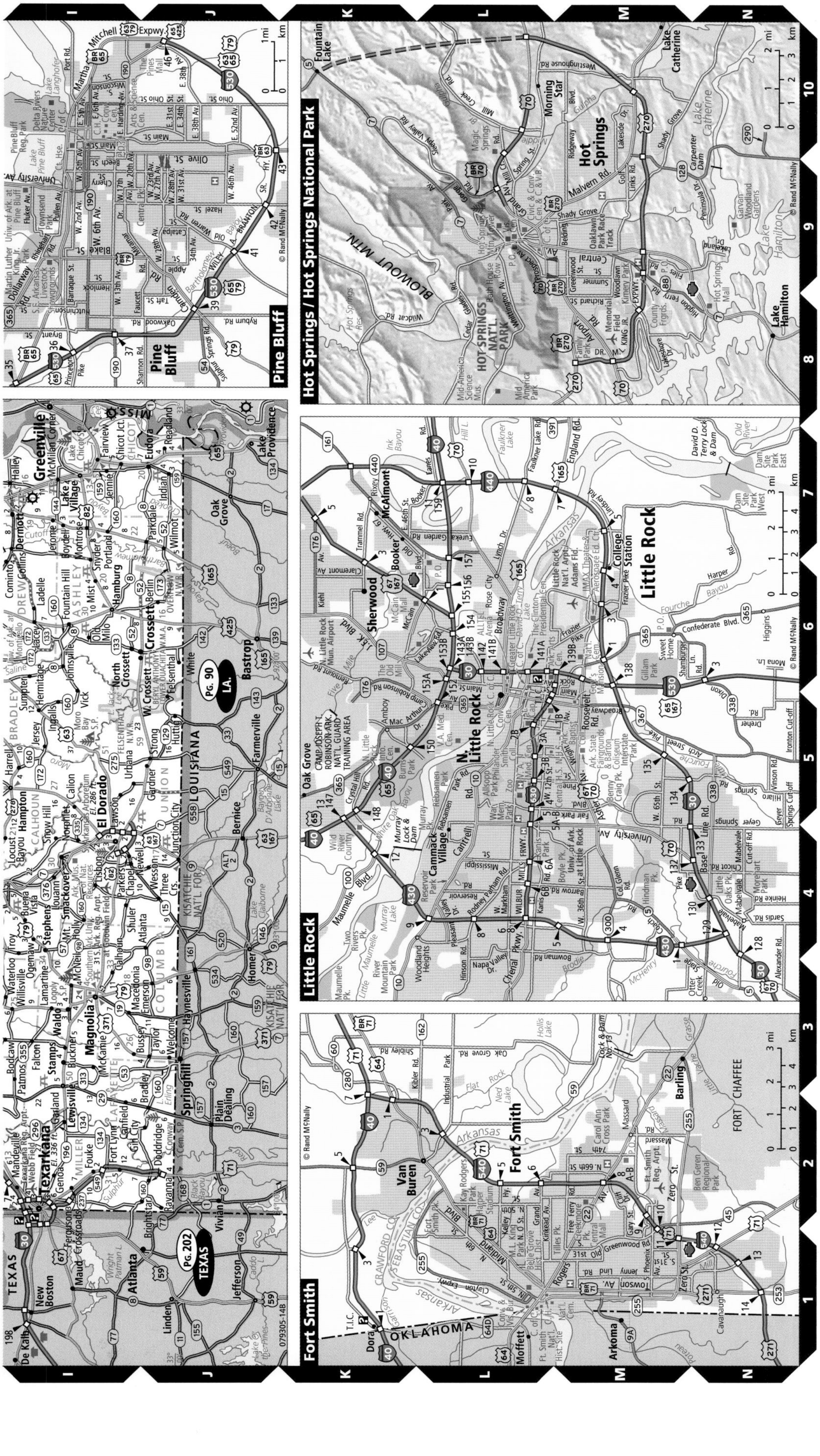

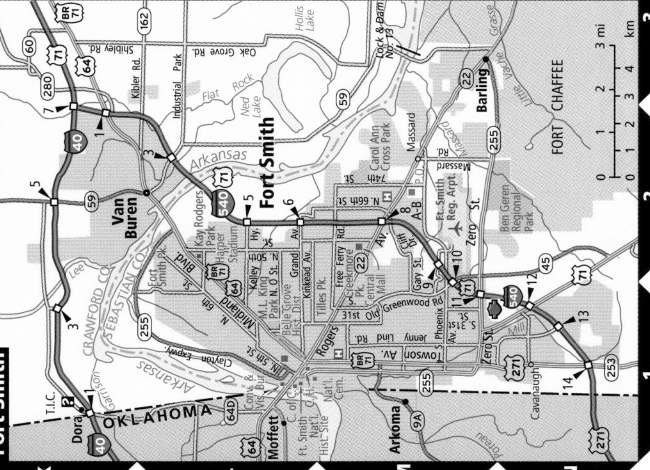
Fort Smith
Van Buren
Barling
FORT CHAFFEE
OKLAHOMA
Arkoma
Moffett
Dora
© Rand McNally

SYMBOLS

Featured ride

Scenic route

Point of interest

Long-term construction

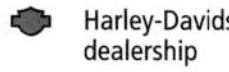

Harley-Davidson dealership

ARKANSAS MOTORCYCLE LAWS

Helmet use:
Required under age 21

Riding two abreast:
No reference in administrative code or statutes

Eye protection:
Required by law

Speed limit:
Primary roads: 70 mph
Secondary roads: 55 mph

ARKANSAS RESOURCES

Road conditions or construction:
(800) 245-1672
(501) 569-2374
www.arkansashighways.com

Highway Emergency Numbers:
911

Tourism:
(800) 628-8725
www.arkansas.com

State motor vehicle information:
(501) 618-8000
www.asp.state.ar.us

CITY-TO-CITY MILEAGE

	EL DORADO	FAYETTEVILLE	FORT SMITH	HARRISON	JONESBORO	LITTLE ROCK	TEXARKANA	WEST MEMPHIS
El Dorado		310	275	255	248	117	90	244
Fayetteville	310		61	88	294	195	239	316
Fort Smith	275	61		150	259	160	180	281
Harrison	255	88	150		170	140	272	261
Jonesboro	248	294	259	170		133	273	63
Little Rock	117	195	160	140	133		140	129
Pine Bluff	91	235	200	180	173	42	151	135
Texarkana	90	239	180	272	273	140		269
West Memphis	244	316	281	261	63	129	269	

HARLEY-DAVIDSON DEALERSHIPS

Old Ft. Harley-Davidson of Ft. Smith, D-1
6304 S 36th St. **Fort Smith**
(479) 648-1666
Lat N 35.322 **Lon** W 94.396

Jones Harley-Davidson Shop of Hot Springs, F-4
4446 Central Ave. **Hot Springs**
(501) 520-4442
Lat N 34.452 **Lon** W 93.077

Harley-Davidson of Jonesboro, C-8
4500 Oliver St. **Jonesboro**
(870) 932-0780
Lat N 35.811 **Lon** W 90.643

Jones Harley-Davidson, F-5
10210 I-30 **Little Rock**
(501) 568-3160
Lat N 34.675 **Lon** W 92.351

Jones Harley-Davidson Shop of North Little Rock, F-5
4300 Landers Rd. **North Little Rock**
(501) 945-4206
Lat N 34.794 **Lon** W 92.221

Pig Trail Harley-Davidson, B-2
2409 W Hudson Rd. **Rogers**
(479) 636-9797
Lat N 36.356 **Lon** W 94.152

Distance scale
One inch represents about 26 miles
0 10 20 30 mi
0 10 20 30 40 km

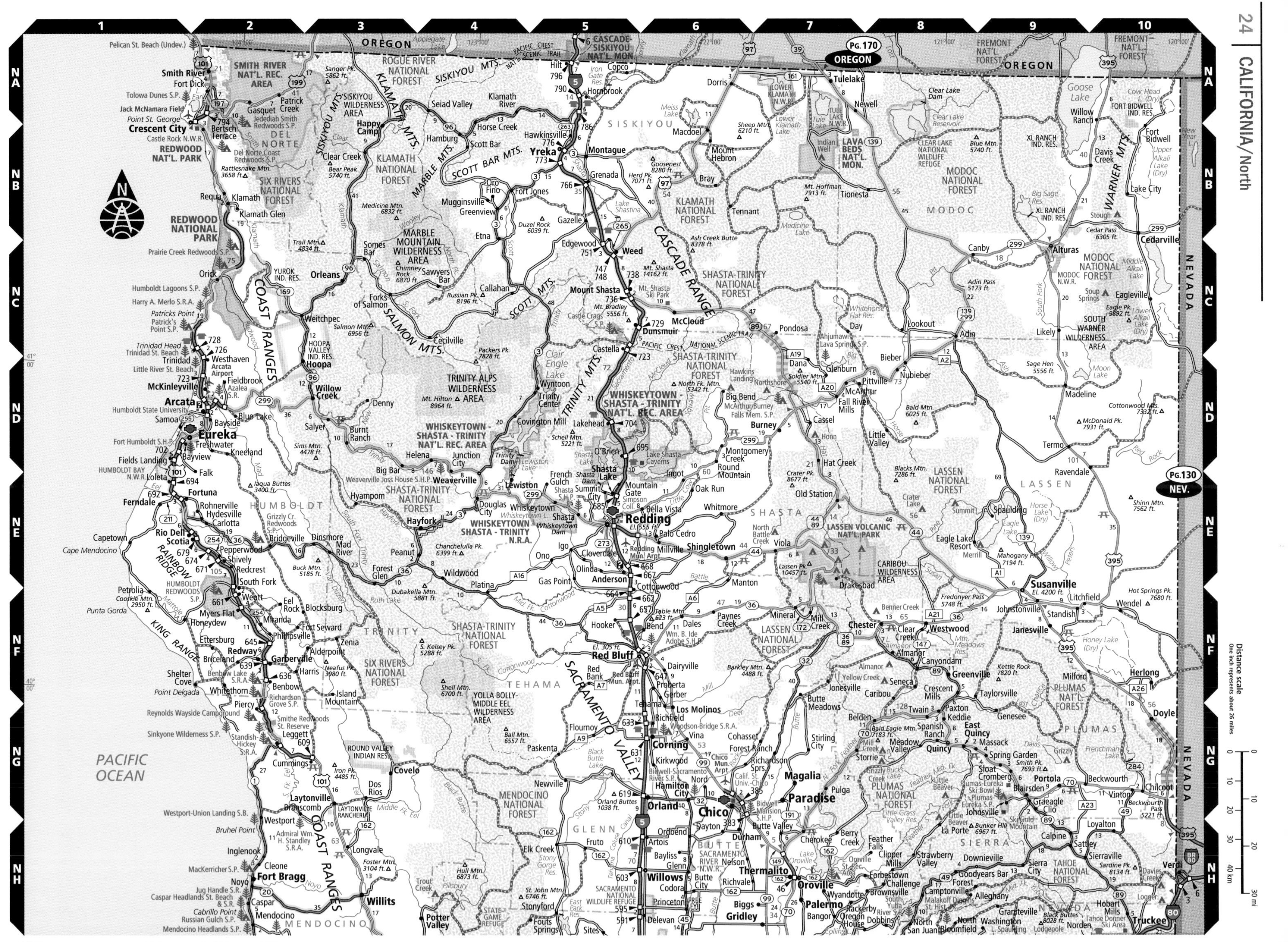
NEVADA
OREGON
PACIFIC OCEAN
PG. 130 NEV.
PG. 170 OREGON
Crescent City
Eureka
Arcata
Fortuna
Redding
Red Bluff
Chico
Paradise
Oroville
Susanville
Alturas
Yreka
Weed
Mount Shasta
Orland
Willows
Corning
Willits
Fort Bragg
Truckee
SACRAMENTO VALLEY
CASCADE RANGE
COAST RANGES
TRINITY MTS.
SALMON MTS.
KLAMATH MTS.
MODOC NATIONAL FOREST
LASSEN NATIONAL FOREST
SHASTA-TRINITY NATIONAL FOREST
KLAMATH NATIONAL FOREST
MENDOCINO NATIONAL FOREST
PLUMAS NAT'L FOREST
SIX RIVERS NATIONAL FOREST
REDWOOD NATIONAL PARK
LASSEN VOLCANIC NAT'L PARK
LAVA BEDS NAT'L MON.
KING RANGE

How to determine distance

2 10 18 4 4 12 16 20

Mileages in red between red arrowheads; in black, between intersections.

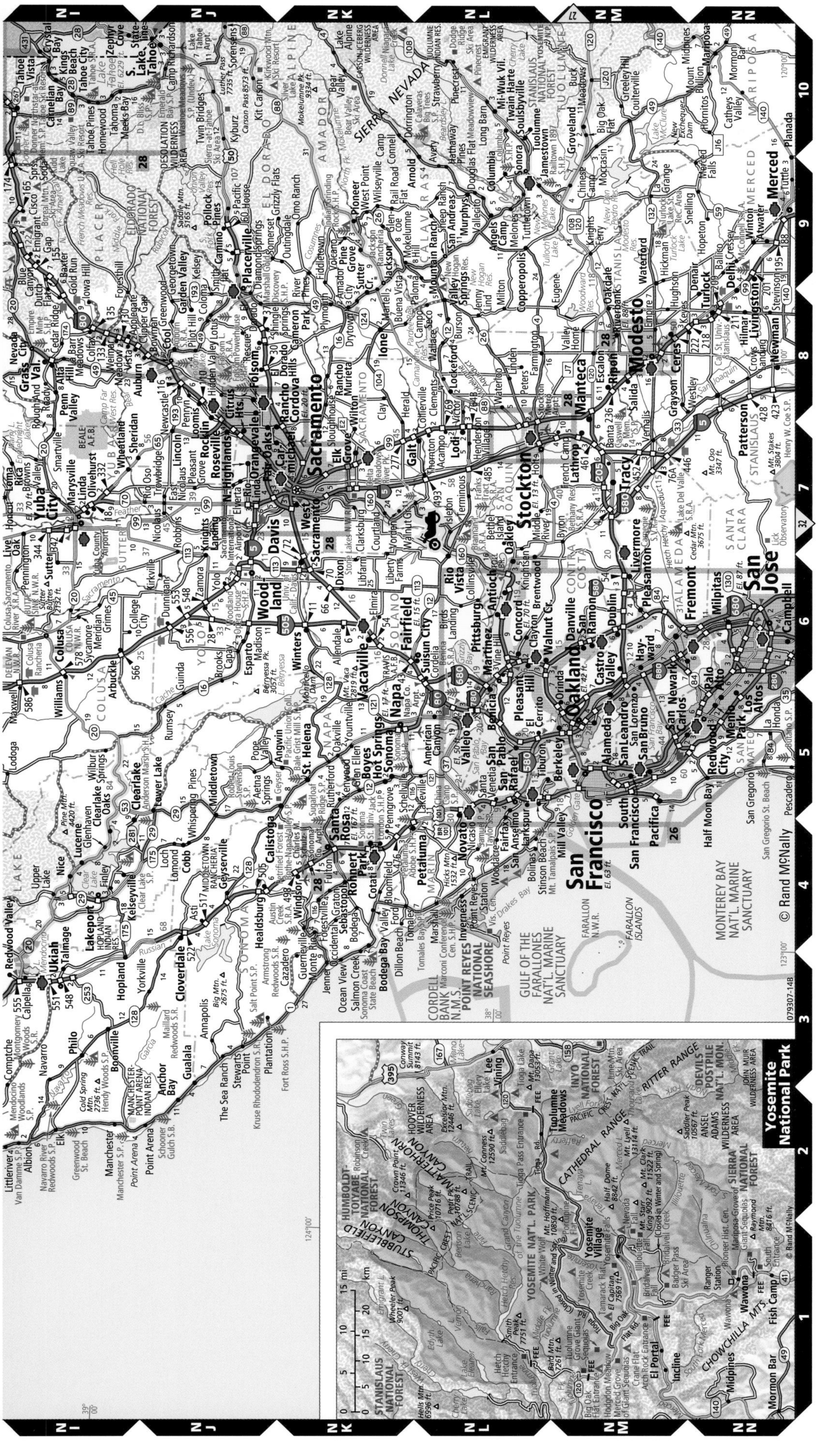

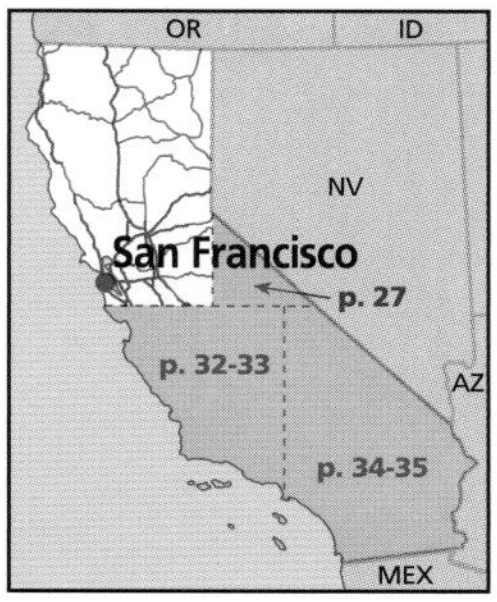

OR ID NV AZ MEX

San Francisco

p. 27

p. 32-33

p. 34-35

SYMBOLS

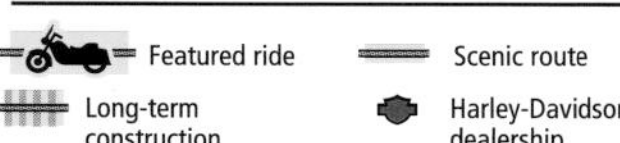

Featured ride — Scenic route

Long-term construction — Harley-Davidson dealership

For California ride, see page R10.

HARLEY-DAVIDSON DEALERSHIPS

For the Bay Area, please see dealer listings on page 27; for northern cities, please see dealer listings on page 29.

Auburn Harley-Davidson, NJ-8
12075 Locksley Ln. **Auburn**
(530) 885-7161
Lat N 38.950 **Lon** W 121.099

Hall's Harley-Davidson, NG-6
1501 Mangrove Ave. **Chico**
(530) 893-1918
Lat N 39.746 **Lon** W 121.841

Michael's Harley-Davidson, NK-4
7601 Redwood Dr. **Cotati**
(707) 793-9180
Lat N 38.334 **Lon** W 122.713

Harley-Davidson of Elk Grove Shop, NK-7
10291 E Stockton Blvd. **Elk Grove**
(916) 714-6952
Lat N 38.380 **Lon** W 121.366

Redwood Harley-Davidson, ND-1
2500 6th St. **Eureka**
(707) 444-0111
Lat N 40.803 **Lon** W 124.150

Harley-Davidson of Folsom, NJ-8
115 Woodmere Rd. **Folsom**
(916) 608-9922
Lat N 38.656 **Lon** W 121.185

Jamestown Harley-Davidson, NL-9
18275 Hwy. 108 **Jamestown**
(209) 984-4888
Lat N 37.963 **Lon** W 120.408

Hangtown Harley-Davidson Shop, NJ-8
629 Main St. **Placerville**
(530) 344-0401
Lat N 38.730 **Lon** W 120.793

Redding Harley-Davidson, NE-5
1268 Twin View Blvd. **Redding**
(530) 241-7117
Lat N 40.624 **Lon** W 122.365

Harley-Davidson of Rocklin, NJ-8
4425 Granite Dr. **Rocklin**
(916) 624-9211
Lat N 38.798 **Lon** W 121.215

Harley-Davidson of Ukiah, NI-3
2501 N State St. **Ukiah**
(707) 462-1672
Lat N 39.183 **Lon** W 123.209

Vacaville Harley-Davidson, NK-6
100 Auto Center Dr. **Vacaville**
(707) 455-7000
Lat N 38.380 **Lon** W 121.942

Guideras Harley-Davidson, NI-7
720 W Onstott Rd. **Yuba City**
(530) 673-3548
Lat N 39.134 **Lon** W 121.635

Distance scale
One inch represents about 26 miles
0 10 20 30 mi
0 10 20 30 40 km

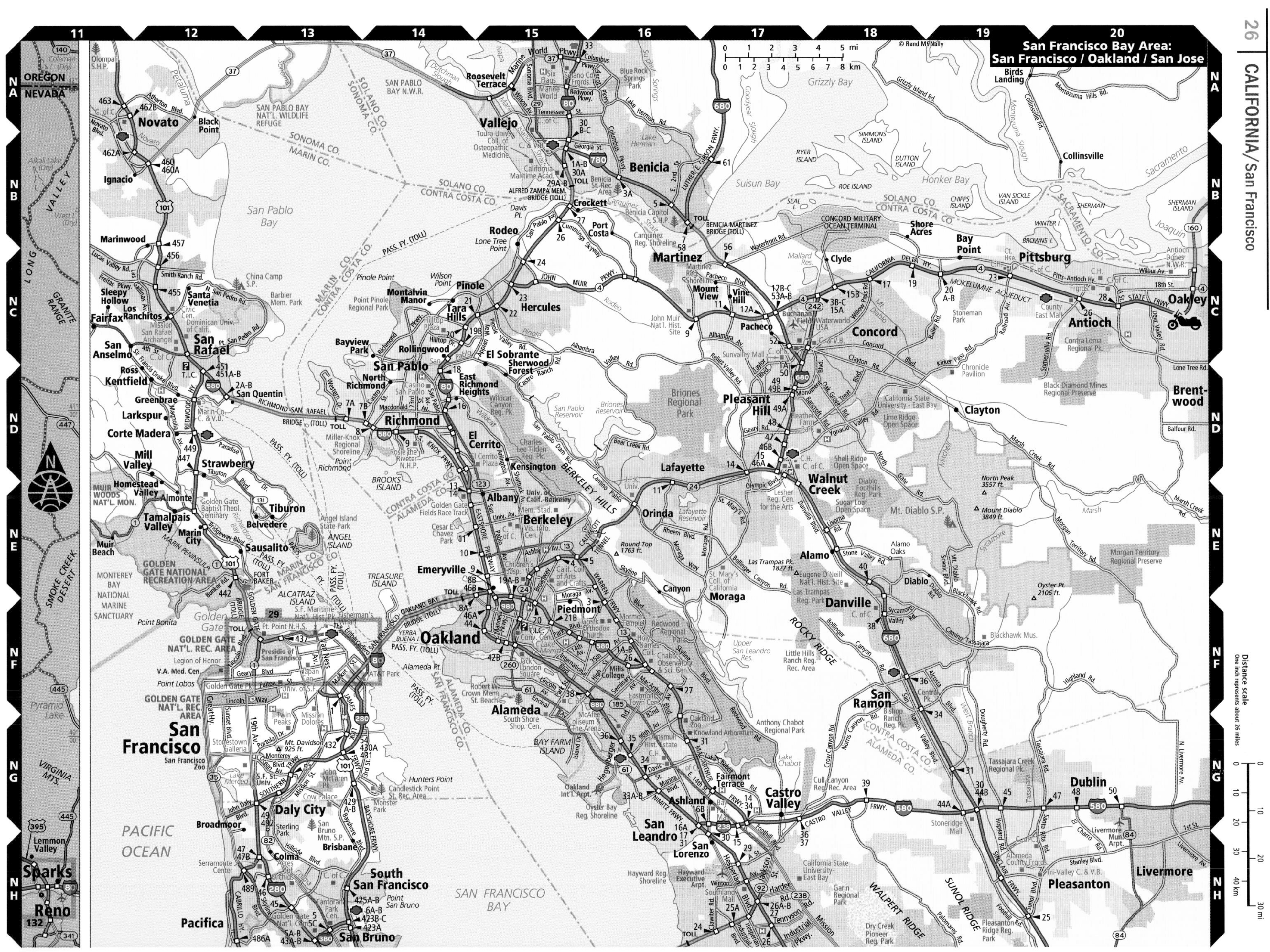

San Francisco Bay Area:
San Francisco / Oakland / San Jose
San Francisco
Oakland
Berkeley
Richmond
Concord
Walnut Creek
Antioch
Pittsburg
Livermore
Pleasanton
Dublin
San Leandro
Alameda
Daly City
South San Francisco
San Rafael
Novato
Vallejo
Benicia
Martinez
Danville
San Ramon
Castro Valley
SAN FRANCISCO BAY
San Pablo Bay
PACIFIC OCEAN
Reno
Sparks
© Rand McNally

How to determine distance

Mileages in red between red arrowheads; in black, between intersections.

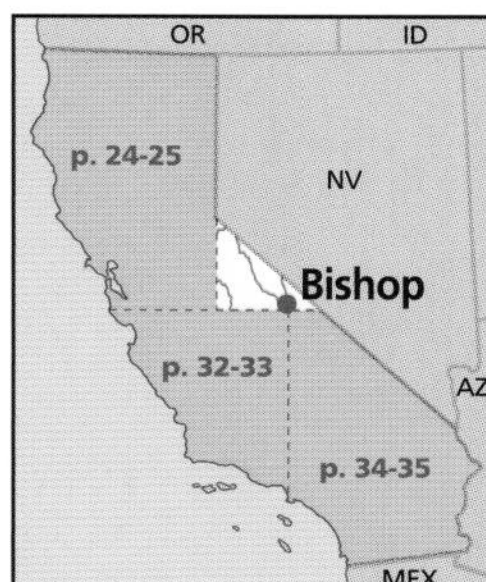

OR
ID
p. 24-25
NV
Bishop
p. 32-33
AZ
p. 34-35
MEX

SYMBOLS

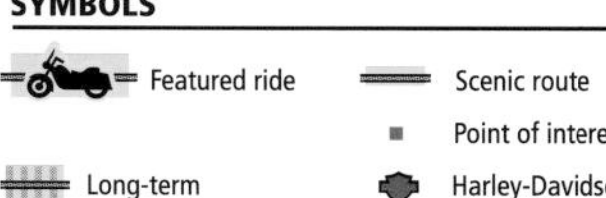

Featured ride
Scenic route
Point of interest
Long-term construction
Harley-Davidson dealership

HARLEY-DAVIDSON DEALERSHIPS

Golden Gate Harley-Davidson, ND-12
13 San Clemente Dr. **Corte Madera**
(415) 927-4464
Lat N 37.922 **Lon** W 122.510

Harley-Davidson of Fremont, NJ-18
41315 Albrae St. **Fremont**
(510) 657-7200
Lat N 37.517 **Lon** W 121.980

Livermore Harley-Davidson, NM-6
7576 Southfront Rd. **Livermore**
(925) 606-0100
Lat N 37.715 **Lon** W 121.704

Golden Gate Harley-Davidson Shop, NB-11
7077 Redwood Blvd. **Novato**
(415) 878-4988
Lat N 38.100 **Lon** W 122.568

Bob Dron Harley-Davidson, NG-16
151 Hegenberger Rd. **Oakland**
(510) 635-0100
Lat N 37.731 **Lon** W 122.199

Devil Mountain Harley-Davidson Shop, NC-20
2240 Loveridge Rd. **Pittsburg**
(925) 427-2700
Lat N 38.009 **Lon** W 121.871

Peninsula Harley-Davidson, NJ-15
380 Convention Way **Redwood City**
(650) 568-0800
Lat N 37.495 **Lon** W 122.231

Dudley Perkins Co. Harley-Davidson, NF-13
2595 Taylor St. **San Francisco**
(415) 776-7781
Lat N 37.806 **Lon** W 122.415

San Jose Harley-Davidson, NM-19
1551 Parkmoor Ave. **San Jose**
(408) 998-1464
Lat N 37.317 **Lon** W 121.917

McGuire Harley-Davidson Shop, NF-18
2000 San Ramon Valley Blvd. **San Ramon**
(925) 838-4647
Lat N 37.785 **Lon** W 121.980

Dudley Perkins Co. Harley-Davidson, NH-13
333 E Corey Way **South San Francisco**
(650) 737-5467
Lat N 37.645 **Lon** W 122.402

Harley-Davidson of Vallejo, NB-15
1600 Sonoma Blvd. (Hwy. 29) **Vallejo**
(707) 643-1413
Lat N 38.100 **Lon** W 122.255

McGuire Harley-Davidson, ND-17
1425 Parkside Dr. **Walnut Creek**
(925) 945-6500
Lat N 37.912 **Lon** W 122.064

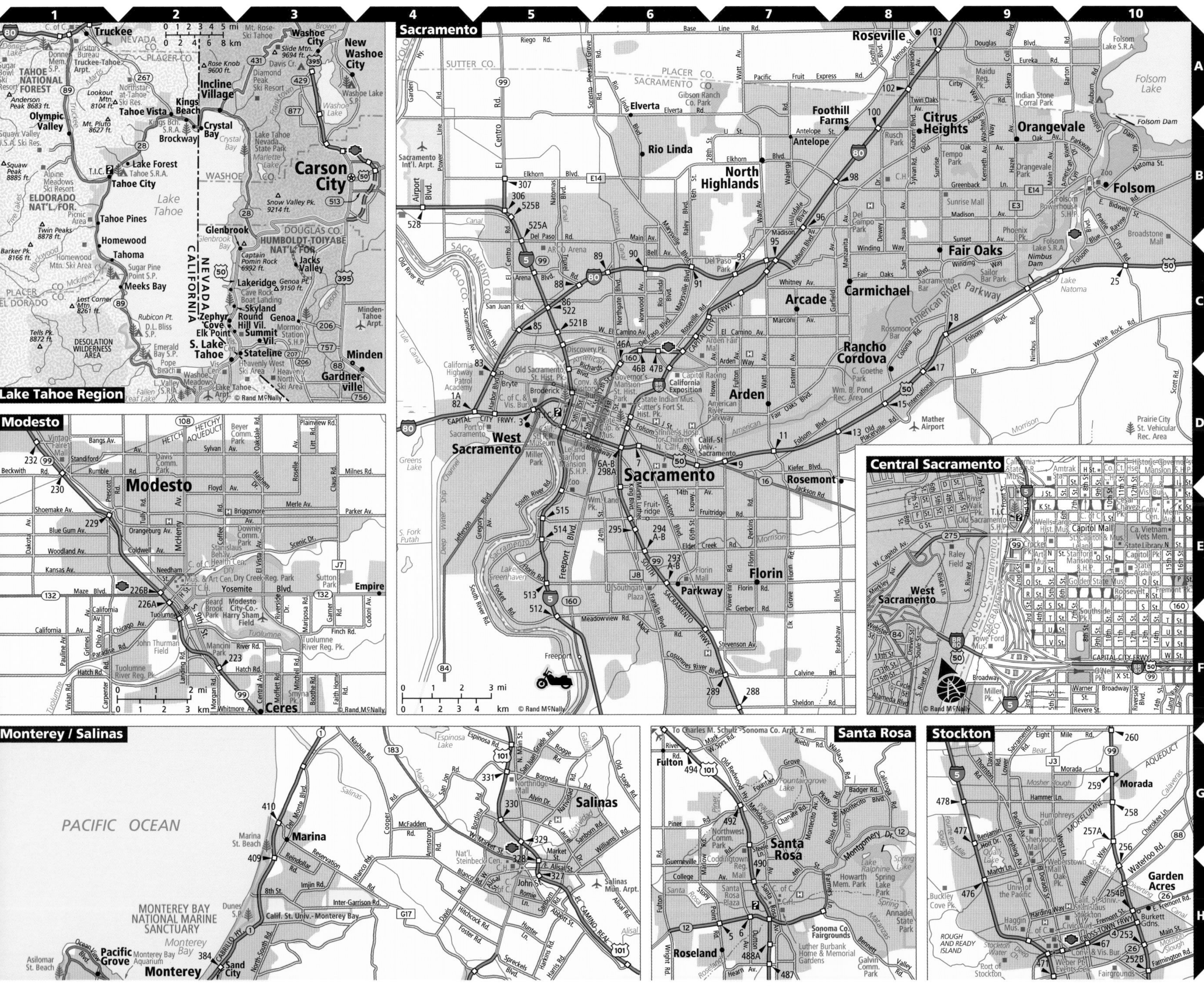
Lake Tahoe Region
Sacramento
Modesto
Central Sacramento
Monterey / Salinas
Santa Rosa
Stockton
Truckee
Olympic Valley
Tahoe Vista
Kings Beach
Incline Village
Crystal Bay
Brockway
Lake Forest
Tahoe City
Tahoe Pines
Homewood
Tahoma
Meeks Bay
Carson City
Washoe City
New Washoe City
Glenbrook
Lakeridge
Zephyr Cove
Round Hill Vil.
Elk Point
Skyland
Summit Vil.
Genoa
Stateline
S. Lake Tahoe
Minden
Gardnerville
NEVADA
CALIFORNIA
Lake Tahoe
Roseville
Elverta
Rio Linda
Foothill Farms
Antelope
North Highlands
Citrus Heights
Orangevale
Folsom
Fair Oaks
Arcade
Carmichael
Rancho Cordova
Arden
West Sacramento
Sacramento
Rosemont
Florin
Parkway
Modesto
Empire
Ceres
PACIFIC OCEAN
Marina
MONTEREY BAY NATIONAL MARINE SANCTUARY
Pacific Grove
Monterey
Sand City
Salinas
Fulton
Santa Rosa
Roseland
Morada
Garden Acres
© Rand McNally

How to determine distance

Mileages in red between red arrowheads; in black, between intersections.

Stockton

Rohnert Park

Seaside

Central San Francisco

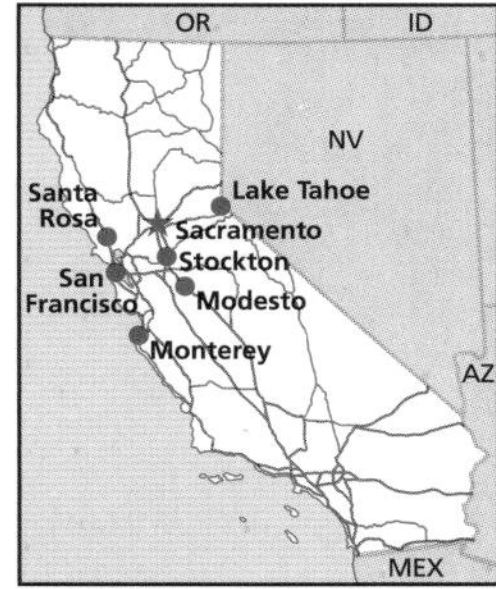
OR
ID
NV
Lake Tahoe
Santa Rosa
Sacramento
Stockton
San Francisco
Modesto
Monterey
AZ
MEX

SYMBOLS

Featured ride
Scenic route
Point of interest
Long-term construction
Harley-Davidson dealership

CALIFORNIA MOTORCYCLE LAWS

Helmet use:
Required

Riding two abreast:
No reference in administrative code or statutes

Eye protection:
Not required

Speed limit:
Primary roads: 70 mph
Secondary roads: 65 mph

CALIFORNIA RESOURCES

Road conditions or construction:
511 (San Francisco Bay and Sacramento areas)
(800) 427-7623 (in CA)
(916) 445-7623
www.dot.ca.gov
www.511.org

Highway Emergency Numbers:
911

Tourism:
(916) 444-4429
(800) 862-2543 (to request travel materials only)
www.visitcalifornia.com

State motor vehicle information:
(800) 777-0133
www.dmv.ca.gov

HARLEY-DAVIDSON DEALERSHIPS

Carson City Harley-Davidson, B-3
2749 N Carson St. **Carson City, NV**
(775) 882-7433
Lat N 39.185 **Lon** W 119.77

Mitchell's Modesto Harley-Davidson, E-2
500 N Carpenter Rd. **Modesto**
(209) 522-1061
Lat N 37.643 **Lon** W 121.030

Harley-Davidson of Sacramento, C-6
1000 Arden Way **Sacramento**
(916) 929-4680
Lat N 38.606 **Lon** W 121.444

Valley Harley-Davidson, H-9
711 E Miner Ave. **Stockton**
(209) 941-0420
Lat N 37.957 **Lon** W 121.283

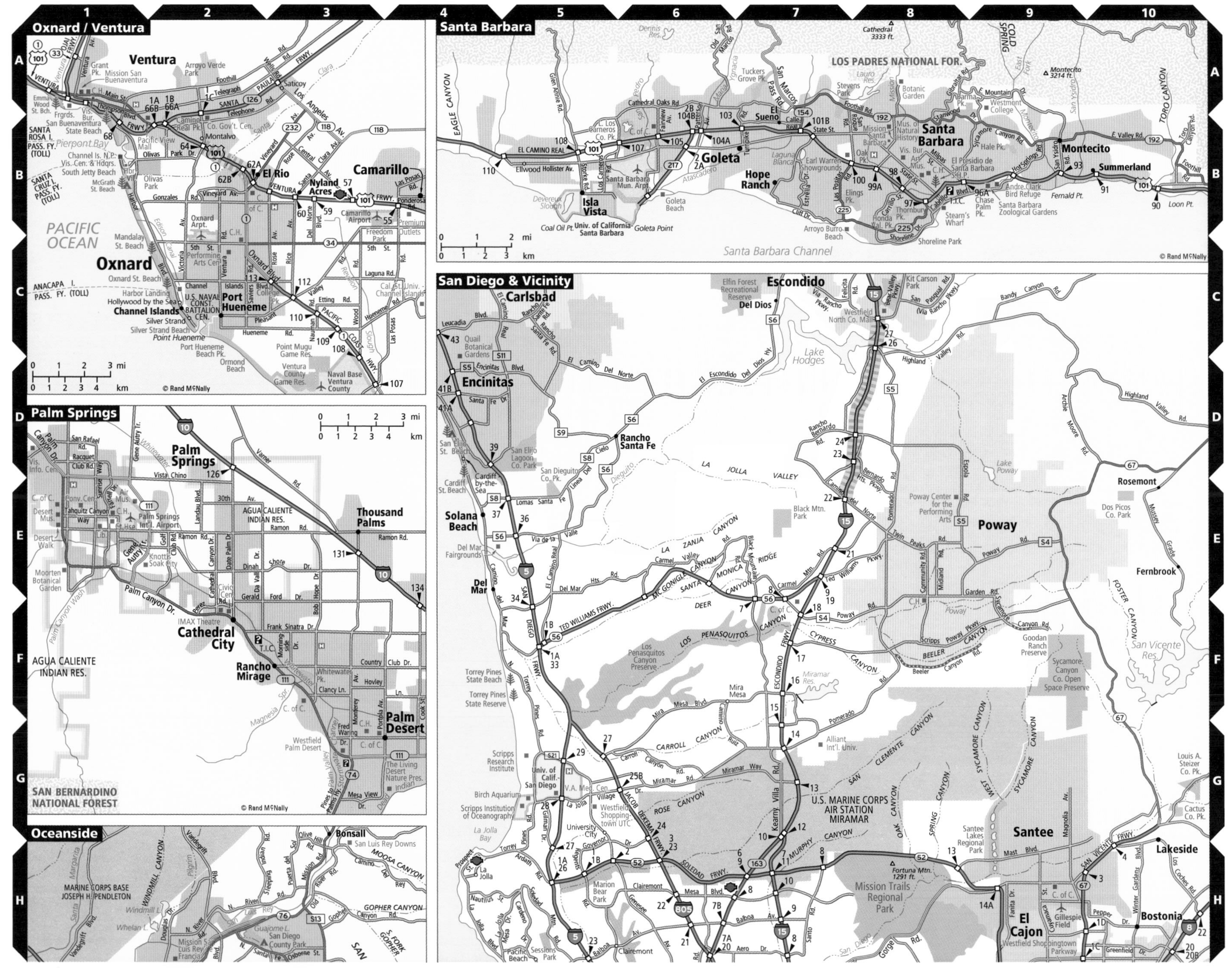
Oxnard / Ventura
Ventura
Oxnard
Camarillo
El Rio
Nyland Acres
Port Hueneme
PACIFIC OCEAN
Santa Barbara
LOS PADRES NATIONAL FOR.
Santa Barbara Channel
Goleta
Isla Vista
Hope Ranch
Montecito
Summerland
San Diego & Vicinity
Carlsbad
Encinitas
Escondido
Rancho Santa Fe
Solana Beach
Del Mar
Poway
Rosemont
Fernbrook
U.S. MARINE CORPS AIR STATION MIRAMAR
Mission Trails Regional Park
Santee
Lakeside
El Cajon
Bostonia
Palm Springs
Palm Springs
Thousand Palms
Cathedral City
Rancho Mirage
Palm Desert
AGUA CALIENTE INDIAN RES.
SAN BERNARDINO NATIONAL FOREST
Oceanside
Bonsall
MARINE CORPS BASE JOSEPH H. PENDLETON
© Rand McNally

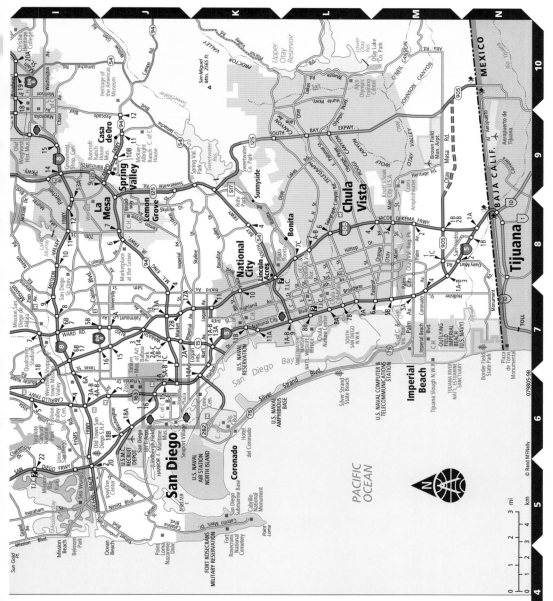

How to determine distance

Mileages in red between red arrowheads; in black, between intersections.

San Diego
Chula Vista
National City
La Mesa
Spring Valley
Lemon Grove
Imperial Beach
Coronado
Tijuana
Bonita
Sunnyside
Casa de Oro
Lincoln Acres
PACIFIC OCEAN
MEXICO
BAJA CALIF.
San Diego Bay
© Rand McNally

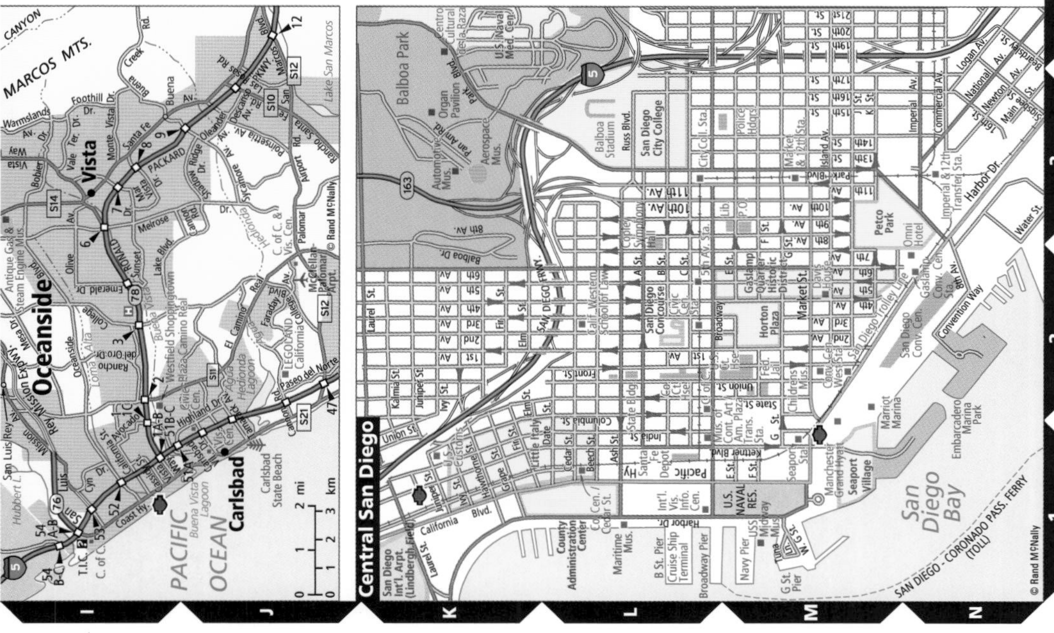
Oceanside
Vista
Carlsbad
PACIFIC OCEAN
Central San Diego
Balboa Park
San Diego Bay
© Rand McNally

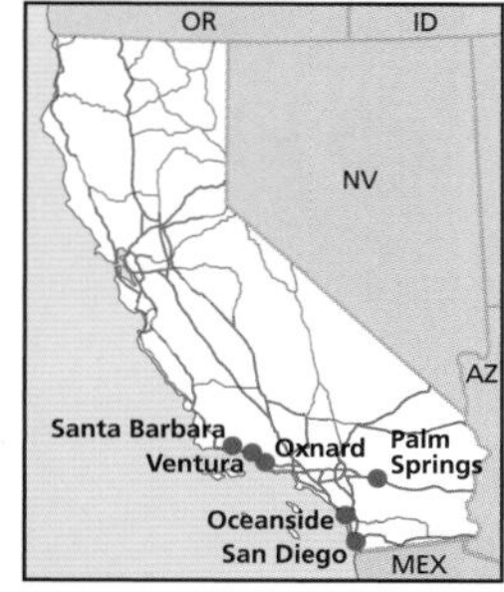
OR
ID
NV
AZ
Santa Barbara
Ventura
Oxnard
Palm Springs
Oceanside
San Diego
MEX

SYMBOLS

- Featured ride
- Scenic route
- Point of interest
- Long-term construction
- Harley-Davidson dealership

CITY-TO-CITY MILEAGE

	BISHOP	EUREKA	REDDING	SACRAMENTO	SAN FRANCISCO	SAN JOSE	SOUTH LAKE TAHOE	VALLEJO
Alturas	385	300	146	307	359	388	239	331
Bishop		556	402	273	297	286	180	298
Crescent City	623	82	217	378	363	406	477	346
Eureka	556		154	296	281	324	398	264
Oakland	289	281	209	83	8	43	185	24
Oroville	333	233	98	72	149	178	155	121
Redding	402	154		165	217	246	267	189
Sacramento	273	296	165		91	116	102	63
San Francisco	297	281	217	91		44	193	32
San Jose	286	324	246	116	44		218	63
Santa Rosa	347	223	226	100	58	101	202	52
South Lake Tahoe	180	398	267	102	193	218		165
Stockton	237	342	211	47	80	69	149	68
Susanville	288	268	114	197	269	298	142	241
Ukiah	421	162	189	148	119	162	250	102
Vallejo	298	264	189	63	32	63	165	
Yosemite N.P.	139	463	336	171	190	179	187	191
Yreka	458	214	97	260	312	341	312	284

HARLEY-DAVIDSON DEALERSHIPS

Ventura Harley-Davidson, B-4
1326 Del Norte Rd. **Camarillo**
(805) 981-9904
Lat N 34.224 **Lon** W 119.104

El Cajon Harley-Davidson, I-9
621 El Cajon Blvd. **El Cajon**
(619) 444-1123
Lat N 32.789 **Lon** W 116.973

San Diego Harley-Davidson La Jolla, H-4
1145 Prospect St. **La Jolla**
(858) 551-6800
Lat N 32.849 **Lon** W 117.273

Sweetwater Harley-Davidson, K-7
3201 Hoover Ave. **National City**
(619) 477-4477
Lat N 32.654 **Lon** W 117.102

San Diego Harley-Davidson Co., H-6
5600 Kearny Mesa Rd. **San Diego**
(858) 616-6999
Lat N 32.835 **Lon** W 117.139

San Diego Harley-Davidson Shop, K-1
2400 Kettner Blvd. Ste. 101 **San Diego**
(619) 233-6677
Lat N 32.729 **Lon** W 117.172

San Diego Harley-Davidson, M-1
861 W Harbor Dr. **San Diego**
(619) 234-5780
Lat N 32.711 **Lon** W 117.169

Distance scale
One inch represents about 26 miles
0 10 20 30 mi
0 10 20 30 40 km

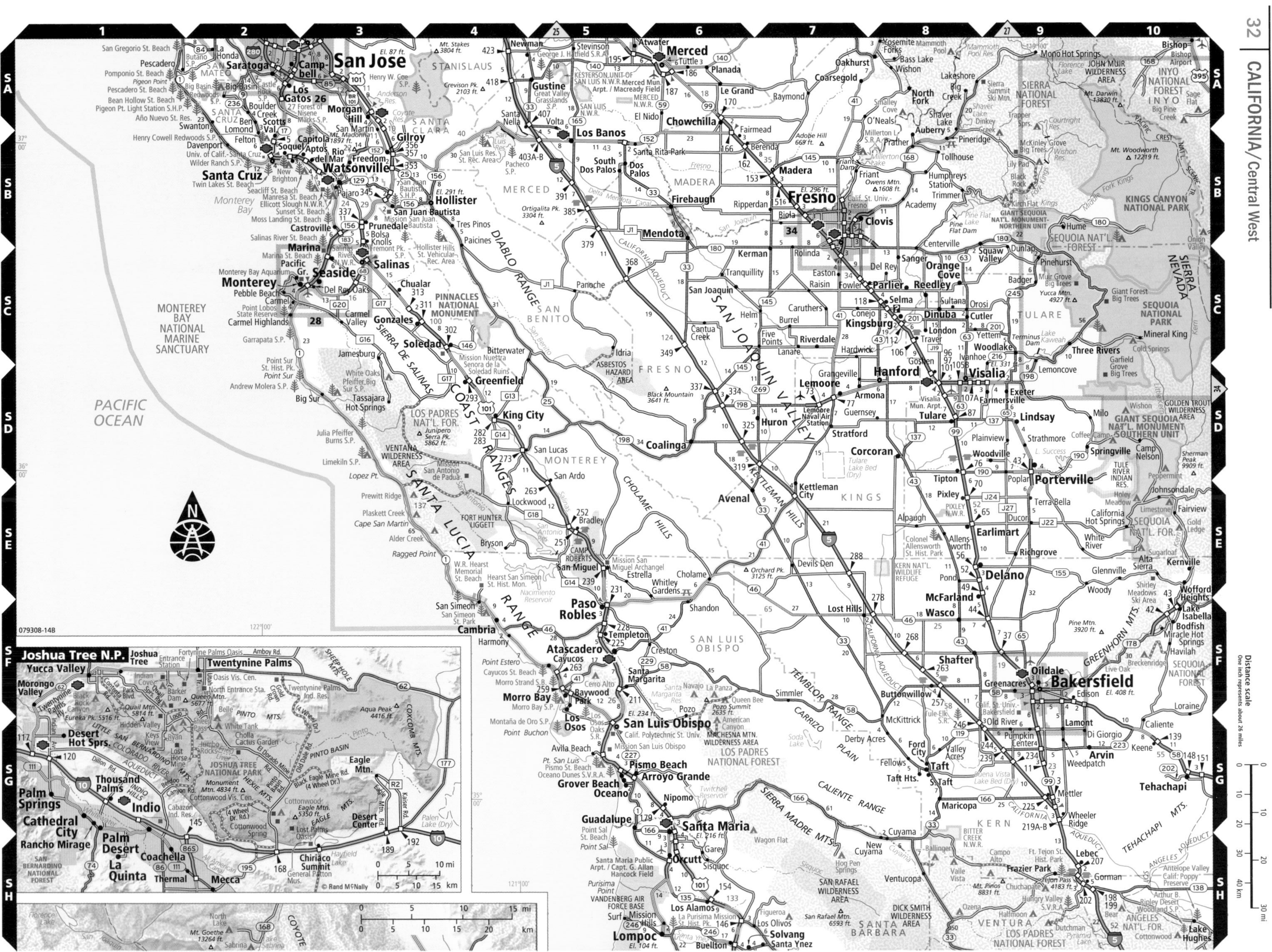
San Jose
Fresno
Bakersfield
Salinas
Monterey
Santa Cruz
Visalia
Merced
Hanford
Porterville
Santa Maria
San Luis Obispo
Paso Robles
Lompoc
Coalinga
Tulare
Delano
Madera
Clovis
SAN JOAQUIN VALLEY
SIERRA NEVADA
PACIFIC OCEAN
MONTEREY BAY NATIONAL MARINE SANCTUARY
KINGS CANYON NATIONAL PARK
SEQUOIA NATIONAL PARK
SANTA LUCIA RANGE
DIABLO RANGE
TEMBLOR RANGE
SIERRA MADRE MTS.
TEHACHAPI MTS.
Joshua Tree N.P.
Palm Springs
Twentynine Palms
Indio
© Rand McNally
079308-14B

How to determine distance

Mileages in red between red arrowheads; in black, between intersections.

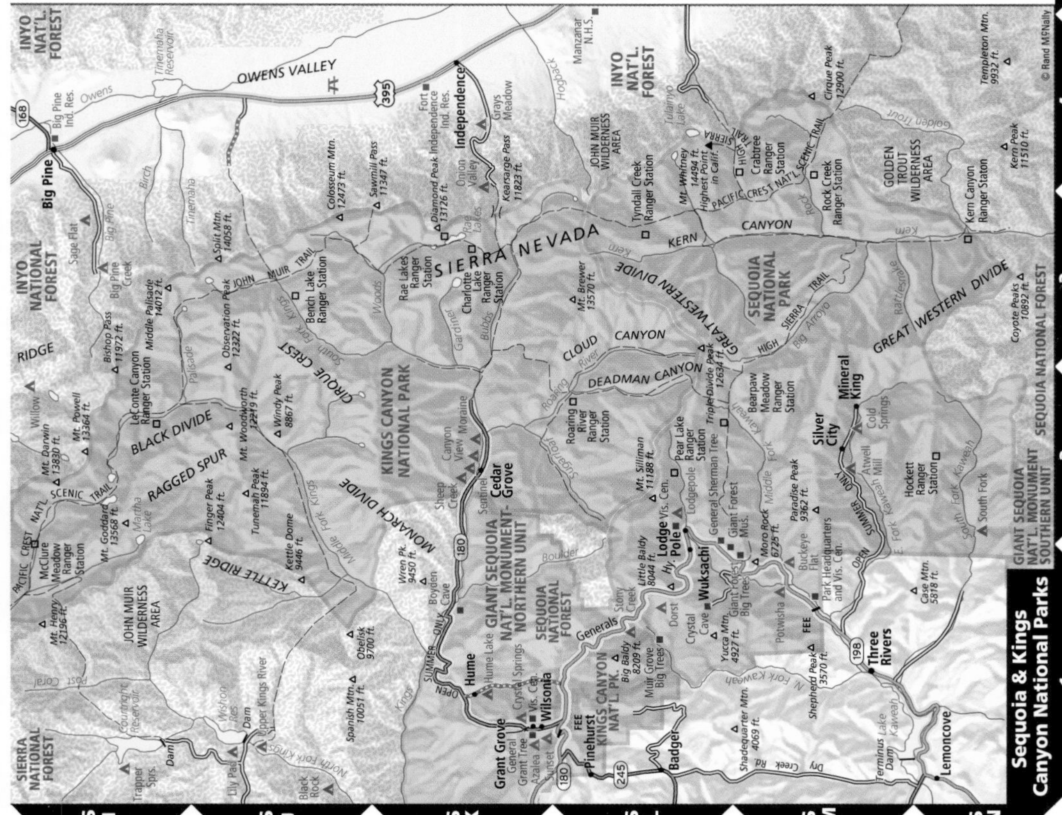
Sequoia & Kings Canyon National Parks
SIERRA NEVADA
KINGS CANYON NATIONAL PARK
SEQUOIA NATIONAL PARK
INYO NAT'L FOREST
OWENS VALLEY
Independence
Big Pine
Cedar Grove
Three Rivers
Lemoncove
Mineral King
Grant Grove
Wilsonia
Hume

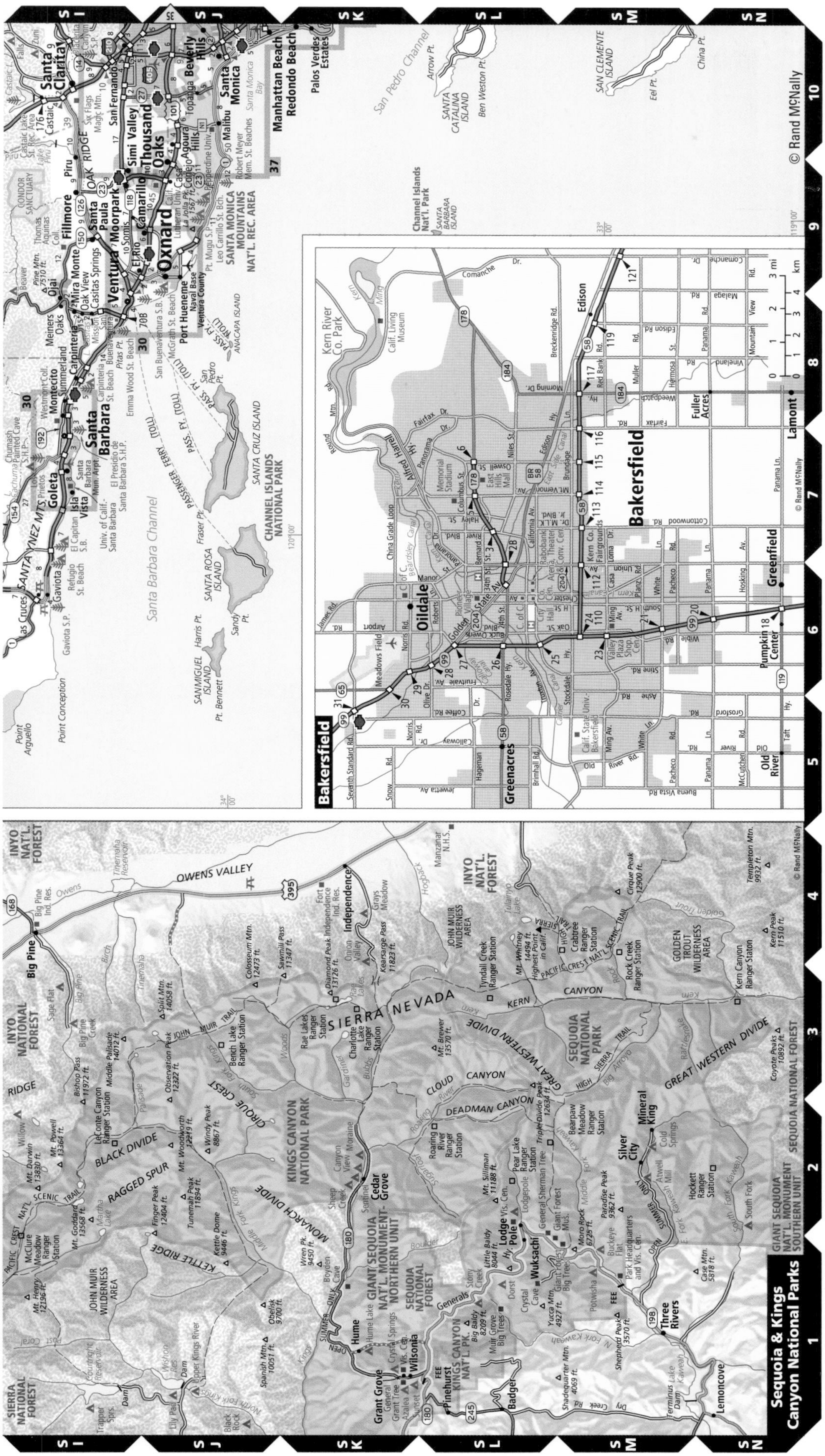

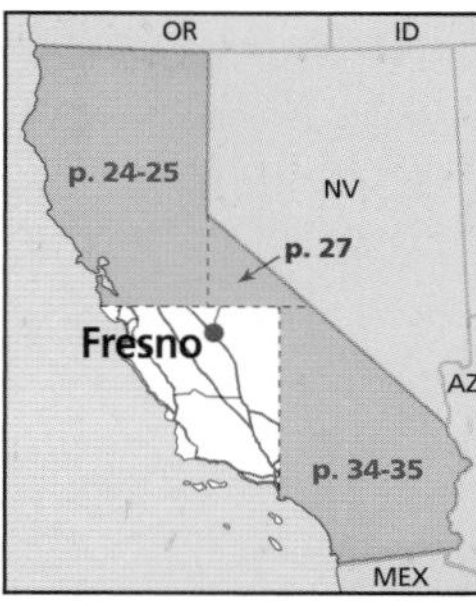
OR
ID
NV
p. 24-25
p. 27
Fresno
AZ
p. 34-35
MEX

HARLEY-DAVIDSON DEALERSHIPS

For the Bay Area, please see dealer listings on page 27; for the Los Angeles Vicinity/West, please see page 37.

- **Gary Bang Harley-Davidson, SF-5**
  7935 San Luis Ave. **Atascadero**
  (805) 461-1818
  Lat N 35.479 **Lon** W 120.670
- **Bakersfield Harley-Davidson, SF-9**
  35088 7th Standard Rd. **Bakersfield**
  (661) 325-3644
  Lat N 35.441 **Lon** W 119.081
- **Santa Barbara Harley-Davidson, SI-8**
  3501 Via Real **Carpinteria (Santa Barbara)**
  (805) 745-1911
  Lat N 34.414 **Lon** W 119.556
- **Harley-Davidson of Fresno, SB-7**
  4345 W Shaw Ave. **Fresno**
  (559) 275-8586
  Lat N 36.808 **Lon** W 119.870
- **Mathews Harley-Davidson, SB-7**
  548 N Blackstone Ave. **Fresno**
  (559) 233-5279
  Lat N 36.751 **Lon** W 119.790
- **Golden Valley Harley-Davidson Shop, SB-5**
  1415 Badger Flat Rd. **Los Banos**
  (209) 827-5900
  Lat N 37.075 **Lon** W 120.876
- **Yosemite Harley-Davidson of Merced, SA-6**
  1645 W Hwy. 140 **Merced**
  (209) 723-9702
  Lat N 37.303 **Lon** W 120.503
- **Simi Valley Harley-Davidson, SI-9**
  6190 Condor Dr. **Moorpark**
  (805) 552-9555
  Lat N 34.291 **Lon** W 118.857
- **House of Thunder Harley-Davidson, SA-3**
  16175 Condit Rd. **Morgan Hill**
  (408) 776-1900
  Lat N 37.121 **Lon** W 121.625
- **Warren's Harley-Davidson, SC-3**
  333 N Main St. **Salinas**
  (831) 424-1909
  Lat N 36.683 **Lon** W 121.653
- **Santa Cruz Harley-Davidson, SB-2**
  1148 Soquel Ave. **Santa Cruz**
  (831) 421-9600
  Lat N 36.979 **Lon** W 122.011
- **Santa Maria Harley-Davidson, SG-6**
  2022 N Preisker Ln. **Santa Maria**
  (805) 928-3668
  Lat N 34.977 **Lon** W 120.430
- **Visalia Harley-Davidson, SD-8**
  30681 Hwy. 99 **Visalia**
  (559) 733-4647
  Lat N 36.350 **Lon** W 119.427
- **Green Valley Harley-Davidson Shop, SB-3**
  1059 S Green Valley Rd. **Watsonville**
  (831) 768-9500
  Lat N 36.918 **Lon** W 121.784

Distance scale
One inch represents about 26 miles
0 10 20 30 mi
0 10 20 30 40 km

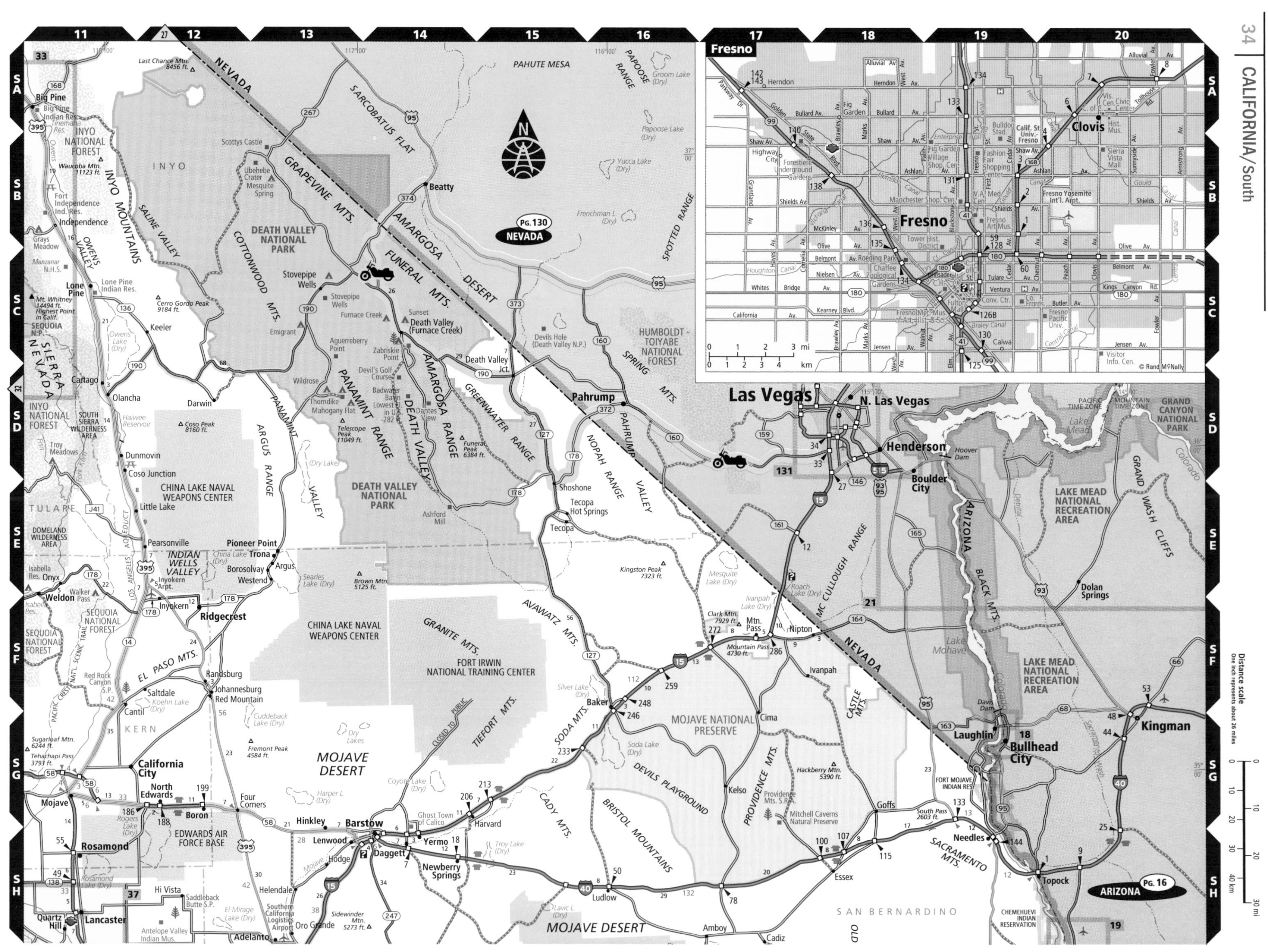
Fresno
Clovis
Las Vegas
N. Las Vegas
Henderson
Boulder City
Kingman
Bullhead City
Laughlin
Needles
Topock
Pahrump
Beatty
Shoshone
Tecopa
Baker
Barstow
Daggett
Yermo
Newberry Springs
Ridgecrest
Inyokern
Lone Pine
Independence
Big Pine
Mojave
Rosamond
Lancaster
California City
Boron
NEVADA
ARIZONA
DEATH VALLEY NATIONAL PARK
MOJAVE NATIONAL PRESERVE
MOJAVE DESERT
LAKE MEAD NATIONAL RECREATION AREA
CHINA LAKE NAVAL WEAPONS CENTER
FORT IRWIN NATIONAL TRAINING CENTER
EDWARDS AIR FORCE BASE
INYO NATIONAL FOREST
SEQUOIA NATIONAL FOREST
HUMBOLDT-TOIYABE NATIONAL FOREST
SIERRA NEVADA
INYO MOUNTAINS
PANAMINT RANGE
AMARGOSA RANGE
FUNERAL MTS.
GRAPEVINE MTS.
SPRING MTS.
NOPAH RANGE
PROVIDENCE MTS.
BLACK MTS.
GRAND WASH CLIFFS
SAN BERNARDINO
Pg. 130 NEVADA
Pg. 16 ARIZONA

How to determine distance

Mileages in red between red arrowheads; in black, between intersections.

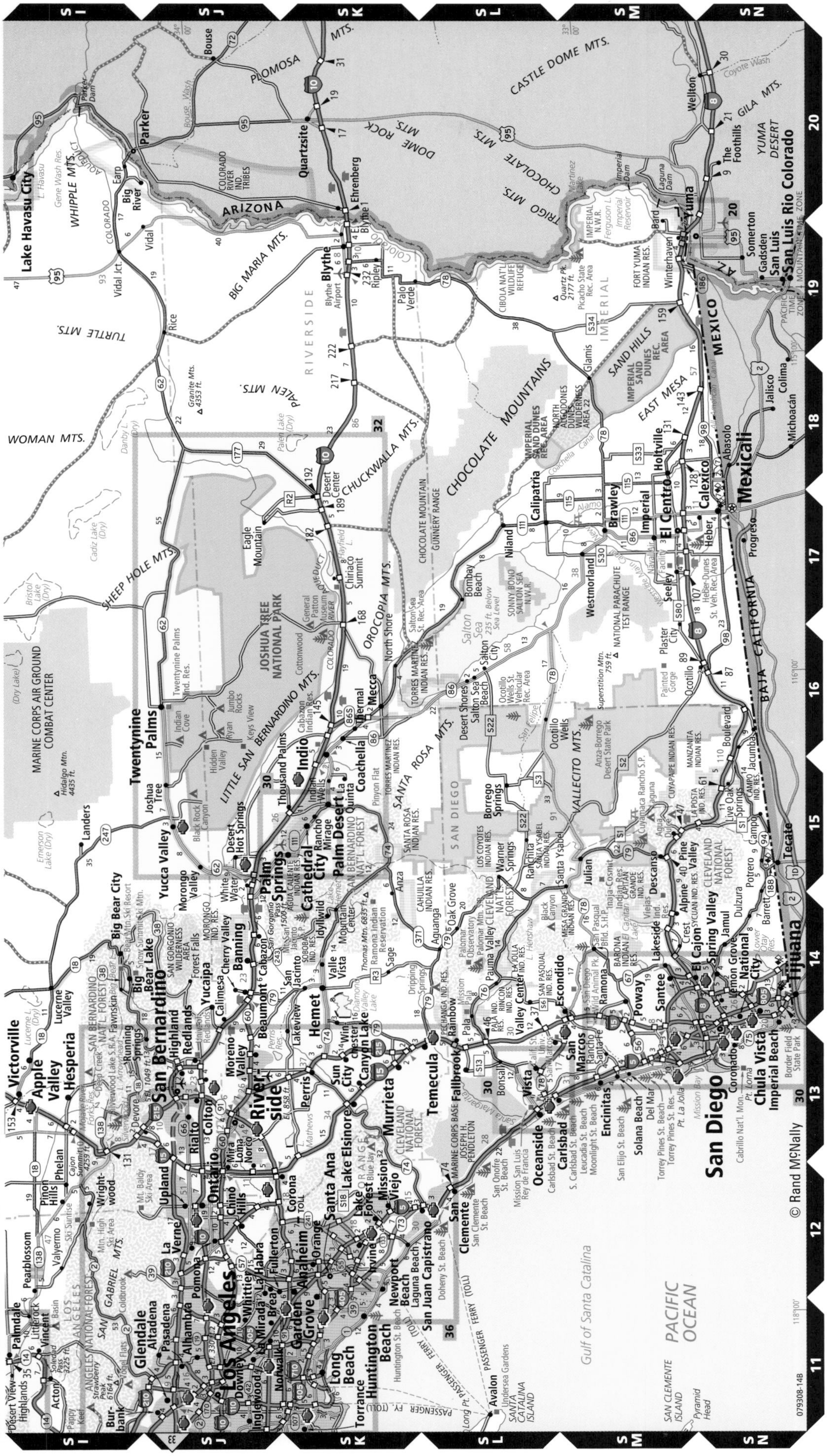

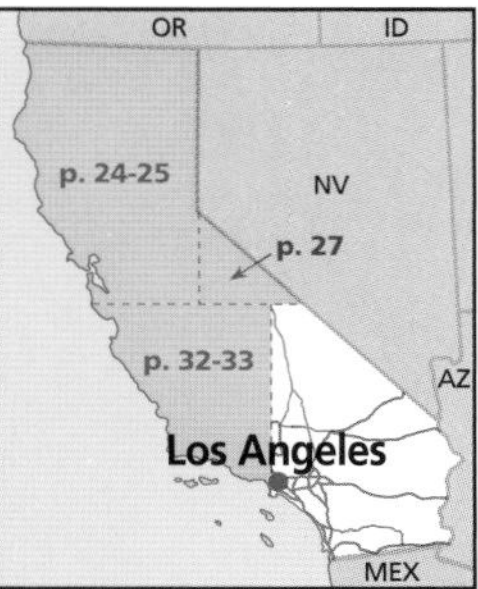
OR
ID
p. 24-25
NV
p. 27
p. 32-33
AZ
Los Angeles
MEX

SYMBOLS

Featured ride
Scenic route
Point of interest
Long-term construction
Harley-Davidson dealership

For Nevada/California ride, see page R24.

HARLEY-DAVIDSON DEALERSHIPS

For southern cities, please see dealer listings on page 31; for the Los Angeles Vicinity/West, please see page 37; for L.A. Vicinity/East, please see page 39.

Antelope Valley Harley-Davidson, SH-11
1759 W Ave. J-12 **Lancaster**
(661) 948-5959
Lat N 34.694 **Lon** W 118.150

Palm Springs Harley-Davidson, SJ-15
19465 N Indian Ave. **North Palm Springs**
(760) 329-1448
Lat N 33.914 **Lon** W 116.549

Biggs Harley-Davidson Shop, SL-13
1555 S Coast Hwy. **Oceanside**
(760) 433-2060
Lat N 33.179 **Lon** W 117.366

Palm Springs Harley-Davidson Shop, SK-15
39101 Leopard St. **Palm Desert**
(760) 200-1775
Lat N 33.765 **Lon** W 116.307

Capistrano Harley-Davidson, SL-12
32421 Calle Perfecto **San Juan Capistrano**
(949) 388-3000
Lat N 33.484 **Lon** W 117.672

Biggs Harley-Davidson, SM-13
717 Center Dr. **San Marcos**
(760) 481-7300
Lat N 33.134 **Lon** W 117.124

Quaid Temecula Harley-Davidson, SL-13
28964 Old Town Front St. **Temecula**
(951) 506-6903
Lat N 33.489 **Lon** W 117.145

Victor Valley Harley-Davidson, SI-13
14522 Valley Center Dr. **Victorville**
(760) 951-1119
Lat N 34.515 **Lon** W 117.320

Hutchins Harley-Davidson, SJ-15
55405 29 Palms Hwy. **Yucca Valley**
(760) 365-6311
Lat N 34.111 **Lon** W 116.475

079308-14B

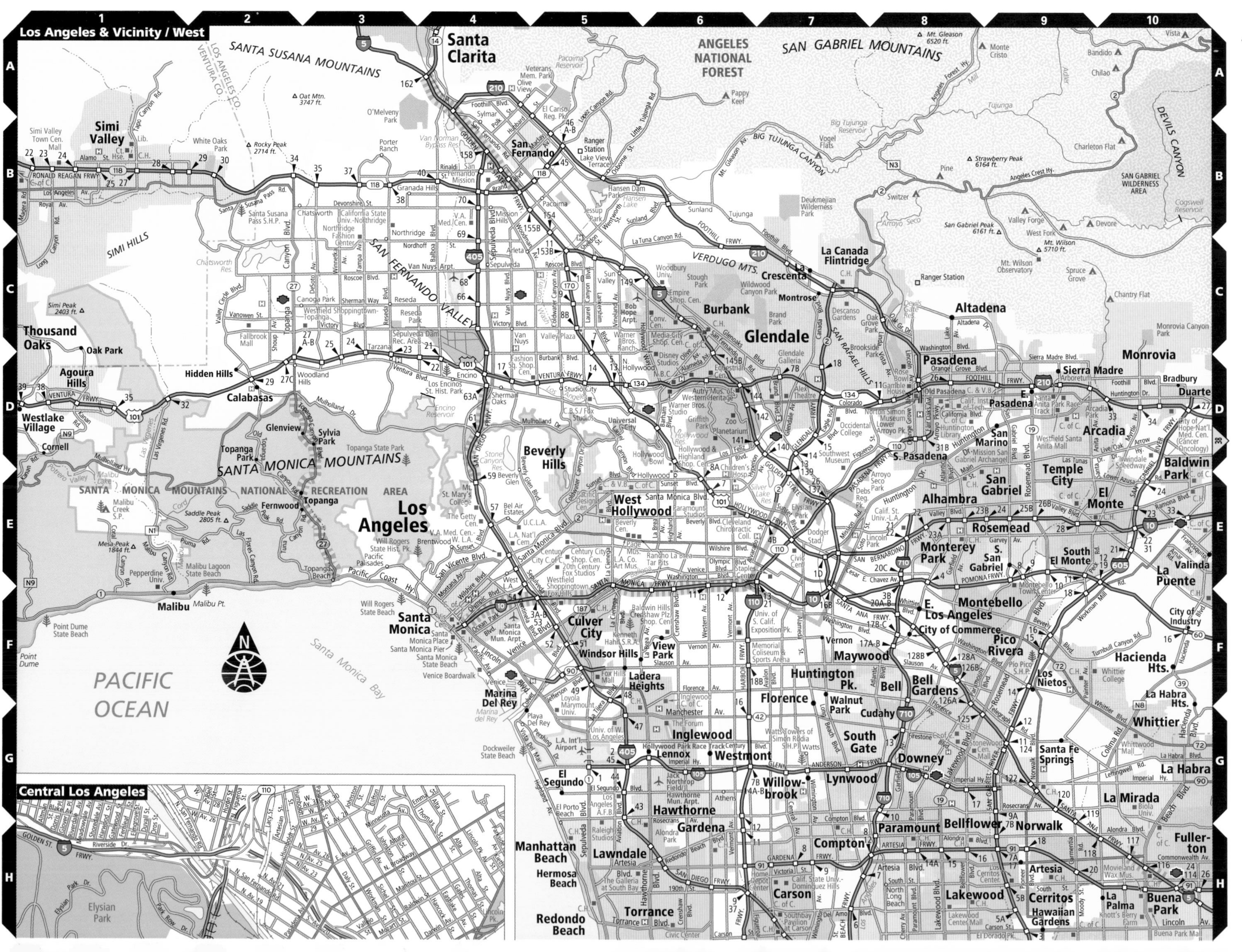
Los Angeles & Vicinity / West
Central Los Angeles
PACIFIC OCEAN
Santa Monica Bay
SAN GABRIEL MOUNTAINS
ANGELES NATIONAL FOREST
SANTA SUSANA MOUNTAINS
SANTA MONICA MOUNTAINS
SANTA MONICA MOUNTAINS NATIONAL RECREATION AREA
SAN FERNANDO VALLEY
VERDUGO MTS.
SAN RAFAEL HILLS
SIMI HILLS
DEVILS CANYON
BIG TUJUNGA CANYON
LOS ANGELES CO.
VENTURA CO.
Los Angeles
Santa Clarita
Simi Valley
Thousand Oaks
Westlake Village
Agoura Hills
Calabasas
Hidden Hills
Malibu
Santa Monica
Beverly Hills
West Hollywood
Culver City
Glendale
Burbank
Pasadena
Altadena
La Canada Flintridge
Monrovia
Arcadia
Sierra Madre
Duarte
Baldwin Park
El Monte
Temple City
San Marino
San Gabriel
Alhambra
Rosemead
Monterey Park
South El Monte
Montebello
E. Los Angeles
Pico Rivera
Whittier
La Habra
Fullerton
La Mirada
Norwalk
Downey
Bell Gardens
Bell
Maywood
Huntington Pk.
South Gate
Lynwood
Compton
Paramount
Bellflower
Lakewood
Cerritos
Artesia
Inglewood
Hawthorne
Gardena
Carson
Torrance
Lawndale
Redondo Beach
Hermosa Beach
Manhattan Beach
El Segundo
Marina Del Rey
Topanga
San Fernando
Crescenta
Montrose

How to determine distance

Mileages in red between red arrowheads; in black, between intersections.

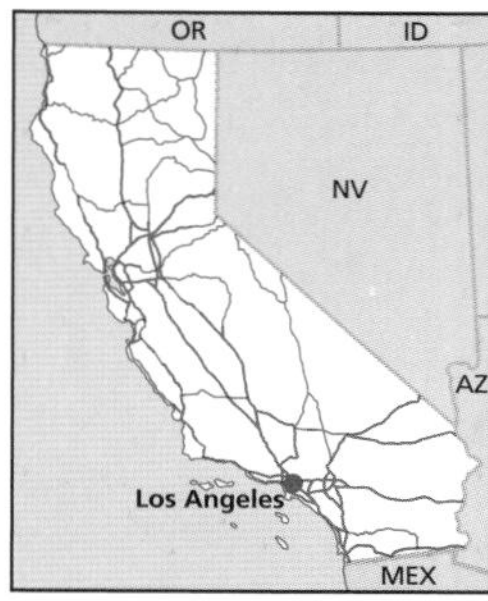
OR
ID
NV
AZ
Los Angeles
MEX

CALIFORNIA MOTORCYCLE LAWS

Helmet use: Required

Riding two abreast:
No reference in administrative code or statutes

Eye protection: Not required

Speed limit:
Primary roads: 70 mph
Secondary roads: 65 mph

CALIFORNIA RESOURCES

Road conditions or construction:
511 (San Francisco Bay and Sacramento areas)
(800) 427-7623 (in CA)
(916) 445-7623
www.dot.ca.gov
www.511.org

Highway Emergency Numbers: 911

Tourism:
(916) 444-4429
www.visitcalifornia.com

State motor vehicle information:
(800) 777-0133
www.dmv.ca.gov

HARLEY-DAVIDSON DEALERSHIPS

Laidlaw's Harley-Davidson Sales, E-10
1919 Puente Ave. **Baldwin Park**
(626) 851-0412
Lat N 34.069 **Lon** W 117.963

Barger Harley-Davidson, C-2
22107 Sherman Way **Canoga Park**
(818) 999-3355
Lat N 34.201 **Lon** W 118.608

Harley-Davidson of Anaheim-Fullerton, H-10
2635 W Orangethorpe Ave. **Fullerton**
(714) 871-6563
Lat N 33.859 **Lon** W 117.974

Harley-Davidson of Glendale, D-7
3717 San Fernando Rd. **Glendale**
(818) 246-5618
Lat N 34.125 **Lon** W 118.256

California Harley-Davidson, I-6
1517 W Pacific Coast Hwy. **Harbor City**
(310) 539-3366
Lat N 33.789 **Lon** W 118.303

Bartels' Harley-Davidson, F-4
4141 Lincoln Blvd. (Rte. 1) **Marina Del Ray**
(310) 823-1112
Lat N 33.988 **Lon** W 118.446

Los Angeles Harley-Davidson, G-8
13300 Paramount Blvd. **South Gate**
(562) 408-6088
Lat N 33.915 **Lon** W 118.159

Hollywood Harley-Davidson, D-5
1000 Universal Studios Blvd. Ste. V112
Universal City
(818) 754-6200
Lat N 34.136 **Lon** W 118.351

Van Nuys Harley-Davidson, C-4
7630 Van Nuys Blvd. **Van Nuys**
(818) 989-2230
Lat N 34.209 **Lon** W 118.449

Harley-Davidson of Westminster, I-10
13031 Goldenwest St. **Westminster**
(714) 893-6274
Lat N 33.773 **Lon** W 118.007

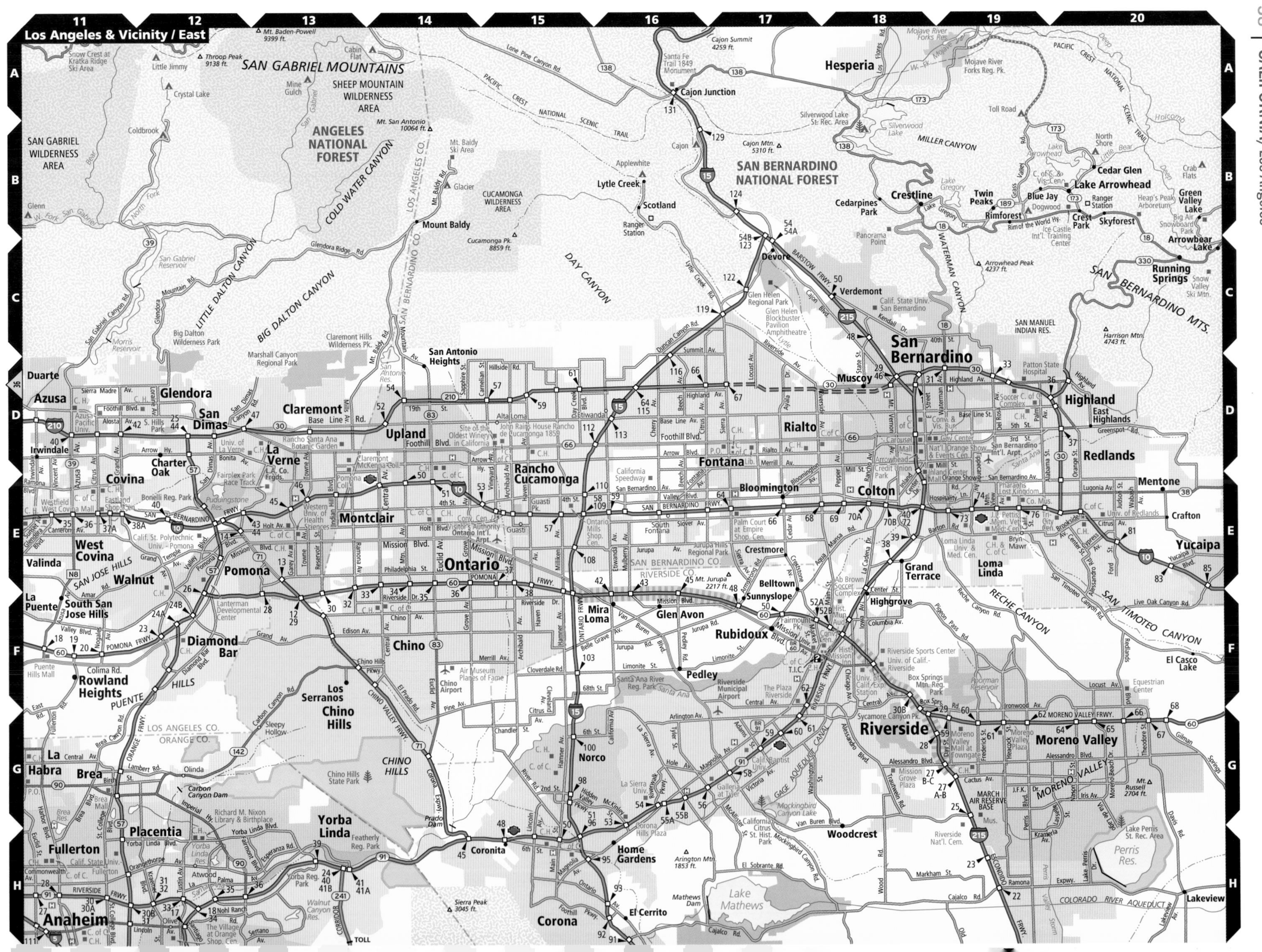
Los Angeles & Vicinity / East
SAN GABRIEL MOUNTAINS
SHEEP MOUNTAIN WILDERNESS AREA
ANGELES NATIONAL FOREST
SAN GABRIEL WILDERNESS AREA
CUCAMONGA WILDERNESS AREA
SAN BERNARDINO NATIONAL FOREST
SAN BERNARDINO MTS.
DAY CANYON
BIG DALTON CANYON
LITTLE DALTON CANYON
COLD WATER CANYON
WATERMAN CANYON
MILLER CANYON
RECHE CANYON
SAN TIMOTEO CANYON
Hesperia
Cajon Junction
Lytle Creek
Scotland
Mount Baldy
Devore
Verdemont
Crestline
Cedarpines Park
Twin Peaks
Rimforest
Blue Jay
Cedar Glen
Lake Arrowhead
Crest Park
Skyforest
Green Valley Lake
Arrowbear Lake
Running Springs
San Bernardino
Muscoy
Highland
East Highlands
Redlands
Mentone
Crafton
Yucaipa
Loma Linda
Grand Terrace
Colton
Rialto
Fontana
Bloomington
Rancho Cucamonga
San Antonio Heights
Upland
Claremont
La Verne
San Dimas
Glendora
Azusa
Duarte
Irwindale
Covina
Charter Oak
West Covina
Valinda
Walnut
Pomona
Montclair
Ontario
Chino
Mira Loma
Glen Avon
Crestmore
Belltown
Sunnyslope
Rubidoux
Pedley
Highgrove
Riverside
Moreno Valley
Woodcrest
Norco
Home Gardens
Corona
Coronita
El Cerrito
Lakeview
Lake Mathews
Perris Res.
La Puente
South San Jose Hills
Diamond Bar
Rowland Heights
Los Serranos
Chino Hills
Yorba Linda
Placentia
Brea
La Habra
Fullerton
Anaheim

How to determine distance

Mileages in red between red arrowheads; in black, between intersections.

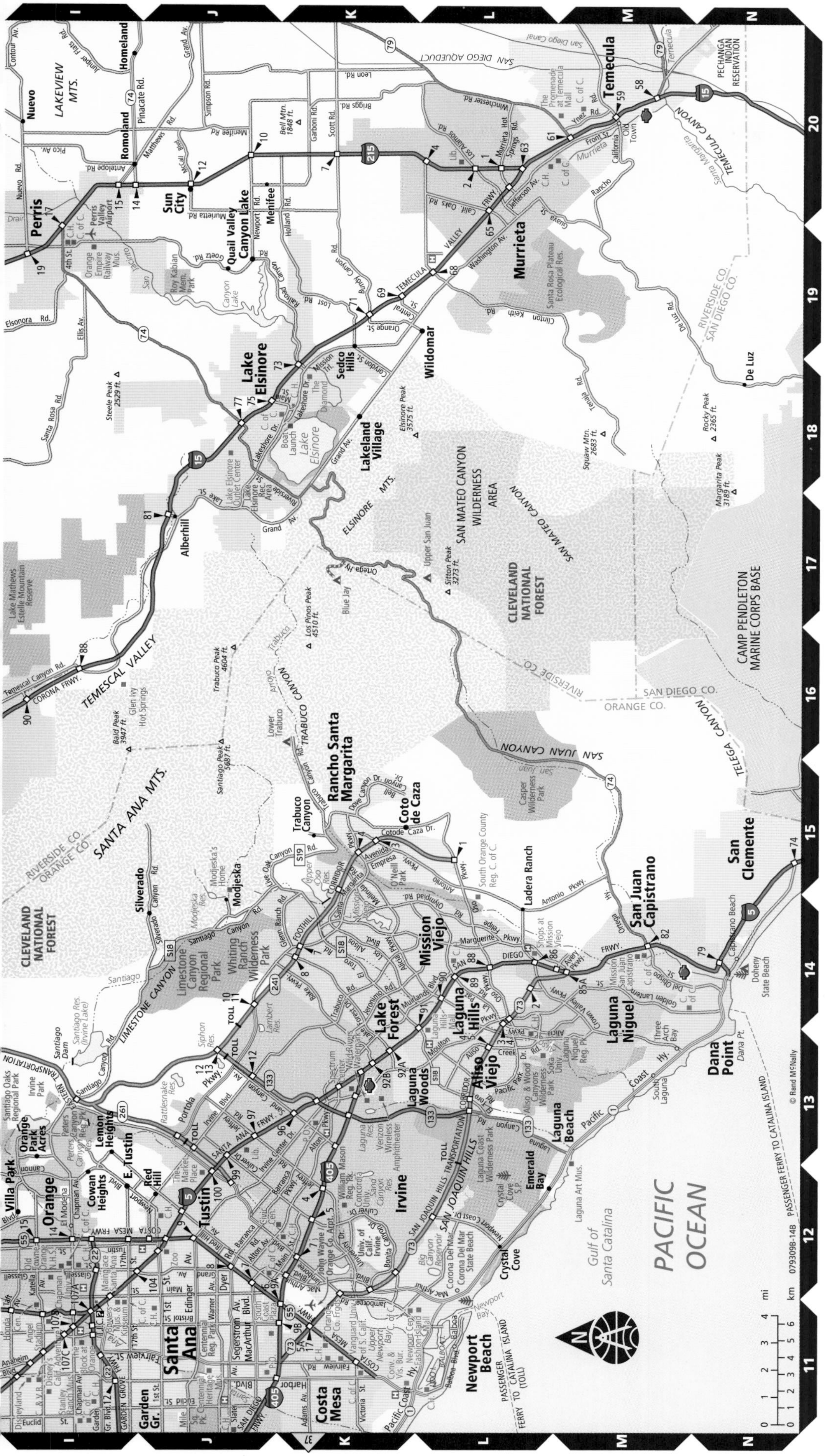

OR
ID
NV
AZ
Los Angeles
MEX

SYMBOLS

- Featured ride
- Scenic route
- Point of interest
- Long-term construction
- Harley-Davidson dealership

CITY-TO-CITY MILEAGE

	BAKERSFIELD	FRESNO	LOS ANGELES	MONTEREY	PALM SPRINGS	RIVERSIDE	SAN DIEGO	SANTA BARBARA
Bakersfield		107	112	226	226	168	236	148
Barstow	136	243	120	362	128	81	180	212
Blythe	335	438	223	548	116	165	223	315
El Centro	331	434	219	544	110	161	114	311
Fresno	107		215	158	329	271	339	251
Las Vegas, NV	287	394	275	513	283	236	335	367
Los Angeles	112	215		325	114	56	124	92
Monterey	226	158	325		439	381	449	246
Needles	280	387	264	506	187	225	324	356
Palm Springs	226	329	114	439		56	131	206
Riverside	168	271	56	381	56		99	148
Sacramento	271	164	379	186	493	435	503	383
San Bernardino	161	268	63	388	57	10	109	155
San Diego	236	339	124	449	131	99		216
San Francisco	282	183	381	111	495	437	505	332
San Luis Obispo	125	127	195	143	309	251	319	103
Santa Barbara	148	251	92	246	206	148	216	
Sequoia N.P.	125	94	233	252	347	289	357	269

HARLEY-DAVIDSON DEALERSHIPS

Corona Harley-Davidson, H-15
2410 Wardlow Rd. Ste. 105-106 **Corona**
(866) 577-2437
Lat N 33.882 **Lon** W 117.612

Orange County Harley-Davidson, K-13
8677 Research Dr. **Irvine**
(949) 727-4464
Lat N 33.645 **Lon** W 117.741

Quaid Harley-Davidson, E-19
25160 Redlands Blvd. **Loma Linda**
(909) 796-8399
Lat N 34.063 **Lon** W 117.257

Pomona Valley Harley-Davidson, E-13
8710 Central Ave. **Montclair**
(909) 981-9500
Lat N 34.095 **Lon** W 117.690

Skip Fordyce Harley-Davidson Sales, G-17
7688 Indiana Ave. **Riverside**
(951) 785-0100
Lat N 33.933 **Lon** W 117.407

0793098-148

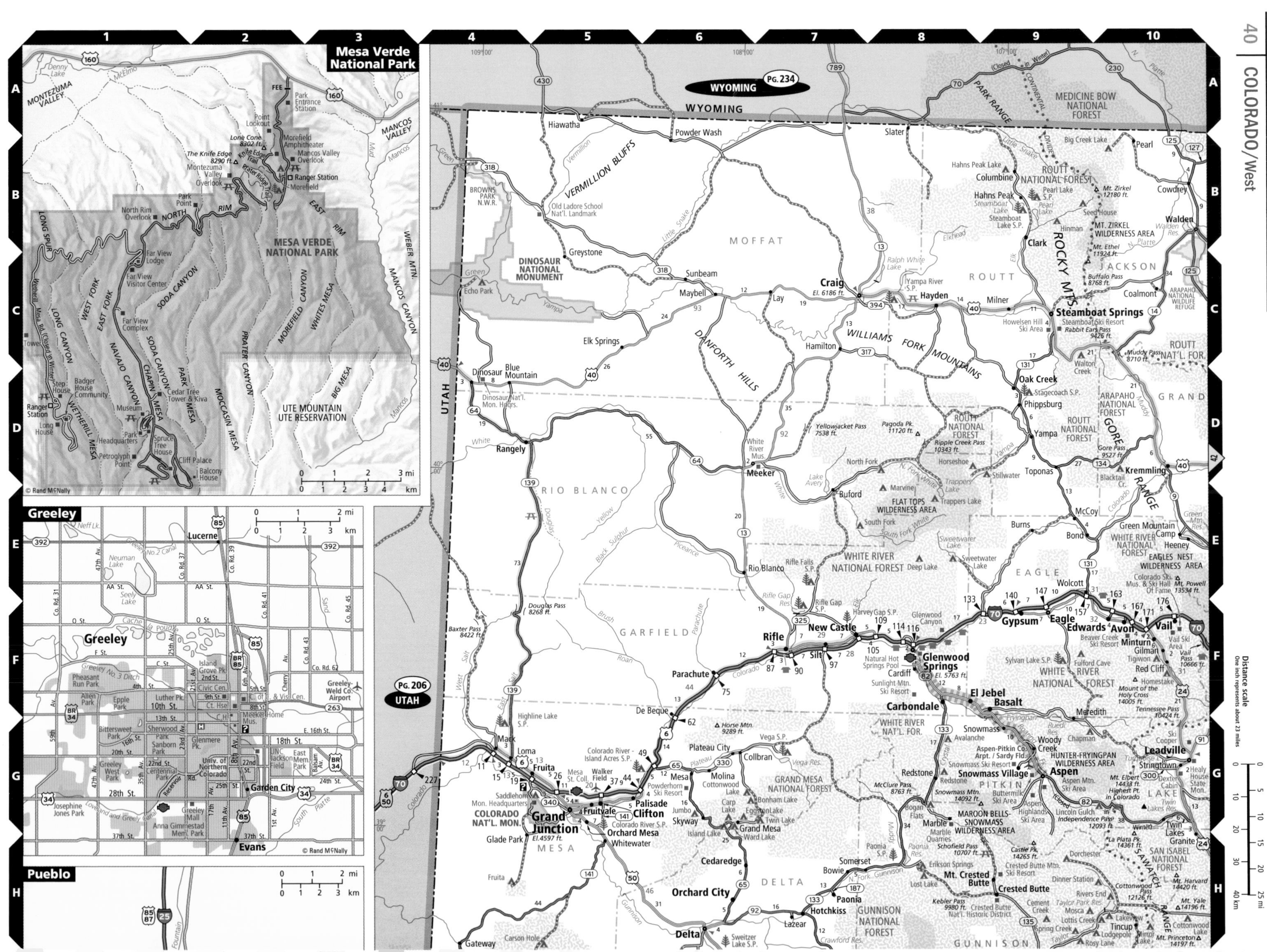
Distance scale
One inch represents about 23 miles
0 5 10 15 20 25 mi
0 10 20 30 40 km
WYOMING
Pg. 234
UTAH
Pg. 206
MOFFAT
ROUTT
JACKSON
GRAND
EAGLE
GARFIELD
RIO BLANCO
MESA
PITKIN
DELTA
GUNNISON
ROCKY MTS.
GORE RANGE
PARK RANGE
SAWATCH RANGE
WILLIAMS FORK MOUNTAINS
DANFORTH HILLS
VERMILLION BLUFFS
DINOSAUR NATIONAL MONUMENT
MEDICINE BOW NATIONAL FOREST
ROUTT NATIONAL FOREST
WHITE RIVER NATIONAL FOREST
GRAND MESA NATIONAL FOREST
GUNNISON NATIONAL FOREST
SAN ISABEL NATIONAL FOREST
FLAT TOPS WILDERNESS AREA
MT. ZIRKEL WILDERNESS AREA
EAGLES NEST WILDERNESS AREA
HUNTER-FRYINGPAN WILDERNESS AREA
MAROON BELLS-SNOWMASS WILDERNESS AREA
COLORADO NAT'L. MON.
Steamboat Springs
Craig
Hayden
Meeker
Rangely
Dinosaur
Rifle
New Castle
Glenwood Springs
Carbondale
Basalt
El Jebel
Aspen
Snowmass Village
Eagle
Gypsum
Vail
Avon
Edwards
Minturn
Leadville
Kremmling
Walden
Grand Junction
Fruita
Palisade
Clifton
Delta
Orchard City
Cedaredge
Paonia
Hotchkiss
Parachute
De Beque
Silt
Mt. Crested Butte
Crested Butte
Mesa Verde National Park
MESA VERDE NATIONAL PARK
UTE MOUNTAIN UTE RESERVATION
MANCOS CANYON
SODA CANYON
NAVAJO CANYON
WETHERILL MESA
LONG CANYON
CHAPIN MESA
PARK MESA
MOCCASIN MESA
PRATER CANYON
MOREFIELD CANYON
WHITES MESA
BIG MESA
Far View Lodge
Far View Visitor Center
Park Entrance Station
Morefield
Cliff Palace
Balcony House
Spruce Tree House
© Rand McNally
Greeley
Evans
Garden City
Lucerne
Pueblo

How to determine distance

Mileages in red between red arrowheads; in black, between intersections.

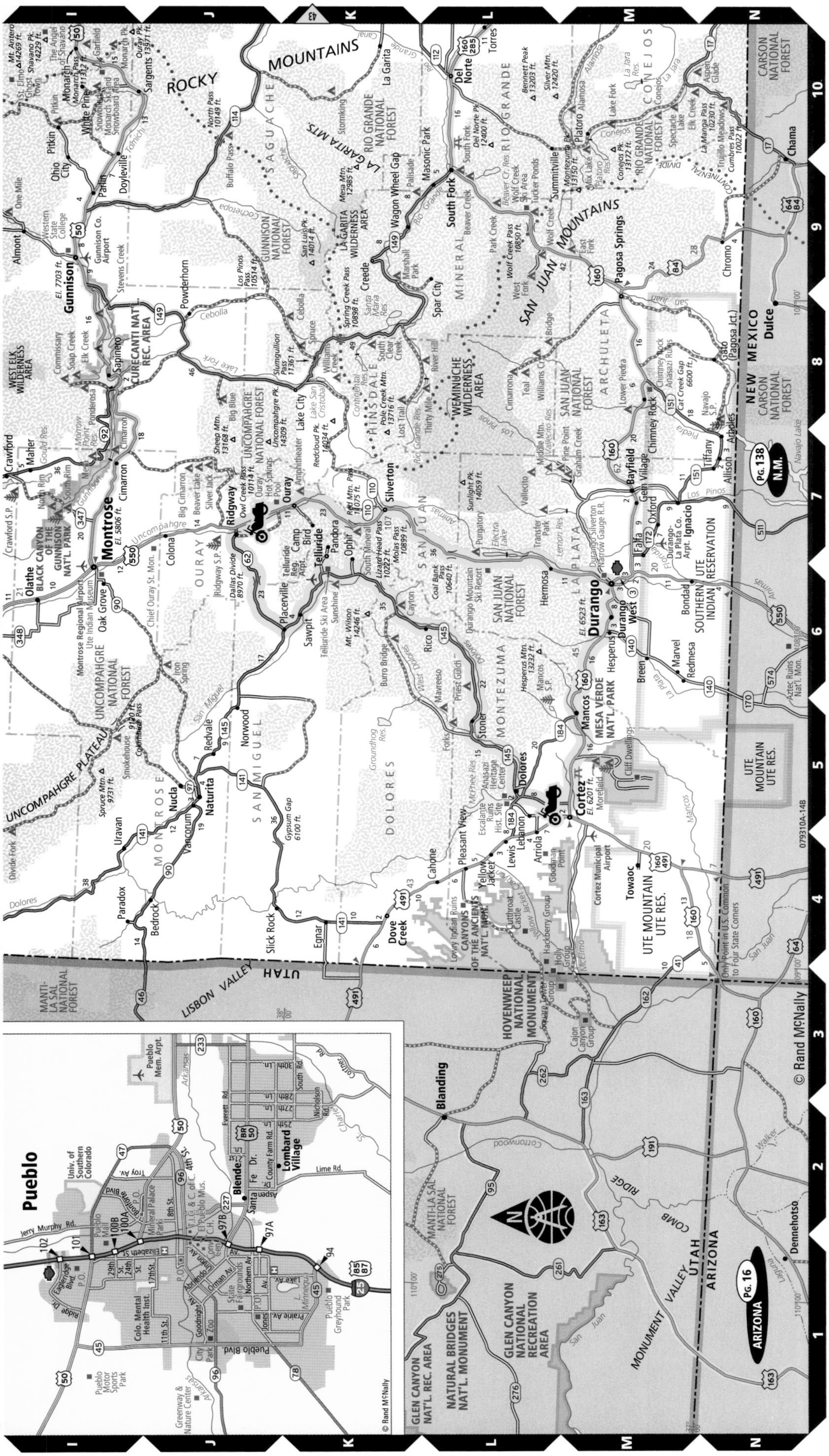

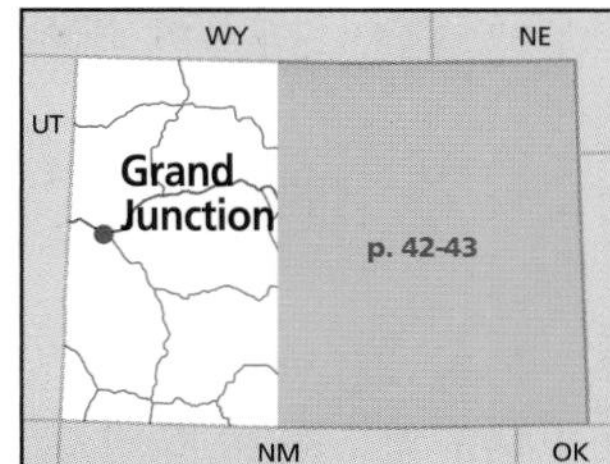
WY
NE
UT
Grand Junction
p. 42-43
NM
OK

SYMBOLS

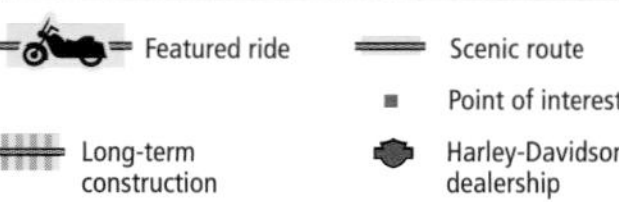
Featured ride
Scenic route
Point of interest
Long-term construction
Harley-Davidson dealership

For Colorado ride, see page R11.

COLORADO MOTORCYCLE LAWS

Helmet use:
Not required

Riding two abreast:
Yes. See state law for specifics

Eye protection:
Required by law

Speed limit:
Primary roads: 75 mph
Secondary roads: 65 mph

COLORADO RESOURCES

Road conditions or construction:
511
(877) 315-7623 (in CO)
(303) 639-1111
www.cotrip.org

Highway Emergency Numbers:
911
*277
(303) 329-4501

Tourism:
(800) 265-6723
www.colorado.com

State motor vehicle information:
(303) 205-5600
www.revenue.state.co.us/mv_dir/home.asp

HARLEY-DAVIDSON DEALERSHIPS

Durango Harley-Davidson, M-6
750 S Camino Del Rio (US 550) **Durango**
(970) 259-0778
Lat N 37.246 **Lon** W 107.874

Aspen Valley Harley-Davidson, F-8
2922 S Glen Ave. **Glenwood Springs**
(970) 928-7493
Lat N 39.522 **Lon** W 107.321

Grand Junction Harley-Davidson, G-5
2747 Crossroads Blvd. **Grand Junction**
(970) 245-0812
Lat N 39.116 **Lon** W 108.545

079310A-14B

Distance scale
One inch represents about 23 miles
0 5 10 15 20 25 mi
0 10 20 30 40 km

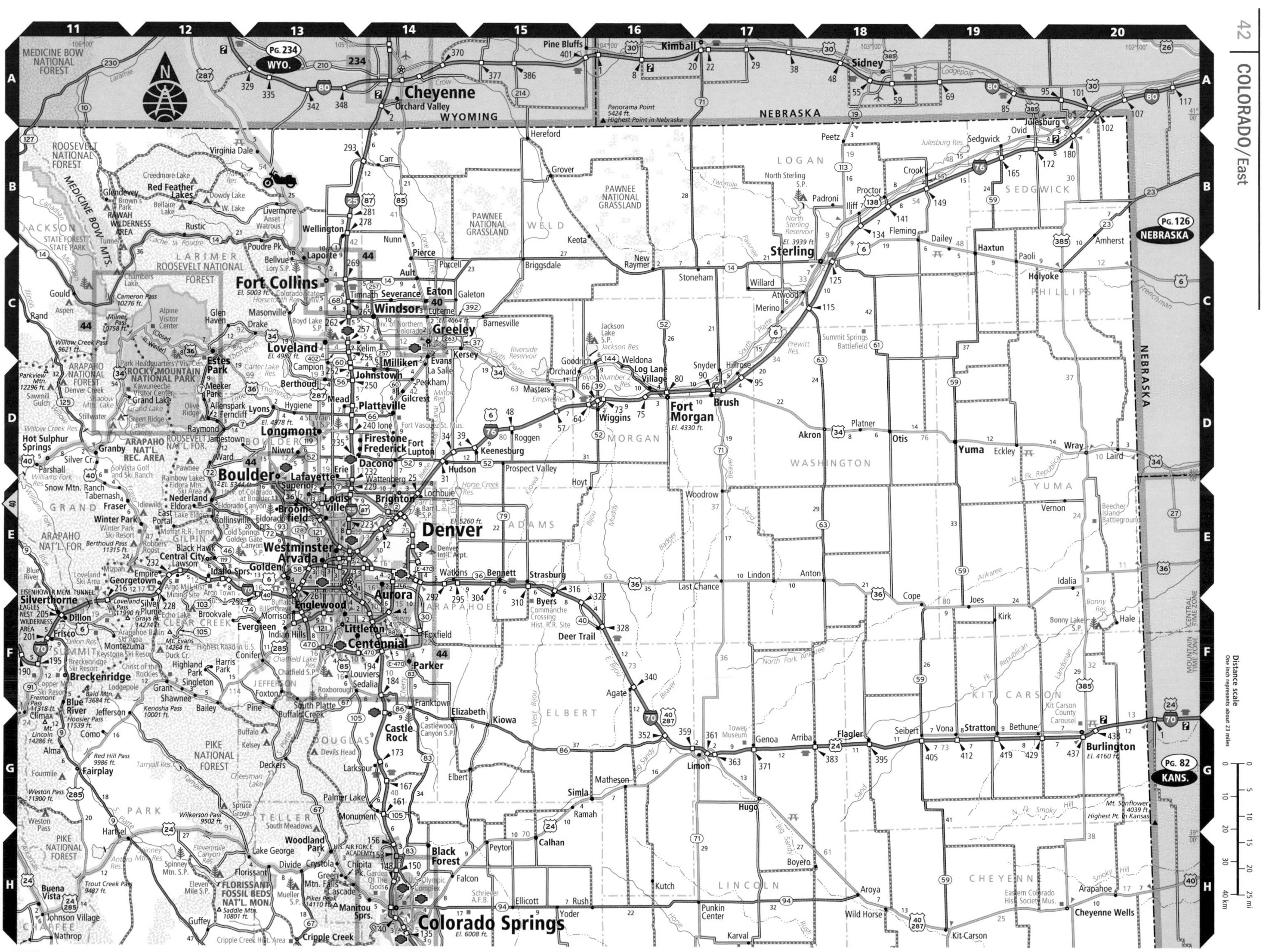
NEBRASKA
WYOMING
Cheyenne
Fort Collins
Greeley
Loveland
Longmont
Boulder
Denver
Aurora
Westminster
Arvada
Lakewood
Littleton
Centennial
Parker
Castle Rock
Colorado Springs
Sterling
Fort Morgan
Brush
Burlington
Limon
Julesburg
Holyoke
Wray
Yuma
Akron
Kimball
Sidney
Pine Bluffs
ROCKY MOUNTAIN NATIONAL PARK
PAWNEE NATIONAL GRASSLAND
PIKE NATIONAL FOREST
ROOSEVELT NATIONAL FOREST
MEDICINE BOW MTS.
LOGAN
SEDGWICK
PHILLIPS
YUMA
WASHINGTON
MORGAN
WELD
ADAMS
ARAPAHOE
ELBERT
LINCOLN
KIT CARSON
CHEYENNE
DOUGLAS
TELLER
Cheyenne Wells
Kit Carson
Flagler
Stratton
Hugo
Breckenridge
Silverthorne
Dillon
Frisco
Georgetown
Idaho Springs
Estes Park
Fairplay
Woodland Park
Manitou Springs
Cripple Creek
Buena Vista

How to determine distance

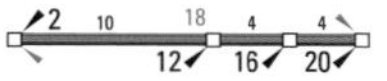

Mileages in red between red arrowheads; in black, between intersections.

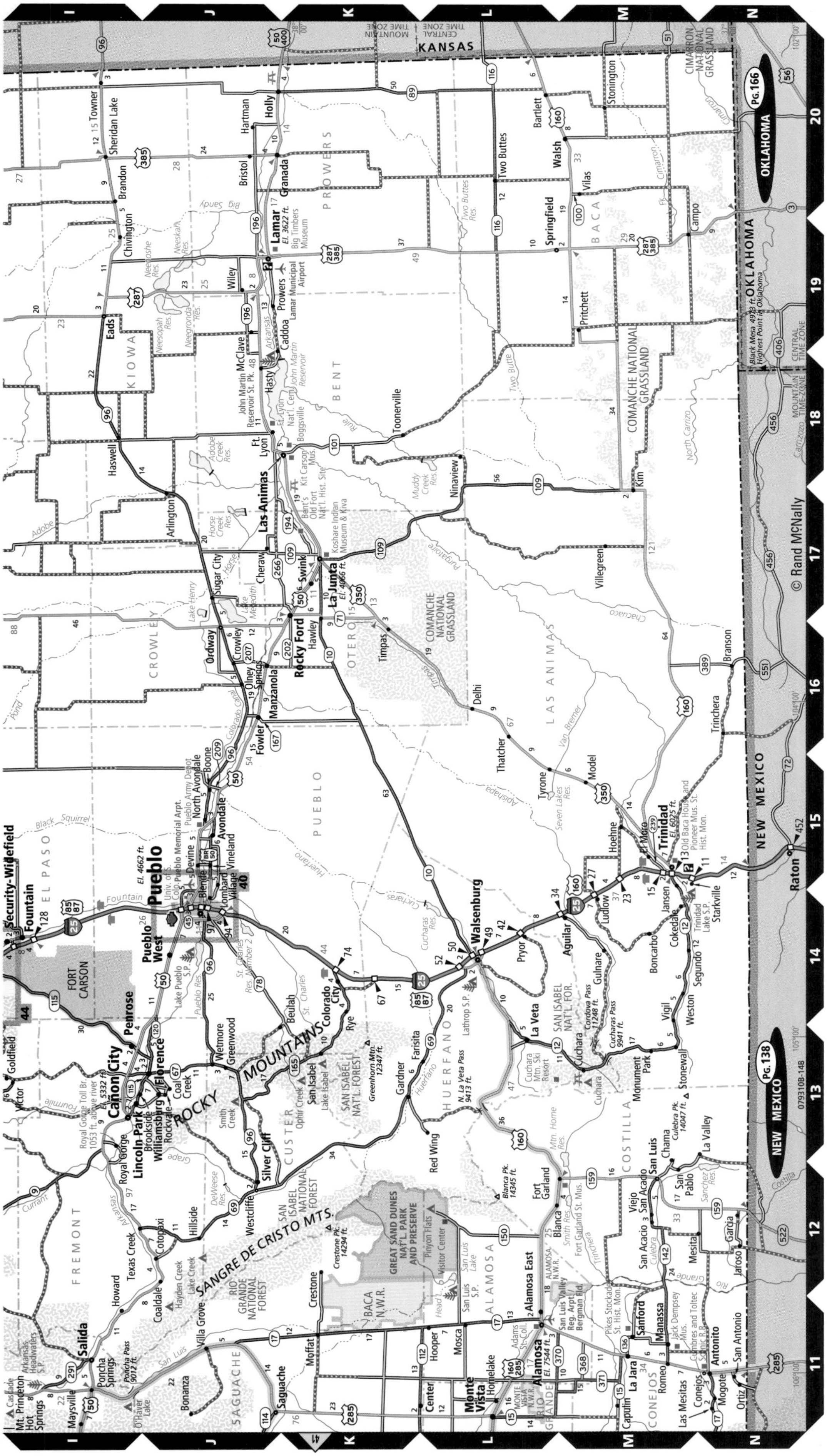

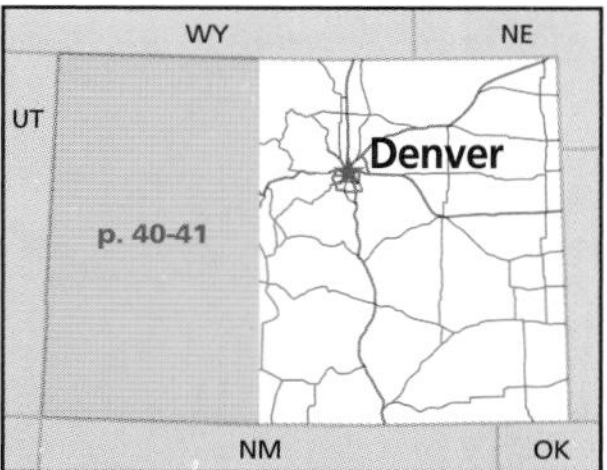
WY
NE
UT
Denver
p. 40-41
NM
OK

SYMBOLS

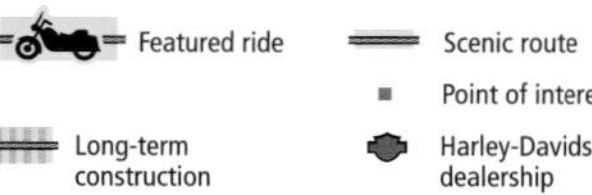
Featured ride
Scenic route
Point of interest
Long-term construction
Harley-Davidson dealership

For Wyoming/Colorado ride, see page R40.

HARLEY-DAVIDSON DEALERSHIPS

Mile High Harley-Davidson, E-14
16565 E 33rd Dr. **Aurora**
(303) 343-3300
Lat N 39.765 **Lon** W 104.795

Boulder Harley-Davidson Shop, D-13
2901 55th St. **Boulder**
(303) 545-6777
Lat N 40.028 **Lon** W 105.225

Rocky Mountain Harley-Davidson Shop, F-14
970 Park St. **Castle Rock**
(303) 327-7799
Lat N 39.380 **Lon** W 104.866

Pike's Peak Harley-Davidson, H-14
5867 N Nevada Ave. at I-25 **Colorado Springs**
(719) 278-2300
Lat N 38.916 **Lon** W 104.766

Colorado Springs Harley-Davidson Shop, H-14
2180 Victor Place **Colorado Springs**
(719) 591-7594
Lat N 38.863 **Lon** W 104.721

Freedom Harley-Davidson, E-13
8020 W Colfax Ave. **Denver**
(303) 238-0425
Lat N 39.740 **Lon** W 105.086

Mile High Harley-Davidson, E-14
8900 Peña Blvd. **Denver**
(303) 342-9021
Lat N 39.852 **Lon** W 104.677

Pike's Peak Harley-Davidson at Ft. Carson, H-14
6110 Martinez St. **Ft. Carson**
(719) 576-0278
Lat N 38.740 **Lon** W 104.797

High Country Harley-Davidson, D-14
3761 Monarch St. **Frederick**
(303) 833-6777
Lat N 40.081 **Lon** W 104.982

Greeley Harley-Davidson, C-14
3010 W 29th St. **Greeley**
(970) 351-8150
Lat N 40.390 **Lon** W 104.727

Rocky Mountain Harley-Davidson, F-13
2885 W County Line Rd. **Littleton**
(303) 703-2885
Lat N 39.566 **Lon** W 105.021

Thunder Mountain Harley-Davidson, C-13
4250 Byrd Dr. **Loveland**
(970) 292-0400
Lat N 40.437 **Lon** W 104.996

Outpost Harley-Davidson, J-14
5001 N Elizabeth St. **Pueblo**
(719) 542-6032
Lat N 38.324 **Lon** W 104.616

Sun Harley-Davidson, E-13
8858 N Pearl St. **Thornton**
(303) 287-7567
Lat N 39.857 **Lon** W 104.979

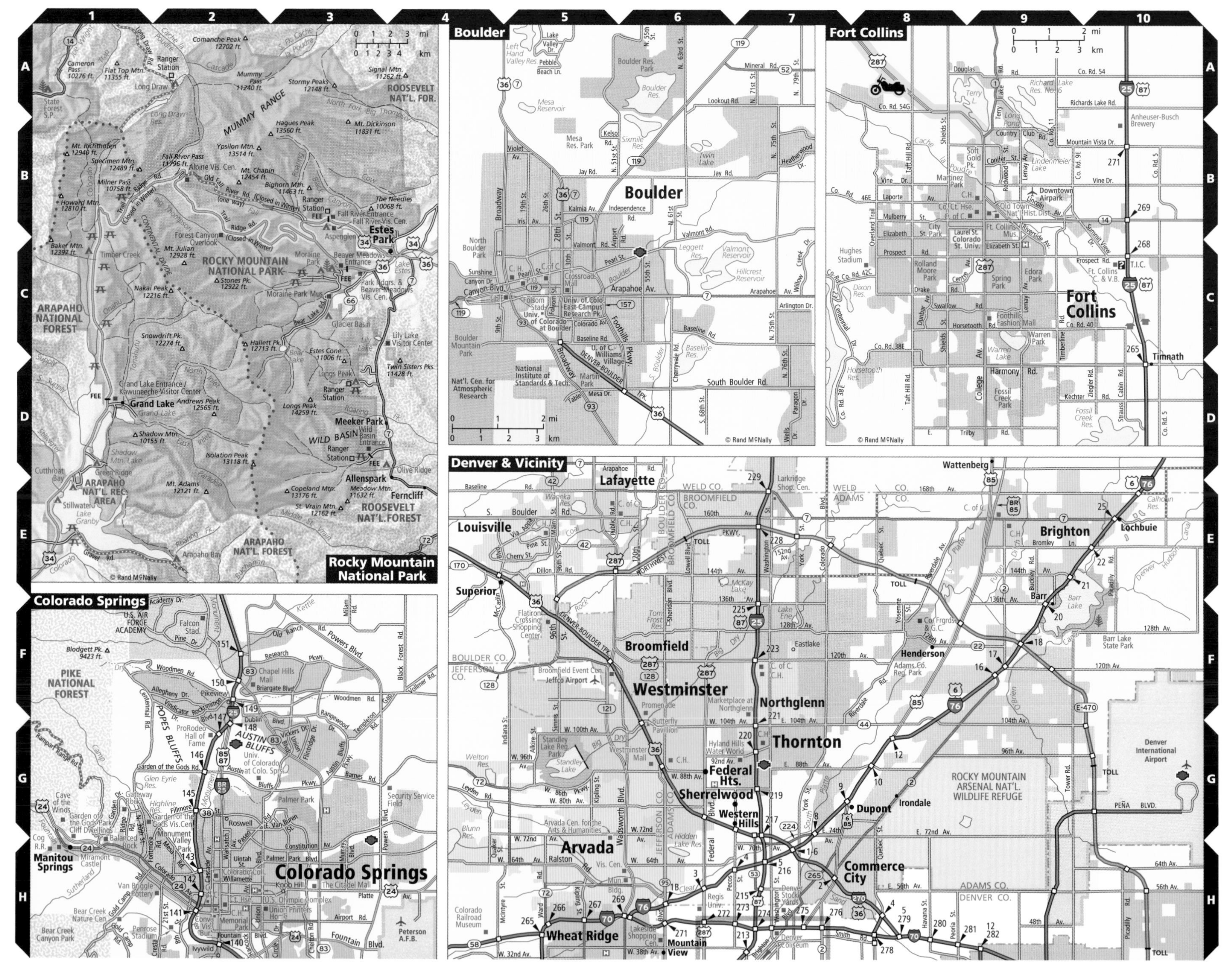
Rocky Mountain National Park
Boulder
Fort Collins
Denver & Vicinity
Colorado Springs

How to determine distance

Mileages in red between red arrowheads; in black, between intersections.

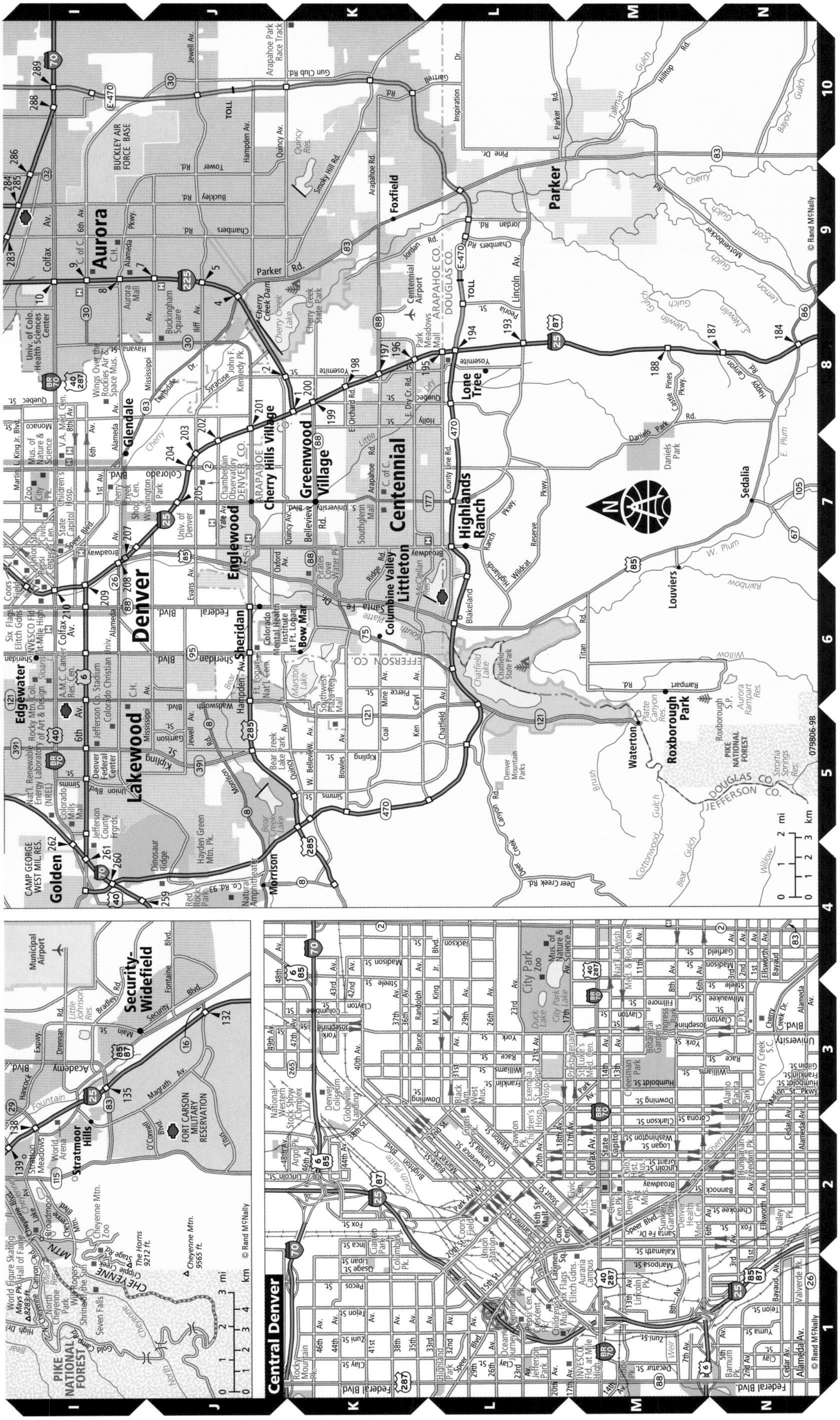

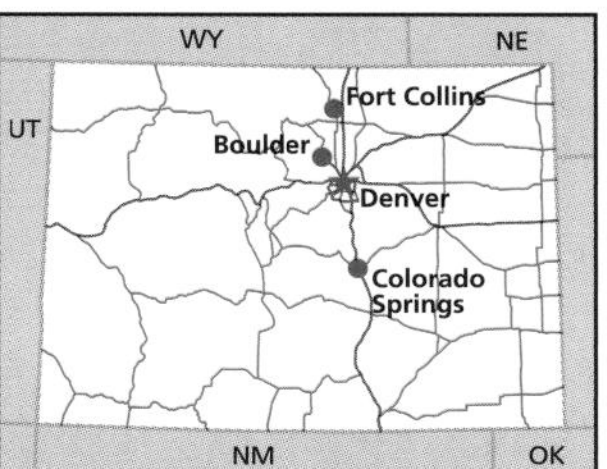
WY
NE
UT
Fort Collins
Boulder
Denver
Colorado Springs
NM
OK

SYMBOLS

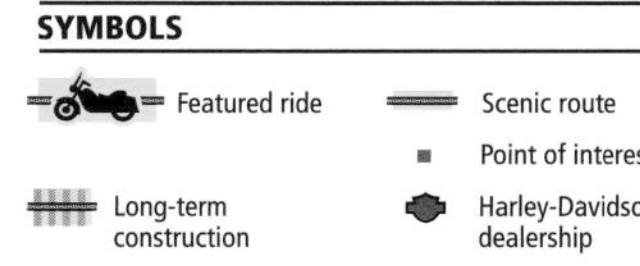
Featured ride
Scenic route
Point of interest
Long-term construction
Harley-Davidson dealership

COLORADO MOTORCYCLE LAWS

Helmet use:
Not required

Riding two abreast:
Yes. See state law for specifics

Eye protection:
Required by law

Speed limit:
Primary roads: 75 mph
Secondary roads: 65 mph

COLORADO RESOURCES

Road conditions or construction:
511
(877) 315-7623 (in CO)
(303) 639-1111
www.cotrip.org

Highway Emergency Numbers:
911
*277
(303) 329-4501

Tourism:
(800) 265-6723
www.colorado.com

State motor vehicle information:
(303) 205-5600
www.revenue.state.co.us/mv_dir/home.asp

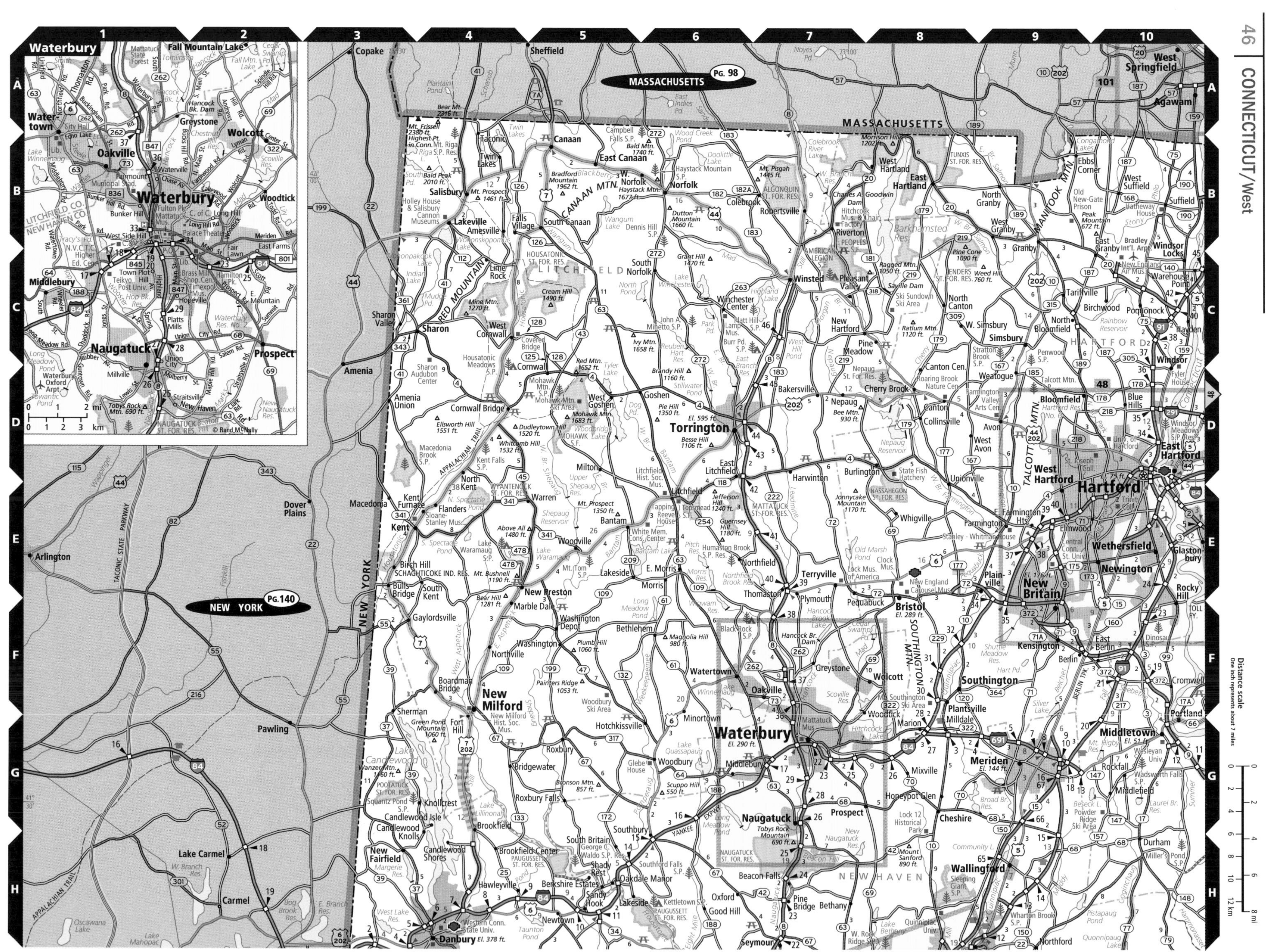

Distance scale
One inch represents about 7 miles
0 2 4 6 8 mi
0 2 4 6 8 10 12 km
MASSACHUSETTS
PG. 98
NEW YORK
PG. 140
Hartford
Waterbury
Torrington
New Britain
Meriden
Middletown
Bristol
Danbury
New Milford
Naugatuck
Waterbury
© Rand McNally

How to determine distance
2 10 18 4 4
12 16 20
Mileages in red between red arrowheads;
in black, between intersections.

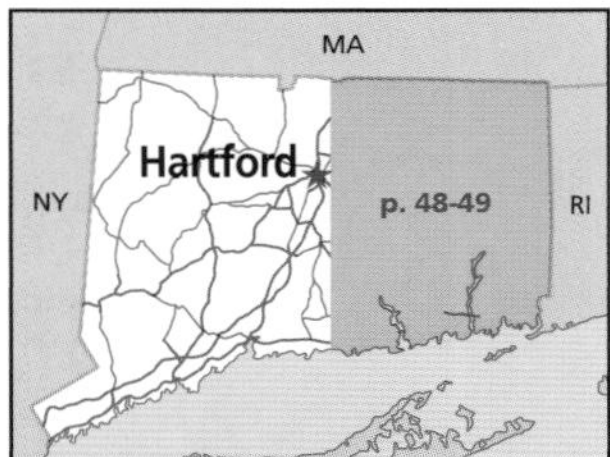
MA
NY
Hartford
p. 48-49
RI

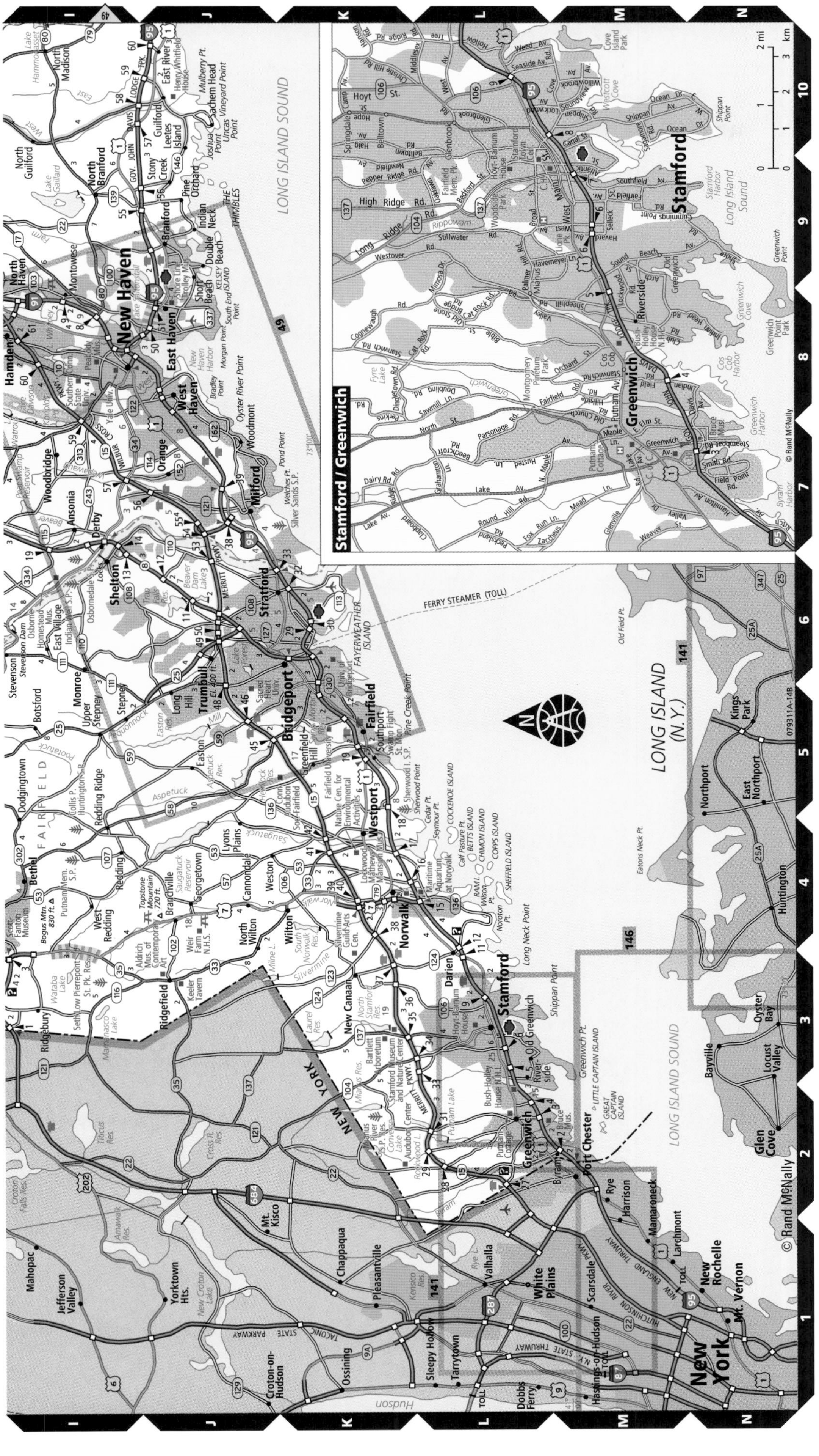

SYMBOLS

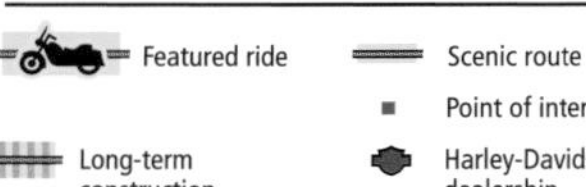
Featured ride
Scenic route
Point of interest
Long-term construction
Harley-Davidson dealership

CONNECTICUT MOTORCYCLE LAWS

Helmet use:
Required under age 18, and for instructional permit holders

Riding two abreast:
Yes. See state law for specifics

Eye protection:
Required unless equipped with windscreen

Speed limit:
Primary roads: 65 mph
Secondary roads: 55 mph

CONNECTICUT RESOURCES

Road conditions or construction:
(800) 443-6817 (in CT)
(860) 594-2650
www.ct.gov/dot

Highway Emergency Numbers:
911

Tourism:
(800) 282-6863
www.ctbound.org

State motor vehicle information:
(860) 263-5700
www.ct.gov/dmv

HARLEY-DAVIDSON DEALERSHIPS

Brothers' Harley-Davidson, J-9
557 W Main St. **Branford**
(203) 315-4759
Lat N 41.279 **Lon** W 72.845

Yankee Harley-Davidson, E-8
488 Farmington Ave. (Rte. 6) **Bristol**
(860) 583-8484
Lat N 41.690 **Lon** W 72.927

Harley-Davidson of Danbury, H-4
51 Federal Rd. **Danbury**
(203) 730-2453
Lat N 41.406 **Lon** W 73.430

Gengras Harley-Davidson, D-10
221 Governor St. **East Hartford**
(860) 528-7200
Lat N 41.771 **Lon** W 72.653

Fritz's Harley-Davidson of Stamford, L-3
575-579 Pacific St. **Stamford**
(203) 975-1985
Lat N 41.046 **Lon** W 73.537

Bridgeport Harley-Davidson, K-6
155 Research Dr. **Stratford**
(203) 380-2600
Lat N 41.173 **Lon** W 73.154

Distance scale
One inch represents about 7 miles
0 2 4 6 8 mi
0 2 4 6 8 10 12 km

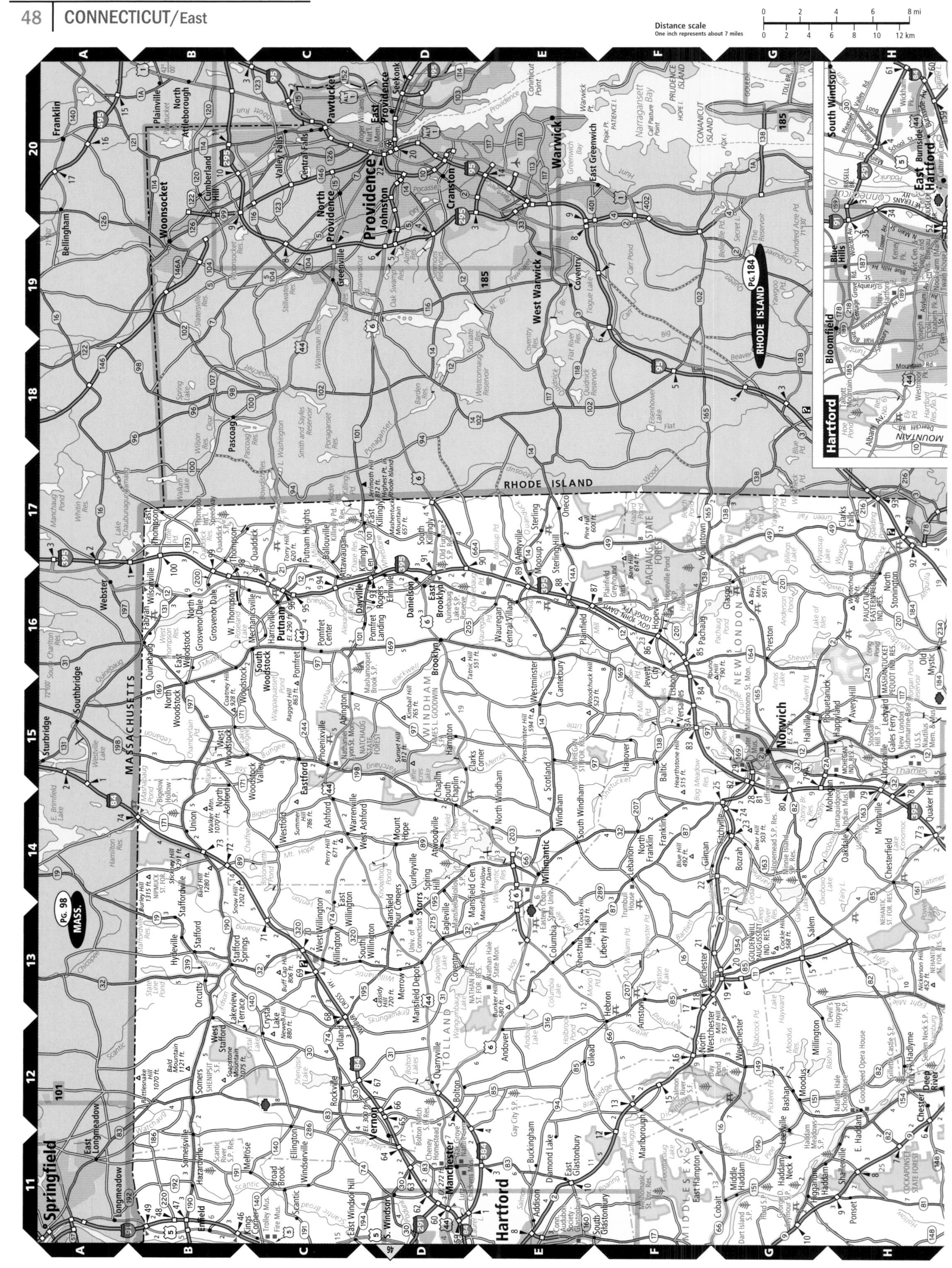

How to determine distance

Mileages in red between red arrowheads; in black, between intersections.

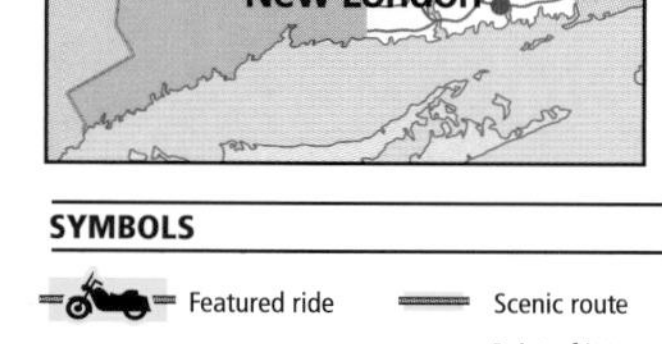
MA
NY
RI
p. 46-47
New London

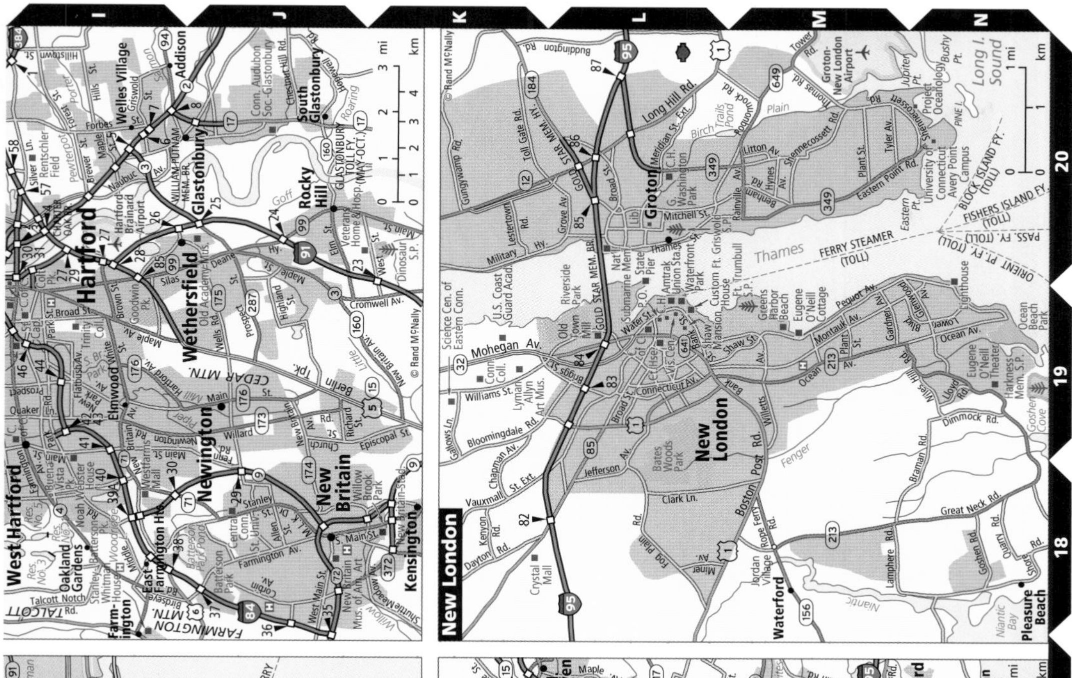
Hartford
West Hartford
Wethersfield
Glastonbury
Newington
New Britain
Kensington
Rocky Hill
© Rand McNally
New London
Groton
Waterford
Pleasure Beach

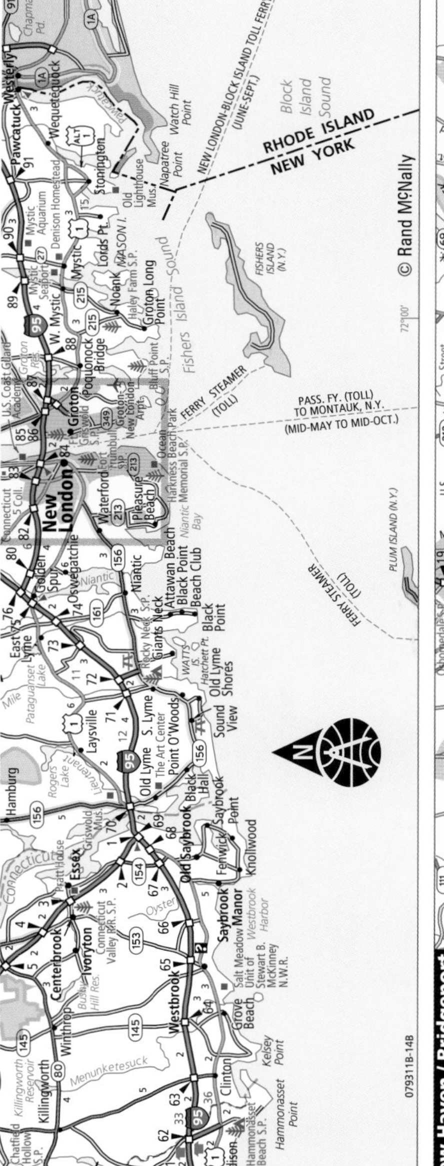
RHODE ISLAND
NEW YORK
© Rand McNally
New London
Groton
Old Saybrook
Clinton
Madison
Westbrook
Long Island Sound
079311B-14B

New Haven / Bridgeport
New Haven
East Haven
West Haven
Hamden
Milford
Stratford
Bridgeport
Fairfield
Trumbull
Shelton
Derby
Ansonia
Orange
Woodbridge
Long Island Sound
© Rand McNally

SYMBOLS

- Featured ride
- Scenic route
- Point of interest
- Long-term construction
- Harley-Davidson dealership

CITY-TO-CITY MILEAGE

	BRIDGEPORT	DANBURY	HARTFORD	NEW HAVEN	NEW LONDON	PUTNAM	TORRINGTON	WATERBURY
Bridgeport		29	57	19	69	112	51	31
Canaan	75	53	43	69	89	122	26	44
Clinton	41	57	40	22	30	73	67	47
Danbury	29		61	35	85	107	49	29
Hartford	57	61		40	46	46	36	32
Meriden	42	44	24	25	56	68	35	15
Middletown	45	54	17	28	44	70	45	25
New Haven	19	35	40		50	93	45	25
New London	69	85	46	50		49	89	69
New York, NY	54	61	111	73	123	166	105	85
Norwich	76	100	41	57	13	39	77	71
Providence, RI	125	146	87	106	56	33	123	117
Putnam	112	107	46	93	49		82	78
Springfield, MA	83	87	26	66	72	63	51	58
Stamford	22	31	79	41	91	134	73	53
Torrington	51	49	36	45	89	82		20
Waterbury	31	29	32	25	69	78	20	
Willimantic	83	91	30	66	28	31	66	62

HARLEY-DAVIDSON DEALERSHIPS

T.S.I. Columbia Harley-Davidson, E-13
8 Commerce Dr. **Columbia**
(860) 423-3116
Lat N 41.717 **Lon** W 72.247

T.S.I. Harley-Davidson Sales & Service, C-12
398 Somers Rd. (Rte. 83) **Ellington**
(860) 875-6663
Lat N 41.929 **Lon** W 72.456

Mike's Famous Harley-Davidson of Groton, I-15
1416 Gold Star Hwy. (Rte. 184) **Groton**
(860) 445-9745
Lat N 41.352 **Lon** W 72.051

Distance scale
One inch represents about 10 miles

0 2 4 6 mi
0 2 4 6 8 km

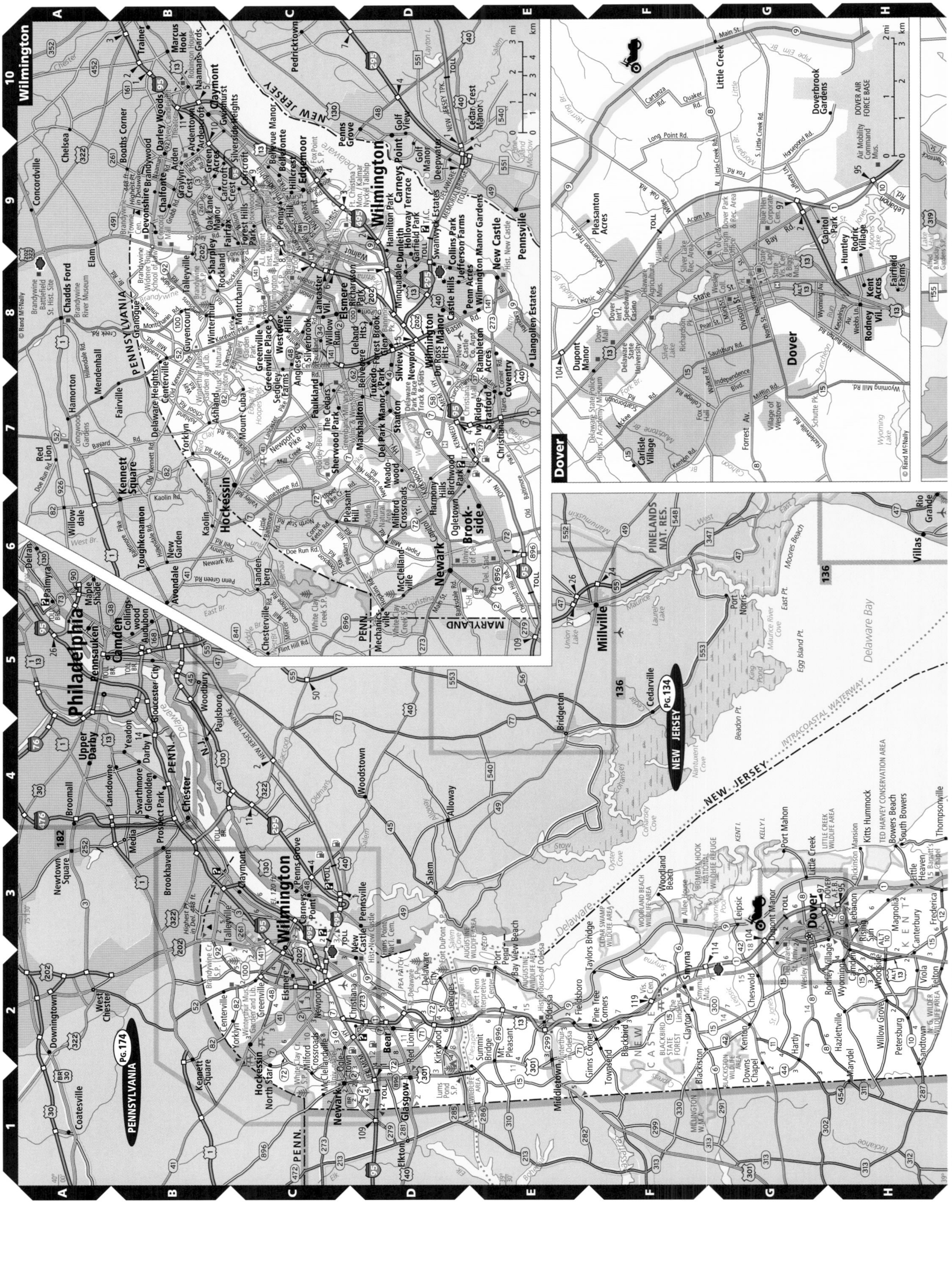

Wilmington

Dover

Philadelphia

Wilmington

Dover

PENNSYLVANIA

NEW JERSEY

MARYLAND

Delaware Bay

Pg. 174

Pg. 134

© Rand McNally

How to determine distance

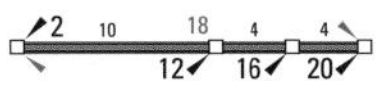

Mileages in red between red arrowheads; in black, between intersections.

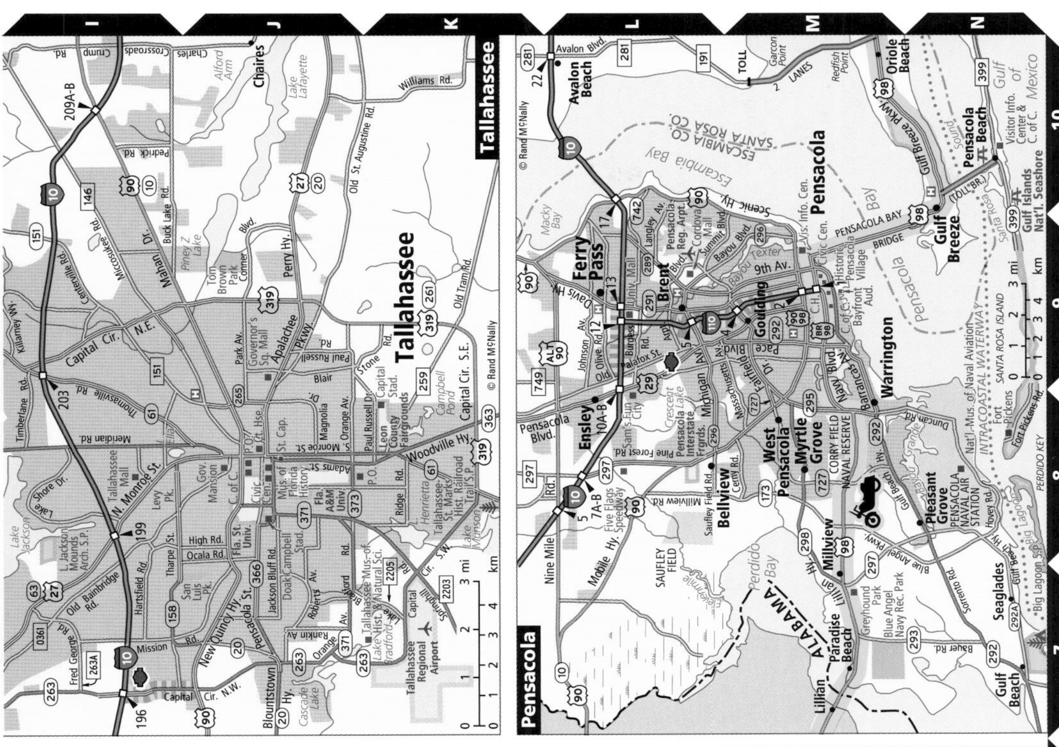
Tallahassee
Pensacola
© Rand McNally

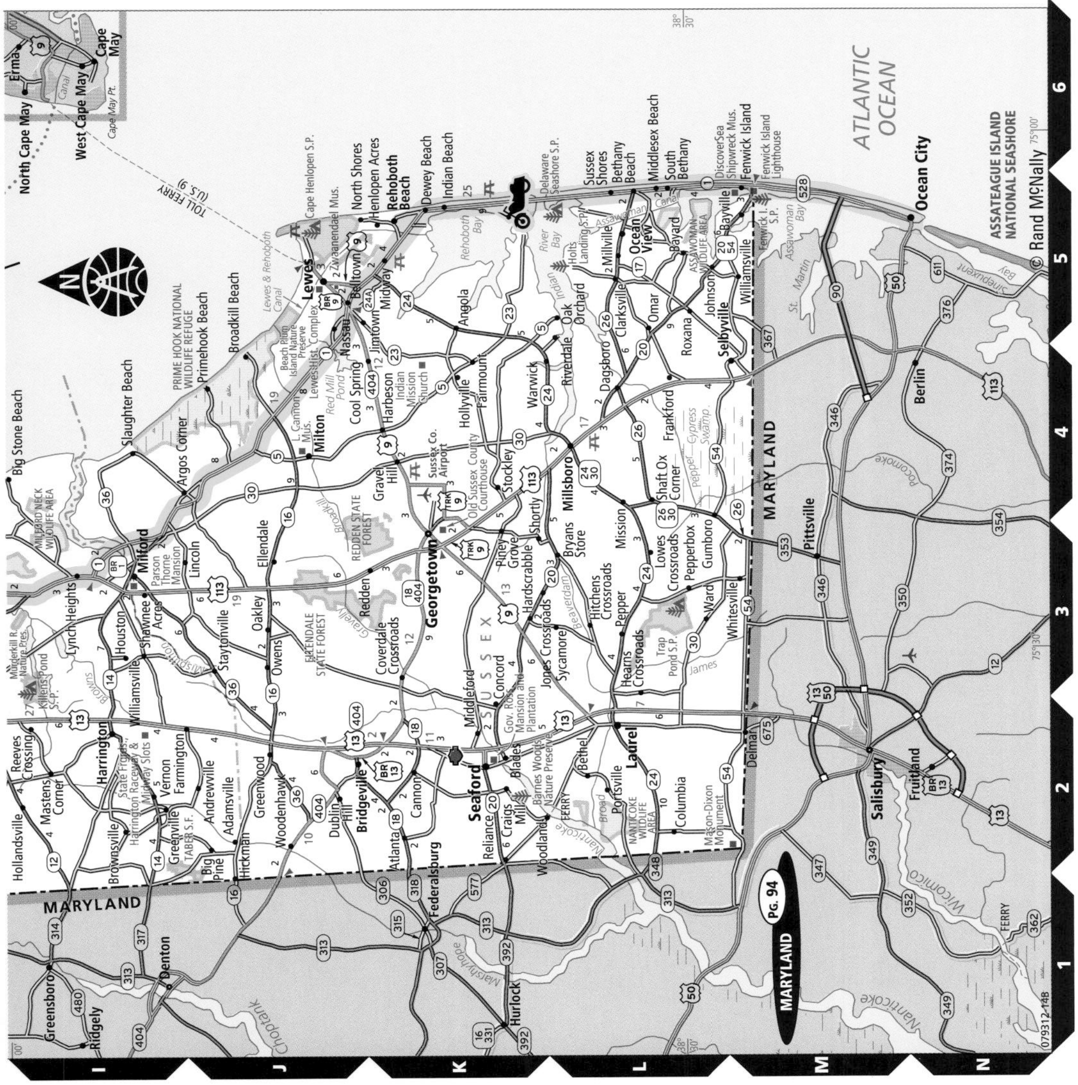

SYMBOLS

Featured ride

Scenic route

Point of interest

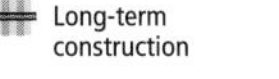
Long-term construction

Harley-Davidson dealership

For Maryland/Delaware ride, see page R18-19.

DELAWARE MOTORCYCLE LAWS

Helmet use:
Required under age 19, and required for instructional permit holders, and reflectorization required, and must have in possession

Riding two abreast:
No reference in administrative code or statutes

Eye protection:
Required by law

Speed limit:
Primary roads: 65 mph
Secondary roads: 55 mph

DELAWARE RESOURCES

Road conditions or construction:
www.deldot.net

Highway Emergency Numbers:
911

Tourism:
(866) 284-7483
(302) 739-4271
www.visitdelaware.com

State motor vehicle information:
(302) 434-3200
www.dmv.de.gov

CITY-TO-CITY MILEAGE

	Dover	Georgetown	Lewes	Milford	Newark	Salisbury, MD	Selbyville	Wilmington
Dover		35	38	19	46	56	55	47
Georgetown	35		14	16	83	27	21	84
Lewes	38	14		20	86	41	33	87
Milford	19	16	20		67	42	36	68
Newark	46	83	86	67		104	103	13
Salisbury, MD	56	27	41	42	104		24	105
Selbyville	55	21	33	36	103	24		104
Wilmington	47	84	87	68	13	105	104	

HARLEY-DAVIDSON DEALERSHIPS - DE

Mike's Famous Harley-Davidson, D-2
2160 New Castle Ave. **New Castle**
(302) 658-8800
Lat N 39.692 **Lon** W 75.555

Harley-Davidson of Seaford, Del., K-2
22586 Sussex Hwy. **Seaford**
(302) 629-6161
Lat N 38.671 **Lon** W 75.593

Mike's Famous Harley-Davidson Shop of Smyrna, F-2
450 Stadium St. **Smyrna**
(302) 659-6400
Lat N 39.249 **Lon** W 75.593

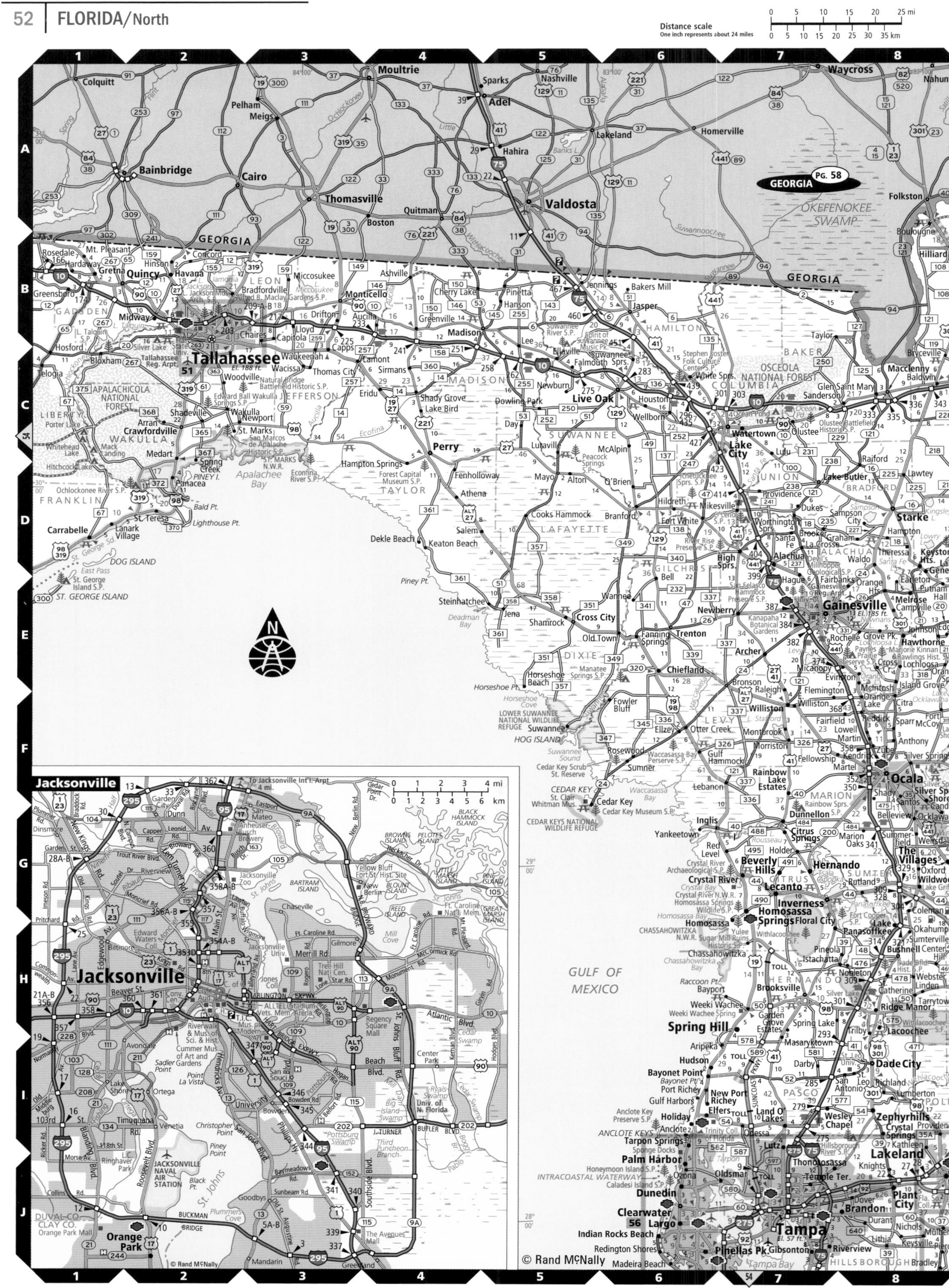
Distance scale
One inch represents about 24 miles
0 5 10 15 20 25 mi
0 5 10 15 20 25 30 35 km
GEORGIA PG. 58
GEORGIA
Moultrie
Valdosta
Thomasville
Bainbridge
Tallahassee
Live Oak
Lake City
Perry
Gainesville
Ocala
Spring Hill
Lakeland
Tampa
Clearwater
OKEFENOKEE SWAMP
Apalachee Bay
GULF OF MEXICO
Jacksonville
© Rand McNally

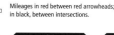

How to determine distance

Mileages in red between red arrowheads; in black, between intersections.

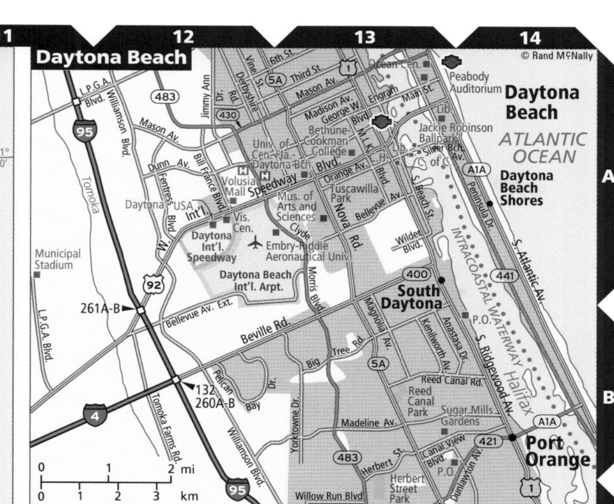
Daytona Beach
Daytona Beach
ATLANTIC OCEAN
Daytona Beach Shores
South Daytona
Port Orange
Daytona Int'l. Speedway
Daytona Beach Int'l. Arpt.
Embry-Riddle Aeronautical Univ.
Mus. of Arts and Sciences
Volusia Mall
Municipal Stadium
Peabody Auditorium
Jackie Robinson Ballpark
Tuscawilla Park
Reed Canal Park
Sugar Mills Gardens
Herbert Street Park
INTRACOASTAL WATERWAY
Halifax
© Rand McNally

Titusville
Titusville
La Grange
South Lake
Fox Lake
ST. JOHN'S N.W.R.
MERRITT ISLAND N.W.R.
CANAVERAL NATIONAL SEASHORE
Nat'l. Wildlife Refuge Headquarters
Shuttle Landing Facility
Shuttle Launch Viewing Area
Miracle City Mall
Indian
INTRACOASTAL WATERWAY
JOHN F. KENNEDY SPACE CENTER
NASA Pkwy.
NASA Visitor Center
U.S. Astronaut Hall of Fame
Space Coast Reg. Arpt.
Enchanted Forest Sanctuary
© Rand McNally

HARLEY-DAVIDSON DEALERSHIPS

For the Orlando area, please see dealer listings on page 55; for the Tampa/St. Petersburg/Lakeland area, see page 57.

Harley-Davidson Shop of Clermont, H-9
2480 S Hwy. 27 **Clermont**
(352) 243-7111
Lat N 28.534 **Lon** W 81.743

Bruce Rossmeyers Harley-Davidson Shop, F-11
290 N Beach St. **Daytona Beach**
(386) 253-2453
Lat N 29.217 **Lon** W 81.022

Daytona Harley-Davidson, F-11
250 N Atlantic Ave. Ste. 111 **Daytona Beach**
(386) 271-2400
Lat N 29.231 **Lon** W 81.010

Gainesville Harley-Davidson, E-7
4125 NW 97th Blvd. **Gainesville**
(352) 331-6363
Lat N 29.690 **Lon** W 82.451

Harley-Davidson of Crystal River, G-7
1785 SE Hwy. 19 **Homosassa**
(352) 563-9900
Lat N 28.800 **Lon** W 82.579

Adamec Harley-Davidson at Regency, C-9
10399 Atlantic Blvd. **Jacksonville**
(904) 641-3735
Lat N 30.348 **Lon** W 81.499

Adamec Harley-Davidson of Jacksonville, C-9
8909 Baymeadows Rd. **Jacksonville**
(904) 493-1931
Lat N 30.221 **Lon** W 81.574

Ridge Harley-Davidson Shop, J-9
1501 Longleaf Blvd. **Lake Wales**
(863) 734-0050
Lat N 27.876 **Lon** W 81.598

Gator Harley-Davidson, G-9
1745 E Main St. **Leesburg**
(352) 787-8050
Lat N 28.817 **Lon** W 81.847

Pineda Harley-Davidson Shop, I-12
6030 N US Hwy. 1 **Melbourne**
(321) 259-1311
Lat N 28.209 **Lon** W 80.664

Gulf Coast Harley-Davidson, I-6
5817 State Rd. 54 **New Port Richey**
(727) 842-4547
Lat N 28.217 **Lon** W 82.718

Bruce Rossmeyers Harley-Davidson, G-11
1899 State Rd. 44 **New Smyrna Beach**
(386) 409-3034
Lat N 29.014 **Lon** W 80.945

Harley-Davidson of Ocala, F-8
5331 N Hwy. 44 **Ocala**
(352) 732-2488
Lat N 29.226 **Lon** W 82.156

Adamec Harley-Davidson of Orange Park, C-9
1520 Wells Rd. **Orange Park**
(904) 215-1931
Lat N 30.190 **Lon** W 81.712

Bruce Rossmeyers Harley-Davidson, F-11
1637 N US Hwy. 1 **Ormond Beach**
(386) 671-7100
Lat N 29.288 **Lon** W 81.105

Space Coast Harley-Davidson, J-12
1440 Executive Circle NE **Palm Bay**
(321) 259-1311
Lat N 28.033 **Lon** W 80.652

Harley-Davidson of St. Augustine, D-10
2575 State Rte. 16 **St. Augustine**
(904) 829-8782
Lat N 29.920 **Lon** W 81.416

Capital City Harley-Davidson, B-2
1745 Capital Circle NW **Tallahassee**
(850) 205-4294
Lat N 30.477 **Lon** W 84.363

079314A-14B

Distance scale
One inch represents about 24 miles

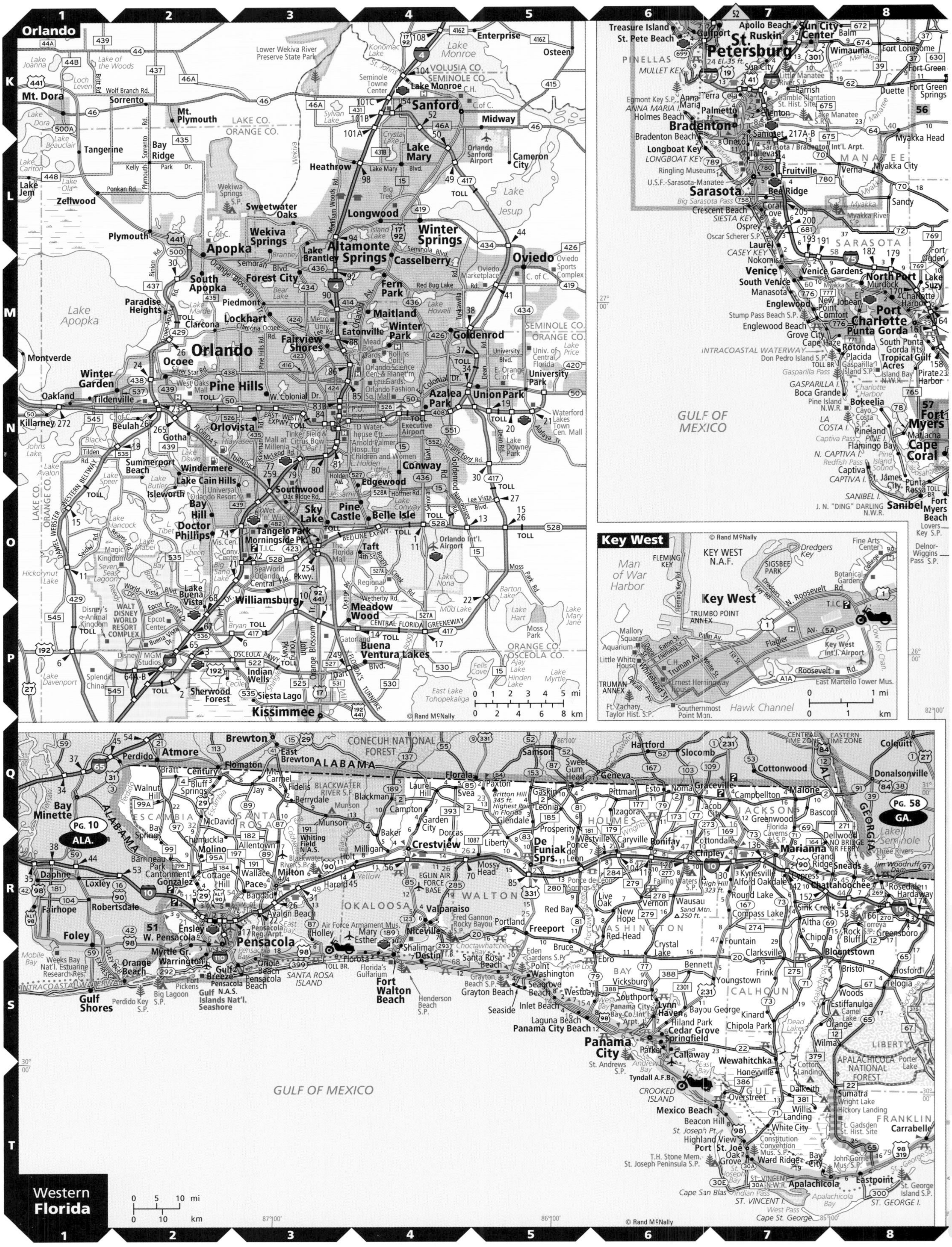

Orlando

Key West

Western Florida

GULF OF MEXICO

© Rand McNally

How to determine distance

Mileages in red between red arrowheads; in black, between intersections.

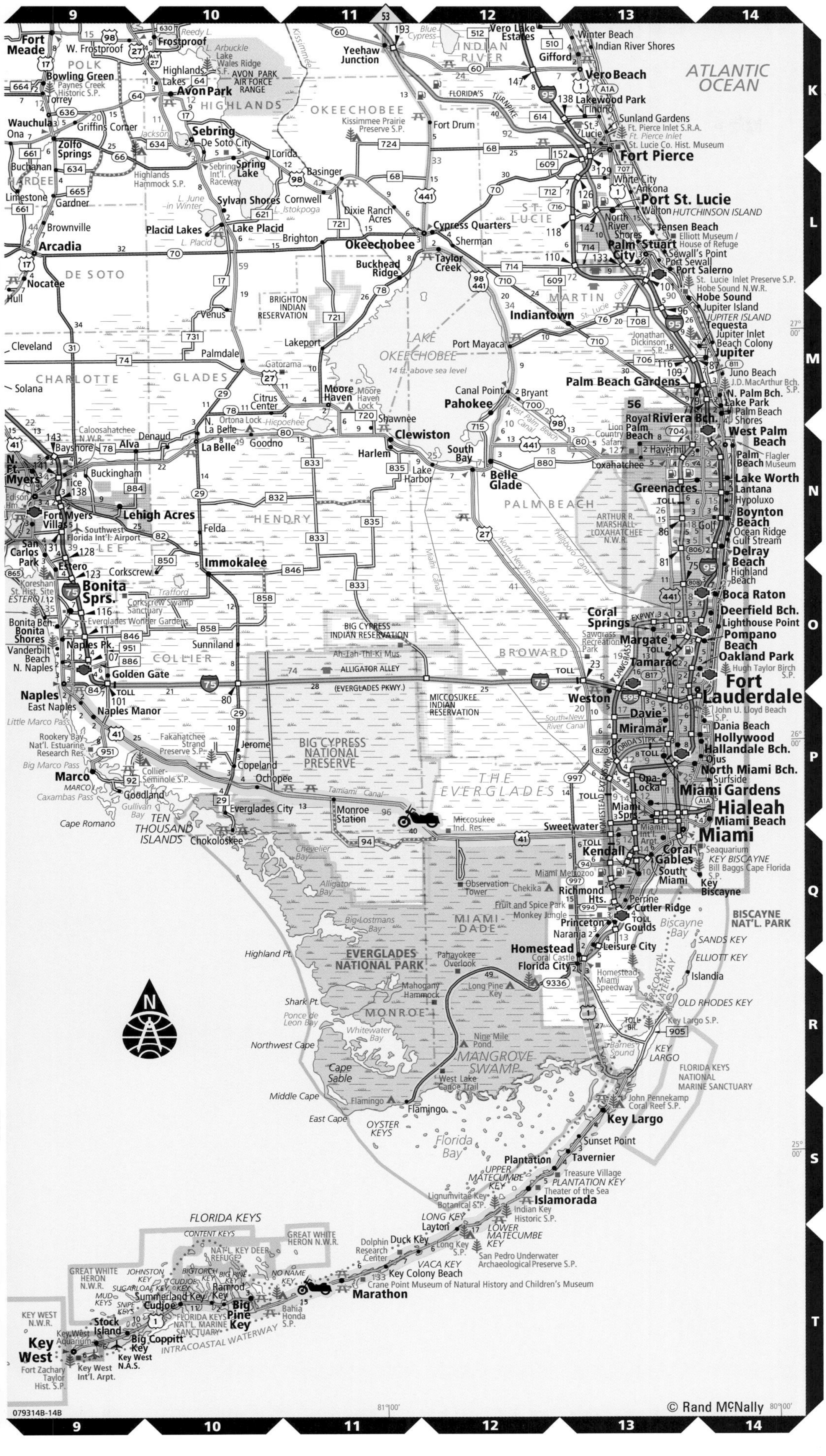

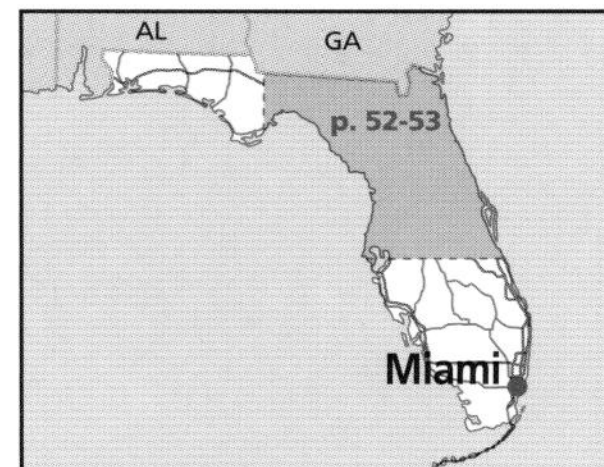
AL
GA
p. 52-53
Miami

For Alabama/Florida ride, see page R6-7.
For Florida ride, see page R12.

FLORIDA MOTORCYCLE LAWS

Helmet use:
Not required over 21 with a minimum of $10,000 medical insurance

Riding two abreast:
Yes. See state law for specifics

Eye protection: Required by law

Speed limit:
Primary roads: 70 mph; Secondary roads: 65 mph

FLORIDA RESOURCES

Road conditions or construction: 511
www.fl511.com; www.511tampabay.com

Highway Emergency Numbers: *FHP

State motor vehicle information:
(850) 922-9000; www.hsmv.state.fl.us

HARLEY-DAVIDSON DEALERSHIPS

For the Miami, Tampa/St. Petersburg, and Ft. Myers areas, please see dealer listings on page 57.

Harley-Davidson of Ft. Walton Beach, S-4
788 N Beal Pkway. **Ft. Walton Beach**
(850) 862-4706
Lat N 30.446 **Lon** W 86.639

Orlando Harley-Davidson South Shop, P-3
5881 W Irlo Bronson Hwy. **Kissimmee**
(407) 944-3700
Lat N 28.333 **Lon** W 81.520

Orlando Harley-Davidson, P-2
1590 E Buena Vista Dr. Bldg One **Lake Buena Vista**
(407) 938-0522
Lat N 28.371 **Lon** W 81.513

Peterson's Harley-Davidson South, Q-13
19825 S Dixie Hwy. **Miami**
(305) 235-4023
Lat N 25.584 **Lon** W 80.365

Harley-Davidson of Naples, O-9
3645 Gateway Ln. **Naples**
(239) 594-5504
Lat N 26.212 **Lon** W 81.745

Orlando Harley-Davidson, M-3
3770 37th St. **Orlando**
(407) 423-0346
Lat N 28.505 **Lon** W 81.425

Orlando Harley-Davidson East, M-3
11898 Lake Underhill Rd. **Orlando**
(407) 447-7400
Lat N 28.547 **Lon** W 81.212

Orlando Harley Gear Store, M-3
8000 International Dr. at Sand Lake Rd. **Orlando**
(407) 351-3302
Lat N 28.461 **Lon** W 81.477

Orlando Harley-Davidson Airport Stores, M-3
9331-9347 Airport Blvd. **Orlando**
(407) 825-3470
Lat N 28.429 **Lon** W 81.302

Harley-Davidson of Pensacola, R-2
6385 Pensacola Blvd. (Hwy. 29) **Pensacola**
(850) 494-1224
Lat N 30.481 **Lon** W 87.255

Harley-Davidson of Port Charlotte, M-8
2224 El Jobean Rd. **Port Charlotte**
(941) 883-8000
Lat N 27.001 **Lon** W 82.181

Seminole Harley-Davidson, K-4
620 Hickman Circle **Sanford**
(407) 831-7888
Lat N 28.816 **Lon** W 80.213

Treasure Coast Harley-Davidson of Stuart, L-13
4967 SE Federal Hwy. **Stuart**
(772) 287-3871
Lat N 27.143 **Lon** W 80.213

079314B-14B

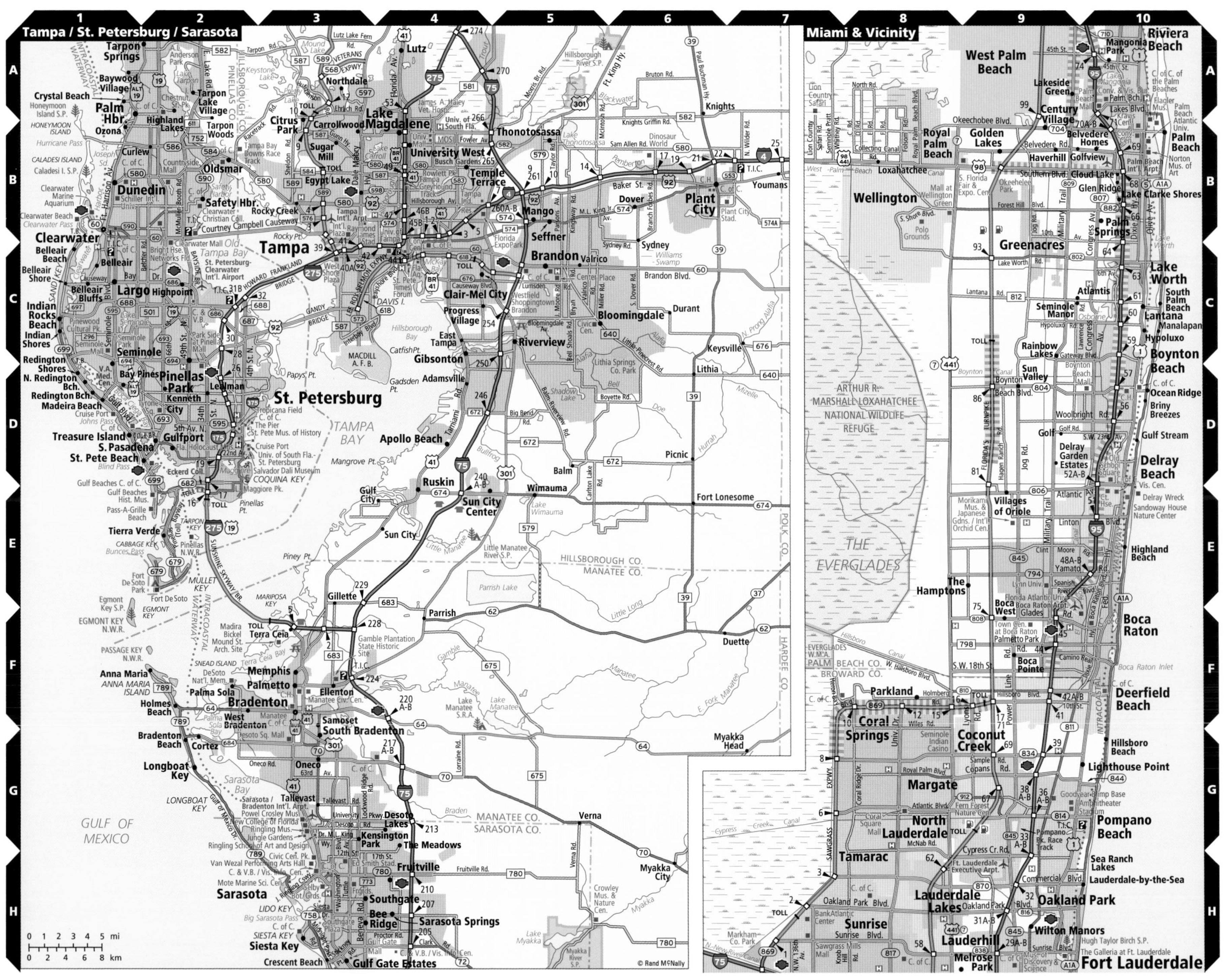
Tampa / St. Petersburg / Sarasota
Miami & Vicinity
Tampa
St. Petersburg
Clearwater
Sarasota
Bradenton
West Palm Beach
Boca Raton
Fort Lauderdale
GULF OF MEXICO
TAMPA BAY
THE EVERGLADES
ARTHUR R. MARSHALL LOXAHATCHEE NATIONAL WILDLIFE REFUGE
© Rand McNally

How to determine distance

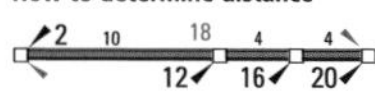
2
10
18
4
4
12
16
20

Mileages in red between red arrowheads; in black, between intersections.

ATLANTIC OCEAN
Hollywood
Hallandale Beach
N. Miami Beach
Sunny Isles Beach
Bal Harbour
Bay Harbor Islands
Miami Beach
Miami
Key Biscayne
Coral Gables
S. Miami
Kendall
Hialeah
Miami Gardens
Pembroke Pines
Miramar
Plantation
Davie
Weston
Southwest Ranches
Cooper City
Westchester
Sweetwater
© Rand McNally

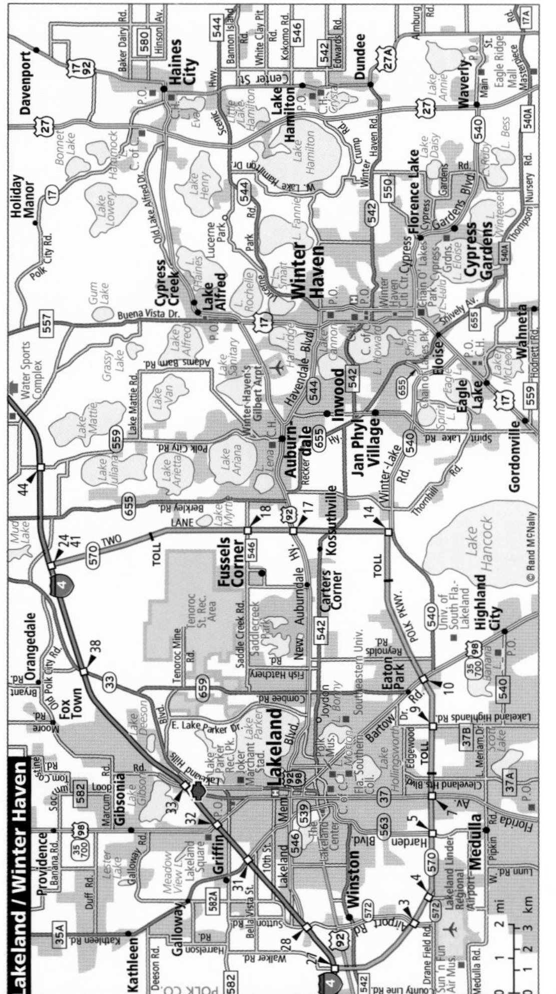
Lakeland / Winter Haven
Lakeland
Winter Haven
Haines City
Davenport
Lake Hamilton
Dundee
Lake Alfred
Auburndale
Polk City
Bartow
Eagle Lake
Fort Meade
© Rand McNally

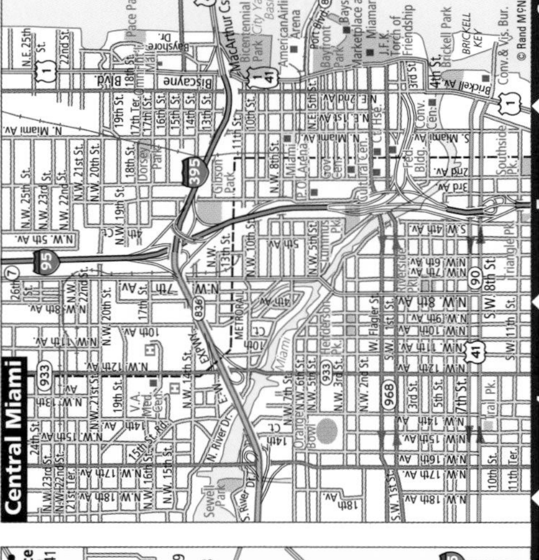
Central Miami
© Rand McNally

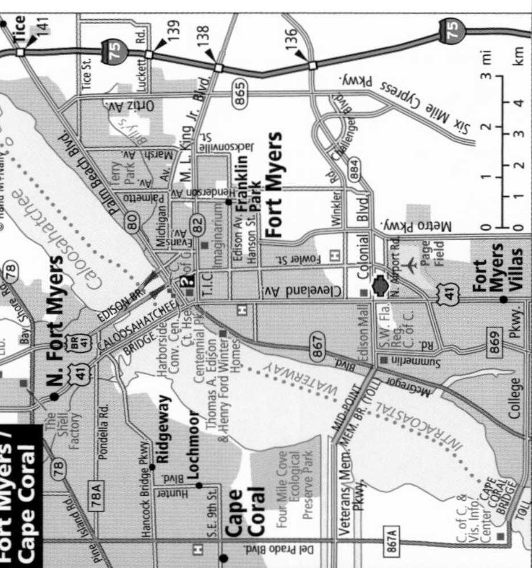
Fort Myers / Cape Coral
Fort Myers
N. Fort Myers
Cape Coral
Fort Myers Villas
Caloosahatchee
© Rand McNally

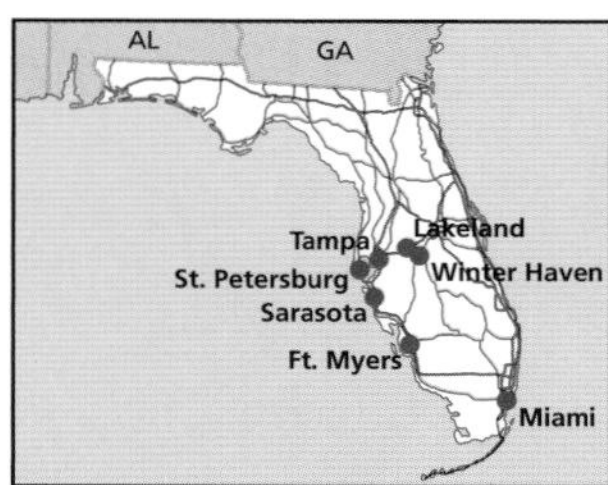
AL
GA
Tampa
Lakeland
St. Petersburg
Winter Haven
Sarasota
Ft. Myers
Miami

SYMBOLS

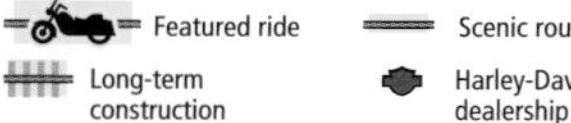
Featured ride
Scenic route
Long-term construction
Harley-Davidson dealership

HARLEY-DAVIDSON DEALERSHIPS

Bruce Rossmeyers Harley-Davidson, F-9
5100 Town Center Circle Ste. 223 **Boca Raton**
Lat N 26.362 **Lon** W 80.122

Manatee River Harley-Davidson, F-3
624 67th St. Circle East **Bradenton**
(941) 745-2429
Lat N 27.494 **Lon** W 82.475

Fletcher's Harley-Davidson Sales, B-1
17129 US Hwy. 19 N **Clearwater**
(727) 535-1844
Lat N 27.928 **Lon** W 82.730

Fletcher's Clearwater Beach Harley-Davidson, B-1
389 Mandalay Ave. **Clearwater Beach**
(727) 446-1844
Lat N 27.979 **Lon** W 82.827

Bruce Rossmeyers Harley-Davidson, H-9
2871 N Federal Hwy. **Ft. Lauderdale**
(954) 491-0300
Lat N 26.164 **Lon** W 80.116

Harley-Davidson of Ft. Myers, M-2
2160 Colonial Blvd. **Ft. Meyers**
(239) 275-4647
Lat N 26.597 **Lon** W 81.868

Harley-Davidson of Lakeland, J-2
4202 Lakeland Hills Blvd. **Lakeland**
(863) 802-1971
Lat N 28.095 **Lon** W 81.952

Peterson's Harley-Davidson of Miami, J-8
19400 NW 2nd Ave. **Miami**
(305) 651-4811
Lat N 25.952 **Lon** W 80.206

Bruce Rossmeyers Harley-Davidson Shop, G-9
2900 Center Point Circle **Pompano Beach**
(954) 545-3200
Lat N 26.265 **Lon** W 80.132

Jim's On the Beach, D-2
6600 Gulf Blvd. **St. Pete Beach**
(727) 363-1333
Lat N 27.737 **Lon** W 82.748

Jim's Harley-Davidson of St. Petersburg, D-3
2805 54th Ave. N **St. Petersburg**
(727) 527-9672
Lat N 27.821 **Lon** W 82.671

Rossiter's Harley-Davidson, H-3
330 Cattlemen Rd. **Sarasota**
(941) 951-6103
Lat N 27.334 **Lon** W 82.449

Sunrise Harley-Davidson, H-7
201 N International Pkwy. **Sunrise**
(954) 414-4135
Lat N 26.123 **Lon** W 80.341

Harley-Davidson of Tampa, C-3
6920 N Dale Mabry Hwy. **Tampa**
(813) 886-7433
Lat N 28.011 **Lon** W 82.505

Brandon Harley-Davidson Shop, C-3
9841 E Adamo Dr. **Tampa**
(813) 740-9898
Lat N 27.948 **Lon** W 82.344

Harley-Davidson of Palm Beach, A-9
2955 45th St. **West Palm Beach**
(561) 659-4131
Lat N 26.759 **Lon** W 80.098

Distance scale
One inch represents about 23 miles
0 5 10 15 20 25 mi
0 5 10 15 20 25 30 35 40 km

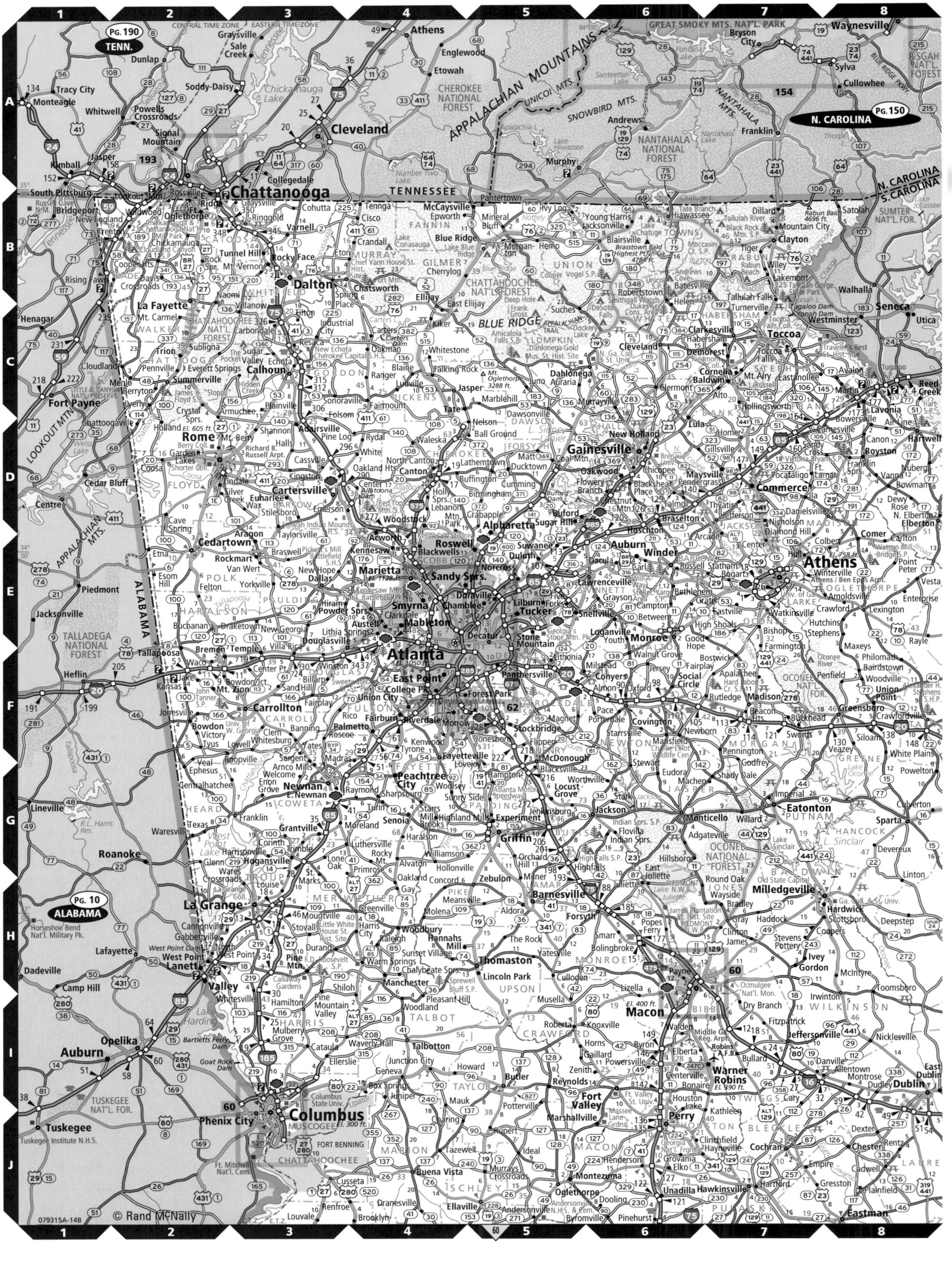

TENN. PG. 190
N. CAROLINA PG. 150
ALABAMA PG. 10

CENTRAL TIME ZONE
EASTERN TIME ZONE
GREAT SMOKY MTS. NAT'L. PARK
APPALACHIAN MOUNTAINS
UNICOI MTS.
SNOWBIRD MTS.
NANTAHALA MTS.
CHEROKEE NATIONAL FOREST
NANTAHALA NATIONAL FOREST
PISGAH NAT'L. FOREST
SUMTER NAT'L. FOR.
CHATTAHOOCHEE NAT'L FOREST
BLUE RIDGE
LOOKOUT MTN.
APPALACHIAN MTS.
TALLADEGA NATIONAL FOREST
OCONEE NATIONAL FOREST
TUSKEGEE NAT'L. FOR.
TENNESSEE
N. CAROLINA
S. CAROLINA
ALABAMA

Chattanooga
Cleveland
Athens
Dalton
Rome
Cartersville
Gainesville
Marietta
Roswell
Alpharetta
Sandy Sprs.
Atlanta
East Point
Decatur
Athens
Carrollton
Newnan
Peachtree City
Griffin
La Grange
Columbus
Phenix City
Macon
Warner Robins
Milledgeville
Dublin
Auburn
Opelika
Tuskegee
Toccoa
Seneca
Franklin
Murphy

079315A-14B

How to determine distance

Mileages in red between red arrowheads; in black, between intersections.

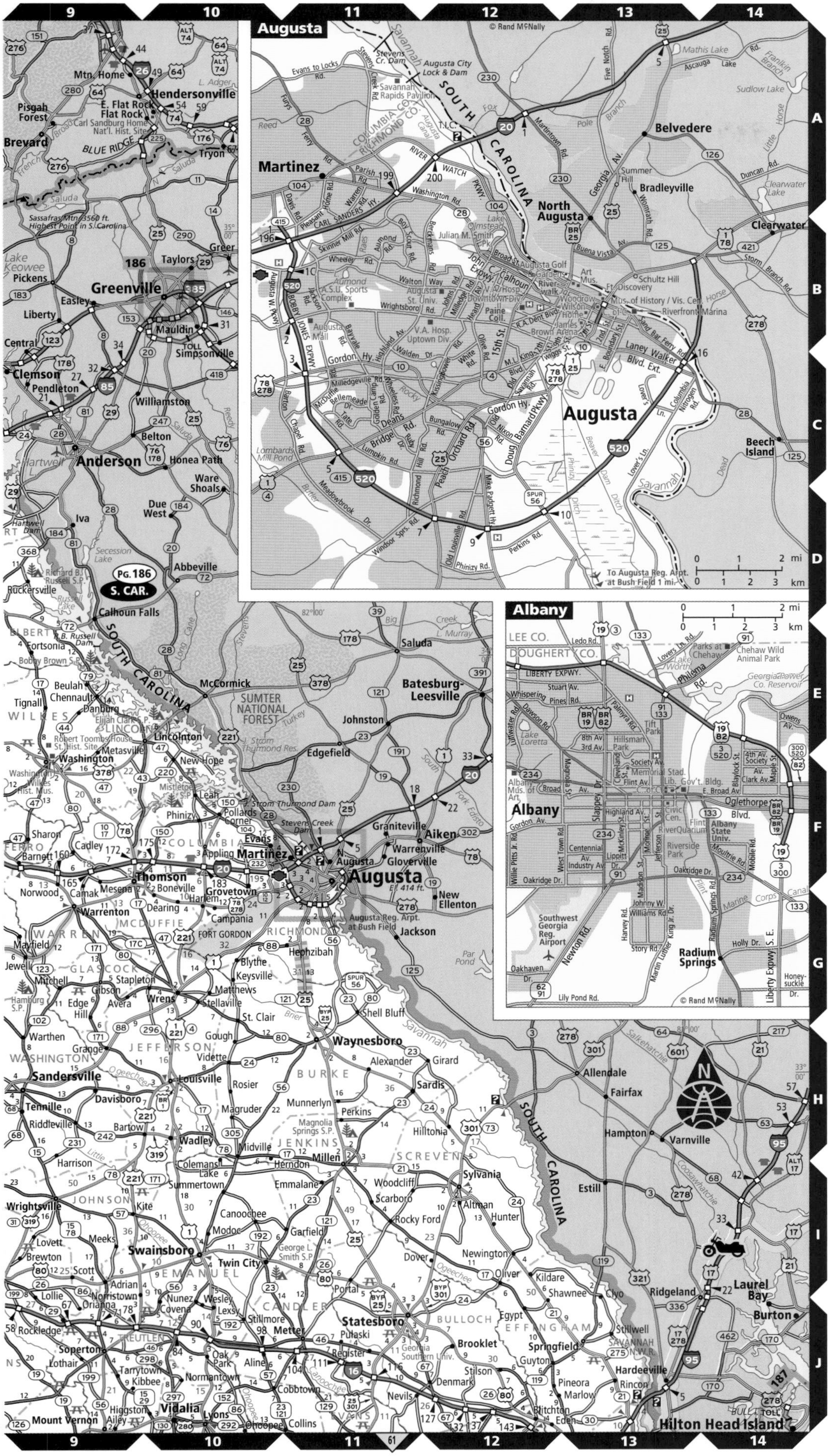

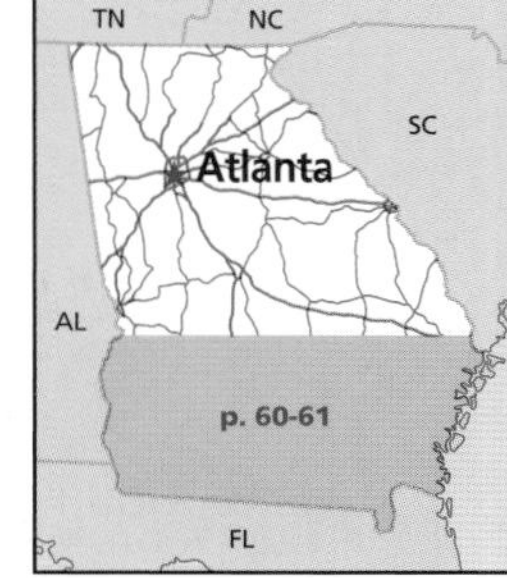
TN
NC
SC
Atlanta
AL
FL
p. 60-61

SYMBOLS

- Featured ride
- Scenic route
- Point of interest
- Long-term construction
- Harley-Davidson dealership

For Georgia/South Carolina ride, see page R13.

HARLEY-DAVIDSON DEALERSHIPS

Augusta Harley-Davidson, F-11
4200 Belair Frontage Rd. **Augusta**
(706) 651-0444
Lat N 33.484 **Lon** W 82.108

Harley-Davidson of Athens, E-7
4225 Atlanta Hwy. **Bogart**
(706) 549-6890
Lat N 33.941 **Lon** W 83.481

Frazier's Harley-Davidson, D-6
4699 Friendship Rd. **Buford**
(770) 945-6011
Lat N 34.140 **Lon** W 83.949

Harley-Davidson of Cartersville, D-3
2281 Hwy. 411 NE **Cartersville**
(678) 721-0203
Lat N 34.238 **Lon** W 84.778

Chattahoochee Harley-Davidson, I-3
7373 Fortson Rd. **Columbus**
(706) 324-4294
Lat N 32.554 **Lon** W 84.948

Granite Mountain Harley-Davidson, F-5
900 Dogwood Dr. SE **Conyers**
(770) 785-3999
Lat N 33.658 **Lon** W 84.018

Mountain Creek Harley-Davidson Shop, B-3
1001 Market St. Ste. 37 **Dalton**
(706) 370-7433
Lat N 34.759 **Lon** W 85.000

Stone Mountain Harley-Davidson, E-5
2060 Ross Rd. **Lilburn**
(770) 979-7999
Lat N 33.835 **Lon** W 84.080

Harley-Davidson of Atlanta, E-4
501 Thornton Rd. **Lithia Springs**
(770) 944-1340
Lat N 33.791 **Lon** W 84.628

Harley-Davidson of Macon, H-6
5000 Mercer University Dr. **Macon**
(478) 474-3344
Lat N 32.831 **Lon** W 83.725

Earl Small's Harley-Davidson, E-4
993 S Cobb Dr. **Marietta**
(770) 919-0000
Lat N 33.929 **Lon** W 84.551

Harley-Davidson of Clayton County, F-5
1384 Southlake Pkwy. **Morrow**
(770) 960-6000
Lat N 33.575 **Lon** W 84.345

Great South Harley-Davidson, G-3
168 Hwy. 16 **Newnan**
OPENING IN 2007
Lat N 33.330 **Lon** W 84.776

Killer Creek Harley-Davidson, E-5
11480 Alpharetta Hwy. **Roswell**
(770) 777-1000
Lat N 34.060 **Lon** W 84.325

Distance scale
One inch represents about 23 miles
0 5 10 15 20 25 mi
0 5 10 15 20 25 30 35 40 km

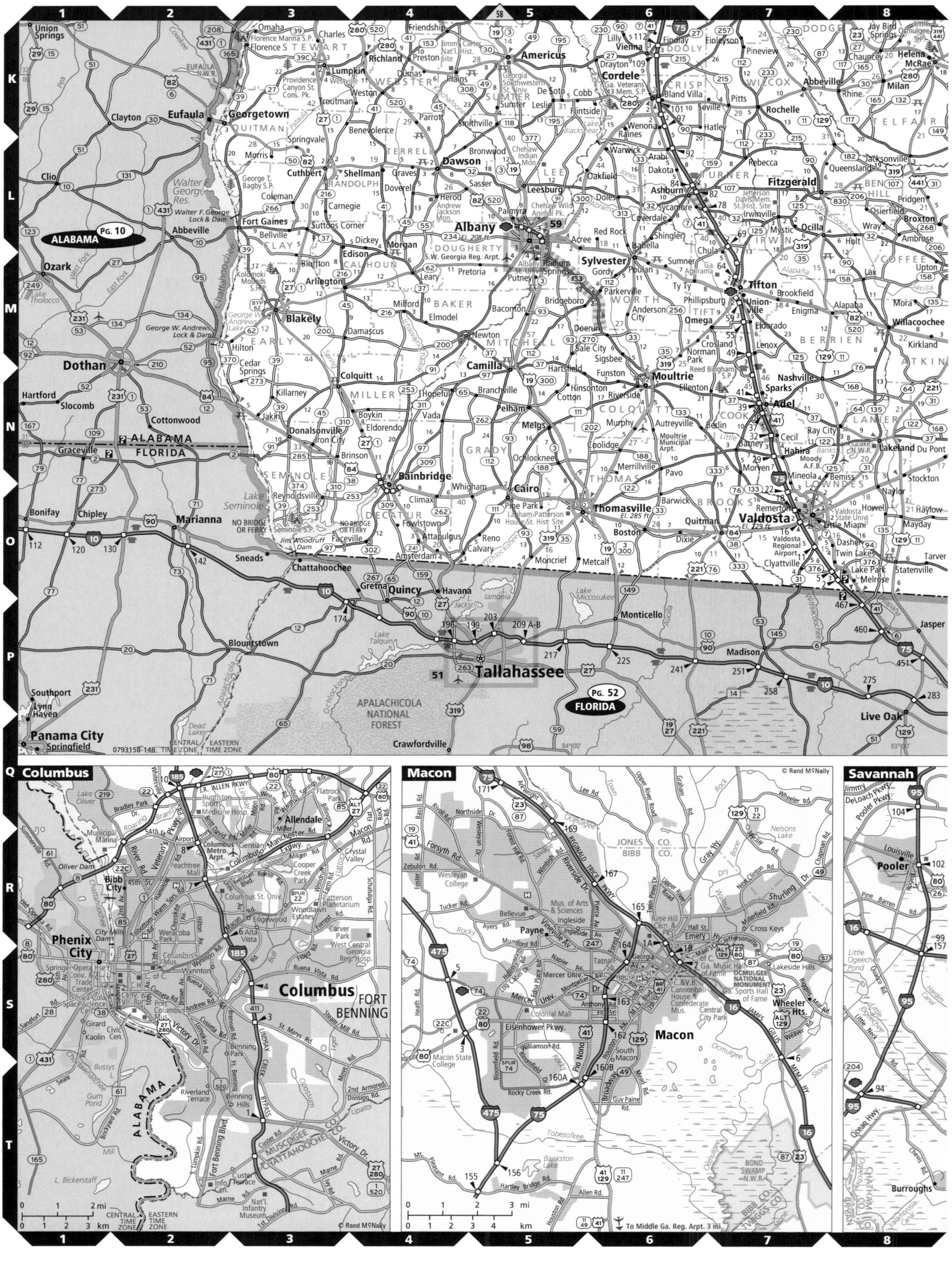

ALABAMA PG. 10

FLORIDA PG. 52

Albany, Americus, Cordele, Tifton, Valdosta, Thomasville, Moultrie, Bainbridge, Dothan, Tallahassee, Panama City, Marianna, Eufaula, Fitzgerald, Douglas

APALACHICOLA NATIONAL FOREST

CENTRAL TIME ZONE / EASTERN TIME ZONE

079315B-14B

Columbus

Phenix City
Columbus
FORT BENNING

© Rand McNally

0 1 2 mi
0 1 2 3 km

Macon

Macon

© Rand McNally

0 1 2 3 mi
0 1 2 3 4 km

To Middle Ga. Reg. Arpt. 3 mi.

Savannah

Pooler
Burroughs

How to determine distance

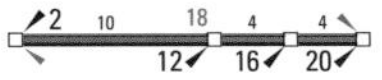

Mileages in red between red arrowheads; in black, between intersections.

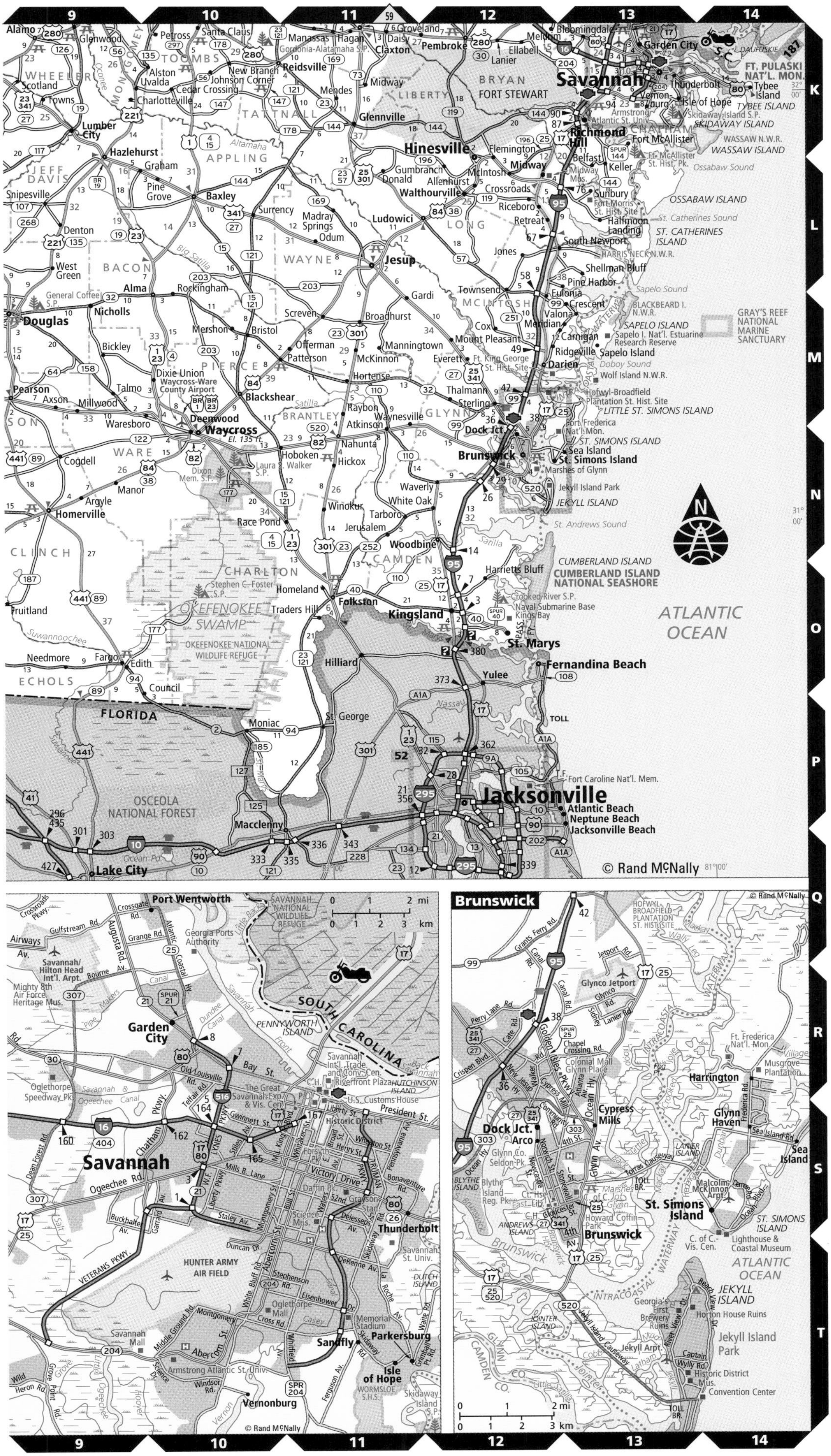

ATLANTIC OCEAN

© Rand McNally

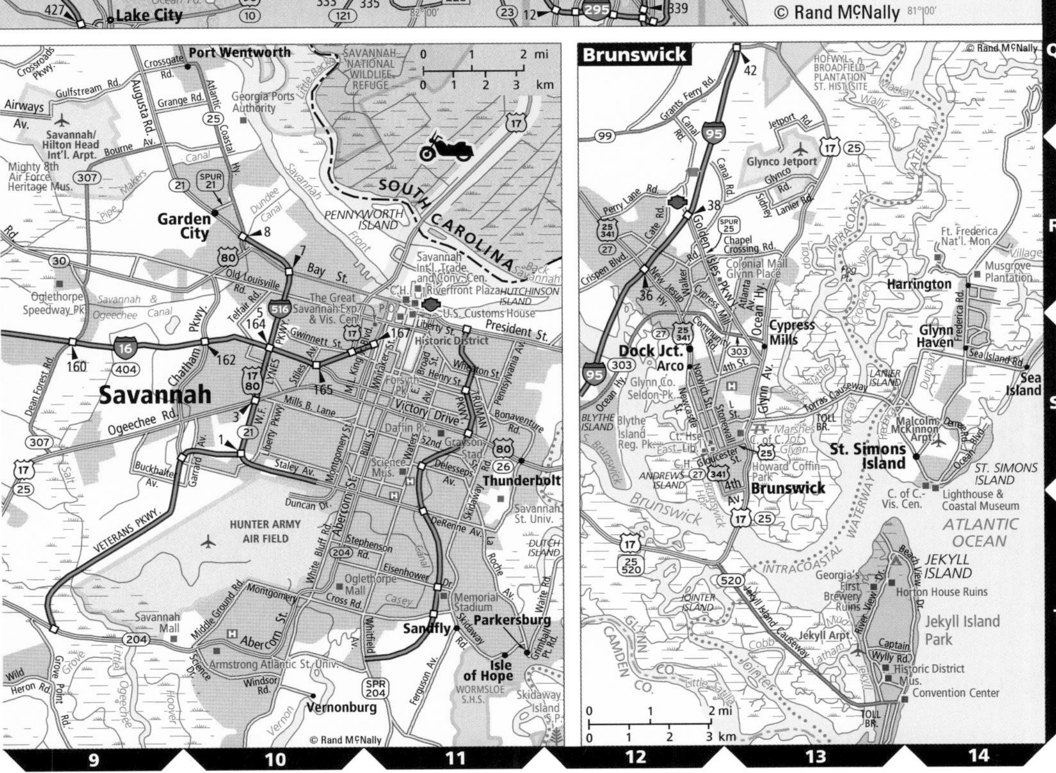
Savannah
Port Wentworth
Garden City
Thunderbolt
Isle of Hope
Parkersburg
Sandfly
Vernonburg
HUNTER ARMY AIR FIELD
SOUTH CAROLINA
Brunswick
Dock Jct.
Arco
Cypress Mills
Harrington
Glynn Haven
St. Simons Island
JEKYLL ISLAND
Jekyll Island Park
ATLANTIC OCEAN
© Rand McNally

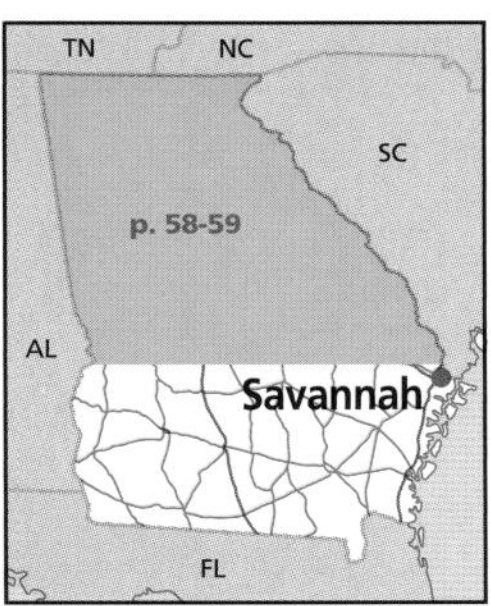
TN
NC
SC
AL
FL
p. 58-59
Savannah

SYMBOLS

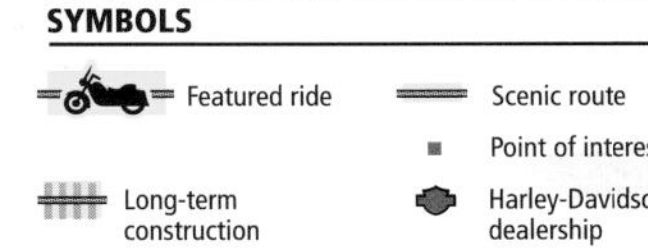
Featured ride
Scenic route
Point of interest
Long-term construction
Harley-Davidson dealership

For Georgia/South Carolina ride, see page R13.

GEORGIA MOTORCYCLE LAWS

Helmet use:
Required

Riding two abreast:
Yes. See state law for specifics

Eye protection:
Required unless equipped with windscreen

Speed limit:
Primary roads: 70 mph
Secondary roads: 65 mph

GEORGIA RESOURCES

Road conditions or construction:
(404) 635-8000
www.dot.state.ga.us

Highway Emergency Numbers:
911

Tourism:
(800) 847-4842
www.georgiaonmymind.org

State motor vehicle information:
(678) 413-8400
www.dds.ga.gov/

HARLEY-DAVIDSON DEALERSHIPS

Flint River Harley-Davidson, L-5
2815 Old Dawson Rd. **Albany**
(229) 639-0035
Lat N 31.614 **Lon** W 84.223

Golden Isles Harley-Davidson Shop, N-12
153 Venture Dr. **Brunswick**
(912) 280-0448
Lat N 31.245 **Lon** W 81.506

Savannah Harley-Davidson, K-13
6 Gateway Blvd. W **Savannah**
(912) 925-0005
Lat N 32.006 **Lon** W 81.286

Savannah Harley-Davidson on River St., K-13
503 River St. **Savannah**
(912) 231-8000
Lat N 32.069 **Lon** W 81.093

Little River Harley-Davidson Shop, M-7
49 Casseta Dr. **Tifton**
(877) 387-8855
Lat N 31.439 **Lon** W 83.527

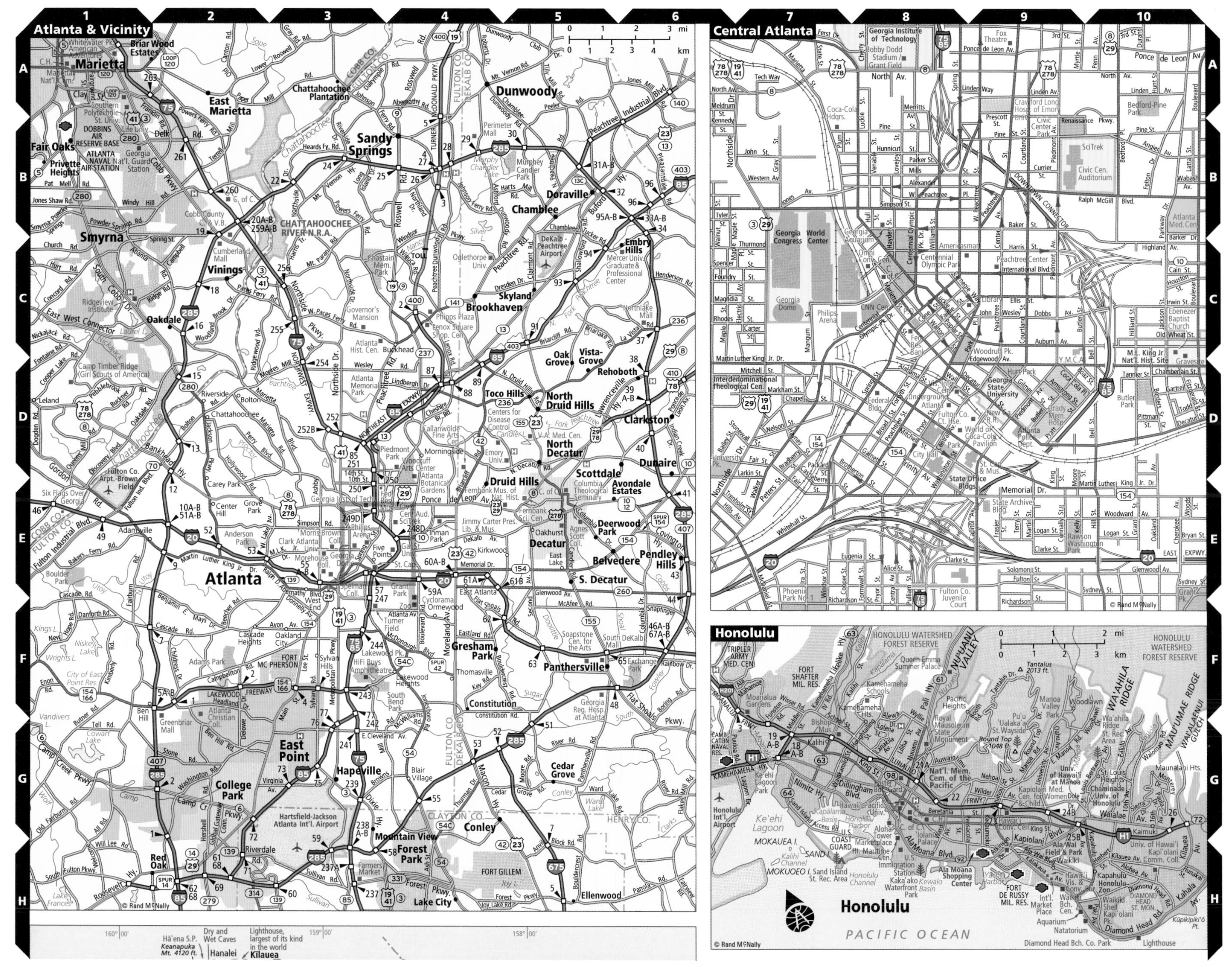
Atlanta & Vicinity
Marietta
Dunwoody
Sandy Springs
Smyrna
Atlanta
East Point
College Park
Decatur
Central Atlanta
Honolulu
PACIFIC OCEAN
© Rand McNally

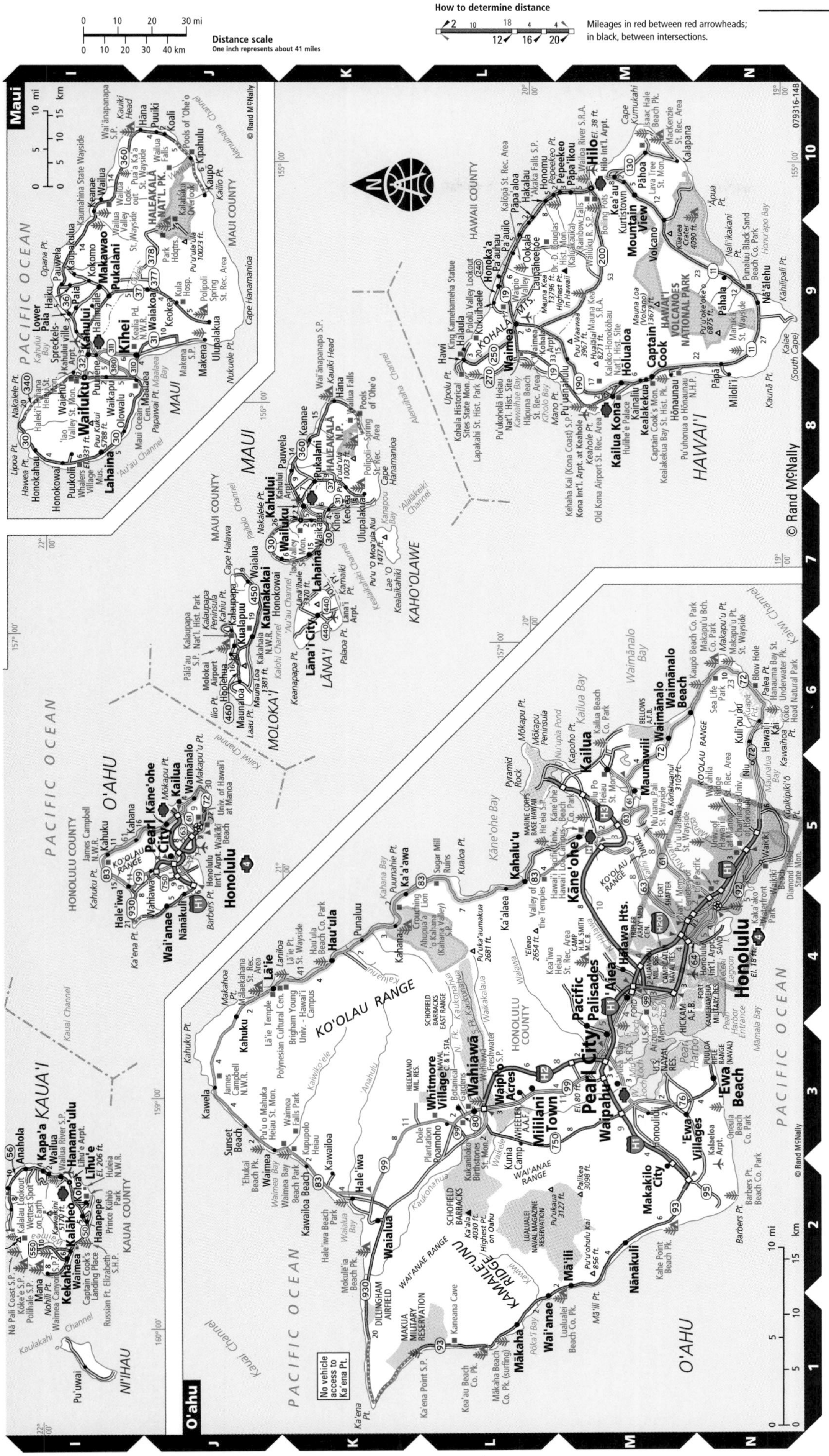

Distance scale
One inch represents about 41 miles

0 10 20 30 mi
0 10 20 30 40 km

How to determine distance

Mileages in red between red arrowheads; in black, between intersections.

SYMBOLS

Featured ride

Scenic route
Point of interest
Long-term construction
Harley-Davidson dealership

HAWAII MOTORCYCLE LAWS

Helmet use:
Required under age 18
Reflectorization required

Riding two abreast:
Yes. See state law for specifics

Eye protection:
Required unless equipped with windscreen

Speed limit:
Primary roads: 60 mph
Secondary roads: 50 mph

HAWAII RESOURCES

Road conditions or construction:
(808) 536-6566
www.hawaii.gov/dot

Highway Emergency Numbers:
911

Tourism:
(800) 464-2924
www.gohawaii.com

State motor vehicle information:
(808) 692-7650
www.state.hi.us/dot/highways/hwy-v/mvso.htm

HARLEY-DAVIDSON DEALERSHIPS

Hilo Harley-Davidson, M-10
200 Kanoelehua Ave. **Hilo**
(808) 934-9090
Lat N 19.720 **Lon** W 155.065

Cycle City Ltd., N-4
600 Puuloa Rd. **Honolulu**
(808) 831-2600
Lat N 21.336 **Lon** W 157.901

Pacific Harley-Davidson Motorclothes & Collectibles, N-4
2333 Kalakaua Ave. **Honolulu**
(808) 971-3500
Lat N 21.278 **Lon** W 157.827

Pacific Harley-Davidson Motorclothes & Collectibles, N-4
2005 Kalia Rd. **Honolulu**
(808) 973-4630
Lat N 21.285 **Lon** W 157.836

Pacific Harley-Davidson Motorclothes & Collectibles, N-4
1450 Ala Moana Blvd. #303 **Honolulu**
(808) 973-2300
Lat N 21.289 **Lon** W 157.843

Maui Harley-Davidson, I-8
150 Dairy Rd. **Kahului**
(808) 877-RIDE
Lat N 20.879 **Lon** W 156.458

Kona Harley-Davidson, M-8
74-5615 E Luhia St. **Kailua Kona**
(808) 326-9887
Lat N 19.685 **Lon** W 155.978

Domenicos Motorcycles, M-5
46-162 Kahuhipa St. **Kāne'ohe**
(808) 235-8711
Lat N 21.41676 **Lon** W 157.805

Kauai Harley-Davidson, I-2
3-1866 Kaumualii Hwy. **Līhu'e**
(808) 241-7020
Lat N 21.966 **Lon** W 159.396

South Seas Cycle Exchange, M-3
94-896 Moloalo St. **Waipahu**
(808) 671-6711
Lat N 21.385 **Lon** W 158.002

Distance scale
One inch represents about 41 miles

0 10 20 30 mi
0 10 20 30 40 km

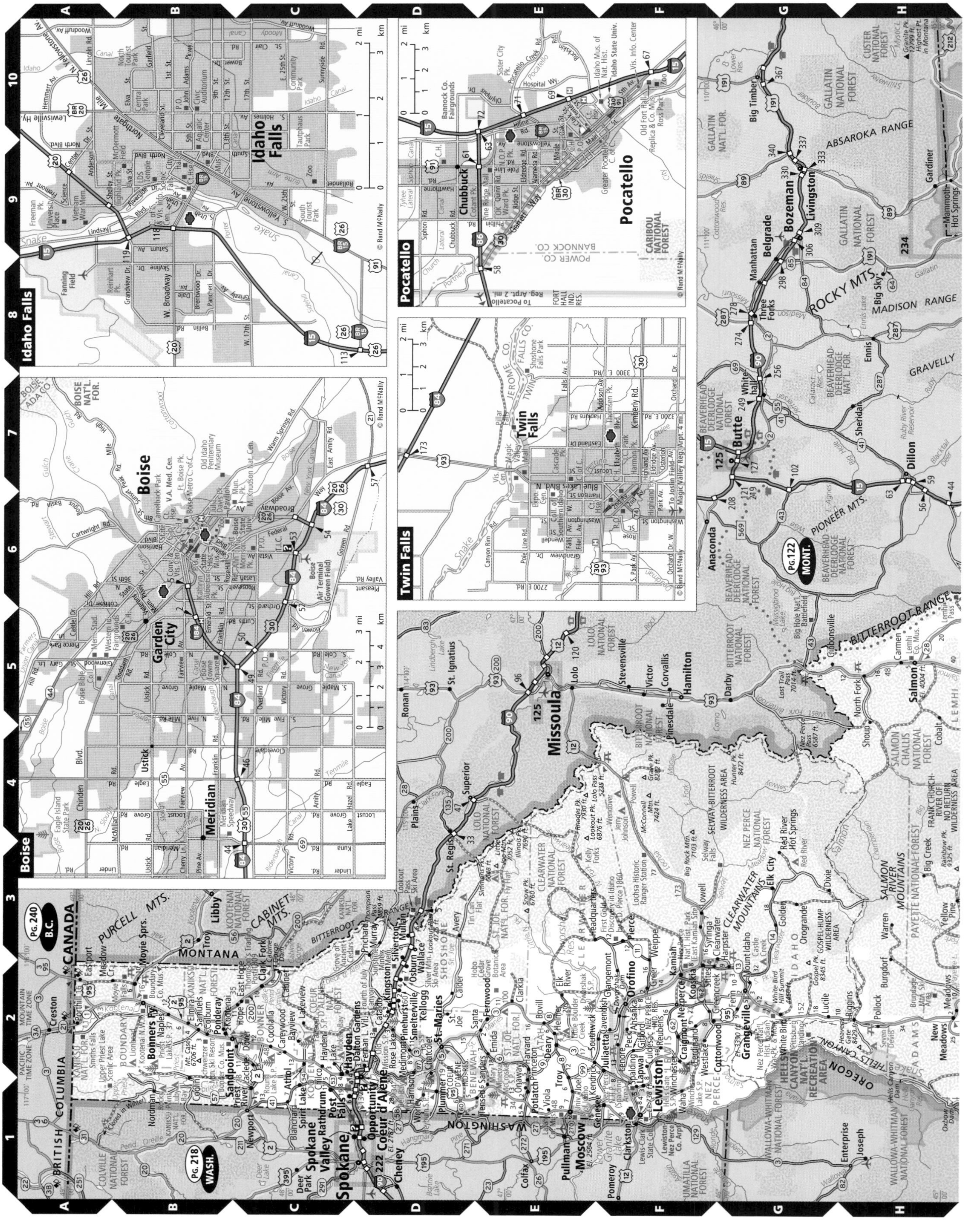

Boise

Idaho Falls

Pocatello

Twin Falls

© Rand McNally

How to determine distance

Mileages in red between red arrowheads; in black, between intersections.

IDAHO
WYOMING
MONTANA
UTAH
NEVADA
OREGON
Boise
Idaho Falls
Pocatello
Twin Falls
Blackfoot
Rexburg
Mountain Home
Nampa
Caldwell
Meridian
Ketchum
Sun Valley
Hailey
Jackson
Logan
SNAKE RIVER PLAINS
ROCKY MOUNTAINS
SAWTOOTH NAT'L. REC. AREA
CRATERS OF THE MOON NAT'L. MON. AND PRESERVE
YELLOWSTONE NATIONAL PARK
GRAND TETON NAT'L. PARK
PG. 234 WYOMING
PG. 206 UTAH
PG. 130 NEVADA
PG. 170 ORE.
© Rand McNally

SYMBOLS

- Featured ride
- Scenic route
- Point of interest
- Long-term construction
- Harley-Davidson dealership

IDAHO MOTORCYCLE LAWS

Helmet use:
Required under age 18

Riding two abreast:
No reference in administrative code or statutes

Eye protection:
Not required

Speed limit:
Primary roads: 75 mph
Secondary roads: 75 mph

IDAHO RESOURCES

Road conditions or construction:
511
(888) 432-7623
www.state.id.us/itd/

Highway Emergency Numbers:
911 or *477

Tourism:
(800) 847-4843
www.visitid.org

State motor vehicle information:
(208) 334-8000
www.itd.idaho.gov/dmv

CITY-TO-CITY MILEAGE

	Boise	Coeur d'Alene	Lewiston	Missoula, MT	Mountain Home	Pocatello	Salmon	Twin Falls
Boise		454	276	371	45	237	255	130
Coeur d'Alene	454		119	168	494	528	308	579
Lewiston	276	119		218	325	517	337	410
Missoula, MT	371	168	218		420	360	143	471
Mountain Home	45	494	325	420		193	294	86
Pocatello	237	528	517	360	193		212	115
Salmon	255	308	337	143	294	212		247
Twin Falls	130	579	410	471	86	115	247	

HARLEY-DAVIDSON DEALERSHIPS

High Desert Harley-Davidson, K-2
3602 Chinden Blvd. **Boise**
(208) 338-5599
Lat N 43.625 **Lon** W 116.242

High Desert Harley-Davidson BoDo District Downtown, K-2
734 West Broad Buiding 7 Ste. 734 **Boise**
(208) 426-8888
Lat N 43.613 **Lon** W 116.205

Birds of Prey Harley-Davidson Shop, K-1
721 Hannibal **Caldwell**
(208) 455-8049
Lat N 43.673 **Lon** W 116.680

Grand Teton Harley-Davidson, K-7
848 Houston Ave. **Idaho Falls**
(208) 523-1464
Lat N 43.497 **Lon** W 112.071

Shumate Harley-Davidson Shop, F-1
2408 North & South Hwy. **Lewiston**
(208) 746-7735
Lat N 46.428 **Lon** W 116.998

Eagle Rock Harley-Davidson Shop, L-7
1444 Yellowstone Ave. **Pocatello**
(208) 237-7433
Lat N 42.901 **Lon** W 112.451

Snake Harley-Davidson, M-4
2404 Addison Ave. E **Twin Falls**
(208) 734-8400
Lat N 42.563 **Lon** W 114.436

Distance scale
One inch represents about 20 miles
0 5 10 15 20 mi
0 5 10 15 20 25 30 km

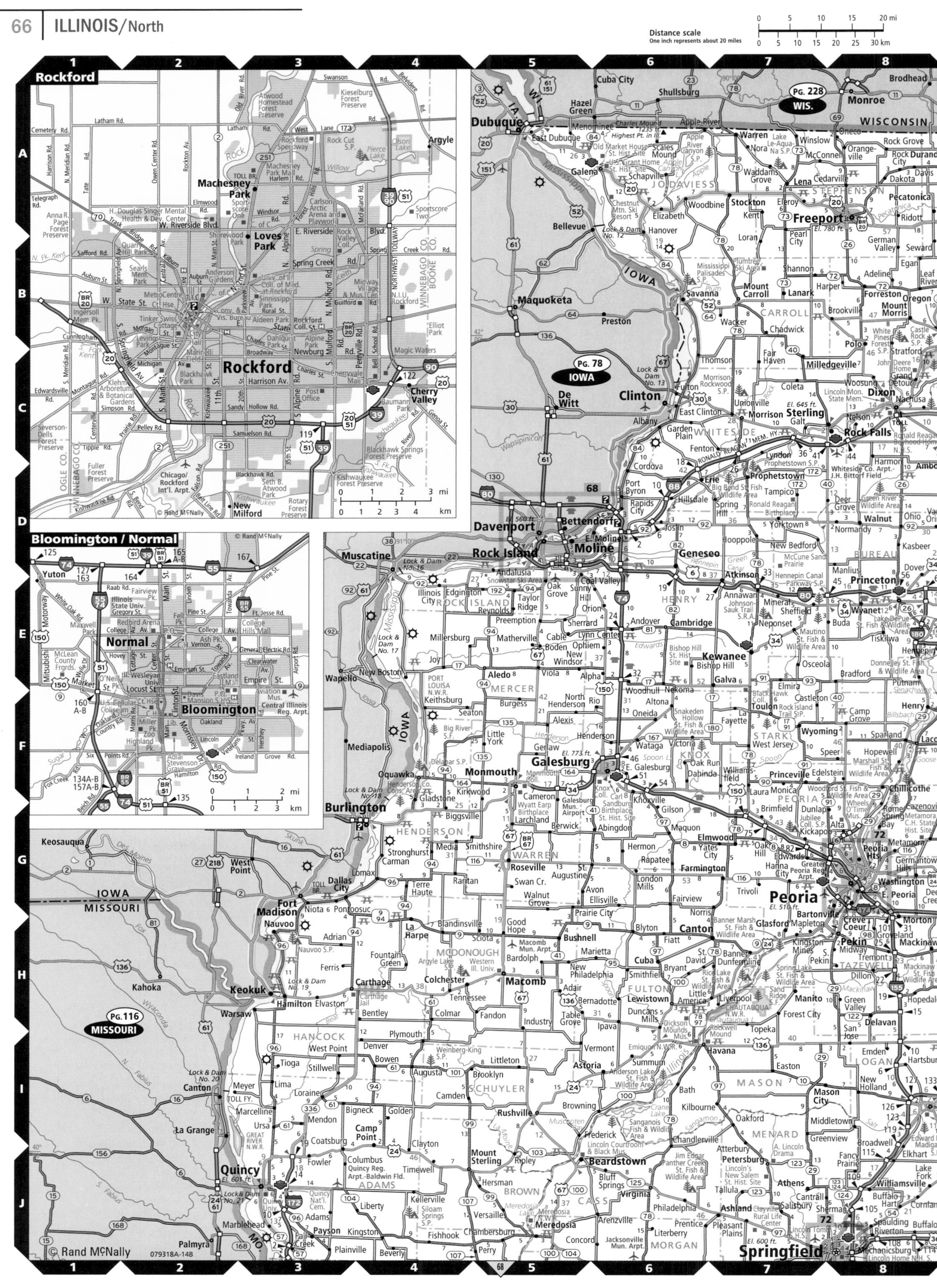
Rockford
Bloomington / Normal
PG. 228 WIS.
WISCONSIN
PG. 78 IOWA
PG. 116 MISSOURI
IOWA
MISSOURI
Dubuque
Galena
Freeport
Rockford
Loves Park
Machesney Park
Cherry Valley
Rock Falls
Sterling
Dixon
Clinton
Davenport
Bettendorf
Rock Island
Moline
Muscatine
Geneseo
Kewanee
Princeton
Galesburg
Monmouth
Burlington
Fort Madison
Keokuk
Macomb
Canton
Peoria
Pekin
East Peoria
Quincy
Springfield
Normal
Bloomington
JO DAVIESS
STEPHENSON
CARROLL
WHITESIDE
ROCK ISLAND
HENRY
BUREAU
MERCER
KNOX
STARK
PEORIA
HENDERSON
WARREN
McDONOUGH
FULTON
TAZEWELL
HANCOCK
SCHUYLER
MASON
LOGAN
ADAMS
BROWN
CASS
MENARD
MORGAN
Mississippi
El. 560 ft.
El. 773 ft.
El. 516 ft.
El. 601 ft.
El. 600 ft.
© Rand McNally
079318A-14B

How to determine distance

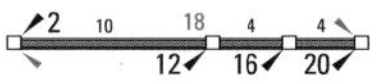

Mileages in red between red arrowheads; in black, between intersections.

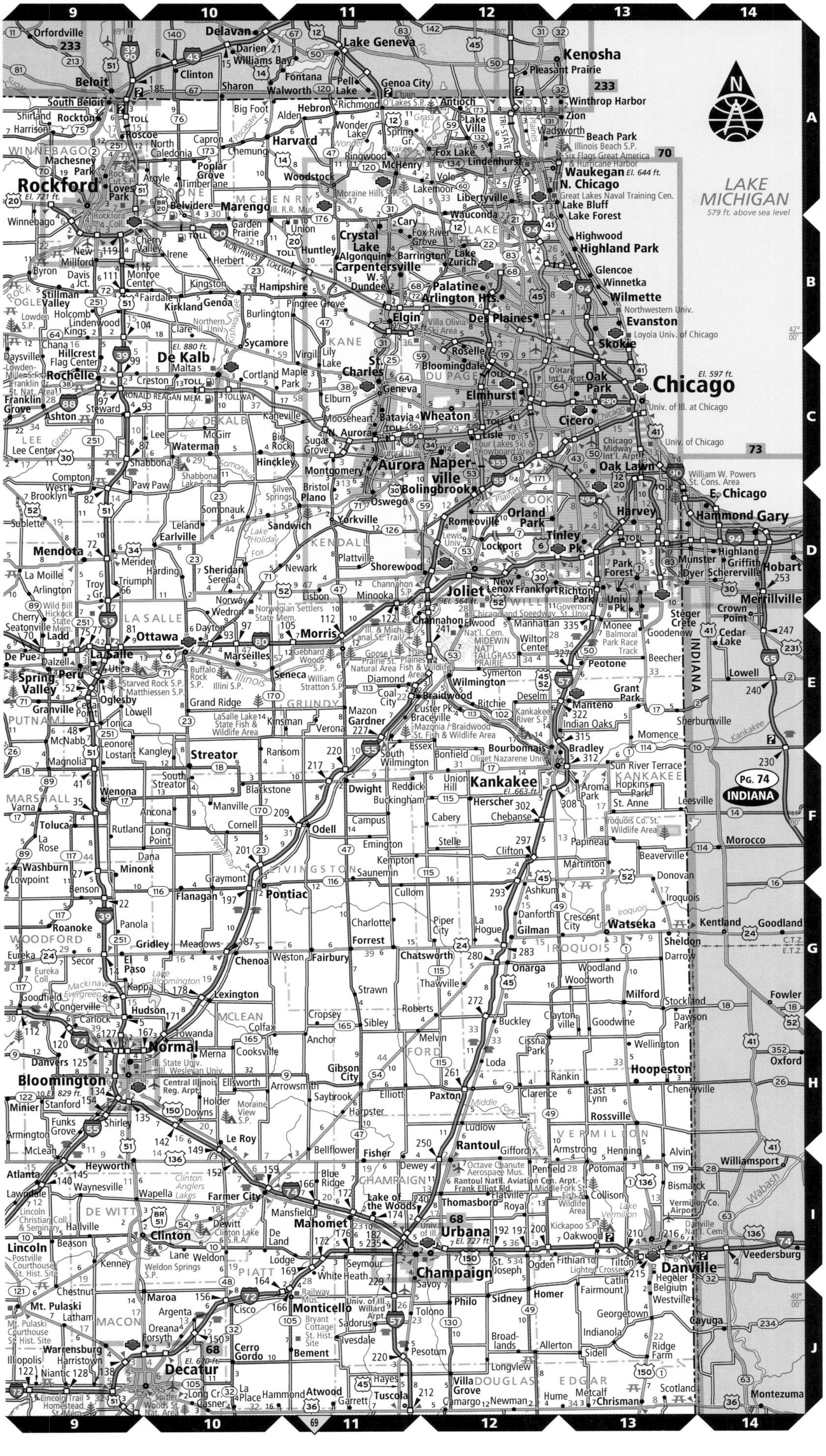

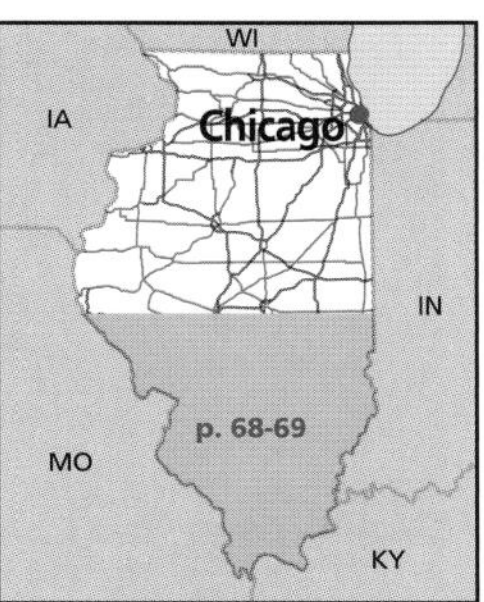
WI
IA
Chicago
IN
MO
p. 68-69
KY

SYMBOLS

- Featured ride
- Scenic route
- Point of interest
- Long-term construction
- Harley-Davidson dealership

HARLEY-DAVIDSON DEALERSHIPS

For Chicagoland, please see dealer listings on page 71; for Peoria and Springfield, see page 73.

Chuck's Harley-Davidson, H-9
2027 Ireland Grove Rd. **Bloomington**
(309) 662-1648
Lat N 40.459 **Lon** W 88.968

Harley-Davidson of Crete, D-13
3445 Eagle Nest Dr. **Crete**
(708) 672-6601
Lat N 41.467 **Lon** W 87.578

Gutteridge Harley-Davidson, I-13
1606 Georgetown Rd. **Danville**
(217) 446-4555
Lat N 40.097 **Lon** W 87.636

Pierce Harley-Davidson Sales, C-10
969 Peace Rd. **DeKalb**
(815) 756-4558
Lat N 41.944 **Lon** W 88.716

Coziahr Harley-Davidson, J-9
150 W Marion Ave. **Forsyth**
(217) 877-7115
Lat N 39.922 **Lon** W 88.959

Harley-Davidson Shop of Galena, A-5
939 Galena Square Dr. **Galena**
(815) 777-9800
Lat N 42.424 **Lon** W 90.443

Nees Harley-Davidson, F-6
2365 Grand Ave. **Galesburg**
(309) 342-3910
Lat N 40.934 **Lon** W 90.334

Reiman's Harley-Davidson, E-7
623 N Main St. **Kewanee**
(309) 854-6661
Lat N 41.249 **Lon** W 89.925

Shreffler's Land of Lincoln Harley-Davidson, E-13
291 N Cypress St. **Manteno**
(815) 468-8673
Lat N 41.253 **Lon** W 87.849

Starved Rock Harley-Davidson, E-10
750 Centennial Dr. **Ottawa**
(815) 431-1900
Lat N 41.375 **Lon** W 88.825

Dant's Harley-Davidson, E-8
230 Backbone Rd. E **Princeton**
(815) 875-8350
Lat N 41.393 **Lon** W 89.464

TNT Harley-Davidson, J-3
5101 Oak St. (off I-72) **Quincy**
(217) 224-1004
Lat N 39.937 **Lon** W 91.336

Workman Harley-Davidson, C-8
1903 Harley-Davidson Dr. (Rte. 40) **Rock Falls**
(815) 626-1213
Lat N 41.763 **Lon** W 89.689

Kegel Harley-Davidson, A-9
7125 Harrison Ave. **Rockford**
(815) 332-7125
Lat N 42.241 **Lon** W 88.977

Andrae's Harley-Davidson, I-12
2010 N Lincoln Ave. **Urbana**
(217) 328-2092
Lat N 40.132 **Lon** W 88.22

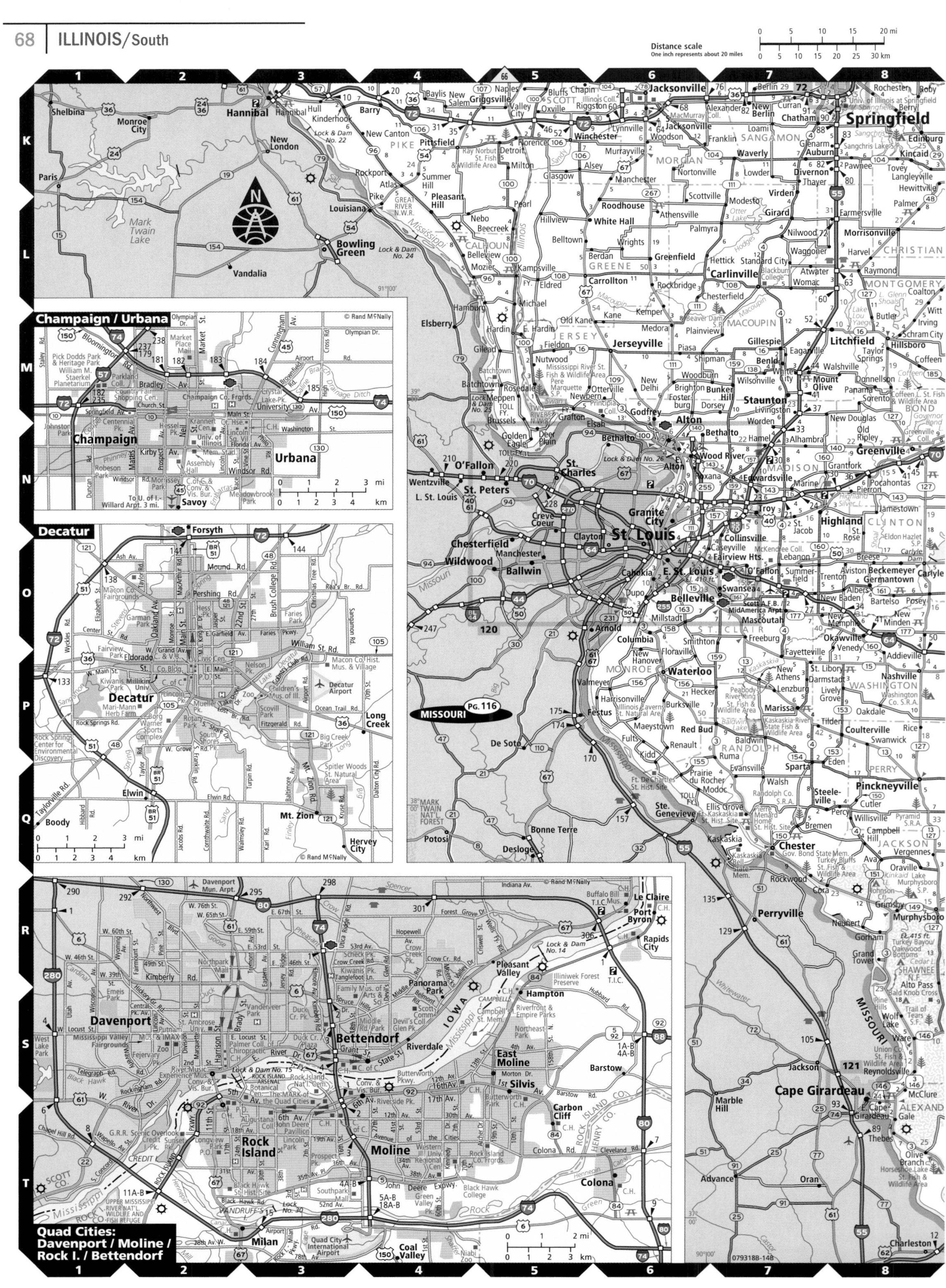
Distance scale
One inch represents about 20 miles
Champaign / Urbana
Decatur
Quad Cities: Davenport / Moline / Rock I. / Bettendorf
Springfield
St. Louis
MISSOURI PG. 116
© Rand McNally
079318B-14B

How to determine distance

Mileages in red between red arrowheads; in black, between intersections.

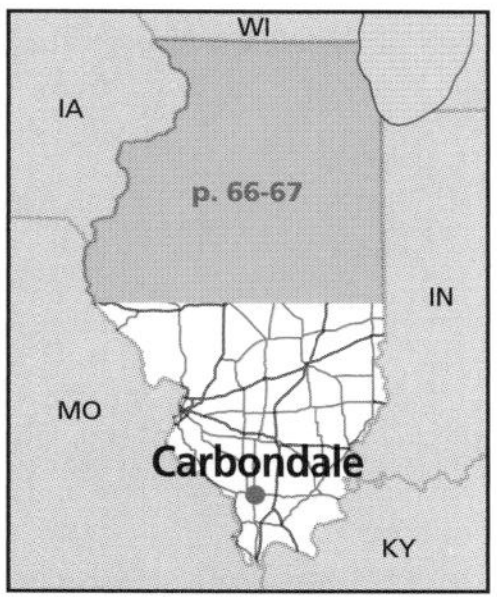

SYMBOLS

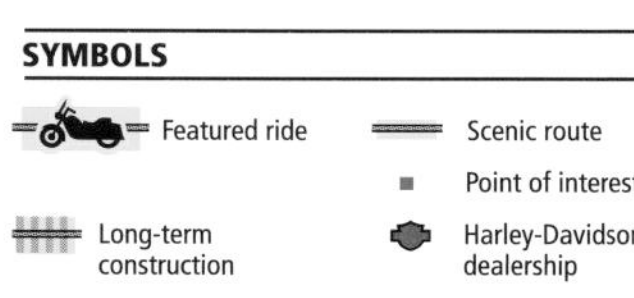
Featured ride
Scenic route
Point of interest
Long-term construction
Harley-Davidson dealership

CITY-TO-CITY MILEAGE

	CARBONDALE	CHAMPAIGN	CHICAGO	MOLINE	PEORIA	ROCKFORD	ST. LOUIS, MO	SPRINGFIELD
Bloomington	249	51	136	132	40	136	164	64
Cairo	59	244	375	410	318	426	169	248
Carbondale		202	333	340	248	384	108	178
Champaign	202		135	182	90	186	182	85
Chicago	333	135		165	170	84	300	200
Decatur	185	47	178	169	77	179	118	38
De Kalb	370	172	66	103	129	44	282	182
Dubuque, IA	415	257	175	74	167	91	337	237
Effingham	124	78	209	256	164	260	104	89
Elgin	369	171	38	152	153	48	307	207
Galesburg	297	139	198	48	49	150	219	119
Kankakee	274	76	56	153	121	138	254	157
Lawrenceville	149	127	250	305	213	309	147	154
Moline	340	182	165		92	117	262	162
Mt. Vernon	58	148	279	314	222	330	82	152
Peoria	248	90	170	92		143	170	70
Quincy	231	195	310	147	130	267	133	110
Rockford	384	186	84	117	143		296	196
St. Louis, MO	108	182	300	262	170	296		100
Springfield	178	85	200	162	70	196	100	
Waukegan	377	179	40	189	198	71	328	228

HARLEY-DAVIDSON DEALERSHIPS

Ted's Harley-Davidson of Alton, N-6
4103 Humbert Rd. **Alton**
(618) 462-3030
Lat N 38.936 **Lon** W 90.156

Frieze Harley-Davidson Sales, O-7
517 S Illinois St. **Belleville**
(618) 277-8864
Lat N 38.509 **Lon** W 89.984

Legacy Harley-Davidson, M-11
1315 Althoff Ave. **Effingham**
(217) 342-3494
Lat N 39.118 **Lon** W 88.568

Campbell's Harley-Davidson, R-10
2400 Williamson County Pkwy. **Marion**
(618) 997-4577
Lat N 37.743 **Lon** W 88.97

Dale's Harley-Davidson, P-10
205 N 44th St. **Mt. Vernon**
(618) 244-4116
Lat N 38.313 **Lon** W 88.949

Frieze Harley-Davidson of O'Fallon, O-7
1607 W Hwy. 50 **O'Fallon**
(618) 622-0045
Lat N 38.593 **Lon** W 89.955

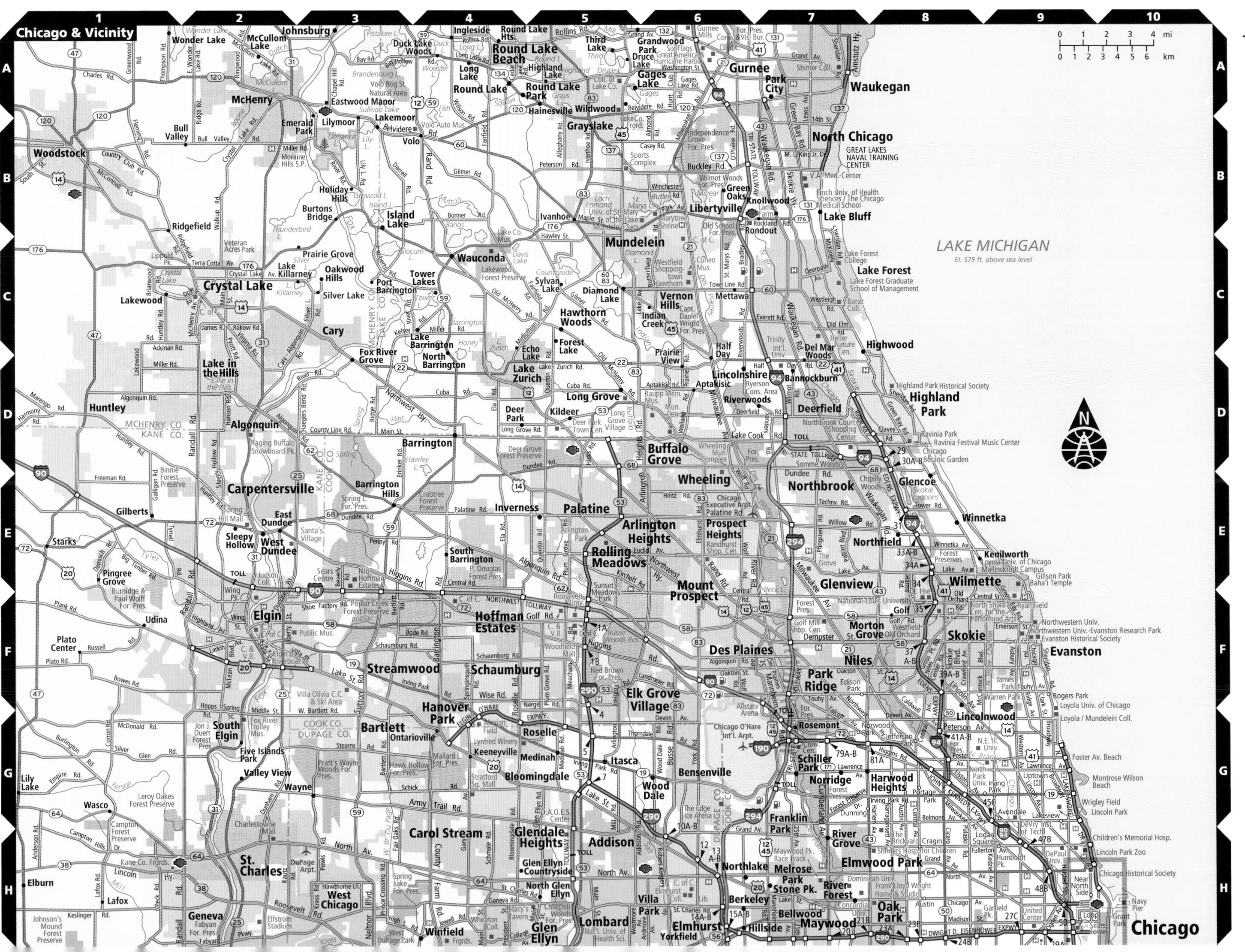
Chicago & Vicinity
LAKE MICHIGAN
El. 579 ft. above sea level
Chicago
Evanston
Skokie
Waukegan
North Chicago
Highland Park
Des Plaines
Schaumburg
Elgin
Arlington Heights
Palatine
Hoffman Estates
Crystal Lake
Woodstock
St. Charles
Oak Park
Chicago O'Hare Int'l. Arpt.

How to determine distance

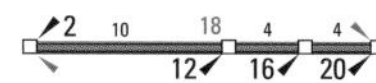
2
10
18
4
4
12
16
20

Mileages in red between red arrowheads; in black, between intersections.

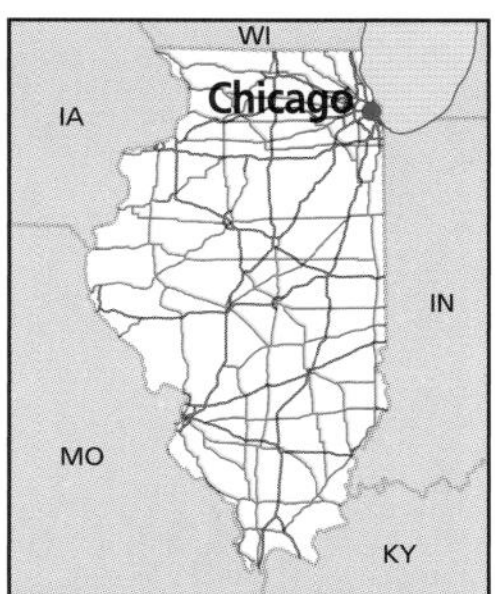
WI
IA
Chicago
IN
MO
KY

SYMBOLS

Featured ride — Scenic route

Long-term construction — Harley-Davidson dealership

HARLEY-DAVIDSON DEALERSHIPS

Illinois Harley-Davidson, I-8
1301 S Harlem Ave. **Berwyn**
(708) 788-1300
Lat N 41.863 **Lon** W 87.804

Chicago Harley-Davidson, F-9
6868 N Western Ave. **Chicago**
(773) 338-6868
Lat N 42.006 **Lon** W 87.69

Chicago Harley-Davidson Downtown, H-10
66 E Ohio St. **Chicago**
(312) 274-9666
Lat N 41.893 **Lon** W 87.626

Chicago Harley-Davidson Shop of Glenview, E-7
2929 Patriot Blvd. **Glenview**
(847) 679-2929
Lat N 42.107 **Lon** W 87.822

Lake Shore Harley-Davidson, B-6
14000 Rockland Rd. (Rte. 176) **Libertyville**
(847) 662-4500
Lat N 42.28 **Lon** W 87.905

Heritage Harley-Davidson, J-4
2595 Ogden Ave. **Lisle**
(630) 420-1942
Lat N 41.797 **Lon** W 88.104

McHenry Harley-Davidson Shop, A-3
2103 Rte. 120 **McHenry**
(815) 344-9300
Lat N 42.331 **Lon** W 88.218

Oak Lawn Harley-Davidson, K-8
11040 S Cicero Ave. **Oak Lawn**
(708) 423-9005
Lat N 41.692 **Lon** W 87.74

Suburban Harley-Davidson, D-5
2200 N Rand Rd. **Palatine**
(847) 358-2112
Lat N 42.15 **Lon** W 88.034

Zylstra Harley-Davidson, H-1
131 S Randall Rd. **St. Charles**
(630) 584-8000
Lat N 41.912 **Lon** W 88.341

Conrad's Harley-Davidson, N-3
19356 NE Frontage Rd. **Shorewood**
(815) 725-2000
Lat N 41.523 **Lon** W 88.186

Chi-Town Harley-Davidson, M-7
17801 S La Grange Rd. **Tinley Park**
(708) 623-6000
Lat N 41.565 **Lon** W 87.852

Wild Fire Harley-Davidson, H-6
120 W North Ave. **Villa Park**
(800) 400-RIDE
Lat N 41.905 **Lon** W 87.981

Woodstock Harley-Davidson, B-1
2050 S Eastwood Dr. **Woodstock**
(815) 337-3511
Lat N 42.293 **Lon** W 88.433

079319A-14B

Central Chicago

Peoria

South Bend

Springfield

Fort Wayne

Indianapolis

How to determine distance

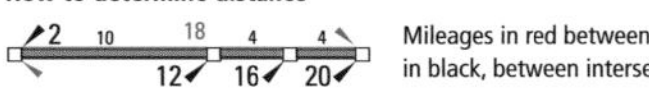
Mileages in red between red arrowheads; in black, between intersections.

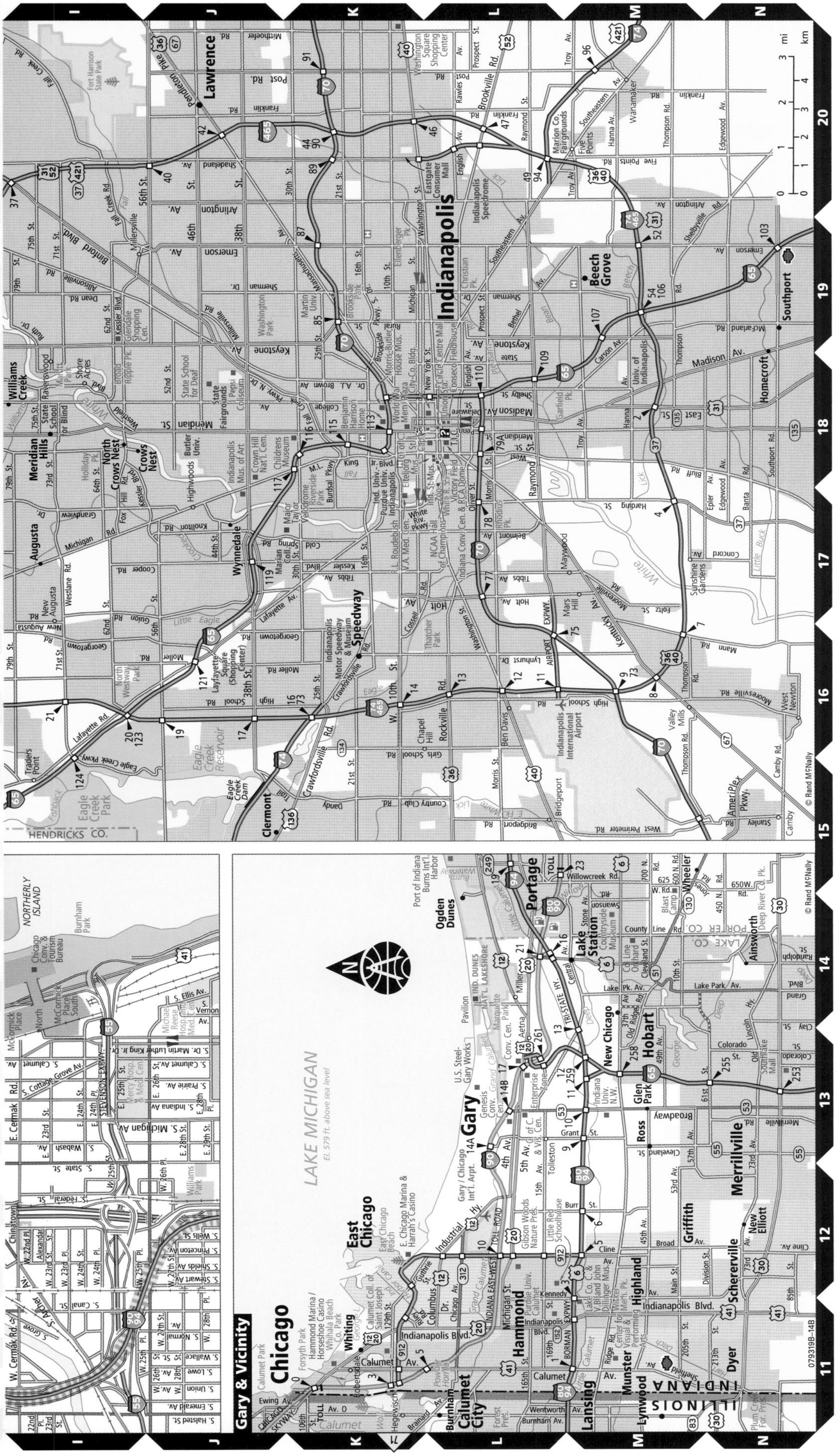

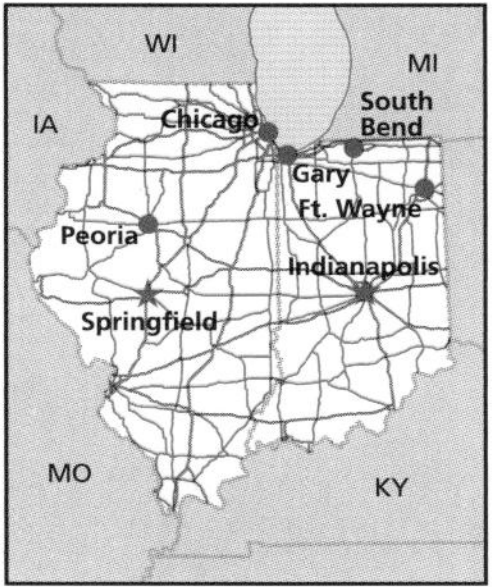
WI
MI
IA
Chicago
South Bend
Gary
Ft. Wayne
Peoria
Indianapolis
Springfield
MO
KY

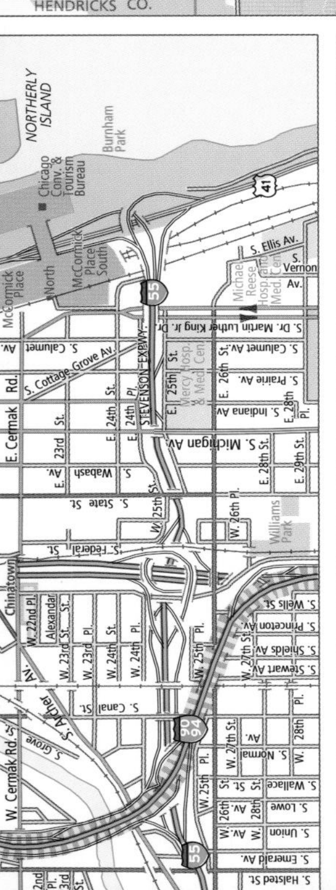

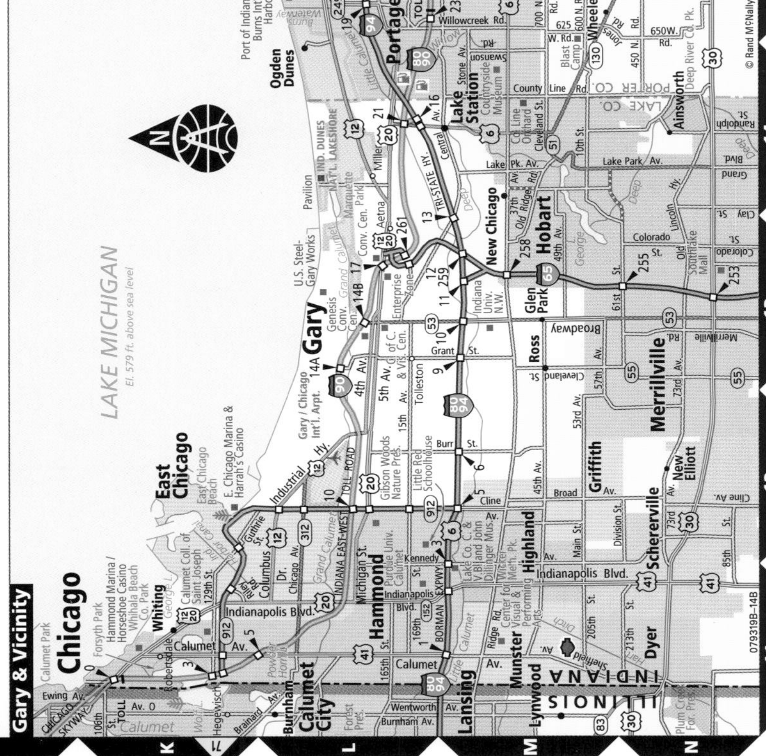
Gary & Vicinity
Chicago
LAKE MICHIGAN
El. 579 ft. above sea level

SYMBOLS

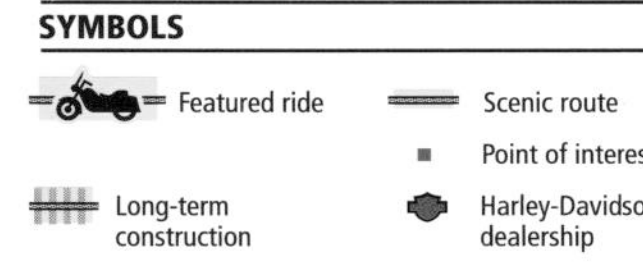
Featured ride
Scenic route
Point of interest
Long-term construction
Harley-Davidson dealership

ILLINOIS MOTORCYCLE LAWS

Helmet use: Not Required

Riding two abreast:
No reference in administrative code or statutes

Eye protection:
Required unless equipped with windscreen

Speed limit:
Primary roads: 65 mph; Secondary roads: 55 mph

ILLINOIS RESOURCES

Road conditions or construction:
(800) 452-4368; (312) 368-4636
www.dot.state.il.us
www.illinoisroads.info

Highway Emergency Numbers: 911

Tourism:
(800) 226-6632; www.enjoyillinois.com

State motor vehicle information:
(217) 782-6212; (312) 814-2975 (Chicago Metro)
www.cyberdriveillinois.com

INDIANA MOTORCYCLE LAWS

Helmet use:
Required under age 18 and for instructional permit holders

Riding two abreast:
Yes. See state law for specifics

Eye protection: Required under age 18

Speed limit:
Primary roads: 70 mph; Secondary roads: 55 mph

INDIANA RESOURCES

Road conditions or construction:
(800) 261-7623
www.in.gov/dot

Highway Emergency Numbers: 911

Tourism:
(888) 365-6946
www.enjoyindiana.com

State motor vehicle information:
(317) 233-6000
www.in.gov/bmv

HARLEY-DAVIDSON DEALERSHIPS

Walters Bros. Harley-Davidson, G-8
615 S Maxwell Rd. **Peoria**
(309) 697-1917
Lat N 40.688 **Lon** W 89.693

Hall's Harley-Davidson, J-8
2301 N Dirksen Pkwy. **Springfield**
(217) 528-8356
Lat N 39.833 **Lon** W 89.605

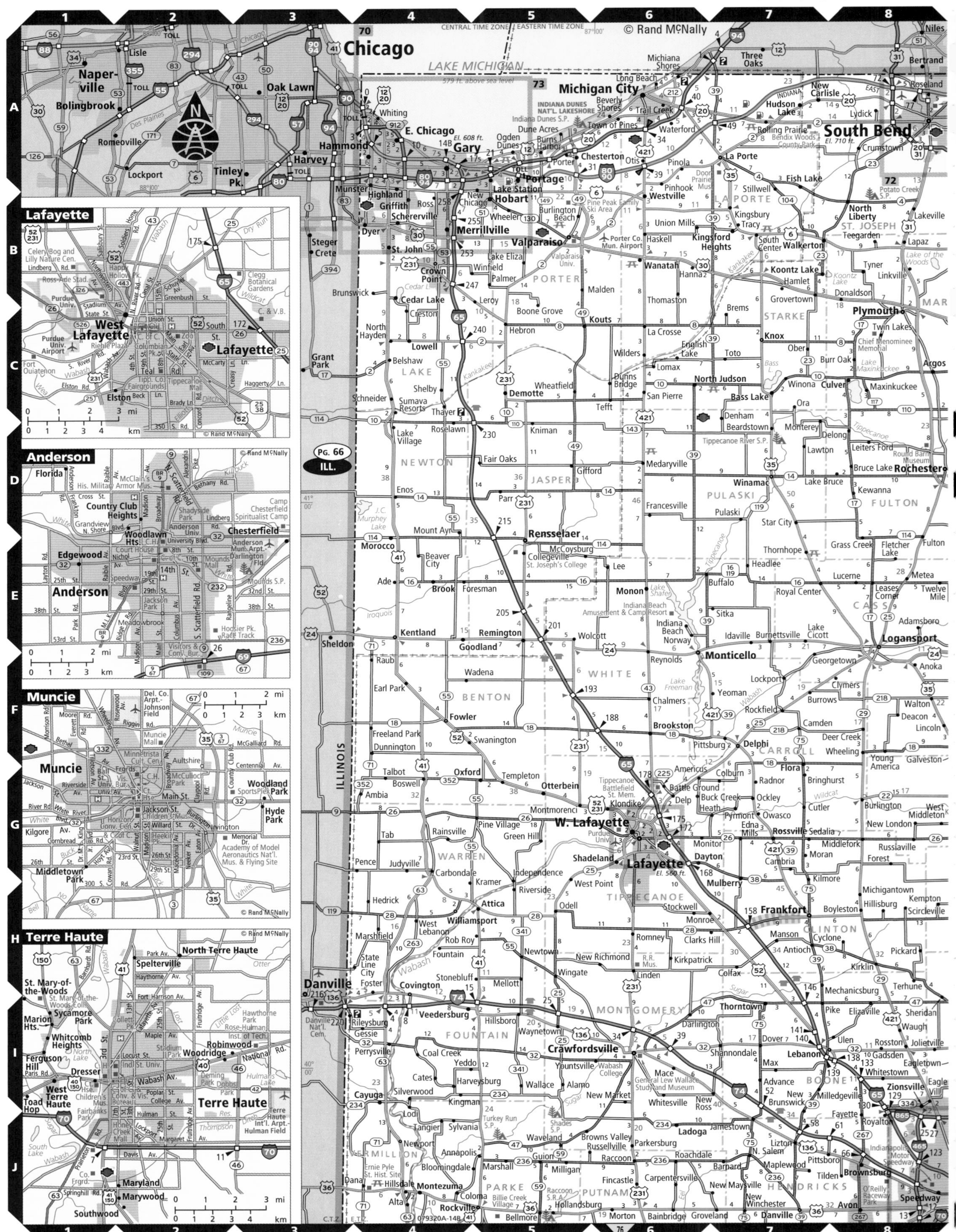

Distance scale
One inch represents about 15 miles
© Rand McNally
Chicago
LAKE MICHIGAN
Michigan City
South Bend
Gary
Lafayette
Anderson
Muncie
Terre Haute
Danville
W. Lafayette
Logansport
Crawfordsville
Frankfort
Valparaiso
Merrillville
Hammond
Rensselaer
Monticello
ILLINOIS

How to determine distance

Mileages in red between red arrowheads; in black, between intersections.

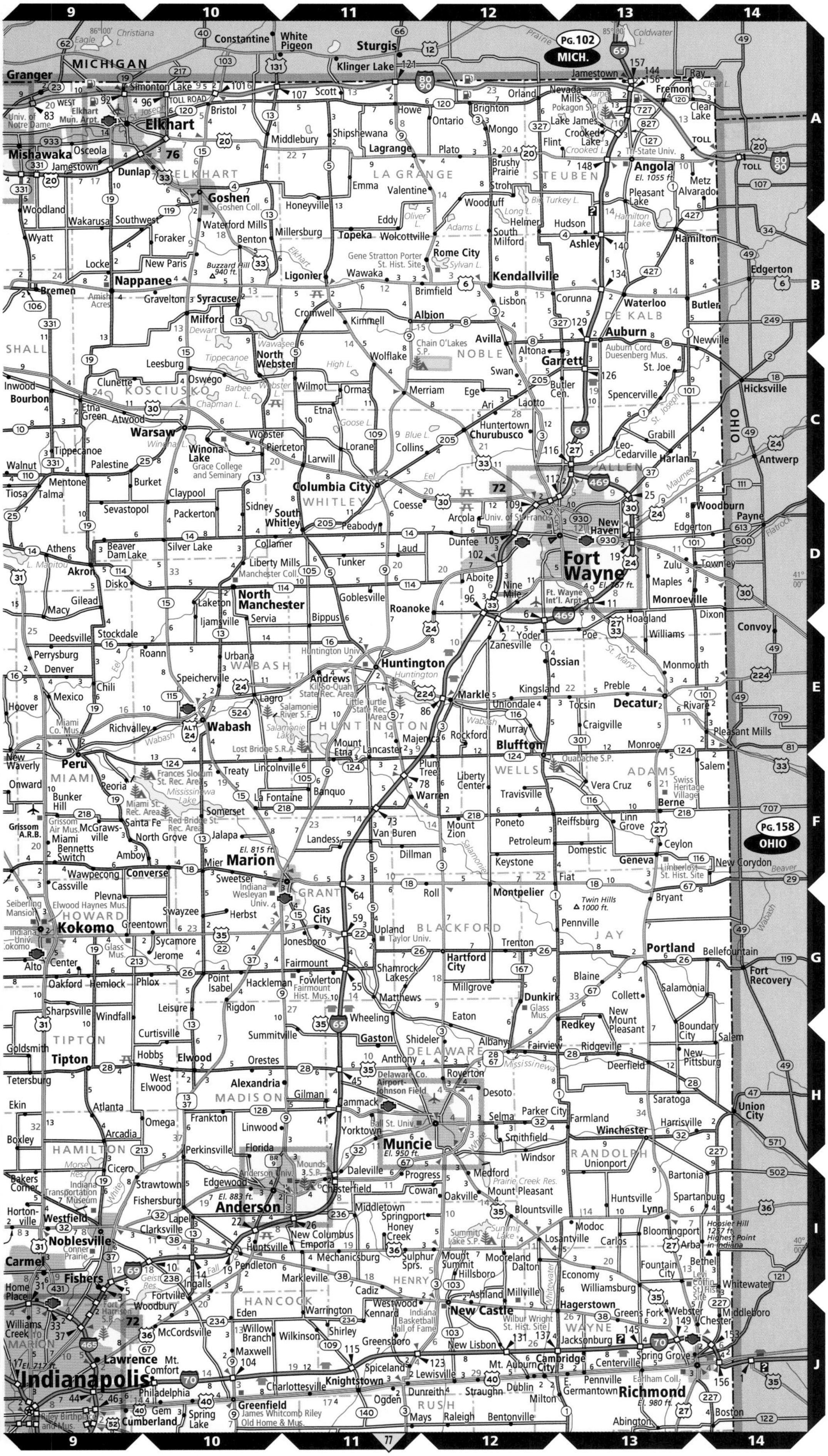

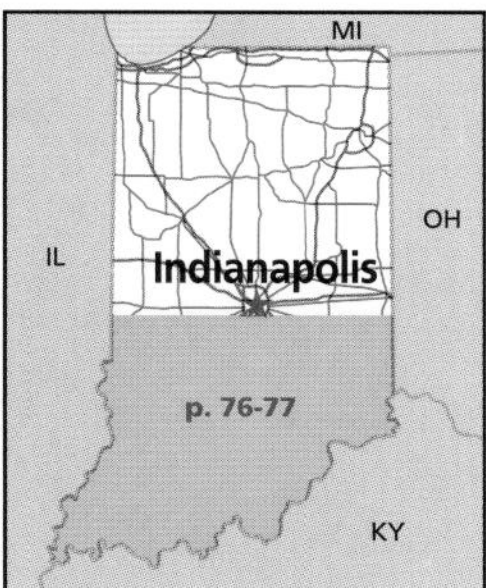
MI
OH
IL
Indianapolis
p. 76-77
KY

SYMBOLS

- Featured ride
- Scenic route
- Long-term construction
- Harley-Davidson dealership

HARLEY-DAVIDSON DEALERSHIPS

Hoosier Harley-Davidson, A-9
720 W Bristol St. **Elkhart**
(574) 262-2735
Lat N 41.703 **Lon** W 85.986

Jim Bailey's Harley-Davidson, D-12
6315 Illinois Rd. **Fort Wayne**
(260) 489-2464
Lat N 41.075 **Lon** W 85.222

River City Harley-Davidson, D-13
5525 Hwy. 930 E **Fort Wayne**
(260) 493-9900
Lat N 41.07 **Lon** W 85.106

Harley-Davidson of Indianapolis, J-9
4146 E 96th St. **Indianapolis**
(317) 815-1800
Lat N 39.927 **Lon** W 86.1

Harley-Davidson of Kokomo, G-9
335 S County Rd. OOE/W **Kokomo**
(765) 864-9999
Lat N 40.449 **Lon** W 86.129

Eagle Harley-Davidson, G-6
702 Navco Dr. **Lafayette**
(765) 448-9132
Lat N 40.41 **Lon** W 86.853

Stone's Harley-Davidson, G-11
6333 E Steltzer Dr. **Marion**
(765) 664-1331
Lat N 40.53 **Lon** W 85.655

The Harley-Davidson Shop of Michigan City, A-6
2968 N US Hwy. 421 **Michigan City**
(219) 878-8885
Lat N 41.615 **Lon** W 86.894

Benson Motorcyles, H-12
6410 W McGalliard (Rte. 332) **Muncie**
(765) 288-1817
Lat N 40.219 **Lon** W 85.461

Calumet Harley-Davidson, B-4
10350 Calumet Ave. **Munster**
(219) 934-6366
Lat N 41.526 **Lon** W 87.509

Harley-Davidson Center, J-13
2240 Chester Blvd. **Richmond**
(765) 962-0596
Lat N 39.864 **Lon** W 84.889

McDaniel's Harley-Davidson, A-8
1910 Lincoln Way E **South Bend**
(574) 289-6650
Lat N 41.658 **Lon** W 86.218

Harley-Davidson of Valparaiso, B-5
1151 US 30 **Valparaiso**
(219) 462-2223
Lat N 41.481 **Lon** W 87.111

Brandt's Harley-Davidson, E-10
1400 N Cass St. **Wabash**
(260) 563-6443
Lat N 40.815 **Lon** W 85.838

Kersting's Harley-Davidson Sales, C-6
8774 W 700 N **Winamac**
(574) 896-2974
Lat N 41.157 **Lon** W 86.772

Distance scale
One inch represents about 15 miles
0 2 4 6 8 10 12 14 mi
0 4 8 12 16 20 km

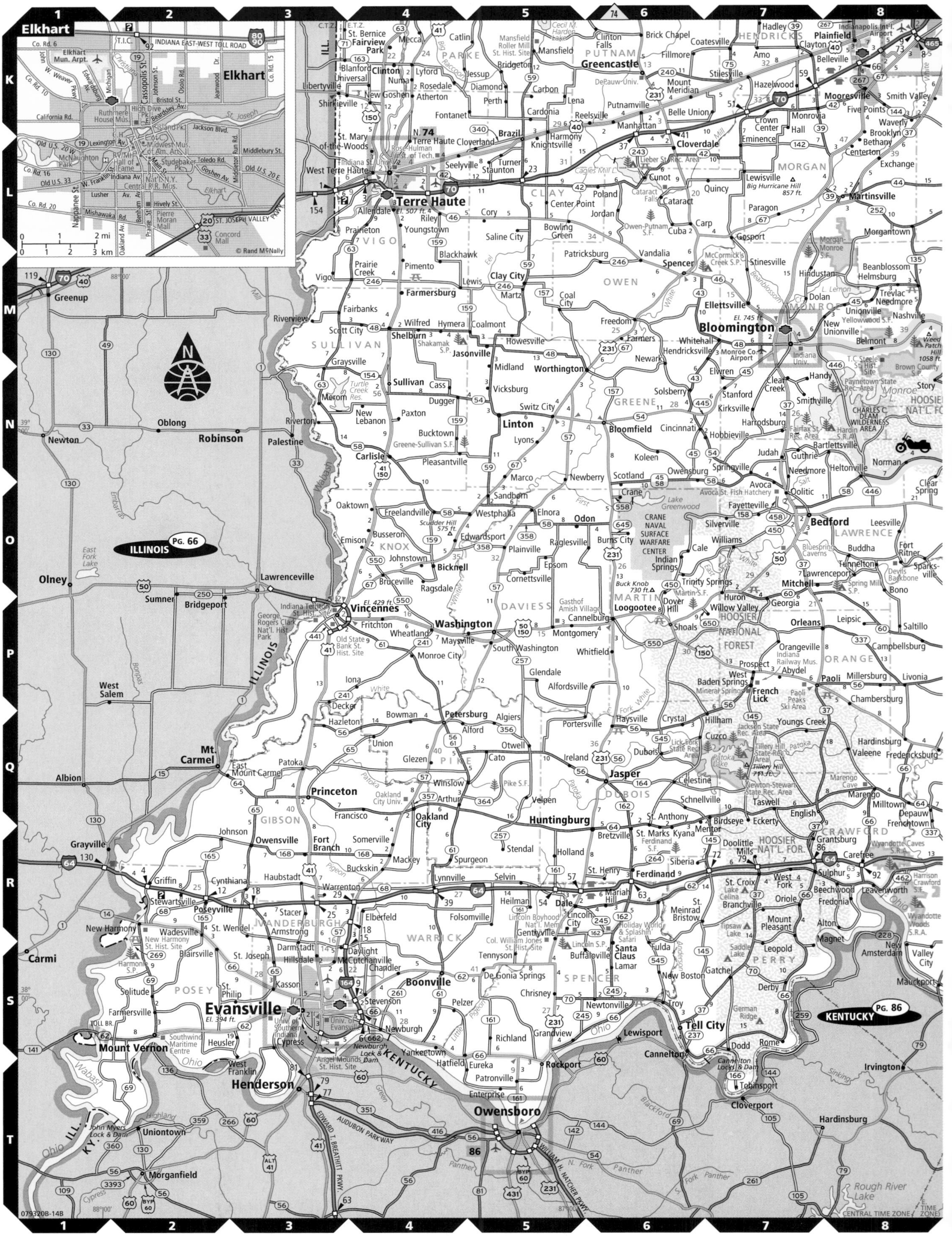

Elkhart

T.I.C. INDIANA EAST-WEST TOLL ROAD 80 90
Elkhart Mun. Arpt.
Elkhart
Ruthmere House Mus.
Midwest Mus. of Am. Art
RV/MH Hall of Fame
Studebaker Pk.
Nat'l N.Y. Central R.R. Mus.
Pierre Moran Mall
Concord Mall
ST. JOSEPH VALLEY PKWY.
0 1 2 mi
0 1 2 3 km
© Rand McNally

Terre Haute
Bloomington
Indianapolis Int'l. Airport
Plainfield
Mooresville
Martinsville
Greencastle
Brazil
Clinton
Spencer
Bedford
Linton
Sullivan
Vincennes
Washington
Jasper
Huntingburg
Princeton
Evansville
Henderson
Owensboro
Mount Vernon
Tell City
Paoli
French Lick
Mitchell
Loogootee
Odon
Bloomfield
Boonville
Rockport
Ferdinand
Santa Claus
Poseyville
New Harmony
Mt. Carmel
Robinson
Olney
Lawrenceville
Palestine
Carmi
Grayville
Morganfield
Uniontown
Cannelton
Cloverport
Hardinsburg
Irvington

PARKE
PUTNAM
HENDRICKS
VIGO
CLAY
OWEN
MORGAN
MONROE
SULLIVAN
GREENE
LAWRENCE
KNOX
DAVIESS
MARTIN
ORANGE
PIKE
DUBOIS
GIBSON
CRAWFORD
VANDERBURGH
WARRICK
SPENCER
PERRY
POSEY

HOOSIER NATIONAL FOREST
CRANE NAVAL SURFACE WARFARE CENTER

ILLINOIS PG. 66
KENTUCKY PG. 86

CENTRAL TIME ZONE | TIME ZONE

079320B-14B

How to determine distance

Mileages in red between red arrowheads; in black, between intersections.

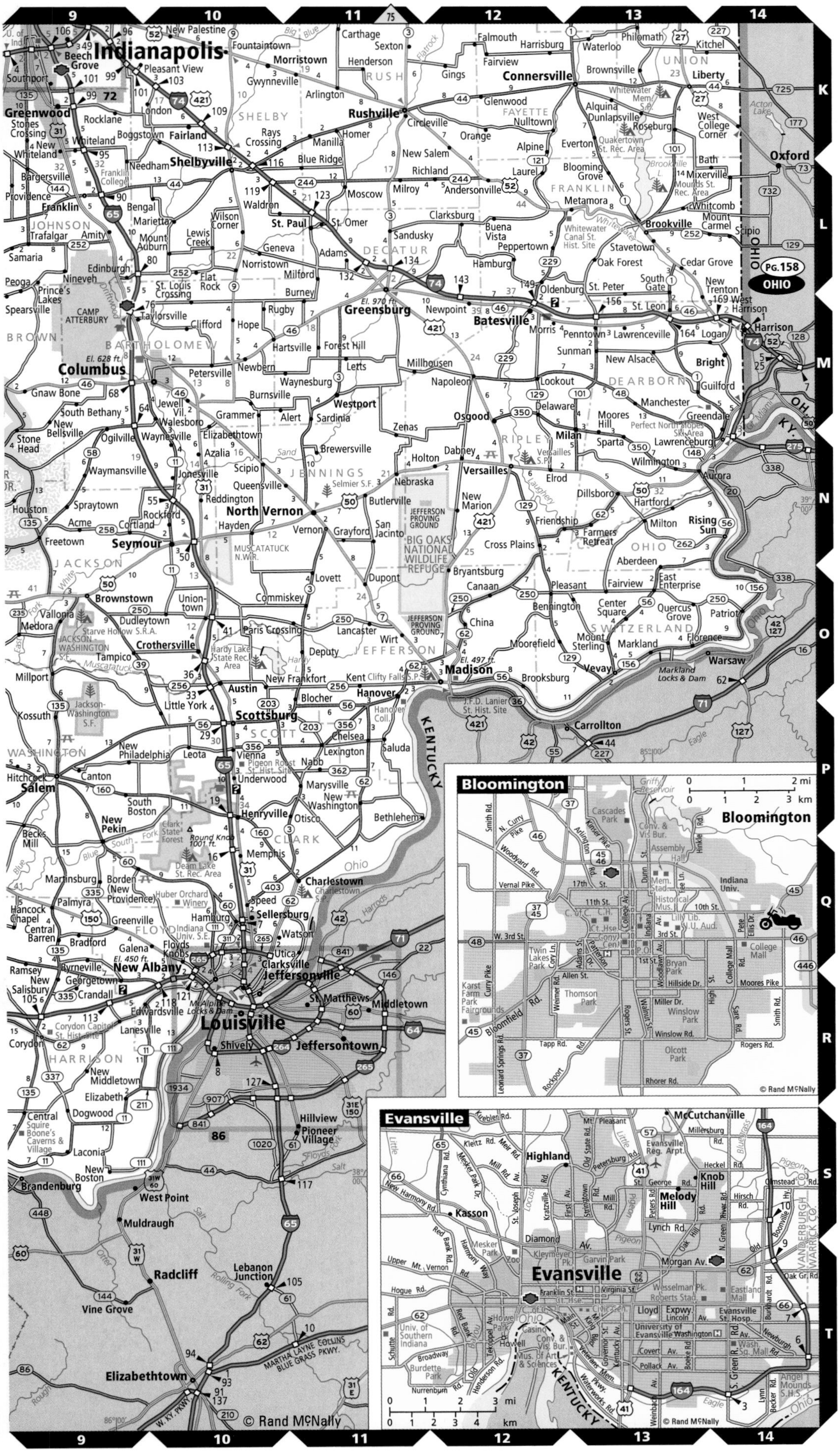

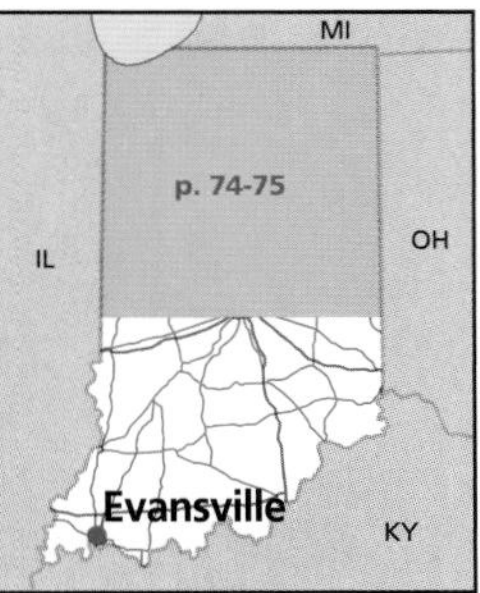
MI
p. 74-75
IL
OH
Evansville
KY

SYMBOLS

- Featured ride
- Scenic route
- Point of interest
- Long-term construction
- Harley-Davidson dealership

For Indiana ride, see page R14.

CITY-TO-CITY MILEAGE

	EVANSVILLE	FORT WAYNE	GARY	INDIANAPOLIS	NEW ALBANY	RICHMOND	SOUTH BEND	TERRE HAUTE
Anderson	234	89	182	48	157	59	142	126
Angola	353	42	135	167	276	140	76	245
Bloomington	134	180	199	50	89	120	198	57
Chicago, IL	294	164	28	179	298	250	87	182
Columbus	179	175	202	48	71	115	192	121
Crawfordsville	178	168	120	56	166	129	133	57
Danville, IL	169	208	130	96	206	169	173	57
Evansville		319	278	186	111	259	326	112
Fort Wayne	319		135	133	242	95	92	211
Gary	278	135		150	269	221	58	166
Greensburg	198	152	202	50	90	67	186	123
Indianapolis	186	133	150		115	73	140	78
Kokomo	239	90	136	53	172	104	91	131
Lafayette	203	120	92	62	181	133	107	92
Michigan City	298	118	26	170	289	241	34	186
Muncie	248	85	196	62	171	43	141	140
New Albany	111	242	269	115		182	259	188
Richmond	259	95	221	73	182		191	151
South Bend	326	92	58	140	259	191		218
Terre Haute	112	211	166	78	188	151	218	
Vincennes	54	265	224	132	137	205	272	58

HARLEY-DAVIDSON DEALERSHIPS

Harley-Davidson of Bloomington, M-7
522 W Gourley Pike **Bloomington**
(800) 667-7939
Lat N 39.185 **Lon** W 86.538

Mann's Harley-Davidson, M-9
3250 W Market Place Dr. **Edinburgh**
(812) 526-3485
Lat N 39.312 **Lon** W 85.965

Bud's Harley-Davidson Sales, S-3
4700 E Morgan Ave. **Evansville**
(812) 473-2837
Lat N 37.991 **Lon** W 87.496

Bud's Harley-Davidson Shop, S-3
2124 W Franklin St. **Evansville**
(812) 425-7687
Lat N 37.981 **Lon** W 87.596

Indianapolis Southside Harley-Davidson, K-9
4930 Southport Crossing Pl. **Indianapolis**
(317) 885-5180
Lat N 39.665 **Lon** W 86.084

Indy West Harley-Davidson, K-8
6201 Cambridge Way **Plainfield**
(317) 279-0062
Lat N 39.673 **Lon** W 86.369

Wabash Valley Harley-Davidson, L-4
3912 S US Hwy. 41 **Terre Haute**
(812) 232-7821
Lat N 39.419 **Lon** W 87.416

Bloomington

Evansville

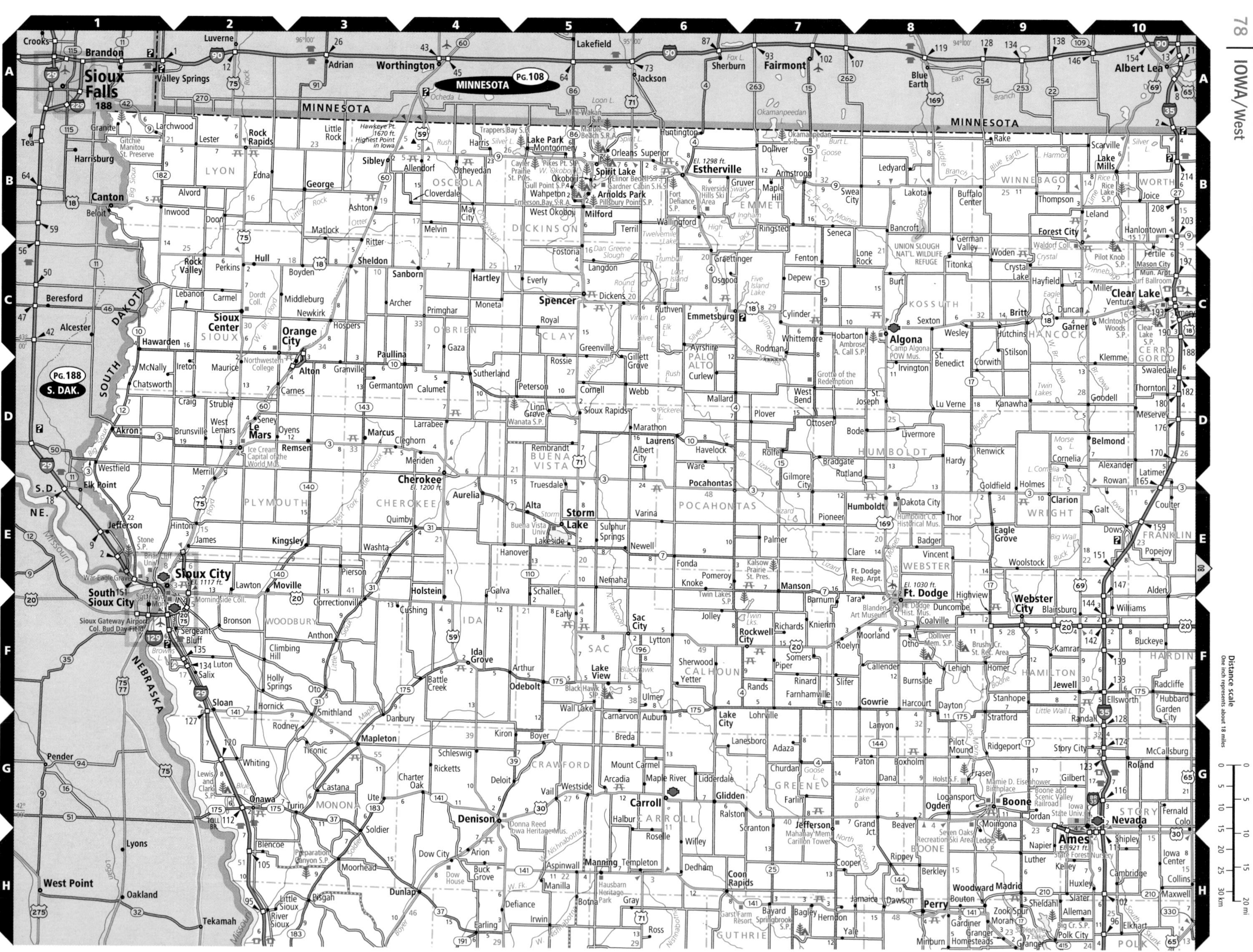
Distance scale
One inch represents about 18 miles
0 5 10 15 20 mi
0 5 10 15 20 25 30 km
MINNESOTA
NEBRASKA
SOUTH DAKOTA
PG. 108 MINNESOTA
PG. 188 S. DAK.
Sioux Falls
Sioux City
South Sioux City
Albert Lea
Worthington
Fairmont
Estherville
Spencer
Spirit Lake
Algona
Clear Lake
Mason City
Ft. Dodge
Webster City
Humboldt
Storm Lake
Cherokee
Le Mars
Orange City
Sioux Center
Carroll
Denison
Boone
Ames
Nevada
Jefferson
Ida Grove
Onawa
Pocahontas
Sac City
Emmetsburg
Garner
Clarion
Eagle Grove

How to determine distance

Mileages in red between red arrowheads; in black, between intersections.

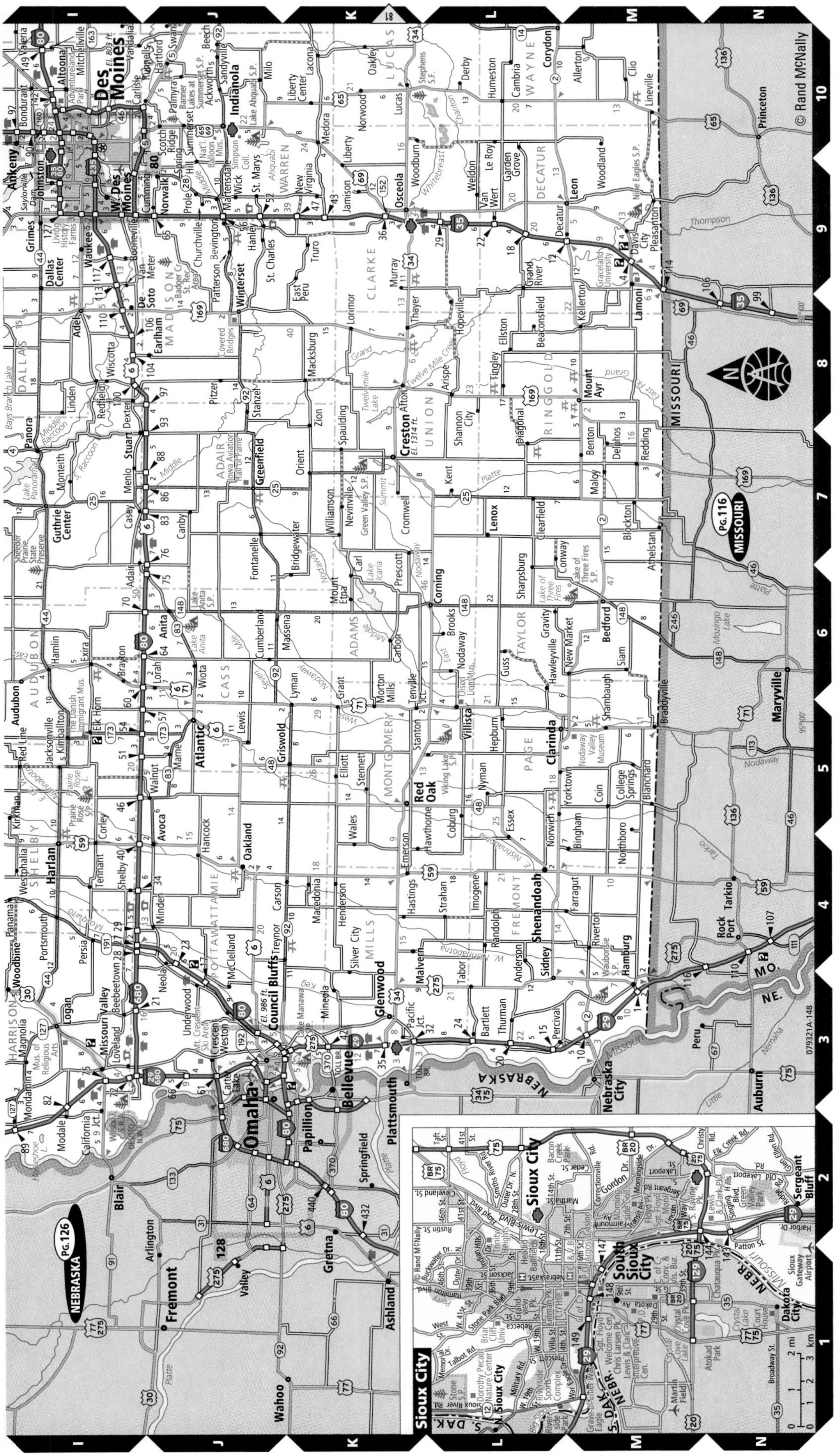

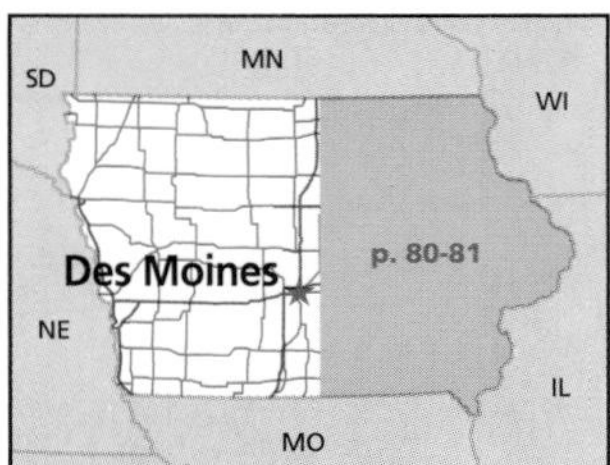
MN
SD
WI
Des Moines
p. 80-81
NE
IL
MO

SYMBOLS

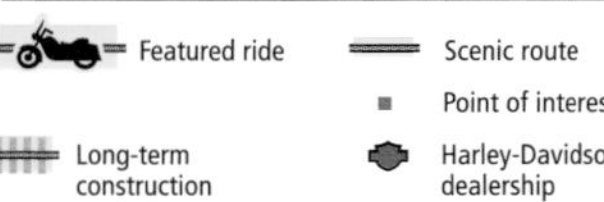
Featured ride
Scenic route
Point of interest
Long-term construction
Harley-Davidson dealership

IOWA MOTORCYCLE LAWS

Helmet use: Not Required

Riding two abreast:
Yes. See state law for specifics

Eye protection: Not required

Speed limit:
Primary roads: 70 mph
Secondary roads: 55 mph

IOWA RESOURCES

Road conditions or construction:
511
(800) 288-1047
www.511ia.org

Highway Emergency Numbers: 911, *55

Tourism:
(800) 345-4692 (to request travel materials only)
(888) 472-6035
(515) 242-4705
www.traveliowa.com

State motor vehicle information:
(515) 244-9124
www.dot.state.ia.us/mvd/ods

HARLEY-DAVIDSON DEALERSHIPS

Ernie's Harley-Davidson, C-8
2613 Hwy. 18 E **Algona**
(515) 295-7951
Lat N 43.083 **Lon** W 94.202

Zylstra Harley-Davidson, G-10
1930 E 13th St. **Ames**
(515) 232-6223
Lat N 42.035 **Lon** W 93.587

Harley-Davidson of Carroll, G-6
1327 Plaza Dr. (Hwy. 30 E) **Carroll**
(712) 792-1610
Lat N 42.064 **Lon** W 94.848

Zook's Harley-Davidson, I-10
81 NW 49th Pl. **Des Moines**
(515) 265-4444
Lat N 41.65 **Lon** W 93.619

Route 65 Harley-Davidson Shop, J-10
1300 S Jefferson Way **Indianola**
(515) 962-2160
Lat N 41.349 **Lon** W 93.558

Chipps Harley-Davidson Shop, K-9
1301 Southwest Blvd. **Osceola**
(641) 342-7494
Lat N 41.025 **Lon** W 93.798

Walker's Harley-Davidson, K-3
57408 190th St. Exit 35 **Pacific Junction**
(712) 622-4000
Lat N 41.031 **Lon** W 95.807

Rooster's Harley-Davidson, E-1
1930 N Lewis Blvd. **Sioux City**
(712) 252-2750
Lat N 42.51 **Lon** W 96.374

Rooster's Harley-Davidson, E-1
4400 Sargent Rd. Ste. 120 **Sioux City**
(712) 252-2750
Lat N 42.447 **Lon** W 96.347

Distance scale
One inch represents about 18 miles

0 5 10 15 20 mi
0 5 10 15 20 25 30 km

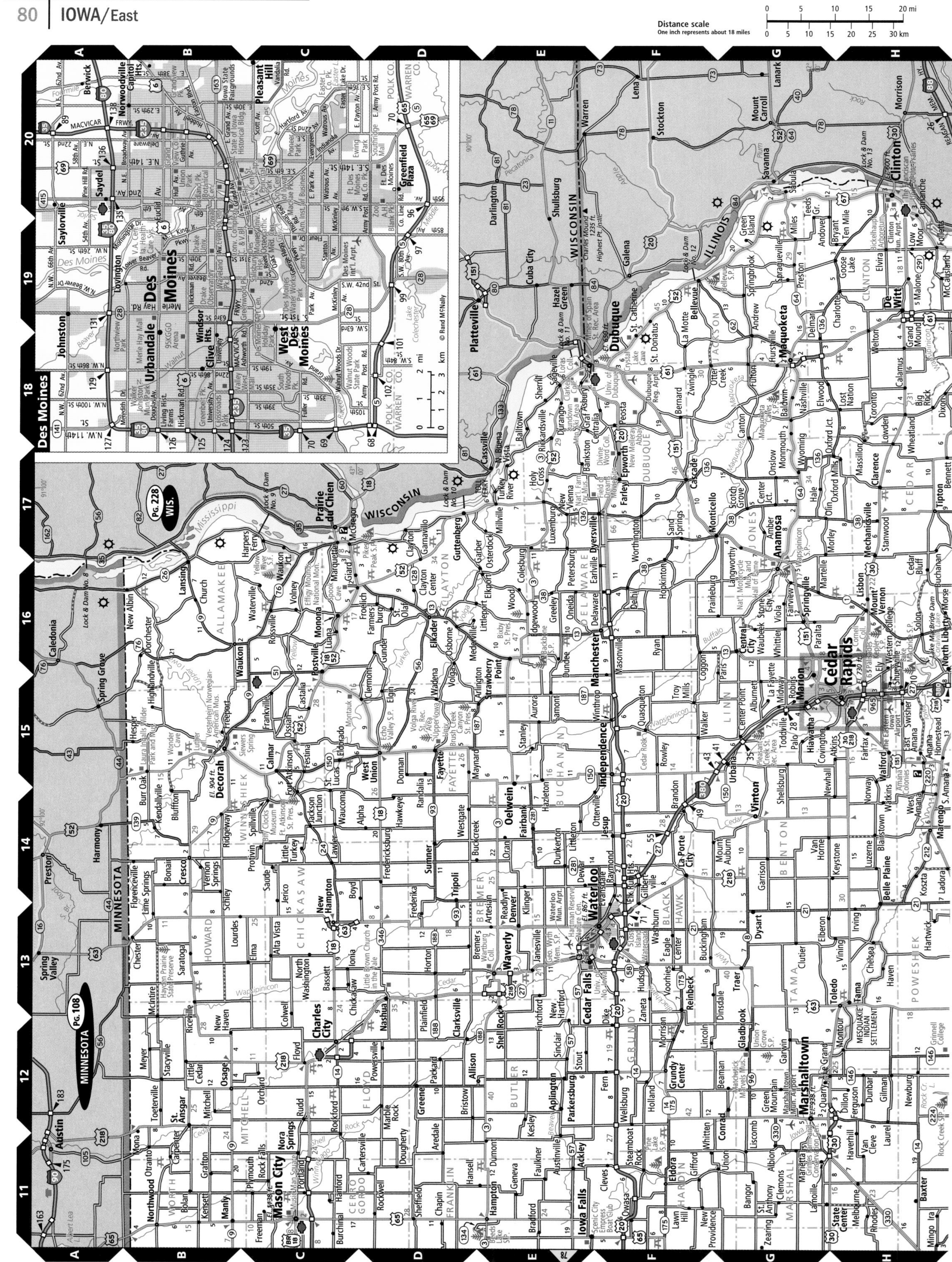
Des Moines
West Des Moines
Urbandale
Johnston
Clive
Windsor Hts.
Saylorville
Pleasant Hill
Norwoodville
MINNESOTA
WISCONSIN
ILLINOIS
Mississippi
Austin
Mason City
Charles City
Decorah
Waukon
Prairie du Chien
Dubuque
Cedar Rapids
Waterloo
Cedar Falls
Marshalltown
Independence
Manchester
Maquoketa
Clinton
Oelwein
Iowa Falls
Platteville
PG. 108
PG. 228 WIS.
© Rand McNally

How to determine distance

Mileages in red between red arrowheads; in black, between intersections.

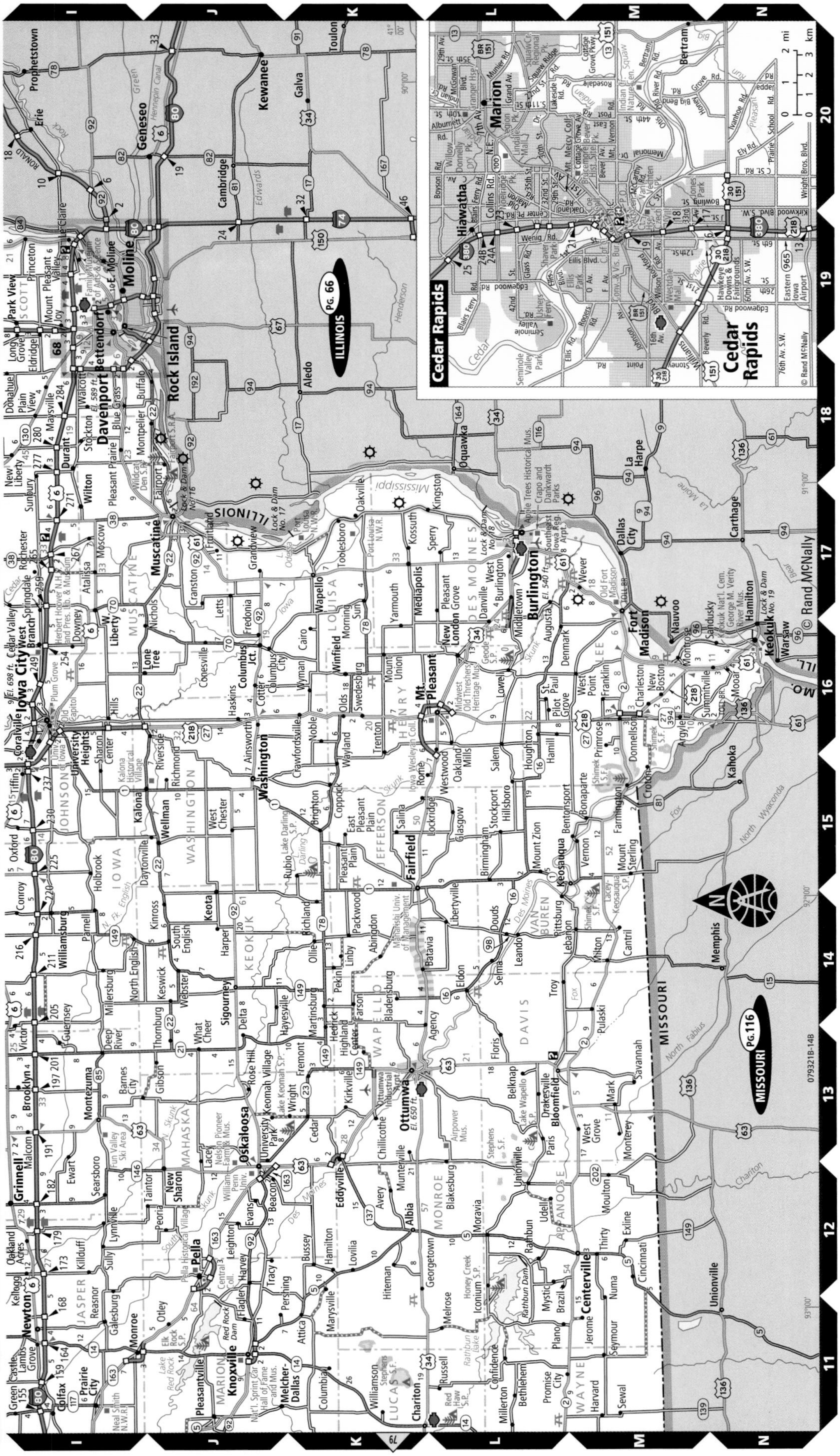

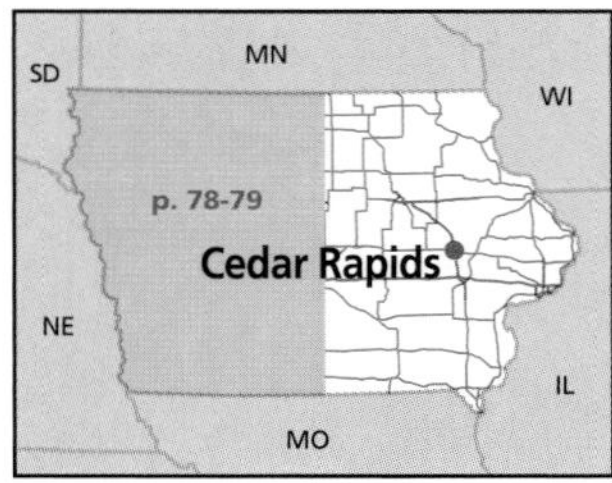
MN
SD
WI
p. 78-79
Cedar Rapids
NE
IL
MO

SYMBOLS

- Featured ride
- Scenic route
- Long-term construction
- Harley-Davidson dealership

CITY-TO-CITY MILEAGE

	BURLINGTON	CEDAR RAPIDS	COUNCIL BLUFFS	DAVENPORT	DES MOINES	DUBUQUE	SIOUX CITY	WATERLOO
Ames	208	106	162	190	33	187	176	99
Burlington		100	314	79	185	151	386	158
Cedar Rapids	100		256	82	127	72	328	58
Council Bluffs	314	256		296	127	329	95	237
Davenport	79	82	296		167	70	368	140
Decorah	210	110	337	175	208	105	309	79
Des Moines	185	127	127	167		200	199	108
Dubuque	151	72	329	70	200		325	93
Fort Dodge	273	174	158	255	98	209	123	114
Iowa City	77	26	240	57	111	85	312	84
Keokuk	42	118	332	121	203	191	404	176
Mason City	239	139	250	221	121	174	213	81
Ottumwa	77	113	217	129	90	186	289	131

HARLEY-DAVIDSON DEALERSHIPS

Heartland Harley-Davidson, L-17
155 S Roosevelt Ave. **Burlington**
(319) 754-1100
Lat N 40.809 **Lon** W 91.141

Metro Harley-Davidson, H-15
2415 Westdale Dr. SW **Cedar Rapids**
(319) 362-9496
Lat N 41.955 **Lon** W 91.723

C & C Harley-Davidson, K-11
130 E Lincoln Ave. **Chariton**
(641) 774-7400
Lat N 41.004 **Lon** W 93.292

Cedar River Harley-Davidson Shop, C-12
1750 Cedar View Rd. **Charles City**
(641) 228-2192
Lat N 43.097 **Lon** W 92.719

Clinton Harley-Davidson, H-20
2519 Lincolnway **Clinton**
(563) 242-1901
Lat N 41.816 **Lon** W 90.247

Hawkeye Harley-Davidson, I-15
2812 Commerce Dr. **Coralville**
(319) 545-7495
Lat N 41.696 **Lon** W 91.614

Wiebler's Quad Cities Harley-Davidson, I-19
5320 Corporate Park Dr. **Davenport**
(563) 355-6437
Lat N 41.575 **Lon** W 90.517

Wilwert's Harley-Davidson Sales, E-18
145 N Crescent Ridge **Dubuque**
(563) 557-8040
Lat N 42.488 **Lon** W 90.718

Harley-Davidson of Mason City, C-11
706 S Federal Ave. **Mason City**
(641) 423-6007
Lat N 43.145 **Lon** W 93.201

Lentner Cycle Company, K-13
2021 Albia Rd. **Ottumwa**
(641) 682-0493
Lat N 41.009 **Lon** W 92.459

Silver Eagle Harley-Davidson, F-13
4022 Sergeant Rd. **Waterloo**
(319) 235-6505
Lat N 42.469 **Lon** W 92.395

Waukon Harley-Davidson, B-16
208 Hwy. 9 SW **Waukon**
(563) 568-3471
Lat N 43.241 **Lon** W 91.577

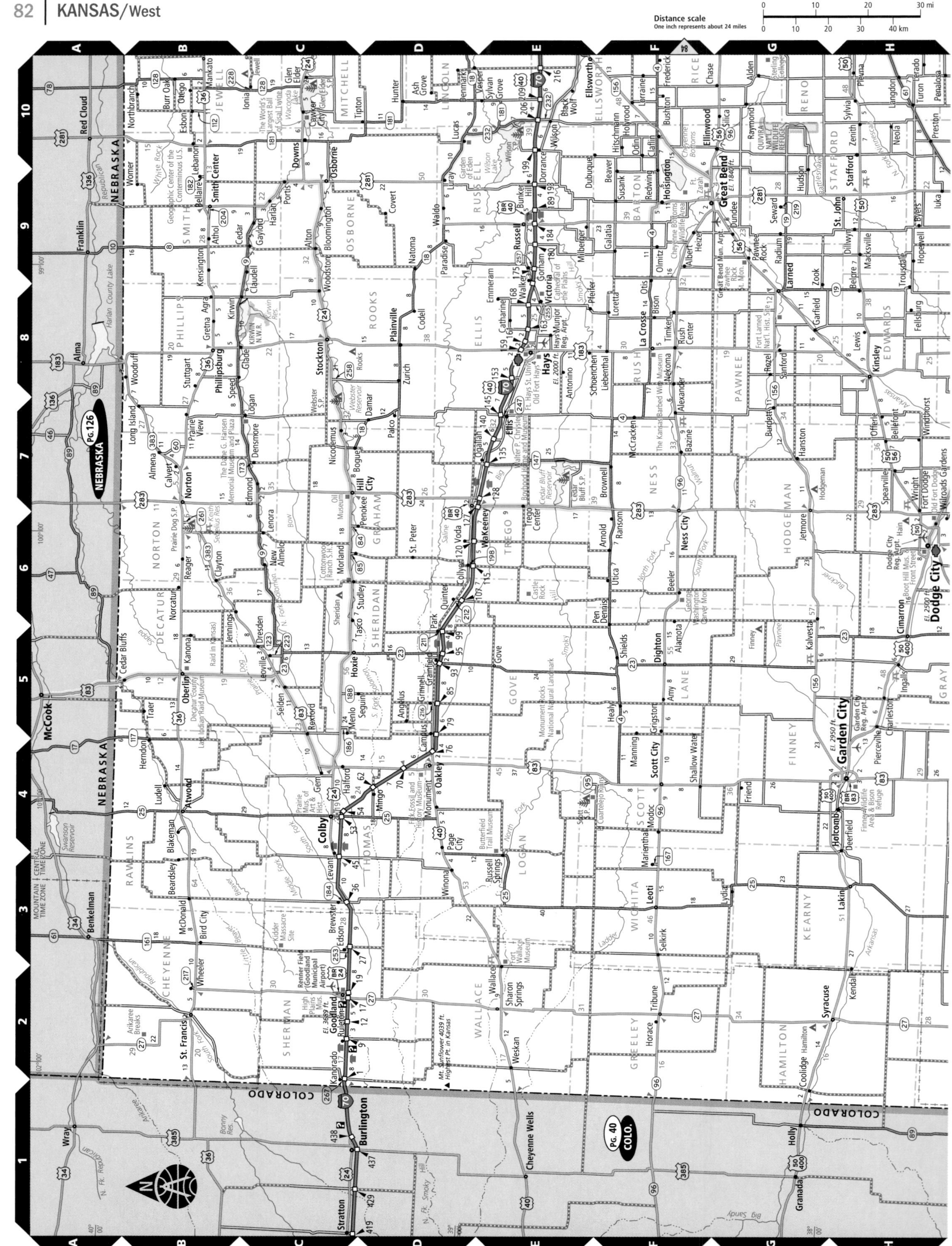
Distance scale
One inch represents about 24 miles
0 10 20 30 mi
0 10 20 30 40 km
NEBRASKA
COLORADO
PG. 126 NEBRASKA
PG. 40 COLO.
MOUNTAIN TIME ZONE
CENTRAL TIME ZONE
CHEYENNE
RAWLINS
DECATUR
NORTON
PHILLIPS
SMITH
JEWELL
SHERMAN
THOMAS
SHERIDAN
GRAHAM
ROOKS
OSBORNE
MITCHELL
LINCOLN
RUSSELL
ELLIS
TREGO
GOVE
LOGAN
WALLACE
GREELEY
WICHITA
SCOTT
LANE
NESS
RUSH
BARTON
ELLSWORTH
RICE
PAWNEE
STAFFORD
RENO
EDWARDS
HODGEMAN
FINNEY
KEARNY
HAMILTON
GRAY

How to determine distance

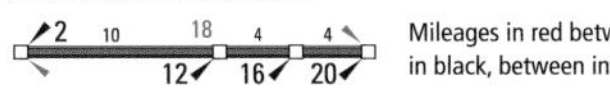

2 10 18 4 4
12 16 20

Mileages in red between red arrowheads; in black, between intersections.

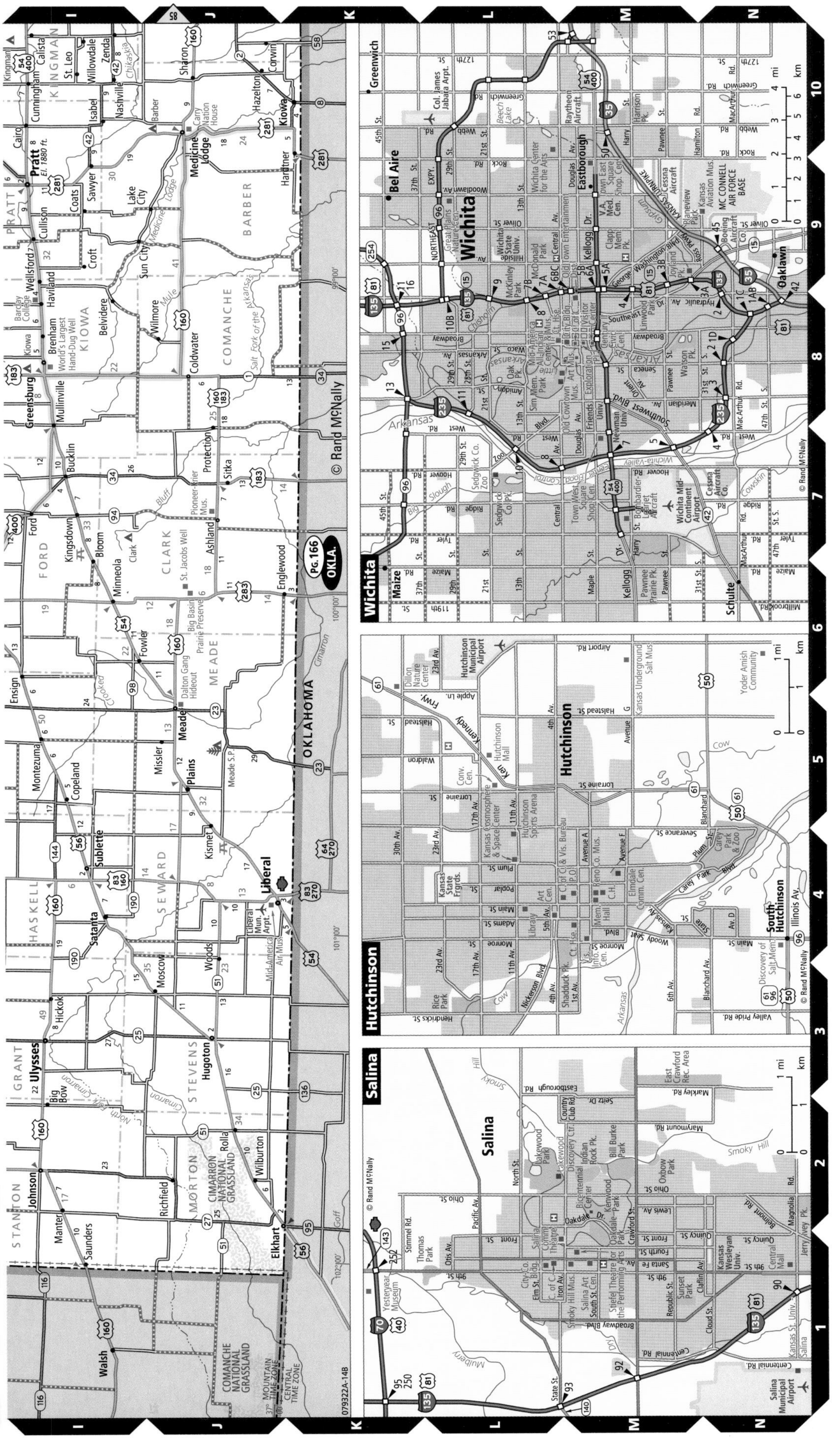

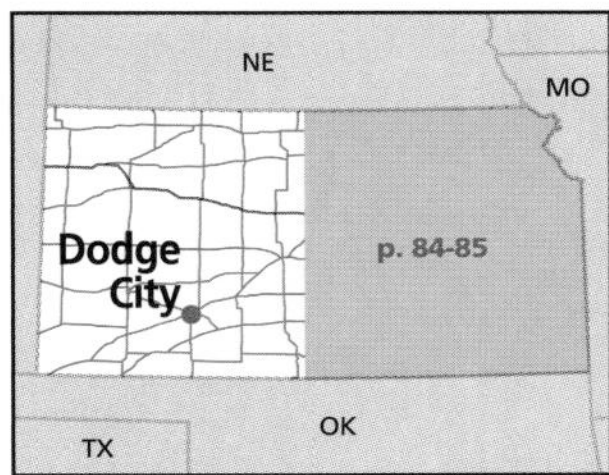

NE
MO
Dodge City
p. 84-85
TX
OK

SYMBOLS

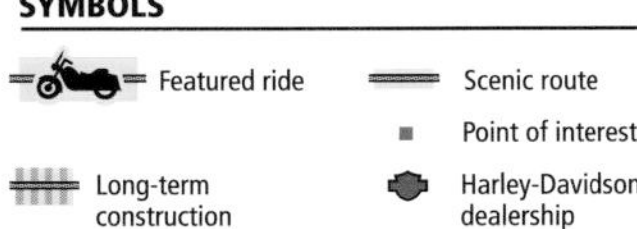

Featured ride
Scenic route
Point of interest
Long-term construction
Harley-Davidson dealership

KANSAS MOTORCYCLE LAWS

Helmet use:
Required under age 18

Riding two abreast:
Yes. See state law for specifics

Eye protection:
Required unless equipped with windscreen

Speed limit:
Primary roads: 70 mph
Secondary roads: 70 mph

KANSAS RESOURCES

Road conditions or construction:
511
(800) 585-7623
511.ksdot.org

Highway Emergency Numbers:
911 or *47

Tourism:
(800) 252-6727
www.travelks.com

State motor vehicle information:
(785) 296-3963
www.ksrevenue.org/vehicle.htm

HARLEY-DAVIDSON DEALERSHIPS

Dodge City Harley-Davidson, H-6
1312 S Second Ave. **Dodge City**
(620) 227-6351
Lat N 37.73 **Lon** W 100.019

Doerfler's Harley-Davidson, E-8
1100 E 43rd St. **Hays**
(785) 625-2022
Lat N 38.901 **Lon** W 99.342

Liberal Harley-Davidson, J-4
1009 S Kansas Ave. **Liberal**
(620) 624-5588
Lat N 37.024 **Lon** W 100.922

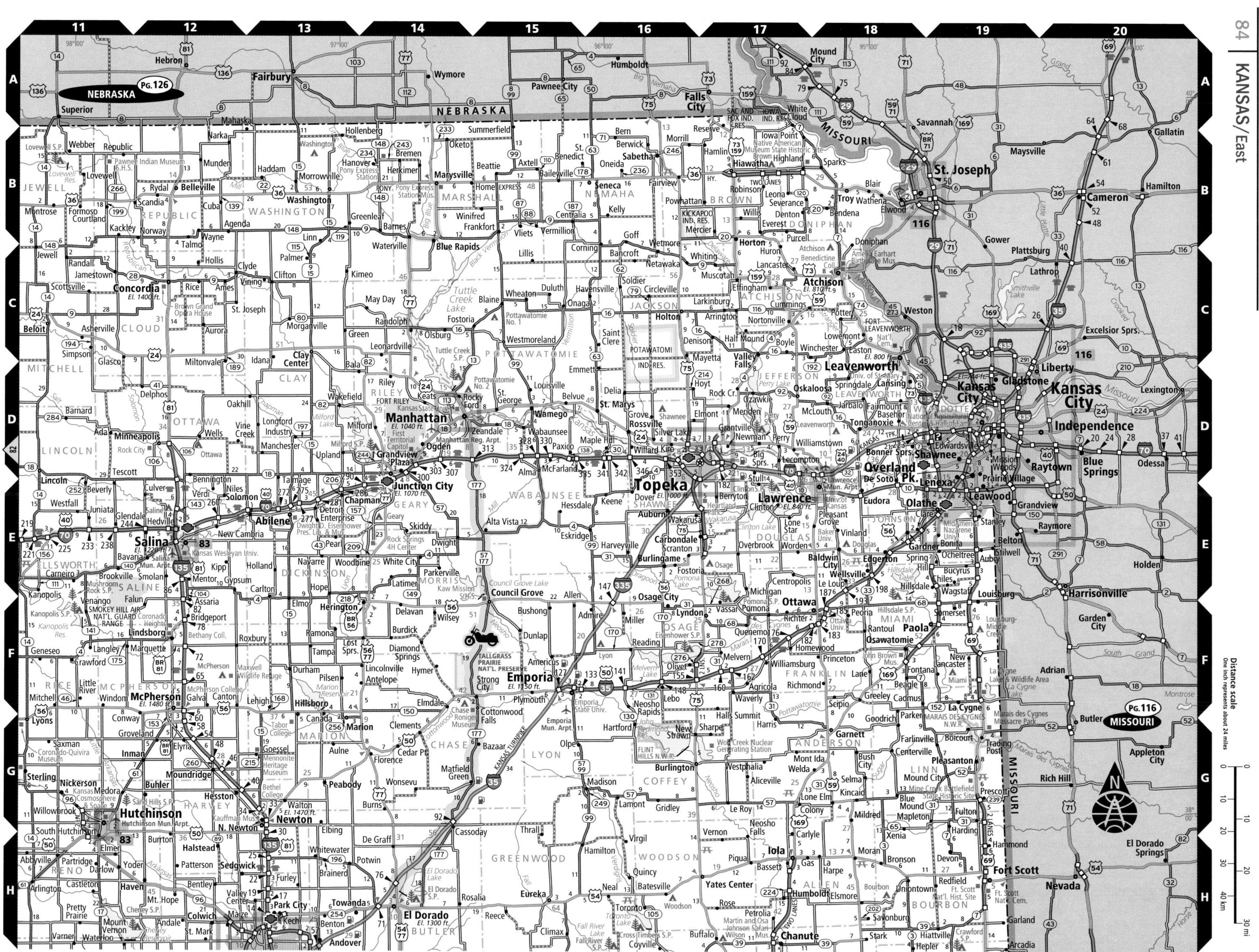
Distance scale
One inch represents about 24 miles
0 10 20 30 mi
0 10 20 30 40 km
NEBRASKA
MISSOURI
PG. 126 NEBRASKA
PG. 116 MISSOURI
KANSAS TURNPIKE
Kansas City
Topeka
Lawrence
Manhattan
Salina
Emporia
Hutchinson
Leavenworth
Olathe
Overland Pk.
Junction City
Abilene
McPherson
Newton
El Dorado
St. Joseph
Independence
Ottawa
Atchison

How to determine distance

Mileages in red between red arrowheads; in black, between intersections.

NE
MO
p. 82-83
Wichita
TX
OK

SYMBOLS

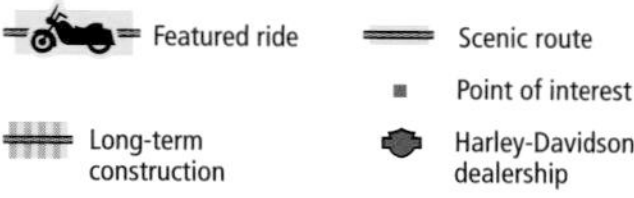
Featured ride
Scenic route
Point of interest
Long-term construction
Harley-Davidson dealership

For Kansas ride, see page R15.

CITY-TO-CITY MILEAGE

	DODGE CITY	GOODLAND	HUTCHINSON	JOPLIN, MO	KANSAS CITY	SALINA	TOPEKA	WICHITA
Arkansas City	211	385	120	157	225	153	177	61
Atchison	328	398	235	196	54	162	52	192
Coffeyville	300	459	194	68	171	227	158	138
Dodge City		193	125	345	338	166	277	154
Emporia	239	349	109	175	103	117	61	85
Fort Scott	306	481	205	59	89	245	134	152
Goodland	193		268	512	408	236	347	324
Great Bend	85	207	63	307	253	81	192	119
Hays	104	145	127	371	267	95	206	183
Hutchinson	125	268		247	212	73	184	59
Joplin, MO	345	512	247		148	280	193	191
Kansas City	338	408	212	148		172	61	188
Liberal	83	208	192	434	401	250	353	213
Manhattan	231	301	138	251	119	65	58	129
Oakley	134	59	211	455	351	179	290	267
Salina	166	236	73	280	172		111	92
Topeka	277	347	184	193	61	111		140
Wichita	154	324	59	191	188	92	140	

HARLEY-DAVIDSON DEALERSHIPS

City Cycle Sales, E-14
1021 Golden Belt Blvd. **Junction City**
(785) 238-3411
Lat N 39.002 **Lon** W 96.85

Central Harley-Davidson South, E-19
725 N Rawhide Rd. **Olathe**
(913) 764-7433
Lat N 38.891 **Lon** W 94.79

Harley-Davidson of Salina, E-12
2200 N Ohio St. **Salina**
(785) 823-3767
Lat N 38.878 **Lon** W 97.594

Central Harley-Davidson Shop, D-19
6801 Hedge Lane Terrace **Shawnee**
(913) 422-3400
Lat N 39.007 **Lon** W 94.859

Topeka Harley-Davidson, D-17
2047 SW Topeka Blvd. **Topeka**
(785) 234-6174
Lat N 39.031 **Lon** W 95.683

Alef's Harley-Davidson, H-13
5427 N Chuzy Dr. **Wichita**
(316) 721-3500
Lat N 37.784 **Lon** W 97.324

Lawrence

Topeka

Manhattan

Distance scale
One inch represents about 18 miles
0 5 10 15 20 mi
0 5 10 15 20 25 30 km

Owensboro
Bowling Green
Louisville
Western Kentucky
Jeffersonville
New Albany
Clarksville
Jeffersontown
Paducah
Mayfield
Cape Girardeau
Evansville
PG. 66 ILL.
PG. 116 MISSOURI
PG. 190 TENN.
PG. 74 INDIANA
For continuation see main map
© Rand McNally

How to determine distance

Mileages in red between red arrowheads; in black, between intersections.

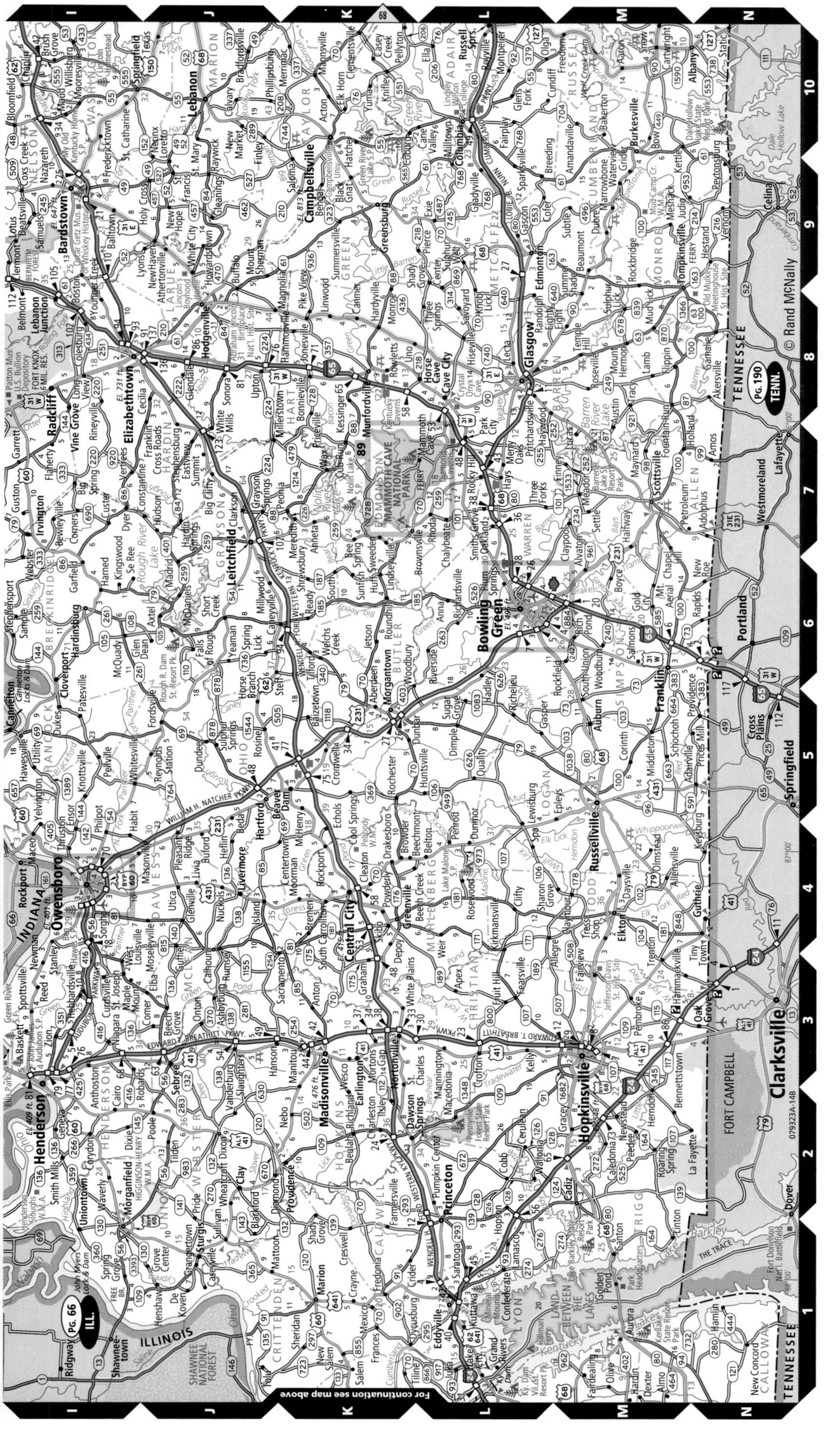

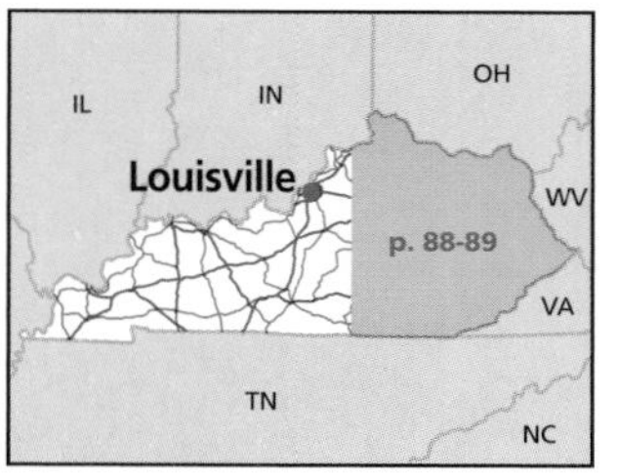

p. 88-89

SYMBOLS

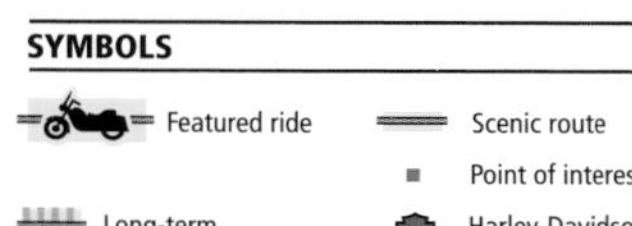
Featured ride
Scenic route
Point of interest
Long-term construction
Harley-Davidson dealership

KENTUCKY MOTORCYCLE LAWS

Helmet use:
Required for novice riders, those under age 21, and for instructional permit holders

Riding two abreast:
No reference in administrative code or statutes

Eye protection:
Required by law

Speed limit:
Primary roads: 65 mph
Secondary roads: 65 mph

KENTUCKY RESOURCES

Road conditions or construction:
511 (Cincinnati/northern Kentucky area)
(866) 737-3767
www.ky.gov

Highway Emergency Numbers:
911 or (800) 222-5555

Tourism:
(800) 225-8747
(502) 564-4930
www.kentuckytourism.com

State motor vehicle information
(502) 564-6800
www.kytc.state.ky.us/drlic

HARLEY-DAVIDSON DEALERSHIPS

Harley-Davidson Bowling Green, L-6
251 Cumberland Trace Rd. **Bowling Green**
(270) 846-4488
Lat N 36.933 **Lon** W 86.415

Louisville Harley-Davidson, G-8
1700 Arthur St. **Louisville**
(502) 634-1340
Lat N 38.222 **Lon** W 85.751

Bluegrass Harley-Davidson, G-9
11701 Gateworth Way **Louisville**
(502) 244-8095
Lat N 38.225 **Lon** W 85.542

Sills Harley-Davidson, E-3
1212 Brown St. **Paducah**
(270) 443-5636
Lat N 37.065 **Lon** W 88.597

For continuation see map above

Distance scale
One inch represents about 18 miles
0 5 10 15 20 mi
0 5 10 15 20 25 30 km

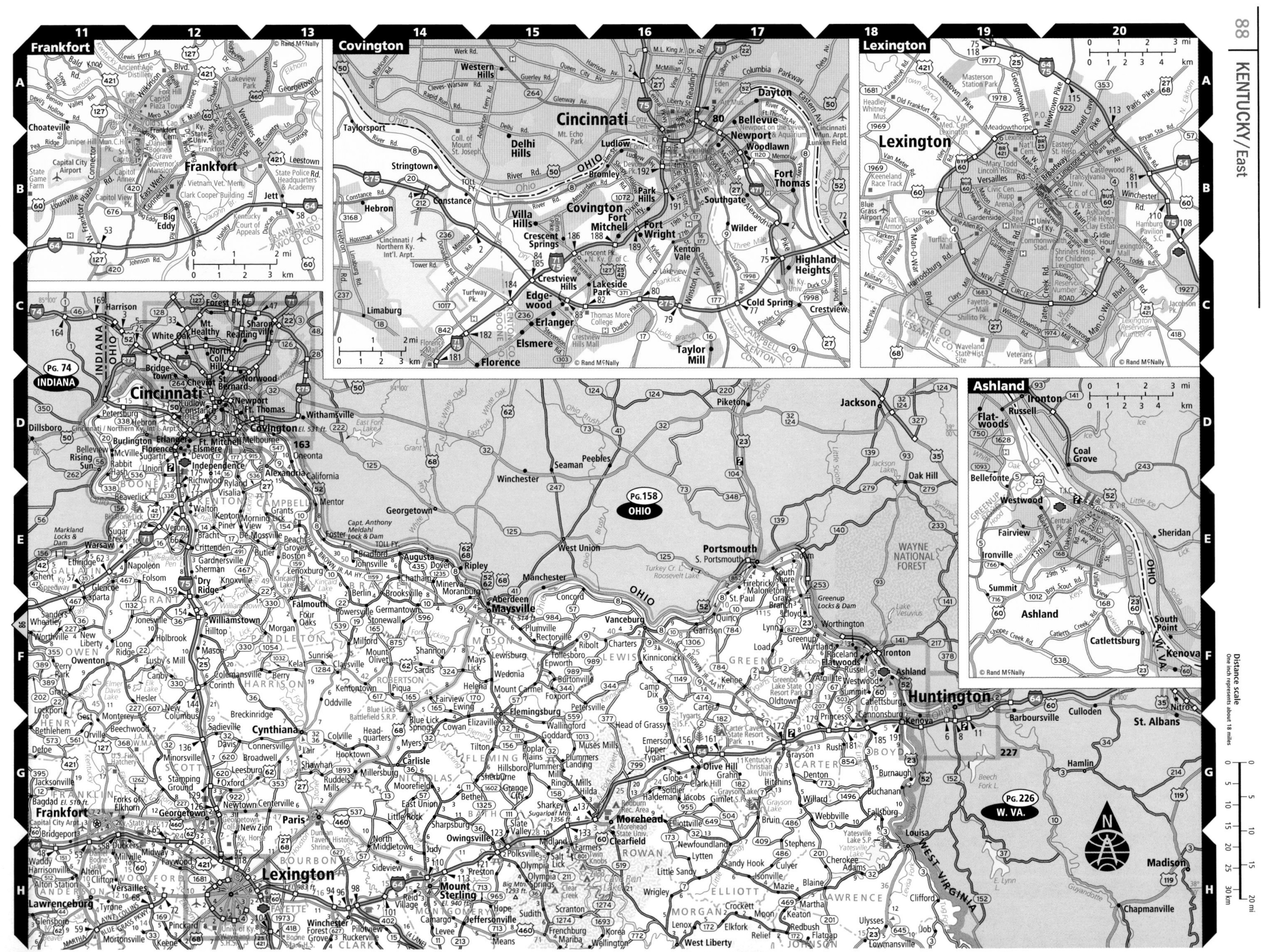

Frankfort
Covington
Lexington
Ashland
Cincinnati
Huntington
Maysville
Portsmouth
Morehead
Paris
Georgetown
Winchester
Mount Sterling
Flemingsburg
Cynthiana
Carlisle
Grayson
Olive Hill
Vanceburg
Ironton
Jackson
Peebles
Ripley
Aberdeen
Manchester
West Union
Piketon
Lawrenceburg
Versailles
Owenton
Williamstown
Dry Ridge
Falmouth
Alexandria
Independence
Florence
Burlington
Erlanger
Newport
Warsaw
Rising Sun
Dillsboro
Louisa
St. Albans
Madison
Hamlin
Barboursville
Culloden
Chapmanville
WAYNE NATIONAL FOREST
WEST VIRGINIA
OHIO
INDIANA
PG. 158 OHIO
PG. 226 W. VA.
PG. 74 INDIANA
© Rand McNally

How to determine distance

Mileages in red between red arrowheads; in black, between intersections.

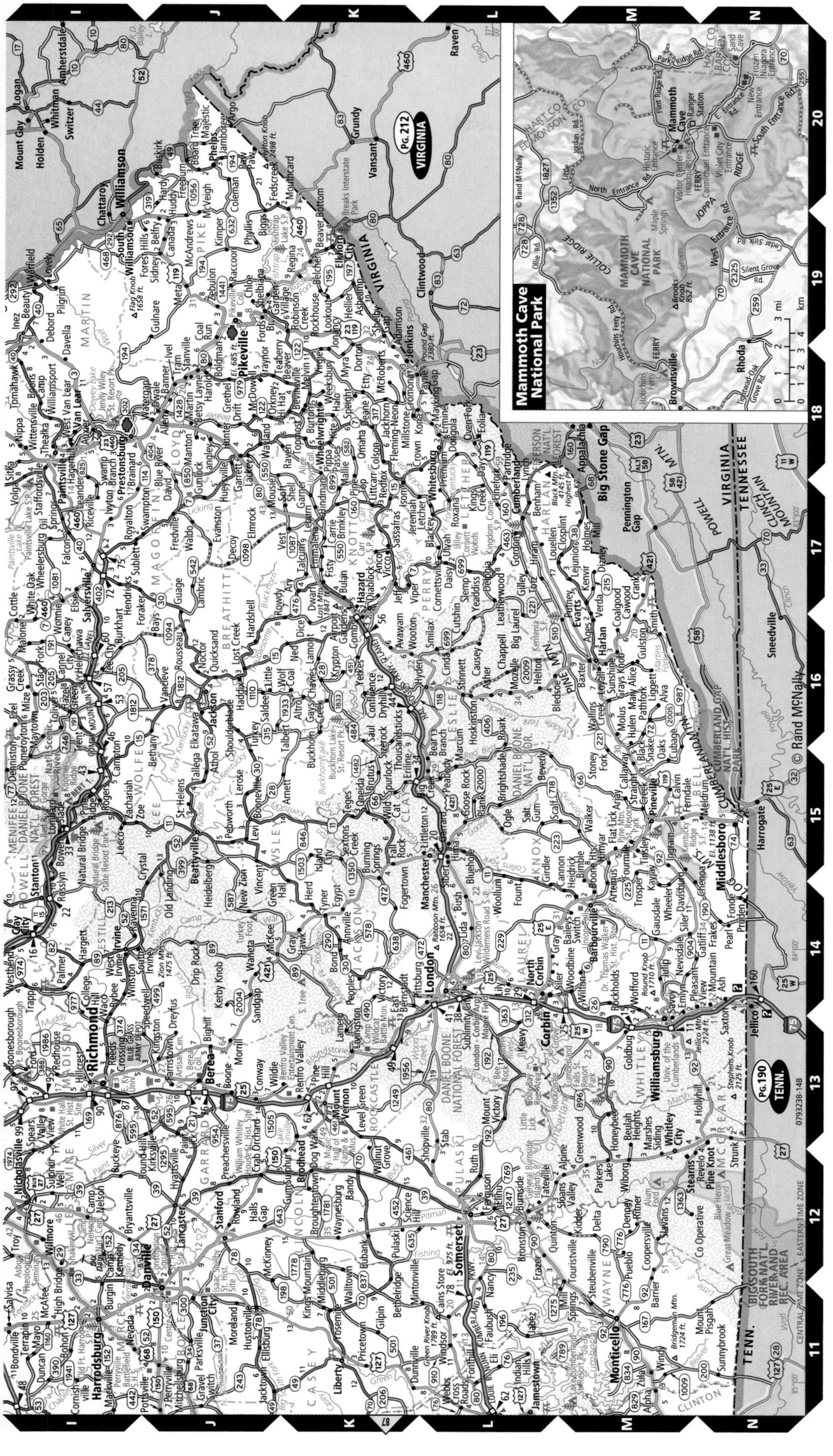

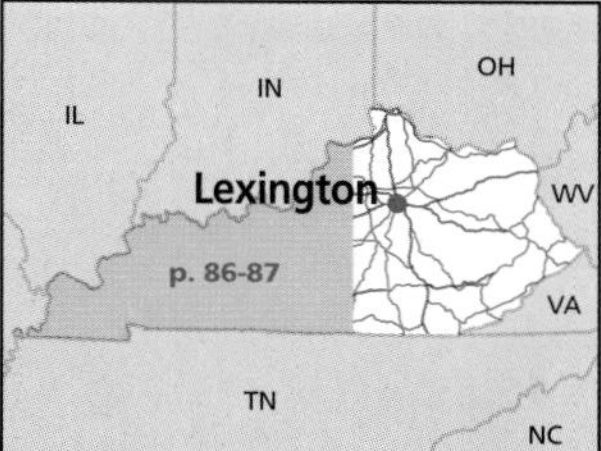
IL
IN
OH
Lexington
WV
p. 86-87
VA
TN
NC

SYMBOLS

- Featured ride
- Scenic route
- Point of interest
- Long-term construction
- Harley-Davidson dealership

CITY-TO-CITY MILEAGE

	ASHLAND	BOWLING GREEN	COVINGTON	HOPKINSVILLE	LEXINGTON	LOUISVILLE	OWENSBORO	PADUCAH
Ashland		278	135	334	123	197	303	385
Bardstown	183	95	137	151	60	40	120	202
Bowling Green	278		218	63	155	116	71	153
Cave City	250	30	190	97	127	88	108	190
Covington	135	218		274	82	102	208	325
Elizabethtown	209	71	147	127	86	45	96	178
Frankfort	146	145	89	201	23	52	170	252
Hopkinsville	334	63	274		211	172	99	76
Huntington, WV	18	282	139	338	127	201	307	389
Lexington	123	155	82	211		74	180	262
London	176	145	154	212	78	152	223	305
Louisville	197	116	102	172	74		106	223
Mayfield	394	162	334	85	271	232	159	24
Maysville	80	227	53	283	66	135	252	334
Owensboro	303	71	208	99	180	106		150
Paducah	385	153	325	76	262	223	150	
Pikeville	100	263	218	353	142	216	322	404
Somerset	179	111	157	178	81	134	189	271

HARLEY-DAVIDSON DEALERSHIPS

Benjy's Harley-Davidson, F-18
500 Winchester Ave. **Ashland**
(606) 326-9074
Lat N 38.485 **Lon** W 82.652

Thoroughbred Harley-Davidson Shop, D-12
8519 Dixie Hwy. **Florence**
(859) 282-2111
Lat N 38.96 **Lon** W 84.619

Harley-Davidson of Lexington, H-13
2073 Bryant Rd. **Lexington**
(859) 253-2461
Lat N 38.016 **Lon** W 84.41

Harley-Davidson of Pikeville, J-19
114 Harley Dr. **Pikeville**
(606) 433-0911
Lat N 37.487 **Lon** W 82.543

Prestonsburg Harley-Davidson, I-18
631 S Lake Dr. **Prestonsburg**
(606) 886-6076
Lat N 37.669 **Lon** W 82.758

Distance scale
One inch represents about 31 miles
0 5 10 15 20 25 30 mi
0 10 20 30 40 km

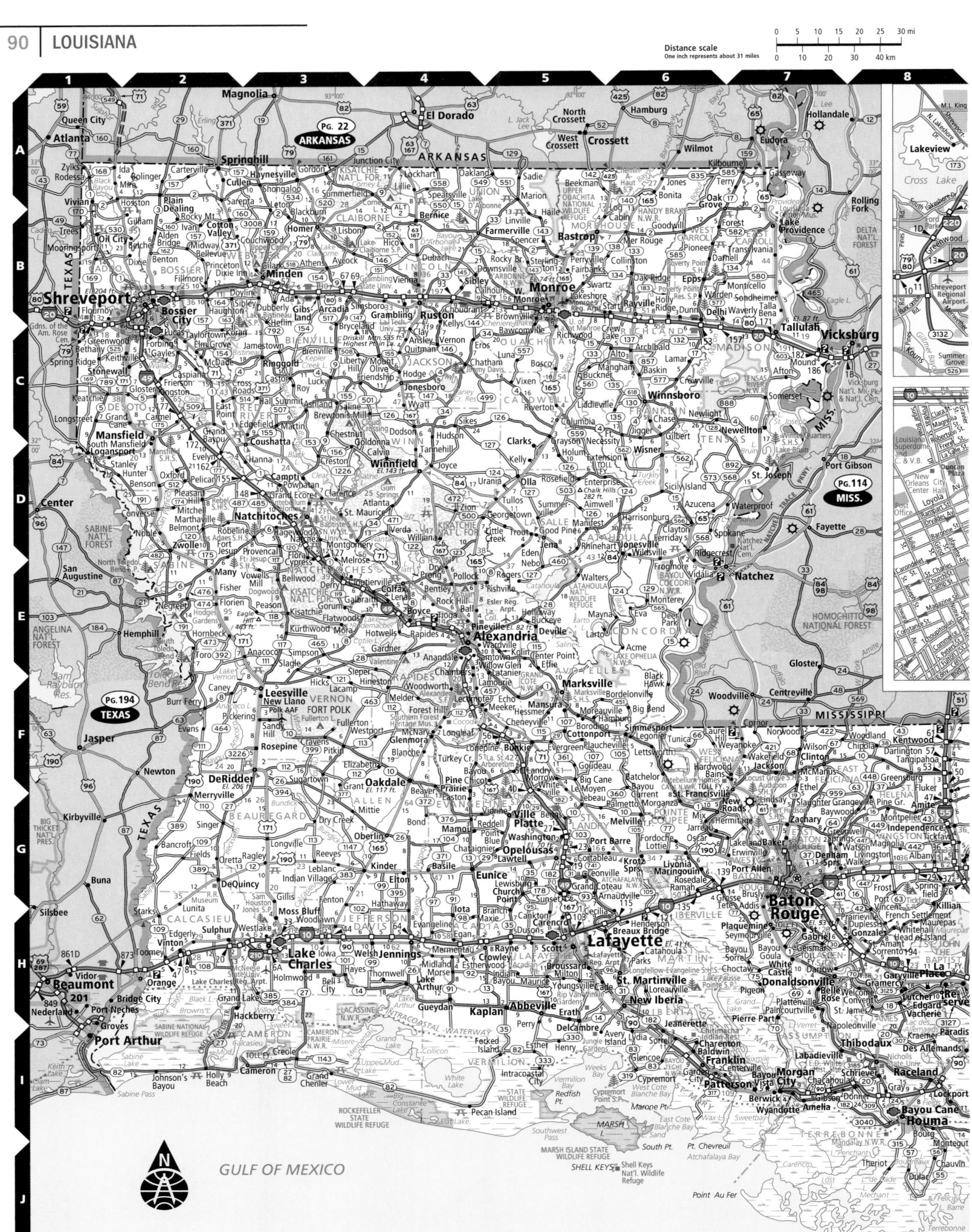

ARKANSAS
PG. 22 ARKANSAS
MISSISSIPPI
PG. 114 MISS.
TEXAS
PG. 194 TEXAS
Shreveport
Bossier City
Monroe
Alexandria
Lafayette
Baton Rouge
Lake Charles
Natchitoches
Ruston
Minden
Vicksburg
Natchez
Beaumont
Port Arthur
Houma
New Iberia
Opelousas
Leesville
DeRidder
Jennings
Crowley
Thibodaux
GULF OF MEXICO
SABINE NAT'L. FOREST
ANGELINA NAT'L. FOREST
HOMOCHITTO NATIONAL FOREST
KISATCHIE NAT'L. FOR.
FORT POLK
ROCKEFELLER STATE WILDLIFE REFUGE
MARSH ISLAND STATE WILDLIFE REFUGE
SABINE NATIONAL WILDLIFE REFUGE
Atchafalaya Bay
Point Au Fer
079324-14B

How to determine distance

Mileages in red between red arrowheads; in black, between intersections.

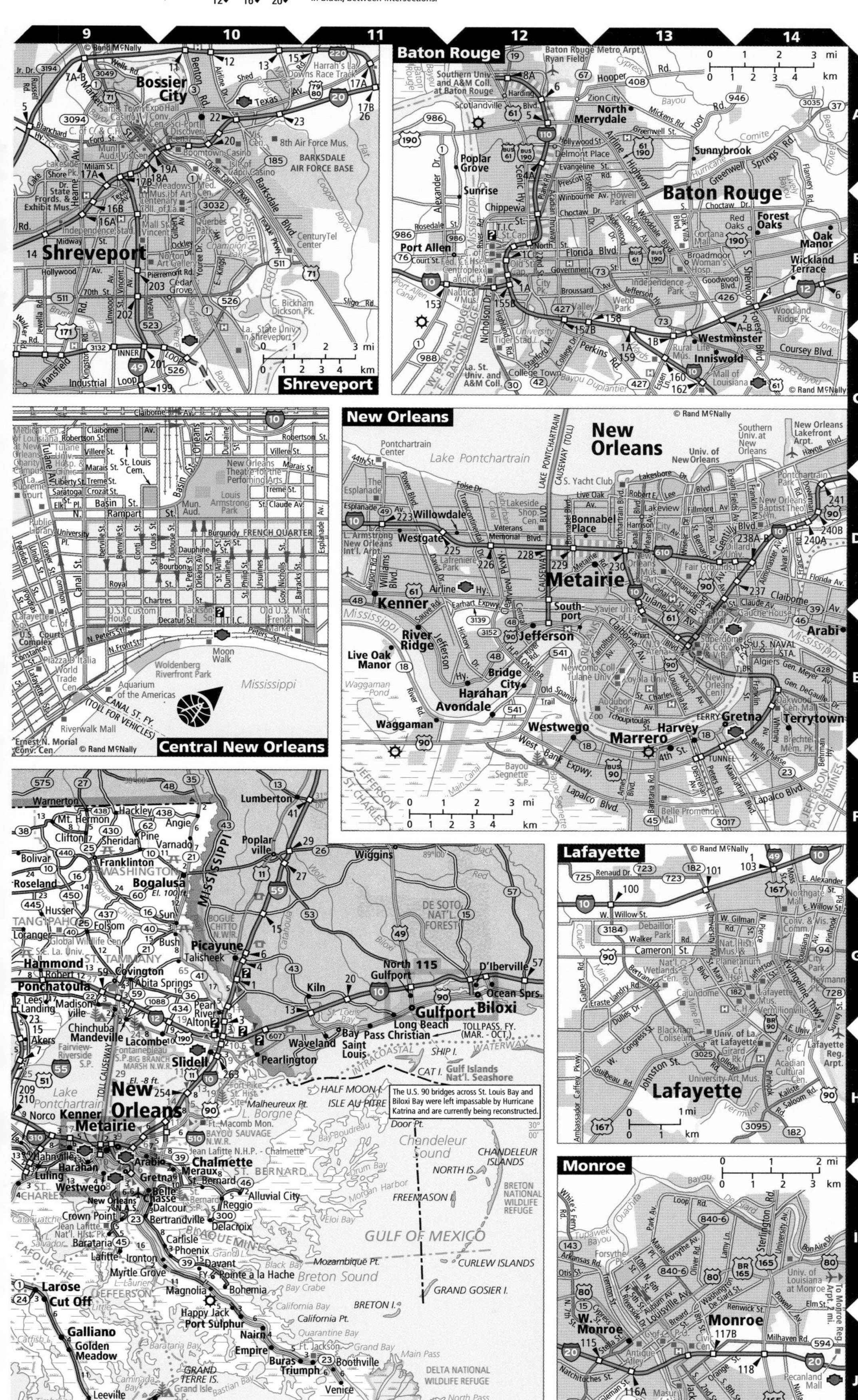
Baton Rouge
Shreveport
Bossier City
Central New Orleans
New Orleans
Metairie
Kenner
Lafayette
Monroe
Gulfport
Biloxi
Slidell
Hammond
Gulf of Mexico
Lake Pontchartrain
© Rand McNally

SYMBOLS

- Featured ride
- Scenic route
- Long-term construction
- Harley-Davidson dealership

LOUISIANA MOTORCYCLE LAWS

Helmet use: Required

Riding two abreast:
Yes. See state law for specifics

Eye protection:
Required unless equipped with windscreen

Speed limit:
Primary roads: 70 mph; Secondary roads: 70 mph

LOUISIANA RESOURCES

Road conditions or construction:
www.511la.org

Highway Emergency Numbers:
911

Tourism:
(800) 334-8626
www.louisianatravel.com

State motor vehicle information:
(877) DMV-LINE
http://omv.dps.state.la.us

HARLEY-DAVIDSON DEALERSHIPS

Renegade Harley-Davidson, E-4
2030 N Mall Dr. **Alexandria**
(318) 448-1509
Lat N 31.277 **Lon** W 92.456

Harley-Davidson of Baton Rouge, G-7
5853 Siegen Ln. **Baton Rouge**
(225) 292-9632
Lat N 30.397 **Lon** W 91.057

Bossier City Harley-Davidson Shop, B-2
3333 E Texas **Bossier City**
(318) 549-1571
Lat N 32.529 **Lon** W 93.695

The Harley-Davidson Shop of New Orleans, I-9
1208 Lafayette St. **Gretna**
(504) 362-4004
Lat N 29.911 **Lon** W 90.057

Mike Bruno's Bayou Country Harley-Davidson, I-8
1740 Martin Luther King Blvd. **Houma**
(985) 872-4380
Lat N 29.612 **Lon** W 90.754

Harley-Davidson of Lake Charles, H-3
2120 Broad St. **Lake Charles**
(337) 436-0022
Lat N 30.228 **Lon** W 93.19

Harley-Davidson of New Orleans, H-9
6015 Airline Dr. **Metarie**
(504) 736-9600
Lat N 29.977 **Lon** W 90.201

Bleu Bayou Harley-Davidson, B-5
6200 Frontage Rd. **Monroe**
(318) 343-1650
Lat N 32.493 **Lon** W 92.047

VooDoo Harley-Davidson, H-9
812 Decatur St. **New Orleans**
(504) 561-0263
Lat N 29.958 **Lon** W 90.062

Cajun Harley-Davidson, H-5
724 I-10 S Frontage Rd. **Scott**
(337) 289-3030
Lat N 30.249 **Lon** W 92.098

Shreveport Harley-Davidson, B-2
805 Brook Hollow Dr. **Shreveport**
(318) 798-1064
Lat N 32.418 **Lon** W 93.725

NorthShore Harley-Davidson, H-10
791 W I-10 Service Rd. **Slidell**
(985) 641-5100
Lat N 30.252 **Lon** W 89.762

Distance scale
One inch represents about 22 miles
0 5 10 15 20 mi
0 5 10 15 20 25 30 km

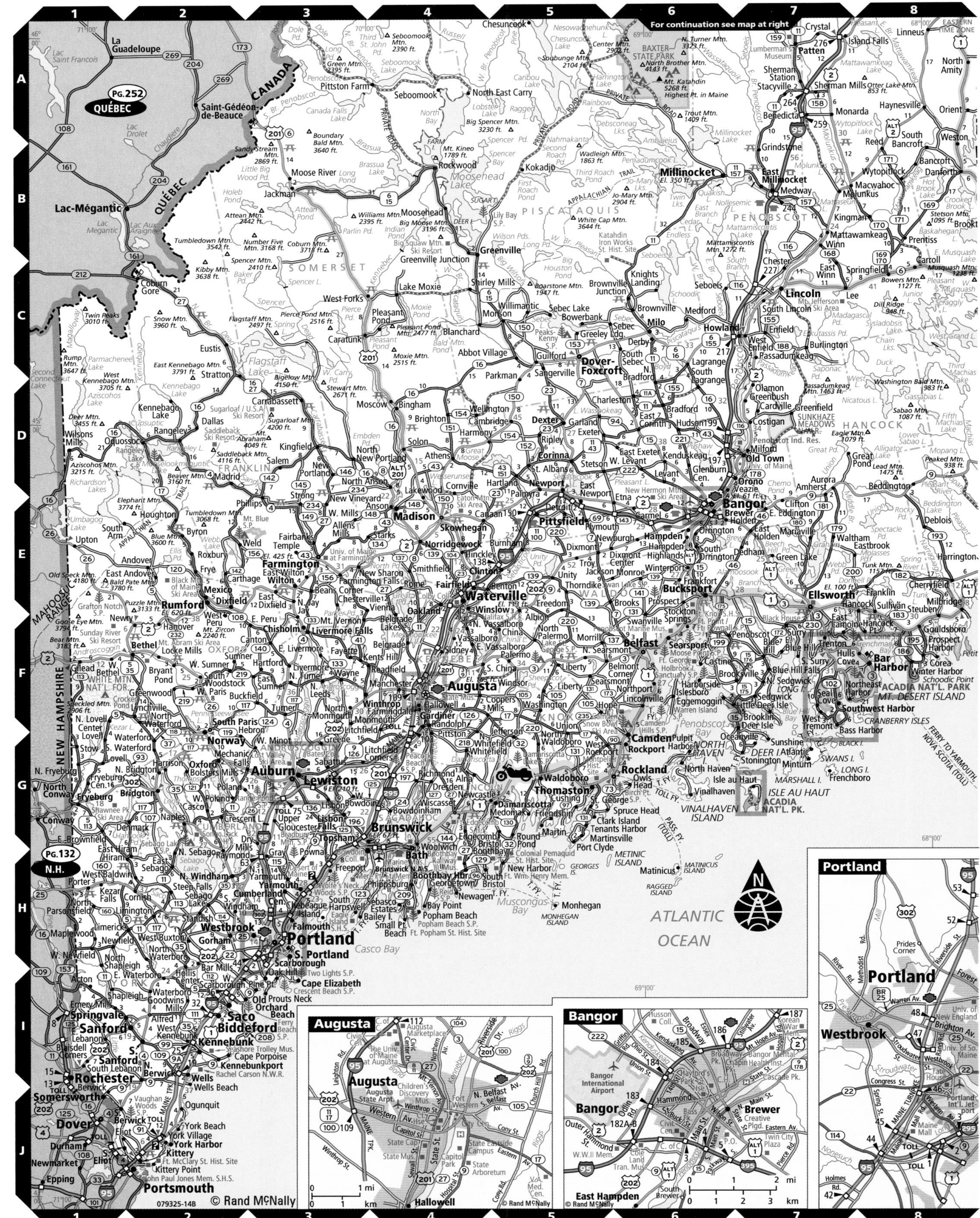
For continuation see map at right
PG.252 QUÉBEC
PG.132 N.H.
CANADA
QUÉBEC
NEW HAMPSHIRE
MAHOOSUC RANGE
ATLANTIC OCEAN
Casco Bay
Penobscot Bay
Muscongus Bay
Moosehead Lake
BAXTER STATE PARK
Mt. Katahdin 5268 ft. Highest Pt. in Maine
ACADIA NAT'L. PARK MT. DESERT ISLAND
ISLE AU HAUT ACADIA NAT'L. PK.
FERRY TO YARMOUTH, NOVA SCOTIA (TOLL)
PISCATAQUIS
PENOBSCOT
SOMERSET
FRANKLIN
HANCOCK
OXFORD
KENNEBEC
WALDO
KNOX
LINCOLN
CUMBERLAND
YORK
ANDROSCOGGIN
SAGADAHOC
Augusta
Portland
Bangor
Lewiston
Auburn
Waterville
Brunswick
Bath
Rockland
Camden
Belfast
Bucksport
Ellsworth
Bar Harbor
Millinocket
Greenville
Skowhegan
Farmington
Rumford
Saco
Biddeford
Sanford
Rochester
Dover
Portsmouth
Kittery
Westbrook
South Portland
Augusta
Bangor
Portland
Bangor International Airport
Brewer
East Hampden
Hallowell
Westbrook
079325-14B © Rand McNally
© Rand McNally
© Rand McNally
1 2 3 4 5 6 7 8
A B C D E F G H I J

How to determine distance

Mileages in red between red arrowheads; in black, between intersections.

Northern Maine
NEW BRUNSWICK PG.254
QUÉBEC PG.252
For continuation see main map
Lewiston / Auburn
Acadia National Park
BAY OF FUNDY
ATLANTIC OCEAN
MOUNT DESERT ISLAND
ACADIA NATIONAL PARK
Bar Harbor
Lewiston
Auburn
Falmouth
South Portland
Calais
St. Stephen
Edmundston
Presque Isle
Caribou
Houlton
© Rand McNally

SYMBOLS

- Featured ride
- Scenic route
- Point of interest
- Long-term construction
- Harley-Davidson dealership

For Maine ride, see page R16-17.

MAINE MOTORCYCLE LAWS

Helmet use:
Required under age 15 with learner's permit, or for 1 year after obtaining license, and for passenger when operator is required to wear helmet

Riding two abreast:
Yes. See state law for specifics

Eye protection:
Not required

Speed limit:
Primary roads: 65 mph
Secondary roads: 65 mph

MAINE RESOURCES

Road conditions or construction:
511
(866) 282-7578
(207) 624-3595
www.state.me.us/mdot/

Highway Emergency Numbers:
911

Tourism:
(888) 624-6345, (225) 342-8100
www.visitmaine.com

State motor vehicle information:
(207) 624-9000
www.state.me.us/sos/bmv

CITY-TO-CITY MILEAGE

	Bangor	East Millinocket	Eastport	Houlton	Portland	Portsmouth, NH	Rangeley	Waterville
Bangor		63	130	121	132	182	122	57
East Millinocket	63		119	60	193	243	183	118
Eastport	130	119		119	261	311	251	186
Houlton	121	60	119		251	301	241	176
Portland	132	193	261	251		50	120	75
Portsmouth, NH	182	243	311	301	50		168	125
Rangeley	122	183	251	241	120	168		77
Waterville	57	118	186	176	75	125	77	

HARLEY-DAVIDSON DEALERSHIPS

North Country Harley-Davidson, F-4
3099 N Belfast Ave. **Augusta**
(207) 622-7994
Lat N 44.327 **Lon** W 69.745

Central Maine Harley-Davidson Shop, E-6
570 Stillwater Ave. **Bangor**
(207) 947-6456
Lat N 44.83 **Lon** W 68.754

Plourdes Harley-Davidson, B-14
11 Laurette St. **Caribou**
(207) 496-3211
Lat N 46.868 **Lon** W 68.005

Central Maine Harley-Davidson, E-6
2387 Rte. 2 **Hermon (Bangor)**
(207) 848-5709
Lat N 44.803 **Lon** W 68.927

L-A Harley-Davidson, G-3
839 Main St. **Lewiston**
(207) 786-2822
Lat N 44.131 **Lon** W 70.198

Big Moose Harley-Davidson, H-3
375 Riverside St. **Portland**
(207) 797-6061
Lat N 43.688 **Lon** W 70.328

Distance scale
One inch represents about 13 miles
0 5 10 15 mi
0 5 10 15 20 km

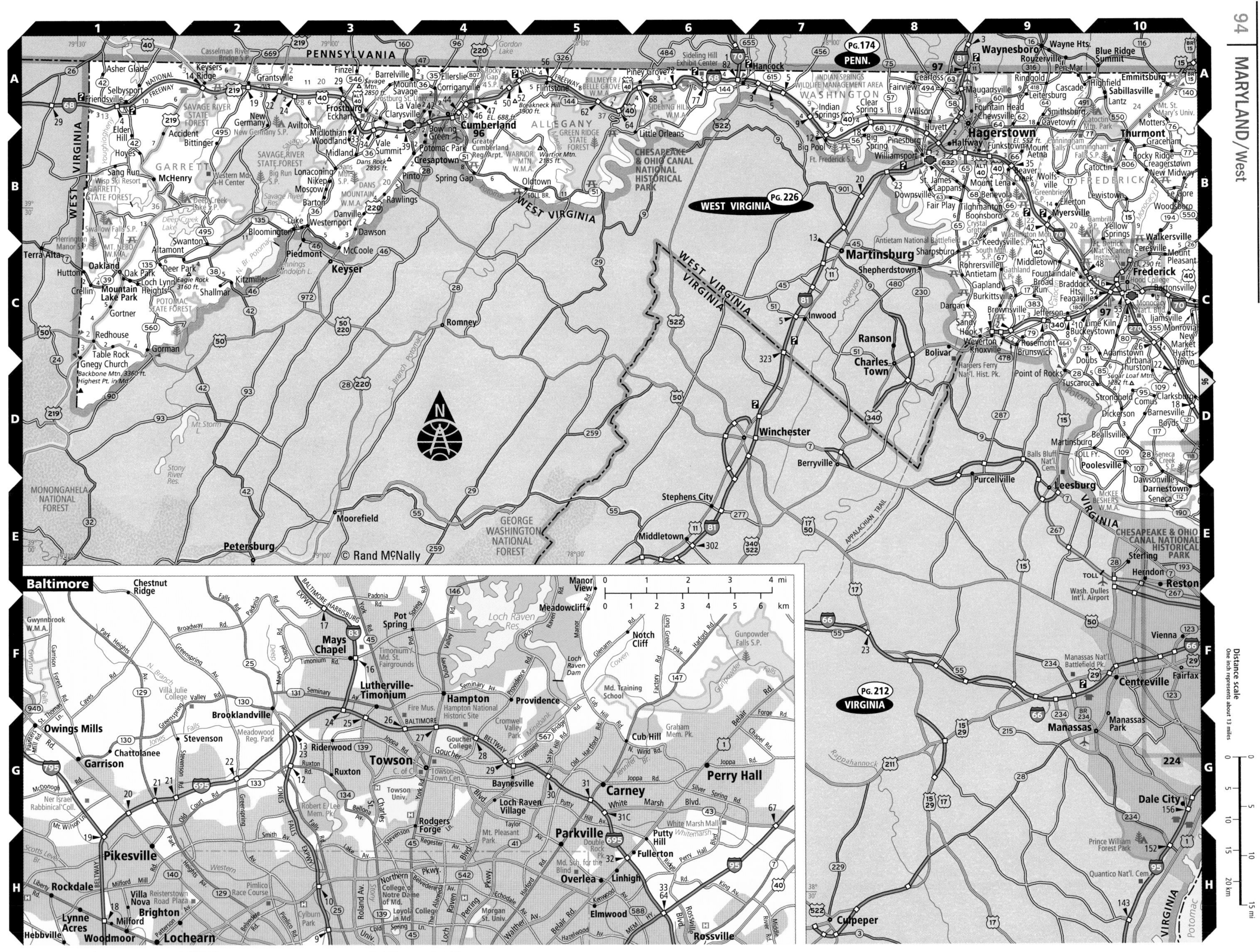

PENNSYLVANIA
WEST VIRGINIA
VIRGINIA
Pg. 174 PENN.
Pg. 226 WEST VIRGINIA
Pg. 212 VIRGINIA
Cumberland
Hagerstown
Frederick
Martinsburg
Winchester
Keyser
Oakland
Frostburg
Hancock
Leesburg
Manassas
Centreville
Culpeper
Romney
Petersburg
Moorefield
Baltimore
Towson
Pikesville
Parkville
Carney
Perry Hall
Lutherville-Timonium
Owings Mills
CHESAPEAKE & OHIO CANAL NATIONAL HISTORICAL PARK
GEORGE WASHINGTON NATIONAL FOREST
MONONGAHELA NATIONAL FOREST
APPALACHIAN TRAIL
© Rand McNally

How to determine distance

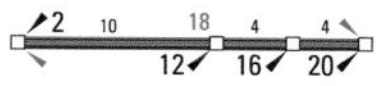

Mileages in red between red arrowheads; in black, between intersections.

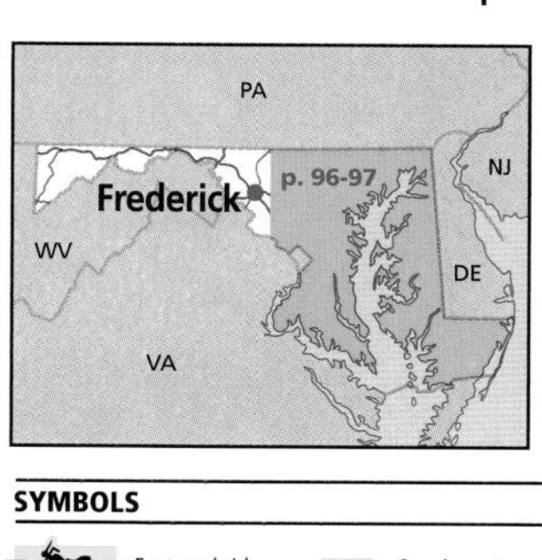
PA
NJ
Frederick
p. 96-97
WV
DE
VA

SYMBOLS

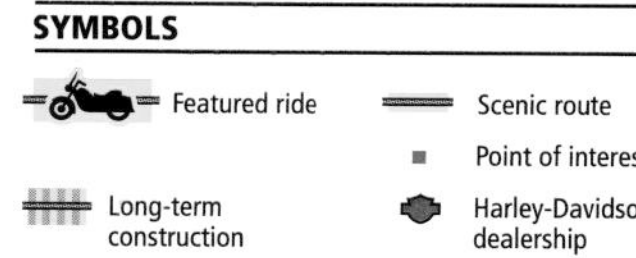
Featured ride
Scenic route
Point of interest
Long-term construction
Harley-Davidson dealership

MARYLAND MOTORCYCLE LAWS

Helmet use:
Required and reflectorization required

Riding two abreast:
Yes. See state law for specifics

Eye protection:
Required unless equipped with windscreen

Speed limit:
Primary roads: 65 mph
Secondary roads: 65 mph

MARYLAND RESOURCES

Road conditions or construction:
(800) 327-3125
(800) 541-9595
(410) 582-5650
www.chart.state.md.us

Highway Emergency Numbers:
911

Tourism:
(800) 634-7386
www.visitmaryland.org

State motor vehicle information:
(301) 729-4550
www.mva.state.md.us

HARLEY-DAVIDSON DEALERSHIPS

Harley-Davidson of Frederick, C-10
5722 Urbana Pike **Frederick**
(301) 694-8177
Lat N 39.389 **Lon** W 77.404

Highland Harley-Davidson Shop, A-4
1285 National Hwy. **La Vale**
(240) 362-0200
Lat N 39.637 **Lon** W 78.843

Harley-Davidson Shop of Williamsport, B-8
10210 Governor Lane Blvd. Ste. 2004
Williamsport
(301) 223-1800
Lat N 39.593 **Lon** W 77.807

Distance scale
One inch represents about 13 miles
0 5 10 15 mi
0 5 10 15 20 km

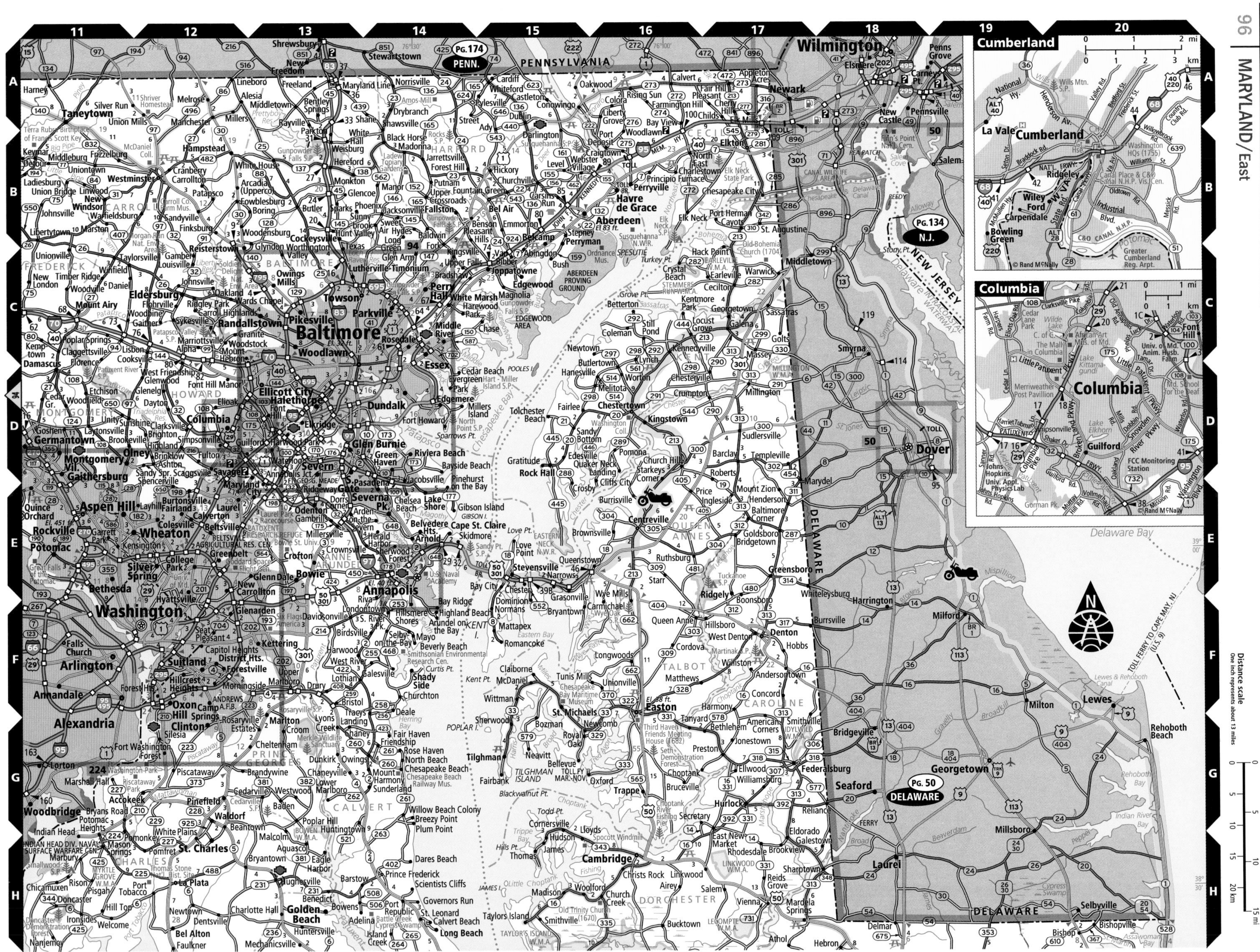
Cumberland
Columbia
PENNSYLVANIA
DELAWARE
NEW JERSEY
Baltimore
Washington
Annapolis
Wilmington
Dover
Delaware Bay
Chesapeake Bay
PG. 174 PENN.
PG. 134 N.J.
PG. 50 DELAWARE
TOLL FERRY TO CAPE MAY, NJ (U.S. 9)

How to determine distance

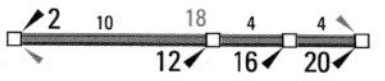

Mileages in red between red arrowheads; in black, between intersections.

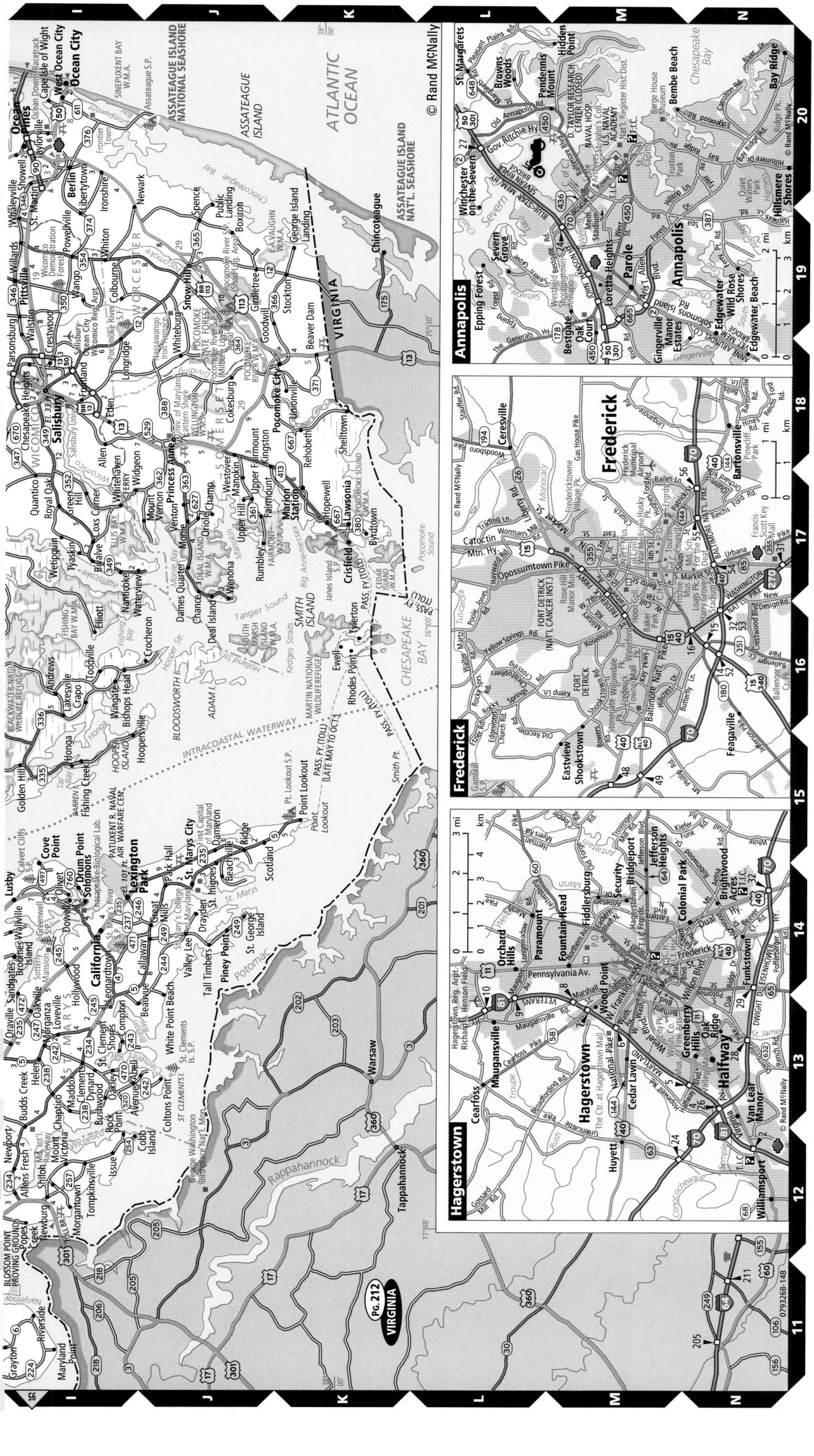

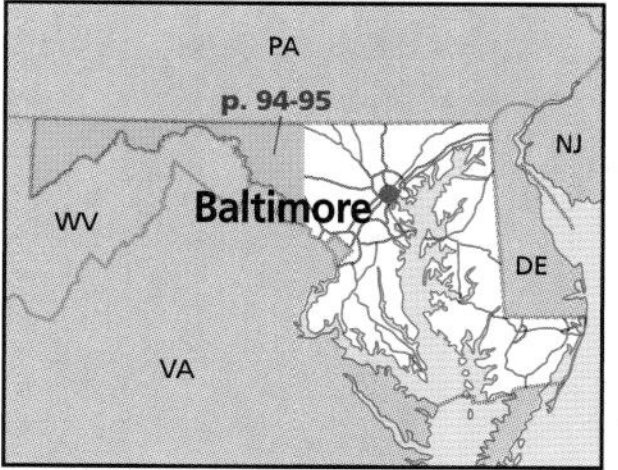
PA
p. 94-95
NJ
WV
Baltimore
DE
VA

SYMBOLS

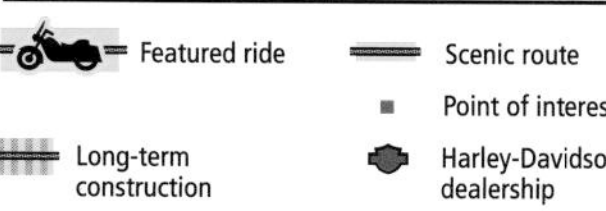
Featured ride
Scenic route
Point of interest
Long-term construction
Harley-Davidson dealership

For Maryland/Delaware ride, see page R18-19.

CITY-TO-CITY MILEAGE

	ABERDEEN	ANNAPOLIS	BALTIMORE	CUMBERLAND	HAGERSTOWN	LEXINGTON PARK	SALISBURY	WASHINGTON, DC
Aberdeen		56	30	175	107	113	121	64
Annapolis	56		28	163	95	72	89	28
Baltimore	30	28		142	74	85	116	38
Cambridge	113	58	85	220	152	129	33	85
Chestertown	65	48	75	210	142	119	85	75
Cumberland	175	163	142		70	210	251	143
Edgewood	11	48	22	167	99	105	141	56
Frederick	83	71	50	93	25	118	159	51
Hagerstown	107	95	74	70		142	183	75
Harrisburg, PA	107	122	88	143	75	179	212	126
Lexington Park	113	72	85	210	142		160	67
Ocean City	134	111	138	273	205	182	29	138
Pocomoke City	149	115	142	277	209	186	26	142
Rockville	73	39	43	121	53	86	127	22
St. Charles	86	43	60	176	108	42	131	33
Salisbury	121	89	116	251	183	160		116
Washington, DC	64	28	38	143	75	67	116	
Wilmington, DE	41	95	69	214	146	152	105	103

HARLEY-DAVIDSON DEALERSHIPS

Harley-Davidson of Annapolis, E-14
30 Hudson St. **Annapolis**
(410) 263-3345
Lat N 38.985 **Lon** W 76.532

The Harley-Davidson Store of Baltimore, C-14
8845 Pulaski Hwy. **Baltimore**
(410) 238-2003
Lat N 39.338 **Lon** W 76.48

Harley-Davidson Shop of Ocean City, I-20
10716 Ocean Gateway **Berlin**
(410) 629-1599
Lat N 38.344 **Lon** W 75.189

Ramsey's Chesapeake Harley-Davidson, A-15
3938 Conowingo Rd. **Darlington**
(410) 457-4541
Lat N 39.647 **Lon** W 76.248

Harley-Davidson of Maryland, D-13
7010 Troy Hill Dr. **Elkridge**
(410) 796-1044
Lat N 39.197 **Lon** W 76.748

Harley-Davidson of Washington, G-12
9407 Livingston Rd. **Ft. Washington**
(301) 248-1200
Lat N 38.761 **Lon** W 76.995

Rockville Harley-Davidson, D-11
7830 Airpark Rd. **Gaithersburg**
(301) 948-4581
Lat N 39.17 **Lon** W 77.16

All American Harley-Davidson, H-13
8126 Leonardtown Rd. **Hughesville**
(301) 884-2800
Lat N 38.54 **Lon** W 76.788

Distance scale
One inch represents about 9 miles

0 2 4 6 8 10 mi
0 2 4 6 8 10 12 14 16 km

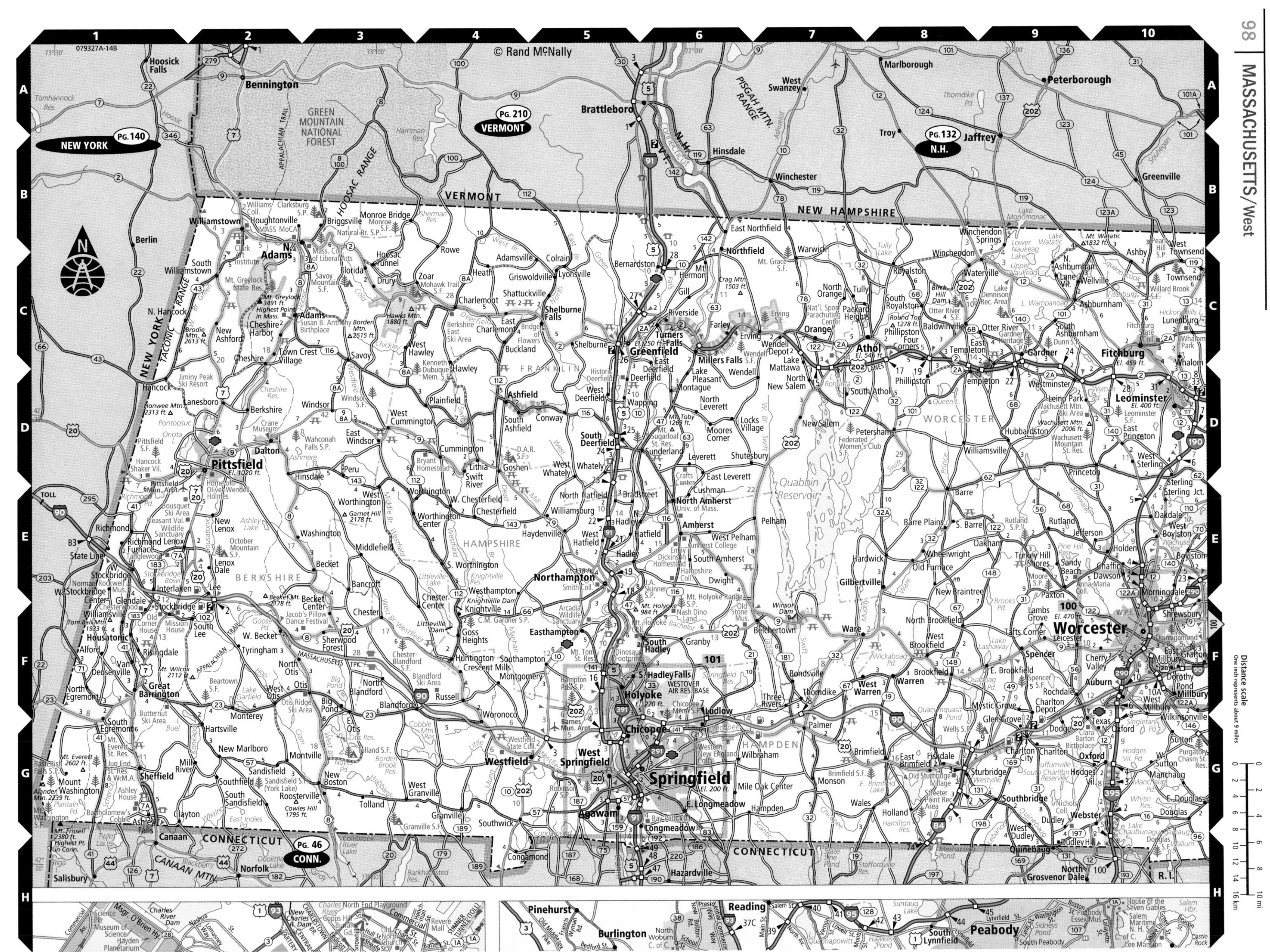
© Rand McNally
079327A-14B
NEW YORK Pg. 140
VERMONT Pg. 210
N.H. Pg. 132
CONN. Pg. 46
NEW YORK
VERMONT
NEW HAMPSHIRE
CONNECTICUT
R.I.
GREEN MOUNTAIN NATIONAL FOREST
HOOSAC RANGE
TACONIC RANGE
PISGAH MTN. RANGE
CANAAN MTN.
BERKSHIRE
HAMPSHIRE
FRANKLIN
HAMPDEN
WORCESTER
Quabbin Reservoir
Worcester
Springfield
Pittsfield
Fitchburg
Leominster
Northampton
Greenfield
Holyoke
Chicopee
Westfield
West Springfield
Athol
Gardner
Brattleboro
Bennington
Peterborough
Jaffrey
Marlborough
Pinehurst
Burlington
Reading
Peabody

How to determine distance

2
10
18
4
4
12
16
20

Mileages in red between red arrowheads; in black, between intersections.

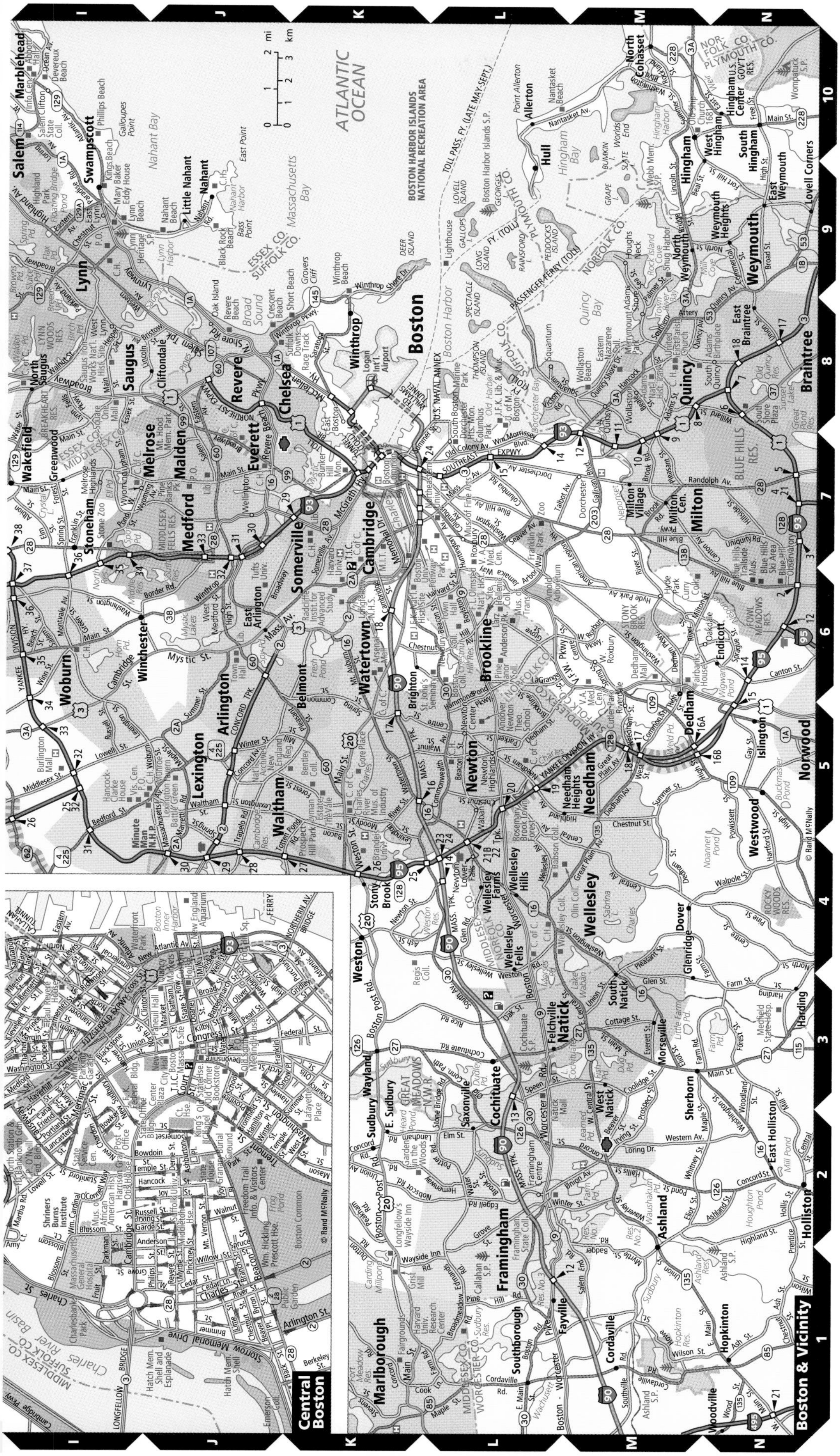

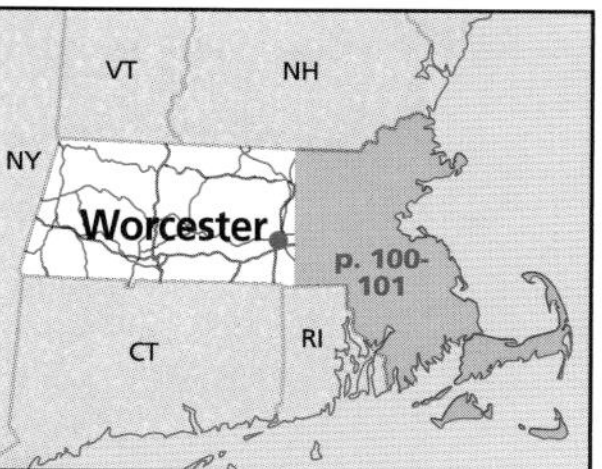
VT
NH
NY
Worcester
p. 100-101
CT
RI

SYMBOLS

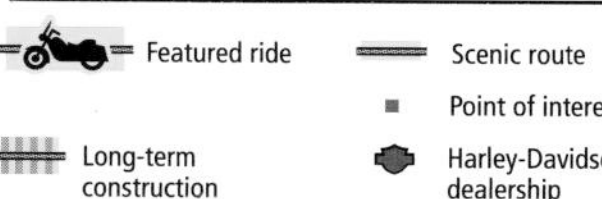
Featured ride
Scenic route
Point of interest
Long-term construction
Harley-Davidson dealership

MASSACHUSETTS MOTORCYCLE LAWS

Helmet use:
Required

Riding two abreast:
Yes. See state law for specifics

Eye protection:
Required for instructional permit holders
Required unless equipped with windscreen

Speed limit:
Primary roads: 65 mph
Secondary roads: 65 mph

MASSACHUSETTS RESOURCES

Road conditions or construction:
(617) 374-1234 (SmarTraveler, Greater Boston only)
www.state.ma.us/eotc/

Highway Emergency Numbers:
911

Tourism:
(800) 227-6277
(617) 973-8500
www.massvacation.com

State motor vehicle information:
(617) 351-4500
www.mass.gov/rmv

HARLEY-DAVIDSON DEALERSHIPS

- **Sheldon's Harley-Davidson, F-10**
  914 Southbridge St. **Auburn**
  (508) 721-9876
  Lat N 42.175 **Lon** W 71.875
- **Aldo's Harley-Davidson, C-6**
  203 South St. **Bernardston**
  (413) 648-9302
  Lat N 42.658 **Lon** W 72.561
- **American Harley-Davidson, D-10**
  1437 Central St. **Leominster**
  (978) 537-6919
  Lat N 42.482 **Lon** W 71.75
- **Ronnie's Harley-Davidson, D-2**
  501 Wahconah St. **Pittsfield**
  (413) 443-0638
  Lat N 42.474 **Lon** W 73.246
- **Easthampton Harley-Davidson, F-5**
  17 College Hwy. **Southampton**
  (413) 527-1556
  Lat N 42.252 **Lon** W 72.7
- **Tibby's Harley-Davidson Sales, G-6**
  227 Berkshire Ave. **Springfield**
  (413) 781-0785
  Lat N 42.129 **Lon** W 72.536

Boston & Vicinity

Central Boston

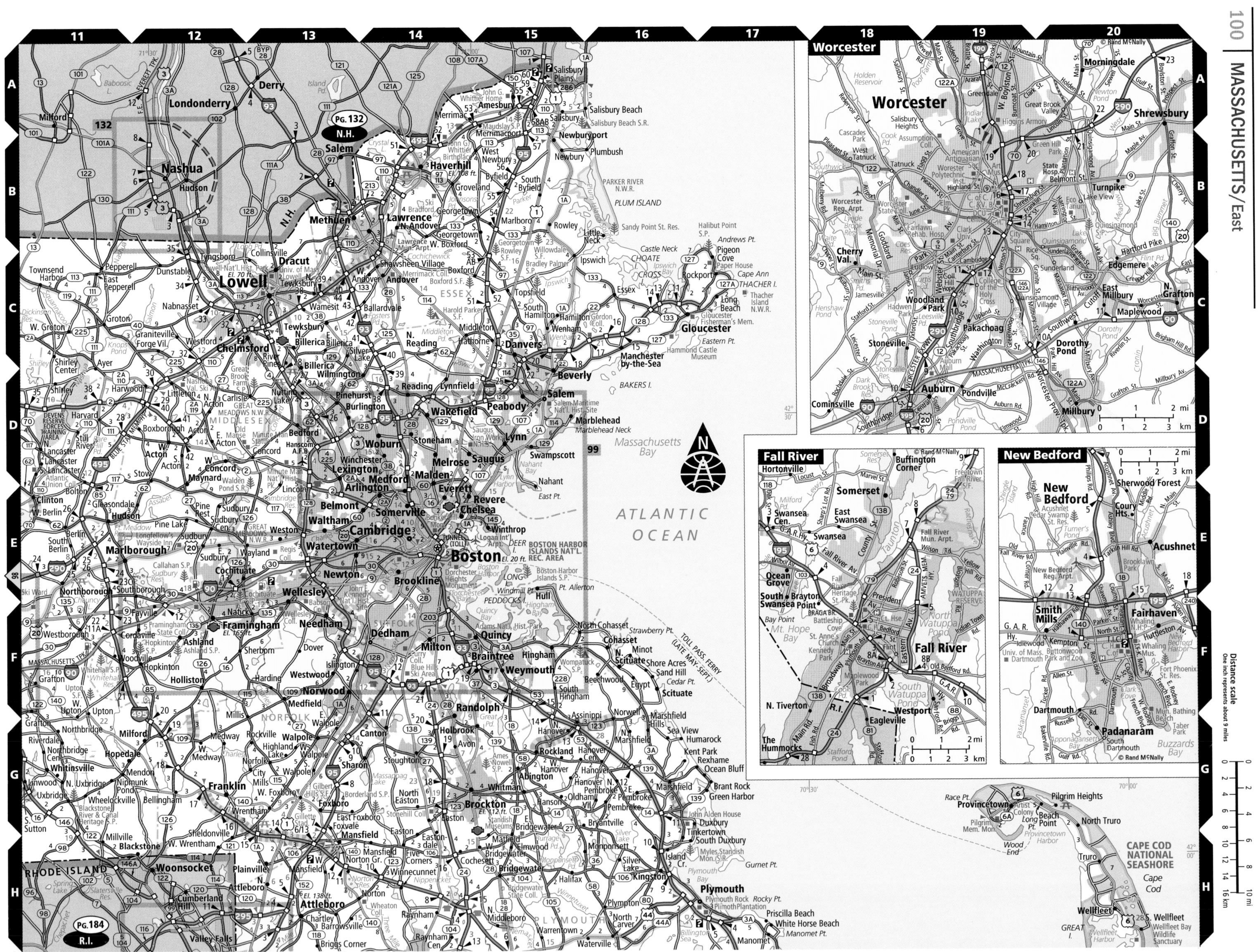
Distance scale
One inch represents about 9 miles
0 2 4 6 8 10 mi
0 2 4 6 8 10 12 14 16 km
Worcester
New Bedford
Fall River
ATLANTIC OCEAN
Massachusetts Bay
CAPE COD NATIONAL SEASHORE
Boston
Cambridge
Lowell
Lawrence
Nashua
Brockton
Plymouth
Gloucester
Salem
Pg. 132 N.H.
Pg. 184 R.I.
© Rand McNally

How to determine distance

Mileages in red between red arrowheads; in black, between intersections.

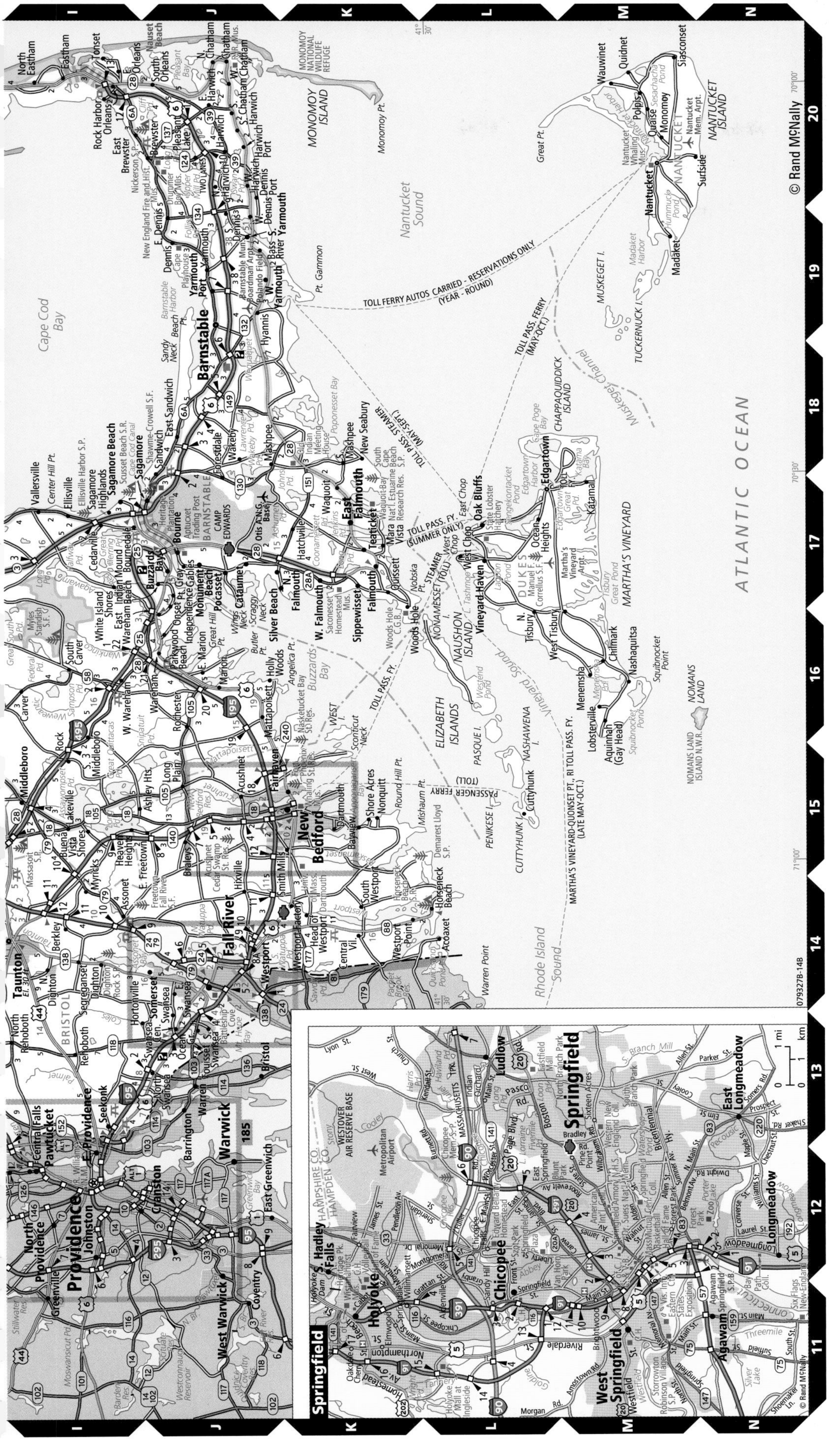

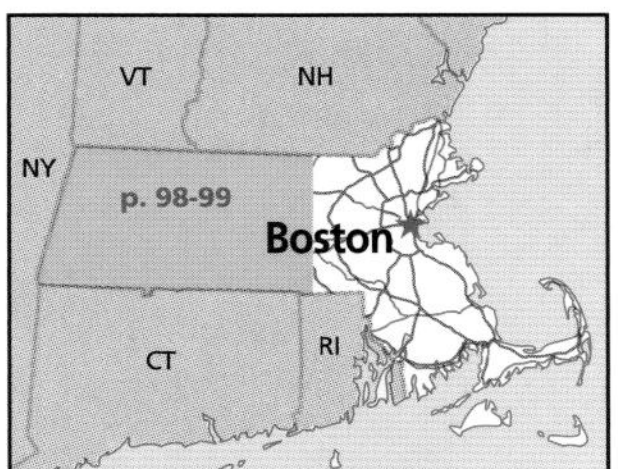
VT
NH
NY
p. 98-99
Boston
CT
RI

SYMBOLS

- Featured ride
- Scenic route
- Point of interest
- Long-term construction
- Harley-Davidson dealership

CITY-TO-CITY MILEAGE

	BOSTON	GLOUCESTER	LOWELL	NEW BEDFORD	PITTSFIELD	PLYMOUTH	SPRINGFIELD	WORCESTER
Albany, NY	166	201	168	199	36	197	83	127
Boston		43	32	58	134	40	90	48
Brockton	24	67	51	37	149	24	105	63
Falmouth	71	114	104	40	186	35	142	103
Fitchburg	51	77	33	93	122	89	78	27
Gloucester	43		49	101	169	83	125	85
Greenfield	99	125	81	154	75	137	38	82
Hartford, CT	102	137	104	119	77	133	26	63
Lowell	32	49		85	136	72	92	41
New Bedford	58	101	85		167	45	123	84
North Adams	163	164	120	196	29	194	80	124
Northampton	102	137	104	135	56	133	19	63
Pittsfield	134	169	136	167		165	51	95
Plymouth	40	83	72	45	165		121	82
Providence, RI	50	93	71	32	131	53	87	43
Provincetown	117	160	149	92	238	81	194	155
Springfield	90	125	92	123	51	121		51
Worcester	48	85	41	84	95	82	51	

HARLEY-DAVIDSON DEALERSHIPS

Boston Harley-Davidson, E-14
1760 Revere Beach Pkwy. (Rte. 16) **Everett**
(617) 389-8888
Lat N 42.402 **Lon** W 71.046

Paramount Harley-Davidson, F-12
266-300 Waverly St. **Framingham**
(508) 879-6666
Lat N 42.278 **Lon** W 71.411

Kelly's House of Harley-Davidson, C-13
1 Chelmsford Rd. **North Billerica**
(978) 663-6298
Lat N 42.584 **Lon** W 71.292

Cape Cod Harley-Davidson, J-17
750 MacArthur Blvd. **Pocasset**
(508) 563-7387
Lat N 41.692 **Lon** W 70.588

Monty's Cycle Shop, G-14
751 N Main St. (Rte. 28) **West Bridgewater**
(508) 583-1172
Lat N 42.041 **Lon** W 71.009

Big Boar Harley-Davidson, J-14
1030 State Rd. (Rte. 6) **Westport**
(508) 674-5780
Lat N 41.647 **Lon** W 71.06

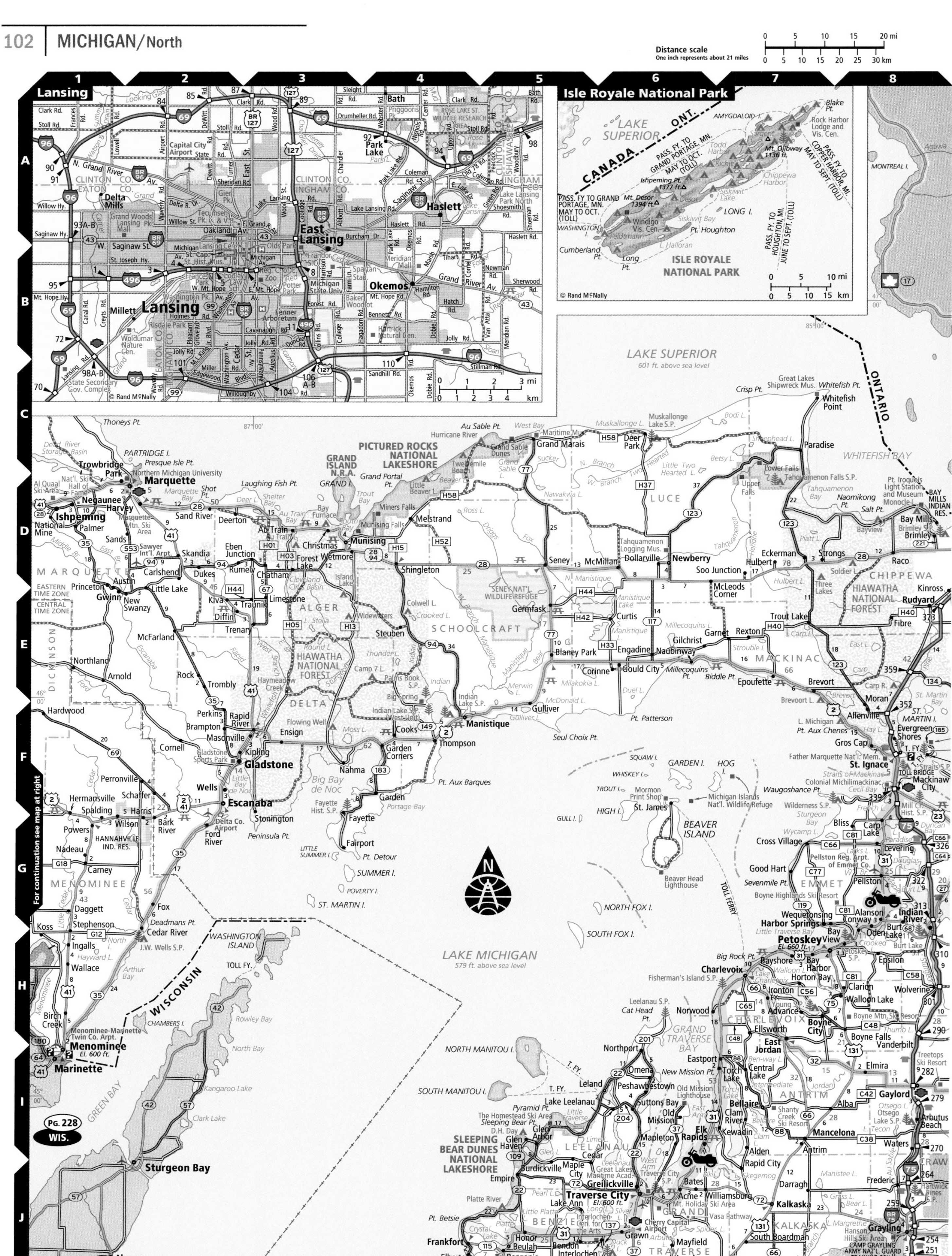
Distance scale
One inch represents about 21 miles
0 5 10 15 20 mi
0 5 10 15 20 25 30 km
Lansing
Isle Royale National Park
LAKE SUPERIOR
CANADA
ONT.
ISLE ROYALE NATIONAL PARK
Mt. Ojibway 1136 ft.
Mt. Desor 1394 ft.
Ishpeming Pt. 1377 ft.
Windigo Vis. Cen.
Rock Harbor Lodge and Vis. Cen.
PASS. FY. TO GRAND PORTAGE, MN. MAY TO OCT. (TOLL)
PASS. FY. TO COPPER HARBOR, MI. MAY TO SEPT. (TOLL)
PASS. FY. TO HOUGHTON, MI. JUNE TO SEPT. (TOLL)
© Rand McNally
East Lansing
Okemos
Haslett
Delta Mills
Millett
Bath
Park Lake
LAKE SUPERIOR
601 ft. above sea level
ONTARIO
WHITEFISH BAY
PICTURED ROCKS NATIONAL LAKESHORE
GRAND ISLAND N.R.A.
HIAWATHA NATIONAL FOREST
SENEY NAT'L WILDLIFE REFUGE
MARQUETTE
ALGER
SCHOOLCRAFT
LUCE
DELTA
MACKINAC
CHIPPEWA
MENOMINEE
DICKINSON
EMMET
CHARLEVOIX
ANTRIM
LEELANAU
BENZIE
GRAND TRAVERSE
KALKASKA
EASTERN TIME ZONE
CENTRAL TIME ZONE
Marquette
Ishpeming
Negaunee
Munising
Manistique
Gladstone
Escanaba
Menominee
Marinette
Newberry
St. Ignace
Mackinaw City
Petoskey
Charlevoix
Traverse City
Gaylord
Grayling
Sturgeon Bay
Algoma
BEAVER ISLAND
St. James
NORTH FOX I.
SOUTH FOX I.
NORTH MANITOU I.
SOUTH MANITOU I.
WASHINGTON ISLAND
LAKE MICHIGAN
579 ft. above sea level
GREEN BAY
WISCONSIN
SLEEPING BEAR DUNES NATIONAL LAKESHORE
For continuation see map at right
PG. 228 WIS.
079330A-14B
104

How to determine distance

Mileages in red between red arrowheads; in black, between intersections.

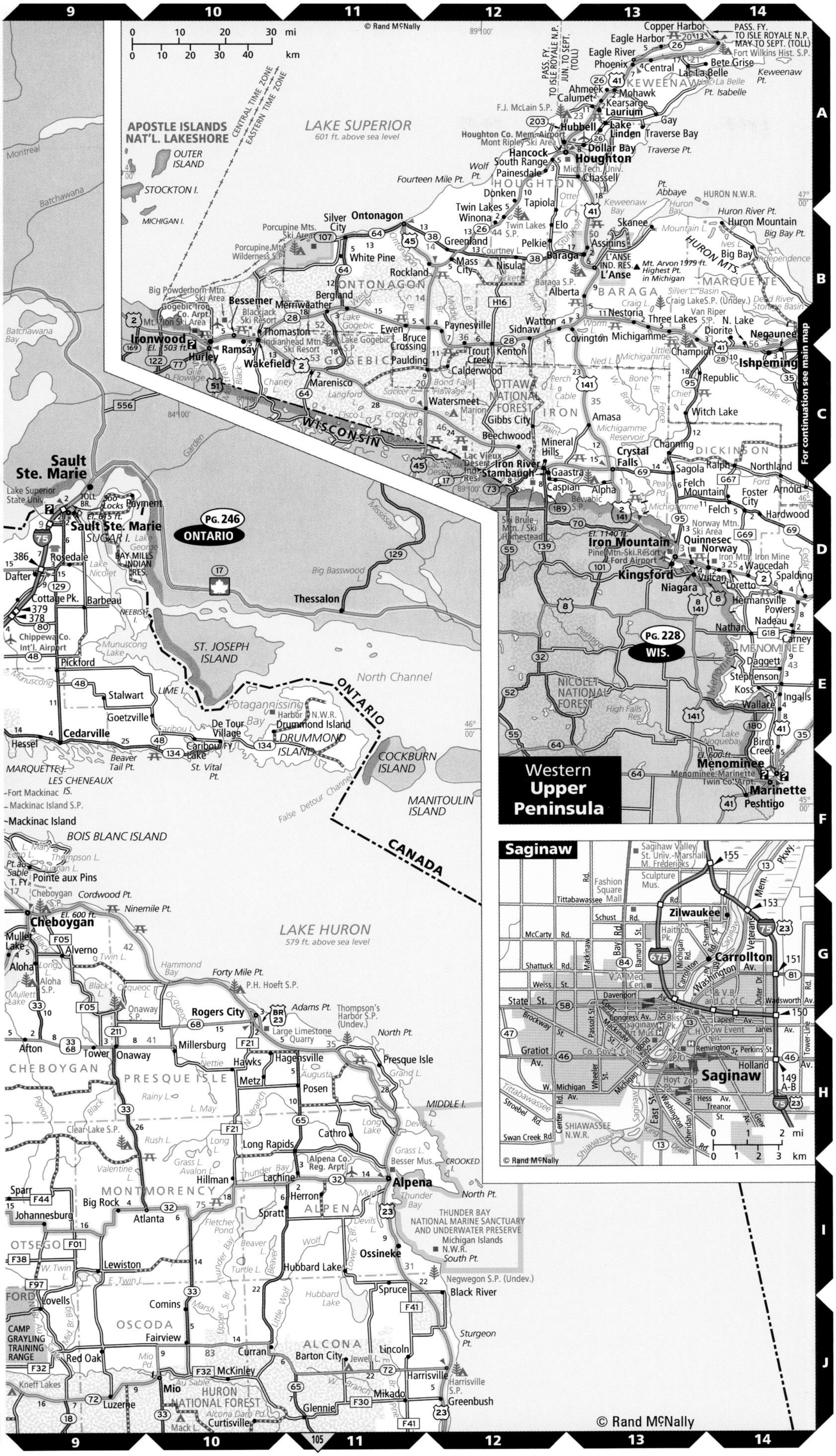

Western Upper Peninsula

Saginaw

For continuation see main map

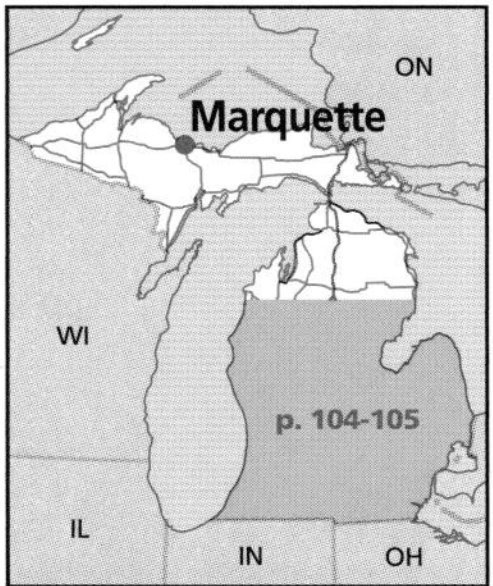

Marquette
ON
WI
p. 104-105
IL
IN
OH

SYMBOLS

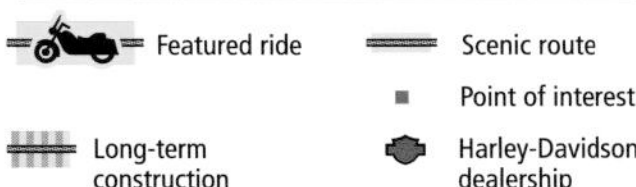

Featured ride
Scenic route
Point of interest
Long-term construction
Harley-Davidson dealership

For Michigan ride, see page R20-21.

MICHIGAN MOTORCYCLE LAWS

Helmet use:
Required

Riding two abreast:
Yes. See state law for specifics

Eye protection:
Required unless equipped with windscreen
Required at speeds over 35 mph

Speed limit:
Primary roads: 70 mph
Secondary roads: 65 mph

MICHIGAN RESOURCES

Road conditions or construction:
(800) 381-8477
(888) 305-7283 (for west and southwest Michigan)
(800) 641-6368 (Metro Detroit)
www.michigan.gov/mdot/

Highway Emergency Numbers:
911

Tourism:
(888) 784-7328
www.michigan.org

State motor vehicle information:
(517) 322-1460
www.michigan.gov/sos

HARLEY-DAVIDSON DEALERSHIPS

Northwoods Harley-Davidson, I-8
980 S Wisconsin Ave. **Gaylord**
(989) 732-8000
Lat N 45.018 **Lon** W 84.682

Northwoods Harley-Davidson, F-8
276 S Huron Ave. **Mackinaw City**
(231) 436-5331
Lat N 45.779 **Lon** W 84.726

Bald Eagle Harley-Davidson, D-2
2080 US 41 W **Marquette**
(906) 228-5330
Lat N 46.53 **Lon** W 87.397

Classic Motor Sports Harley-Davidson, J-6
3939 S Blue Star Dr. **Traverse City**
(231) 943-9344
Lat N 44.694 **Lon** W 85.656

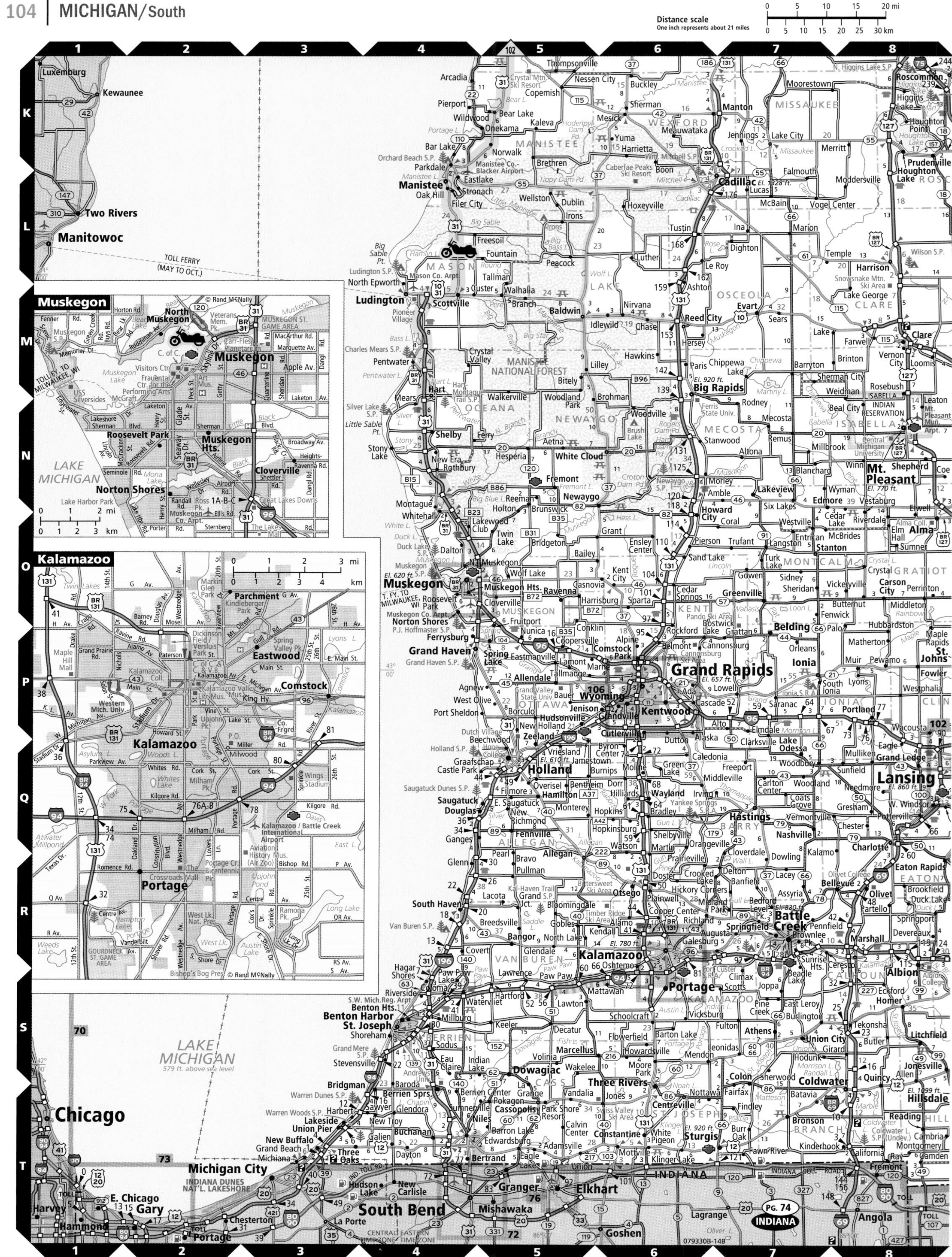
Distance scale
One inch represents about 21 miles
0 5 10 15 20 mi
0 5 10 15 20 25 30 km
Muskegon
© Rand McNally
Kalamazoo
LAKE MICHIGAN
579 ft. above sea level
Chicago
Manitowoc
Two Rivers
Kewaunee
Luxemburg
TOLL FERRY (MAY TO OCT.)
Ludington
Manistee
Muskegon
Grand Haven
Holland
Grand Rapids
El. 657 ft.
Lansing
Mt. Pleasant
Big Rapids
Cadillac
Kalamazoo
Portage
Battle Creek
Benton Harbor
St. Joseph
South Haven
Michigan City
South Bend
Elkhart
Goshen
Mishawaka
Gary
Hammond
Angola
Sturgis
Coldwater
Hillsdale
MANISTEE NATIONAL FOREST
INDIANA
PG. 74 INDIANA
CENTRAL TIME ZONE
EASTERN TIME ZONE
INDIANA DUNES NAT'L. LAKESHORE
079330B-14B

How to determine distance

Mileages in red between red arrowheads; in black, between intersections.

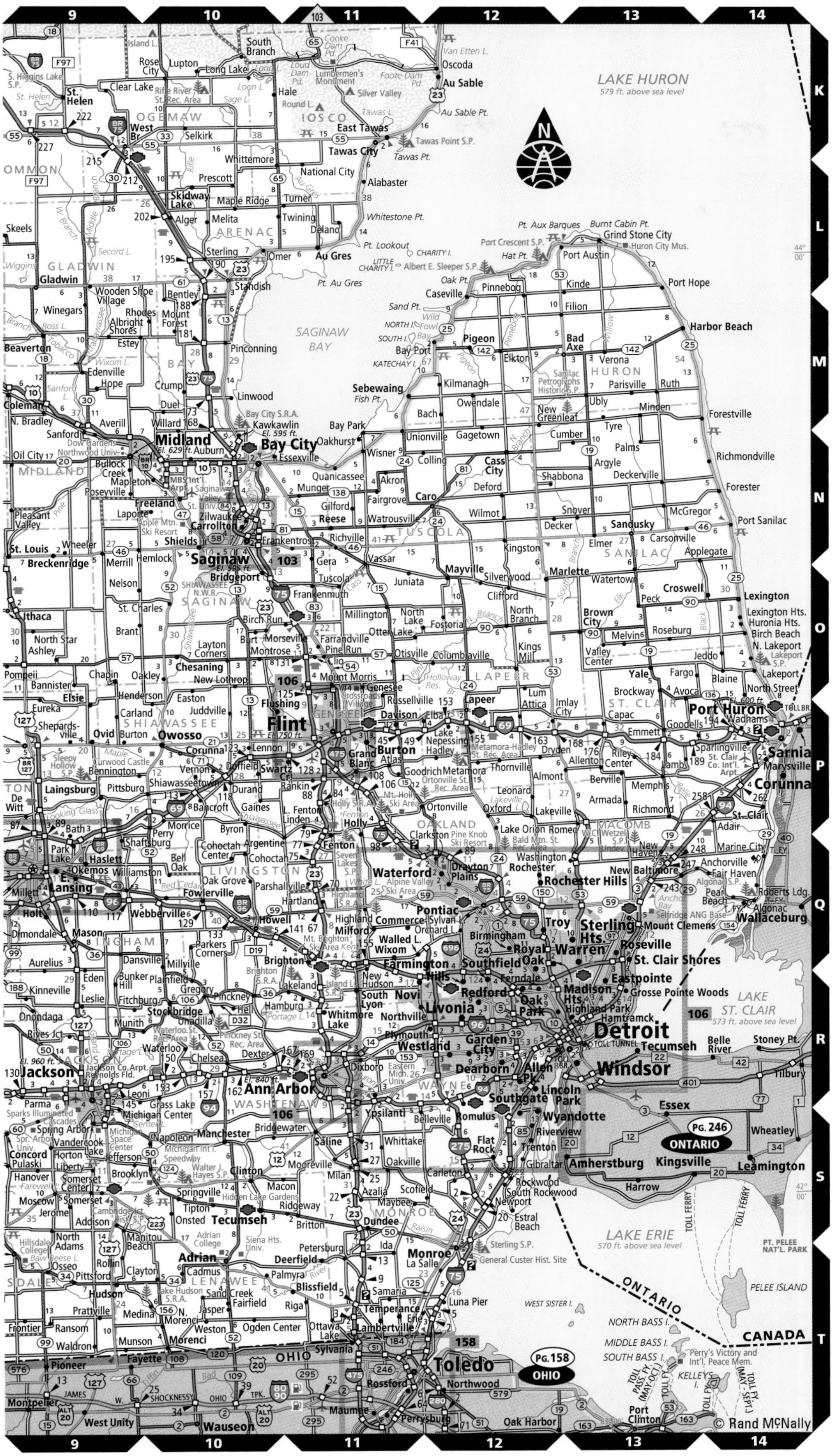

ON
p. 102-103
WI
Detroit
IL
IN
OH

For Michigan ride, see page R20-21.

HARLEY-DAVIDSON DEALERSHIPS

For Ann Arbor, Detroit metro, Flint, and Grand Rapids areas, please see dealer listings on page 107.

- **Battle Creek Harley-Davidson, R-7**
  5738 Beckley Rd. **Battle Creek**
  (269) 979-2233
  Lat N 42.261 **Lon** W 85.183
- **Saginaw Valley Harley-Davidson, N-10**
  3850 S Huron Rd. **Bay City**
  (989) 686-0400
  Lat N 43.629 **Lon** W 83.915
- **Shiawassee Harley-Davidson, O-11**
  11901 N Beyer Rd. **Birch Run**
  (989) 624-4400
  Lat N 43.267 **Lon** W 83.794
- **Brighton Harley-Davidson, Q-11**
  5942 Whitmore Lake Rd. **Brighton**
  (810) 225-2915
  Lat N 42.517 **Lon** W 83.759
- **Town & Country Sports Harley-Davidson, S-9**
  US 12 & US 127 **Cement City**
  (517) 547-3333
  Lat N 42.061 **Lon** W 84.354
- **Capitol Harley-Davidson, Inc., Q-8**
  9550 Woodlane Dr. **Dimondale**
  (517) 646-2345
  Lat N 42.681 **Lon** W 84.650
- **Harley-Davidson at Birchwood Mall, P-14**
  4350 24th Ave. Unit 102 **Fort Gratiot**
  (810) 385-3763
  Lat N 43.036 **Lon** W 82.456
- **Sandy's Harley-Davidson Sport Center, N-5**
  11940 N Maple Island Rd. **Fremont**
  (231) 924-3020
  Lat N 43.466 **Lon** W 86.039
- **Wild Boar Harley-Davidson, P-5**
  2977 Corporate Grove Dr. **Hudsonville**
  (616) 896-0111
  Lat N 42.848 **Lon** W 85.857
- **Perry Harley-Davidson, R-6**
  5331 S Sprinkle Rd. **Kalamazoo**
  (269) 329-3450
  Lat N 42.24 **Lon** W 85.537
- **Ray C's Harley-Davidson of Lapeer, P-12**
  1422 Imlay City Rd. **Lapeer**
  (810) 664-9261
  Lat N 43.048 **Lon** W 83.288
- **C & S Harley-Davidson, N-8**
  4741 E Pickard St. (M-20) **Mt. Pleasant**
  (989) 772-5513
  Lat N 43.612 **Lon** W 84.753
- **Hot Rod Harley-Davidson, O-4**
  590 Ottawa St. **Muskegon**
  (231) 722-3653
  Lat N 43.242 **Lon** W 86.241
- **Gilbert's Harley-Davidson, P-14**
  3350 Lapeer Rd. **Port Huron**
  (810) 982-4351 (24 hours)
  Lat N 42.979 **Lon** W 82.466
- **Hamlin's Harley-Davidson, T-6**
  68951 White School Rd. **Sturgis**
  (269) 651-3424
  Lat N 41.797 **Lon** W 85.448
- **Biker Bob's Harley-Davidson Motown, S-12**
  14100 Telegraph Rd. **Taylor**
  (734) 947-4647
  Lat N 42.204 **Lon** W 83.269
- **Tecumseh Harley-Davidson Shop, S-10**
  8080 Matthews Hwy. **Tecumseh**
  (517) 423-3333
  Lat N 42.008 **Lon** W 83.985
- **Gildner's Harley-Davidson, K-9**
  2723 S M-76 **West Branch**
  (989) 345-1330
  Lat N 44.254 **Lon** W 84.21

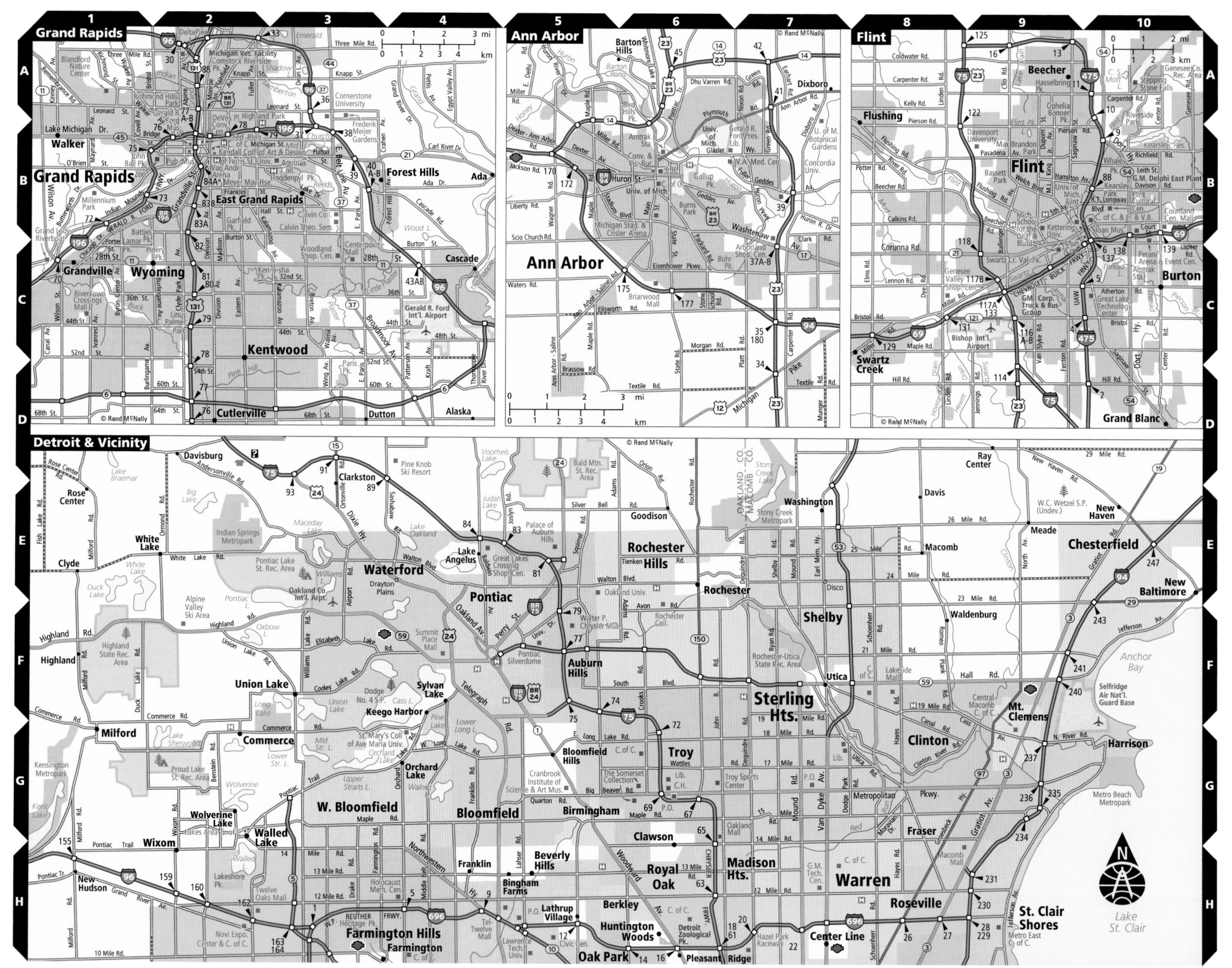
Grand Rapids
Ann Arbor
Flint
Detroit & Vicinity
© Rand McNally
Walker
Grand Rapids
East Grand Rapids
Forest Hills
Ada
Cascade
Grandville
Wyoming
Kentwood
Cutlerville
Dutton
Alaska
Barton Hills
Dixboro
Ann Arbor
Flushing
Beecher
Flint
Burton
Swartz Creek
Grand Blanc
Davisburg
Clarkston
Rose Center
White Lake
Clyde
Waterford
Lake Angelus
Pontiac
Rochester Hills
Rochester
Washington
Shelby
Davis
Macomb
Ray Center
New Haven
Chesterfield
New Baltimore
Highland
Milford
Union Lake
Commerce
Sylvan Lake
Keego Harbor
Orchard Lake
Auburn Hills
Utica
Sterling Hts.
Troy
Clinton
Mt. Clemens
Harrison
Wolverine Lake
Walled Lake
Wixom
W. Bloomfield
Bloomfield
Bloomfield Hills
Birmingham
Clawson
Fraser
Franklin
Beverly Hills
Bingham Farms
Royal Oak
Madison Hts.
Warren
Roseville
New Hudson
Farmington Hills
Farmington
Lathrup Village
Berkley
Huntington Woods
Oak Park
Pleasant Ridge
Center Line
St. Clair Shores
Lake St. Clair

How to determine distance

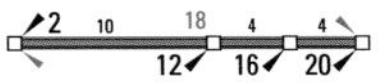

Mileages in red between red arrowheads; in black, between intersections.

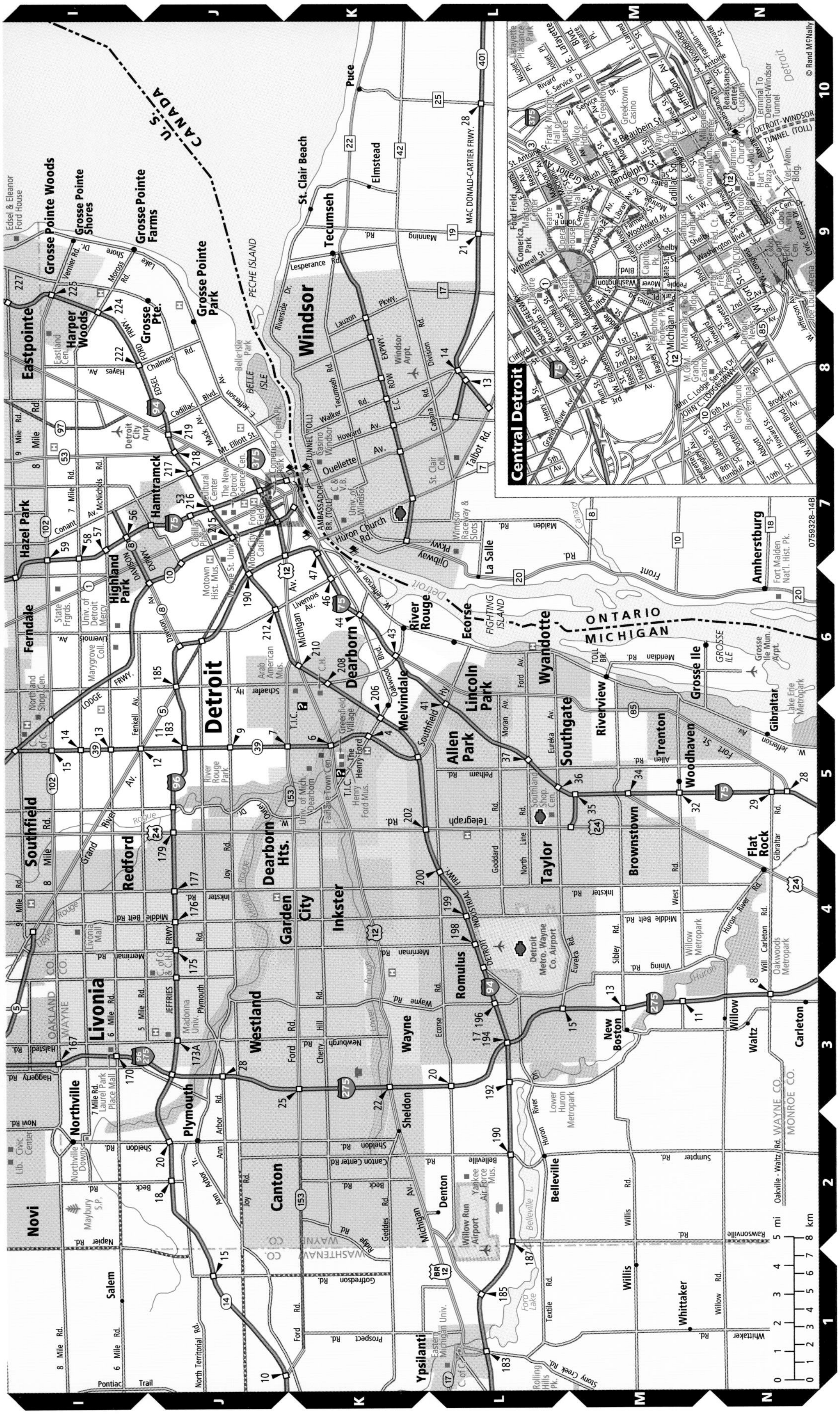

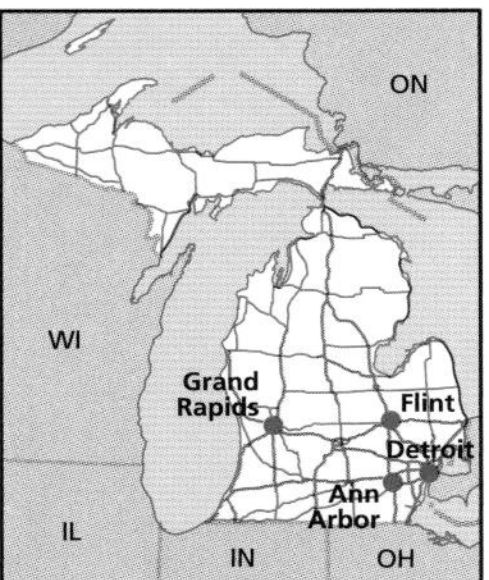
ON
WI
Grand Rapids
Flint
Detroit
Ann Arbor
IL
IN
OH

SYMBOLS

- Featured ride
- Scenic route
- Point of interest
- Long-term construction
- Harley-Davidson dealership

HARLEY-DAVIDSON DEALERSHIPS

American Harley-Davidson, B-5
5436 Jackson Rd. **Ann Arbor**
(734) 747-8008
Lat N 42.288 **Lon** W 83.836

Cummings Harley-Davidson Sales, B-10
5350 Davison Rd. **Burton**
(810) 234-6646
Lat N 43.033 **Lon** W 83.602

Detroit Harley-Davidson, H-7
25152 Van Dyke Rd. **Center Line**
(586) 756-1284
Lat N 42.479 **Lon** W 83.027

Wolverine Harley-Davidson, F-9
44660 N Gratiot Ave. **Clinton Township**
(586) 463-7700
Lat N 42.626 **Lon** W 82.863

Motown Harley-Davidson, L-4
830 Metro Airport 6-2B **Detroit**
(734) 229-5755
Lat N 42.22 **Lon** W 83.347

Motor City Harley-Davidson, H-3
34900 Grand River Ave. **Farmington Hills**
(248) 473-7433
Lat N 42.469 **Lon** W 83.391

A.B.C. Harley-Davidson, F-3
4405 Highland Rd. (M-59) **Waterford**
(248) 674-3175
Lat N 42.644 **Lon** W 83.354

Distance scale
One inch represents about 23 miles
0 5 10 15 20 25 mi
0 5 10 15 20 25 30 35 40 km

Winnipeg 244
Sainte-Anne-des-Chênes
Steinbach
Kenora
Keewatin
MANITOBA
ONTARIO
CANADA
PG. 244 MANITOBA
Angle Inlet
RED LAKE INDIAN RESERVATION
NORTHWEST ANGLE S.F.
Lake of the Woods
Duluth / Superior
Duluth International Airport
Duluth
Proctor
Pembina
Noyes
St. Vincent
Humboldt
Northcote
Hallock
Lancaster
KITTSON
Lake Bronson
Kennedy
Drayton
Pinecreek
Ross
Roseau
ROSEAU
Warroad
Roosevelt
Williams
Baudette
Rainy River
Clementson
Birchdale
Indus
Loman
KOOCHICHING
LAKE OF THE WOODS
Greenbush
Wannaska
Karlstad
Strandquist
Stephen
Argyle
MARSHALL
Newfolden
Middle River
Gatzke
AGASSIZ NATIONAL WILDLIFE REFUGE
Grygla
RED LAKE WILDLIFE MANAGEMENT AREA
BELTRAMI
Warren
Alvarado
Oslo
Thief River Falls
Upper Red Lake
Lower Red Lake
RED LAKE INDIAN RESERVATION
Waskish
Grand Falls
Big Falls
Margie
Grand Forks
East Grand Forks
NORTH DAKOTA
PENNINGTON
POLK
RED LAKE
Red Lake Falls
Crookston
Redlake
Kelliher
Northome
Gemmell
Effie
Bigfork
Bergville
CHIPPEWA NAT'L FOR.
Fosston
CLEARWATER
Bemidji
Bagley
Cass Lake
Blackduck
Hillsboro
NORMAN
Ada
MAHNOMEN
Mahnomen
WHITE EARTH IND. RES.
HUBBARD
Park Rapids
LEECH LAKE INDIAN RESERVATION
Walker
Longville
Deer River
Grand Rapids
Zemple
Cohasset
Fargo
Moorhead
West Fargo
CLAY
BECKER
Detroit Lakes
Hawley
Barnesville
Glyndon
Frazee
Perham
OTTER TAIL
WADENA
Menahga
Sebeka
Pequot Lakes
Crosslake
CASS
CROW WING
PG. 156 N.D.

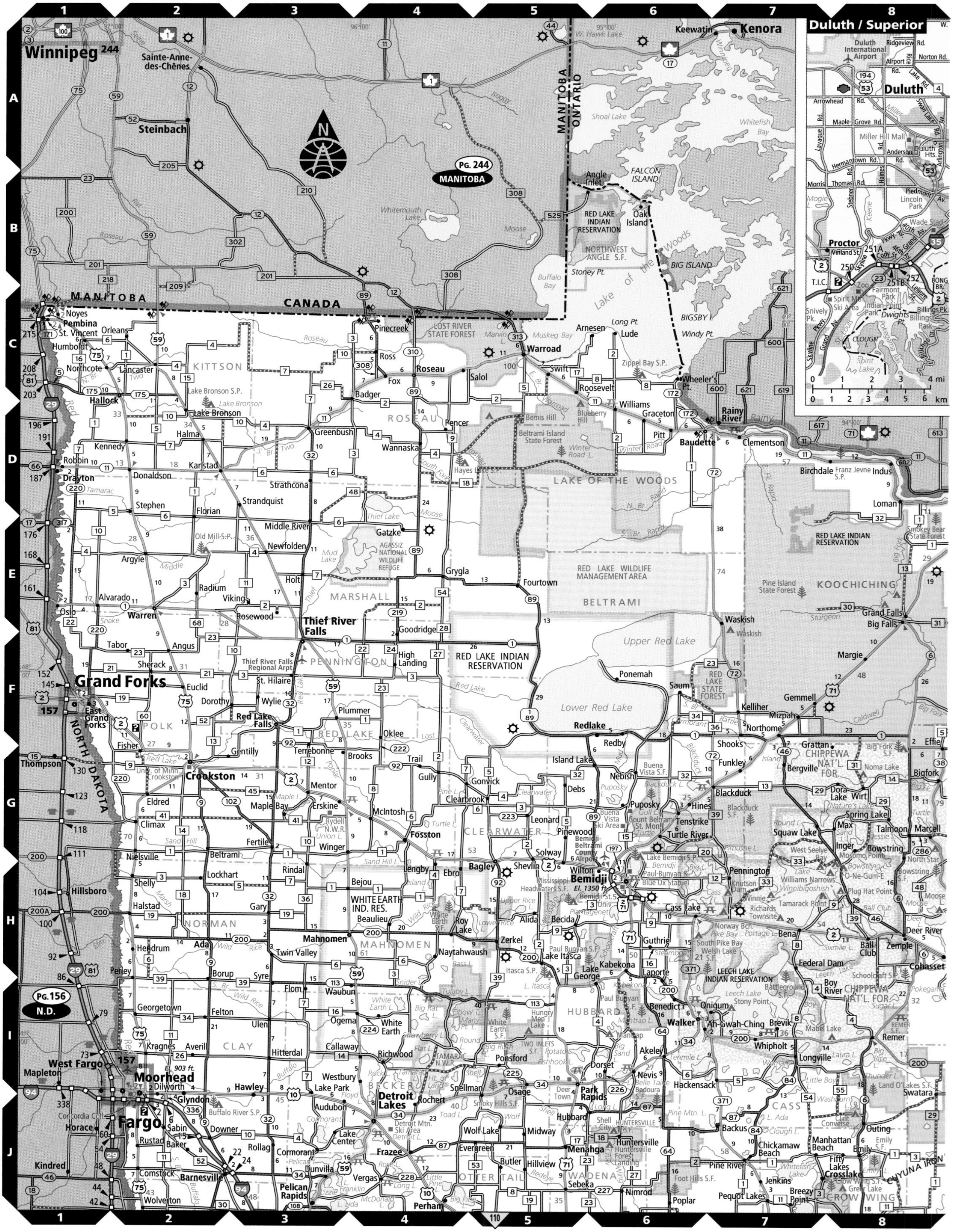

How to determine distance

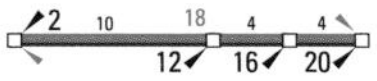

Mileages in red between red arrowheads; in black, between intersections.

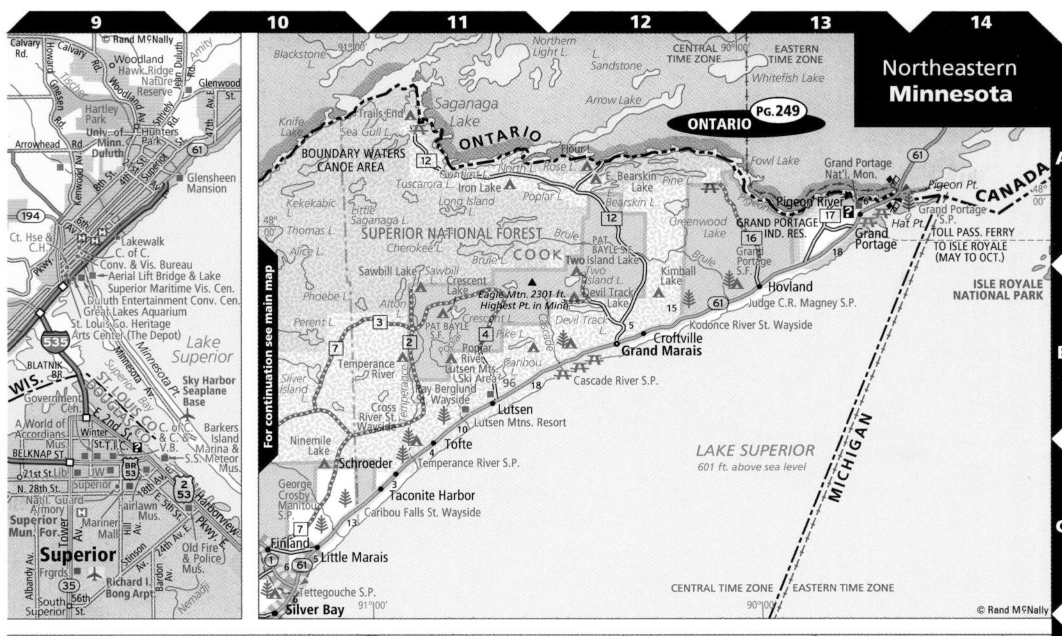
Northeastern Minnesota
ONTARIO PG. 249
BOUNDARY WATERS CANOE AREA
SUPERIOR NATIONAL FOREST
COOK
GRAND PORTAGE IND. RES.
Grand Portage
Grand Marais
Lutsen
Tofte
Schroeder
Taconite Harbor
Little Marais
Finland
Silver Bay
LAKE SUPERIOR
601 ft. above sea level
ISLE ROYALE NATIONAL PARK
CANADA
MICHIGAN
TOLL PASS. FERRY TO ISLE ROYALE (MAY TO OCT.)
Eagle Mtn. 2301 ft. Highest Pt. in Minn.
CENTRAL TIME ZONE
EASTERN TIME ZONE
For continuation see main map
Duluth
Superior
Lake Superior
© Rand McNally

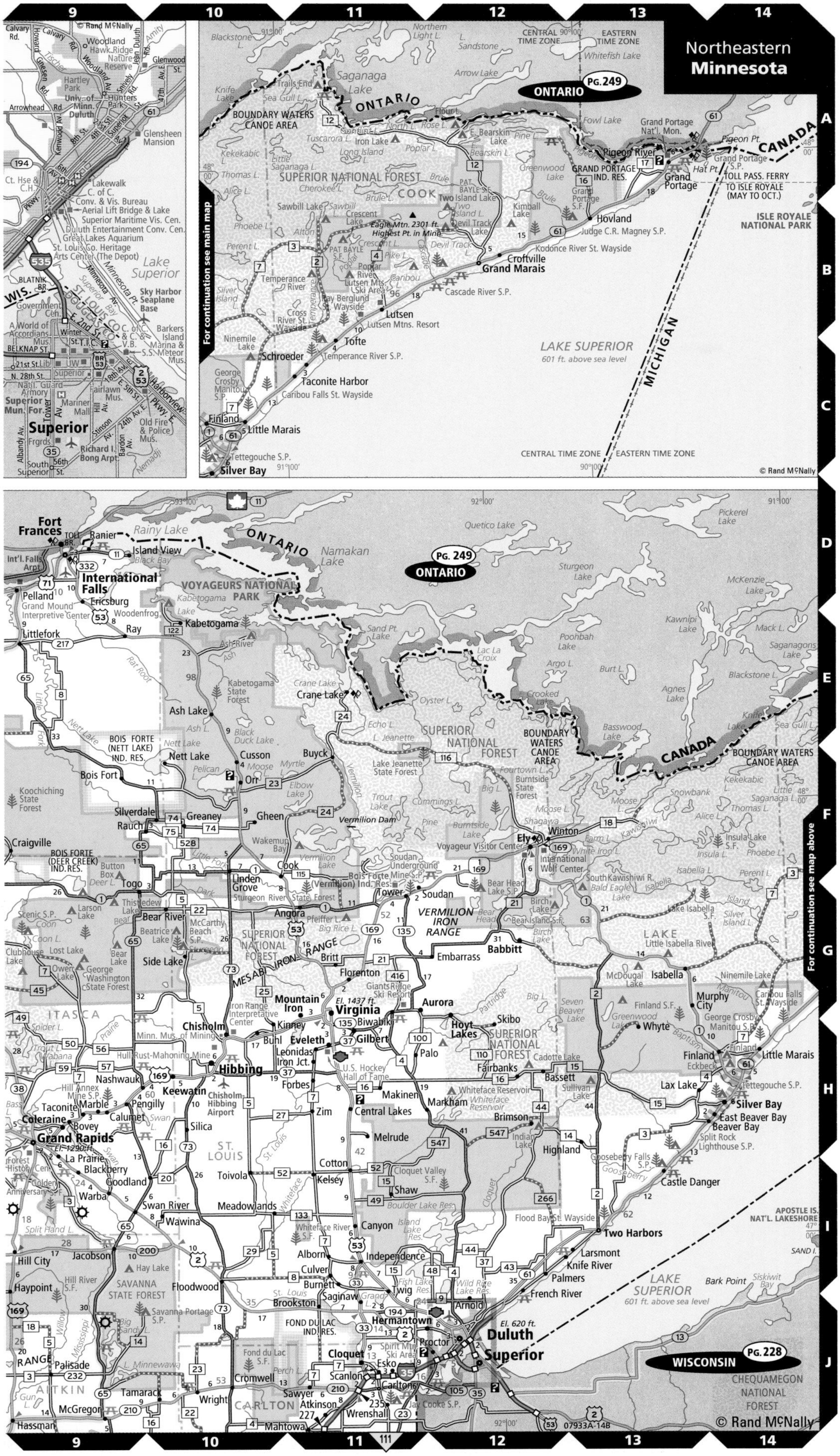

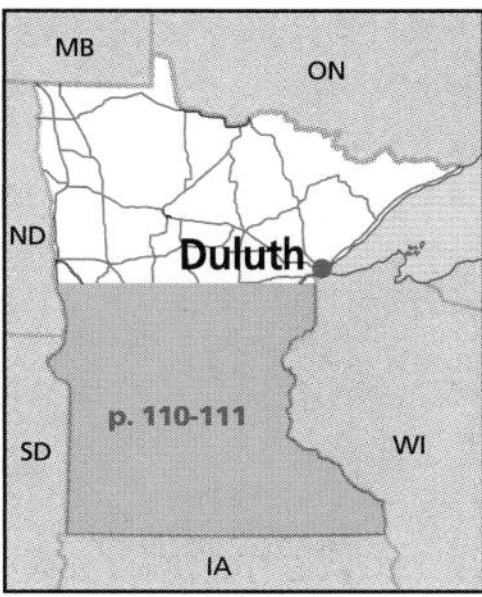
MB
ON
ND
Duluth
p. 110-111
SD
WI
IA

SYMBOLS

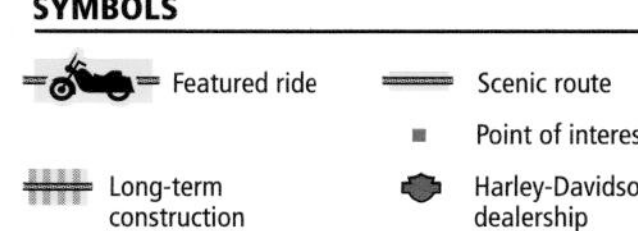
Featured ride
Scenic route
Point of interest
Long-term construction
Harley-Davidson dealership

MINNESOTA MOTORCYCLE LAWS

Helmet use:
Required under age 18 and for instructional permit holders

Riding two abreast:
Yes. See state law for specifics

Eye protection:
Required by law

Speed limit:
Primary roads: 70 mph
Secondary roads: 65 mph

MINNESOTA RESOURCES

Road conditions or construction:
511
(800) 542-0220
www.dot.state.mn.org

Highway Emergency Numbers:
911

Tourism:
(800) 657-3700
(651) 296-5029
www.exploreminnesota.com

State motor vehicle information:
(651) 296-6911
www.dps.state.mn.us/dvs

HARLEY-DAVIDSON DEALERSHIPS

Harley-Davidson Sport Center, J-12
4355 Stebner Rd. **Duluth**
(218) 729-9600
Lat N 46.827 **Lon** W 92.196

Five Seasons Sports Center, H-11
Box 360 Hwy. 53 **Eveleth**
(218) 744-5871
Lat N 47.428 **Lon** W 92.517

For continuation see map above

ONTARIO PG. 249

WISCONSIN PG. 228

111

Distance scale
One inch represents about 23 miles

0 5 10 15 20 25 mi
0 5 10 15 20 25 30 35 40 km

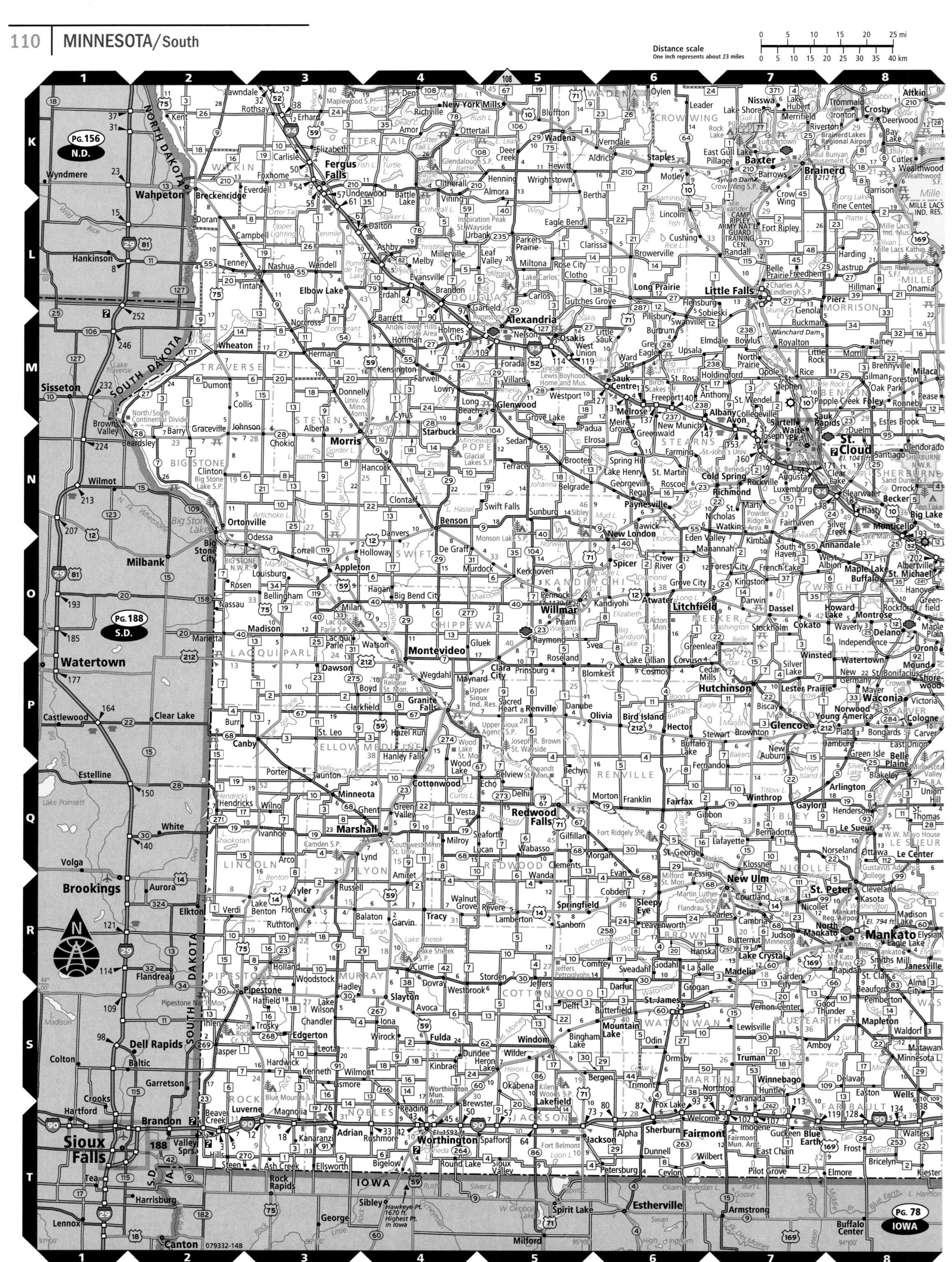
1 2 3 4 5 6 7 8
K L M N O P Q R S T
108
Pg. 156 N.D.
Pg. 188 S.D.
Pg. 78 IOWA
NORTH DAKOTA
SOUTH DAKOTA
IOWA
Wahpeton
Breckenridge
Fergus Falls
Alexandria
Morris
Wheaton
Ortonville
Benson
Willmar
Montevideo
Marshall
Redwood Falls
New Ulm
Mankato
St. Peter
Hutchinson
Litchfield
St. Cloud
Little Falls
Brainerd
Baxter
Staples
Long Prairie
Sauk Centre
Glenwood
Madison
Granite Falls
Pipestone
Luverne
Worthington
Windom
Jackson
Fairmont
Blue Earth
Sioux Falls
Brookings
Watertown
Sisseton
Milbank
Spirit Lake
Estherville
Canton
079332-14B

How to determine distance

Mileages in red between red arrowheads; in black, between intersections.

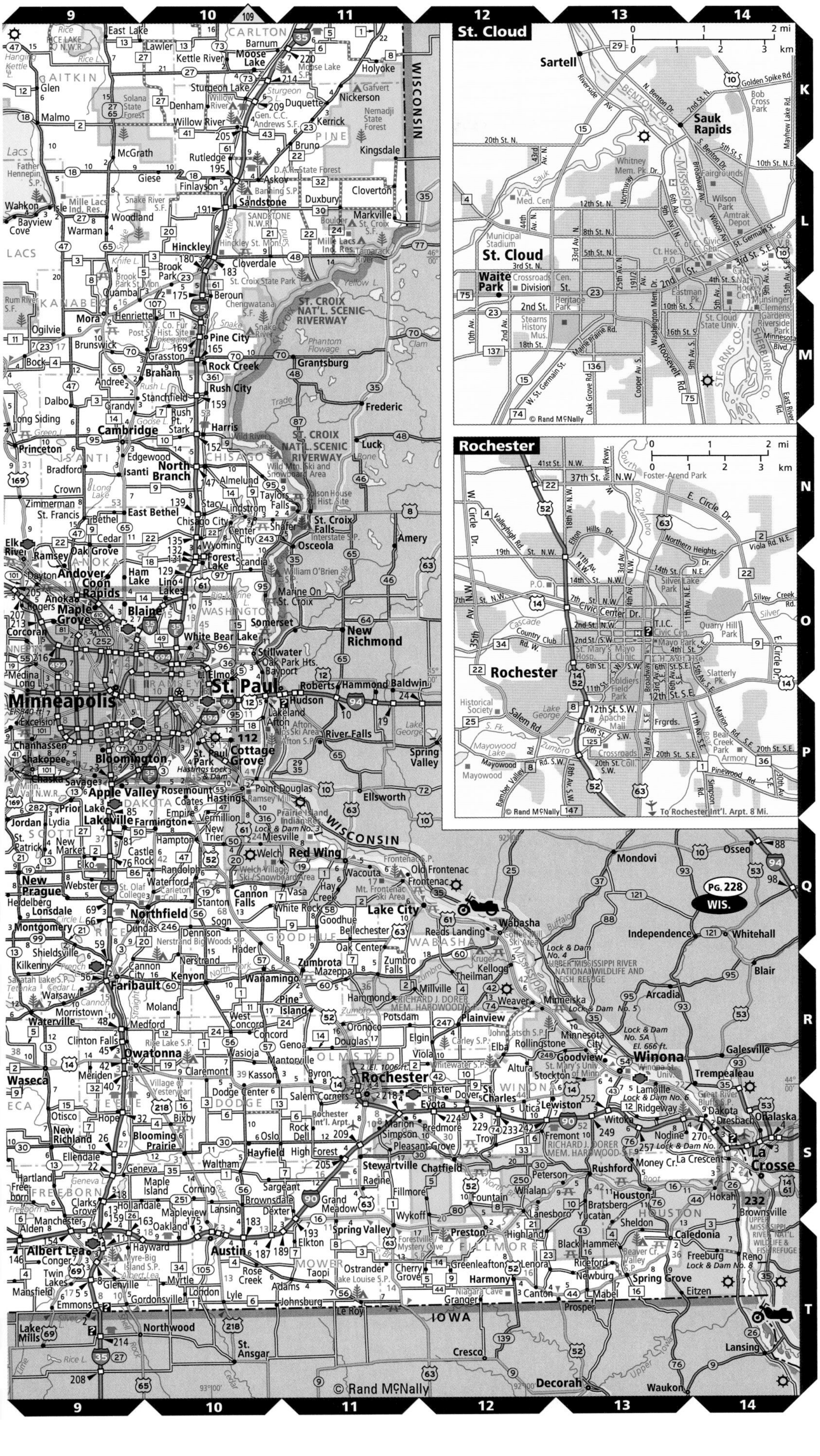

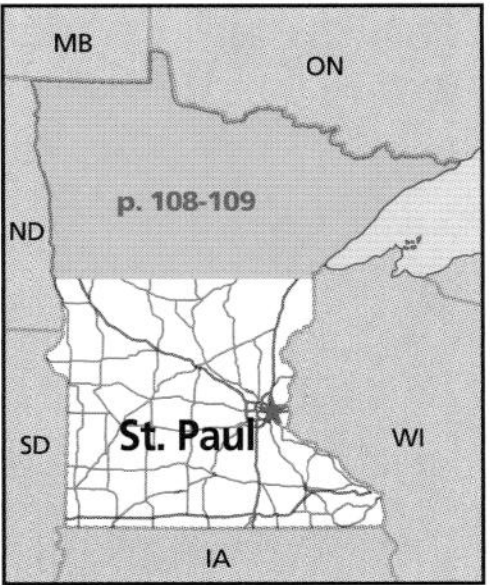
MB
ON
ND
p. 108-109
SD
St. Paul
WI
IA

SYMBOLS

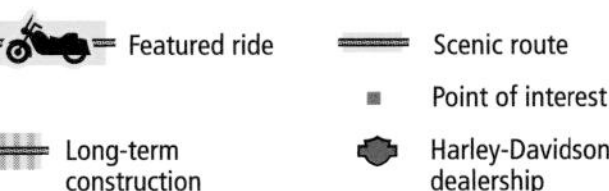
Featured ride
Scenic route
Point of interest
Long-term construction
Harley-Davidson dealership

For Wisconsin/Minnesota ride, see page R38-39.

HARLEY-DAVIDSON DEALERSHIPS

For the Minneapolis/St. Paul metro area, please see dealer listings on page 113.

Bergdale Harley-Davidson, T-9
905 Plaza St. **Albert Lea**
(507) 373-5236
Lat N 43.661 **Lon** W 93.372

Apol's Harley-Davidson, M-5
1515 42nd Ave. West **Alexandria**
(888) 544-1791
Lat N 45.890 **Lon** W 95.366

Donahue Harley-Davidson Shop of Brainerd, K-7
15808 Edgewood **Baxter**
(218) 822-4434
Lat N 46.384 **Lon** W 94.257

Donahue Harley-Davidson, O-8
4354 US Hwy. 12 SE **Delano**
(763) 972-2677
Lat N 45.04 **Lon** W 93.796

Zylstra Harley-Davidson, N-9
19600 Evans St. NW **Elk River**
(763) 241-2000
Lat N 45.329 **Lon** W 93.56

Faribault Harley-Davidson, R-9
2704 W Airport Dr. **Faribault**
(507) 334-5130
Lat N 44.299 **Lon** W 93.29

Twin Cities Harley-Davidson, P-9
10770 165th St. W **Lakeville**
(952) 898-4515
Lat N 44.71 **Lon** W 93.283

Mankato Harley-Davidson, R-8
1200 N River Dr. **Mankato**
(507) 345-6077
Lat N 44.183 **Lon** W 94.008

Apol's Harley-Davidson Shop, O-5
Hwy. 23 **Raymond**
(320) 967-4511
Lat N 45.018 **Lon** W 95.209

Rochester Harley-Davidson, S-11
7180 Hwy. 14 E **Rochester**
(507) 288-9050
Lat N 44.003 **Lon** W 92.336

Donahue Harley-Davidson, N-7
3555 Shadowwood Dr. NE **Sauk Rapids**
(320) 251-6980
Lat N 45.582 **Lon** W 94.09

Harley-Davidson Shop of Winona, R-13
1845 Mobile Dr. **Winona**
(507) 454-4578
Lat N 44.026 **Lon** W 91.606

Minneapolis / St. Paul & Vicinity
© Rand McNally
Minneapolis
St. Paul
Anoka
Coon Rapids
Blaine
Lino Lakes
Centerville
Hugo
Lexington
Circle Pines
Mounds View
Spring Lake Pk.
Fridley
Columbia Heights
Hilltop
New Brighton
Arden Hills
Shoreview
North Oaks
Vadnais Heights
Little Canada
Roseville
Lauderdale
Falcon Hts.
St. Anthony
Maplewood
North St. Paul
Oakdale
Woodbury
Landfall
Gem Lake
White Bear Lake
Birchwood Village
Willernie
Mahtomedi
Grant
Dellwood
White Bear Beach
Bald Eagle
Pine Springs
Lake Elmo
West St. Paul
South St. Paul
Lilydale
Mendota
Mendota Heights
Richfield
Edina
Hopkins
Minnetonka
St. Louis Park
Golden Valley
Robbinsdale
Crystal
New Hope
Brooklyn Center
Brooklyn Park
Osseo
Champlin
Dayton
Maple Grove
Plymouth
Medicine Lake
Wayzata
Woodland
Deephaven

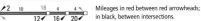

How to determine distance

Mileages in red between red arrowheads; in black, between intersections.

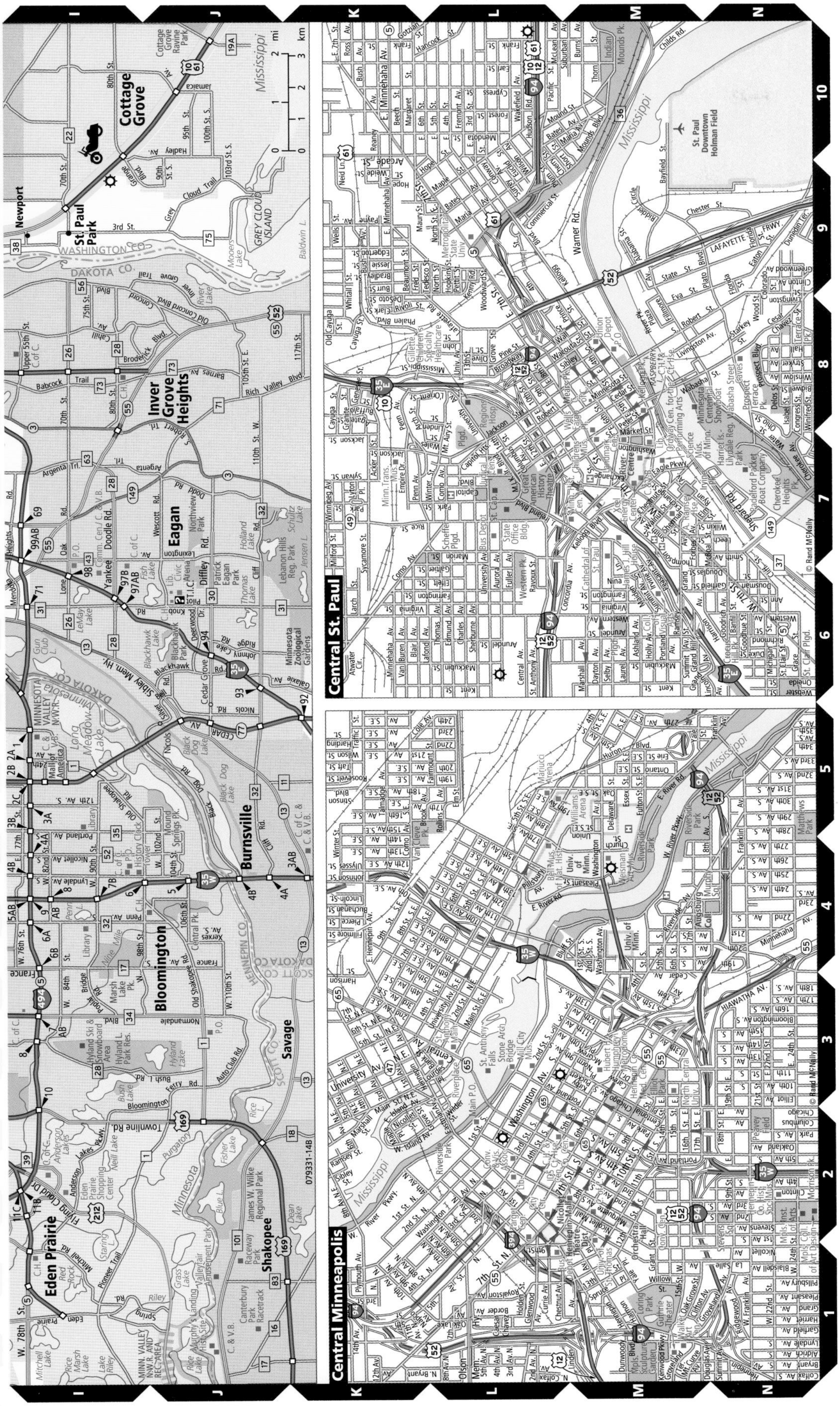

Central St. Paul

Central Minneapolis

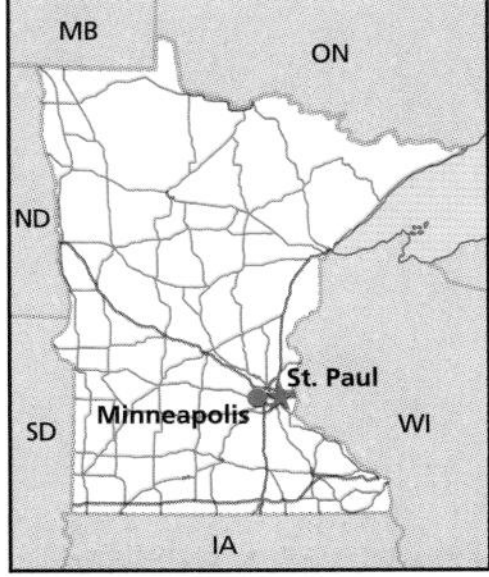
MB
ON
ND
St. Paul
Minneapolis
SD
WI
IA

SYMBOLS

Featured ride

Scenic route

Point of interest

Long-term construction

Harley-Davidson dealership

CITY-TO-CITY MILEAGE

	BEMIDJI	DULUTH	MINNEAPOLIS	MOORHEAD	ROCHESTER	ST. CLOUD	ST. PAUL	SIOUX FALLS, SD
Albert Lea	315	251	97	330	64	165	100	175
Austin	319	255	101	334	39	169	104	197
Bemidji		153	222	142	315	150	231	384
Brainerd	99	114	133	140	226	61	142	274
Duluth	153		157	254	235	143	151	423
Fairmont	296	306	152	357	119	146	155	121
Fergus Falls	141	211	184	55	277	120	193	236
Grand Forks, ND	113	264	318	80	411	254	327	318
Hibbing	108	76	196	216	274	178	190	462
International Falls	116	164	299	256	377	250	293	498
La Crosse, WI	389	239	164	400	72	235	154	297
Mankato	272	237	80	283	82	122	86	155
Marshall	261	276	155	202	193	133	161	90
Minneapolis	222	157		237	94	72	10	269
Moorhead	142	254	237		330	173	246	244
Red Wing	280	198	60	295	49	130	50	283
Rochester	315	235	94	330		165	84	236
St. Cloud	150	143	72	173	165		81	221
St. Paul	231	151	10	246	84	81		272
Sioux Falls, SD	384	423	269	244	236	221	272	
Willmar	194	209	96	174	186	66	106	156

HARLEY-DAVIDSON DEALERSHIPS

Twin Cities Harley-Davidson North, C-5
1441 85th Ave. NE **Blaine**
(763) 786-9079
Lat N 45.125 **Lon** W 93.234

St. Paul Harley-Davidson, G-9
2899 Hudson Blvd. **St. Paul**
(651) 738-2168
Lat N 44.949 **Lon** W 92.978

Twin Cities Harley-Davidson / Minneapolis-St. Paul International Airport, H-6
4300 Glumack Dr. **St. Paul**
(407) 447-3178
Lat N 44.883 **Lon** W 93.206

Distance scale
One inch represents about 29 miles

0 10 20 mi
0 10 20 30 km

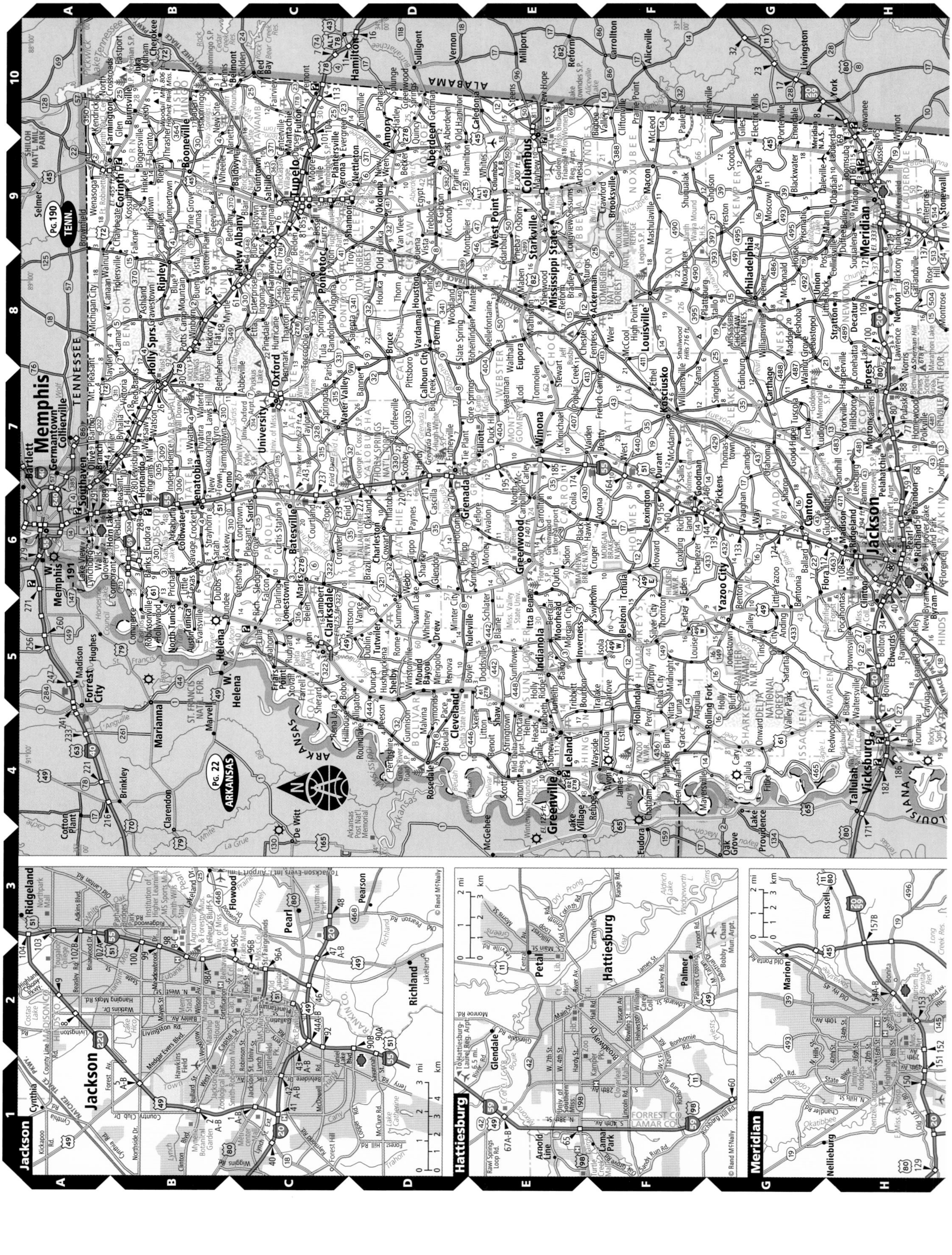

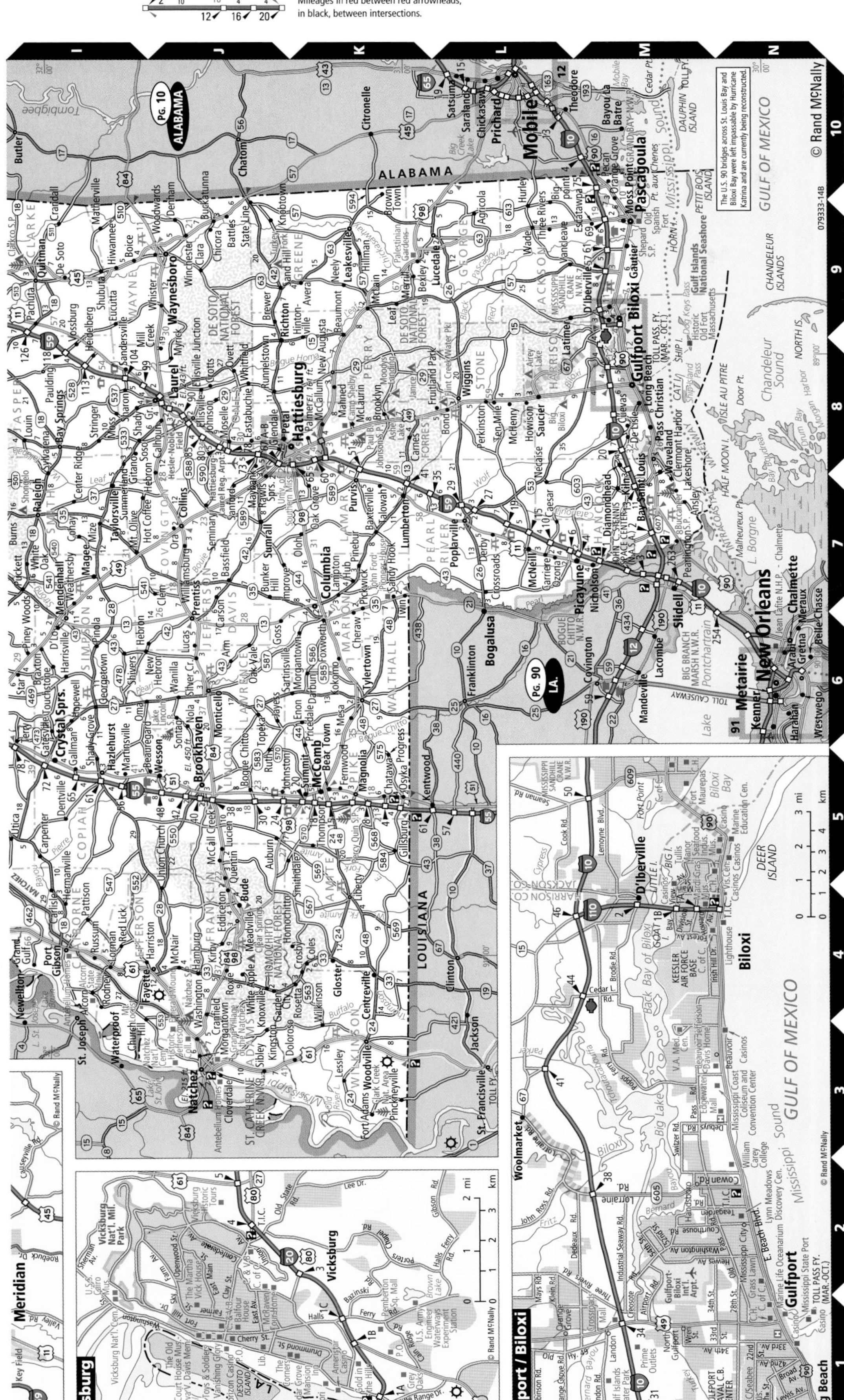
How to determine distance
Mileages in red between red arrowheads; in black, between intersections.
ALABAMA
LOUISIANA
GULF OF MEXICO
Vicksburg
Gulfport / Biloxi
Meridian
The U.S. 90 bridges across St. Louis Bay and Biloxi Bay were left impassable by Hurricane Katrina and are currently being reconstructed.
© Rand McNally

SYMBOLS

Featured ride
Scenic route
Point of interest
Long-term construction
Harley-Davidson dealership

MISSISSIPPI MOTORCYCLE LAWS

Helmet use:
Required

Riding two abreast:
No reference in administrative code or statutes

Eye protection:
Not required

Speed limit:
Primary roads: 70 mph
Secondary roads: 70 mph

MISSISSIPPI RESOURCES

Road conditions or construction:
(601) 987-1211
(601) 359-7301
www.mdot.state.ms.us

Highway Emergency Numbers:
911

Tourism:
(800) 927-6378
(601) 359-3297
www.visitmississippi.org

State motor vehicle information:
(601) 987-1200
www.dps.state.ms.us

CITY-TO-CITY MILEAGE

	Biloxi	Greenville	Jackson	Memphis, TN	Meridian	New Orleans, LA	Tupelo	Vicksburg
Biloxi		290	170	378	168	87	312	215
Greenville	290		120	147	192	300	193	101
Jackson	170	120		212	93	180	225	45
Memphis, TN	378	147	212		230	392	107	254
Meridian	168	192	93	230		196	144	138
Natchez	223	153	114	326	207	175	339	74
New Orleans, LA	87	300	180	392	196		340	225
Tupelo	312	193	225	107	144	340		267
Vicksburg	215	101	45	254	138	225	267	

HARLEY-DAVIDSON DEALERSHIPS

Mississippi Coast Harley-Davidson, M-9
941 Cedar Lake Rd. **Biloxi**
(228) 388-8700
Lat N 30.445 **Lon** W 88.934

Southern Thunder Harley-Davidson, A-6
6935 Windchase Dr. **Horn Lake**
(662) 349-1099
Lat N 34.955 **Lon** W 90.049

Harley-Davidson of Jackson, H-6
3509 I-55 S **Jackson**
(601) 372-5770
Lat N 32.252 **Lon** W 90.214

Chunky River Harley-Davidson, H-9
584 Bonita Lakes Dr. **Meridian**
(601) 482-4131
Lat N 32.36 **Lon** W 88.672

Distance scale
One inch represents about 26 miles

0 10 20 30 mi
0 10 20 30 40 km

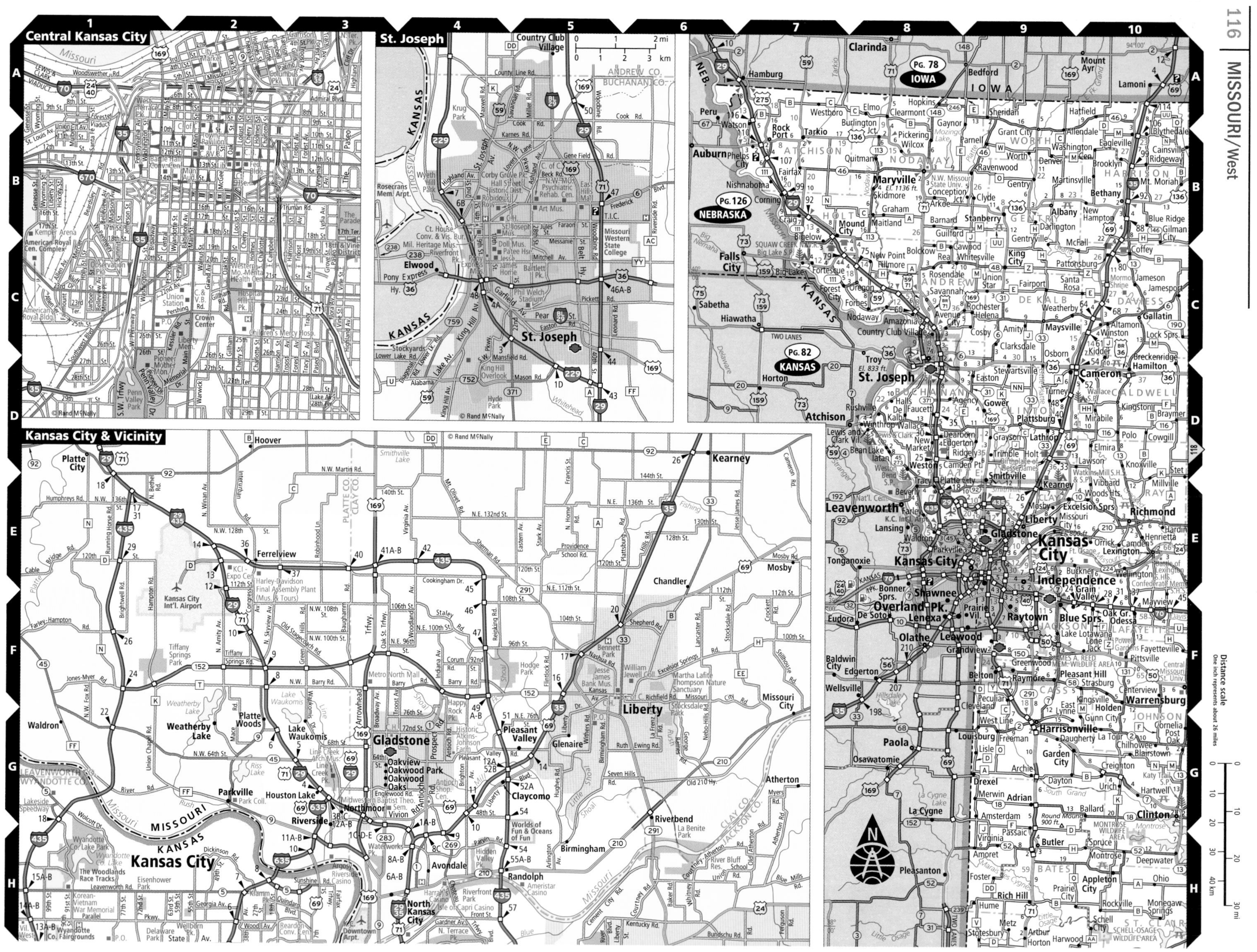
Central Kansas City
St. Joseph
Kansas City & Vicinity
PG. 78 IOWA
PG. 82 KANSAS
PG. 126 NEBRASKA
118
Kansas City
St. Joseph
Independence
Leavenworth
Liberty
Gladstone
Overland Pk.
Olathe
Lenexa
Shawnee
Blue Sprs.
Raytown
Harrisonville
Warrensburg
Clinton
Cameron
Maryville
Bethany
Richmond
Atchison
Kearney
Paola
Clarinda
Hamburg
Auburn
Falls City
© Rand McNally

How to determine distance

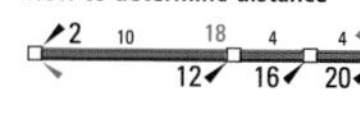
2
10
18
4
4
12
16
20

Mileages in red between red arrowheads; in black, between intersections.

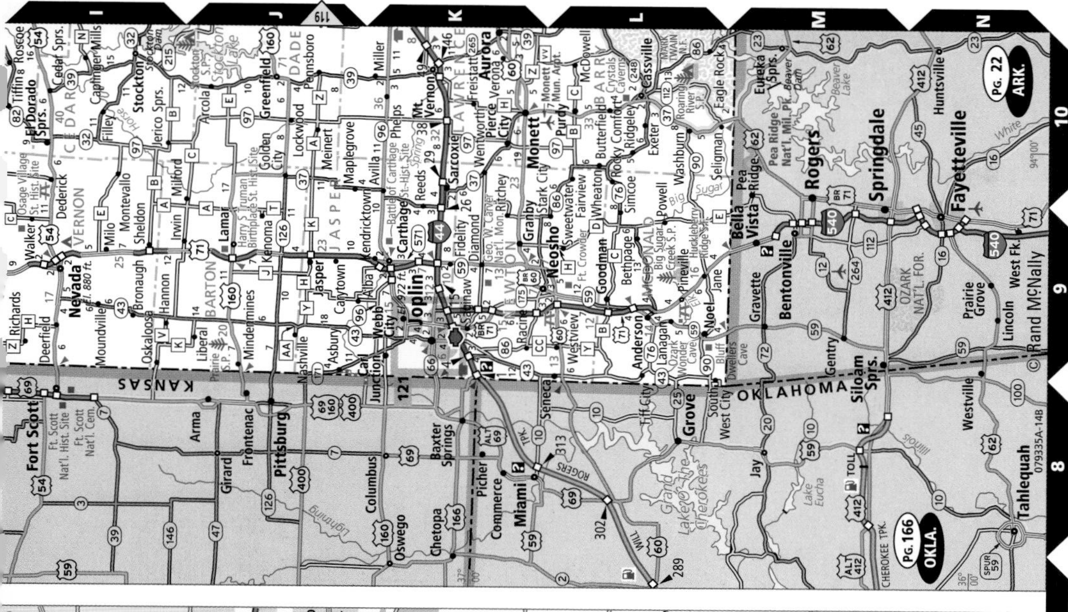

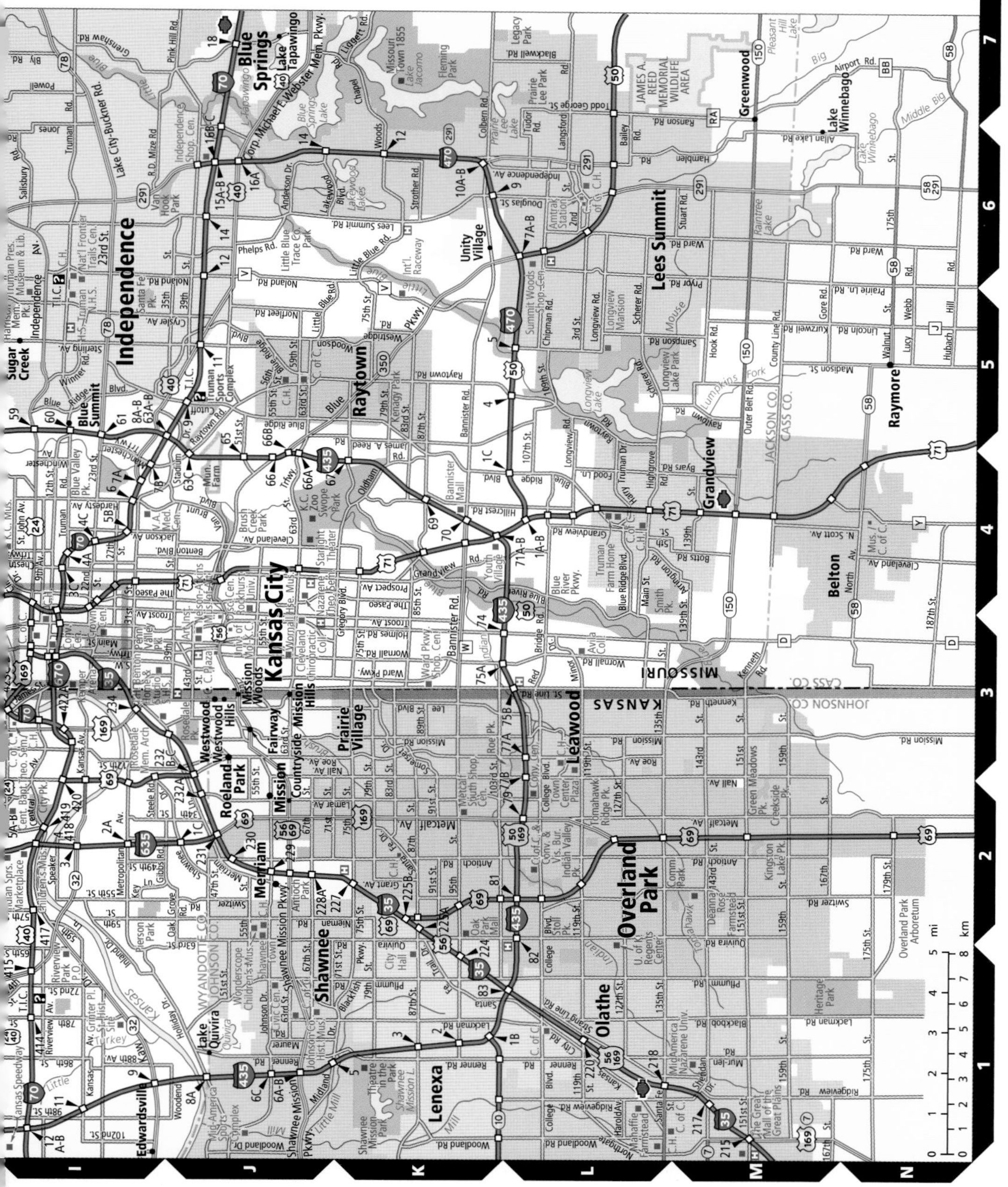

IA
IL
Kansas City
KS
p. 118-119
OK
AR
TN

SYMBOLS

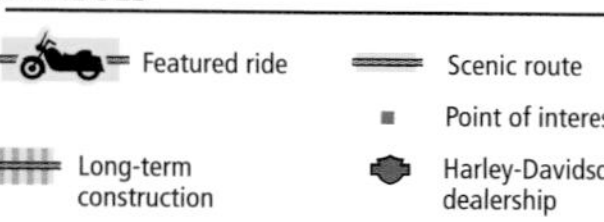
Featured ride
Scenic route
Point of interest
Long-term construction
Harley-Davidson dealership

MISSOURI MOTORCYCLE LAWS

Helmet use:
Required

Riding two abreast:
No reference in administrative code or statutes

Eye protection:
Not required

Speed limit:
Primary roads: 70 mph
Secondary roads: 60 mph

MISSOURI RESOURCES

Road conditions or construction:
(800) 222-6400 (in MO)
www.modot.mo.gov

Highway Emergency Numbers:
911 or *55

Tourism:
(800) 810-5500 (to request travel materials only)
(573) 751-4133
www.visitmo.com

State motor vehicle information:
(573) 751-4600
www.dor.mo.gov/mvdl/drivers

HARLEY-DAVIDSON DEALERSHIPS

Blue Springs Harley-Davidson, F-9
3100 NW Jefferson St. **Blue Springs**
(816) 224-5005
Lat N 39.035 **Lon** W 94.3

Worth Harley-Davidson North, E-9
6609 N Oak Traffic Way **Gladstone**
(816) 420-9000
Lat N 39.214 **Lon** W 94.576

Gail's Harley-Davidson, F-9
5900 E Hwy. 150 **Grandview**
(816) 966-2222
Lat N 38.882 **Lon** W 94.521

Cycle Connection Harley-Davidson, K-9
5014 Hearnes Blvd. **Joplin**
(417) 623-1054
Lat N 37.043 **Lon** W 94.515

St. Joe Harley-Davidson, D-8
4020 S 169 Hwy. **St. Joseph**
(816) 233-9061
Lat N 39.733 **Lon** W 94.821

Distance scale
One inch represents about 26 miles

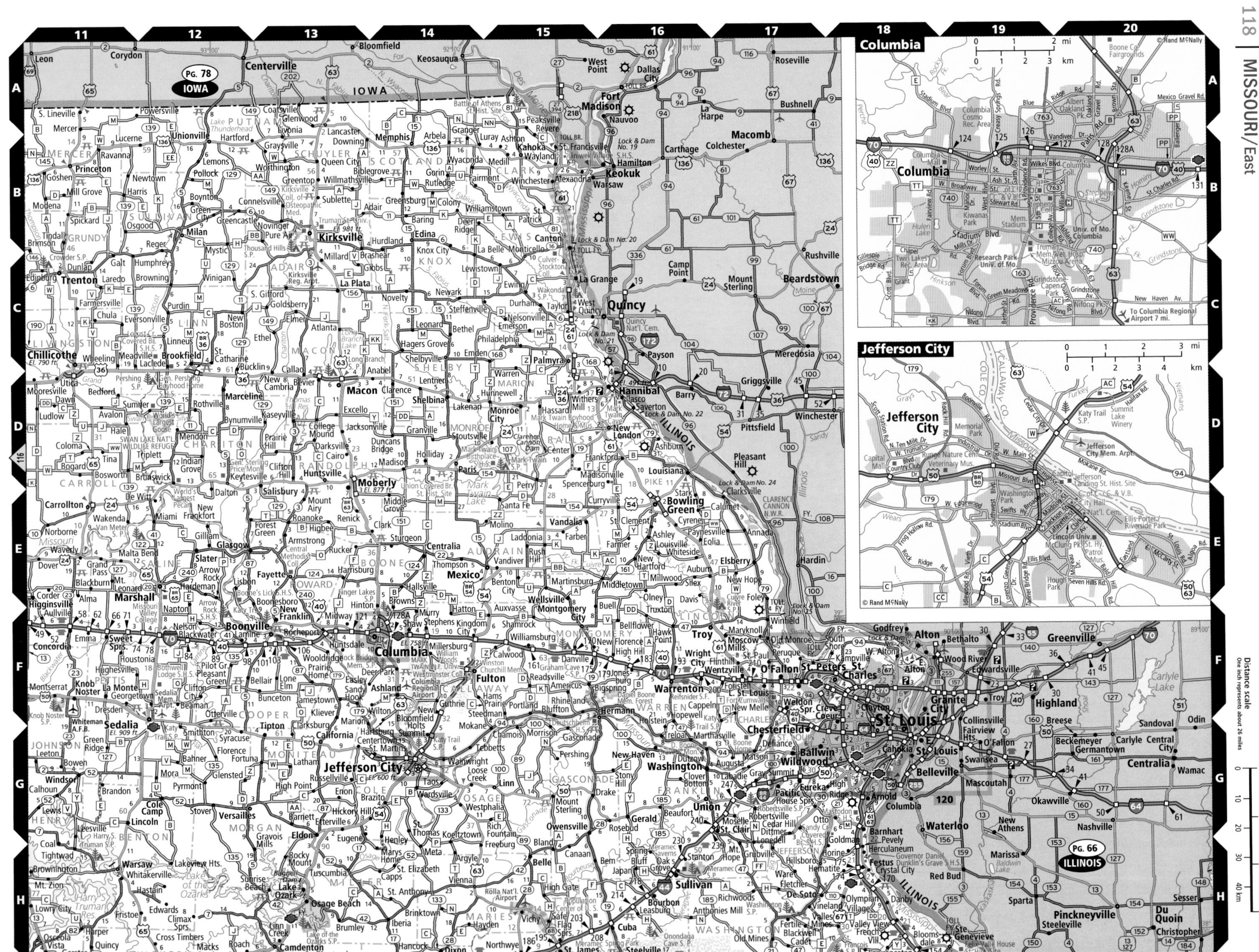
Columbia
Jefferson City
St. Louis
Quincy
Hannibal
Kirksville
Sedalia
Fulton
Mexico
PG. 78 IOWA
PG. 66 ILLINOIS
© Rand McNally

How to determine distance

Mileages in red between red arrowheads; in black, between intersections.

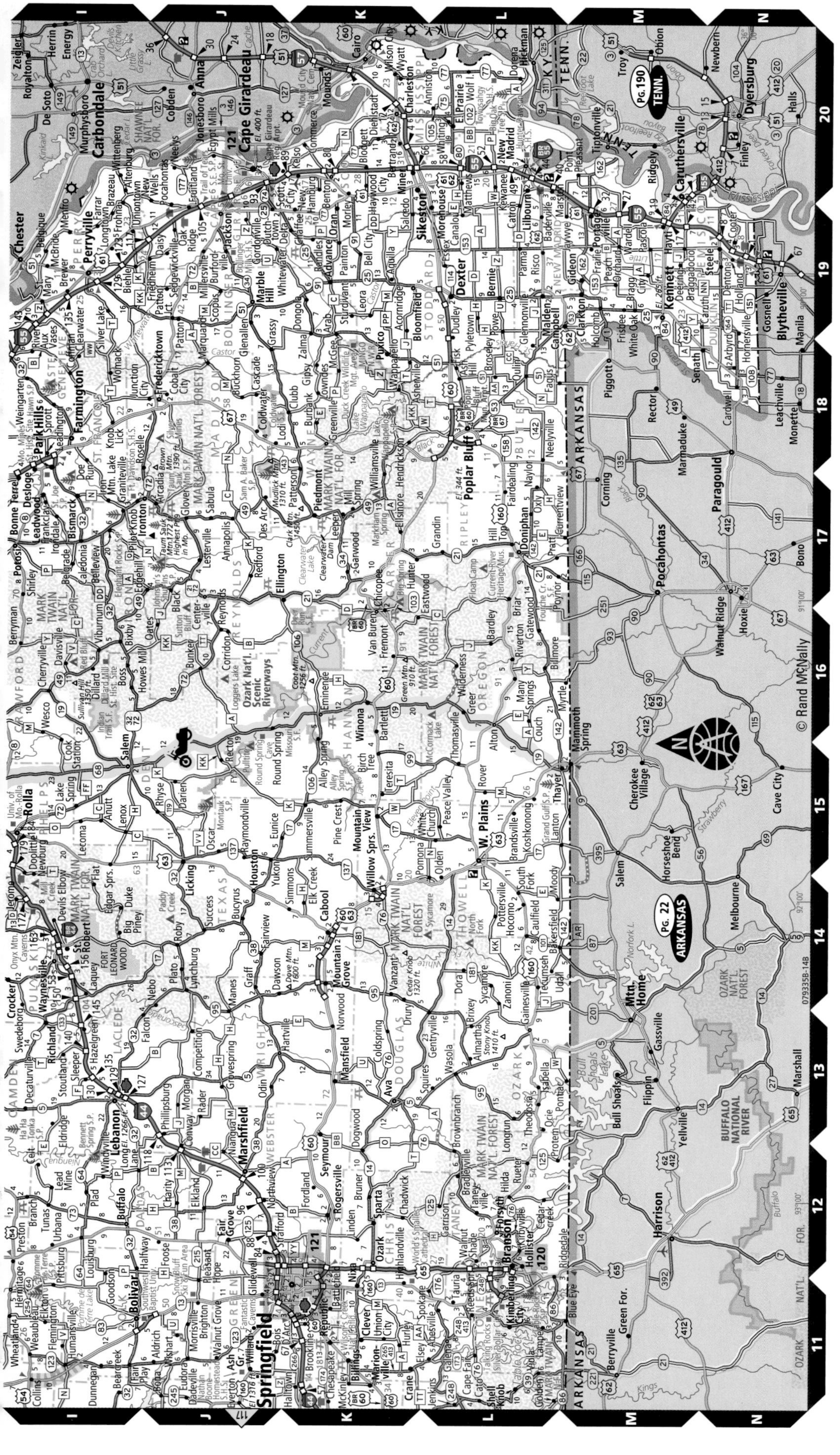

IA
IL
p. 116-117
St. Louis
KS
OK
AR
TN

SYMBOLS

- Featured ride
- Scenic route
- Point of interest
- Long-term construction
- Harley-Davidson dealership

For Missouri ride, see page R22-23.

CITY-TO-CITY MILEAGE

	CAPE GIRARDEAU	COLUMBIA	JOPLIN	KANSAS CITY	POPLAR BLUFF	ST. JOSEPH	ST. LOUIS	SPRINGFIELD
Branson	342	205	112	211	219	265	250	42
Brookfield	320	97	274	117	357	100	217	200
Cape Girardeau		227	374	356	84	412	114	304
Columbia	227		237	129	264	185	124	167
Hannibal	219	97	312	213	256	196	116	242
Hayti	81	304	326	433	63	489	191	256
Jefferson City	236	31	206	160	222	216	133	136
Joplin	374	237		150	263	202	282	72
Kansas City	356	129	150		393	54	253	169
Kirksville	320	97	315	158	357	141	217	260
Maryville	452	225	242	94	489	42	349	263
Osage Beach	257	76	161	173	230	229	165	91
Poplar Bluff	84	264	263	393		449	151	193
Rolla	197	93	178	222	170	278	105	108
St. Joseph	412	185	202	54	449		309	223
St. Louis	114	124	282	253	151	309		212
Springfield	304	167	72	169	193	223	212	
West Plains	186	192	180	279	102	333	204	110

HARLEY-DAVIDSON DEALERSHIPS

For the St. Louis metro area, please see dealer listings on page 121.

Mid America Harley-Davidson, F-14
5704 Freedom Dr. **Columbia**
(573) 875-4444
Lat N 38.962 **Lon** W 92.252

Gary Surdyke Harley-Davidson, H-18
2435 Hwy. 67 S **Festus**
(636) 931-8700
Lat N 38.178 **Lon** W 90.446

Ozark Harley-Davidson, I-13
2300 Evergreen Pkwy. **Lebanon**
(417) 532-2900
Lat N 37.636 **Lon** W 92.48

Lake of the Ozarks Harley-Davidson Shop, H-13
6482 Hwy. 54 **Osage Beach**
(573) 302-7600
Lat N 38.099 **Lon** W 92.685

Minor's Harley-Davidson Sales, J-20
2100 E Outer Rd. N (Exit 91) **Scott City**
(800) 474-0516
Lat N 37.227 **Lon** W 89.559

Yeager Cycle Sales, G-12
3001 S Limit (Hwy. 65) **Sedalia**
(660) 826-2925
Lat N 38.686 **Lon** W 93.251

Denney's Harley-Davidson of Springfield, K-11
3980 W Sunshine St. **Springfield**
(417) 882-0100
Lat N 37.181 **Lon** W 93.361

Bourbeuse Valley Harley-Davidson, G-17
1418 Hwy. AT **Villa Ridge**
(636) 742-2707
Lat N 38.459 **Lon** W 90.879

St. Louis & Vicinity

Central St. Louis

Branson

© Rand McNally

How to determine distance

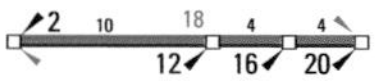

Mileages in red between red arrowheads; in black, between intersections.

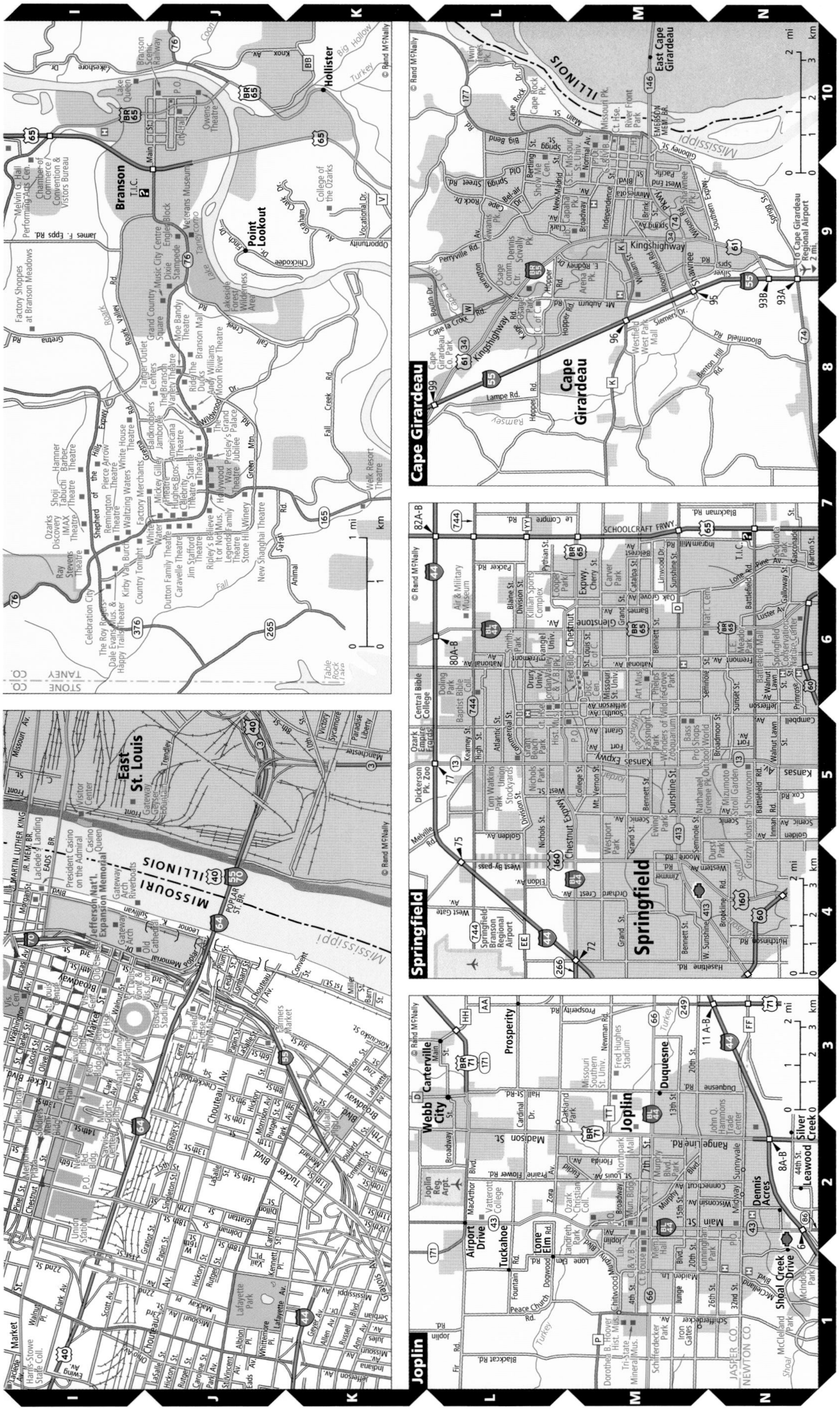

Branson

Cape Girardeau

Springfield

Joplin

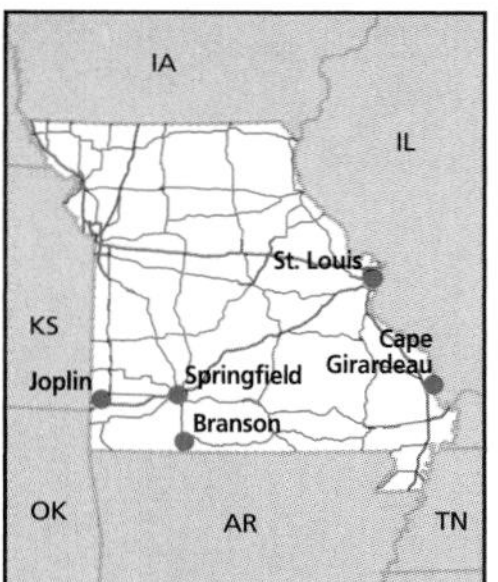
IA
IL
St. Louis
KS
Joplin
Springfield
Cape Girardeau
Branson
OK
AR
TN

SYMBOLS

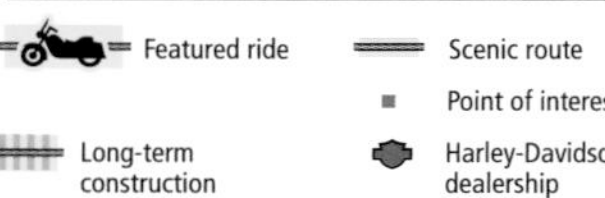
Featured ride
Scenic route
Point of interest
Long-term construction
Harley-Davidson dealership

MISSOURI MOTORCYCLE LAWS

Helmet use:
Required

Riding two abreast:
No reference in administrative code or statutes

Eye protection:
Not required

Speed limit:
Primary roads: 70 mph
Secondary roads: 60 mph

MISSOURI RESOURCES

Road conditions or construction:
(800) 222-6400 (in MO)
www.modot.mo.gov

Highway Emergency Numbers:
911 or *55

Tourism:
(573) 751-4133
www.visitmo.com

State motor vehicle information:
(573) 751-4600
www.dor.mo.gov/mvdl/drivers

HARLEY-DAVIDSON DEALERSHIPS

Doc's Harley-Davidson Motorcycle Sales & Service, F-4
930 S Kirkwood Rd. **Kirkwood**
(314) 965-0166
Lat N 38.568 **Lon** W 90.407

Bob Schultz Harley-Davidson, C-3
3830 W Clay St. **St. Charles**
(636) 946-6487
Lat N 38.792 **Lon** W 90.56

Gateway to the West Harley-Davidson, G-6
3600 LeMay Ferry Rd. **St. Louis**
(314) 845-9900
Lat N 38.511 **Lon** W 90.32

Distance scale
One inch represents about 31 miles
0 10 20 30 mi
0 10 20 30 40 km

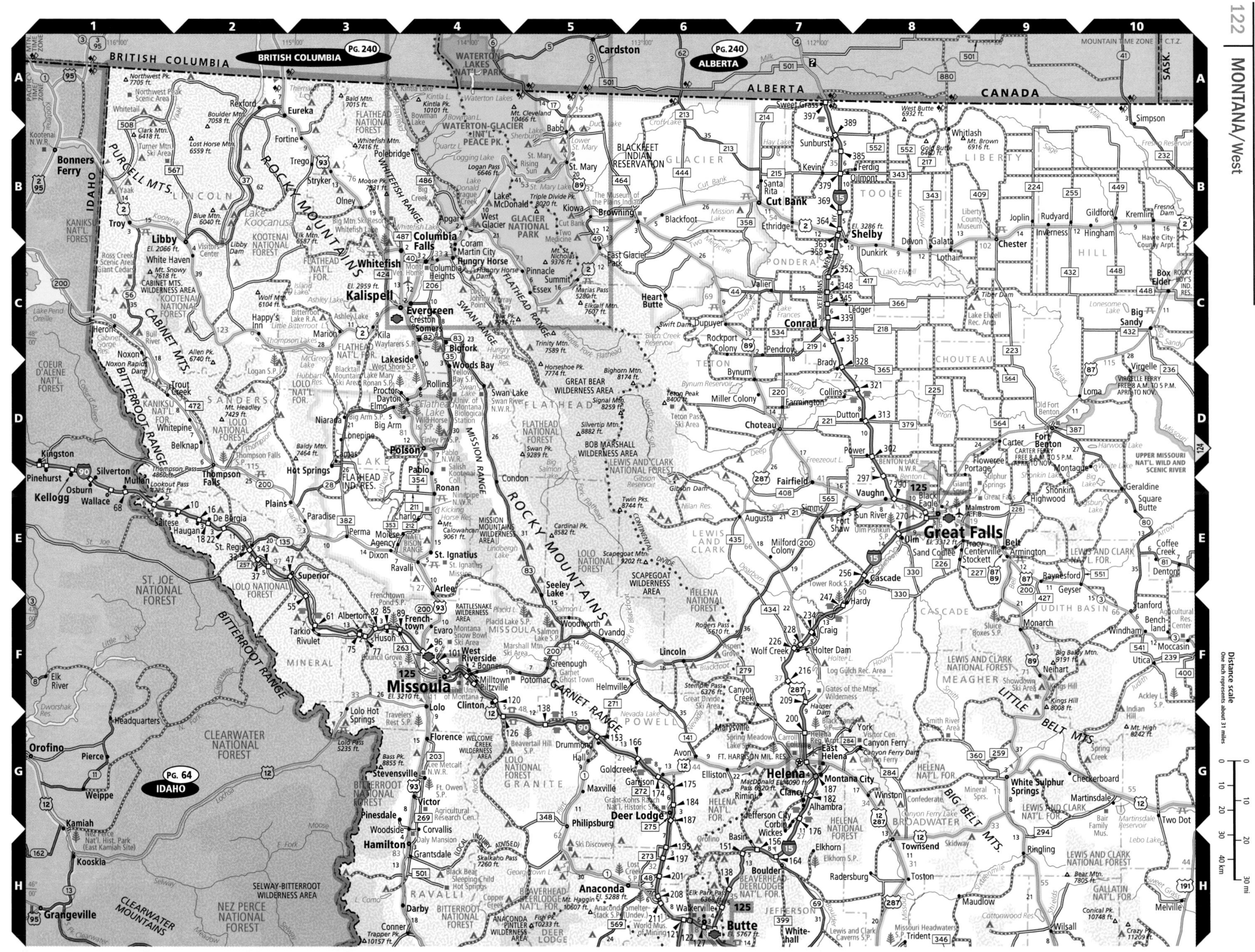
BRITISH COLUMBIA
ALBERTA
CANADA
IDAHO
PG. 240 BRITISH COLUMBIA
PG. 240 ALBERTA
PG. 64 IDAHO
Great Falls
Missoula
Helena
Butte
Kalispell
Shelby
Cut Bank
Conrad
Choteau
Whitefish
Columbia Falls
Polson
Hamilton
Anaconda
Deer Lodge
Libby
Eureka
Browning
Big Sandy
Fort Benton
Chester
Lincoln
Seeley Lake
Thompson Falls
Superior
ROCKY MOUNTAINS
LITTLE BELT MTS.
BIG BELT MTS.
CABINET MTS.
PURCELL MTS.
BITTERROOT RANGE
GARNET RANGE
MISSION RANGE
SWAN RANGE
FLATHEAD RANGE
WHITEFISH RANGE
GLACIER NATIONAL PARK
WATERTON-GLACIER INT'L PEACE PK.
BLACKFEET INDIAN RESERVATION
FLATHEAD IND. RES.
BOB MARSHALL WILDERNESS AREA
SCAPEGOAT WILDERNESS AREA
GREAT BEAR WILDERNESS AREA
CLEARWATER NATIONAL FOREST
ST. JOE NATIONAL FOREST
NEZ PERCE NATIONAL FOREST
SELWAY-BITTERROOT WILDERNESS AREA
CLEARWATER MOUNTAINS
CONTINENTAL DIVIDE

How to determine distance

Mileages in red between red arrowheads; in black, between intersections.

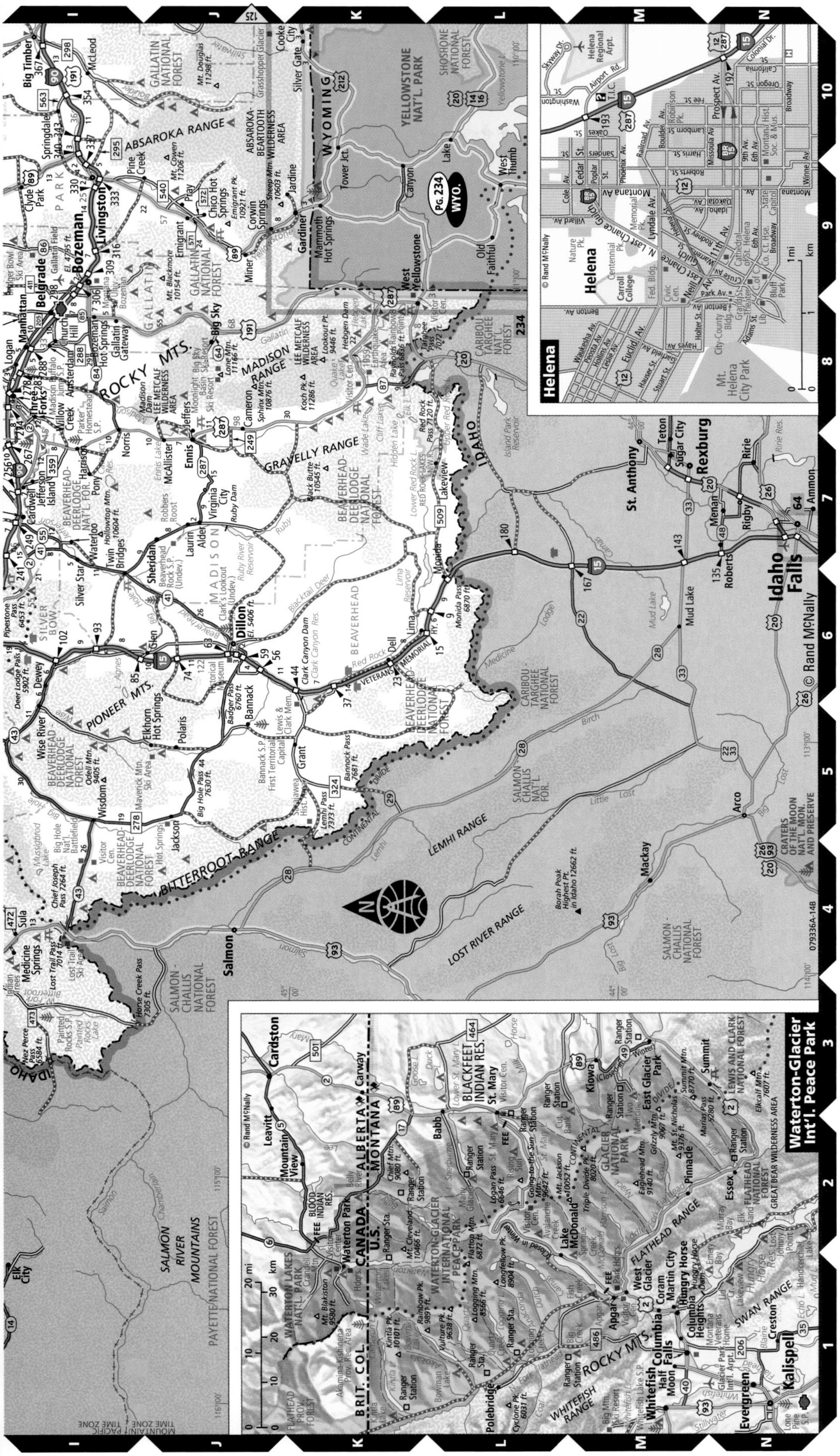

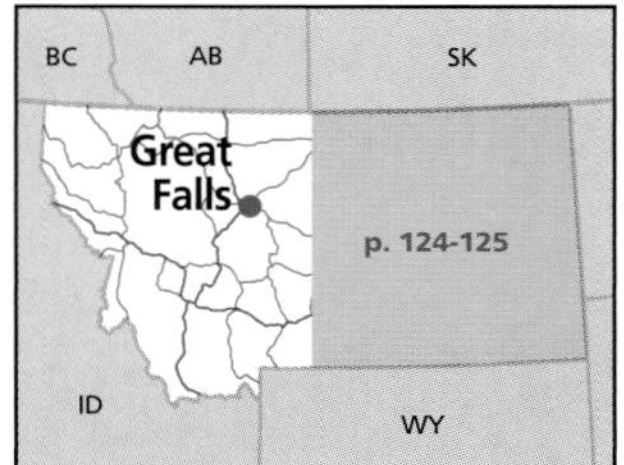
BC
AB
SK
Great Falls
p. 124-125
ID
WY

SYMBOLS

- Featured ride
- Scenic route
- Point of interest
- Long-term construction
- Harley-Davidson dealership

MONTANA MOTORCYCLE LAWS

Helmet use:
Required under age 18

Riding two abreast:
Yes. See state law for specifics

Eye protection:
Not required

Speed limit:
Primary roads: 75 mph
Secondary roads: 65 mph

MONTANA RESOURCES

Road conditions or construction:
511
(800) 226-7623
www.mdt.mt.gov/travelinfo/

Highway Emergency Numbers:
911

Tourism:
(800) 847-4868
(406) 841-2870
www.visitmt.com

State motor vehicle information:
(406) 444-3288
www.doj.state.mt.us/driving

HARLEY-DAVIDSON DEALERSHIPS

Yellowstone Harley-Davidson of Belgrade, I-8
540 Alaska Frontage Rd. **Belgrade**
(406) 388-7684
Lat N 45.761 **Lon** W 111.166

Thunderbolt Harley-Davidson, H-6
34 Olympic Way **Butte**
(406) 782-5601
Lat N 45.962 **Lon** W 112.477

Big Sky Harley-Davidson, E-8
4258 10th Ave. S **Great Falls**
(406) 727-2161
Lat N 47.494 **Lon** W 111.234

Montana Harley-Davidson Shop, C-4
2480 Hwy. 93 S **Kalispell**
(406) 752-6843
Lat N 48.221 **Lon** W 114.235

Montana Harley-Davidson, F-4
5106 E Harrier Blvd. **Missoula**
(406) 721-2154
Lat N 46.934 **Lon** W 114.087

Distance scale
One inch represents about 31 miles
0 10 20 30 mi
0 10 20 30 40 km

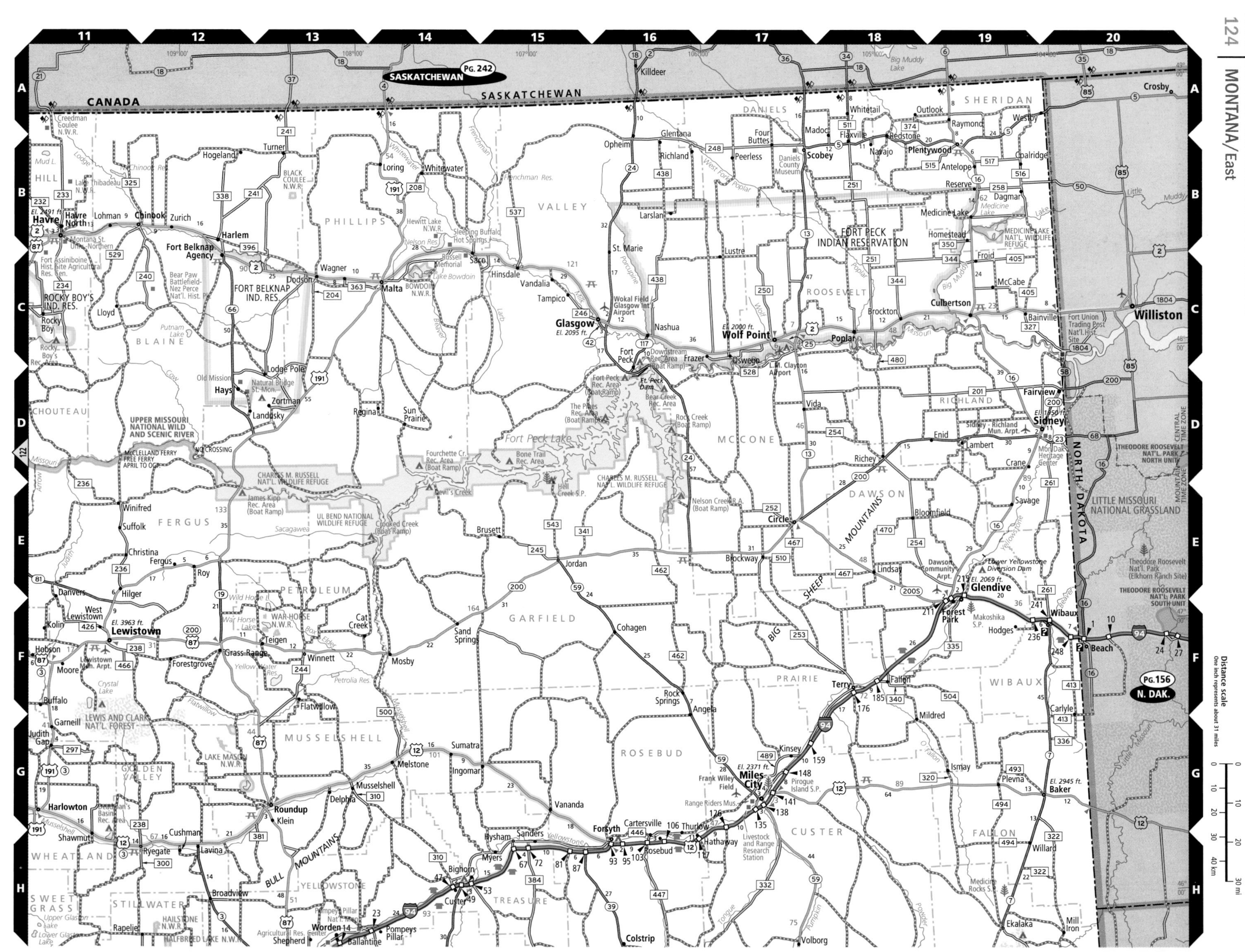
CANADA
SASKATCHEWAN
PG. 242 SASKATCHEWAN
NORTH DAKOTA
PG. 156 N. DAK.
Williston
Crosby
Sidney
Glendive
Wibaux
Beach
Baker
Plevna
Ekalaka
Terry
Fallon
Miles City
Forsyth
Colstrip
Rosebud
Hysham
Custer
Roundup
Lewistown
Havre
Chinook
Harlem
Malta
Glasgow
Wolf Point
Poplar
Culbertson
Plentywood
Scobey
Fort Peck
Jordan
Circle
Winnett
Grass Range
Harlowton
Hobson
Moore
FORT PECK INDIAN RESERVATION
FORT BELKNAP IND. RES.
ROCKY BOY'S IND. RES.
CHARLES M. RUSSELL NAT'L. WILDLIFE REFUGE
UL BEND NATIONAL WILDLIFE REFUGE
UPPER MISSOURI NATIONAL WILD AND SCENIC RIVER
LITTLE MISSOURI NATIONAL GRASSLAND
THEODORE ROOSEVELT NAT'L. PARK NORTH UNIT
THEODORE ROOSEVELT NAT'L. PARK SOUTH UNIT
LEWIS AND CLARK NAT'L. FOREST
LAKE MASON N.W.R.
WAR HORSE N.W.R.
BIG SHEEP MOUNTAINS
BULL MOUNTAINS
SHERIDAN
DANIELS
ROOSEVELT
RICHLAND
DAWSON
WIBAUX
FALLON
PRAIRIE
CUSTER
MCCONE
VALLEY
PHILLIPS
BLAINE
HILL
CHOUTEAU
FERGUS
PETROLEUM
GARFIELD
ROSEBUD
TREASURE
MUSSELSHELL
GOLDEN VALLEY
WHEATLAND
STILLWATER
SWEET GRASS
YELLOWSTONE
CENTRAL TIME ZONE
MOUNTAIN TIME ZONE
Fort Peck Lake
Yellowstone
Missouri
Milk
122

How to determine distance

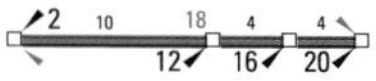

Mileages in red between red arrowheads; in black, between intersections.

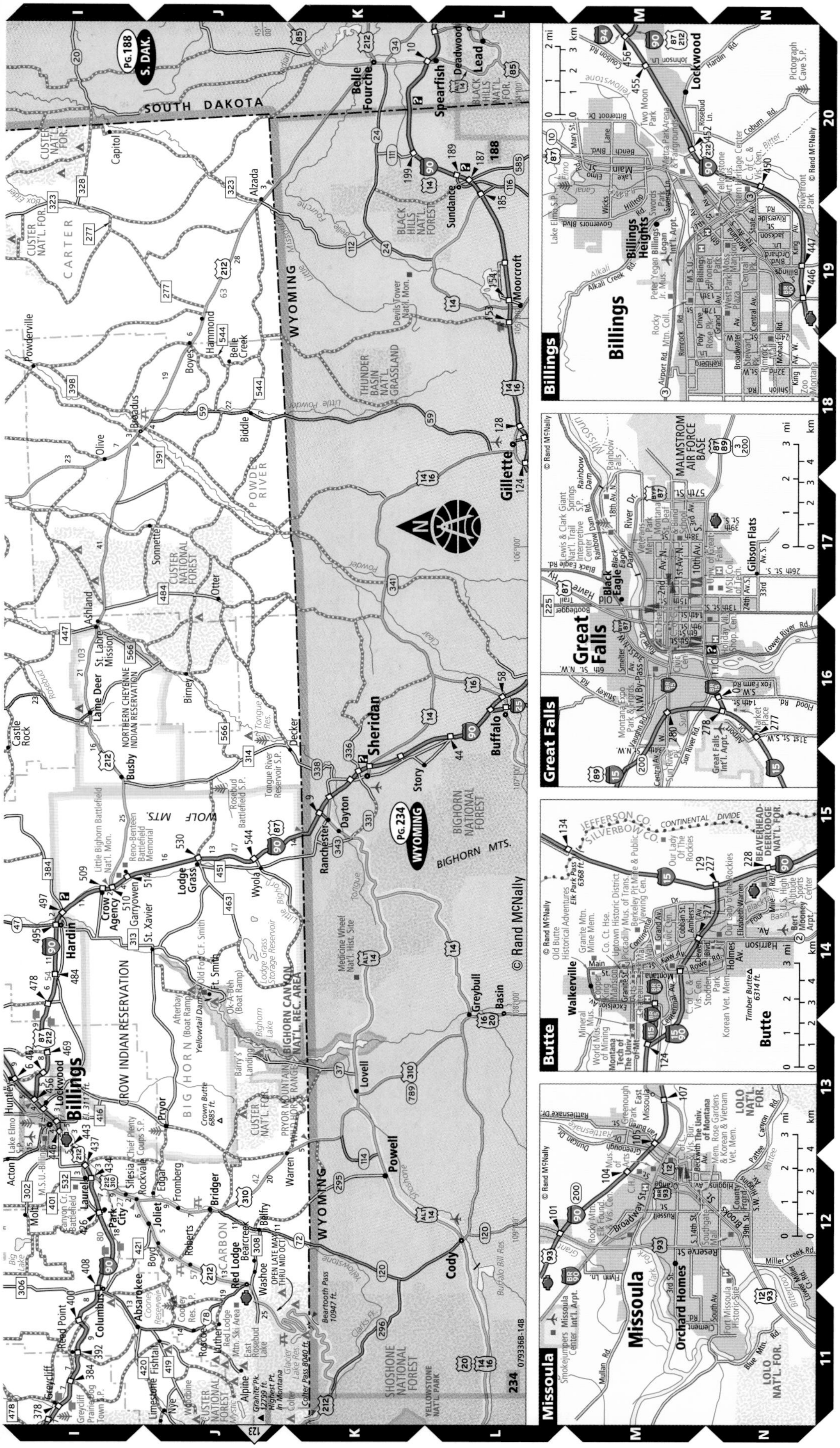

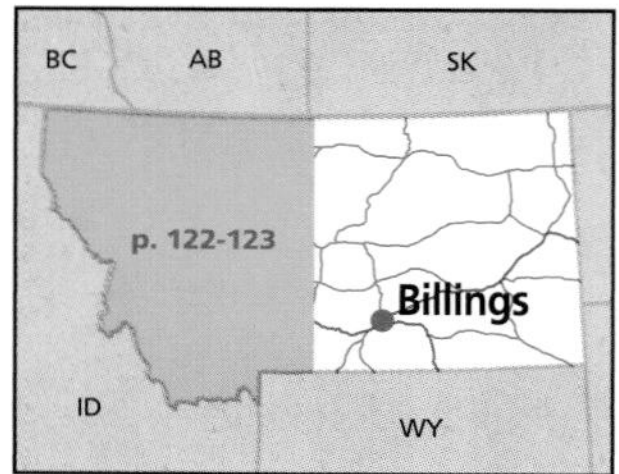
BC
AB
SK
p. 122-123
Billings
ID
WY

SYMBOLS

- Featured ride
- Scenic route
- Point of interest
- Long-term construction
- Harley-Davidson dealership

CITY-TO-CITY MILEAGE

	BILLINGS	BOZEMAN	BUTTE	GREAT FALLS	HELENA	KALISPELL	MILES CITY	MISSOULA
Billings		140	221	222	239	463	144	340
Bozeman	140		82	190	100	324	286	201
Butte	221	82		155	65	242	367	119
Dillon	254	115	67	222	132	295	400	172
Glasgow	278	367	431	276	367	425	222	443
Great Falls	222	190	155		91	233	327	167
Havre	249	305	270	115	206	264	344	282
Helena	239	100	65	91		198	385	111
Kalispell	463	324	242	233	198		609	123
Lewistown	126	162	243	106	195	340	221	274
Libby	532	393	311	324	289	91	678	192
Miles City	144	286	367	327	385	609		486
Missoula	340	201	119	167	111	123	486	
St. Mary	387	306	271	164	207	86	492	209
Shelby	309	271	236	86	172	160	414	227
Sheridan, WY	127	269	350	349	368	592	201	469
Sidney	271	413	494	379	512	565	129	613
West Yellowstone	229	89	148	269	179	390	375	267

HARLEY-DAVIDSON DEALERSHIPS

Beartooth Harley-Davidson, I-13
6900 S Frontage Rd. **Billings**
(406) 252-2888
Lat N 45.739 **Lon** W 108.589

Beartooth Harley-Davidson of Red Lodge, J-11
213 N Broadway **Red Lodge**
(406) 446-9856
Lat N 45.195 **Lon** W 109.309

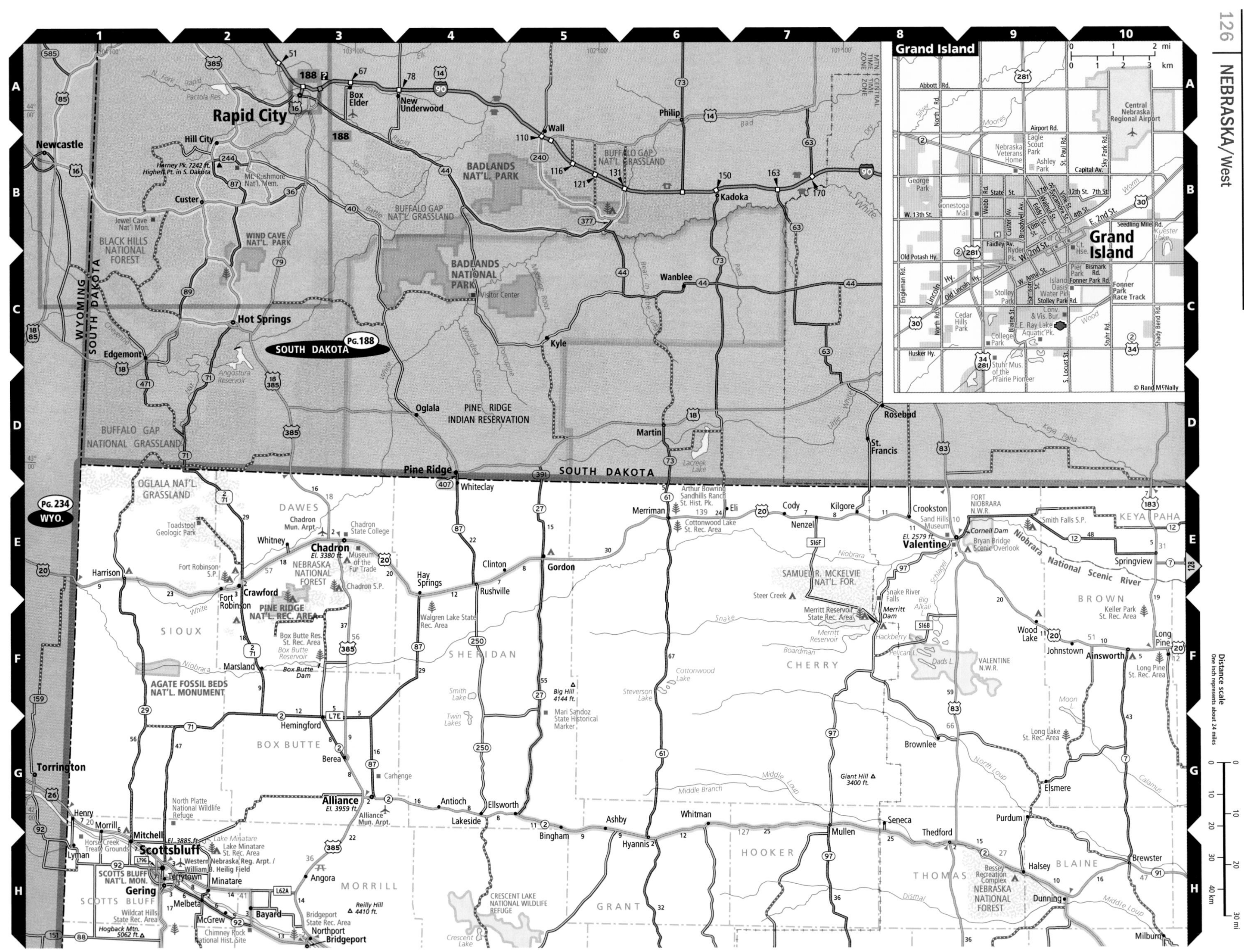

Distance scale
One inch represents about 24 miles
0 10 20 30 mi
0 10 20 30 40 km
Grand Island
© Rand McNally
SOUTH DAKOTA
WYOMING
Rapid City
Hot Springs
Pine Ridge
Valentine
Chadron
Alliance
Scottsbluff
Gering
Torrington
Newcastle
BADLANDS NAT'L. PARK
WIND CAVE NAT'L. PARK
BLACK HILLS NATIONAL FOREST
BUFFALO GAP NATIONAL GRASSLAND
PINE RIDGE INDIAN RESERVATION
OGLALA NAT'L. GRASSLAND
AGATE FOSSIL BEDS NAT'L. MONUMENT
SCOTTS BLUFF NAT'L. MON.
NEBRASKA NATIONAL FOREST
SAMUEL R. MCKELVIE NAT'L. FOR.
VALENTINE N.W.R.
CRESCENT LAKE NATIONAL WILDLIFE REFUGE
Niobrara National Scenic River
PG. 188 SOUTH DAKOTA
PG. 234 WYO.

How to determine distance

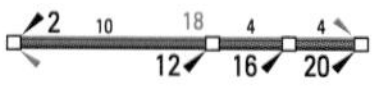

Mileages in red between red arrowheads; in black, between intersections.

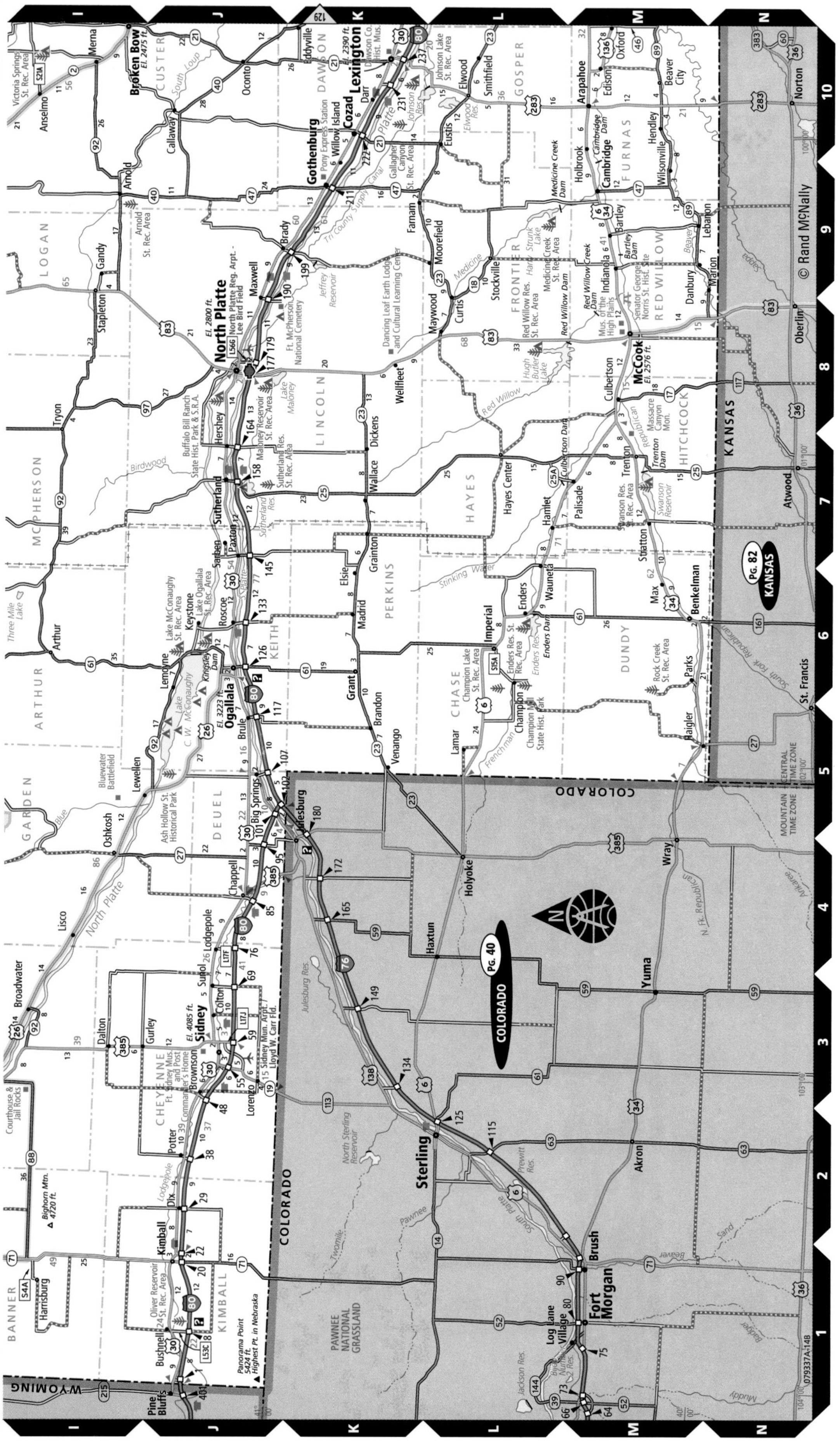

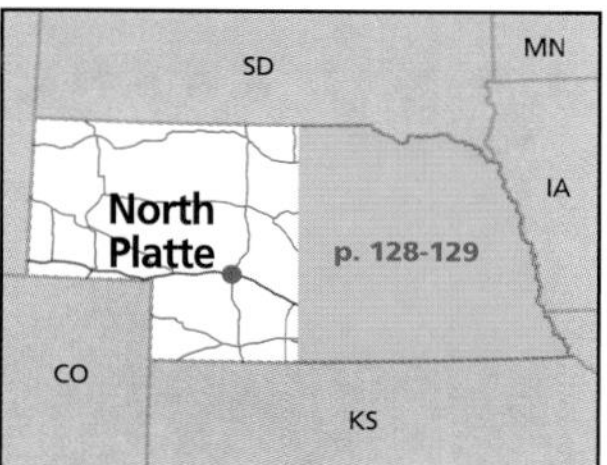

SD
MN
IA
North Platte
p. 128-129
CO
KS

SYMBOLS

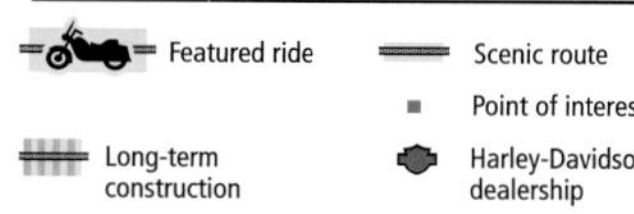

Featured ride
Scenic route
Point of interest
Long-term construction
Harley-Davidson dealership

NEBRASKA MOTORCYCLE LAWS

Helmet use:
Required

Riding two abreast:
Yes. See state law for specifics

Eye protection:
Not required

Speed limit:
Primary roads: 75 mph
Secondary roads: 65 mph

NEBRASKA RESOURCES

Road conditions or construction:
511
(800) 906-9069
(402) 471-4533
www.511nebraska.org

Highway Emergency Numbers:
911

Tourism:
(877) 632-7275
(800) 228-4307
(402) 471-3796
www.visitnebraska.org

State motor vehicle information:
(402) 471-2281
www.dmv.state.ne.us

HARLEY-DAVIDSON DEALERSHIPS

Budke's Harley-Davidson, J-8
695 E Halligan Dr. **North Platte**
(308) 532-4339
Lat N 41.111 **Lon** W 100.756

Distance scale
One inch represents about 24 miles
0 10 20 30 mi
0 10 20 30 40 km

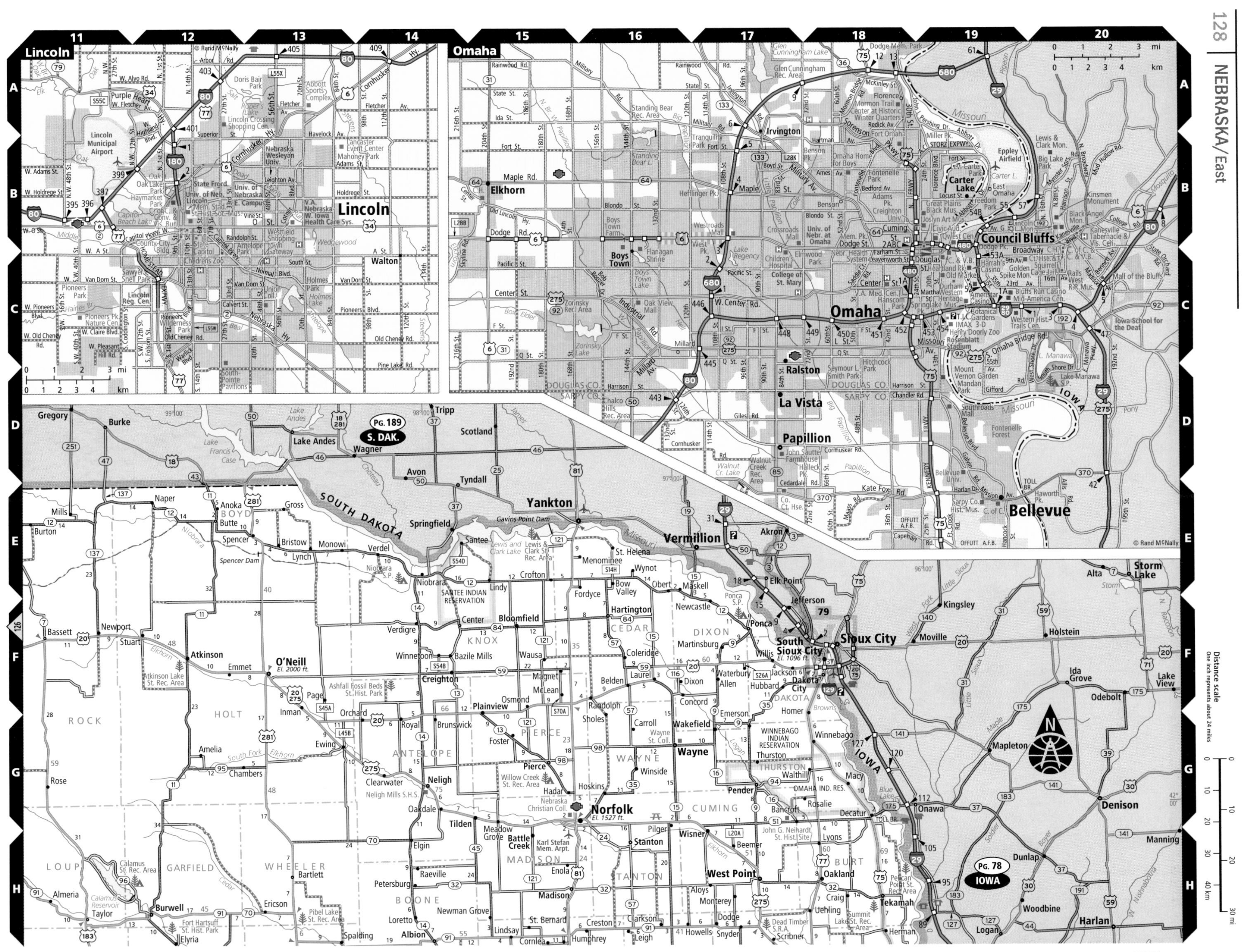
Lincoln
Omaha
Council Bluffs
Bellevue
Papillion
La Vista
Ralston
Boys Town
Elkhorn
Irvington
Carter Lake
Sioux City
South Sioux City
Norfolk
Yankton
Vermillion
Wayne
West Point
O'Neill
Tekamah
Denison
Harlan
Storm Lake
SOUTH DAKOTA
IOWA
PG. 189 S. DAK.
PG. 78 IOWA
© Rand McNally

How to determine distance

Mileages in red between red arrowheads; in black, between intersections.

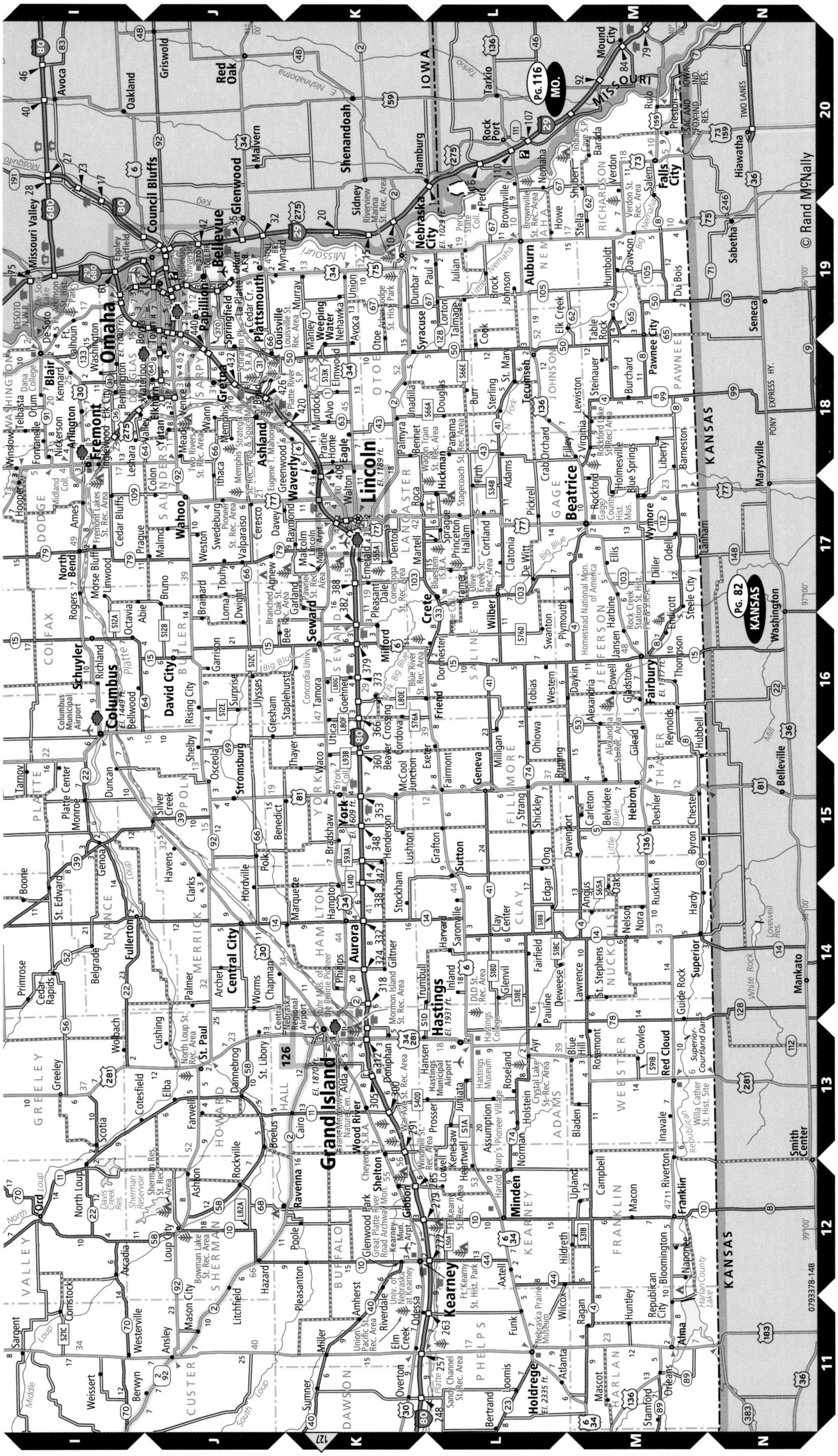

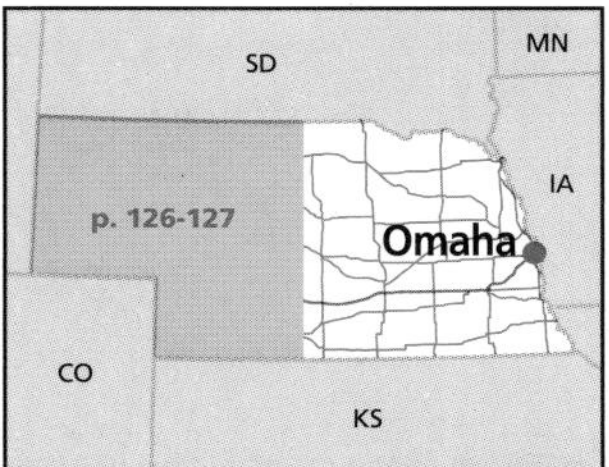
SD
MN
IA
p. 126-127
Omaha
CO
KS

SYMBOLS

- Featured ride
- Scenic route
- Point of interest
- Long-term construction
- Harley-Davidson dealership

CITY-TO-CITY MILEAGE

	GRAND ISLAND	LINCOLN	NORFOLK	NORTH PLATTE	OGALLALA	OMAHA	SCOTTSBLUFF	VALENTINE
Alliance	321	400	329	177	123	455	57	164
Beatrice	134	40	161	263	314	98	436	343
Chadron	379	458	324	235	181	513	99	138
Cheyenne, WY	365	444	474	221	169	499	109	352
Columbus	63	78	46	210	261	88	383	232
Grand Island		97	109	147	198	152	320	211
Kearney	51	130	160	100	151	185	273	195
Lincoln	97		124	226	277	58	399	306
McCook	155	234	264	68	118	289	240	199
Nebraska City	145	49	154	274	325	44	447	354
Norfolk	109	124		256	307	112	429	186
North Platte	147	226	256		54	281	176	131
Ogallala	198	277	307	54		332	122	185
Omaha	152	58	112	281	332		454	299
O'Neill	111	207	75	194	248	188	329	123
Scottsbluff	320	399	429	176	122	454		218
Sioux City, IA	179	155	74	378	429	98	453	235
Valentine	211	306	186	131	185	299	218	

HARLEY-DAVIDSON DEALERSHIPS

Harley-Davidson Sales, I-16
410 23rd St. **Columbus**
(402) 564-8733
Lat N 41.439 **Lon** W 97.331

Dillon Brothers Harley-Davidson Shop, I-18
2440 E 23rd St. (Hwy. 30) **Fremont**
(402) 721-2007
Lat N 41.451 **Lon** W 96.468

Harley-Davidson Central, K-13
2719 S Locust St. **Grand Island**
(308) 382-7020
Lat N 40.896 **Lon** W 98.34

Frontier Harley-Davidson, K-17
205 NW 40th St. **Lincoln**
(402) 466-9100
Lat N 40.812 **Lon** W 96.778

Elworth's Harley-Davidson Sales & Service, G-15
2311 Riverside Blvd. **Norfolk**
(402) 371-6210
Lat N 42.059 **Lon** W 97.425

Dillon Brothers Harley-Davidson, I-18
3838 N HWS Cleveland Blvd. **Omaha**
(402) 289-5556
Lat N 41.296 **Lon** W 96.159

Harley-Davidson of Omaha, J-19
7337 L St. **Omaha**
(402) 331-0022
Lat N 41.212 **Lon** W 96.026

Distance scale
One inch represents about 40 miles
0 10 20 30 mi
0 10 20 30 40 km

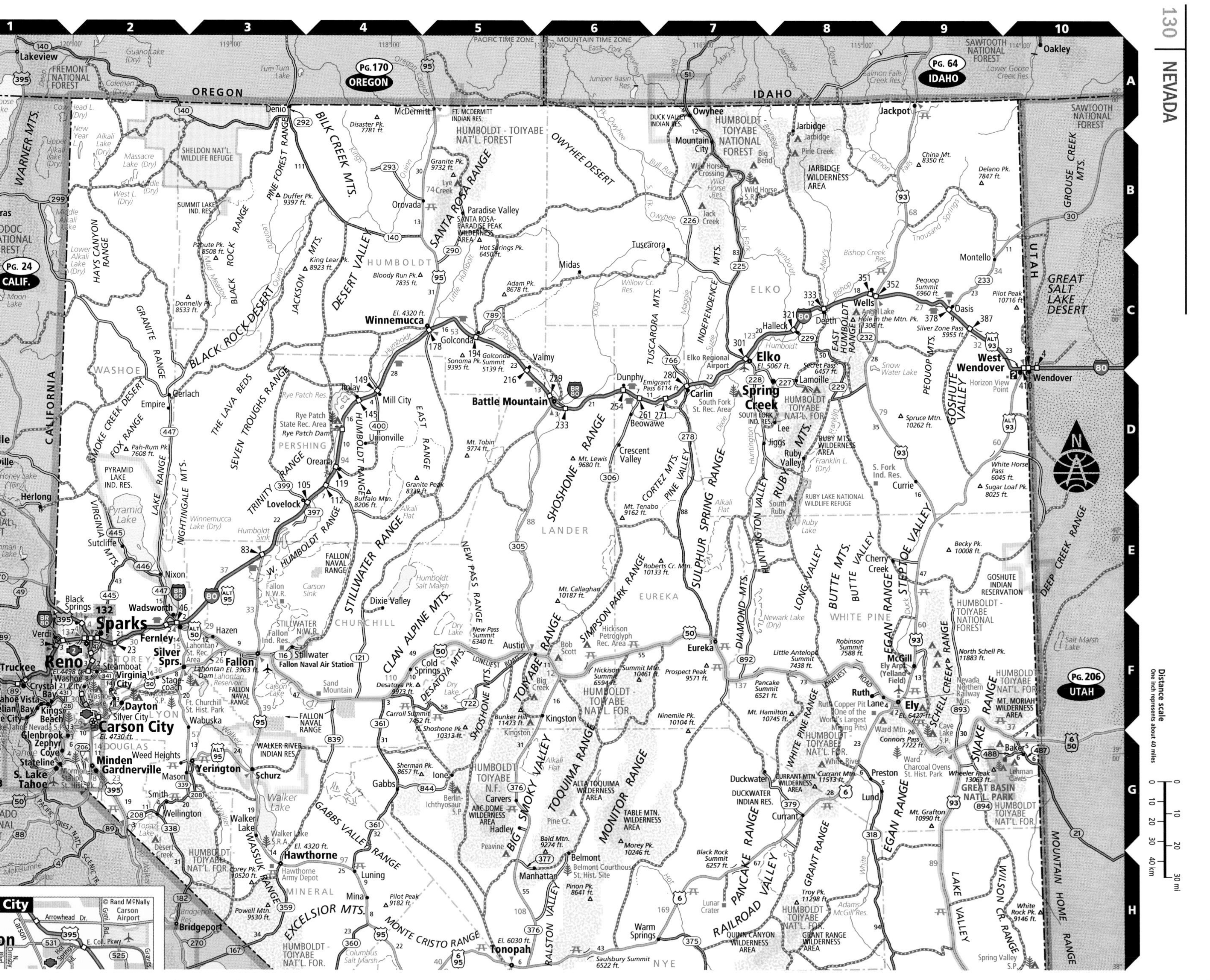
OREGON
IDAHO
UTAH
CALIFORNIA
PG. 170 OREGON
PG. 64 IDAHO
PG. 24 CALIF.
PG. 206 UTAH
Lakeview
Oakley
Alturas
Susanville
Janesville
Herlong
Portola
Truckee
Tahoe City
S. Lake Tahoe
Bridgeport
Denio
McDermitt
Owyhee
Jackpot
Jarbidge
Mountain City
Tuscarora
Midas
Orovada
Paradise Valley
Montello
Wells
Oasis
West Wendover
Wendover
Winnemucca
Golconda
Valmy
Battle Mountain
Dunphy
Carlin
Elko
Spring Creek
Lamoille
Halleck
Deeth
Gerlach
Empire
Imlay
Mill City
Unionville
Lovelock
Oreana
Nixon
Wadsworth
Sutcliffe
Reno
Sparks
Verdi
Fernley
Hazen
Silver Springs
Fallon
Stillwater
Virginia City
Dayton
Carson City
Minden
Gardnerville
Yerington
Schurz
Wabuska
Smith
Wellington
Walker Lake
Hawthorne
Luning
Mina
Gabbs
Ione
Austin
Eureka
Kingston
Carvers
Hadley
Manhattan
Belmont
Tonopah
Warm Springs
Currie
Cherry Creek
McGill
Ely
Ruth
Lane
Preston
Lund
Duckwater
Currant
Baker
Beowawe
Crescent Valley
Dixie Valley
Jiggs
Lee
Ruby Valley
OWYHEE DESERT
BLACK ROCK DESERT
SMOKE CREEK DESERT
THE LAVA BEDS
WARNER MTS.
HAYS CANYON RANGE
GRANITE RANGE
FOX RANGE
LAKE RANGE
VIRGINIA MTS.
NIGHTINGALE MTS.
SEVEN TROUGHS RANGE
TRINITY RANGE
HUMBOLDT RANGE
W. HUMBOLDT RANGE
EAST RANGE
STILLWATER RANGE
CLAN ALPINE MTS.
DESATOYA MTS.
NEW PASS RANGE
SHOSHONE MTS.
SHOSHONE RANGE
TOIYABE RANGE
BIG SMOKY VALLEY
TOQUIMA RANGE
MONITOR RANGE
SIMPSON PARK RANGE
SULPHUR SPRING RANGE
DIAMOND MTS.
CORTEZ MTS.
PINE VALLEY
TUSCARORA MTS.
INDEPENDENCE MTS.
RUBY MTS.
EAST HUMBOLDT RANGE
PEQUOP MTS.
GOSHUTE VALLEY
HUNTINGTON VALLEY
LONG VALLEY
BUTTE MTS.
BUTTE VALLEY
EGAN RANGE
STEPTOE VALLEY
SCHELL CREEK RANGE
SNAKE RANGE
DEEP CREEK RANGE
GREAT SALT LAKE DESERT
GROUSE CREEK MTS.
MOUNTAIN HOME RANGE
WILSON CR. RANGE
LAKE VALLEY
WHITE PINE RANGE
GRANT RANGE
PANCAKE RANGE
RAILROAD VALLEY
RALSTON VALLEY
MONTE CRISTO RANGE
EXCELSIOR MTS.
GABBS VALLEY RANGE
WASSUK RANGE
BILK CREEK MTS.
PINE FOREST RANGE
JACKSON MTS.
BLACK ROCK RANGE
DESERT VALLEY
SANTA ROSA RANGE
WASHOE
HUMBOLDT
PERSHING
CHURCHILL
LANDER
EUREKA
ELKO
WHITE PINE
NYE
MINERAL
LYON
DOUGLAS
STOREY
GREAT BASIN NAT'L. PARK
Carson City
© Rand McNally

How to determine distance

Mileages in red between red arrowheads; in black, between intersections.

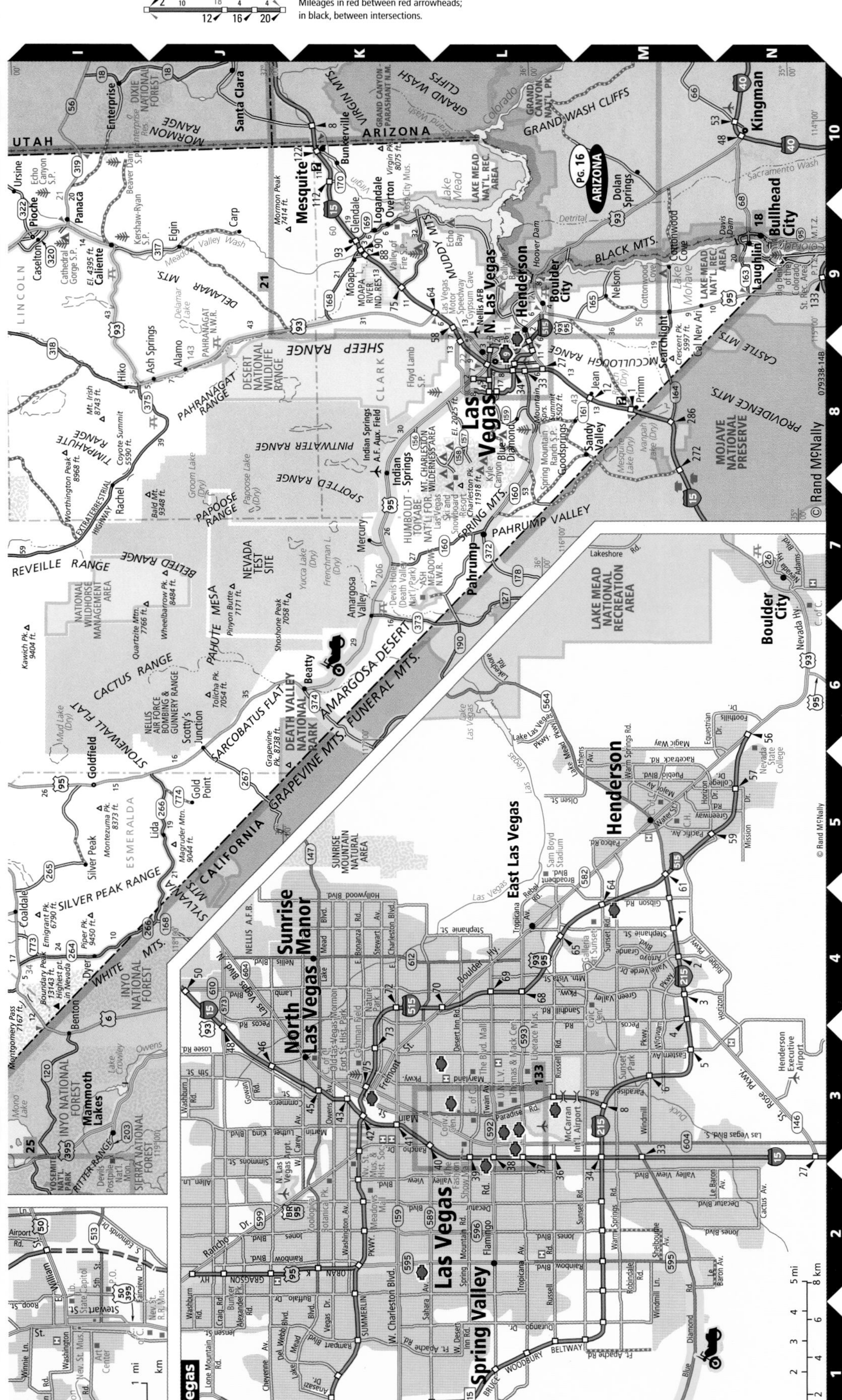
UTAH
ARIZONA
CALIFORNIA
Las Vegas
North Las Vegas
Henderson
Boulder City
Mesquite
Laughlin
Bullhead City
Kingman
Pahrump
Beatty
Goldfield
Mammoth Lakes
Sunrise Manor
East Las Vegas
Spring Valley
NEVADA TEST SITE
DEATH VALLEY NATIONAL PARK
MOJAVE NATIONAL PRESERVE
LAKE MEAD NATIONAL RECREATION AREA
© Rand McNally

SYMBOLS

- Featured ride
- Scenic route
- Point of interest
- Long-term construction
- Harley-Davidson dealership

For Nevada/California ride, see page R24.

NEVADA MOTORCYCLE LAWS

Helmet use: Required

Riding two abreast:
Yes. See state law for specifics

Eye protection:
Required unless equipped with windscreen

Speed limit:
Primary roads: 75 mph; Secondary roads: 65 mph

NEVADA RESOURCES

Road conditions or construction:
(877) 687-6237
www.nevadadot.com

Highway Emergency Numbers:
911 or *647

Tourism:
(800) 638-2328
www.travelnevada.com

State motor vehicle information:
(877) 368-7828
www.dmvnv.com

HARLEY-DAVIDSON DEALERSHIPS

Carson City Harley-Davidson, F-2
2749 N Carson St. **Carson City**
(775) 882-7433
Lat N 39.185 **Lon** W 119.77

Henderson Harley-Davidson, L-9
1010 W Warm Springs Rd. **Henderson**
(702) 456-1666
Lat N 36.056 **Lon** W 115.029

Las Vegas Harley-Davidson, L-8
2605 S Eastern Ave. **Las Vegas**
(702) 431-8500
Lat N 36.142 **Lon** W 115.119

Las Vegas Harley-Davidson, L-8
7100 W Sahara Ave. **Las Vegas**
(702) 876-2884
Lat N 36.144 **Lon** W 115.247

Las Vegas Harley-Davidson, L-8
3799 Las Vegas Blvd. S **Las Vegas**
(702) 795-7073
Lat N 36.101 **Lon** W 115.17

Las Vegas Harley-Davidson, L-8
5757 Wayne Newton Blvd. **Las Vegas**
(702) 736-9493
Lat N 36.084 **Lon** W 115.149

Las Vegas Harley-Davidson, L-8
328 E Fremont St. **Las Vegas**
(702) 383-1010
Lat N 36.17 **Lon** W 115.143

Las Vegas Harley-Davidson, L-8
3645 S Las Vegas Blvd. **Las Vegas**
(702) 893-7773
Lat N 36.112 **Lon** W 115.173

Las Vegas Harley-Davidson, L-8
3700 W Flamingo Rd. **Las Vegas**
(702) 252-5130
Lat N 36.115 **Lon** W 115.187

Las Vegas Harley-Davidson, L-8
3790 Las Vegas Blvd. S **Las Vegas**
(702) 891-0530
Lat N 36.102 **Lon** W 115.173

Las Vegas Harley-Davidson, L-8
3150 Paradise Rd. **Las Vegas**
(702) 943-6822
Lat N 36.132 **Lon** W 115.155

Reno Harley-Davidson, F-2
2295 Market St. **Reno**
(775) 329-2913
Lat N 39.516 **Lon** W 119.783

Reno Harley-Davidson at Silver Legacy, F-2
407 N Virginia St. **Reno**
(775) 329-2913
Lat N 39.530 **Lon** W 119.814

Distance scale
One inch represents about 15 miles
0 5 10 mi
0 5 10 15 km

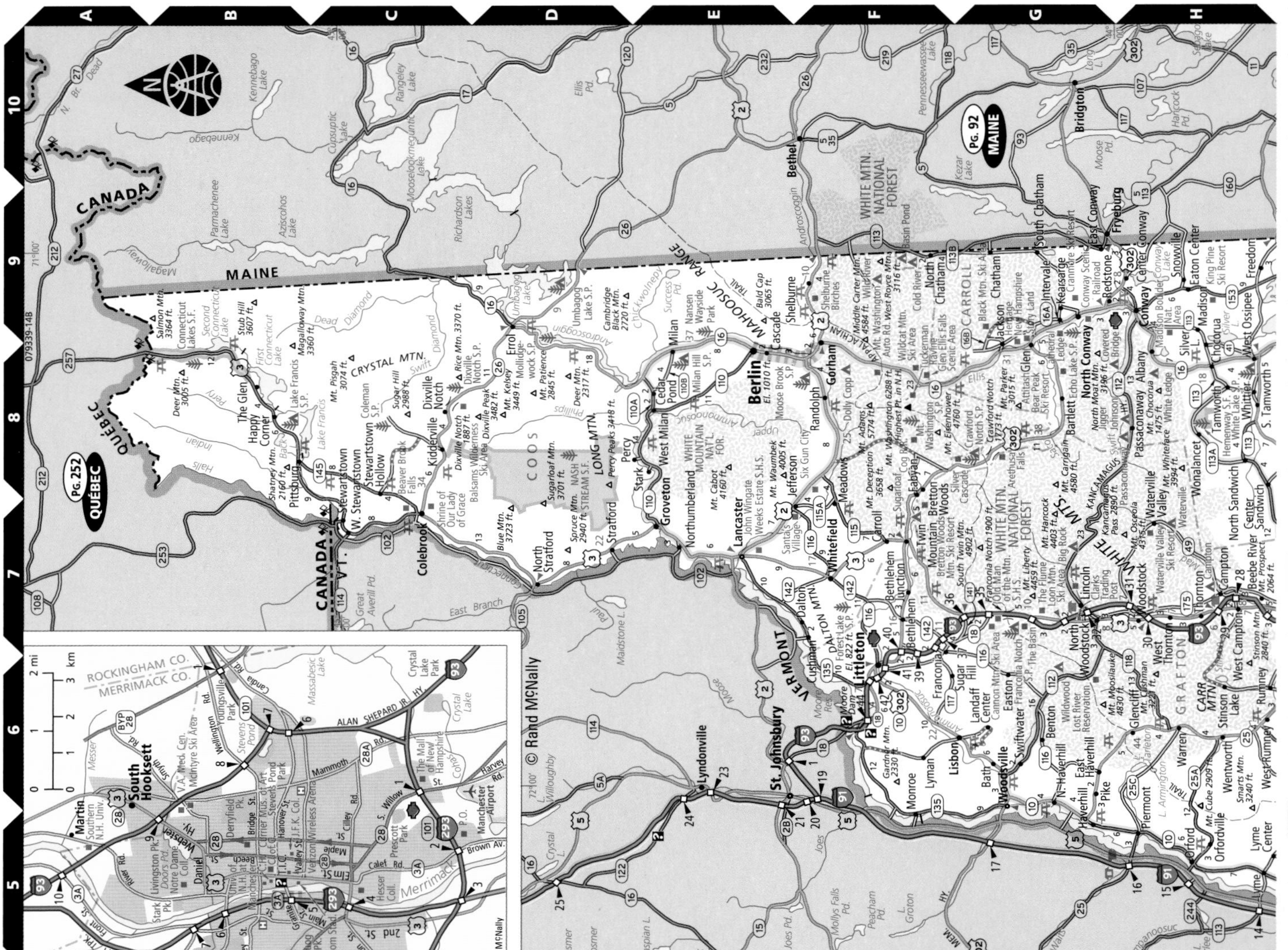

A B C D E F G H

10 9 8 7 6 5 4 3 2 1

QUÉBEC
CANADA
MAINE
VERMONT
WHITE MTN. NATIONAL FOREST
Pg. 252 QUÉBEC
Pg. 92 MAINE
Pg. 210 VERMONT
© Rand McNally

Manchester
Concord
Nashua
Reno

How to determine distance

2
10
18
4
4
12
16
20

Mileages in red between red arrowheads; in black, between intersections.

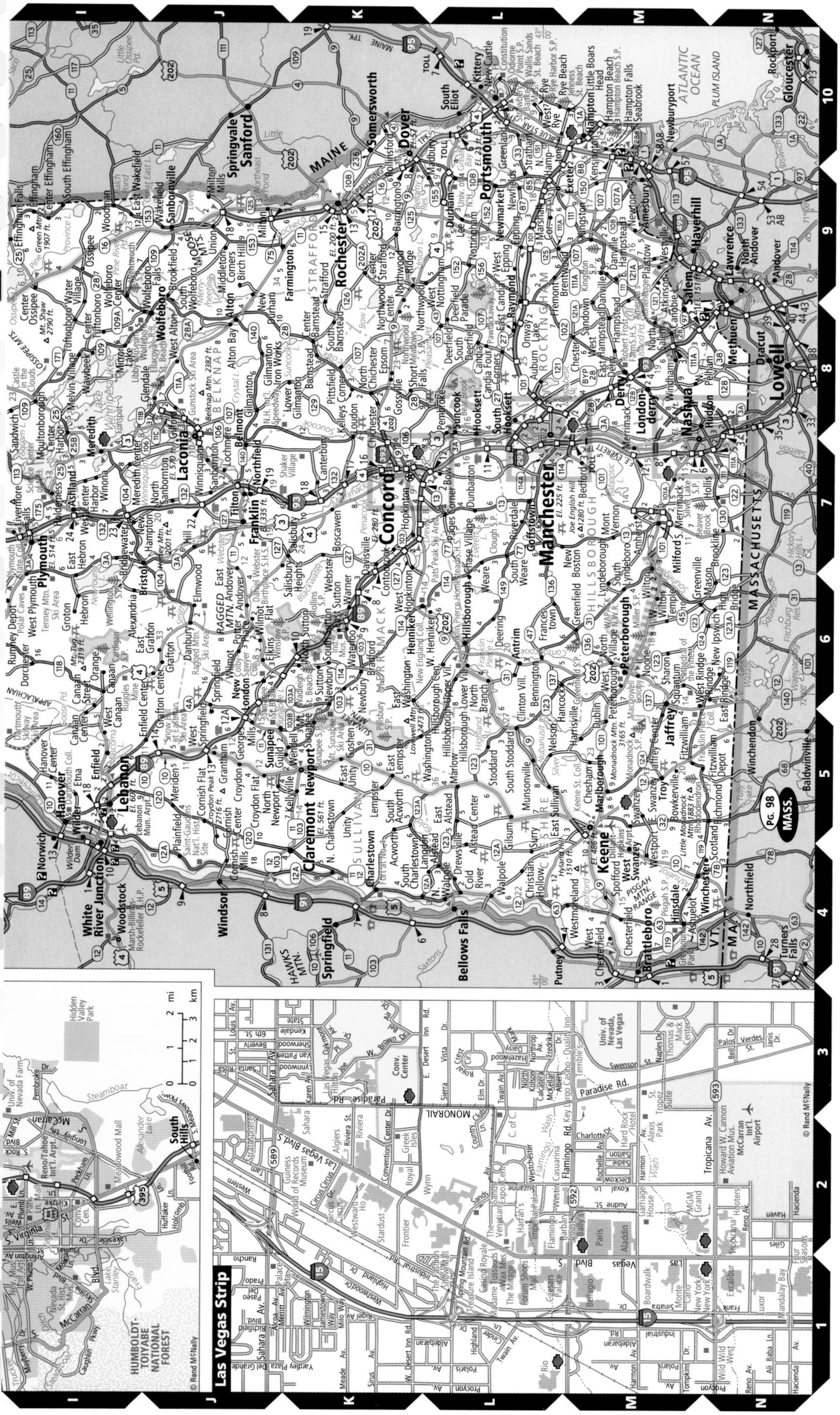

SYMBOLS

Featured ride

Scenic route

Point of interest

Long-term construction

Harley-Davidson dealership

NEW HAMPSHIRE MOTORCYCLE LAWS

Helmet use:
Required under age 18

Riding two abreast:
Yes. See state law for specifics

Eye protection:
Required unless equipped with windscreen

Speed limit:
Primary roads: 65 mph
Secondary roads: 65 mph

NEW HAMPSHIRE RESOURCES

Road conditions or construction:
511
(866) 282-7579
www.511nh.com

Highway Emergency Numbers:
911

Tourism:
(800) 386-4664
(603) 271-2665
www.visitnh.gov

State motor vehicle information:
(603) 271-7000
www.nh.gov/safety/division/dmv

HARLEY-DAVIDSON DEALERSHIPS

Littleton Harley-Davidson, F-6
1341 Whitefield Rd. **Bethlehem**
(603) 444-1300
Lat N 44.319 **Lon** W 71.712

Heritage Harley-Davidson, K-7
142 Manchester St. **Concord**
(603) 224-3268
Lat N 43.188 **Lon** W 71.503

Meredith Harley-Davidson Shop of Conway, H-9
1275 White Mountain Hwy. (Rte. 16) **Conway**
(603) 356-7775
Lat N 44.014 **Lon** W 71.113

Monadnock Harley-Davidson, M-5
588 Monadnock Hwy. **East Swanzey**
(603) 352-1472
Lat N 42.875 **Lon** W 72.231

Twin States Harley-Davidson, I-5
351 Miracle Mile **Lebanon**
(603) 448-4664
Lat N 43.637 **Lon** W 72.286

Manchester Harley-Davidson, L-8
115 John E Devine Dr. **Manchester**
(603) 622-2461
Lat N 42.959 **Lon** W 71.444

Meredith Harley-Davidson, I-7
239 Daniel Webster Hwy. (Rte. 3) **Meredith**
(603) 279-4526
Lat N 43.655 **Lon** W 71.497

Nashua Harley-Davidson, M-7
717 Rte. 101A **Merrimack**
(603) 578-9400
Lat N 42.805 **Lon** W 71.547

Seacoast Harley-Davidson, M-10
17 Lafayette Rd. (US Rte. 1) **North Hampton**
(603) 964-9959
Lat N 42.961 **Lon** W 70.834

Distance scale
One inch represents about 9 miles
0 5 10 mi
0 5 10 15 km

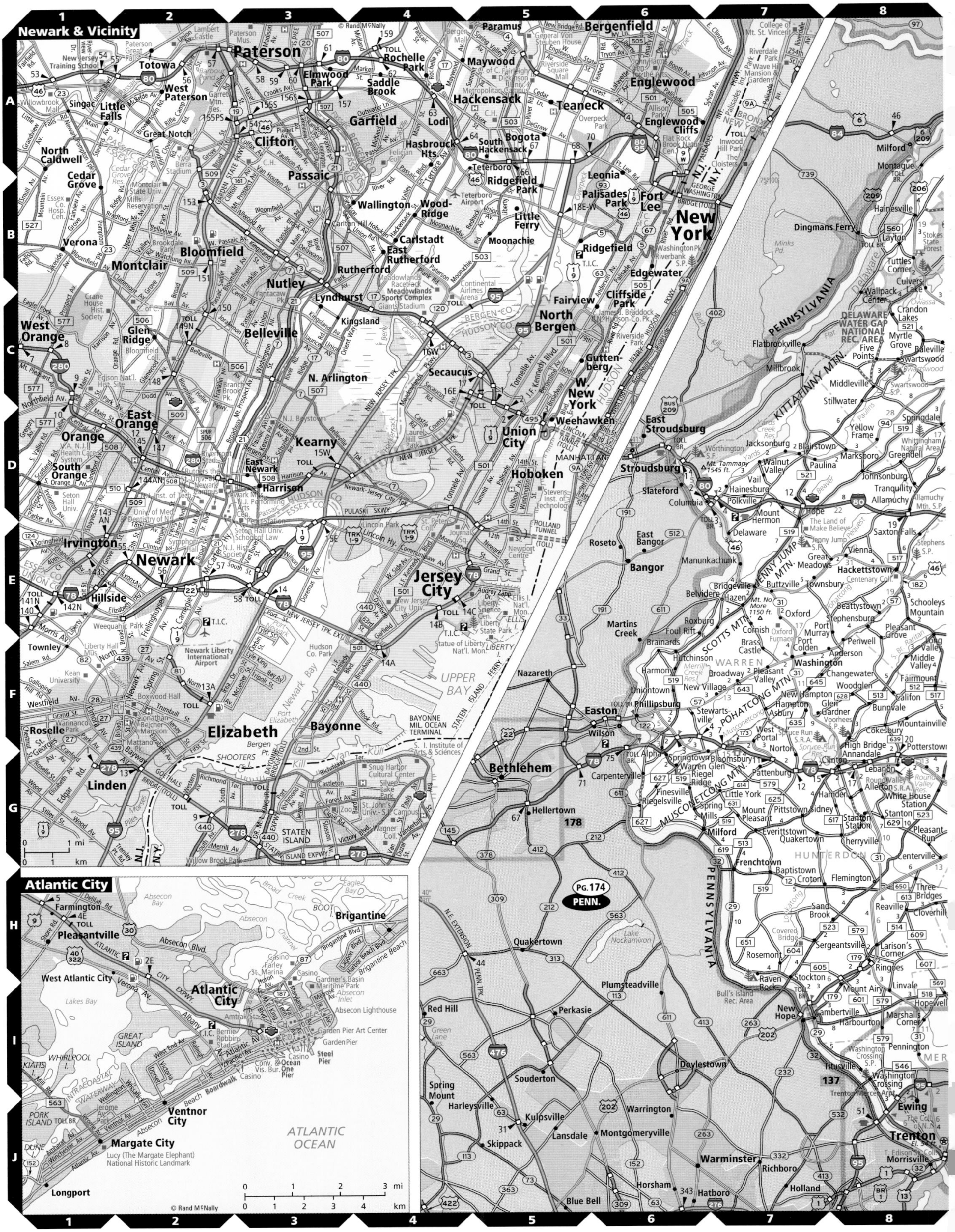

1 2 3 4 5 6 7 8

Newark & Vicinity

Paterson
Totowa
West Paterson
Little Falls
Singac
Great Notch
North Caldwell
Cedar Grove
Verona
Montclair
Bloomfield
Glen Ridge
West Orange
East Orange
Orange
South Orange
Irvington
Newark
Hillside
Townley
Kean University
Westfield
Roselle
Roselle Park
Linden
Elizabeth
Bayonne
Jersey City
Hoboken
Union City
Weehawken
West New York
Guttenberg
North Bergen
Secaucus
Kearny
East Newark
Harrison
North Arlington
Kingsland
Belleville
Nutley
Lyndhurst
Rutherford
East Rutherford
Carlstadt
Wallington
Wood-Ridge
Passaic
Clifton
Garfield
Elmwood Park
Saddle Brook
Rochelle Park
Paramus
Maywood
Lodi
Hackensack
Hasbrouck Hts.
South Hackensack
Teterboro
Bogota
Ridgefield Park
Little Ferry
Moonachie
Bergenfield
Teaneck
Englewood
Englewood Cliffs
Leonia
Palisades Park
Fort Lee
Ridgefield
Fairview
Cliffside Park
Edgewater
New York
Manhattan
Staten Island
Newark Liberty International Airport
Upper Bay
Statue of Liberty Nat'l. Mon.
Meadowlands Sports Complex
Giants Stadium
Holland Tunnel (Toll)
Lincoln Tunnel (Toll)
George Washington Bridge (Toll)
Goethals Bridge (Toll)
Bayonne Bridge (Toll)
New Jersey Tpk.
Garden State Pkwy.
Bergen Co.
Hudson Co.
Essex Co.
Union Co.
Passaic Co.
0 1 mi
0 1 km
© Rand McNally

Atlantic City

Farmington
Pleasantville
West Atlantic City
Atlantic City
Brigantine
Absecon Bay
Absecon Lighthouse
Lakes Bay
Great Island
Whirlpool I.
Garden Pier Art Center
Steel Pier
Conv. & Vis. Bur.
Ocean One Pier
Ventnor City
Margate City
Lucy (The Margate Elephant) National Historic Landmark
Longport
Atlantic Ocean
0 1 2 3 mi
0 1 2 3 4 5 km
© Rand McNally

Pennsylvania
Delaware Water Gap National Rec. Area
Kittatinny Mtn.
Milford
Montague
Dingmans Ferry
Hainesville
Layton
Stokes State Forest
Tuttles Corner
Culvers Lake
Wallpack Center
Crandon Lakes
Myrtle Grove
Baleville
Swartswood
Five Points
Flatbrookville
Millbrook
Middleville
Stillwater
Springdale
Yellow Frame
Blairstown
Jacksonburg
Greendell
Marksboro
Walnut Valley
Paulina
Johnsonburg
Tranquility
Allamuchy
East Stroudsburg
Stroudsburg
Mt. Tammany 1545 ft.
Slateford
Columbia
Vail
Hainesburg
Polkville
Hope
Mount Hermon
Delaware
Saxton Falls
Roseto
East Bangor
Bangor
Manunkachunk
Vienna
Great Meadows
Hackettstown
Jenny Jump Mtn.
Buttzville
Townsbury
Bridgeville
Belvidere
Hazen
Oxford
Beattystown
Schooleys Mountain
Martins Creek
Foul Rift
Roxburg
Scotts Mtn.
Port Murray
Stephensburg
Pleasant Grove
Brainards
Brass Castle
Port Colden
Penwell
Long Valley
Middle Valley
Hutchinson
Harmony
Washington
Anderson
Changewater
Fairmount
Warren
Broadway
Pleasant Valley
New Village
Woodglen
Califon
Uniontown
Phillipsburg
Pohatcong Mtn.
New Hampton
Glen Gardner
Bunnvale
Nazareth
Easton
Stewartsville
Asbury
Voorhees S.P.
Mountainville
Cokesbury
Wilson
West Portal
High Bridge
Potterstown
Annandale
Alpha
Norton
Bethlehem
Carpentersville
Springtown
Bloomsbury
Warren Glen
Riegel Ridge
Pattenburg
Clinton
Lebanon
Finesville
Riegelsville
Musconetcong Mtn.
Little York
Allerton
Hamden
White House Station
Hellertown
Spring Mills
Pittstown
Sidney
Mount Pleasant
Stanton
Stanton Station
Milford
Everittstown
Quakertown
Cherryville
Pleasant Run
Frenchtown
Hunterdon
Centerville
Baptistown
Croton
Flemington
Three Bridges
Sand Brook
Reaville
Cloverhill
Covered Bridge
Sergeantsville
Larison's Corner
Rosemont
Ringoes
Stockton
Raven Rock
Mount Airy
Linvale
Hopewell
Bull's Island Rec. Area
New Hope
Lambertville
Harbourton
Marshalls Corner
Pennington
Washington Crossing S.P.
Titusville
Washington Crossing
Trenton-Mercer Arpt.
Ewing
Trenton
Morrisville
Richboro
Holland
Warminster
Hatboro
Horsham
Quakertown
Lake Nockamixon
Plumsteadville
Perkasie
Red Hill
Green Lane Res.
Souderton
Doylestown
Spring Mount
Harleysville
Kulpsville
Skippack
Lansdale
Montgomeryville
Warrington
Blue Bell
N.E. Extension Penn. Tpk.

PG. 174 PENN.
178
137

A B C D E F G H I J

How to determine distance

Mileages in red between red arrowheads; in black, between intersections.

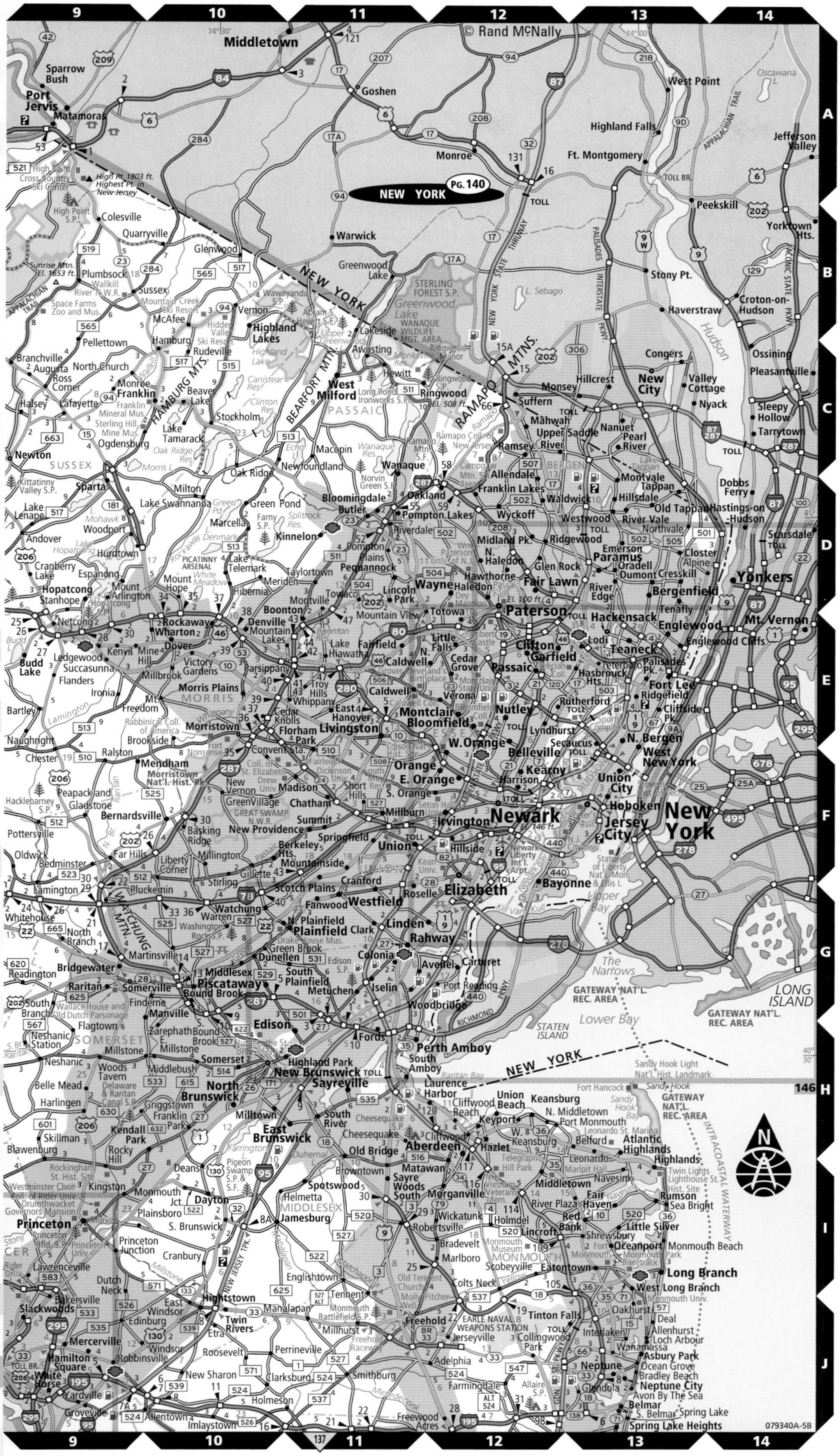

© Rand McNally

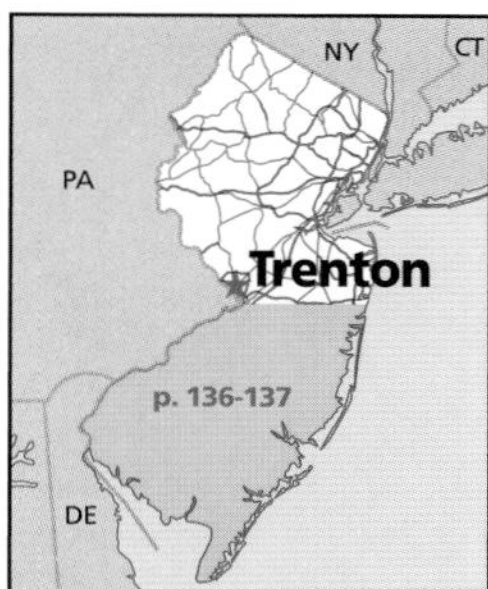
NY
CT
PA
Trenton
p. 136-137
DE

NEW JERSEY MOTORCYCLE LAWS

Helmet use:
Required and reflectorization required

Riding two abreast:
No reference in administrative code or statutes

Eye protection:
Required for instructional permit holders
Required unless equipped with windscreen

Speed limit:
Primary roads: 65 mph; Secondary roads: 55 mph

NEW JERSEY RESOURCES

Road conditions or construction:
(732) 247-0900, then 2 (turnpike)
(800) 336-5875 (turnpike)
(732) 727-5929 (Garden State Parkway)
www.state.nj.us/njcommuter/
www.state.nj.us/turnpike/

Highway Emergency Numbers: 911

Tourism:
(800) 847-4865
(609) 777-0885
www.visitnj.org

State motor vehicle information:
(609) 292-6500
www.state.nj.us/mvc

HARLEY-DAVIDSON DEALERSHIPS

- **Harley-Davidson of Essex, F-12**
  168 Bloomfield Ave. **Bloomfield**
  (973) 748-2500
  Lat N 40.78 **Lon** W 74.19
- **Trenton World-Class Harley-Davidson, J-9**
  960 US Rte. 130 & I-195 **Hamilton**
  (609) 689-0200
  Lat N 40.214 **Lon** W 74.614
- **Harley-Davidson of Edison, H-11**
  211 Woodbridge Ave. **Highland Park**
  (732) 985-7546
  Lat N 40.501 **Lon** W 74.413
- **Tramontin Harley-Davidson, E-7**
  Rte. 80 W Exit 12 **Hope**
  (908) 459-4101
  Lat N 40.911 **Lon** W 74.968
- **Kosco Harley-Davidson, D-11**
  1149 Rte. 23 S **Kinnelon**
  (973) 838-8800
  Lat N 40.993 **Lon** W 74.366
- **Williams Harley-Davidson, G-8**
  1100 US Hwy. 22 W **Lebanon**
  (908) 236-0767
  Lat N 40.645 **Lon** W 74.812
- **Legends Harley-Davidson, E-9**
  1895 Rte. 46 W **Ledgewood**
  (973) 347-0258
  Lat N 40.883 **Lon** W 74.659
- **Harley-Davidson of Long Branch, I-13**
  671 Broadway **Long Branch**
  (732) 229-8518
  Lat N 40.299 **Lon** W 74.006
- **Liberty Harley-Davidson, G-11**
  12 W Milton Ave. **Rahway**
  (732) 381-2400
  Lat N 40.606 **Lon** W 74.278
- **Harley-Davidson of Bergen County, E-13**
  124 Essex St. **Rochelle Park**
  (201) 843-6930
  Lat N 40.893 **Lon** W 74.074

079340A-5B

Distance scale
One inch represents about 9 miles
0 5 10 mi
0 5 10 15 km

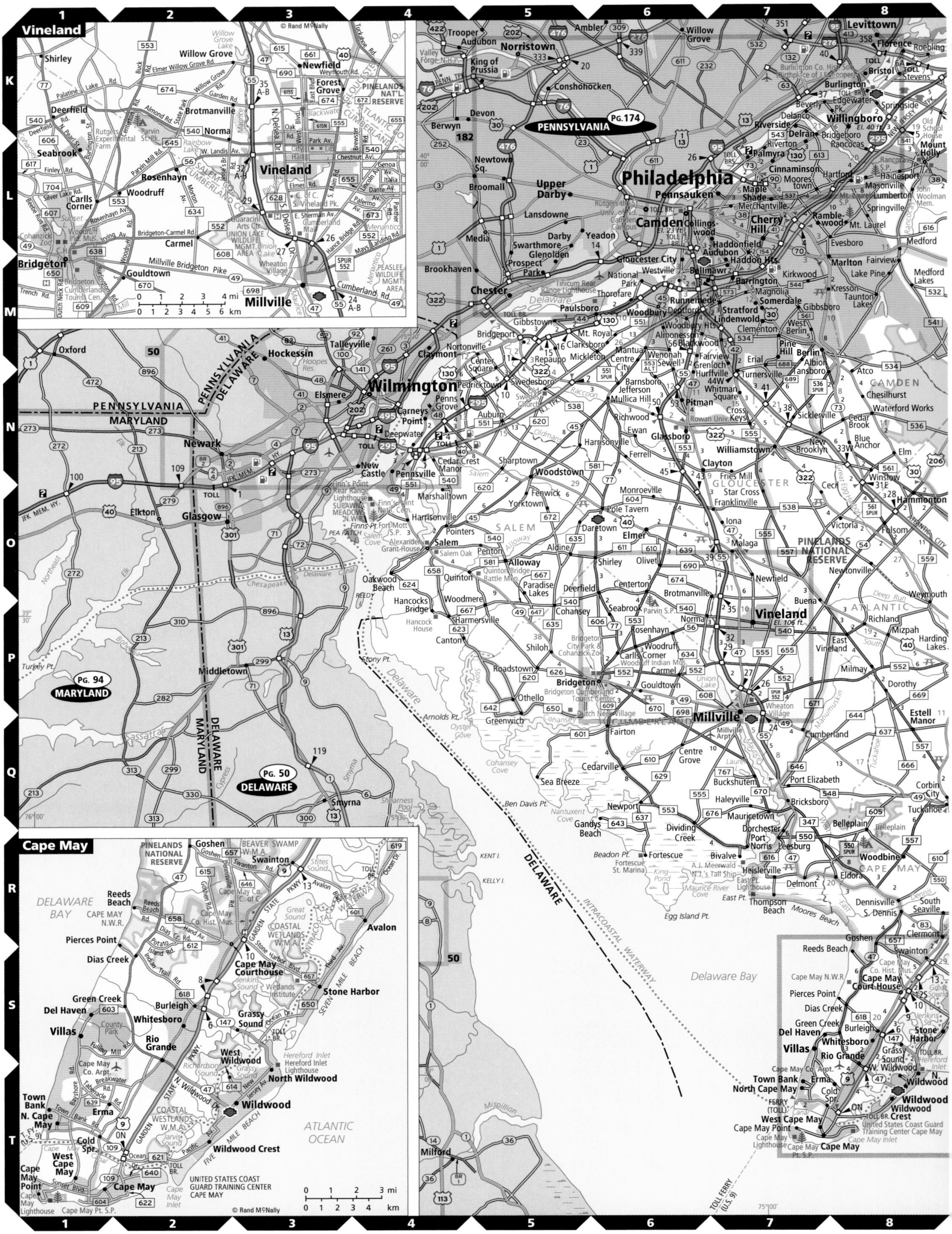

Vineland

Shirley
Willow Grove
Newfield
Forest Grove
PINELANDS NAT'L. RESERVE
Deerfield
Brotmanville
Norma
Seabrook
Vineland
Rosenhayn
Woodruff
Carls Corner
Carmel
Bridgeton
Gouldtown
Millville
UNION LAKE WILDLIFE MGMT. AREA
PEASLEE WILDLIFE MGMT. AREA
© Rand McNally
0 1 2 3 4 mi
0 1 2 3 4 5 6 km

Philadelphia
Camden
Wilmington
Norristown
Chester
Salem
Bridgeton
Vineland
Millville
Glassboro
Woodstown
Pennsville
New Castle
Newark
Elkton
Middletown
Smyrna
Milford
PENNSYLVANIA
MARYLAND
DELAWARE
SALEM
GLOUCESTER
CUMBERLAND
CAMDEN
ATLANTIC
CAPE MAY
PINELANDS NATIONAL RESERVE
Delaware Bay
INTRACOASTAL WATERWAY

PENNSYLVANIA PG. 174
PG. 94 MARYLAND
PG. 50 DELAWARE

Cape May

PINELANDS NATIONAL RESERVE
Goshen
Swainton
Reeds Beach
DELAWARE BAY
CAPE MAY N.W.R.
Pierces Point
Dias Creek
Cape May Courthouse
Avalon
Stone Harbor
Green Creek
Del Haven
Burleigh
Whitesboro
Villas
Rio Grande
West Wildwood
North Wildwood
Wildwood
Town Bank
N. Cape May
Erma
Cold Spr.
West Cape May
Cape May Point
Cape May
Wildwood Crest
ATLANTIC OCEAN
UNITED STATES COAST GUARD TRAINING CENTER CAPE MAY
Cape May Pt. S.P.
© Rand McNally
0 1 2 3 mi
0 1 2 3 4 km

How to determine distance

Mileages in red between red arrowheads; in black, between intersections.

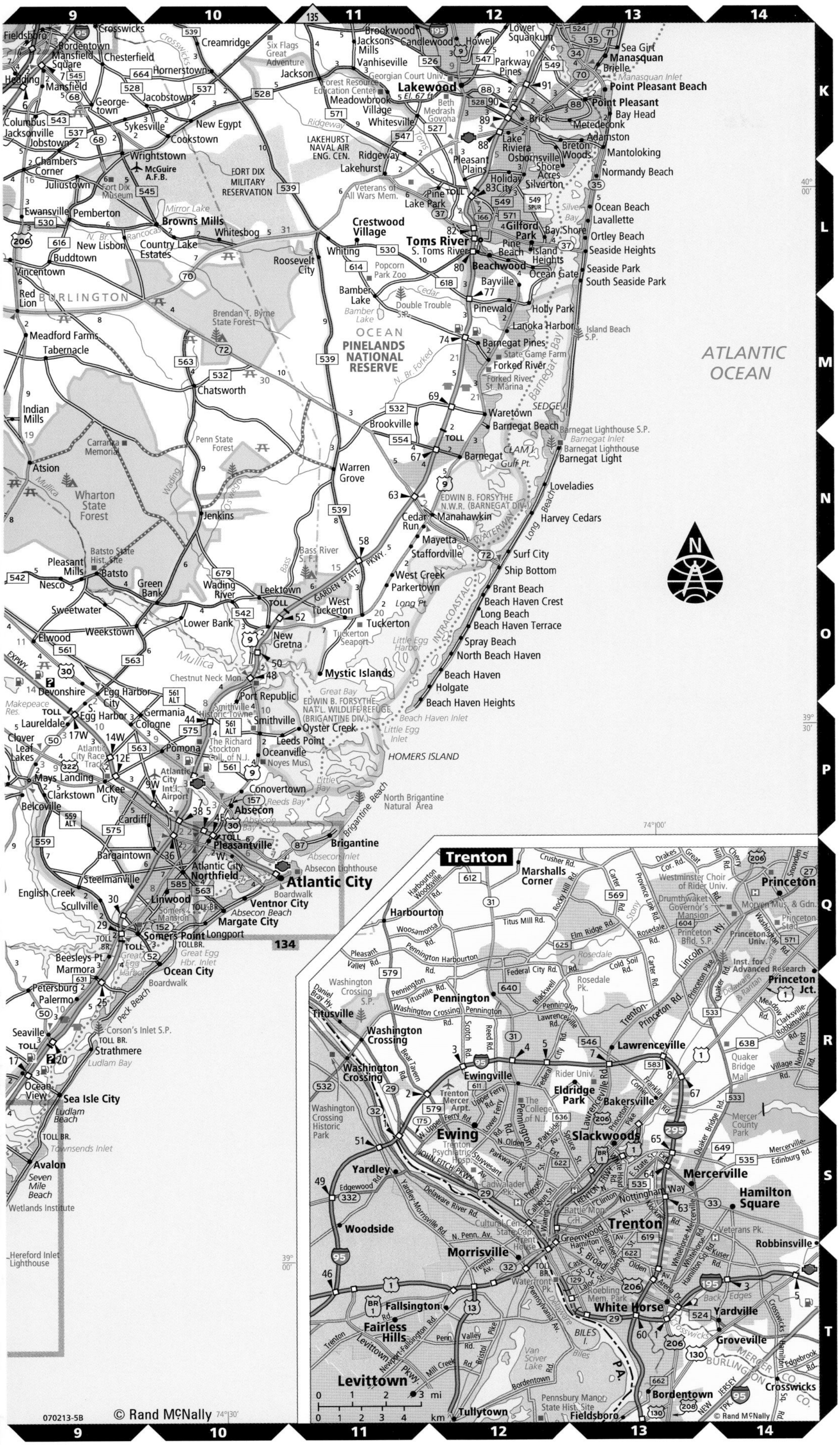

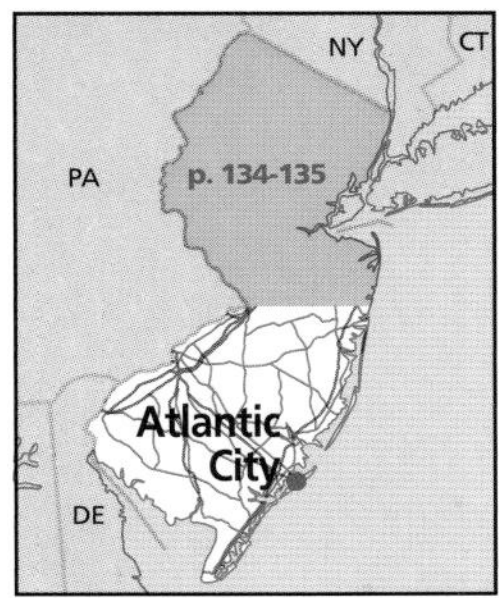
NY
CT
PA
p. 134-135
Atlantic City
DE

SYMBOLS

	Featured ride		Scenic route
			Point of interest
	Long-term construction		Harley-Davidson dealership

CITY-TO-CITY MILEAGE

	Atlantic City	Camden	Newark	New Brunswick	Paterson	Phillipsburg	Trenton	Wilmington, DE
Atlantic City		60	117	95	129	145	81	86
Camden	60		82	63	94	85	37	36
Cape May	49	93	151	129	163	178	114	93
Cherry Hill	55	6	78	59	90	91	33	43
Elizabeth	114	79	5	22	22	63	52	114
Jersey City	122	87	5	30	15	68	60	122
Long Branch	81	77	46	33	58	86	50	112
Newark	117	82		25	19	63	55	117
New Brunswick	95	63	25		37	52	36	98
New York, NY	140	107	25	50	31	88	80	142
Paterson	129	94	19	37		66	67	129
Phillipsburg	145	85	63	52	66		57	100
Point Pleasant	64	71	56	38	68	96	44	106
Port Jervis, NY	182	147	75	90	54	76	107	162
Princeton	93	48	41	18	58	56	12	79
Somerville	119	70	34	14	41	39	31	101
Toms River	51	55	66	44	78	106	46	88
Trenton	81	37	55	36	67	57		68
Vineland	37	38	115	96	127	123	70	44
Willingboro	70	14	68	49	80	70	20	51
Wilmington, DE	86	36	117	98	129	100	68	

HARLEY-DAVIDSON DEALERSHIPS

Atlantic County Harley-Davidson, P-10
219 E White Horse Pike (Rte. 30) **Absecon** (Galloway)
(609) 652-5555
Lat N 39.448 **Lon** W 74.531

Atlantic City Harley-Davidson, Q-10
101 N Michigan Ave. **Atlantic City**
(609) 344-6464
Lat N 39.361 **Lon** W 74.437

Mills Harley-Davidson Sales, K-8
612 Tyler St. **Burlington**
(609) 386-1871
Lat N 40.073 **Lon** W 74.852

Salem County Harley-Davidson Sales, O-6
354 Rte. 77 **Elmer**
(856) 358-8188
Lat N 39.608 **Lon** W 75.235

Harley-Davidson of Ocean County, K-12
300 Rte. 70 **Lakewood**
(732) 367-7000
Lat N 40.049 **Lon** W 74.209

Harley-Davidson of Millville, Q-7
1131 S 2nd St. **Millville**
(856) 327-0266
Lat N 39.379 **Lon** W 75.028

Barb's Harley-Davidson, M-6
926 Black Horse Pike **West Collingswood Heights**
(856) 456-4141
Lat N 39.89 **Lon** W 75.09

The Harley Shop of Wildwood, T-8
127 W Rio Grande Ave. **Wildwood**
(609) 522-7151
Lat N 38.984 **Lon** W 74.825

070213-5B

Distance scale
One inch represents about 40 miles

0 10 20 30 mi

0 10 20 30 40 km

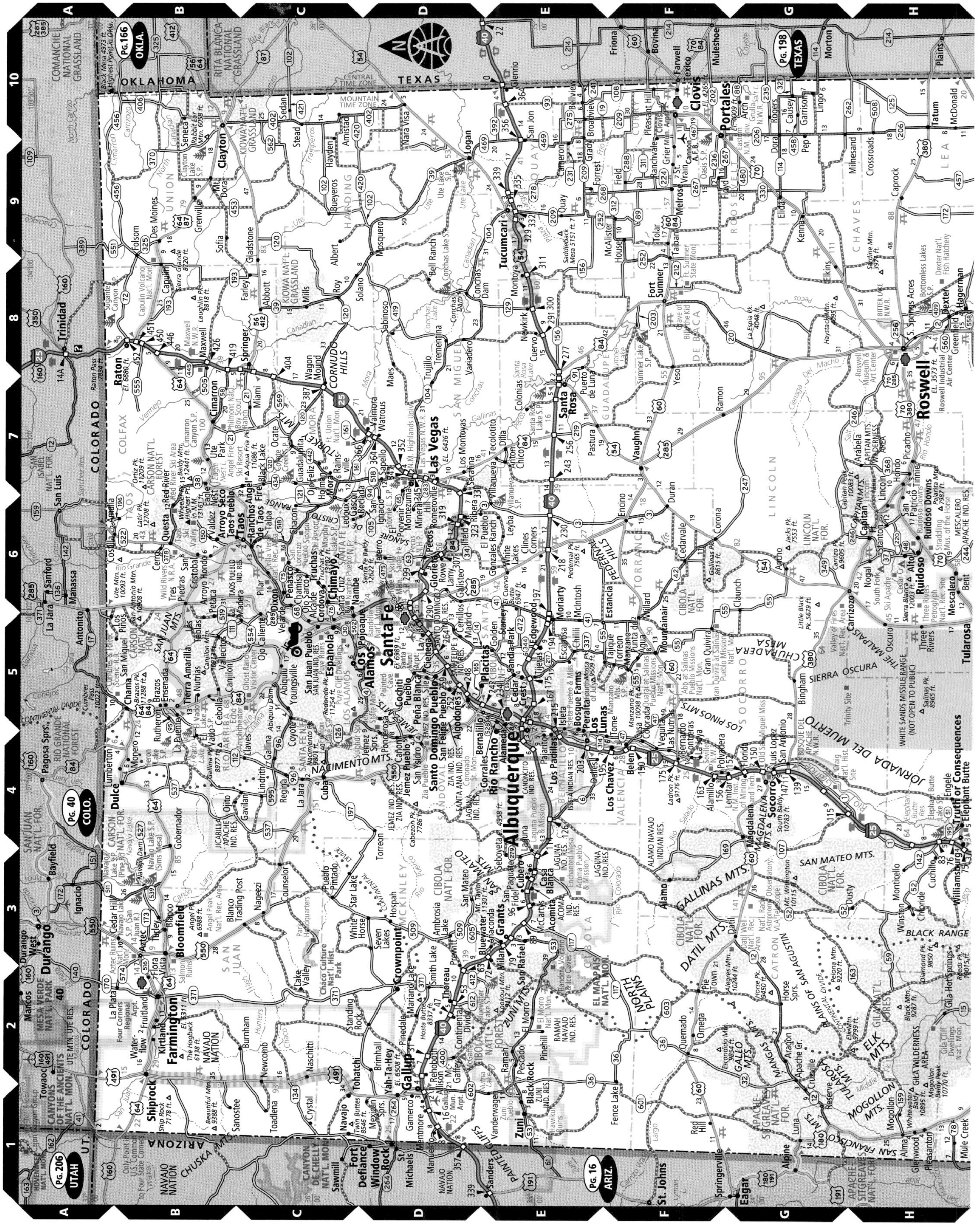

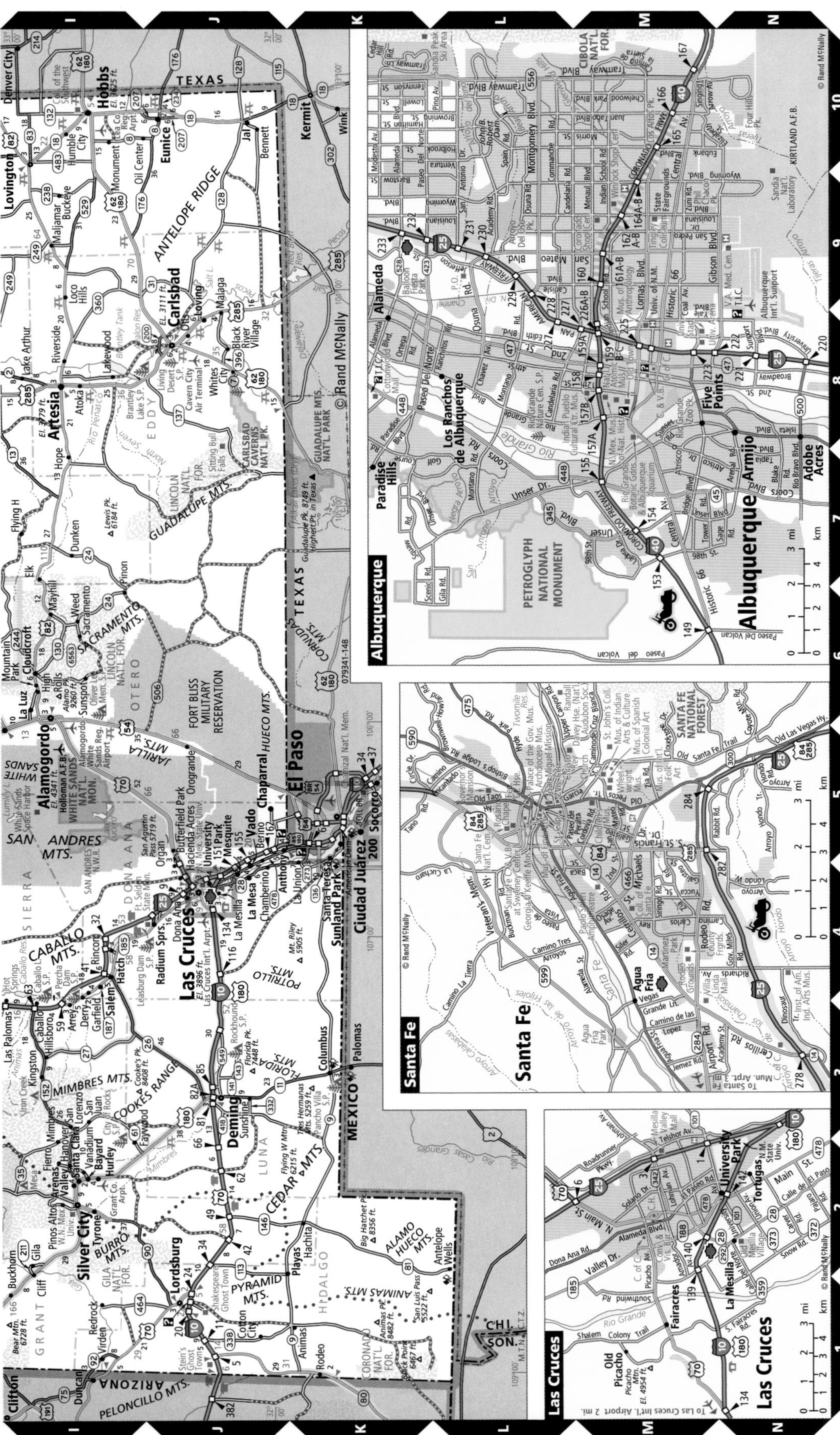
How to determine distance
Mileages in red between red arrowheads; in black, between intersections.
Albuquerque
Santa Fe
Las Cruces
© Rand McNally

SYMBOLS

- Featured ride
- Scenic route
- Point of interest
- Long-term construction
- Harley-Davidson dealership

For New Mexico ride, see page R26-27.

NEW MEXICO MOTORCYCLE LAWS

Helmet use:
Required under age 18 and reflectorization required

Riding two abreast:
No reference in administrative code or statutes

Eye protection:
Required unless equipped with windscreen

Speed limit:
Primary roads: 75 mph; Secondary roads: 75 mph

NEW MEXICO RESOURCES

Road conditions or construction:
(800) 432-4269
www.nmshtd.state.nm.us

Highway Emergency Numbers:
911

Tourism:
(800) 733-6396
www.newmexico.org

State motor vehicle information:
(888) 683-4636
www.state.nm.us/tax/mvd

CITY-TO-CITY MILEAGE

	ALBUQUERQUE	CARLSBAD	CLOVIS	GALLUP	LAS CRUCES	SANTA FE	TRINIDAD, CO	TUCUMCARI
Alamogordo	210	146	229	324	69	217	345	236
Albuquerque		275	217	139	224	58	246	174
Carlsbad	275		179	414	208	267	381	242
Clovis	217	179		356	298	209	255	82
El Paso, TX	267	165	314	381	46	325	430	321
Farmington	182	447	389	122	406	208	298	346
Gallup	139	414	356		338	197	385	313
Grants	79	354	296	61	278	137	325	253
Hobbs	315	70	127	454	257	307	382	200
Las Cruces	224	208	298	338		282	470	305
Las Vegas	118	253	165	257	342	63	128	122
Lordsburg	294	324	416	303	118	352	540	468
Raton	224	359	233	363	448	169	22	177
Roswell	198	77	111	337	187	190	304	165
Santa Fe	58	267	209	197	282		191	166
Silver City	240	317	408	270	111	298	486	414
Socorro	78	240	246	192	146	136	324	252
Taos	126	328	240	265	350	69	118	197
Truth or Consequences	150	280	318	264	75	208	396	324
Tucumcari	174	242	82	313	305	166	199	

HARLEY-DAVIDSON DEALERSHIPS

Thunderbird Harley-Davidson, E-5
5000 Alameda Blvd. NE **Albuquerque**
(505) 856-1600
Lat N 35.184 **Lon** W 106.59

High Plains Harley-Davidson, F-10
4400 Mabry Dr. **Clovis**
(505) 769-1000
Lat N 34.394 **Lon** W 103.149

Four Corners Harley-Davidson, B-2
6520 E Main St. **Farmington**
(505) 325-6710
Lat N 36.778 **Lon** W 108.126

Barnetts Las Cruces Harley-Davidson, J-4
2600 Lakeside Dr. **Las Cruces**
(505) 541-1440
Lat N 32.291 **Lon** W 106.806

Champion Harley-Davidson, H-8
2801 W 2nd St. **Roswell**
(505) 624-0151
Lat N 33.394 **Lon** W 104.563

Santa Fe Harley-Davidson, D-5
3501 Cerrillos Rd. **Santa Fe**
(505) 471-3808
Lat N 35.646 **Lon** W 106.006

Distance scale
One inch represents about 15 miles
0 5 10 15 mi
0 5 10 15 20 km

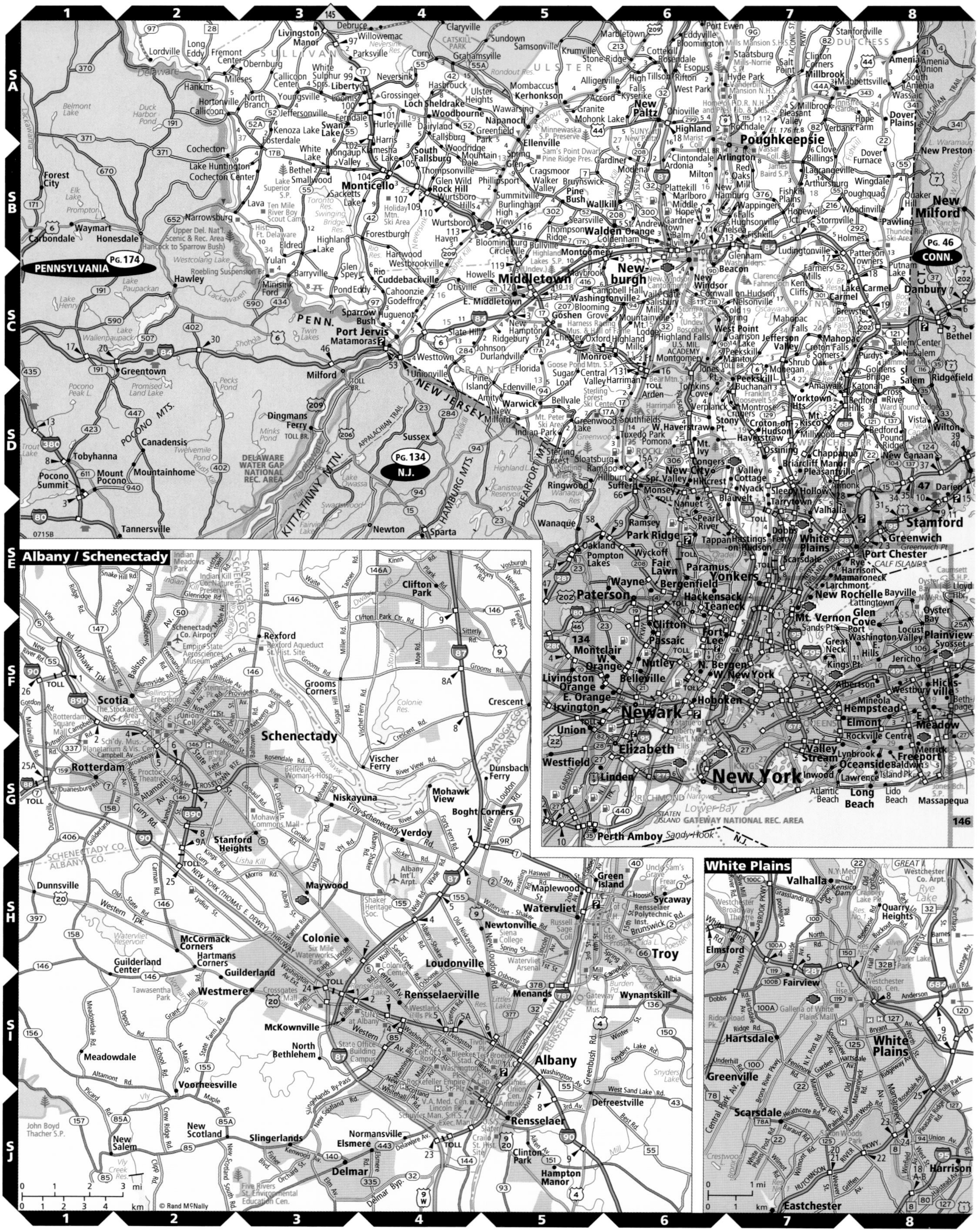

1 2 3 4 5 6 7 8
SA SB SC SD SE SF SG SH SI SJ
SULLIVAN
ULSTER
DUTCHESS
PUTNAM
ORANGE
ROCKLAND
WESTCHESTER
NASSAU
PENNSYLVANIA
PG. 174
PG. 46
CONN.
PG. 134
N.J.
NEW JERSEY
PENN.
Livingston Manor
Liberty
Monticello
Middletown
Newburgh
New Paltz
Poughkeepsie
Port Jervis
Matamoras
Milford
Honesdale
Carbondale
Hawley
Greentown
Tannersville
Sparta
Newton
Warwick
Goshen
Monroe
Beacon
Peekskill
Ossining
Danbury
New Milford
Stamford
Greenwich
Port Chester
White Plains
Yonkers
Paterson
Newark
Elizabeth
New York
Long Beach
Massapequa
Perth Amboy
Hempstead
Hicksville
GATEWAY NATIONAL REC. AREA
DELAWARE WATER GAP NATIONAL REC. AREA
POCONO MTS.
KITTATINNY MTN.
HAMBURG MTS.
APPALACHIAN TRAIL
Albany / Schenectady
Schenectady
Scotia
Rotterdam
Rexford
Clifton Park
Niskayuna
Colonie
Loudonville
Watervliet
Troy
Green Island
Menands
Albany
Rensselaer
Delmar
Guilderland
Westmere
Voorheesville
Slingerlands
New Scotland
New Salem
Elsmere
Normansville
Defreestville
Maywood
Wynantskill
Hampton Manor
Clinton Park
Albany Int'l. Arpt.
NEW YORK (THOMAS E. DEWEY) THRUWAY
SCHENECTADY CO.
ALBANY CO.
White Plains
Valhalla
Elmsford
Fairview
Hartsdale
Greenville
Scarsdale
Eastchester
Harrison
Quarry Heights
© Rand McNally
146

How to determine distance

Mileages in red between red arrowheads; in black, between intersections.

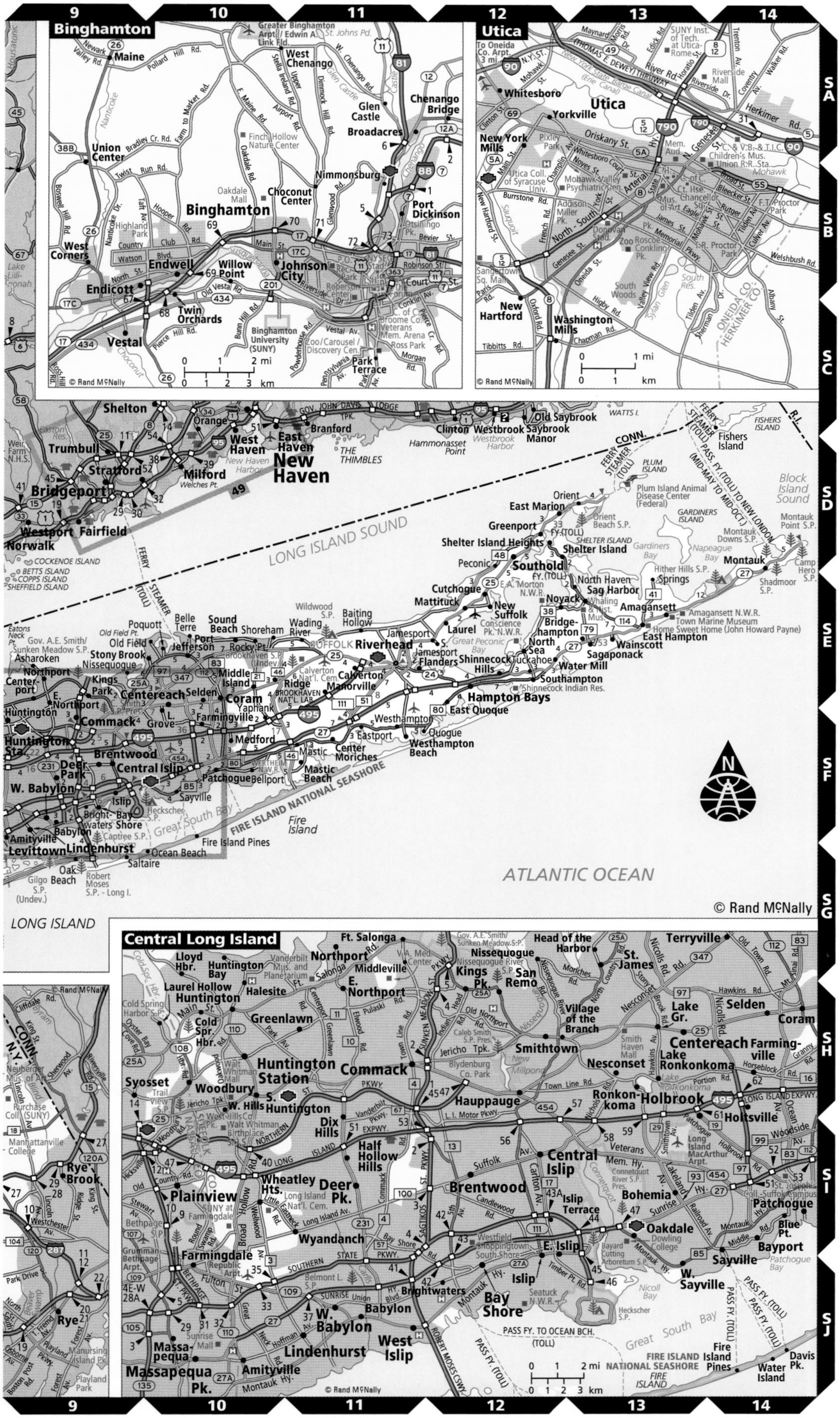

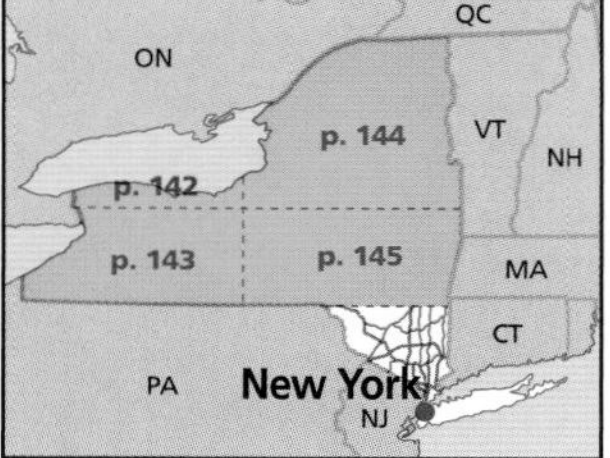
QC
ON
VT
NH
p. 144
p. 142
p. 143
p. 145
MA
CT
PA
New York
NJ

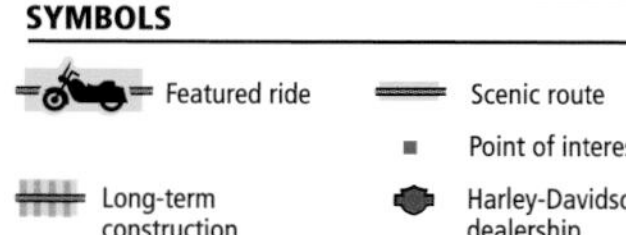
SYMBOLS
Featured ride
Scenic route
Point of interest
Long-term construction
Harley-Davidson dealership

HARLEY-DAVIDSON DEALERSHIPS

Harley-Davidson of Nassau County, SF-8
2428 Sunrise Hwy. **Bellmore**
(516) 409-9200
Lat N 40.666 **Lon** W 73.537

Brooklyn Harley-Davidson, SG-6
3449 Fort Hamilton Pkwy. **Brooklyn**
(718) 851-6666
Lat N 40.646 **Lon** W 73.986

Prestige Harley-Davidson, SD-7
205 Rte. 9 W **Congers**
(845) 268-6651
Lat N 41.151 **Lon** W 73.941

Miracle Mile Harley-Davidson, SF-7
215 Northern Blvd. **Great Neck**
(516) 466-8800
Lat N 40.777 **Lon** W 73.729

Lighthouse Harley-Davidson, SF-9
670 E Jericho Turnpike **Huntington Station**
(631) 427-0382
Lat N 40.834 **Lon** W 73.386

Harley-Davidson of New York, SF-7
42-11 Northern Blvd. **Long Island City**
(718) 707-9300
Lat N 40.753 **Lon** W 73.921

NewRoc Harley-Davidson, SE-7
8 Industrial Ln. **New Rochelle**
(914) 632-6743
Lat N 40.898 **Lon** W 73.794

Moroney's Harley-Davidson Sales, SC-6
833 Union Ave. **New Windsor**
(845) 564-5400
Lat N 41.492 **Lon** W 74.076

Harley-Davidson of New York, SF-6
686 Lexington Ave. **New York**
(212) 355-3003
Lat N 40.761 **Lon** W 73.969

Suffolk County Harley-Davidson, SI-13
4020 Sunrise Hwy. **Oakdale**
(631) 244-9000
Lat N 40.748 **Lon** W 73.141

Eastern Harley-Davidson, SE-11
1570 Old Country Rd. **Riverhead**
(631) 727-4700
Lat N 40.925 **Lon** W 72.696

Lombardi's Staten Island Harley-Davidson, SG-6
440-442 Bay St. **Staten Island**
(718) 447-4009
Lat N 40.632 **Lon** W 74.076

Reggie Pink, SE-7
295 Central Ave. **White Plains**
(914) 946-6622
Lat N 41.035 **Lon** W 73.784

H-D Military Sales, SF-8
100 Crossways Park West **Woodbury**
(516) 921-2800
Lat N 40.809 **Lon** W 73.489

O'Tooles Harley-Davidson, SB-5
4 Sullivan St. P.O. Box 837 **Wurtsboro**
(845) 888-2426
Lat N 41.572 **Lon** W 74.476

Distance scale
One inch represents about 18 miles
0 5 10 15 20 mi
0 5 10 15 20 25 30 km

Buffalo / Niagara Falls
Rochester
Syracuse
Elmira
Niagara Falls
Lockport
South Lockport
Tonawanda
N. Tonawanda
Grand Island
Amherst
Williamsville
Kenmore
Eggertsville
Cheektowaga
Buffalo
West Seneca
Lackawanna
Lancaster
Depew
Fort Erie
Crystal Beach
Chippawa
LAKE ERIE
CANADA
ONTARIO
Irondequoit
Greece
Gates
Brighton
E. Rochester
Chili Center
W. Webster
Lake Ontario
North Syracuse
Liverpool
Mattydale
Solvay
Fairmount
Westvale
De Witt
Camillus
Horseheads
LAKE ONTARIO
245 ft. above sea level
© Rand McNally

How to determine distance

Mileages in red between red arrowheads; in black, between intersections.

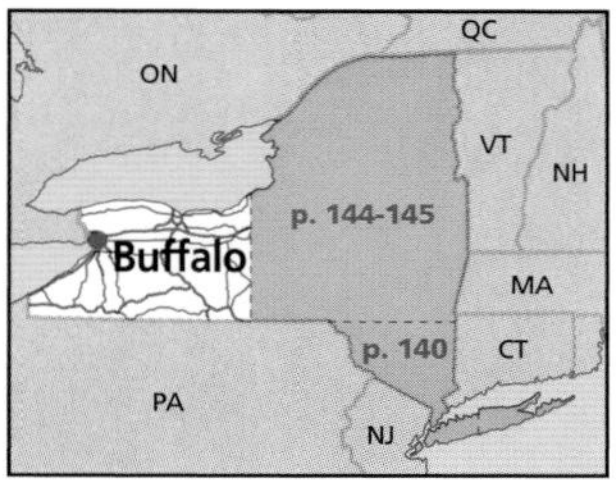

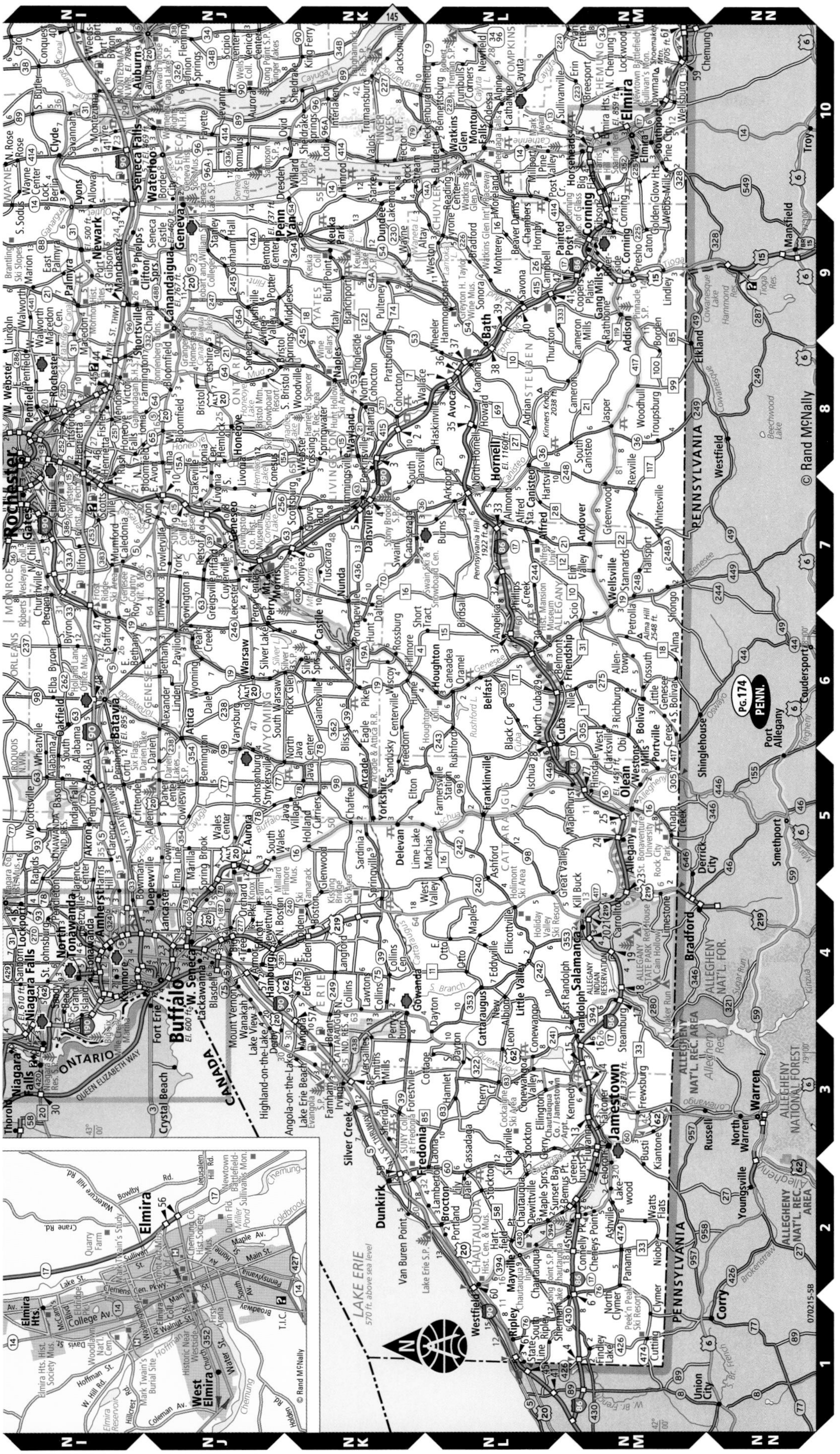

SYMBOLS

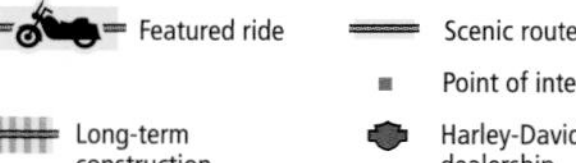
Featured ride
Scenic route
Point of interest
Long-term construction
Harley-Davidson dealership

HARLEY-DAVIDSON DEALERSHIPS

Buffalo Harley-Davidson, NI-4
4220 Bailey Ave. **Amherst**
(716) 832-7159
Lat N 42.97 **Lon** W 78.814

Arkport Harley-Davidson, NK-7
1 Main St. **Arkport**
(607) 295-7426
Lat N 42.462 **Lon** W 77.772

Stan's Harley-Davidson, NI-6
4425 W Saile Dr. **Batavia**
(585) 343-9598
Lat N 43.029 **Lon** W 78.191

Ithaca Harley-Davidson, NL-10
6033 Rte. 13 (at jct. of Rte. 224) **Cayuta**
(607) 594-3536
Lat N 42.294 **Lon** W 76.713

American Twin Harley-Davidson, NM-9
26 Bridge St. **Corning**
(607) 937-8351
Lat N 42.148 **Lon** W 77.061

Geneva Harley-Davidson Sales & Service, NJ-9
1103 Rtes. 5 & 20 **Geneva**
(315) 789-7976
Lat N 42.859 **Lon** W 77.03

Gowanda Harley-Davidson, NK-3
2535 Gowanda Zoar Rd. **Gowanda**
(716) 532-4584
Lat N 42.461 **Lon** W 78.908

Harley-Davidson of Jamestown, NM-2
2950 N Main St. Ext. (Exit 12 I-86) **Jamestown**
(716) 484-0113
Lat N 42.094 **Lon** W 79.245

Harv's Harley-Davidson, NI-8
3120 Kittering Rd. **Macedon**
(585) 377-0711
Lat N 43.119 **Lon** W 77.369

American Harley-Davidson, NI-3
1940 Military Rd. **Niagara Falls**
(716) 298-4849
Lat N 43.097 **Lon** W 78.974

American Harley-Davidson, NI-4
1149 Erie Ave. **North Tonawanda**
(716) 692-7200
Lat N 43.05 **Lon** W 78.848

Harley-Davidson of Rochester, NI-7
2600 W Henrietta Rd. (Rte. 15) **Rochester**
(585) 424-2120
Lat N 43.101 **Lon** W 77.629

Wyoming County Harley-Davidson, NJ-5
Rtes. 20A & 98 **Varysburg**
(585) 535-7900
Lat N 42.745 **Lon** W 78.321

Distance scale
One inch represents about 18 miles

0 5 10 15 20 mi
0 5 10 15 20 25 30 km

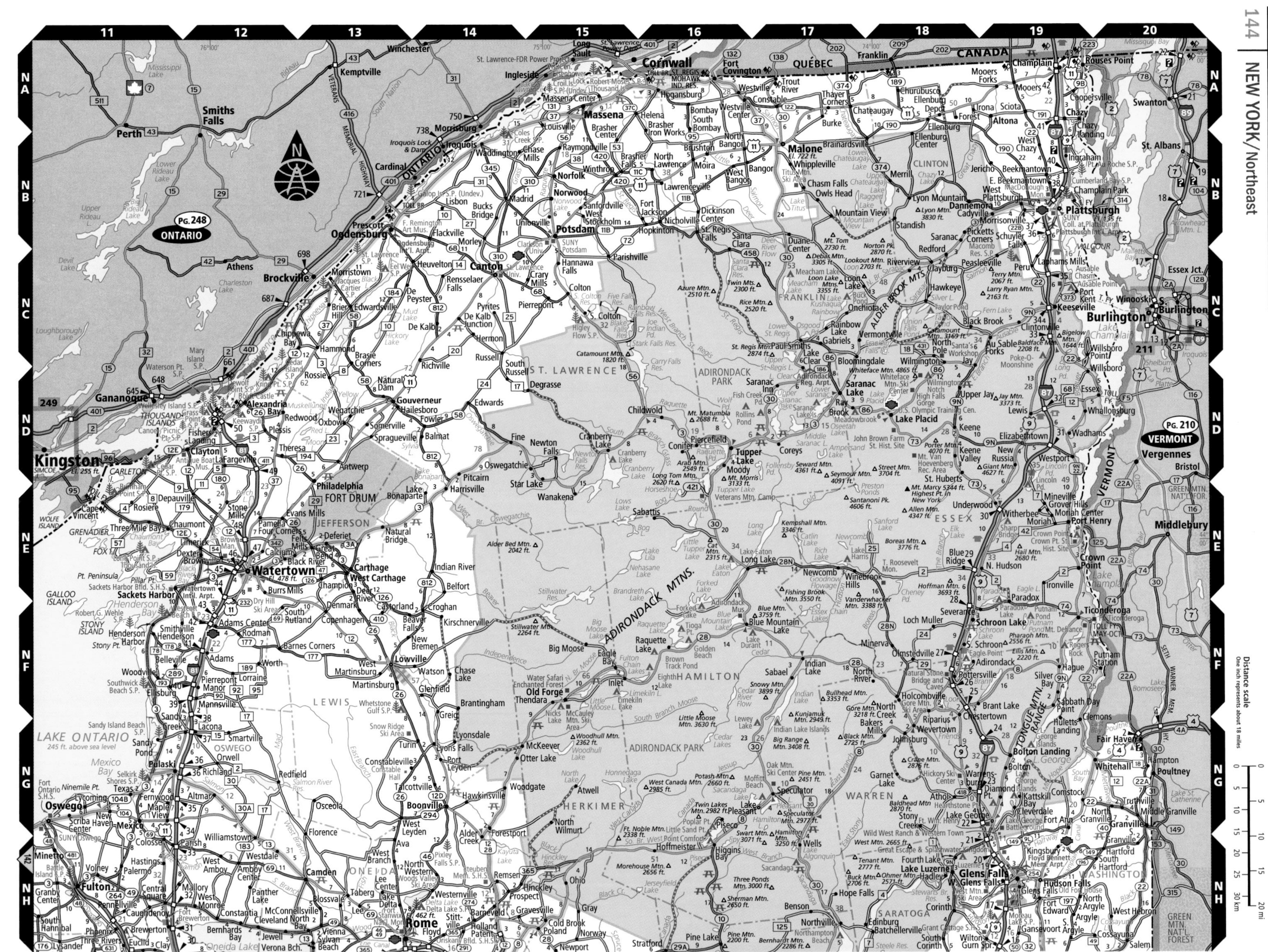
CANADA
QUÉBEC
ONTARIO
VERMONT
Pg. 210 VERMONT
Pg. 248 ONTARIO
Cornwall
Massena
Potsdam
Canton
Malone
Plattsburgh
Burlington
Ogdensburg
Brockville
Gananoque
Kingston
Watertown
Lake Placid
Saranac Lake
Tupper Lake
Old Forge
Glens Falls
Rome
Oswego
Fulton
Perth
Smiths Falls
Kemptville
ADIRONDACK MTNS.
ADIRONDACK PARK
LAKE ONTARIO
CLINTON
FRANKLIN
ESSEX
ST. LAWRENCE
HAMILTON
HERKIMER
WARREN
JEFFERSON
LEWIS
ONEIDA
OSWEGO
SARATOGA
FORT DRUM
THOUSAND ISLANDS
Mt. Marcy 5344 ft. Highest Pt. in New York

How to determine distance

Mileages in red between red arrowheads; in black, between intersections.

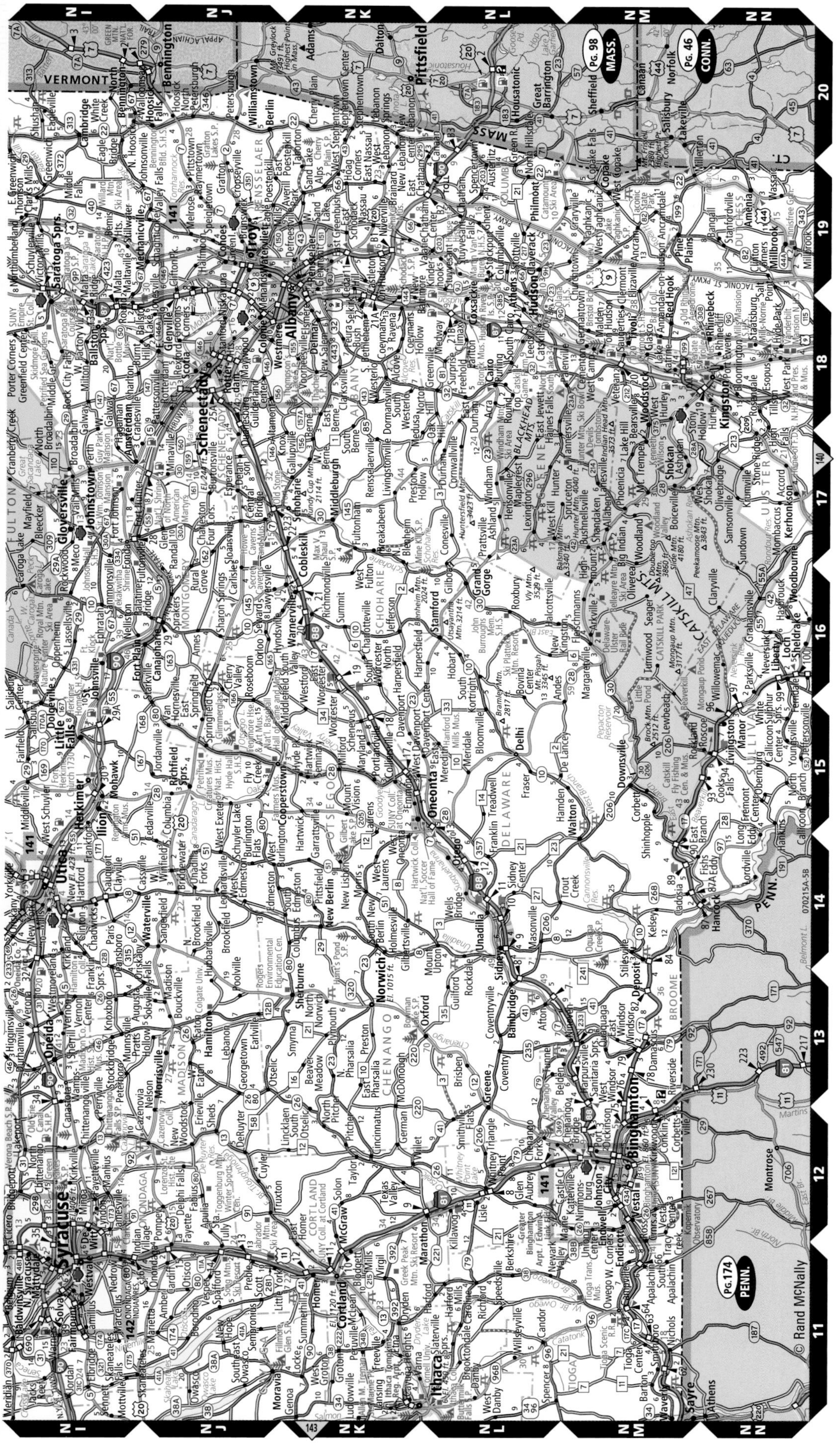

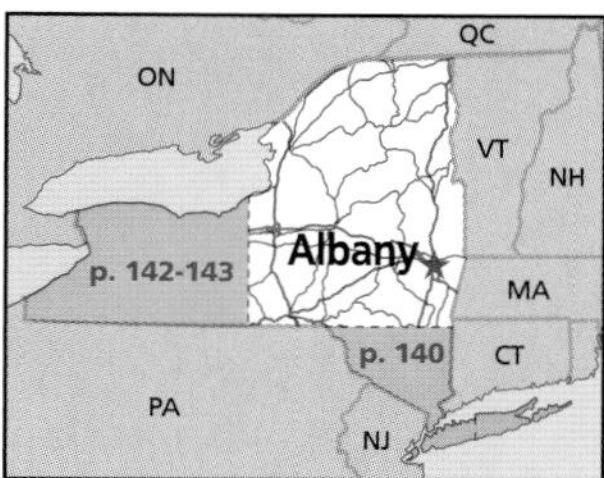
QC
ON
VT
NH
MA
CT
PA
NJ
p. 142-143
Albany
p. 140

SYMBOLS

Featured ride
Scenic route
Point of interest
Long-term construction
Harley-Davidson dealership

HARLEY-DAVIDSON DEALERSHIPS

Iron Block Harley-Davidson, NF-12
17890 Goodnough St. **Adams Center**
(315) 583-6177
Lat N 43.865 **Lon** W 76.015

Spitzie's Motorcycle Center, NJ-18
1970 Central Ave. **Albany**
(518) 456-RIDE (7433)
Lat N 42.741 **Lon** W 73.86

Southern Tier Harley-Davidson, NM-12
1152 Front St. **Binghamton**
(607) 773-0264
Lat N 42.15 **Lon** W 75.899

Tom McDermott Motorcycle Sales, NH-20
4294 State Rte. 4 **Fort Ann**
(518) 746-9303
Lat N 43.384 **Lon** W 73.503

Van's Harley-Davidson, NI-17
432 S Main St. **Gloversville**
(518) 725-3698
Lat N 43.035 **Lon** W 74.356

Woodstock Harley-Davidson, NM-18
949 Rte. 28 **Kingston**
(845) 338-2800
Lat N 41.98 **Lon** W 74.086

Lake City Harley-Davidson, ND-18
2534 Main St. **Lake Placid**
(518) 523-8737
Lat N 44.287 **Lon** W 73.985

Harley-Davidson of Utica, NI-14
4870 Commercial Dr. **New York Mills**
(315) 797-5570
Lat N 43.1 **Lon** W 75.301

North End Harley-Davidson, NB-19
594 Rte. 3 **Plattsburgh**
(518) 563-4360
Lat N 44.696 **Lon** W 73.506

Sovie's Harley-Davidson, NC-15
590 Ames Rd. **Potsdam**
(315) 265-4297
Lat N 44.631 **Lon** W 75.084

Dick's Harley-Davidson, NH-14
725 Erie Blvd. **Rome**
(315) 337-9160
Lat N 43.216 **Lon** W 75.473

Spitzie's Harley-Davidson of Saratoga Springs, NI-18
514 Broadway **Saratoga Springs**
(518) 581-8777
Lat N 43.085 **Lon** W 73.784

Performance Harley-Davidson, NI-11
807 N Geddes St. **Syracuse**
(315) 471-1157
Lat N 43.056 **Lon** W 76.17

Brunswick Harley-Davidson, NJ-19
1130 Hoosick Rd. (NY-7) **Troy**
(518) 279-1145
Lat N 42.759 **Lon** W 73.602

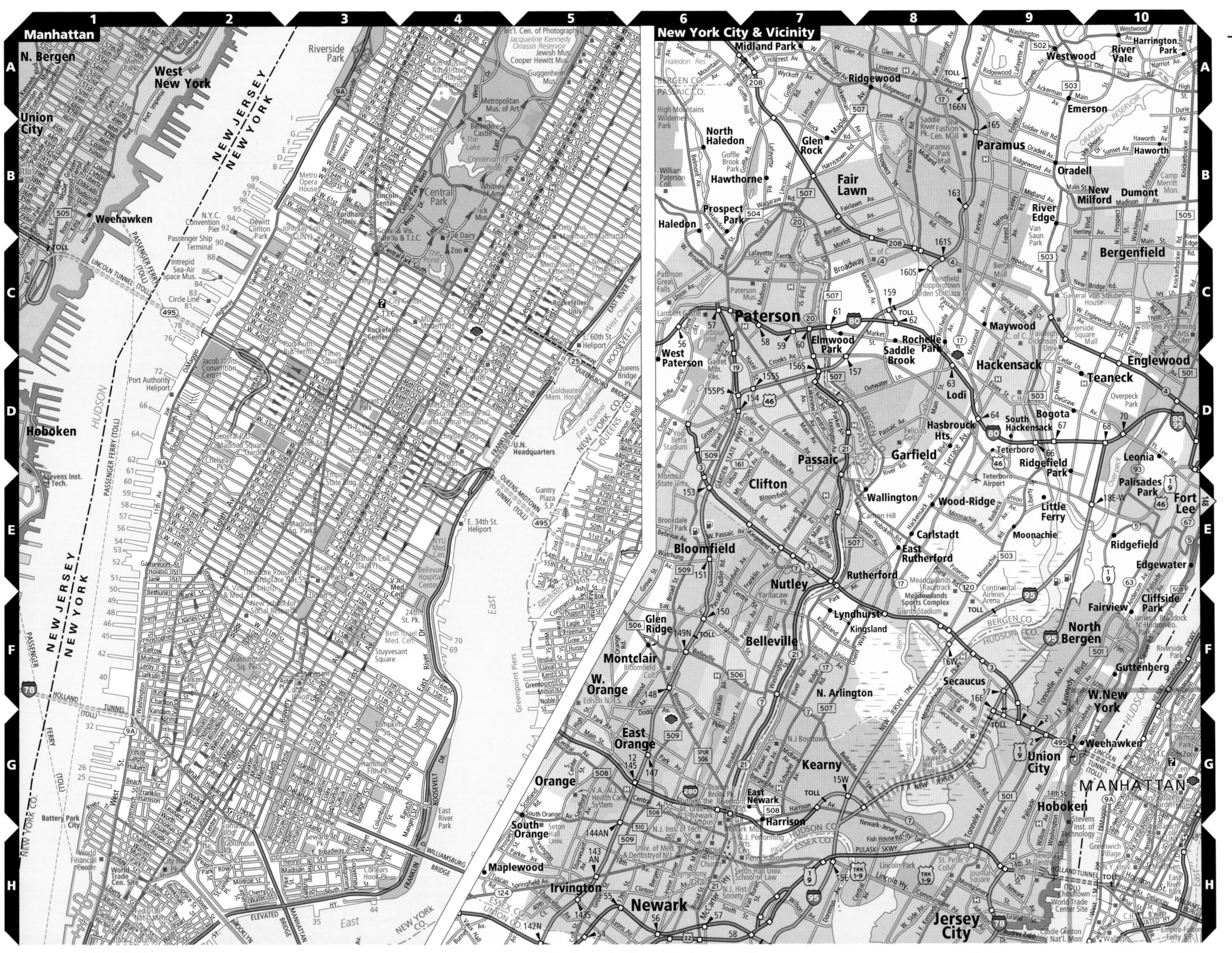
Manhattan
New York City & Vicinity
N. Bergen
West New York
Union City
Weehawken
Hoboken
Riverside Park
Central Park
Times Square
U.N. Headquarters
East
HUDSON
NEW JERSEY
NEW YORK
Paterson
Passaic
Clifton
Hackensack
Teaneck
Englewood
Fort Lee
Paramus
Ridgewood
Fair Lawn
Bergenfield
Secaucus
North Bergen
Kearny
Harrison
Belleville
Nutley
Bloomfield
Montclair
East Orange
Orange
Irvington
Maplewood
Lyndhurst
Rutherford
Garfield
Lodi
Newark
Jersey City
MANHATTAN

How to determine distance

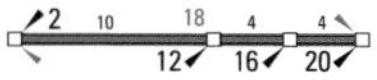

Mileages in red between red arrowheads; in black, between intersections.

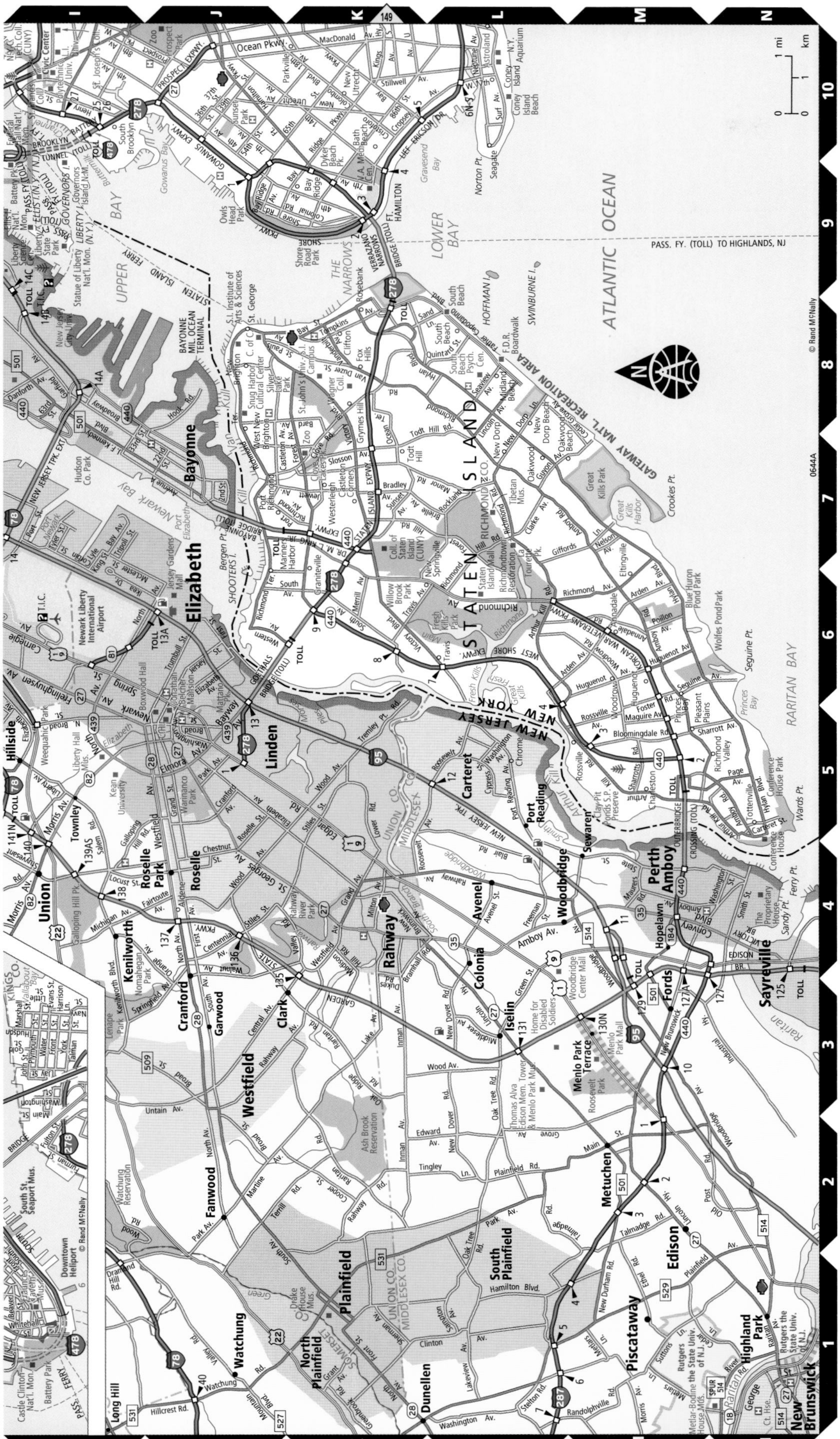

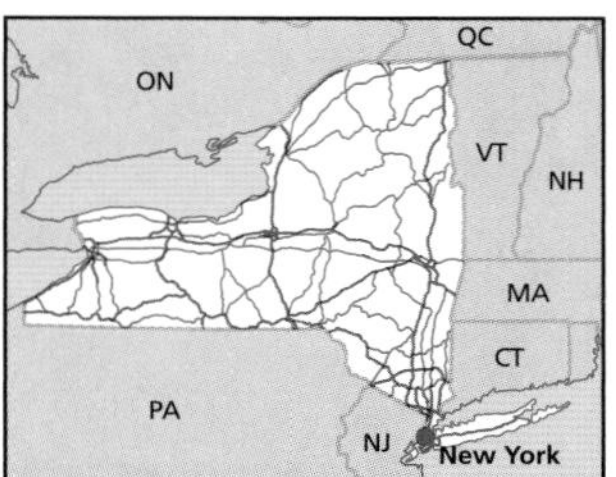
QC
ON
VT
NH
MA
CT
PA
NJ
New York

SYMBOLS

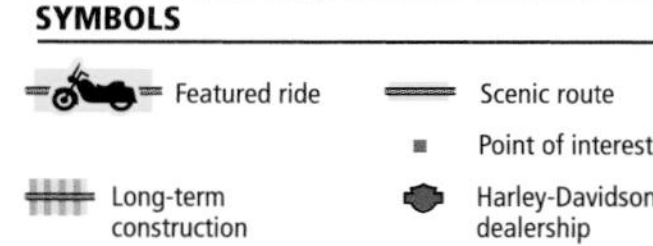
Featured ride
Scenic route
Point of interest
Long-term construction
Harley-Davidson dealership

NEW YORK MOTORCYCLE LAWS

Helmet use:
Required and reflectorization required

Riding two abreast:
Yes. See state law for specifics

Eye protection:
Required by law

Speed limit:
Primary roads: 65 mph
Secondary roads: 65 mph

NEW YORK RESOURCES

Road conditions or construction:
(800) 847-8929 (thruway)
www.thruway.state.ny.us (thruway)
www.dot.state.ny.us (all other roads)

Highway Emergency Numbers:
911

Tourism:
(800) 225-5697
(518) 474-4116
www.iloveny.com

State motor vehicle information:
(518) 473-5595
www.nydmv.state.ny.us

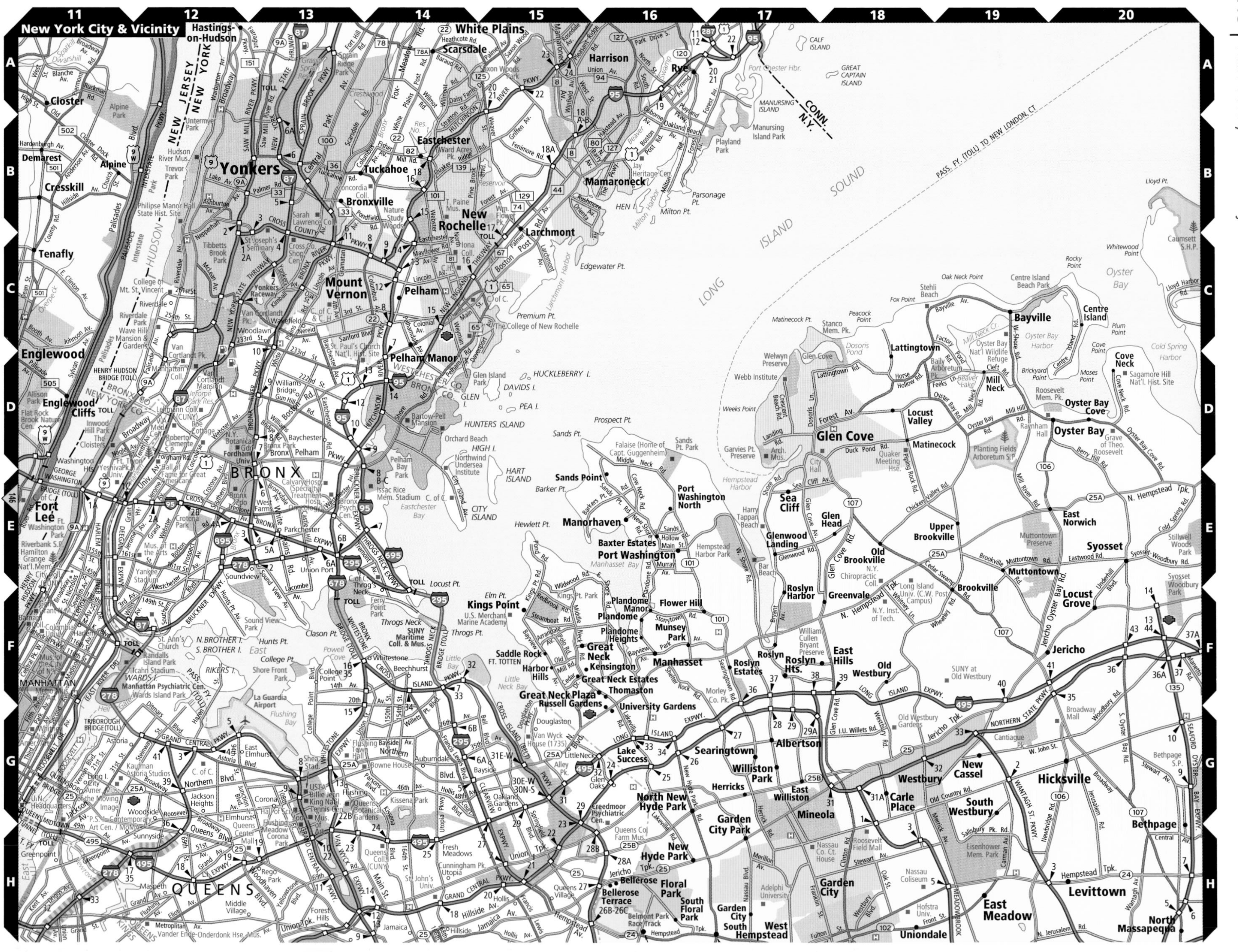
New York City & Vicinity
Long Island Sound
Oyster Bay
Glen Cove
Bayville
Lattingtown
Locust Valley
Matinecock
Syosset
Jericho
Hicksville
Bethpage
Levittown
North Massapequa
East Meadow
Westbury
Uniondale
Garden City
Mineola
Albertson
Roslyn
Port Washington
Manhasset
Great Neck
Lake Success
New Hyde Park
Floral Park
West Hempstead
Sands Point
Kings Point
White Plains
Scarsdale
Harrison
Rye
Mamaroneck
Larchmont
New Rochelle
Eastchester
Tuckahoe
Bronxville
Pelham
Pelham Manor
Mount Vernon
Yonkers
Hastings-on-Hudson
Bronx
Queens
Manhattan
La Guardia Airport
Fort Lee
Englewood
Englewood Cliffs
Tenafly
Cresskill
Demarest
Closter
Alpine
Hudson
New York
New Jersey
Conn.
N.Y.

How to determine distance

Mileages in red between red arrowheads; in black, between intersections.

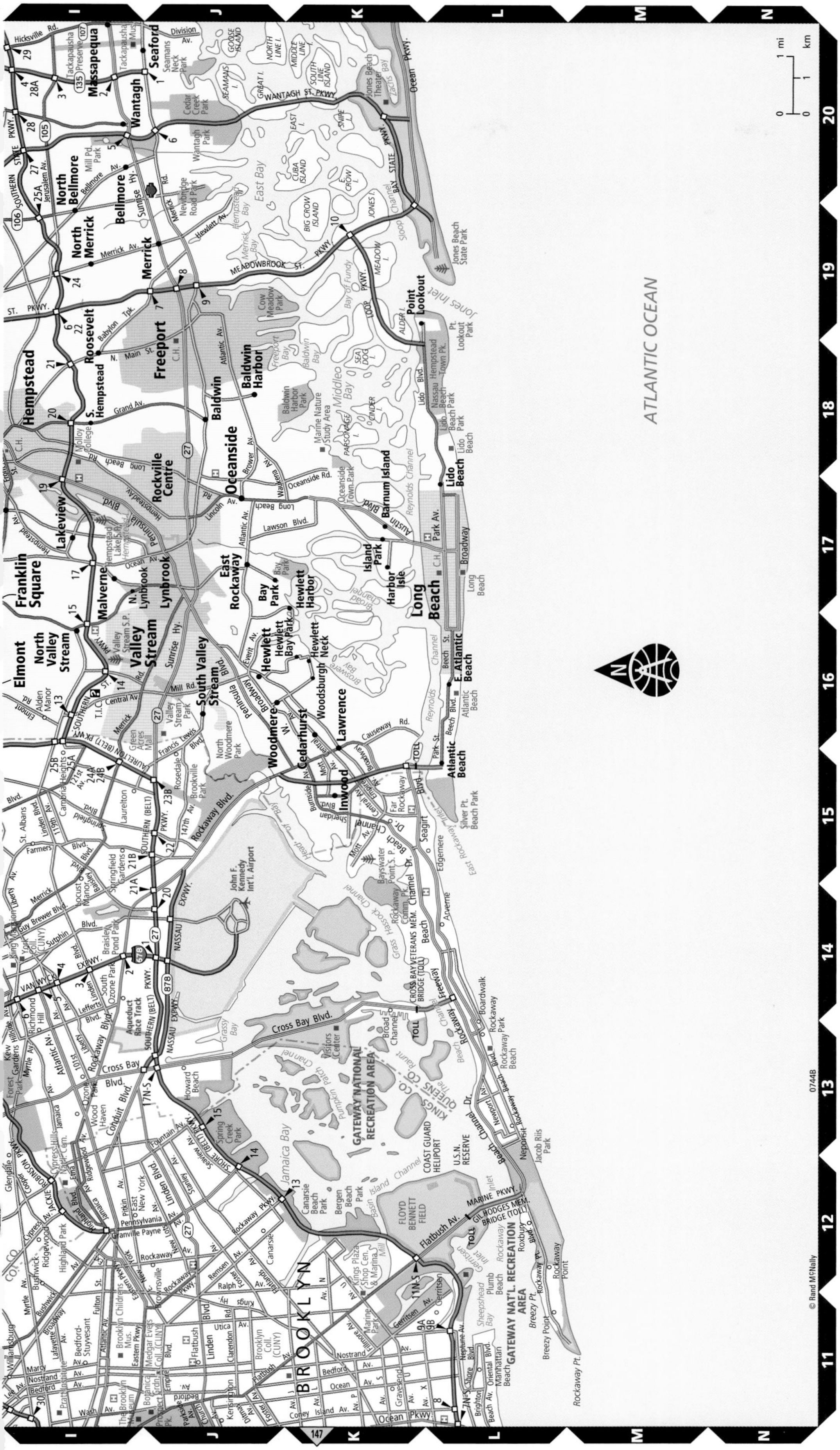

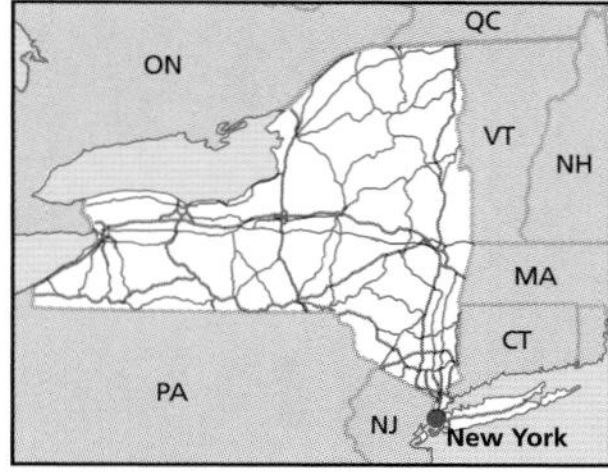
ON
QC
VT
NH
MA
CT
PA
NJ
New York

SYMBOLS

- Featured ride
- Scenic route
- Point of interest
- Long-term construction
- Harley-Davidson dealership

CITY-TO-CITY MILEAGE

	ALBANY	BINGHAMTON	BUFFALO	JAMESTOWN	PLATTSBURGH	ROCHESTER	SYRACUSE	UTICA
Albany		134	295	357	161	231	147	95
Auburn	176	90	128	193	259	64	27	85
Binghamton	134		230	224	282	166	76	93
Buffalo	295	230		71	378	78	154	204
Elmira	192	59	148	166	340	121	92	147
Glens Falls	58	179	313	402	110	249	165	113
Ithaca	176	51	154	191	287	90	58	113
Jamestown	357	224	71		505	143	219	269
Kingston	54	134	345	356	214	281	197	145
Lake Placid	142	263	347	412	49	283	201	164
Massena	221	242	312	377	87	248	166	161
New York	159	195	417	417	319	359	269	250
Niagara Falls	309	244	22	93	392	92	168	218
Olean	304	171	77	56	452	118	191	241
Oneonta	80	56	277	279	228	213	123	62
Oswego	176	116	159	224	259	77	40	85
Plattsburgh	161	282	378	505		314	230	188
Rochester	231	166	78	143	314		90	140
Syracuse	147	76	154	219	230	90		56
Utica	95	93	204	269	188	140	56	
Watertown	208	148	218	283	170	154	72	84

Distance scale
One inch represents about 21 miles

0 5 10 15 20 mi
0 5 10 15 20 25 30 km
VIRGINIA
TENNESSEE
SOUTH CAROLINA
Pg. 212 VIRGINIA
Pg. 190 TENN.
Pg. 186 S. CAR.
For continuation see main below
JEFFERSON NATIONAL FOREST
MT. ROGERS NATIONAL RECREATION AREA
Mt. Rogers 5729 ft. Highest Pt. in Virginia
CHEROKEE NAT'L FOR.
PISGAH NAT'L FOR.
NATIONAL FOREST
FORT BRAGG
APPALACHIAN MOUNTAINS
HOLSTON MTN.
IRON MTS.
BRUSHY MTS.
BLUE RIDGE
Abingdon
Bristol
Kingsport
Johnson City
Erwin
Marion
Galax
Martinsville
Danville
Mount Airy
Boone
North Wilkesboro
Wilkesboro
Lenoir
Morganton
Hickory
Asheville
Black Mountain
Hendersonville
Forest City
Rutherfordton
Shelby
Gastonia
Lincolnton
Statesville
Mooresville
Salisbury
Kannapolis
Concord
Charlotte
Monroe
Albemarle
Lexington
Thomasville
High Point
Winston-Salem
Greensboro
Burlington
Chapel Hill
Carrboro
Asheboro
Sanford
Pinehurst
Southern Pines
Rockingham
Laurinburg
Hamlet
Wadesboro
Spartanburg
Greenville
Gaffney
York
Rock Hill
Lancaster
Chester
Union
Cheraw
Chesterfield
Catawba
Broad

How to determine distance

Mileages in red between red arrowheads; in black, between intersections.

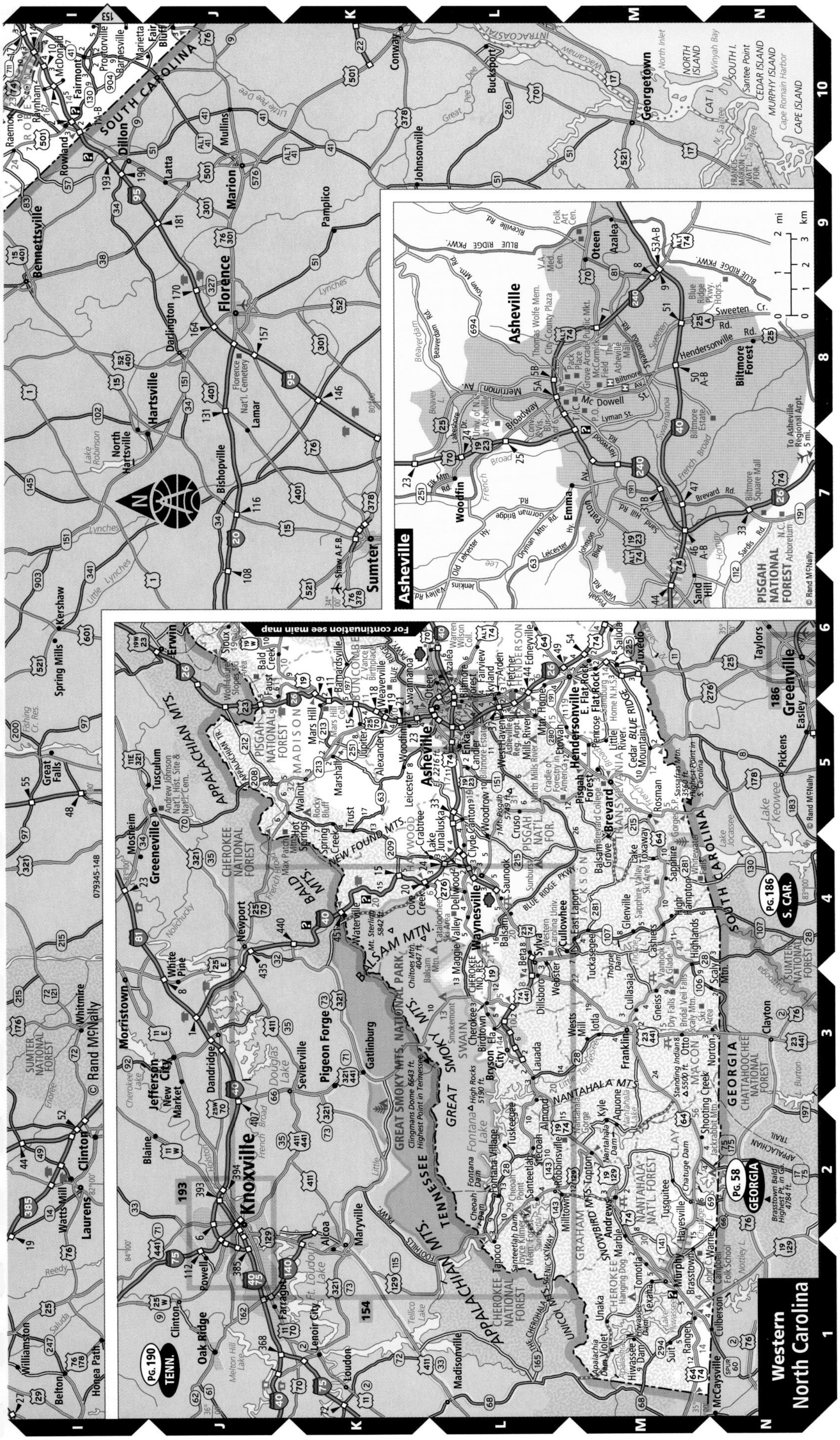

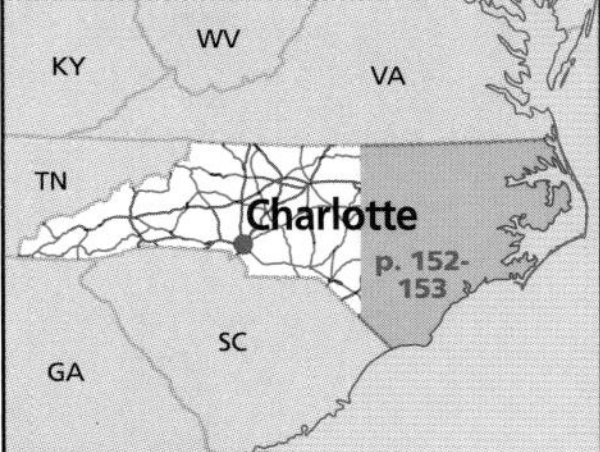

KY
WV
VA
TN
Charlotte
p. 152-153
SC
GA

NORTH CAROLINA MOTORCYCLE LAWS

Helmet use: Required

Riding two abreast:
Yes. See state law for specifics

Eye protection: Not required

Speed limit:
Primary roads: 70 mph; Secondary roads: 70 mph

NORTH CAROLINA RESOURCES

Road conditions or construction:
511
(877) 511-4662
www.ncsmartlink.org

Highway Emergency Numbers: 911

Tourism:
(800) 847-4862; (919) 733-8372
www.visitnc.com

State motor vehicle information:
(919) 715-7000
www.ncdot.org/dmv/driver_services

HARLEY-DAVIDSON DEALERSHIPS

For Charlotte and Winston-Salem/Greensboro areas, please see dealer listings on page 155.

Cox's Harley-Davidson, E-8
2795 NC Hwy. 134 **Asheboro**
(336) 629-2415
Lat N 35.615 **Lon** W 79.823

Davis' Harley-Davidson, D-9
2215 Hanford Rd. **Burlington**
(336) 227-1261
Lat N 36.062 **Lon** W 79.434

Pat Rogers Speedway Harley-Davidson, F-6
10049 Weddington Rd. **Concord**
(704) 979-7433
Lat N 35.363 **Lon** W 80.713

Carolina Harley-Davidson, F-4
2830 E Franklin Blvd. **Gastonia**
(704) 867-2855
Lat N 35.26 **Lon** W 81.128

Blue Ridge Harley-Davidson, E-4
2002 13th Ave. Dr. SE **Hickory**
(828) 327-3030
Lat N 35.711 **Lon** W 81.305

Sandhill Harley-Davidson, G-9
7540 NC Hwy. 15-501 S **Pinehurst**
(910) 295-9033
Lat N 35.195 **Lon** W 79.464

Wolf Creek Harley-Davidson, C-9
2014 Barnes St. **Reidsville**
OPENING IN 2007
Lat N 36.330 **Lon** W 79.648

Tilley's Harley-Davidson Shop, E-6
1509 E Innes St. **Salisbury**
(704) 638-6044
Lat N 35.653 **Lon** W 80.456

Tilley Harley-Davidson, E-5
1226 Morland Dr. **Statesville**
(704) 872-3883
Lat N 35.77 **Lon** W 80.86

Gene Lummus Harley-Davidson, E-1
20 Patton Cove Rd. **Swannanoa**
(828) 298-1683
Lat N 35.6 **Lon** W 82.403

Ghost Town Harley-Davidson, L-4
82 Locust Rd. **Waynesville**
(828) 454-0066
Lat N 35.476 **Lon** W 83.011

Crossroads Harley-Davidson, C-4
1921 US Hwy. 421 **Wilkesboro**
(336) 667-1003
Lat N 36.15 **Lon** W 81.185

Western North Carolina

Distance scale
One inch represents about 21 miles
0 5 10 15 20 mi
0 5 10 15 20 25 30 km

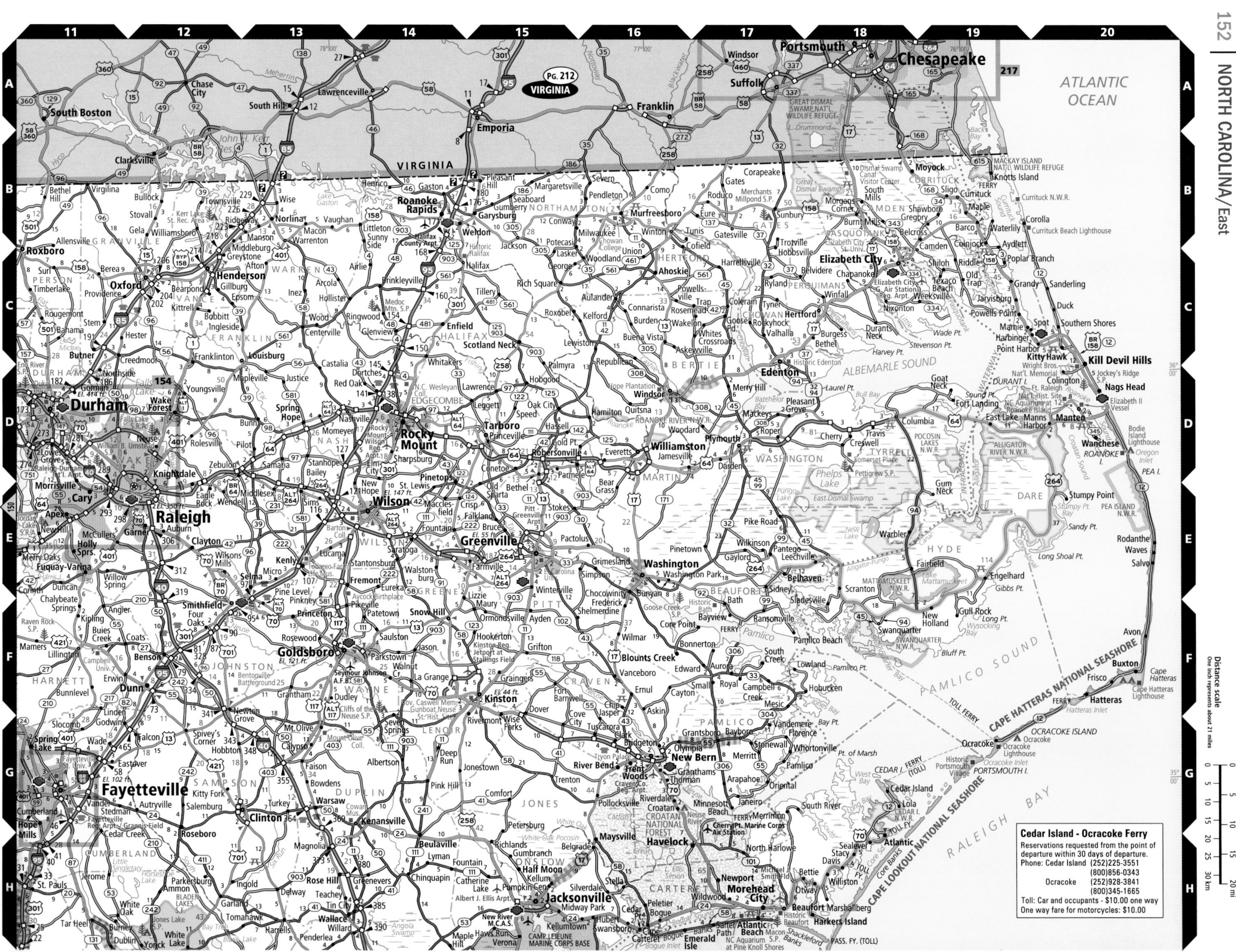
ATLANTIC OCEAN
VIRGINIA
PG. 212 VIRGINIA
ALBEMARLE SOUND
PAMLICO SOUND
RALEIGH BAY
CAPE HATTERAS NATIONAL SEASHORE
CAPE LOOKOUT NATIONAL SEASHORE
OCRACOKE ISLAND
Cedar Island - Ocracoke Ferry
Reservations requested from the point of departure within 30 days of departure.
Phone: Cedar Island (252)225-3551
(800)856-0343
Ocracoke (252)928-3841
(800)345-1665
Toll: Car and occupants - $10.00 one way
One way fare for motorcycles: $10.00
Raleigh
Durham
Cary
Fayetteville
Rocky Mount
Wilson
Greenville
Goldsboro
Kinston
New Bern
Jacksonville
Washington
Elizabeth City
Chesapeake
Portsmouth
Suffolk
Franklin
Emporia
Roanoke Rapids
Henderson
Oxford
Tarboro
Williamston
Edenton
Plymouth
Morehead City
Kill Devil Hills
Nags Head
Manteo
Hatteras
Ocracoke

How to determine distance

Mileages in red between red arrowheads; in black, between intersections.

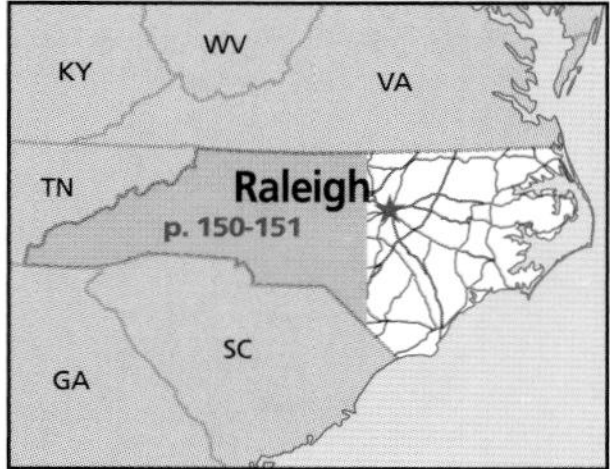
KY
WV
VA
TN
Raleigh
p. 150-151
SC
GA

SYMBOLS

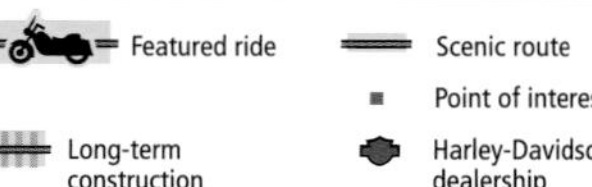
Featured ride
Scenic route
Point of interest
Long-term construction
Harley-Davidson dealership

HARLEY-DAVIDSON DEALERSHIPS

For the Raleigh/Durham area, please see dealer listings on page 155.

Outer Banks Harley-Davidson, C-18
1223 US Hwy. 17 **Elizabeth City**
(252) 338-8866
Lat N 36.296 **Lon** W 76.246

Cape Fear Harley-Davidson, G-11
3950 Sycamore Dairy Rd. **Fayetteville**
(910) 864-1200
Lat N 35.077 **Lon** W 78.951

Shelton's Harley-Davidson, F-13
606 Corporate Dr. **Goldsboro**
(919) 731-2776
Lat N 35.4 **Lon** W 77.984

Kitty Hawk Harley-Davidson Shop, C-20
8739 Hwy. 158 **Harbinger**
(252) 491-2091
Lat N 36.102 **Lon** W 75.814

New River Harley-Davidson Shop, H-15
2394 Wilmington Hwy. **Jacksonville**
(910) 346-9997
Lat N 34.739 **Lon** W 77.482

Nags Head Harley-Davidson, D-20
4104 S Virginia Dare Trail #22 **Nags Head**
(252) 255-5922
Lat N 35.954 **Lon** W 75.622

Harley-Davidson of New Bern, G-16
1613 Hwy. 70 E **New Bern**
(252) 633-4060
Lat N 35.075 **Lon** W 77.028

Collier Harley-Davidson, B-14
316 Premier Blvd. **Roanoke Rapids**
(252) 537-6493
Lat N 36.43 **Lon** W 77.641

Rocky Mount Harley-Davidson, D-14
928 N Winstead Ave. **Rocky Mount**
(252) 446-7292
Lat N 35.979 **Lon** W 77.844

Shelton's Harley-Davidson Mall Shop, F-12
1043 Industrial Park Dr. **Smithfield**
(919) 938-1592
Lat N 35.509 **Lon** W 78.313

Carolina Coast Harley-Davidson, J-14
6620 Market St. **Wilmington**
(910) 791-9997
Lat N 34.257 **Lon** W 77.84

J & E Harley-Davidson, E-15
2300 Elaines' Way **Winterville**
(252) 439-1345
Lat N 35.536 **Lon** W 77.408

Gastonia

Wilmington

Fayetteville

ATLANTIC OCEAN

ONSLOW BAY

LONG BAY

079345-148

Raleigh / Durham / Chapel Hill
Durham
Chapel Hill
Carrboro
Raleigh
Cary
Morrisville
Apex
Garner
Wake Forest
Forestville
Bayleaf
Falls
Neuse
New Hope
Wendell
Knightdale
Bethesda
Lowes Grove
Parkwood
Research Triangle Park
Raleigh-Durham Int'l. Arpt.
William B. Umstead St. Park
Carpenter
Green Level
Macedonia
Farrington
Fearrington
Wilsonville
B. Everett Jordan Lake
Jordan Lake St. Rec. Area
Falls Lake
Falls Lake St. Rec. Area
Duke Forest
Duke Univ.
Univ. of N.C.
N.C. State Univ.
Koka Booth Amphitheatre
Crabtree Valley Mall
Durham Co.
Wake Co.
Orange Co.
Chatham Co.
McAdenville
Belmont
Lake Wylie
S. CAR.
Daniel J. Stowe Botanical Garden
© Rand McNally
Great Smoky Mountains National Park
Knoxville
Kodak
Newport
Clevenger
Chestnut Hill
Bridgeport
Del Rio
Marbledale
Kimberlin Heights
Boyds Creek
Oak City
Seymour
Trundel Crossroad
Newell Station
Sevierville
Millican Grove
Harrisburg
Cherokee Hills
Jones Cove
East Fork
Cosby
Hartford
Waterville
Louisville
Rockford
Alcoa
Maryville
Wildwood
Miser Station
Binfield
Knob Creek
Du Pont
Walden Creek
Pigeon Forge
Wear Valley
Walland
Townsend
Gatlinburg
Pittman Center
Elkmont
Cades Cove
Tallassee
Tapoco
Fontana Village
Yellow Creek
Tuskeegee
Stecoah
Almond
Santeetlah
Robbinsville
Bryson City
Ela
Whittier
Birdtown
Cherokee
Lauada
Dillsboro
Barkers Creek
Beta
Sylva
Webster
Balsam
Saunook
Waynesville
Dellwood
Maggie Valley
Cove Creek
English Mountain
Snow Mountain
Chilhowee Mountain
Appalachian Mountains
Great Smoky Mountains
Balsam Mountain
Welch Ridge
Plott Balsams
Unicoi Mountains
Cheoah Mountains
Cowee Mountains
Tennessee
North Carolina
Great Smoky Mountains Nat'l. Pk.
Cherokee National Forest
Pisgah Nat'l. For.
Nantahala National Forest
Cherokee Indian Reservation
Clingmans Dome 6643 ft.
Mt. Le Conte 6593 ft.
Mt. Guyot 6621 ft.
Mt. Sterling 5842 ft.
Newfound Gap 5048 ft.
Fontana Lake
Stanleyville
Arcadia
Enterprise
Welcome
Arnold

How to determine distance

2 10 18 4 4 12 16 20

Mileages in red between red arrowheads; in black, between intersections.

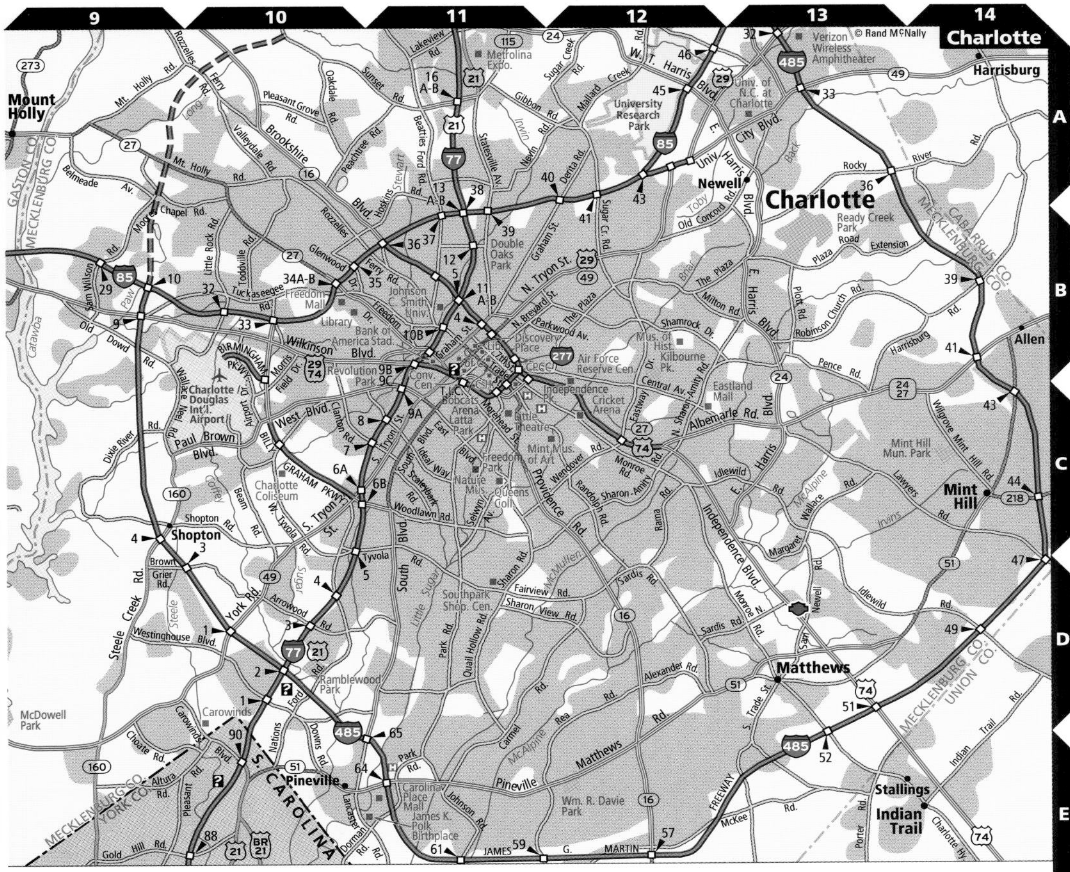
Charlotte
© Rand McNally
Mount Holly
Harrisburg
Newell
Charlotte
Allen
Mint Hill
Shopton
Matthews
Pineville
Stallings
Indian Trail
McDowell Park
Carowinds
University Research Park
Charlotte Douglas Int'l. Airport
Charlotte Coliseum
Southpark Shop. Cen.
Eastland Mall
Carolina Place Mall
GASTON CO.
MECKLENBURG CO.
CABARRUS CO.
UNION CO.
YORK CO.
S. CAROLINA

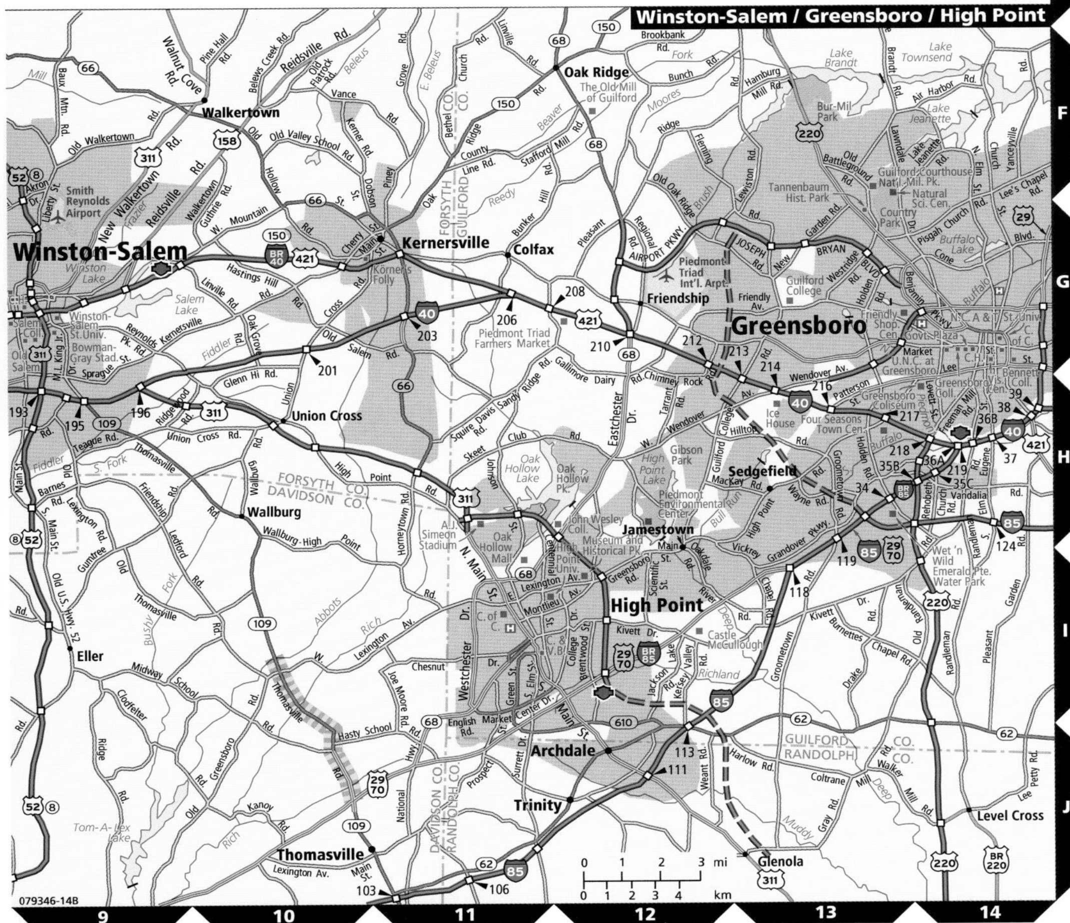
Winston-Salem / Greensboro / High Point
Walkertown
Oak Ridge
Kernersville
Colfax
Winston-Salem
Smith Reynolds Airport
Piedmont Triad Int'l. Arpt.
Friendship
Greensboro
Union Cross
Wallburg
Sedgefield
Jamestown
High Point
Eller
Archdale
Trinity
Thomasville
Glenola
Level Cross
FORSYTH CO.
GUILFORD CO.
DAVIDSON CO.
RANDOLPH CO.
079346-148
0 1 2 3 mi
0 1 2 3 4 km

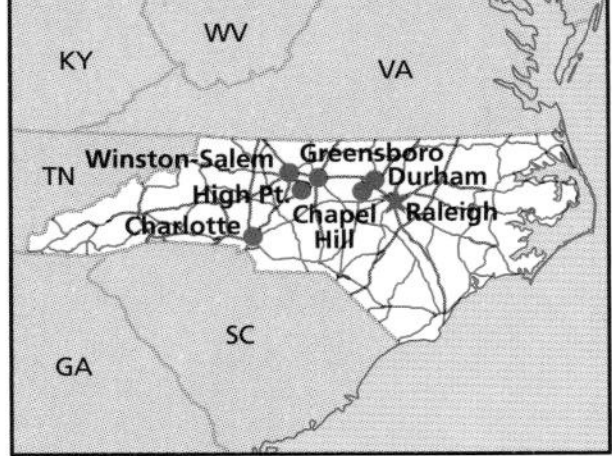
KY
WV
VA
TN
Winston-Salem
Greensboro
Durham
High Pt.
Charlotte
Chapel Hill
Raleigh
SC
GA

SYMBOLS

- Featured ride
- Scenic route
- Point of interest
- Long-term construction
- Harley-Davidson dealership

CITY-TO-CITY MILEAGE

	ASHEVILLE	CHARLOTTE	FAYETTEVILLE	GREENSBORO	GREENVILLE	RALEIGH	WILMINGTON	WINSTON-SALEM
Asheville		126	261	168	325	247	328	144
Boone	85	118	206	113	270	192	321	89
Charlotte	126		139	97	247	169	204	83
Durham	221	143	92	53	105	27	156	81
Elizabeth City	409	331	206	241	96	164	213	269
Fayetteville	261	139		98	109	66	118	121
Greensboro	168	97	98		157	79	208	28
Greenville	325	247	109	157		80	137	185
Hickory	73	63	192	99	256	178	307	75
Knoxville, TN	115	229	373	280	437	359	431	256
Nags Head	444	366	241	276	131	199	239	304
New Bern	358	280	130	190	46	112	90	218
Raleigh	247	169	66	79	80		130	107
Roanoke Rapids	306	228	128	138	80	86	192	166
Rockingham	199	75	64	90	174	97	129	109
Rocky Mt.	299	221	96	131	38	54	160	159
Wilmington	328	204	118	208	137	130		236
Winston-Salem	144	83	121	28	185	107	236	

HARLEY-DAVIDSON DEALERSHIPS

Shelton's Harley-Davidson of Durham, A-3
300 Muldee St. **Durham**
(919) 596-9511
Lat N 35.994 **Lon** W 78.863

Harley-Davidson of Greensboro, H-14
538 Farragut St. **Greensboro**
(336) 273-1101
Lat N 36.033 **Lon** W 79.806

Harley-Davidson Shop of High Point, I-12
2001 Brentwood St. **High Point**
(336) 883-1105
Lat N 35.940 **Lon** W 79.979

Harley-Davidson of Charlotte, D-13
9205 E Independence Blvd. **Matthews**
(704) 847-4647
Lat N 35.141 **Lon** W 80.719

Ray Price Harley-Davidson, D-6
1126 S Saunders St. **Raleigh**
(919) 832-2261
Lat N 35.766 **Lon** W 78.649

Curly's Harley-Davidson, G-9
3441 Myer Lee Dr. **Winston-Salem**
(336) 722-3106
Lat N 36.109 **Lon** W 80.171

Distance scale
One inch represents about 32 miles
0 10 20 mi
0 10 20 30 km

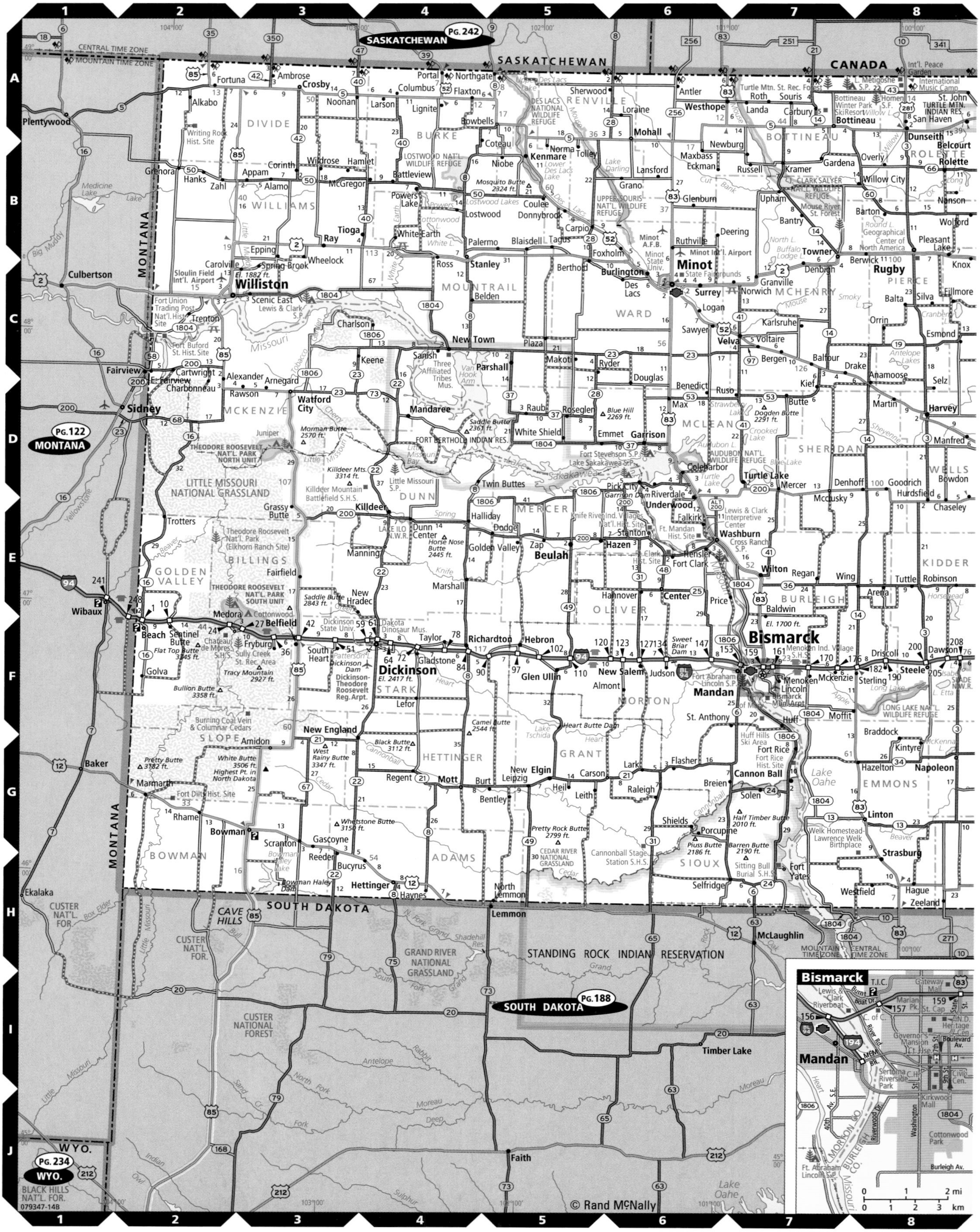

SASKATCHEWAN PG. 242
CANADA
MONTANA PG. 122
SOUTH DAKOTA PG. 188
WYO. PG. 234

CENTRAL TIME ZONE
MOUNTAIN TIME ZONE

DIVIDE
BURKE
RENVILLE
BOTTINEAU
ROLETTE
WILLIAMS
MOUNTRAIL
WARD
MCHENRY
PIERCE
MCKENZIE
MCLEAN
SHERIDAN
WELLS
DUNN
MERCER
BILLINGS
GOLDEN VALLEY
OLIVER
BURLEIGH
KIDDER
STARK
MORTON
SLOPE
HETTINGER
GRANT
EMMONS
BOWMAN
ADAMS
SIOUX

Fortuna
Ambrose
Crosby
Noonan
Columbus
Portal
Northgate
Flaxton
Larson
Lignite
Bowbells
Sherwood
Antler
Westhope
Roth
Souris
Landa
Carbury
Bottineau
Dunseith
Belcourt
Rolette
St. John
San Haven
Alkabo
Plentywood
Writing Rock Hist. Site
Columbus
Coteau
Niobe
Kenmare
Norma
Tolley
Loraine
Mohall
Maxbass
Eckman
Newburg
Russell
Kramer
Gardena
Overly
Willow City
Grenora
Hanks
Zahl
Appam
Corinth
Alamo
Wildrose
Hamlet
McGregor
Battleview
Powers Lake
Lostwood
Coulee
Donnybrook
Carpio
Lansford
Grano
Glenburn
Upham
Bantry
Barton
Nanson
Wolford
Tioga
Ray
Epping
Wheelock
Spring Brook
Carolville
White Earth
Palermo
Blaisdell
Tagus
Foxholm
Burlington
Des Lacs
Minot
Deering
Ruthville
Towner
Pleasant Lake
Rugby
Knox
Berwick
Denbigh
Granville
Surrey
Norwich
Logan
Sawyer
Velva
Voltaire
Bergen
Balfour
Drake
Anamoose
Balta
Silva
Fillmore
Orrin
Esmond
Selz
Harvey
Martin
Kief
Manfred
Culbertson
Williston
Scenic East
Stanley
Ross
Belden
Berthold
Plaza
Makoti
Ryder
Douglas
Benedict
Ruso
Max
Butte
Fairview
Sidney
Trenton
Fort Union Trading Post Nat'l. Hist. Site
Fort Buford St. Hist. Site
Cartwright
Charbonneau
Alexander
Arnegard
Rawson
Watford City
Keene
Charlson
New Town
Sanish
Parshall
Mandaree
Raub
Roseglen
White Shield
Emmet
Garrison
Coleharbor
Turtle Lake
Mercer
Denhoff
Goodrich
Hurdsfield
Bowdon
Chaseley
McClusky
Fort Stevenson S.P.
Lake Sakakawea S.P.
Pick City
Riverdale
Underwood
Falkirk
Washburn
Wilton
Regan
Wing
Tuttle
Robinson
Juniper
Theodore Roosevelt Nat'l. Park North Unit
Little Missouri National Grassland
Killdeer
Killdeer Mountain Battlefield S.H.S.
Little Missouri S.P.
Twin Buttes
Halliday
Dodge
Dunn Center
Golden Valley
Zap
Beulah
Hazen
Stanton
Fort Clark
Hensler
Grassy Butte
Trotters
Theodore Roosevelt Nat'l. Park (Elkhorn Ranch Site)
Manning
Fairfield
New Hradec
Marshall
Hannover
Center
Price
Baldwin
Arena
Bismarck
Wibaux
Beach
Sentinel Butte
Medora
Theodore Roosevelt Nat'l. Park South Unit
Belfield
Fryburg
South Heart
Dickinson
Gladstone
Taylor
Richardton
Hebron
Glen Ullin
New Salem
Judson
Mandan
Menoken
McKenzie
Sterling
Driscoll
Dawson
Steele
Golva
Almont
Lefor
St. Anthony
Moffit
Braddock
Kintyre
Napoleon
Hazelton
Baker
Marmarth
Fort Dilts Hist. Site
Amidon
New England
Regent
Mott
Burt
New Leipzig
Elgin
Carson
Lark
Flasher
Breien
Cannon Ball
Solen
Rhame
Bowman
Scranton
Gascoyne
Reeder
Bucyrus
Hettinger
Haynes
Bentley
Heil
Leith
Raleigh
Shields
Porcupine
Fort Yates
Selfridge
Linton
Strasburg
Hague
Zeeland
Westfield
North Lemmon
Lemmon
McLaughlin
Ekalaka
Timber Lake
Faith
Custer Nat'l. For.
Grand River National Grassland
Custer National Forest
Standing Rock Indian Reservation
Cave Hills
Black Hills Nat'l. For.
Lostwood Nat'l. Wildlife Refuge
Des Lacs National Wildlife Refuge
Upper Souris Nat'l. Wildlife Refuge
J. Clark Salyer Nat'l. Wildlife Refuge
Audubon Nat'l. Wildlife Refuge
Long Lake Nat'l. Wildlife Refuge
Fort Berthold Indian Res.
Three Affiliated Tribes Mus.
Turtle Mtn. Indian Res.
International Peace Garden
Geographical Center of North America
Lake Sakakawea
Lake Oahe
Missouri
Minot A.F.B.

Bismarck
Mandan

079347-14B

How to determine distance

Mileages in red between red arrowheads; in black, between intersections.

9
10
11
12
13
14
A
B
C
D
E
F
G
H
I
J
MANITOBA
PG.244
PG.108
MINN.
MINNESOTA
SOUTH DAKOTA
Crystal City
Altona
Piney
Pembina
Langdon
Cavalier
Grafton
Devils Lake
Grand Forks
East Grand Forks
Thief River Falls
Red Lake Falls
Crookston
New Rockford
Cooperstown
Mayville
Hillsboro
Valley City
Jamestown
Fargo
Moorhead
West Fargo
Wahpeton
Breckenridge
Fergus Falls
Ellendale
Wishek
Ashley
Edgeley
La Moure
Lisbon
Forman
Kindred
Casselton
Carrington
Cando
Rolla
Warren
Hawley
Barnesville
Pelican Rapids
Wheaton
Eureka
Britton
Bismarck
Grand Forks
Fargo
© Rand McNally

SYMBOLS

- Featured ride
- Scenic route
- Point of interest
- Long-term construction
- Harley-Davidson dealership

NORTH DAKOTA MOTORCYCLE LAWS

Helmet use:
Required under age 18, and reflectorization required

Riding two abreast:
Yes. See state law for specifics

Eye protection:
Not required

Speed limit:
Primary roads: 75 mph
Secondary roads: 75 mph

NORTH DAKOTA RESOURCES

Road conditions or construction:
511
(866) 696-3511
www.state.nd.us/dot/divisions/maintenance/511-nd.html

Highway Emergency Numbers:
911 or *2121

Tourism:
(800) 435-5663
(701) 328-2525
www.ndtourism.com

State motor vehicle information:
(701) 328-2500
www.dot.nd.gov/dlts.html

CITY-TO-CITY MILEAGE

	Bismarck	Devils Lake	Dickinson	Fargo	Garrison	Grand Forks	Minot	Williston
Bismarck		179	99	193	76	269	111	230
Devils Lake	179		275	163	168	89	121	249
Dickinson	99	275		289	148	365	183	131
Fargo	193	163	289		266	78	263	420
Garrison	76	168	148	266		257	47	141
Grand Forks	269	89	365	78	257		210	338
Minot	111	121	183	263	47	210		126
Williston	230	249	131	420	141	338	126	

HARLEY-DAVIDSON DEALERSHIPS

Andy's Harley-Davidson, C-13
2756 N Washington St. **Grand Forks**
(701) 775-6098
Lat N 47.948 **Lon** W 97.068

Stutsman Harley-Davidson, F-10
1202 12th Ave. SE **Jamestown**
(701) 252-5271
Lat N 46.897 **Lon** W 98.692

Roughrider Harley-Davidson, F-7
3708 Memorial Hwy. (I-94) **Mandan**
(701) 663-2220
Lat N 46.816 **Lon** W 100.845

Rough Rider Harley-Davidson Minot, C-6
515 20th Ave. SE **Minot**
(701) 839-6330
Lat N 48.211 **Lon** W 101.286

Fargo Harley-Davidson Sales & Service, F-13
600 W Main Ave. **West Fargo**
(701) 277-1000
Lat N 46.877 **Lon** W 96.909

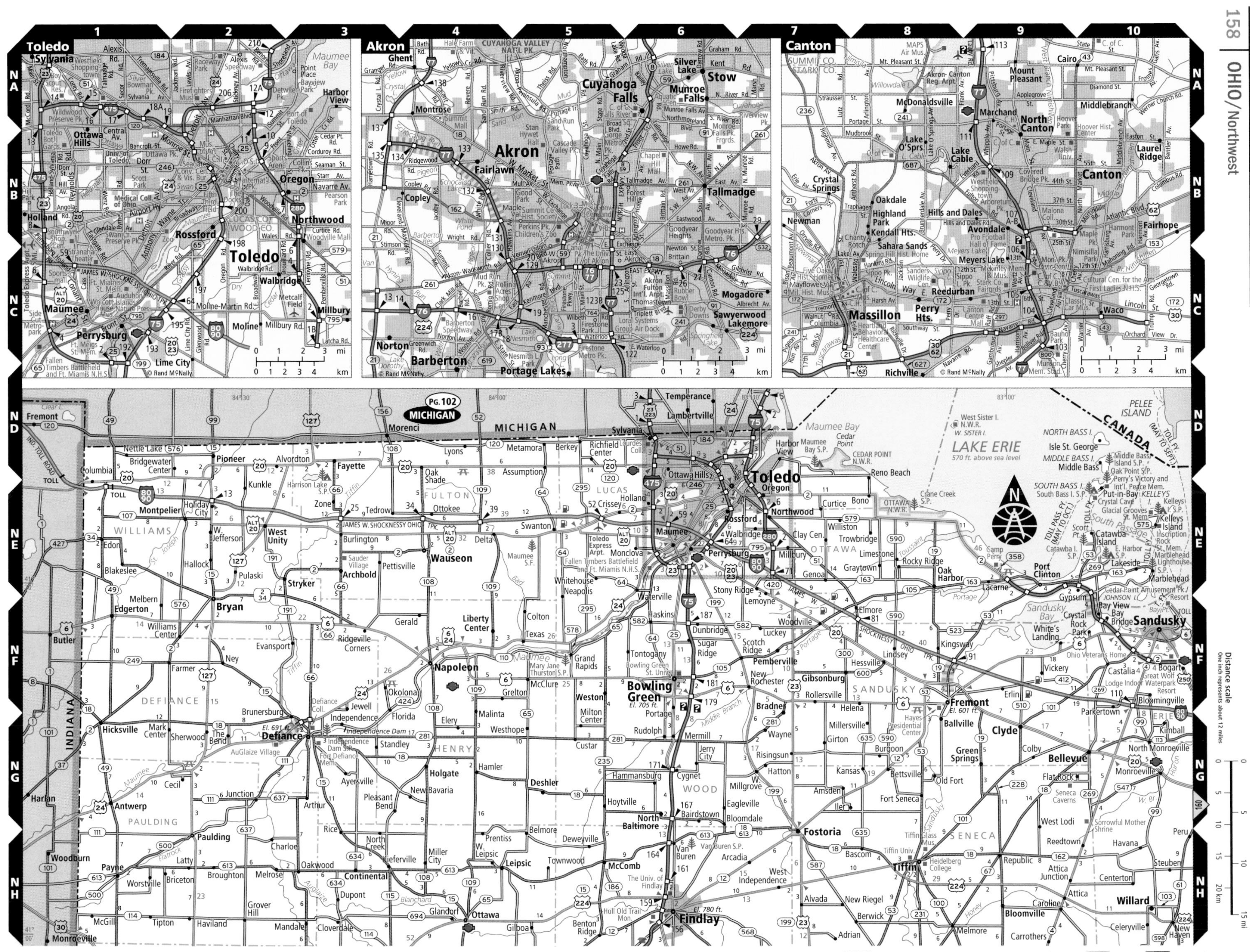
Distance scale
One inch represents about 12 miles
0 5 10 15 mi
0 5 10 15 20 km
Toledo
Akron
Canton
LAKE ERIE
570 ft. above sea level
PELEE ISLAND
CANADA
MICHIGAN
INDIANA
PG. 102 MICHIGAN
WILLIAMS
DEFIANCE
PAULDING
FULTON
LUCAS
HENRY
WOOD
OTTAWA
SANDUSKY
SENECA
Sandusky
Fremont
Bowling Green
Findlay
Napoleon
Defiance
Bryan
Wauseon
Fostoria
Tiffin
Perrysburg
Maumee
© Rand McNally

How to determine distance

Mileages in red between red arrowheads; in black, between intersections.

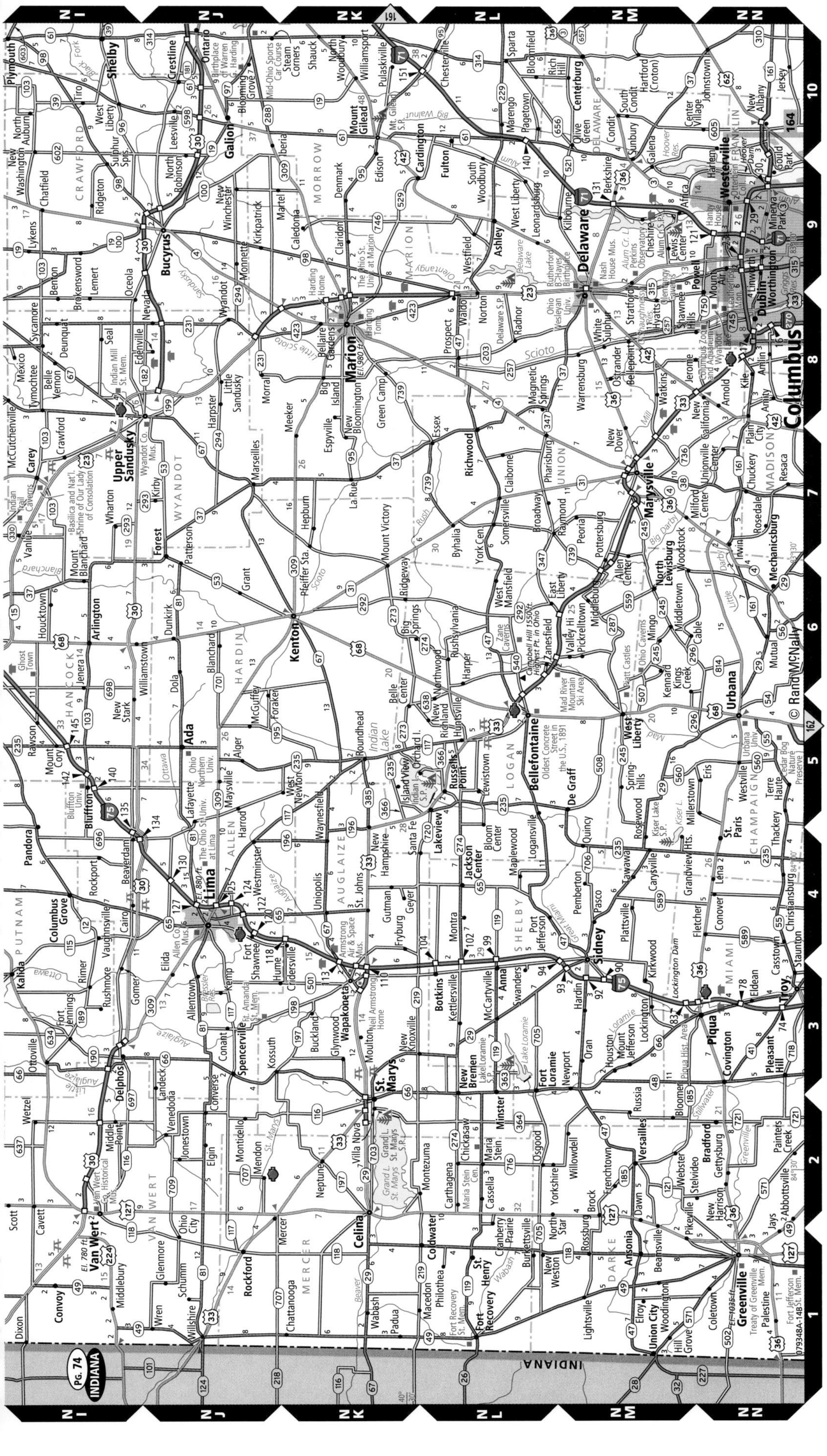

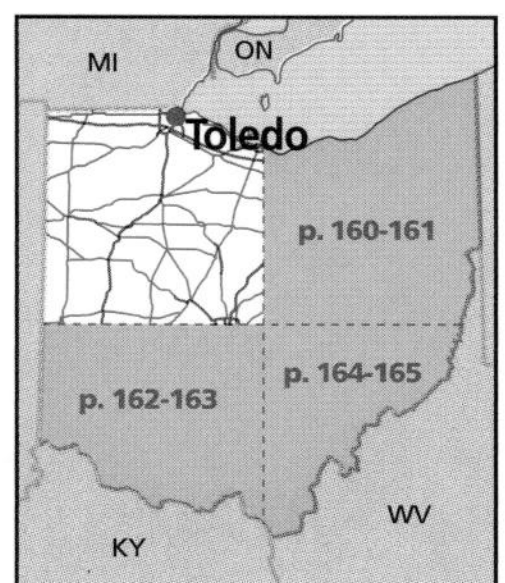
MI
ON
Toledo
p. 160-161
p. 162-163
p. 164-165
KY
WV

SYMBOLS

- Featured ride
- Scenic route
- Point of interest
- Long-term construction
- Harley-Davidson dealership

HARLEY-DAVIDSON DEALERSHIPS

High Point Harley-Davidson, NL-5
288 Stockyard Rd. (TR-217) **Bellefontaine**
(937) 599-4550
Lat N 40.382 **Lon** W 83.76

Harley-Davidson of Lima, NJ-4
3255 Fort Shawnee Industrial Dr. **Lima**
(419) 331-3027
Lat N 40.688 **Lon** W 84.124

Jim's Harley-Davidson Sales, NJ-2
7172 Rte. 707 **Mendon**
(419) 795-4185
Lat N 40.671 **Lon** W 84.524

Roeder Harley-Davidson Shop, NG-10
3684 US 20 W **Monroeville**
(419) 465-2546
Lat N 41.239 **Lon** W 82.703

Harley-Davidson Sales & Service, NF-4
862 American Rd. **Napoleon**
(419) 592-7123
Lat N 41.363 **Lon** W 84.084

Ben Breece Harley-Davidson, NH-4
242 W 4th St. **Ottawa**
(419) 523-4274
Lat N 41.021 **Lon** W 84.05

Signature Harley-Davidson, NE-6
1176 Professional Dr. **Perrysburg**
(419) 873-2453
Lat N 41.55 **Lon** W 83.607

Gover Harley-Davidson, NN-3
1501 E Ash St. (US Rte. 36) **Piqua**
(937) 773-8733
Lat N 40.154 **Lon** W 84.243

C & A Harley-Davidson, NN-8
7610 Commerce Place **Plain City**
(614) 873-4604
Lat N 40.124 **Lon** W 83.189

Roeder Harley-Davidson, NF-10
5316 Milan Rd. **Sandusky**
(419) 621-1046
Lat N 41.397 **Lon** W 82.653

Toledo Harley-Davidson, ND-6
7960 W Central Ave. **Toledo**
(419) 843-7892
Lat N 41.674 **Lon** W 83.734

Thiel's Wheels Harley-Davidson, NI-8
350 Tarhe Trail **Upper Sandusky**
(419) 294-4951
Lat N 40.856 **Lon** W 83.274

Distance scale
One inch represents about 12 miles
0 5 10 15 mi
0 5 10 15 20 km

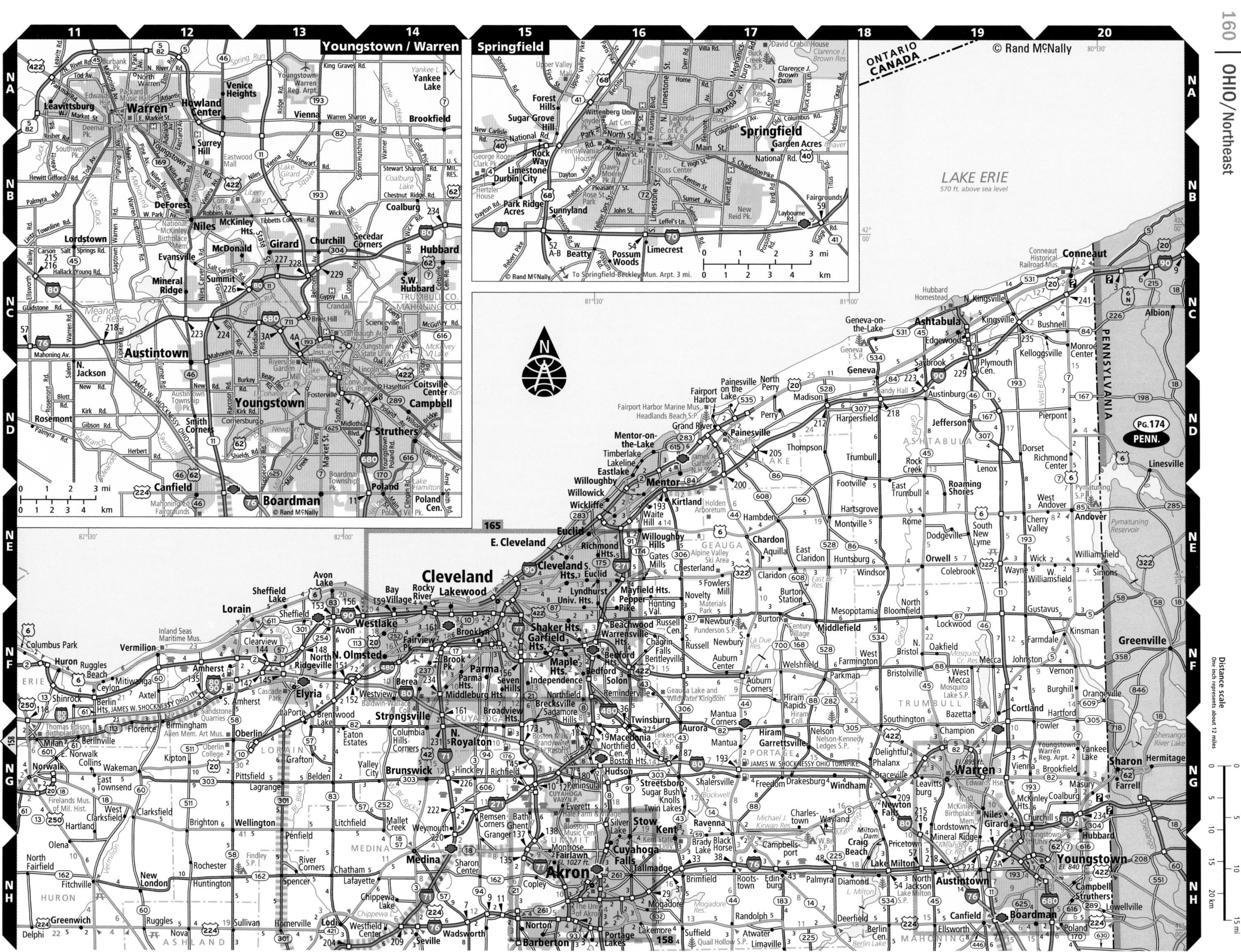

LAKE ERIE
570 ft. above sea level
ONTARIO
CANADA
PENNSYLVANIA
PG. 174 PENN.
Cleveland
Akron
Youngstown
Warren
Youngstown / Warren
Springfield
© Rand McNally

How to determine distance

Mileages in red between red arrowheads; in black, between intersections.

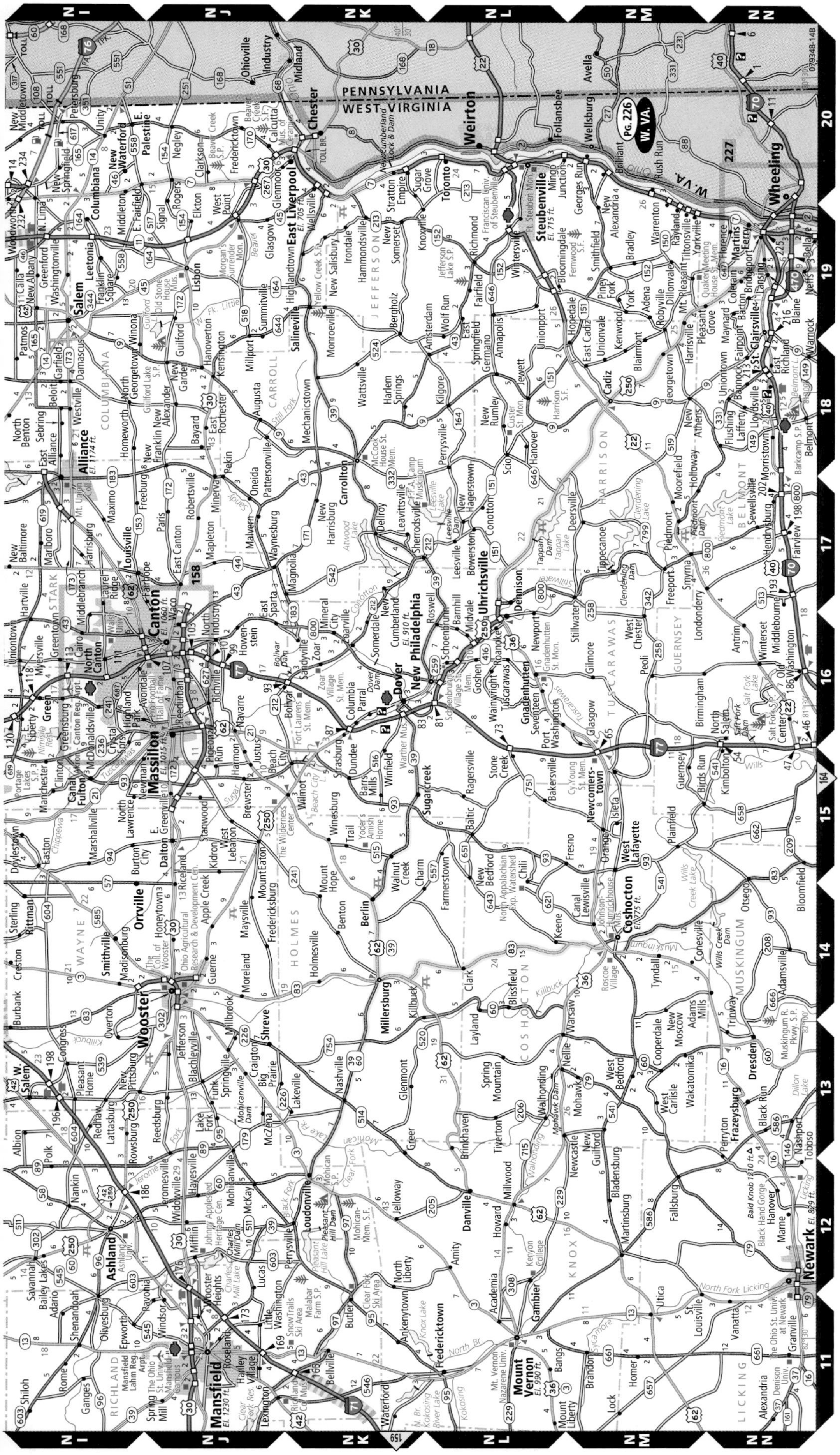

MI
ON
Cleveland
p. 158-159
p. 162-163
p. 164-165
KY
WV

SYMBOLS

- Featured ride
- Scenic route
- Point of interest
- Long-term construction
- Harley-Davidson dealership

HARLEY-DAVIDSON DEALERSHIPS

Liberty Harley-Davidson of Akron, NH-16
32 E Cuyahoga Falls **Akron**
(330) 535-9900
Lat N 41.105 **Lon** W 81.514

Lake Erie Harley-Davidson Shop, NF-13
38401 Chester Rd. **Avon**
(440) 934-5000
Lat N 41.467 **Lon** W 82.051

South East Harley-Davidson Sales, NF-16
23105 Aurora Rd. **Bedford Heights**
(440) 439-5300
Lat N 41.417 **Lon** W 81.514

Liberty Harley-Davidson North Shop, NG-16
334 E Hines Hill Rd. **Boston Heights**
(330) 650-2799
Lat N 41.263 **Lon** W 81.502

Harley-Davidson of Youngstown, NH-19
4478 Boardman-Canfield Rd. **Canfield**
(330) 702-1010
Lat N 41.025 **Lon** W 80.733

Harley-Davidson Sales, NF-14
14550 Lorain Ave. **Cleveland**
(216) 252-3111
Lat N 41.454 **Lon** W 81.796

Warren Harley-Davidson Sales, NF-19
2102 Elm Rd. **Cortland**
(330) 395-4700
Lat N 41.316 **Lon** W 80.733

Adventure Harley-Davidson, NK-16
1465 Rte. 39 NW **Dover**
(330) 364-6519
Lat N 40.536 **Lon** W 81.478

Elyria Harley-Davidson Sales, NF-13
561 Cleveland St. **Elyria**
(440) 365-7354
Lat N 41.376 **Lon** W 82.08

Hale's Harley-Davidson, NJ-11
1400 Harrington Memorial Rd. **Mansfield**
(419) 522-8602
Lat N 40.794 **Lon** W 82.513

Carlton Harley-Davidson, NG-17
11771 State Rte. 44 **Mantua**
(330) 274-3141
Lat N 41.309 **Lon** W 81.222

Century Harley-Davidson, NH-14
3053 Eastpointe Circle **Medina**
(330) 721-1702
Lat N 41.137 **Lon** W 81.797

Western Reserve Harley-Davidson, ND-16
8567 Tyler Blvd. **Mentor**
(440) 974-6900
Lat N 41.686 **Lon** W 81.333

Freedom Harley-Davidson, NI-16
7233 Sunset Strip Ave. NW **North Canton**
(330) 494-2453
Lat N 40.887 **Lon** W 81.433

Neidengard's Harley-Davidson, NL-19
284 Canton Rd. (Rte. 43) **Wintersville**
(740) 266-6188
Lat N 40.381 **Lon** W 80.708

Distance scale
One inch represents about 12 miles
0 5 10 15 mi
0 5 10 15 20 km

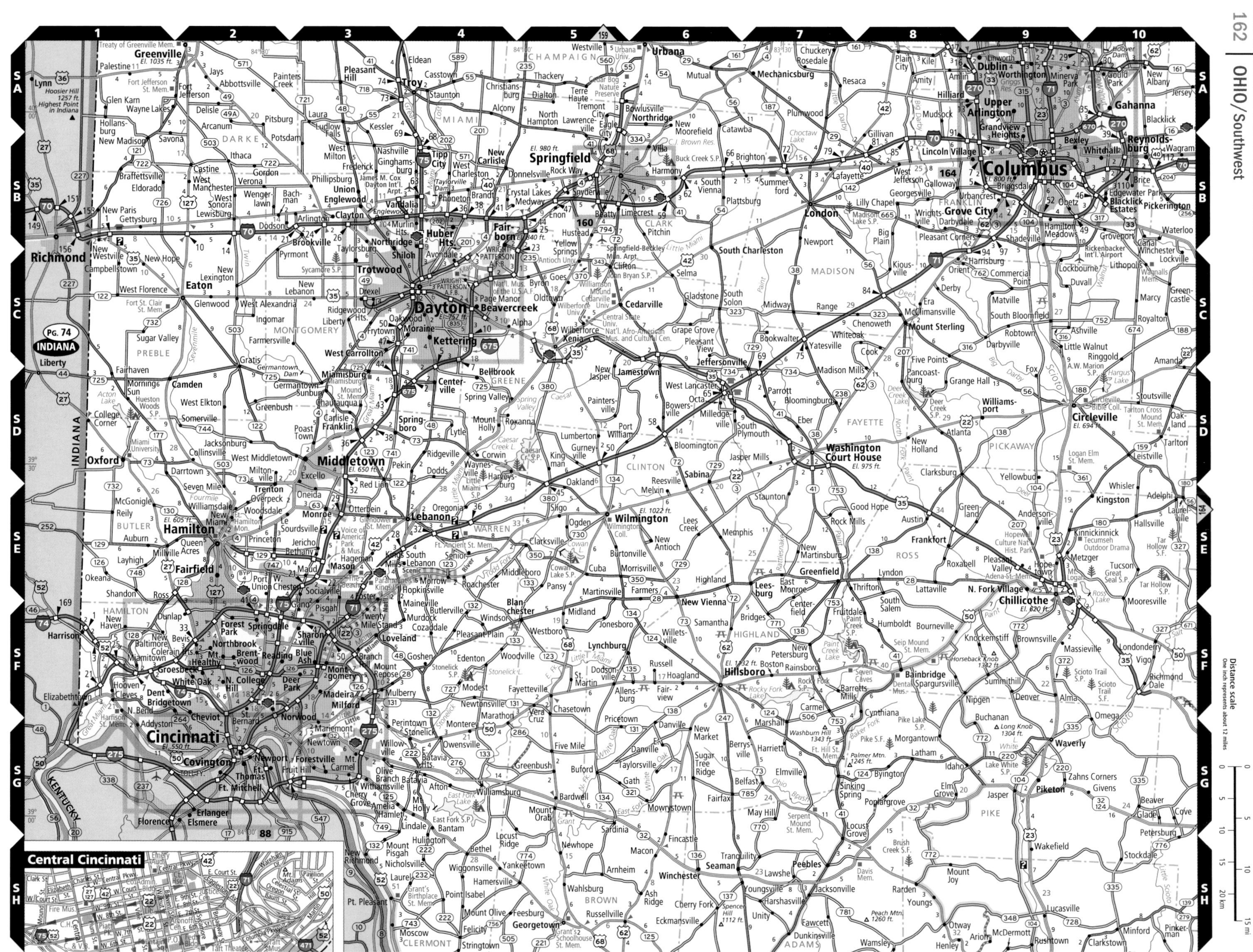

Columbus
Dayton
Springfield
Cincinnati
Hamilton
Middletown
Chillicothe
Circleville
Washington Court House
Wilmington
Xenia
Lebanon
Hillsboro
Greenville
Eaton
Oxford
Richmond
Urbana
London
Central Cincinnati
INDIANA
KENTUCKY
PG. 74 INDIANA

How to determine distance

Mileages in red between red arrowheads; in black, between intersections.

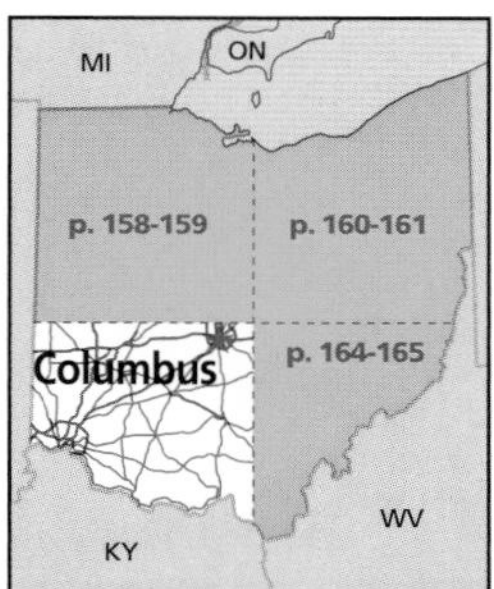
MI
ON
p. 158-159
p. 160-161
Columbus
p. 164-165
KY
WV

HARLEY-DAVIDSON DEALERSHIPS

Harley-Davidson of Chillicothe, SE-9
818 Eastern Ave. **Chillicothe**
(740) 773-8826
Lat N 39.324 **Lon** W 82.957

Harley-Davidson of Cincinnati-Eastgate, SG-3
699 Old SR 74 **Cincinnati (Eastgate)**
(513) 528-1400
Lat N 39.071 **Lon** W 84.277

Harley-Davidson of Cincinnati, SF-2
1799 Tennessee Ave. **Cincinnati**
(513) 641-1188
Lat N 39.167 **Lon** W 84.466

A.D. Farrow Harley-Davidson, SB-9
491 W Broad St. **Columbus**
(614) 228-6353
Lat N 39.961 **Lon** W 83.013

F & S Harley-Davidson, SC-4
7220 N Dixie Dr. **Dayton**
(937) 898-8084
Lat N 39.835 **Lon** W 84.199

Tri-County Harley-Davidson, SE-2
5960 Dixie Hwy. **Fairfield**
(513) 874-4343
Lat N 39.328 **Lon** W 84.514

Aces & Eights Harley-Davidson, SE-3
2383 Kings Center Ct. **Mason**
(513) 459-1777
Lat N 39.356 **Lon** W 84.26

Centennial Park Harley-Davidson, SA-10
12477 Broad St. SW **Pataskala**
(740) 964-2205
Lat N 39.995 **Lon** W 82.724

Mid-Ohio Harley-Davidson, SB-6
2100 Quality Ln. **Springfield**
(937) 322-3590
Lat N 39.894 **Lon** W 83.734

Buckminn's Harley-Davidson, SC-5
1213 Cincinnati Ave. **Xenia**
(937) 376-3344
Lat N 39.67 **Lon** W 83.944

Distance scale
One inch represents about 12 miles
0 5 10 15 mi
0 5 10 15 20 km

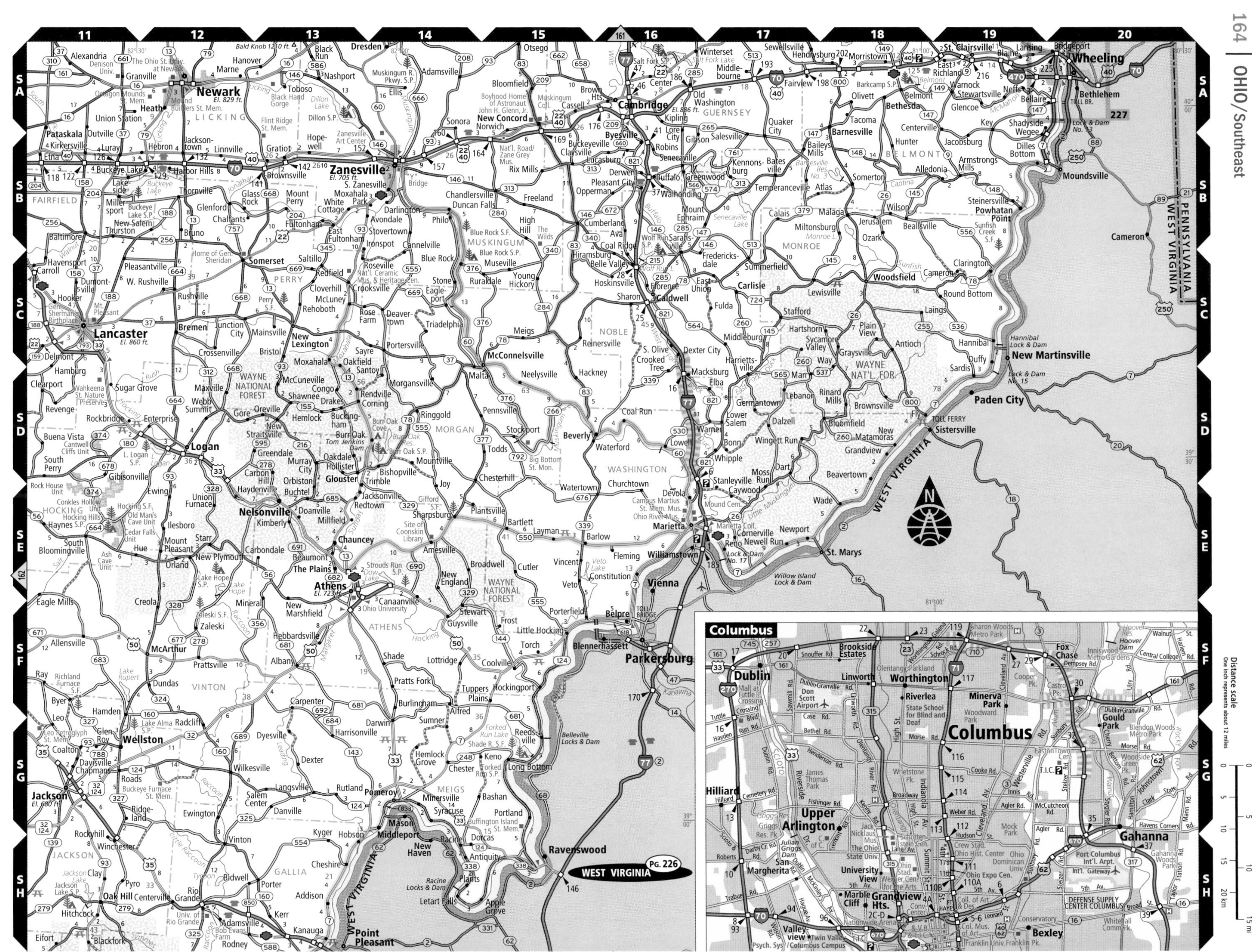
PENNSYLVANIA
WEST VIRGINIA
Wheeling
Bethlehem
Moundsville
New Martinsville
Paden City
Sistersville
St. Marys
Cambridge
Zanesville
Newark
Lancaster
Logan
Nelsonville
Athens
Marietta
Parkersburg
Vienna
Williamstown
Belpre
Caldwell
McConnelsville
New Lexington
Somerset
Woodsfield
Barnesville
St. Clairsville
Bellaire
Jackson
Wellston
Pomeroy
Point Pleasant
Ravenswood
Columbus
Worthington
Dublin
Hilliard
Upper Arlington
Grandview Hts.
Bexley
Gahanna
WAYNE NATIONAL FOREST
PG. 226

How to determine distance

2 10 18 4 4 12 16 20 — Mileages in red between red arrowheads; in black, between intersections.

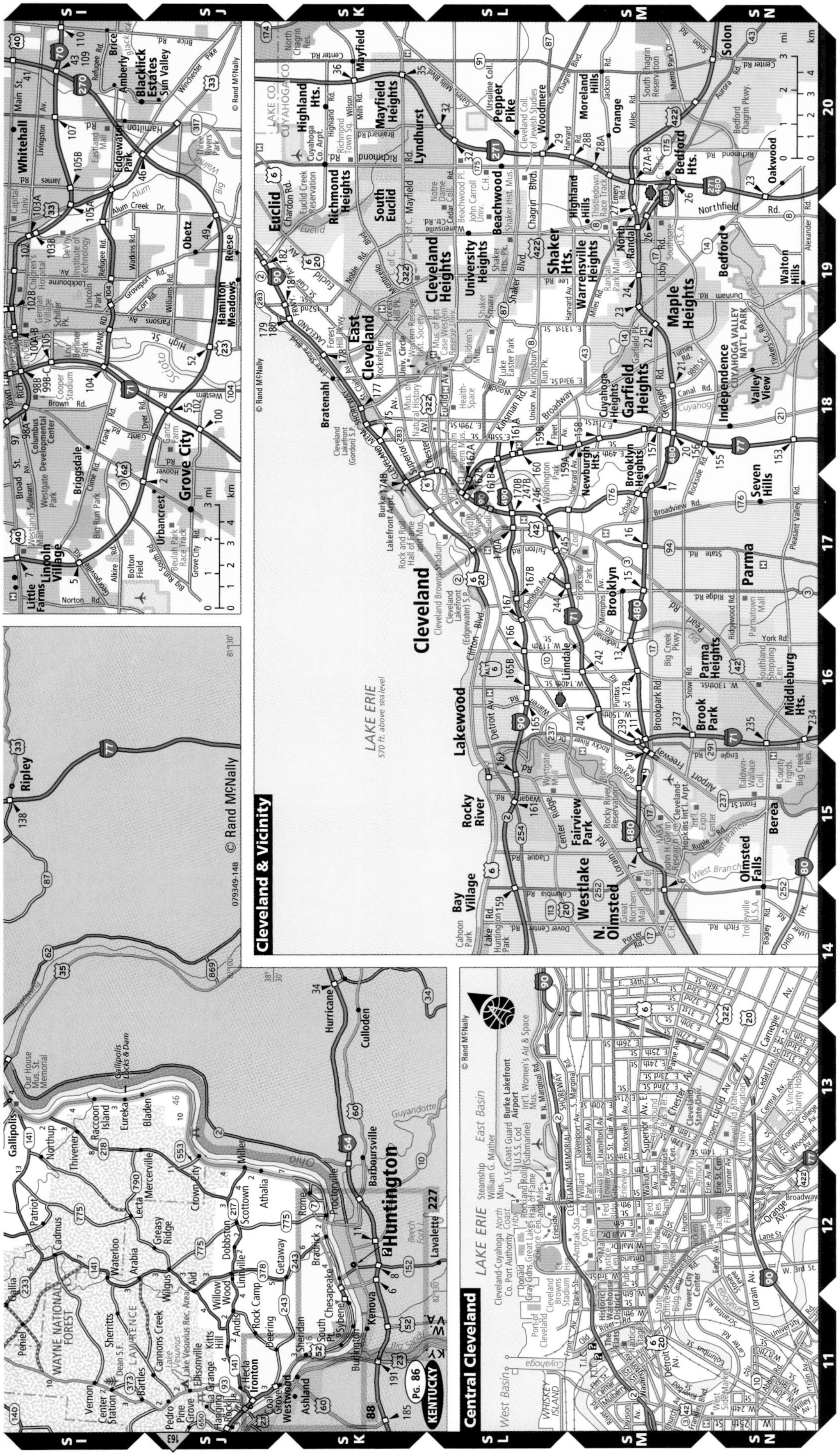

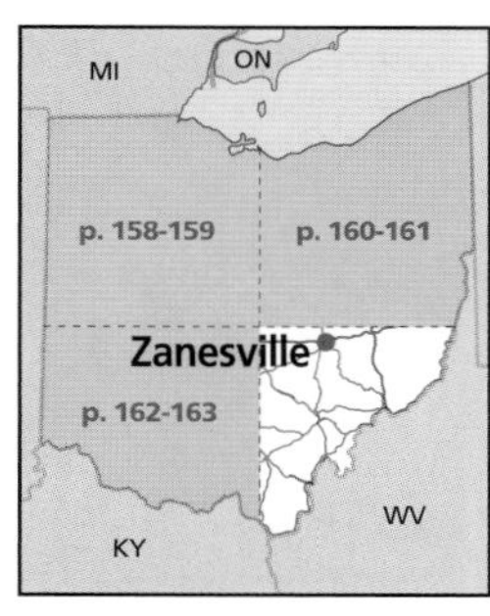
MI
ON
p. 158-159
p. 160-161
Zanesville
p. 162-163
KY
WV

SYMBOLS

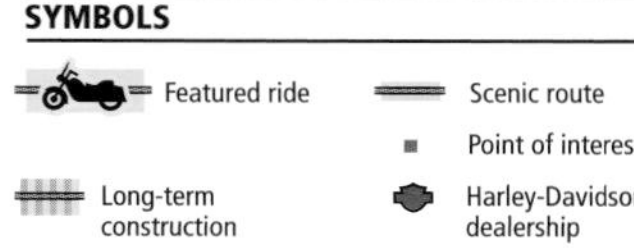
Featured ride
Scenic route
Point of interest
Long-term construction
Harley-Davidson dealership

OHIO MOTORCYCLE LAWS

Helmet use:
Required under age 18, and required for novice riders

Riding two abreast:
Yes. See state law for specifics

Eye protection:
Required unless equipped with windscreen

Speed limit:
Primary roads: 65 mph
Secondary roads: 65 mph

OHIO RESOURCES

Road conditions or construction:
511 (Cincinnati/northern Kentucky area)
(888) 264-7623 (in OH)
(614) 644-7013
(440) 234-2030 (turnpike)
(888) 876-7453 (turnpike)
www.buckeyetraffic.org
www.ohioturnpike.org
www.artimis.org (Cincinnati/northern Kentucky area)

Highway Emergency Numbers:
911

Tourism:
(800) 282-5393
www.ohiotourism.com

State motor vehicle information:
(614) 752-7500
www.ohiobmv.com

HARLEY-DAVIDSON DEALERSHIPS

Athens Harley-Davidson, SE-13
165 Columbus Rd. **Athens**
(740) 592-1692
Lat N 39.353 **Lon** W 82.099

Valley Harley-Davidson Shop, SA-18
41255 Reco Rd. **Belmont**
(740) 695-9591
Lat N 40.058 **Lon** W 81.052

Baxter Harley-Davidson, SH-13
1900 Jackson Pike **Bidwell**
(740) 446-6336
Lat N 38.843 **Lon** W 82.271

Joe Carson Harley-Davidson, SC-11
2930 Helena Dr. **Carroll**
(740) 756-1900
Lat N 39.77 **Lon** W 82.684

Marietta Cycle Center, SE-17
1100 Pike St. **Marietta**
(740) 374-7070
Lat N 39.403 **Lon** W 81.411

Fink's Harley-Davidson, SB-14
2650 Maysville Pike **Zanesville**
(740) 454-0010
Lat N 39.898 **Lon** W 82.036

Cleveland & Vicinity

Central Cleveland

Distance scale
One inch represents about 26 miles
0 10 20 30 mi
0 10 20 30 40 km

KANSAS
TEXAS
COLORADO
NEW MEXICO
Pg. 82 KANSAS
Pg. 40 COLORADO
Pg. 138 N. MEX.
Tulsa
Guymon
Woodward
Elk City
Clinton
Weatherford
Liberal
Alva
Boise City
Perryton
Shamrock
Wellington
Broken Arrow
Sand Springs
Jenks
Owasso
Catoosa
Sapulpa
OSAGE INDIAN RESERVATION
BLACK KETTLE NAT'L. GRASSLAND
RITA BLANCA NATIONAL GRASSLAND
CIMARRON NATIONAL GRASSLAND
COMANCHE NATIONAL GRASSLAND
© Rand McNally

How to determine distance

Mileages in red between red arrowheads; in black, between intersections.

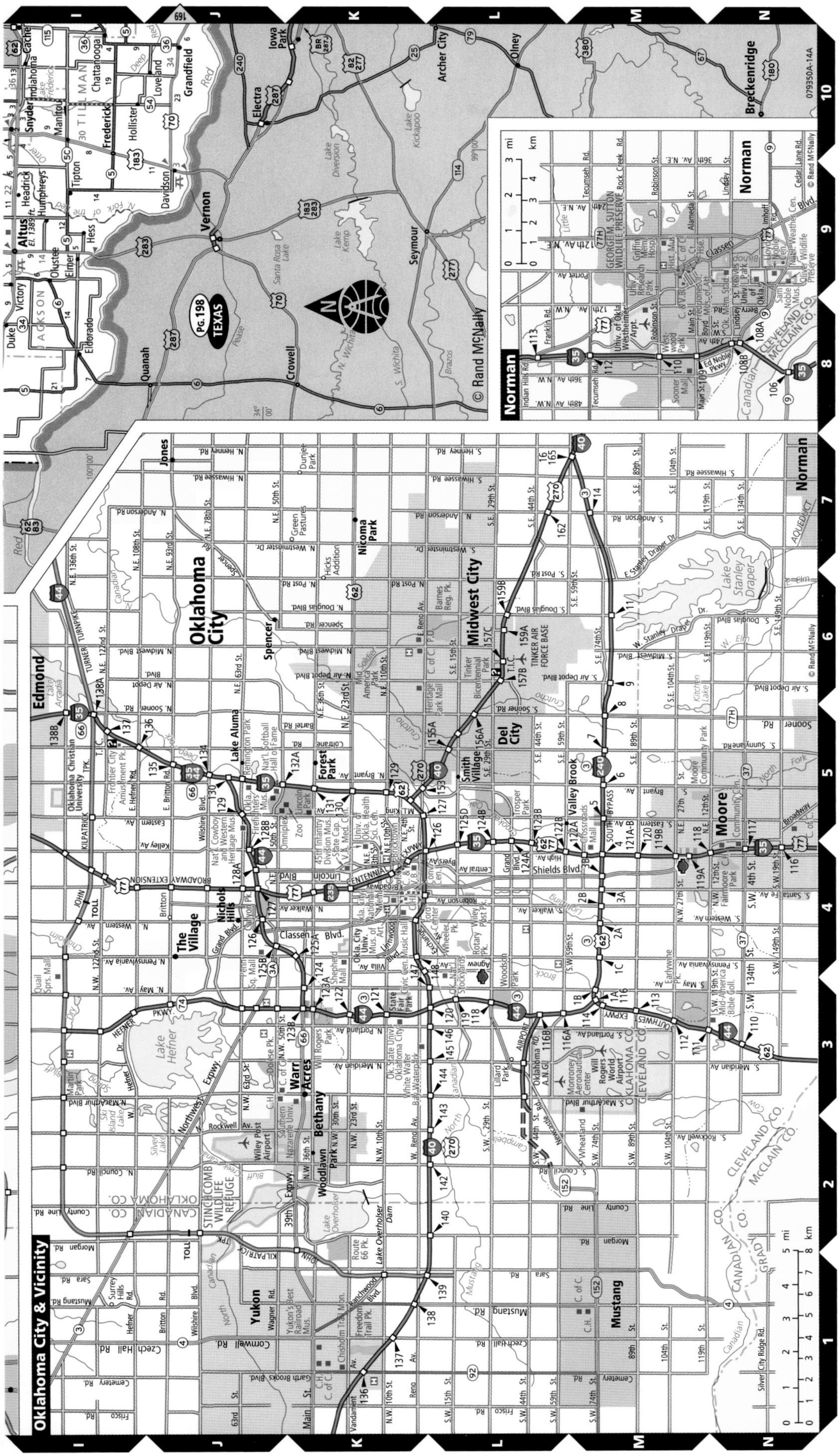

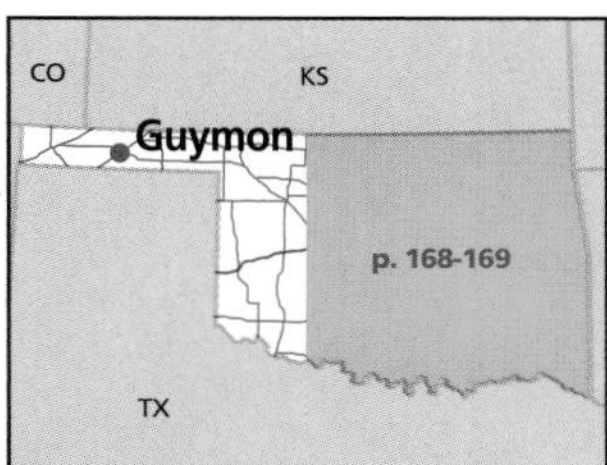
CO
KS
Guymon
p. 168-169
TX

SYMBOLS

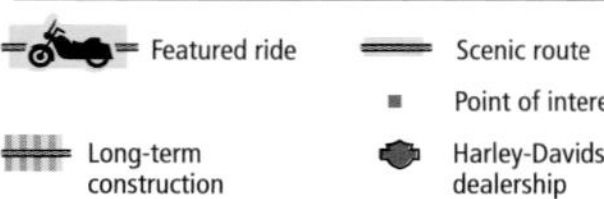
Featured ride
Scenic route
Point of interest
Long-term construction
Harley-Davidson dealership

OKLAHOMA MOTORCYCLE LAWS

Helmet use:
Required under age 18

Riding two abreast:
No reference in administrative code or statutes

Eye protection:
Required unless equipped with windscreen

Speed limit:
Primary roads: 75 mph
Secondary roads: 70 mph

OKLAHOMA RESOURCES

Road conditions or construction:
(405) 425-2385
(888) 425-2385
www.okladot.state.ok.us

Highway Emergency Numbers:
911

Tourism:
(800) 652-6552
www.travelok.com

State motor vehicle information:
(405) 425-2026
www.dps.state.ok.us/

Oklahoma City & Vicinity

Norman

Distance scale
One inch represents about 26 miles
0 10 20 30 mi
0 10 20 30 40 km

OKLAHOMA
KANSAS
ARKANSAS
MO
Tulsa
Oklahoma City
Muskogee
Bartlesville
Stillwater
Enid
Ponca City
Shawnee
Norman
Fort Smith
Joplin
Fayetteville
McAlester
© Rand McNally

How to determine distance

Mileages in red between red arrowheads; in black, between intersections.

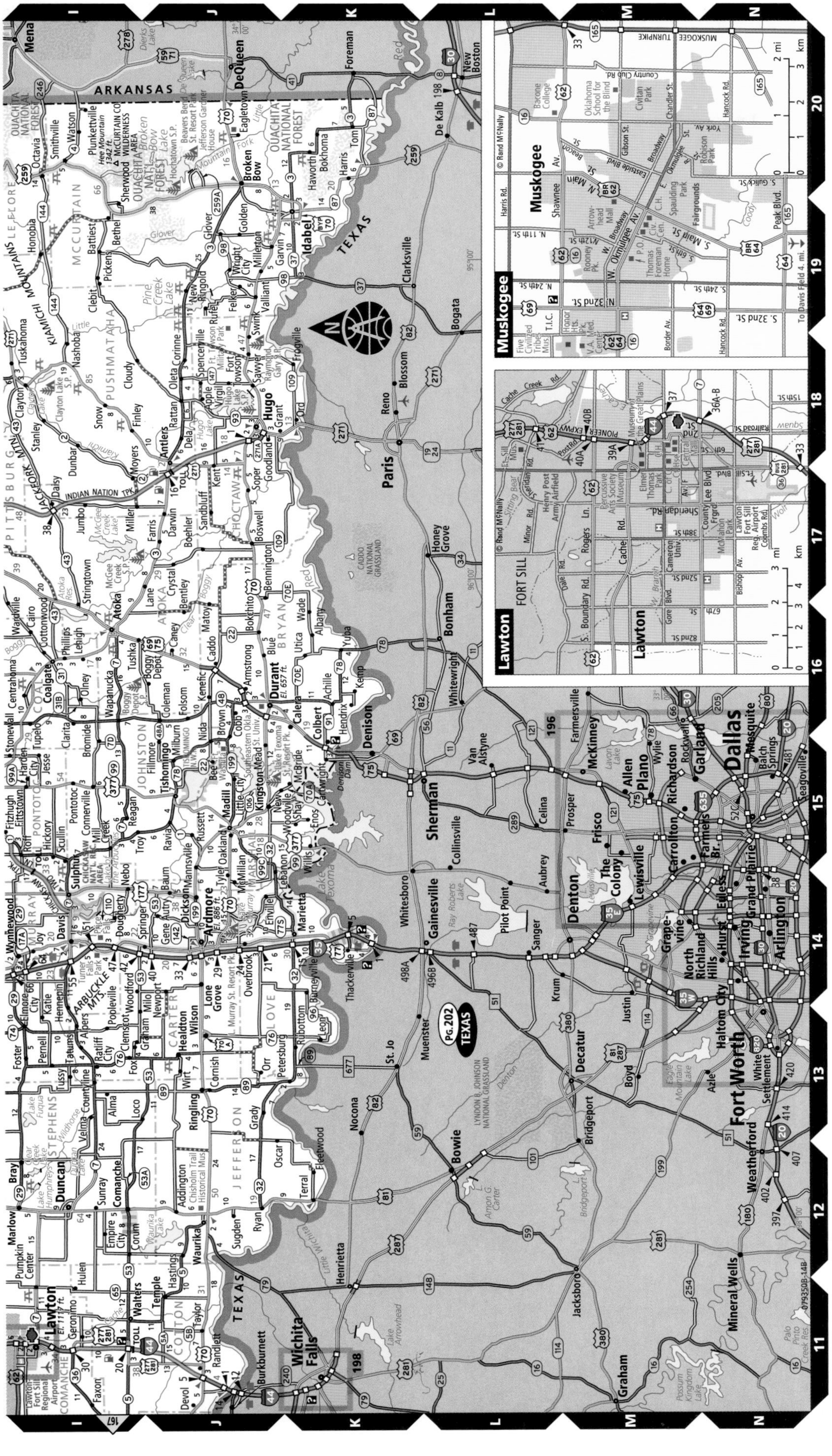

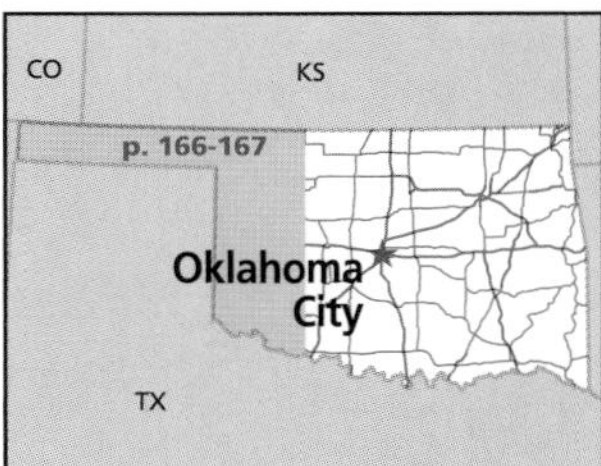
CO
KS
p. 166-167
Oklahoma City
TX

SYMBOLS

- Featured ride
- Scenic route
- Point of interest
- Long-term construction
- Harley-Davidson dealership

CITY-TO-CITY MILEAGE

	ARDMORE	ELK CITY	ENID	LAWTON	MUSKOGEE	OKLAHOMA CITY	TULSA	WICHITA FALLS, TX
Altus	160	59	195	55	274	140	246	85
Ardmore		210	196	106	191	98	203	91
Bartlesville	248	263	132	238	91	150	45	291
Dallas, TX	112	320	306	187	238	208	262	134
Elk City	210		151	108	250	112	218	144
Enid	196	151		145	164	98	115	198
Ft. Smith, AR	233	292	231	263	71	180	116	316
Guymon	362	185	213	297	377	264	328	317
Joplin, MO	315	330	229	305	119	217	114	358
Lawton	106	108	145		221	87	193	53
McAlester	120	240	204	211	67	128	93	264
Muskogee	191	250	164	221		138	49	274
Oklahoma City	98	112	98	87	138		105	140
Ponca City	203	218	69	193	141	105	92	246
Stillwater	163	178	65	153	120	65	71	206
Tulsa	203	218	115	193	49	105		246
Wichita Falls, TX	91	144	198	53	274	140	246	
Woodward	236	79	87	171	251	138	202	224

HARLEY-DAVIDSON DEALERSHIPS

Bartlesville Cycle Sports, C-17
1400 Tuxedo Blvd. **Bartlesville**
(918) 336-3800
Lat N 36.757 **Lon** W 95.956

Harley-Davidson World Shop, F-13
3433 S Broadway **Edmond**
(405) 478-4024
Lat N 35.622 **Lon** W 97.488

ProTeam Harley-Davidson, I-11
301 SE Interstate Dr. **Lawton**
(580) 353-5088
Lat N 34.603 **Lon** W 98.378

Bryan Harley-Davidson, G-13
2624 N Moore Ave. **Moore**
(405) 793-8877
Lat N 35.362 **Lon** W 97.497

Harley-Davidson World, F-13
2823 S Agnew Ave. **Oklahoma City**
(405) 631-8680
Lat N 35.437 **Lon** W 97.555

Forman Harley-Davidson, E-14
3512 S Boomer Rd. **Stillwater**
(405) 377-0045
Lat N 36.085 **Lon** W 97.053

Route 66 Harley-Davidson, D-17
3637 S Memorial Dr. **Tulsa**
(918) 622-1340
Lat N 36.111 **Lon** W 95.886

Myers-Duren Harley-Davidson, D-17
4848 S Peoria Ave. **Tulsa**
(918) 743-4440
Lat N 36.094 **Lon** W 95.976

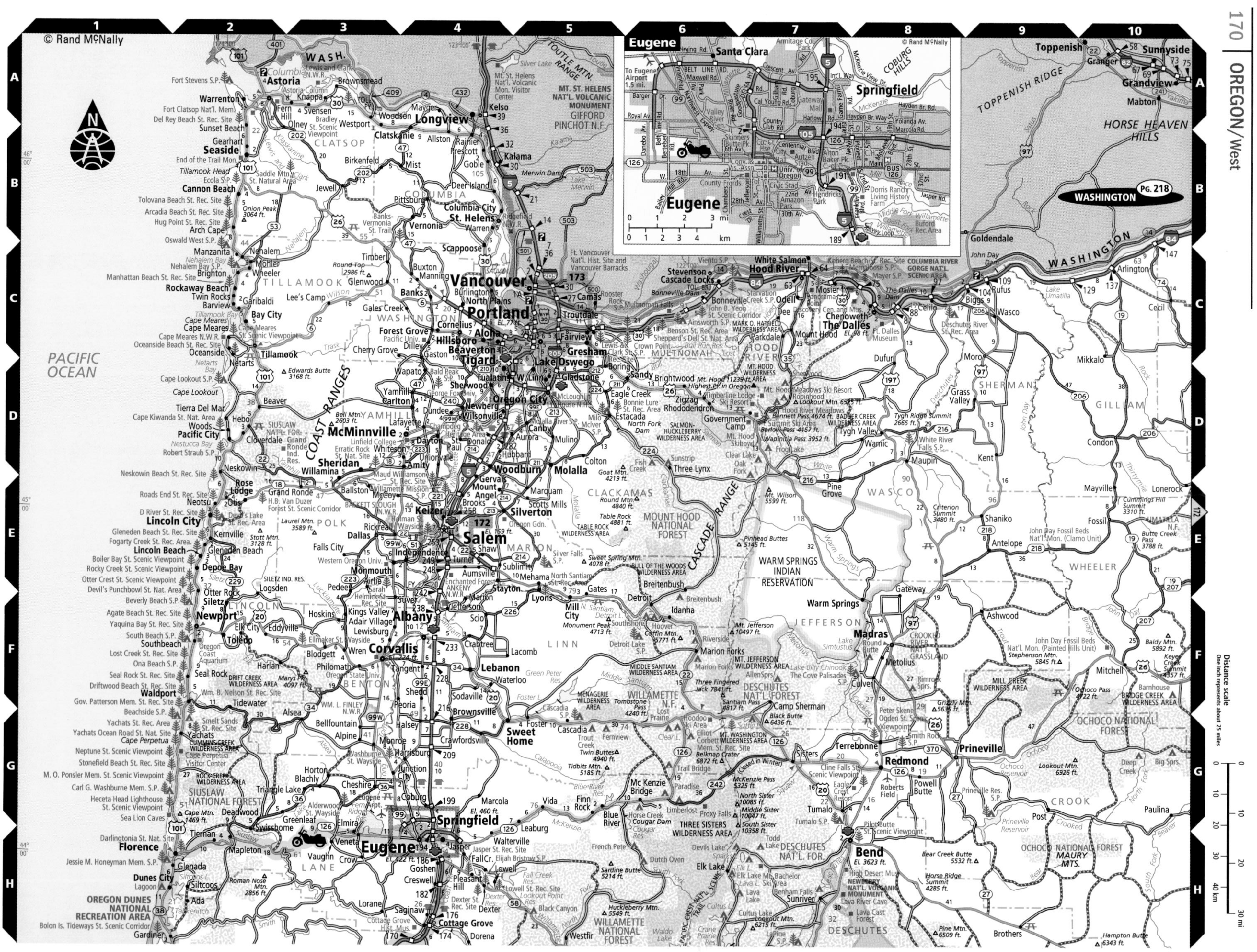
© Rand McNally
Distance scale
One inch represents about 25 miles
0 10 20 30 mi
0 10 20 30 40 km
PACIFIC OCEAN
WASHINGTON
WASH.
PG. 218
Eugene
Springfield
Santa Clara
COBURG HILLS
Portland
Vancouver
Salem
Astoria
Seaside
Tillamook
McMinnville
Lincoln City
Newport
Corvallis
Albany
Florence
The Dalles
Hood River
Madras
Redmond
Bend
Prineville
Toppenish
Sunnyside
Grandview
HORSE HEAVEN HILLS
TOPPENISH RIDGE
COAST RANGES
CASCADE RANGE
WARM SPRINGS INDIAN RESERVATION
MOUNT HOOD NATIONAL FOREST
WILLAMETTE NATIONAL FOREST
DESCHUTES NAT'L FOR.
OCHOCO NATIONAL FOREST
SIUSLAW NATIONAL FOREST
OREGON DUNES NATIONAL RECREATION AREA

How to determine distance

Mileages in red between red arrowheads; in black, between intersections.

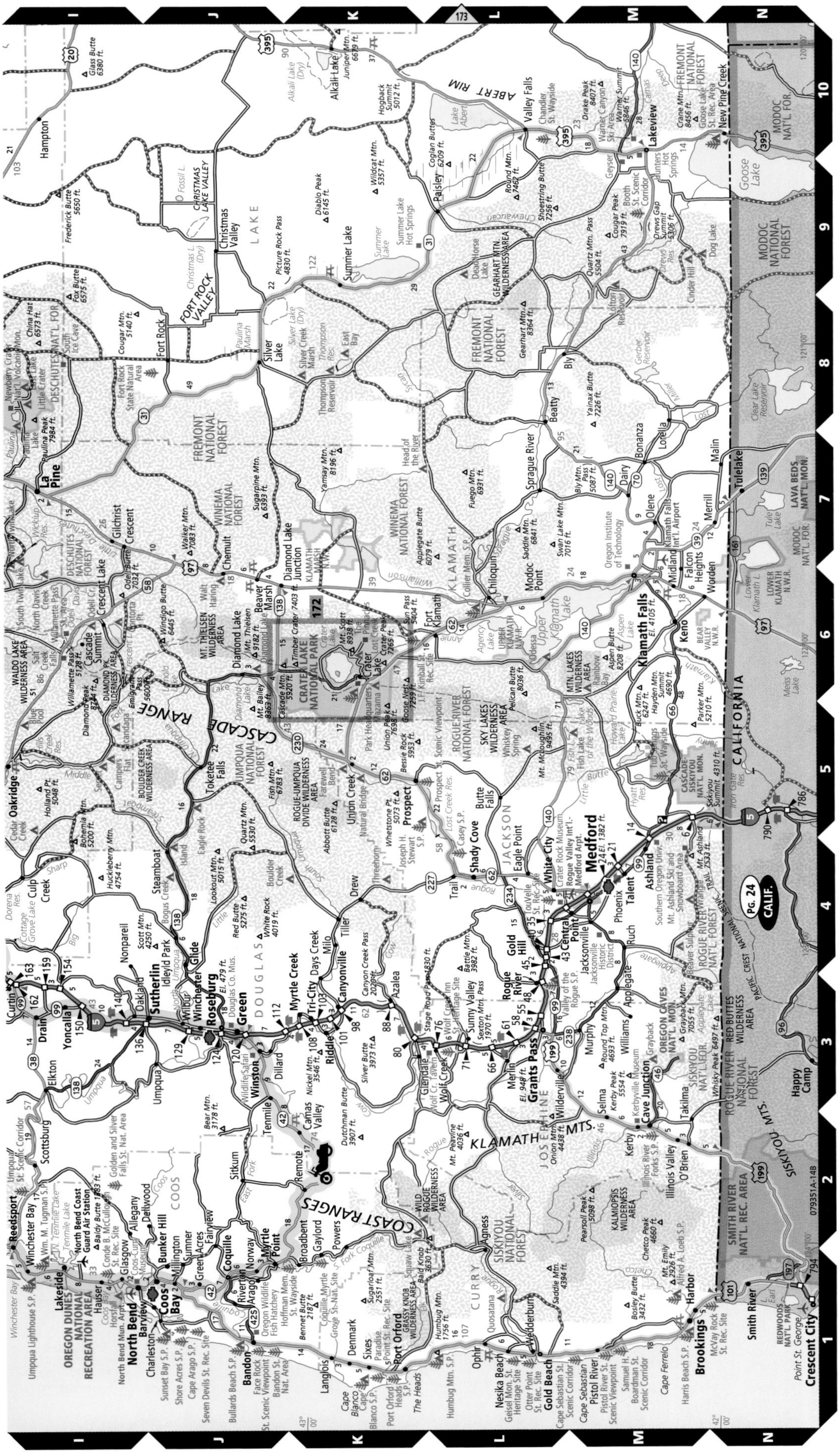

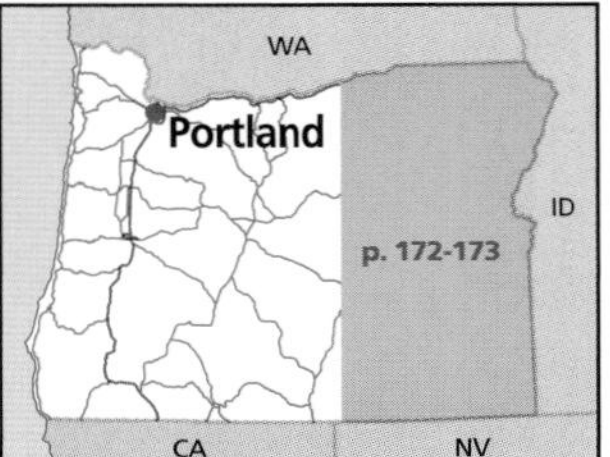
WA
Portland
ID
p. 172-173
CA
NV

SYMBOLS

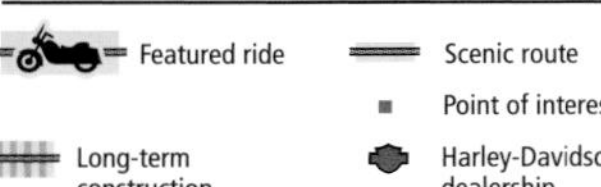
Featured ride
Scenic route
Point of interest
Long-term construction
Harley-Davidson dealership

For Oregon ride, see page R30-31.

OREGON MOTORCYCLE LAWS

Helmet use: Required

Riding two abreast:
Yes. See state law for specifics

Eye protection: Not required

Speed limit:
Primary roads: 65 mph
Secondary roads: 55 mph

OREGON RESOURCES

Road conditions or construction:
511
(800) 977-6368
(503) 588-2941
www.tripcheck.com

Highway Emergency Numbers: 911

Tourism:
(800) 547-7842
www.traveloregon.com

State motor vehicle information:
(503) 945-5000
www.oregon.gov/odot/dmv

HARLEY-DAVIDSON DEALERSHIPS

American Motorcycle Classics Harley-Davidson, F-4
1600 Century Dr. NE **Albany**
(541) 928-6234
Lat N 44.656 **Lon** W 123.06

Cascade Harley-Davidson, H-7
63028 Sherman Rd. **Bend**
(541) 330-6228
Lat N 44.088 **Lon** W 121.303

Highway 101 Harley-Davidson of Coos Bay, J-1
536 S 2nd St. **Coos Bay**
(541) 266-7051
Lat N 43.364 **Lon** W 124.215

Doyle's Harley-Davidson, H-4
86441 College View Rd. **Eugene**
(541) 747-1033
Lat N 44.011 **Lon** W 123.022

Latus Motors Harley-Davidson, D-5
870 E Berkeley St. **Gladstone**
(503) 249-8653
Lat N 45.383 **Lon** W 122.581

D & S Harley-Davidson, M-4
3846 S Pacific Hwy. **Medford**
(541) 535-5515
Lat N 42.284 **Lon** W 122.828

Doyle's Harley-Davidson Shop, J-3
2675 NW Edenbower Blvd. **Roseburg**
(541) 440-1088
Lat N 43.242 **Lon** W 123.361

Salem Harley-Davidson, E-4
3601 Silverton Rd. NE **Salem**
(503) 363-0634
Lat N 44.969 **Lon** W 122.989

Paradise Harley-Davidson, C-4
10770 SW Cascade Ave. **Tigard**
(503) 924-3700
Lat N 45.442 **Lon** W 122.78

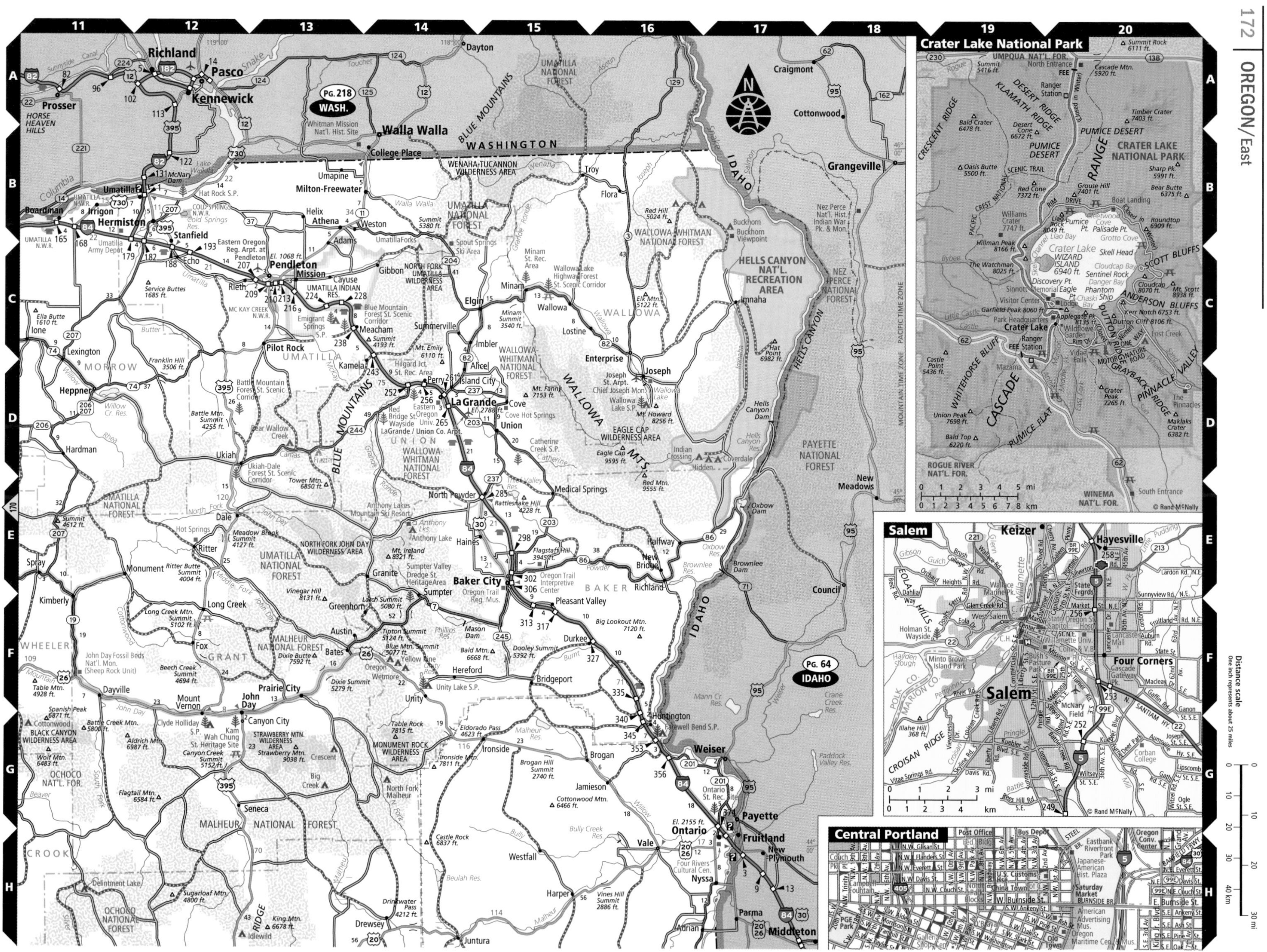
Crater Lake National Park
CRATER LAKE NATIONAL PARK
Crater Lake
WIZARD ISLAND
PUMICE DESERT
CASCADE
RANGE
ROGUE RIVER NAT'L. FOR.
WINEMA NAT'L. FOR.
UMPQUA NAT'L. FOR.
Salem
Keizer
Hayesville
Four Corners
Central Portland
WASHINGTON
IDAHO
BLUE MOUNTAINS
WALLOWA MTS.
HELLS CANYON NAT'L. RECREATION AREA
PAYETTE NATIONAL FOREST
UMATILLA NATIONAL FOREST
WALLOWA-WHITMAN NATIONAL FOREST
MALHEUR NATIONAL FOREST
OCHOCO NATIONAL FOREST
EAGLE CAP WILDERNESS AREA
Richland
Pasco
Kennewick
Prosser
Walla Walla
College Place
Milton-Freewater
Hermiston
Umatilla
Boardman
Pendleton
Heppner
La Grande
Baker City
Enterprise
Joseph
Ontario
John Day
Prairie City
Grangeville
Weiser
Payette
Fruitland
Middleton
Pg. 218 WASH.
Pg. 64 IDAHO
PACIFIC TIME ZONE
MOUNTAIN TIME ZONE
Distance scale
One inch represents about 25 miles
© Rand McNally

How to determine distance

2 10 18 4 4
12 16 20

Mileages in red between red arrowheads; in black, between intersections.

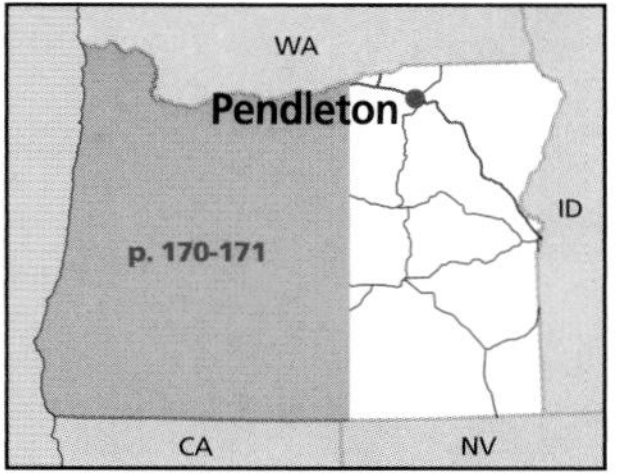
WA
Pendleton
ID
p. 170-171
CA
NV

SYMBOLS

- Featured ride
- Scenic route
- Point of interest
- Long-term construction
- Harley-Davidson dealership

CITY-TO-CITY MILEAGE

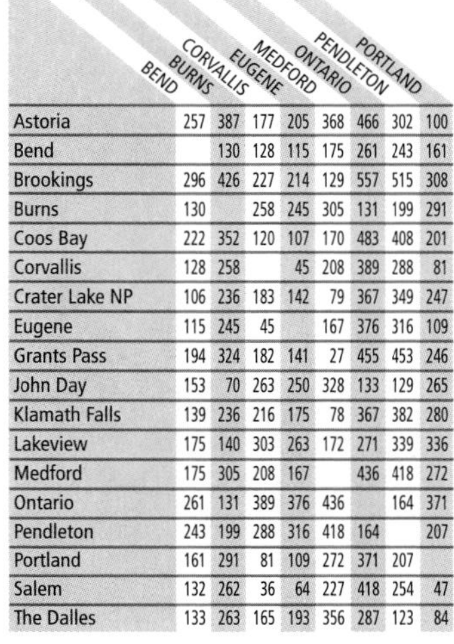

	BEND	BURNS	CORVALLIS	EUGENE	MEDFORD	ONTARIO	PENDLETON	PORTLAND
Astoria	257	387	177	205	368	466	302	100
Bend		130	128	115	175	261	243	161
Brookings	296	426	227	214	129	557	515	308
Burns	130		258	245	305	131	199	291
Coos Bay	222	352	120	107	170	483	408	201
Corvallis	128	258		45	208	389	288	81
Crater Lake NP	106	236	183	142	79	367	349	247
Eugene	115	245	45		167	376	316	109
Grants Pass	194	324	182	141	27	455	453	246
John Day	153	70	263	250	328	133	129	265
Klamath Falls	139	236	216	175	78	367	382	280
Lakeview	175	140	303	263	172	271	339	336
Medford	175	305	208	167		436	418	272
Ontario	261	131	389	376	436		164	371
Pendleton	243	199	288	316	418	164		207
Portland	161	291	81	109	272	371	207	
Salem	132	262	36	64	227	418	254	47
The Dalles	133	263	165	193	356	287	123	84

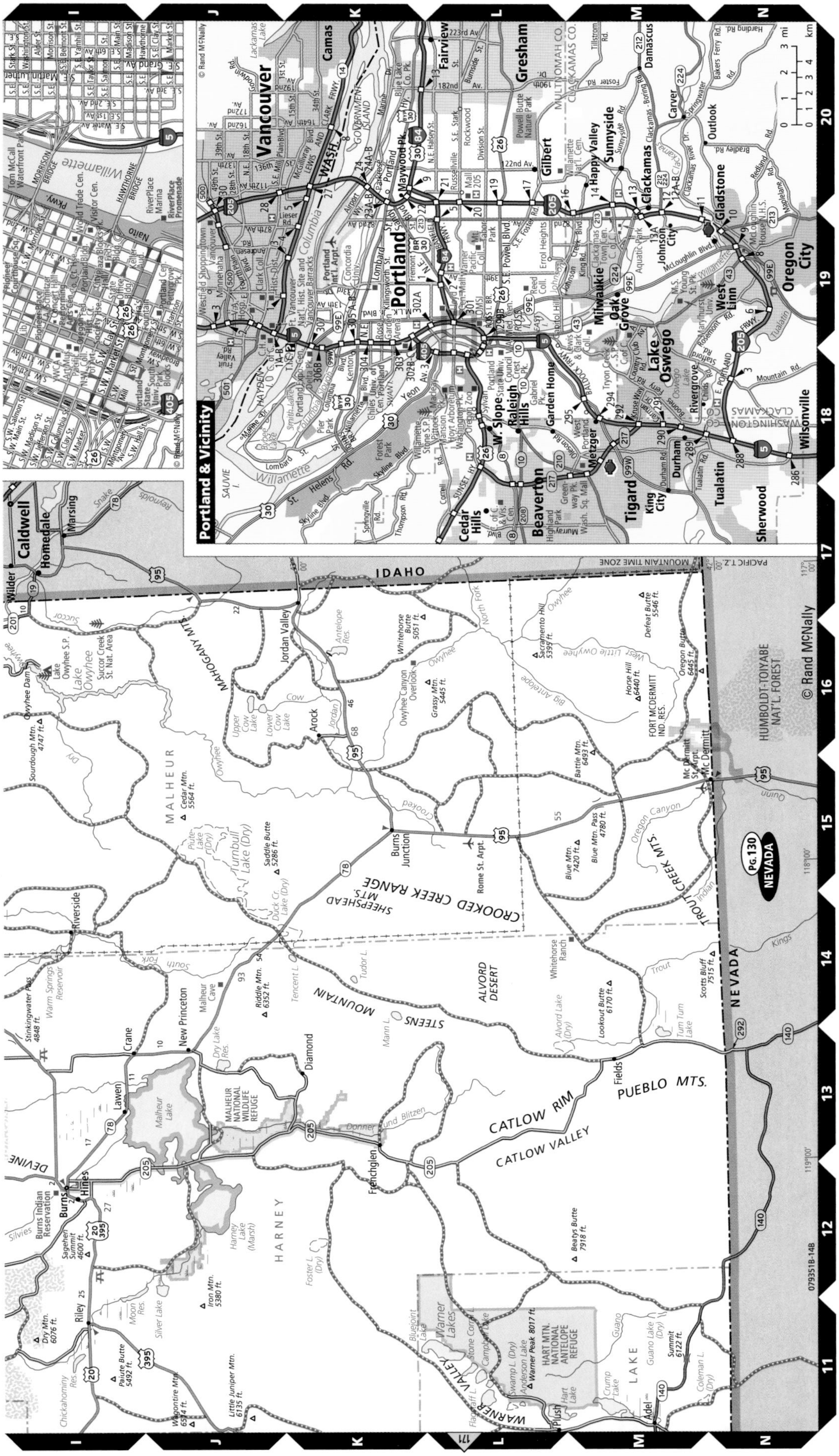

Distance scale
One inch represents about 12 miles
0 5 10 mi
0 5 10 15 km

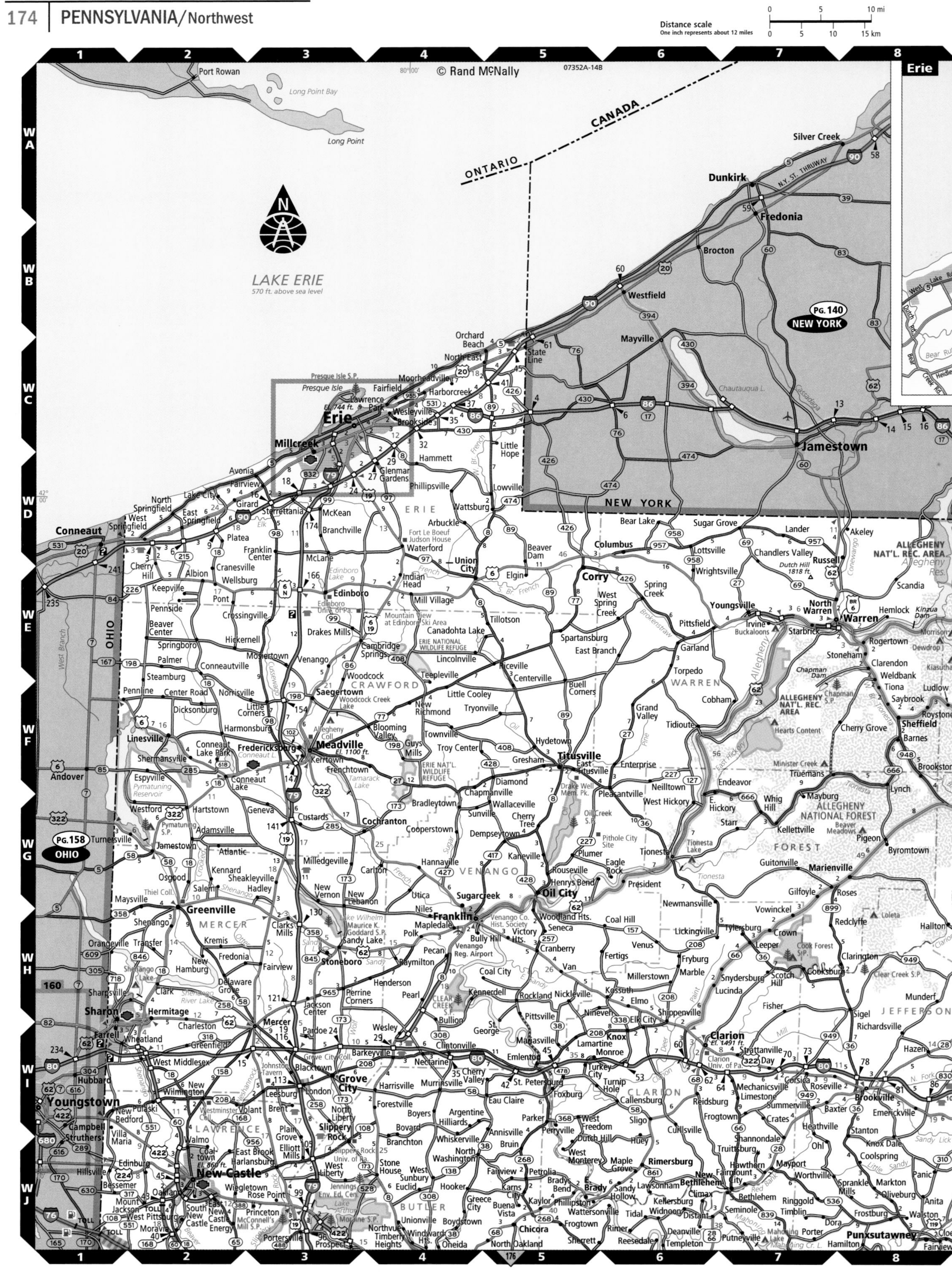
© Rand McNally
07352A-14B
Port Rowan
Long Point Bay
Long Point
ONTARIO
CANADA
LAKE ERIE
570 ft. above sea level
Erie
Silver Creek
Dunkirk
N.Y. ST. THRUWAY
Fredonia
Brocton
Westfield
Mayville
Chautauqua L.
Jamestown
NEW YORK
PG. 140
NEW YORK
Orchard Beach
North East
State Line
Presque Isle S.P.
Presque Isle
Fairfield
Lawrence Park
Moorheadville
Harborcreek
Wesleyville
Brookside
Millcreek
Hammett
Little Hope
Glenmar Gardens
Avonia
Fairview
Lake City
North Springfield
West Springfield
East Springfield
Girard
Sterrettania
McKean
Conneaut
Phillipsville
Lowville
Wattsburg
Arbuckle
Fort Le Boeuf
Judson House
Waterford
Union City
Beaver Dam
Elgin
Corry
Columbus
Bear Lake
Sugar Grove
Lander
Akeley
ALLEGHENY NAT'L. REC. AREA
Russell
Chandlers Valley
Lottsville
Wrightsville
Scandia
Youngsville
Irvine
North Warren
Warren
Hemlock
Starbrick
Kinzua Dam
Cherry Hill
Albion
Cranesville
Wellsburg
Franklin Center
McLane
Edinboro
Keepville
Pennside
Pont
Crossingville
Beaver Center
Springboro
Palmer
Steamburg
Conneautville
Hickernell
Drakes Mills
Mosiertown
Venango
Cambridge Springs
Mountain View at Edinboro Ski Area
Canadohta Lake
ERIE NATIONAL WILDLIFE REFUGE
Lincolnville
Mill Village
Tillotson
Spartansburg
East Branch
Pittsfield
Garland
Torpedo
Rogertown
Clarendon
Stoneham
Chapman Dam
Weldbank
Tiona
Ludlow
Saybrook
Sheffield
Barnes
Roystone
Pennline
Center Road
Dicksonburg
Norrisville
Little Corners
Harmonsburg
Woodcock
Saegertown
CRAWFORD
Teepleville
Little Cooley
Tryonville
Riceville
Centerville
Buell Corners
Grand Valley
Tidioute
Cobham
WARREN
Cherry Grove
Hearts Content
Linesville
Conneaut Lake Park
Fredericksburg
Meadville
El. 1100 ft.
Kerrtown
Frenchtown
Shermansville
Espyville
Pymatuning Reservoir
Andover
Blooming Valley
Guys Mills
Townville
Troy Center
Hydetown
Titusville
Gresham
East Titusville
Enterprise
Neilltown
Endeavor
Truemans
Brookston
Lynch
Westford
Hartstown
Conneaut Lake
Geneva
Custards
Cochranton
Bradleytown
Diamond
Chapmanville
Wallaceville
Sunville
Cherry Tree
Pleasantville
West Hickory
E. Hickory
Whig Hill
Mayburg
ALLEGHENY NATIONAL FOREST
Starr
Kellettville
Pigeon
Byromtown
Turnersville
Jamestown
Adamsville
Atlantic
Cooperstown
Dempseytown
Pithole City Site
Oil Creek S.P.
Plumer
Tionesta
Tionesta Lake
PG. 158
OHIO
Osgood
Kennard
Sheakleyville
Milledgeville
Hannaville
Kaneville
VENANGO
Rouseville
Eagle Rock
Henrys Bend
President
Guitonville
Marienville
Maysville
Thiel Coll.
Salem
Hadley
New Vernon
New Lebanon
Carlton
Utica
Sugarcreek
Oil City
Gilfoyle
Roses
Greenville
Shenango
MERCER
Kremis
Clarks Mills
Niles
Franklin
Mapledale
Polk
Woodland Hts.
Seneca
Coal Hill
Newmansville
Vowinckel
Redclyffe
Halton
Orangeville
Transfer
Fredonia
New Hamburg
Lake Wilhelm
Maurice K. Goddard S.P.
Sandy Lake
Stoneboro
Fairview
Bully Hill
Victory Hts.
Venango Reg. Airport
Pecan
Raymilton
Cranberry
Venus
Lickingville
Tylersburg
Leeper
Crown
Cook Forest S.P.
Clarington
Sharpsville
Clark
Delaware Grove
Henderson
Coal City
Van
Fertigs
Fryburg
Marble
Millerstown
Snydersburg
Scotch Hill
Cooksburg
Sharon
Hermitage
Jackson Center
Perrine Corners
Pearl
Kennerdell
Rockland
Nickleville
Kossuth
Elmo
Lucinda
Shippenville
Fisher
Munderf
Farrell
Wheatland
Charleston
Mercer
Pardoe
Wesley
Bullion
St. George
Pittsville
Nineveh
Elk City
Sigel
JEFFERSON
Richardsville
Greenfield
Barkeyville
Clintonville
Emlenton
Marnasville
Lamartine
Knox
Monroe
Clarion
Hazen
Youngstown
West Middlesex
Hubbard
New Wilmington
Grove City
Harrisville
Nectarine
Murrinsville
Cherry Valley
St. Petersburg
Turkey City
Turnip Hole
Strattanville
Day
Corsica
Roseville
Brookville
Campbell
Struthers
New Bedford
Pulaski
Volant
LAWRENCE
Leesburg
London
Forestville
Boyers
Argentine
Hilliards
Eau Claire
Parker
Foxburg
Callensburg
Sligo
Reidsburg
Frogtown
Mechanicsville
Limestone
Summerville
Baxter
Emerickville
Villa Maria
Walmo
Brent
North Liberty
Slippery Rock
Plain Grove
Elliott Mills
Bovard
Branchton
Whiskerville
Annisville
Bruin
Perryville
West Freedom
Dutch Hill
Huey
Curllsville
Shannondale
Heathville
Stanton
Hillsville
Edinburg
Coal-town
East Brook
Harlansburg
New Castle
El. 860 ft.
West Liberty
Stone House
West Sunbury
North Washington
Hooker
Fairview
Petrolia
West Monterey
Maple Grove
Rimersburg
Truittsburg
Hawthorn
Mayport
Ohl
Knox Dale
Coolspring
Bessemer
Mount Jackson
West Pittsburg
Moravia
Oakland
South New Castle
New Castle
Energy
Wiegletown
Rose Point
Princeton
McConnell's Mill S.P.
Euclid
BUTLER
Greece City
Karns City
Buena Vista
Bradys Bend
E. Brady
Sandy Hollow
Lawsonham
New Bethlehem
Fairmount City
Worthville
Sprankle Mills
Markton
Panic
Jennings Env. Ed. Ctr.
Lake Arthur
Moraine S.P.
Portersville
Prospect
Northvue
Timberly Heights
Unionville
Windward Hts.
Boydstown
Oneida
Chicora
North Oakland
Kaylor
Phillipston
Wattersonville
Frogtown
Sherrett
Tidal
Widnoon
Distant
Climax
Red Bank
Bethlehem
Seminole
Kellersburg
Rimer
Reesedale
Deanville
Templeton
Putneyville
Mahoning Lake
Ringgold
Timblin
Oliveburg
Frostburg
Dora
Porter
Hamilton
Walston
Anita
Punxsutawney
Fairview

How to determine distance

Mileages in red between red arrowheads; in black, between intersections.

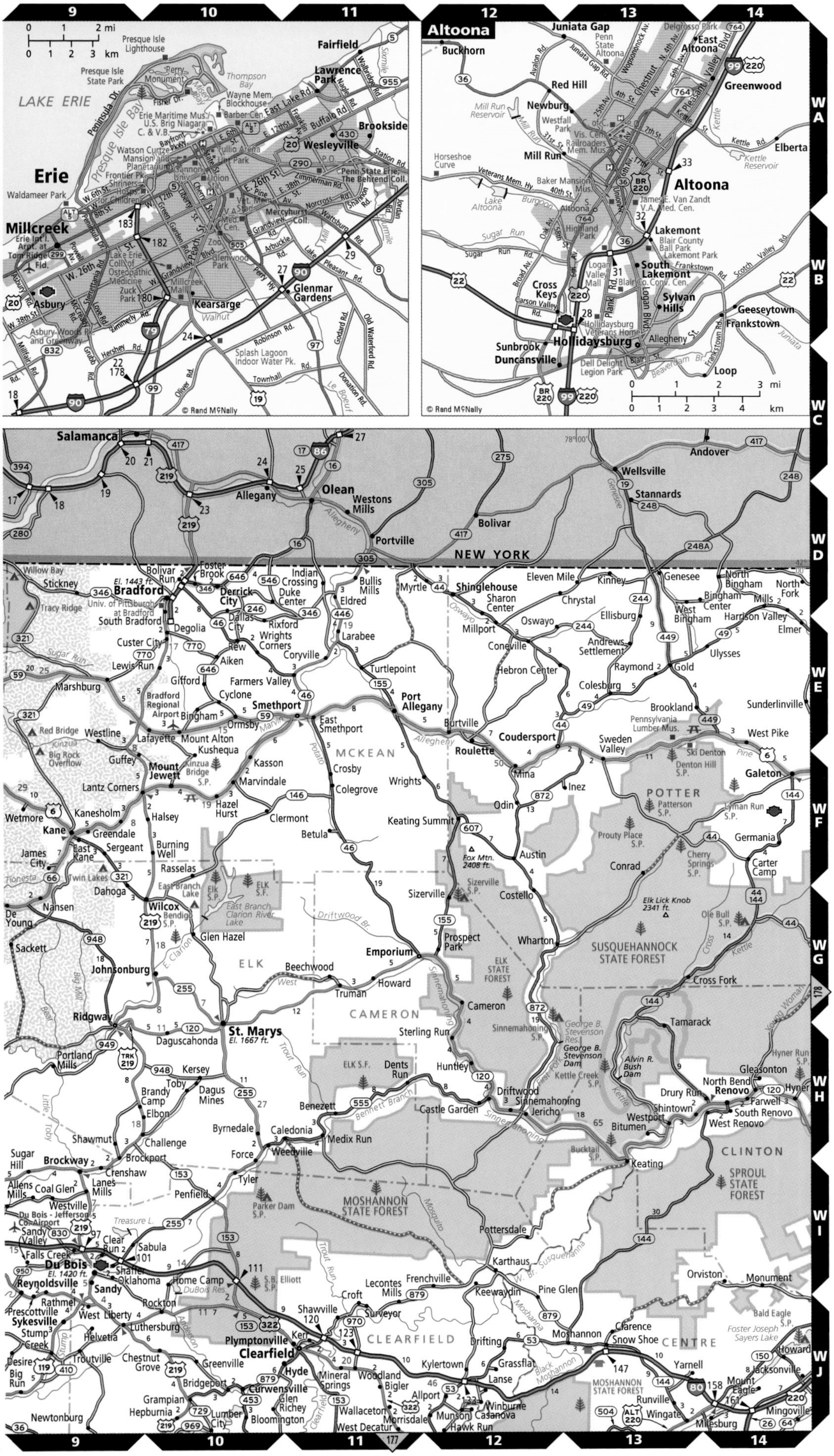

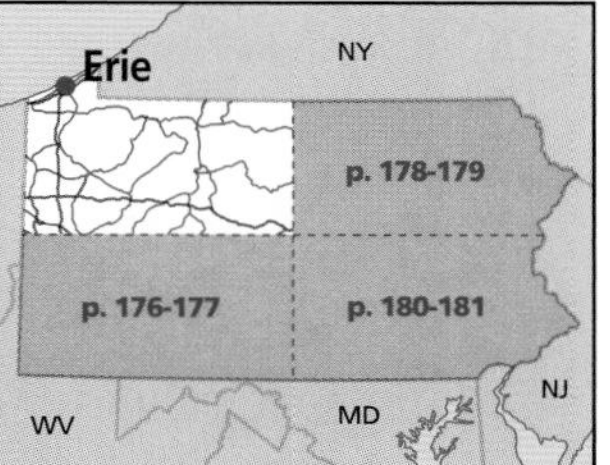
Erie
NY
p. 178-179
p. 176-177
p. 180-181
WV
MD
NJ

SYMBOLS

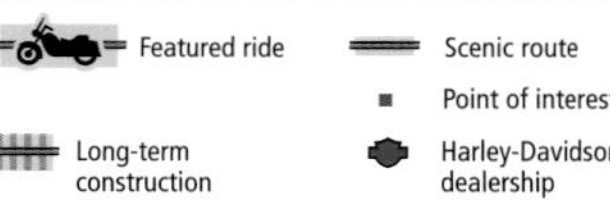
Featured ride
Scenic route
Point of interest
Long-term construction
Harley-Davidson dealership

PENNSYLVANIA MOTORCYCLE LAWS

Helmet use:
Required under 21

Riding two abreast:
Yes. See state law for specifics

Eye protection:
Required by law

Speed limit:
Primary roads: 65 mph
Secondary roads: 55 mph

PENNSYLVANIA RESOURCES

Road conditions or construction:
(888) 783-6783 (in PA)
(215) 567-5678 (SmarTraveler, Camden/Philadelphia area)
www.dot.state.pa.us

Highway Emergency Numbers:
911

Tourism:
(800) 847-4872
www.visitpa.com

State motor vehicle information:
(717) 391-6190
www.dmv.state.pa.us

HARLEY-DAVIDSON DEALERSHIPS

Street Track N Trail Harley-Davidson, WF-3
13723 Conneaut Lake Rd. **Conneaut Lake**
(814) 382-4821
Lat N 41.614 **Lon** W 80.259

Du Bois Harley-Davidson, WI-9
101 W Du Bois Ave. (Rte. 219) **Du Bois**
(814) 371-5750
Lat N 41.128 **Lon** W 78.759

Harley-Davidson of Erie, WD-3
4575 W Ridge Rd. **Erie**
(814) 838-1356
Lat N 42.075 **Lon** W 80.177

Larry's Harley-Davidson, WF-14
US 6 West Pike **Galeton**
(814) 435-6548
Lat N 41.695 **Lon** W 77.678

New Castle Harley-Davidson, WJ-2
4655 US Rte. 422 **New Castle**
(724) 924-2310
Lat N 40.992 **Lon** W 80.33

Thunder Harley-Davidson, WH-1
1344 E State St. **Sharon**
(724) 981-7282
Lat N 41.233 **Lon** W 80.484

Distance scale
One inch represents about 12 miles
0 5 10 mi
0 5 10 15 km

PENNSYLVANIA

OHIO

WEST VIRGINIA

MARYLAND

PG. 226 W. VA.

079352B-14B

Johnstown

Gettysburg / Gettysburg National Military Park

York

How to determine distance

Mileages in red between red arrowheads; in black, between intersections.

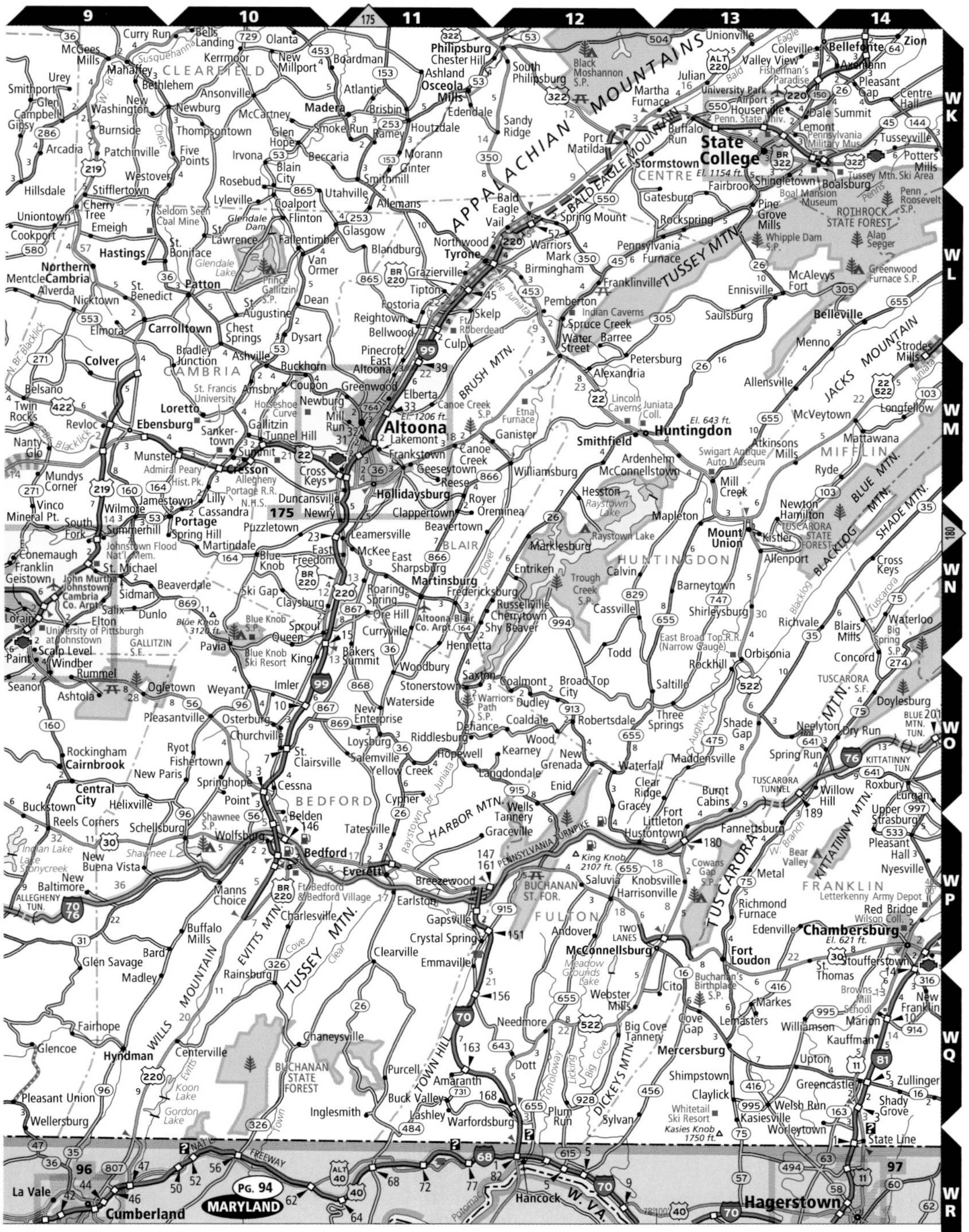

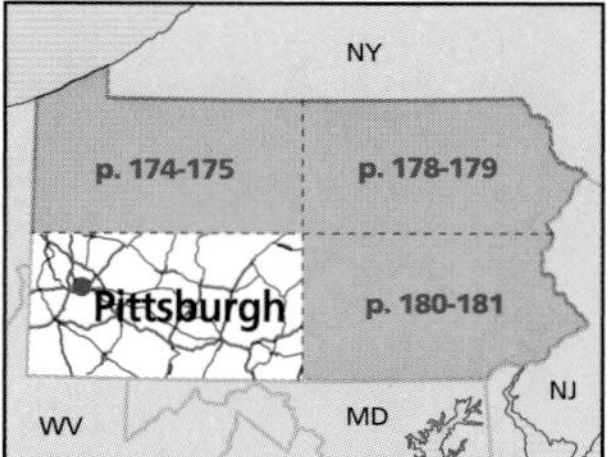
NY
p. 174-175
p. 178-179
Pittsburgh
p. 180-181
WV
MD
NJ

SYMBOLS

- Featured ride
- Scenic route
- Point of interest
- Long-term construction
- Harley-Davidson dealership

HARLEY-DAVIDSON DEALERSHIPS

For the Pittsburgh metro area, please see dealer listings on page 183.

Apple Harley-Davidson, WM-11
495 Municipal Dr. **Altoona (Duncansville)**
(814) 696-7433
Lat N 40.446 **Lon** W 78.433

McMahon's Harley-Davidson, WK-2
613 7th Ave. **Beaver Falls**
(724) 846-6251
Lat N 40.739 **Lon** W 80.329

Cerini Harley-Davidson, WO-4
4325 State Rte. 51 N **Belle Vernon**
(724) 930-8443
Lat N 40.16 **Lon** W 79.78

Zanotti Motor Co., WK-4
170 Pittsburgh Rd. (Rte. 8) **Butler**
(724) 283-2777
Lat N 40.837 **Lon** W 79.92

No. 1 Cycle Center Harley-Davidson, WK-14
107 Yearicks Blvd. **Centre Hall**
(814) 364-1340
Lat N 40.789 **Lon** W 77.71

M & S Harley-Davidson, WP-14
160 Falling Spring Rd. **Chambersburg**
(717) 709-9650
Lat N 39.926 **Lon** W 77.635

Z & M Harley-Davidson Sales, WN-6
Rural Rte. 6 Box 224 (Rte. 30) **Greensburg**
(724) 837-9404
Lat N 40.294 **Lon** W 79.501

Zepka Harley-Davidson, WN-9
960 Eisenhower Blvd. **Johnstown**
(814) 262-7777
Lat N 40.268 **Lon** W 78.861

Highland Harley-Davidson, WP-8
802 N Center Ave. **Somerset**
(814) 444-1903
Lat N 40.016 **Lon** W 79.078

Gatto Harley-Davidson, WL-5
139 E 6th Ave. **Tarentum**
(724) 224-0500
Lat N 40.602 **Lon** W 79.756

Gatto Cycle Shop, WL-5
562 Pittsburg Mills Circle **Tarentum**
(724) 274-4474
Lat N 40.616 **Lon** W 79.784

Cerini's National Road Harley-Davidson, WP-5
69 Romeo Ln. **Uniontown**
(724) 439-8888
Lat N 39.915 **Lon** W 79.724

Steel City Harley-Davidson, WO-3
1375 Washington Rd. **Washington**
(724) 225-7020
Lat N 40.211 **Lon** W 80.197

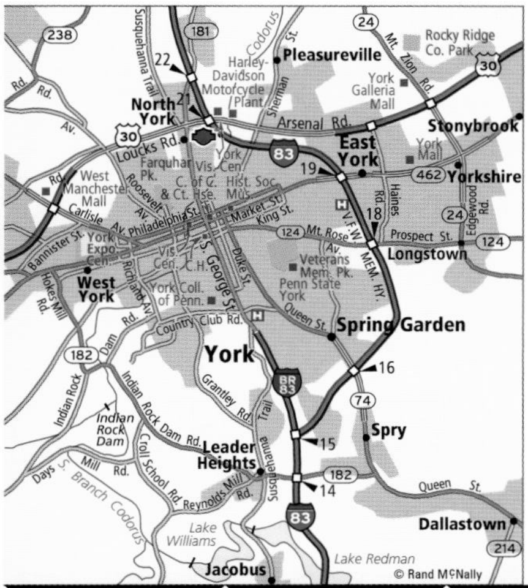

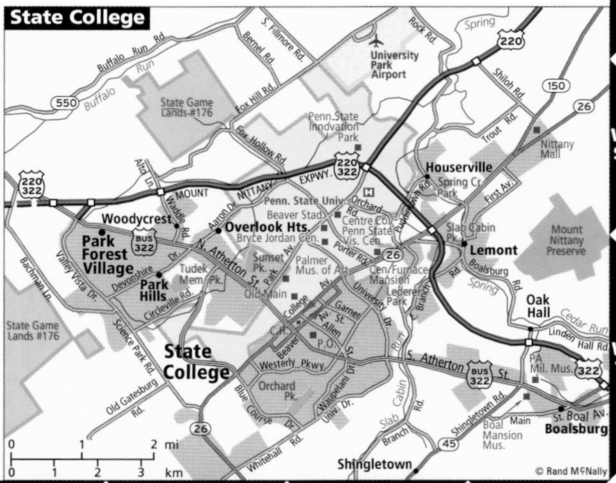

Distance scale
One inch represents about 12 miles

0 5 10 mi
0 5 10 15 km

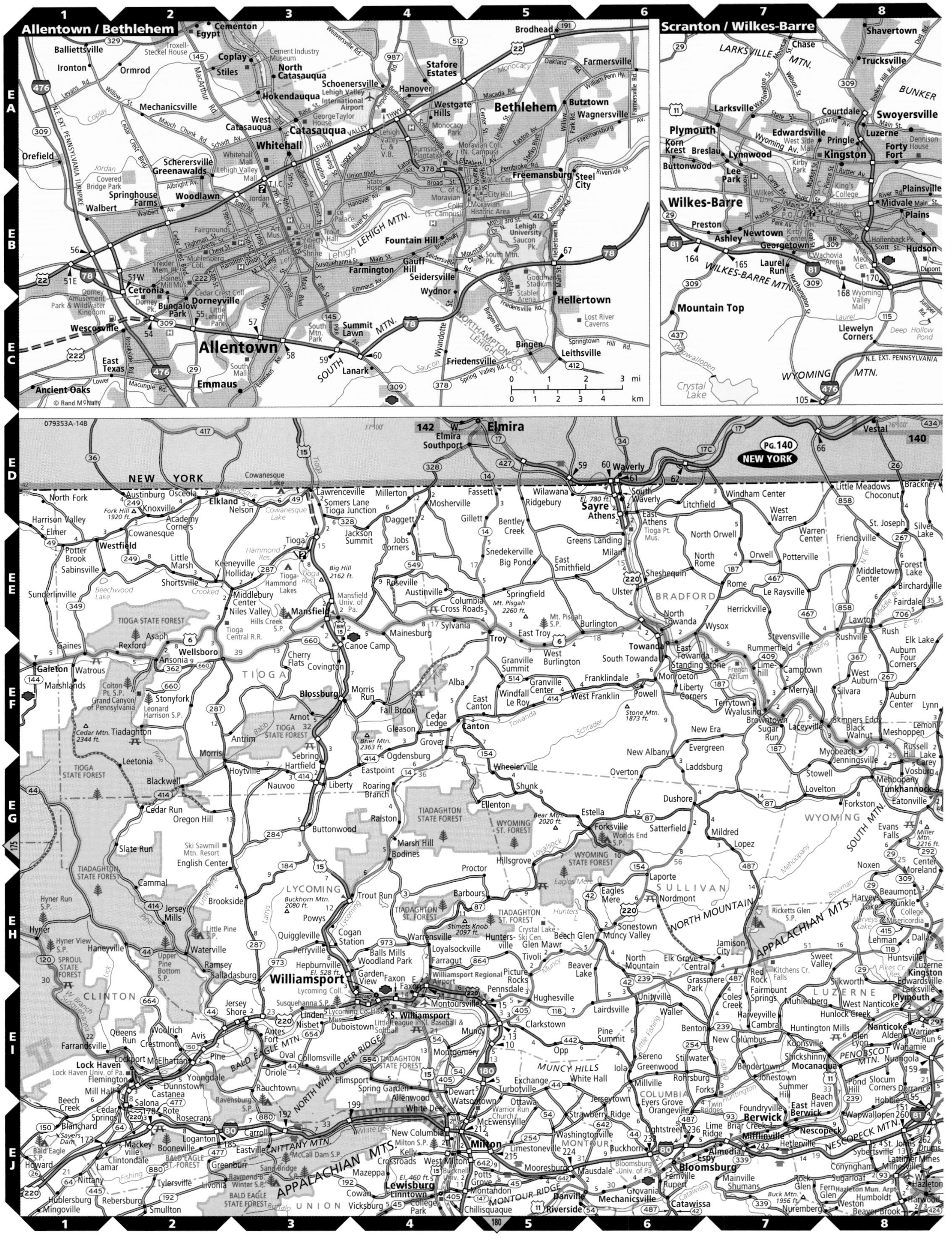

Allentown / Bethlehem

Scranton / Wilkes-Barre

079353A-14B

Pg. 140 NEW YORK

How to determine distance

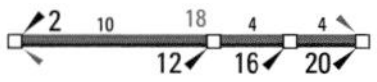

Mileages in red between red arrowheads; in black, between intersections.

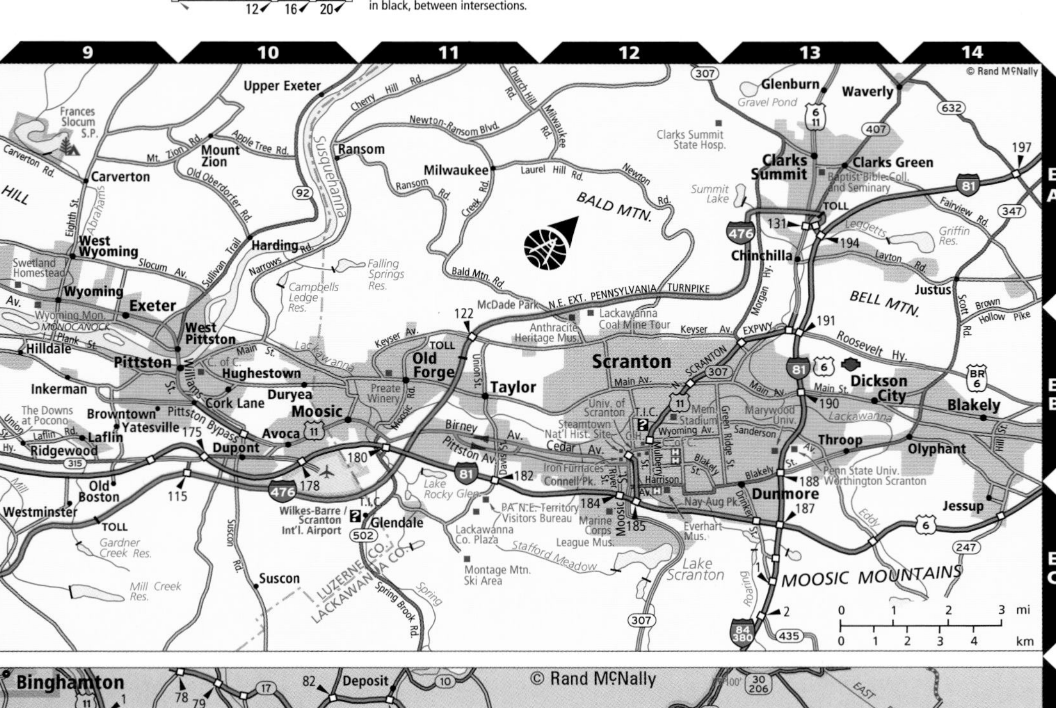

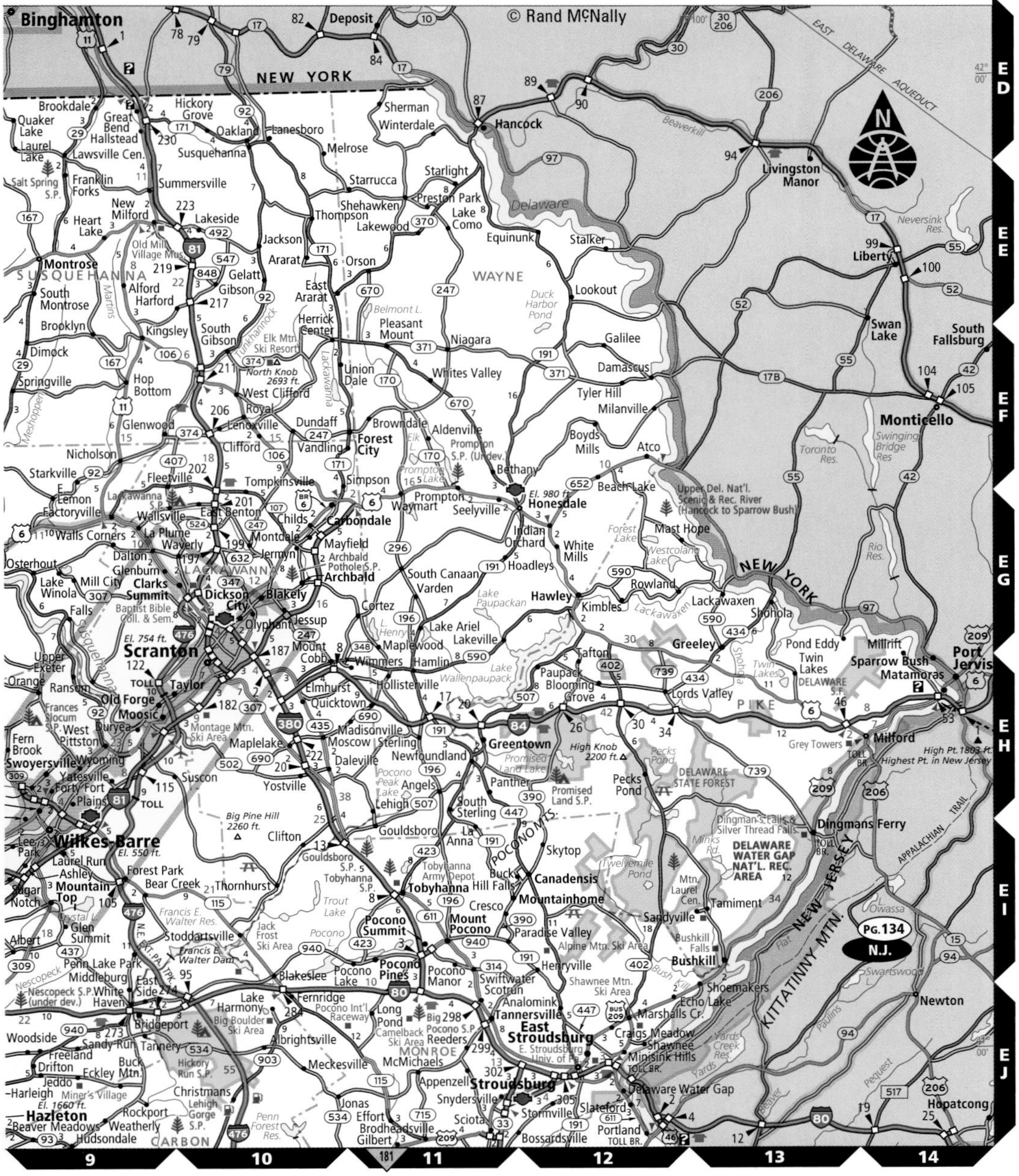

Scranton
Clarks Summit
Dickson City
Dunmore
Pittston
Old Forge
Taylor
Moosic
Wilkes-Barre / Scranton Int'l. Airport
BALD MTN.
BELL MTN.
MOOSIC MOUNTAINS
© Rand McNally

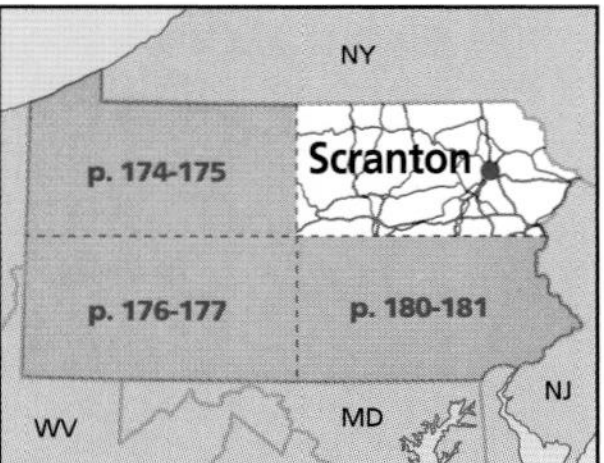

NY
Scranton
p. 174-175
p. 176-177
p. 180-181
WV
MD
NJ

SYMBOLS

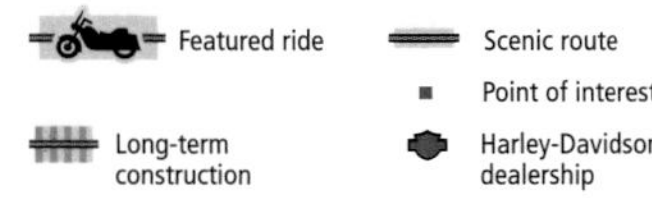

Featured ride
Scenic route
Point of interest
Long-term construction
Harley-Davidson dealership

PENNSYLVANIA MOTORCYCLE LAWS

Helmet use:
Required under age 21

Riding two abreast:
Yes. See state law for specifics

Eye protection:
Required by law

Speed limit:
Primary roads: 65 mph
Secondary roads: 55 mph

PENNSYLVANIA RESOURCES

Road conditions or construction:
(888) 783-6783 (in PA)
(215) 567-5678 (SmarTraveler, Camden/Philadelphia area)
www.dot.state.pa.us

Highway Emergency Numbers:
911

Tourism:
(800) 847-4872
www.visitpa.com

State motor vehicle information:
(717) 391-6190
www.dmv.state.pa.us

HARLEY-DAVIDSON DEALERSHIPS

- **Vreeland's Harley-Davidson, EJ-6**
  317 Montour Blvd. **Bloomsburg**
  (570) 784-2453
  Lat N 40.979 **Lon** W 76.496
- **Electric City Harley-Davidson, EG-10**
  1534 Rte. 6 Scranton/Carbondale Hwy.
  Dickson City (Scranton)
  (570) 483-0883
  Lat N 41.439 **Lon** W 75.662
- **Baer Sport Center, EG-11**
  Rte. 6 East **Honesdale**
  (570) 253-2000
  Lat N 41.587 **Lon** W 75.254
- **Cox's Northern Tier Harley-Davidson, EE-3**
  2911 S Main St. (Rte. 15 S) **Mansfield**
  (570) 659-5000
  Lat N 41.781 **Lon** W 77.069
- **Noto's Harley-Davidson Shop, EI-9**
  1022 Hwy. Rte. 315 **Plains**
  (570) 831-5001
  Lat N 41.239 **Lon** W 75.854
- **Schoch Harley-Davidson, EJ-12**
  4300 Manor Dr. **Stroudsburg**
  (570) 992-7500
  Lat N 40.96 **Lon** W 75.266
- **Horsepower Harley-Davidson, EI-4**
  1910 E 3rd St. **Williamsport**
  (570) 320-0630
  Lat N 41.249 **Lon** W 76.963

© Rand McNally

Pg. 134 N.J.

181

Distance scale
One inch represents about 12 miles

0 5 10 mi
0 5 10 15 km

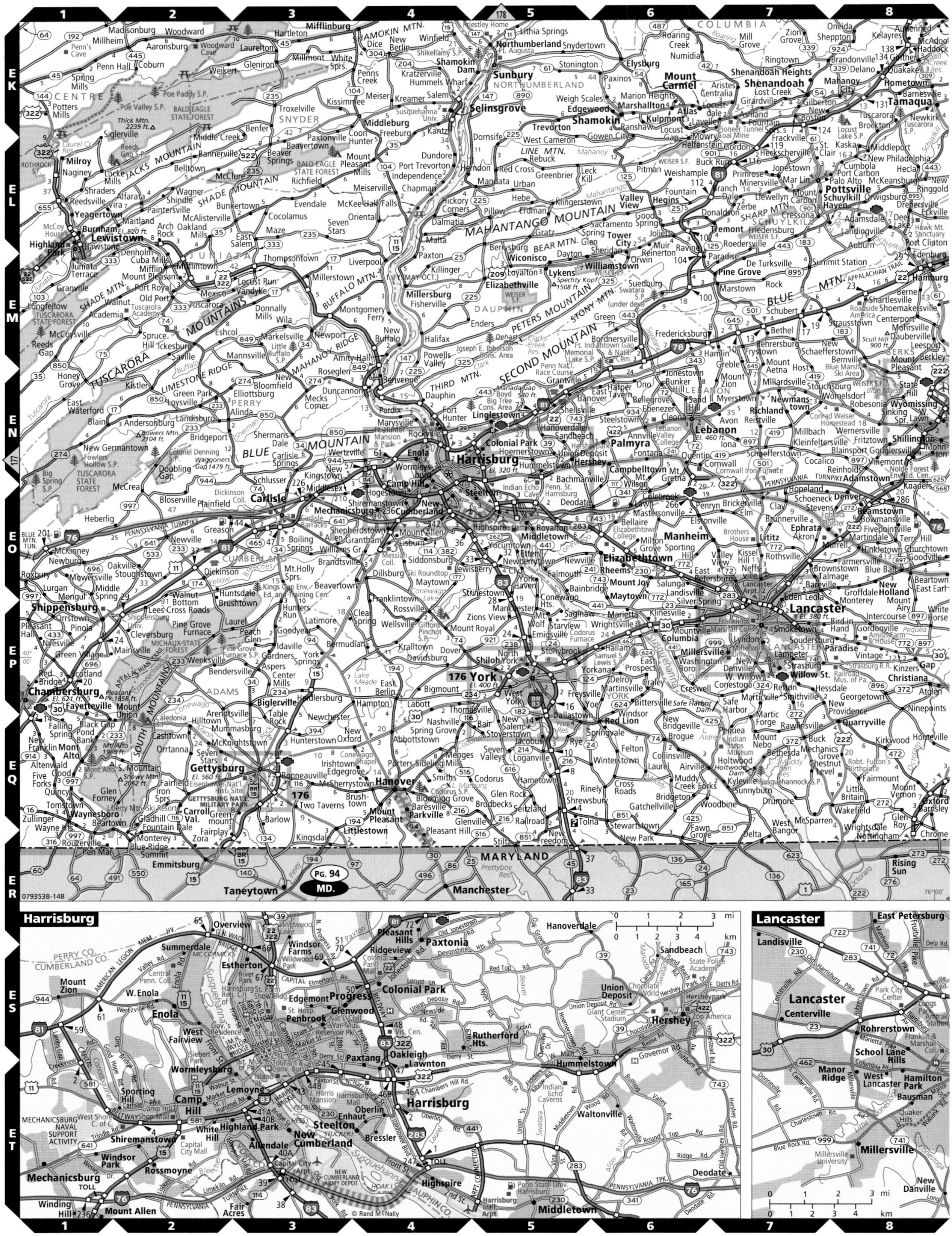

PG. 94
MD.

079353B-14B

Harrisburg

Lancaster

How to determine distance

Mileages in red between red arrowheads; in black, between intersections.

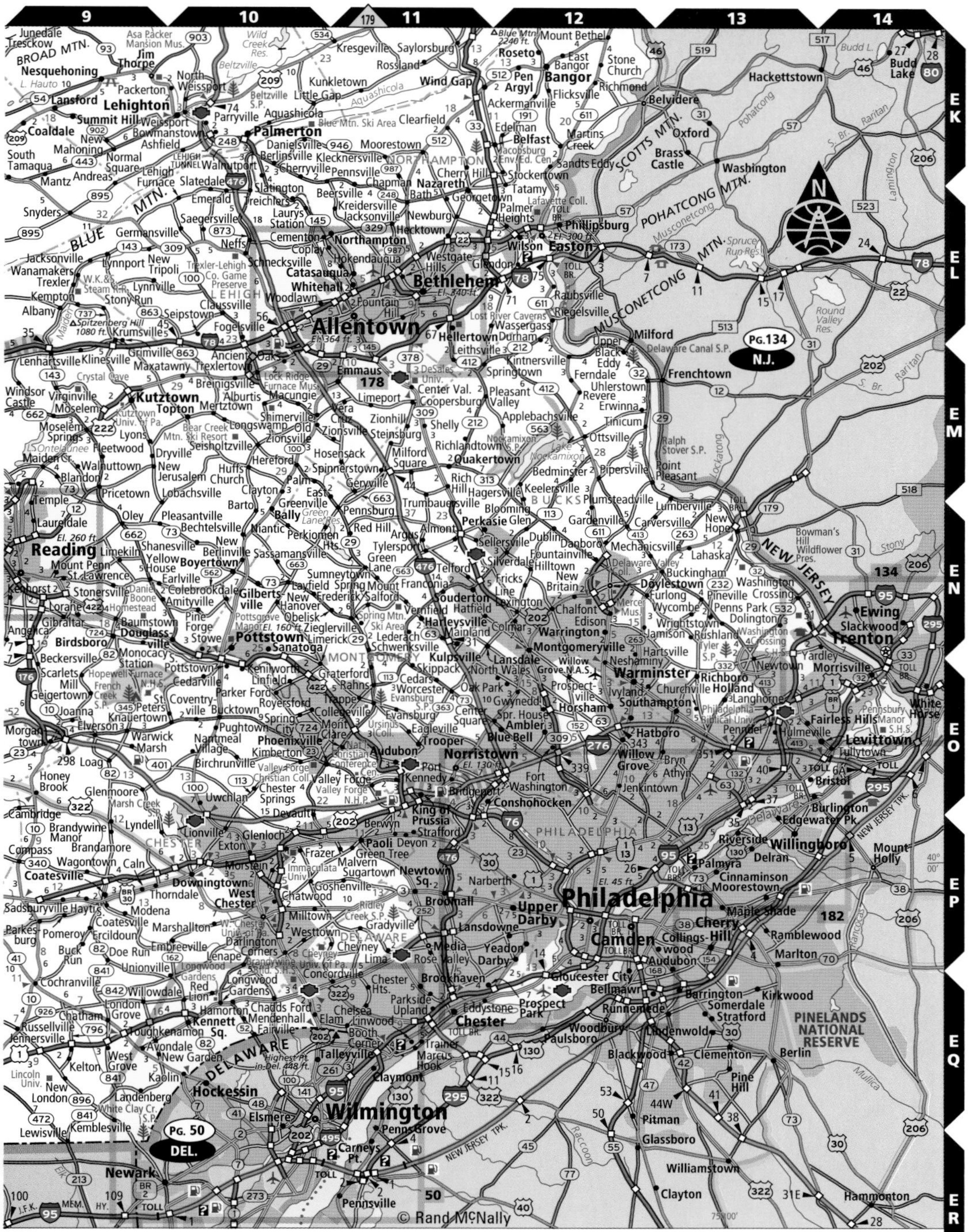

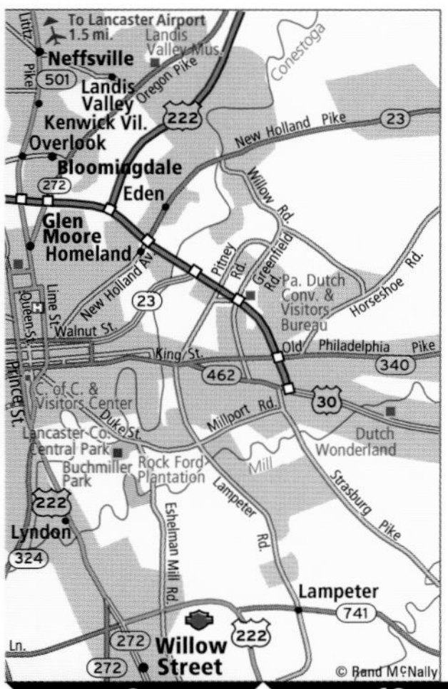

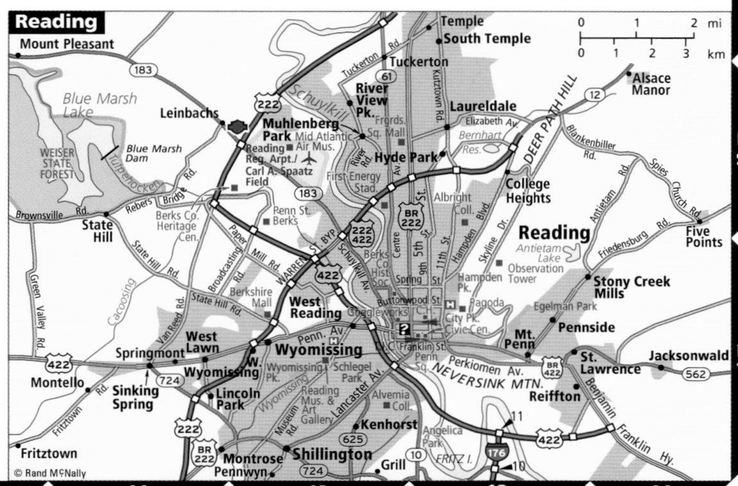

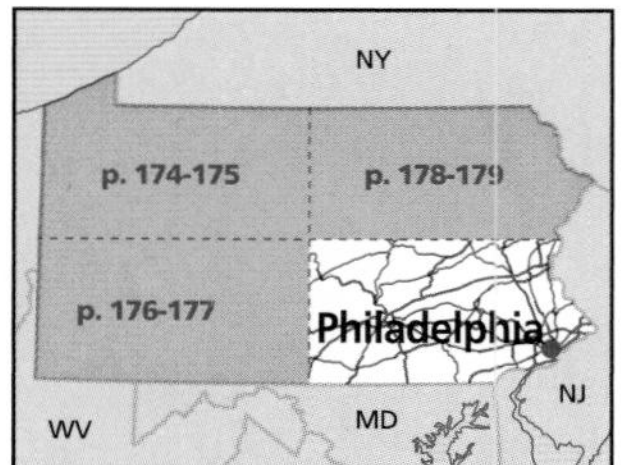
NY
p. 174-175
p. 178-179
p. 176-177
Philadelphia
WV
MD
NJ

SYMBOLS

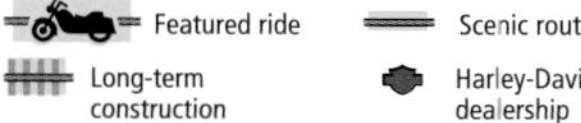
Featured ride
Scenic route
Long-term construction
Harley-Davidson dealership

HARLEY-DAVIDSON DEALERSHIPS

For the Philadelphia metro area, please see dealer listings on page 183.

- **Crossroads Harley-Davidson, EM-11**
  5118 Rte. 309 S **Center Valley**
  (610) 797-7979
  Lat N 40.538 **Lon** W 75.411
- **Harley-Davidson Shop of Chadds Ford, EQ-10**
  1241 Baltimore Pike **Chadds Ford**
  (610) 558-3331
  Lat N 39.879 **Lon** W 75.552
- **Smaltz's Harley-Davidson, EO-10**
  12 Pottstown Pike (Rte. 100) **Eagle**
  (610) 458-9004
  Lat N 40.077 **Lon** W 75.688
- **Battlefield Harley-Davidson, EQ-3**
  21 Cavalry Field Rd. **Gettysburg**
  (717) 337-9005
  Lat N 39.847 **Lon** W 77.182
- **Susquehanna Valley Harley-Davidson, EN-5**
  6300 Allentown Blvd. (Rte. 22) **Harrisburg**
  (717) 810-1993
  Lat N 40.338 **Lon** W 76.784
- **Brian's Harley-Davidson, EO-13**
  600 S Flowers Mill Rd. **Langhorne**
  (215) 752-9400
  Lat N 40.169 **Lon** W 74.899
- **White's Harley-Davidson, EN-7**
  1515 E Cumberland St. **Lebanon**
  (717) 272-4986
  Lat N 40.349 **Lon** W 76.386
- **Classic Harley-Davidson, EN-8**
  983 James Dr. (Rte. 183) **Leesport**
  (610) 916-7777
  Lat N 40.392 **Lon** W 75.996
- **Iron Valley Harley-Davidson Shop, EO-6**
  3091 Lebanon Rd. **Manheim**
  (717) 664-0888
  Lat N 40.237 **Lon** W 76.436
- **Appalachian Harley-Davidson, EO-4**
  6695 Carlisle Pike **Mechanicsburg**
  (800) 369-7743
  Lat N 40.241 **Lon** W 77.05
- **Hannum's Harley-Davidson Sales, EP-11**
  1011 W Baltimore Pike **Media**
  (610) 566-5562
  Lat N 39.915 **Lon** W 75.426
- **Valley Forge Harley-Davidson, EO-11**
  1217-19 S Trooper Rd. **Norristown**
  (610) 666-5122
  Lat N 40.114 **Lon** W 75.419
- **Schaeffer's Harley-Davidson Sales & Service, EL-8**
  1123 Brick Hill Rd. **Orwigsburg**
  (570) 366-0143
  Lat N 40.645 **Lon** W 76.083
- **Blocker Harley-Davidson, EK-10**
  770 State Rd. **Parryville**
  (610) 377-0440
  Lat N 40.821 **Lon** W 75.686
- **Dean's Harley-Davidson, EN-11**
  3255 State Rd. (Rte. 152) **Sellersville**
  (215) 257-6112
  Lat N 40.345 **Lon** W 75.306
- **Lancaster Harley-Davidson, EP-7**
  Rtes. 222 & 741 **Willow Street**
  (717) 464-2703
  Lat N 39.964 **Lon** W 76.271
- **Laugerman's Harley-Davidson Sales, EP-5**
  Rte. 30 & I-83 **York**
  (717) 854-3214
  Lat N 39.968 **Lon** W 76.769

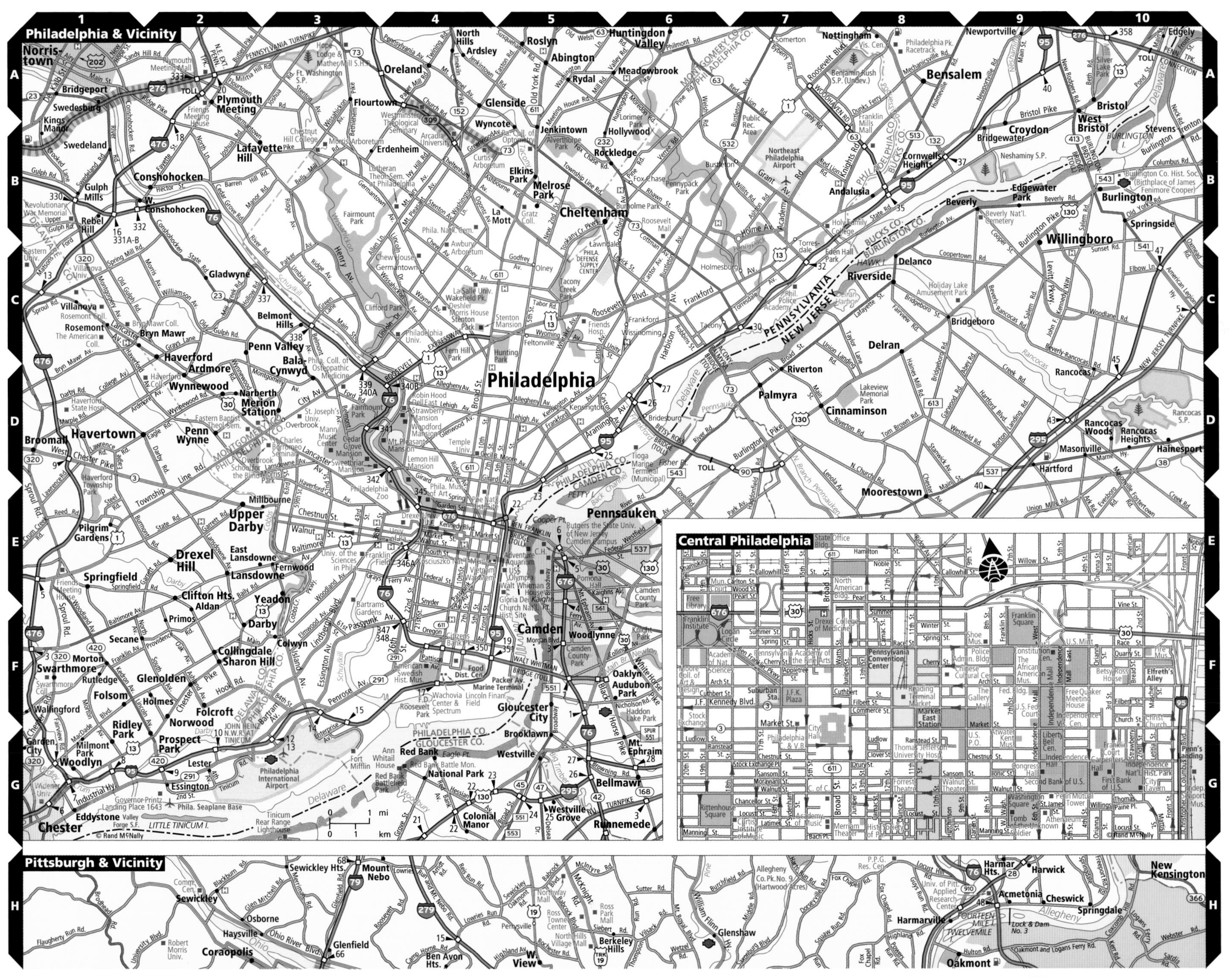
Philadelphia & Vicinity
Central Philadelphia
Pittsburgh & Vicinity
Philadelphia
Camden
Pennsauken
Cheltenham
Upper Darby
Drexel Hill
Chester
Willingboro
Bensalem
Bristol
Burlington
© Rand McNally

How to determine distance

Mileages in red between red arrowheads; in black, between intersections.

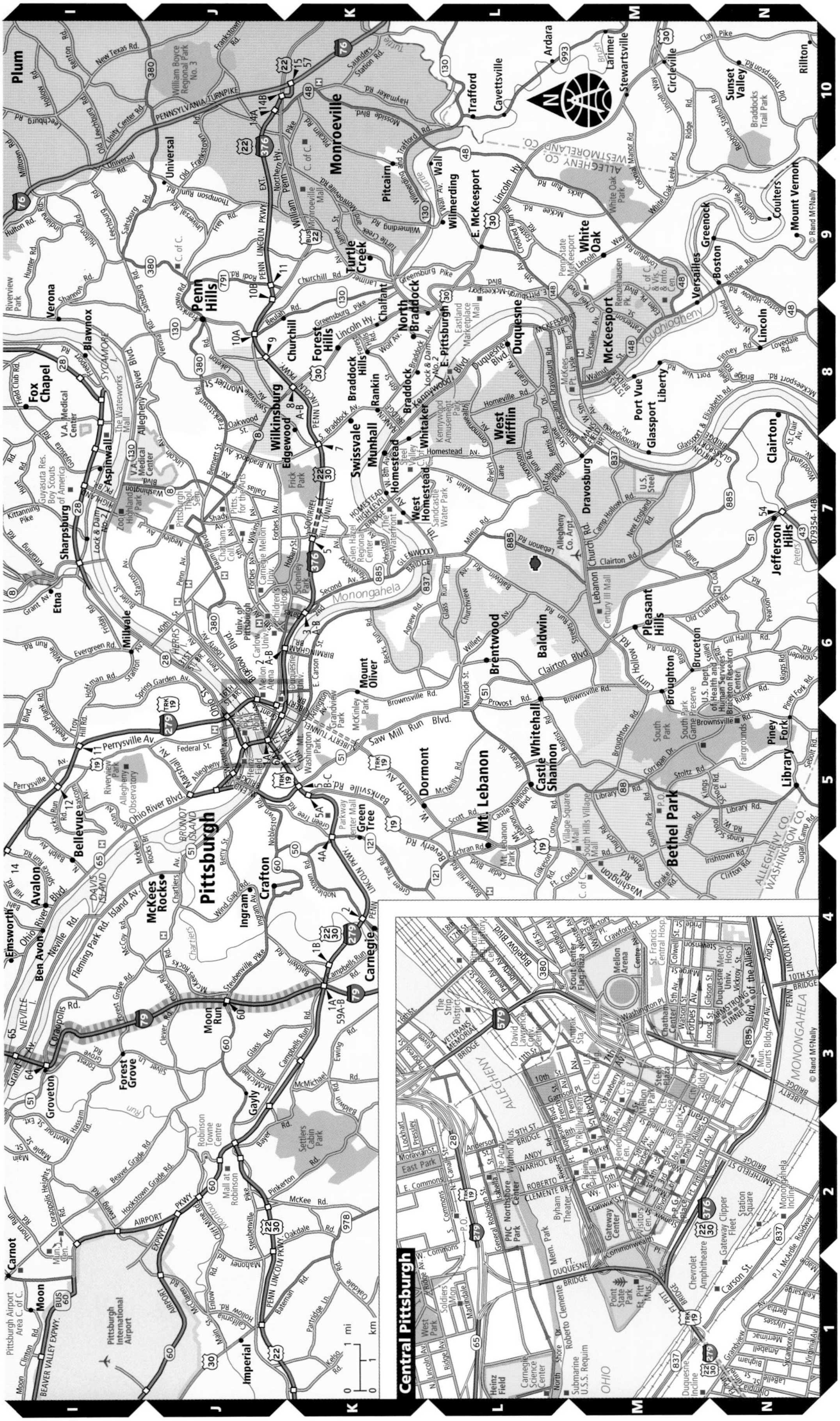

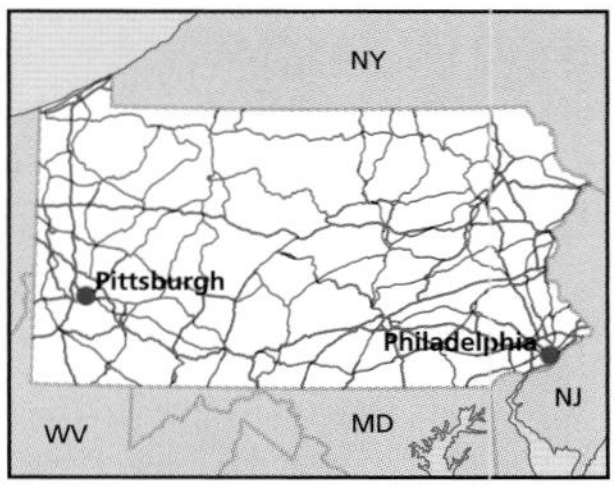

SYMBOLS

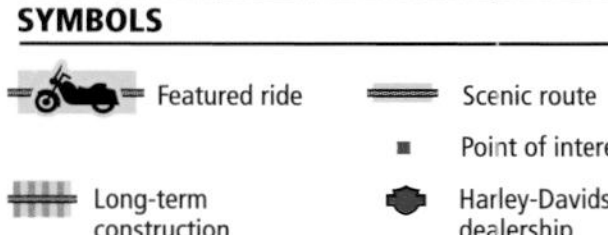
Featured ride
Scenic route
Point of interest
Long-term construction
Harley-Davidson dealership

PENNSYLVANIA MOTORCYCLE LAWS

Helmet use:
Required under age 21

Riding two abreast:
Yes. See state law for specifics

Eye protection:
Required by law

Speed limit:
Primary roads: 65 mph
Secondary roads: 55 mph

PENNSYLVANIA RESOURCES

Road conditions or construction:
(888) 783-6783 (in PA)
(215) 567-5678 (SmarTraveler, Camden/Philadelphia area)
www.dot.state.pa.us

Highway Emergency Numbers:
911

Tourism:
(800) 847-4872
www.visitpa.com

State motor vehicle information:
(717) 391-6190
www.dmv.state.pa.us

HARLEY-DAVIDSON DEALERSHIPS

Spirit Harley-Davidson, H-6
1463 Glenn Ave. **Glenshaw**
(412) 487-3377
Lat N 40.529 **Lon** W 79.953

Barb's Harley-Davidson, G-2
8800 Essington Ave. **Philadelphia**
(856) 456-4141
Lat N 40.06 **Lon** W 75.048

Heritage Harley-Davidson, L-7
1122 Lebanon Rd. (Rte. 885) **West Mifflin**
(412) HOG-WILD
Lat N 40.36 **Lon** W 79.933

Central Pittsburgh

Distance scale
One inch represents about 6 miles

0 1 2 3 4 mi
0 1 2 3 4 5 6 km

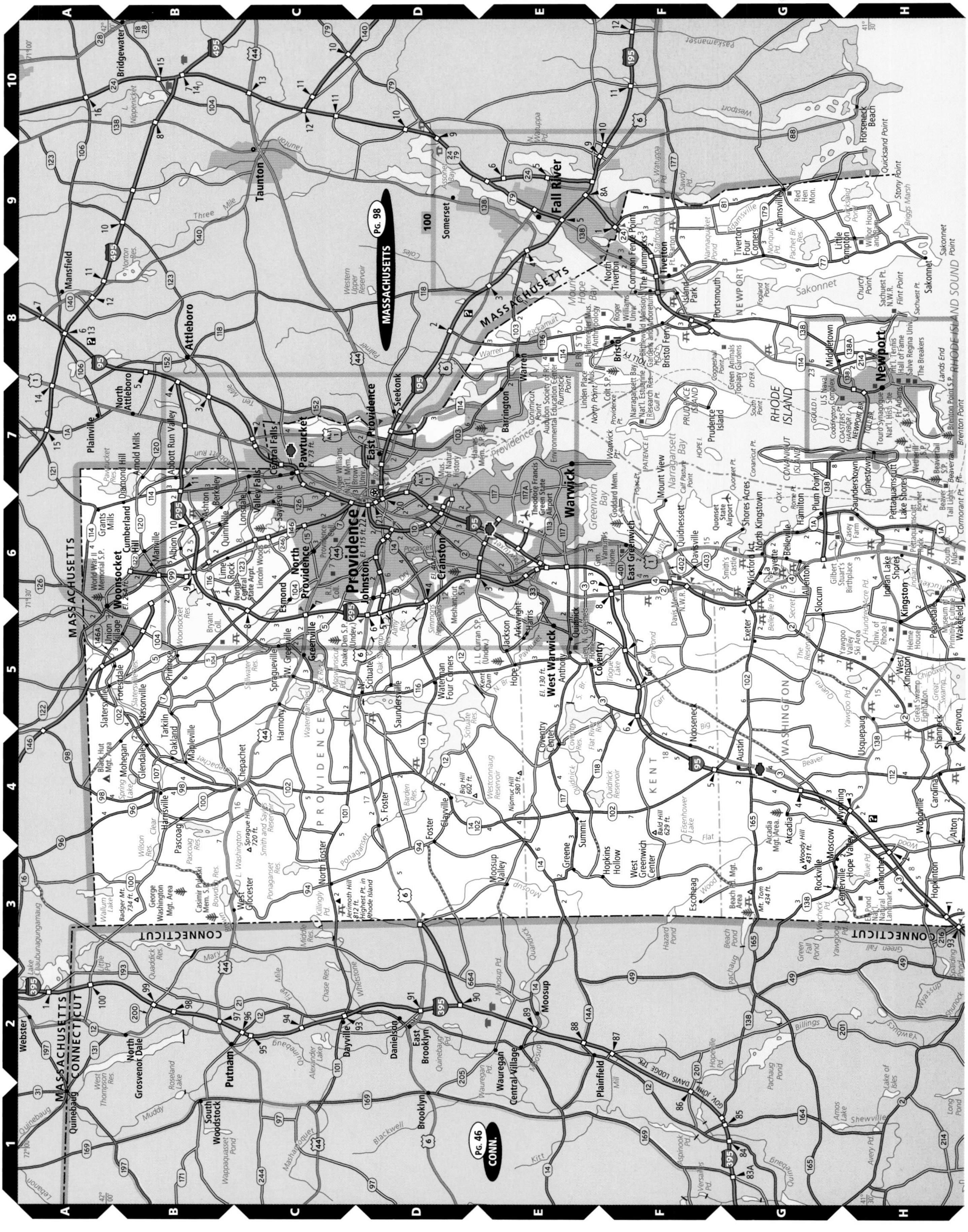

How to determine distance

Mileages in red between red arrowheads; in black, between intersections.

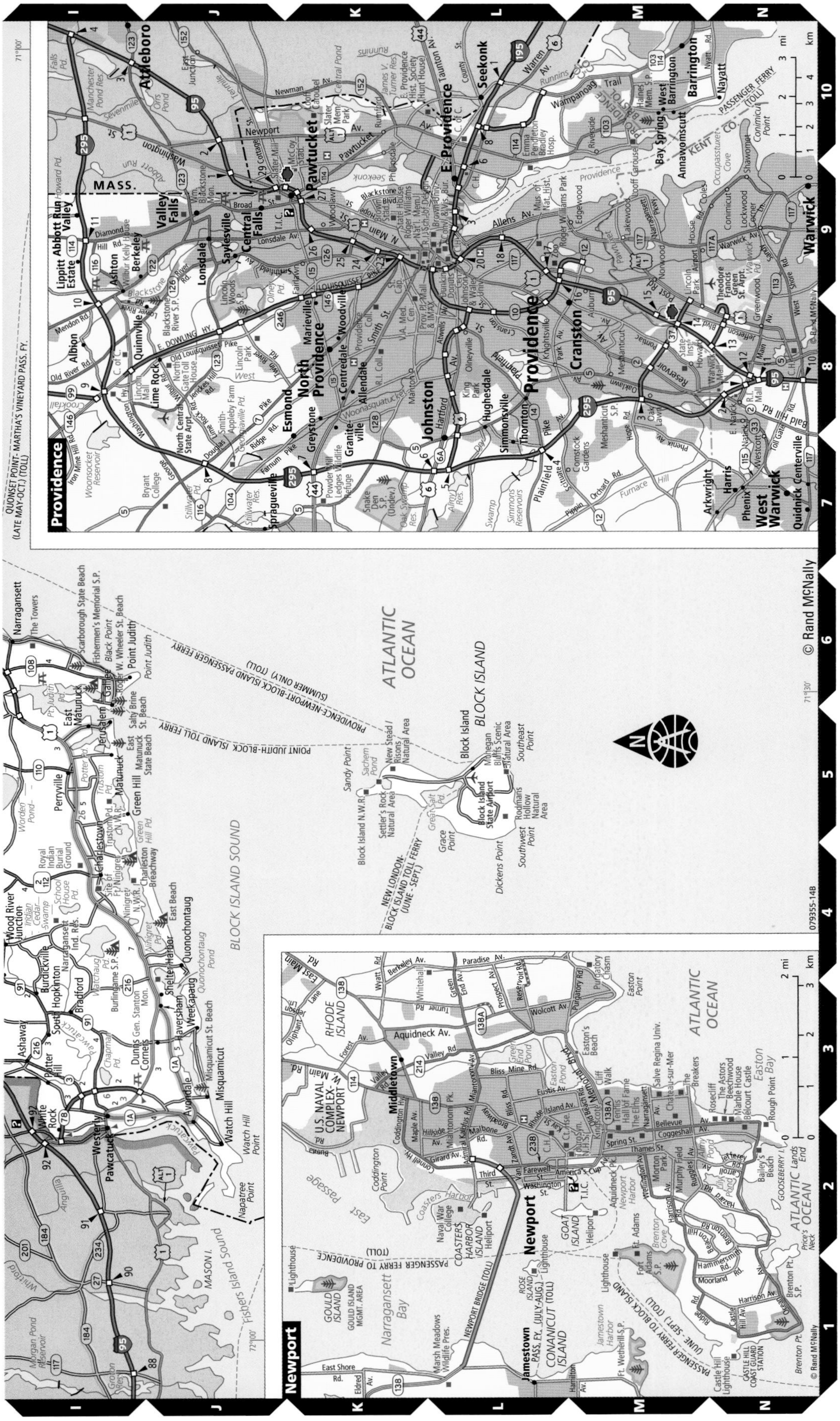

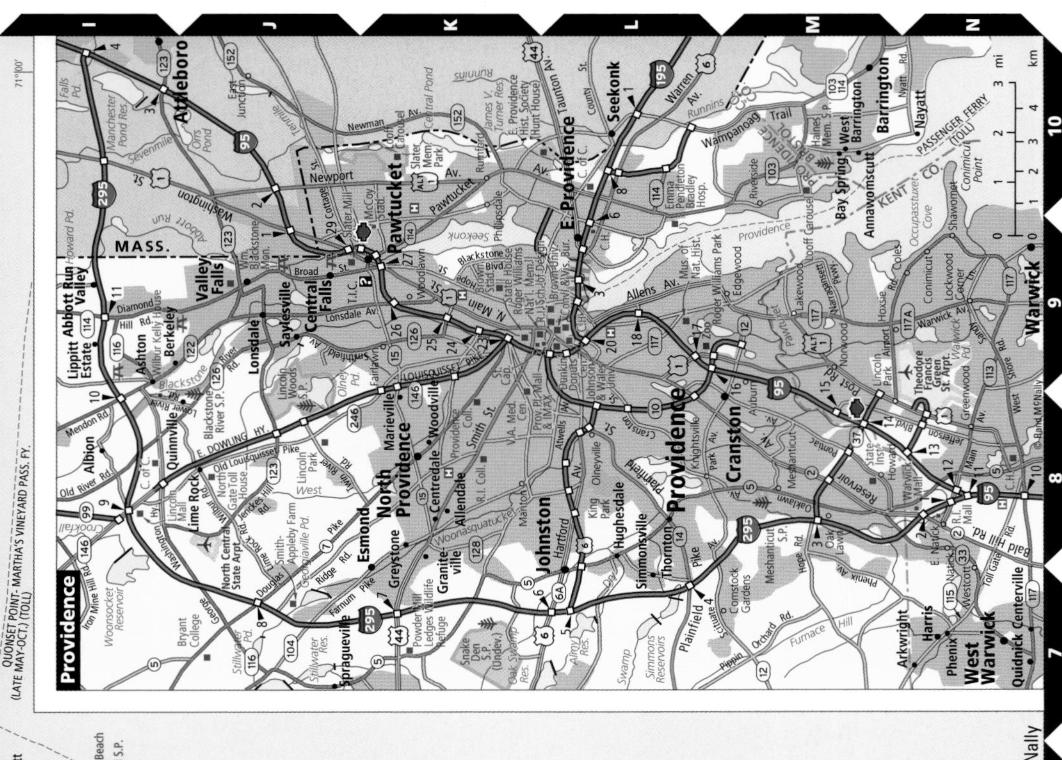

SYMBOLS

 Featured ride
Scenic route
Point of interest
 Long-term construction
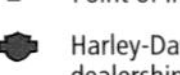 Harley-Davidson dealership

RHODE ISLAND MOTORCYCLE LAWS

Helmet use:
Required under age 21, and for novice riders, and for passengers

Riding two abreast:
Yes. See state law for specifics

Eye protection:
Required by law

Speed limit:
Primary roads: 65 mph
Secondary roads: 55 mph

RHODE ISLAND RESOURCES

Road conditions or construction:
511
www.tmc.state.ri.us

Highway Emergency Numbers:
911

Tourism:
(888) 886-9463
(800) 556-2484
(401) 222-2601
www.visitrhodeisland.com

State motor vehicle information:
(401) 588-3020
www.drive.state.ri.us

CITY-TO-CITY MILEAGE

	FALL RIVER, MA	KINGSTON	NEWPORT	PROVIDENCE	WARWICK	WESTERLY	WOONSOCKET	WORCESTER, MA
Chepachet	36	44	46	20	27	56	17	37
Fall River, MA		37	23	16	26	58	32	59
Kingston	37		16	30	25	24	47	74
Newport	23	16		32	27	37	49	76
Providence	16	30	32		10	42	16	43
Warwick	26	25	27	10		37	26	53
Westerly	58	24	37	42	37		59	70
Woonsocket	32	47	49	16	26	59		32
Worcester, MA	59	74	76	43	53	70	32	

HARLEY-DAVIDSON DEALERSHIPS

Ocean State Harley-Davidson Shop, G-4
435 Nooseneck Hill Rd. (Rte 3) **Exeter**
(401) 392-1162
Lat N 41.572 **Lon** W 71.656

Precision Harley-Davidson, C-7
269 Armistice Blvd. **Pawtucket**
(401) 724-0010
Lat N 41.881 **Lon** W 71.366

Ocean State Harley-Davidson, E-6
5 Albany Rd. **Warwick**
(401) 781-6866
Lat N 41.75 **Lon** W 71.437

Distance scale
One inch represents about 25 miles
0 5 10 15 20 mi
0 5 10 15 20 25 30 km

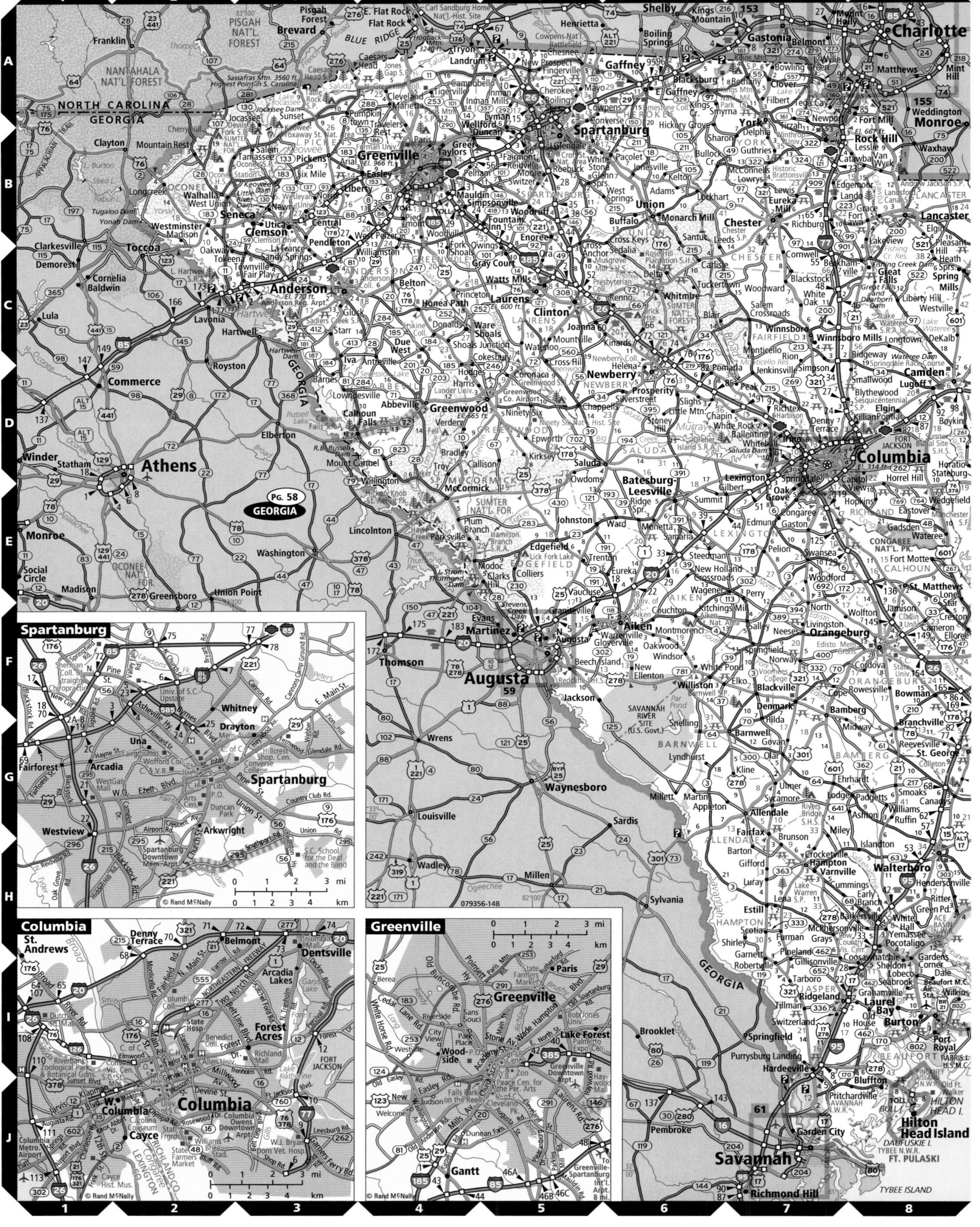
NORTH CAROLINA
GEORGIA
Charlotte
Spartanburg
Greenville
Anderson
Athens
Columbia
Augusta
Savannah
Hilton Head Island
Rock Hill
Monroe
Gastonia
Orangeburg
Aiken
Greenwood
Walterboro
Beaufort
PG. 58
GEORGIA
Spartanburg
Columbia
Greenville
© Rand McNally
079356-14B

How to determine distance

Mileages in red between red arrowheads; in black, between intersections.

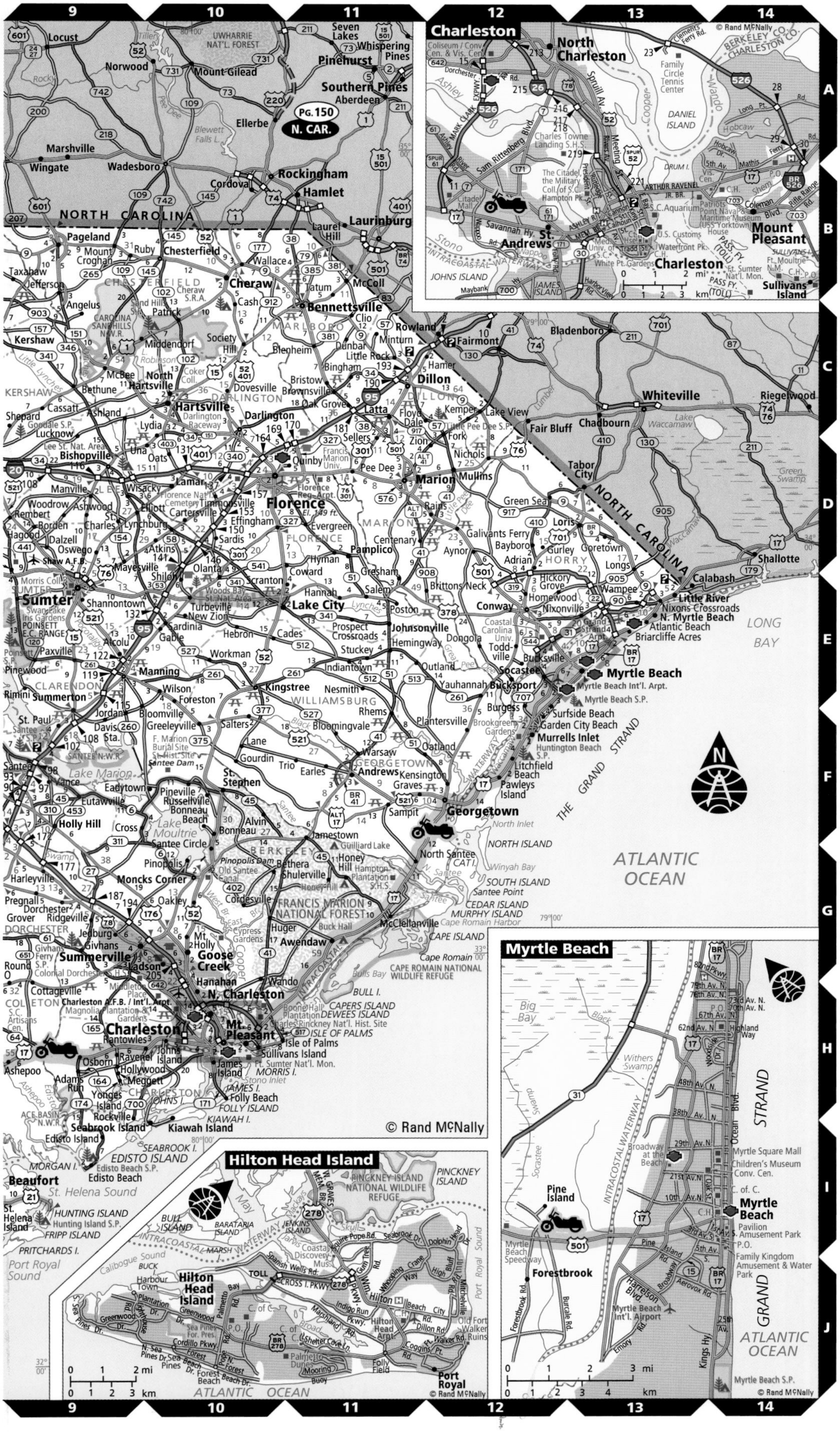

SYMBOLS

Featured ride

Scenic route

Point of interest

Long-term construction

Harley-Davidson dealership

For Georgia/South Carolina ride, see page R13.

SOUTH CAROLINA MOTORCYCLE LAWS

Helmet use:
Required under age 21, and reflectorization required

Riding two abreast:
Yes. See state law for specifics

Eye protection:
Required under age 21
Required unless equipped with windscreen

Speed limit:
Primary roads: 70 mph
Secondary roads: 70 mph

SOUTH CAROLINA RESOURCES

Road conditions or construction:
www.dot.state.sc.us

Highway Emergency Numbers: 911

Tourism:
(888) 727-6453 (to request travel materials only)
(803) 734-1700
www.discoversouthcarolina.com

State motor vehicle information:
(803) 896-5000
www.scdmvonline.com

HARLEY-DAVIDSON DEALERSHIPS

Timms Harley-Davidson, C-3
4110 Clemson Blvd. **Anderson**
(864) 224-1531
Lat N 34.56 **Lon** W 82.692

Low Country Harley-Davidson, H-10
4707 Dorchester Rd. **Charleston**
(843) 554-1847
Lat N 32.854 **Lon** W 80.02

The Harley Shop, H-10
57 S Market St. **Charleston**
(843) 722-9472
Lat N 32.781 **Lon** W 79.929

Thunder Tower Harley-Davidson, D-8
190 Pontiac Business Center Dr. **Elgin**
(803) 461-1121
Lat N 34.106 **Lon** W 80.837

Doug's Harley-Davidson, D-10
2207 T.V. Rd. **Florence**
(843) 669-9961
Lat N 34.239 **Lon** W 79.749

Harley-Davidson of Greenville, B-4
30 Chrome Dr. **Greenville**
(864) 234-1340
Lat N 34.836 **Lon** W 82.296

Harley Haven, D-7
941 Western Ln. **Irmo**
(803) 794-4887
Lat N 34.12 **Lon** W 81.195

Myrtle Beach Harley-Davidson, E-12
4710 S Kings Hwy. **Myrtle Beach**
(843) 369-5555
Lat N 33.647 **Lon** W 78.942

Myrtle Beach Harley-Davidson, E-13
913A N Ocean Blvd. **Myrtle Beach**
(843) 946-9499
Lat N 33.692 **Lon** W 78.88

Myrtle Beach Harley-Davidson at Broadway at the Beach, E-13
1316 Celebrity Circle **Myrtle Beach**
(843) 293-5555
Lat N 33.719 **Lon** W 78.882

The Harley-Davidson Shop at the Beach, E-13
4002 Hwy. 17 S **North Myrtle Beach**
(843) 663-5555
Lat N 33.802 **Lon** W 78.729

Cox's Harley-Davidson of Rock Hill, B-7
1093 Albright Rd. **Rock Hill**
(803) 327-1183
Lat N 34.906 **Lon** W 81.024

Spartanburg Harley-Davidson, A-5
365 Sha Ln. **Spartanburg**
(864) 583-8840
Lat N 35.028 **Lon** W 81.871

Distance scale
One inch represents about 35 miles
0 5 10 15 20 25 30 mi
0 10 20 30 40 km

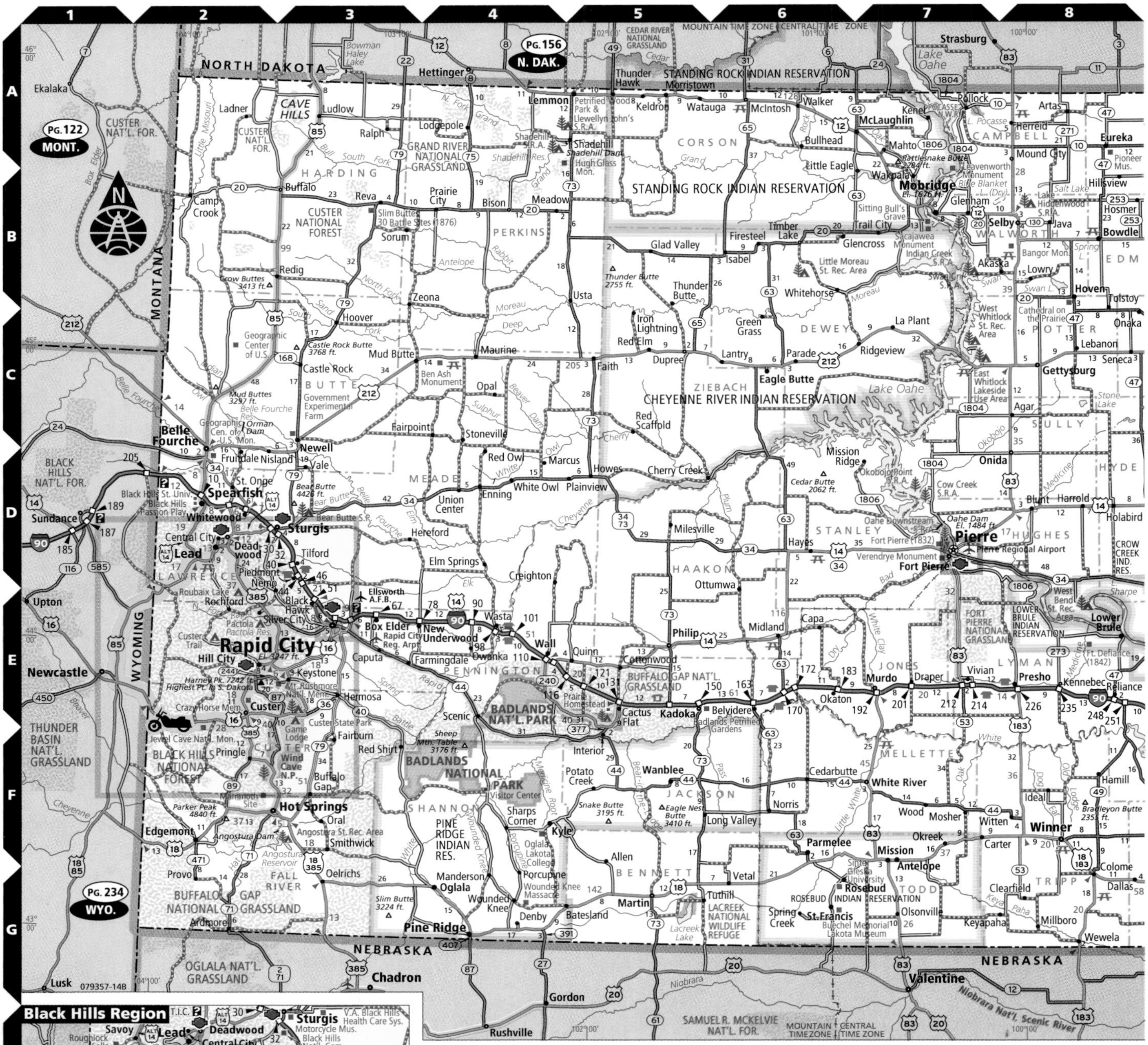

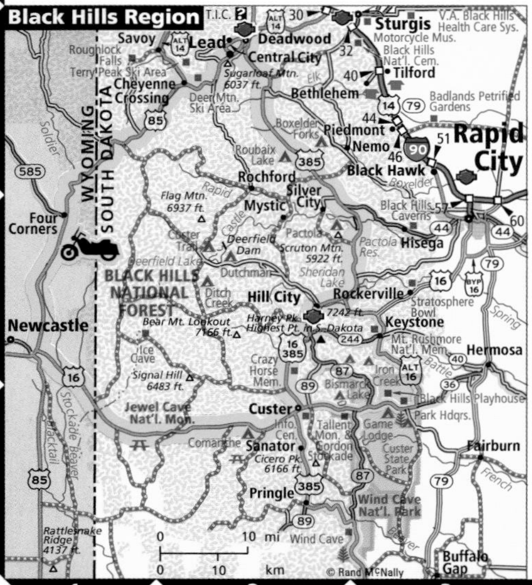

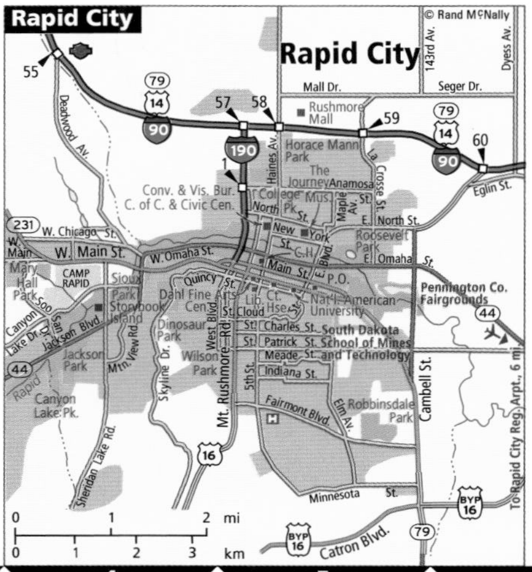

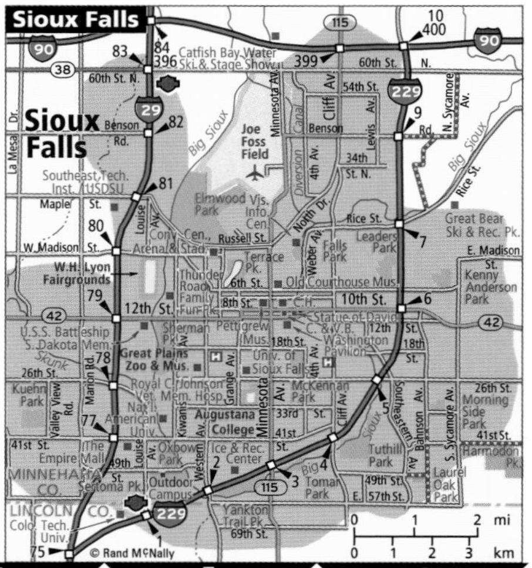

NORTH DAKOTA
MONTANA
WYOMING
NEBRASKA

PG. 156 N. DAK.
PG. 122 MONT.
PG. 234 WYO.

STANDING ROCK INDIAN RESERVATION
CHEYENNE RIVER INDIAN RESERVATION
BADLANDS NATIONAL PARK
PINE RIDGE INDIAN RES.

079357-148

Black Hills Region

0 10 mi
0 10 km

Rapid City

0 1 2 mi
0 1 2 3 km

Sioux Falls

0 1 2 mi
0 1 2 3 km

How to determine distance

2 10 18 4 4 12 16 20

Mileages in red between red arrowheads; in black, between intersections.

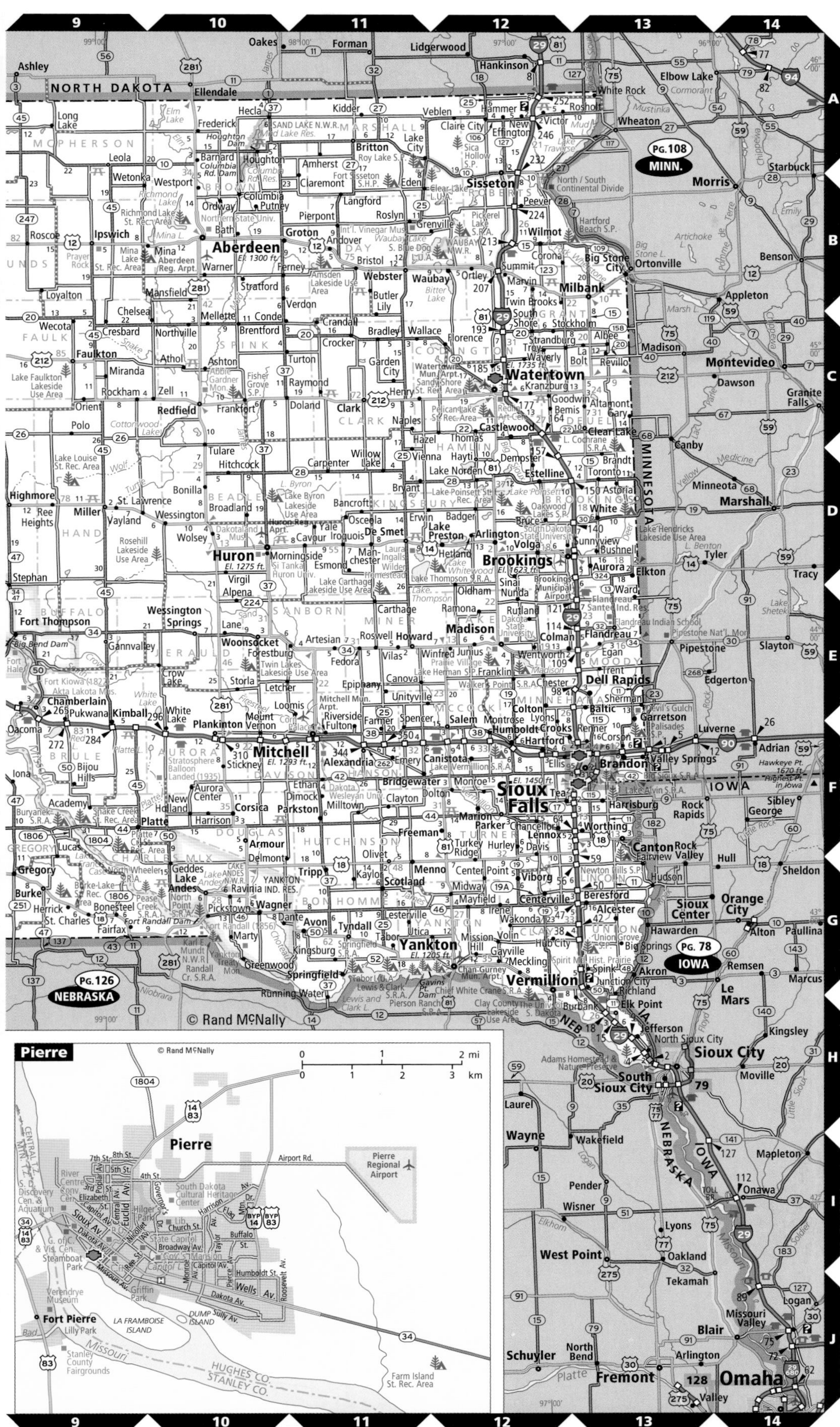
NORTH DAKOTA
MINNESOTA
NEBRASKA
IOWA
PG. 108 MINN.
PG. 78 IOWA
PG. 126 NEBRASKA
Aberdeen
Watertown
Brookings
Huron
Mitchell
Sioux Falls
Yankton
Vermillion
Sioux City
Omaha
© Rand McNally
Pierre

SYMBOLS

- Featured ride
- Scenic route
- Point of interest
- Long-term construction
- Harley-Davidson dealership

For South Dakota/Wyoming ride, see page R32-33.

SOUTH DAKOTA MOTORCYCLE LAWS

Helmet use:
Required under age 18

Riding two abreast:
Yes. See state law for specifics

Eye protection:
Required unless equipped with windscreen

Speed limit:
Primary roads: 75 mph
Secondary roads: 75 mph

SOUTH DAKOTA RESOURCES

Road conditions or construction:
511
(866) 697-3511
www.sddot.com/511

Highway Emergency Numbers:
911

Tourism:
(800) 732-5682
(605) 773-3301
www.travelsd.com

State motor vehicle information:
(800) 952-3696
www.state.sd.us/dps/dl

CITY-TO-CITY MILEAGE

	Aberdeen	Belle Fourche	Mobridge	Pierre	Rapid City	Sioux City, IA	Sioux Falls	Watertown
Aberdeen		312	100	159	350	285	204	105
Belle Fourche	312		213	247	60	485	404	365
Mobridge	100	213		109	241	385	304	205
Pierre	159	247	109		191	306	225	190
Rapid City	350	60	241	191		429	348	406
Sioux City, IA	285	485	385	306	429		85	185
Sioux Falls	204	404	304	225	348	85		104
Watertown	105	365	205	190	406	185	104	

HARLEY-DAVIDSON DEALERSHIPS

Deadwood Harley-Davidson, D-2
645 Main St. **Deadwood**
(605) 722-2675
Lat N 44.377 **Lon** W 103.730

Hill City Harley-Davidson, E-2
347 Main St. **Hill City**
(605) 574-3636
Lat N 43.932 **Lon** W 103.576

Petersen Motors Harley-Davidson, D-7
422 S Fort St. **Pierre**
(605) 224-4242
Lat N 44.366 **Lon** W 100.357

Black Hills Harley-Davidson, E-3
2820 Harley Dr. **Rapid City**
(605) 342-9362
Lat N 44.124 **Lon** W 103.296

J & L Harley-Davidson, F-13
2601 W 60th St. N **Sioux Falls**
(605) 334-2721
Lat N 43.602 **Lon** W 96.762

J & L Harley-Davidson, F-13
5019 S Louise Ave. **Sioux Falls**
(605) 271-2100
Lat N 43.5 **Lon** W 96.771

Sturgis Harley-Davidson, D-2
1040 Junction Ave. **Sturgis**
(605) 347-2056
Lat N 44.414 **Lon** W 103.509

Glacial Lakes Harley-Davidson Shop, C-12
1000 19th St. SE **Watertown**
(605) 886-3448
Lat N 44.912 **Lon** W 97.118

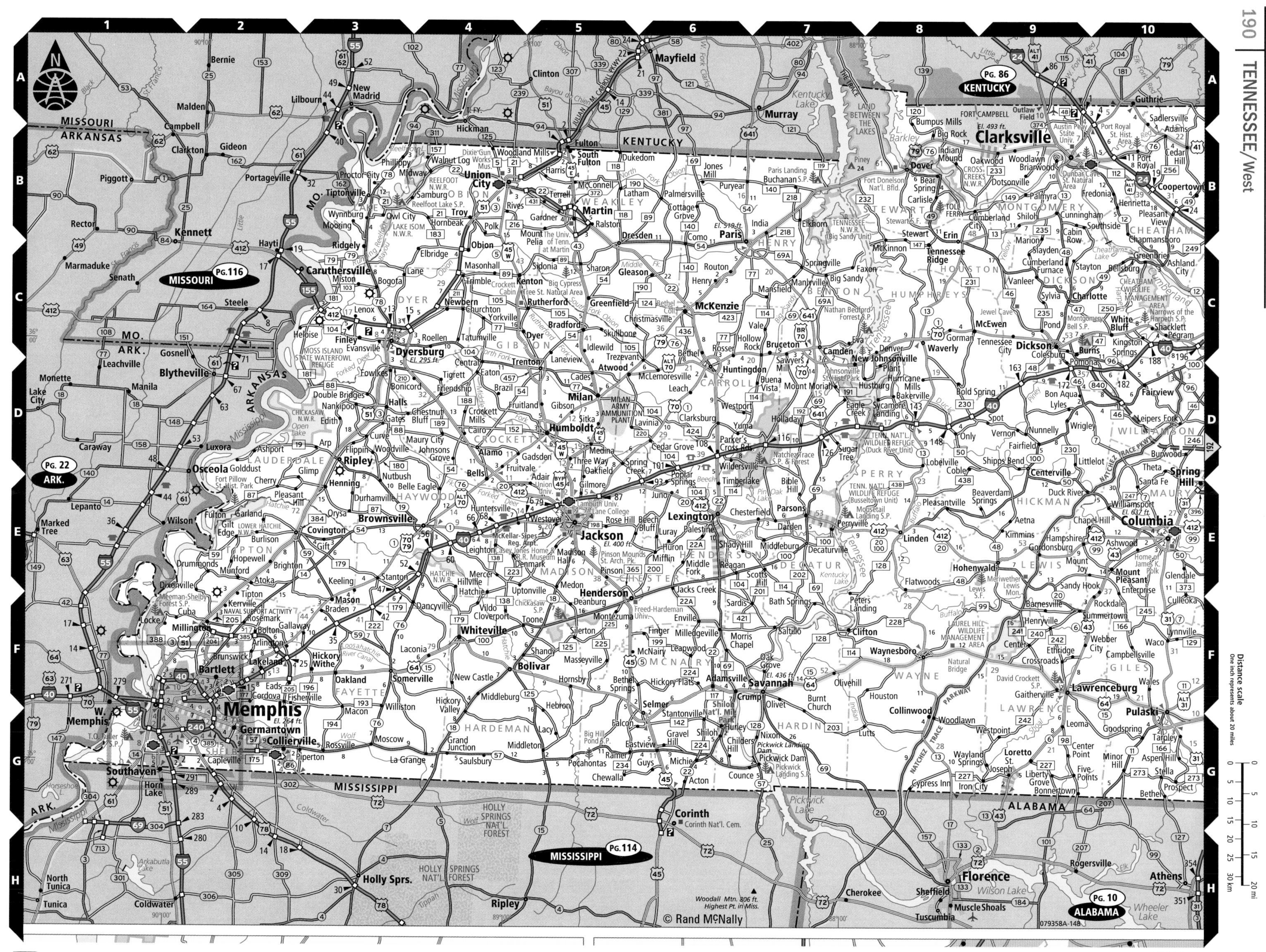
Distance scale
One inch represents about 20 miles
0 5 10 15 20 mi
0 5 10 15 20 25 30 km
KENTUCKY
MISSOURI
ARKANSAS
MISSISSIPPI
ALABAMA
PG. 86 KENTUCKY
PG. 116 MISSOURI
PG. 22 ARK.
PG. 114 MISSISSIPPI
PG. 10 ALABAMA
Memphis
Jackson
Clarksville
Columbia
Woodall Mtn. 806 ft. Highest Pt. in Miss.
© Rand McNally
079358A-14B

How to determine distance

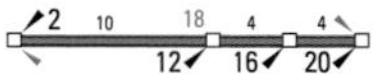

2 10 18 4 4 12 16 20

Mileages in red between red arrowheads; in black, between intersections.

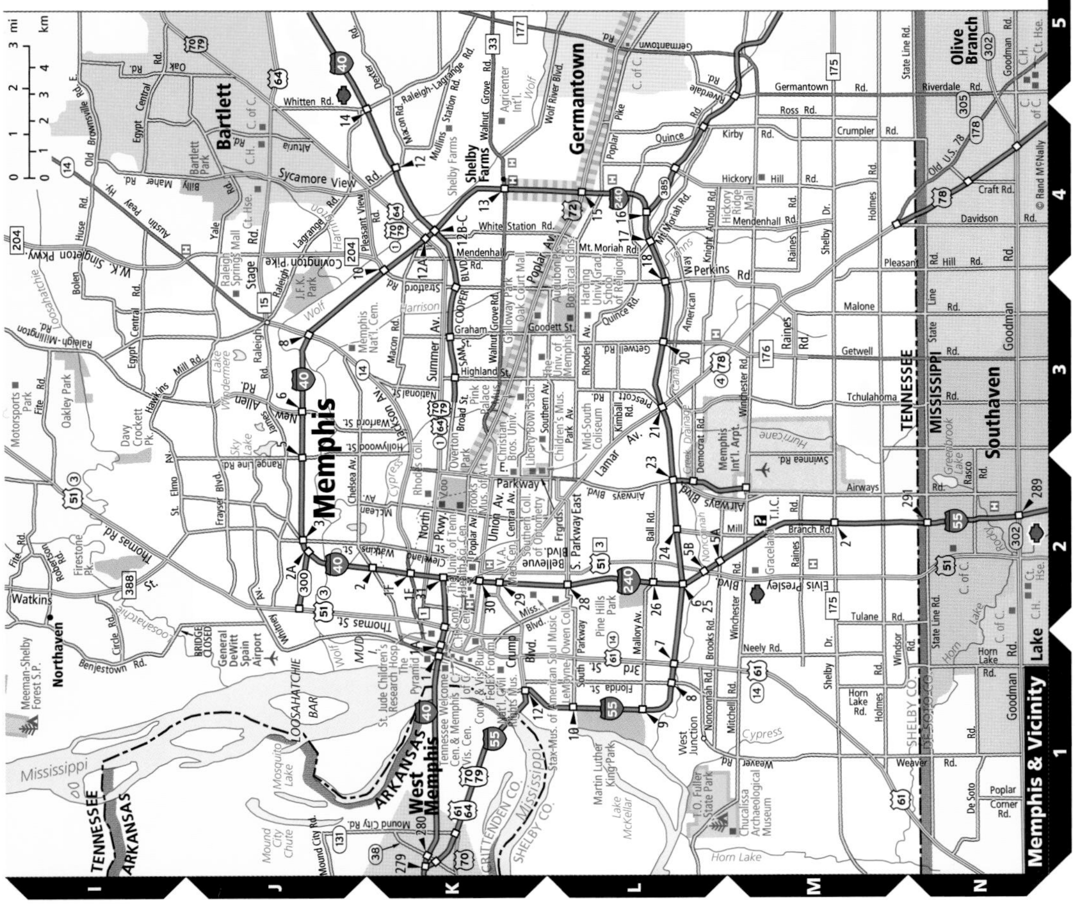

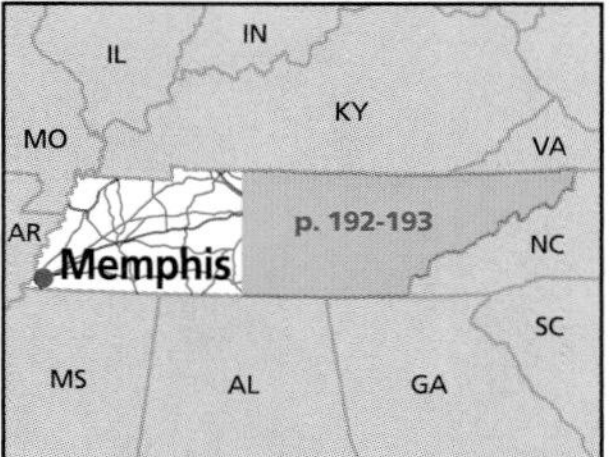
IL
IN
KY
MO
VA
AR
Memphis
p. 192-193
NC
SC
MS
AL
GA

SYMBOLS

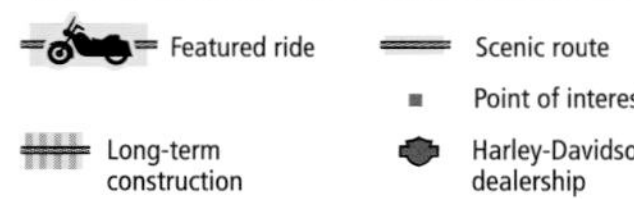
Featured ride
Scenic route
Point of interest
Long-term construction
Harley-Davidson dealership

TENNESSEE MOTORCYCLE LAWS

Helmet use:
Required

Riding two abreast:
Yes. See state law for specifics

Eye protection:
Required unless equipped with windscreen

Speed limit:
Primary roads: 70 mph
Secondary roads: 70 mph

TENNESSEE RESOURCES

Road conditions or construction:
(800) 342-3258
(800) 858-6349
www.tdot.state.tn.us/travel.htm

Highway Emergency Numbers:
911

Tourism:
(800) 462-8366 (to request travel materials only)
(615) 741-2159
www.tnvacation.com

State motor vehicle information:
(615) 253-5221
www.state.tn.us/safety

HARLEY-DAVIDSON DEALERSHIPS

- **Appleton's Harley-Davidson, B-9**
  2501 Hwy. 41A Bypass **Clarksville**
  (931) 648-1607
  Lat N 36.502 **Lon** W 87.286
- **Bumpus Harley-Davidson Shop of Collierville, G-2**
  325 S Byhalia Rd. **Collierville**
  (901) 316-1121
  Lat N 35.037 **Lon** W 89.689
- **Harley-Davidson Shop of Columbia, E-10**
  1028 Nashville Hwy. **Columbia**
  (931) 540-0099
  Lat N 35.635 **Lon** W 87.018
- **Bumpus Harley-Davidson of Jackson, E-5**
  326 Carriage House Dr. **Jackson**
  (731) 422-5508
  Lat N 35.667 **Lon** W 88.842
- **Bumpus Harley-Davidson of Memphis, F-2**
  2160 Whitten Rd. **Memphis**
  (901) 372-1121
  Lat N 35.185 **Lon** W 89.836
- **Graceland Harley-Davidson, G-1**
  3727 Elvis Presley Blvd. **Memphis**
  (877) 803-5847
  Lat N 35.047 **Lon** W 90.025
- **Abernathy's Motorcycle Sales, B-4**
  1704 W Main St. **Union City**
  (731) 885-1792
  Lat N 36.428 **Lon** W 89.077

Nashville

Memphis & Vicinity

Distance scale
One inch represents about 20 miles
0 5 10 15 20 mi
0 5 10 15 20 25 30 km

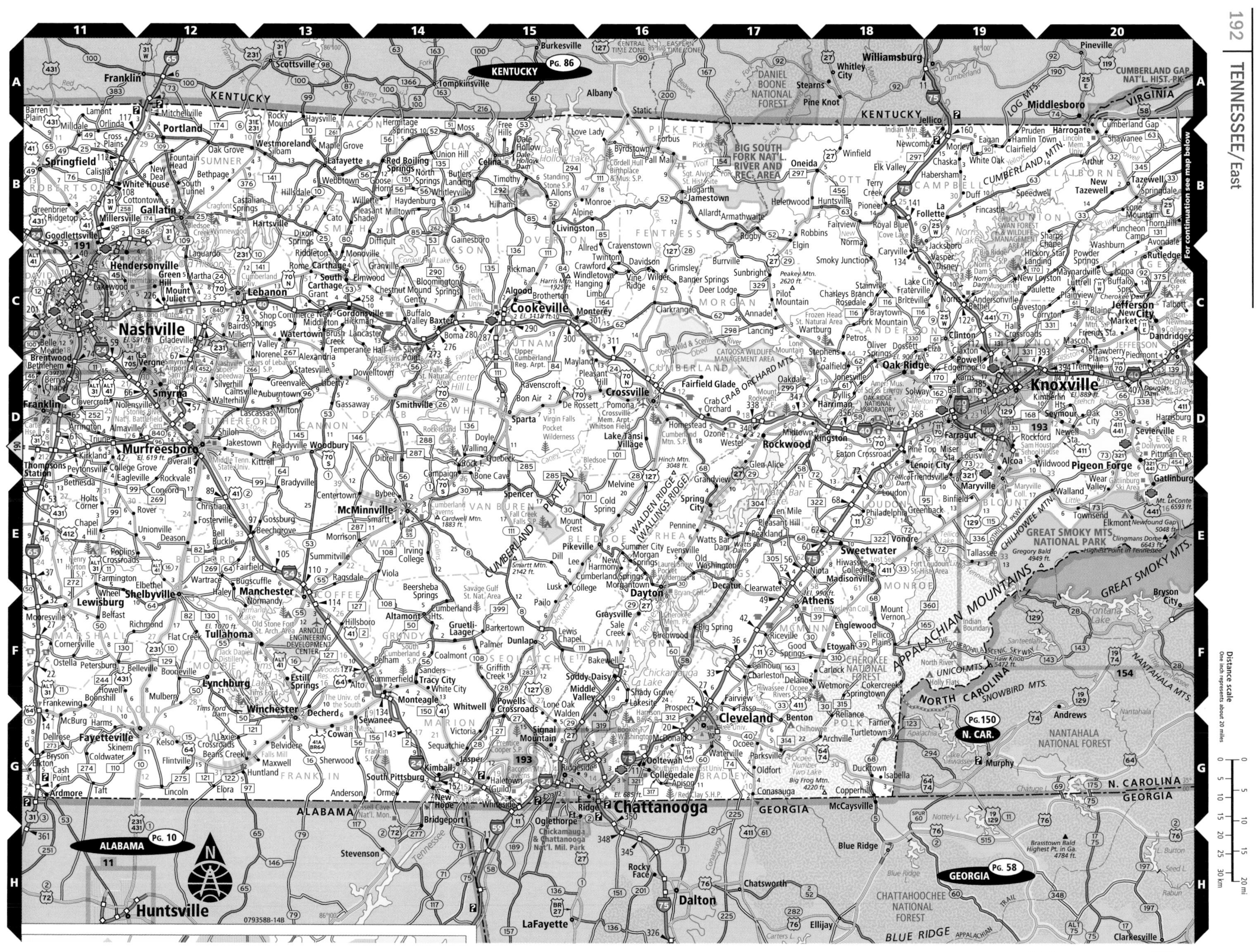
For continuation see map below
KENTUCKY
VIRGINIA
NORTH CAROLINA
GEORGIA
ALABAMA
Knoxville
Nashville
Chattanooga
Murfreesboro
Cookeville
Crossville
Cleveland
Huntsville
Dalton
Middlesboro
Williamsburg
Gatlinburg
Pigeon Forge
Oak Ridge
McMinnville
Tullahoma
Manchester
Shelbyville
Lebanon
Franklin
Gallatin
Hendersonville
Smyrna
Athens
Maryville
Sweetwater
Dayton
GREAT SMOKY MOUNTAINS NATIONAL PARK
CHATTAHOOCHEE NATIONAL FOREST
NANTAHALA NATIONAL FOREST
DANIEL BOONE NATIONAL FOREST
BIG SOUTH FORK NAT'L RIVER AND REC. AREA
CUMBERLAND GAP NAT'L HIST. PK.
Pg. 86
Pg. 150
Pg. 58
Pg. 10
CENTRAL TIME ZONE
EASTERN TIME ZONE
0793588-148

How to determine distance

Mileages in red between red arrowheads; in black, between intersections.

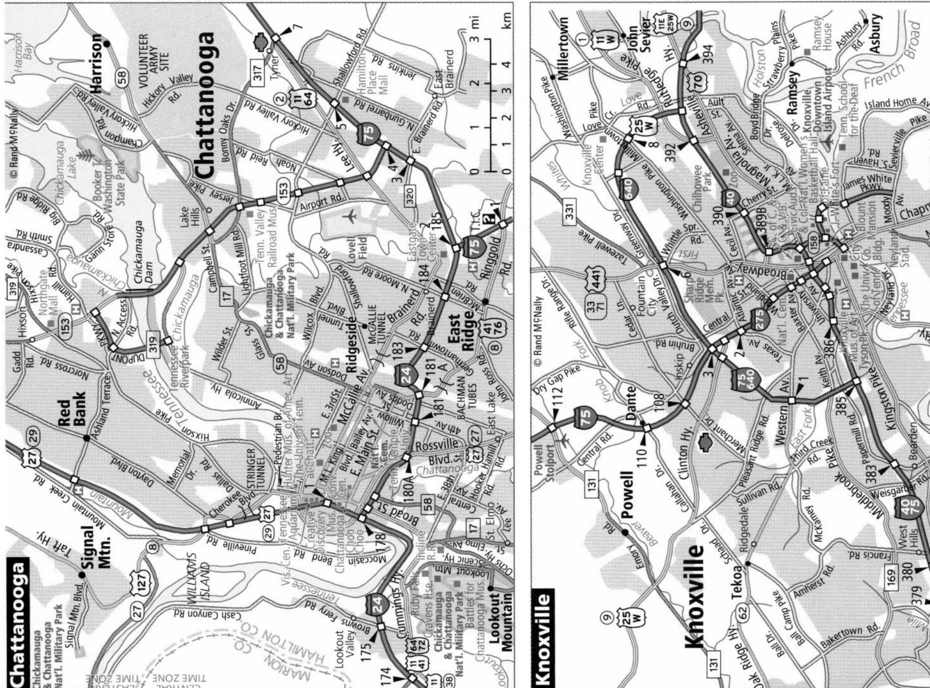
Chattanooga
Knoxville

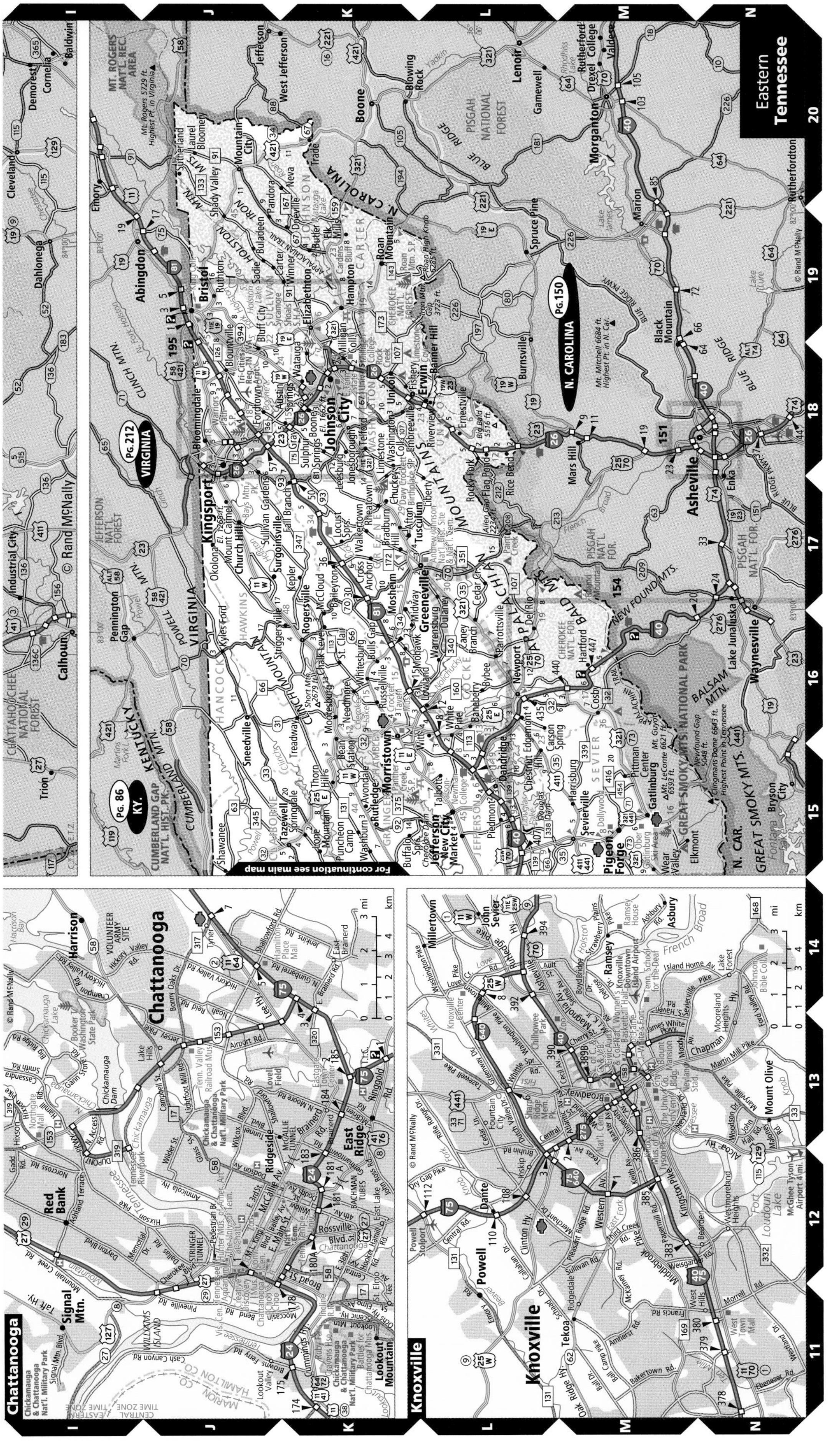

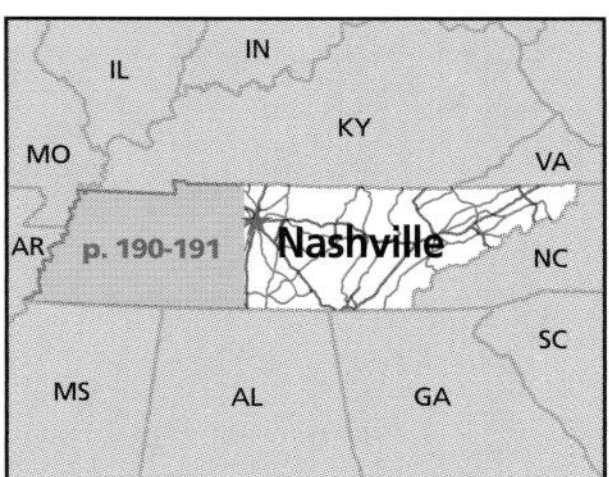
IL
IN
KY
MO
VA
AR
p. 190-191
Nashville
NC
SC
MS
AL
GA

SYMBOLS

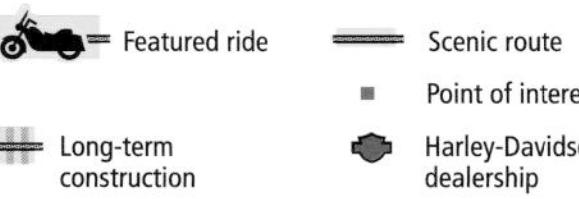
Featured ride
Scenic route
Point of interest
Long-term construction
Harley-Davidson dealership

HARLEY-DAVIDSON DEALERSHIPS

Thunder Creek Harley-Davidson, G-16
7720 Lee Hwy. **Chattanooga**
(423) 892-4888
Lat N 35.061 **Lon** W 85.133

Boswell's Harley-Davidson Shop of Cookeville, C-15
1424 Interstate Dr. **Cookeville**
(931) 526-3139
Lat N 36.138 **Lon** W 85.513

Harley-Davidson of Cool Springs, D-11
7128 S Springs Dr. **Franklin**
(615) 771-7775
Lat N 35.952 **Lon** W 86.816

Smoky Mountain Harley-Davidson, E-20
530 Parkway **Gatlinburg**
(865) 430-1602
Lat N 35.714 **Lon** W 83.511

Smith Brothers Harley-Davidson Sales, K-18
3518 Bristol Hwy. **Johnson City**
(423) 283-0422
Lat N 36.373 **Lon** W 82.374

Knoxville Harley-Davidson, D-19
5800 Clinton Hwy. **Knoxville**
(865) 689-2454
Lat N 36.007 **Lon** W 83.989

Knoxville Harley-Davidson West Shop, D-19
605 Lovell Rd. **Knoxville**
(865) 671-2454
Lat N 35.909 **Lon** W 84.149

Boswell's Harley-Davidson Shop, C-11
2200 Gallatin Pike N **Madison**
(615) 855-1001
Lat N 36.305 **Lon** W 86.689

Smoky Mountain Harley-Davidson, D-19
1820 W Lamar Alexander Pkwy. **Maryville**
(865) 977-1669
Lat N 35.755 **Lon** W 84.02

Colboch Harley-Davidson Sales, K-16
1830 N Davy Crockett Pkwy. **Morristown**
(423) 586-5343
Lat N 36.243 **Lon** W 83.266

Bumpus Harley-Davidson of Murfreesboro, D-12
2250 NW Broad St. **Murfreesboro**
(615) 849-8025
Lat N 35.883 **Lon** W 86.431

Boswell's Harley-Davidson, C-11
401 Fesslers Ln. **Nashville**
(615) 242-6067
Lat N 36.149 **Lon** W 86.743

C & S Harley-Davidson of Nashville, C-11
4600 Delaware Ave. **Nashville**
(615) 297-7500
Lat N 36.154 **Lon** W 86.842

Smoky Mountain Harley-Davidson, D-20
2530 Parkway, Ste. 3 **Pigeon Forge**
(865) 774-3445
Lat N 35.806 **Lon** W 83.577

Houston & Vicinity

Galveston

079808-9A

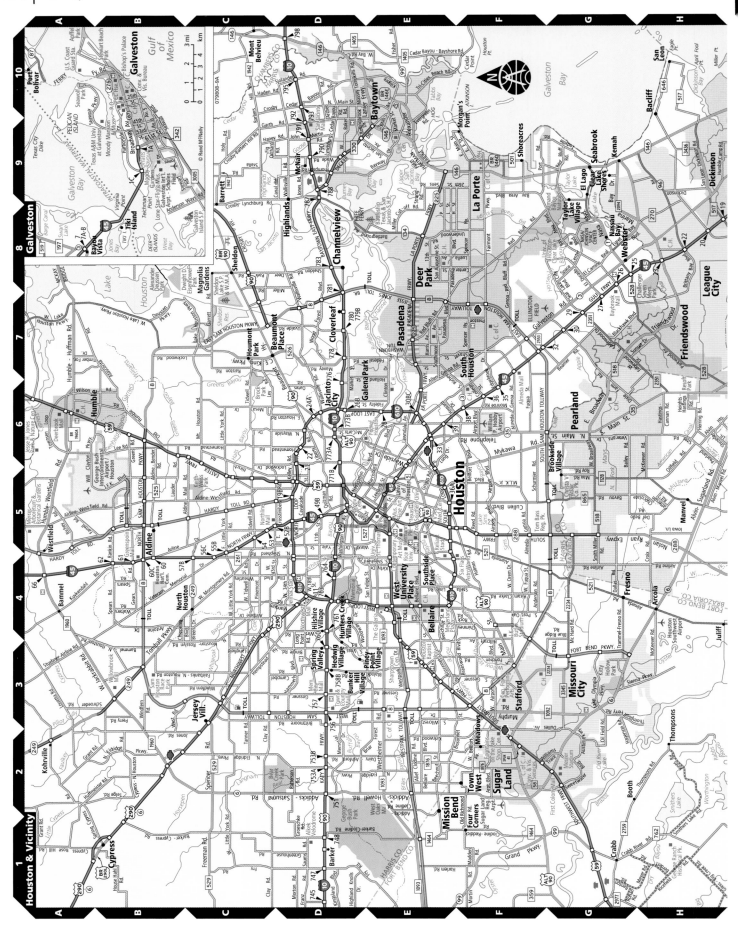

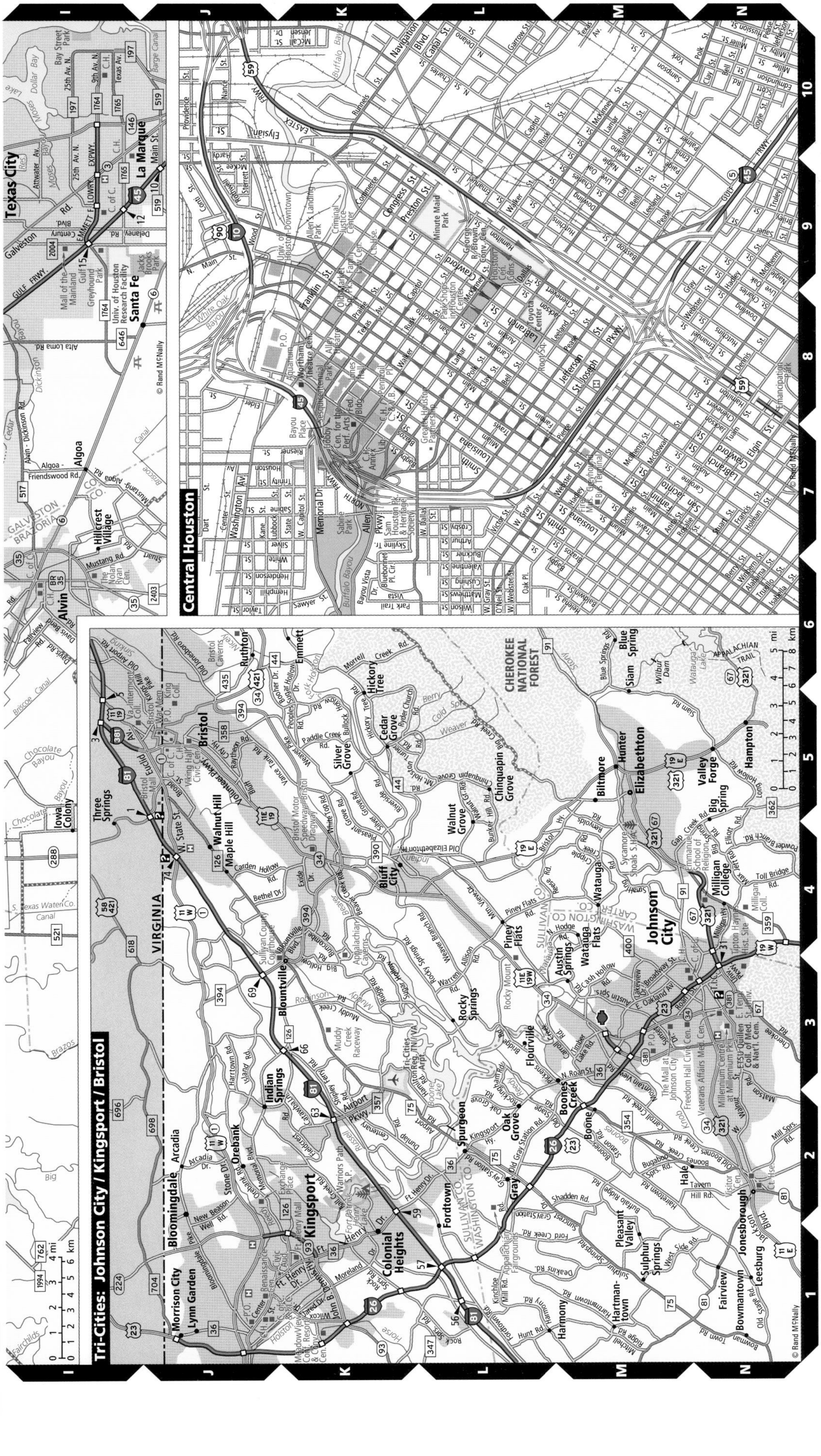

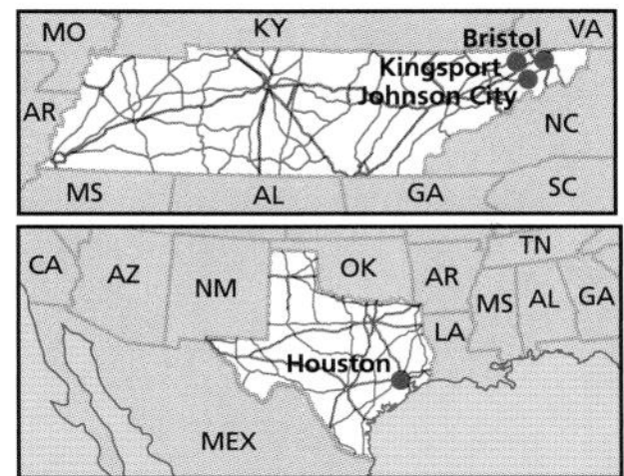
MO
KY
VA
Bristol
Kingsport
Johnson City
AR
NC
MS
AL
GA
SC

SYMBOLS

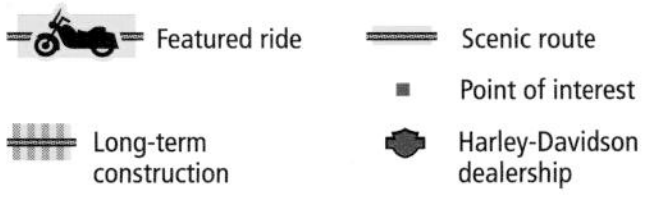

- Featured ride
- Scenic route
- Point of interest
- Long-term construction
- Harley-Davidson dealership

HARLEY-DAVIDSON DEALERSHIPS

Mancuso Harley-Davidson Central, D-5
535 North Loop **Houston**
(713) 880-5666
Lat N 29.814 **Lon** W 95.393

Mancuso Harley-Davidson, B-2
12710 Crossroads Park Dr. **Houston**
(281) 970-9700
Lat N 29.915 **Lon** W 95.609

Stubbs Harley-Davidson, E-6
4400 Telephone Rd. **Houston**
(713) 644-7535
Lat N 29.7 **Lon** W 95.303

San Jacinto Harley-Davidson, F-7
3636 E Sam Houston Pkwy. S **Pasadena**
(281) 991-4275
Lat N 29.657 **Lon** W 95.157

Republic Harley-Davidson, F-2
12707 Southwest Frwy. **Stafford**
(281) 295-1000
Lat N 29.637 **Lon** W 95.583

Central Houston

Tri-Cities: Johnson City / Kingsport / Bristol

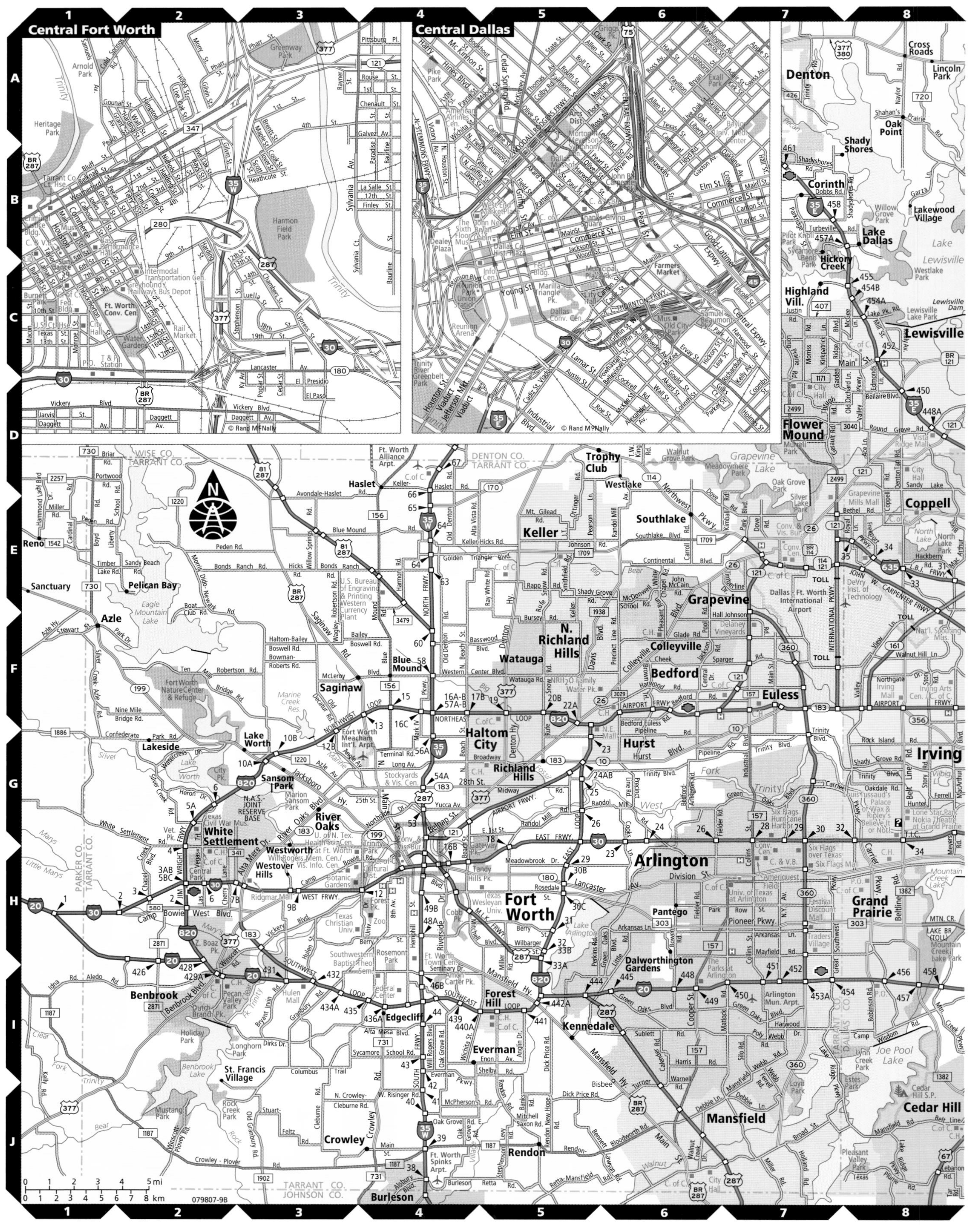
Central Fort Worth
Central Dallas
Denton
Corinth
Lake Dallas
Hickory Creek
Highland Vill.
Lewisville
Flower Mound
Coppell
Trophy Club
Westlake
Southlake
Keller
Grapevine
Colleyville
Haslet
N. Richland Hills
Watauga
Bedford
Euless
Irving
Blue Mound
Saginaw
Reno
Sanctuary
Pelican Bay
Azle
Lake Worth
Lakeside
Sansom Park
Haltom City
Richland Hills
Hurst
River Oaks
White Settlement
Westworth
Westover Hills
Arlington
Fort Worth
Pantego
Grand Prairie
Dalworthington Gardens
Benbrook
Edgecliff
Forest Hill
Kennedale
Everman
St. Francis Village
Crowley
Rendon
Mansfield
Cedar Hill
Burleson
Dallas / Ft. Worth International Airport
Ft. Worth Alliance Arpt.
Ft. Worth Meacham Int'l. Arpt.
Arlington Mun. Arpt.
Ft. Worth Spinks Arpt.
Eagle Mountain Lake
Grapevine Lake
Lewisville Lake
Lake Arlington
Benbrook Lake
Joe Pool Lake
Mountain Creek Lake
WISE CO.
TARRANT CO.
DENTON CO.
DALLAS CO.
PARKER CO.
JOHNSON CO.
© Rand McNally
079807-9B

Dallas / Fort Worth & Vicinity

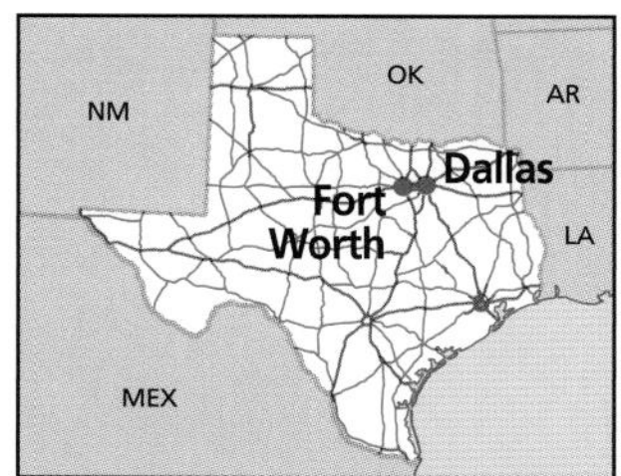
NM
OK
AR
Fort Worth
Dallas
LA
MEX

SYMBOLS

- Featured ride
- Scenic route
- Point of interest
- Long-term construction
- Harley-Davidson dealership

HARLEY-DAVIDSON DEALERSHIPS

Harley-Davidson of Dallas, B-12
304 Central Expy. S (US 75) **Allen**
(214) 495-0259
Lat N 33.099 **Lon** W 96.679

Texas Harley-Davidson, F-6
1839 Airport Frwy. **Bedford**
(817) 267-2646
Lat N 32.837 **Lon** W 97.137

Harley-Davidson of North Texas, D-9
1910 Old Denton Rd. **Carrollton**
(972) 245-1492
Lat N 32.965 **Lon** W 96.913

American Eagle Harley-Davidson, B-7
5920 S I-35 E **Corinth**
(940) 498-5000
Lat N 33.153 **Lon** W 97.062

Ft. Worth Harley-Davidson, H-2
3025 W Loop 820 S **Fort Worth**
(817) 696-9090
Lat N 32.73 **Lon** W 97.481

Dallas Harley-Davidson, F-12
1334 W Centerville Rd. **Garland**
(972) 270-3962
Lat N 32.857 **Lon** W 96.648

Longhorn Harley-Davidson, H-7
2618 W I-20 **Grand Prairie**
(972) 988-1903
Lat N 32.673 **Lon** W 97.024

Distance scale
One inch represents about 33 miles
0 5 10 15 20 25 30 35 mi
0 10 20 30 40 50 km

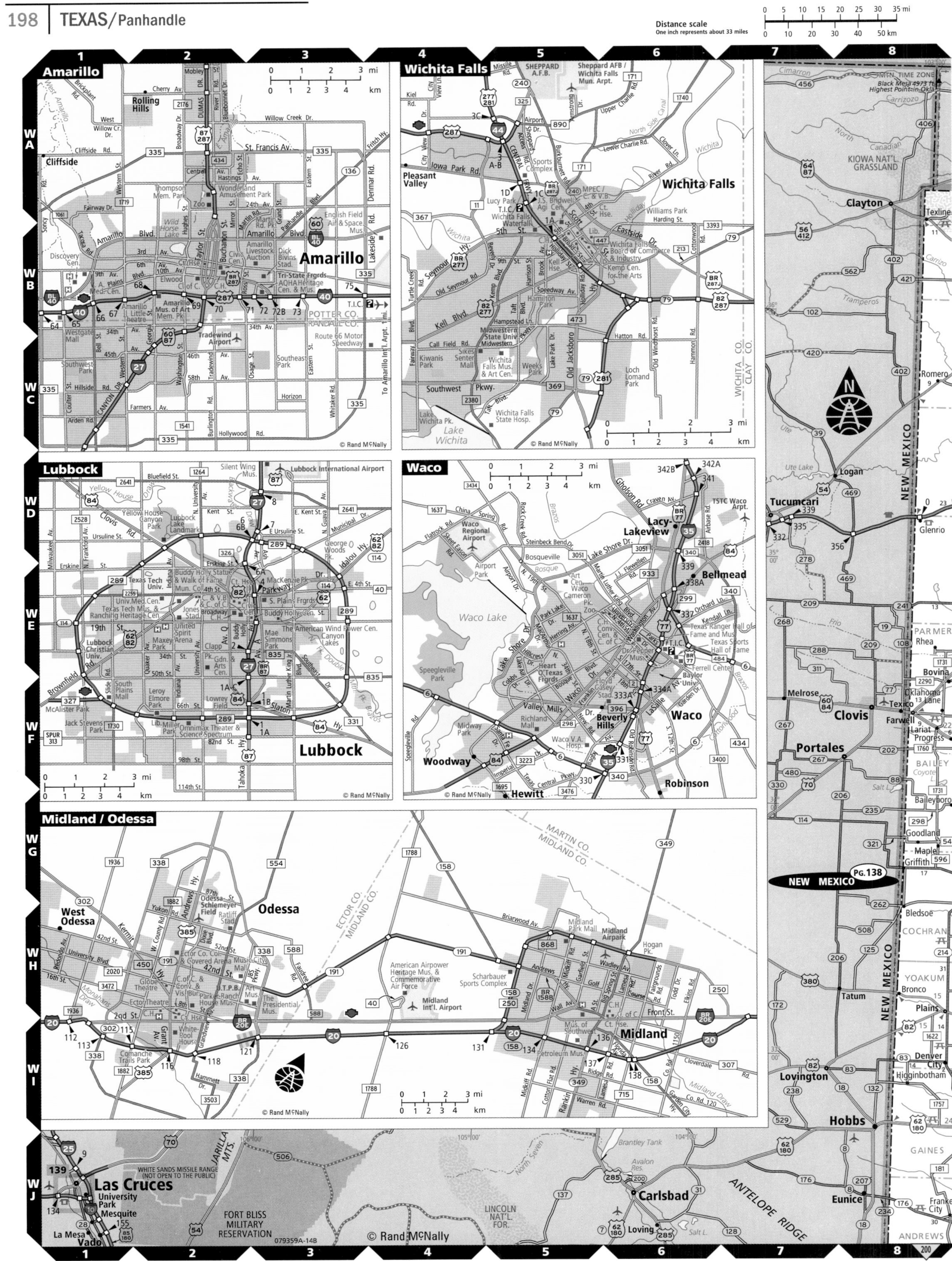

Amarillo
Wichita Falls
Lubbock
Waco
Midland / Odessa
Las Cruces
Carlsbad
Hobbs
Clovis
Portales
Tucumcari
Clayton
Lovington
Eunice
Logan
NEW MEXICO
NEW MEXICO PG. 138
KIOWA NAT'L. GRASSLAND
FORT BLISS MILITARY RESERVATION
WHITE SANDS MISSILE RANGE (NOT OPEN TO THE PUBLIC)
LINCOLN NAT'L. FOR.
ANTELOPE RIDGE
West Odessa
Odessa
Midland
Lacy-Lakeview
Bellmead
Woodway
Hewitt
Robinson
Beverly Hills
Pleasant Valley
Cliffside
Rolling Hills
© Rand McNally
079359A-14B

How to determine distance

Mileages in red between red arrowheads; in black, between intersections.

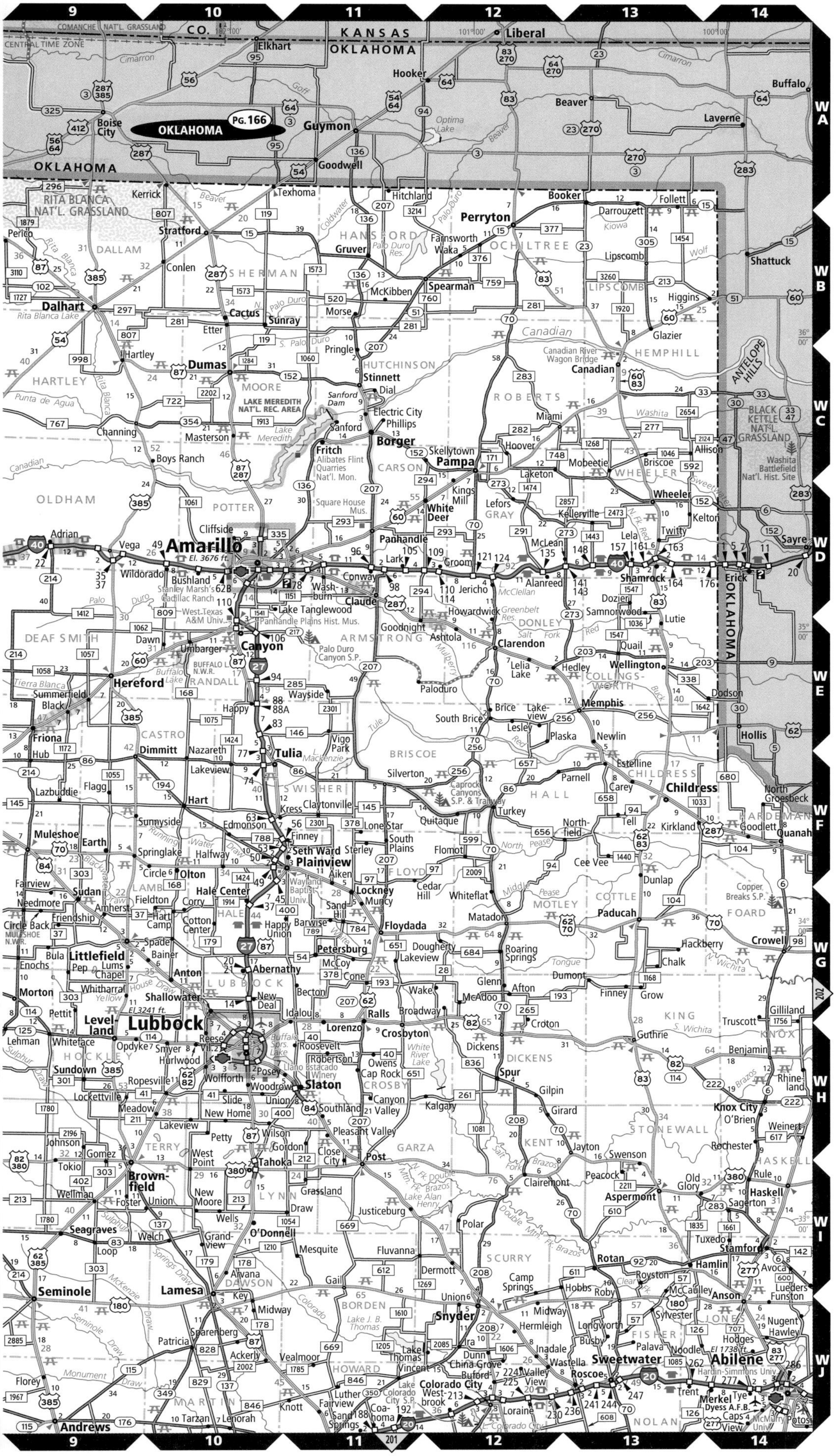

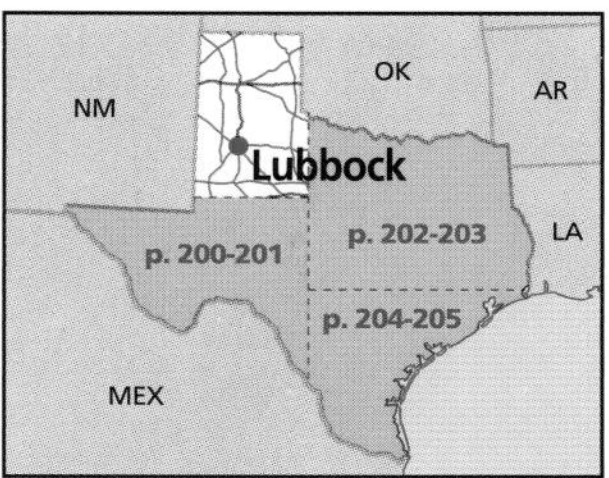
NM
OK
AR
Lubbock
p. 200-201
p. 202-203
LA
p. 204-205
MEX

SYMBOLS

- Featured ride
- Scenic route
- Point of interest
- Long-term construction
- Harley-Davidson dealership

TEXAS MOTORCYCLE LAWS

Helmet use:
Required under age 21; not required over 21 with successful completion of rider training or $10,000 medical insurance

Riding two abreast:
No reference in administrative code or statutes

Eye protection:
Not required

Speed limit:
Primary roads: 75 mph
Secondary roads: 70 mph

TEXAS RESOURCES

Road conditions or construction:
(800) 452-9292
www.dot.state.tx.us

Highway Emergency Numbers:
911

Tourism:
(800) 888-8839 (to request travel materials only)
www.traveltex.com

State motor vehicle information:
(512) 424-2600
www.txdps.state.tx.us

HARLEY-DAVIDSON DEALERSHIPS

Kent's Harley-Davidson Sales, WJ-14
3106 S Clack **Abilene**
(325) 673-7103
Lat N 32.415 **Lon** W 99.778

Tripp's Harley-Davidson, WD-10
6040 I-40 W **Amarillo**
(806) 352-2021
Lat N 35.19 **Lon** W 101.905

Wild West Harley-Davidson, WH-10
5702 58th St. **Lubbock**
(866) 791-4597
Lat N 33.541 **Lon** W 101.937

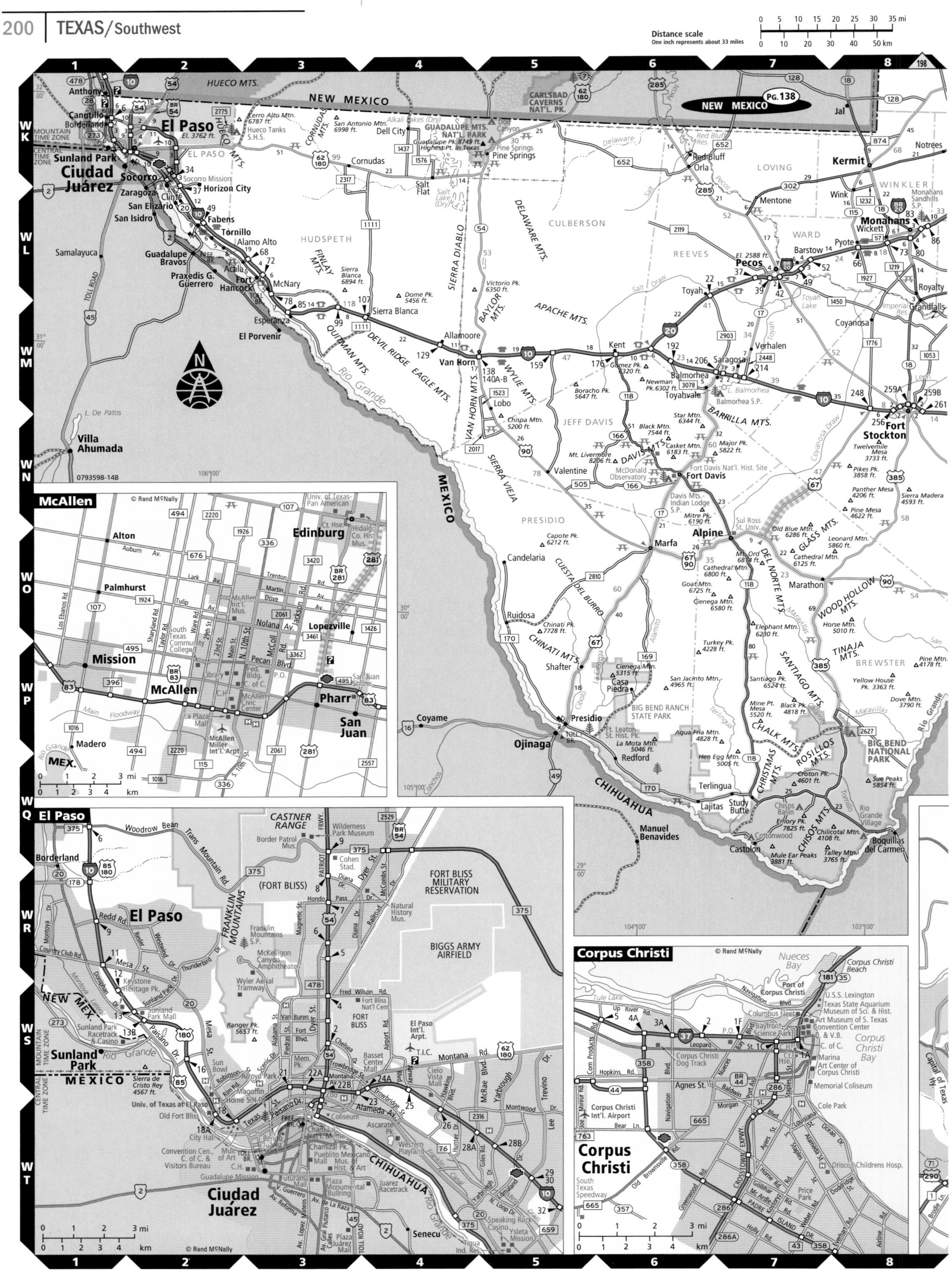
Distance scale
One inch represents about 33 miles
0 5 10 15 20 25 30 35 mi
0 10 20 30 40 50 km
198
NEW MEXICO
NEW MEXICO PG. 138
HUECO MTS.
CARLSBAD CAVERNS NAT'L. PK.
GUADALUPE MTS. NAT'L. PARK
Guadalupe Pk. 8749 ft. Highest Pt. in Texas
Pine Springs
Dell City
Cornudas
Salt Flat
Anthony
Canutillo
Borderland
El Paso
El. 3762 ft.
Sunland Park
Ciudad Juárez
Socorro
Horizon City
Zaragoza
Clint
San Elizario
San Isidro
Fabens
Tornillo
Alamo Alto
Guadalupe Bravos
Praxedis G. Guerrero
Acala
Fort Hancock
McNary
Esperanza
El Porvenir
Samalayuca
Sierra Blanca
Allamoore
Van Horn
Lobo
Valentine
Kent
Toyah
Pecos
El. 2588 ft.
Barstow
Pyote
Wickett
Monahans
Kermit
Wink
Mentone
Orla
Red Bluff
Jal
Notrees
Royalty
Grandfalls
Coyanosa
Verhalen
Saragosa
Balmorhea
Toyahvale
Balmorhea S.P.
Fort Stockton
Fort Davis
Fort Davis Nat'l. Hist. Site
McDonald Observatory
Davis Mts. Indian Lodge S.P.
Alpine
Sul Ross St. Univ.
Marfa
Marathon
Candelaria
Ruidosa
Shafter
Presidio
Ojinaga
Casa Piedra
Redford
Lajitas
Terlingua
Study Butte
Castolon
Rio Grande Village
Boquillas del Carmen
Manuel Benavides
Coyame
Villa Ahumada
BIG BEND RANCH STATE PARK
BIG BEND NATIONAL PARK
HUDSPETH
CULBERSON
LOVING
WINKLER
WARD
REEVES
JEFF DAVIS
PRESIDIO
BREWSTER
MEXICO
CHIHUAHUA
Rio Grande
DELAWARE MTS.
SIERRA DIABLO
BAYLOR MTS.
APACHE MTS.
VAN HORN MTS.
WYLIE MTS.
DEVIL RIDGE
EAGLE MTS.
QUITMAN MTS.
FINLAY MTS.
CORNUDAS MTS.
SIERRA VIEJA
DAVIS MTS.
BARRILLA MTS.
CUESTA DEL BURRO
CHINATI MTS.
DEL NORTE MTS.
GLASS MTS.
WOOD HOLLOW MTS.
SANTIAGO MTS.
TINAJA MTS.
CHALK MTS.
CHRISTMAS MTS.
ROSILLOS MTS.
CHISOS MTS.
McAllen
Edinburg
Alton
Palmhurst
Mission
Lopezville
Pharr
San Juan
Madero
MEX.
El Paso
FORT BLISS MILITARY RESERVATION
BIGGS ARMY AIRFIELD
FRANKLIN MOUNTAINS
CASTNER RANGE
Ciudad Juárez
Sunland Park
MEXICO
CHIHUAHUA
Senecu
Corpus Christi
Corpus Christi Bay
Nueces Bay
Corpus Christi Beach
U.S.S. Lexington
Texas State Aquarium
Corpus Christi Int'l. Airport
© Rand McNally

How to determine distance

Mileages in red between red arrowheads; in black, between intersections.

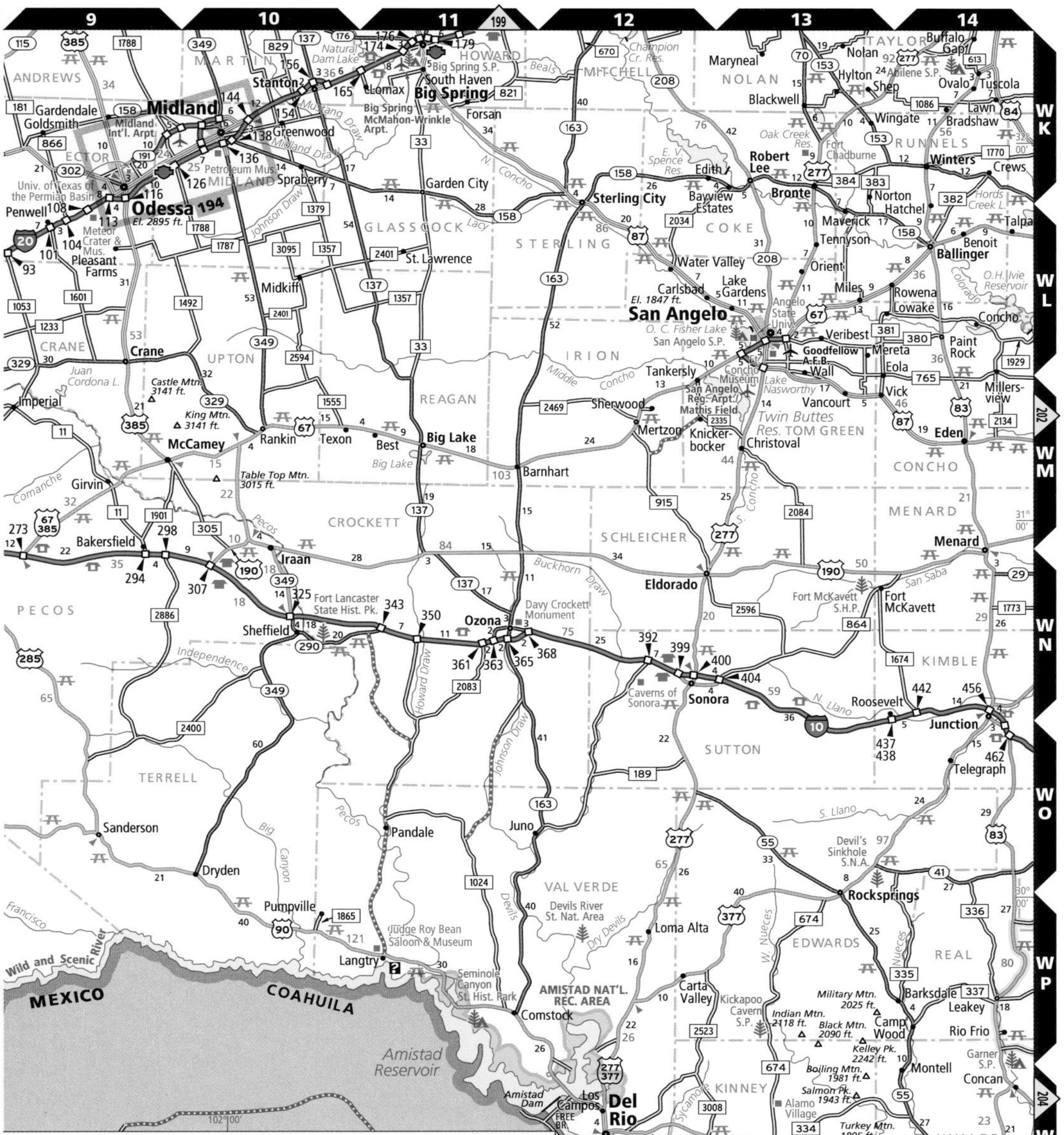

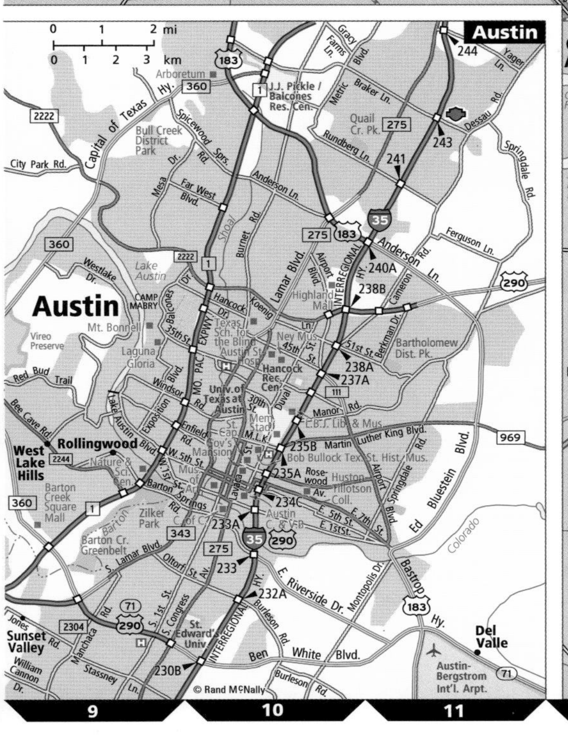

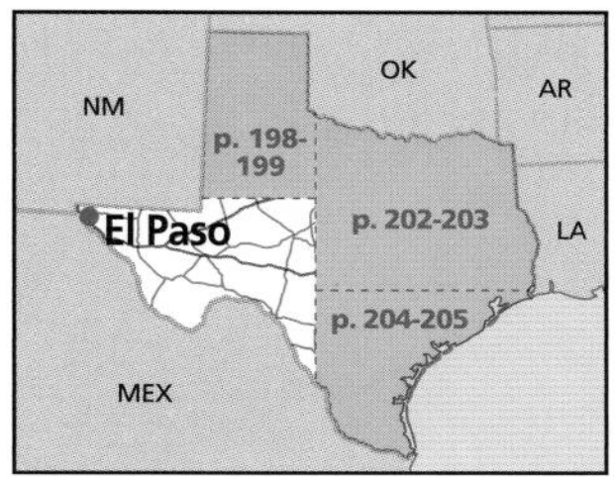

NM
OK
AR
p. 198-199
El Paso
p. 202-203
LA
p. 204-205
MEX

SYMBOLS

- Featured ride
- Scenic route
- Point of interest
- Long-term construction
- Harley-Davidson dealership

CITY-TO-CITY MILEAGE

	ABILENE	AMARILLO	DALLAS	EL PASO	LUBBOCK	ODESSA	SAN ANGELO	SAN ANTONIO
Abilene		283	185	447	165	168	92	261
Amarillo	283		359	432	118	258	300	512
Big Bend NP	379	469	565	324	351	213	290	446
Big Spring	108	225	294	340	107	61	86	299
Carlsbad, NM	276	296	462	165	179	139	255	458
Childress	155	117	242	556	147	277	226	417
Clovis, NM	269	103	455	314	104	203	286	498
Dallas	185	359		633	351	354	262	277
Del Rio	247	449	425	424	331	250	155	151
Eagle Pass	302	504	416	479	386	305	210	139
El Paso	447	432	633		344	281	402	558
Fort Stockton	252	342	438	238	224	86	163	319
Houston	347	605	247	753	519	546	363	199
Lubbock	165	118	351	344		140	182	394
Midland	147	235	333	301	117	22	111	331
Odessa	168	258	354	281	140		131	351
Pecos	242	332	428	207	214	76	205	374
Perryton	307	121	396	524	239	379	378	569
San Angelo	92	300	262	402	182	131		213
San Antonio	261	512	277	558	394	351	213	
Van Horn	328	418	514	119	300	162	283	439

HARLEY-DAVIDSON DEALERSHIPS

The Harley-Davidson Shop, WK-11
908 W 3rd St. **Big Spring**
(432) 263-2322
Lat N 32.249 **Lon** W 101.486

Barnett Harley-Davidson, WK-2
8272 Gateway Blvd. E **El Paso**
(915) 592-5804
Lat N 31.742 **Lon** W 106.329

Legacy Harley-Davidson, WK-9
12100 W Hwy. 80 E **Odessa**
(432) 561-8991
Lat N 31.907 **Lon** W 102.247

Distance scale
One inch represents about 33 miles
0 5 10 15 20 25 30 35 mi
0 10 20 30 40 50 km

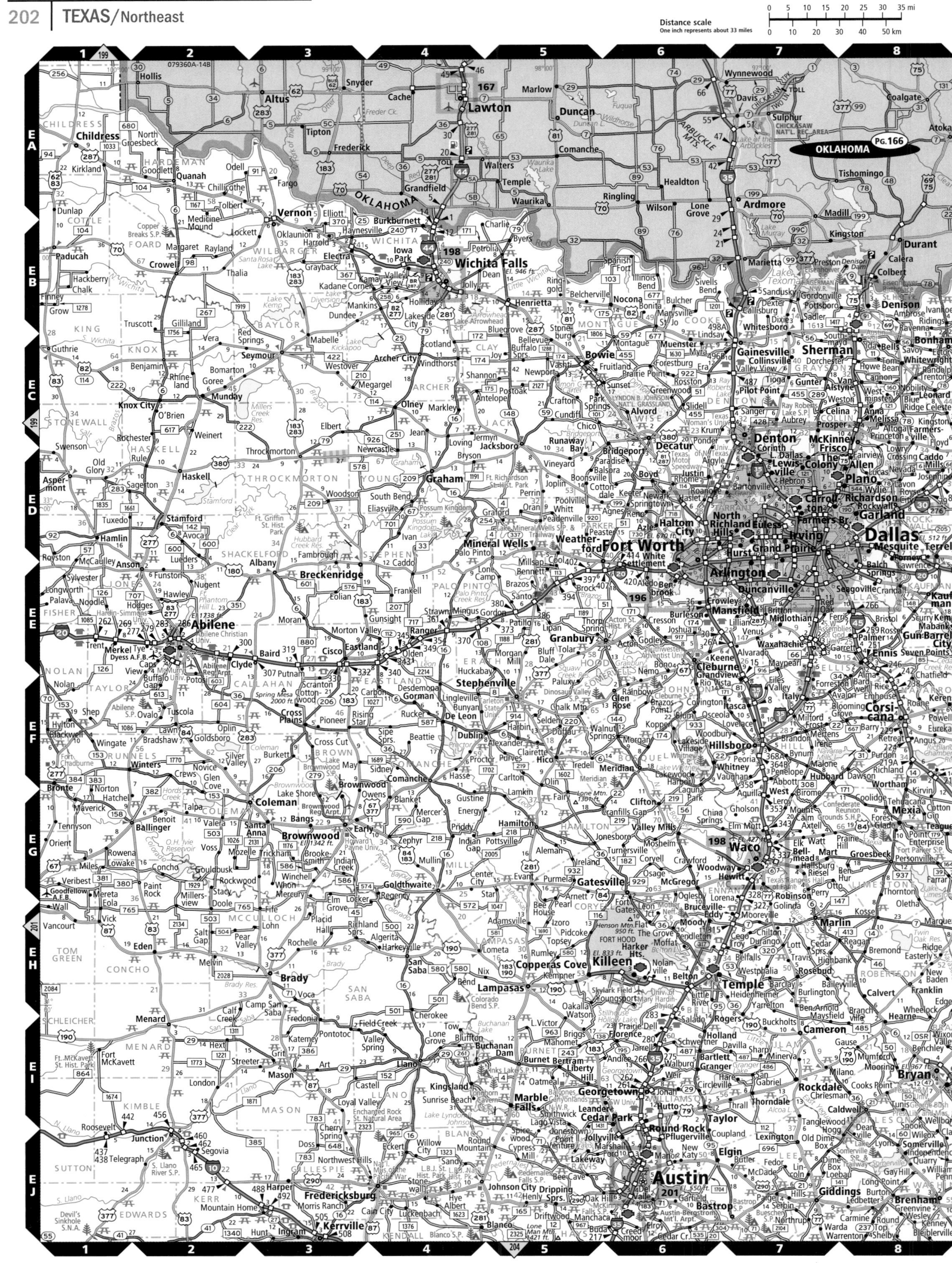
OKLAHOMA
PG. 166
Lawton
Wichita Falls
Abilene
Fort Worth
Dallas
Arlington
Denton
Sherman
Waco
Temple
Killeen
Austin
Brownwood
San Angelo
Childress
Vernon
Graham
Stephenville
Mineral Wells
Weatherford
Granbury
Cleburne
Hillsboro
Corsicana
Ennis
Waxahachie
Mexia
Lampasas
Brady
Llano
Fredericksburg
Kerrville
Junction
Georgetown
Round Rock
Bastrop
Giddings
Bryan
Ardmore
Duncan
Altus

How to determine distance

Mileages in red between red arrowheads; in black, between intersections.

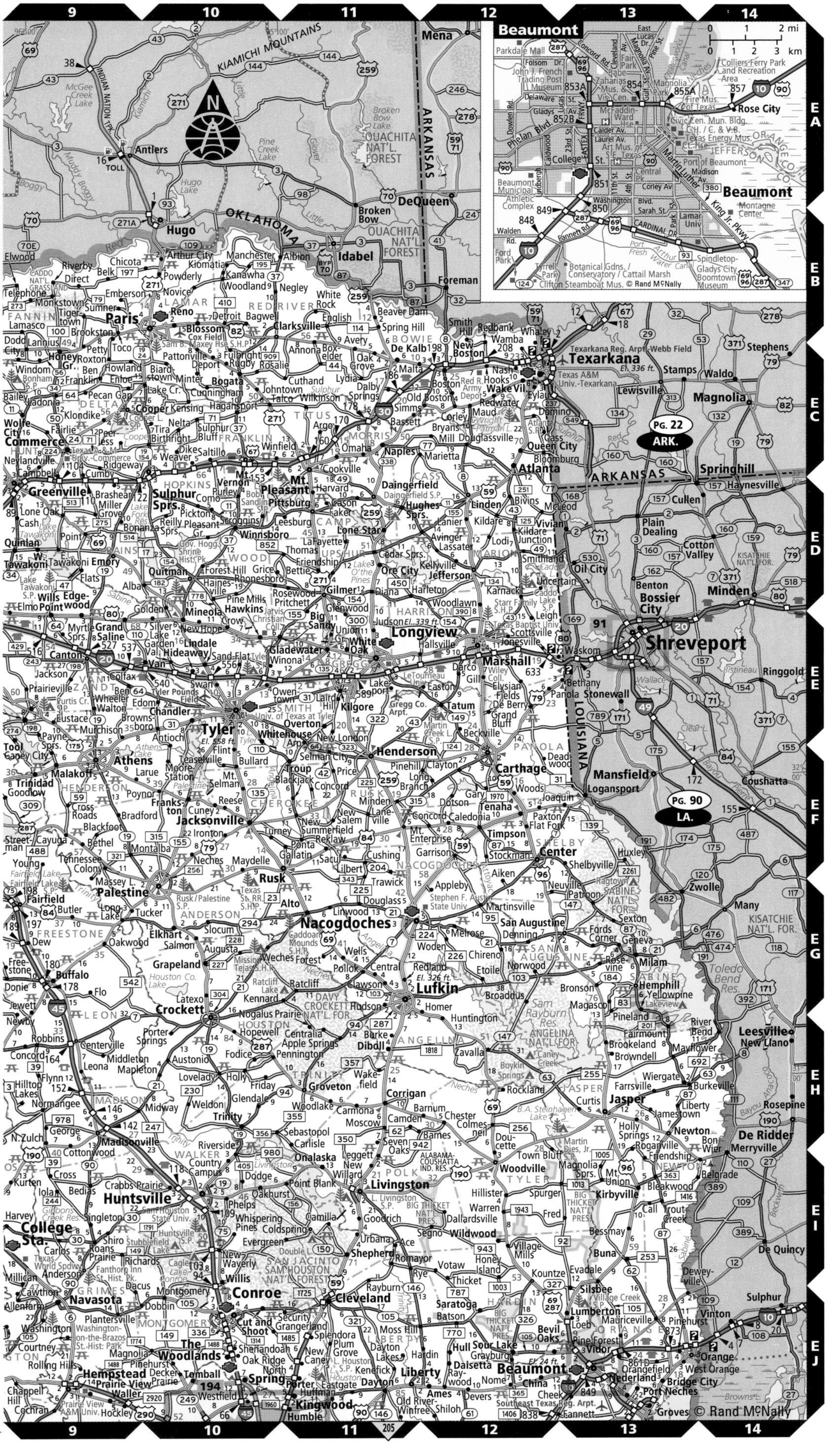

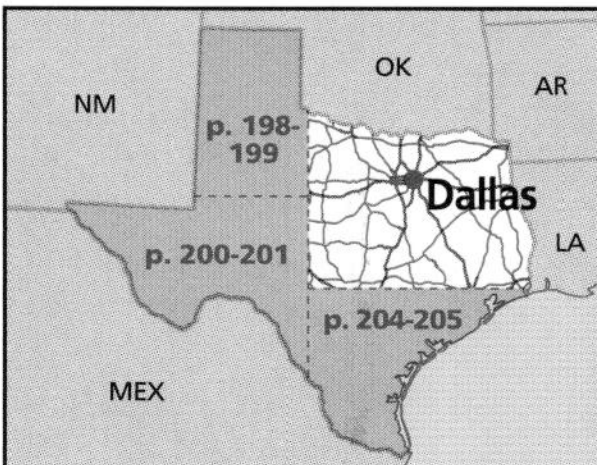
NM
OK
AR
p. 198-199
Dallas
LA
p. 200-201
p. 204-205
MEX

HARLEY-DAVIDSON DEALERSHIPS

For the Dallas/Fort Worth metro area, please see dealer listings on page 197.

- **Central Texas Harley-Davidson, EJ-6**
  804 E Braker Ln. (Exit 243) **Austin**
  (512) 973-8521
  Lat N 30.377 **Lon** W 97.675
- **Cowboy Harley-Davidson, EJ-6**
  10917 S I-35 (Exit 225) **Austin**
  (512) 448-4294
  Lat N 30.14 **Lon** W 97.765
- **Cowboy Harley-Davidson of Beaumont, EJ-13**
  1150 I-10 S **Beaumont**
  (409) 840-6969
  Lat N 30.065 **Lon** W 94.175
- **Independence Harley-Davidson, EI-9**
  4101 State Hwy. 6 S **College Station**
  (979) 690-1669
  Lat N 30.576 **Lon** W 96.278
- **Texan Harley-Davidson, EJ-10**
  2111 N Frazier St. **Conroe**
  (936) 539-1726
  Lat N 30.334 **Lon** W 95.467
- **Ft. Hood Harley-Davidson, EH-6**
  875 W Central Texas Expy. **Harker Heights**
  (254) 680-4747
  Lat N 31.075 **Lon** W 97.684
- **The Harley Shop, EE-11**
  3400 N 4th St. **Longview**
  (903) 663-3838
  Lat N 32.544 **Lon** W 94.731
- **Texas Thunder Harley-Davidson Shop, EG-11**
  2518 NW Stallings Dr. **Nacogdoches**
  (936) 715-0100
  Lat N 31.624 **Lon** W 94.684
- **Paris Harley-Davidson, EB-10**
  2875 NE Loop 286 **Paris**
  (903) 784-6392
  Lat N 33.675 **Lon** W 95.523
- **Texoma Harley-Davidson, EB-8**
  4000 N US Hwy. 75 **Sherman**
  (903) 892-2530
  Lat N 33.653 **Lon** W 96.607
- **Horny Toad Harley-Davidson, EH-6**
  720 N Gen Bruce Dr. **Temple**
  (254) 773-2243
  Lat N 31.109 **Lon** W 97.357
- **Doolins Harley-Davidson, EC-12**
  4810 W 7th **Texarkana**
  (903) 832-4366
  Lat N 33.418 **Lon** W 94.105
- **Harley-Davidson of the Woodlands, EJ-10**
  25545 I-45 N **The Woodlands**
  (281) 681-0099
  Lat N 30.141 **Lon** W 95.468
- **Lone Star Harley-Davidson, EE-10**
  1211 SSE Loop 323 **Tyler**
  (903) 597-1488
  Lat N 32.335 **Lon** W 95.266
- **Harley-Davidson of Waco, EG-7**
  4201 S Jack Kultgen Fwy. **Waco**
  (254) 753-0393
  Lat N 31.506 **Lon** W 97.144
- **Red River Harley-Davidson, EB-4**
  4514 US 287 NW Fwy. **Wichita Falls**
  (940) 264-7743
  Lat N 33.950 **Lon** W 98.554

Distance scale
One inch represents about 33 miles
0 5 10 15 20 25 30 35 mi
0 10 20 30 40 50 km

San Antonio
Corpus Christi
Laredo
Nuevo Laredo
Monterrey
San Nicholas de los Garzas
Guadalupe
Reynosa
Matamoros
Brownsville
McAllen
Harlingen
Victoria
New Braunfels
San Marcos
Seguin
Uvalde
Kingsville
Alice
Beeville
Pleasanton
Floresville
Cuero
Yoakum
Gonzales
Lockhart
Luling
Kyle
Edinburg
Weslaco
Mission
Pharr
Rio Grande City
Roma
Zapata
Hebbronville
Falfurrias
Raymondville
Port Isabel
South Padre Island
Rockport
Aransas Pass
Port Aransas
Ingleside
Portland
Sinton
Mathis
George West
Three Rivers
Pearsall
Dilley
Cotulla
Carrizo Springs
Crystal City
Hondo
Castroville
Boerne
Comfort
Bandera
Schulenburg
Hallettsville
Edna
Port Lavaca
Goliad
Refugio
Freer
Premont
MEXICO
COAHUILA
NUEVO LEÓN
TAMAULIPAS
MATAGORDA ISLAND
SAN JOSE ISLAND
PADRE ISLAND NATIONAL SEASHORE
PADRE ISLAND
© Rand McNally
079360B-14B

How to determine distance

Mileages in red between red arrowheads; in black, between intersections.

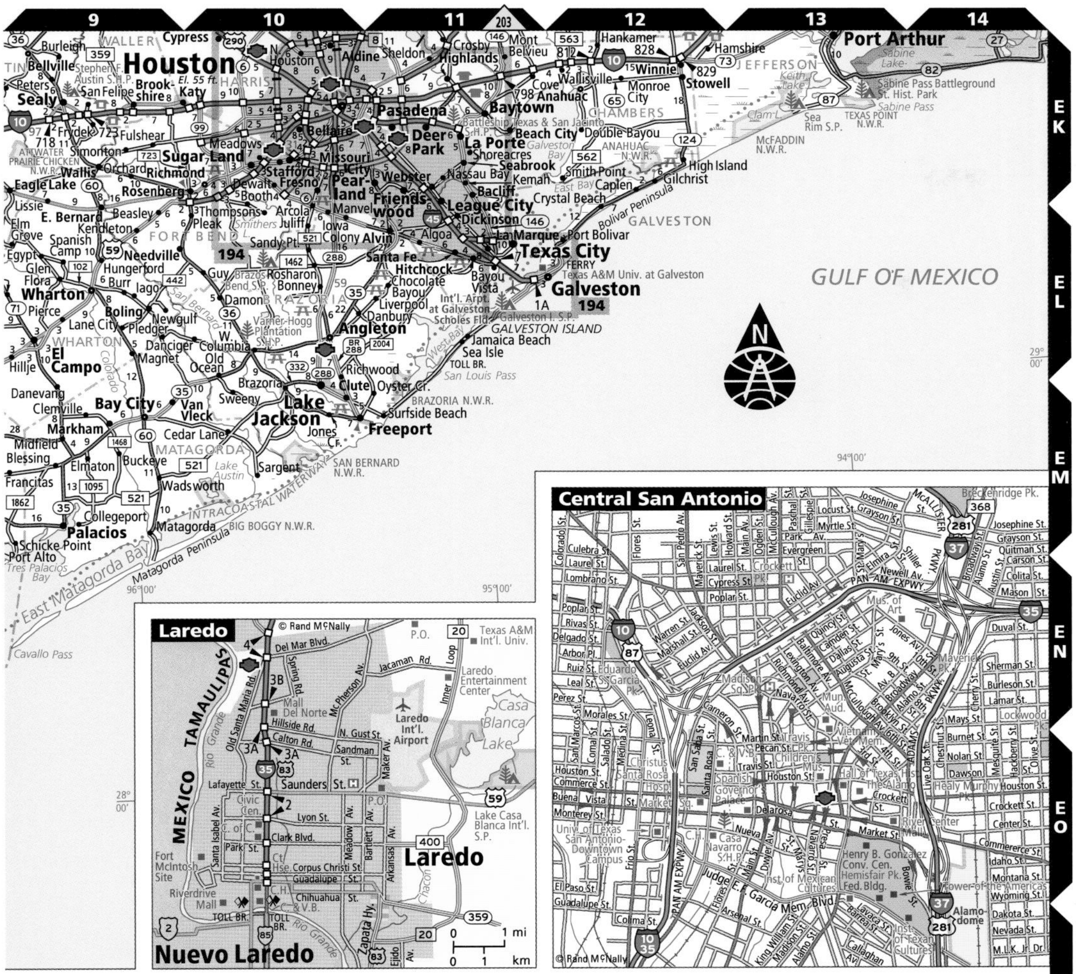

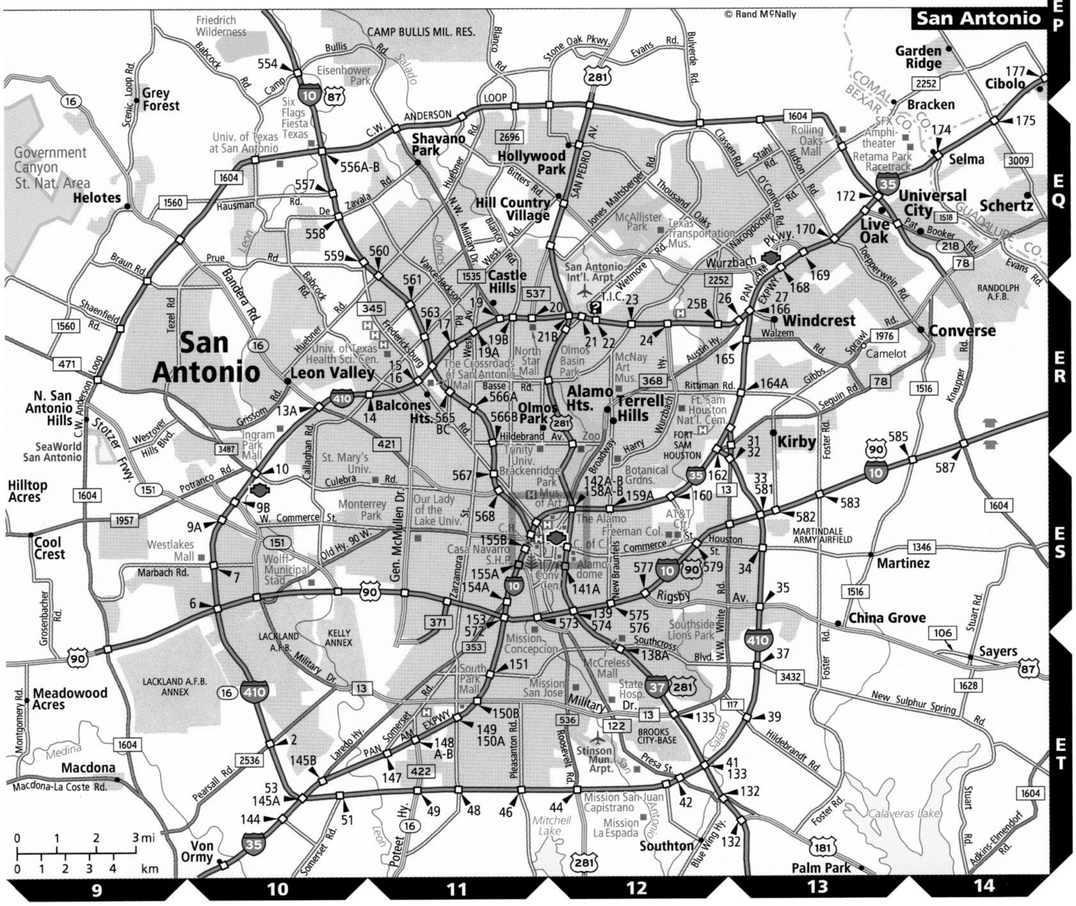

Central San Antonio

Laredo

San Antonio

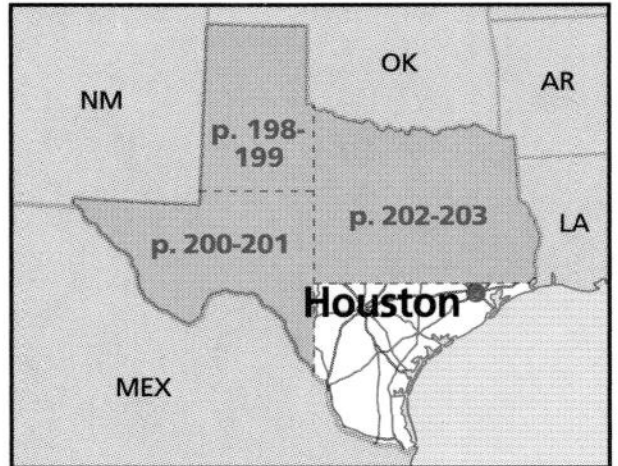
NM
OK
AR
p. 198-199
p. 202-203
p. 200-201
LA
Houston
MEX

SYMBOLS

Featured ride — Scenic route — Long-term construction — Harley-Davidson dealership

CITY-TO-CITY MILEAGE

	ABILENE	AUSTIN	BROWNSVILLE	CORPUS CHRISTI	DALLAS	HOUSTON	SAN ANTONIO	SHREVEPORT, LA
Abilene		230	539	405	185	347	261	373
Austin	230		352	218	195	162	82	327
Beaumont	467	246	443	303	294	88	283	195
Brownsville	539	352		159	547	355	278	593
Corpus Christi	405	218	159		413	215	144	453
Dallas	185	195	547	413		247	277	186
Fort Worth	155	190	542	408	30	267	272	216
Galveston	394	209	386	232	294	47	246	286
Houston	347	162	355	215	247		199	239
Laredo	409	232	203	141	427	349	150	559
Lufkin	359	222	473	333	182	119	313	119
McAllen	497	310	60	152	505	348	236	586
Paris	294	304	656	522	109	310	386	150
San Angelo	92	206	491	357	262	363	213	450
San Antonio	261	82	278	144	277	199		409
Shreveport, LA	373	327	593	453	186	239	409	
Texarkana	362	372	646	506	177	292	454	71
Tyler	285	228	580	446	98	206	310	99
Waco	191	99	451	317	96	188	181	228

HARLEY-DAVIDSON DEALERSHIPS

For the Houston metro area, please see dealer listings on page 195.

Goe Harley-Davidson, EL-10
1350 S Hwy. 288-B **Angleton**
(979) 849-3681
Lat N 29.17 **Lon** W 95.452

Javelina Harley-Davidson, EK-4
29078 W I-10 **Boerne**
(800) 860-9696
Lat N 29.818 **Lon** W 98.72

Corpus Christi Harley-Davidson, EP-6
502 S Padre Island Dr. **Corpus Christi**
(361) 854-3146
Lat N 27.758 **Lon** W 97.462

Laredo Harley-Davidson, EP-2
7080 San Bernardo **Laredo**
(956) 717-8763
Lat N 27.57 **Lon** W 99.504

Gruene Harley-Davidson, EK-5
1288 Loop 337 **New Braunfels**
(830) 624-2473
Lat N 29.725 **Lon** W 98.110

RGV Harley-Davidson, ES-5
1007 E Expy. 83 **Pharr**
(956) 782-4243
Lat N 26.206 **Lon** W 98.17

Alamo City Harley-Davidson, EL-5
11005 I-35 N **San Antonio**
(210) 646-0499
Lat N 29.539 **Lon** W 98.381

Alamo City Harley-Davidson, EL-4
111 W Crockett St. Ste. 206 **San Antonio**
(210) 212-4461
Lat N 29.425 **Lon** W 98.489

Caliente Harley-Davidson, EL-4
7230 NW Loop 410 **San Antonio**
(210) 681-2254
Lat N 29.452 **Lon** W 98.63

Roadrunner Harley-Davidson Shop, ES-6
3515 W Expy. 83 **San Benito**
(956) 399-4244
Lat N 26.123 **Lon** W 97.634

Victoria Harley-Davidson, EM-7
608 N Moody St. **Victoria**
(361) 575-7881
Lat N 28.804 **Lon** W 97.007

Ogden
Provo
© Rand McNally
WYOMING
IDAHO
NEVADA
PG. 64 IDAHO
PG. 234 WY.
PG. 130 NEVADA
Salt Lake City
Ogden
Provo
Orem
Logan
Evanston
Tooele
Wendover
West Wendover
Great Salt Lake
4212 ft. Above Sea Level
GREAT SALT LAKE DESERT
DUGWAY PROVING GROUND (NO PUBLIC ACCESS)
TEST AND TRAINING RANGE (NO PUBLIC ACCESS)
LAKESIDE MTS.
HOGUP MTS.
CEDAR MTS.
DUGWAY RANGE
DEEP CREEK RANGE
FISH SPRINGS RANGE
GROUSE CREEK MTS.
NEWFOUNDLAND MTS.
TERRACE MTS.
HANSEL MTS.
UINTA MTS.
WASATCH RANGE
UINTAH AND OURAY INDIAN RESERVATION
GOSHUTE INDIAN RES.
SKULL VALLEY IND. RES.
HILL AIR FORCE BASE
DWIGHT D. EISENHOWER HY.
Bear Lake
Utah Lake
Bountiful
Farmington
Kaysville
Layton
Clearfield
Roy
Brigham City
Tremonton
Park City
Heber City
Sandy
Draper
Lehi
American Fk.
Pleasant Grove
Springville
Spanish Fk.
Payson
Nephi
Price
Delta
Ephraim
Manti
Castle Dale
Huntington
Helper
Coalville
Morgan
Kamas
Eureka
Distance scale
One inch represents about 28 miles

How to determine distance

Mileages in red between red arrowheads; in black, between intersections.

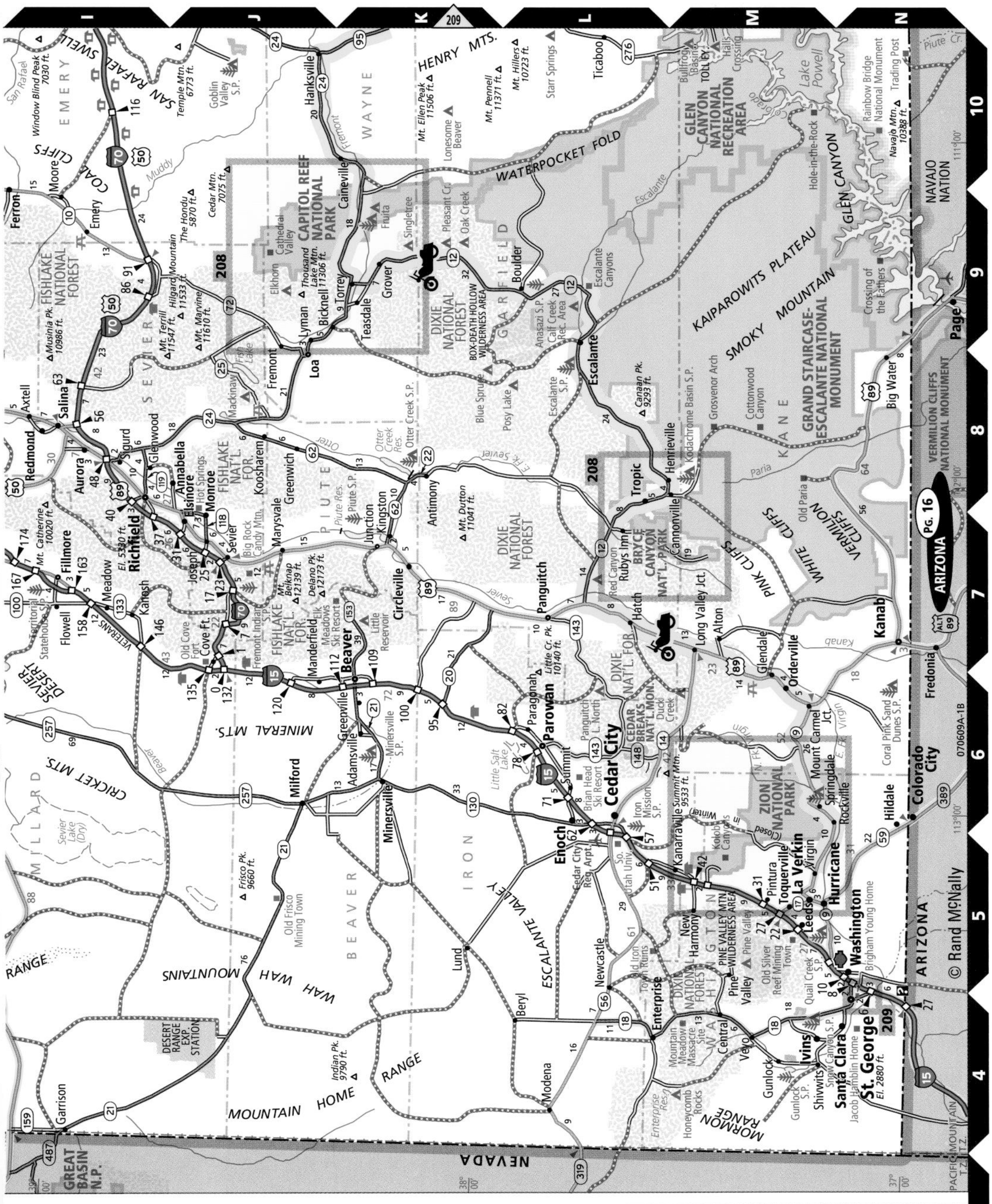

Salt Lake City

p. 208-209

SYMBOLS

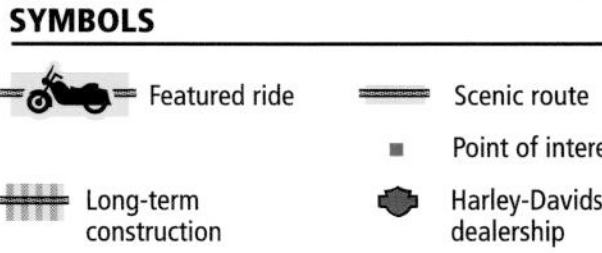
Featured ride
Scenic route
Point of interest
Long-term construction
Harley-Davidson dealership

For Utah ride, see page R34.

UTAH MOTORCYCLE LAWS

Helmet use:
Required under age 18

Riding two abreast:
Yes. See state law for specifics

Eye protection:
Not required

Speed limit:
Primary roads: 75 mph
Secondary roads: 65 mph

UTAH RESOURCES

Road conditions or construction:
511
(800) 492-2400
(866) 511-8824
www.utahcommuterlink.com

Highway Emergency Numbers:
911

Tourism:
(800) 200-1160
(801) 538-1030
www.utah.com

State motor vehicle information:
(801) 965-4437
www.driverlicense.utah.gov

HARLEY-DAVIDSON DEALERSHIPS

Saddleback Harley-Davidson Shop, B-8
2359 N Main St. **Logan**
(435) 787-8100
Lat N 41.775 **Lon** W 111.834

Harley-Davidson of Northern Utah, C-8
892 W Riverdale Rd. **Ogden**
(801) 394-4464
Lat N 41.178 **Lon** W 112

Timpanogos Harley-Davidson, E-8
350 W 800 North **Orem**
(801) 434-4647
Lat N 40.312 **Lon** W 111.704

Park City Harley-Davidson, D-9
324 Main St. **Park City**
(435) 214-5099
Lat N 40.642 **Lon** W 111.495

Harley-Davidson of Salt Lake City, D-8
2928 S State St. **Salt Lake City**
(801) 487-4647
Lat N 40.707 **Lon** W 111.888

South Valley Harley-Davidson Shop, E-8
8886 S Sandy Pkwy. Dr. **Sandy**
(801) 563-1100
Lat N 40.58 **Lon** W 111.886

Zion Harley-Davidson Shop, N-5
2345 N Coral Canyon Blvd. **Washington**
(435) 673-5100
Lat N 37.153 **Lon** W 113.46

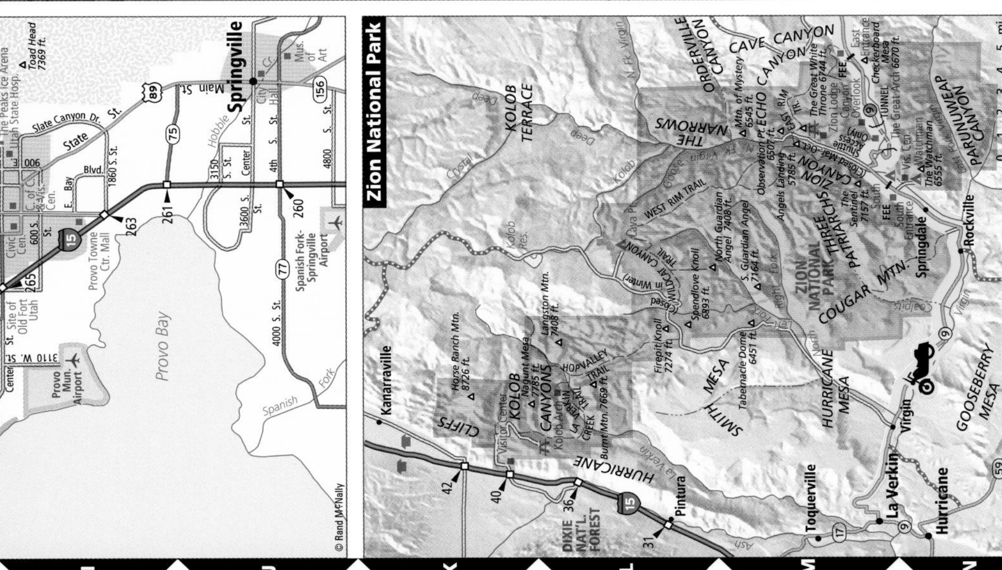
Zion National Park
Springville

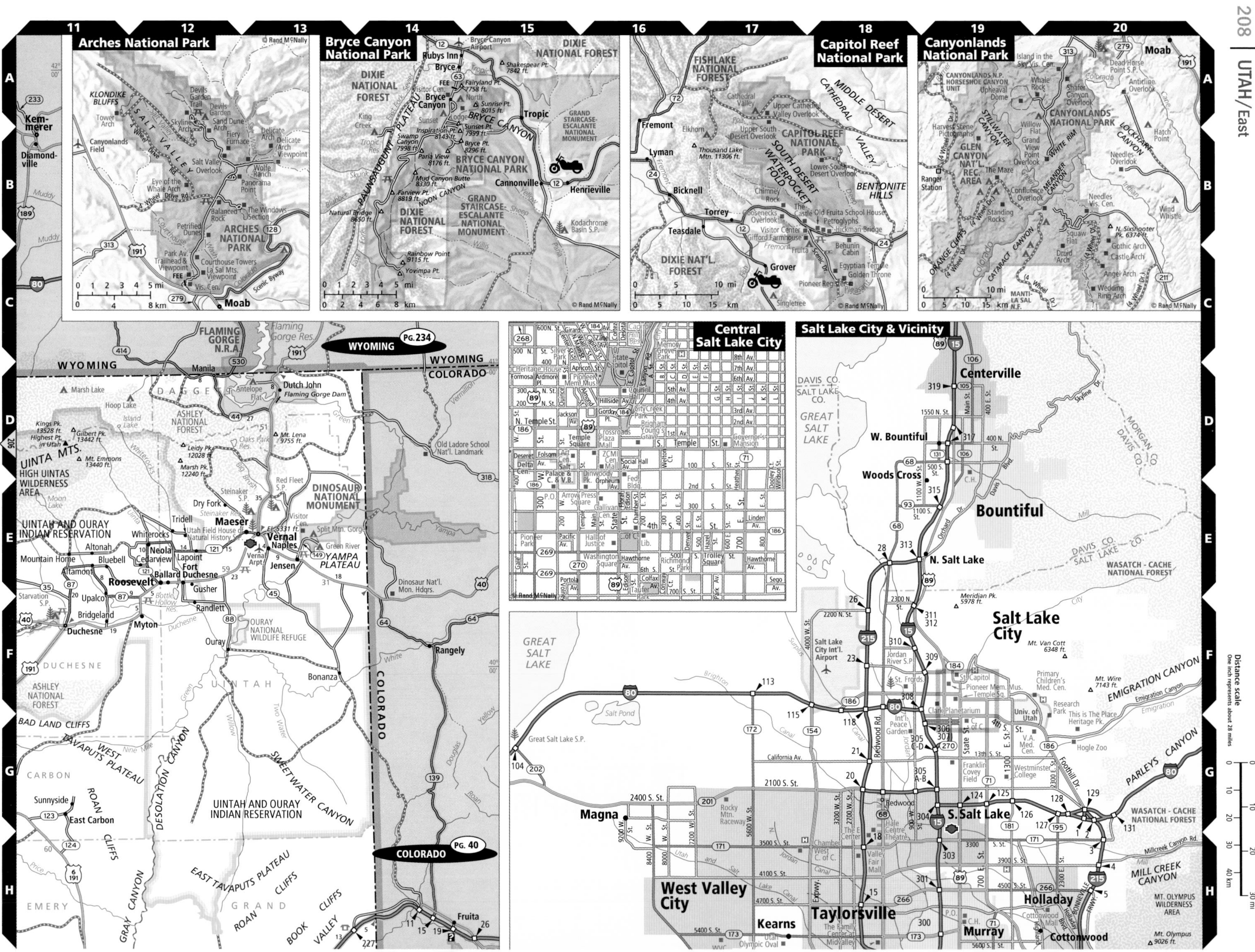
Arches National Park
Bryce Canyon National Park
Capitol Reef National Park
Canyonlands National Park
Central Salt Lake City
Salt Lake City & Vicinity
Moab
Salt Lake City
Bountiful
Centerville
N. Salt Lake
W. Bountiful
Woods Cross
S. Salt Lake
Holladay
Cottonwood
Murray
Taylorsville
West Valley City
Kearns
Magna
GREAT SALT LAKE
WYOMING
COLORADO
UINTAH AND OURAY INDIAN RESERVATION
DINOSAUR NATIONAL MONUMENT
FLAMING GORGE N.R.A.
Vernal
Roosevelt
Duchesne
Rangely
Fruita
PG. 234
PG. 40
Distance scale
One inch represents about 28 miles
© Rand McNally

How to determine distance

Mileages in red between red arrowheads; in black, between intersections.

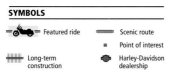

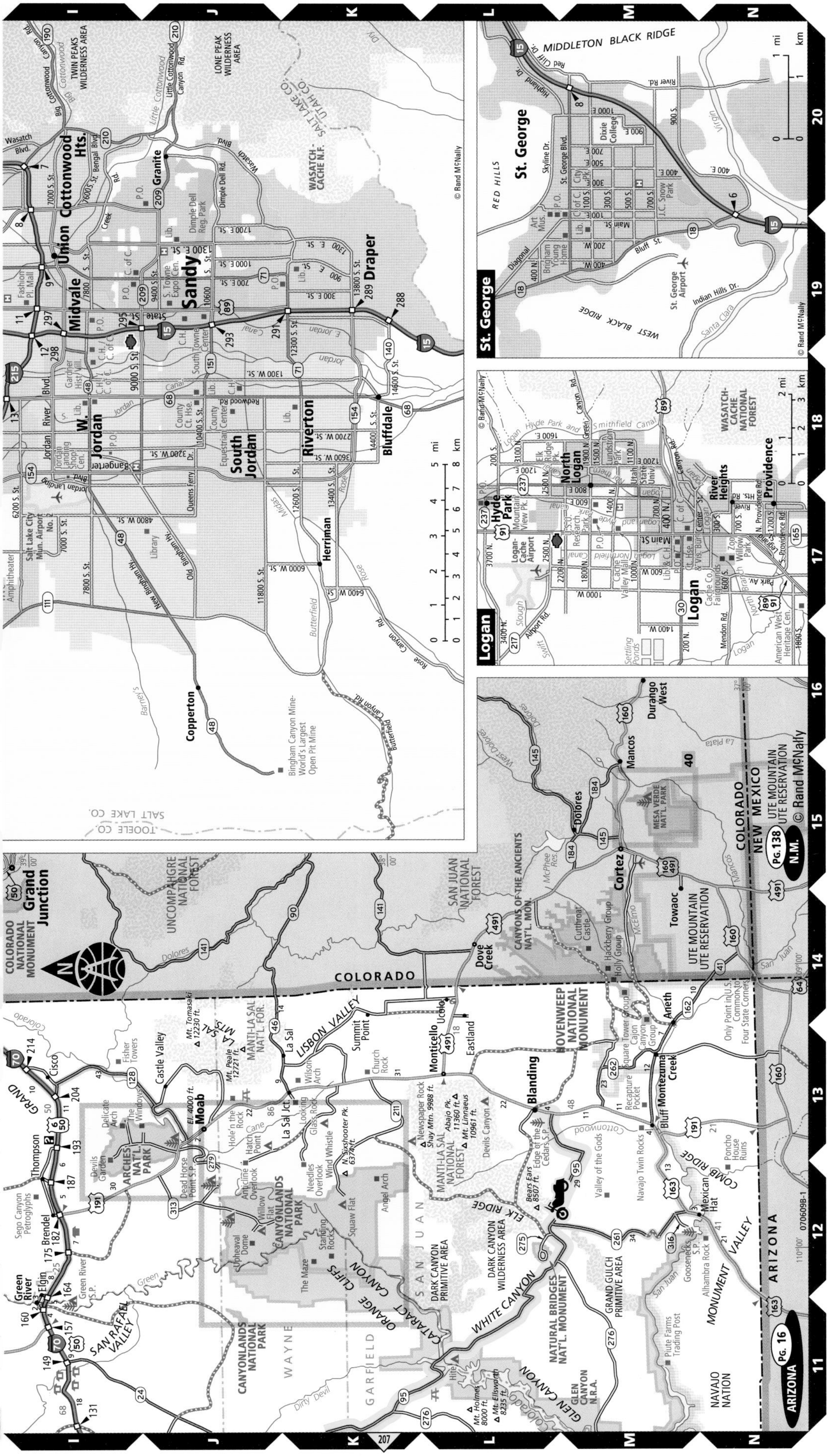

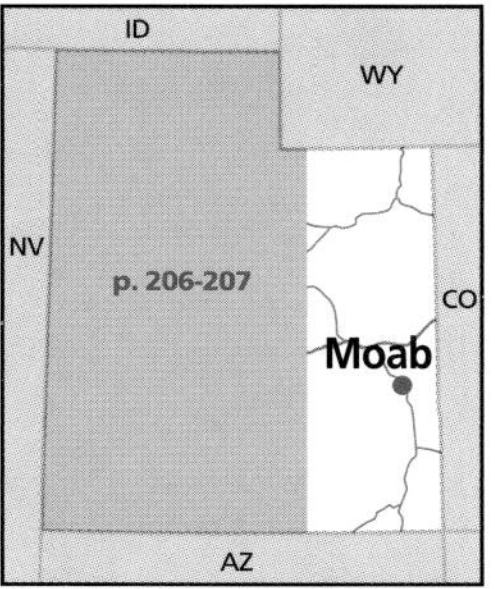
ID
WY
NV
p. 206-207
CO
Moab
AZ

SYMBOLS

Featured ride
Scenic route
Point of interest
Long-term construction
Harley-Davidson dealership

For Utah ride, see page R34.

CITY-TO-CITY MILEAGE

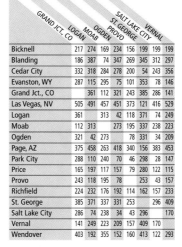

	GRAND JCT., CO	LOGAN	MOAB	OGDEN	PROVO	ST. GEORGE	SALT LAKE CITY	VERNAL
Bicknell	217	274	169	234	156	199	199	199
Blanding	186	387	74	347	269	345	312	297
Cedar City	332	318	284	278	200	54	243	356
Evanston, WY	287	115	295	75	101	353	78	146
Grand Jct., CO		361	112	321	243	385	286	141
Las Vegas, NV	505	491	457	451	373	121	416	529
Logan	361		313	42	118	371	74	249
Moab	112	313		273	195	337	238	223
Ogden	321	42	273		78	331	34	209
Page, AZ	375	458	263	418	340	156	383	453
Park City	288	110	240	70	46	298	28	147
Price	165	197	117	157	79	280	122	115
Provo	243	118	195	78		253	43	157
Richfield	224	232	176	192	114	162	157	233
St. George	385	371	337	331	253		296	409
Salt Lake City	286	74	238	34	43	296		170
Vernal	141	249	223	209	157	409	170	
Wendover	403	192	355	152	160	413	122	293

HARLEY-DAVIDSON DEALERSHIPS

Beers Harley-Davidson, E-13
2029 W Hwy. 40 **Vernal**
(435) 789-5196
Lat N 40.438 **Lon** W 109.567

Distance scale
One inch represents about 14 miles

0 5 10 mi

0 5 10 15 km

PG. 132
PG. 250
PG. 140

MAINE
NEW HAMPSHIRE
QUÉBEC
CANADA
NEW HAMPSHIRE
NEW YORK
N.Y.

WHITE MOUNTAIN NATIONAL FOREST
WHITE MTS.
GREEN MTS.
GREEN MOUNTAIN NAT'L FOR.
LONG MTN.
CRYSTAL MTN.
MAHOOSUC RANGE
CARR MTN.
TACONIC RANGE
TONGUE MTN. RANGE

ESSEX
ORLEANS
CALEDONIA
FRANKLIN
GRAND ISLE
CHITTENDEN
LAMOILLE
WASHINGTON
ORANGE
ADDISON
RUTLAND

Montpelier / Barre

Major towns: Berlin, Newport, St. Johnsbury, Lyndonville, Burlington, Montpelier, Barre, Middlebury, Vergennes, Rutland, Randolph, Hanover, Lebanon, White River Junction, Woodstock, Littleton, Lancaster, North Conway, Plattsburgh, Champlain, St. Albans, Morrisville, Stowe, Waterbury

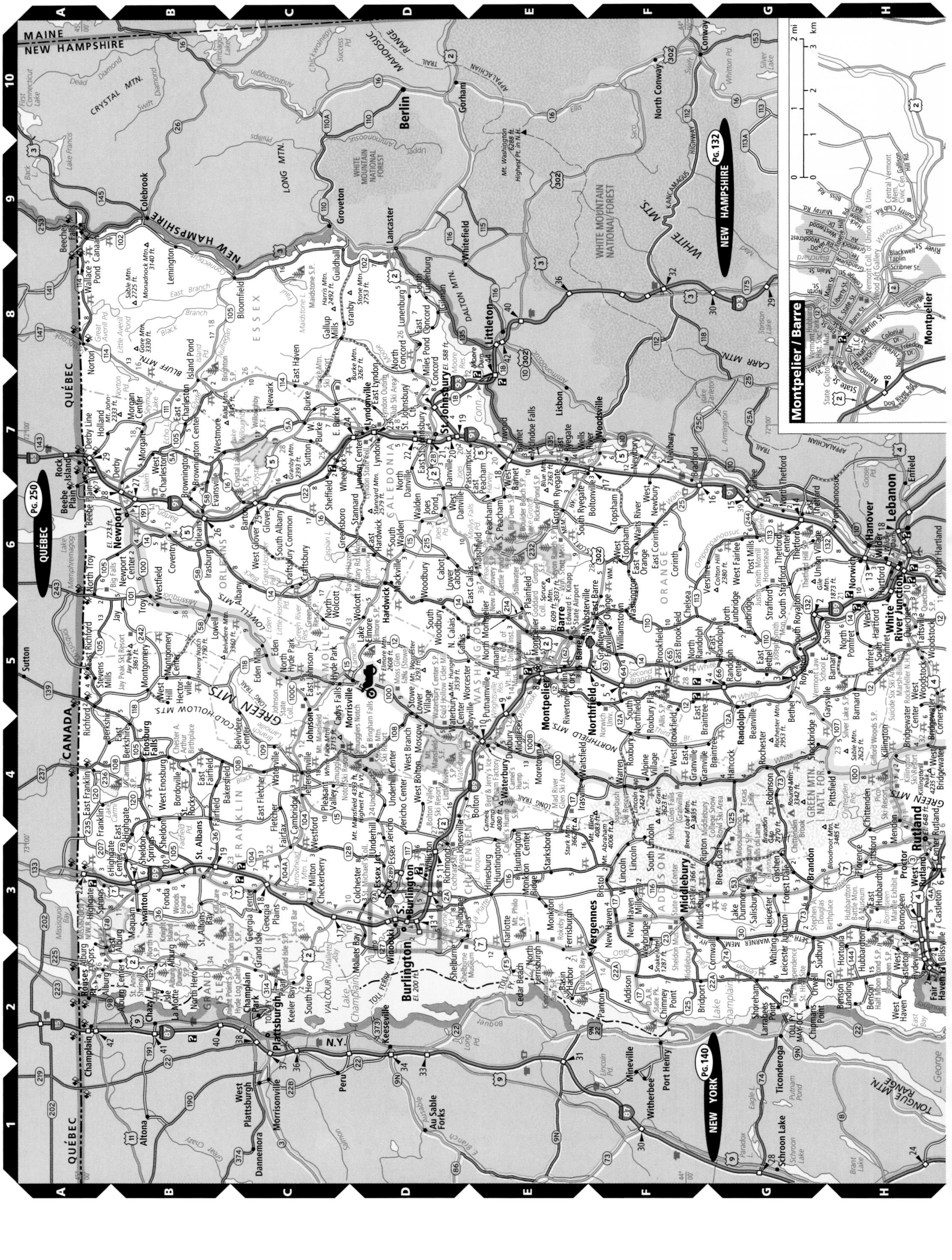

How to determine distance

Mileages in red between red arrowheads; in black, between intersections.

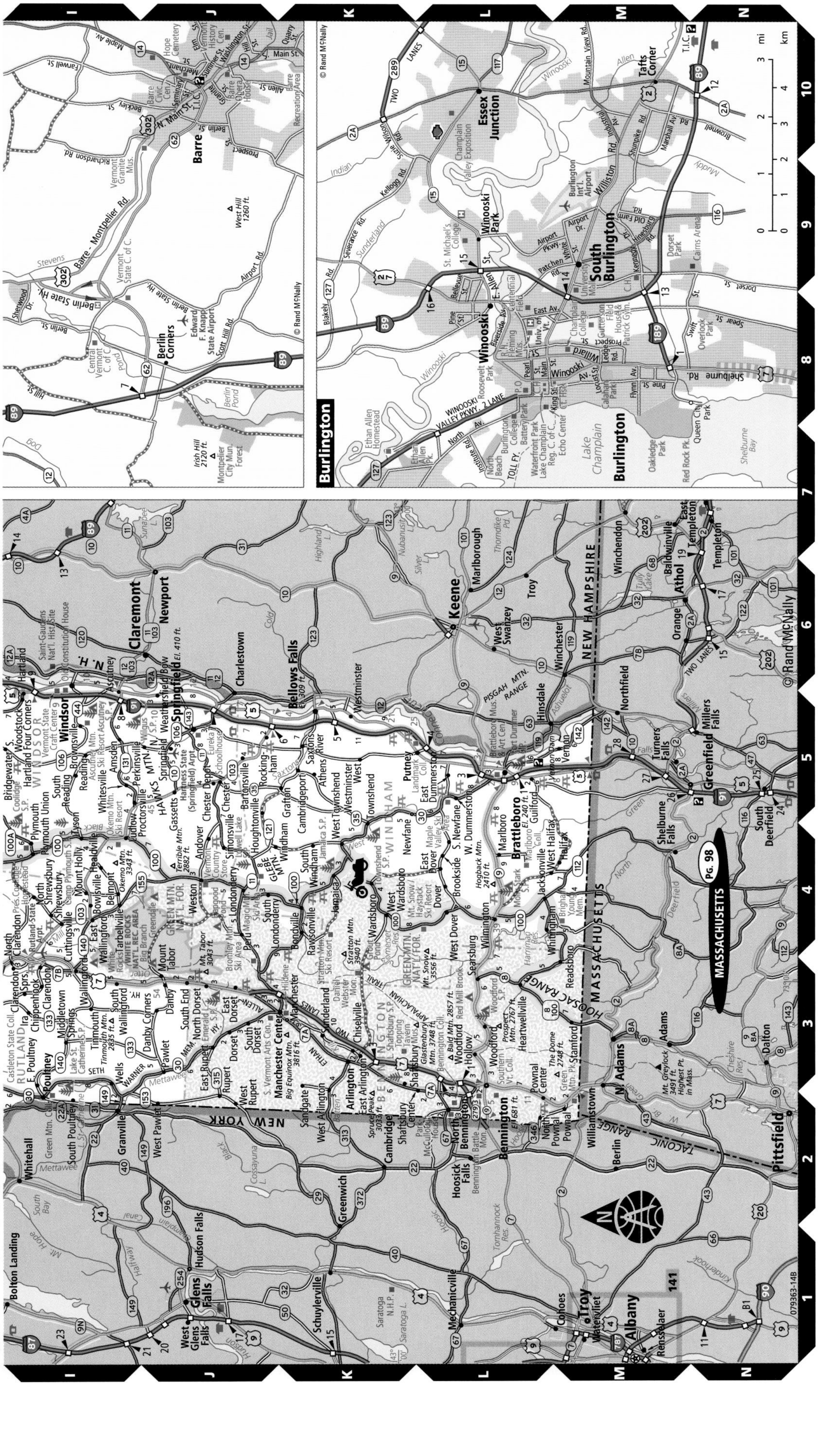

SYMBOLS

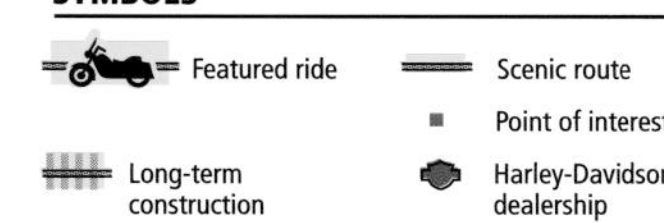
Featured ride
Scenic route
Point of interest
Long-term construction
Harley-Davidson dealership

For Vermont ride, see page R35.

VERMONT MOTORCYCLE LAWS

Helmet use:
Reflectorization required

Riding two abreast:
No. See state law for specifics

Eye protection:
Required unless equipped with windscreen

Speed limit:
Primary roads: 65 mph
Secondary roads: 55 mph

VERMONT RESOURCES

Road conditions or construction:
511
(800) 429-7623
www.aot.state.vt.us/travelinfo.htm
www.511vt.com

Highway Emergency Numbers:
911

Tourism:
(800) 837-6668
www.vermontvacation.com

State motor vehicle information:
(802) 828-2000
www.dmv.state.vt.us

CITY-TO-CITY MILEAGE

	ALBANY, NY	BRATTLEBORO	BURLINGTON	MONTPELIER	NEWPORT	RUTLAND	ST. JOHNSBURY	WHITE RIVER JUNCTION
Albany, NY		81	152	162	246	96	202	145
Brattleboro	81		154	117	166	77	122	65
Burlington	152	154		39	75	67	77	91
Montpelier	162	117	39		80	66	38	54
Newport	246	166	75	80		146	44	101
Rutland	96	77	67	66	146		102	45
St. Johnsbury	202	122	77	38	44	102		57
White River Junction	145	65	91	54	101	45	57	

HARLEY-DAVIDSON DEALERSHIPS

Wilkins Harley-Davidson, F-5
663 S Barre Rd. **Barre**
(802) 476-6104
Lat N 44.168 **Lon** W 72.51

Green Mountain Harley-Davidson, D-3
157 Pearl St. **Essex Junction**
(802) 878-4778
Lat N 44.498 **Lon** W 73.128

Distance scale
One inch represents about 18 miles

0 5 10 15 20 mi
0 5 10 15 20 25 30 km

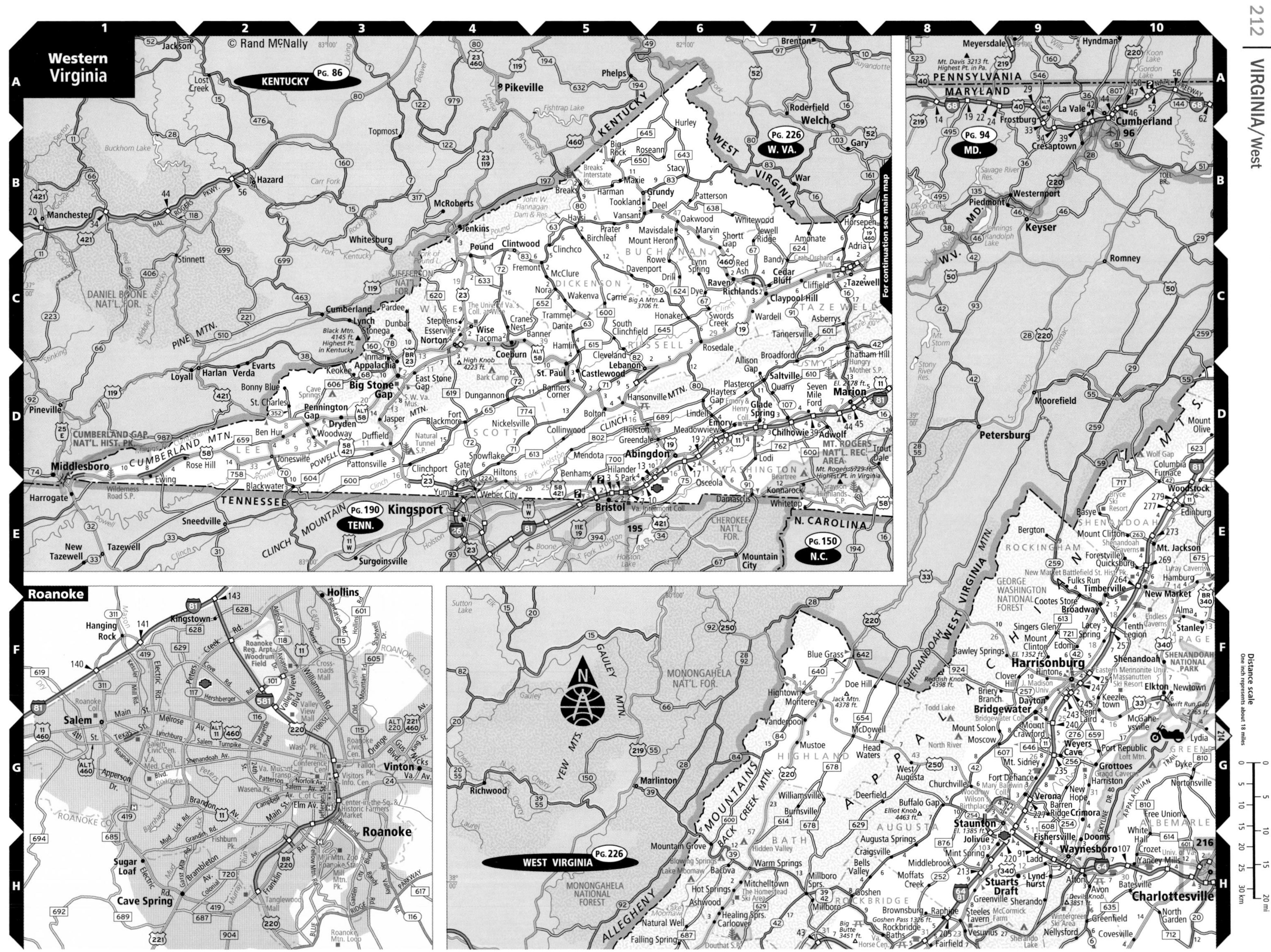
Western Virginia
Roanoke
© Rand McNally
KENTUCKY PG. 86
PG. 226 W. VA.
PG. 94 MD.
PG. 150 N.C.
PG. 190 TENN.
PG. 226 WEST VIRGINIA
214
For continuation see main map
PENNSYLVANIA
MARYLAND
WEST VIRGINIA
TENNESSEE
N. CAROLINA
Cumberland
Keyser
Petersburg
Moorefield
Romney
Harrisonburg
Staunton
Waynesboro
Charlottesville
Woodstock
New Market
Elkton
Bridgewater
Pikeville
Hazard
Middlesboro
Big Stone Gap
Norton
Wise
Kingsport
Bristol
Abingdon
Marion
Lebanon
Tazewell
Welch
Grundy
Salem
Roanoke
Vinton
Hollins
Cave Spring
GEORGE WASHINGTON NATIONAL FOREST
MONONGAHELA NATIONAL FOREST
JEFFERSON NAT'L. FOR.
DANIEL BOONE NAT'L. FOR.
CHEROKEE NAT'L. FOR.
CUMBERLAND GAP NAT'L. HIST. PK.
MT. ROGERS NAT'L. REC. AREA
SHENANDOAH NATIONAL PARK
ALLEGHENY MOUNTAINS
SHENANDOAH MTN.

How to determine distance

Mileages in red between red arrowheads; in black, between intersections.

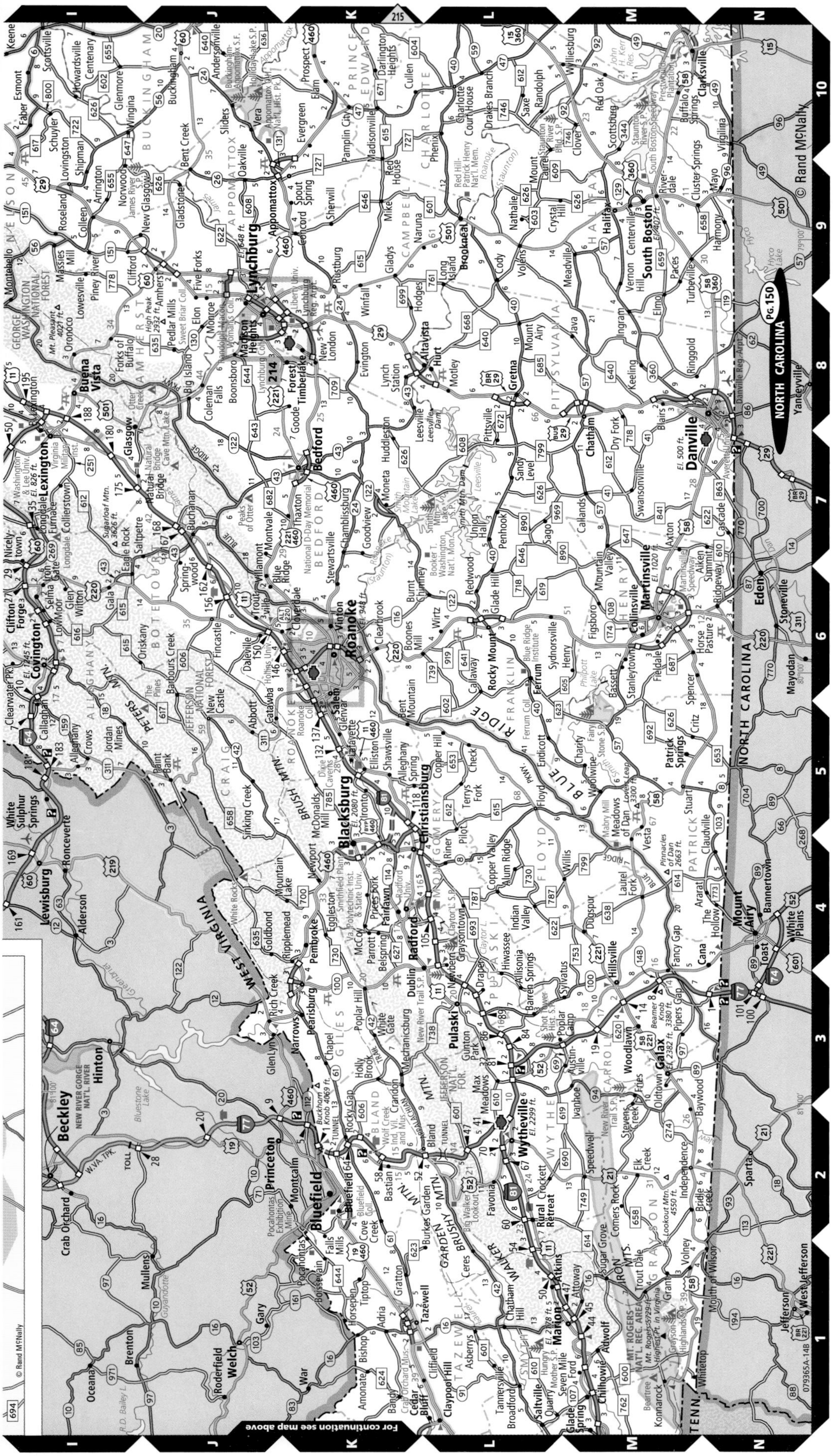

For continuation see map above

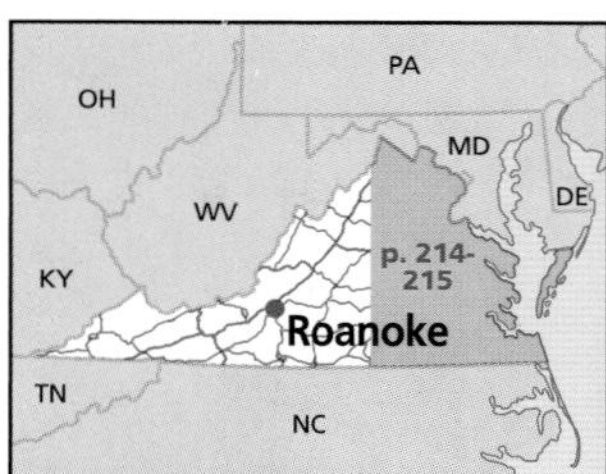
PA
OH
MD
WV
DE
KY
p. 214-215
Roanoke
TN
NC

SYMBOLS

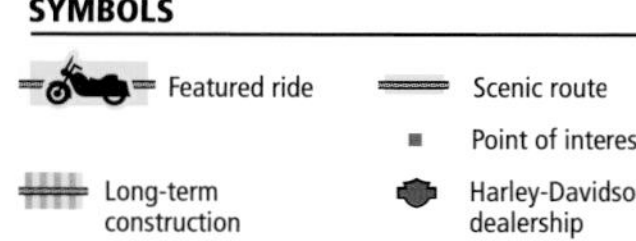
Featured ride
Scenic route
Point of interest
Long-term construction
Harley-Davidson dealership

For Virginia ride, see page R36.

VIRGINIA MOTORCYCLE LAWS

Helmet use:
Required

Riding two abreast:
No. See state law for specifics

Eye protection:
Required unless equipped with windscreen

Speed limit:
Primary roads: 65 mph
Secondary roads: 65 mph

VIRGINIA RESOURCES

Road conditions or construction:
511
(800) 367-7623
(800) 578-4111
www.511virginia.org

Highway Emergency Numbers:
911

Tourism:
(800) 321-3244
(800) 847-4882
www.virginia.org

State motor vehicle information:
(866) 368-5463
www.dmvnow.com

HARLEY-DAVIDSON DEALERSHIPS

- **Black Wolf Harley-Davidson, D-6**
  18100 Black Wolf Dr. **Abingdon**
  (276) 628-5822
  Lat N 36.655 **Lon** W 81.893
- **Thunder Road Harley-Davidson, N-7**
  4960 Riverside Dr. **Danville**
  (434) 822-2453
  Lat N 36.592 **Lon** W 79.462
- **Harley-Davidson of Lynchburg, K-8**
  20452 Timberlake Rd. **Lynchburg**
  (434) 237-2381
  Lat N 37.342 **Lon** W 79.236
- **Roanoke Valley Harley-Davidson, K-6**
  1925 Peters Creek Rd. **Roanoke**
  (540) 562-5424
  Lat N 37.3 **Lon** W 80.007
- **Shenandoah Harley-Davidson, H-9**
  213 Rolling Thunder Ln. **Staunton**
  (540) 213-RIDE
  Lat N 38.105 **Lon** W 79.073
- **Harley-Davidson Shop of Wytheville, L-2**
  430 Lithia Rd. **Wytheville**
  (276) 228-9000
  Lat N 36.951 **Lon** W 81.055

Distance scale
One inch represents about 18 miles
0 5 10 15 20 mi
0 5 10 15 20 25 30 km

Lynchburg
© Rand McNally
Baltimore
Washington
Annapolis
Alexandria
Arlington
Frederick
Hagerstown
Martinsburg
Winchester
Fredericksburg
Charlottesville
Culpeper
Salisbury
Cambridge
Easton
Georgetown
Lewes
PENNSYLVANIA
MARYLAND
DELAWARE
Pg. 50 DEL.
Pg. 94 MD.
Pg. 174 PENN.
Pg. 226 W. VA.

How to determine distance

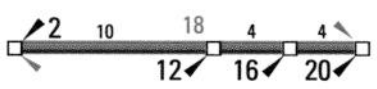

Mileages in red between red arrowheads; in black, between intersections.

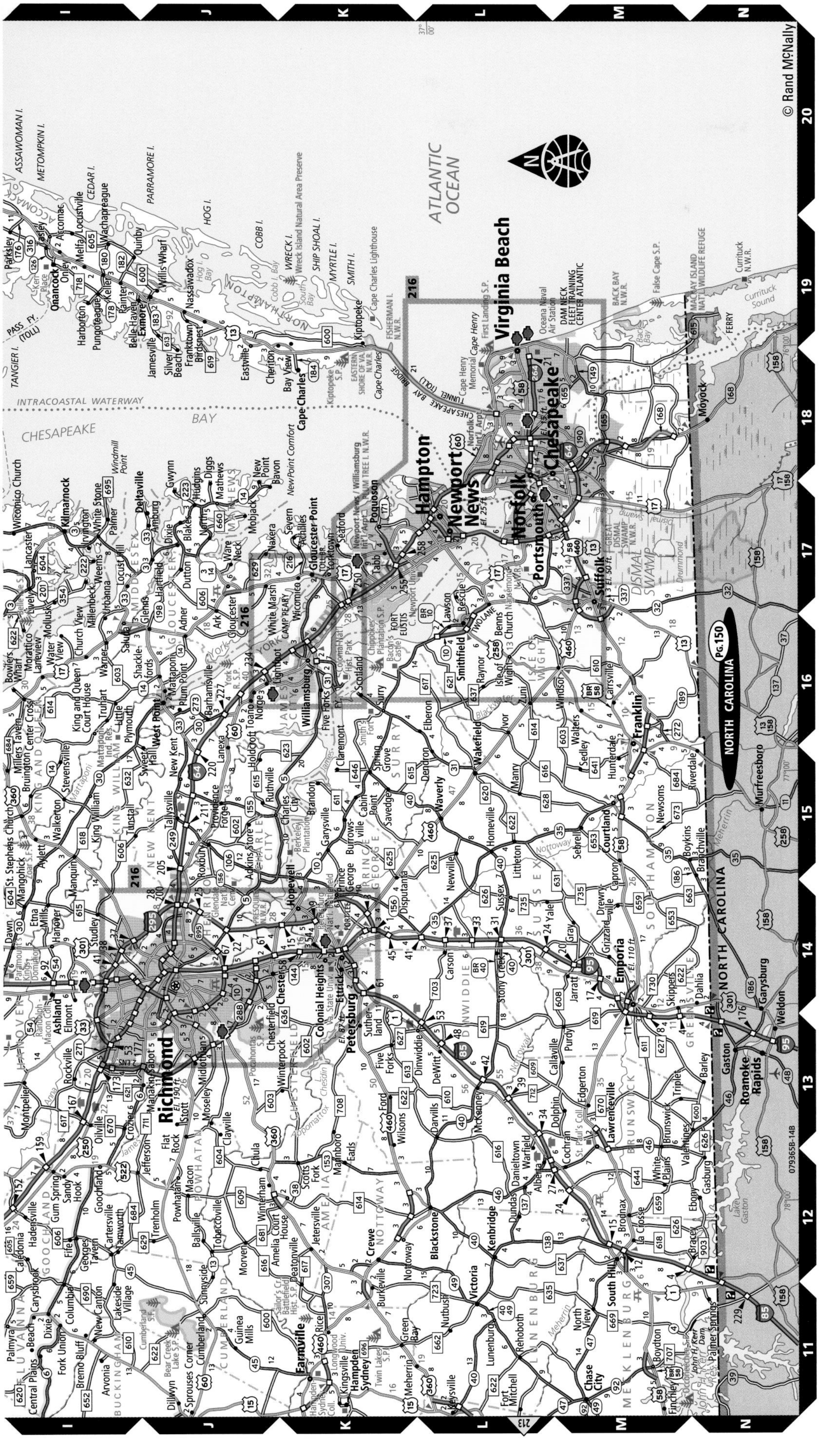

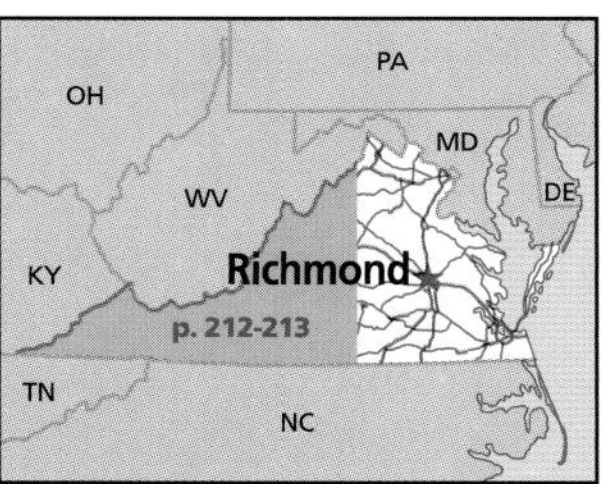
PA
OH
MD
WV
DE
KY
Richmond
p. 212-213
TN
NC

SYMBOLS

- Featured ride
- Scenic route
- Long-term construction
- Harley-Davidson dealership

For Virginia ride, see page R36.

CITY-TO-CITY MILEAGE

	CHARLOTTESVILLE	EMPORIA	NORFOLK	RICHMOND	ROANOKE	WASHINGTON, DC	WINCHESTER	WYTHEVILLE
Bristol	252	341	418	324	146	374	313	69
Charlottesville		138	168	74	114	122	125	182
Chincoteague	261	180	105	186	373	161	242	441
Danville	126	113	186	149	82	250	220	120
Emporia	138		74	64	178	170	198	271
Fredericksburg	80	119	145	55	194	54	82	262
Hagerstown, MD	167	235	261	171	217	75	42	285
Harrisonburg	59	195	225	131	109	129	68	177
Lynchburg	63	127	194	118	54	185	157	132
Manassas	95	156	182	92	209	37	53	277
Norfolk	168	74		93	280	196	224	348
Richmond	74	64	93		186	106	134	254
Roanoke	114	178	280	186		236	175	76
Virginia Beach	180	88	17	105	292	208	236	360
Washington, DC	122	170	196	106	236		77	304
Williamsburg	126	106	46	51	238	154	182	306
Winchester	125	198	224	134	175	77		243
Wytheville	182	271	348	254	76	304	243	

HARLEY-DAVIDSON DEALERSHIPS

For the Richmond and Williamsburg areas, please see dealer listings on page 217.

East Coast Harley-Davidson, F-14
17975 Main St. (US 1) **Dumfries**
(703) 221-3757
Lat N 38.563 **Lon** W 77.331

Patriot Harley-Davidson, D-14
9739 Lee Hwy. **Fairfax**
(703) 352-5400
Lat N 38.864 **Lon** W 77.281

Richmond Harley-Davidson, I-14
10441 Washington Hwy. **Glen Allen**
(804) 550-9280
Lat N 37.695 **Lon** W 77.463

Whitt's Harley-Davidson Sales, E-14
9321 Center St. **Manassas**
(703) 631-3750
Lat N 38.751 **Lon** W 77.480

Waugh Enterprises Harley-Davidson, G-12
385 Waugh Blvd. **Orange**
(540) 672-5550
Lat N 38.243 **Lon** W 78.097

Bayside Harley-Davidson, L-17
3403 High St. **Portsmouth**
(757) 397-5550
Lat N 36.834 **Lon** W 76.344

Southside Harley-Davidson, L-18
385 N Witchduck Rd. **Virginia Beach**
(757) 499-8964
Lat N 36.849 **Lon** W 76.155

Harley Haven, L-19
1920 Atlantic Ave. **Virginia Beach**
(757) 425-2458
Lat N 36.847 **Lon** W 75.975

Virginia Beach Harley-Davidson, L-19
237 Laskin Rd. **Virginia Beach**
(757) 417-7197
Lat N 36.859 **Lon** W 75.979

Grove's Winchester Harley-Davidson, C-12
140 Independence Dr. **Winchester**
(540) 662-4468
Lat N 39.14 **Lon** W 78.125

Hampton Roads Harley-Davidson, K-17
6450 George Washington Hwy. (Rte. 17) **Yorktown**
(757) 872-7223
Lat N 37.17 **Lon** W 76.473

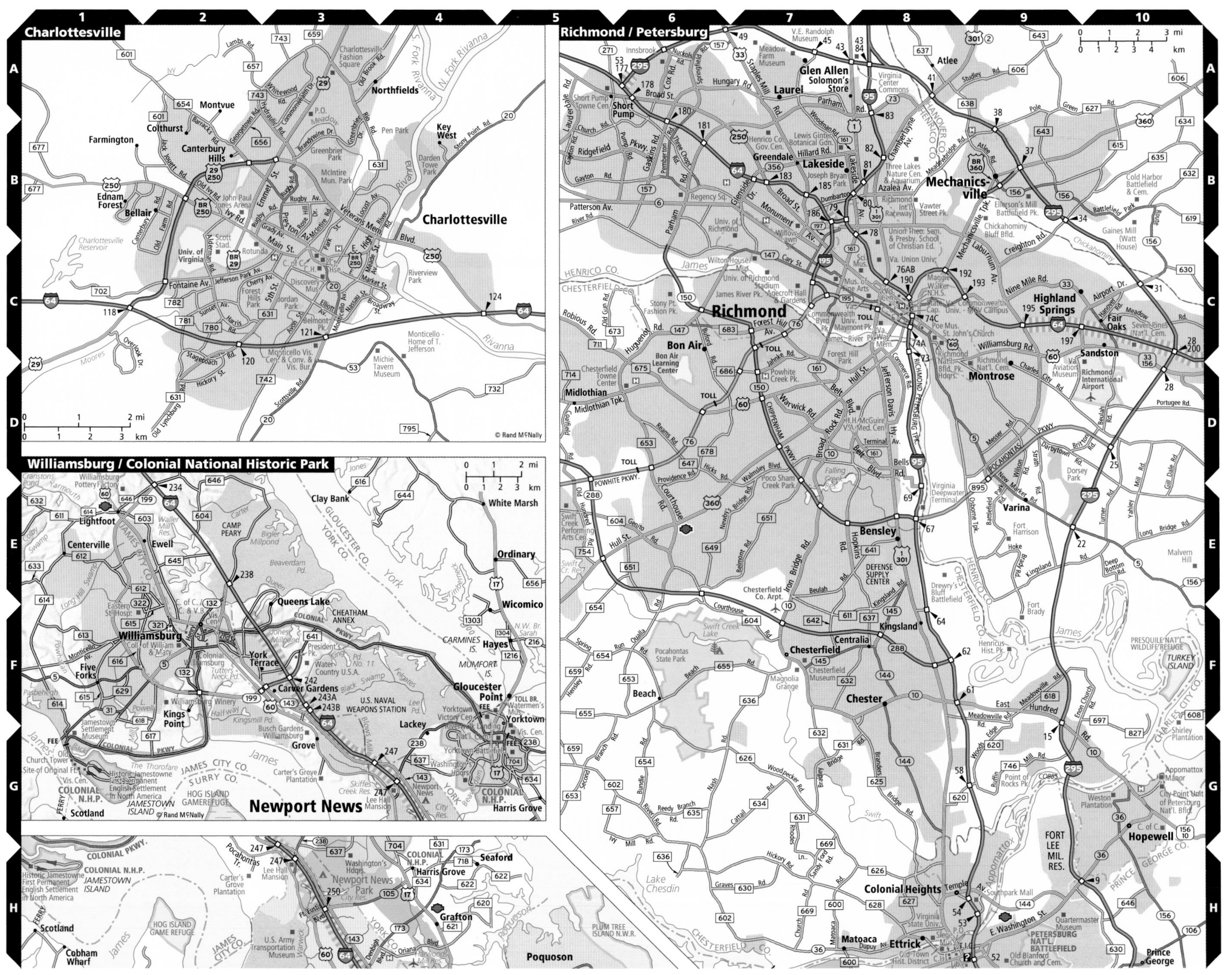
Charlottesville
Richmond / Petersburg
Williamsburg / Colonial National Historic Park
Richmond
Charlottesville
Williamsburg
Newport News
Yorktown
Hopewell
Colonial Heights
Mechanicsville
Highland Springs
Chester
Chesterfield
Petersburg Nat'l Battlefield
Fort Lee Mil. Res.
Poquoson
© Rand McNally

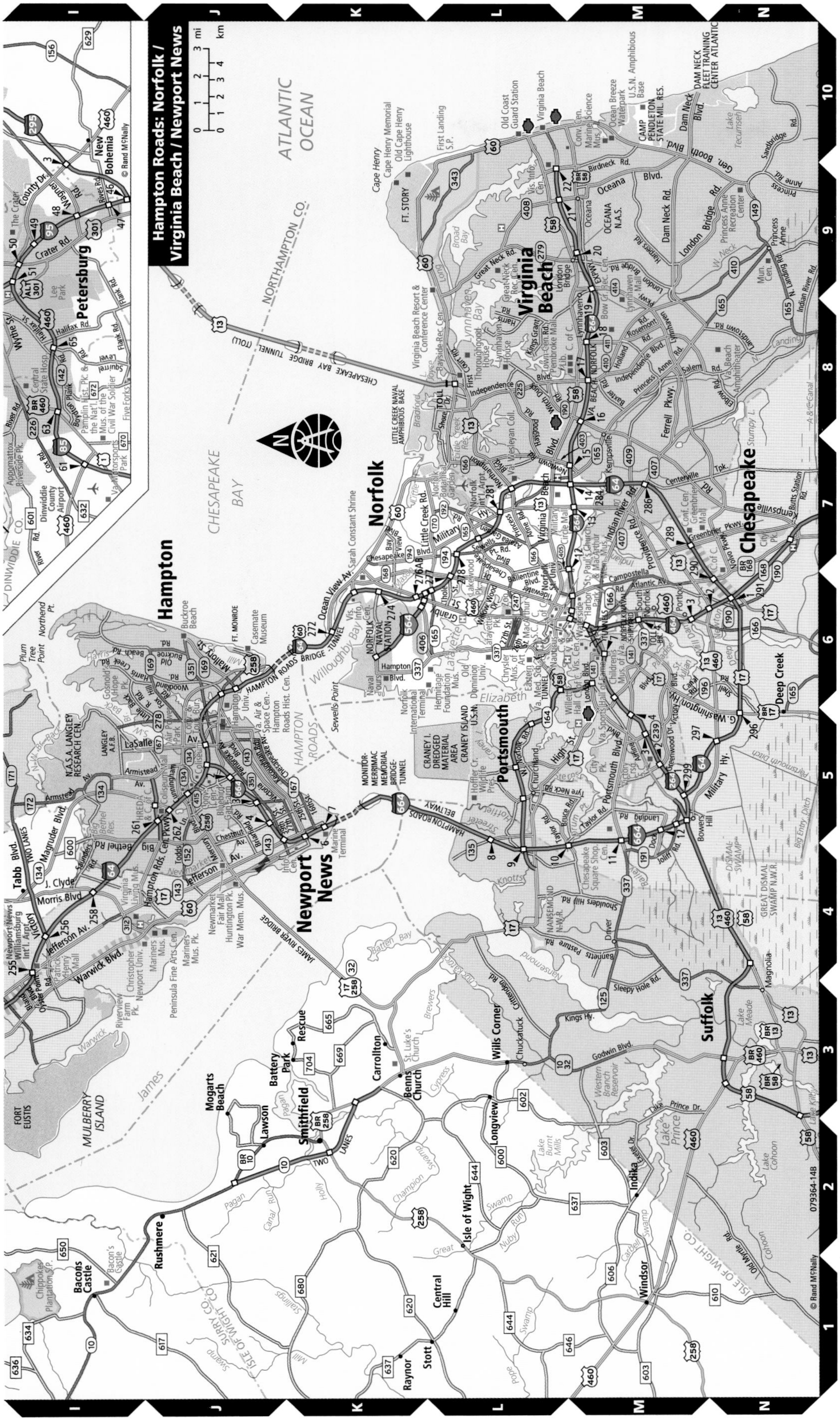

Hampton Roads: Norfolk / Virginia Beach / Newport News

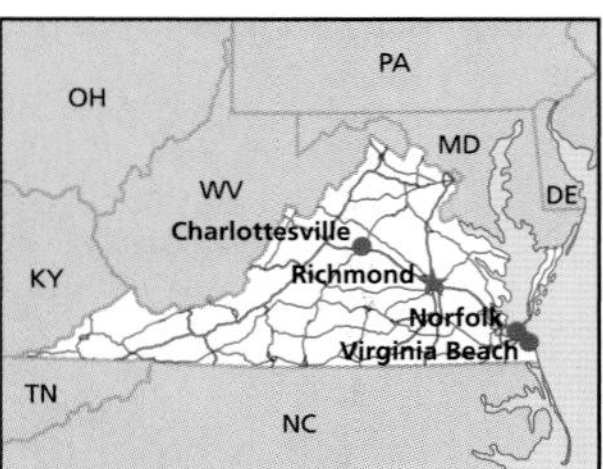
PA
OH
MD
WV
DE
Charlottesville
Richmond
KY
Norfolk
Virginia Beach
TN
NC

SYMBOLS

- Featured ride
- Scenic route
- Point of interest
- Long-term construction
- Harley-Davidson dealership

VIRGINIA MOTORCYCLE LAWS

Helmet use:
Required

Riding two abreast:
No. See state law for specifics

Eye protection:
Required unless equipped with windscreen

Speed limit:
Primary roads: 65 mph
Secondary roads: 65 mph

VIRGINIA RESOURCES

Road conditions or construction:
511
(800) 367-7623
(800) 578-4111
www.511virginia.org

Highway Emergency Numbers:
911

Tourism:
(800) 321-3244
(800) 847-4882
www.virginia.org

State motor vehicle information:
(866) 368-5463
www.dmvnow.com

HARLEY-DAVIDSON DEALERSHIPS

Colonial Harley-Davidson, H-8
1701 Temple Pkwy. **Prince George**
(804) 861-4700
Lat N 37.251 **Lon** W 77.372

South Richmond Harley-Davidson Shop, E-6
10011 Hull St. Rd. **Richmond**
(804) 745-3445
Lat N 37.444 **Lon** W 77.579

Revolutionary Harley-Davidson, E-1
6401 Richmond Rd. Store 71 **Williamsburg**
(757) 565-5122
Lat N 37.339 **Lon** W 76.754

Distance scale
One inch represents about 21 miles

0 5 10 15 20 25 mi
0 10 20 30 40 km

How to determine distance

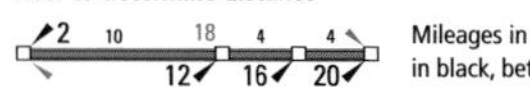
2
10
18
4
4
12
16
20

Mileages in red between red arrowheads; in black, between intersections.

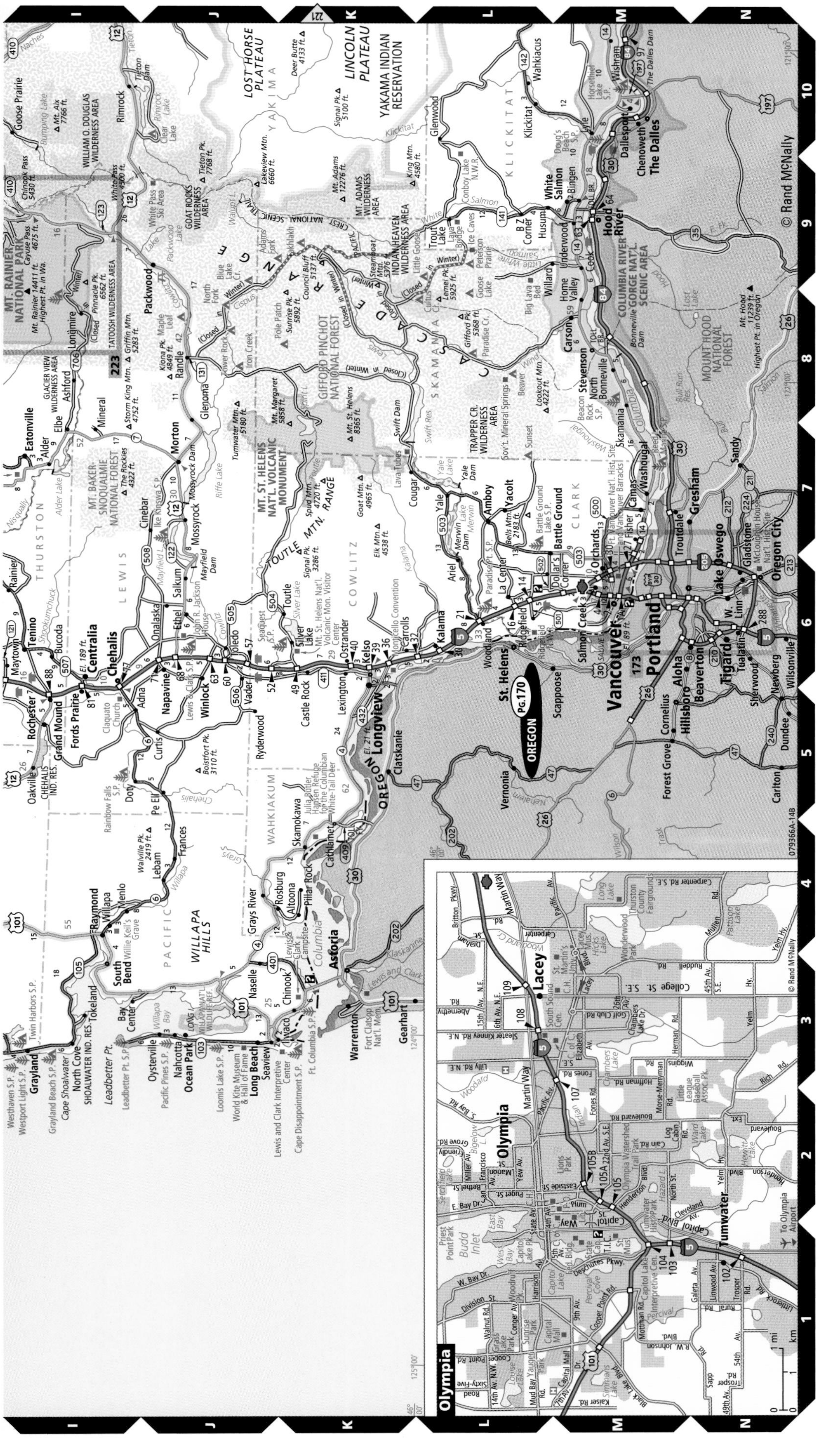

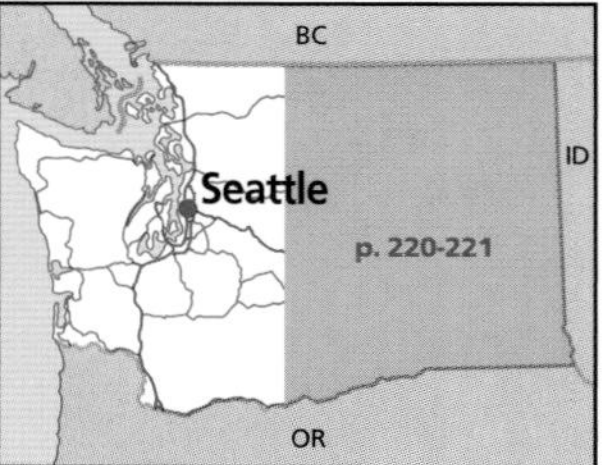
BC
Seattle
ID
p. 220-221
OR

SYMBOLS

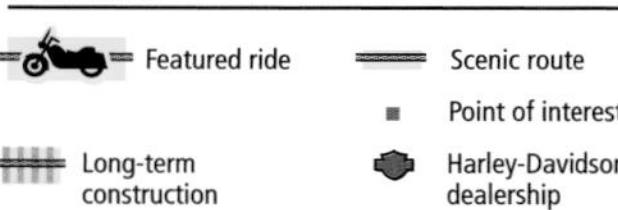
Featured ride
Scenic route
Point of interest
Long-term construction
Harley-Davidson dealership

WASHINGTON MOTORCYCLE LAWS

Helmet use:
Required

Riding two abreast:
Yes. See state law for specifics

Eye protection:
Required unless equipped with windscreen

Speed limit:
Primary roads: 70 mph
Secondary roads: 60 mph

WASHINGTON RESOURCES

Road conditions or construction:
511
(800) 695-7623
www.wsdot.wa.gov/traffic/

Highway Emergency Numbers:
911

Tourism:
(800) 544-1800
www.experiencewashington.com

State motor vehicle information:
(360) 902-3600
www.dol.wa.gov/drivers.htm

HARLEY-DAVIDSON DEALERSHIPS

For the Seattle/Tacoma metro area, please see dealer listings on page 223.

Harley-Davidson of Bellingham, B-7
1419 N State St. **Bellingham**
(360) 671-7575
Lat N 48.75 **Lon** W 122.475

Skagit Harley-Davidson, C-7
1337 Goldenrod Rd. **Burlington**
(360) 757-1515
Lat N 48.463 **Lon** W 122.343

Northwest Harley-Davidson, H-6
8000 Freedom Ln. NE **Lacey**
(360) 705-8515
Lat N 47.062 **Lon** W 122.769

Harley-Davidson of Seattle, E-7
5711 188th St. SE **Lynnwood**
(425) 921-1100
Lat N 47.828 **Lon** W 122.31

Sound Harley-Davidson, D-8
16212 Smokey Point Blvd. **Marysville**
(360) 454-5000
Lat N 48.144 **Lon** W 122.183

Destination Harley-Davidson Shop, H-7
18810 Meridian Ave. E (Hwy. 161) **Puyallup**
(253) 693-5700
Lat N 47.085 **Lon** W 122.294

Legend Harley-Davidson, F-6
9625 Provost Rd. NW **Silverdale**
(360) 698-3700
Lat N 47.653 **Lon** W 122.707

Columbia Motorcycle Harley-Davidson, M-6
1314 NE 102nd St. **Vancouver**
(360) 695-8831
Lat N 45.713 **Lon** W 122.631

Distance scale
One inch represents about 21 miles
0 5 10 15 20 25 mi
0 10 20 30 40 km

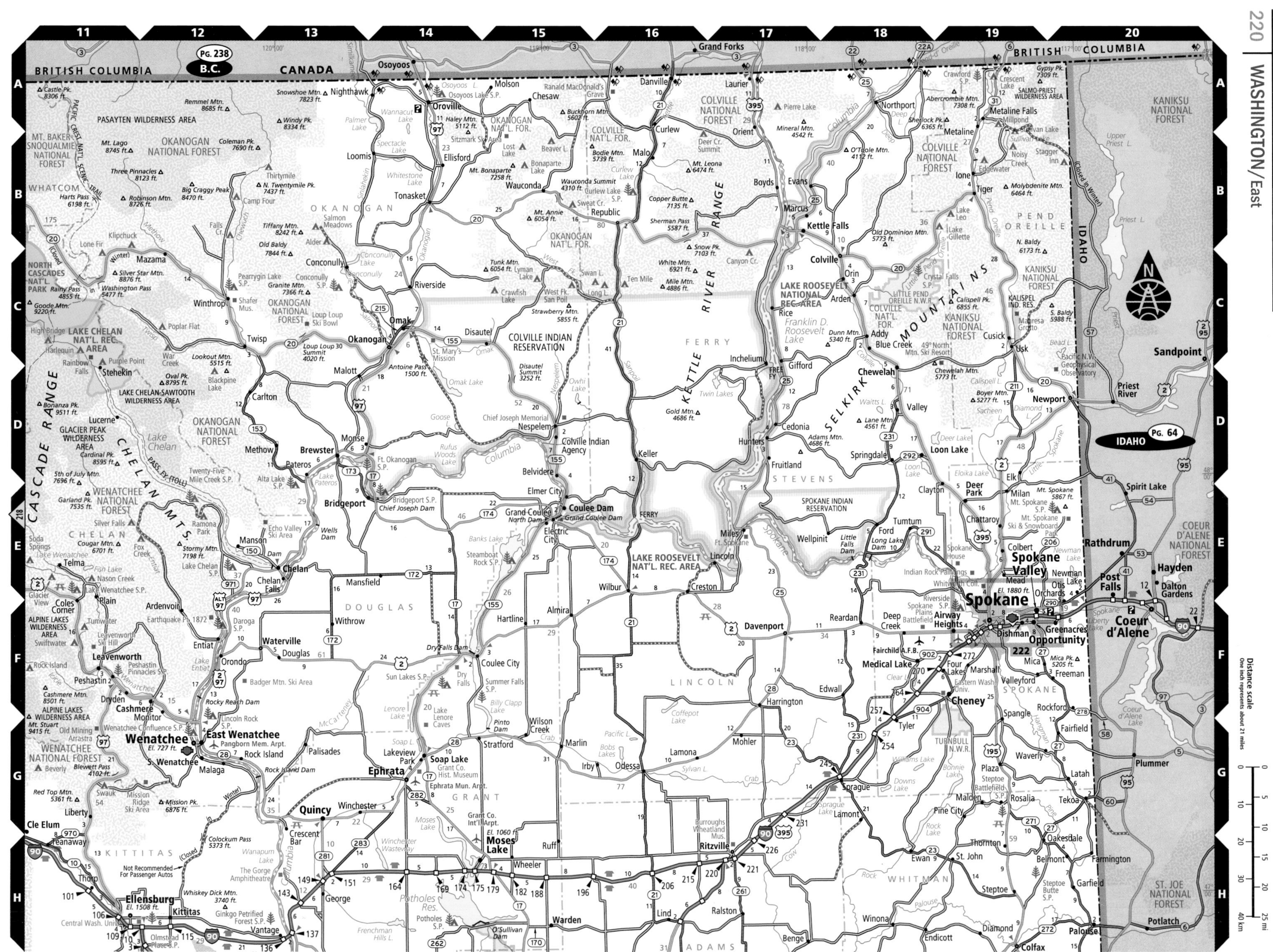

BRITISH COLUMBIA
CANADA
IDAHO
PG. 64
PG. 238
B.C.
Spokane
Spokane Valley
Coeur d'Alene
Wenatchee
East Wenatchee
Ellensburg
Moses Lake
Sandpoint
Colville
Omak
Okanogan
Chelan
Ephrata
Cheney
Ritzville
Oroville
Republic
Davenport
Grand Coulee
Coulee Dam
Newport
Leavenworth
Quincy
Soap Lake
Kittitas
Cle Elum
COLVILLE NATIONAL FOREST
OKANOGAN NATIONAL FOREST
WENATCHEE NATIONAL FOREST
KANIKSU NATIONAL FOREST
LAKE ROOSEVELT NAT'L. REC. AREA
COLVILLE INDIAN RESERVATION
SPOKANE INDIAN RESERVATION
PASAYTEN WILDERNESS AREA
LAKE CHELAN-SAWTOOTH WILDERNESS AREA
GLACIER PEAK WILDERNESS AREA
ALPINE LAKES WILDERNESS AREA
SELKIRK MOUNTAINS
KETTLE RIVER RANGE
CASCADE RANGE
CHELAN MTS.
PACIFIC CREST NAT'L. SCENIC TRAIL

How to determine distance

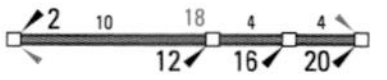

2 10 18 4 4 12 16 20 — Mileages in red between red arrowheads; in black, between intersections.

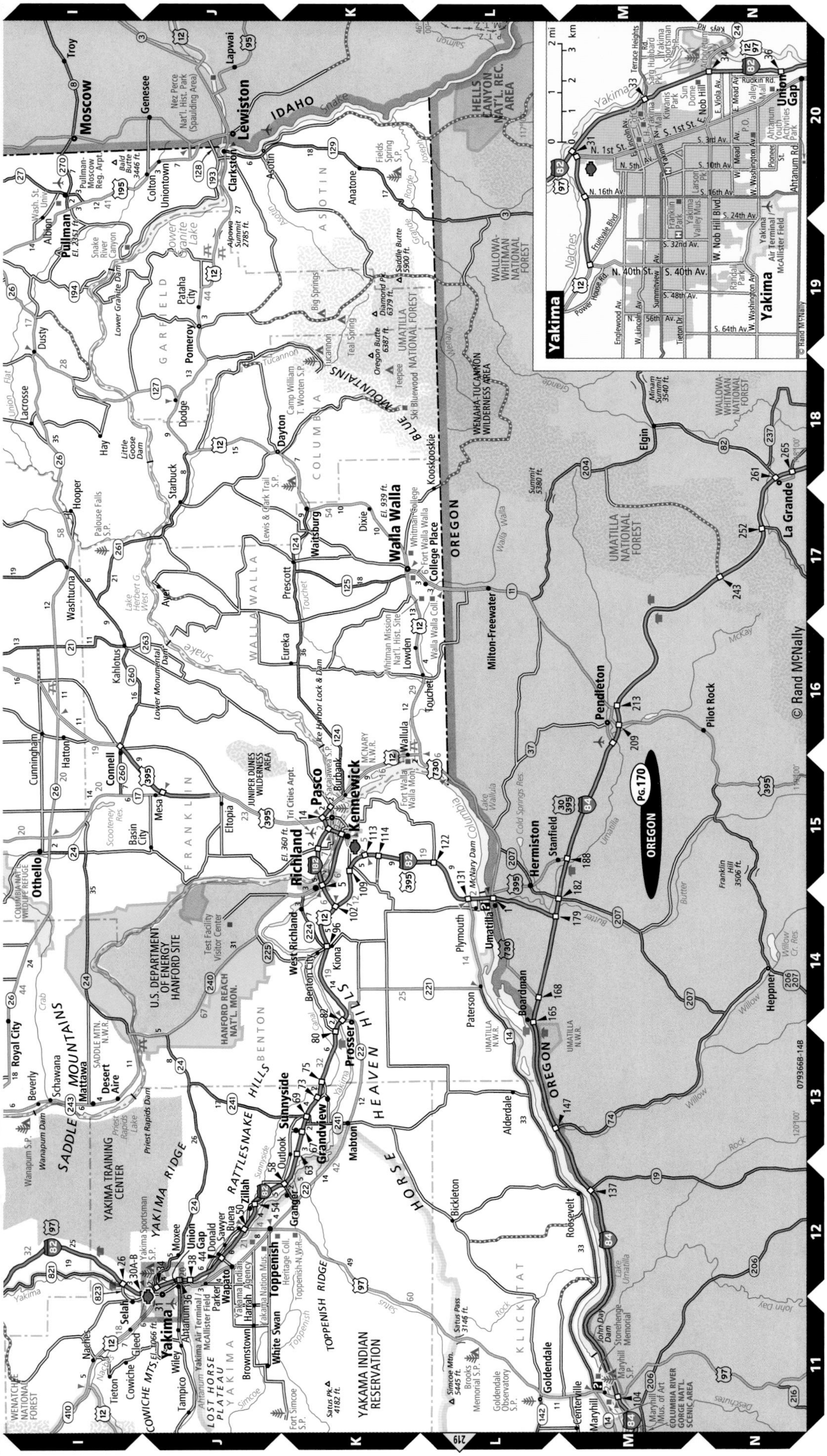

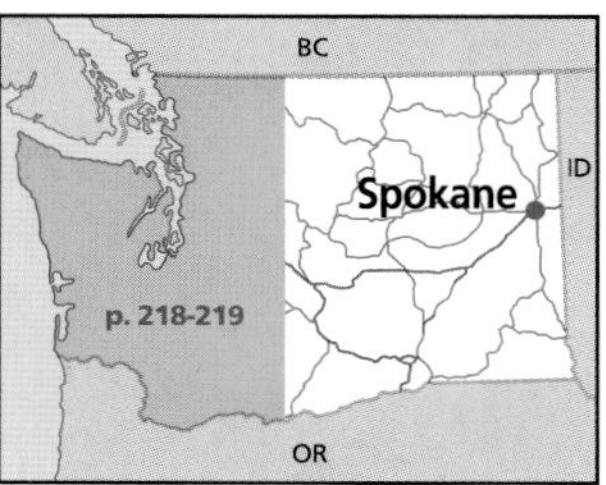
BC
Spokane
ID
p. 218-219
OR

SYMBOLS

- Featured ride
- Scenic route
- Point of interest
- Long-term construction
- Harley-Davidson dealership

CITY-TO-CITY MILEAGE

	BELLINGHAM	KENNEWICK	PORTLAND, OR	SEATTLE	SPOKANE	TACOMA	THE DALLES, OR	YAKIMA
Aberdeen	197	286	145	109	373	78	222	207
Bellingham		302	262	88	365	119	324	223
Bremerton	152†	265†	174	64†	328†	33	251	186†
Colville	326	210	423	353	71	366	339	273
Kennewick	302		213	219	139	232	129	79
Lewiston, ID	397	122	334	314	109	327	250	200
Longview	217	255	49	129	371	98	126	169
Olympia	147	260	115	59	323	28	192	181
Omak	208	189	377	241	138	254	293	192
Port Angeles	124†	338	232	82†	401†	106†	309	259†
Portland, OR	262	213		174	352	143	84	185
Seattle	88	219	174		282	31	241	140
Spokane	365	139	352	282		295	268	202
Tacoma	119	232	143	31	295		220	153
The Dalles, OR	324	129	84	241	268	220		101
Vancouver, BC	55	357	317	143	420	174	379	278
Wenatchee	185	140	291	153	172	166	207	106
Yakima	223	79	185	140	202	153	101	

† Via ferry

HARLEY-DAVIDSON DEALERSHIPS

Shumate Harley-Davidson, K-15
3305 W 19th Ave. **Kennewick**
(509) 735-9775
Lat N 46.192 **Lon** W 119.167

Shumate Harley-Davidson Spokane, F-19
6815 E Trent Ave. **Spokane Valley**
(509) 928-6811
Lat N 47.675 **Lon** W 117.313

Wenatchee Harley-Davidson, G-12
708 S Wenatchee Ave. **Wenatchee**
(509) 662-3434
Lat N 47.415 **Lon** W 120.304

Owens Harley-Davidson, J-12
1707 N 1st St. **Yakima**
(509) 575-1916
Lat N 46.622 **Lon** W 120.512

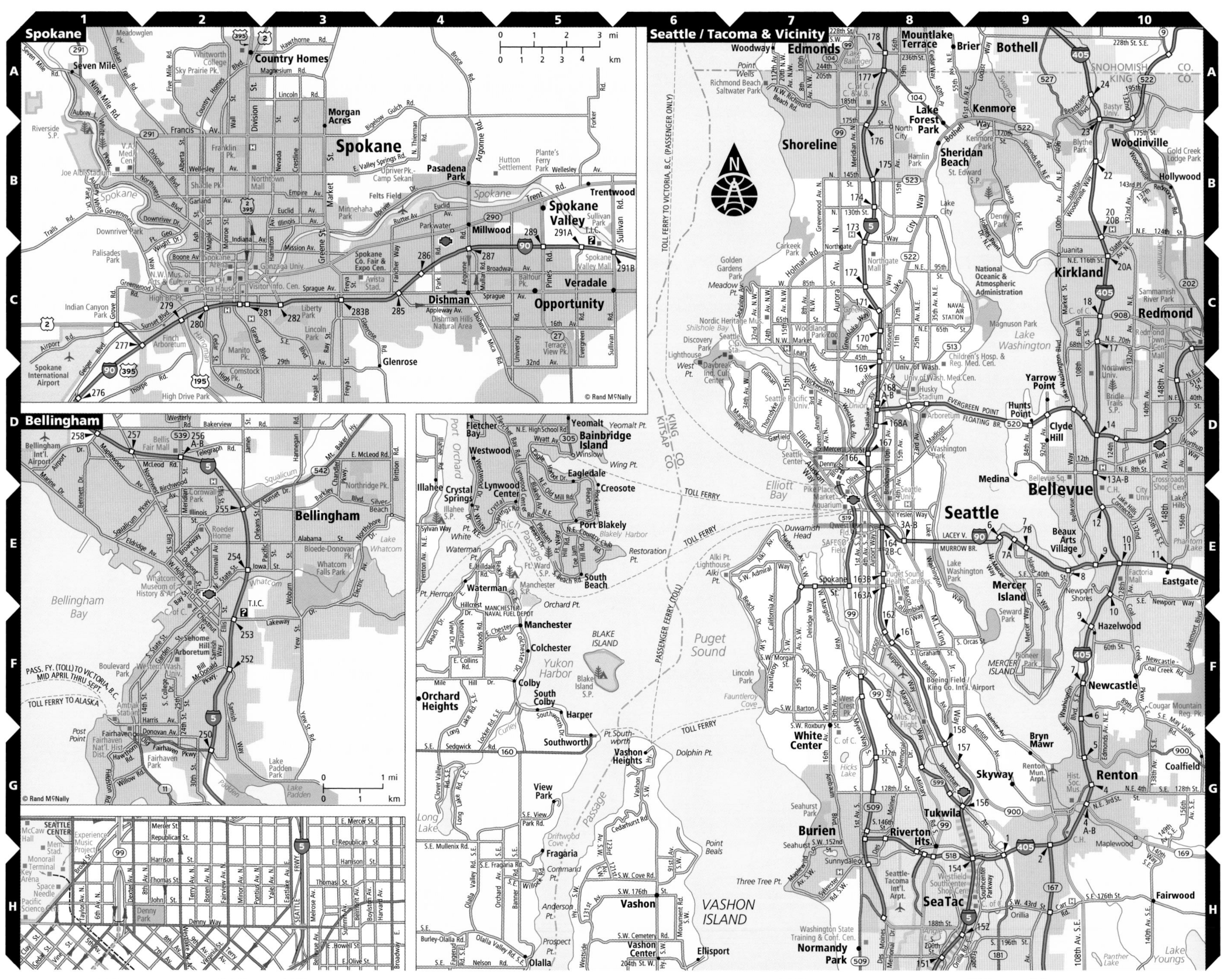
Spokane
Seattle / Tacoma & Vicinity
Bellingham
Spokane Valley
Opportunity
Veradale
Dishman
Millwood
Country Homes
Morgan Acres
Pasadena Park
Trentwood
Seven Mile
Glenrose
Edmonds
Shoreline
Bothell
Kenmore
Woodinville
Kirkland
Redmond
Bellevue
Seattle
Mercer Island
Renton
Newcastle
Tukwila
SeaTac
Burien
White Center
Bainbridge Island
Port Orchard
Manchester
Vashon Island
Puget Sound
Elliott Bay
Lake Washington
Bellingham Bay
© Rand McNally

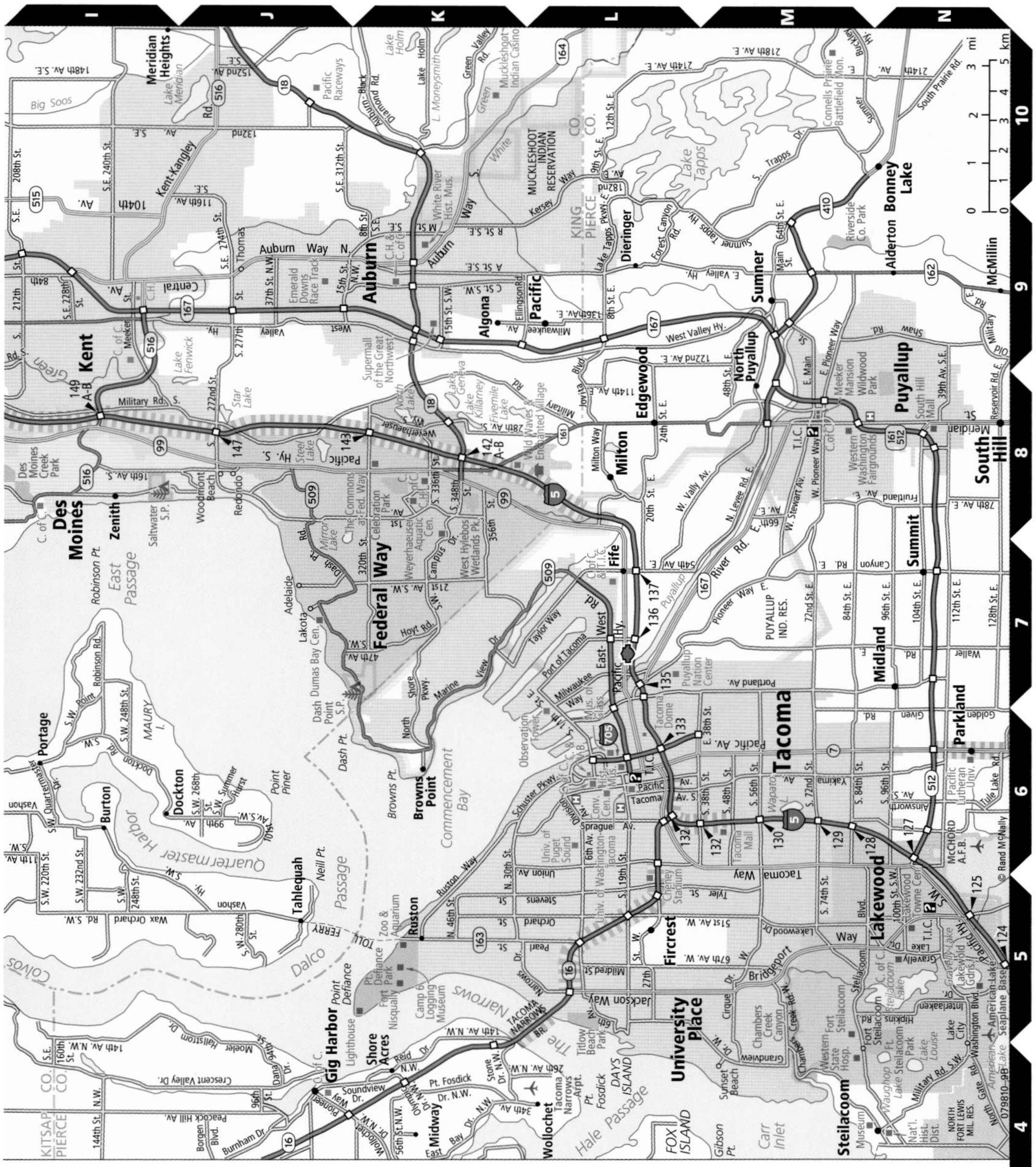

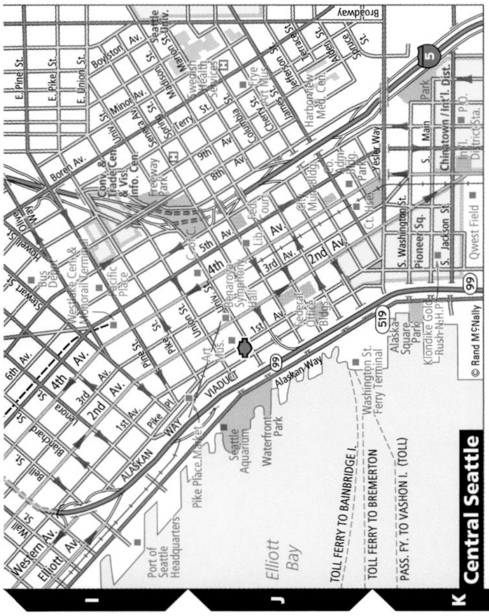

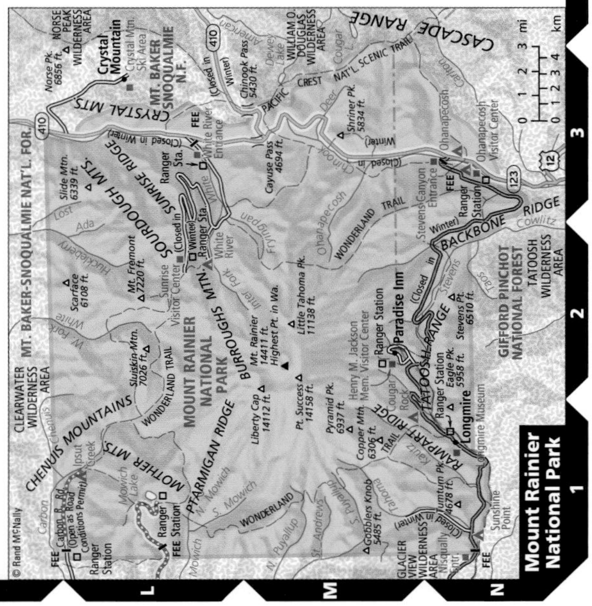

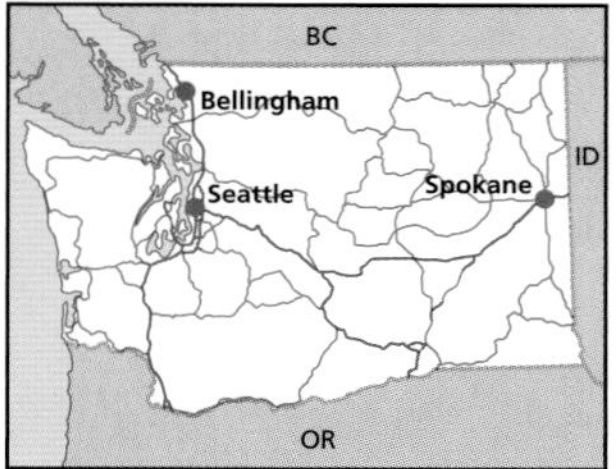
BC
Bellingham
Seattle
Spokane
ID
OR

SYMBOLS

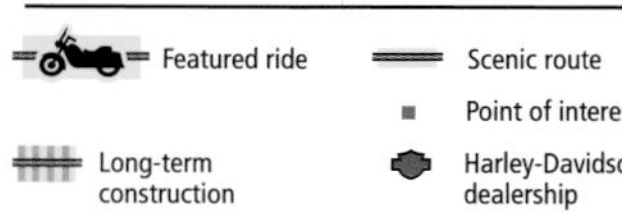
Featured ride
Scenic route
Point of interest
Long-term construction
Harley-Davidson dealership

WASHINGTON MOTORCYCLE LAWS

Helmet use:
Required

Riding two abreast:
Yes. See state law for specifics

Eye protection:
Required unless equipped with windscreen

Speed limit:
Primary roads: 70 mph
Secondary roads: 60 mph

WASHINGTON RESOURCES

Road conditions or construction:
511
(800) 695-7623
www.wsdot.wa.gov/traffic/

Highway Emergency Numbers:
911

Tourism:
(800) 544-1800
www.experiencewashington.com

State motor vehicle information:
(360) 902-3600
www.dol.wa.gov/drivers.htm

HARLEY-DAVIDSON DEALERSHIPS

Eastside Harley-Davidson, D-10
14408 NE 20th St. **Bellevue**
(425) 702-2000
Lat N 47.628 **Lon** W 122.148

Destination Harley-Davidson, L-7
2302 Pacific Hwy. E **Fife (Tacoma)**
(253) 922-3700
Lat N 47.243 **Lon** W 122.397

Downtown Harley-Davidson, E-8
1305 1st Ave. **Seattle**
(206) 448-5661
Lat N 47.607 **Lon** W 122.338

Downtown Harley-Davidson, G-8
13001 48th Ave. S **Tukwila**
(206) 243-5000
Lat N 47.486 **Lon** W 122.269

Central Seattle

Mount Rainier National Park

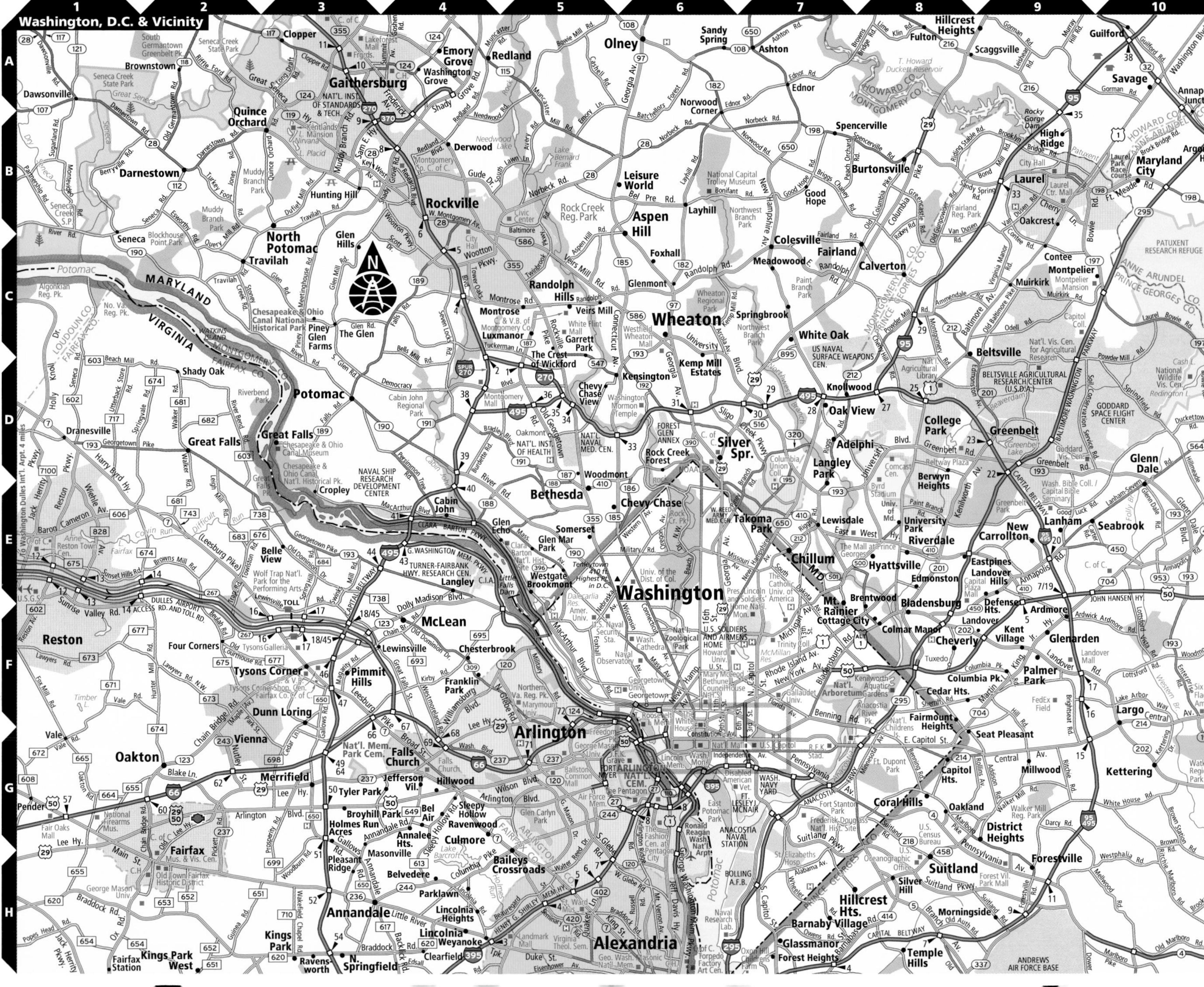
Washington, D.C. & Vicinity
Washington
Alexandria
Arlington
Bethesda
Silver Spr.
Rockville
Gaithersburg
Wheaton
Laurel
Greenbelt
Potomac
McLean
Reston
Fairfax
Annandale
Olney
Falls Church
Tysons Corner
Chevy Chase
College Park
Bowie
Suitland
MARYLAND
VIRGINIA

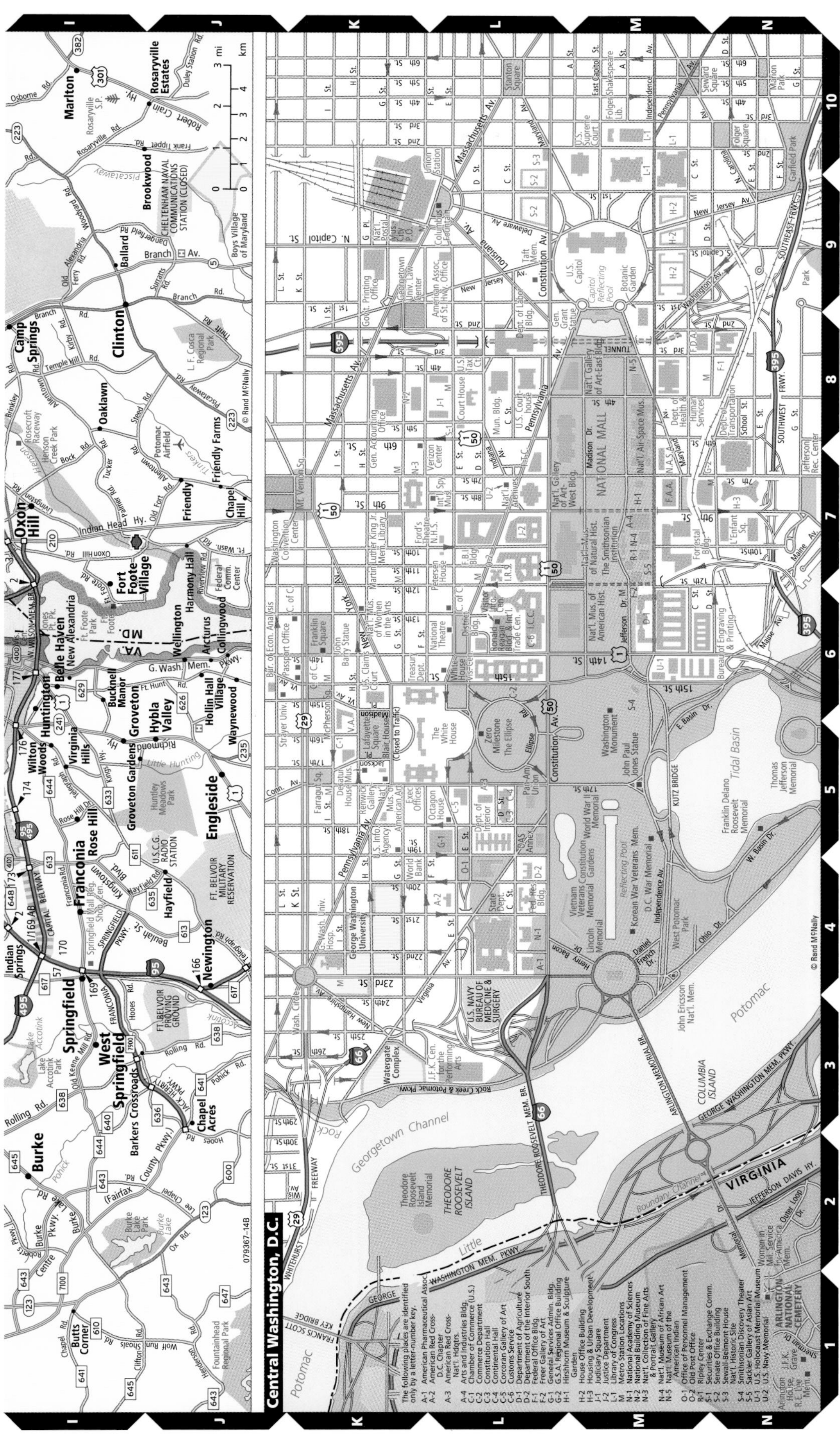
Central Washington, D.C.
NATIONAL MALL
U.S. Capitol
The White House
Washington Monument
Tidal Basin
Potomac
THEODORE ROOSEVELT ISLAND
COLUMBIA ISLAND
VIRGINIA
ARLINGTON NATIONAL CEMETERY
Springfield
Franconia
Clinton
Oxon Hill
© Rand McNally

SYMBOLS

Featured ride
Scenic route
Point of interest
Long-term construction
Harley-Davidson dealership

WASHINGTON, D.C. MOTORCYCLE LAWS

Helmet use:
Required

Riding two abreast:
No reference in administrative code or statutes

Eye protection:
Required unless equipped with windscreen

Speed limit:
Primary roads: 55 mph
Secondary roads: N/A

WASHINGTON, D.C. RESOURCES

Road conditions or construction:
www.ddot.dc.gov

Highway Emergency Numbers:
911

Tourism:
(800) 422-8644 (to request travel materials only)
(202) 789-7000
www.washington.org

State motor vehicle information:
(202) 727-5000
http://dmv.washingtondc.gov

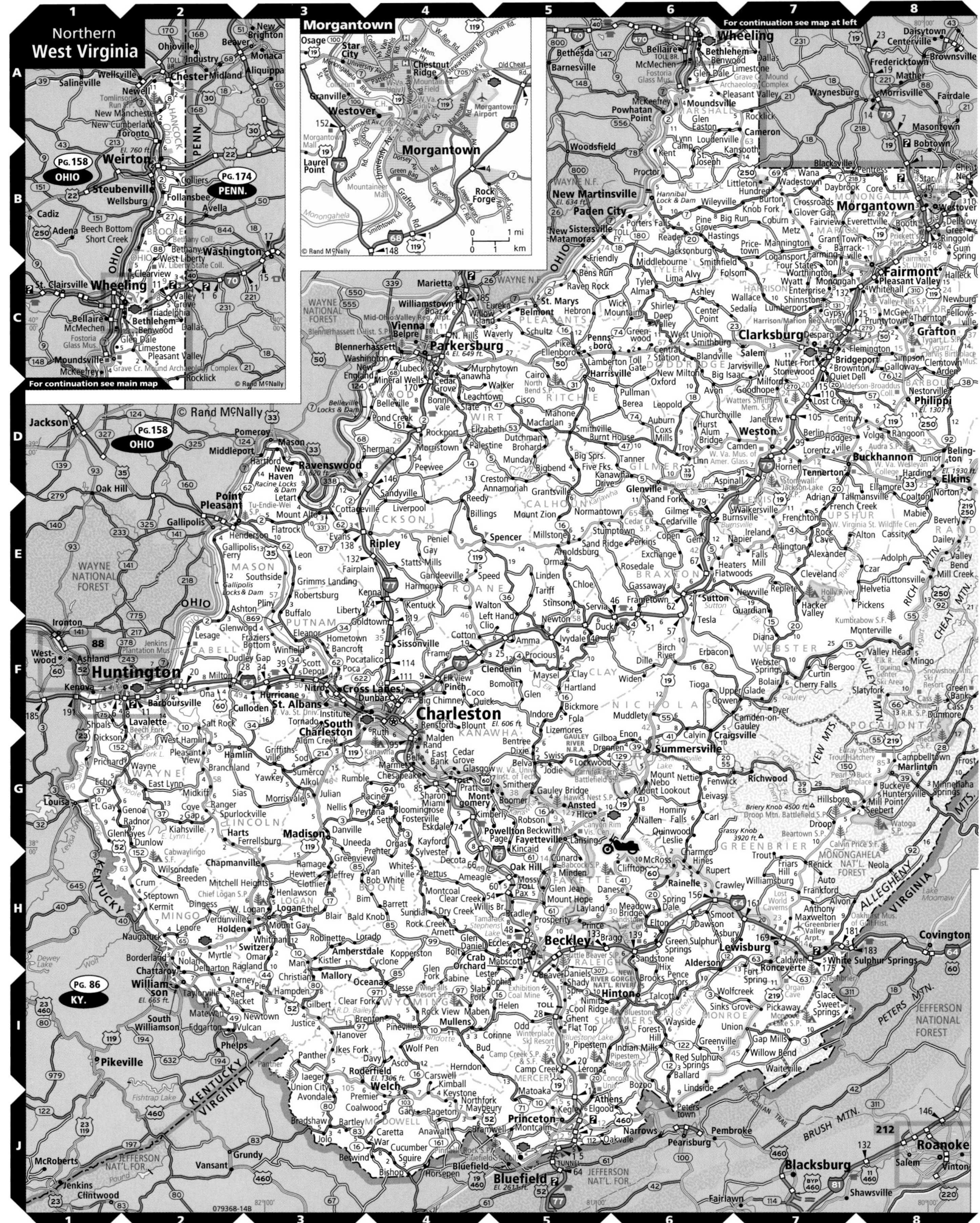
Distance scale
One inch represents about 21 miles
0 5 10 15 20 mi
0 5 10 15 20 25 30 km
Northern West Virginia
Morgantown
For continuation see map at left
For continuation see main map
© Rand McNally
Wheeling
Parkersburg
Charleston
Huntington
Clarksburg
Morgantown
Fairmont
Beckley
Bluefield
Princeton
Lewisburg
White Sulphur Springs
Weirton
Steubenville
Blacksburg
Roanoke
PG. 158 OHIO
PG. 174 PENN.
PG. 86 KY.
WAYNE NATIONAL FOREST
JEFFERSON NAT'L. FOR.
MONONGAHELA NAT'L. FOREST
079368-14B

How to determine distance

Mileages in red between red arrowheads; in black, between intersections.

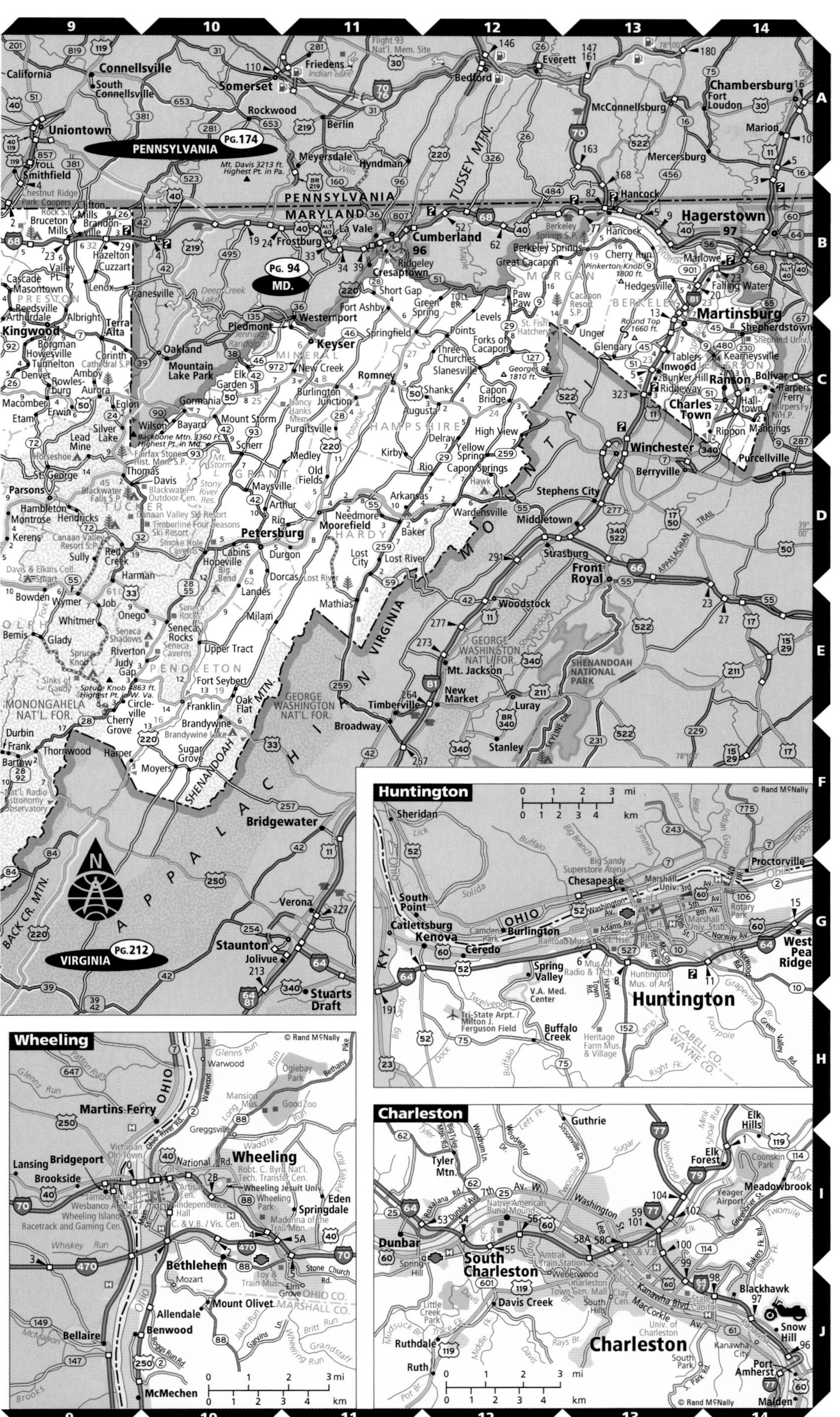
PENNSYLVANIA
PG. 174
MD.
PG. 94
VIRGINIA
PG. 212
Connellsville
Somerset
Uniontown
Bedford
Chambersburg
Hagerstown
Cumberland
Martinsburg
Morgantown
Kingwood
Keyser
Petersburg
Winchester
Charles Town
Front Royal
Harrisonburg
Staunton
Bridgewater
Mt. Jackson
New Market
Luray
Elkins
MONONGAHELA NAT'L. FOR.
GEORGE WASHINGTON NAT'L. FOR.
SHENANDOAH NATIONAL PARK
APPALACHIAN MTN.
Spruce Knob 4863 ft. Highest Pt. in W. Va.
Mt. Davis 3213 ft. Highest Pt. in Pa.
Backbone Mtn. 3360 Ft. Highest Pt. in Md.
Huntington
© Rand McNally
Wheeling
© Rand McNally
Charleston
© Rand McNally
South Charleston
Martins Ferry
Bellaire
Bethlehem
McMechen
Kenova
Ceredo
Proctorville
Dunbar
Kanawha City

SYMBOLS

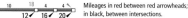

- Featured ride
- Scenic route
- Point of interest
- Long-term construction
- Harley-Davidson dealership

For West Virginia ride, see page R37.

WEST VIRGINIA MOTORCYCLE LAWS

Helmet use:
Reflectorization required

Riding two abreast:
No reference in administrative code or statutes

Eye protection:
Required by law

Speed limit:
Primary roads: 70 mph
Secondary roads: 55 mph

WEST VIRGINIA RESOURCES

Road conditions or construction:
(877) 982-7623
www.wvdot.com

Highway Emergency Numbers:
911

Tourism:
(800) 225-5982
www.callwva.com

State motor vehicle information:
(304) 558-3900
www.wvdot.com/6_motorists/dmv

CITY-TO-CITY MILEAGE

	Beckley	Charleston	Cumberland, MD	Huntington	Morgantown	Parkersburg	Wheeling	White Sulphur Springs
Beckley		60	241	111	169	135	236	60
Charleston	60		227	51	155	75	176	125
Cumberland, MD	241	227		278	72	181	146	193
Huntington	111	51	278		206	126	227	176
Morgantown	169	155	72	206		109	74	201
Parkersburg	135	75	181	126	109		105	200
Wheeling	236	176	146	227	74	105		301
White Sulphur Sprs.	60	125	193	176	201	200	301	

HARLEY-DAVIDSON DEALERSHIPS

Cole Harley-Davidson, J-5
1804 Bland St. (Rte. 52 N) **Bluefield**
(304) 324-8116
Lat N 37.276 **Lon** W 81.219

Mike's Harley-Davidson Sales, I-2
US Hwy. 119 Preece Bottom Rd. **Delbarton**
(304) 475-0123
Lat N 37.788 **Lon** W 81.154

New River Gorge Harley-Davidson Shop, G-6
52489 Midland Trail **Hico**
(304) 658-3300
Lat N 38.106 **Lon** W 80.958

Benjy's Harley-Davidson, F-2
408 4th St. **Huntington**
(304) 523-1340
Lat N 38.419 **Lon** W 82.452

Triple S Harley-Davidson, B-8
308 Cheat Rd. **Morgantown**
(304) 284-8244
Lat N 39.651 **Lon** W 79.909

B & B Harley-Davidson Cycle Sales, C-7
100 Alexander Ave. **Nutter Fort (Clarksburg)**
(304) 623-0484
Lat N 39.275 **Lon** W 80.359

Harley-Davidson of West Virginia, F-3
4924 MacCorkle Ave. SW **South Charleston**
(304) 768-1600
Lat N 38.355 **Lon** W 81.732

Valley Harley-Davidson, A-6
1034 E Bethlehem **Wheeling**
(304) 243-9300
Lat N 40.039 **Lon** W 80.677

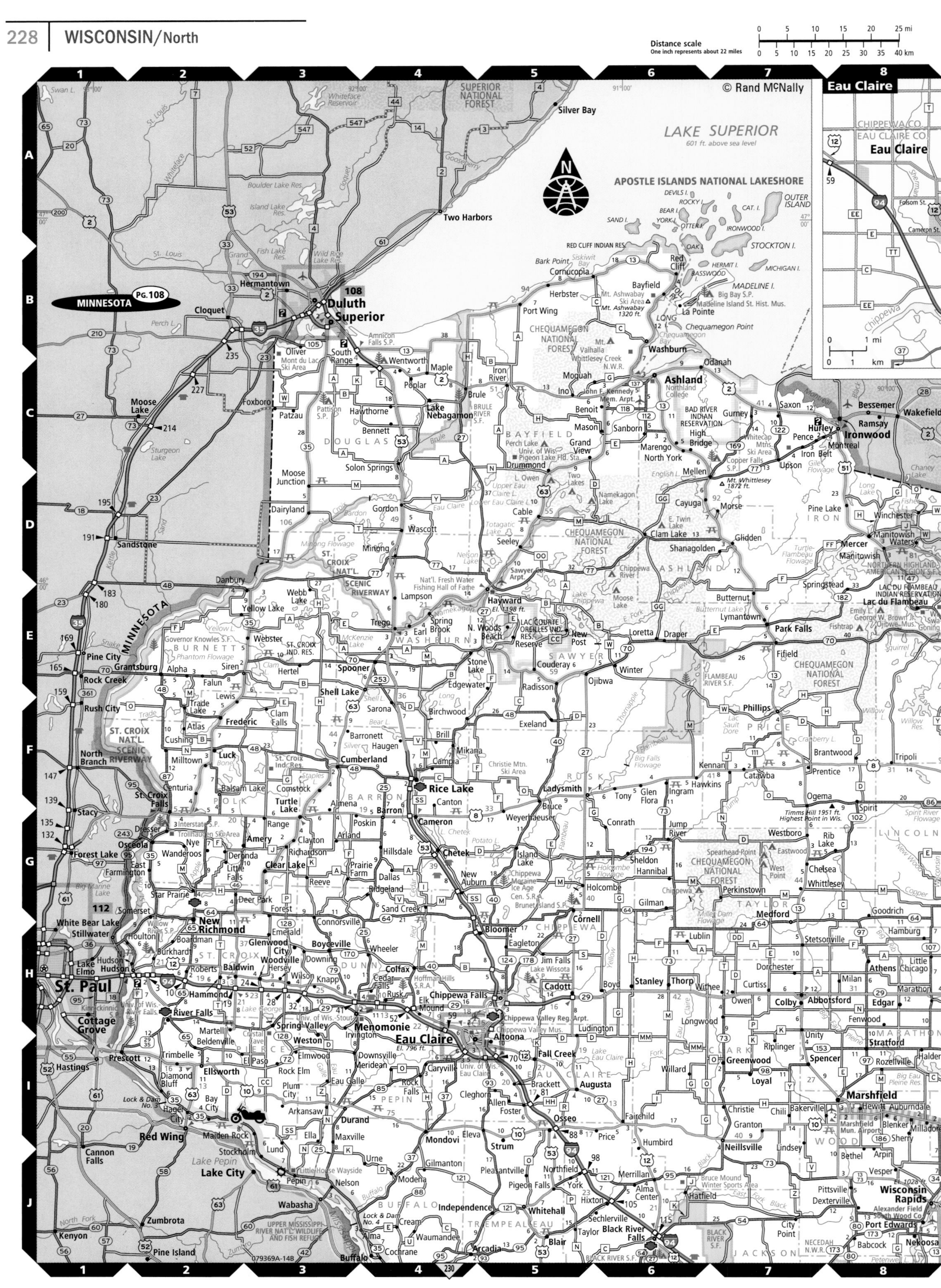
Distance scale
One inch represents about 22 miles
0 5 10 15 20 25 mi
0 5 10 15 20 25 30 35 40 km
© Rand McNally
Eau Claire
LAKE SUPERIOR
601 ft. above sea level
APOSTLE ISLANDS NATIONAL LAKESHORE
SUPERIOR NATIONAL FOREST
MINNESOTA PG. 108
Silver Bay
Two Harbors
Duluth
Superior
Cloquet
Hermantown
Moose Lake
Sandstone
Pine City
Rush City
North Branch
Stacy
Forest Lake
White Bear Lake
Stillwater
St. Paul
Cottage Grove
Hastings
Red Wing
Cannon Falls
Lake City
Wabasha
Zumbrota
Kenyon
Pine Island
Bayfield
Washburn
Ashland
Red Cliff
La Pointe
Cornucopia
Herbster
Port Wing
Iron River
Brule
Lake Nebagamon
Solon Springs
Gordon
Minong
Hayward
Cable
Drummond
Mellen
Hurley
Ironwood
Bessemer
Wakefield
Saxon
Montreal
Mercer
Manitowish Waters
Lac du Flambeau
Park Falls
Phillips
Butternut
Springstead
Danbury
Webster
Siren
Grantsburg
Frederic
Luck
St. Croix Falls
Osceola
Amery
Spooner
Shell Lake
Trego
Rice Lake
Cumberland
Barron
Cameron
Chetek
Ladysmith
Bruce
Hawkins
Medford
Prentice
New Richmond
Hudson
River Falls
Prescott
Ellsworth
Menomonie
Baldwin
Glenwood City
Boyceville
Bloomer
Cornell
Chippewa Falls
Eau Claire
Altoona
Fall Creek
Augusta
Osseo
Mondovi
Durand
Pepin
Alma
Buffalo
Arcadia
Independence
Whitehall
Blair
Black River Falls
Neillsville
Greenwood
Loyal
Spencer
Marshfield
Stratford
Colby
Abbotsford
Athens
Stanley
Thorp
Owen
Withee
Wisconsin Rapids
Port Edwards
Nekoosa
Pittsville
Dexterville
CHEQUAMEGON NATIONAL FOREST
ST. CROIX NAT'L. SCENIC RIVERWAY
BAYFIELD
DOUGLAS
BURNETT
WASHBURN
SAWYER
ASHLAND
IRON
PRICE
RUSK
BARRON
POLK
ST. CROIX
DUNN
CHIPPEWA
TAYLOR
CLARK
EAU CLAIRE
PEPIN
PIERCE
BUFFALO
TREMPEALEAU
JACKSON
WOOD
MARATHON
LINCOLN
UPPER MISSISSIPPI RIVER NAT'L. WILDLIFE AND FISH REFUGE
Timms Hill 1951 ft. Highest Point in Wis.
Mt. Whittlesey 1872 ft.
079369A-148

How to determine distance

Mileages in red between red arrowheads; in black, between intersections.

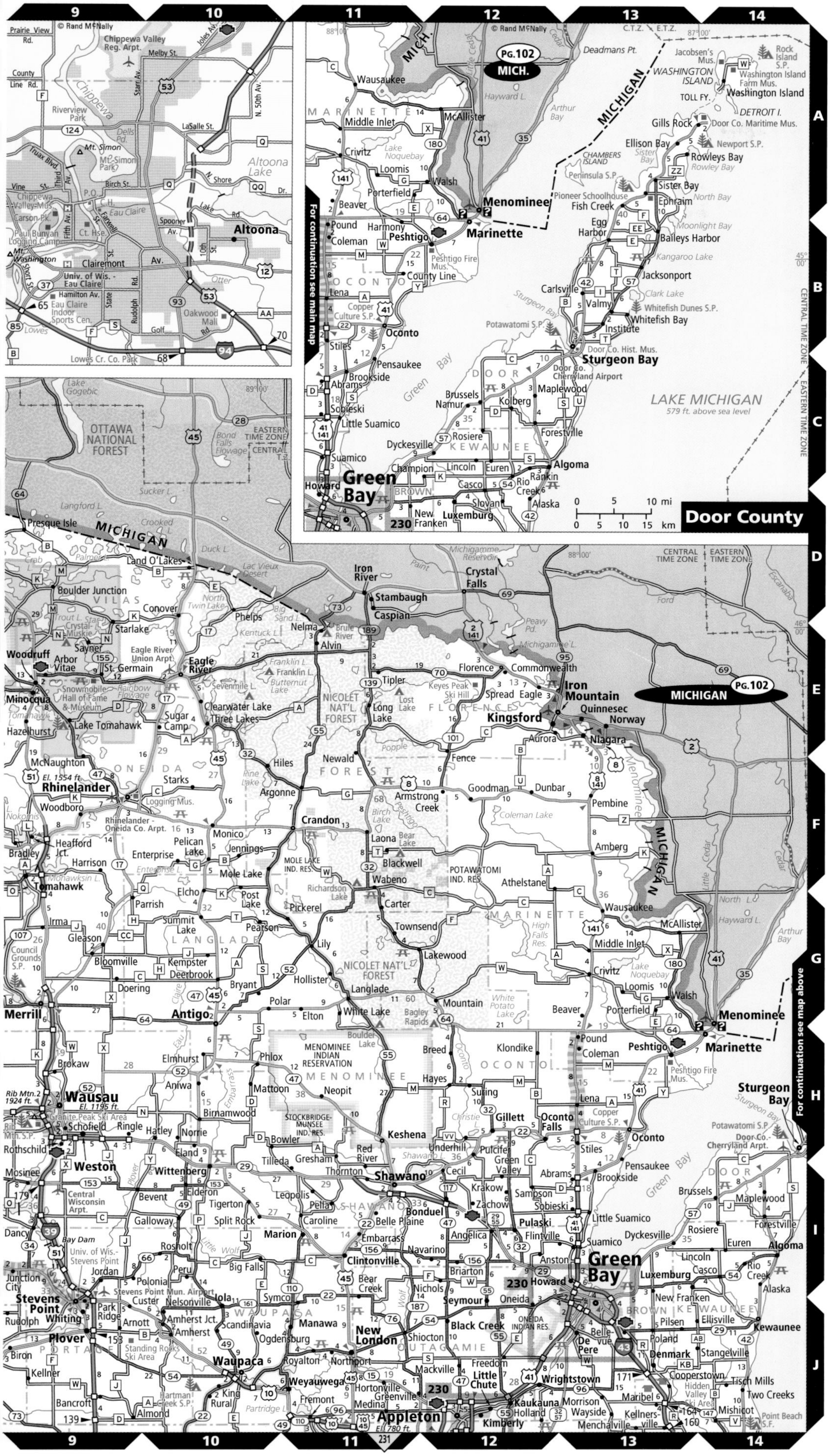

Door County

For continuation see main map

For continuation see map above

MN
MI
Green Bay
p. 230-231
IA
IL

SYMBOLS

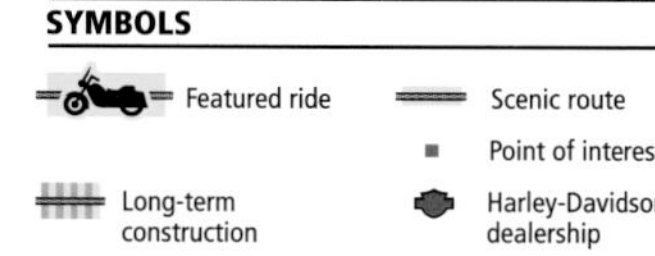
Featured ride
Scenic route
Point of interest
Long-term construction
Harley-Davidson dealership

For Wisconsin/Minnesota ride, see page R38-39.

WISCONSIN MOTORCYCLE LAWS

Helmet use:
Required under age 18, and for instructional permit holders

Riding two abreast:
Yes. See state law for specifics

Eye protection:
Required for instructional permit holders
Required unless equipped with windscreen which is 15" or higher above handlebars

Speed limit:
Primary roads: 65 mph
Secondary roads: 65 mph

HARLEY-DAVIDSON DEALERSHIPS

Harley-Davidson Appleton, J-12
5322 Clairemont Dr. **Appleton**
(920) 757-1651
Lat N 44.285 **Lon** W 88.487

Northern Lights Harley-Davidson, E-9
1700 Hwy. 51 **Arbor Vitae**
(715) 358-5054
Lat N 45.922 **Lon** W 89.683

Al Muth Harley-Davidson Sales, J-6
N6630 Cty. Hwy. A **Black River Falls**
(715) 284-4725
Lat N 44.283 **Lon** W 90.822

Doc's Harley-Davidson of Shawano, I-12
W2709 State Hwy. 29 **Bondeul**
(715) 758-9080
Lat N 44.703 **Lon** W 88.369

Sport Motors Harley-Davidson, H-5
2452 Hallie Rd. (US Hwy. 53) **Chippewa Falls**
(715) 723-7433
Lat N 44.875 **Lon** W 91.433

McCoy's Harley-Davidson Green Bay, J-13
2728 Manitowoc Rd. **Green Bay**
(920) 406-3900
Lat N 44.465 **Lon** W 87.947

St. Croix Harley-Davidson, G-2
2060 Hwy. 65 N **New Richmond**
(715) 246-2959
Lat N 45.160 **Lon** W 92.529

Vandervest Harley-Davidson, H-13
810 Frontage Rd. **Peshtigo**
(715) 582-8843
Lat N 45.053 **Lon** W 87.733

Rice Lake Harley-Davidson, F-4
2801 S Wisconsin Ave. **Rice Lake**
(715) 234-5400
Lat N 45.495 **Lon** W 91.745

St. Croix Harley-Davidson Shop, H-2
883 Hwy. 65 **River Falls**
(715) 426-0199
Lat N 44.859 **Lon** W 92.629

Wausau Harley-Davidson, H-9
1570 County Rd. XX **Rothschild**
(715) 355-4464
Lat N 44.858 **Lon** W 89.635

Distance scale
One inch represents about 22 miles

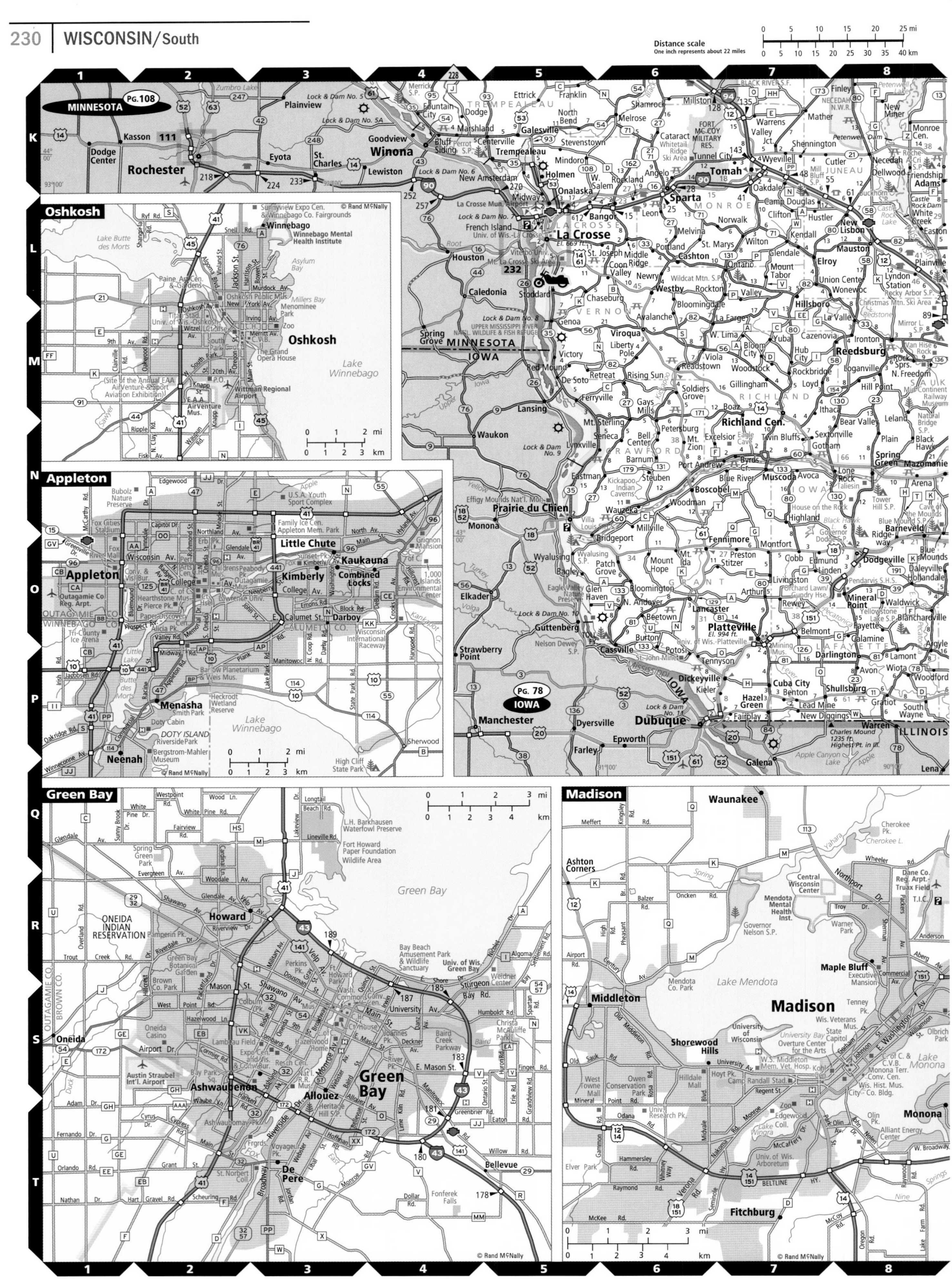

MINNESOTA PG. 108
Rochester
Winona
La Crosse
Tomah
Sparta
Onalaska
Prairie du Chien
Platteville
Dubuque
Reedsburg
Richland Cen.
Dodgeville
Viroqua
MINNESOTA
IOWA
PG. 78 IOWA
ILLINOIS
Oshkosh
Lake Winnebago
Appleton
Little Chute
Kaukauna
Kimberly
Combined Locks
Menasha
Neenah
Green Bay
Howard
Ashwaubenon
Allouez
De Pere
Bellevue
Madison
Middleton
Shorewood Hills
Maple Bluff
Monona
Fitchburg
Waunakee
Lake Mendota
© Rand McNally

How to determine distance

Mileages in red between red arrowheads; in black, between intersections.

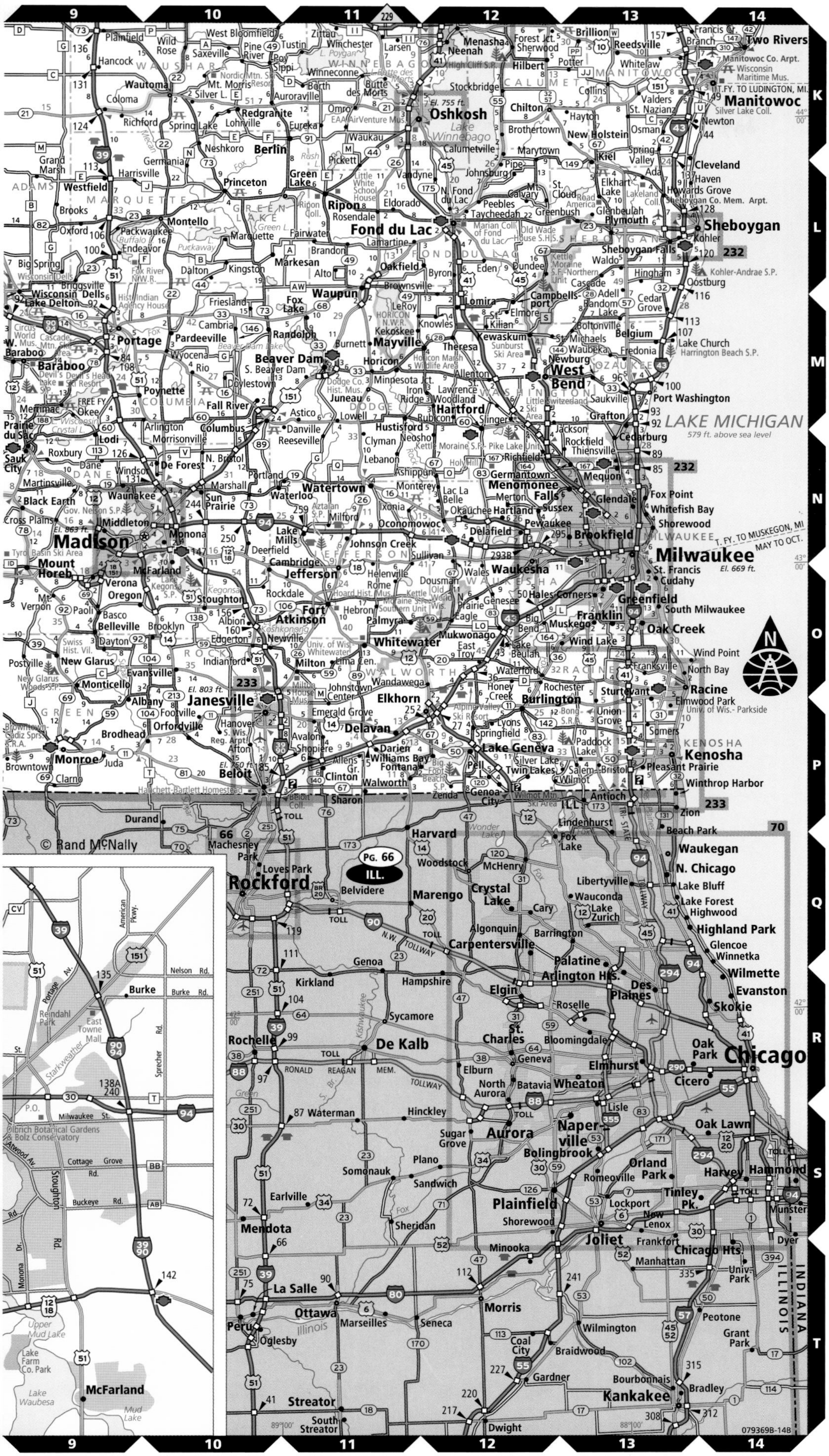

MN
MI
p. 228-229
Milwaukee
IA
IL

SYMBOLS

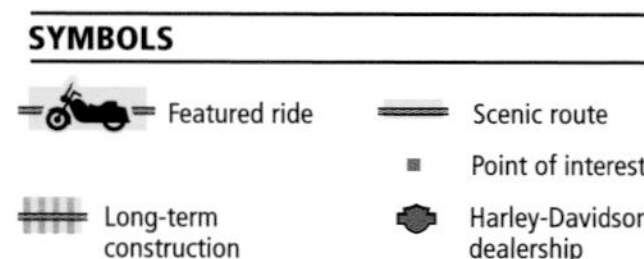
Featured ride
Scenic route
Point of interest
Long-term construction
Harley-Davidson dealership

For Wisconsin/Minnesota ride, see page R38-39.

HARLEY-DAVIDSON DEALERSHIPS

For Milwaukee and Racine/Kenosha area dealers, please see listings on page 233.

Mischler's Harley-Davidson, M-11
N8131 Kellom Rd. **Beaver Dam**
(920) 887-8425
Lat N 43.481 **Lon** W 88.820

Bob's Harley-Davidson, L-12
24 S Rolling Meadows Dr. **Fond du Lac**
(920) 921-2344
Lat N 43.776 **Lon** W 88.483

Hartford Harley-Davidson Shop, M-12
427 Sumner St. (Hwy. 60 W) **Hartford**
(262) 670-1000
Lat N 43.317 **Lon** W 88.369

Kutter Harley-Davidson, P-10
3223 N Pontiac Dr. **Janesville**
(608) 757-0880
Lat N 42.721 **Lon** W 88.989

Capital City Harley-Davidson, N-10
6200 Millpond Rd. **Madison**
(608) 221-2761
Lat N 43.044 **Lon** W 89.273

Stock's Harley-Davidson, K-14
3206 Menasha Ave. **Manitowoc**
(920) 684-0237
Lat N 44.119 **Lon** W 87.688

Bala's Harley-Davidson, L-8
N 4833 Hwy. 58 **Mauston**
(608) 847-7702
Lat N 43.801 **Lon** W 90.049

Kutter Harley-Davidson Shop, P-9
129 W 6th St. **Monroe**
(608) 329-4884
Lat N 42.607 **Lon** W 89.658

Wisconsin Harley-Davidson, N-12
1280 Blue Ribbon Dr. **Oconomowoc**
(262) 569-8500
Lat N 43.064 **Lon** W 88.472

La Crosse Area Harley-Davidson, L-5
1116 Oak Forest Dr. **Onalaska**
(608) 783-6112
Lat N 43.871 **Lon** W 91.220

Sauk Prairie Harley-Davidson, N-9
836 Phillips Blvd. **Sauk City**
(608) 643-3735
Lat N 43.271 **Lon** W 89.737

Route 43 Harley-Davidson, L-13
3736 S Taylor Dr. **Sheboygan**
(920) 458-0777
Lat N 43.716 **Lon** W 87.759

West Bend Harley-Davidson, M-12
2910 W Washington St. **West Bend**
(262) 338-8761
Lat N 43.427 **Lon** W 88.223

Bala's Harley-Davidson of Wisconsin Dells, M-8
524 Wisconsin Dells Pkwy. **Wisconsin Dells**
(608) 253-2252
Lat N 43.595 **Lon** W 89.794

079369B-14B

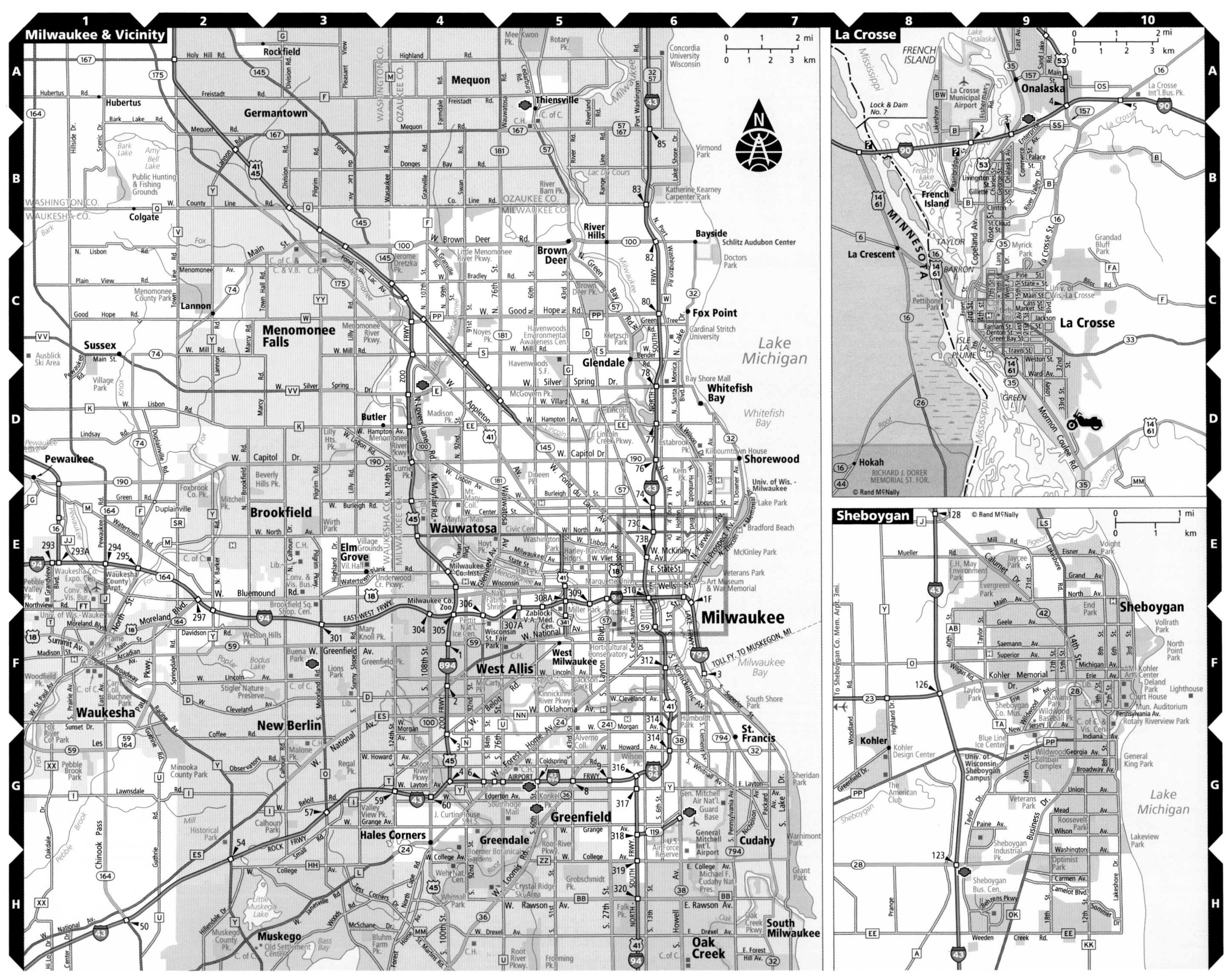
La Crosse
Sheboygan
Milwaukee & Vicinity
La Crosse
Onalaska
French Island
La Crescent
Hokah
MINNESOTA
Mississippi
Lake Michigan
Sheboygan
Kohler
© Rand McNally
Milwaukee
Shorewood
Whitefish Bay
Fox Point
Bayside
River Hills
Brown Deer
Glendale
Thiensville
Mequon
Germantown
Rockfield
Hubertus
Colgate
Menomonee Falls
Lannon
Sussex
Pewaukee
Butler
Wauwatosa
Brookfield
Elm Grove
Waukesha
New Berlin
West Allis
West Milwaukee
Greenfield
Greendale
Hales Corners
Muskego
St. Francis
Cudahy
South Milwaukee
Oak Creek

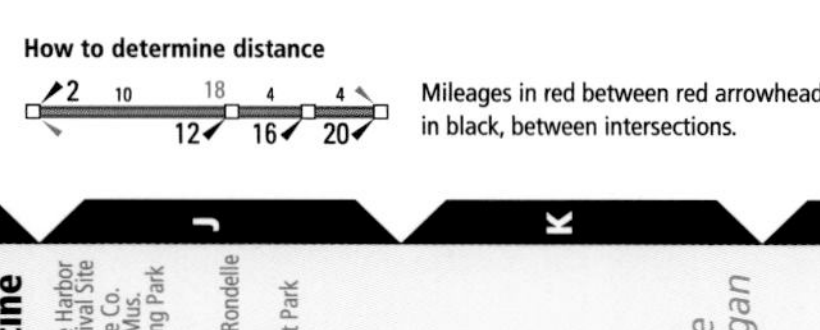
How to determine distance
Mileages in red between red arrowheads; in black, between intersections.

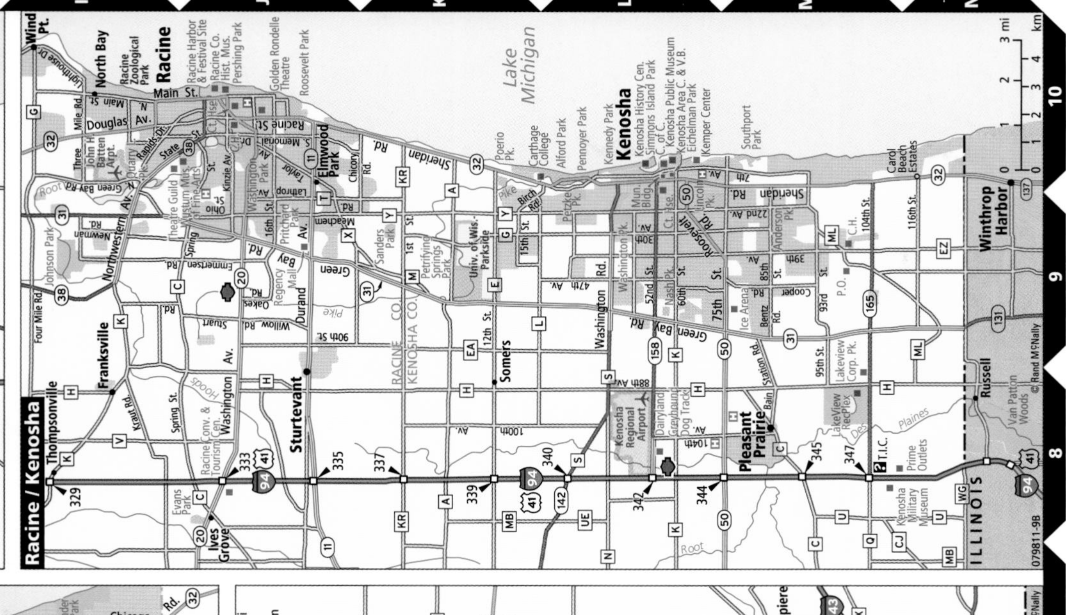
Racine / Kenosha
Lake Michigan
Racine
Kenosha
Sturtevant
Pleasant Prairie
Somers
ILLINOIS

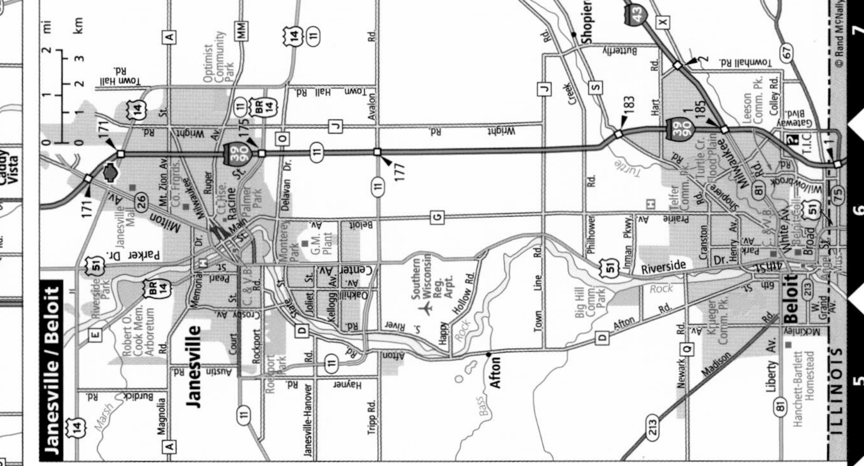
Janesville / Beloit
Janesville
Beloit
Afton
Shopiere
ILLINOIS

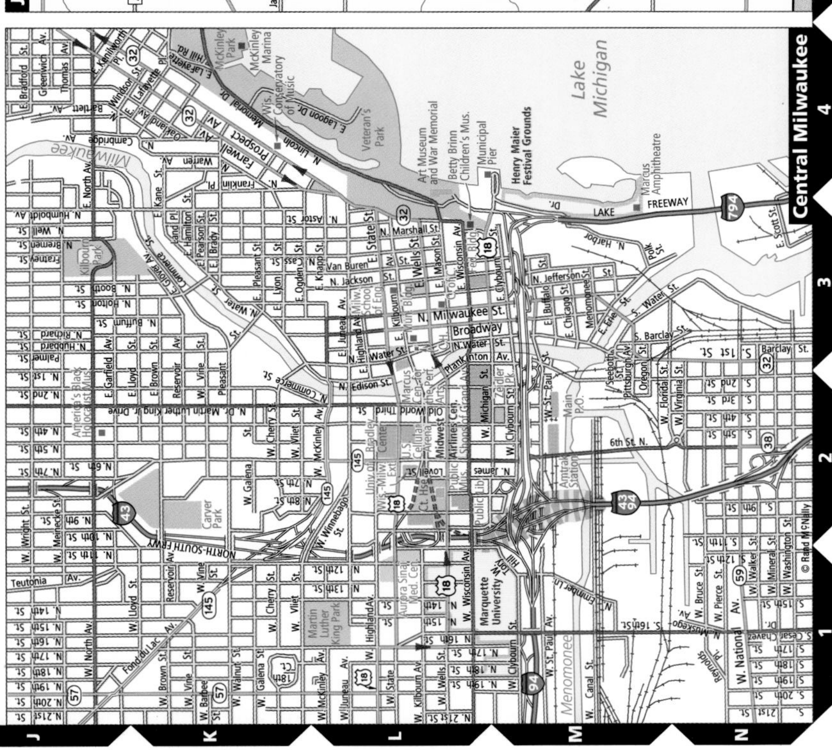
Central Milwaukee
Franklin
Lake Michigan
Big Muskego Lake
Big Bend

MN
MI
IA
IL
La Crosse
Sheboygan
Milwaukee
Janesville
Racine
Beloit
Kenosha

SYMBOLS

- Featured ride
- Scenic route
- Point of interest
- Long-term construction
- Harley-Davidson dealership

WISCONSIN MOTORCYCLE LAWS

Helmet use:
Required under age 18, and for instructional permit holders

Riding two abreast:
Yes. See state law for specifics

Eye protection:
Required for instructional permit holders
Required unless equipped with windscreen which is 15" or higher above handlebars

Speed limit:
Primary roads: 65 mph
Secondary roads: 65 mph

WISCONSIN RESOURCES

Road conditions or construction:
(800) 762-3947
www.dot.state.wi.us

Highway Emergency Numbers:
911

Tourism:
(800) 432-8747
www.travelwisconsin.com

State motor vehicle information:
(608) 266-2353
www.dot.wisconsin.gov/drivers

HARLEY-DAVIDSON DEALERSHIPS

Uke's Harley-Davidson, L-8
5995 120th Ave. **Kenosha**
(262) 857-UKES
Lat N 42.582 **Lon** W 87.952

House of Harley-Davidson, G-5
6221 W Layton Ave. **Milwaukee**
(414) 282-2211
Lat N 42.959 **Lon** W 87.992

House of Harley-Davidson Airport, G-6
5300 S Howell Ave. **Milwaukee**
(414) 747-5384
Lat N 42.948 **Lon** W 87.910

Milwaukee Harley-Davidson, D-4
11310 W Silver Spring Rd. **Milwaukee**
(414) 461-4444
Lat N 43.119 **Lon** W 88.052

Hal's Harley-Davidson, F-3
1925 S Moorland Rd. **New Berlin**
(262) 860-2060
Lat N 43.009 **Lon** W 88.108

Racine Harley-Davidson, J-9
1155 Oakes Rd. **Racine**
(262) 884-0123
Lat N 42.720 **Lon** W 87.870

Suburban Motors Harley-Davidson, A-5
139 N Main St. **Thiensville**
(262) 242-2464
Lat N 43.232 **Lon** W 87.984

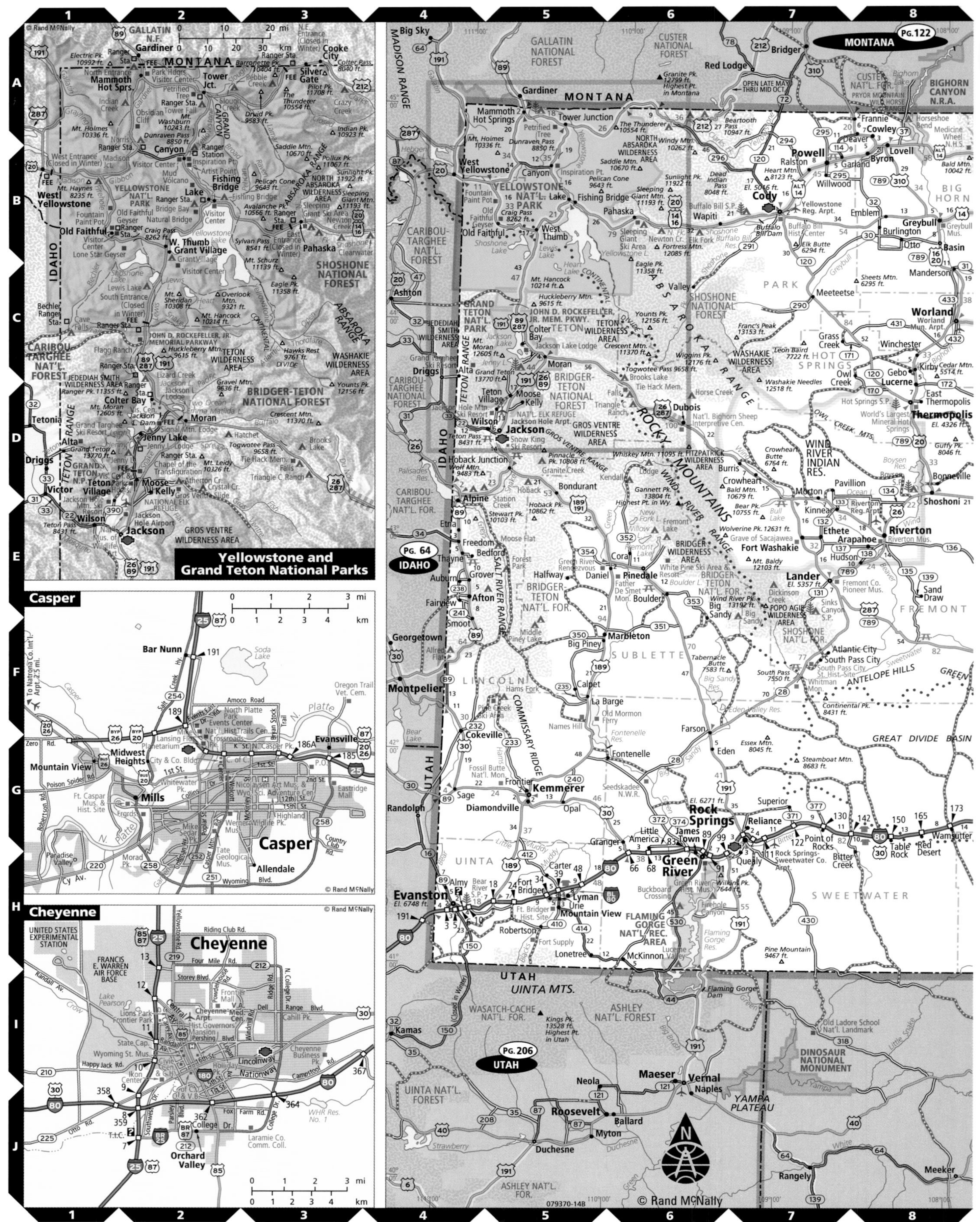
Distance scale
One inch represents about 40 miles
MONTANA
PG. 122
IDAHO
PG. 64
UTAH
PG. 206
Yellowstone and Grand Teton National Parks
Casper
Cheyenne
Cody
Jackson
Rock Springs
Green River
Evanston
Riverton
Lander
Thermopolis
Worland
Powell
Kemmerer
Pinedale
© Rand McNally

How to determine distance

2 10 18 4 4 / 12 16 20 — Mileages in red between red arrowheads; in black, between intersections.

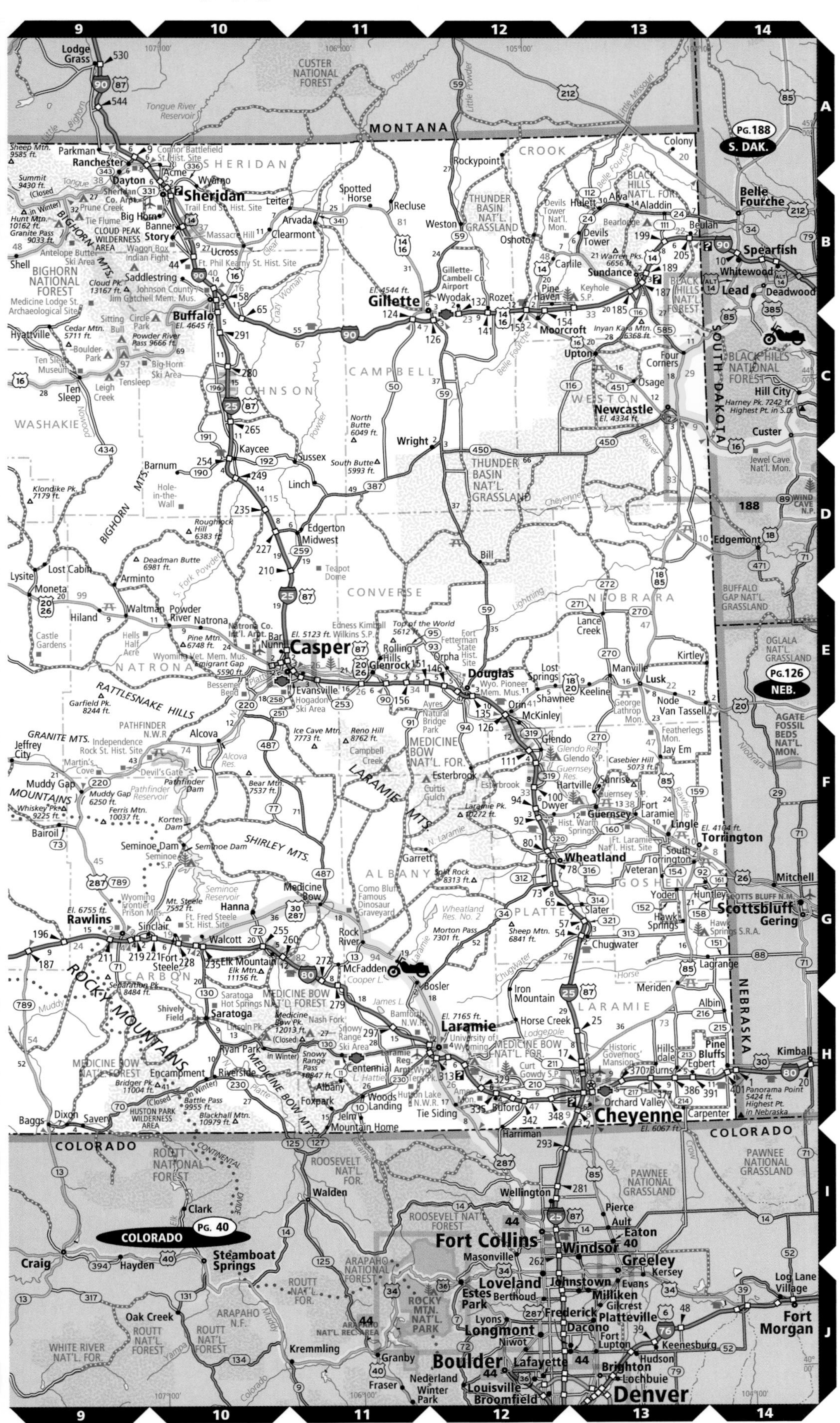
MONTANA
S. DAK.
PG. 188
SOUTH DAKOTA
NEBRASKA
PG. 126
NEB.
COLORADO
PG. 40
SHERIDAN
CROOK
JOHNSON
CAMPBELL
WESTON
CONVERSE
NIOBRARA
NATRONA
GOSHEN
PLATTE
ALBANY
LARAMIE
CARBON
WASHAKIE
Sheridan
Buffalo
Gillette
Casper
Douglas
Newcastle
Sundance
Spearfish
Lead
Deadwood
Belle Fourche
Rawlins
Laramie
Cheyenne
Wheatland
Torrington
Scottsbluff
Fort Collins
Greeley
Loveland
Longmont
Boulder
Denver
Steamboat Springs
Craig
Fort Morgan
BIGHORN NATIONAL FOREST
THUNDER BASIN NAT'L. GRASSLAND
MEDICINE BOW NAT'L. FOR.
BLACK HILLS NAT'L. FOREST
LARAMIE MTS.
ROCKY MOUNTAINS
BIGHORN MTS.
RATTLESNAKE HILLS
SHIRLEY MTS.
ROCKY MTN. NAT'L. PARK

SYMBOLS

- Featured ride
- Scenic route
- Point of interest
- Long-term construction
- Harley-Davidson dealership

For Wyoming/Colorado ride, see page R40.
For South Dakota/Wyoming ride, see page R32-33.

WYOMING MOTORCYCLE LAWS

Helmet use:
Required under age 18

Riding two abreast:
Yes. See state law for specifics

Eye protection:
Not required

Speed limit:
Primary roads: 75 mph
Secondary roads: 60 mph

WYOMING RESOURCES

Road conditions or construction:
511
(888) 996-7623 (in WY)
(307) 772-0824
www.dot.state.wy.us

Highway Emergency Numbers:
911

Tourism:
(800) 225-5996
www.wyomingtourism.org

State motor vehicle information:
(307) 777-4800
www.dot.state.wy.us

CITY-TO-CITY MILEAGE

	Casper	Cheyenne	Cody	Jackson	Riverton	Rock Springs	Sheridan	Spearfish, SD
Casper		180	214	282	119	226	152	223
Cheyenne	180		395	436	275	258	329	295
Cody	214	395		178	139	282	148	346
Jackson	282	436	178		166	178	326	509
Riverton	119	275	139	166		143	217	346
Rock Springs	226	258	282	178	143		378	449
Sheridan	152	329	148	326	217	378		199
Spearfish, SD	223	295	346	509	346	449	199	

HARLEY-DAVIDSON DEALERSHIPS

Deluxe Harley-Davidson, E-11
831 N Glenn Rd. **Casper**
(307) 265-3211
Lat N 42.859 **Lon** W 106.339

Cheyenne Harley-Davidson, H-13
3320 E Lincoln Way **Cheyenne**
(307) 638-8307
Lat N 41.138 **Lon** W 104.776

Beartooth Harley-Davidson, B-7
1137 Sheridan Ave. **Cody**
(307) 527-7776
Lat N 44.526 **Lon** W 109.065

Deluxe Harley-Davidson Shop, C-12
3300 Conestoga Dr. **Gillette**
(307) 687-2001
Lat N 44.295 **Lon** W 105.454

Jackson Hole Harley-Davidson, D-5
40 S Millward **Jackson**
(307) 739-1500
Lat N 43.479 **Lon** W 110.765

Laramie Harley-Davidson Shop, H-11
2061 Snowy Range Rd. **Laramie**
(307) 721-1024
Lat N 41.294 **Lon** W 106.016

Flaming Gorge Harley-Davidson, G-7
2401 Foothill Blvd. **Rock Springs**
(307) 382-9099
Lat N 41.579 **Lon** W 109.264

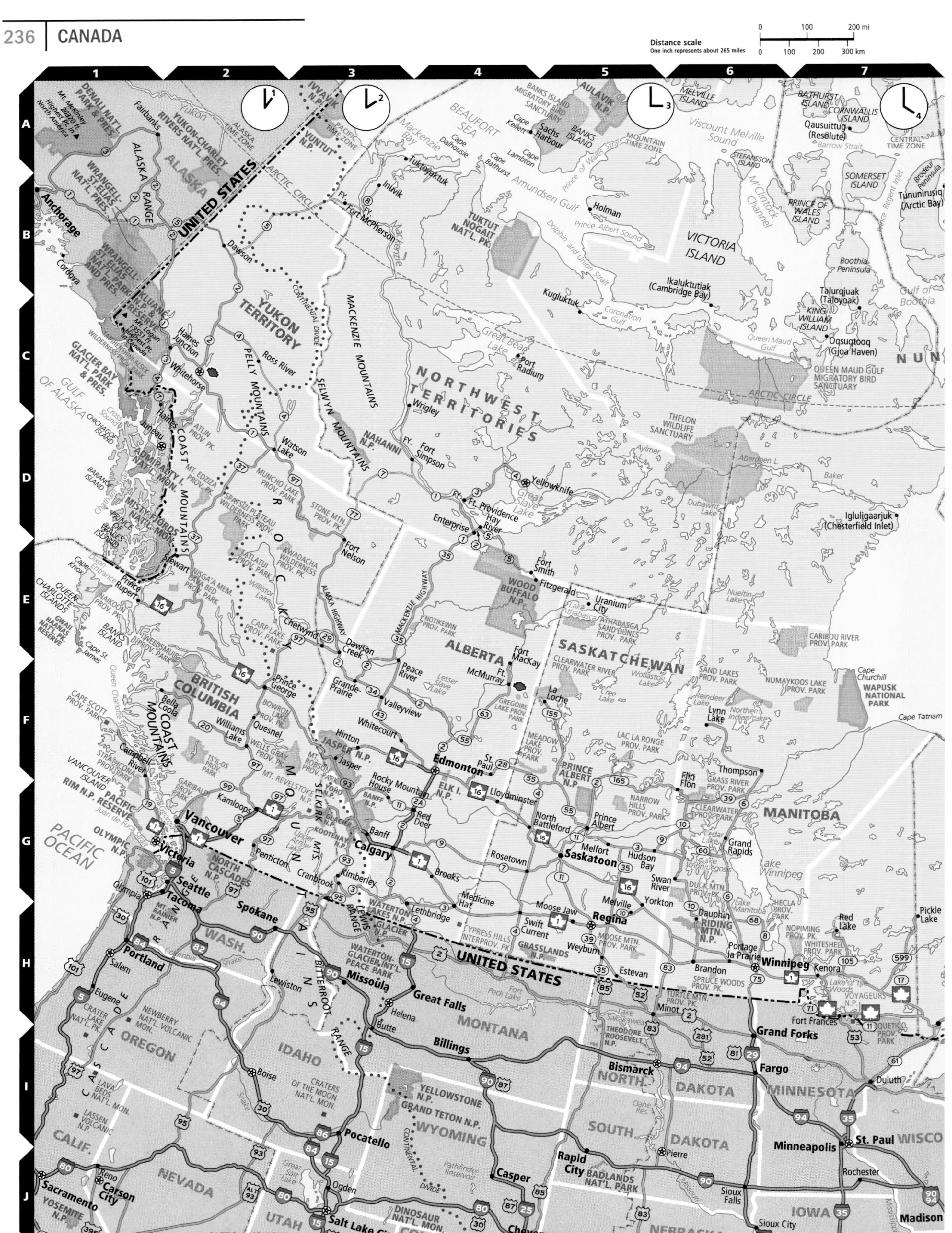
Distance scale
One inch represents about 265 miles
0 100 200 mi
0 100 200 300 km

How to determine distance

Kilometers in blue and mileages in red between red arrowheads; mileages in black between intersections.

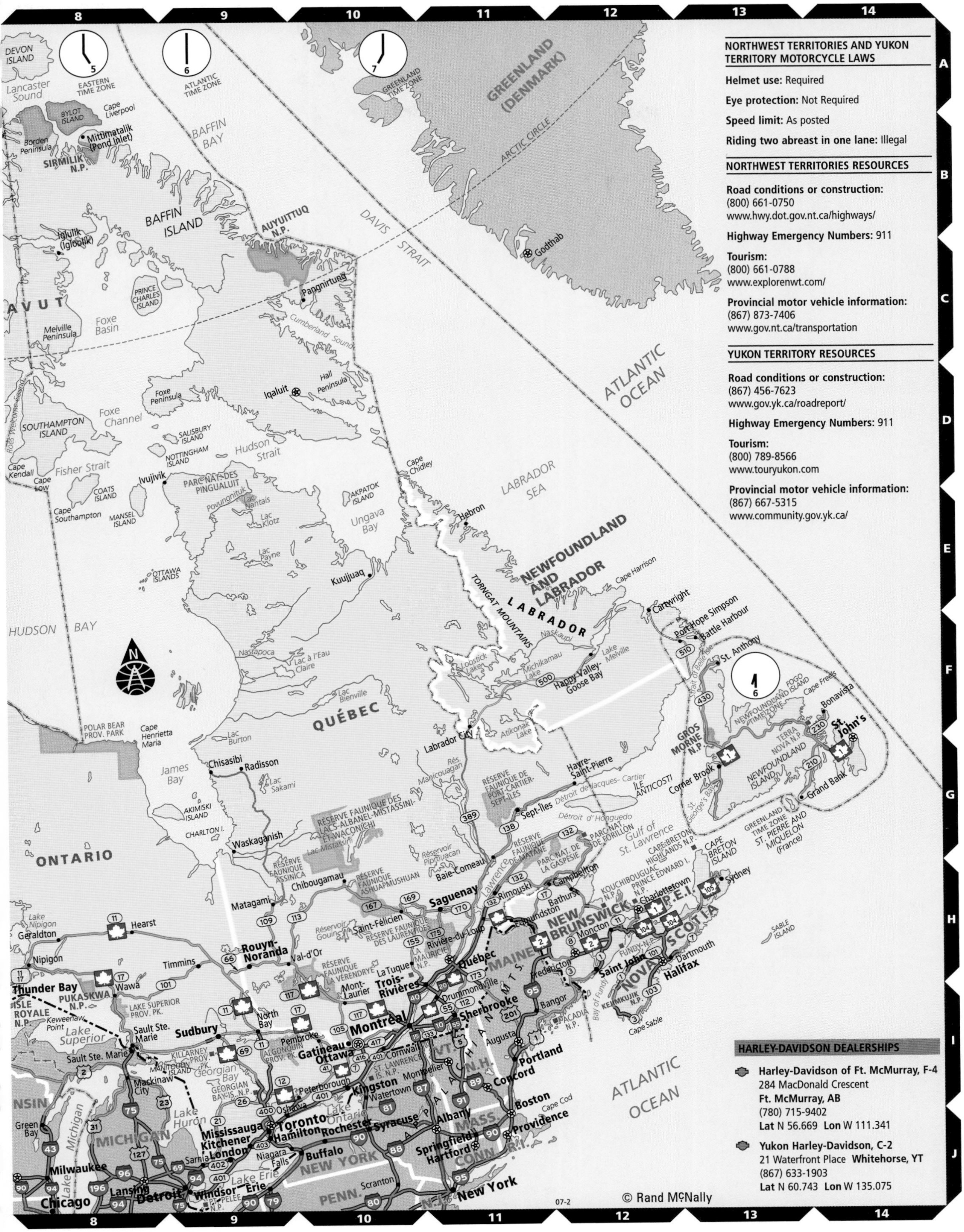

NORTHWEST TERRITORIES AND YUKON TERRITORY MOTORCYCLE LAWS

Helmet use: Required

Eye protection: Not Required

Speed limit: As posted

Riding two abreast in one lane: Illegal

NORTHWEST TERRITORIES RESOURCES

Road conditions or construction:
(800) 661-0750
www.hwy.dot.gov.nt.ca/highways/

Highway Emergency Numbers: 911

Tourism:
(800) 661-0788
www.explorenwt.com/

Provincial motor vehicle information:
(867) 873-7406
www.gov.nt.ca/transportation

YUKON TERRITORY RESOURCES

Road conditions or construction:
(867) 456-7623
www.gov.yk.ca/roadreport/

Highway Emergency Numbers: 911

Tourism:
(800) 789-8566
www.touryukon.com

Provincial motor vehicle information:
(867) 667-5315
www.community.gov.yk.ca/

HARLEY-DAVIDSON DEALERSHIPS

Harley-Davidson of Ft. McMurray, F-4
284 MacDonald Crescent
Ft. McMurray, AB
(780) 715-9402
Lat N 56.669 Lon W 111.341

Yukon Harley-Davidson, C-2
21 Waterfront Place Whitehorse, YT
(867) 633-1903
Lat N 60.743 Lon W 135.075

07-2

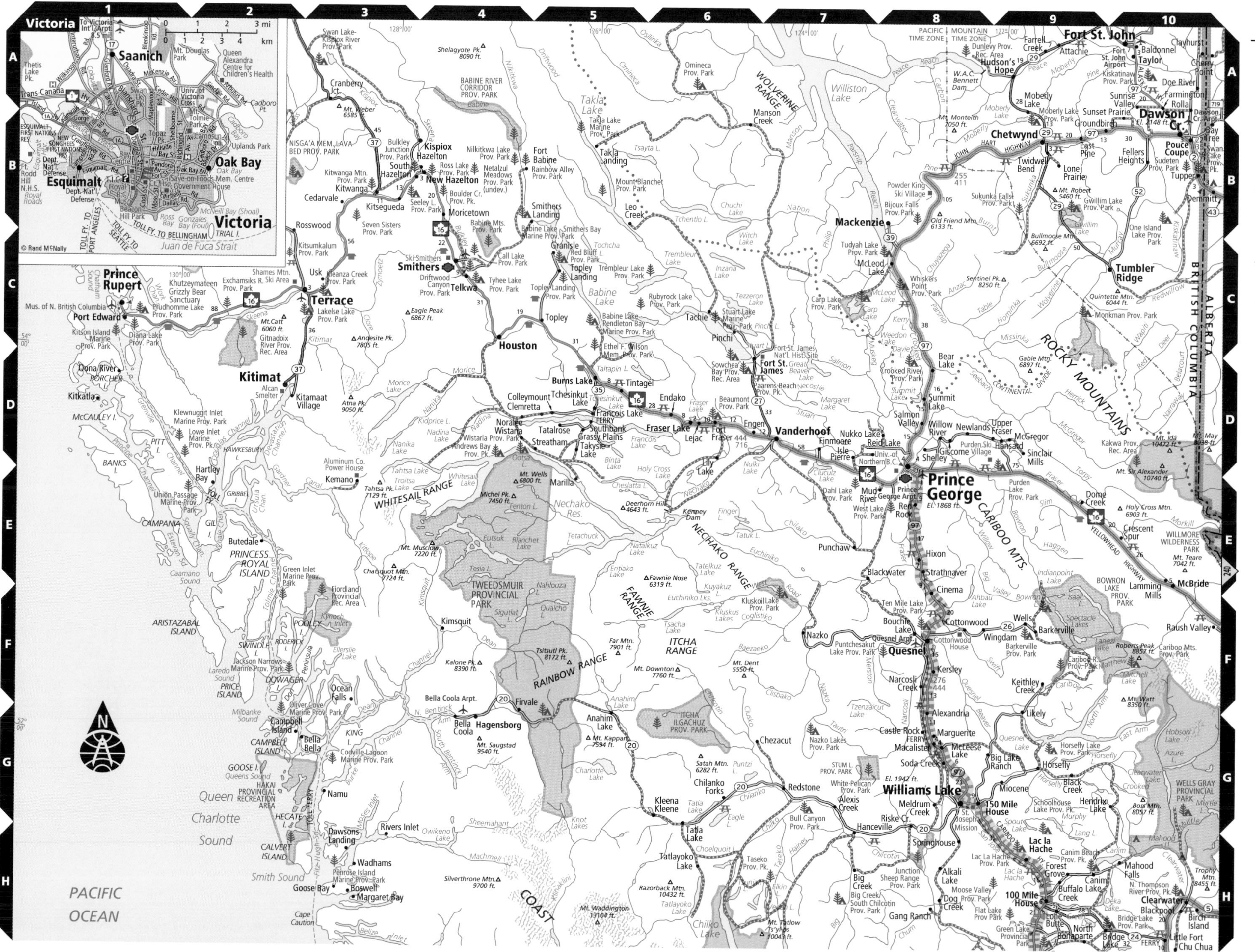
ALBERTA
BRITISH COLUMBIA
ROCKY MOUNTAINS
CARIBOO MTS.
Fort St. John
Dawson Cr.
Chetwynd
Tumbler Ridge
Mackenzie
Prince George
Vanderhoof
Quesnel
Williams Lake
100 Mile House
Smithers
Houston
Burns Lake
Terrace
Kitimat
Prince Rupert
TWEEDSMUIR PROVINCIAL PARK
NECHAKO RANGE
RAINBOW RANGE
WHITESAIL RANGE
Queen Charlotte Sound
PACIFIC OCEAN
Victoria
Saanich
Oak Bay
Esquimalt
Juan de Fuca Strait
© Rand McNally

Distance scale
One inch represents about 47 miles

0 10 20 30 40 mi
0 10 20 30 40 50 60 km

YT
NT
BC
AB
SK
p. 240-241
Vancouver
Victoria
WA
ID
MT

SYMBOLS

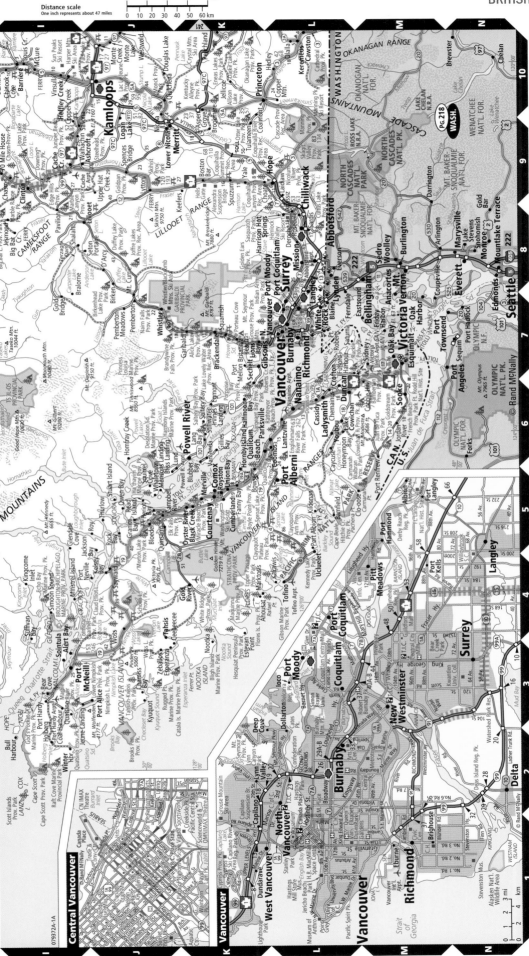

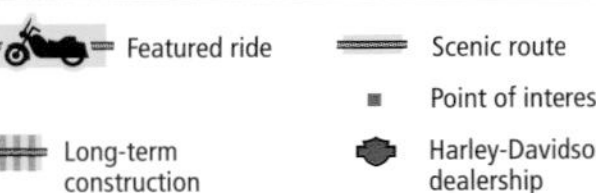
Featured ride
Scenic route
Point of interest
Long-term construction
Harley-Davidson dealership

BRITISH COLUMBIA MOTORCYCLE LAWS

Helmet use: Required

Eye protection: Not Required

Speed limit: As posted

Riding two abreast in one lane: Illegal

BRITISH COLUMBIA RESOURCES

Road conditions or construction:
(604) 660-9770
www.gov.bc.ca/tran/

Highway Emergency Numbers: 911

Tourism:
(800) 435-5622
www.hellobc.com

Provincial motor vehicle information:
(604) 661-2255
www.icbc.com/licensing

HARLEY-DAVIDSON DEALERSHIPS

Harley-Davidson of Chilliwack, L-8
44768 Yale Rd. West **Chilliwack, BC**
(604) 792-7820
Lat N 49.145 **Lon** W 121.987

Kamloops Harley-Davidson, J-10
1465 Iron Mask Rd., Exit 366 **Kamloops, BC**
(250) 828-0622
Lat N 50.660 **Lon** W 120.403

Barnes Harley-Davidson, L-7
20091 Logan Ave. **Langley, BC**
(604) 534-6044
Lat N 49.111 **Lon** W 122.666

Cariboo Motorcycles, L-7
3066 St. Johns St. **Port Moody, BC**
(604) 461-3458
Lat N 49.277 **Lon** W 122.844

Harley-Davidson of Prince George, E-8
2626 Vance Rd. **Prince George, BC**
(250) 564-6667
Lat N 53.881 **Lon** W 122.774

Harley-Davidson of Smithers, C-4
Hwy. 16 West, Box 1086 **Smithers, BC**
(250) 847-5473
Lat N 54.780 **Lon** W 127.169

Trev Deeley Motorcycles, L-7
2375 Boundary Rd. **Vancouver, BC**
(604) 291-2453
Lat N 49.263 **Lon** W 123.024

Steve Drane Harley-Davidson, M-7
735 Cloverdale Ave. **Victoria, BC**
(250) 475-1345
Lat N 48.450 **Lon** W 123.372

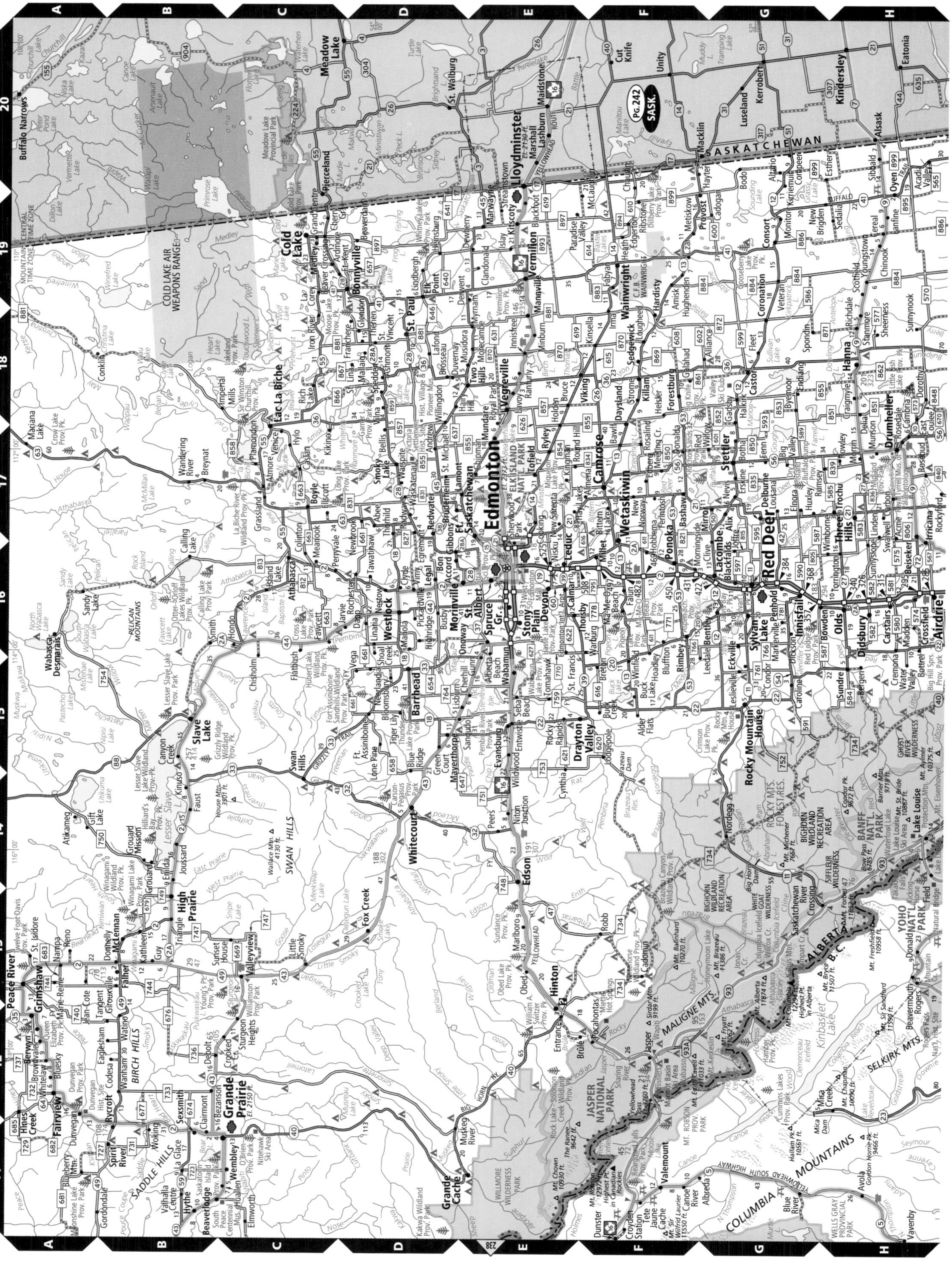

Edmonton
Red Deer
Lloydminster
Grande Prairie
Cold Lake
Lac La Biche
Slave Lake
High Prairie
Peace River
Meadow Lake
Kindersley
Hinton
Edson
Whitecourt
Camrose
Wetaskiwin
Stettler
Drumheller
Airdrie
Vermilion
Wainwright
JASPER NATIONAL PARK
BANFF NAT'L. PARK
YOHO NAT'L. PARK
SASKATCHEWAN
ALBERTA
B.C.
COLUMBIA MOUNTAINS
SELKIRK MTS.
MALIGNE MTS.
SWAN HILLS
BIRCH HILLS
SADDLE HILLS
PELICAN MOUNTAINS
COLD LAKE AIR WEAPONS RANGE
MOUNTAIN TIME ZONE
CENTRAL TIME ZONE
Pg. 242 SASK.

Distance scale
One inch represents about 47 miles

YT
NT
BC
AB
SK
Edmonton
p. 238-239
Calgary
WA
ID
MT

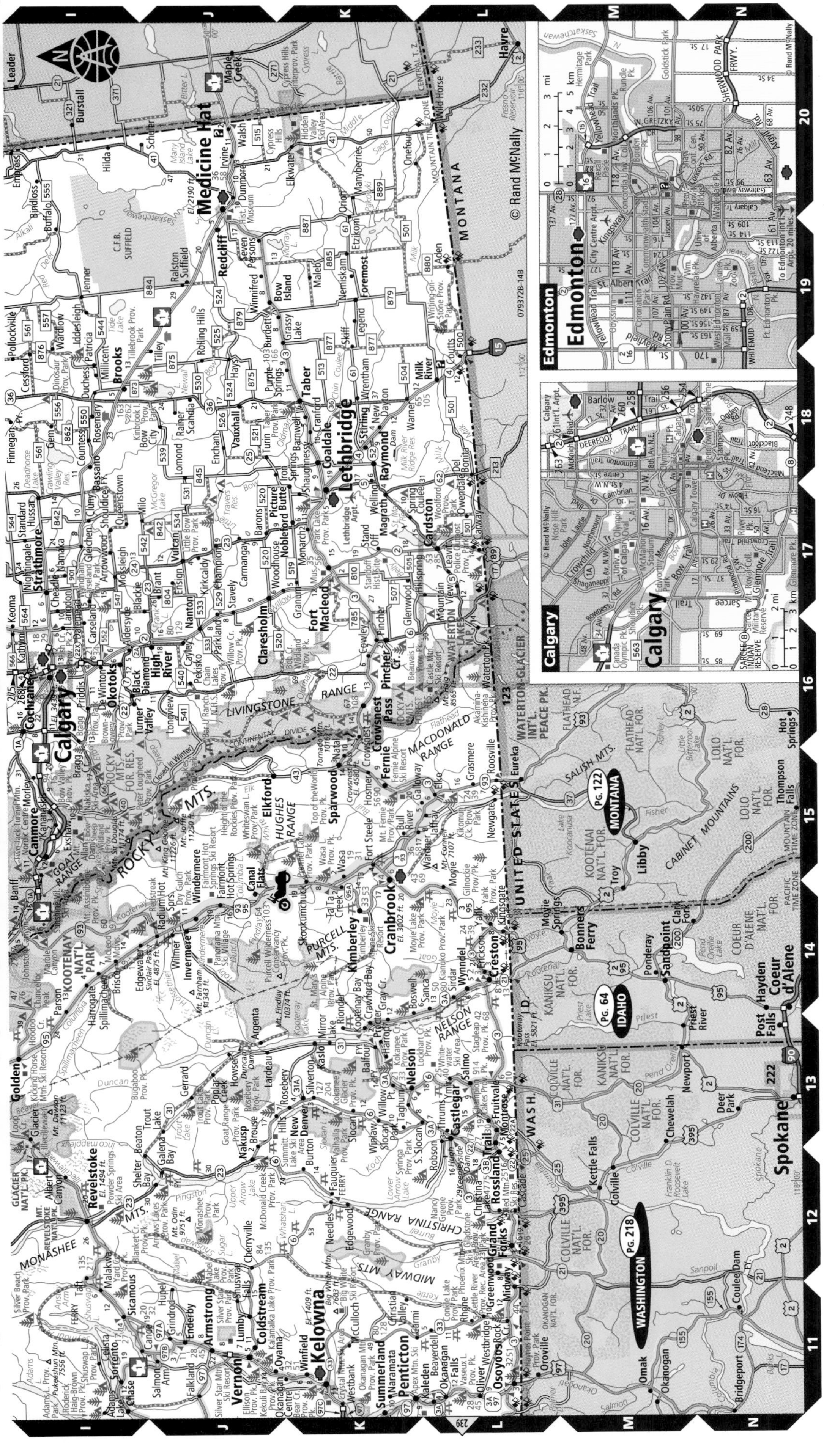

SYMBOLS

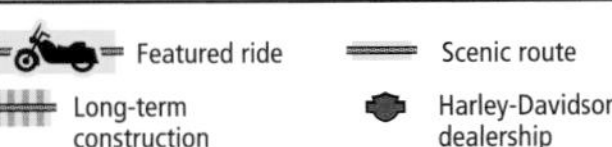

Featured ride
Scenic route
Long-term construction
Harley-Davidson dealership

For Alberta/British Columbia ride, see page R8.

ALBERTA MOTORCYCLE LAWS

Helmet use: Required

Eye protection: Not Required

Speed limit: As posted

Riding two abreast in one lane: Illegal

ALBERTA RESOURCES

Road conditions or construction:
(403) 246-5853
www.trans.gov.ab.ca

Highway Emergency Numbers: 911

Tourism:
(800) 252-3782
www.travelalberta.com

Provincial motor vehicle information:
(780) 427-2731
www.infratrans.gov.ab.ca

HARLEY-DAVIDSON DEALERSHIPS

Calgary Harley-Davidson, I-16
2245 Pegasus Rd. N.E. **Calgary, AB**
(403) 250-3141
Lat N 51.094 **Lon** W 114.010

Calgary Harley-Davidson, I-16
2000 Airport Trail N.E. **Calgary, AB**
(403) 398-3637
Lat N 51.131 **Lon** W 114.009

Kane's Motor Cycle Shop, I-16
914 11th St. S.E. **Calgary, AB**
(403) 269-8577
Lat N 51.042 **Lon** W 114.037

Harley-Davidson of Cranbrook, K-15
1817 Cranbrook St. North **Cranbrook, BC**
(250) 426-6606
Lat N 49.529 **Lon** W 115.748

Harley-Davidson of Medicine Hat, J-20
Hwy. 1, Box 150 1923 2nd Ave. **Dunmore, AB**
(403) 527-9235
Lat N 49.968 **Lon** W 110.587

Harley-Davidson Motorcycles of Edmonton, E-16
12506 124th St. **Edmonton, AB**
(780) 451-7857
Lat N 53.582 **Lon** W 113.536

Heritage Harley-Davidson, E-16
9743 51st Ave. **Edmonton, AB**
(780) 430-7200
Lat N 53.488 **Lon** W 113.476

Harley-Davidson Grande Prairie, C-11
12401 99 St. **Grande Prairie, AB**
(780) 814-5771
Lat N 55.193 **Lon** W 118.791

Kane's Harley-Davidson, K-11
1075 McCurdy Rd. **Kelowna, BC**
(250) 765-6666
Lat N 49.901 **Lon** W 119.405

Lethbridge Harley-Davidson, K-17
1505 2nd Ave. South **Lethbridge, AB**
(403) 320-1903
Lat N 49.698 **Lon** W 112.82

Redline Harley-Davidson Shop Lloydminster, E-20
4810 50th Ave. **Lloydminster, AB**
(780) 875-3373
Lat N 53.282 **Lon** W 110.006

Gasoline Alley Harley-Davidson, G-16
37423 Hwy. 2 South **Red Deer, AB**
(403) 341-3040
Lat N 52.223 **Lon** W 113.814

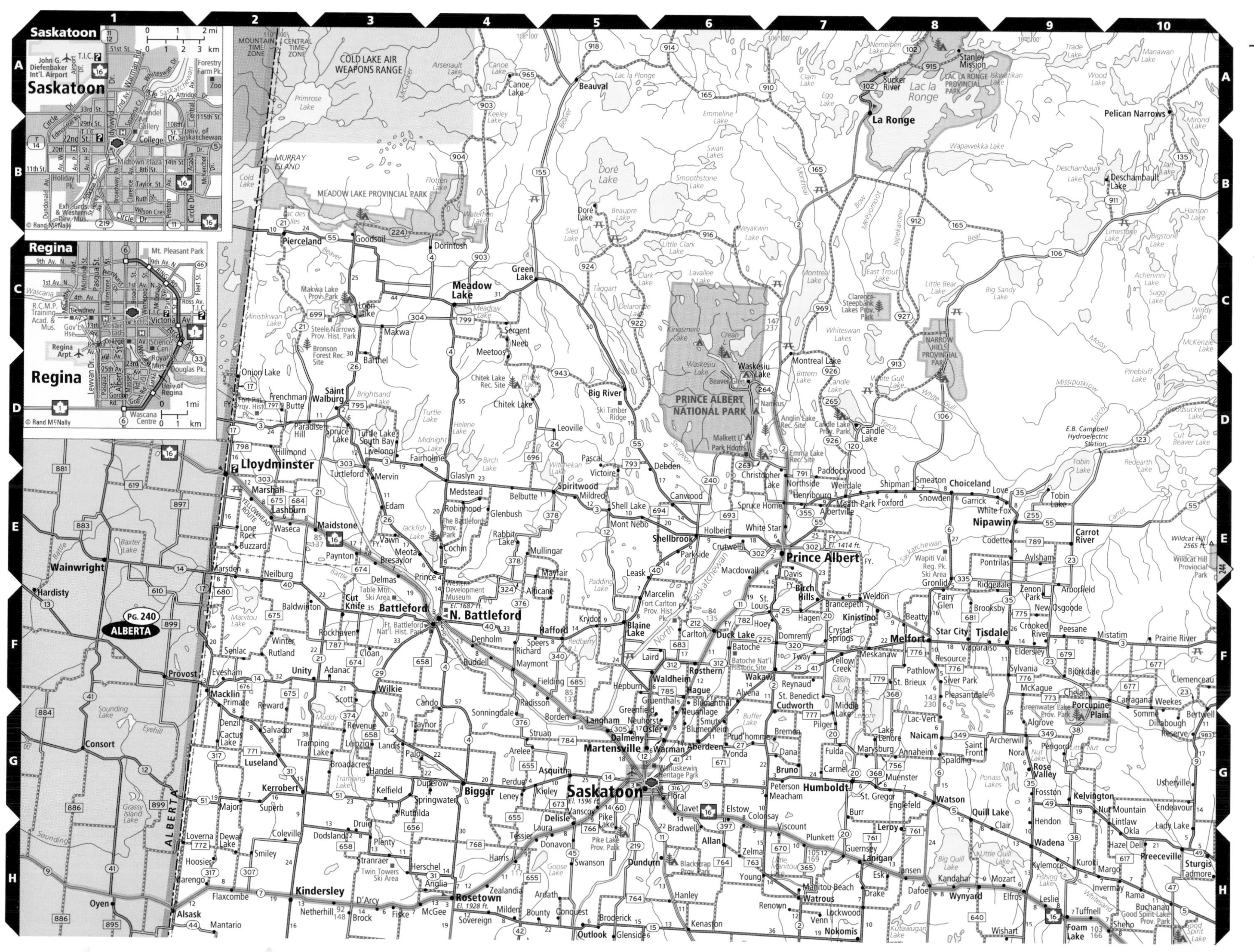

Saskatoon
Regina
Prince Albert
N. Battleford
Battleford
Lloydminster
Meadow Lake
La Ronge
Nipawin
Melfort
Tisdale
Humboldt
Kindersley
Rosetown
Biggar
Wilkie
Unity
Watson
Wadena
Wynyard
Nokomis
Outlook
Wainwright
Hardisty
Provost
Consort
Oyen
Alsask
PRINCE ALBERT NATIONAL PARK
LAC LA RONGE PROVINCIAL PARK
NARROW HILLS PROVINCIAL PARK
MEADOW LAKE PROVINCIAL PARK
COLD LAKE AIR WEAPONS RANGE
Lac la Ronge
ALBERTA
PG. 240
© Rand McNally

Distance scale
One inch represents about 37 miles
0 10 20 30 mi
0 10 20 30 40 km

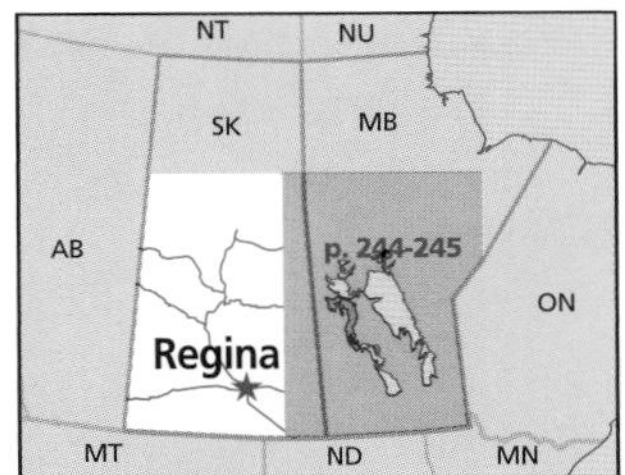
NT
NU
SK
MB
AB
ON
Regina
P. 244-245
MT
ND
MN

SYMBOLS

- Featured ride
- Scenic route
- Point of interest
- Long-term construction
- Harley-Davidson dealership

SASKATCHEWAN MOTORCYCLE LAWS

Helmet use: Required

Eye protection:
Required unless equipped with windscreen

Speed limit: As posted

Riding two abreast in one lane: Illegal

SASKATCHEWAN RESOURCES

Road conditions or construction:
(306) 787-7623 (Regina and surrounding areas, areas outside of province)
(306) 933-8333 (Saskatoon and surrounding areas)
(888) 335-7623 (All other areas)
www.highways.gov.sk.ca

Highway Emergency Numbers: 911

Tourism:
(877) 237-2273
www.sasktourism.com

Provincial motor vehicle information:
(306) 751-1200
www.sgi.sk.ca/

SASKATCHEWAN CITY-TO-CITY MILEAGE

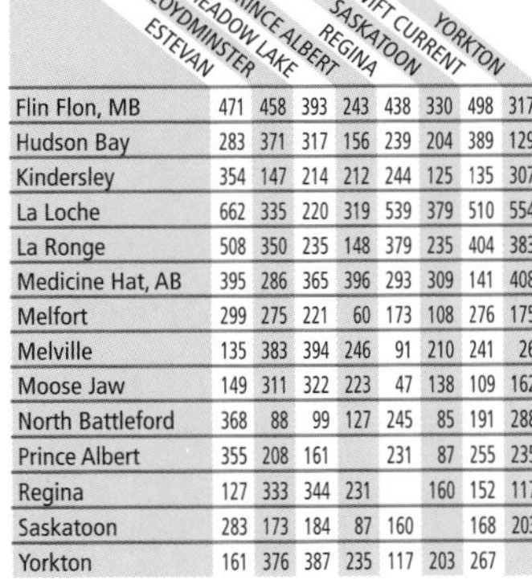

	ESTEVAN	LLOYDMINSTER	MEADOW LAKE	PRINCE ALBERT	REGINA	SASKATOON	SWIFT CURRENT	YORKTON
Flin Flon, MB	471	458	393	243	438	330	498	317
Hudson Bay	283	371	317	156	239	204	389	129
Kindersley	354	147	214	212	244	125	135	307
La Loche	662	335	220	319	539	379	510	554
La Ronge	508	350	235	148	379	235	404	383
Medicine Hat, AB	395	286	365	396	293	309	141	408
Melfort	299	275	221	60	173	108	276	175
Melville	135	383	394	246	91	210	241	26
Moose Jaw	149	311	322	223	47	138	109	162
North Battleford	368	88	99	127	245	85	191	288
Prince Albert	355	208	161		231	87	255	235
Regina	127	333	344	231		160	152	117
Saskatoon	283	173	184	87	160		168	203
Yorkton	161	376	387	235	117	203	267	

HARLEY-DAVIDSON DEALERSHIPS

Prairie Motorcycle, K-8
1355 McIntyre St. **Regina, SK**
(306) 522-1747
Lat N 50.458 **Lon** W 104.616

Redline Harley-Davidson, G-5
102 23rd St. East **Saskatoon, SK**
(306) 934-2750
Lat N 52.131 **Lon** W 106.664

Harley-Davidson of Yorkton, I-10
86 7th Ave. South **Yorkton, SK**
(306) 783-1999
Lat N 51.207 **Lon** W 102.453

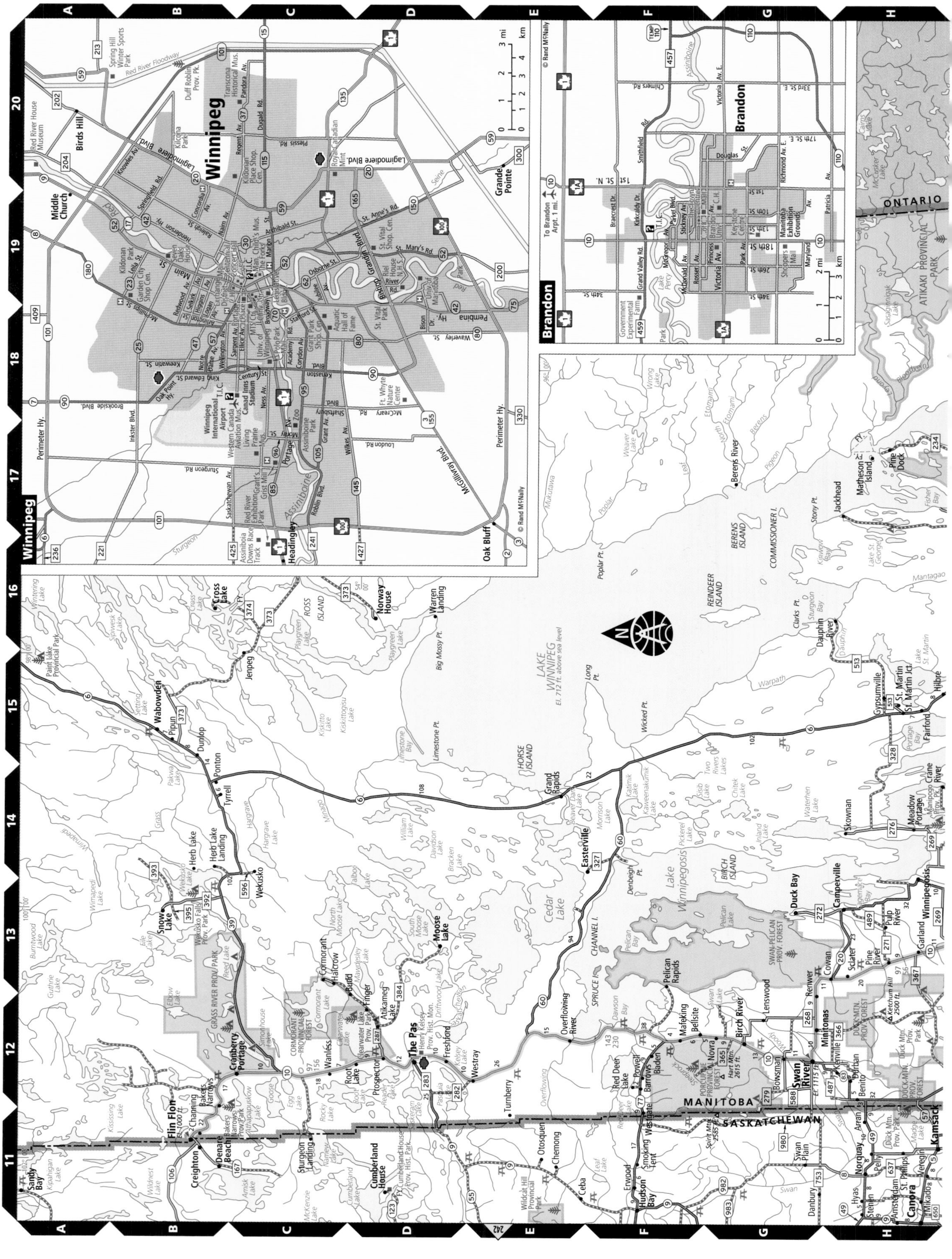

Winnipeg

© Rand McNally

Brandon

© Rand McNally

LAKE WINNIPEG
El. 712 ft. above sea level

MANITOBA

SASKATCHEWAN

ONTARIO

Lake Winnipegosis

Cedar Lake

The Pas

Flin Flon

Swan River

Grand Rapids

Norway House

Berens River

ATIKAKI PROVINCIAL PARK

Distance scale
One inch represents about 37 miles

0 10 20 30 mi
0 10 20 30 40 km

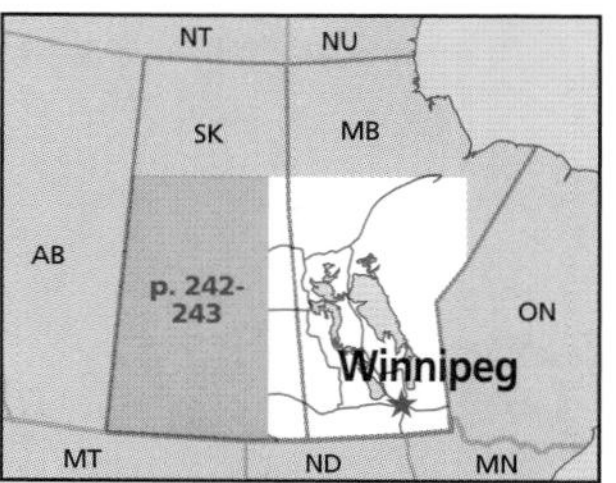
NT
NU
SK
MB
AB
p. 242-243
Winnipeg
ON
MT
ND
MN

SYMBOLS

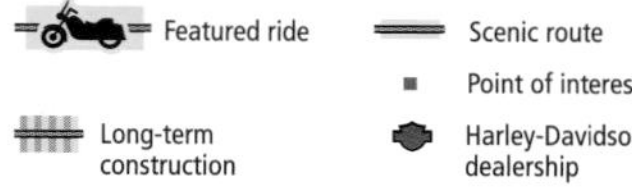
Featured ride
Scenic route
Point of interest
Long-term construction
Harley-Davidson dealership

MANITOBA MOTORCYCLE LAWS

Helmet use: Required

Eye protection: Not Required

Speed limit: As posted

Riding two abreast in one lane: Illegal

MANITOBA RESOURCES

Road conditions or construction:
(877) 627-6237 (in MB)
(204) 945-3704
www.gov.mb.ca/roadinfo

Highway Emergency Numbers: 911

Tourism:
(800) 665-0040
www.travelmanitoba.com

Provincial motor vehicle information:
(800) 665-2410
www.mpi.mb.ca

MANITOBA CITY-TO-CITY MILEAGE

	BRANDON	DAUPHIN	FLIN FLON	MORDEN	PORTAGE LA PRAIRIE	SWAN RIVER	VIRDEN	WINNIPEG
Ashern	199	125	366	180	117	232	246	111
Brandon		104	445	133	80	209	50	134
Dauphin	104		343	209	138	107	151	192
Grand Rapids	354	280	255	335	272	213	401	266
Killarney	62	166	507	86	120	271	105	147
Minnedosa	34	75	416	152	81	180	81	135
Pine Falls	214	266	543	163	132	369	259	80
Portage la Prairie	80	138	483	69		245	127	52
Riverton	203	170	449	153	121	277	250	75
Russell	113	91	344	236	164	108	73	218
Selkirk	157	209	488	101	75	314	204	23
The Pas	353	251	92	454	391	144	325	385
Thompson	557	483	241	538	475	385	566	469
Winnipeg	134	192	477	75	52	52	181	

HARLEY-DAVIDSON DEALERSHIPS

Gaslight Harley-Davidson, M-16
999 Thornhill St. **Morden, MB**
(204) 822-5877
Lat N 49.192 **Lon** W 98.128

Northland Leisure Products, D-12
17th St. Settee **The Pas, MB**
(204) 623-3504
Lat N 53.826 **Lon** W 101.256

Harley-Davidson Winnipeg, L-17
1377 Niakwa Rd. East **Winnipeg, MB**
(204) 254-3974
Lat N 49.857 **Lon** W 97.039

Lone Star Motorcycles, K-17
231 Oak Point Hwy. **Winnipeg, MB**
(204) 633-2453
Lat N 49.933 **Lon** W 97.215

079373B-148

Distance scale
One inch represents about 28 miles
0 10 20 30 mi
0 10 20 30 40 km

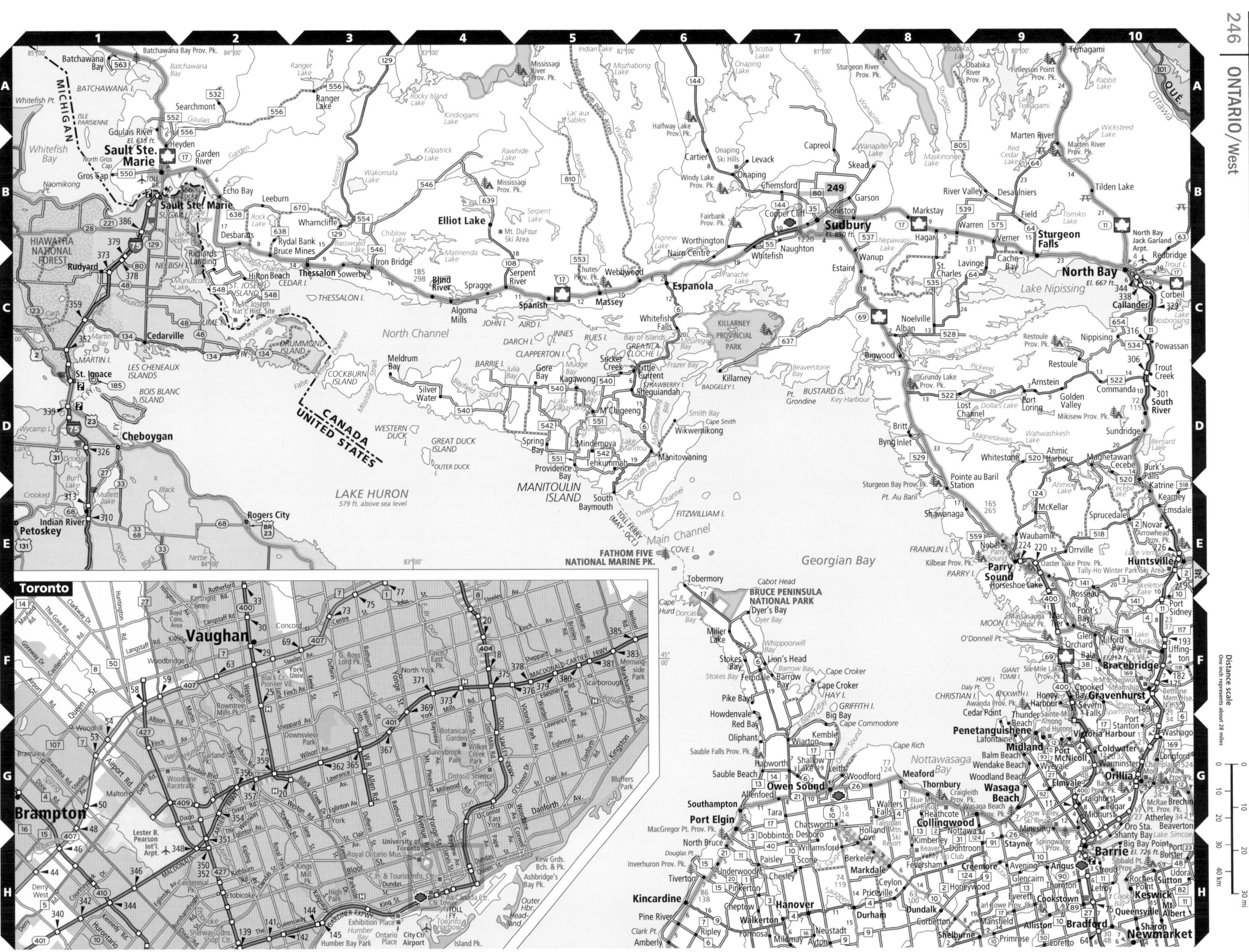

Georgian Bay
LAKE HURON
579 ft. above sea level
North Channel
Main Channel
Lake Nipissing
MANITOULIN ISLAND
BRUCE PENINSULA NATIONAL PARK
FATHOM FIVE NATIONAL MARINE PK.
KILLARNEY PROVINCIAL PARK
HIAWATHA NATIONAL FOREST
CANADA
UNITED STATES
MICHIGAN
QUÉ.
Sault Ste. Marie
Elliot Lake
Blind River
Espanola
Sudbury
Sturgeon Falls
North Bay
Cheboygan
Petoskey
Parry Sound
Huntsville
Bracebridge
Gravenhurst
Orillia
Barrie
Penetanguishene
Midland
Wasaga Beach
Collingwood
Owen Sound
Port Elgin
Kincardine
Hanover
Durham
Keswick
Bradford
Newmarket
Toronto
Vaughan
Brampton

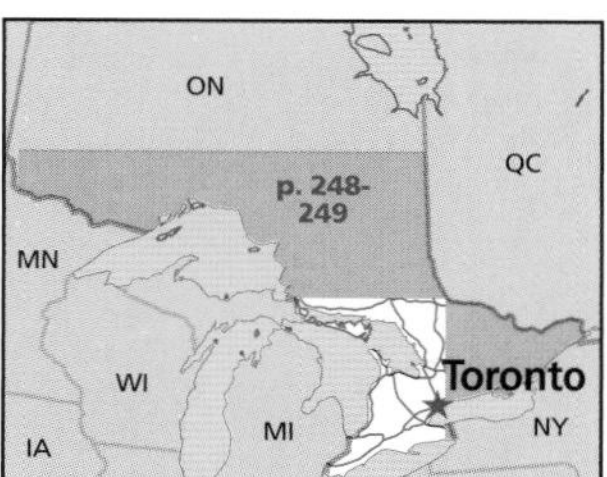

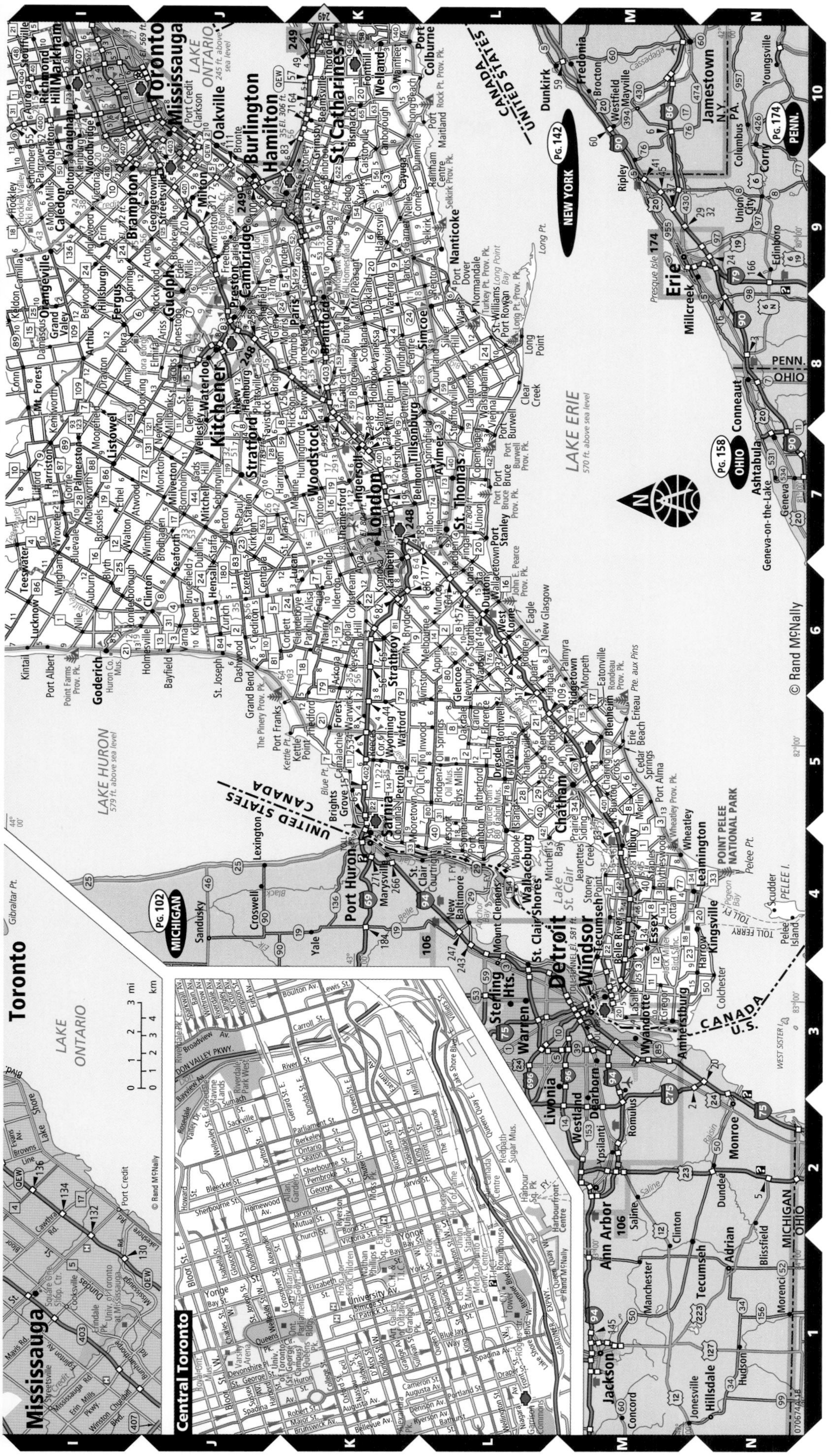

ON
QC
p. 248-249
MN
WI
MI
Toronto
IA
NY

ONTARIO MOTORCYCLE LAWS

Helmet use: Required

Eye protection: Not Required

Speed limit: As posted

Riding two abreast in one lane: Illegal

ONTARIO RESOURCES

Road conditions or construction:
(800) 268-4686 (in ON)
(416) 235-4686 (in Toronto)
www.mto.gov.on.ca

Highway Emergency Numbers: 911

Tourism:
(800) 668-2746
www.ontariotravel.net

Provincial motor vehicle information:
(416) 235-4686
www.mto.gov.on.ca

HARLEY-DAVIDSON DEALERSHIPS

Barrie Harley-Davidson, H-10
311 Byrne Dr. **Barrie**
(705) 728-5322
Lat N 44.337 **Lon** W 79.688

Dukes Harley-Davidson, M-5
Five Classic Car Dr. **Blenheim**
(519) 354-0650
Lat N 42.327 **Lon** W 81.999

Clare's Cycle & Sports, K-10
799 Hwy. 20 West **Fenwick**
(905) 892-2664
Lat N 43.084 **Lon** W 79.352

Poole's Cycle, K-9
215 Parkdale Ave. North **Hamilton**
(905) 545-0687
Lat N 43.243 **Lon** W 79.789

Kitchener Harley-Davidson, J-8
2295 Kingsway Dr. **Kitchener**
(519) 893-0493
Lat N 43.434 **Lon** W 80.450

The Shop, B-7
112 Fielding Rd. **Lively**
(705) 682-4463
Lat N 46.441 **Lon** W 81.098

Rocky's Harley-Davidson of London, K-7
900 Wilton Grove Rd. **London**
(519) 438-1450
Lat N 42.928 **Lon** W 81.195

Jacox Harley-Davidson, J-9
2815 Argentia Rd. **Mississauga**
(905) 858-0966
Lat N 43.600 **Lon** W 79.774

Fox Harley-Davidson, G-7
123003 Story Book Park Rd. **Owen Sound**
(519) 371-6666
Lat N 44.564 **Lon** W 80.857

Davies Harley-Davidson, I-10
8779 Yonge St. **Richmond Hill**
(905) 709-1340
Lat N 43.843 **Lon** W 79.430

Motorsport Custom Accessories, K-5
1375 Confederation St. **Sarnia**
(519) 337-5601
Lat N 42.960 **Lon** W 82.355

Harley-Davidson of Toronto, I-10
578 Front St. West **Toronto**
(416) 703-HOGS
Lat N 43.641 **Lon** W 79.401

Thunder Road Harley-Davidson, M-3
2139 Huron Church Rd. **Windsor**
(519) 966-1520
Lat N 42.276 **Lon** W 83.051

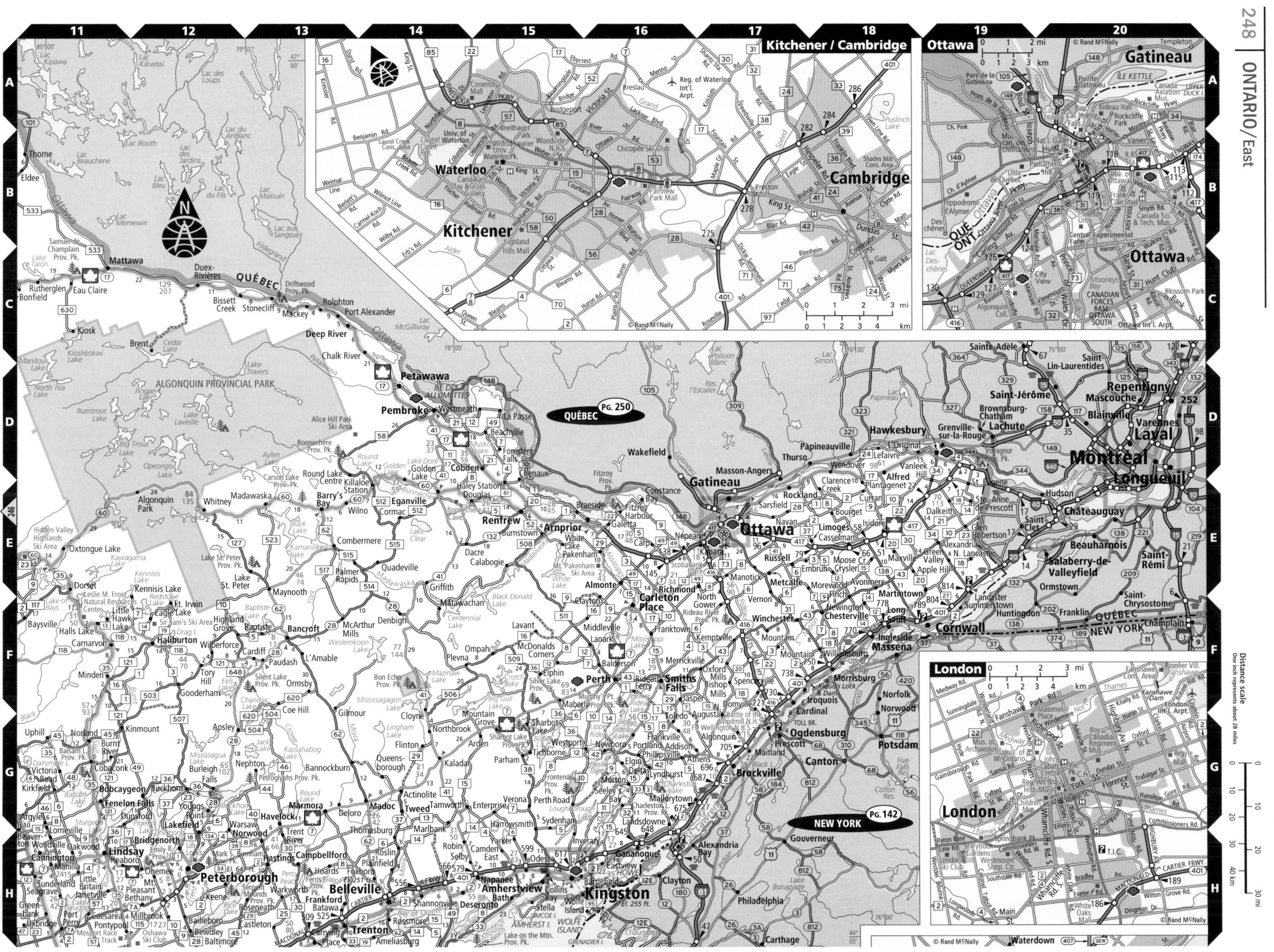

Distance scale
One inch represents about 28 miles
0 10 20 30 mi
0 10 20 30 40 km
Kitchener / Cambridge
Ottawa
London
Gatineau
Kitchener
Waterloo
Cambridge
Montréal
Laval
Longueuil
Ottawa
Gatineau
Kingston
Belleville
Peterborough
Cornwall
Pembroke
Petawawa
ALGONQUIN PROVINCIAL PARK
QUÉBEC
PG. 250
NEW YORK
PG. 142
© Rand McNally

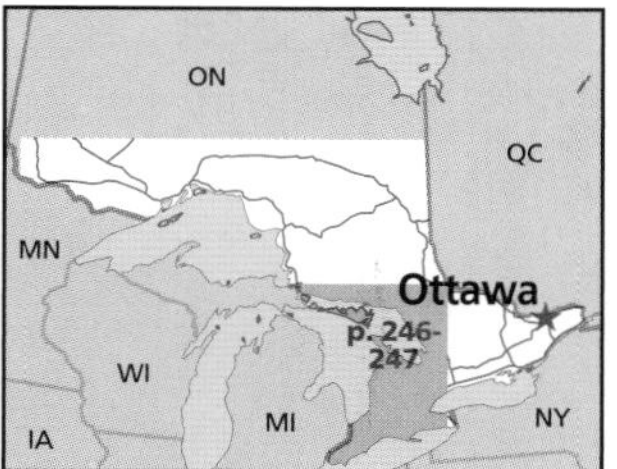
ON
QC
MN
WI
MI
IA
NY
Ottawa
p. 246-247

SYMBOLS

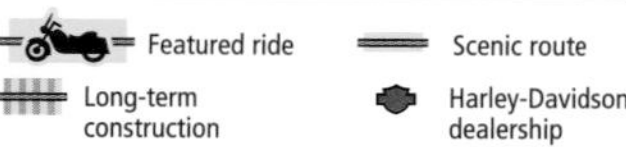
Featured ride
Scenic route
Long-term construction
Harley-Davidson dealership

CITY-TO-CITY MILEAGE

	KINGSTON	LONDON	NIAGARA FALLS	OTTAWA	SUDBURY	THUNDER BAY	TORONTO	WINDSOR
Barrie	210	160	132	269	189	806	62	272
Hamilton	206	85	48	294	281	898	47	197
Kenora	1304	1274	1246	1225	930	307	1176	1386
Kingston		275	247	117	380	997	161	387
London	275		138	363	350	967	125	120
Montréal, QC	187	456	428	133	441	1002	342	568
Niagara Falls	247	138		335	322	939	88	250
Ottawa	117	363	335		308	918	249	475
Owen Sound	285	144	163	343	253	870	121	275
Pembroke	156	361	333	95	208	818	247	473
Peterborough	122	196	168	171	258	875	82	308
Sarnia	341	71	204	429	416	1033	191	99
Sault Ste. Marie	557	527	499	494	183	440	429	639
Sudbury	380	350	322	308		623	252	462
Thunder Bay	997	967	939	918	623		869	1079
Timmins	516	533	505	455	181	519	435	645
Toronto	161	125	88	249	252	869		237
Windsor	387	120	250	475	462	1079	237	

HARLEY-DAVIDSON DEALERSHIPS

Goulet Motosports, D-19
189 John St. **Hawkesbury**
(613) 632-3462
Lat N 45.611 **Lon** W 74.605

MotoSport Plus Kingston, H-15
295 Dalton Ave. **Kingston**
(613) 544-4600
Lat N 44.268 **Lon** W 76.511

Freedom Harley-Davidson, E-16
1450 Merivale Rd. **Nepean (Ottawa)**
(613) 228-9449
Lat N 45.363 **Lon** W 75.733

Mackie Harley-Davidson, I-11
880 Champlain Ave. **Oshawa**
(905) 434-6550
Lat N 43.874 **Lon** W 78.887

Harley-Davidson of Ottawa, E-17
505 Industrial Ave. **Ottawa**
(613) 736-8899
Lat N 45.412 **Lon** W 75.645

Pete's Sales & Service, D-14
2107 Petawawa Blvd. **Pembroke**
(613) 735-3711
Lat N 45.829 **Lon** W 77.109

Cameron Motorcycle Sales, F-15
R.R. 7, 6 mi. west of Perth **Perth**
(613) 267-3873
Lat N 44.916 **Lon** W 76.352

Longley Harley-Davidson of Peterborough, H-12
1097 Hwy. 7 East **Peterborough**
(705) 745-0421
Lat N 44.322 **Lon** W 78.264

Thunder Bay Harley-Davidson, M-15
636 Arthur St. West **Thunder Bay**
(807) 577-6221
Lat N 48.381 **Lon** W 89.297

Thunder Bay Harley-Davidson, M-15
1330 Rosslyn Rd. **Thunder Bay**
(807) 577-6221
Lat N 48.363 **Lon** W 89.323

Distance scale
One inch represents about 38 miles

0 10 20 30 mi
0 10 20 30 40 km

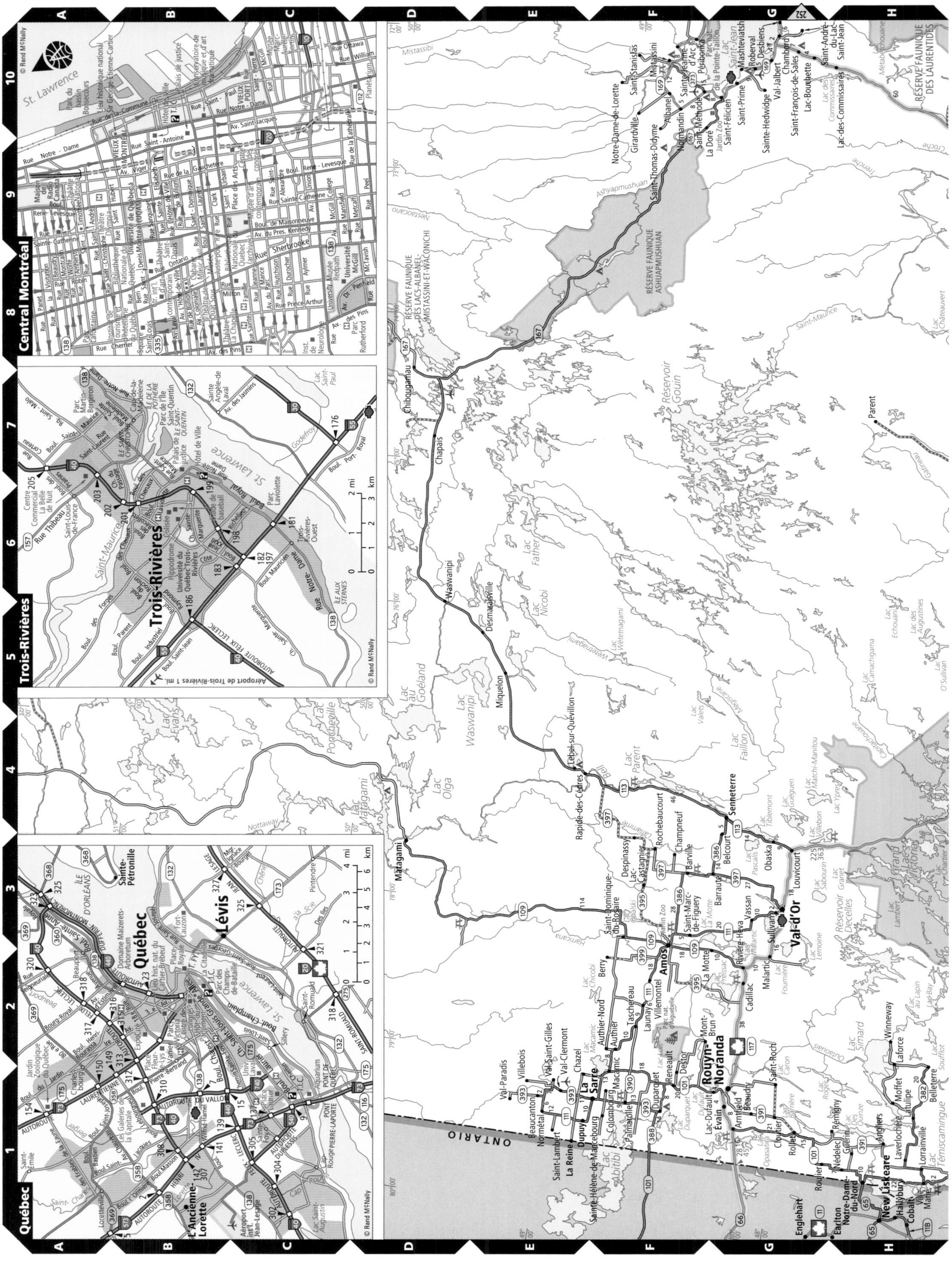

Québec

Trois-Rivières

Central Montréal

© Rand McNally

Québec · Lévis · Trois-Rivières · Val-d'Or · Rouyn-Noranda · Amos · La Sarre · Chibougamau · Chapais · Matagami · Lebel-sur-Quévillon · Senneterre · Malartic · New Liskeard · Mistassini · Dolbeau · Roberval

Réservoir Gouin

Réserve Faunique Ashuapmushuan

Réserve Faunique des Lacs-Albanel-Mistassini-et-Waconichi

Réserve Faunique des Laurentides

ONTARIO

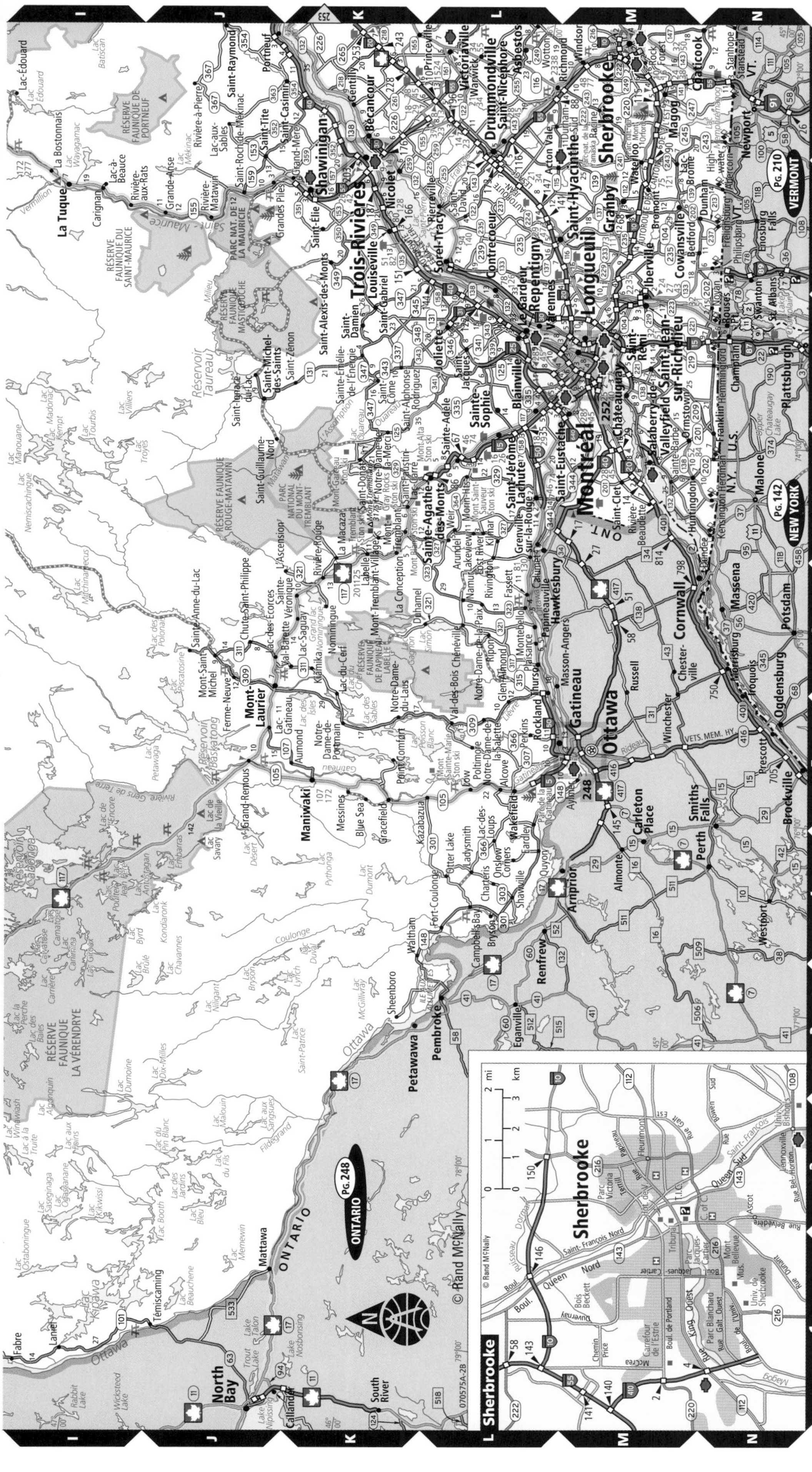

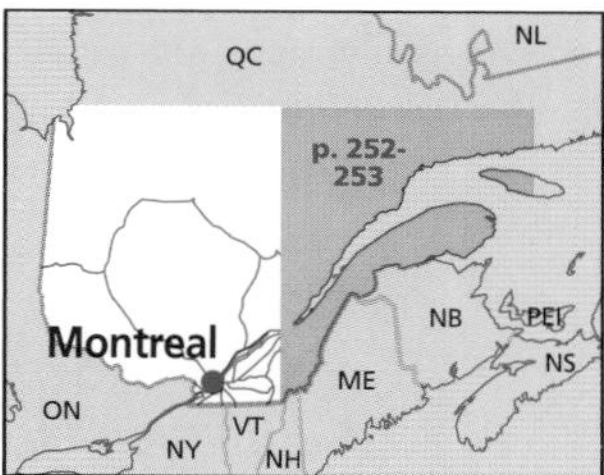
QC
NL
p. 252-253
Montreal
ON
NY
VT
NH
ME
NB
PEI
NS

SYMBOLS

- Featured ride
- Scenic route
- Point of interest
- Long-term construction
- Harley-Davidson dealership

HARLEY-DAVIDSON DEALERSHIPS

Boileau Moto Service Enrg., L-10
888 Route 116 Ouest **Acton Vale**
(450) 549-4341
Lat N 45.579 **Lon** W 72.468

Centre de Moto Harley-Davidson, M-8
8705 Boul. Taschereau **Brossard**
(450) 674-3986
Lat N 45.440 **Lon** W 73.473

Harley-Davidson de L'Outaouais, M-5
22 Boul. Mont-Bleu **Gatineau**
(819) 772-8008
Lat N 45.462 **Lon** W 75.745

L'Ami Denis, M-10
2 Rue Queen **Lennoxville**
(819) 565-1376
Lat N 45.363 **Lon** W 71.856

Harley-Davidson Montréal, L-8
6695 St.-Jacques West **Montréal**
(514) 483-6686
Lat N 45.459 **Lon** W 73.628

Blanchette (The Shop), L-8
515 Rue Leclerc **Repentigny**
(450) 582-2442
Lat N 45.748 **Lon** W 73.451

N.J.N. Motosport, G-10
450 Rue Principal **Saint-Prime**
(418) 251-4830
Lat N 48.588 **Lon** W 72.330

Shawinigan Harley-Davidson, K-9
6033 Boul. de Hêtre **Shawinigan**
(819) 539-1450
Lat N 46.571 **Lon** W 72.724

Sherbrooke Harley-Davidson, M-10
4203 King Ouest **Sherbrooke**
(819) 563-0707
Lat N 45.386 **Lon** W 71.963

Bibeau Moto Sport, G-3
372 Rue Gareau **Val d'Or (Jacola)**
(819) 824-2541
Lat N 48.108 **Lon** W 77.815

Sport Boutin, M-7
2000 Boul. Hébert **Valleyfield**
(450) 373-6565
Lat N 45.269 **Lon** W 74.097

G.P. Motosports, L-10
12 Bl. Arthabaska (Route 116) **Victoriaville**
(819) 758-8830
Lat N 46.088 **Lon** W 71.980

Moto Sport Blanchette, K-9
4350 Arsenault **Ville de Becancourt**
(819) 233-3303
Lat N 46.269 **Lon** W 72.488

Distance scale
One inch represents about 38 miles
0 10 20 30 mi
0 10 20 30 40 km

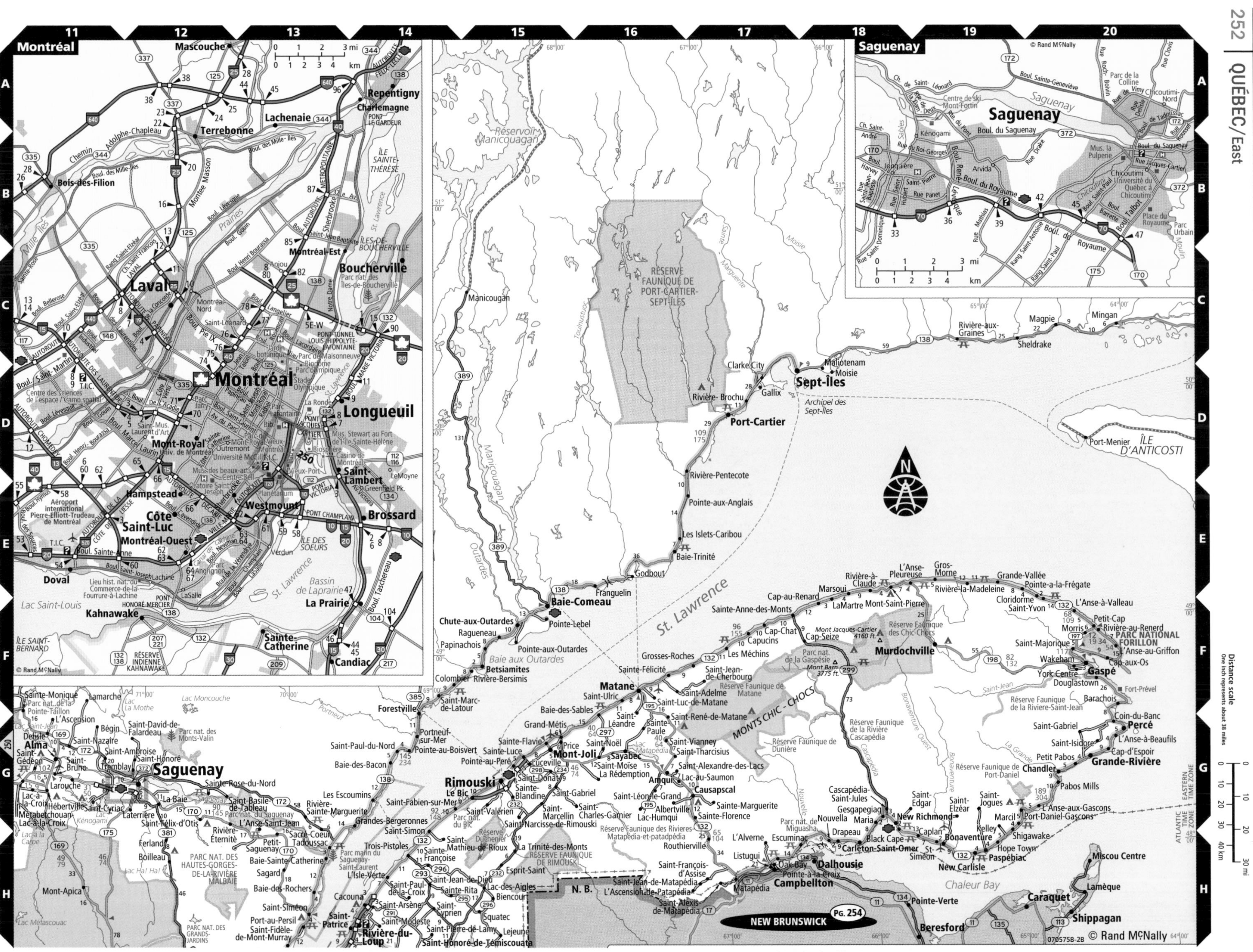
Montréal
Saguenay
Laval
Montréal
Longueuil
Boucherville
Brossard
Saguenay
Baie-Comeau
Sept-Îles
Port-Cartier
St. Lawrence
ÎLE D'ANTICOSTI
RÉSERVE FAUNIQUE DE PORT-CARTIER-SEPT-ÎLES
Rimouski
Matane
Mont-Joli
Murdochville
Gaspé
Percé
Grande-Rivière
Campbellton
Dalhousie
Chaleur Bay
NEW BRUNSWICK
Pg. 254
© Rand McNally

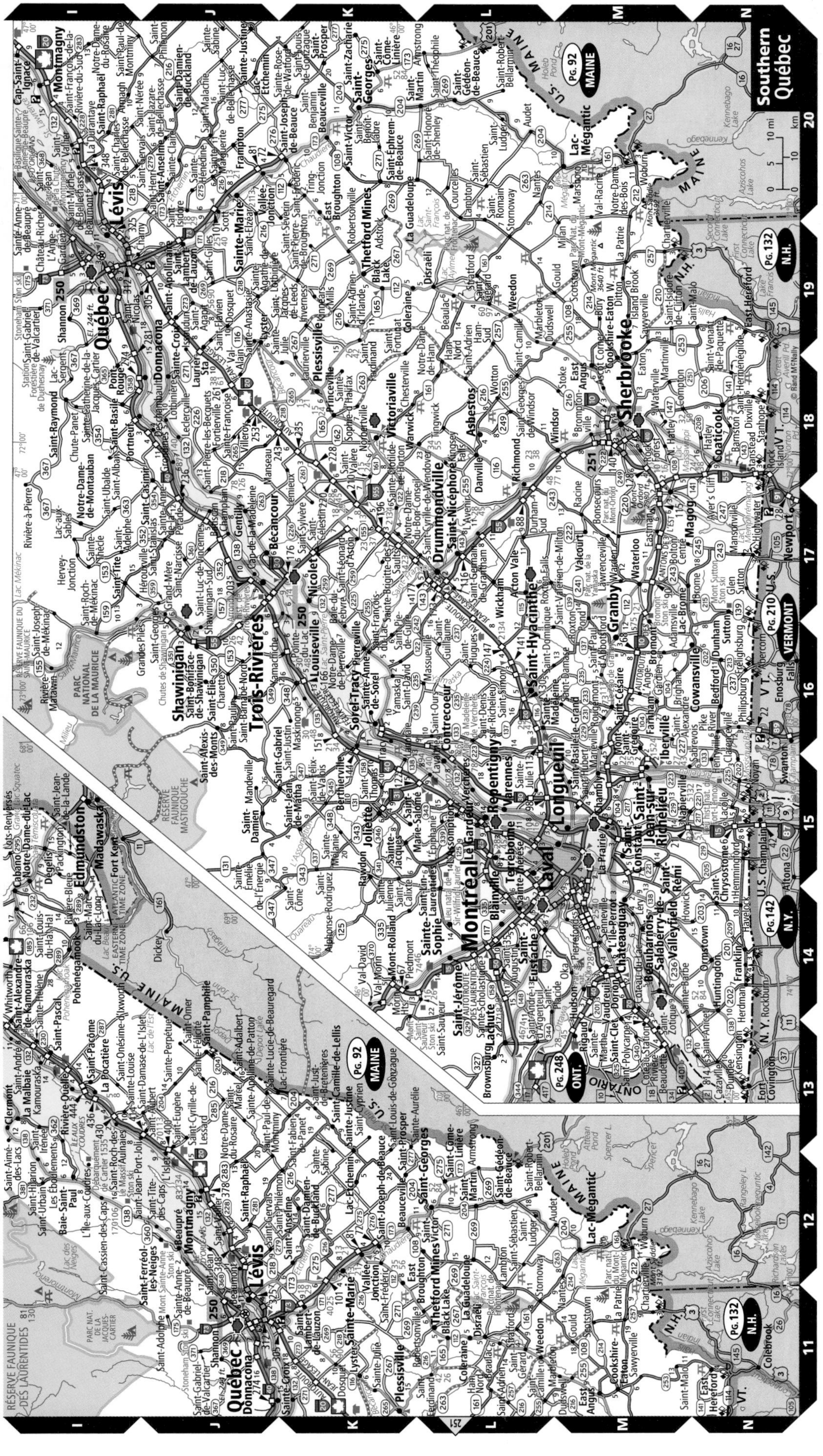

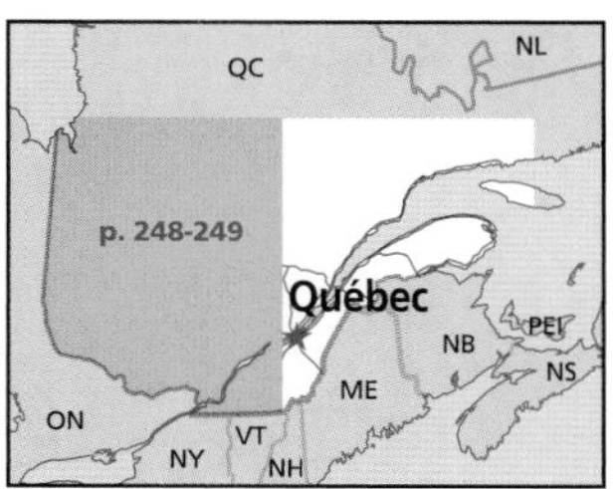
QC
NL
p. 248-249
Québec
PEI
NB
NS
ME
ON
NY
VT
NH
0 5 10 mi
0 5 10 km

SYMBOLS

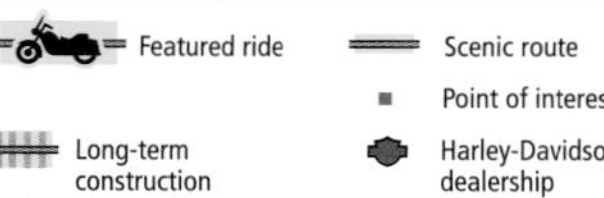
Featured ride
Scenic route
Point of interest
Long-term construction
Harley-Davidson dealership

QUÉBEC MOTORCYCLE LAWS

Helmet use: Required

Eye protection: Not Required

Speed limit: As posted

Riding two abreast in one lane: Illegal

QUÉBEC RESOURCES

Road conditions or construction:
(888) 355-0511
(877) 393-2363 (in Québec)
www.mtq.gouv.qc.ca/en/index.asp (English)

Highway Emergency Numbers: 911

Tourism:
(877) 266-5687
www.bonjourquebec.com

Provincial motor vehicle information:
(418) 643-7620
www.saaq.gouv.qc.ca/en/index.html

HARLEY-DAVIDSON DEALERSHIPS

Hamilton & Bourassa, F-15
324 Boul. Lasalle **Baie Comeau**
(418) 296-9191
Lat N 49.214 **Lon** W 68.194

RPM Moto Plus, G-12
2510 Rue Dubose **Jonquière**
(418) 699-7766
Lat N 48.402 **Lon** W 71.159

Harley-Davidson Laval, L-14
4501 Autoroute Laval West **Laval**
(450) 973-4501
Lat N 45.560 **Lon** W 73.791

New Richmond Mécanique Sport, G-18
162 Route 132 East **New Richmond**
(418) 392-5281
Lat N 48.256 **Lon** W 65.719

Atelier de Mécanique Prémont, J-11
2495 Boul. Hamel Ouest **Québec**
(418) 683-1340
Lat N 46.806 **Lon** W 71.300

Harley-Davidson of Rimouski, G-15
424 Montée Industrielle **Rimouski**
(418) 724-0883
Lat N 48.449 **Lon** W 68.495

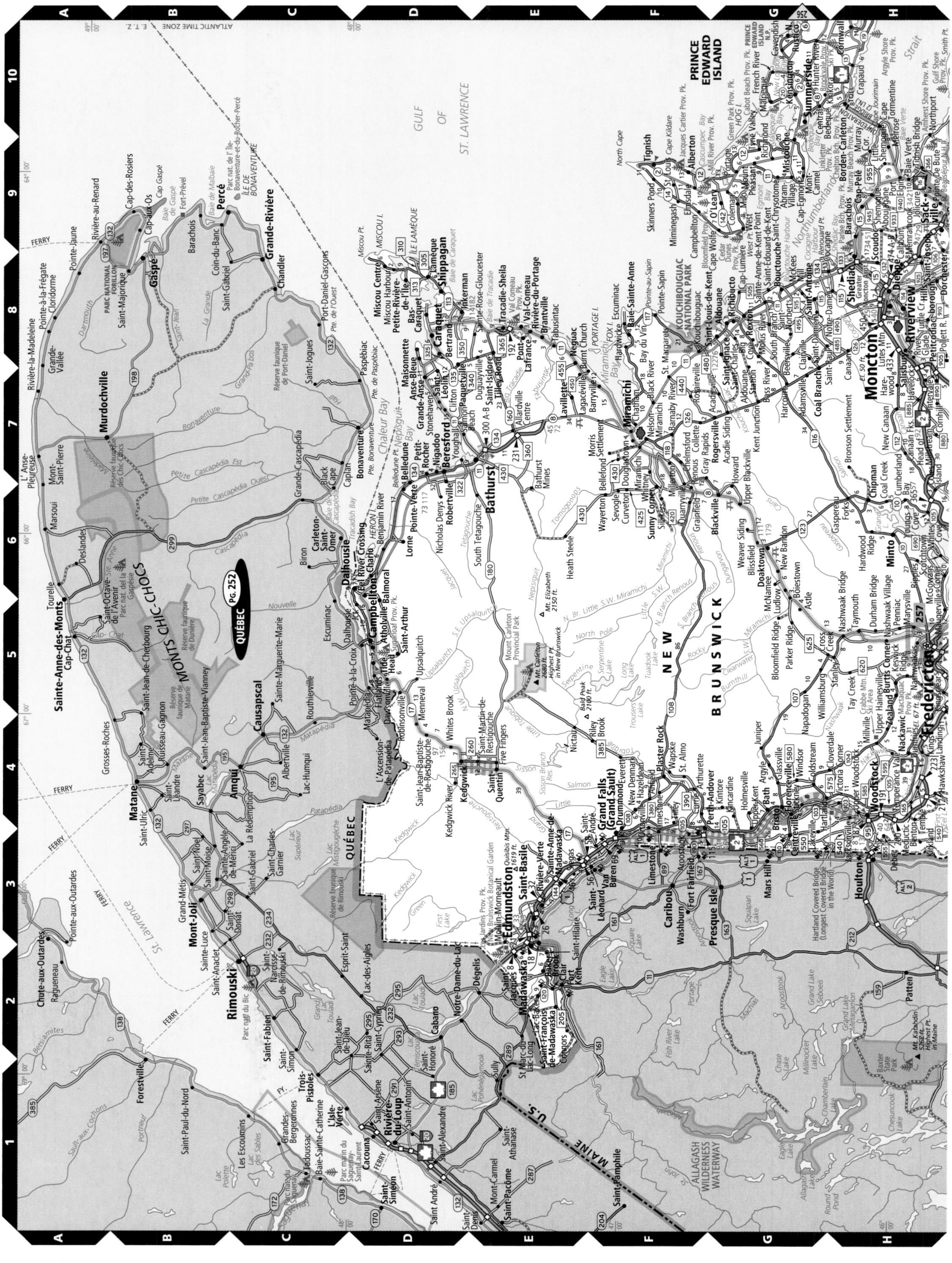

QUÉBEC

NEW BRUNSWICK

PRINCE EDWARD ISLAND

MAINE

U.S.

GULF OF ST. LAWRENCE

MONTS CHIC-CHOCS

ATLANTIC TIME ZONE

E.T.Z.

Pg. 252

Chaleur Bay

Northumberland Strait

Rimouski

Matane

Gaspé

Percé

Campbellton

Dalhousie

Bathurst

Miramichi

Moncton

Fredericton

Edmundston

Woodstock

Presque Isle

Houlton

Caribou

Rivière-du-Loup

Summerside

ALLAGASH WILDERNESS WATERWAY

KOUCHIBOUGUAC NATIONAL PARK

PARC NATIONAL FORILLON

Distance scale
One inch represents about 33 miles
0 10 20 30 mi
0 10 20 30 40 km

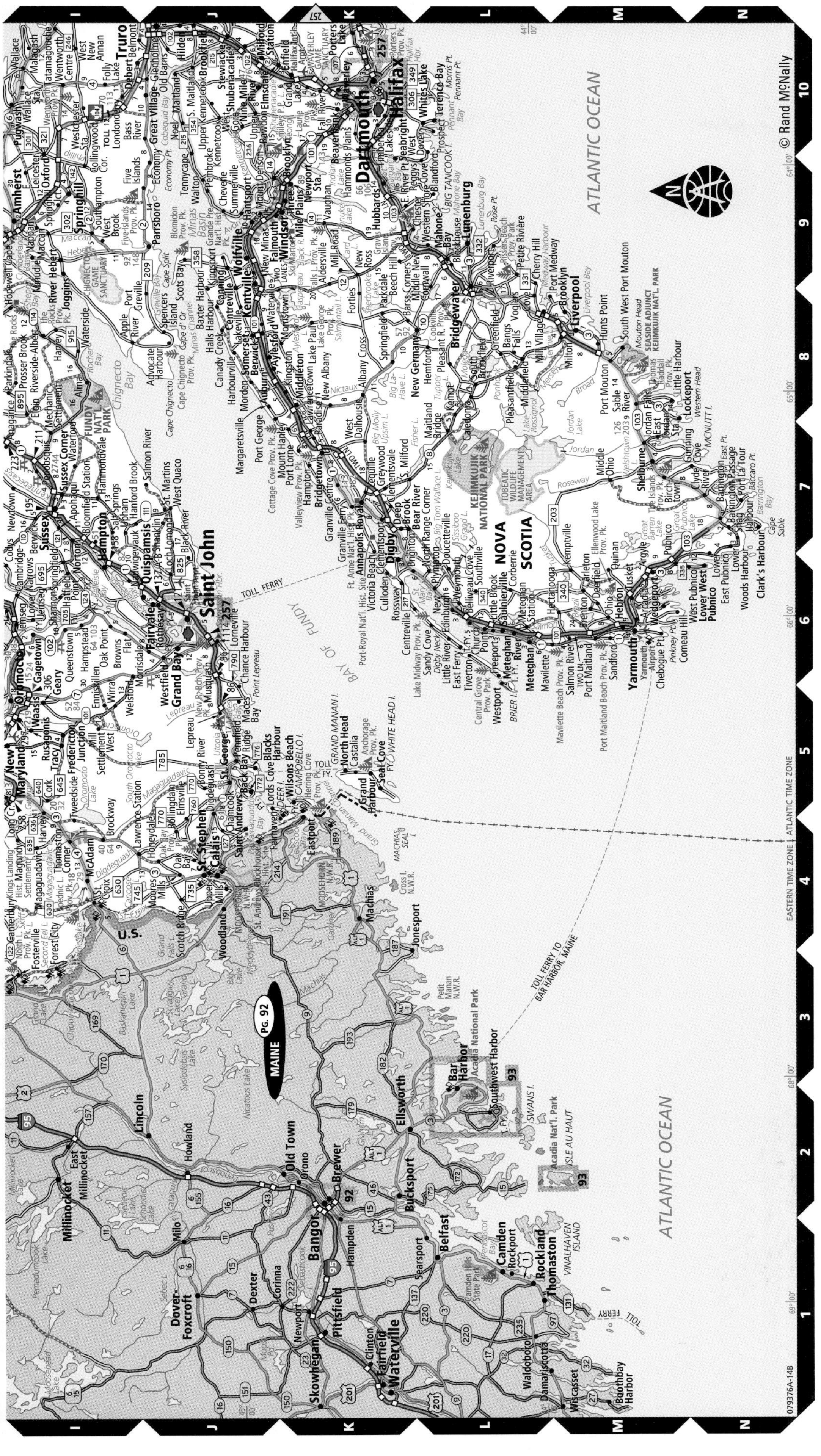

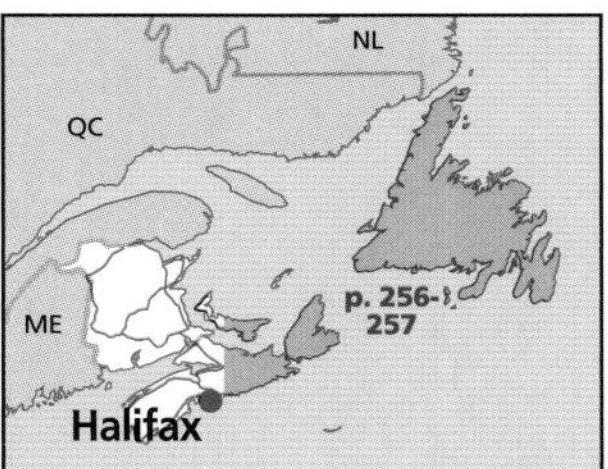
NL
QC
ME
p. 256-257
Halifax

SYMBOLS

- Featured ride
- Scenic route
- Point of interest
- Long-term construction
- Harley-Davidson dealership

NEW BRUNSWICK, NOVA SCOTIA, AND PRINCE EDWARD ISLAND MOTORCYCLE LAWS

Helmet use: Required

Eye protection: Not Required

Speed limit: As posted

Riding two abreast in one lane:
New Brunswick: Illegal
Nova Scotia and Prince Edward Island: Illegal

NEW BRUNSWICK RESOURCES

Road conditions or construction:
(800) 561-4063 (in NB)
www.gnb.ca/0113

Highway Emergency Numbers: 911

Tourism:
(800) 561-0123
www.tourismnbcanada.com

Provincial motor vehicle information:
(506) 684-7901
www.snb.ca

NOVA SCOTIA RESOURCES

Road conditions or construction:
(800) 307-7669 (in NS)
(902) 424 3933
www.gov.ns.ca/tran

Highway Emergency Numbers: 911

Tourism:
(800) 565-0000
novascotia.com

Provincial motor vehicle information:
(902) 424-5200
www.gov.ns.ca/snsmr/rmv

PRINCE EDWARD ISLAND RESOURCES

Road conditions or construction:
(902) 368-4770
www.gov.pe.ca/roadconditions

Highway Emergency Numbers: 911

Tourism:
(888) 734-7529
www.peiplay.com

Provincial motor vehicle information:
(902) 368-5228
www.gov.pe.ca/tpwpei

HARLEY-DAVIDSON DEALERSHIPS

Privateers Harley-Davidson, K-10
100 Susie Lake Crescent, Unit 10 **Halifax, NS**
(902) 444-HOGS
Lat N 44.651 **Lon** W 63.677

J.H. Stewart, F-7
564 Water St. **Miramichi, NB**
(506) 622-3405
Lat N 47.002 **Lon** W 65.546

Toys for Big Boys, H-8
633 Salisbury Rd. **Moncton, NB**
(506) 858-8088
Lat N 46.070 **Lon** W 64.831

Eldridge's Harley-Davidson, J-6
1230 Fairville Blvd. **Saint John, NB**
(506) 635-1223
Lat N 45.253 **Lon** W 66.098

079376A-14B

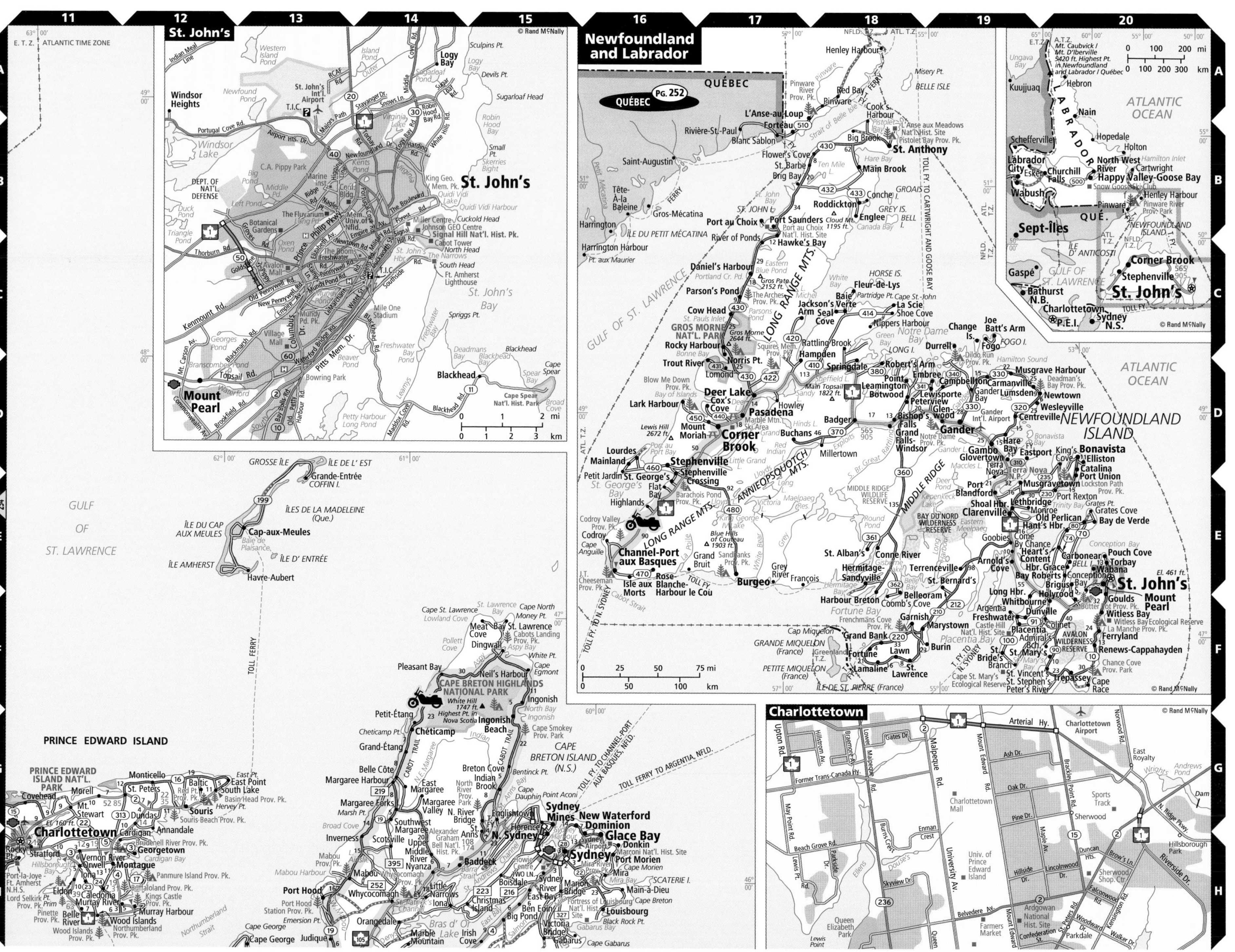
St. John's
Newfoundland and Labrador
Charlottetown
QUÉBEC
Pg. 252
PRINCE EDWARD ISLAND
GULF OF ST. LAWRENCE
ATLANTIC OCEAN
NEWFOUNDLAND ISLAND
LABRADOR
CAPE BRETON HIGHLANDS NATIONAL PARK
CAPE BRETON ISLAND (N.S.)
LONG RANGE MTS.
ÎLES DE LA MADELEINE (Que.)
ATLANTIC TIME ZONE
TOLL FY. TO CARTWRIGHT AND GOOSE BAY
TOLL FERRY TO ARGENTIA, NFLD.
TOLL FY. TO CHANNEL-PORT AUX BASQUES, NFLD.
Corner Brook
Gander
Stephenville
Channel-Port aux Basques
Sydney
Glace Bay
Mount Pearl
© Rand McNally

Distance scale
One inch represents about 33 miles

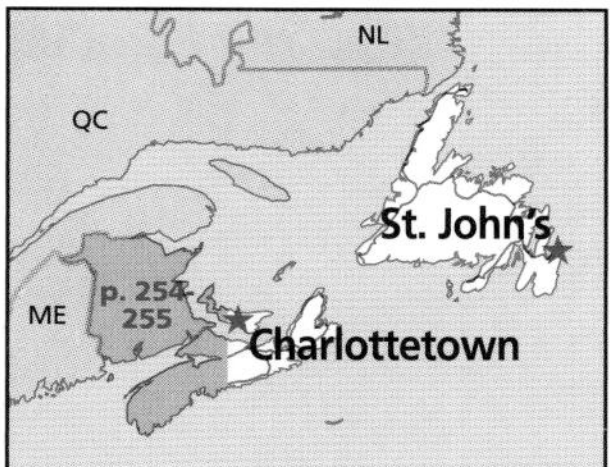
NL
QC
St. John's
ME
p. 254-255
Charlottetown

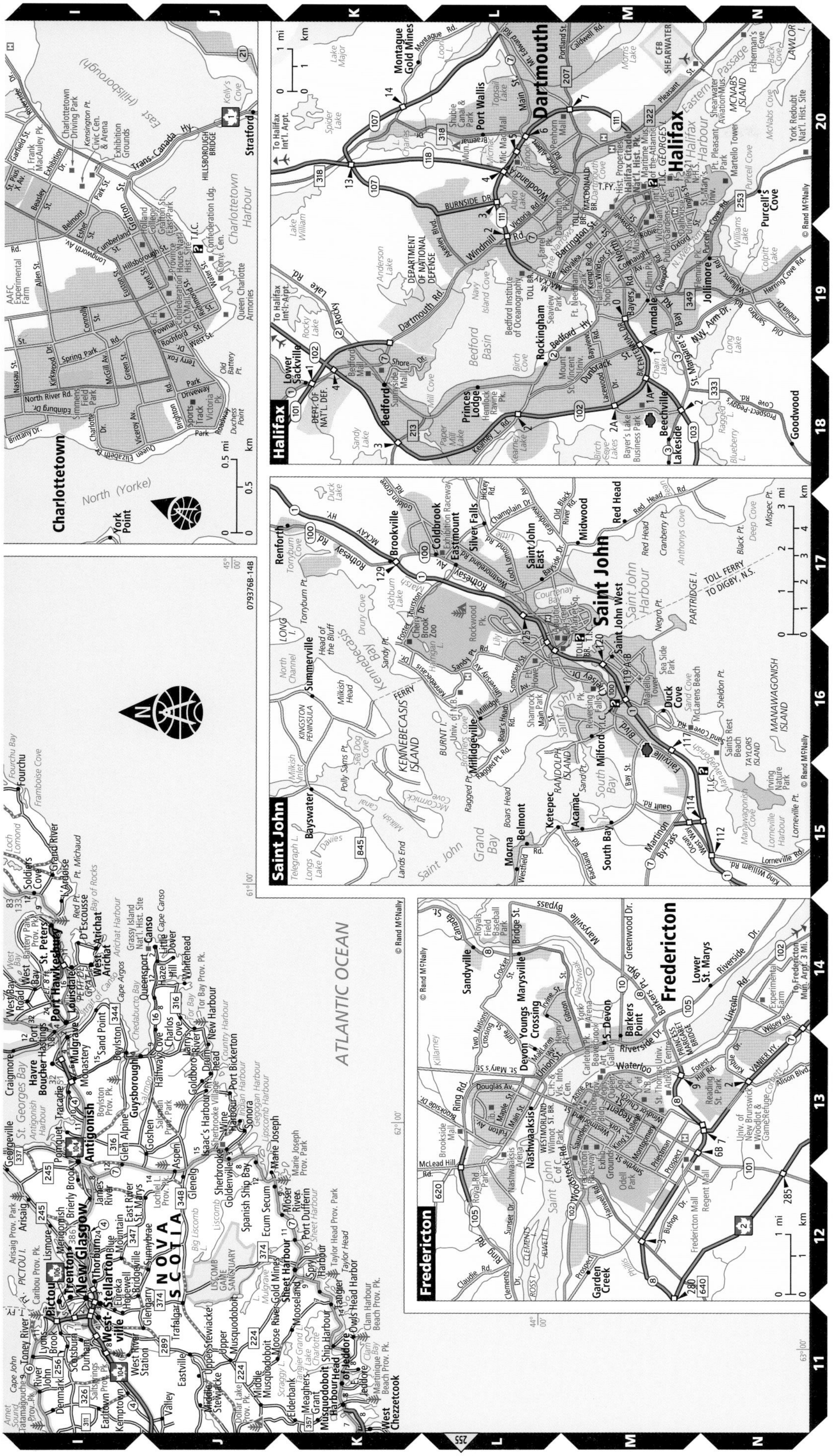

SYMBOLS

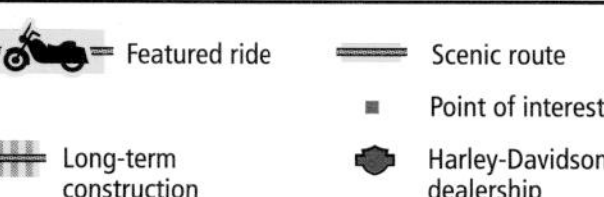
Featured ride
Scenic route
Point of interest
Long-term construction
Harley-Davidson dealership

For Newfoundland & Labrador ride, see page R25.
For Nova Scotia ride, see page R28-29.

NEWFOUNDLAND & LABRADOR MOTORCYCLE LAWS

Helmet use: Required

Eye protection:
Required unless equipped with windscreen

Speed limit: As posted

Riding two abreast in one lane: Illegal

NEWFOUNDLAND & LABRADOR RESOURCES

Road conditions or construction:
www.roads.gov.nf.ca
www.roads.gov.nl.ca

Highway Emergency Numbers: 911

Tourism:
(800) 563-6353
(709) 729-2830
www.gov.nf.ca/tourism

Provincial motor vehicle information:
(709) 729-2519
www.gov.nl.ca/services/transport.stm

CITY-TO-CITY MILEAGE

	CHARLOTTETOWN, PE	EDMUNDSTON, NB	FREDERICTON, NB	HALIFAX, NS	MONCTON, NB	SAINT JOHN, NB	ST. JOHN'S, NL	SYDNEY, NS
Amherst, NS	93	336	158	135	38	136	945†	263
Bathurst, NB	249	193	158	306	131	229	1116†	434
Campbellton, NB	319	129	238	386	211	309	1196†	514
Charlottetown, PE		417†	239†	157†	119	218	597	247
Corner Brook, NL	482	860†	682	519†	562†	660†	427	267†
Edmundston, NB	422		177	471	294	246	1281†	599
Fredericton, NB	241	177		293	116	70	1103†	421
Gander, NL	688	1080†	902	739†	782†	880†	201	487†
Grand Falls, NB	384	37	139	433	256	208	1243	561
Halifax, NS	164	471	293		173	271	940†	258
Moncton, NB	119	294	116	173		94	983†	301
New Glasgow, NS	67	446	268	105	148	246	837†	155
Saint John, NB	218	246	70	271	94		1081†	399
St. John's, NL	597	1281†	1103†	940†	983†	1081†		688†
St. Stephen, NB	321	220	79	341	164	70	1151†	469
Sydney, NS	247	599	421	258	301	399	688†	
Truro, NS	104	409	231	64	111	209	878†	196
Yarmouth, NS	326	356	180	186	365	110	1132	450

† Via ferry

HARLEY-DAVIDSON DEALERSHIPS

Cycle City and Recreation, E-20
1073 Topsail Rd. **Mount Pearl, NL**
(709) 364-9051
Lat N 47.525 **Lon** W 52.808

Ramsay's Harley-Davidson, H-15
616 Keltic Dr. **Sydney, NS**
(902) 539-1730 or 7644
Lat N 46.127 **Lon** W 60.252

Red Rock Harley-Davidson, G-11
5 Campbell Rd. **Winsloe (Charlottetown), PEI**
(902) 368-8324
Lat N 46.295 **Lon** W 63.179

Distance scale
One inch represents about 153 miles
0 25 50 75 100 125 mi
0 50 100 150 200 km

Mexico City
Ciudad de México
(Mexico City)
Naucalpan
Tlalnepantla
Coacalco
Ecatepec
Tulpetla
Texcoco
Ciudad Netzahualcóyotl
Chimalhuacán
Cuautlalpan
Los Reyes
Ixtapaluca
Chalco
Xochimilco
Tlalpan
Cuajimalpa
Tepexpan
Vaso del Lago de Texcoco (Dry)
Aeropuerto Int. Benito Juárez
Ciudad Universitaria
Estadio Azteca
Parque Nacional Desierto de los Leones
Cerro San Miguel 12382 ft.
Volcán Ajusco 12894 ft.
Cerro Mezontépetl 11407 ft.
Cerro Teuhtli 8898 ft.
© Rand McNally
0 1 2 3 4 5 mi
0 2 4 6 8 km

PACIFIC OCEAN

079377-14B

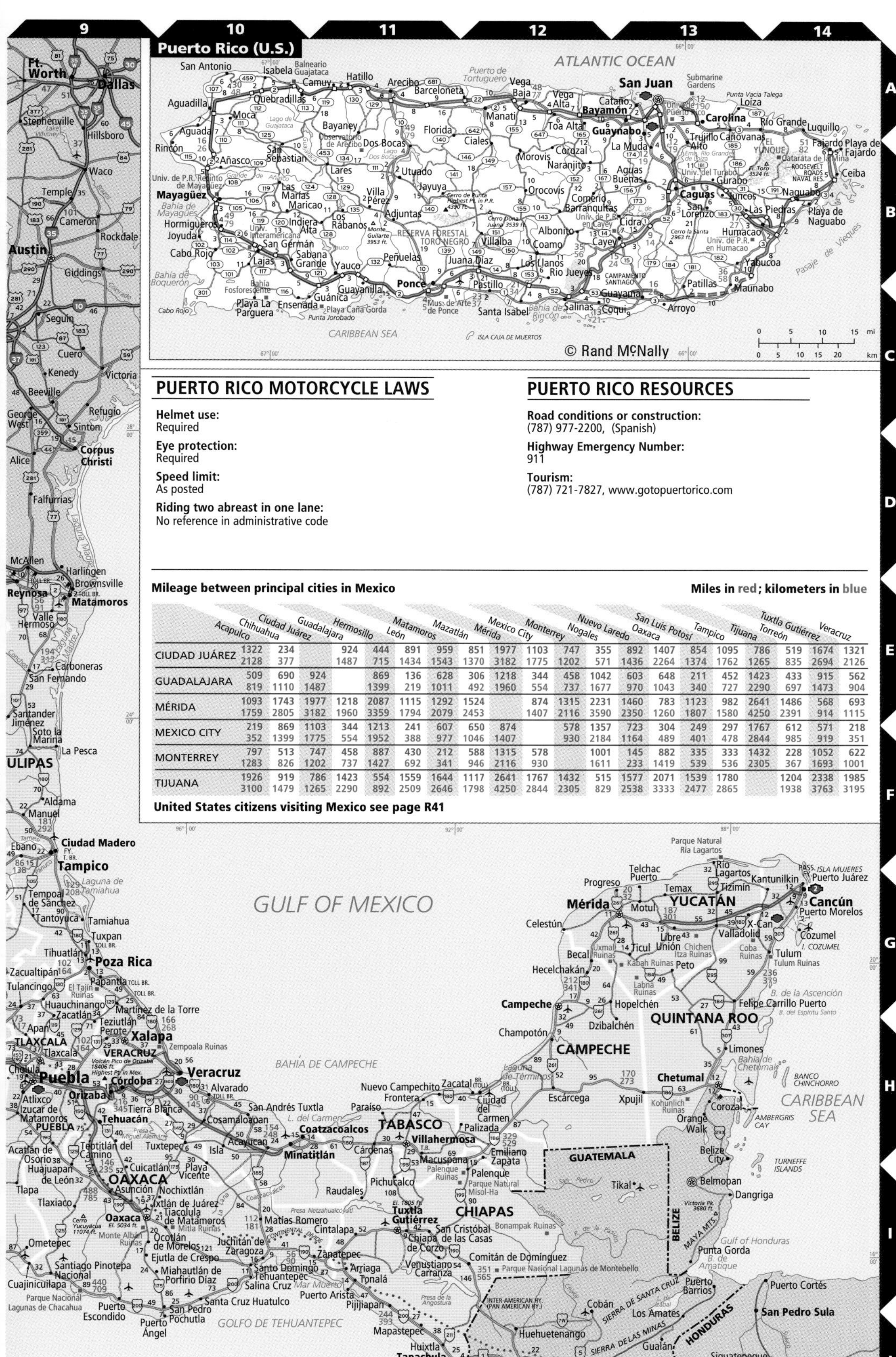
Puerto Rico (U.S.)
ATLANTIC OCEAN
San Juan
Bayamón
Guaynabo
Carolina
Caguas
Arecibo
Mayagüez
Aguadilla
Ponce
Guayama
Humacao
Fajardo
CARIBBEAN SEA
© Rand McNally
GULF OF MEXICO
BAHÍA DE CAMPECHE
CARIBBEAN SEA
YUCATÁN
CAMPECHE
QUINTANA ROO
TABASCO
CHIAPAS
OAXACA
GUATEMALA
BELIZE
HONDURAS
EL SALVADOR
Mérida
Cancún
Campeche
Chetumal
Villahermosa
Coatzacoalcos
Veracruz
Puebla
Oaxaca
Tuxtla Gutiérrez
Tapachula
Guatemala
Tegucigalpa
San Pedro Sula
Tampico
Poza Rica
Xalapa
Dallas
Ft. Worth
Austin
Corpus Christi
Matamoros
Reynosa
GOLFO DE TEHUANTEPEC
© Rand McNally

PUERTO RICO MOTORCYCLE LAWS

Helmet use:
Required

Eye protection:
Required

Speed limit:
As posted

Riding two abreast in one lane:
No reference in administrative code

PUERTO RICO RESOURCES

Road conditions or construction:
(787) 977-2200, (Spanish)

Highway Emergency Number:
911

Tourism:
(787) 721-7827, www.gotopuertorico.com

Mileage between principal cities in Mexico

Miles in red; kilometers in blue

	Acapulco	Chihuahua	Ciudad Juárez	Guadalajara	Hermosillo	León	Matamoros	Mazatlán	Mérida	Mexico City	Monterrey	Nogales	Nuevo Laredo	Oaxaca	San Luis Potosí	Tampico	Tijuana	Torreón	Tuxtla Gutiérrez	Veracruz
CIUDAD JUÁREZ	1322 / 2128	234 / 377		924 / 1487	444 / 715	891 / 1434	959 / 1543	851 / 1370	1977 / 3182	1103 / 1775	747 / 1202	355 / 571	892 / 1436	1407 / 2264	854 / 1374	1095 / 1762	786 / 1265	519 / 835	1674 / 2694	1321 / 2126
GUADALAJARA	509 / 819	690 / 1110	924 / 1487		869 / 1399	136 / 219	628 / 1011	306 / 492	1218 / 1960	344 / 554	458 / 737	1042 / 1677	603 / 970	648 / 1043	211 / 340	452 / 727	1423 / 2290	433 / 697	915 / 1473	562 / 904
MÉRIDA	1093 / 1759	1743 / 2805	1977 / 3182	1218 / 1960	2087 / 3359	1115 / 1794	1292 / 2079	1524 / 2453		874 / 1407	1315 / 2116	2231 / 3590	1460 / 2350	783 / 1260	1123 / 1807	982 / 1580	2641 / 4250	1486 / 2391	568 / 914	693 / 1115
MEXICO CITY	219 / 352	869 / 1399	1103 / 1775	344 / 554	1213 / 1952	241 / 388	607 / 977	650 / 1046	874 / 1407		578 / 930	1357 / 2184	723 / 1164	304 / 489	249 / 401	297 / 478	1767 / 2844	612 / 985	571 / 919	218 / 351
MONTERREY	797 / 1283	513 / 826	747 / 1202	458 / 737	887 / 1427	430 / 692	212 / 341	588 / 946	1315 / 2116	578 / 930		1001 / 1611	145 / 233	882 / 1419	335 / 539	333 / 536	1432 / 2305	228 / 367	1052 / 1693	622 / 1001
TIJUANA	1926 / 3100	919 / 1479	786 / 1265	1423 / 2290	554 / 892	1559 / 2509	1644 / 2646	1117 / 1798	2641 / 4250	1767 / 2844	1432 / 2305	515 / 829	1577 / 2538	2071 / 3333	1539 / 2477	1780 / 2865		1204 / 1938	2338 / 3763	1985 / 3195

United States citizens visiting Mexico see page R41

SYMBOLS

Featured ride
Scenic route
Point of interest
Long-term construction
Harley-Davidson dealership

MEXICO HARLEY-DAVIDSON DEALERSHIPS

Harley-Davidson Veracruz, H-10
Avenida Viveros Lote 1, Colonia Jardines de Virginia **Boca Del Rio, VE**
(52) 229-927-2560

Harley-Davidson Los Cabos, F-3
Av. Lazaro Cardenas, Plaza Puerto Paraiso, Local 40 **Cabo San Lucas, BCS**
(52) 624-143-3337

Harley-Davidson Motorclothes, G-14
Kukulkan Plaza, Blvd. Kukulkan Km 13.5, Local 119–125, Zona Hotelera **Cancun, QR**
(52) 555-520-3390

Harley-Davidson Motorclothes, G-14
Forum Plaza, Blvd. Kukulkan Km 9, Local A-19, Zona Hotelera **Cancun, QR**
(52) 998-883-4850

Harley-Davidson Leon, G-7
Av. Cerro Gordo No. 111, Col. Valle del Campestre **León, GT**
(52) 477-781-1400

Harley-Davidson Mexico, H-8
Bolivar No. 482, Col. Algarin **Mexico City, DF**
(52) 55-5519-6389

Harley-Davidson Mexico, H-8
Carretera Picacho Ajusco No. 486, Col. Heroes De Padierna **Mexico City, DF**
(52) 55-5644-4421

Harley-Davidson Santa Fe, H-8
Prol. Paseo de la Reforma No. 71, Manzana 4 Lote 6, Col. Paseo de las Lomas, Santa Fe **Mexico City, DF**
(52) 555-292-4733

Motocicletas de Milwaukee, E-8
Rio Tamazunchale 404 Norte, Col. Del Valle, San Pedro Garza Garcia **Monterrey, NL**
(52) 818-356-5680

Harley-Davidson Satelite, G-1
Blvd. Manuel Avila Camacho 2170, Ciudad Satelite Poniente **Naucalpan, DF**
(52) 555-374-2302

Harley-Davidson Motorclothes, G-14
Paseo del Carmen, Calle 10 Av. Sur, Local 44 **Playa del Carmen, QR**
(52) 9984-803-3956

Harley-Davidson Puebla, S.A., H-9
31 Pte. No. 1707, Col. Volcanes **Puebla, PU**
(52) 222-211-2249

Harley-Davidson Jalisco, G-6
Av. Patria 1848-A, Col. Santa Isabel **Zapopan, JA**
(52) 33-3642-1560

PUERTO RICO HARLEY-DAVIDSON DEALERSHIPS

Motor Sport, Inc., A-13
Acuarela St. #92 **Guaynabo**
(787) 790-4900

Harley-Davidson Boutique, A-13
Plaza del Sheraton Hotel, Waterfront **San Juan**
(787) 721-4202

Alabama
Map pp. 10-13

Abbeville, 2963 M-11
Adamsville, 4845 F-6
Addison, 713 C-5
Akron, 514 H-4
Alabaster, 27517 G-6
Albertville, 18615 C-8
Aldrich, 600 G-6
Alexander City, 14957 H-9
Aliceville, 2465 G-2
Allgood, 693 E-7
Altoona, 970 D-8
Andalusia, 8691 N-7
Anniston, 23741 E-9
Arab, 7498 C-7
Ardmore, 1106 A-6
Ariton, 755 M-10
Ashford, 1932 N-11
Ashland, 1885 G-9
Ashville, 2429 E-8
Athens, 20972 A-6
Atmore, 7530 O-4
Attalla, 6474 D-8
Auburn, 49928 I-10
AUTAUGA CO., 48612 J-7
Autaugaville, 865 J-7
Avon, 470 N-11
Axis, 950 O-3
Babbie, 626 N-8
BALDWIN CO., 162586 P-4
BARBOUR CO., 28414 L-11
Bay Minette, 7808 O-3
Bayou La Batre, 2725 Q-2
Bayview, 600 F-6
Bear Cr., 1021 C-4
Beatrice, 403 L-5
Bellamy, 750 J-2
Berry, 1226 E-4
Bessemer, 28641 F-6
BIBB CO., 21516 H-6
Birmingham, 231483 F-6
BLOUNT CO., 55725 D-8
Blountsville, 1923 D-7
Boaz, 7893 C-8
Bon Secour, 900 R-3
Brantley, 909 M-8
Brent, 4129 H-5
Brewton, 5373 O-6
Bridgeport, 2693 A-10
Brighton, 3416 S-10
Brilliant, 733 D-3
Brookside, 1355 P-10
Brookwood, 1466 G-5
Brundidge, 2327 L-9
BULLOCK CO., 11055 K-10
BUTLER CO., 20766 L-7
Butler, 1780 K-2
Bynum, 1863 F-9
Cahaba Hts., 5203 S-13
Calera, 6707 G-7
CALHOUN CO., 112141 E-10
Calvert, 540 N-3
Camden, 2228 K-5
Camp Hill, 1199 H-10
Carbon Hill, 2047 E-4
Carrollton, 956 G-2
Castleberry, 560 N-6
Cedar Bluff, 1537 C-10
Center Pt., 22784 E-7
Centre, 3316 D-10
Centreville, 2507 H-5
Chalkville, 3829 E-7
CHAMBERS CO., 35460 H-11
Chatom, 1178 M-2
Chelsea, 3635 G-7
CHEROKEE CO., 24522 C-10
Cherokee, 1183 A-3
Chickasaw, 6000 P-2
Childersburg, 5000 G-8
CHILTON CO., 41744 H-7
CHOCTAW CO., 14807 K-2
Chunchula, 750 O-2
Citronelle, 3686 O-2
Clanton, 8336 H-7
CLARKE CO., 27269 M-3
CLAY CO., 13964 G-10
Clayhatchee, 498 N-10
Claysville, 650 C-8
Clayton, 1402 L-11
CLEBURNE CO., 14460 F-11
Cleveland, 1363 D-7
Clio, 2216 L-10
Cloverdale, 700 A-3
Coaling, 1103 G-5
Coden, 1050 Q-2
COFFEE CO., 45567 M-9
Coffeeville, 354 L-2
Coker, 789 G-4
COLBERT CO., 54660 B-3
Colbert Hts., 600 B-4
Coldwater, 600 F-9
Collinsville, 1667 C-9
Columbia, 823 N-12
Columbiana, 3664 G-7
Concord, 1809 F-6
CONECUH CO., 13257 N-6
COOSA CO., 11162 H-8
Coosada, 1484 J-8
Cordova, 2336 E-5
Cottondale, 2150 G-4
Cottonwood, 1171 O-11
Courtland, 765 B-5
COVINGTON CO., 37003 N-8
Cowarts, 1592 N-11
CRENSHAW CO., 13727 M-8
Creola, 2058 O-2
Crossville, 1449 C-9
Crumley Chapel, 1630 Q-10
Cuba, 334 J-2
CULLMAN CO., 79886 D-7
Cullman, 14735 D-6
Dadeville, 3145 H-10
DALE CO., 48748 M-10
Daleville, 4545 N-10
DALLAS CO., 44366 J-5
Daphne, 18581 P-3
Dauphin Island, 1533 R-2
De Armanville, 580 F-10
Decatur, 54909 B-6
DEKALB CO., 67271 B-10
Demopolis, 7555 J-3
Docena, 1000 Q-10
Dora, 2391 E-6
Dothan, 62713 N-11
Double Sprs., 983 D-5
Dozier, 393 M-8
E. Brewton, 2424 O-6
Eastern Valley, 2000 T-10
Eclectic, 1112 I-9
Edgewater, 730 R-10
Elba, 4181 N-9
Elberta, 583 Q-4
Elkmont, 493 A-6
ELMORE CO., 73937 I-9
Elmore, 465 I-8
Elrod, 450 G-3
Enterprise, 22892 N-9
ESCAMBIA CO., 38082 O-5
ETOWAH CO., 103189 D-9
Eufaula, 13463 L-12
Eutaw, 1800 I-3
Evergreen, 3442 M-6
Excel, 601 N-5
Fairfield, 11696 F-6
Fairhope, 15391 Q-3
Falkville, 1177 C-6
Fayette, 4761 E-3
FAYETTE CO., 18228 E-4
Flomaton, 1560 O-5
Florala, 1893 O-8
Florence, 36480 A-4
Foley, 11419 Q-4
Forestdale, 10509 Q-11
Forkland, 616 I-3
Ft. Deposit, 1229 K-7
Ft. Mitchell, 750 J-12
Ft. Payne, 13573 C-10
FRANKLIN CO., 30737 B-3
Frisco City, 1397 M-5
Fruitdale, 520 N-1
Fultondale, 6853 F-6
Fyffe, 1020 C-9
Gadsden, 37405 D-9
Gallant, 720 D-8
Garden City, 587 D-7
Gardendale, 12830 E-6
GENEVA CO., 25735 O-10
Geneva, 4379 O-9
Georgiana, 1636 M-7
Geraldine, 816 C-9
Glencoe, 5265 D-9
Good Hope, 2029 D-6
Goodsprings, 450 E-5
Goodwater, 1494 H-9
Gordo, 1596 G-3
Gordon, 416 N-12
Grand Bay, 3918 Q-2
Grant, 677 B-8
Graysville, 2452 F-6
GREENE CO., 9661 H-3
Greenhill, 600 A-4
Green Pond, 650 G-5
Greensboro, 2616 I-4
Greenville, 7104 L-7
Grove Hill, 1383 L-3
Guin, 2246 D-3
Gulf Shores, 7263 R-4
Guntersville, 7721 C-8
Gurley, 854 B-8
Hackleburg, 1475 C-3
HALE CO., 18316 I-4
Haleyville, 4159 C-4
Hamilton, 6496 D-3
Hammondville, 529 B-10
Hanceville, 3127 D-6
Harpersville, 1630 G-7
Hartford, 2372 O-10
Hartselle, 13080 C-6
Harvest, 3054 A-7
Hayneville, 1141 K-7
Hazel Green, 3805 A-7
Headland, 3714 N-11
Heflin, 3308 E-10
Helena, 13237 G-6
Henagar, 2507 B-9
HENRY CO., 16610 M-12
Hillview, 3080 Q-11
Hobson City, 860 F-9
Hokes Bluff, 4317 D-9
Holly Pond, 709 D-7
Hollywood, 929 A-9
Holt, 4020 G-4
Homewood, 23963 F-6
Hoover, 67469 F-6
HOUSTON CO., 94249 O-12
Hueytown, 15192 F-6
Huntsville, 166313 B-7
Hurtsboro, 558 J-11
Ider, 688 B-10
Indian Sprs. Vil., 2417 T-12
Inverness, 2528 T-13
Irondale, 9531 R-13
Irvington, 1000 Q-2
Jackson, 5285 M-3
JACKSON CO., 53650 A-9
Jacksonville, 8862 E-10
Jasper, 14088 E-5
JEFFERSON CO., 657229 E-7
Jemison, 2487 H-7
Kennedy, 511 F-3
Kent, 500 I-9
Killen, 1124 A-4
Kimberly, 2321 E-6
Kinsey, 1905 N-11
Kinston, 612 N-8
Laceys Chapel, 500 T-10
Laceys Spr., 600 B-7
Ladonia, 3229 J-12
Lafayette, 3102 H-11
LAMAR CO., 14962 E-3
Lanett, 7590 H-11
LAUDERDALE CO., 87691 A-4
LAWRENCE CO., 34605 B-5
LEE CO., 123254 I-11
Leeds, 11053 F-7
Leighton, 835 B-4
Level Plains, 1529 N-10
Lexington, 830 A-5
Lillian, 900 Q-4
LIMESTONE CO., 70469 A-6
Lincoln, 4921 F-8
Linden, 2336 J-3
Lineville, 2389 G-10
Lipscomb, 2318 T-10
Lisman, 602 K-2
Littleville, 947 B-4
Livingston, 3048 J-2
Lockhart, 542 O-8
Louisville, 580 L-10
LOWNDES CO., 13076 K-7
Loxley, 1435 P-3
Luverne, 2668 L-8
Lynn, 719 D-4
MACON CO., 22810 J-10
MADISON CO., 298192 A-7
Madison, 35893 B-7
Magnolia Sprs., 1300 Q-3
Malvern, 1202 O-10
Maplesville, 687 I-6
MARENGO CO., 21879 K-4
Margaret, 1241 E-7
Marion, 3428 I-5
MARION CO., 30154 D-4
MARSHALL CO., 85634 B-8
Maytown, 438 R-9
McCalla, 1000 G-6
McDonald Chapel, 1054 R-10
McKenzie, 623 M-7
Meadowbrook, 4697 T-14
Mentone, 472 B-10
Meridianville, 4117 A-7
Midfield, 5319 F-6
Midland City, 1798 N-10
Midway, 433 K-10
Millbrook, 14805 J-8
Millport, 1062 F-2
Millry, 604 M-2
Minor, 1116 R-10
MOBILE CO., 401427 P-2
Mobile, 191544 P-2
MONROE CO., 23733 M-5
Monroeville, 6690 M-5
Montevallo, 5092 G-6
Montgomery, 200127 J-8
MONTGOMERY CO., 221619 K-9
Montrose, 110 Q-3
Moody, 10764 F-7
MORGAN CO., 113740 C-7
Morris, 1868 E-6
Moulton, 3276 B-5
Moundville, 2188 H-4
Mtn. Brook, 20821 F-7
Mt. Meigs, 700 J-9
Mt. Olive, 3957 E-6
Mt. Vernon, 819 O-3
Munford, 2446 F-9
Muscle Shoals, 12523 A-4
Muscoda, 550 T-10
New Brockton, 1236 N-9
New Hope, 2671 B-8
New Market, 1864 A-7
New Site, 828 H-10
Newton, 1679 N-10
Newville, 539 N-11
Northport, 21216 G-4
Notasulga, 851 I-10
Oak Grove, 448 G-8
Oakman, 948 E-5
Odenville, 1203 E-8
Ohatchee, 1211 E-9
Oneonta, 6537 D-7
Opelika, 23804 I-11
Opp, 6658 N-8
Orange Beach, 5055 R-4
Overton, 1500 R-13
Owens Cross Roads, 1313 B-7
Oxford, 19981 F-9
Ozark, 14833 M-10
Palmerdale, 570 E-7
Parrish, 1259 E-5
Pawnee, 300 P-13
Pea Ridge, 800 G-6
Pelham, 19450 G-6
Pell City, 11010 F-8
Perdido, 1200 O-4
PERRY CO., 11371 I-5
Peterman, 300 M-5
Peterson, 950 G-4
Phenix City, 29460 J-12
Phil Campbell, 1050 C-4
PICKENS CO., 20178 G-3
Piedmont, 4969 D-10
PIKE CO., 29639 L-10
Pinckard, 642 N-10
Pinedale Shores, 800 E-8
Pine Hill, 923 K-4
Pinson, 5033 E-7
Pisgah, 702 B-9
Plantersville, 750 I-6
Pleasant Gr., 10312 F-6
Port Birmingham, 480 F-5
Pt. Clear, 1876 Q-3
Powell, 959 B-9
Prattville, 30043 J-7
Priceville, 2233 B-6
Prichard, 27963 P-2
Ragland, 2027 E-8
Raimund, 400 T-10
Rainbow City, 8880 D-9
Rainsville, 4782 B-9
Ramer, 500 K-8
Ranburne, 471 F-11
RANDOLPH CO., 22717 G-11
Red Bay, 3282 C-2
Red Level, 550 N-7
Reece City, 608 D-9
Reform, 1858 F-3
River Falls, 613 N-7
Riverside, 1749 F-8
Roanoke, 6650 G-11
Robertsdale, 4681 Q-4
Robinwood, 1000 Q-13
Rockford, 405 H-8
Rock Mills, 676 G-11
Roebuck Plaza Q-14
Rogersville, 1186 A-5
RUSSELL CO., 49326 J-12
Russellville, 8793 B-4
Rutledge, 508 L-8
Saginaw, 700 G-6
ST. CLAIR CO., 72330 E-8
St. Elmo, 1050 Q-2
Samson, 2025 O-9
Saraland, 12683 P-2
Sardis City, 1918 D-8
Satsuma, 5951 P-2
Sayre, 600 E-6
Scottsboro, 14840 B-9
Section, 763 B-9
Selma, 19401 J-6
Semmes, 2350 P-2
Shannon, 1000 T-11
Sheffield, 9228 A-4
Shelby, 1000 G-7
SHELBY CO., 171465 G-7
Shorter, 337 J-9
Silverhill, 695 Q-3
Sipsey, 548 E-5
Skyline, 839 A-8
Slocomb, 2033 O-10
Smiths, 4477 I-12
Snead, 817 D-8
Southside, 7838 D-9
Spanish Ft., 5642 P-3
Springville, 3054 E-7
Spruce Pine, 600 C-4
Stapleton, 1300 P-3
Steele, 1154 D-8
Sterrett, 600 F-7
Stevenson, 2138 A-9
Sulligent, 2033 E-2
Sumiton, 2582 E-6
Summerdale, 673 Q-4
SUMTER CO., 13819 J-2
Sycamore, 1000 G-8
Sylacauga, 12956 G-8
Sylvania, 1238 B-9
Sylvan Springs, 1510 R-9
Talladega, 17149 F-8
TALLADEGA CO., 80457 F-9
TALLAPOOSA CO., 40717 H-10
Tallassee, 5032 I-9
Tanner, 750 B-6
Tarrant, 6691 F-6
Taylor, 1943 N-11
Theodore, 6811 Q-2
Thomaston, 375 J-4
Thomasville, 4552 L-4
Thorsby, 1981 H-7
Tillmans Corner, 15685 P-2
Town Cr., 1209 B-5
Townley, 550 E-4
Trinity, 1842 B-6
Troy, 13935 L-9
Trussville, 16760 F-7
TUSCALOOSA CO., 168908 F-4
Tuscaloosa, 81358 G-4
Tuscumbia, 8170 B-4
Tuskegee, 11590 J-10
Union Sprs., 3443 K-10
Uniontown, 1520 J-4
Uriah, 500 N-4
Valhermoso Sprs., 500 B-7
Valley, 9000 H-11
Valley Head, 639 B-10
Verbena, 550 I-7
Vernon, 1984 E-2
Vestavia Hills, 31022 F-6
Vincent, 1950 F-8
Vinemont, 462 C-6
Vredenburgh, 320 L-5
Wadley, 648 G-10
WALKER CO., 70117 E-5
Walnut Gr., 702 D-8
Warrior, 3037 E-6
WASHINGTON CO., 17773 N-2
Weaver, 2555 E-9
Webb, 1337 N-11
Wedowee, 824 G-10
W. Blocton, 1418 G-5
Westwood, 1630 Q-10
Wetumpka, 6905 I-8
Whatley, 400 M-4
WILCOX CO., 12937 L-5
Wilmer, 400 P-1
Wilsonville, 1742 G-7
Wilton, 609 H-6
Winfield, 4673 D-3
WINSTON CO., 24498 C-5
Woodville, 755 B-8
York, 2625 J-2

Alaska
Map pp. 14-15

Adak Station, 600 J-9
Akiachak, 585 G-5
Akutan, 784 I-11
Alakanuk, 697 E-4
Anchorage, 275043 G-8
Anchor Point, 1845 G-7
Anderson, 324 E-8
Angoon, 481 H-12
Aniak, 581 F-5
Barrow, 4218 A-7
Bethel, 6262 G-5
Big Delta, 749 E-9
Big Lake, 2635 F-8
Chevak, 819 F-4
College, 11402 A-1
Copper Center, 362 F-9
Cordova, 2327 G-9
Craig, 1217 I-13
Delta Jct., 897 E-9
Denali Nat'l Park, 142 E-8
Dillingham, 2468 H-6
Emmonak, 823 E-4
Fairbanks, 31324 E-9
Ft. Yukon, 561 C-9
Galena, 641 E-6
Gambell, 653 D-2
Glennallen, 554 F-9
Haines, 1811 G-12
Healy, 1000 E-8
Homer, 5364 G-7
Hoonah, 751 H-12
Hooper Bay, 1085 F-4
Houston, 1614 F-8
Hydaburg, 351 I-13
Juneau, 30987 H-12
Kake, 667 H-13
Kasigluk, 543 F-4
Kasilof, 471 G-8
Kenai, 7464 G-8
Ketchikan, 7410 I-14
Kiana, 411 C-6
King Cove, 748 J-4
King Salmon, 442 H-6
Kipnuk, 644 G-4
Klawock, 767 I-13
Kodiak, 6273 H-7
Kotlik, 635 E-4
Kotzebue, 3237 C-5
Kwethluk, 726 G-5
Manokotak, 400 H-5
McGrath, 379 F-6
Metlakatla, 1375 I-14
Mountain Village, 808 F-4
Naknek, 678 H-6
Nenana, 371 E-8
New Stuyahok, 472 G-6
Nikiski, 4327 G-8
Ninilchik, 772 G-7
Nome, 3590 D-4
Noorvik, 672 C-5
North Pole, 1778 E-9
Nuiqsut, 386 A-8
Nulato, 318 D-6
Nunapitchuk, 474 G-4
Old Hbr., 217 I-7
Palmer, 6920 F-8
Petersburg, 3010 I-13
Pilot Sta., 590 F-5
Pt. Hope, 704 B-4
Quinhagak, 563 G-5
St. Marys, 536 F-4
Sand Pt., 951 J-5
Savoonga, 648 E-3
Selawik, 819 C-6
Seldovia, 300 H-7
Seward, 3016 G-8
Shishmaref, 565 C-4
Sitka, 8986 I-12
Skagway, 828 G-12
Soldotna, 4087 G-8
Stebbins, 552 E-5
Tanana, 290 D-7
Togiak, 810 H-5
Tok, 1393 E-10
Toksook Bay, 542 G-4
Tuluksak, 428 F-5
Unalakleet, 752 E-5
Unalaska, 4347 I-11
Valdez, 4015 G-9
Wainwright, 507 A-6
Wasilla, 8471 F-8
Wrangell, 2117 I-13
Yakutat, 680 G-11

Arizona
Map pp. 16-21

* City keyed to pp. 20-21

Aguila, 140 I-5
Ajo, 3705 M-6
Alpine, 350 I-14
APACHE CO., 69343 E-13
Apache Jct., 32297 J-9
Arizona City, 4385 L-8
Ash Fork, 457 E-7
Avondale, 66706 I-7
Bagdad, 1578 G-5
Bapchule, 100 K-8
Benson, 4934 N-11
Bisbee, 6177 O-12
Black Canyon City, 2697 H-7
Bouse, 615 I-3
Bowie, 550 M-13
Buckeye, 9619 J-6
Bullhead City, 39101 F-2
Bylas, 600 K-12
Camp Verde, 10155 G-8
Carefree, 3706 I-8
Casa Grande, 32855 K-8
Catalina, 7025 L-10
Cave Cr., 4884 I-8
Central Hts., 2000 J-10
Chambers, 250 E-13
Chandler, 234939 J-8
Chinle, 5366 C-13
Chino Valley, 9710 G-7
Chloride, 225 E-3
Chuichu, 339 L-8
Cibecue, 1331 H-11
Clarkdale, 3753 G-8
Claypool, 1794 J-10
Clay Sprs., 250 H-11
Clifton, 2265 K-13
COCHISE CO., 126106 M-13
COCONINO CO., 123866 C-8
Colorado City, 4371 A-6
Concho, 400 G-13
Congress, 1717 H-6
Coolidge, 8154 K-9
Cornville, 3335 G-8
Cortaro, 250 M-10
Cottonwood, 10894 G-8
Dennehotso, 734 A-12
Dewey, 700 G-7
Dilkon, 1265 E-11
Dolan Sprs., 1867 D-3
Douglas, 16791 O-13
Dudleyville, 1323 K-10
Duncan, 713 L-14
Eagar, 4126 H-13
Ehrenberg, 1357 I-2
Elfrida, 600 N-13
El Mirage, 22171 *C-3
Eloy, 10855 L-9
Flagstaff, 57391 F-8
Florence, 17053 K-9
Ft. Apache, 200 I-12
Ft. Defiance, 4061 D-14
Fountain Hills, 23217 J-8
Fredonia, 1051 A-7
Gadsden, 953 L-2
Ganado, 1505 D-13
Gila Bend, 2055 K-6
Gilbert, 173989 J-8
Glendale, 239435 J-7
Globe, 7187 J-10
Goodyear, 43941 J-7
GRAHAM CO., 33073 K-13
Grand Canyon, 1460 C-7
Greasewood, 581 E-12
GREENLEE CO., 7521 J-13
Green Valley, 17283 N-10
Guadalupe, 5258 *E-6
Hayden, 843 K-10
Heber, 300 G-11
Higley, 1000 *F-8
Holbrook, 5126 F-12
Hotevilla, 600 D-10
Houck, 1087 E-13
Huachuca City, 1890 O-11
Humboldt, 1300 G-7
Jerome, 343 G-7
Joseph City, 1100 F-11
Kaibito, 1607 B-10
Kayenta, 4922 B-11
Keams Canyon, 260 D-11
Kearny, 2765 K-10
Kingman, 25547 F-3
Komatke, 1000 J-7
Kykotsmovi Vil., 776 D-11
Lake Havasu City, 55338 G-3
Lake Montezuma, 3344 G-8
LA PAZ CO., 20238 I-4
Laveen, 1200 J-7
Litchfield Park, 4523 I-7
Mammoth, 2167 L-11
Many Farms, 1548 C-13
Marana, 26098 L-9
Maricopa, 1040 K-8
MARICOPA CO., 3635528 I-6
Mayer, 1408 H-7
McNary, 349 H-12
Meadview, 1000 C-3
Mesa, 442780 J-8
Miami, 1841 J-10
Moenkopi, 901 C-9
MOHAVE CO., 187200 F-4
Morenci, 1879 K-13
Mountainaire, 1014 F-8
Mt. Lemmon, 100 M-10
Naco, 833 O-12
NAVAJO CO., 108432 E-11
Nazlini, 397 D-13
Nogales, 20833 O-10
Oracle, 3563 L-10
Oro Valley, 38438 M-10
Overgaard, 400 H-11
Page, 6794 A-9
Palominas O-12
Paradise Valley, 14558 *C-6
Parker, 3222 H-3
Patagonia, 825 O-10
Paulden, 3420 F-7
Payson, 14729 H-9
Peach Sprs., 600 E-5
Peoria, 138200 J-7
Peridot, 1266 J-11
Phoenix, 1461575 J-8
Picacho, 500 L-9
Pima, 1965 K-12
PIMA CO., 924786 M-8
PINAL CO., 229549 L-9
Pine, 1931 H-9
Pinetop-Lakeside, 4156 H-12
Pinon, 1190 C-11
Pirtleville, 1550 O-13
Plantsite, 600 K-13
Polacca, 700 D-11
Prescott, 40360 G-7
Prescott Valley, 33068 G-7
Quartzsite, 3397 I-3
Queen Cr., 16628 J-8
Red Rock, 300 B-13
Rillito, 400 M-9
Rio Rico, 1400 O-10
Rio Verde, 1419 I-8
Rock Pt., 724 B-13
Rough Rock, 469 C-12
Round Rock, 601 B-13
Sacaton, 1584 K-8
Safford, 8932 K-13
Sahuarita, 9007 N-10
St. David, 1744 N-12
St. Johns, 3538 G-13
St. Michaels, 1295 D-14
Salome, 1690 I-4
San Carlos, 3716 J-11
Sanders, 550 E-13
San Luis, 21646 L-2
San Manuel, 4375 L-11
San Simon, 260 M-14
SANTA CRUZ CO., 42009 O-10
Santa Maria, 350 *E-4
Santa Rosa, 438 M-8
Sawmill, 612 D-14
Scottsdale, 226013 J-8
Second Mesa, 814 D-11
Sedona, 11220 F-8
Seligman, 456 E-6
Sells, 2799 N-8
Shonto, 568 B-10
Show Low, 10000 H-12
Sierra Vista, 41908 O-11
Skull Valley G-6
Snowflake, 4958 G-12
Solomon, 530 L-13
Somerton, 10071 L-2
S. Tucson, 5562 M-10
Springerville, 1956 H-13
Stanfield, 651 K-8
Steamboat Canyon, 350 D-12
Sun City, 38309 J-7
Sun City W., 26344 I-7
Sun Lakes, 11936 K-8
Sunsites N-12
Supai, 423 C-6
Superior, 3158 J-10
Surprise, 74411 I-7
Tacna, 555 L-4
Taylor, 3807 G-12
Teec Nos Pos, 799 A-13
Tempe, 161143 J-8
Thatcher, 4121 K-12
Tolleson, 5974 *E-4
Tombstone, 1569 N-12
Topock G-3
Tsaile, 1078 C-13
Tuba City, 8225 C-9
Tucson, 515526 M-10
Tusayan, 562 D-7
Wellton, 1862 L-3
Wenden, 556 I-4
Whiteriver, 5220 I-12
Wickenburg, 6224 I-6
Wikieup G-4
Wilhoit, 664 H-6
Willcox, 3769 M-12
Williams, 3094 E-7
Window Rock, 3059 D-14
Winkelman, 444 K-10
Winslow, 9931 F-10
Wittmann, 1050 I-7
Woodruff, 200 G-12
Yarnell, 645 H-6
YAVAPAI CO., 198701 F-6
Young, 561 H-10
Youngtown, 4021 *C-3
YUMA CO., 181277 K-3
Yuma, 84688 L-2

Arkansas
Map pp. 22-23

Alma, 4734 D-1
Altheimer, 1161 G-6
Altus, 835 D-2
Amity, 741 G-3
Arkadelphia, 10548 G-4
ARKANSAS CO., 20073 G-7
Arkansas City, 549 H-7
Ashdown, 4592 H-1
Ash Flat, 998 B-6
ASHLEY CO., 23178 I-6
Atkins, 2890 D-4
Augusta, 2456 D-7
Bald Knob, 3316 D-7
Barling, 4318 D-1
Batesville, 9556 C-6
Bauxite, 442 F-5
BAXTER CO., 40330 B-5
Bay, 1953 C-9
Bearden, 1047 H-5
Beebe, 5623 E-6
Bella Vista, 16582 B-1
Belleville, 371 E-3
BENTON CO., 186938 B-1
Benton, 25673 F-5
Bentonville, 29538 B-1
Berryville, 4935 B-3
Biggers, 354 B-8
Biscoe, 447 E-7
Black Rock, 690 B-7
Blytheville, 16638 C-10
Bonanza, 530 D-1
Bono, 1540 C-8
BOONE CO., 35793 B-4
Booneville, 4162 E-2
Bradford, 828 D-7
BRADLEY CO., 12192 I-5
Bradley, 553 I-2
Brinkley, 3520 E-7
Brookland, 1442 C-8
Bryant, 13185 F-5
Bull Shoals, 2060 B-5
Cabot, 21039 E-6
CALHOUN CO., 5589 I-4
Calico Rock, 1025 B-5
Calion, 496 I-5
Camden, 12204 H-4
Cammack Vil., 784 L-4
Caraway, 1355 C-9
Carlisle, 2419 F-6
CARROLL CO., 26999 B-3
Carthage, 416 G-5
Cave City, 1980 C-7
Cave Sprs., 1424 B-1
Charleston, 3025 D-2
Cherokee Vil., 4633 B-7
Cherry Valley, 702 D-8
CHICOT CO., 13027 I-7
Clarendon, 1835 F-7
CLARK CO., 22916 G-3
Clarksville, 8311 D-3
CLAY CO., 16578 B-9
CLEBURNE CO., 25391 D-6
CLEVELAND CO., 8903 H-5
Clinton, 2475 D-5
Coal Hill, 1040 D-2
College Station, 766 M-6
COLUMBIA CO., 24695 J-3
Conway, 51999 E-5
CONWAY CO., 20739 D-4
Corning, 3456 B-8
Cotter, 1032 B-5
Cotton Plant, 895 E-7
Cove, 383 F-1
CRAIGHEAD CO., 86735 C-8
CRAWFORD CO., 57630 D-1
Crawfordsville, 498 D-9
CRITTENDEN CO., 51882 E-9
CROSS CO., 19237 D-8
Crossett, 5802 J-6
Cushman, 467 C-6
DALLAS CO., 8524 H-4
Danville, 2442 E-3
Dardanelle, 4337 E-3
Decatur, 1352 B-1
DeQueen, 5953 G-1
Dermott, 3463 I-7
Des Arc, 1821 E-7
Desha, 750 C-6
DESHA CO., 14358 H-7
De Valls Bluff, 743 F-7
De Witt, 3414 G-7
Diamond City, 760 B-4
Diaz, 1200 D-7
Dierks, 1252 G-2
Dover, 1359 D-4
DREW CO., 18693 I-6
Dumas, 4862 H-7
Dyer, 609 D-2
Dyess, 480 D-9
Earle, 2895 D-9
East Camden, 835 H-4
Edmondson, 493 E-9
Elaine, 777 G-8
El Dorado, 20467 I-4
Elkins, 1890 C-2
Emmet, 450 H-3
England, 3028 F-6
Eudora, 2571 J-7
Eureka Sprs., 2350 B-2
Fairfield Bay, 2502 D-5
Farmington, 4376 C-1
FAULKNER CO., 97147 E-5
Fayetteville, 66655 B-2
Flippin, 1396 B-5
Fordyce, 4409 H-5
Foreman, 1071 H-1
Forrest City, 14078 E-8
Ft. Smith, 82481 D-1
Fouke, 851 I-2
FRANKLIN CO., 18218 D-2
FULTON CO., 11934 B-6
Garland, 356 I-2
GARLAND CO., 93551 F-3
Gassville, 1931 B-5
Gentry, 2613 B-1
Gillett, 787 G-7
Gilmore, 287 D-9
Glenwood, 2057 G-3
Gosnell, 3661 C-10
Gould, 1210 G-7
Grady, 479 G-6
GRANT CO., 17348 F-5
Gravette, 2275 B-1
Greenbrier, 3615 E-5
GREENE CO., 39401 B-8
Green Forest, 2859 B-3
Greenland, 1061 C-2
Greenwood, 7914 E-1
Greers Ferry, 966 D-5
Grubbs, 410 C-8
Gurdon, 2233 H-3
Hackett, 726 E-1
Hamburg, 2844 I-6
Hampton, 1512 I-5
Hardy, 779 B-7
Harrisburg, 2165 D-8
Harrison, 12764 B-4
Hartford, 779 E-1
Hartman, 620 D-3
Haskell, 3016 F-4
Hatfield, 389 F-1
Hazen, 1562 F-7
Heber Sprs., 7016 D-6
Hector, 517 D-4
Helena, 5687 F-8
HEMPSTEAD CO., 23383 H-2
Hermitage, 762 I-5
Hickory Ridge, 365 D-8
Holly Gr., 639 F-7
Hope, 10467 H-3
Horatio, 1025 H-1
Horseshoe Bend, 2287 B-6
HOT SPRING CO., 31264 G-4
Hot Springs, 37847 F-4
Hot Springs Vil., 8397 F-4
HOWARD CO., 14552 G-2
Hoxie, 2717 C-8
Hughes, 1762 E-9
Humphrey, 787 F-6
Huntington, 696 E-1
Huntsville, 2207 B-2
Huttig, 716 J-5
Imboden, 643 B-7
INDEPENDENCE CO., 34737 C-6
IZARD CO., 13430 B-6
JACKSON CO., 17601 D-7
Jacksonville, 30367 E-6
Jasper, 494 C-3
JEFFERSON CO., 81700 G-6
JOHNSON CO., 24042 D-3
Joiner, 506 D-9
Jonesboro, 59358 C-8
Judsonia, 2087 D-6
Junction City, 691 J-4
Keiser, 763 C-9
Kensett, 1708 D-6
Kibler, 1019 D-1
Kingsland, 454 H-5
Knoxville, 628 D-3
LAFAYETTE CO., 8027 I-2
Lake City, 2002 C-9
Lake Hamilton, 1609 F-4
Lakeview, 806 B-5
Lake View, 494 F-8
Lake Vil., 2608 I-7
Lamar, 1542 D-3
Lavaca, 2059 D-1
LAWRENCE CO., 17153 C-7
Leachville, 1847 C-9
LEE CO., 11545 F-8
Leola, 536 G-5
Lepanto, 2079 D-9
Leslie, 464 C-5
Lewisville, 1200 I-3
Lincoln, 1904 C-1
LINCOLN CO., 14262 G-6
LITTLE RIVER CO., 13227 H-1
Little Rock, 184564 F-5
Lockesburg, 733 G-1
LOGAN CO., 22944 E-2
London, 955 D-3
Lonoke, 4552 F-6
LONOKE CO., 60658 F-6
Lowell, 7042 B-2
Luxora, 1243 C-10
Macon, 960 E-5
Madison, 919 E-8
MADISON CO., 14962 C-3
Magazine, 910 E-2
Magnolia, 10478 I-3
Malvern, 9068 G-4
Mammoth Spr., 1157 A-7
Mandeville, 520 I-2
Manila, 2813 C-9
Mansfield, 1107 E-1
Marianna, 4792 F-8
Marion, 9792 D-9
MARION CO., 16735 B-4
Marked Tree, 2720 D-9
Marmaduke, 1163 B-9
Marshall, 1255 C-4
Marvell, 1250 F-8
Maumelle, 14318 E-5
Mayflower, 1900 E-5
McAlmont, 1922 K-7
McCrory, 1688 D-7
McGehee, 4233 H-7
McNeil, 638 I-3
McRae, 681 E-6
Melbourne, 1700 C-6
Mena, 5608 F-1
MILLER CO., 43162 I-2
Mineral Sprs., 1293 H-2
MISSISSIPPI CO., 47911 C-9
Mitchellville, 512 H-7
Monette, 1189 C-9
MONROE CO., 9302 F-7
MONTGOMERY CO., 9274 F-2
Monticello, 9327 H-6
Montrose, 525 I-7
Morrilton, 6607 E-4
Mountainburg, 713 D-2
Mtn. Home, 11896 B-5
Mtn. Pine, 827 F-3
Mtn. View, 2998 C-6
Mt. Ida, 971 F-2
Mt. Pleasant, 407 C-6
Mulberry, 1696 D-2
Murfreesboro, 1713 G-2
Nashville, 4929 H-2
NEVADA CO., 9550 H-3
Newark, 1233 C-7
Newport, 7281 D-7
NEWTON CO., 8452 C-3
Norman, 422 F-2
Norphlet, 807 I-4
N. Crossett, 3581 I-6
N. Little Rock, 58803 F-5
Oak Grove, 660 K-5
Ola, 1206 E-3
Osceola, 8128 C-10
OUACHITA CO., 27102 H-4
Oxford, 653 B-6
Ozark, 3586 D-2
Palestine, 736 E-8
Pangburn, 661 D-6
Paragould, 23775 B-9
Paris, 3707 D-2
Parkdale, 365 J-7
Parkers Chapel, 500 I-4
Parkin, 1548 D-9
Patterson, 434 D-7
Pea Ridge, 3344 B-2
PERRY CO., 10468 E-4
Perryville, 1471 E-4
PHILLIPS CO., 24107 F-8
Piggott, 3661 B-9
PIKE CO., 11038 G-3
Pine Bluff, 52693 G-6
Plainview, 756 E-3
Plumerville, 873 E-4
Pocahontas, 6765 B-8
POINSETT CO., 25349 D-8
POLK CO., 20176 F-1
POPE CO., 56580 D-4
Portland, 528 I-7
PRAIRIE CO., 9113 E-6
Prairie Gr., 2996 C-1
Prescott, 4285 H-3
PULASKI CO., 366463 F-5
Quitman, 741 D-5
RANDOLPH CO., 18465 B-7
Rector, 1856 B-9
Redfield, 1173 F-5
Reed, 263 H-7
Reyno, 483 B-8
Rison, 1340 H-5
Rogers, 48353 B-2
Roland, 200 E-5
Russellville, 25520 D-3
ST. FRANCIS CO., 27902 E-8
Salem, 1587 B-6
Salesville, 465 B-5
SALINE CO., 91188 F-4
SCOTT CO., 11150 E-2
Searcy, 20663 D-6
SEARCY CO., 7969 C-4
SEBASTIAN CO., 118750 E-1
SEVIER CO., 16456 H-1
Shannon Hills, 2651 F-5
SHARP CO., 17397 C-7
Sheridan, 4349 G-5
Sherwood, 23149 K-6
Siloam Sprs., 13604 B-1
Smackover, 1929 I-4
Sparkman, 535 H-4
Springdale, 60096 B-2
Stamps, 1984 I-3
Star City, 2321 H-6
Stephens, 1066 I-4
STONE CO., 11716 C-5
Strong, 637 J-5
Stuttgart, 9376 F-7
Subiaco, 448 D-2
Sulphur Sprs., 689 A-1
Summit, 585 B-4
Sunset, 333 D-9
Swifton, 811 C-7
Taylor, 545 J-3
Texarkana, 30006 I-2
Thornton, 505 H-5
Tontitown, 1621 B-1
Traskwood, 552 F-4
Trumann, 6922 C-9
Tuckerman, 1721 C-7
Turrell, 912 D-9
Tyronza, 890 D-9
UNION CO., 44186 J-5
VAN BUREN CO., 16529 D-5
Van Buren, 21249 D-1
Vilonia, 2719 E-5
Wabbaseka, 311 G-6
Waldo, 1490 I-3
Waldron, 3555 E-2
Walnut Ridge, 4724 B-8
Ward, 3271 E-6
Warren, 6263 H-6
WASHINGTON CO., 180357 C-1
Weiner, 755 D-8
W. Crossett, 1664 I-6
W. Fork, 2195 C-1
W. Helena, 7876 F-8
W. Memphis, 28181 E-9
Wheatley, 348 E-7
WHITE CO., 71332 D-6
White Hall, 5114 G-6
Wickes, 678 G-1
Wilmar, 559 H-6
Wilmot, 742 J-7
Wilson, 854 D-10
Wilton, 431 H-1
WOODRUFF CO., 8098 E-7
Woodson, 445 F-5
Wrightsville, 1521 F-5
Wynne, 8569 E-8
YELL CO., 21391 E-3
Yellville, 1348 B-4

California
Map pp. 24-39

Index keys NA to NN refer to Northern CA, pp. 24-27, SA to SN refer to Southern CA, pp. 32-35.
* City keyed to pp. 28-29
† City keyed to pp. 30-31
‡ City keyed to pp. 36-39

Acton, 2390 SI-11
Adelanto, 24360 SH-13
Agoura Hills, 22765 SJ-10
Ahwahnee, 650 NN-11
ALAMEDA CO., 1448905 NM-7
Alameda, 70576 NM-5
Alamo, 15626 NE-18
Albany, 15994 NE-15
Alhambra, 87410 SJ-11
Allendale, 1000 NK-6
Alpaugh, 761 SE-8
Alpine, 13143 SM-14
ALPINE CO., 1159 NJ-11
Altadena, 42610 SJ-11
Alta Hill, 850 NJ-8
Alturas, 2902 NC-9
AMADOR CO., 38471 NK-10
Anaheim, 331804 SK-12
Anchor Bay, 1000 NJ-2
Anderson, 10528 NE-5
Angels Camp, 3761 NL-9
Angwin, 3148 NK-5
Antioch, 100631 NL-6
Apple Valley, 65156 SI-13
Aptos, 9396 SB-3
Arbuckle, 2332 NI-6
Arcade, 42000 *C-7
Arcadia, 56153 ‡D-9
Arcata, 16914 ND-2
Arden, 55000 *D-7
Argus, 300 SE-13
Armona, 3239 SD-7
Arnold, 4218 NL-9
Arroyo Grande, 16315 SG-5
Artesia, 16672 ‡H-9
Arvin, 14724 SG-9
Ashland, 20793 NG-17
Atascadero, 27130 SF-5
Atherton, 7177 NK-16
Atwater, 27107 NN-9
Auberry, 2053 SB-8
Auburn, 12912 NJ-8
Avalon, 3334 SL-11
Avenal, 16631 SE-6
Avery, 672 NL-9
Azusa, 47120 ‡D-11
Baker, 860 SF-16
Bakersfield, 295536 SF-9
Baldwin Park, 78861 ‡D-10
Banning, 29308 SJ-14
Barstow, 23737 SH-14
Bay Point, 21534 NC-19
Bayview, 2359 ND-2
Bayview Park NC-14
Baywood Park, 6000 SF-5
Beaumont, 20530 SJ-14
Bell, 37521 †F-8
Bellflower, 74570 ‡G-8
Bell Gardens, 45135 †F-8
Belltown, 1750 ‡E-17
Belmont, 24522 NJ-15
Belvedere, 2072 NE-13
Benicia, 26489 NL-5
Ben Lomond, 2364 SA-2
Berkeley, 100744 NM-5
Bertsch Ter., 975 NB-2
Bethel Island, 2312 NL-7
Beverly Hills, 35078 SJ-10
Big Bear City, 5779 SI-14
Big Bear Lake, 6158 SI-14
Big Creek, 260 SA-8
Biggs, 1803 NH-7
Big Pine, 1350 SA-11
Big River, 1266 SI-20
Biola, 1037 SB-7
Bishop, 3606 NN-14
Bloomington, 19318 ‡E-17
Blue Lake, 1128 ND-2
Blythe, 22130 SK-19
Bodfish, 1823 SF-10
Bolinas, 1246 NL-4
Bolsa Knolls, 1950 SB-3
Bonita, 12401 †L-8
Bonsall, 3401 SL-13
Boonville, 1200 NI-3
Boron, 2025 SG-12
Borrego Sprs., 2535 SL-15
Bostonia, 15169 †H-10
Boulder Cr., 4081 SA-2
Bowman, 1100 NJ-8
Boyes Hot Sprs., 6665 NK-5
Bradbury, 1014 ‡D-10
Brawley, 22433 SM-17
Brea, 38465 SJ-12
Brentwood, 43794 NL-6
Bridgeport, 600 NK-13
Brisbane, 3556 NH-13
Broadmoor, 4026 NG-12
Buellton, 4293 SH-6
Buena Park, 79174 ‡H-10
Burbank, 104108 SJ-11
Burlingame, 27380 NI-14
Burney, 3217 ND-7
BUTTE CO., 214185 NH-6
Buttonwillow, 1266 SF-8
Byron, 916 NM-7
Cabazon, 2229 SJ-14
Calabasas, 21908 ‡D-2
CALAVERAS CO., 46871 NL-9
Calexico, 36005 SN-17
California City, 11790 SG-11
Calimesa, 7491 SJ-14
Calipatria, 7725 SL-17
Calistoga, 5190 NK-5
Camarillo, 61576 SJ-9
Cambria, 6232 SF-4
Cambrian Park, 3258 NN-19
Cameron Park, 14549 NJ-8
Camino, 1200 NJ-9
Campbell, 37042 NN-6
Canyon Lake, 11287 SK-13
Capitola, 9553 SB-2
Carlsbad, 90773 SL-13
Carmel, 3994 SC-2
Carmel Highlands, 940 SC-2
Carmel Point, 500 *J-1
Carmel Valley, 4700 SC-3
Carmel Woods, 1200 *I-1
Carmichael, 49742 NJ-7
Carnelian Bay, 650 NI-10
Carpinteria, 13549 SI-8
Carson, 93955 †H-7
Caruthers, 2103 SC-7
Casa Conejo, 3180 SJ-9
Casa de Oro, 12000 †J-9
Casitas Sprs., 800 SI-8
Castaic, 1200 SI-10
Castro Valley, 57292 NM-6
Castroville, 6724 SB-3
Cathedral City, 51713 SK-15
Cayucos, 2943 SF-5
Cedar Glen, 2100 ‡B-20
Cedarville, 700 NB-10
Ceres, 40571 NM-8
Cerritos, 52561 ‡H-9
Challenge, 250 NH-8
Channel Islands, 3142 †C-2
Charter Oak, 9027 ‡D-12
Cherry Valley, 5891 SJ-14
Chester, 2316 NF-8
Chico, 71427 NG-6
Chino, 77578 ‡F-14
Chino Hills, 75722 ‡G-13
Chowchilla, 16525 SA-6
Chula Vista, 210497 SN-14
Citrus Hts., 86272 NJ-7
City of Commerce, 13455 ‡F-8
Claremont, 35182 ‡D-13
Clayton, 11142 NL-6
Clearlake, 14728 NI-4
Clearlake Oaks, 2402 NI-4
Cloverdale, 8016 NJ-4
Clovis, 86527 SB-7
Coachella, 32432 SK-16
Coalinga, 17350 SD-6
Coarsegold, 2000 SA-7
Cobb, 1638 NJ-4
Colfax, 1720 NI-8
Colma, 1394 NH-13
Colton, 51350 SJ-13
Columbia, 2405 NL-9
COLUSA CO., 21095 NI-6
Colusa, 5826 NI-6
Compton, 95659 ‡H-7
Concord, 123252 NL-6
CONTRA COSTA CO., 1017787 NM-7
Cool, 1200 NJ-8
Copperopolis, 2363 NL-9
Corcoran, 22456 SD-8
Corning, 7140 NG-6
Corona, 149387 SK-12
Coronado, 26424 SN-13
Coronita, 2400 ‡H-15
Corte Madera, 9120 ND-12
Costa Mesa, 109830 ‡K-11
Cotati, 7138 NK-4
Cottonwood, 2960 NF-5
Covelo, 1175 NG-3
Covina, 47850 ‡E-11
Cowan Hts., 4000 ‡I-12
Crescent City, 7825 NA-1
Crest, 2716 SM-14
Crestline, 10218 ‡B-18
Crockett, 3194 NB-15
Cudahy, 25004 ‡G-8
Culver City, 39603 †F-5
Cupertino, 52171 NM-17
Cutler, 4491 SC-8
Cypress, 47383 ‡H-9
Daggett, 450 SH-14
Daly City, 100339 NG-13
Dana Pt., 35867 ‡N-14
Danville, 41852 NM-6
Davis, 60709 NK-6
Death Valley, 31 SC-14
Delano, 45531 SE-8
Delhi, 8022 NN-8
Del Mar, 4378 SM-13
DEL NORTE CO., 28705 NB-2
Del Rey, 950 SC-8
Del Rey Oaks, 1584 SC-3
Denair, 3446 NN-8
Derby Acres, 376 SG-8
Descanso, 850 SM-15
Desert Hot Sprs., 20492 SJ-15
Desert View Highlands, 2337 SI-11
Devore SJ-13
Diablo, 988 NE-19
Diamond Bar, 57975 ‡F-12
Diamond Sprs., 4888 NJ-8
Dinuba, 19308 SC-8
Dixon, 17330 NK-6
Dorris, 875 NA-6
Dos Palos, 5036 SB-5
Downey, 109718 SJ-11
Downieville, 200 NH-8
Doyle, 800 NG-10
Duarte, 22194 ‡D-10
Dublin, 39328 NM-6
Dunsmuir, 1870 NC-5
Durham, 5220 NH-6
Eagle Mtn., 580 SJ-17
Earlimart, 6583 SE-8
Earp, 70 SJ-20
E. Blythe, 3 SK-19
E. Foothills, 8133 NL-20
E. Los Angeles, 124283 ‡F-8
Easton, 1966 SC-7
E. Palo Alto, 32242 NK-17
E. Pasadena, 6045 ‡D-9
E. Quincy, 2398 NG-8
E. Richmond Hts., 3357 ND-14
E. Tustin, 11000 ‡I-12
El Cajon, 92487 SN-14
El Centro, 39636 SM-17
El Cerrito, 4590 ‡H-16
El Cerrito, 22868 NL-5
El Dorado, 1100 NJ-8
EL DORADO CO., 176841 NJ-10
El Dorado Hills, 18016 NJ-8
El Granada, 5724 NJ-13
Elk Grove, 59984 NK-7
El Monte, 122513 ‡E-10
El Portal, 520 NM-11
El Rio, 6193 SI-9
El Segundo, 16517 ‡G-5
El Sobrante, 12260 NC-15
Elverta, 1130 NJ-7
Emerald Bay, 1100 ‡L-12
Emeryville, 8528 NE-15
Empire, 3903 NM-8
Encinitas, 59525 SM-13
Escalon, 7171 NM-8
Escondido, 134085 SM-14
Esparto, 1858 NJ-6
Etna, 796 NB-4
Eureka, 25579 ND-1
Exeter, 9974 SD-9
Fairfax, 7106 NL-5
Fairfield, 104476 NL-6
Fair Oaks, 28008 NJ-7
Fallbrook, 29100 SL-13
Fall River Mills, 648 ND-7
Farmersville, 9918 SD-9
Fawnskin, 500 SI-14
Fellows, 153 SG-8
Felton, 1051 SB-2
Ferndale, 1394 NE-1
Fieldbrook, 1000 ND-2
Fillmore, 14895 SI-9
Firebaugh, 7001 SB-6
Florence, 25000 ‡F-7
Florin, 27653 *E-7
Folsom, 65611 NJ-8
Fontana, 163860 ‡D-16
Foothill Farms, 17426 *B-8
Ford City, 3512 SG-8
Foresthill, 1791 NI-8

Forestville, 2370 NK-4
Ft. Bragg, 6814 NH-2
Fortuna, 11155 NE-1
Foster City, 28756 NI-15
Fountain Valley, 55942 ‡J-10
Fowler, 4713 SC-7
Frazier Park, 2348 SH-9
Freedom, 6000 SB-3
Fremont, 200468 NM-6
French Camp, 4109 NM-7
Fresno, 461116 SB-7
FRESNO CO., 877584 SD-6
Fullerton, 132787 SJ-12
Fulton, 1300 NK-4
Galt, 23173 NL-7
Garberville, 800 NF-2
Gardena, 59891 ‡H-6
Garden Acres, 9747 *H-10
Garden Grove, 166075 SK-12
Garden Valley, 700 NJ-8
Georgetown, 962 NJ-8
Gerber, 1100 NF-6
Geyserville, 1000 NJ-4
Gilroy, 45718 SB-3
Glen Avon, 14853 ‡F-16
Glendale, 200065 SJ-11
Glendora, 50540 ‡D-12
Glen Ellen, 992 NK-5
GLENN CO., 27759 NH-5
Goleta, 55204 SI-7
Gonzales, 8498 SC-3
Goshen, 2394 SD-8
Grand Ter., 12342 ‡E-18
Grant Grove SK-1
Grass Valley, 12449 NI-8
Graton, 1815 NK-4
Greeley Hill, 250 NM-10
Greenacres, 7379 SF-9
Greenbrae, 3400 ND-12
Greenfield, 13330 SD-4
Greenville, 1160 NF-8
Gridley, 5588 NH-7
Grover Beach, 12887 SG-5
Guadalupe, 6346 SG-5
Gualala, 1500 NJ-3
Guerneville, 2441 NK-4
Gustine, 5324 SA-5
Hacienda Hts., 53122 ‡F-10
Half Moon Bay, 12203 NN-5
Hamilton City, 1903 NG-6
Hanford, 47485 SD-8
Happy Camp, 1200 NB-3
Hathaway Pines, 350 NL-9
Hawaiian Gardens, 15398 ‡H-9
Hawthorne, 85697 ‡G-6
Hayfork, 2315 NE-4
Hayward, 140293 NM-6
Healdsburg, 11051 NJ-4
Heber, 2988 SN-17
Hemet, 68063 SK-14
Hercules, 24109 NC-15
Herlong, 1000 NF-10
Hermosa Beach, 19500 ‡H-5
Hesperia, 77984 SI-13
Hidden Hills, 1994 ‡D-2
Hidden Valley, 1400 NJ-8
Highgrove, 3445 ‡F-18
Highland, 50892 SJ-13
Hillsborough, 10615 NI-14
Hilmar, 4807 NN-8
Hinkley, 1000 SG-13
Hollister, 35941 SB-4
Holtville, 5470 SM-18
Home Gardens, 9461 ‡H-16
Homeland, 3710 ‡I-20
Homestead Valley, 3500 NE-12
Hoopa, 1200 ND-2
Hope Ranch, 1600 †B-7
Hopland, 630 NI-3
Hughson, 5705 NM-8
HUMBOLDT CO., 128376 NE-2
Huntington Beach, 194457 SK-11
Huntington Park, 62491 ‡F-7
Huron, 7187 SD-7
Hydesville, 1209 NE-2
Idyllwild, 2200 SK-14
Ignacio NB-12
IMPERIAL CO., 155823 SM-19
Imperial, 9707 SM-17
Imperial Beach, 26374 SN-14
Independence, 574 SB-11
Indian Wells, 4933 SK-15
Indio, 70542 SK-16
Inglewood, 114467 SJ-11
Inverness, 1421 NL-4
INYO CO., 18156 SB-12
Inyokern, 984 SF-12
Ione, 7607 NK-8
Irvine, 186852 SK-12
Irwindale, 1480 ‡D-11
Isla Vista, 21069 SI-7
Isleton, 820 NL-7
Ivanhoe, 4474 SC-9
Jackson, 4303 NK-9
Jamestown, 3017 NL-9
Jamul, 5920 SN-14
Janesville, 1000 NF-9
Joshua Tree, 4207 SJ-15
Julian, 1621 SM-15
June Lake, 600 NM-12
Kelseyville, 2928 NI-4
Kensington, 4936 ND-15
Kentfield, 6351 ND-12
Kenwood, 900 NK-5
Kerman, 11223 SC-7
KERN CO., 756825 SG-9
Kernville, 1736 SE-10
Kettleman City, 1499 SE-7
Keyes, 4575 NN-8
King City, 11004 SD-4
KINGS CO., 143420 SE-7
Kings Beach, 4037 NI-10
Kingsburg, 11148 SC-8
Klamath, 651 NB-2
Knights Ldg., 1250 NJ-6
La Canada Flintridge, 20998 ‡C-7
La Crescenta, 13000 ‡C-7
Ladera, 1540 NL-16
Ladera Hts., 6568 ‡F-5
Lafayette, 24767 ND-16
Laguna Beach, 24127 SK-12
Laguna Hills, 32198 ‡L-14
Laguna Niguel, 64664 ‡M-14
Laguna Woods, 18293 ‡L-13
La Habra, 59326 SJ-12
La Habra Hts., 5970 ‡F-10
La Honda, 900 NN-5
LAKE CO., 65147 NI-4
Lake Arrowhead, 8934 ‡B-20
Lake Elsinore, 39258 SK-13
Lake Forest, 76412 SK-12
Lake Forest, 500 *B-2
Lake Hughes, 300 SH-10
Lake Isabella, 3315 SF-10
Lakeland Village, 5626 ‡K-18
Lakeport, 5241 NI-4
Lakeside, 19560 SM-14
Lakeview, 1619 SK-13
Lakewood, 80467 ‡H-8
La Mesa, 53081 †I-8
La Mirada, 49640 SJ-11
Lamont, 13296 SG-9
Lancaster, 134032 SH-11
Landers, 2300 SI-15
La Palma, 15805 ‡H-10
La Puente, 41762 ‡E-10
La Quinta, 38232 SK-15
Larkspur, 11724 NL-5
LASSEN CO., 34751 NE-9
Lathrop, 13116 NM-7
La Verne, 33185 SJ-12
Lawndale, 32193 ‡H-5
Laytonville, 1301 NG-3
Lebec, 1285 SH-9
Lee Vining, 300 NL-12
Leggett, 100 NG-2
Le Grand, 1760 SA-6
Lemon Gr., 24124 SN-14
Lemon Hts., 2800 ‡I-13
Lemoore, 22699 SD-7
Lennox, 22950 ‡G-6
Lenwood, 3222 SH-13
Lewiston, 1305 NE-4
Lincoln, 32804 NJ-7
Lincoln Acres, 1650 †K-8
Linda, 13474 NI-7
Linden, 1103 NL-8
Lindsay, 10767 SD-9
Littlerock, 1402 SI-11
Live Oak, 7128 NI-7
Livermore, 78409 NM-6
Livingston, 12585 NN-9
Lockeford, 3179 NL-8
Lodi, 62133 NL-7
Loleta, 600 NE-1
Loma Linda, 20901 SJ-13
Loma Rica, 2075 NI-7
Lomita, 20515 ‡I-6
Lompoc, 39985 SH-6
London, 1848 SC-8
Lone Pine, 1655 SC-11
Long Beach, 474014 SK-11
Loomis, 6577 NJ-8
Los Alamitos, 11657 ‡I-9
Los Alamos, 1372 SH-6
Los Altos, 27096 NN-5
Los Altos Hills, 8164 NL-17
Los Angeles, 3844829 SJ-11
LOS ANGELES CO., 9935475 SH-10
Los Banos, 33506 SB-5
Los Gatos, 28029 SA-2
Los Molinos, 1952 NG-6
Los Nietos, 8200 ‡F-9
Los Osos, 5000 SF-5
Los Ranchitos, 425 NC-12
Lost Hills, 1938 SF-7
Lower Lake, 1755 NJ-5
Loyalton, 817 NH-10
Lucerne, 2870 NI-4
Lucerne Valley, 2100 SI-14
Lynwood, 71208 ‡G-7
Lytle Creek, 530 ‡B-16
Madera, 52147 SB-7
MADERA CO., 142788 SB-6
Magalia, 10569 NG-7
Malibu, 13208 SJ-10
Mammoth Lakes, 7156 NM-13
Manhattan Beach, 36481 SJ-10
Manteca, 62651 NM-8
Maricopa, 1160 SG-8
MARIN CO., 246960 NL-5
Marina, 19006 SC-3
Marina Del Rey, 8176 ‡G-4
Marin City, 2500 NE-12
Marinwood, 2300 NB-12
MARIPOSA CO., 18069 NN-10
Mariposa, 1373 NN-10
Martinez, 35916 NL-6
Marysville, 12131 NI-7
Maxwell, 850 NI-5
Maywood, 28600 ‡F-7
McCloud, 1343 NC-6
McFarland, 11875 SE-8
McKinleyville, 13599 ND-2
Meadow Vista, 3096 NI-8
Mecca, 5402 SK-16
Meiners Oaks, 3750 SI-8
MENDOCINO CO., 88161 NH-3
Mendocino, 824 NH-2
Mendota, 8942 SB-6
Menlo Park, 29661 NN-5
Mentone, 7803 ‡E-20
MERCED CO., 241706 SB-4
Merced, 73767 NN-9
Middletown, 1020 NJ-5
Midway City, 5900 ‡J-10
Millbrae, 20342 NI-13
Mill Valley, 13286 NL-5
Milpitas, 63383 NN-6
Mira Loma, 17617 SJ-12
Mira Monte, 7177 SI-8
Mission Hills, 3142 SH-6
Mission Viejo, 94982 SK-12
Mi-Wuk Village, 1485 NL-10
Modesto, 207011 NM-8
MODOC CO., 9524 NB-8
Mojave, 3836 SG-11
MONO CO., 12509 NL-12
Monrovia, 37954 ‡D-10
Montague, 1504 NB-5
Montalvin Manor, 2000 NC-14
Montara, 2950 NJ-12
Montclair, 35474 ‡E-13
Montebello, 63290 ‡F-8
Montecito, 10000 SI-8
Monterey, 29217 SC-2
MONTEREY CO., 412104 SD-5
Monterey Park, 62065 ‡E-8
Monte Rio, 1104 NK-4
Monte Sereno, 3462 NN-18
Montgomery Creek, 96 ND-6
Montrose, 4100 ‡C-7
Moorpark, 35844 SI-9
Morada, 3726 *G-10
Moraga, 16869 NE-17
Moreno Valley, 178367 SJ-13
Morgan Hill, 34852 SA-3
Morongo Valley, 1929 SJ-15
Morro Bay, 10208 SF-5
Moss Beach, 1953 NJ-12
Mtn. Pass SF-17
Mtn. View, 69276 NL-17
Mt. Shasta, 3623 NC-5
Mount View, 1500 NC-17
Murphys, 2061 NL-9
Murrieta, 82778 SK-13
Muscoy, 8919 ‡D-18
NAPA CO., 132764 NK-5
Napa, 74782 NK-5
National City, 61419 SN-14
Needles, 5348 SH-19
NEVADA CO., 98394 NH-9
Nevada City, 3032 NI-8
Newark, 41956 NM-6
Newberry Sprs., 1500 SH-14
Newcastle, 2200 NJ-8
Newman, 9623 NN-8
Newport Beach, 79834 SK-12
Nice, 2509 NI-4
Niland, 1143 SL-17
Nipomo, 12626 SG-6
Norco, 26960 SJ-12
N. Edwards, 1227 SG-12
N. Fair Oaks, 15440 NK-16
N. Fork, 500 SA-8
N. Highlands, 44187 NJ-7
N. Richmond, 2200 ND-14
Norwalk, 105834 SJ-11
Novato, 50335 NL-5
Noyo NH-2
Nuevo, 4135 ‡I-20
Nyland Acres, 2200 †B-3
Oakdale, 18561 NM-8
Oakhurst, 2868 NN-11
Oakland, 395274 NM-5
Oakley, 27177 NL-6
Oak View, 4199 SI-8
Oceano, 7260 SG-5
Oceanside, 166108 SL-13
Oildale, 27885 SF-9
Ojai, 7945 SI-8
Olivehurst, 11061 NI-7
Olympic Valley, 800 *B-1
Ontario, 172679 SJ-12
Orange, 134950 SK-12
ORANGE CO., 2988072 SK-12
Orange Cove, 9578 SC-8
Orange Park Acres, 1000 ‡I-13
Orangevale, 26705 NJ-8
Orcutt, 28830 SH-6
Orinda, 18259 NM-5
Orland, 6757 NG-6
Orleans, 375 NC-3
Oro Grande, 310 SH-13
Orosi, 7318 SC-8
Oroville, 13468 NH-7
Oxnard, 183628 SJ-9
Pacheco, 3562 NC-17
Pacifica, 37092 NM-5
Pacific Gr., 15091 SC-2
Pajaro, 3420 SB-3
Palermo, 5720 NH-7
Palmdale, 134570 SI-11
Palm Desert, 47058 SK-15
Palm Sprs., 47082 SK-15
Palo Alto, 56982 NN-5
Palo Cedro, 1247 NE-6
Palomar Park, 530 NK-15
Palos Verdes Estates, 13812 SK-10
Paradise, 26517 NG-7
Paramount, 56540 ‡H-8
Parkway, 14280 *E-6
Parlier, 13025 SC-8
Pasadena, 143731 SJ-11
Paso Robles, 27477 SF-5
Patterson, 15500 NN-8
Pearblossom, 700 SI-12
Pebble Beach, 2200 SC-2
Pedley, 11207 ‡F-16
Penn Valley, 1387 NI-8
Perris, 45671 SK-13
Petaluma, 54846 NK-4
Philo, 250 NI-3
Pico Rivera, 64679 ‡F-9
Piedmont, 10559 NF-15
Pine Gr., 1000 NK-9
Pine Valley, 1501 SM-15
Pinole, 19061 NC-14
Pioneer, 700 NK-9
Pioneer Pt., 1000 SE-13
Piru, 1196 SI-9
Pismo Beach, 8419 SG-5
Pittsburg, 62547 NL-6
Pixley, 2586 SE-8
Placentia, 49795 ‡H-12
PLACER CO., 317028 NI-9
Placerville, 10184 NJ-8
Planada, 4369 NN-9
Pleasant Hill, 33153 NL-6
Pleasanton, 65950 NM-6
PLUMAS CO., 21477 NG-10
Plymouth, 1072 NK-8
Point Reyes Station, 818 NL-4
Pollock Pines, 4728 NJ-9
Pomona, 153787 SJ-12
Poplar, 1496 SD-9
Porterville, 44959 SD-9
Port Hueneme, 22032 SJ-9
Portola, 2242 NG-9
Portola Valley, 4417 NL-16
Potter Valley, 1025 NH-4
Poway, 48476 SM-14
Prunedale, 16514 SB-3
Pumpkin Cen., 520 SG-9
Quail Valley, 1639 ‡J-19
Quartz Hill, 9890 SH-11
Quincy, 1879 NG-8
Ramona, 15691 SM-14
Rancho Cordova, 55060 NJ-7
Rancho Cucamonga, 169353 ‡D-15
Rancho Mirage, 16514 SK-15
Rancho Palos Verdes, 41949 ‡J-5
Rancho Rinconada NM-18
Rancho Santa Fe, 3252 SM-13
Rancho Santa Margarita, 50682 ‡K-15
Red Bluff, 14059 NF-5
Redding, 89641 NE-5
Red Hill, 2800 ‡J-12
Redlands, 69995 SJ-13
Redondo Beach, 66824 SK-10
Redway, 1188 NF-2
Redwood City, 73114 NN-5
Redwood Valley, 1900 NI-3
Reedley, 22368 SC-8
Rialto, 99513 SJ-13
Richgrove, 2723 SE-9
Richmond, 102186 ND-14
Ridgecrest, 25974 SF-12
Rio Dell, 3158 NE-1
Rio Del Mar, 9198 SB-3
Rio Linda, 10466 NJ-7
Rio Vista, 7077 NL-6
Ripon, 13658 NM-8
Riverbank, 19727 NM-8
Riverdale, 2416 SC-7
Riverside, 290086 SJ-13
RIVERSIDE CO., 1946419 SK-19
Rocklin, 49626 NJ-8
Rodeo, 8717 NB-15
Rohnert Park, 41101 NK-4
Rolling Hills, 1933 ‡I-6
Rolling Hills Estates, 8105 ‡I-6
Rollingwood, 2900 NC-14
Romoland, 2764 ‡I-20
Roosevelt Terrace NA-15
Rosamond, 14349 SH-11
Roseland, 6369 *H-7
Rosemead, 55119 ‡E-9
Rosemont, 22904 *D-8
Rosemont, 800 †E-10
Roseville, 105940 NJ-7
Ross, 2283 ND-12
Rossmoor, 10298 ‡I-9
Rough and Ready, 230 NI-8
Round Mtn., 122 ND-6
Rowland Hts., 48553 ‡F-11
Rubidoux, 29180 ‡F-17
Running Springs, 5125 SJ-13
Rutherford, 500 NK-5
SACRAMENTO CO., 1363482 NK-8
Sacramento, 456441 NK-7
St. Helena, 5938 NK-5
Salida, 12560 NM-8
Salinas, 146431 SC-3
Salton City, 978 SL-16
Salyer, 500 ND-3
San Andreas, 2615 NL-9
San Anselmo, 12018 NL-5
San Antonio Hts., 3122 ‡D-14
SAN BENITO CO., 55936 SC-5
SAN BERNARDINO CO., 1963535 SH-18
San Bernardino, 198550 SJ-13
San Bruno, 39752 NM-5
San Carlos, 26821 NM-5
San Clemente, 60235 SL-12
SAN DIEGO CO., 2933462 SL-15
San Diego, 1255540 SN-13
San Dimas, 35850 ‡D-12
San Fernando, 24207 SI-10
San Francisco, 739426 NM-5
SAN FRANCISCO CO., 739426 NM-5
San Gabriel, 41056 ‡E-9
Sanger, 22041 SC-8
San Jacinto, 30253 SK-14
San Joaquin, 3579 SC-6
SAN JOAQUIN CO., 664116 NL-7
San Jose, 912332 NN-6
San Juan Bautista, 1652 SB-3
San Juan Capistrano, 34673 SL-12
San Leandro, 78178 NM-5
San Lorenzo, 21898 NM-5
SAN LUIS OBISPO CO., 255478 SF-6
San Luis Obispo, 43509 SG-5
San Marcos, 73487 SL-13
San Marino, 13165 ‡D-9
San Martin, 4230 SA-3
San Mateo, 91081 NI-14
SAN MATEO CO., 699610 SA-2
San Miguel, 1427 SE-5
San Pablo, 31004 NL-5
San Rafael, 55716 NL-5
San Ramon, 49999 NM-6
Santa Ana, 340368 SK-12
SANTA BARBARA CO., 400762 SH-7
Santa Barbara, 85899 SI-7
SANTA CLARA CO., 1699052 NN-7
Santa Clara, 105402 NL-18
Santa Clarita, 168253 SI-10
SANTA CRUZ CO., 249666 SA-2
Santa Cruz, 54760 SB-2
Santa Fe Sprs., 17058 ‡G-9
Santa Margarita, 1200 SF-5
Santa Maria, 84346 SG-6
Santa Monica, 87800 SJ-10
Santa Paula, 28478 SI-9
Santa Rosa, 153158 NK-4
Santa Venetia, 4298 NL-5
Santa Ynez, 4584 SH-7
Santee, 52306 SM-14
Saratoga, 29663 SA-2
Sausalito, 7184 NE-12
Scotia, 850 NE-2
Scotts Valley, 11154 SB-2
Seal Beach, 24295 ‡J-9
Seaside, 34214 SC-3
Sebastopol, 7598 NK-4
Sedco Hills, 3078 ‡K-19
Seeley, 1624 SM-17
Selma, 22261 SC-8
Shafter, 14569 SF-8
SHASTA CO., 179904 NE-7
Shasta, 950 NE-5
Shasta Lake, 10233 NE-5
Sheridan, 1100 NI-7
Sherwood Forest, 2600 ND-15
Shingle Springs, 2643 NJ-8
Shore Acres, 4000 NB-18
SIERRA CO., 3434 NH-9
Sierra City, 250 NH-9
Sierra Madre, 10988 ‡D-9
Signal Hill, 10851 ‡I-8
Silverado, 800 ‡J-14
Simi Valley, 118687 SI-9
SISKIYOU CO., 45259 NB-6
Skyforest, 750 ‡B-20
Sleepy Hollow, 2400 NC-11
Smith River, 950 NA-2
Solana Beach, 12716 SM-13
SOLANO CO., 411593 NK-6
Soledad, 27210 SC-4
Solvang, 5141 SH-6
Somis, 1000 SI-9
SONOMA CO., 466477 NJ-4
Sonoma, 9885 NK-5
Sonora, 4668 NL-9
Soquel, 5081 SB-2
Soulsbyville, 1729 NL-10
S. Dos Palos, 1385 SB-5
S. El Monte, 21666 ‡E-9
S. Gate, 98897 ‡G-7
S. Lake Tahoe, 24016 NJ-10
S. Pasadena, 24889 ‡D-8
S. San Francisco, 60735 NM-5
S. San Gabriel, 7595 ‡E-9
S. San Jose Hills, 20218 ‡F-11
S. Taft, 1898 SG-8
Spr. Valley, 26663 SN-14
Springville, 1109 SD-9
Squaw Valley, 2691 SB-8
Stanford, 13315 NK-16
STANISLAUS CO., 505505 SA-4
Stanton, 37661 ‡I-10
Stinson Beach, 751 NL-4
Stockton, 286926 NL-7
Stratford, 1264 SD-7
Strathmore, 2584 SD-9
Strawberry, 5302 ND-12
Suisun City, 26762 NL-6
Sultana, 750 SC-8
Summerland, 1545 SI-8
Summit City NE-5
Sun City, 17773 SK-13
Sunnyside, 1000 †K-8
Sunnyslope, 4437 ‡F-17
Sunnyvale, 128902 NL-18
Sunol, 1332 NI-19
Sunset Beach, 1000 ‡J-9
Susanville, 18101 NF-9
Sutter, 2885 NI-6
SUTTER CO., 88876 NI-7
Sutter Cr., 2748 NK-8
Taft, 9106 SG-8
Taft Hts., 1865 SG-8
Tahoe City, 700 NI-10
Tahoe Vista, 1668 NI-10
Talmage, 1141 NI-3
Tamalpais Valley, 7000 NE-12
Tara Hills, 5332 NC-14
Tehachapi, 11752 SG-10
TEHAMA CO., 61197 NF-5
Temecula, 85799 SL-13
Temple City, 37363 ‡E-9
Templeton, 4687 SF-5
Terra Bella, 3466 SE-9
Thermal, 1400 SK-16
Thermalito, 6045 NH-7
Thornton, 1100 NL-7
Thousand Oaks, 124359 SJ-9
Thousand Palms, 5120 SK-15
Three Rivers, 2248 SC-9
Tiburon, 8671 NL-5
Tipton, 1790 SD-8
Topanga, 700 SJ-10
Torrance, 142384 ‡H-5
Tracy, 79964 NM-7
Tranquillity, 813 SC-6
TRINITY CO., 13622 NF-3
Trinity Center, 320 ND-5
Trona, 500 SE-13
Truckee, 15737 NI-10
TULARE CO., 410874 SC-9
Tulare, 50127 SD-8
Tulelake, 1010 NA-7
TUOLUMNE CO., 59380 NL-11
Tuolumne, 1865 NL-10
Turlock, 67669 NN-8
Tustin, 69096 ‡J-12
Twain Harte, 2586 NL-10
Twentynine Palms, 28409 SJ-16
Twin Peaks, 2100 ‡B-19
Ukiah, 15463 NI-3
Union City, 69176 NI-18
Upland, 73589 SJ-12
Upper Lake, 989 NI-4
Vacaville, 92985 NK-6
Valinda, 21776 ‡E-10
Vallecito, 427 NL-9
Vallejo, 117483 NL-5
Valle Vista, 10488 SK-14
Valley Center, 7323 SL-14
Venice ‡F-4
VENTURA CO., 796106 SH-9
Ventura, 104017 SI-8
Victorville, 91264 SI-13
View Park, 5500 ‡F-6
Villa Park, 6026 ‡I-12
Vine Hill, 3260 NL-6
Visalia, 108669 SD-8
Vista, 90402 SL-13
Walnut, 31424 ‡E-11
Walnut Cr., 64196 NL-6
Walnut Gr., 669 NL-7
Walnut Park, 16180 ‡F-7
Wasco, 23874 SF-8
Waterford, 8161 NM-9
Watsonville, 47927 SB-3
Weaverville, 3554 NE-4
Weed, 3114 NC-5
Weedpatch, 2726 SG-9
Weimar, 850 NI-8
W. Covina, 108185 ‡E-11
Westhaven, 370 ND-2
W. Hollywood, 36732 ‡E-5
Westlake Vil., 8585 ‡D-1
Westley, 747 NM-8
Westminster, 89523 ‡J-10
Westmont, 31623 ‡G-6
Westmorland, 2266 SM-17
W. Point, 746 NK-9
W. Sacramento, 41744 NK-7
Westwood, 1998 NF-8
Wheatland, 3638 NI-7
Whittier, 84473 SJ-11
Wildomar, 14064 ‡L-19
Williams, 4755 NI-6
Willits, 5066 NH-3
Willowbrook, 34138 ‡G-7
Willow Cr., 1743 ND-3
Willows, 6296 NH-6
Winchester, 2155 SK-14
Windsor, 24968 NK-4
Windsor Hills, 5000 ‡F-5
Winterhaven, 529 SM-19
Winters, 6764 NK-6
Winton, 8832 NN-9
Wofford Hts., 2276 SE-10
Woodacre, 1393 NL-4
Woodcrest, 8342 ‡H-18
Woodlake, 7215 SC-9
Woodland, 51020 NJ-6
Woodside, 5463 NK-15
Woodville, 1678 SD-9
Wrightwood, 3837 SI-12
Yermo, 1000 SH-14
YOLO CO., 184932 NJ-6
Yolo, 450 NJ-6
Yorba Linda, 64476 ‡G-13
Yountville, 3307 NK-5
Yreka, 7295 NB-5
YUBA CO., 67153 NI-7
Yuba City, 58628 NI-7
Yucaipa, 49100 SJ-14
Yucca Valley, 19696 SJ-15

Colorado

Map pp. 40-45

* City keyed to pp. 44-45

ADAMS CO., 399426 E-15
Aguilar, 578 M-14
Akron, 1575 D-18
Alamosa, 8682 L-11
ALAMOSA CO., 15282 L-12
Alamosa E., 1528 L-11
Allenspark, 496 D-12
Almont, 70 I-9
Antonito, 850 M-11
ARAPAHOE CO., 529090 F-14
ARCHULETA CO., 11886 M-18
Arriba, 226 G-18
Arvada, 103966 E-13
Aspen, 5804 G-9
Ault, 1425 C-14
Aurora, 297235 E-14
Avon, 6349 F-10
Avondale, 754 J-15
BACA CO., 4069 M-19
Basalt, 3007 F-9
Bayfield, 1639 M-7
Bellvue, 400 C-13
Bennett, 2536 E-15
BENT CO., 5558 K-18
Berthoud, 5055 D-13
Beulah, 280 J-13
Black Forest, 13247 H-14
Black Hawk, 107 E-12
Blanca, 372 L-12
Blende, 1500 J-14
Boone, 333 J-15
Boulder, 91685 D-13
BOULDER CO., 280440 D-13
Bow Mar, 808 *K-6
Breckenridge, 2680 F-11
Brighton, 28013 E-14
Bristol, 130 J-20
BROOMFIELD CO., 43478 E-13
Broomfield, 43478 E-13
Brush, 5186 D-17
Buena Vista, 2174 H-11
Burlington, 3493 G-20
Byers, 1233 E-15
Calhan, 876 H-15
Campion, 1832 D-13
Cañon City, 16000 I-13
Carbondale, 5825 F-8
Cascade, 500 H-13
Castle Rock, 35745 G-14
Cedaredge, 2148 H-6
Centennial, 98243 F-14
Center, 2497 L-11
Central City, 491 E-12
CHAFFEE CO., 16968 H-11
Chama, 245 M-13
Cheraw, 212 J-17
Cherry Hills Vil., 6138 *J-7
CHEYENNE CO., 1953 H-19
Cheyenne Wells, 873 H-20
Clark B-9
CLEAR CREEK CO., 9197 F-12
Clifton, 17345 G-5
Collbran, 408 G-6
Colorado Sprs., 369815 H-14
Columbine Valley, 1220 *K-6
Commerce City, 34189 *H-8
CONEJOS CO., 8512 M-10
Conifer, 200 F-13
Cortez, 8244 M-5
COSTILLA CO., 3424 M-13
Craig, 9143 C-7
Crawford, 386 I-7
Creede, 412 K-9
Crested Butte, 1546 H-9
Cripple Cr., 1065 H-13
Crowley, 180 J-16
CROWLEY CO., 5401 J-16
CUSTER CO., 3860 K-13
Dacono, 3529 D-14
De Beque, 472 F-6
Deer Trail, 577 F-16
Del Norte, 1569 L-10
DELTA CO., 29947 H-7
Delta, 8135 H-6
DENVER CO., 557917 E-14
Denver, 557917 E-13
Dillon, 774 F-11
Dinosaur, 340 D-4
Divide, 50 H-13
DOLORES CO., 1827 K-5
Dolores, 863 L-5
DOUGLAS CO., 249416 G-13
Dove Cr., 683 K-4
Dupont, 3650 *G-8
Durango, 15501 M-6
Eads, 651 I-19
Eagle, 4276 F-9
EAGLE CO., 47530 E-9
Eastlake *F-7
Eaton, 3932 C-14
Eckley, 273 D-19
Edgewater, 5211 *I-6
ELBERT CO., 22788 F-15
Eldorado Sprs., 557 E-13
Elizabeth, 1513 G-14
El Jebel, 4488 F-8
EL PASO CO., 565582 I-15
Empire, 339 E-12
Englewood, 32350 F-13
Erie, 12351 D-13
Estes Park, 5812 C-12
Evans, 17470 C-14
Evergreen, 9216 F-13
Fairplay, 677 G-11
Federal Hts., 11706 *G-6
Flagler, 590 G-18
Fleming, 444 B-18
Florence, 3685 J-13
Ft. Collins, 128026 C-13
Ft. Garland, 432 M-12
Ft. Lupton, 7121 D-14
Ft. Morgan, 10844 D-16
Fountain, 19081 I-14
Fowler, 1138 J-16
Foxfield, 892 F-14
Fraser, 899 E-11
Frederick, 6620 D-14
FREMONT CO., 47766 I-12
Frisco, 2418 F-11
Fruita, 6878 G-4
Fruitvale, 6936 G-5
Garden City, 342 G-2
GARFIELD CO., 49810 F-6
Gateway H-4
Genoa, 195 G-17
Georgetown, 1068 E-12
Gilcrest, 1149 D-14
GILPIN CO., 4932 E-12
Glendale, 4771 *I-7
Glenwood Sprs., 8564 F-8
Golden, 17366 E-13
Granada, 611 J-20
Granby, 1685 D-11
GRAND CO., 13211 D-10
Grand Jct., 45299 G-5
Grand Lake, 438 D-11
Greeley, 87596 C-14
Green Mtn. Falls, 784 H-13
Greenwood Vil., 12817 *K-7
GUNNISON CO., 14226 H-9
Gunnison, 5298 I-9
Gypsum, 4964 F-9
Haxtun, 995 C-19
Hayden, 1539 C-8
Henderson, 600 *F-8
Highlands Ranch, 70931 *L-7
HINSDALE CO., 765 K-8
Hoehne, 85 M-15
Holly, 997 J-20
Holyoke, 2289 C-20
Hotchkiss, 1043 H-7
Hot Sulphur Sprs., 512 D-11
Hudson, 1587 D-14
HUERFANO CO., 7771 L-13
Hugo, 799 G-17
Hygiene, 400 D-13
Idaho Sprs., 1807 E-12
Ignacio, 679 M-7
Indian Hills, 1197 F-13
Irondale, 440 *G-8
JACKSON CO., 1448 C-10
Jamestown, 233 D-12
Jansen, 210 M-15
JEFFERSON CO., 526801 F-13
Johnson Vil., 270 H-11
Johnstown, 7250 D-14
Julesburg, 1335 A-20
Keenesburg, 1141 D-15
Kersey, 1401 C-14
KIOWA CO., 1422 I-18
Kiowa, 596 G-15
Kit Carson, 225 H-19
KIT CARSON CO., 7642 F-19
Kremmling, 1554 D-10
Lafayette, 23884 E-13
La Jara, 831 M-11
La Junta, 7260 K-17
LAKE CO., 7738 G-10
Lake City, 359 K-8
Lake George, 120 H-13
Lakewood, 140671 *I-5
Lamar, 8414 J-19
LA PLATA CO., 47452 M-7
Laporte, 2691 C-13
LARIMER CO., 271927 C-12
La Salle, 1895 D-14
LAS ANIMAS CO., 15446 L-16
Las Animas, 2543 K-18
La Veta, 887 L-13
Lawson, 320 E-12
Leadville, 2688 G-10
Limon, 1879 G-17
LINCOLN CO., 5618 H-17
Lincoln Park, 3904 I-13
Littleton, 40396 F-13
Lochbuie, 3588 E-14
LOGAN CO., 20719 B-17
Log Lane Vil., 1020 D-16
Loma, 400 G-4
Lombard Vil., 600 J-15
Longmont, 81818 D-13
Louisville, 18358 E-13
Louviers, 237 F-13
Loveland, 59563 C-13
Lucerne, 160 C-14
Lyons, 1624 D-13
Manassa, 1024 M-11
Mancos, 1183 M-5
Manitou Sprs., 5039 H-14
Manzanola, 496 J-16
Masonville, 140 C-13
Meeker, 2222 D-6
Meeker Park, 120 D-12
Merino, 279 C-17
MESA CO., 129872 H-5
Milliken, 5593 D-14
MINERAL CO., 932 L-9
Minturn, 1097 F-10
MOFFAT CO., 13417 B-7
Monte Vista, 4212 L-11
MONTEZUMA CO., 24778 L-5
MONTROSE CO., 37482 J-5
Montrose, 15479 I-7
Monument, 2508 G-14
MORGAN CO., 27995 D-16
Morrison, 410 F-13
Mtn. View, 529 *H-6
Naturita, 665 J-5
Nederland, 1337 E-12
New Castle, 3017 F-7
Niwot, 4160 D-13
Northglenn, 32906 *F-7
Norwood, 460 J-5
Nucla, 739 J-5
Nunn, 521 B-14
Oak Cr., 797 D-9
Olathe, 1679 I-6
Olney Sprs., 377 J-16
Orchard City, 3053 H-6
Orchard Mesa, 6456 G-5
Ordway, 1178 J-16
OTERO CO., 19495 K-16
Otis, 512 D-18
OURAY CO., 4260 J-7
Ouray, 877 K-7
Ovid, 316 B-19
Pagosa Sprs., 1628 M-8
Palisade, 2683 G-5
Palmer Lake, 2271 G-14
Paonia, 1584 H-7
Parachute, 1094 F-6
PARK CO., 16949 G-12
Parker, 38428 F-14
Penrose, 4070 I-13
PHILLIPS CO., 4586 C-20
Pierce, 872 C-14
Pine, 150 F-13
PITKIN CO., 14914 G-9
Platteville, 2598 D-14
Poncha Sprs., 465 I-11
PROWERS CO., 13892 K-20
PUEBLO CO., 151322 K-15
Pueblo, 103495 J-14
Pueblo W., 16899 J-14
Rangely, 2038 D-4
Red Cliff, 306 F-10
Ridgway, 752 J-7
Rifle, 8038 F-7
RIO BLANCO CO., 5973 E-5
RIO GRANDE CO., 12227 L-10
Rockvale, 438 J-13
Rocky Ford, 4121 K-17
Rollinsville, 150 E-12
Romeo, 371 M-11
ROUTT CO., 21313 C-9
Roxborough Park, 4446 *M-6
Saguache, 606 J-11
SAGUACHE CO., 7031 J-10
Salida, 5476 I-11
Sanford, 802 M-11
SAN JUAN CO., 577 L-7
San Luis, 697 M-12
SAN MIGUEL CO., 7213 J-5
Security, 4400 H-14
Sedalia, 211 F-14
SEDGWICK CO., 2529 B-20
Sheridan, 5483 *J-6
Sherrelwood, 17657 *G-7
Silt, 2260 F-7
Silver Cliff, 575 J-12
Silverthorne, 3610 F-11
Silverton, 548 K-7
Simla, 728 G-16
Snowmass Village, 1767 G-9
South Fork, 575 L-9
Springfield, 1363 L-19
Steamboat Sprs., 9354 C-9
Sterling, 12589 C-18
Strasburg, 1402 E-15
Stratmoor Hills, 2350 *I-2
Stratton, 626 G-19
Sugar City, 265 J-17
SUMMIT CO., 24892 F-11
Superior, 10308 E-13
Swink, 683 K-17
Tabernash, 165 E-11
TELLER CO., 21918 G-13
Telluride, 2303 K-7
Thornton, 105182 *G-7
Timnath, 214 C-13
Towaoc, 1097 M-4
Trinidad, 9077 M-15
Uravan I-4
Vail, 4589 F-10
Victor, 419 I-13
Walden, 646 B-10
Walsenburg, 3946 L-14
Walsh, 682 M-20
WASHINGTON CO., 4633 D-18
Watkins, 300 E-14
Wattenberg, 330 E-14
WELD CO., 228943 B-15
Wellington, 3469 B-13
Westcliffe, 456 J-12
Western Hills, 2600 *G-6
Westminster, 105084 E-13
Wheat Ridge, 31242 *H-5
Widefield, 4200 H-14
Wiggins, 951 D-16
Wiley, 476 J-19
Windsor, 14874 C-14
Winter Park, 705 E-12
Woodland Park, 6660 H-13
Woody Cr., 260 G-9
Wray, 2147 D-20
Yampa, 416 D-9
Yuma, 3231 D-19
YUMA CO., 9789 E-20

Connecticut

Map pp. 46-49

Addison, 800 E-11
Ansonia, 18744 I-7
Avon, 1800 D-9
Baltic, 2000 F-15
Beacon Falls, 1650 H-7
Berlin, 1230 F-9
Bethany, 1280 H-7
Bethel, 9137 I-4
Bethlehem, 2022 F-6
Bloomfield, 7500 D-9
Blue Hills, 3020 D-10
Branford, 5735 J-9
Bridgeport, 139008 K-6
Bristol, 61353 E-8
Broad Brook, 3469 C-11
Brookfield, 1650 G-4
Brookfield Cen., 1550 H-4
Brooklyn, 1650 D-16
Canaan, 1288 B-5
Candlewood Shores, 1800 H-4
Cannondale, 1500 J-4
Canton, 1565 D-8
Centerbrook, 1000 I-12
Central Vil., 1800 E-16
Cheshire, 5789 G-8
Chester, 1546 H-12
Clinton, 3516 J-11
Colchester, 4500 F-13
Collinsville, 2686 D-8
Coventry, 2914 D-13
Cromwell, 2500 F-10
Danbury, 78736 H-4
Danielson, 4285 D-16
Darien, 19607 L-3
Dayville, 1650 D-16
Deep River, 2470 H-12
Derby, 12536 I-7
Durham, 2773 H-10
E. Berlin, 1100 F-10
E. Brooklyn, 1473 D-16
E. Canaan, 1000 B-5
E. Granby, 1300 C-10
E. Hampton, 2254 F-11
E. Hartford, 49575 D-10
E. Haven, 28189 J-8
E. Lyme, 1330 I-14
E. River, 3800 J-10
E. Villlage, 100 I-6
E. Windsor, 2100 C-10
Ellington, 1700 C-12
Enfield, 45441 B-11
Essex, 2573 I-12
Fairfield, 57300 K-5
FAIRFIELD CO., 902775 I-4
Farmington, 3100 E-9
Gales Ferry, 1200 H-15
Georgetown, 1650 J-4
Giants Neck, 1330 I-14
Glastonbury, 7157 E-10
Granby, 2453 B-9
Greenwich, 61100 L-2
Groton, 9493 I-15
Groton Long Pt., 680 I-15
Guilford, 2603 J-10
Haddam, 1300 G-11
Hamden, 56900 H-8
HARTFORD CO., 877393 C-9
Hartford, 124397 D-10
Harwinton, 3242 D-7
Hazardville, 4900 B-11
Higganum, 1671 G-11
Honeypot Glen, 1200 G-8
Indian Neck, 2500 J-9
Ivoryton, 2600 I-12
Jewett City, 3001 F-16
Kensington, 8541 F-9
Lakeside, 1340 H-5
Lakeville, 1900 B-4
Litchfield, 1340 E-6
LITCHFIELD CO., 190071 C-5
Madison, 2222 J-11
Manchester, 54700 D-11
Mansfield Cen., 973 D-14
Marion, 850 G-8
Marlborough, 1048 F-12
Meriden, 59653 G-9
Middlebury, 4200 G-6
MIDDLESEX CO., 163214 F-11
Middletown, 47438 G-10
Milford, 53045 J-7
Milldale, 900 G-8
Mixville, 1400 G-8
Montville, 610 H-14
Moodus, 1263 G-12
Moosup, 3237 E-16
Mystic, 4001 I-16
Naugatuck, 31864 G-7
New Britain, 71254 F-9
New Canaan, 17864 K-3
New Fairfield, 5200 H-3
New Hartford, 1049 C-7
New Haven, 124791 I-8
NEW HAVEN CO., 846766 H-7
Newington, 29306 E-10
NEW LONDON CO., 266618 G-16
New London, 26174 I-15
New Milford, 6633 F-4
New Preston, 1120 E-4
Newtown, 1835 H-5
Niantic, 3085 I-14
Noank, 1830 I-16
Norfolk, 1430 B-6
N. Branford, 7400 I-9
Northford, 3600 H-9
N. Grosvenor Dale, 1424 B-16
N. Haven, 23035 H-8
Norwalk, 84437 K-4
Norwich, 36598 G-15
Oakdale, 910 H-14
Oakville, 8618 F-7
Old Saybrook, 1962 J-12
Orange, 13233 J-7
Oxford, 2100 H-6
Pawcatuck, 5474 I-17
Pine Bridge, 1000 H-7
Pine Orchard, 950 J-9
Plainfield, 2638 E-16
Plainville, 17392 E-9
Plantsville, 6000 F-8
Pleasure Beach, 1450 I-14
Plymouth, 1200 E-7
Poquonock, 1100 C-10
Poquonock Bridge, 1592 I-15
Portland, 5534 G-10
Prospect, 7775 G-7
Putnam, 6746 C-16
Quaker Hill, 1700 H-15
Quinebaug, 1122 B-16
Ridgefield, 7212 J-3
Rocky Hill, 16554 F-10
Salisbury, 1700 B-4
Sandy Hook, 1200 H-5
Seymour, 14288 H-7
Sharon, 1200 C-4
Shelton, 39477 I-6
Short Beach, 200 J-9
Simsbury, 5603 C-9
Somers, 1626 B-12
Somersville, 1300 B-11
Southbury, 3400 H-6
S. Glastonbury, 2000 E-11
Southington, 42077 F-8
S. Windham, 1278 E-14
S. Windsor, 14000 D-11
S. Woodstock, 1211 C-16
Stafford Sprs., 4900 B-13
Stamford, 120045 L-3
Stonington, 1054 I-16
Storrs, 11106 D-13
Stratford, 49976 K-6
Suffield, 1244 B-10
Tariffville, 1371 C-9
Terryville, 5360 E-7
Thomaston, 4000 E-7
Tolland, 1350 C-12
TOLLAND CO., 147634 D-12
Torrington, 35995 D-6
Trumbull, 34243 J-6
Uncasville, 1420 H-15
Unionville, 4400 E-8
Upper Stepney, 1000 I-5
Vernon, 28100 D-11
Wallingford, 17509 H-9
Waterbury, 107902 G-7
Waterford, 2935 I-14
Watertown, 6300 F-6
Wauregan, 1085 E-16
Weatogue, 2805 D-9
Wequetequock, 850 I-16
Westbrook, 2238 J-12
W. Hartford, 61046 E-9
W. Haven, 52923 J-8
W. Mystic, 3595 I-16
Weston, 1460 J-4
Westport, 25749 K-4
W. Simsbury, 2395 C-8
Wethersfield, 26271 E-10
Willimantic, 15823 E-14
Wilton, 7500 K-4
WINDHAM CO., 115826 D-15
Windsor, 18800 D-10
Windsor Locks, 12043 C-10
Winsted, 7321 C-7
Wolcott, 6400 F-8
Woodbridge, 7860 I-7
Woodbury, 1298 G-6
Woodmont, 1757 J-7

Delaware

Map pp. 50-51

Bear, 17593 D-2
Bellefonte, 1288 C-9
Bellevue Manor, 200 C-9
Belvedere, 800 D-8
Birchwood Park, 400 D-7
Blades, 999 K-2
Brandywood, 800 B-9
Bridgeville, 1578 J-2
Brookside, 14806 E-6
Camden, 2281 H-2
Carrcroft, 500 C-9
Carrcroft Crest, 900 B-9
Castle Hills, 2000 D-8
Chalfonte, 1400 B-9
Claymont, 9220 C-3
Clayton, 1400 F-2
Cleland Hts., 900 D-8
Collins Park, 1500 D-8
Coventry, 1500 E-7
Darley Woods, 1300 B-9
Delaware City, 1510 D-2
Delmar, 1483 M-2
Del Park Manor, 1100 D-7
Devonshire, 2200 B-9
Dover, 34288 G-3
Dunleith, 2400 D-8
Dupont Manor, 300 G-3
Du Ross Hts., 900 D-8
Edgemoor, 5992 C-9
Elsmere, 5722 C-2
Fairfax, 1600 C-9
Faulkland, 1300 C-7
Felton, 838 H-2
Forest Brook Glen, 400 D-8
Forest Hills Park, 650 C-9
Fox Hall F-7
Frankford, 754 L-4
Frederica, 697 H-3
Garfield Park, 400 D-8
Georgetown, 4911 K-3
Graylyn Crest, 450 B-9
Green Acres, 1100 B-9
Greenville, 2332 C-2
Greenville Place, 1000 C-8
Greenwood, 883 J-2
Gwinhurst, 400 B-10
Harmony Hills, 800 D-7
Harrington, 3236 I-2
Hockessin, 12902 C-2
Holloway Ter., 1200 D-9
Ivy Ridge, 1800 E-7
Jefferson Farms, 2000 D-8
KENT CO., 143968 H-3
Lancaster Vil., 1100 C-8
Laurel, 3822 L-2
Lewes, 3116 J-5
Llangollen Estates, 1400 E-8
Marshallton, 1800 D-7
Meadowood, 600 D-7
Middletown, 9121 E-2
Milford, 7201 I-3
Millsboro, 2505 L-4
Milton, 1791 J-4
Minquadale, 650 D-8
Naamans Gardens, 600 B-10
Newark, 30060 C-1
New Castle, 4836 D-2
NEW CASTLE CO., 523008 F-2
Newport, 1106 C-2
North Star, 8277 C-1
Oak Lane Manor, 950 B-9
Penn Acres, 2000 D-8
Penny Hill, 600 C-9
Rambleton Acres, 1500 E-8
Rehoboth Beach, 1556 K-5
Richardson Park, 500 D-8
Rising Sun, 250 H-3
Rodney Vil., 1606 H-3
Seaford, 6997 K-2
Selbyville, 1742 M-4
Sharpley, 1400 B-8
Sherwood Park, 2000 C-7
Silview, 1500 D-8
Smyrna, 7413 F-2
Stanton, 2000 D-7
Stratford, 1100 E-7
SUSSEX CO., 176548 K-3
Swanwyck Estates, 800 D-8
Talleyville, 800 B-3
Tuxedo Park, 1300 D-7
Westover Hills, 1200 C-8
Willow Run, 500 C-8
Wilmington, 72786 C-3
Wilmington Manor, 8262 D-8
Wilmington Manor Gardens, 1800 E-8
Wyoming, 1242 H-2
Yorklyn, 300 C-2

District of Columbia

Map pp. 224-225

Washington, 550521 E-6

Florida

Map pp. 52-57

* City keyed to pp. 56-57
† City keyed to p. 51

Alachua, 7557 D-7
ALACHUA CO., 223852 D-8
Altamonte Sprs., 41057 H-10
Andover Lake Estates, 1500 *J-8
Anna Maria, 1867 K-6
Anthony, 1150 F-8
Apalachicola, 2340 T-8
Apollo Beach, 7444 K-7
Apopka, 34728 H-10
Arcadia, 7151 L-9
Archer, 1288 E-7
Atlantic Beach, 13436 C-10
Auburndale, 12381 J-9
Aventura, 29391 *J-9
Avon Park, 8872 K-10
Azalea Park, 11073 N-4
Babson Park, 1182 J-10
Bagdad, 1490 R-3
BAKER CO., 24569 C-7
Baldwin, 1589 C-8
Bal Harbour, 3272 *K-9
Bartow, 16278 J-9
BAY CO., 161558 S-6
Bay Hbr. Islands, 5093 *K-9
Bay Hill, 5177 O-2
Bayonet Pt., 23577 I-6
Bay Pines, 3065 *D-1
Bay Ridge, 155 L-2
Baywood Village *A-1
Bee Ridge, 8744 L-7
Belleair, 4170 *C-1
Belleair Beach, 1628 *C-1
Belleair Bluffs, 2224 *C-1
Belle Glade, 15423 N-12
Belle Isle, 6431 O-4
Belleview, 3856 G-8
Bellview, 21201 †L-8
Belvedere Homes, 4000 *B-10
Beverly Hills, 8317 G-7
Big Coppitt Key, 2595 T-9
Big Pine Key, 5032 T-10
Biscayne Gardens, 1150 *K-8
Biscayne Park, 3128 *K-9
Bithlo, 4626 H-11
Blountstown, 2433 S-7
Boca Pointe, 3302 *F-9
Boca Raton, 86632 O-14
Boca West, 2100 *F-9
Bonifay, 2711 R-6
Bonita Shores, 2000 O-9
Bonita Sprs., 37992 O-9
Bowling Green, 2928 K-9
Boynton Beach, 66885 N-14
Bradenton, 53917 K-7
Bradenton Beach, 1561 L-6
BRADFORD CO., 28118 D-8
Bradley, 600 J-8
Brandon, 77871 J-8
Brent, 22257 †L-9
BREVARD CO., 531250 J-12
Brooksville, 7637 H-7
BROWARD CO., 1777638 O-12
Brownsville, 14393 *L-8
Buccaneer Estates, 1000 *J-8
Buckhead Ridge, 1390 L-11
Buena Venture Lakes, 14000 P-4
Bunche Park, 3972 *K-8
Bunnell, 1479 E-10
Bushnell, 2119 H-8
CALHOUN CO., 13290 S-7
Callahan, 951 B-9
Callaway, 14437 S-6
Campbell, 2677 I-10
Canal Pt., 525 M-12
Canova Beach, 150 I-12
Cantonment, 2800 R-2
Cape Canaveral, 10523 I-12
Cape Coral, 140010 N-8
Carrabelle, 1290 D-1
Carrollwood, 3100 *B-3
Casselberry, 24298 H-10
Century, 1799 Q-2
Century Village, 7616 *B-9
Chaires, 100 B-3
CHARLOTTE CO., 157536 M-9
Chattahoochee, 3720 R-8
Chiefland, 2095 E-6
Chipley, 3682 R-6
Chuluota, 1921 H-11
CITRUS CO., 134370 G-7
Citrus Sprs., 4157 G-7
Clair-Mel City, 7500 *C-4
Clarcona, 800 M-2

CLAY CO., 171095......D-9
Clearwater, 108687......J-6
Clermont, 11617......H-9
Clewiston, 7173......N-11
Cocoa, 16898......I-12
Cocoa Beach, 12435......I-12
Coconut Cr., 49017......*G-9
COLLIER CO., 307242......O-10
COLUMBIA CO., 64040......C-7
Conway, 14394......H-10
Cooper City, 30022......*I-8
Coral Cove, 1160......L-7
Coral Gables, 42871......Q-13
Coral Sprs., 128804......O-13
Coral Way Vil., 3200......*M-7
Cottondale, 879......R-7
Crawfordville, 1400......C-2
Crescent City, 1817......E-10
Crestview, 17707......R-4
Cross City, 1808......E-5
Crystal Beach, 1350......*A-1
Crystal River, 3600......G-7
Cudjoe......T-10
Cutler Ridge, 24781......Q-13
Cypress Creek......*J-4
Cypress Gardens, 8844......*K-5
Cypress Quarters, 1150......L-12
Dade City, 6823......I-8
Dania Beach, 28782......P-14
Davenport, 2017......J-9
Davie, 84204......P-13
Daytona Beach, 64421......F-11
Daytona Beach Shores, 4817......F-11
Debary, 16413......G-10
Deerfield Beach, 76348......O-14
De Funiak Sprs., 5038......R-5
DeLand, 24375......G-10
De Leon Sprs., 2358......F-10
Delray Beach, 64757......N-14
Deltona, 82788......G-10
DESOTO CO., 35406......L-9
Desoto Lakes, 3198......*G-4
Destin, 12423......S-4
DIXIE CO., 14647......E-5
Doctor Phillips, 9548......O-2
Dover, 2798......J-8
Dundee, 3064......J-9
Dunedin, 36690......J-6
Dunnellon, 1971......G-7
DUVAL CO., 826436......C-9
Eagle Lake, 2489......*K-4
E. Naples, 2050......P-9
E. Palatka, 1707......E-9
Eastpoint, 2158......T-8
Eatonville, 2390......M-3
Edgewater, 21132......G-11
Edgewood, 2098......N-4
Egypt Lake, 3500......*B-3
Elfers, 13161......I-6
Ellenton, 3142......K-7
El Portal, 2427......*L-9
Englewood, 16196......M-7
Ensley, 18752......R-2
ESCAMBIA CO., 296772......Q-2
Eustis, 17683......G-9
Fairview Shores, 13898......M-3
Fellsmere, 4800......J-12
Fernandina Beach, 11264......B-10
Fern Park, 8318......M-4
Ferry Pass, 27176......†L-9
FLAGLER CO., 76410......E-10
Flagler Beach, 3179......E-11
Floral City, 4989......H-8
Florida City, 8913......R-13
Forest City, 12612......M-3
Ft. Lauderdale, 167380......O-14
Ft. McCoy, 300......F-8
Ft. Meade, 5742......K-9
Ft. Myers, 58428......N-9
Ft. Myers Beach, 6834......O-8
Ft. Myers Villas, 5600......N-9
Ft. Pierce, 38552......K-13
Ft. Walton Beach, 19817......S-4
FRANKLIN CO., 10177......D-1
Frostproof, 2950......K-10
Fruitland Park, 3578......G-9
Fruitville, 12741......L-7
GADSDEN CO., 46428......B-1
Gainesville, 108184......E-7
Gibsonia, 4507......*I-1
Gibsonton, 8752......J-7
Gifford, 7599......K-13
GILCHRIST CO., 16402......D-6
GLADES CO., 11252......M-10
Glenvar Heights, 16243......*M-7
Golden Gate, 20951......O-9
Golden Lakes, 6694......*B-9
Goldenrod, 12871......M-4
Goodland, 320......P-9
Goulding, 4484......†M-9
Goulds, 7453......Q-13
Graceville, 2423......Q-6
Greenacres, 32525......N-14
Green Cove Sprs., 6085......D-9
Greenville, 829......B-4
Gretna, 1699......B-1
Grove City, 2092......M-7
Groveland, 5205......H-9
GULF CO., 13975......T-7
Gulf Breeze, 6455......S-3
Gulf City, 550......*E-4
Gulf Gate Estates, 11647......*H-3
Gulf Harbors, 3300......I-6
Gulfport, 12661......K-6
Gulf Stream, 751......N-14
Haines City, 16371......I-9
Hallandale Beach, 37083......P-14
HAMILTON CO., 13983......B-6
HARDEE CO., 28286......L-8
Harlem, 2730......N-11
Havana, 1701......B-2
Haverhill, 1621......N-14
Hawthorne, 1443......E-8
Heathrow, 4068......G-10
HENDRY CO., 39561......N-10
Hernando, 8253......G-7
HERNANDO CO., 158409......H-7
Hialeah, 220485......P-13
Highland City, 2051......J-9
Highland Lakes......*A-2
HIGHLANDS CO., 95496......K-10
Highpoint, 2300......*C-2
High Sprs., 4157......D-7
Hiland Park, 999......S-6
Hilliard, 2913......B-8
Hillsboro Beach, 2329......*G-10
HILLSBOROUGH CO., 1132152......J-8
Hobe Sound, 11376......M-13
Holiday, 21904......I-6
Holly Hill, 12630......F-11
Hollywood, 145629......P-14
HOLMES CO., 19264......Q-6
Holmes Beach, 5100......K-6
Homestead, 44494......Q-13
Homosassa, 2294......G-7
Homosassa Sprs., 12458......G-7
Hudson, 12765......I-6
Immokalee, 19763......O-10
Indialantic, 3076......I-12
Indian Harbour Beach, 8441......I-12
INDIAN RIVER CO., 128594......K-12
Indian Rocks Beach, 5265......J-6
Indian Shores, 1787......*C-1
Indiantown, 5588......M-13
Indian Wells......P-3
Inverness, 7295......G-7
Inwood, 6925......J-4
Islamorada, 6606......S-12
Ives Estates, 17586......*J-9
JACKSON CO., 48985......Q-7
Jacksonville, 782623......C-9
Jacksonville Beach, 21770......C-10
Jan Phyl Village, 5633......*K-4
Jasper, 1817......B-6
JEFFERSON CO., 14490......C-3
Jensen Beach, 11100......L-13
June Park, 4367......J-12
Juno Beach, 3395......M-14
Jupiter, 47909......M-14
Kathleen, 3280......I-8
Kendall, 75226......Q-13
Kenneth City, 4419......*D-2
Kensington Park, 3720......*G-3
Key Biscayne, 10158......Q-14
Key Largo, 11886......S-13
Keystone Hts., 1427......D-8
Key West, 23935......T-9
Kissimmee, 59364......I-10
La Belle, 4551......N-10
Lacoochee, 1345......H-8
Lady Lake, 13244......G-8
LAFAYETTE CO., 7953......D-5
LAKE CO., 277035......I-9
Lake Alfred, 3930......J-9
Lake Brantley, 3000......L-3
Lake Butler, 1967......D-7
Lake Cain Hills, 1600......N-3
Lake City, 10970......C-7
Lake Clarke Shores, 3460......*B-10
Lake Hamilton, 1414......J-9
Lake Helen, 2816......G-10
Lakeland, 88713......J-8
Lake Magdalene, 28873......*B-4
Lake Mary, 14638......G-10
Lake Panasoffkee, 3413......H-8
Lake Park, 9039......M-14
Lake Placid, 1784......L-10
Lakeside Green, 3311......*A-9
Lake Suzy, 1040......M-8
Lake Wales, 12964......J-9
Lakewood Park, 10458......K-13
Lake Worth, 36342......N-14
Land O'Lakes, 20971......I-7
Lantana, 10498......N-14
Largo, 74473......J-6
Lauderdale-by-the-Sea, 5990......*H-10
Lauderdale Lakes, 31826......*H-8
Lauderhill, 59621......*H-8
Laurel, 8393......L-7
Lealman, 4200......*D-2
LEE CO., 544758......N-9
Leesburg, 19086......G-9
Lehigh Acres, 33430......N-9
Leisure City, 22152......Q-13
LEON CO., 245756......B-3
LEVY CO., 37998......F-7
LIBERTY CO., 7773......C-1
Lighthouse Pt., 11262......O-14
Live Oak, 6922......C-6
Lockhart, 12944......M-3
Longboat Key, 7583......L-6
Longwood, 13580......H-10
Loughman, 1385......I-9
Loxahatchee, 120......N-13
Lutz, 17081......I-7
Lynn Haven, 15677......S-6
Macclenny, 5186......C-8
Madeira Beach, 4464......J-6
MADISON CO., 19092......C-4
Madison, 3190......B-5
Maitland, 14125......H-10
MANATEE CO., 306779......L-8
Mangonia Park, 1283......*A-10
Marathon, 9822......T-11
Marco, 16109......P-9
Margate, 56002......O-13
Marianna, 6275......R-7
MARION CO., 303442......F-7
MARTIN CO., 139728......M-13
Mary Esther, 4086......S-4
Mascotte, 4647......H-9
Matlacha, 735......N-8
Mayo, 1032......D-5
Meadow Wood, 11286......P-3
Medulla, 6637......*K-4
Melbourne, 76646......J-12
Melbourne Beach, 3314......J-12
Melrose, 1100......E-8
Melrose Park, 7114......*I-8
Memphis, 7264......*F-3
Merritt Island, 36090......I-12
Mexico Beach, 1192......T-7
Miami, 386417......Q-13
Miami Beach, 87925......P-14
MIAMI-DADE CO., 2376014......Q-12
Miami Gardens, 99438......P-13
Miami Lakes, 22676......*K-7
Miami Shores, 10040......*K-9
Miami Sprs., 13170......P-13
Middleburg, 10338......D-9
Midway, 1585......B-2
Midway, 1714......G-10
Millview, 1100......†M-7
Milton, 8131......R-3
Mims, 9147......H-11
Minneola, 8665......H-9
Miramar, 106623......P-13
Mission City, 1700......G-11
Molino, 1312......R-2
MONROE CO., 76329......R-11
Monticello, 2546......B-3
Moore Haven, 1751......M-11
Morningside Park, 500......O-3
Mt. Dora, 11474......G-9
Mulberry, 3233......J-8
Myrtle Gr., 17211......R-2
Nalcrest, 500......J-10
Naples, 21709......O-9
Naples Park, 6741......O-9
Naranja, 4034......Q-13
Narcoossee, 200......I-10
NASSAU CO., 64746......B-9
Neptune Beach, 7018......C-10
Newberry, 3804......E-7
New Port Richey, 16928......I-6
New Smyrna Beach, 22356......G-11
Niceville, 12582......R-4
Nocatee, 1600......L-9
Nokomis, 3334......M-7
Norland, 22995......*K-8
N. Bay Village, 7615......*L-9
Northdale......*A-3
N. Fort Myers, 40214......N-9
N. Lauderdale, 42262......*G-8
N. Miami, 57654......*K-9
N. Miami Beach, 39442......P-13
N. Naples, 400......O-9
N. Palm Beach, 12633......M-14
N. Port, 42253......M-8
N. Redington Beach, 1517......*D-1
North River Shores, 3101......L-13
Oak Hill, 1484......G-11
Oakland Park, 31713......O-14
Ocala, 49745......F-8
Ocean Ridge, 1699......N-14
Ocklawaha, 860......G-8
Ocoee, 29849......H-9
Ojus, 16642......P-14
OKALOOSA CO., 182172......R-4
OKEECHOBEE CO., 39836......K-11
Okeechobee, 5900......L-12
Oldsmar, 13552......J-7
Oneco, 3200......L-7
Opa Locka, 15763......P-13
ORANGE CO., 1023023......I-11
Orange City, 7862......G-10
Orange Park, 9205......C-9
Orlando, 213223......H-10
Orlovista, 6047......H-10
Ormond Beach, 38613......F-11
Ormond By The Sea, 8430......F-11
OSCEOLA CO., 231578......I-11
Osprey, 4143......L-7
Osteen, 550......G-11
Oviedo, 29848......H-10
Ozona, 1900......J-6
Pace, 7393......R-3
Pahokee, 6554......M-12
Palatka, 10942......E-9
Palma Sola, 3100......*F-2
Palm Bay, 92833......J-12
PALM BEACH CO., 1268548......N-12
Palm Beach, 9852......N-14
Palm Beach Gardens, 48989......M-14
Palm Beach Shores, 1515......M-14
Palm City, 20097......L-13
Palm Coast, 60952......E-10
Palmetto, 13510......K-7
Palm Hbr., 59248......J-6
Palm Sprs., 15267......*B-10
Palm Springs North, 5460......*K-7
Panacea, 900......D-2
Panama City, 37188......S-6
Panama City Beach, 11477......S-6
Parker, 4672......S-6
PASCO CO., 429065......I-7
Pembroke Park, 5487......*J-9
Pembroke Pines, 150380......*J-7
Pensacola, 54055......R-2
Pensacola Beach, 1200......S-3
Perrine, 1370......Q-13
Perry, 6734......C-4
Pierson, 2604......F-10
Pine Castle, 8803......O-4
Pine Hills, 41764......H-10
Pine Island Ridge, 5199......*I-8
PINELLAS CO., 928032......K-6
Pinellas Park, 47352......J-6
Pinewood Park, 3400......*K-8
Placid Lakes, 3054......L-10
Plantation, 85989......*I-8
Plantation, 1900......S-12
Plant City, 31450......J-8
Playland Isles, 1000......*I-8
Pleasant Grove, 1000......†N-8
Plymouth, 1250......H-9
POLK CO., 542912......I-8
Pompano Beach, 104179......O-14
Ponte Vedra Beach, 3000......C-10
Port Charlotte, 46451......M-8
Port Orange, 53746......F-11
Port Richey, 3333......I-6
Port St. Joe, 3602......T-7
Port St. John, 12112......H-12
Port St. Lucie, 131692......L-13
Port Salerno, 10141......L-13
Princeton, 10090......Q-13
Progress Vil., 2482......*C-4
Punta Gorda, 17111......M-8
PUTNAM CO., 73568......E-9
Quincy, 6993......B-1
Rainbow Lakes, 1550......*C-9
Redington Beach, 1525......*D-1
Redington Shores, 2065......J-6
Richmond Hts., 8479......Q-13
Ridge Manor, 4108......H-8
Riverview, 12040......J-7
Riviera Beach, 33772......M-14
Rockledge, 24245......I-12
Royal Palm Beach, 30886......N-13
Ruskin, 8321......K-7
Safety Hbr., 17517......*B-2
St. Augustine, 12263......D-10
St. Augustine Beach, 5753......D-10
St. Augustine Shores, 4922......D-10
St. Cloud, 22508......I-10
St. James City, 4105......N-8
ST. JOHNS CO., 161525......D-10
St. Leo, 936......I-8
ST. LUCIE CO., 241305......L-12
St. Pete Beach, 10173......K-6
St. Petersburg, 249079......K-7
Salt Sprs., 600......F-9
Samoset, 3440......K-7
San Carlos Park, 16317......N-9
Sanford, 47257......G-10
Sanibel, 6072......O-8
San Mateo, 1100......E-9
SANTA ROSA CO., 143105......Q-3
Santa Rosa Beach, 600......S-5
SARASOTA CO., 366256......L-8
Sarasota, 53711......L-7
Sarasota Springs, 15875......*H-4
Satellite Beach, 9811......I-12
Sebastian, 19643......J-12
Sebring, 10431......K-10
Seffner, 5467......*B-5
SEMINOLE CO., 401619......H-11
Seminole, 18505......*C-1
Seminole Manor, 2546......*G-9
Seville, 530......F-10
Sharpes, 3415......H-12
Siesta Key, 7150......*H-3
Silver Sprs., 1050......F-8
Silver Springs Shores, 6690......F-8
Sky Lake, 5651......O-3
Sneads, 1943......R-8
Solana, 1011......M-8
S. Apopka, 5800......M-2
S. Bay, 4059......N-12
S. Bradenton, 21587......*G-3
S. Daytona, 13733......F-11
Southgate, 7455......*H-3
S. Miami, 11147......Q-13
S. Pasadena, 5715......*D-2
Southport, 1500......S-6
S. Venice, 13539......M-7
Southwest Ranches, 7388......*I-7
Southwood, 1700......O-3
Springfield, 9043......S-6
Spring Hill, 69078......H-7
Starke, 5844......D-8
Stock Island, 4410......T-9
Stuart, 15764......L-13
Sugar Mill......*B-3
SUMTER CO., 64182......G-8
Sun City Cen., 9000......K-7
Sunny Isles, 15424......*K-9
Sunrise, 90589......*H-8
Sun Valley, 1300......*D-9
Surfside, 4710......P-14
SUWANNEE CO., 38624......C-5
Sweetwater, 13741......Q-13
Sweetwater Oaks, 1100......L-3
Sylvan Shores, 2424......L-10
Taft, 1938......I-10
Taft, 1938......O-4
Tallahassee, 158500......B-2
Tamarac, 59923......O-13
Tampa, 325989......J-7
Tangelo Park, 2430......O-3
Tangerine, 826......G-9
Tarpon Lake Village......*A-2
Tarpon Sprs., 22651......I-6
Tavares, 11621......G-9
Tavernier, 2173......S-13
TAYLOR CO., 19622......D-4
Taylor Creek, 4289......L-12
Temple Ter., 21978......J-7
Tequesta, 5989......M-14
The Hamptons......*E-9
The Meadows, 4423......*G-4
The Villages, 8333......G-8
Thonotosassa, 6091......J-7
Tice, 4538......N-9
Titusville, 43767......H-11
Treasure Island, 7542......K-6
Trenton, 1793......E-6
Uleta, 2300......*K-9
Umatilla, 2647......G-9
UNION CO., 14916......D-7
Union Park, 10191......H-10
University West......*B-4
Valparaiso, 6365......R-4
Venice, 20974......M-7
Venice Gardens, 7466......M-7
Vero Beach, 17078......K-13
Viera, 200......I-12
Villages of Oriole, 4758......*E-9
Virginia Gardens, 2260......*L-7
VOLUSIA CO., 490055......G-11
WAKULLA CO., 28212......C-2
Waldo, 776......D-8
WALTON CO., 50324......R-5
Warrington, 15207......S-2
WASHINGTON CO., 22299......R-6
Wauchula, 4450......K-9
Waverly, 1927......J-9
Weirsdale, 840......G-8
Wekiva Springs, 23169......L-3
Wellington, 53583......*B-8
West Bradenton, 4444......*F-2
Westchester, 30271......*M-7
W. Melbourne, 15054......J-12
W. Miami, 5829......*M-7
Weston, 65679......O-13
W. Palm Beach, 97498......N-14
W. Pensacola, 21939......R-2
Westwood Lakes, 12005......*M-7
Wewahitchka, 1691......S-7
White City, 4221......L-13
Wildwood, 3428......G-8
Williamsburg, 6736......O-3
Williston, 2508......F-7
Wilton Manors, 12858......*H-9
Wimauma, 4246......K-8
Windermere, 2003......H-10
Winter Garden, 25500......H-9
Winter Haven, 29501......J-9
Winter Park, 28179......H-10
Winter Springs, 32583......L-4
Woodville, 3006......C-2
Yalaha, 1175......H-9
Zellwood, 2540......H-9
Zephyrhills, 12258......I-8
Zolfo Sprs., 1666......K-9

Georgia

Map pp. 58-62

* City keyed to p. 62

Abbeville, 2471......K-7
Acworth, 18428......E-4
Adairsville, 3090......D-3
Adel, 5434......N-7
Adrian, 574......I-9
Ailey, 540......J-9
Alamo, 2451......K-9
Alapaha, 694......M-8
Albany, 75394......L-5
Allenhurst, 707......L-11
Alma, 3361......M-10
Alpharetta, 40128......D-5
Alto, 887......C-7
Americus, 16873......K-5
APPLING CO., 17954......L-10
Aragon, 1058......E-3
Arlington, 1505......M-3
Ashburn, 4397......L-6
Athens, 103238......E-7
ATKINSON CO., 8030......M-8
Atlanta, 470688......E-4
Auburn, 7134......E-6
Augusta, 190782......F-11
Austell, 6566......E-4
Avondale Estates, 2623......*E-5
BACON CO., 10379......L-9
Baconton, 968......M-5
Bainbridge, 11874......O-4
BAKER CO., 4154......M-4
BALDWIN CO., 45230......G-7
Baldwin, 2818......C-7
Ball Ground, 811......D-5
BANKS CO., 16055......D-7
Barnesville, 5808......H-5
BARROW CO., 59954......E-6
BARTOW CO., 89229......D-3
Baxley, 4402......L-10
Belvedere, 6000......*E-5
BEN HILL CO., 17316......L-8
Berlin, 613......N-6
BERRIEN CO., 16708......M-7
BIBB CO., 154918......I-6
Bibb City......R-2
Blackshear, 3421......M-10
Blacksville, 4......G-5
Blackwells, 5000......E-4
Blairsville, 683......B-6
Blakely, 5476......M-3
BLECKLEY CO., 12141......J-7
Bloomingdale, 2677......K-13
Blue Ridge, 1089......B-5
Bogart, 1094......E-7
Bonaire, 900......I-7
Boston, 1449......O-6
Bowdon, 1963......F-2
Bowdon Jct., 400......F-2
Bowman, 987......D-8
BRANTLEY CO., 15491......M-11
Bremen, 5350......F-2
Brookhaven, 7000......*C-4
Brooklet, 1176......J-12
BROOKS CO., 16327......O-7
Broxton, 1468......L-8
Brunswick, 15956......N-12
BRYAN CO., 28549......K-12
Buchanan, 1018......E-2
Buena Vista, 1697......J-4
Buford, 10972......D-5
BULLOCH CO., 61454......J-11
BURKE CO., 23299......H-11
Butler, 1888......I-5
BUTTS CO., 21045......G-5
Byromville, 420......J-6
Byron, 3251......I-6
Cairo, 9389......O-5
Calhoun, 13570......C-3
CALHOUN CO., 5972......M-4
CAMDEN CO., 45759......N-11
Camilla, 5616......N-5
CANDLER CO., 10321......J-11
Canon, 806......D-8
Canton, 17685......D-4
Carnesville, 617......D-8
CARROLL CO., 105453......F-3
Carrollton, 21837......F-3
Cartersville, 17653......D-3
Cataula, 550......I-3
CATOOSA CO., 60813......B-2
Cave Spr., 997......D-2
Cedar Gr., 2000......*G-5
Cedartown, 9771......E-2
Centerville, 6624......I-7
Chamblee, 9763......E-5
CHARLTON CO., 10790......O-10
CHATHAM CO., 238410......K-13
Chatsworth, 3924......B-3
CHATTAHOOCHEE CO., 14679......J-3
CHATTOOGA CO., 26570......C-2
CHEROKEE CO., 184211......D-4
Chickamauga, 2497......B-2
Chicopee, 750......D-6
Clarkdale, 500......E-4
CLARKE CO., 104439......E-7
Clarkesville, 1505......C-7
Clarkston, 7078......*D-6
Claxton, 2400......K-11
CLAY CO., 3242......L-3
CLAYTON CO., 267966......F-4
Clayton, 2100......B-7
Cleveland, 2360......C-6
CLINCH CO., 6996......N-9
COBB CO., 663818......E-4
Cochran, 4721......I-7
COFFEE CO., 39674......L-9
Colbert, 515......E-8
College Park, 20181......F-4
Collins, 552......J-11
COLQUITT CO., 43915......N-6
Colquitt, 1889......N-3
COLUMBIA CO., 103812......F-10
Columbus, 185271......J-3
Comer, 1156......E-8
Commerce, 5856......D-7
Conley, 6188......*G-4
Constitution, 600......*F-4
Conyers, 12205......F-5
COOK CO., 16366......N-7
Coolidge, 558......N-6
Cordele, 11493......K-6
Cornelia, 3771......C-7
Covington, 13856......F-6
COWETA CO., 109903......G-3
CRAWFORD CO., 12874......I-5
Crawford, 813......E-8
Crawfordville, 502......F-8
CRISP CO., 22017......K-6
Cumming, 5802......D-5
Cusseta, 9805......J-3
Cuthbert, 3491......L-3
Dacula, 4425......E-6
DADE CO., 16040......B-2
Dahlonega, 4519......C-6
Dallas, 8667......E-3
Dalton, 32140......B-3
Danville, 358......I-7
Darien, 1713......M-12
Dasher, 807......O-8
DAWSON CO., 19731......D-5
Dawson, 4859......L-4
Dearing, 446......G-10
Decatur, 17884......E-5
DECATUR CO., 28618......O-4
Deenwood, 1836......N-10
Deerwood Park, 3000......*E-5
DE KALB CO., 677959......F-5
Demorest, 1777......C-7
Dexter, 533......I-8
Dock Jct., 6951......N-12
DODGE CO., 19574......J-7
Doerun, 848......M-6
Donalsonville, 2702......N-3
DOOLY CO., 11749......K-6
Doraville, 9872......E-5
DOUGHERTY CO., 94882......L-4
DOUGLAS CO., 112760......F-3
Douglas, 10978......M-9
Douglasville, 27568......F-3
Druid Hills, 12741......*E-4
Dublin, 16924......I-8
Duluth, 24482......E-5
Dunaire, 8000......*D-6
Dunwoody, 32808......*A-4
EARLY CO., 12056......M-3
E. Dublin, 2711......I-9
Eastman, 5441......J-8
East Marietta, 12000......*A-2
E. Newnan, 1305......G-3
E. Point, 40680......F-4
Eatonton, 6758......G-7
ECHOLS CO., 4253......O-8
Echota, 650......C-3
Eden, 750......J-12
Edison, 1236......L-3
EFFINGHAM CO., 46924......J-12
ELBERT CO., 20799......E-8
Elberta, 950......I-6
Elberton, 4714......D-8
Ellaville, 1758......J-5
Ellijay, 1519......C-4
EMANUEL CO., 22108......I-10
Embry Hills, 1600......*C-6
Emerson, 1302......D-3
Enigma, 886......M-7
Euharlee, 3859......D-3
EVANS CO., 11443......J-11
Evans, 17727......F-10
Experiment, 3233......G-5
Fairburn, 8564......F-4
Fairmount, 785......C-4
Fair Oaks, 8443......*B-1
FANNIN CO., 21887......B-4
Fargo, 383......O-9
FAYETTE CO., 104248......G-4
Fayetteville, 14363......F-4
Fitzgerald, 8920......L-7
Five Forks, 3200......E-5
Flowery Branch, 2087......D-6
FLOYD CO., 94198......D-2
Folkston, 3270......O-11
Forest Park, 22201......F-4
Forsyth, 4259......H-6
FORSYTH CO., 140393......D-5
Ft. Gaines, 1059......L-3
Ft. Oglethorpe, 8964......B-2
Ft. Valley, 8197......I-6
Franklin, 897......G-3
FRANKLIN CO., 21590......C-7
Franklin Sprs., 781......D-8
FULTON CO., 915623......F-4
Gainesville, 32444......D-6
Garden City, 9550......K-13
Garden Lakes, 4000......D-2
Georgetown, 912......K-2
Gibson, 741......G-9
GILMER CO., 27335......B-4
GLASCOCK CO., 2705......G-9
Glennville, 5031......K-11
Glenwood, 850......K-9
GLYNN CO., 71874......M-12
Gordon, 2119......H-7
GORDON CO., 50279......C-3
GRADY CO., 24466......N-5
Grantville, 2407......G-3
Gray, 2109......H-7
GREENE CO., 15693......F-8
Greensboro, 3303......F-8
Greenville, 938......H-4
Gresham Park, 9215......*F-4
Griffin, 23286......G-5
Grovetown, 7483......F-10
Guyton, 1707......J-12
GWINNETT CO., 726273......E-6
HABERSHAM CO., 39603......C-7
Haddock, 750......H-7
Hagan, 1028......K-11
Hahira, 1915......N-7
HALL CO., 165771......D-6
Hamilton, 527......I-3
Hampton, 4743......G-5
HANCOCK CO., 9643......G-8
Hapeville, 6085......*G-3
HARALSON CO., 28338......E-2
Hardwick, 4800......H-7
Harlem, 1818......G-10
HARRIS CO., 27779......I-3
HART CO., 24036......D-8
Hartwell, 4288......D-8
Hawkinsville, 4212......J-7
Hazlehurst, 3729......K-9
HEARD CO., 11346......G-2
Helena, 2523......K-8
HENRY CO., 167848......F-5
Hephzibah, 4210......G-11
Hiawassee, 844......B-6
Highland Mills, 700......G-5
Hinesville, 28615......K-12
Hiram, 1762......E-3
Hoboken, 512......N-10
Hogansville, 2823......G-3
Holly Sprs., 5328......D-4
Homeland, 809......O-11
Homer, 1085......D-7
Homerville, 2811......N-9
Hoschton, 1455......D-6
HOUSTON CO., 126163......J-6
Ideal, 490......J-5
IRWIN CO., 10093......L-7
Irwinton, 584......I-8
Isle of Hope, 2605......K-13
Jackson, 4358......G-6
JASPER CO., 13147......G-6
Jasper, 2837......C-4
JEFF DAVIS CO., 13083......L-9
JEFFERSON CO., 16926......H-9
Jefferson, 5599......D-7
Jeffersonville, 1219......I-7
JENKINS CO., 8729......H-11
Jesup, 9851......L-11
JOHNSON CO., 9538......I-9
JONES CO., 26836......H-7
Jonesboro, 3922......F-5
Kennesaw, 30522......E-4
Kingsland, 12063......O-12
Kingston, 668......D-3
La Fayette, 6753......B-2
La Grange, 27362......H-3
Lake City, 2776......*H-4
Lakeland, 2769......N-8
Lake Park, 633......O-7
LAMAR CO., 16378......H-5
LANIER CO., 7553......N-8
LAURENS CO., 46896......I-8
Lavonia, 1982......C-8
Lawrenceville, 28393......E-6
Leary, 620......M-4
LEE CO., 31099......L-5
Leesburg, 2777......L-5
Lenox, 902......M-7
Leslie, 440......K-5
LIBERTY CO., 57544......K-11
Lilburn, 11416......E-5
LINCOLN CO., 8207......E-9
Lincoln Park, 1122......H-5
Lincolnton, 1515......E-10
Lindale, 4088......D-2
Lithia Sprs., 2072......E-4
Lithonia, 2197......F-5
Lizella, 600......I-6
Locust Gr., 3434......G-5
Loganville, 8881......E-6
LONG CO., 11083......L-12
Lookout Mtn., 1570......B-2
Louisville, 2643......H-10
LOWNDES CO., 96705......N-7
Ludowici, 1558......L-12
Lula, 1878......D-6
Lumber City, 1209......K-9
LUMPKIN CO., 24324......C-5
Lumpkin, 1265......K-3
Lyerly, 513......C-2
Lyons, 4384......J-10
Mableton, 29733......E-4
Macon, 94316......H-6
MACON CO., 13745......J-5
MADISON CO., 27289......D-7
Madison, 3833......F-7
Manchester, 3719......H-4
Marietta, 61261......E-4
MARION CO., 7244......J-4
Marshallville, 1286......J-6
Martinez, 27749......F-11
Maysville, 1520......D-7
McCaysville, 936......B-5
McDonough, 15523......F-5
MCDUFFIE CO., 21743......G-9
MCINTOSH CO., 11068......M-12
McRae, 4283......K-8
Meigs, 1105......N-5
Menlo, 509......C-2
MERIWETHER CO., 22919......H-3
Metter, 4143......J-11
Midville, 472......H-10
Midway, 1008......L-12
Milan, 762......K-8
Milledgeville, 19397......H-8
Millen, 3526......I-11
MILLER CO., 6228......N-4
Milstead, 1500......F-5
MITCHELL CO., 23791......M-5
MONROE CO., 23785......H-5
Monroe, 12329......E-6
Montezuma, 3997......J-5
MONTGOMERY CO., 8909......K-9
Monticello, 2565......G-6
MORGAN CO., 17492......F-7
Morrow, 5283......F-5
Morven, 623......N-7
Moultrie, 14913......N-6
Mtn. City, 779......B-7
Mtn. View, 1100......*G-3
Mt. Airy, 665......C-7
Mt. Berry, 500......D-2
Mt. Vernon, 2162......J-9
Mt. Zion, 1492......F-2
MURRAY CO., 40812......B-4
Murrayville, 800......C-6
MUSCOGEE CO., 185271......J-3
Nahunta, 1044......N-11
Nashville, 4841......N-7
Nelson, 761......D-5
New Holland, 1200......D-6
Newnan, 24654......G-3
NEWTON CO., 86713......F-6
Newton, 867......M-4
Nicholls, 2557......M-9
Norcross, 9887......E-5
Norman Park, 859......M-6
N. Decatur, 15270......*D-5
N. Druid Hills, 18852......*D-5
N. West Point, 700......H-2
Oakdale, 1100......*C-2
Oak Gr., 2850......*D-5
Oakwood, 3408......D-6
Ochlocknee, 619......N-5
Ocilla, 3417......L-7
OCONEE CO., 29748......E-7
OGLETHORPE CO., 13609......E-8
Oglethorpe, 1157......J-5
Omega, 1360......M-7
Oxford, 2214......F-6
Palmetto, 4676......F-4
Panthersville, 11791......F-5
Patterson, 662......M-10
PAULDING CO., 112411......E-3
Pavo, 713......N-6
PEACH CO., 24794......I-6
Peachtree City, 34524......G-4
Pearson, 1901......M-9
Pelham, 3914......N-5
Pembroke, 2503......K-12
Pendley Hills, 5000......*E-6
Perry, 11018......J-6
Phillipsburg, 887......M-7
PICKENS CO., 28442......C-4
PIERCE CO., 17119......M-10
PIKE CO., 16128......H-4
Pine Mtn., 1231......H-3
Pine Mtn. Valley, 950......H-3
Pineview, 533......K-7
Plains, 614......K-4
POLK CO., 40479......E-2
Pooler, 10019......Q-9
Portal, 595......I-11
Porterdale, 1569......F-6
Port Wentworth, 3238......S-8
Poulan, 926......M-6
Powder Sprs., 14507......E-4
PULASKI CO., 9737......J-7
PUTNAM CO., 19829......G-7
Putney, 2998......M-5
QUITMAN CO., 2467......K-3
Quitman, 4520......O-7
RABUN CO., 16087......B-7
Radium Sprs., 1400......M-5
RANDOLPH CO., 7310......L-3
Ray City, 763......N-8
Red Oak, 2800......*H-2
Rehoboth, 1300......*D-6
Reidsville, 2400......K-10
Remerton, 1001......O-7
Reynolds, 1031......I-5
Rhine, 421......K-8
Richland, 1673......K-4
RICHMOND CO., 195769......G-10
Richmond Hill, 9187......K-13
Rincon, 6349......J-13
Ringgold, 2793......B-3
Riverdale, 15475......F-4
Roberta, 776......I-5
Rochelle, 1418......K-7
ROCKDALE CO., 78545......F-5
Rockmart, 4310......E-3
Rocky Face, 1000......B-3
Rome, 35816......D-2
Rossville, 3416......B-2
Roswell, 85920......E-5
Royston, 2678......D-8
Rutledge, 757......F-7
St. Marys, 16404......O-12
St. Simons Island, 13381......N-12
Sandersville, 6031......H-9
Sandy Sprs., 85781......E-4
Sardis, 1217......H-11
Sargent, 900......F-3
Savannah, 128453......K-13
SCHLEY CO., 4122......J-4
Scottdale, 9803......*D-6
SCREVEN CO., 15430......H-11
Screven, 756......M-11
Sea Island, 700......N-13
SEMINOLE CO., 9226......N-3
Senoia, 2719......G-4
Shannon, 1682......D-3
Shellman, 1084......L-4
Skyland, 2500......*C-5
Smithville, 920......K-5
Smyrna, 47643......E-4
Snellville, 19238......E-5
Social Circle, 4053......F-6
Soperton, 2747......J-9
S. Decatur, 19400......*E-5
SPALDING CO., 61289......G-5
Sparks, 1781......N-7
Sparta, 1374......G-8
Springfield, 2034......J-13
Statenville, 650......O-8
Statesboro, 24612......I-11
Statham, 2555......E-7
STEPHENS CO., 25060......C-7
STEWART CO., 4882......K-3
Stillmore, 755......J-10
Stockbridge, 13140......F-5
Stone Mtn., 7080......E-5
Sugar Hill, 15696......D-5
Sugar Valley, 300......C-3
Summerville, 4853......C-2
SUMTER CO., 32912......K-5
Suwanee, 12553......E-5
Swainsboro, 7162......I-10
Sylvania, 2591......I-12
Sylvester, 5924......M-6
TALBOT CO., 6709......I-4
Talbotton, 1022......I-4
TALIAFERRO CO., 1826......F-8
Tallapoosa, 3031......F-2
Tate, 1000......C-4
TATTNALL CO., 23211......K-10
TAYLOR CO., 8887......I-4
TELFAIR CO., 13205......K-8
Temple, 3910......F-3
Tennille, 1480......H-9
TERRELL CO., 10711......L-4
THOMAS CO., 44692......N-6
Thomaston, 9265......H-5
Thomasville, 18725......O-5
Thomson, 6866......F-9
Thunderbolt, 2467......K-13
TIFT CO., 40793......M-7
Tifton, 16327......M-7
Tignall, 642......E-9
Toccoa, 9103......C-7
Toco Hills, 3200......*D-5
TOOMBS CO., 27274......K-10
Toomsboro, 617......H-8
TOWNS CO., 10315......B-6
Trenton, 2155......B-2
TREUTLEN CO., 6753......J-9
Trion, 2048......C-2
TROUP CO., 62015......G-3
Tucker, 26532......E-5
Tunnel Hill, 1072......B-3
TURNER CO., 9474......L-7
TWIGGS CO., 10299......I-7
Twin City, 1752......I-10
Twin Lakes, 950......O-8
Tybee Island, 3614......K-14
Tyrone, 5789......F-4
Ty Ty, 763......M-6
Unadilla, 2879......J-6
UNION CO., 19782......B-5
Union City, 15382......F-4
Union Pt., 1645......F-8
Unionville, 2074......M-7
UPSON CO., 27679......H-5
Uvalda, 551......K-9
Valdosta, 45205......O-7
Vidalia, 11037......J-10
Vienna, 2952......K-6
Villa Rica, 9897......F-3
Vinings, 9677......*C-2
Vista Grove, 3000......*D-5
Waco, 506......F-2
Wadley, 2016......H-10
Waleska, 816......D-4
WALKER CO., 63890......C-2
Walthourville, 3631......L-12
WALTON CO., 75647......E-6
WARE CO., 34492......N-9
Warner Robins, 57907......I-7
WARREN CO., 6101......G-9
Warrenton, 2012......G-9
Warwick, 419......L-6
Washington, 4150......F-9
WASHINGTON CO., 20118......H-9
Watkinsville, 2535......E-7
Waverly Hall, 774......I-3
Waycross, 15112......N-10
WAYNE CO., 28390......L-11
Waynesboro, 5999......H-11
WEBSTER CO., 2289......K-4
W. Point, 3360......H-2
WHEELER CO., 6706......K-9
Whigham, 612......O-5
White, 716......D-4
WHITE CO., 24055......C-6
Whitesburg, 583......F-3
WHITFIELD CO., 90889......B-3
WILCOX CO., 8721......K-7
WILKES CO., 10457......E-9
WILKINSON CO., 10143......I-8
Willacoochee, 1506......M-8
Winder, 12451......E-6
Winterville, 1059......E-7
Woodbine, 1353......N-12
Woodbury, 1091......H-4
Woodland, 421......I-4
Woodstock, 19602......D-4
WORTH CO., 21996......M-6
Wrens, 2261......G-10
Wrightsville, 3183......I-9
Young Harris, 542......B-6
Zebulon, 1194......H-5

Hawaii

Map pp. 62-63

'Aiea, 9019......M-4
Anahola, 1932......I-2
Captain Cook, 3206......M-8
'Ewa Beach, 14650......N-3
'Ewa Villages, 4741......M-3
Hālawa Hts., 4000......M-4
Hale'iwa, 2225......L-3
Halimaile, 895......I-9
Hanamaulu, 3272......I-2
Hanapepe, 2153......I-2
Hau'ula, 3651......K-4
HAWAII CO., 167293......L-10
Hawi, 938......L-8
Hilo, 40759......M-10
Hōlualoa, 6107......M-8
Hōnaunau......M-8
Honoka'a, 2233......L-9
Honolulu, 377379......L-5
HONOLULU CO., 905266......L-5
Ka'a'awa, 1324......K-4
Kahalu'u, 2935......L-5
Kahuku, 2097......J-5
Kahului, 20146......K-7
Kailua, 36513......L-5
Kailua Kona, 9870......M-8
Kalāheo, 3913......I-2
Kāne'ohe, 34970......L-5
Kapa'a, 9472......I-2
KAUAI CO., 62640......I-2
Kaunakakai, 2726......I-6
Kea'au, 2010......M-10
Kealakekua, 1645......M-8
Kekaha, 3175......I-2
Keokea......K-8
Kīhei, 16749......K-7
Kīlauea, 2092......I-2
Koloa, 1942......I-2
Kurtistown, 1157......M-10
Lahaina, 9118......K-7
Lā'ie, 4585......J-4
Lān'ai City, 3164......K-7
Līhu'e, 5674......I-2
Lower Paia, 220......I-9
Mā'ili, 5943......M-2
Mākaha, 7753......L-1
Makakilo City, 13156......M-2
MAUI CO., 139884......J-7
Maunawili, 4869......M-5
Mililani Town, 28608......L-3
Nā'ālehu, 919......N-9
Nānākuli, 10814......J-4
Pa'auilo, 571......J-9
Pacific Palisades, 5600......M-3
Pāhala, 1378......N-9
Pāhoa, 962......M-10
Paia, 2499......I-9
Pāpa'ikou, 1414......M-10
Pearl City, 30976......J-5
Pukalani, 7380......K-8
Sunset Beach, 660......J-3
Volcano, 2231......M-9
Wahiawā, 16151......J-5
Waiakoa, 900......I-9
Waialua, 3761......K-2
Wai'anae, 10506......J-4
Wailua, 2083......I-2
Wailuku, 12296......K-7
Waimānalo, 3664......J-5
Waimānalo Beach, 4271......M-6
Waimea, 1787......I-2
Waimea, 7028......L-9
Waipahu, 33108......M-3
Waipi'o Acres, 5298......L-1
Whitmore Vil., 4057......L-3

Idaho

Map pp. 64-65

Aberdeen, 1828......L-6
ADA CO., 344727......K-2
ADAMS CO., 3591......H-2
Albion, 258......M-5
American Falls, 4162......L-6
Ammon, 10925......K-8
Arco, 989......K-6
Arimo, 319......M-7
Ashton, 1105......J-8
Athol, 707......C-2
Bancroft, 363......L-8
BANNOCK CO., 78155......L-7
Basalt, 427......K-7
Bayview, 350......C-2
BEAR LAKE CO., 6176......N-9
Bellevue, 2203......K-5
BENEWAH CO., 9218......D-2
BINGHAM CO., 43739......L-6
Blackfoot, 10828......L-7
BLAINE CO., 21166......L-6
BOISE CO., 7535......J-3
Boise, 193161......K-2
BONNER CO., 40908......C-2
Bonners Ferry, 2725......B-2
BONNEVILLE CO., 91856......K-8
BOUNDARY CO., 10619......B-2
Bovill, 285......E-2
Buhl, 4015......M-4
Burley, 9131......M-5
BUTTE CO., 2808......K-6
Caldwell, 34433......K-1
CAMAS CO., 1050......K-4
Cambridge, 354......I-2
CANYON CO., 164593......K-1
Carey, 511......K-5
CARIBOU CO., 7131......L-8
Cascade, 1005......I-2
CASSIA CO., 21324......M-5
Challis, 844......I-5
Chubbuck, 10707......L-7
CLARK CO., 943......I-7
Clark Fk., 578......C-2
CLEARWATER CO., 8373......E-3
Cobalt......H-5
Coeur d'Alene, 40059......D-2
Cottonwood, 1070......F-2
Council, 742......I-2
Craigmont, 548......F-2
Culdesac, 375......F-2
CUSTER CO., 4077......J-5
Dalton Gardens, 2400......C-2
Dayton, 463......N-8
Deary, 515......E-2
Declo, 332......M-5
Downey, 577......M-7
Driggs, 1197......K-9
Dubois, 642......J-7
Eagle, 17338......K-2
Eden, 416......M-5
Elk City, 300......G-3
Elk River, 142......E-2
ELMORE CO., 28634......L-3
Emmett, 6124......J-2
Fairfield, 392......K-4
Fernwood, 425......E-2
Filer, 1768......M-4
Firth, 417......K-7
Ft. Hall, 1200......L-7
FRANKLIN CO., 12371......M-8
Franklin, 673......N-8
FREMONT CO., 12242......J-8
Fruitland, 4406......J-1
Garden City, 11424......B-5
GEM CO., 16273......J-2
Genesee, 879......F-1
Georgetown, 494......M-8
Glenns Ferry, 1451......L-3
GOODING CO., 14461......L-4
Gooding, 3320......L-4
Grace, 972......M-8
Grand View, 477......L-2
Grangeville, 3151......G-2
Greenleaf, 890......K-1
Hagerman, 838......L-4
Hailey, 7583......K-5
Hammett, 300......L-3
Hansen, 961......M-5
Harrison, 282......D-2
Hayden, 11906......C-2
Hayden Lake, 540......C-2
Hazelton, 720......M-5
Headquarters, 35......E-3
Heyburn, 2755......M-5
Homedale, 2577......K-1
Horseshoe Bend, 834......J-2
IDAHO CO., 15697......G-3
Idaho City, 488......K-3
Idaho Falls, 52338......K-7
Inkom, 686......L-7
Iona, 1256......K-8
JEFFERSON CO., 21580......J-7
Jerome, 8503......M-4
JEROME CO., 19638......L-5
Juliaetta, 561......F-2
Kamiah, 1148......F-2
Kellogg, 2298......D-2
Kendrick, 344......E-2
Ketchum, 3145......K-4
Kimberly, 2686......M-4
Kingston, 800......C-2
Kooskia, 665......F-2
Kootenai, 480......B-2
KOOTENAI CO., 127668......C-2
Kuna, 10153......K-2
Laclede, 400......C-2
Lapwai, 1116......F-1
LATAH CO., 34714......E-2
Lava Hot Sprs., 504......M-8
LEMHI CO., 7909......H-5
LEWIS CO., 3750......F-2
Lewiston, 31081......F-1
Lewisville, 497......K-7
LINCOLN CO., 4545......L-5
Lincoln, 500......K-8
Mackay, 529......J-5
MADISON CO., 30975......K-8
Malad City, 2124......M-7
Marsing, 976......K-1
Marysville, 180......J-8
McCall, 2415......I-2
McCammon, 789......M-7
Melba, 544......K-2
Menan, 726......K-8
Meridian, 52240......K-2
Middleton, 4409......K-2
MINIDOKA CO., 19014......L-5
Montpelier, 2507......M-8
Moreland, 500......L-7
Moscow, 21862......E-1
Mtn. Home, 11565......L-3
Moyie Sprs., 722......B-2
Mullan, 788......D-3
Nampa, 71713......K-2
Newdale, 360......J-8
New Meadows, 492......H-2
New Plymouth, 1403......J-1
NEZ PERCE CO., 37931......F-1
Nezperce, 514......F-2
Notus, 540......K-1
Oakley, 663......M-5
ONEIDA CO., 4209......M-6
Orofino, 3145......F-2
Osburn, 1458......D-2
OWYHEE CO., 11073......M-2
Paris, 518......M-8
Parker, 321......J-8
Parma, 1799......K-1
Paul, 947......M-5
Payette, 7560......J-1
PAYETTE CO., 22197......J-2
Pierce, 551......F-3
Pinehurst, 1588......D-2
Plummer, 985......D-1
Pocatello, 53372......L-7
Ponderay, 807......B-2
Post Falls, 23162......C-1
Potlatch, 735......E-1
POWER CO., 7753......M-7
Preston, 5019......N-8
Priest River, 1909......C-1
Rathdrum, 5740......C-1
Rexburg, 26265......J-8
Richfield, 437......L-5
Rigby, 3245......K-8
Riggins, 404......H-2
Ririe, 531......K-8
Roberts, 665......K-7
Rockland, 330......M-6
Rupert, 5225......M-5
St. Anthony, 3348......J-8
St. Maries, 2634......D-2
Salmon, 3072......H-5
Sandpoint, 8105......B-2
Shelley, 4131......K-7
SHOSHONE CO., 13157......D-3
Shoshone, 1574......L-4
Silverton, 300......D-3
Smelterville, 618......D-2
Soda Sprs., 3256......M-8
Spirit Lake, 1500......C-1
Star, 2767......K-2
Stites, 229......F-2
Sugar City, 1479......J-8
Sun Valley, 1444......K-4
TETON CO., 7467......K-8
Teton, 573......J-8
Troy, 744......E-2
TWIN FALLS CO., 69419......M-4
Twin Falls, 38630......M-4
Ucon, 1015......K-8
VALLEY CO., 8332......I-3
Victor, 1365......K-9
Wallace, 907......D-3
WASHINGTON CO., 10098......I-1
Weippe, 390......F-3
Weiser, 5420......I-1
Wendell, 2396......L-4
Weston, 450......N-8
Wilder, 1451......K-1
Winchester, 308......F-2

Illinois

Map pp. 66-73

* City keyed to pp. 70-73
‡ City keyed to p. 120

Abingdon, 3379......G-6
ADAMS CO., 67040......J-4
Addison, 36811......*H-5
Albany, 904......C-6
Albers, 994......O-8
Albion, 1892......P-12
Aledo, 3535......E-5
ALEXANDER CO., 8927......T-8
Alexis, 823......F-5
Algonquin, 29022......B-11
Alorton, 2620......‡F-8
Alpha, 704......E-6
Alsip, 19072......*K-8
Altamont, 2259......M-10
Alton, 29433......N-6
Amboy, 2570......C-8
Andalusia, 1059......D-5
Anna, 5070......S-9
Annawan, 919......E-7
Antioch, 12353......A-12
Arbury Hills, 1770......*M-7
Arcola, 2662......K-11
Argenta, 852......J-10
Arlington Hts., 74620......B-12
Aroma Park, 802......F-13
Arthur, 2180......K-11
Ashland, 1376......J-7
Ashton, 1195......C-9
Assumption, 1231......K-9
Astoria, 1160......I-6
Athens, 1800......I-7
Atkinson, 975......E-7
Atlanta, 1671......I-9
Atwood, 1250......I-11
Auburn, 4274......K-7
Aurora, 168181......C-11
Ava, 654......Q-8
Aviston, 1540......O-8
Avon, 881......G-5
Bannockburn, 1609......*D-7
Barrington, 10179......B-12
Barrington Hills, 4258......*E-3
Barry, 1330......K-4
Bartlett, 38479......*G-3

2000 Census populations or latest available estimate.
Index to Canada and Mexico cities and towns, pages 274-275.

Bartonville, 6146 G-8
Batavia, 27172 C-11
Beach Park, 12486 A-12
Beardstown, 5876 J-5
Beckemeyer, 1071 O-8
Beecher, 2769 E-13
Belleville, 41143 O-7
Bellevue, 1808 *C-15
Bellwood, 19517 *H-7
Belvidere, 24593 A-10
Bement, 1739 J-11
Benld, 1491 M-7
Bensenville, 20514 *G-6
Benton, 6930 Q-10
Berkeley, 5006 *H-6
Berwyn, 51409 *I-8
Bethalto, 9660 N-6
Bethany, 1261 K-10
Bismarck, 551 I-13
Blandinsville, 719 H-4
Bloomingdale, 21924 C-12
Bloomington, 69749 H-9
Blue Island, 22788 *L-9
Blue Mound, 1056 K-9
Bluffs, 729 K-5
Bolingbrook, 68365 D-12
BOND CO., 18027 M-8
BOONE CO., 50483 A-10
Bourbonnais, 16875 E-12
Bradford, 765 E-8
Bradley, 13812 F-13
Braidwood, 6320 E-12
Brandywine, 3100 *I-6
Breese, 4202 O-8
Bridgeport, 2148 N-13
Bridgeview, 14933 *J-7
Brighton, 2324 M-6
Brimfield, 900 G-7
Broadview, 7856 *I-7
Brookfield, 18462 *I-7
Brookport, 1061 T-10
BROWN CO., 6835 J-5
Brownstown, 708 M-10
Buffalo Gr., 43115 *D-6
Bunker Hill, 1795 M-7
Burbank, 27634 *J-8
BUREAU CO., 35330 D-8
Burnham, 4080 *L-10
Burr Ridge, 10949 *J-6
Bushnell, 3022 H-5
Butterfield, 3750 *I-5
Byron, 3582 B-9
Cahokia, 15608 O-6
Cairo, 3342 T-9
CALHOUN CO., 5163 L-4
Calumet City, 37795 *L-10
Calumet Park, 8124 *L-9
Cambria, 1338 R-9
Cambridge, 2121 E-6
Camp Pt., 1191 I-4
Canton, 14938 H-7
Capron, 1326 A-10
Carbon Cliff, 1681 T-5
Carbondale, 24806 R-9
Carlinville, 5768 L-7
Carlyle, 3377 O-8
Carmi, 5414 Q-12
Carol Stream, 40040 *H-4
Carpentersville, 37204 B-11
Carrier Mills, 1841 R-10
CARROLL CO., 16086 B-7
Carrollton, 2519 L-5
Carterville, 5099 R-9
Carthage, 2548 H-3
Cary, 19115 B-11
Casey, 2948 L-12
Caseyville, 4297 O-6
CASS CO., 13898 J-6
Catlin, 2051 I-13
Cedarville, 705 A-8
Central City, 1342 O-9
Centralia, 13600 O-9
Centreville, 5837 ‡F-8
Cerro Gordo, 1385 J-10
CHAMPAIGN CO., 184905 I-11
Champaign, 71568 I-11
Chandlerville, 716 I-6
Channahon, 12218 D-12
Charleston, 20189 L-12
Chatham, 9787 K-7
Chatsworth, 1221 G-11
Chebanse, 1101 F-12
Chenoa, 1805 G-10
Cherry Valley, 2228 B-9
Chester, 7872 Q-7
Chicago, 2842518 C-13
Chicago Hts., 31373 D-13
Chicago Ridge, 13668 *K-8
Chillicothe, 5781 F-8
Chrisman, 1259 J-13
CHRISTIAN CO., 35176 L-8
Christopher, 2833 Q-9
Cicero, 82741 C-13
Cisne, 662 O-11
Cissna Park, 774 H-12
Clarendon Hills, 8397 *I-6
CLARK CO., 16976 L-13
CLAY CO., 14122 N-11
Clay City, 961 N-11
Clayton, 841 J-4
Clifton, 1279 F-12
CLINTON CO., 36095 N-8
Clinton, 7261 I-9
Coal City, 5170 E-11
Coal Valley, 3904 D-5
Cobden, 1102 S-9
Coffeen, 708 M-8
Colchester, 1394 H-4
COLES CO., 51065 K-11
Colfax, 991 H-10
Collinsville, 25487 N-7
Colona, 5275 T-6
Columbia, 8902 O-6
COOK CO., 5303683 D-12
Cottage Hills, 980 ‡A-8
Coulterville, 1189 P-8
Country Club Hills, 16534 *M-8
Countryside, 5831 *J-7
CRAWFORD CO., 19898 M-13
Creal Sprs., 718 R-10
Crest Hill, 19438 *M-4
Crestwood, 11207 *L-8
Crete, 8772 D-13
Creve Coeur, 5261 G-8
Crossville, 746 P-12
Crystal Lake, 40922 B-11
Crystal Lawns, 2933 *M-4
Cuba, 1382 H-6
CUMBERLAND CO., 10973 L-11
Dallas City, 1011 G-3
Danvers, 1132 H-9
Danville, 32920 I-13
Darien, 22730 *J-5
Decatur, 77836 J-10
Deer Cr., 700 G-8
Deerfield, 19471 *D-7
Deer Park, 3253 *D-4
DEKALB CO., 97665 C-10
De Kalb, 42085 C-10
Delavan, 1777 H-8
De Pue, 1791 E-9
De Soto, 1583 R-9
Des Plaines, 56551 B-12
DE WITT CO., 16617 I-9
Diamond, 2105 E-11
Diamond Lake, 1500 *C-5
Divernon, 1145 K-8
Dixmoor, 3813 *L-9
Dixon, 15372 C-8
Dolton, 24504 *L-10
Dongola, 803 S-9
DOUGLAS CO., 19950 K-11
Downers Gr., 49094 *I-5
Downs, 745 H-10
Dunlap, 904 G-8
DUPAGE CO., 929113 C-12
Dupo, 3957 O-6
Du Quoin, 6412 Q-9
Durand, 1077 A-8
Dwight, 4360 F-11
Earlville, 1821 D-10
E. Alton, 6609 N-6
E. Dubuque, 1985 A-5
E. Dundee, 3138 *E-2
E. Galesburg, 799 F-6
E. Hazel Crest, 1570 *M-9
E. Moline, 21250 D-6
E. Peoria, 22536 G-8
E. St. Louis, 29843 O-6
EDGAR CO., 19157 K-13
Edinburg, 1140 K-8
EDWARDS CO., 6784 O-12
Edwardsville, 24047 N-7
Effingham, 12440 M-11
EFFINGHAM CO., 34581 M-10
Elburn, 4236 C-11
Eldorado, 4416 R-11
Elgin, 98645 B-11
Elizabeth, 673 A-6
Elk Grove Vil., 34025 *F-5
Elkville, 939 Q-9
Elmhurst, 44976 C-12
Elmwood, 1893 G-7
Elmwood Pk., 24499 *H-7
El Paso, 2748 G-9
Elsah, 640 M-6
Elwood, 2237 E-12
Energy, 1177 R-9
Enfield, 625 Q-11
Equality, 687 R-11
Erie, 1573 D-6
Eureka, 5084 G-9
Evanston, 75236 B-13
Evansville, 697 Q-7
Evergreen Pk., 19876 *K-8
Fairbury, 3919 G-11
Fairfield, 5230 P-11
Fairmont, 2563 *M-4
Fairmont City, 2324 ‡E-8
Fairmount, 642 J-13
Fairview Hts., 16471 O-7
Farmer City, 2005 I-10
Farmingdale, 970 *J-6
Farmington, 2514 G-7
FAYETTE CO., 21713 M-9
Findlay, 685 K-10
Fisher, 1654 I-11
Flanagan, 1061 G-10
Flora, 4855 O-11
Flossmoor, 9390 *M-9
FORD CO., 14157 H-11
Ford Hts., 3294 *N-10
Forest Homes, 1700 ‡A-8
Forest Lake, 1530 *C-5
Forest Park, 15197 *I-7
Forest View, 739 *I-8
Forrest, 1202 G-11
Forreston, 1515 B-8
Fox Lake, 10736 A-12
Fox River Gr., 5084 B-11
Frankfort, 15819 D-12
FRANKLIN CO., 39723 Q-10
Franklin Gr., 1019 C-9
Franklin Pk., 18490 *G-7
Freeburg, 4092 O-7
Freeport, 25612 A-8
Fulton, 3853 C-6
FULTON CO., 37708 H-6
Gages Lake, 10415 *A-5
Galatia, 988 R-10
Galena, 3405 A-6
Galesburg, 32017 F-6
GALLATIN CO., 6152 R-12
Galva, 2705 E-7
Gardner, 1436 E-11
Geneseo, 6524 D-6
Geneva, 23424 C-11
Genoa, 4671 B-10
Georgetown, 3516 J-13
Germantown, 1105 O-8
Gibson City, 3281 H-11
Gifford, 999 I-12
Gilberts, 4869 *E-1
Gillespie, 3278 M-7
Gilman, 1788 G-12
Girard, 2237 L-7
Glasford, 1038 H-7
Glen Carbon, 11932 ‡C-9
Glencoe, 8979 B-13
Glendale Hts., 32465 *H-4
Glen Ellyn, 27193 *H-5
Glen Ellyn Countryside, 2500 *H-4
Glenview, 45989 *E-7
Glenview Countryside, 1950 *F-7
Glenwood, 8663 *M-10
Godfrey, 16996 M-6
Golconda, 668 S-11
Goreville, 970 S-9
Grafton, 692 M-5
Grand Tower, 589 R-8
Grandview, 1445 *F-17
Granite City, 30796 N-6
Grant Park, 1557 E-13
Granville, 1388 E-9
Grayslake, 21099 *B-5
Grayville, 1638 P-12
GREENE CO., 14581 L-5
Greenfield, 1142 L-6
Green Oaks, 3914 *B-6
Greenup, 1494 L-12
Green Valley, 702 H-8
Greenview, 823 I-7
Greenville, 7067 N-8
Gridley, 1398 G-10
Griggsville, 1215 K-5
GRUNDY CO., 43838 E-10
Gurnee, 30772 *A-6
Hamilton, 2838 H-3
HAMILTON CO., 8301 Q-11
Hampshire, 4077 B-11
Hampton, 1746 S-5
HANCOCK CO., 19153 I-3
Hanna City, 988 G-7
Hanover, 797 A-6
Hanover Pk., 37229 *G-4
HARDIN CO., 4718 S-11
Hardin, 952 M-5
Harrisburg, 9628 R-11
Harristown, 1259 J-9
Hartford, 1492 ‡B-8
Harvard, 9104 A-10
Harvey, 28771 D-13
Harwood Hts., 8188 *G-7
Havana, 3476 I-6
Hawthorn Woods, 7176 *C-5
Hazel Crest, 14415 *M-9
Hebron, 1141 A-11
HENDERSON CO., 7972 G-4
Henry, 2530 F-8
HENRY CO., 50591 E-6
Herrin, 11688 R-9
Herscher, 1554 F-12
Heyworth, 2470 I-9
Hickory Hills, 13542 *K-7
Highland, 9200 N-7
Highland Hills, 200 *I-5
Highland Pk., 31380 B-13
Highwood, 5468 B-13
Hillcrest, 1295 C-9
Hillsboro, 4272 M-8
Hillside, 7771 *H-6
Hinckley, 2050 C-10
Hinsdale, 17898 *I-6
Hodgkins, 2073 *J-7
Hoffman Estates, 52046 *F-3
Holiday Hills, 813 *B-3
Hollywood Hts., 1060 ‡E-9
Homer, 1157 J-12
Homer Glen, 24736 *L-6
Hometown, 4241 *K-8
Homewood, 18917 *M-9
Hoopeston, 5753 H-13
Hopedale, 913 H-8
Hudson, 1664 H-9
Huntley, 17674 B-11
Hurst, 791 R-9
Illiopolis, 867 J-9
Indian Head Park, 3656 *J-6
Ingalls Park, 3082 *N-5
Ingleside, 1700 *A-4
Inverness, 7343 *E-5
IROQUOIS CO., 30677 G-12
Island Lake, 8419 *B-3
Itasca, 8444 *G-5
JACKSON CO., 57954 Q-8
Jacksonville, 19470 K-6
JASPER CO., 10020 M-12
JEFFERSON CO., 40434 O-9
Jerome, 1327 *G-16
JERSEY CO., 22456 M-5
Jerseyville, 8187 M-6
JO DAVIESS CO., 22580 A-6
JOHNSON CO., 13169 S-10
Johnston City, 3476 R-10
Joliet, 136208 D-12
Jonesboro, 1843 S-9
Justice, 12692 *J-7
KANE CO., 482113 B-11
KANKAKEE CO., 107972 F-13
Kankakee, 26642 F-13
Kansas, 826 K-12
Keithsburg, 713 F-4
KENDALL CO., 79514 D-11
Kenilworth, 2445 *E-8
Kewanee, 12655 E-7
Kildeer, 4004 *D-5
Kincaid, 1468 K-8
Kinmundy, 871 N-10
Kirkland, 1607 B-10
Kirkwood, 724 F-5
Knollwood, 1500 *B-7
KNOX CO., 53309 F-6
Knoxville, 3005 F-6
Lacon, 1923 F-8
Ladd, 1305 E-9
La Grange, 15482 *I-7
La Grange Highlands, 3650 *J-6
La Grange Pk., 12726 *I-7
La Harpe, 1323 H-4
LAKE CO., 702682 B-12
Lake Barrington, 5033 *C-4
Lake Bluff, 6251 A-13
Lake Forest, 21123 B-13
Lake in the Hills, 28786 *D-2
Lakemoor, 5085 A-12
Lake Villa, 8492 A-12
Lakewood, 3502 *C-1
Lake Zurich, 20045 B-12
La Moille, 760 D-9
Lanark, 1483 B-7
Lansing, 27324 *M-10
La Salle, 9510 E-9
LA SALLE CO., 112604 E-9
LAWRENCE CO., 15930 O-13
Lawrenceville, 4513 N-13
Lebanon, 3749 O-7
LEE CO., 35669 C-8
Leland, 942 D-10
Leland Gr., 1481 *F-16
Lemont, 15146 *K-5
Lena, 2854 A-7
Le Roy, 3391 H-10
Lewistown, 2448 H-6
Lexington, 1866 G-10
Libertyville, 21760 A-12
Lincoln, 14971 I-8
Lincolnshire, 6841 *D-6
Lincolnwood, 12026 *F-8
Lindenhurst, 14403 A-12
Lisle, 23376 C-12
Litchfield, 6771 M-8
Livingston, 797 M-7
LIVINGSTON CO., 39186 F-10
Lockport, 22161 D-12
LOGAN CO., 30603 I-8
Lombard, 42816 *H-5
Long Gr., 7833 *D-5
Long Lake, 3356 *A-4
Louisville, 1256 N-11
Loves Park, 22983 A-9
Lovington, 1196 K-10
Lyndon, 546 C-7
Lynwood, 7655 *N-10
Lyons, 10466 *I-7
Machesney Pk., 21846 A-9
Mackinaw, 1614 H-8
Macomb, 18587 H-5
MACON CO., 110167 J-9
Macon, 1151 K-9
MACOUPIN CO., 49111 M-7
MADISON CO., 264309 N-7
Madison, 4558 ‡D-7
Mahomet, 5714 I-11
Malta, 963 C-10
Manhattan, 5169 E-12
Manito, 1702 H-7
Mansfield, 939 I-11
Manteno, 7955 E-13
Maple Park, 1132 C-10
Marengo, 7381 B-10
Marine, 940 N-7
MARION CO., 40144 O-10
Marion, 17104 R-10
Marissa, 2044 P-7
Markham, 12304 *L-9
Maroa, 1563 J-10
Marseilles, 4860 E-10
Marshall, 3724 L-13
MARSHALL CO., 13217 F-8
Martinsville, 1230 L-13
Maryville, 6629 ‡D-10
Mascoutah, 5824 O-7
MASON CO., 15741 I-7
Mason City, 2473 I-7
MASSAC CO., 15348 T-10
Matherville, 780 E-5
Matteson, 15675 *N-8
Mattoon, 17385 L-11
Maywood, 25777 *H-7
Mazon, 918 E-11
McClure, 600 S-8
McCullom Lake, 1037 *A-2
MCDONOUGH CO., 31966 H-4
McHenry, 24863 A-11
MCHENRY CO., 303990 A-10
MCLEAN CO., 159013 G-10
McLean, 783 I-9
McLeansboro, 2776 Q-11
Meadowbrook, 1000 ‡A-9
Melrose Park, 22512 *H-7
MENARD CO., 12738 I-7
Mendon, 875 I-3
Mendota, 7077 D-9
MERCER CO., 16912 E-5
Meredosia, 996 J-5
Merrionette Park, 2047 *K-9
Metamora, 3067 G-8
Metropolis, 6468 T-10
Midlothian, 13949 *L-8
Milan, 5237 T-3
Milford, 1310 G-13
Milledgeville, 946 C-7
Millstadt, 3067 O-6
Minier, 1255 H-9
Minonk, 2158 F-9
Minooka, 8403 D-11
Mitchell, 1300 ‡C-8
Moecherville, 1320 *J-2
Mokena, 17396 *M-6
Moline, 42892 D-5
Momence, 3066 E-13
Monee, 4629 E-13
Monmouth, 9198 F-5
MONROE CO., 31040 P-6
Montgomery, 11959 C-11
MONTGOMERY CO., 30396 L-8
Monticello, 5275 J-11
MORGAN CO., 35722 J-6
Morris, 12939 E-11
Morrison, 4318 C-7
Morrisonville, 1050 L-8
Morton, 15761 G-8
Morton Gr., 22202 *F-8
MOULTRIE CO., 14510 K-10
Mound City, 633 T-9
Mounds, 1008 T-9
Mt. Carmel, 7690 O-13
Mt. Carroll, 1704 B-7
Mt. Morris, 3066 B-8
Mt. Olive, 2100 M-7
Mt. Prospect, 54482 *F-6
Mt. Pulaski, 1632 J-9
Mt. Sterling, 2011 J-4
Mt. Vernon, 16344 P-10
Mt. Zion, 5032 K-10
Moweaqua, 1845 K-9
Mulberry Gr., 675 N-9
Mundelein, 32774 *C-5
Murphysboro, 8288 R-8
Naperville, 141579 C-12
Nashville, 3083 P-8
Nauvoo, 1155 H-3
Neoga, 1770 L-11
Newark, 1031 D-11
New Athens, 2011 P-7
New Baden, 3048 O-7
New Berlin, 1129 K-7
New Boston, 643 E-4
New Lenox, 23197 D-12
Newman, 936 J-12
Newton, 3038 M-12
New Windsor, 707 E-5
Niantic, 690 J-9
Niles, 29330 *F-7
Noble, 713 N-12
Nokomis, 2317 L-9
Normal, 49927 H-9
Norridge, 14054 *G-7
Norris City, 1059 Q-11
N. Aurora, 14394 C-11
N. Barrington, 3207 *C-4
Northbrook, 34190 *E-7
N. Chicago, 33376 A-12
Northfield, 5543 *E-8
N. Glen Ellyn, 1400 *H-5
Northlake, 11358 *H-6
N. Riverside, 6382 *I-7
Oak Brook, 8835 *I-6
Oakbrook Ter., 2249 *I-6
Oak Forest, 28116 *L-8
Oak Gr., 721 E-5
Oakland, 943 K-12
Oak Lawn, 53991 C-13
Oak Park, 50757 C-13
Oakwood, 1466 I-13
Oakwood Hills, 2348 *C-3
Oblong, 1554 M-12
Odell, 1022 F-11
Odin, 1082 O-9
O'Fallon, 25155 O-7
Ogden, 737 I-12
OGLE CO., 54290 B-9
Oglesby, 3621 E-9
Okawville, 1333 O-8
Olney, 8470 N-12
Olympia Fields, 4673 *N-9
Onarga, 1396 G-12
Oneida, 717 F-6
Oquawka, 1473 F-4
Oreana, 951 J-10
Oregon, 4163 B-8
Orion, 1703 E-6
Orland Hills, 7273 *M-7
Orland Park, 55461 D-12
Oswego, 23330 D-11
Ottawa, 18824 E-10
Palatine, 67232 B-12
Palestine, 1342 M-13
Palmyra, 730 L-7
Palos Hts., 12561 *L-7
Palos Hills, 17258 *K-7
Palos Park, 4757 *K-7
Pana, 5529 L-9
Paris, 8834 K-13
Park City, 6775 *A-7
Park Forest, 23036 D-13
Park Ridge, 36983 *F-7
Pawnee, 2569 K-8
Paw Paw, 857 D-9
Paxton, 4534 H-12
Pecatonica, 2161 A-8
Pekin, 33331 H-8
PEORIA CO., 182328 F-7
Peoria, 112685 G-8
Peoria Hts., 6298 G-8
Peotone, 3981 E-13
Percy, 942 Q-8
PERRY CO., 22815 Q-8
Peru, 9815 E-9
Petersburg, 2240 J-7
Philo, 1532 J-12
Phoenix, 2069 *L-9
PIATT CO., 16680 I-10
PIKE CO., 17099 K-4
Pinckneyville, 5452 Q-8
Piper City, 749 G-12
Pittsfield, 4599 K-4
Plainfield, 28162 D-12
Plano, 7338 D-11
Pleasant Hill, 1012 L-4
Pleasant Plains, 738 J-7
Pocahontas, 728 N-8
Polo, 2507 B-8
Pontiac, 11457 G-10
Pontoon Beach, 6046 ‡D-8
POPE CO., 4211 S-11
Poplar Gr., 3077 A-10
Port Byron, 1623 D-6
Posen, 4929 *L-9
Potomac, 666 I-13
Prairie Du Rocher, 589 Q-6
Preston Hts., 2527 *N-4
Princeton, 7554 E-8
Princeville, 1574 F-7
Prophetstown, 1960 D-7
Prospect Hts., 16387 *E-6
PULASKI CO., 6794 T-9
PUTNAM CO., 6094 E-8
Quincy, 39841 J-3
Ramsey, 1063 M-9
RANDOLPH CO., 33122 P-7
Rankin, 599 H-12
Rantoul, 12483 I-12
Rapids City, 980 D-6
Raymond, 922 L-8
Red Bud, 3522 P-7
RICHLAND CO., 15798 O-12
Richmond, 2215 A-11
Richton Park, 12998 D-13
Ridge Farm, 877 J-13
Ridgway, 885 R-12
Riverdale, 14588 *L-9
River Forest, 11289 *H-7
River Gr., 10216 *H-7
Riverside, 8485 *I-7
Riverton, 3043 J-8
Riverwoods, 4100 *D-7
Roanoke, 1988 G-9
Robbins, 6375 *L-9
Robinson, 6471 M-13
Rochelle, 9712 C-9
Rochester, 3004 K-8
Rockdale, 2018 *N-4
Rock Falls, 9470 C-8
Rockford, 152916 A-9
Rock Island, 38702 D-5
ROCK ISLAND CO., 147808 E-4
Rockton, 5348 A-9
Rolling Meadows, 23909 *E-5
Rome, 1776 G-8
Romeoville, 36396 D-12
Roodhouse, 2217 L-6
Roscoe, 6355 A-9
Roselle, 23240 B-12
Rosemont, 4037 *G-7
Roseville, 998 G-5
Rosewood Hts., 4262 ‡A-8
Rosiclare, 1168 S-11
Rossville, 1183 H-13
Round Lake, 14803 *A-4
Round Lake Beach, 28253 *A-4
Round Lake Hts., 2370 *A-4
Round Lake Park, 6224 *A-4
Roxana, 1504 N-6
Royalton, 1171 Q-9
Rushville, 3162 I-5
St. Anne, 1214 F-13
St. Charles, 32332 C-11
ST. CLAIR CO., 260067 O-6
St. David, 568 H-6
St. Elmo, 1435 M-10
St. Francisville, 751 O-13
St. Jacob, 892 N-7
St. Joseph, 3629 I-12
Salem, 7574 O-10
SALINE CO., 26072 Q-11
Sandoval, 1362 O-9
Sandwich, 7018 D-10
SANGAMON CO., 192789 K-7
Sauk Vil., 10486 *N-10
Savanna, 3288 B-6
Savoy, 4839 J-11
Saybrook, 736 H-11
Schaumburg, 72805 *F-4
Schiller Park, 11597 *G-7
Schram City, 631 M-8
SCHUYLER CO., 7073 I-4
SCOTT CO., 5412 K-5
Seneca, 2057 E-10
Sesser, 2136 Q-9
Shabbona, 943 C-10
Shannon, 799 B-7
Shawneetown, 1345 R-12
Sheffield, 957 E-7
SHELBY CO., 22322 K-10
Shelbyville, 4739 L-10
Sheldon, 1178 G-13
Sheridan, 2226 D-10
Sherman, 3465 J-8
Sherrard, 671 E-5
Shiloh, 10367 ‡F-10
Shorewood, 12114 D-12
Sidney, 1103 J-12
Signal Hill, 1160 ‡F-8
Silvis, 7489 S-5
Skokie, 64678 B-13
Sleepy Hollow, 3695 *E-2
Smithton, 2870 O-7
Somonauk, 1492 D-10
S. Barrington, 3935 *E-4
S. Beloit, 5421 A-9
S. Chicago Heights, 3873 *N-9
S. Elgin, 20758 *G-2
Southern View, 1682 *G-16
S. Holland, 21552 *M-10
S. Jacksonville, 3329 K-6
S. Roxana, 1826 ‡B-8
S. Streator, 500 F-10
S. Wilmington, 625 E-11
Sparta, 4395 Q-7
Springfield, 115668 J-8
Spring Valley, 5380 E-9
Stanford, 644 H-9
STARK CO., 6169 F-7
State Park Place, 2600 ‡E-9
Staunton, 5109 M-7
Steeleville, 2058 Q-7
Steger, 10409 D-13
STEPHENSON CO., 47965 A-7
Sterling, 15381 C-8
Stewardson, 730 L-10
Stickney, 5899 *I-8
Stillman Valley, 1097 B-9
Stockton, 1820 A-7
Stone Park, 4905 *H-7
Stonington, 924 K-9
Streamwood, 37312 *F-3
Streator, 13899 F-10
Stronghurst, 846 G-4
Sugar Gr., 8416 C-11
Sullivan, 4323 K-10
Summit, 10348 *J-7
Sumner, 1820 N-13
Swansea, 12274 O-7
Sycamore, 14831 B-10
Tallula, 630 J-7
Tamaroa, 732 P-9
Tamms, 1150 T-9
Tampico, 745 D-7
Taylor Sprs., 581 M-8
Taylorville, 11240 K-9
TAZEWELL CO., 129999 H-8
Teutopolis, 1634 M-11
Thayer, 705 K-7
Thomasboro, 1222 I-12
Thornton, 2458 *M-10
Tilden, 902 P-7
Tilton, 2847 I-13
Tinley Park, 57477 D-13
Tiskilwa, 768 E-8
Toledo, 1143 L-11
Tolono, 2776 J-11
Toluca, 1311 F-9
Tonica, 698 E-9
Toulon, 1368 F-7
Tower Hill, 602 L-9
Tower Lakes, 1329 *C-4
Tremont, 2065 H-8
Trenton, 2651 O-7
Tri-State Vil., 1200 *J-6
Troy, 9374 N-7
Tuscola, 4583 J-11
UNION CO., 18202 S-9
University Park, 8102 D-13
Urbana, 38463 I-12
Utica, 984 E-9
Valier, 660 Q-9
Valley View, 700 *G-2
Vandalia, 6811 M-9
Venice, 2448 ‡E-7
VERMILION CO., 82344 H-13
Vermont, 781 H-5
Vernon Hills, 23957 *C-6
Vienna, 1304 S-10
Villa Gr., 2507 J-12
Villa Hills, 1410 ‡G-8
Villa Park, 22616 *H-5
Viola, 966 E-5
Virden, 3472 K-7
Virginia, 1730 J-6
WABASH CO., 12570 O-13
Wadsworth, 3651 A-12
Walnut, 1421 D-8
Wamac, 1297 O-9
WARREN CO., 17558 G-5
Warren, 1421 A-7
Warrensburg, 1209 J-9
Warrenville, 13217 *I-3
Warsaw, 1648 H-3
Washburn, 1107 F-9
WASHINGTON CO., 14922 P-8
Washington, 12759 G-8
Washington Park, 5740 ‡E-8
Wataga, 810 F-6
Waterloo, 9225 P-6
Waterman, 1214 C-10
Watseka, 5547 G-13
Wauconda, 10903 A-12
Waukegan, 91396 A-12
Waverly, 1272 K-7
WAYNE CO., 16796 O-11
Wayne, 2355 *G-3
Wayne City, 1075 P-11
Wenona, 1077 F-9
Westchester, 16177 *I-6
W. Chicago, 26554 *H-3
W. City, 737 Q-10
W. Dundee, 7875 B-11
Western Sprs., 12530 *I-6
Westfield, 669 L-12
W. Frankfort, 8285 Q-10
Westmont, 24863 *J-5
W. Peoria, 4710 *C-16
W. Salem, 977 O-12
Westville, 3058 J-13
Wheaton, 54700 C-12
Wheeling, 36641 *E-6
WHITE CO., 15284 P-11
White Hall, 2609 L-5
WHITESIDE CO., 59863 C-7
Wildwood, 40 *A-5
WILL CO., 642813 D-12
WILLIAMSON CO., 63617 R-10
Williamsville, 1396 J-8
Willowbrook, 8893 *J-5
Willow Sprs., 6011 *K-7
Wilmette, 26922 B-13
Wilmington, 5957 E-12
Winchester, 1609 K-5
Windsor, 1074 L-10
Winfield, 9844 *H-4
Winnebago, 3065 A-9
WINNEBAGO CO., 288695 A-9
Winnetka, 12452 B-13
Winthrop Hbr., 7090 A-13
Witt, 986 L-8
Wonder Lake, 2751 A-11
Wood Dale, 13419 *G-6
WOODFORD CO., 37448 G-9
Woodhull, 810 E-6
Woodridge, 34058 *J-5
Wood River, 10985 N-6
Woodstock, 21985 A-11
Worden, 997 N-7
Worth, 10652 *K-8
Wyanet, 1010 E-8
Wyoming, 1390 F-7
Yates City, 691 G-7
York Cen., 4818 *I-5
Yorkfield, 1500 *I-6
Yorkville, 10791 D-11
Zeigler, 1682 Q-9
Zion, 24303 A-13

Indiana

Map pp. 72-77

* City keyed to pp. 72-73

ADAMS CO., 33849 F-13
Advance, 582 I-7
Akron, 1045 D-9
Albany, 2315 H-12
Albion, 2323 B-11
Alexandria, 5868 H-11
ALLEN CO., 344006 C-13
Anderson, 57500 I-10
Andrews, 1267 E-11
Angola, 7890 A-13
Arcadia, 1794 H-9
Ardmore, 2200 *B-18
Argos, 1833 C-8
Arlington, 500 K-11
Ashley, 999 B-13
Atlanta, 820 H-9
Attica, 3385 H-5
Auburn, 12687 B-13
Aurora, 4064 N-13
Austin, 4694 O-10
Avilla, 2359 B-12
Bainbridge, 785 J-6
Bargersville, 2461 L-9
BARTHOLOMEW CO., 73540 M-9
Bass Lake, 1249 C-7
Batesville, 6407 M-12
Battle Ground, 1356 G-6
Bedford, 13551 O-7
Beech Gr., 14069 K-9
BENTON CO., 9039 F-5
Berne, 4157 F-13
Beverly Shores, 711 A-6
Bicknell, 3284 O-4
Birdseye, 472 Q-7
BLACKFORD CO., 13849 G-12
Blackhawk, 80 M-4
Blanford, 300 K-3
Bloomfield, 2542 N-6
Bloomington, 69017 M-7
Bluffton, 9460 F-12
Boggstown, 400 K-10
BOONE CO., 52061 I-7
Boonville, 6782 S-4
Boswell, 783 G-4
Bourbon, 1788 C-9
Brazil, 8214 L-5
Bremen, 4569 B-9
Bristol, 1635 A-10
Brook, 1009 E-4
Brooklyn, 1540 K-8
Brookston, 1632 F-6
Brookville, 2933 L-13
BROWN CO., 15154 M-8
Brownsburg, 18290 J-8
Brownstown, 3050 O-9
Bruceville, 457 O-4
Bunker Hill, 1017 F-9
Burlington, 449 G-8
Burlington Beach, 900 B-5
Burns Hbr., 820 A-5
Butler, 2714 B-13
Cambridge City, 2027 J-12
Camden, 570 F-7
Campbellsburg, 585 P-8
Cannelton, 1168 S-6
Carlisle, 694 N-4
Carmel, 59243 I-9
CARROLL CO., 20426 F-7
Carthage, 880 K-11
CASS CO., 40130 E-8
Cayuga, 1116 I-4
Cedar Lake, 9901 B-4
Centerville, 2590 J-13
Chalmers, 485 F-6
Chandler, 3065 S-4
Charlestown, 8052 Q-11
Chesterton, 12032 A-5
Chrisney, 539 S-5
Churubusco, 1773 C-12
Cicero, 4368 I-9
CLARK CO., 101592 Q-10
Clarks Hill, 660 H-7
Clarksville, 21060 R-10
CLAY CO., 27142 L-5
Clay City, 1036 M-5
Clayton, 817 K-7
Clermont, 1461 *J-15
Clinton, 4906 K-4
CLINTON CO., 34091 H-7
Cloverdale, 2262 L-6
Coatesville, 566 K-7
Colfax, 780 H-7
Collegeville, 865 E-5
Columbia City, 8024 C-11
Columbus, 39380 M-9
Connersville, 14368 K-13
Converse, 1116 F-10
Corydon, 2787 R-9
Covington, 2465 H-4
CRAWFORD CO., 11216 R-8
Crawfordsville, 15155 I-6
Crothersville, 1544 O-10
Crown Pt., 22697 B-4
Culver, 1526 C-8
Cynthiana, 670 R-3
Dale, 1539 R-5
Daleville, 1573 I-11
Dana, 679 J-4
Danville, 7425 J-7
Darlington, 847 I-6
Darmstadt, 1475 S-3
DAVIESS CO., 30466 P-5
Dayton, 1149 G-6
DEARBORN CO., 49082 M-13
DECATUR CO., 25184 L-11
Decatur, 9547 E-13
DE KALB CO., 41659 B-13
DELAWARE CO., 116362 H-12
Delphi, 2980 F-7
Demotte, 3785 C-5
Denver, 521 E-9
Dillsboro, 1455 N-13
Dublin, 671 J-12
DUBOIS CO., 40858 Q-6
Dubois, 600 Q-6
Dugger, 959 N-4
Dunkirk, 2639 G-12
Dunlap, 5887 A-10
Dyer, 15071 B-4
E. Chicago, 30946 A-4
Eaton, 1515 H-12
Edgewood, 1883 I-10
Edinburgh, 4517 L-9
Elberfeld, 648 R-4
Elizabethtown, 405 M-10
Elkhart, 52270 A-9
ELKHART CO., 195362 A-10
Ellettsville, 5294 M-7
Elnora, 743 O-5
Elwood, 9167 H-10
English, 695 Q-7
Etna Green, 639 C-9
Evansville, 115918 S-3
Fairland, 1276 K-10
Fairmount, 2814 G-11
Fairview Park, 1501 K-4
Farmersburg, 1208 M-4
Farmland, 1396 H-13
FAYETTE CO., 24885 K-12
Ferdinand, 2299 R-6
Fillmore, 565 K-6
Fishers, 57220 I-9
Fish Lake, 1300 A-7
Flora, 2161 F-7
Florida, 100 D-1
FLOYD CO., 71997 Q-9
Floyds Knobs, 800 Q-10
Ft. Branch, 2342 R-3
Fortville, 3626 J-10
Ft. Wayne, 223341 D-13
FOUNTAIN CO., 17462 I-4
Fountain City, 705 I-13
Fowler, 2271 F-4
Francesville, 869 D-6
Francisco, 547 Q-4
Frankfort, 16432 H-7
FRANKLIN CO., 23085 L-13
Franklin, 21747 L-9
Frankton, 1864 H-10
Freelandville, 630 O-4
Freetown, 700 N-9
Fremont, 1659 A-13
French Lick, 1923 P-7
FULTON CO., 20665 D-8
Galena, 1831 Q-10
Galveston, 1441 F-9
Garrett, 5760 B-13
Gary, 98715 A-4
Gas City, 5819 G-11
Gaston, 963 H-11
Geneva, 1330 F-13
Georgetown, 2682 R-9
GIBSON CO., 33408 Q-3
Gilmer Park, 2100 *C-19
Goodland, 1047 E-4
Goshen, 31269 A-10
Gosport, 748 L-7
Grabill, 1152 C-13
Grandview, 684 S-5
Granger, 28284 A-9
GRANT CO., 70557 G-11
Greencastle, 10065 K-6
Greendale, 4357 M-14
GREENE CO., 33479 N-6
Greenfield, 16654 J-10
Greensburg, 10536 L-11
Greentown, 2459 G-9
Greenville, 586 Q-9
Greenwood, 42236 K-9
Griffith, 16666 B-4
Hagerstown, 1673 J-12
HAMILTON CO., 240685 H-9
Hamilton, 1504 B-13
Hamlet, 768 B-7
Hammond, 79217 A-4
HANCOCK CO., 63138 J-10
Hanna, 500 B-6
Hanover, 3768 O-11
Harlan, 1200 C-13
Harmony, 627 K-5
HARRISON CO., 36827 R-9
Hartford City, 6684 G-12
Hatfield, 700 S-4
Haubstadt, 1537 R-3
Hebron, 3570 C-5
Heltonville, 500 N-8
HENDRICKS CO., 127483 J-7
HENRY CO., 47244 I-11
Henryville, 1545 P-10
Highland, 4107 S-12
Highland, 23172 A-4
Hillsboro, 479 I-5
Hillsdale, 180 J-4
Hoagland, 675 D-13
Hobart, 27768 B-5
Holland, 699 R-5
Home Place, 1300 J-9
Hope, 2185 M-10
HOWARD CO., 84977 G-9
Howe, 900 A-11
Hudson Lake, 1300 A-7
Huntertown, 2136 C-12
Huntingburg, 5929 R-6
Huntington, 17011 E-11
HUNTINGTON CO., 38236 E-11
Hymera, 823 M-4
Idaville, 500 E-7
Indianapolis, 784118 J-9
Ingalls, 1454 I-10
JACKSON CO., 42237 N-9
Jamestown, 957 J-7
Jasonville, 2508 M-5
JASPER CO., 31876 D-5
Jasper, 13767 Q-6
JAY CO., 21606 G-13
JEFFERSON CO., 32430 O-11
Jeffersonville, 28621 R-10
JENNINGS CO., 28427 N-11
Jewell Vil., 700 M-10
JOHNSON CO., 128436 L-9
Jonesboro, 1759 G-11
Kendallville, 10018 B-12
Kentland, 1747 E-4
Kewanna, 619 D-8
Kingman, 532 I-4
Kingsford Hts., 1407 B-7
Kirklin, 779 H-8
Klondike B-1
Knightstown, 2026 J-11
Knightsville, 635 L-5
KNOX CO., 38366 O-4
Knox, 3667 C-7
Kokomo, 46178 G-9
Koontz Lake, 1554 B-7
KOSCIUSKO CO., 76072 C-10
Kouts, 1766 C-5
La Crosse, 561 C-6
Ladoga, 1038 J-6
Lafayette, 60459 G-6
La Fontaine, 859 F-10
Lagrange, 2972 A-11
LAGRANGE CO., 36875 A-11
Lagro, 436 E-10
LAKE CO., 493297 C-4
Lake Eliza, 600 B-5
Lake James, 800 A-13
Lake Sta., 13565 A-5
Laketon, 250 D-10
Lake Vil., 855 D-4
Lakeville, 557 B-8
Landess, 100 F-11
Lanesville, 630 R-9
Lapaz, 489 B-8
Lapel, 1846 I-10
La Porte, 21092 A-7
LA PORTE CO., 110512 B-7
Laurel, 580 L-12
LAWRENCE CO., 46403 O-8
Lawrence, 40959 J-9
Lawrenceburg, 4750 N-14
Lebanon, 14633 I-7
Leesburg, 613 C-10
Leo-Cedarville, 2902 C-13
Liberty, 1940 K-13
Ligonier, 4423 B-11
Linden, 696 H-6
Linton, 5808 N-5
Logansport, 19211 E-8
Long Beach, 1554 A-6
Loogootee, 2680 P-6
Lowell, 8039 C-4
Lydick, 800 A-8
Lynn, 1095 I-13
Lynnville, 819 R-4
Lyons, 753 N-5
MADISON CO., 130412 H-10
Madison, 12443 O-12
Maple Lane, 2100 *B-20
Marengo, 862 Q-8
MARION CO., 863133 J-8
Marion, 30644 F-11
Markle, 1101 E-12
MARSHALL CO., 46945 B-8
MARTIN CO., 10386 P-6
Martinsville, 11657 L-8
Maryland, 800 J-2
Marywood, 600 J-2
Matthews, 558 G-11
McCordsville, 1266 J-10
Medaryville, 549 D-6
Medora, 553 O-9
Melody Hill, 3066 S-13
Memphis, 400 Q-10
Mentone, 891 C-9
Merrillville, 31525 B-4
Mexico, 984 E-9
MIAMI CO., 35620 F-9
Michigan City, 32205 A-6
Michigantown, 407 H-8
Middlebury, 3150 A-10
Middletown, 2384 I-11
Middletown Park, 850 G-1
Milan, 1806 M-13
Milford, 1535 B-10
Millersburg, 909 B-10
Milltown, 931 Q-8
Milroy, 850 L-11
Milton, 610 J-12
Mishawaka, 48497 A-9
Mitchell, 4626 O-7
Monon, 1654 E-6
MONROE CO., 121407 M-7
Monroe, 778 E-13
Monroe City, 531 P-4
Monroeville, 1277 D-13
Monrovia, 624 K-7
Montezuma, 1151 J-4
MONTGOMERY CO., 38239 I-6
Monticello, 5462 F-6
Montpelier, 1857 F-12
Mooreland, 375 I-12
Moores Hill, 652 N-13
Mooresville, 11111 K-8
MORGAN CO., 69778 L-7
Morgantown, 966 L-8
Morocco, 1159 E-4
Morristown, 1218 K-10
Mt. Vernon, 7238 S-2
Mulberry, 1461 G-7
Muncie, 66164 H-12
Munster, 22347 A-4
Nappanee, 6955 B-9
Nashville, 804 M-8
New Albany, 36772 R-10
Newburgh, 3298 S-4
New Carlisle, 1629 A-7
New Castle, 18718 J-12
New Chicago, 2036 B-5
New Elliott, 800 *N-12
New Goshen, 500 K-4
New Harmony, 885 R-2
New Haven, 13676 D-13
New Market, 654 I-6
New Palestine, 1826 K-10
New Paris, 1006 B-10
Newport, 557 J-4
New Salisbury, 400 R-9
NEWTON CO., 14456 D-4
New Washington, 547 P-11
New Whiteland, 4431 K-9
NOBLE CO., 47448 C-12
Noblesville, 38825 I-9
N. Judson, 1867 C-6
N. Liberty, 1362 B-8
N. Manchester, 5980 D-10
N. Salem, 636 J-7
N. Terre Haute, 4606 L-4
N. Vernon, 6433 N-11
N. Webster, 1057 C-10
Norway, 437 E-6
Oakland City, 2596 Q-4
Oaktown, 610 O-4
Odon, 1418 O-5
Ogden Dunes, 1275 A-5
OHIO CO., 5874 N-13
Oldenburg, 645 L-12
Oolitic, 1123 O-7
ORANGE CO., 19770 P-8
Orestes, 326 H-10
Orleans, 2294 P-7
Osceola, 1811 A-9
Osgood, 1655 M-12
Ossian, 2908 E-12
Otterbein, 1242 G-5
Otwell, 400 Q-5
OWEN CO., 22823 M-6
Owensville, 1339 R-3
Oxford, 1208 G-5
Palmyra, 716 Q-9
Paoli, 3947 P-7
Paragon, 642 L-7
PARKE CO., 17362 J-5
Parker City, 1359 H-12
Patoka, 794 Q-3
Pendleton, 3859 I-10
Pennville, 740 G-12
PERRY CO., 19032 S-7
Peru, 12732 E-9
Petersburg, 2501 Q-4
Pierceton, 686 C-10
PIKE CO., 12766 Q-4
Pittsboro, 2245 J-7
Plainfield, 23532 K-8
Pleasant Lake, 500 A-13
Plymouth, 10876 C-8
Portage, 35687 A-5
Porter, 5217 A-5
PORTER CO., 157772 B-5
Portland, 6191 G-13
POSEY CO., 26852 S-2
Poseyville, 1151 R-2
Prince's Lakes, 1538 L-9
Princeton, 8652 Q-3
PULASKI CO., 13783 D-7
PUTNAM CO., 36957 K-6
RANDOLPH CO., 26684 H-13
Redkey, 1418 G-12
Reelsville, 150 K-6
Remington, 1262 E-5
Rensselaer, 6234 E-5
Reynolds, 524 F-6
Richland, 500 S-5
Richmond, 37560 J-13
Ridgeville, 818 H-13
RIPLEY CO., 27710 N-12
Rising Sun, 2405 N-14
Roachdale, 976 J-6
Roanoke, 1468 D-12
Rochester, 6451 D-8
Rockport, 2091 T-5
Rockville, 2701 J-5
Rolling Prairie, 500 A-7
Rome City, 1645 B-12
Rosedale, 759 K-4
Roseland, 626 A-8
Ross, 1100 B-4
Rossville, 1540 G-7
Royal Cen., 817 E-7
Royerton, 900 H-12
RUSH CO., 17823 K-11
Rushville, 5679 K-11
Russiaville, 1186 G-8
St. Bernice, 800 K-3
St. John, 10783 B-4
ST. JOSEPH CO., 266160 B-8
St. Leon, 515 M-13
St. Mary-of-the-Woods, 300 L-4
St. Meinrad, 500 R-6
St. Paul, 1016 L-11
St. Wendel, 500 R-3
Salem, 6453 P-9
Sandborn, 436 O-5
Santa Claus, 2283 S-6
Schererville, 28394 B-4
SCOTT CO., 23820 P-10
Scottsburg, 6060 P-10
Seelyville, 1148 L-4
Sellersburg, 6028 Q-10
Selma, 830 H-12
Seymour, 18890 N-10
Shadeland, 1613 G-6
Sharpsville, 620 G-9
Shelburn, 1279 M-4
Shelby, 750 C-4
SHELBY CO., 43766 K-10
Shelbyville, 18063 L-10
Sheridan, 2661 I-8
Shipshewana, 530 A-11
Shirley, 837 J-11
Shoals, 817 P-6
Silver Lake, 537 D-10
Simonton Lake, 4053 A-9
Smith Valley, 1800 K-8
S. Bend, 105262 A-8
Southport, 1729 K-9
S. Whitley, 1847 D-11
Speed, 300 Q-10
Speedway, 12408 J-8
Spelterville, 500 H-2
SPENCER CO., 20528 S-5
Spencer, 2549 M-6
Spiceland, 900 J-11
Star City, 377 D-7
STARKE CO., 22933 C-7
Staunton, 563 L-5
STEUBEN CO., 33773 A-12
Stockwell, 500 H-6
SULLIVAN CO., 21763 M-3
Sullivan, 4537 N-4
Summitville, 1052 H-11
Sunman, 803 M-13
Swayzee, 935 G-10
Sweetser, 842 F-10
SWITZERLAND CO., 9718 O-13
Syracuse, 3030 B-10
Taylorsville, 936 M-9
Tell City, 7690 S-6
Terre Haute, 56893 L-4
Thorntown, 1573 I-7
TIPPECANOE CO., 153875 H-6
Tipton, 5254 H-9
TIPTON CO., 16385 H-9
Topeka, 1194 B-11
Town of Pines, 793 A-6
Trafalgar, 936 L-9
Trail Creek, 2205 A-6
Troy, 393 S-6
UNION CO., 7208 K-13
Union City, 3471 H-14
Upland, 3735 G-11
Utica, 637 Q-11
Vallonia, 500 O-9
Valparaiso, 29102 B-5
Van Buren, 870 F-11
VANDERBURGH CO., 173187 R-3
Veedersburg, 2228 I-4
VERMILLION CO., 16562 J-4
Versailles, 1766 N-12
Vevay, 1655 O-13
VIGO CO., 102592 L-3
Vincennes, 18077 P-3
WABASH CO., 33843 E-10
Wabash, 11209 E-10
Wakarusa, 1666 B-9
Waldron, 800 L-10
Walkerton, 2200 B-7
Walton, 1028 F-8
Wanatah, 990 B-6
WARREN CO., 8785 G-4
Warren, 1248 F-11
WARRICK CO., 56362 R-4
Warsaw, 12735 C-10
WASHINGTON CO., 27885 P-9
Washington, 11357 P-5
Waterloo, 2198 B-13
Waveland, 412 J-5
WAYNE CO., 69192 J-13
Waynetown, 900 I-5
WELLS CO., 28085 F-12
W. Baden Sprs., 615 P-7
W. College Corner, 605 K-14
Westfield, 12322 I-9
W. Lafayette, 28599 G-6
W. Lebanon, 789 H-4
Westpoint, 250 G-5
Westport, 1502 M-11
W. Terre Haute, 2255 L-4
Westville, 5219 B-6
Wheatfield, 865 C-5
Wheeler, 500 B-5
WHITE CO., 24463 F-6
Whiteland, 4271 K-9
Whitestown, 688 I-8
Whiting, 4893 A-4
WHITLEY CO., 32323 D-11
Williamsburg, 360 I-13
Williamsport, 1928 H-4
Winamac, 2436 D-7
Winchester, 4845 H-13
Windfall, 696 G-9
Winona Lake, 4235 C-10
Winslow, 856 Q-5
Wolcott, 939 E-5
Wolcottville, 953 B-12
Woodburn, 1635 D-13
Woodland Park, 200 G-3
Woodridge, 700 I-2
Worthington, 1488 N-6
Yorktown, 4966 H-11
Zanesville, 599 E-12
Zionsville, 11853 I-8

Iowa

Map pp. 78-81

Ackley, 1738 E-11
ADAIR CO., 7859 J-7
Adair, 773 I-7
ADAMS CO., 4264 K-6
Adel, 4046 I-8
Afton, 886 K-8
Agency, 648 K-14
Akron, 1467 D-1
Albert City, 696 D-6
Albia, 3679 K-12
Albion, 575 G-11
Alden, 854 E-10

Algona, 5505 C-8
ALLAMAKEE CO., 14709 B-16
Allerton, 560 M-10
Allison, 981 E-12
Alta, 1874 E-5
Alton, 1117 D-3
Altoona, 12938 I-10
Amana, 420 H-15
Ames, 52263 G-10
Anamosa, 5616 G-16
Anita, 1166 J-6
Ankeny, 36681 I-10
Anthon, 634 F-3
Aplington, 1023 E-12
APPANOOSE CO., 13666 L-12
Armstrong, 902 B-7
Arnolds Park, 1211 B-5
Asbury, 3384 E-18
Atkins, 1330 H-15
Atlantic, 6959 J-5
AUDUBON CO., 6457 I-5
Audubon, 2257 I-6
Aurelia, 973 E-4
Avoca, 1562 J-4
Badger, 586 E-8
Bancroft, 752 B-8
Batavia, 496 K-14
Battle Cr., 716 F-4
Baxter, 1063 H-11
Bayard, 527 H-7
Bedford, 1525 M-6
Belle Plaine, 2919 H-14
Bellevue, 2358 F-19
Belmond, 2451 D-10
BENTON CO., 27000 G-14
Bettendorf, 31890 I-19
BLACK HAWK CO., 125891 F-13
Blairstown, 709 H-14
Bloomfield, 2597 L-13
Blue Grass, 1285 I-18
Bondurant, 2203 I-10
BOONE CO., 26602 H-8
Boone, 12831 G-9
Boyden, 669 C-3
BREMER CO., 23677 E-13
Brighton, 693 K-15
Britt, 2011 C-9
Brooklyn, 1389 I-13
BUCHANAN CO., 21019 E-14
BUENA VISTA CO., 20151 D-5
Buffalo, 1275 J-18
Buffalo Cen., 897 B-9
Burlington, 25436 L-17
Burt, 520 C-8
BUTLER CO., 15072 E-12
CALHOUN CO., 10443 F-6
Calmar, 1062 C-15
Camanche, 4260 H-20
Cambridge, 756 H-10
Carlisle, 3544 J-10
CARROLL CO., 21034 G-6
Carroll, 10047 G-6
Carson, 706 K-4
Carter Lake, 3404 J-3
Cascade, 2030 F-17
CASS CO., 14219 J-6
CEDAR CO., 18254 H-17
Cedar Falls, 36471 E-13
Cedar Rapids, 123119 H-15
Center Pt., 2214 G-15
Centerville, 5788 M-12
Central City, 1142 G-16
CERRO GORDO CO., 44645 C-11
Chariton, 4609 K-11
Charles City, 7606 C-12
CHEROKEE CO., 12237 E-3
Cherokee, 5027 D-4
CHICKASAW CO., 12563 C-13
Clarence, 993 H-17
Clarinda, 5523 L-5
Clarion, 2873 E-9
CLARKE CO., 9161 K-9
Clarksville, 1403 D-12
CLAY CO., 16897 C-5
CLAYTON CO., 18337 D-16
Clear Lake, 7913 C-10
Clermont, 708 C-15
Clinton, 27086 H-20
CLINTON CO., 49717 H-19
Clive, 13851 B-18
Coggon, 701 F-16
Colfax, 2228 I-11
Colo, 808 G-10
Columbus Jct., 1835 J-16
Conrad, 1009 G-12
Coon Rapids, 1263 H-6
Coralville, 17811 I-16
Corning, 1688 L-6
Correctionville, 859 F-3
Corydon, 1521 L-10
Council Bluffs, 59568 J-3
CRAWFORD CO., 16889 G-5
Cresco, 3774 B-14
Creston, 7359 K-7
Dakota City, 852 E-8
DALLAS CO., 51762 I-8
Dallas Cen., 1828 I-9
Danville, 859 L-16
Davenport, 98845 I-19
DAVIS CO., 8659 L-13
Dayton, 837 F-8
DECATUR CO., 8605 L-9
Decorah, 8084 B-15
DELAWARE CO., 18025 E-16
Delmar, 505 G-18
Denison, 7374 G-4
Denver, 1642 E-13
Des Moines, 194163 I-10
DES MOINES CO., 40810 L-17
De Soto, 1164 I-8
De Witt, 5204 H-19
Dexter, 803 I-8
DICKINSON CO., 16687 B-5
Dike, 1157 F-12
Donnellson, 923 M-16
Dows, 604 E-10
DUBUQUE CO., 91631 F-17
Dubuque, 57798 E-18
Dumont, 658 E-11
Dunkerton, 768 E-14
Dunlap, 1117 H-4
Durant, 1677 I-18
Dyersville, 4043 F-17
Dysart, 1289 G-13
Eagle Gr., 3515 E-9
Earlham, 1332 J-8
Earlville, 863 F-16
Early, 540 F-5
Eddyville, 1072 K-13
Edgewood, 898 E-16
Eldon, 974 L-14
Eldora, 2847 F-11
Eldridge, 4484 I-19
Elgin, 656 D-15
Elkader, 1383 D-16
Elk Horn, 613 I-5
Elk Run Hts., 1082 F-14
Elma, 577 C-13
EMMET CO., 10534 B-7
Emmetsburg, 3706 C-6
Epworth, 1580 F-17
Essex, 840 L-4
Estherville, 6347 B-6
Evansdale, 4585 F-14
Everly, 645 C-5
Exira, 775 I-6
Fairbank, 1034 E-14
Fairfax, 1512 H-15
Fairfield, 9404 K-15
Farley, 1363 F-17
Farmington, 731 M-15
FAYETTE CO., 21298 D-14
Fayette, 1341 D-15
FLOYD CO., 16443 C-12
Fonda, 588 E-6
Fontanelle, 679 J-7
Forest City, 4250 B-10
Ft. Dodge, 25493 F-8
Ft. Madison, 11048 M-17
FRANKLIN CO., 10732 E-10
Fredericksburg, 903 D-14
Fremont, 690 K-13
FREMONT CO., 7759 L-4
Garnavillo, 744 D-17
Garner, 2975 C-10
Garwin, 549 G-12
George, 1025 B-3
Gilbert, 973 G-9
Gilbertville, 779 F-14
Gilman, 575 H-12
Gilmore City, 515 E-7
Gladbrook, 1021 G-12
Glenwood, 5650 K-3
Glidden, 1228 G-6
Goldfield, 642 E-9
Gowrie, 1045 F-8
Graettinger, 866 C-6
Grand Jct., 927 G-8
Grand Mound, 661 H-18
Granger, 943 H-9
GREENE CO., 9963 G-7
Greene, 1015 D-12
Greenfield, 1984 J-7
Greenfield Plaza D-20
Grimes, 6037 I-9
Grinnell, 9332 I-12
Griswold, 983 K-5
GRUNDY CO., 12329 F-12
Grundy Cen., 2583 F-12
GUTHRIE CO., 11547 H-6
Guthrie Cen., 1617 I-7
Guttenberg, 1943 D-17
Hamburg, 1221 M-3
HAMILTON CO., 16209 F-9
Hampton, 4224 E-11
HANCOCK CO., 11786 C-9
HARDIN CO., 18003 F-10
Harlan, 5170 I-4
HARRISON CO., 15884 I-3
Hartford, 754 J-10
Hartley, 1565 C-4
Hawarden, 2440 C-1
Hazleton, 924 E-15
Hedrick, 828 K-13
HENRY CO., 20246 K-16
Hiawatha, 6596 G-15
Hills, 617 I-16
Hinton, 847 E-2
Holstein, 1415 F-4
Hopkinton, 656 F-17
Hospers, 674 C-3
HOWARD CO., 9700 B-13
Hubbard, 845 F-10
Hudson, 2127 F-13
Hull, 2039 C-2
HUMBOLDT CO., 9973 D-8
Humboldt, 4366 E-8
Humeston, 545 L-10
Huxley, 2347 H-10
IDA CO., 7379 F-4
Ida Gr., 2218 F-4
Independence, 6054 F-15
Indianola, 13944 J-10
Inwood, 874 B-1
IOWA CO., 16055 I-15
Iowa City, 62887 I-16
Iowa Falls, 5112 E-11
Ireton, 592 D-2
JACKSON CO., 20335 F-18
Janesville, 875 E-13
JASPER CO., 37674 I-11
Jefferson, 4407 G-7
JEFFERSON CO., 15972 K-15
Jesup, 2413 F-14
Jewell, 1211 F-9
JOHNSON CO., 117067 I-15
Johnston, 12931 I-9
JONES CO., 20509 G-17
Kalona, 2486 J-15
Kanawha, 691 D-9
Kellogg, 627 I-12
KEOKUK CO., 11157 J-14
Keokuk, 10762 N-16
Keosauqua, 1076 M-15
Keota, 939 J-14
Keystone, 690 H-14
Kingsley, 1248 E-3
Klemme, 558 D-10
Knoxville, 7512 J-11
KOSSUTH CO., 16142 C-8
Lake City, 1693 F-6
Lake Mills, 2060 B-10
Lake Park, 993 B-5
Lake View, 1221 F-5
Lamoni, 2470 M-9
Lansing, 987 B-16
La Porte City, 2301 F-14
Larchwood, 808 B-1
Laurens, 1326 D-6
Lawler, 435 C-14
Le Claire, 3123 I-19
LEE CO., 36705 M-16
Le Grand, 966 G-12
Lehigh, 484 F-8
Le Mars, 9349 D-2
Lenox, 1310 L-7
Leon, 1924 M-9
LINN CO., 198903 G-15
Lisbon, 1944 H-16
Logan, 1319 I-3
Lone Tree, 1081 J-16
LOUISA CO., 11842 K-16
Lovilia, 556 K-12
Lowden, 818 H-18
LUCAS CO., 9672 K-10
LYON CO., 11750 B-2
MADISON CO., 15158 J-8
Madrid, 2420 H-9
MAHASKA CO., 22364 J-12
Malvern, 1342 K-4
Manchester, 5074 F-16
Manilla, 833 H-5
Manly, 1336 B-11
Manning, 1447 H-5
Manson, 1760 E-7
Mapleton, 1230 G-3
Maquoketa, 6054 G-18
Marcus, 1064 D-3
Marengo, 2539 H-14
MARION CO., 32984 J-11
Marion, 30233 G-16
MARSHALL CO., 39418 G-11
Marshalltown, 25977 G-12
Mason City, 27909 C-11
Maxwell, 764 H-10
Maynard, 464 D-15
McGregor, 897 C-17
Mechanicsville, 1177 H-17
Mediapolis, 1587 K-17
Melbourne, 795 H-11
Melcher-Dallas, 1269 J-11
Merrill, 772 E-2
Milford, 2441 B-5
MILLS CO., 15284 K-4
Milo, 828 J-10
Milton, 502 M-14
Missouri Valley, 2932 I-3
MITCHELL CO., 10919 C-11
Mitchellville, 2092 I-10
MONONA CO., 9520 G-3
Monona, 1445 C-16
Monroe, 1838 I-11
MONROE CO., 7835 L-12
Montezuma, 1419 I-13
MONTGOMERY CO., 11313 K-5
Monticello, 3701 G-17
Montrose, 942 M-16
Moravia, 731 L-12
Morning Sun, 857 K-17
Moulton, 683 M-12
Mt. Ayr, 1764 M-8
Mt. Pleasant, 8767 L-16
Mt. Vernon, 4051 H-16
Moville, 1480 E-2
Murray, 786 K-9
Muscatine, 22757 J-17
MUSCATINE CO., 42756 I-16
Mystic, 618 L-12
Nashua, 1574 D-13
Neola, 840 J-4
Nevada, 6129 G-10
New Albin, 529 B-16
Newell, 869 E-5
Newhall, 989 H-14
New Hampton, 3528 C-13
New Hartford, 640 E-12
New London, 1871 L-16
New Sharon, 1307 J-12
Newton, 15607 I-11
Nora Sprs., 1466 C-11
N. English, 1004 I-14
N. Liberty, 8808 H-16
Northwood, 2036 B-11
Norwalk, 7877 J-9
Norway, 618 H-15
Norwoodville, 1200 B-20
Oakland, 1460 J-4
O'BRIEN CO., 14414 C-4
Ocheyedan, 512 B-4
Odebolt, 1045 F-5
Oelwein, 6371 E-15
Ogden, 2019 G-8
Okoboji, 966 B-5
Olin, 714 G-17
Onawa, 2921 G-2
Orange City, 5775 C-2
Osage, 3462 B-12
OSCEOLA CO., 6694 B-4
Osceola, 4783 K-9
Oskaloosa, 11026 J-12
Ossian, 836 C-15
Otho, 543 F-8
Ottumwa, 24798 K-13
Oxford, 645 I-15
Oxford Jct., 561 G-17
Pacific Jct., 518 K-3
PAGE CO., 16253 L-5
PALO ALTO CO., 9697 D-6
Panora, 1214 I-7
Parkersburg, 1881 E-12
Park View, 2169 I-19
Paullina, 1041 D-4
Pella, 10291 J-12
Perry, 8865 H-8
Pleasant Hill, 6229 C-20
Pleasantville, 1607 J-11
PLYMOUTH CO., 24958 E-2
POCAHONTAS CO., 7930 E-6
Pocahontas, 1876 E-6
POLK CO., 401006 I-10
Polk City, 2940 H-9
Pomeroy, 658 E-6
Postville, 2322 C-16
POTTAWATTAMIE CO., 89738 J-4
POWESHIEK CO., 18925 H-13
Prairie City, 1424 I-11
Preston, 946 G-19
Primghar, 841 C-4
Princeton, 931 I-19
Radcliffe, 575 F-10
Raymond, 637 F-14
Readlyn, 767 E-14
Redfield, 965 I-8
Red Oak, 5919 K-5
Reinbeck, 1687 F-13
Remsen, 1735 D-3
Riceville, 834 B-13
Richland, 584 K-14
RINGGOLD CO., 5273 L-7
Riverside, 961 J-16
Robins, 2270 G-15
Rockford, 899 C-12
Rock Rapids, 2598 B-2
Rock Valley, 2852 C-2
Rockwell, 973 D-11
Rockwell City, 2096 F-7
Roland, 1242 G-10
Rolfe, 612 D-7
Russell, 587 L-11
Ruthven, 716 C-6
Sabula, 667 G-20
SAC CO., 10621 F-5
Sac City, 2157 F-6
St. Ansgar, 974 B-12
Sanborn, 1309 C-4
Saydel, 3500 A-20
Saylorville, 3238 A-20
Schaller, 728 E-5
Schleswig, 828 G-4
SCOTT CO., 160998 I-19
Scranton, 561 G-7
Sergeant Bluff, 3819 F-2
Seymour, 787 M-11
Sheffield, 1002 D-11
SHELBY CO., 12634 I-4
Shelby, 675 I-4
Sheldon, 4807 C-3
Shell Rock, 1266 E-13
Shellsburg, 1028 G-15
Shenandoah, 5239 L-4
Sibley, 2690 B-3
Sidney, 1190 L-3
Sigourney, 2168 J-14
SIOUX CO., 32277 C-2
Sioux Cen., 6513 C-2
Sioux City, 83148 E-1
Sioux Rapids, 700 D-5
Slater, 1421 H-9
Sloan, 1022 F-2
Solon, 1352 H-16
Spencer, 11117 C-5
Spirit Lake, 4590 B-5
Springville, 1001 G-16
Stanton, 710 L-5
Stanwood, 651 H-17
State Cen., 1337 G-11
Storm Lake, 9963 E-5
STORY CO., 79952 G-10
Story City, 3141 G-10
Stratford, 737 F-9
Strawberry Pt., 1279 E-16
Stuart, 1750 I-7
Sully, 888 I-12
Sumner, 2042 D-14
Sutherland, 665 D-4
Swea City, 596 B-8
Swisher, 796 H-15
Tabor, 975 L-3
TAMA CO., 17919 G-13
Tama, 2603 H-13
TAYLOR CO., 6614 L-6
Tipton, 3132 H-17
Titonka, 543 C-8
Toledo, 2687 H-13
Traer, 1586 G-13
Treynor, 914 J-4
Tripoli, 1269 D-14
UNION CO., 11972 L-7
University Park, 554 J-13
Urbana, 1344 G-15
Urbandale, 34696 B-19
VAN BUREN CO., 7786 L-14
Van Horne, 750 G-14
Van Meter, 1088 I-9
Ventura, 676 C-10
Victor, 1004 I-14
Villisca, 1300 L-5
Vinton, 5219 G-14
Walcott, 1530 I-18
Walker, 727 F-15
Wall Lake, 766 F-5
Walnut, 750 J-5
WAPELLO CO., 35965 K-13
Wapello, 2042 K-17
WARREN CO., 42981 K-9
Washburn, 1400 F-14
WASHINGTON CO., 21457 J-15
Washington, 7207 J-15
Waterloo, 66483 F-13
Waukee, 9213 I-9
Waukon, 4013 B-16
Waverly, 9298 E-13
Wayland, 944 K-15
WAYNE CO., 6601 L-10
WEBSTER CO., 39003 E-8
Webster City, 8077 F-9
Wellman, 1470 J-15
Wellsburg, 681 F-12
W. Bend, 817 D-7
W. Branch, 2269 I-16
W. Burlington, 3231 L-17
W. Des Moines, 52768 I-9
W. Liberty, 3603 I-17
W. Point, 961 M-16
W. Union, 2485 D-15
What Cheer, 658 J-13
Wheatland, 760 H-18
Whiting, 772 G-2
Whittemore, 492 C-7
Williamsburg, 2751 I-14
Wilton, 2866 I-17
Windsor Hts., 4607 B-18
Winfield, 1105 K-16
WINNEBAGO CO., 11351 B-9
WINNESHIEK CO., 21234 C-14
Winterset, 4877 J-8
Winthrop, 769 F-15
Woodbine, 1624 I-3
WOODBURY CO., 102605 F-2
Woodward, 1305 H-9
WORTH CO., 7768 B-11
WRIGHT CO., 13647 E-9
Wyoming, 623 G-17
Zearing, 536 G-11

Kansas

Map pp. 82-85

* City keyed to pp. 116-117

Abilene, 6409 E-13
ALLEN CO., 13787 H-17
Alma, 764 D-15
Almena, 454 B-7
Altamont, 1065 J-18
Alta Vista, 425 E-15
Altoona, 472 I-17
Americus, 932 F-15
Andale, 808 H-12
ANDERSON CO., 8182 G-17
Andover, 9114 H-13
Anthony, 2302 J-11
Argonia, 500 J-12
Arkansas City, 11581 J-13
Arlington, 440 H-11
Arma, 1495 I-19
Ashland, 943 J-7
Assaria, 444 F-12
ATCHISON CO., 16804 C-17
Atchison, 10169 C-18
Attica, 604 J-11
Atwood, 1139 B-4
Auburn, 1131 E-16
Augusta, 8608 I-14
Axtell, 433 B-15
Baldwin City, 3746 E-18
BARBER CO., 4958 J-9
BARTON CO., 28105 F-9
Basehor, 3287 D-18
Baxter Sprs., 4246 J-19
Bazine, 263 F-7
Bel Aire, 6557 K-9
Belle Plaine, 1618 I-13
Belleville, 1956 B-12
Beloit, 3703 C-11
Bennington, 614 D-12
Benton, 817 H-13
Bird City, 438 B-3
Blue Rapids, 1048 B-14
Bonner Sprs., 6942 D-18
BOURBON CO., 14997 H-18
BROWN CO., 10239 B-17
Bucklin, 734 I-7
Buhler, 1335 G-12
Burden, 553 J-14
Burlingame, 1015 E-16
Burlington, 2707 G-16
Burrton, 913 H-12
BUTLER CO., 62354 H-14
Caldwell, 1215 K-12
Caney, 1975 J-16
Canton, 812 F-12
Carbondale, 1451 E-17
Cawker City, 474 C-10
Cedar Vale, 669 J-15
Centralia, 504 B-15
Chanute, 9006 H-17
Chapman, 1243 E-13
CHASE CO., 3081 G-14
Chase, 467 G-10
CHAUTAUQUA CO., 4109 J-15
Cheney, 1843 I-12
Cherokee, 718 I-19
CHEROKEE CO., 21555 J-18
Cherryvale, 2266 J-17
Chetopa, 1231 J-18
CHEYENNE CO., 2946 B-2
Cimarron, 2029 H-5
Claflin, 688 F-10
CLARK CO., 2283 J-6
CLAY CO., 8629 D-13
Clay Cen., 4378 C-13
Clearwater, 2214 I-12
Clifton, 508 C-13
CLOUD CO., 9759 C-11
Clyde, 709 C-12
COFFEY CO., 8683 G-16
Coffeyville, 10359 J-17
Colby, 5030 C-4
Coldwater, 774 J-8
Colony, 390 G-17
Columbus, 3259 J-19
Colwich, 1328 H-12
COMANCHE CO., 1935 J-8
Concordia, 5371 C-12
Conway Sprs., 1253 I-12
Cottonwood Falls, 959 F-15
Council Gr., 2275 F-15
COWLEY CO., 35298 J-14
CRAWFORD CO., 38222 I-18
Cunningham, 477 I-10
Dearing, 452 J-17
DECATUR CO., 3191 B-5
Deerfield, 892 H-4
Delphos, 449 D-12
Derby, 20543 I-13
De Soto, 5170 D-18
DICKINSON CO., 19209 E-13
Dighton, 1106 F-5
Dodge City, 26104 H-6
DONIPHAN CO., 7816 B-17
DOUGLAS CO., 102914 E-17
Douglass, 1799 I-13
Downs, 938 C-10
Eastborough, 790 M-9
Easton, 357 C-18
Edgerton, 1692 E-18
Edna, 422 J-18
EDWARDS CO., 3292 H-8
Edwardsville, 4503 D-19
Effingham, 582 C-17
El Dorado, 12659 H-14
ELK CO., 3075 I-15
Elkhart, 2036 J-2
Ellinwood, 2119 G-10
ELLIS CO., 26767 D-8
Ellis, 1812 E-7
ELLSWORTH CO., 6343 E-11
Ellsworth, 2887 E-10
Elwood, 1153 B-18
Emporia, 26456 F-15
Enterprise, 811 E-13
Erie, 1167 I-18
Eskridge, 571 E-16
Eudora, 5284 E-18
Eureka, 2739 H-15
Fairway, 3840 *J-3
FINNEY CO., 38988 G-4
Florence, 650 G-14
FORD CO., 33751 I-6
Ft. Scott, 7990 H-19
Fowler, 578 I-6
Frankfort, 795 B-15
Franklin, 350 I-19
FRANKLIN CO., 26247 F-17
Fredonia, 2455 I-16
Frontenac, 3101 I-19
Galena, 3163 J-19
Galva, 773 F-12
Garden City, 27098 H-4
Garden Plain, 823 I-12
Gardner, 14317 E-18
Garnett, 3338 G-18
Gas, 552 H-17
GEARY CO., 24585 E-14
Geneseo, 271 F-11
Girard, 2686 I-19
Glasco, 504 C-11
Glen Elder, 399 C-10
Goddard, 3337 I-12
Goessel, 547 G-13
Goodland, 4485 C-2
GOVE CO., 2763 E-5
GRAHAM CO., 2721 D-6
Grainfield, 298 D-5
Grandview Plaza, 1039 D-14
GRANT CO., 7530 I-3
GRAY CO., 5861 H-5
Great Bend, 15440 F-9
GREELEY CO., 1349 F-2
Greenleaf, 328 B-13
Greensburg, 1398 I-8
GREENWOOD CO., 7338 H-15
Gridley, 365 G-16
Gypsum, 399 E-12
Halstead, 1912 H-12
HAMILTON CO., 2604 G-2
Hanover, 593 B-14
Harper, 1478 J-11
HARPER CO., 6081 J-11
Hartford, 505 G-16
HARVEY CO., 33843 G-12
HASKELL CO., 4232 I-4
Haven, 1170 H-12
Haviland, 574 I-8
Hays, 19632 E-8
Haysville, 9817 I-13
Herington, 2468 F-14
Hesston, 3631 G-12
Hiawatha, 3236 B-17
Highland, 941 B-17
Hill City, 1451 C-7
Hillsboro, 2731 F-13
HODGEMAN CO., 2110 G-6
Hoisington, 2996 F-9
Holcomb, 1888 H-4
Holton, 3400 C-16
Holyrood, 452 F-10
Hope, 367 E-13
Horton, 1843 B-17
Howard, 764 I-15
Hoxie, 1149 C-5
Hoyt, 600 D-16
Hugoton, 3644 J-3
Humboldt, 1921 H-17
Hutchinson, 40961 G-11
Independence, 9284 J-17
Inman, 1194 G-12
Iola, 6008 H-17
JACKSON CO., 13535 C-16
JEFFERSON CO., 19106 D-17
Jetmore, 914 G-7
JEWELL CO., 3352 B-11
Jewell, 439 C-11
Johnson, 1411 I-2
JOHNSON CO., 506562 E-18
Jct. City, 16402 D-14
Kanopolis, 516 E-11
Kansas City, 144210 D-19
KEARNY CO., 4516 G-3
Kensington, 490 B-9
Kingman, 3183 I-11
KINGMAN CO., 8165 I-11
Kinsley, 1547 H-8
Kiowa, 965 K-10
KIOWA CO., 2984 I-8
Kismet, 521 J-5
LABETTE CO., 22169 J-18
La Crosse, 1305 F-8
La Cygne, 1146 F-19
La Harpe, 673 H-18
Lake Quivira, 922 *J-1
Lakin, 2292 H-3
LANE CO., 1894 F-5
Lansing, 10214 D-18
Larned, 3874 G-8
Lawrence, 81816 E-18
Leavenworth, 35213 C-18
LEAVENWORTH CO., 73113 D-18
Leawood, 30145 E-19
Lebanon, 278 B-10
Lebo, 950 F-16
Lecompton, 589 D-17
Lenexa, 43434 D-19
Leon, 648 I-14
Leonardville, 354 C-14
Leoti, 1440 F-3
Le Roy, 579 G-17
Lewis, 475 H-8
Liberal, 20257 J-4
Lincoln, 1263 D-11
LINCOLN CO., 3411 D-11
Lindsborg, 3305 F-12
LINN CO., 9914 G-18
Linn, 388 B-13
Little River, 528 F-11
LOGAN CO., 2794 E-3
Logan, 549 C-7
Longton, 371 I-16
Louisburg, 3313 F-19
Lucas, 422 D-10
Lyndon, 1041 F-17
LYON CO., 35609 G-15
Lyons, 3554 G-11
Macksville, 494 H-9
Madison, 799 G-16
Maize, 2117 H-12
Manhattan, 48668 D-14
Mankato, 843 B-10
Maple Hill, 492 D-16
MARION CO., 12952 G-13
Marion, 2028 G-13
Marquette, 585 F-11
MARSHALL CO., 10405 B-14
Marysville, 3151 B-14
McCune, 424 I-18
McLouth, 849 D-18
MCPHERSON CO., 29523 F-11
McPherson, 13695 F-12
MEADE CO., 4625 J-6
Meade, 1629 J-5
Medicine Lodge, 2028 J-10
Melvern, 430 F-17
Meriden, 708 D-17
Merriam, 10769 *J-2
MIAMI CO., 30496 F-18
Milford, 444 D-14
Miltonvale, 486 C-12
Minneapolis, 2015 D-12
Minneola, 681 I-6
Mission, 9751 *J-2
Mission Hills, 3523 *J-3
MITCHELL CO., 6420 D-11
Moline, 431 I-15
Montezuma, 964 I-5
MONTGOMERY CO., 34570 I-16
Moran, 541 H-18
MORRIS CO., 6049 E-14
MORTON CO., 3196 J-2
Mound City, 820 G-19
Moundridge, 1643 G-12
Mound Valley, 414 J-17
Mt. Hope, 842 H-12
Mulberry, 574 I-19
Mulvane, 5628 I-13
Natoma, 329 D-9
NEMAHA CO., 10443 B-16
Neodesha, 2652 I-17
NEOSHO CO., 16529 I-17
NESS CO., 3009 F-7
Ness City, 1326 F-7
Newton, 18229 G-13
Nickerson, 1164 G-11
N. Newton, 1574 G-13
NORTON CO., 5664 B-6
Norton, 2806 B-7
Nortonville, 598 C-17
Norwich, 522 I-11
Oaklawn, 3000 N-9
Oakley, 1984 D-4
Oberlin, 1811 B-5
Ogden, 1432 D-14
Olathe, 111334 E-19
Olpe, 509 G-15
Onaga, 683 C-15
OSAGE CO., 17150 F-16
Osage City, 2987 F-16
Osawatomie, 4616 F-18
Osborne, 1440 C-9
OSBORNE CO., 4050 C-9
Oskaloosa, 1149 D-17
Oswego, 1996 J-18
Otis, 319 F-9
Ottawa, 12597 F-18
OTTAWA CO., 6123 D-12
Overbrook, 971 E-17
Overland Park, 164811 D-19
Oxford, 1117 J-13
Ozawkie, 574 D-17
Paola, 5292 F-19
Park City, 7173 H-13
Parsons, 11212 I-18
PAWNEE CO., 6739 G-7
Pawnee Rock, 346 G-9
Peabody, 1302 G-13
Perry, 883 D-17
PHILLIPS CO., 5504 B-8
Phillipsburg, 2432 B-8
Pittsburg, 19214 I-19
Plains, 1163 J-5
Plainville, 1889 D-8
Pleasanton, 1368 G-19
Pomona, 942 F-17
POTTAWATOMIE CO., 19129 C-15
Potwin, 438 H-13
Prairie Vil., 21454 D-19
PRATT CO., 9496 H-9
Pratt, 6447 I-9
Pretty Prairie, 600 H-11
Protection, 541 J-7
Quenemo, 455 F-17
Quinter, 846 D-6
Ransom, 292 F-6
RAWLINS CO., 2672 B-3
RENO CO., 63558 H-11
REPUBLIC CO., 5164 B-12
RICE CO., 10452 F-10
Richmond, 514 F-18
RILEY CO., 62826 D-14
Riley, 692 D-14
Riverton, 600 J-19
Roeland Park, 6975 *J-3
Rolla, 445 J-2
ROOKS CO., 5351 D-8
Rose Hill, 3896 I-13
Rossville, 996 D-16
RUSH CO., 3406 F-8
RUSSELL CO., 6845 D-9
Russell, 4342 E-9
Sabetha, 2523 B-16
St. Francis, 1376 B-2
St. John, 1215 H-9
St. Marys, 2253 D-16
St. Paul, 657 I-18
Salina, 45956 E-12
SALINE CO., 53919 E-11
Satanta, 1179 I-4
Scammon, 475 J-19
Scandia, 374 B-12
SCOTT CO., 4600 F-4
Scott City, 3474 F-4
Scranton, 712 E-16
Sedan, 1269 J-16
SEDGWICK CO., 466061 I-12
Sedgwick, 1644 H-12
Seneca, 2068 B-16
Severy, 352 I-15
SEWARD CO., 23274 J-4
Sharon Sprs., 733 E-2
Shawnee, 57628 D-19
SHAWNEE CO., 172365 E-16
SHERIDAN CO., 2591 D-5
SHERMAN CO., 6153 C-2
Silver Lake, 1352 D-16
SMITH CO., 4121 B-9
Smith Cen., 1725 B-9
Solomon, 1056 E-13
S. Haven, 368 J-13
S. Hutchinson, 2481 H-11
Spearville, 858 H-7
Spring Hill, 4494 E-19
Stafford, 1067 H-10
STAFFORD CO., 4488 H-9
STANTON CO., 2245 I-2
Sterling, 2576 G-11
STEVENS CO., 5412 J-3
Stockton, 1453 C-8
Strong City, 583 F-15
Sublette, 1582 I-4
SUMNER CO., 24797 J-12
Syracuse, 1788 H-2
Tecumseh, 650 M-17
Thayer, 500 I-17
THOMAS CO., 7639 D-3
Tonganoxie, 3774 D-18
Topeka, 121946 D-17
Towanda, 1355 H-13
TREGO CO., 3050 E-6
Tribune, 722 F-2
Troy, 1017 B-18
Turon, 436 H-10
Udall, 766 I-13
Ulysses, 5650 I-3
Valley Cen., 5508 H-13
Valley Falls, 1209 C-17
Victoria, 1164 E-8
WABAUNSEE CO., 6919 E-15
WaKeeney, 1773 D-7
Wakefield, 874 D-13
WALLACE CO., 1573 E-2
Wamego, 4243 D-15
WASHINGTON CO., 6009 B-13
Washington, 1145 B-13
Waterville, 628 B-14
Wathena, 1290 B-18
Waverly, 556 F-17
Weir, 752 J-19
Wellington, 8098 J-13
Wellsville, 1631 E-18
Westmoreland, 655 C-15
Westwood, 1483 *J-3
Westwood Hills, 365 *J-3
White City, 499 E-14
Whitewater, 639 H-13
Wichita, 354865 I-13
WICHITA CO., 2309 F-3
Wilroads Gardens, 400 H-6
WILSON CO., 9834 I-16
Wilson, 767 E-10
Winchester, 582 C-17
Winfield, 11861 J-14
WOODSON CO., 3572 H-16
WYANDOTTE CO., 155750 D-18
Yates Cen., 1493 H-17

Kentucky

Map pp. 86-89

ADAIR CO., 17573 L-10
Adairville, 930 N-5
Ages, 500 M-16
Airport Gardens, 700 K-17
Albany, 2288 M-10
Alexandria, 7996 D-13
ALLEN CO., 18706 N-7
Altro, 35 K-16
Anchorage, 2529 G-9
Anco, 360 K-17
ANDERSON CO., 20394 H-11
Argillite, 50 F-18
Arjay, 600 M-15
Arlington, 391 F-2
Artemus, 800 M-14
Ary, 60 K-17
Ashland, 21510 F-18
Auburn, 1489 M-5
Audubon Park, 1535 C-7
Augusta, 1257 E-14
Aurora, 200 M-1
Auxier, 900 I-18
Avawam, 250 K-16
BALLARD CO., 8277 E-2
Banner, 100 J-18
Barbourmeade, 1272 A-9
Barbourville, 3520 M-14
Bardstown, 10984 I-9
Bardwell, 793 F-2
Barlow, 713 E-2
BARREN CO., 40073 L-8
Baskett, 300 I-3
BATH CO., 11626 G-14
Baxter, 800 M-16
Beattyville, 1153 J-15
Beauty, 600 I-19
Beaver, 200 K-18
Beaver Dam, 3113 K-5
Bedford, 740 F-10
Beechmont, 600 K-4
Beechwood Vil., 1170 B-8
Belfry, 600 J-19
BELL CO., 29665 M-15
Bellefonte, 846 E-19
Bellemeade, 873 B-9
Bellevue, 6022 A-17
Benham, 556 L-17
Benton, 4335 F-4
Berea, 13230 J-13
Betsy Layne, 450 J-18
Bloomfield, 873 I-10
Bond, 90 K-14
Bonnieville, 365 K-8
BOONE CO., 106272 D-11
Boone Hts., 800 M-14
Boston, 300 I-9
BOURBON CO., 19833 H-13
Bowling Green, 52272 L-6
BOYD CO., 49594 G-18
BOYLE CO., 28363 J-11
BRACKEN CO., 8670 E-13
Brandenburg, 2214 H-7
BREATHITT CO., 15957 J-16
BRECKINRIDGE CO., 19293 I-6
Brodhead, 1194 K-13
Bromley, 784 B-16
Bronston, 400 L-12
Brooks, 2678 H-8
Brooksville, 609 E-14
Browder, 300 K-4
Brownsboro Farm, 678 A-9
Brownsboro Vil., 316 B-8
Brownsville, 1039 K-7
Buckner, 4000 G-9
Buffalo, 400 J-9
Bulan, 600 K-17
BULLITT CO., 68474 H-9
Burgin, 873 I-11
Burkesville, 1760 M-10
Burlington, 10779 D-12
Burnside, 673 L-12
BUTLER CO., 13414 K-6
Butler, 634 E-13
Cadiz, 2550 M-2
CALDWELL CO., 12973 K-1
Calhoun, 813 J-4
CALLOWAY CO., 35122 N-1
Calvert City, 2749 E-4
Camargo, 963 H-14
CAMPBELL CO., 87251 E-13
Campbellsburg, 714 F-10
Campbellsville, 10906 K-10
Campton, 410 I-15
Canada, 400 J-19
Caneyville, 653 K-6
Cannel City, 250 I-16
Cannonsburg, 700 G-18
CARLISLE CO., 5329 F-2
Carlisle, 2030 G-14
CARROLL CO., 10454 E-10
Carrollton, 3861 F-10
CARTER CO., 27306 G-17
CASEY CO., 16290 K-11
Catlettsburg, 1927 F-18
Cave City, 2054 L-8
Cawood, 850 M-16
Cecilia, 750 J-8
Centertown, 427 K-4
Central City, 5785 K-4
Chaplin, 500 I-10
Cherrywood Vil. B-8
Chloe, 150 J-19
CHRISTIAN CO., 70145 L-3
CLARK CO., 34887 H-13
Clarkson, 826 J-7
CLAY CO., 24146 K-15
Clay, 1180 J-2
Clay City, 1344 I-14
Clearfield, 1300 H-16
Cleaton, 500 K-4
Clinton, 1364 G-2
CLINTON CO., 9559 M-11
Cloverport, 1262 I-6
Cold Spring, 5255 C-17
Colonial Ter. B-9
Columbia, 4174 L-10
Combs, 900 K-16
Corbin, 8230 L-14
Corydon, 773 I-2
Covington, 42811 D-12
Crab Orchard, 866 J-12
Cranks, 120 M-17
Crescent Park C-15
Crescent Sprs., 3975 B-15
Crestview, 459 C-18
Crestview Hills, 3362 C-15
Crestwood, 2250 G-9
Crittenden, 2571 E-12
CRITTENDEN CO., 8984 J-1
Crofton, 825 L-3
Cromona, 400 K-18
Cub Run, 125 K-7
Cumberland, 2330 L-17
CUMBERLAND CO., 7147 M-9
Cunningham, 400 F-3
Custer, 125 I-7
Cynthiana, 6311 G-13
Danville, 15409 J-11
DAVIESS CO., 93060 J-4
Dawson Sprs., 2953 K-2
Dayton, 5556 A-17
Diablock, 200 K-17
Dixon, 611 J-2
Dorton, 250 K-18
Drakesboro, 625 K-4
Drift, 300 J-18
Dry Ridge, 2176 E-12
Dwarf, 100 K-17
Earlington, 1601 K-3
E. Bernstadt, 774 K-14
Eddyville, 2373 L-1
Edgewood, 8913 C-15
EDMONSON CO., 12030 K-7
Edmonton, 1600 L-9
Elizabethtown, 23450 I-8
Elkhorn City, 1030 K-19
Elkton, 1941 M-4
ELLIOTT CO., 6902 H-17
Elsmere, 7948 D-12
Eminence, 2257 G-10
Emlyn, 350 M-14
Eolia, 300 L-18
Erlanger, 16852 D-12
Ermine, 300 L-18
ESTILL CO., 15089 I-14
Evarts, 1052 M-17
Ezel, 300 I-16
Falmouth, 2096 E-13
Fancy Farm, 300 F-3
FAYETTE CO., 268080 H-13
Ferguson, 912 L-12
Flaherty, 250 I-7
Flat Lick, 700 M-15
Flatwoods, 7621 F-18
FLEMING CO., 14610 G-14
Fleming-Neon, 808 K-18
Flemingsburg, 3104 F-15
Florence, 26349 D-12
FLOYD CO., 42218 J-18
Fordsville, 546 J-5
Forest Hills, 507 C-9
Forest Hills, 300 J-19
Ft. Mitchell, 7605 D-12
Ft. Thomas, 15592 D-12
Ft. Wright, 5438 B-16
Fourmile, 450 M-15
Frankfort, 27210 G-11
FRANKLIN CO., 48207 G-11
Franklin, 8079 M-6
Fredonia, 418 K-1
Freeburn, 500 J-20
Frenchburg, 569 H-15
FULTON CO., 7217 G-1
Fulton, 2564 G-2
GALLATIN CO., 8134 E-11
Gamaliel, 431 N-8
Garner, 150 K-17
GARRARD CO., 16579 J-12
Garrett, 500 J-18
Garrison, 600 F-16
Georgetown, 19988 G-12
Ghent, 389 E-11
Gilbertsville, 800 E-4
Glasgow, 14062 L-8
Glendale, 350 J-8
Glenview Hills, 341 A-8
Goshen, 987 G-9
Graham, 700 K-3
Grahn, 550 G-17
Grand Rivers, 339 L-1
GRANT CO., 24610 F-12
GRAVES CO., 37625 F-3
Gray, 750 L-14
Graymoor-Devondale, 2937 B-9
Grays Knob, 300 M-16
Grayson, 3986 G-17
GRAYSON CO., 25189 J-7
GREEN CO., 11588 K-9
Greensburg, 2396 K-9
GREENUP CO., 37184 F-17
Greenup, 1184 F-18
Greenville, 4273 K-4
Guthrie, 1434 N-4
Hagerhill, 150 I-18
HANCOCK CO., 8613 I-5
Hanson, 592 J-3
Hardin, 570 M-1
HARDIN CO., 96947 J-7
Hardinsburg, 2452 I-6
Hardy, 650 J-20
Harlan, 1912 M-16
HARLAN CO., 31614 L-17
Harold, 400 J-18
HARRISON CO., 18527 F-12
Harrodsburg, 8126 I-11
HART CO., 18319 K-8
Hartford, 2652 J-5
Hawesville, 981 I-5
Hazard, 4819 K-17
Hazel, 447 G-4
Hebron, 3500 D-12
Heidrick, 700 M-14
Hellier, 400 K-19
HENDERSON CO., 45573 I-2
Henderson, 27666 I-3
HENRY CO., 15903 G-11
Herndon, 150 M-2
HICKMAN CO., 5075 G-2
Hickman, 2371 G-1
Highland Hts., 5791 C-17
Hillcrest, 300 I-13
Hillview, 7349 H-9
Hima, 250 L-15
Hindman, 772 K-17
Hitchins, 350 G-17
Hodgenville, 2788 J-8
Hollow Cr., 821 D-8
Hollyvilla, 494 H-8
HOPKINS CO., 46705 K-2
Hopkinsville, 28821 M-3
Horse Cave, 2314 L-8
Houston Acres, 491 C-9
Hulen, 300 M-16
Hurstbourne, 3939 B-9
Hustonville, 356 J-11
Hyden, 196 L-16
Independence, 19065 D-12
Indian Hills, 2977 B-8
Inez, 457 I-19
Ironville, 600 E-19
Irvine, 2714 I-14
Irvington, 1359 I-7
Island, 436 J-4
Jackhorn, 500 K-18
JACKSON CO., 13618 K-14
Jackson, 2413 J-16
Jamestown, 1711 L-11
Jeff, 400 K-17
JEFFERSON CO., 699827 H-9
Jeffersontown, 26100 G-9
Jeffersonville, 1882 H-14
Jenkins, 2297 K-18
JESSAMINE CO., 43463 I-12
JOHNSON CO., 24001 H-17
Jonancy, 125 K-18
Junction City, 2175 J-11
KENTON CO., 153665 E-12
Kenton, 175 E-12
Kenvir, 900 M-17
Kevil, 572 E-3
Kingsley, 424 C-8
KNOTT CO., 17561 K-17
Knottsville, 400 I-5
KNOX CO., 32069 L-15
Kuttawa, 631 L-1
La Center, 1034 E-2
La Grange, 6046 G-10
Lake City, 300 L-1
Lakeside Park, 2687 C-16
Lancaster, 4207 J-12
Langley, 400 J-18
LARUE CO., 13699 J-8
LAUREL CO., 56338 L-14
LAWRENCE CO., 16166 H-18
Lawrenceburg, 9403 H-11
Lebanon, 5959 J-10
Lebanon Jct., 1934 I-8
Leburn, 250 K-17
LEE CO., 7709 J-15
Leitchfield, 6462 J-7
Lejunior, 300 M-17
LESLIE CO., 11994 L-16
LETCHER CO., 24434 L-17
LEWIS CO., 13872 F-16
Lewisburg, 918 L-4
Lewisport, 1655 H-5
Lexington, 268080 H-12
Liberty, 1892 K-11
Lily, 500 L-14
LINCOLN CO., 25122 K-12
Lindseyville, 200 K-7
Livermore, 1469 J-4
LIVINGSTON CO., 9760 D-4
Lloyd, 900 F-17
LOGAN CO., 27169 L-5
London, 7787 L-14
Lone Oak, 439 E-3
Long View, 200 I-8
Lookout, 350 K-19
Loretto, 650 J-9
Louisa, 2051 H-18
Louisville, 556429 G-8
Lovely, 700 I-19
Loyall, 723 M-16
Ludlow, 4647 D-12
Lynch, 844 L-17
Lyndon, 10248 B-9
Lynnview, 960 C-7
LYON CO., 8160 L-1
Maceo, 500 I-4
MADISON CO., 77749 I-13
Madisonville, 19273 K-3
Magnolia, 800 J-8
MAGOFFIN CO., 13472 J-17
Majestic, 400 J-20
Manchester, 1968 L-15
Marion, 3033 K-1
MARION CO., 18939 J-10
MARSHALL CO., 30967 F-4
Marshes Siding, 700 M-12
MARTIN CO., 12215 I-19
Martin, 636 J-18
MASON CO., 17140 F-15
Masonville, 1075 I-4
Mayfield, 10288 F-3
Mays Lick, 350 F-14
Maysville, 9136 F-15
McAndrews, 450 J-19
MCCRACKEN CO., 64698 E-3
MCCREARY CO., 17233 N-12
McDaniels, 200 J-6
McDowell, 400 J-18
McHenry, 436 K-5
McKee, 855 J-14
MCLEAN CO., 9926 J-3
McRoberts, 921 K-18
McVeigh, 250 J-19
MEADE CO., 28447 H-7
Melbourne, 453 D-13
Melvin, 250 K-18
MENIFEE CO., 6809 H-15
MERCER CO., 21610 I-11
METCALFE CO., 10197 L-9
Middlesboro, 10164 N-15
Middletown, 6072 G-9
Midway, 1622 H-12
Millersburg, 839 G-13
Millstone, 300 K-18
Milton, 595 E-10
Minor Lane Hts., 1526 D-7
Mitchellsburg, 350 J-11
MONROE CO., 11660 M-9
MONTGOMERY CO., 24256 H-14
Monticello, 6062 M-11
Moorland, 463 B-9
Morehead, 7592 G-16
MORGAN CO., 14334 H-16
Morganfield, 3430 I-1
Morgantown, 2552 K-5
Mortons Gap, 956 K-3
Mt. Olivet, 287 F-14
Mt. Sterling, 6317 H-14
Mt. Vernon, 2599 K-13
Mt. Washington, 8624 H-9
Mousie, 400 J-18
MUHLENBERG CO., 31548 L-4
Muldraugh, 1346 H-8
Munfordville, 1603 K-8
Murray, 15538 G-4
Nazareth, 400 I-9
NELSON CO., 41088 I-9
New Castle, 929 F-10
New Haven, 864 J-9
New Hope, 200 J-9
Newport, 15911 D-12
NICHOLAS CO., 7027 G-14
Nicholasville, 23897 I-12
N. Corbin, 1662 L-14
Northfield, 984 B-8
N. Middletown, 561 H-14
Nortonville, 1252 K-3
Oakdale, 1900 E-4
Oak Grove, 7570 N-3
OHIO CO., 23676 J-5
Oil Sprs., 150 I-17
OLDHAM CO., 53533 G-10
Olive Hill, 1823 G-16
Oneida, 300 K-15
OWEN CO., 11374 F-11
Owensboro, 55459 I-4
Owenton, 1470 F-11
Owingsville, 1564 H-15
OWSLEY CO., 4746 J-15
Paducah, 25575 E-3
Paintsville, 4141 I-18
Paris, 9334 G-13
Park City, 542 L-7
Park Hills, 2803 B-16
Parkway Vil., 706 C-7
Pathfork, 400 M-16
Pembroke, 778 M-3
PENDLETON CO., 15125 F-13
PERRY CO., 29452 K-17
Perryville, 755 J-11
Petersburg, 400 D-11
Pewee Valley, 1546 A-10
Phelps, 1053 J-20
Philpot, 400 I-4
Phyllis, 350 J-19
PIKE CO., 66922 J-19
Pikeville, 6312 J-19
Pilgrim, 150 I-19
Pine Knot, 1680 N-13
Pine Ridge, 125 I-15
Pineville, 2014 M-15
Pioneer Village, 2631 H-9
Pittsburg, 600 L-14
Plantation, 903 B-9
Pleasant Ridge, 200 J-4
Pleasant View, 500 M-14
Pleasureville, 888 G-10
Poole, 400 J-2
Powderly, 843 K-4
POWELL CO., 13687 I-14
Premium, 150 L-17
Prestonsburg, 3706 I-18
Princeton, 6447 L-1
Prospect, 4877 G-9
Providence, 3549 K-2
PULASKI CO., 59200 L-12
Quicksand, 150 J-16
Quincy, 350 F-17
Raccoon, 400 J-19
Raceland, 2477 F-18
Radcliff, 21471 I-8
Ravenna, 676 I-14
Reed, 100 I-3
Reidland, 4353 E-4
Revelo, 700 M-12
Richlawn, 452 B-8

2000 Census populations or latest available estimate.
Index to Canada and Mexico cities and towns, pages 274-275.

Richmond, 30893 .... I-13
Rineyville, 400 .... I-8
Riverwood, 477 .... A-8
Robards, 568 .... I-3
ROBERTSON CO., 2279 .... F-14
Robinson Cr., 400 .... K-19
ROCKCASTLE CO., 16712 .... K-13
Rockhouse, 200 .... K-19
Rockport, 344 .... K-4
Rolling Fields, 653 .... B-8
Rolling Hills, 907 .... A-9
Rosine, 200 .... J-5
ROWAN CO., 22226 .... H-16
Rowletts, 300 .... K-8
Royalton, 200 .... I-17
Russell, 3597 .... F-18
RUSSELL CO., 17020 .... M-10
Russell Sprs., 2537 .... L-10
Russellville, 7271 .... M-5
Sacramento, 515 .... K-3
St. Catharine, 500 .... I-10
St. Charles, 312 .... K-3
St. Dennis C-5
St. Matthews, 17309 .... G-9
St. Regis Park, 1526 .... C-9
Salem, 759 .... K-1
Salt Lick, 355 .... H-15
Salvisa, 250 .... I-11
Salyersville, 1604 .... I-17
Sandgap, 300 .... J-14
Sandy Hook, 687 .... H-17
Sassafras, 950 .... K-17
Science Hill, 653 .... K-12
SCOTT CO., 39380 .... G-12
Scottsville, 4525 .... M-7
Sebree, 1569 .... J-3
Sedalia, 300 .... G-3
Seneca Gardens, 695 .... C-8
Sharpsburg, 312 .... G-14
Shelbiana, 350 .... J-19
SHELBY CO., 38205 .... G-10
Shelbyville, 10730 .... G-10
Shepherdsville, 8874 .... H-8
Shively, 15212 .... G-8
Sidney, 200 .... J-19
Silver Gr., 1174 .... D-13
SIMPSON CO., 17021 .... M-6
Simpsonville, 1369 .... G-10
Smith, 150 .... M-16
Smithland, 395 .... E-4
Smith Mills, 450 .... I-2
Smiths Gr., 752 .... L-7
Somerset, 12136 .... L-12
Southgate, 3356 .... B-17
S. Irvine, 400 .... I-14
S. Portsmouth, 900 .... E-17
S. Shore, 1243 .... E-17
S. Williamson, 1000 .... I-19
SPENCER CO., 15651 .... H-10
Spottsville, 350 .... I-3
Springfield, 2806 .... I-10
Springlee B-8
Staffordsville, 200 .... I-18
Stamping Ground, 631 .... G-12
Stanford, 3452 .... J-12
Stanley, 300 .... I-4
Stanton, 3109 .... I-14
Stanville, 125 .... J-18
Stearns, 1586 .... M-12
Strathmoor Vil., 619 .... C-8
Sturgis, 2008 .... J-1
Sublimity City, 800 .... L-14
Sullivan, 300 .... J-1
Summer Shade, 300 .... M-8
Summersville, 150 .... K-9
Summit, 900 .... F-18
Sunshine, 350 .... M-16
Symsonia, 500 .... F-4
Tateville, 500 .... L-12
TAYLOR CO., 23754 .... K-10
Taylor Mill, 6733 .... C-17
Taylorsville, 1173 .... H-10
Thealka, 400 .... I-18
Tinsley, 100 .... M-15
TODD CO., 11944 .... M-4
Tollesboro, 600 .... F-15
Tompkinsville, 2633 .... M-9
Topmost, 200 .... K-18
Trenton, 419 .... M-3
TRIGG CO., 13349 .... M-2
TRIMBLE CO., 9023 .... F-10
Ulysses, 30 .... H-18
Union, 3379 .... D-12
UNION CO., 15592 .... J-2
Uniontown, 1063 .... I-1
Upton, 629 .... J-8
Utica, 300 .... J-4
Vanceburg, 1698 .... F-16
Van Lear, 1050 .... I-18
Verda, 800 .... M-16
Verona, 600 .... E-12
Versailles, 7728 .... H-12
Villa Hills, 7749 .... B-15
Vine Gr., 3983 .... I-8
Viper, 100 .... K-17
Virgie, 300 .... K-18
Waco, 200 .... I-13
Walton, 2856 .... E-12
Warfield, 274 .... I-19
WARREN CO., 98960 .... L-7
Warsaw, 1838 .... E-11
WASHINGTON CO., 11399 .... I-10
Water Valley, 322 .... G-3
Watterson Park, 1046 .... C-8
Waverly, 292 .... I-2
Wayland, 293 .... J-18
WAYNE CO., 20352 .... M-11
WEBSTER CO., 14161 .... J-2
Weeksbury, 800 .... K-18
Wellington, 556 .... C-8
W. Buechel, 1323 .... C-8
W. Liberty, 3349 .... H-16
W. Point, 1032 .... H-8
Westport, 300 .... F-9
W. Van Lear, 600 .... I-18
Westwood, 4888 .... F-18
Westwood, 614 .... B-9
Wheelwright, 1032 .... K-18
White Plains, 804 .... K-3
Whitesburg, 1512 .... L-18
Whitesville, 596 .... I-5
WHITLEY CO., 38029 .... M-13
Whitley City, 1111 .... M-12
Wickliffe, 790 .... E-2
Wilder, 2981 .... B-17
Williamsburg, 5162 .... M-13
Williamstown, 3423 .... F-12
Wilmore, 5826 .... I-12
Winchester, 16494 .... H-13
Windy Hills, 2504 .... B-8
Wingo, 595 .... G-3
Wittensville, 200 .... I-18
WOLFE CO., 7070 .... I-15
Woodbine, 500 .... M-14
Woodburn, 334 .... M-6
WOODFORD CO., 24246 .... H-11
Woodlawn, 254 .... B-17
Woodlawn Park, 1034 .... B-8
Worthington, 1679 .... F-18
Wurtland, 1046 .... F-18
Zebulon, 200 .... J-19

Louisiana

Map pp. 90-91

Abbeville, 11664 .... H-5
Abita Sprs., 2211 .... G-9
ACADIA PAR., 59552 .... H-4
Addis, 2430 .... H-7
Albany, 1002 .... G-8
Alexandria, 45693 .... E-4
ALLEN PAR., 25270 .... G-3
Amelia, 2423 .... I-7
Amite, 4065 .... G-8
Anacoco, 782 .... E-3
Anandale, 2000 .... E-4
Arabi, 8093 .... H-9
Arcadia, 2854 .... B-3
Arnaudville, 1395 .... G-5
ASCENSION PAR., 90501 .... H-7
ASSUMPTION PAR., 23196 .... I-7
Avondale, 5441 .... E-12
AVOYELLES PAR., 42098 .... E-5
Baker, 13250 .... G-7
Baldwin, 2603 .... I-6
Ball, 3684 .... E-4
Barataria, 1333 .... I-9
Basile, 2382 .... G-4
Bastrop, 12403 .... B-5
Baton Rouge, 222064 .... G-7
Bawcomville, 2300 .... C-5
Bayou Cane, 17046 .... I-8
Bayou Goula, 650 .... H-7
BEAUREGARD PAR., 34562 .... G-2
Belle Chasse, 9848 .... I-9
Belle Rose, 1944 .... H-7
Benton, 2886 .... B-2
Bernice, 1727 .... B-4
Berwick, 4286 .... I-7
BIENVILLE PAR., 15176 .... C-3
Bogalusa, 12964 .... F-10
Boothville, 900 .... J-11
BOSSIER PAR., 105541 .... B-2
Bossier City, 60505 .... B-2
Bourg, 2160 .... I-8
Boyce, 1188 .... E-4
Breaux Bridge, 7902 .... H-5
Bridge City, 8323 .... E-12
Broussard, 6754 .... H-5
Brusly, 2028 .... G-7
Bunkie, 4502 .... F-5
Buras, 1480 .... J-11
CADDO PAR., 251309 .... B-1
CALCASIEU PAR., 185419 .... H-2
CALDWELL PAR., 10563 .... C-5
CAMERON PAR., 9558 .... I-3
Cameron, 1965 .... I-3
Campti, 1054 .... D-3
Carencro, 6097 .... H-5
Carville H-7
Catahoula, 700 .... H-6
CATAHOULA PAR., 10447 .... D-5
Cecilia, 1505 .... H-6
Centerville, 700 .... I-6
Chalmette, 32069 .... H-10
Charenton, 1944 .... I-6
Chatham, 616 .... C-4
Chauvin, 3229 .... J-8
Cheneyville, 884 .... F-5
Choudrant, 580 .... B-4
Church Pt., 4682 .... G-5
CLAIBORNE PAR., 16309 .... B-3
Clarence, 494 .... D-3
Clarks, 1060 .... D-5
Clayton, 791 .... D-6
Clinton, 1922 .... F-7
Colfax, 1676 .... E-4
CONCORDIA PAR., 19273 .... E-6
Cottonport, 2266 .... F-5
Cotton Valley, 1169 .... B-2
Coushatta, 2205 .... D-3
Covington, 9347 .... G-9
Crowley, 13861 .... H-4
Cullen, 1248 .... A-2
Cut Off, 5635 .... I-9
Delcambre, 2146 .... H-5
Delhi, 3055 .... B-6
Denham Sprs., 10206 .... G-7
DeQuincy, 3234 .... G-2
DeRidder, 9976 .... F-3
Des Allemands, 2500 .... I-8
DE SOTO PAR., 26383 .... C-2
Donaldsonville, 7535 .... H-7
Doyline, 831 .... B-2
Dubach, 776 .... B-4
Duson, 1619 .... H-5
EAST BATON ROUGE PAR., 411417 .... G-7
EAST CARROLL PAR., 8756 .... B-7
EAST FELICIANA PAR., 20823 .... F-7
Elton, 1249 .... G-4
Empire, 2211 .... J-10
Epps, 1120 .... B-6
Erath, 2177 .... H-5
Estherwood, 836 .... H-4
Eunice, 11527 .... G-4
EVANGELINE PAR., 35540 .... G-4
Farmerville, 3662 .... B-4
Ferriday, 3568 .... D-6
Florien, 701 .... E-2
Fordoche, 949 .... G-6
Forest Oaks, 1500 .... B-14
FRANKLIN PAR., 20380 .... C-6
Franklin, 7822 .... I-6
Franklinton, 3708 .... F-9
French Settlement, 1053 .... H-8
Galliano, 7356 .... J-9
Garyville, 2775 .... H-8
Gibsland, 1082 .... B-3
Gilbert, 527 .... C-6
Glenmora, 1558 .... F-4
Golden Meadow, 2145 .... J-9
Gonzales, 8499 .... H-8
Grambling, 4522 .... B-4
Gramercy, 3178 .... H-8
Grand Coteau, 1035 .... G-5
Grand Isle, 1594 .... J-9
GRANT PAR., 19503 .... E-4
Gray, 4958 .... I-8
Grayson, 527 .... C-5
Greensburg, 615 .... F-8
Greenwood, 2609 .... C-1
Gretna, 17161 .... I-9
Grosse Tete, 626 .... G-6
Gueydan, 1603 .... H-4
Hackberry, 1699 .... H-2
Hahnville, 2792 .... H-9
Hammond, 18096 .... G-8
Harahan, 9716 .... H-9
Hardwood, 500 .... F-7
Harrisonburg, 728 .... D-6
Harvey, 22226 .... E-13
Haughton, 2791 .... B-2
Hayes, 880 .... H-3
Haynesville, 2540 .... A-3
Henderson, 1544 .... H-6
Hessmer, 650 .... F-5
Hodge, 480 .... C-4
Homer, 3552 .... B-3
Houma, 32105 .... I-8
IBERIA PAR., 74388 .... H-6
IBERVILLE PAR., 32386 .... H-6
Independence, 1718 .... G-8
Inniswold, 4944 .... C-13
Iota, 1399 .... H-4
Iowa, 2591 .... H-3
Jackson, 3774 .... F-7
JACKSON PAR., 15135 .... C-4
Jarreau, 520 .... G-6
Jeanerette, 5945 .... I-6
Jefferson, 11843 .... E-12
JEFFERSON PAR., 452824 .... I-9
JEFFERSON DAVIS PAR., 31272 .... H-3
Jena, 2872 .... D-5
Jennings, 10652 .... H-4
Jonesboro, 3743 .... C-4
Jonesville, 2316 .... D-6
Junction City, 632 .... A-4
Kaplan, 5131 .... H-5
Kenner, 69911 .... H-9
Kentwood, 2171 .... F-8
Killian, 1250 .... G-8
Kinder, 2104 .... G-3
Krotz Sprs., 1239 .... G-6
Labadieville, 1811 .... I-7
Lacombe, 7518 .... H-10
Lafayette, 112030 .... H-5
LAFAYETTE PAR., 197390 .... H-5
Lafitte, 1576 .... I-9
LAFOURCHE PAR., 92179 .... I-8
Lake Arthur, 2912 .... H-4
Lake Charles, 70555 .... H-3
Lake Providence, 4584 .... B-7
Lakeshore, 1400 .... B-5
Lakeview, 1200 .... A-8
La Place, 27684 .... H-8
Larose, 7306 .... I-9
LA SALLE PAR., 14040 .... D-5
Lawtell, 1000 .... G-5
Lecompte, 1338 .... F-4
Leesville, 6160 .... F-3
Leonville, 1014 .... G-5
LINCOLN PAR., 42108 .... B-4
Live Oak Manor, 1900 .... E-11
LIVINGSTON PAR., 109206 .... G-8
Livingston, 1577 .... G-8
Livonia, 1336 .... G-6
Lockport, 2596 .... I-8
Logansport, 1681 .... D-1
Loreauville, 950 .... H-6
Luling, 11512 .... H-9
Lutcher, 3598 .... H-8
Lydia, 1079 .... I-6
MADISON PAR., 12457 .... C-7
Madisonville, 744 .... G-9
Mamou, 3433 .... G-4
Mandeville, 11632 .... G-9
Mangham, 563 .... C-6
Mansfield, 5504 .... C-2
Mansura, 1564 .... F-5
Many, 2809 .... E-2
Maringouin, 1210 .... G-6
Marion, 784 .... A-5
Marksville, 5707 .... F-5
Marrero, 36165 .... E-13
Martin, 620 .... C-3
Melville, 1365 .... G-6
Meraux, 10192 .... H-10
Mermentau, 702 .... H-4
Mer Rouge, 686 .... B-6
Merryville, 1162 .... G-2
Metairie, 146136 .... H-9
Minden, 13281 .... B-3
Monroe, 51914 .... B-5
Montegut, 1803 .... J-8
Montgomery, 823 .... D-3
Mooringsport, 811 .... B-1
Moreauville, 934 .... F-5
MOREHOUSE PAR., 29989 .... B-5
Morgan City, 11930 .... I-7
Morganza, 625 .... G-6
Morse, 749 .... H-4
Moss Bluff, 10535 .... H-3
Nairn, 1000 .... J-10
Napoleonville, 689 .... H-7
NATCHITOCHES PAR., 38541 .... E-3
Natchitoches, 17701 .... D-3
Newellton, 1346 .... C-7
New Iberia, 32495 .... H-6
New Llano, 2160 .... F-3
New Orleans, 454863 .... H-9
New Roads, 4790 .... G-6
Norco, 3579 .... H-9
N. Merrydale, 4000 .... A-13
Oakdale, 7981 .... F-4
Oak Grove, 2044 .... B-6
Oak Manor, 1100 .... B-14
Oberlin, 1869 .... G-4
Oil City, 1189 .... B-1
Olla, 1359 .... D-5
Opelousas, 22897 .... G-5
ORLEANS PAR., 454863 .... H-9
OUACHITA PAR., 148237 .... C-5
Paincourtville, 884 .... H-7
Paradis, 1252 .... I-9
Patterson, 5152 .... I-7
Pearl River, 2044 .... G-10
Pierre Part, 3239 .... H-7
Pine Prairie, 1211 .... F-4
Pineville, 14083 .... E-4
Pitkin, 700 .... F-3
Plain Dealing, 1057 .... A-2
Plaquemine, 6717 .... H-7
PLAQUEMINES PAR., 28995 .... I-10
Pleasant Hill, 719 .... D-2
POINTE COUPEE PAR., 22377 .... G-6
Ponchatoula, 5784 .... G-9
Port Allen, 5062 .... G-7
Port Barre, 2318 .... G-5
Port Sulphur, 3115 .... J-10
Provencal, 704 .... D-3
Raceland, 10224 .... I-8
RAPIDES PAR., 128462 .... F-4
Rayne, 8516 .... H-5
Rayville, 4014 .... B-6
Red Oaks B-14
RED RIVER PAR., 9465 .... C-3
Reserve, 9111 .... H-8
RICHLAND PAR., 20526 .... C-6
Richwood, 2094 .... C-5
Ridgecrest, 734 .... E-6
Ringgold, 1567 .... C-3
River Ridge, 14588 .... E-11
Rosedale, 727 .... G-6
Roseland, 1227 .... G-8
Rosepine, 1321 .... F-3
Ruston, 20667 .... B-4
SABINE PAR., 23786 .... E-2
ST. BERNARD PAR., 65364 .... I-10
ST. CHARLES PAR., 50633 .... I-9
St. Francisville, 1628 .... F-7
ST. HELENA PAR., 10259 .... G-8
ST. JAMES PAR., 21150 .... I-8
ST. JOHN THE BAPTIST PAR., 46393 .... H-8
St. Joseph, 1174 .... D-7
ST. LANDRY PAR., 89937 .... G-5
ST. MARTIN PAR., 50434 .... H-6
St. Martinville, 6947 .... H-6
ST. MARY PAR., 51416 .... I-6
ST. TAMMANY PAR., 220295 .... G-9
Samtown, 3500 .... E-4
Sarepta, 916 .... A-2
Scotlandville G-7
Scott, 8120 .... H-5
Seymourville, 3000 .... H-7
Shreveport, 198874 .... B-2
Sibley, 1087 .... B-3
Simmesport, 2211 .... F-6
Simpson, 522 .... E-3
Simsboro, 664 .... B-4
Slaughter, 997 .... G-7
Slidell, 26840 .... H-10
Sorrento, 1341 .... H-8
Springhill, 5237 .... A-2
Starks, 950 .... H-2
Sterlington, 1246 .... B-5
Stonewall, 1888 .... C-2
Sulphur, 19608 .... H-2
Sunnybrook, 800 .... A-13
Sunset, 2459 .... G-5
Tallulah, 8152 .... C-7
Tangipahoa, 737 .... F-8
TANGIPAHOA PAR., 106502 .... G-8
TENSAS PAR., 6125 .... C-6
TERREBONNE PAR., 107491 .... I-7
Terrytown, 25430 .... E-14
Thibodaux, 14408 .... I-8
Tickfaw, 642 .... G-8
Tioga, 1300 .... E-4
Triumph, 1080 .... J-11
Trout, 200 .... D-5
UNION PAR., 22901 .... A-4
Urania, 685 .... D-5
Vacherie, 2411 .... H-8
VERMILION PAR., 55195 .... I-4
VERNON PAR., 48745 .... F-3
Vidalia, 4210 .... E-6
Ville Platte, 8250 .... G-5
Vinton, 3173 .... H-2
Vivian, 3866 .... A-1
Waggaman, 9435 .... E-11
Walker, 5751 .... G-8
Wardville, 1200 .... E-4
Washington, 1057 .... G-5
WASHINGTON PAR., 44623 .... F-9
Waterproof, 777 .... D-7
WEBSTER PAR., 41356 .... B-2
Welsh, 3310 .... H-4
WEST BATON ROUGE PAR., 21634 .... G-7
WEST CARROLL PAR., 11806 .... B-6
WEST FELICIANA PAR., 15199 .... F-6
Westlake, 4565 .... H-3
Westminster, 2515 .... C-13
W. Monroe, 13038 .... B-5
Westwego, 10489 .... I-9
White Castle, 1850 .... H-7
Wilson, 660 .... F-7
WINN PAR., 15968 .... D-4
Winnfield, 5307 .... D-4
Winnsboro, 4991 .... C-6
Wisner, 1066 .... D-6
Wyandotte, 1200 .... I-7
Youngsville, 5289 .... H-5
Zachary, 12258 .... G-7
Zwolle, 1768 .... D-2

Maine

Map pp. 92-93

Alfred, 600 .... I-2
Andover, 600 .... E-2
ANDROSCOGGIN CO., 108039 .... G-3
Anson, 818 .... E-4
AROOSTOOK CO., 73240 .... B-12
Ashland, 750 .... B-13
Auburn, 23602 .... G-3
Augusta, 18626 .... F-4
Bailey Island, 650 .... H-3
Bangor, 31074 .... E-6
Bar Hbr., 2680 .... F-8
Bass Hbr., 500 .... F-7
Bath, 9257 .... H-4
Belfast, 6872 .... F-6
Berwick, 1993 .... J-1
Bethel, 1200 .... F-2
Biddeford, 22072 .... I-2
Bingham, 856 .... D-4
Blaine, 500 .... C-14
Blue Hill, 800 .... F-7
Boothbay, 450 .... H-4
Boothbay Hbr., 1237 .... H-4
Brewer, 9138 .... E-6
Bridgton, 2359 .... G-2
Brownville, 350 .... C-6
Brownville Jct., 800 .... C-6
Brunswick, 14816 .... H-3
Bucksport, 2970 .... E-6
Calais, 3308 .... C-10
Camden, 3934 .... G-6
Canton, 400 .... F-3
Cape Elizabeth, 8854 .... I-3
Cape Porpoise, 500 .... I-2
Caribou, 8308 .... B-14
Castine, 800 .... F-6
Chisholm, 1399 .... F-3
Clinton, 1305 .... E-5
Corinna, 1100 .... D-5
Cornish, 600 .... H-2
CUMBERLAND CO., 274950 .... G-2
Cumberland Cen., 2596 .... H-3
Damariscotta, 1100 .... G-5
Danforth, 500 .... B-8
Dexter, 2201 .... D-5
Dixfield, 1137 .... E-2
Dover-Foxcroft, 2592 .... C-5
Eagle Lake, 600 .... B-13
E. Corinth, 400 .... D-6
E. Hampden, 1200 .... J-6
E. Machias, 300 .... E-10
E. Millinocket, 1701 .... B-7
Eastport, 1594 .... D-10
Ellsworth, 7021 .... E-7
Fairfield, 2569 .... E-4
Falmouth, 7610 .... H-3
Falmouth Foreside, 1964 .... H-10
Farmingdale, 1935 .... F-4
Farmington, 4098 .... E-3
Ft. Fairfield, 1600 .... B-14
Ft. Kent, 1978 .... A-13
FRANKLIN CO., 29704 .... D-2
Freeport, 1813 .... H-3
Frenchville, 475 .... A-13
Friendship, 600 .... G-5
Fryeburg, 1549 .... G-1
Gardiner, 6237 .... F-4
Gorham, 4164 .... H-2
Grand Isle, 375 .... A-14
Gray, 1100 .... H-3
Greenville, 1319 .... B-4
Greenville Jct., 450 .... B-4
Guilford, 945 .... C-5
Hallowell, 2535 .... F-4
Hampden, 4126 .... E-6
Hampden Highlands, 800 .... E-6
HANCOCK CO., 53660 .... D-7
Harrison, 600 .... G-2
Hartland, 872 .... D-5
Houlton, 5270 .... C-14
Howland, 1210 .... C-7
Island Falls, 600 .... A-7
Jackman, 800 .... B-3
Jay, 600 .... F-3
Jonesport, 1100 .... E-9
KENNEBEC CO., 120986 .... F-4
Kennebunk, 4804 .... I-2
Kennebunkport, 1376 .... I-2
Kezar Falls, 900 .... H-1
Kingfield, 850 .... D-3
Kittery, 4884 .... J-2
Kittery Pt., 1135 .... J-2
KNOX CO., 41219 .... F-5
Lewiston, 36050 .... G-3
Limestone, 1453 .... B-14
LINCOLN CO., 35240 .... G-4
Lincoln, 2933 .... C-7
Lisbon, 1400 .... G-3
Lisbon Falls, 4420 .... G-3
Littleton, 200 .... C-14
Livermore Falls, 1626 .... F-3
Lubec, 800 .... D-10
Machias, 1376 .... E-9
Madawaska, 3326 .... A-13
Madison, 2733 .... E-4
Manchester, 650 .... F-4
Mapleton, 500 .... B-14
Mars Hill, 1200 .... C-14
Mattawamkeag, 650 .... B-7
Mechanic Falls, 2450 .... G-2
Medway, 900 .... B-7
Mexico, 1946 .... E-2
Milbridge, 600 .... E-8
Milford, 2197 .... D-7
Millinocket, 5190 .... B-6
Milo, 1898 .... C-6
Monmouth, 600 .... F-3
Monson, 500 .... C-5
Monticello, 400 .... C-14
Newcastle, 600 .... G-4
New Harbor, 500 .... H-5
Newport, 1754 .... D-5
Norridgewock, 1557 .... E-4
N. Anson, 750 .... D-4
N. Berwick, 1580 .... I-2
N. Bridgton, 500 .... G-2
Northeast Hbr., 650 .... F-8
N. Vassalboro, 900 .... F-4
N. Windham, 4568 .... H-2
Norway, 2623 .... G-2
Oakland, 2758 .... E-4
Ogunquit, 974 .... J-2
Old Orchard Beach, 8856 .... I-2
Old Town, 7792 .... D-7
Orono, 8253 .... D-7
Oxford, 1300 .... G-2
OXFORD CO., 56628 .... F-2
Patten, 1000 .... A-7
PENOBSCOT CO., 147068 .... B-7
Phillips, 750 .... E-3
Pine Pt., 200 .... I-3
PISCATAQUIS CO., 17674 .... B-5
Pittsfield, 3217 .... E-5
Port Clyde, 600 .... G-5
Portland, 63889 .... H-3
Presque Isle, 9377 .... B-14
Princeton, 750 .... C-9
Randolph, 1911 .... F-4
Rangeley, 700 .... D-2
Raymond, 600 .... H-2
Richmond, 1864 .... G-4
Rockland, 7658 .... G-6
Rockport, 1200 .... G-6
Rumford, 4795 .... E-2
Sabattus, 1300 .... G-3
Saco, 18230 .... I-2
SAGADAHOC CO., 36962 .... G-4
Sanford, 10133 .... I-2
Sangerville, 650 .... C-5
Scarborough, 3867 .... H-3
Searsport, 1102 .... F-6
Sebago Lake, 600 .... H-2
Sherman Mills, 450 .... A-7
Skowhegan, 6696 .... E-4
SOMERSET CO., 51667 .... C-3
S. Berwick, 3000 .... J-1
S. Bristol, 500 .... H-4
S. Eliot, 3445 .... J-1
S. Paris, 2237 .... F-2
S. Portland, 23742 .... H-3
S. Sanford, 4173 .... I-2
Southwest Hbr., 1200 .... F-7
S. Windham, 400 .... H-2
Springvale, 3488 .... I-2
Stonington, 800 .... G-7
Stratton, 400 .... C-2
Strong, 700 .... E-3
Thomaston, 2714 .... G-5
Topsham, 6271 .... G-3
Turner, 500 .... F-3
Union, 600 .... G-5
Unity, 486 .... E-5
Van Buren, 2369 .... A-14
Veazie, 1633 .... D-6
Vinalhaven, 800 .... G-6
WALDO CO., 38705 .... E-5
Waldoboro, 1291 .... G-5
Washburn, 1200 .... B-13
WASHINGTON CO., 33448 .... D-9
Waterboro, 750 .... I-2
Waterville, 15621 .... E-4
Wells, 1200 .... I-2
Westbrook, 16108 .... H-3
W. Enfield, 600 .... C-7
W. Kennebunk, 809 .... I-2
W. Paris, 550 .... F-2
W. Peru, 600 .... F-2
W. Scarborough, 900 .... I-2
Wilton, 2290 .... E-3
Winslow, 7743 .... E-4
Winter Hbr., 900 .... F-8
Winterport, 1307 .... E-6
Winthrop, 2893 .... F-3
Wiscasset, 1203 .... G-4
Woodland, 1044 .... C-9
Woolwich, 600 .... G-4
Yarmouth, 3560 .... H-3
YORK CO., 202315 .... I-1
York Beach, 900 .... J-2
York Hbr., 3321 .... J-2

Maryland

Map pp. 94-97

* City keyed to pp. 224-225
‡ Independent city: Not included in any county.

Aberdeen, 14305 .... B-15
Abingdon, 2000 .... C-15
Accokeek, 7349 .... G-12
Adelphi, 14998 .... *D-7
ALLEGANY CO., 73639 .... B-5
Annapolis, 36300 .... E-14
Annapolis Jct., 800 .... E-13
ANNE ARUNDEL CO., 510878 .... E-13
Arbutus, 20116 .... K-2
Arden-on-the-Severn, 1971 .... E-14
Ardmore, 1200 .... *F-9
Arnold, 23422 .... E-14
Arundel Gardens, 1250 .... L-3
Arundel Vil., 2700 .... L-4
Ashton, 1500 .... D-12
Aspen Hill, 50228 .... E-11
Baltimore, 635815 .... ‡C-13
BALTIMORE CO., 786113 .... C-13
Baltimore Highlands, 6700 .... K-3
Barnaby Vil., 5300 .... *H-7
Barton, 464 .... B-3
Bay Ridge, 2200 .... F-14
Bayside Beach, 950 .... D-14
Bel Air, 10014 .... B-15
Belcamp, 6128 .... B-15
Beltsville, 15690 .... E-12
Belvedere Hts., 5600 .... E-14
Bembe Beach, 110 .... M-20
Benedict, 600 .... H-13
Berlin, 3711 .... I-20
Berwyn Hts., 3068 .... *D-8
Bethesda, 55277 .... E-11
Bladensburg, 7918 .... *F-8
Boonsboro, 2982 .... B-9
Bowie, 53878 .... E-13
Bowling Green, 1800 .... B-4
Braddock Hts., 4627 .... C-9
Bradshaw, 500 .... C-14
Brandywine, 1410 .... G-12
Brentwood, 2937 .... *F-8
Bridgeport, 860 .... M-14
Brighton, 5100 .... H-1
Brinklow, 300 .... D-12
Brooklandville, 1700 .... F-2
Brooklyn Park, 10938 .... K-3
Brookmont, 3202 .... *E-5
Brookwood, 2200 .... *I-10
Brunswick, 5242 .... C-9
Bryans Road, 4912 .... G-11
Burtonsville, 7305 .... E-12
Cabin John, 1734 .... *E-4
California, 9300 .... I-14
CALVERT CO., 87925 .... G-13
Calverton, 12610 .... E-12
Cambridge, 11089 .... H-16
Camp Sprs., 17968 .... F-12
Cape Isle of Wight, 750 .... I-20
Cape St. Claire, 8022 .... E-14
Capitol Hts., 4313 .... F-12
Carney, 28264 .... G-5
CAROLINE CO., 31822 .... F-17
CARROLL CO., 168541 .... B-11
Carroll Highlands, 2000 .... C-12
Cascade, 1000 .... A-10
Catonsville, 39820 .... J-1
Catonsville Manor, 2600 .... J-1
Cavetown, 1486 .... A-9
Cearfoss, 300 .... L-13
CECIL CO., 97796 .... B-17
Cedar Hts., 1150 .... *F-8
Cedar Lawn, 400 .... M-13
Centreville, 2660 .... E-16
CHARLES CO., 138822 .... H-11
Charlestown, 1091 .... B-16
Charlotte Hall, 1214 .... H-13
Chase, 920 .... C-15
Chelsea Beach, 3300 .... E-14
Cheltenham, 950 .... G-12
Chesaco Park, 450 .... I-6
Chesapeake Beach, 3463 .... G-14
Chesapeake City, 802 .... B-17
Chesapeake Hts., 550 .... I-18
Chester, 3723 .... E-15
Chestertown, 4673 .... D-16
Cheverly, 6668 .... *F-8
Chevy Chase, 9381 .... *E-5
Chevy Chase View, 888 .... *D-5
Chillum, 34252 .... *E-7
Clarksburg, 1834 .... D-10
Clinton, 26064 .... G-12
Cockeysville, 19388 .... B-13
Colesville, 19810 .... E-12
College Park, 25171 .... E-12
Colmar Manor, 1312 .... *F-8
Colonial Park, 600 .... N-14
Columbia, 88254 .... D-12
Columbia Park, 1000 .... *F-9
Conowingo, 150 .... A-15
Coral Hills, 10720 .... *G-8
Corriganville, 930 .... A-4
Cottage City, 1176 .... *F-8
Cresaptown, 5884 .... B-4
Crisfield, 2808 .... K-17
Crofton, 20091 .... E-13
Crownsville, 1670 .... E-14
Cumberland, 20915 .... A-4
Damascus, 11430 .... D-11
Darlington, 800 .... B-15
Dayton, 800 .... D-12
Deale, 4796 .... F-14
Deal Island, 578 .... J-17
Defense Hts., 2250 .... *E-9
Delmar, 2290 .... H-18
Denton, 3252 .... F-17
Derwood, 2000 .... *B-4
District Hts., 6296 .... F-12
DORCHESTER CO., 31401 .... H-16
Dorsey, 1350 .... M-1
Drum Pt., 1600 .... I-14
Dundalk, 62306 .... D-14
Easton, 13447 .... F-16
Eastpines, 1250 .... *E-8
Eckhart Mines, 1500 .... A-3
Edgemere, 9248 .... D-14
Edgewater, 1400 .... N-19
Edgewood, 23378 .... C-15
Edmonston, 1390 .... *E-8
Eldersburg, 27741 .... C-12
Elkridge, 22042 .... D-13
Elkton, 14466 .... B-17
Ellerslie, 1400 .... A-4
Ellicott City, 56397 .... D-13
Elmwood, 1650 .... H-5
Emmitsburg, 2369 .... A-10
Emory Gr., 5300 .... *A-4
Essex, 39078 .... C-14
Fairland, 21738 .... E-12
Fairmount Hts., 1566 .... *F-8
Fallston, 8427 .... B-14
Feagaville, 220 .... N-16
Federalsburg, 2637 .... G-17
Fell's Point J-4
Ferndale, 16056 .... L-3
Fishing Cr., 700 .... I-15
Font Hill Manor, 2500 .... D-12
Forest Hts., 2679 .... F-12
Forest Hill, 900 .... B-14
Forestville, 12712 .... F-12
Ft. Howard, 890 .... D-14
Ft. Washington Forest, 1200 .... G-12
Fountain Green, 1400 .... B-15
Fountain Head, 1350 .... A-8
Frederick, 57907 .... C-10
FREDERICK CO., 220701 .... B-10
Friendly, 10938 .... *J-7
Friendsville, 518 .... A-1
Frostburg, 7958 .... A-3
Fruitland, 3953 .... I-18
Fullerton, 2400 .... H-5
Fulton, 1150 .... D-12
Funkstown, 960 .... B-9
Gaithersburg, 57698 .... D-11
Galesville, 1000 .... F-14
Gambrills, 1500 .... E-13
Garland, 1800 .... L-3
GARRETT CO., 29909 .... B-2
Garrett Park, 942 .... E-11
Garrison, 7969 .... G-1
Germantown, 55419 .... D-11
Glassmanor, 8800 .... *H-7
Glenarden, 6380 .... F-12
Glen Arm, 730 .... C-14
Glen Burnie, 38922 .... D-13
Glen Hills, 1400 .... *C-3
Glenn Dale, 12609 .... E-13
Glyndon, 900 .... B-13
Golden Beach, 2669 .... H-13
Granite, 950 .... C-12
Grantsville, 593 .... A-2
Grasonville, 2193 .... E-15
Greenbelt, 22242 .... E-12
Green Haven, 17415 .... D-14
Greensboro, 1944 .... E-17
Guilford, 1000 .... D-12
Hagerstown, 38326 .... A-8
Halfway, 10065 .... B-8
Hampstead, 5451 .... B-12
Hancock, 1736 .... A-6
Harewood Pk., 1100 .... C-14
HARFORD CO., 239259 .... B-14
Havre de Grace, 11884 .... B-16
Hebbville, 2500 .... H-1
Hebron, 1022 .... H-18
Herald Hbr., 2313 .... E-14
Hereford, 700 .... B-13
Hernwood Hts., 960 .... H-1
Highland, 1700 .... D-12
High Pt., 3700 .... M-5
High Ridge, 2500 .... *B-9
Hillcrest Hts., 16359 .... F-12
Hillsmere Shores, 2977 .... F-14
Hollywood, 1000 .... I-14
HOWARD CO., 269457 .... D-12
Hughesville, 1537 .... H-13
Hurlock, 2003 .... G-17
Hyattsville, 16677 .... E-12
Indian Head, 3642 .... H-11
Jarrettsville, 2756 .... B-14
Jefferson Hts., 800 .... M-14
Jessup, 7865 .... M-1
Kemp Mill Estates, 3050 .... *C-6
Kensington, 1920 .... E-11
KENT CO., 19899 .... C-16
Kent Village, 2700 .... *F-9
Kenwood, 2500 .... I-6
Kettering, 11008 .... F-13
Kingstown, 1644 .... D-16
Kingsville, 4214 .... C-14
Knollwood, 1250 .... *D-7
Lake Shore, 13065 .... E-14
Landover, 640 .... *F-9
Landover Hills, 1589 .... *E-9
Langley Park, 16214 .... *E-7
Lanham, 5200 .... *E-9
Lansdowne, 8700 .... K-2
La Plata, 8442 .... H-12
Largo, 8408 .... *F-10
Laurel, 22125 .... E-12
La Vale, 4613 .... A-4
Lawsonia, 1326 .... K-17
Layhill, 1600 .... E-12
Leonardtown, 2075 .... I-13
Lewisdale, 3100 .... *E-7
Lexington Park, 11021 .... I-14
Liberty Manor, 920 .... H-1
Libertytown, 750 .... B-11
Linhigh, 2100 .... H-5
Linthicum, 7539 .... L-3
Lochearn, 25269 .... H-1
Lonaconing, 1164 .... B-3
Londontown, 4000 .... F-14
Long Beach, 1100 .... H-14
Long Green, 500 .... B-14
Love Point, 290 .... E-15
Lusby, 1666 .... I-14
Lutherville-Timonium, 15814 .... C-13
Luxmanor, 2500 .... *C-5
Lynne Acres, 6700 .... H-1
Manchester, 3557 .... A-12
Marbury, 1244 .... H-11
Margate, 1500 .... M-4
Marion Sta., 1050 .... K-17
Marley, 1500 .... M-4
Marlton, 7798 .... F-13
Maryland City, 6814 .... E-13
Maugansville, 2295 .... A-8
Meadowood, 1100 .... *C-7
Middle River, 23958 .... C-14
Middletown, 2860 .... C-9
Midland, 457 .... B-3
Milford, 690 .... H-1
Millersville, 950 .... E-13
Millwood, 1100 .... *G-9
MONTGOMERY CO., 927583 .... D-11
Montgomery Vil., 38051 .... D-11
Montpelier, 3600 .... *C-10
Montrose, 1800 .... *C-5
Morningside, 1459 .... F-12
Mtn. Lake Park, 2164 .... C-1
Mt. Airy, 8375 .... C-11
Mt. Hebron, 2000 .... C-12
Mt. Pleasant Beach, 2100 .... M-5
Mt. Rainier, 8751 .... *E-7
Mt. Savage, 1300 .... A-3
New Carrollton, 12818 .... E-12
New Windsor, 1359 .... B-11
N. Beach, 1882 .... G-14
N. East, 2817 .... B-16
N. Potomac, 23044 .... *C-2
Oakcrest, 780 .... *B-9
Oakland, 2500 .... *G-8
Oakland, 2078 .... C-12
Oakland, 1896 .... C-1
Oaklawn, 1600 .... *I-8
Oakmont *D-5
Oak View, 3400 .... *D-7
Ocean City, 7049 .... I-20
Odenton, 20534 .... E-13
Olney, 31438 .... D-11
Orchard Beach, 2200 .... M-5
Orchard Hills, 1250 .... L-14
Overlea, 12148 .... H-5
Owings Mills, 20193 .... G-1
Oxford, 746 .... G-15
Oxon Hill, 35355 .... F-12
Palmer Park, 7019 .... *F-9
Paradise Beach, 350 .... N-8
Paramount, 1450 .... L-14
Parkville, 31118 .... C-14
Parole, 14031 .... M-19
Parsonsburg, 680 .... I-19
Pasadena, 12093 .... E-14
Perry Hall, 28705 .... C-14
Perryman, 2461 .... B-15
Perryville, 3770 .... B-16
Pikesville, 29123 .... C-13
Pinefield, 8800 .... G-12
Pinehurst on the Bay, 570 .... E-14
Piney Glen Farms, 470 .... *C-3
Piney Pt., 1500 .... J-14
Pleasant Hills, 2851 .... B-14
Pocomoke City, 3909 .... K-18
Poolesville, 5498 .... D-10
Port Deposit, 693 .... B-16
Potomac, 44822 .... E-11
Potomac Park, 1600 .... B-4
Powhattan Mill, 2300 .... I-1
Prince Frederick, 1432 .... H-14
PRINCE GEORGE'S CO., 846123 .... G-13
Princess Anne, 2800 .... J-18
Providence, 1400 .... F-4
Pumphrey, 5317 .... L-3
QUEEN ANNE'S CO., 45612 .... E-16
Randallstown, 30870 .... C-13
Randolph Hills, 6150 .... *C-5
Reisterstown, 22438 .... C-12
Ridgely, 1354 .... E-17
Rippling Ridge, 2100 .... L-3
Rising Sun, 1785 .... A-16
Riva, 3966 .... E-14
Riverdale, 6630 .... *E-8
Riviera Beach, 12695 .... D-14
Rockdale, 6700 .... H-1
Rock Hall, 2566 .... D-15
Rock Hill Beach, 1350 .... M-5
Rockville, 57402 .... E-11
Rosedale, 19199 .... C-14
Rossville, 11515 .... I-6
St. Charles, 33379 .... H-12
ST. MARY'S CO., 96518 .... I-13
St. Marys City, 3300 .... J-14
St. Michaels, 1121 .... F-15
Salisbury, 26295 .... I-18
Sandy Spr., 1200 .... D-12
Sandyville, 650 .... B-12
Savage, 8000 .... D-13
Seabrook, 8000 .... *E-9
Seat Pleasant, 5063 .... F-12
Selby-on-the-Bay, 3674 .... F-14
Severn, 35076 .... D-13
Severna Park, 28507 .... E-14
Shady Side, 5559 .... F-14
Sharpsburg, 674 .... C-8
Sharptown, 621 .... H-18
Silver Hill, 1850 .... *H-8
Silver Spr., 76540 .... E-12
Smithsburg, 2859 .... A-9
Snow Hill, 2323 .... J-19
Solomons, 1536 .... I-14
Somerset, 1154 .... *E-5
SOMERSET CO., 25845 .... J-18
S. Gate, 28672 .... D-13
Spencerville, 2850 .... E-12
Springbrook, 1100 .... *C-7
Stevenson, 750 .... G-1
Stevensville, 5880 .... E-15
Suitland, 26750 .... F-12
Sunnybrook, 980 .... B-14
Sykesville, 4440 .... C-12
Takoma Park, 18540 .... *E-7
TALBOT CO., 35683 .... F-16
Taneytown, 5453 .... A-11
Temple Hills, 7792 .... *H-8
The Crest of Wickford, 900 .... *C-5
Thurmont, 6036 .... B-10
Tilghman, 1000 .... G-15
Towson, 51793 .... C-13
Union Bridge, 1085 .... B-11
University Park, 2401 .... *E-8
Upper Marlboro, 683 .... F-13
Van Lear Manor, 1050 .... N-13
Venice on the Bay, 300 .... M-6
Villa Nova, 940 .... H-1
Waldorf, 22312 .... G-12
Walkersville, 5593 .... B-10
WASHINGTON CO., 141895 .... A-7
W. Edmondale, 3450 .... J-1
Westernport, 2020 .... B-3
W. Friendship, 1200 .... C-12
Westminster, 17761 .... B-12
Westover, 800 .... J-18
Wheaton, 134800 .... E-11
White Marsh, 8485 .... C-14
White Oak, 20973 .... *C-7
White Plains, 3560 .... H-12
WICOMICO CO., 90402 .... I-18
Williamsport, 2135 .... B-8
Winchester on the Severn, 700 .... L-19
Woodlawn, 36079 .... C-13
Woodlawn Hts., 2400 .... L-3
Woodmoor, 8400 .... H-1
Woodstock, 850 .... C-12
WORCESTER CO., 48750 .... I-19
Worthington, 2350 .... K-1

Massachusetts

Map pp. 98-101

Abington, 14605 .... G-15
Acton, 2300 .... D-12
Acushnet, 3171 .... J-15
Adams, 5784 .... C-2
Agawam, 28599 .... G-5
Amesbury, 12327 .... A-15
Amherst, 17824 .... E-6
Andover, 7900 .... C-14
Arlington, 42389 .... E-14
Ashburnham, 1500 .... C-9
Ashland, 12066 .... F-12
Assinippi, 1400 .... G-15
Assonet, 1300 .... I-14
Athol, 8370 .... C-8
Attleboro, 43382 .... H-13
Auburn, 15005 .... F-10
Avon, 4558 .... G-14
Ayer, 2960 .... D-11
Baldwinville, 1852 .... C-8
Ballardvale, 1400 .... C-14
BARNSTABLE CO., 226514 .... J-17
Barnstable, 47826 .... J-19
Barre, 1150 .... E-8
Bedford, 12996 .... D-13
Belchertown, 2626 .... F-7
Bellingham, 4497 .... G-12
Belmont, 24194 .... E-13
BERKSHIRE CO., 131868 .... E-2
Beverly, 39876 .... D-15
Billerica, 6850 .... C-13
Blackstone, 5000 .... H-12
Bondsville, 1876 .... F-7
Boston, 559034 .... E-14
Bourne, 1443 .... J-17
Boxford, 2340 .... C-15
Braintree, 33698 .... F-14
Brant Rock, 1800 .... G-17
Brewster, 2212 .... J-20
Bridgewater, 6664 .... H-15
BRISTOL CO., 546331 .... I-13
Brockton, 94632 .... G-14
Brookfield, 1200 .... F-8
Brookline, 57107 .... E-14
Bryantville, 1800 .... G-15
Burlington, 22876 .... D-13
Buzzards Bay, 3549 .... J-17
Byfield, 1300 .... B-15
Cambridge, 100135 .... E-14
Canton, 18530 .... G-14
Carver, 1500 .... I-16
Chaffin, 4000 .... E-10
Charlton City, 1400 .... G-9
Chatham, 1667 .... J-20
Chelmsford, 34200 .... C-13
Chelsea, 32518 .... E-14
Cherry Valley, 1200 .... F-10
Cheshire, 1200 .... C-2
Chicopee, 54680 .... G-5
Clinton, 7884 .... E-11
Cochituate, 6768 .... E-12
Cohasset, 6000 .... F-16
Concord, 4700 .... D-13
Cordaville, 2515 .... F-12
Dalton, 7155 .... D-2
Danvers, 25212 .... C-15
Dedham, 23464 .... F-14
Dennis, 2798 .... J-19
Dennis Port, 3612 .... J-20
Dorothy Pond, 1700 .... F-10
Dover, 2216 .... F-13
Dracut, 25594 .... C-13
Dudley, 3700 .... G-9
DUKES CO., 15592 .... L-17
Duxbury, 1426 .... G-16
E. Billerica, 3850 .... C-13
E. Bridgewater, 3400 .... H-15
E. Brookfield, 1410 .... F-9
E. Dennis, 3299 .... J-19
E. Douglas, 2319 .... G-10
E. Falmouth, 6615 .... K-17
Eastham, 1250 .... I-20
Easthampton, 16004 .... F-5
E. Longmeadow, 13367 .... G-6
E. Millbury, 1000 .... F-10
E. Orleans, 1200 .... I-20
E. Pepperell, 2034 .... C-11
E. Templeton, 1350 .... C-9
E. Walpole, 3800 .... G-13
E. Wareham, 1500 .... J-16
Edgartown, 1500 .... L-17
Egypt, 900 .... F-16
Essex, 1426 .... C-16
ESSEX CO., 738301 .... C-14
Everett, 36837 .... E-14
Fairhaven, 16132 .... K-15
Fall River, 91802 .... J-14
Falmouth, 4115 .... K-17
Fayville, 1000 .... F-12
Feeding Hills G-5
Fiskdale, 2156 .... G-8
Fitchburg, 40045 .... C-10
Foxboro, 5509 .... G-13
Framingham, 66910 .... F-12
FRANKLIN CO., 72334 .... D-5
Franklin, 30893 .... G-12
Gardner, 20908 .... C-9
Georgetown, 2200 .... B-15
Gilbertville, 1050 .... E-8
Gloucester, 30713 .... C-16
Grafton, 1650 .... F-11
Granby, 1344 .... F-6
Graniteville, 1200 .... C-12
Great Barrington, 2459 .... F-1
Greenfield, 13716 .... C-5
Green Hbr., 1500 .... G-17
Groton, 1113 .... C-11
Groveland, 3800 .... B-14
Hamilton, 1000 .... C-15
HAMPDEN CO., 461591 .... G-7
HAMPSHIRE CO., 153339 .... E-4
Hanover, 2500 .... G-16
Hanover Cen., 1000 .... G-15
Hanson, 2044 .... G-15
Harvard, 1200 .... D-11
Harwich, 1832 .... J-20
Harwich Port, 1809 .... J-20
Hatfield, 1298 .... E-5
Haverhill, 60242 .... B-14
Hingham, 5352 .... F-15
Hinsdale, 1050 .... D-2
Holbrook, 10785 .... G-15
Holden, 4200 .... E-10
Holliston, 12926 .... F-12
Holyoke, 39958 .... F-5
Hopedale, 4158 .... G-11
Hopkinton, 2628 .... F-12
Housatonic, 1335 .... F-1
Hudson, 14388 .... E-11
Hull, 11050 .... E-15
Huntington, 1200 .... F-4
Hyannis J-19
Hyannis Port K-19
Ipswich, 4161 .... C-15
Islington, 4800 .... F-13
Kingston, 5380 .... H-16
Lakeville, 2233 .... I-15
Lanesboro, 1000 .... D-2
Lawrence, 71314 .... B-14
Lee, 2021 .... E-2
Leicester, 3200 .... F-9
Lenox, 1667 .... E-1
Leominster, 41804 .... D-10
Lexington, 30355 .... D-13
Lincoln, 2850 .... E-13
Littleton, 2816 .... D-12
Longmeadow, 15633 .... G-5
Lowell, 103111 .... C-13
Ludlow, 18820 .... G-6
Lunenburg, 1695 .... C-10
Lynn, 88792 .... D-15
Lynnfield, 11542 .... D-14
Malden, 55871 .... D-14
Manchaug, 800 .... G-10
Manchester, 5286 .... C-16
Manomet, 1600 .... H-17
Mansfield, 7320 .... H-13
Marblehead, 20377 .... D-15
Marion, 1202 .... J-16
Marlborough, 37444 .... E-11
Marshfield, 4246 .... G-16
Marshfield Hills, 2369 .... G-16
Mattapoisett, 2966 .... J-16
Maynard, 10433 .... D-12
Medfield, 6670 .... F-13
Medford, 53523 .... E-14
Medway, 4000 .... G-12
Melrose, 26365 .... D-14
Mendon, 1000 .... G-11
Merrimac, 2200 .... A-14
Methuen, 44609 .... B-13
Middleboro, 6913 .... I-15
MIDDLESEX CO., 1459011 .... D-12
Middleton, 4921 .... C-14
Mile Oak Center, 2050 .... G-6
Milford, 24230 .... G-12
Millbury, 5000 .... F-10
Millers Falls, 1072 .... C-6
Millis, 3800 .... F-12
Millville, 2236 .... H-11
Milton, 26062 .... F-14
Monson, 2103 .... G-7
Monument Beach, 2438 .... J-17
Morningdale, 1150 .... E-10
Nabnasset, 3600 .... C-12
Nahant, 3632 .... E-15
NANTUCKET CO., 10168 .... M-20
Nantucket, 3830 .... M-20
Natick, 32200 .... F-12
Needham, 28911 .... F-13
New Bedford, 93102 .... K-15
Newburyport, 17414 .... B-15
Newton, 83158 .... E-13
NORFOLK CO., 653595 .... F-13
N. Adams, 14010 .... B-2
N. Amherst, 6019 .... E-6
Northampton, 28715 .... E-5
N. Andover, 22792 .... B-14
N. Attleboro, 16796 .... H-13
N. Billerica, 5500 .... C-13
Northborough, 6257 .... E-11
Northbridge, 3600 .... G-11
N. Brookfield, 2527 .... F-8
N. Dighton, 1250 .... I-14
N. Eastham, 1915 .... I-20
N. Easton, 4500 .... G-14
N. Falmouth, 3355 .... J-17
Northfield, 1141 .... B-6
N. Grafton, 3150 .... F-10
N. Oxford, 1200 .... G-10
N. Pembroke, 2913 .... G-16
N. Reading, 12002 .... C-14
N. Scituate, 5065 .... F-16
N. Sudbury, 2600 .... E-12
N. Swansea, 900 .... J-13
N. Tewksbury, 1200 .... C-13
N. Uxbridge, 1800 .... G-11
Norton, 2618 .... H-13
Norton Gr., 2100 .... H-13
Norwell, 1200 .... G-16
Norwood, 28587 .... F-13
Nutting Lake, 3200 .... D-13
Oak Bluffs, 2000 .... L-17
Ocean Bluff, 2500 .... G-17
Ocean Gr., 3012 .... J-13
Onset, 1292 .... J-17
Orange, 3945 .... C-7
Orleans, 1716 .... I-20
Oxford, 5899 .... G-10
Palmer, 3900 .... G-7
Paxton, 1600 .... E-9
Peabody, 51239 .... D-15
Pembroke, 2100 .... G-16
Pepperell, 2517 .... C-11
Pigeon Cove, 1800 .... C-17
Pinehurst, 6941 .... D-13
Pittsfield, 43860 .... D-2
Plainville, 6871 .... H-13
PLYMOUTH CO., 492409 .... H-15
Plymouth, 7658 .... H-16
Pocasset, 2671 .... J-17
Provincetown, 3561 .... G-19
Quincy, 90250 .... F-14
Randolph, 30963 .... F-14
Raynham, 2100 .... H-14
Raynham Cen., 3633 .... H-14
Reading, 23708 .... D-14
Revere, 45807 .... E-14
River Pines, 3600 .... C-13
Rochdale, 1150 .... F-9
Rockland, 16123 .... G-15
Rockport, 5606 .... C-17
Rowley, 1434 .... B-15
Rutland, 2205 .... E-9
Sagamore, 3544 .... J-17
Salem, 41756 .... D-15
Salisbury, 4484 .... A-15
Sand Hill, 1800 .... F-16
Sandwich, 3058 .... J-18
Saugus, 26078 .... D-14
Scituate, 5069 .... F-16
Seekonk, 13046 .... I-13
Sharon, 5941 .... G-14
Shawsheen Vil., 2600 .... C-14
Sheffield, 1150 .... G-1
Shelburne Falls, 1951 .... C-5
Sherborn, 1400 .... F-12
Shirley, 1427 .... D-11
Shore Acres, 1200 .... F-16
Shrewsbury, 31600 .... F-10
Silver Lake, 2900 .... C-13
Smith Mills, 4432 .... K-15
Somerset, 18234 .... J-14
Somerville, 74963 .... E-14
S. Acton, 3200 .... D-12
S. Amherst, 5039 .... E-6
S. Ashburnham, 1013 .... C-9
Southborough, 1500 .... E-12
Southbridge, 12878 .... G-9
S. Deerfield, 1868 .... D-5
S. Dennis, 3679 .... J-19
S. Duxbury, 3062 .... H-16
S. Easton, 1500 .... G-14
S. Grafton, 2750 .... F-11
S. Hadley, 5500 .... F-6
S. Hadley Falls, 5100 .... F-5
S. Hamilton, 2800 .... C-15
S. Hanover, 1000 .... G-15
S. Hingham, 4000 .... F-15
S. Lancaster, 1742 .... D-11
S. Swansea, 1000 .... J-13
S. Walpole, 1300 .... G-13
S. Wellfleet, 600 .... H-20
Southwick, 1250 .... G-4
S. Yarmouth, 11603 .... J-19
Spencer, 6032 .... F-9
Springfield, 151732 .... G-5
Sterling, 1350 .... D-10
Stockbridge, 1100 .... F-1
Stoneham, 22219 .... D-14
Stoughton, 26777 .... G-14

*, †, ‡, See explanation under state title in this index.
County names are listed in capital letters and in boldface type.

Stow, 1250 D-12
Sturbridge, 2047 G-8
Sudbury, 1950 E-12
Sudbury Cen., 2600 E-12
SUFFOLK CO., 654428 F-14
Swampscott, 14412 D-15
Taunton, 56251 I-14
Teaticket, 1907 K-17
Tewksbury, 11000 C-13
Thorndike, 1150 F-7
Three Rivers, 2939 F-7
Topsfield, 2826 C-15
Touisset, 1500 J-13
Townsend, 1043 C-10
Turners Falls, 4441 C-6
Upton, 1200 F-11
Uxbridge, 3500 G-11
Vineyard Haven, 2048 L-17
Wakefield, 24804 D-14
Walpole, 5867 G-13
Waltham, 59556 E-13
Wamesit, 2700 C-13
Ware, 6174 F-7
Wareham, 2874 J-16
Warren, 1452 F-8
Watertown, 32303 E-13
Wayland, 2500 E-12
Webster, 11600 G-9
Wellesley, 26613 F-13
Wellfleet, 1200 H-20
Wenham, 4212 C-15
W. Acton, 5200 D-12
W. Andover, 2000 C-14
Westborough, 3983 F-11
W. Boylston, 3300 E-10
W. Bridgewater, 2100 H-15
W. Brookfield, 1610 F-8
W. Chatham, 1446 J-20
W. Concord, 5632 D-12
W. Dennis, 2570 J-19
W. Falmouth, 1867 K-17
Westfield, 40525 G-4
Westford, 1400 C-12
W. Foxboro, 1100 G-13
W. Groton, 900 C-11
W. Hanover, 1700 G-15
W. Harwich, 1500 J-20
W. Medway, 2000 G-12
Westminster, 1100 D-9
W. Newbury, 1100 B-15
Weston, 10200 E-13
W. Springfield, 27899 G-5
W. Upton, 1100 F-11
W. Wareham, 1908 I-16
W. Warren, 1300 F-7
Westwood, 6500 F-13
W. Yarmouth, 6460 J-19
Weymouth, 53988 F-15
Whalom, 1400 C-10
White Island Shores, 2133 I-17
Whitinsville, 6340 G-11
Whitman, 13240 G-15
Wilbraham, 3544 G-6
Williamsburg, 1200 E-5
Williamstown, 4754 B-2
Wilmington, 21363 D-14
Winchendon, 4246 C-9
Winchester, 20810 D-14
Winthrop, 18303 E-15
Woburn, 37147 D-14
Woods Hole, 925 K-17
WORCESTER CO., 783262 D-8
Worcester, 175898 F-10
Wrentham, 2250 G-13
Yarmouth Port, 5395 J-19

Michigan

Map pp. 102-107

* City keyed to pp. 106-107

Ada, 2300 P-6
Addison, 611 S-9
Adrian, 21784 T-10
Albion, 9348 R-8
ALCONA CO., 11653 J-11
ALGER CO., 9662 E-3
Algonac, 4598 Q-14
Allegan, 4963 R-5
ALLEGAN CO., 113174 Q-5
Allendale, 11555 P-5
Allen Park, 28083 R-12
Alma, 9260 O-8
Almont, 2874 P-13
Alpena, 10792 I-11
ALPENA CO., 30428 I-11
Amasa, 400 C-13
Ann Arbor, 113271 R-11
ANTRIM CO., 24422 I-7
ARENAC CO., 17154 L-10
Argentine, 2285 Q-11
Armada, 1650 P-13
Athens, 1075 S-7
Atlanta, 757 I-10
Auburn, 2057 N-10
Auburn Hills, 21011 *F-5
Au Gres, 982 L-11
Augusta, 852 R-7
Au Sable, 1533 K-12
Bad Axe, 3246 M-13
Baldwin, 1157 M-5
Bancroft, 609 P-10
Bangor, 1882 R-5
Baraga, 1252 B-13
BARAGA CO., 8746 B-13
Baroda, 893 S-4
Barron Lake, 1570 T-5
BARRY CO., 59892 Q-7
Bath, 730 Q-9
Battle Creek, 53202 R-7
BAY CO., 109029 M-10
Bay City, 34879 N-10
Beadle Lake, 1550 R-7
Beaverton, 1118 M-9
Beecher, 12793 *A-9
Beechwood, 30 C-12
Beechwood, 2963 Q-5
Belding, 5895 P-7
Bellaire, 1146 I-7
Belleville, 3853 S-11
Bellevue, 1375 R-8
Belmont, 730 P-6
Benton Hbr., 10749 S-4
Benton Heights, 5458 S-4
BENZIE CO., 17644 J-5
Bergland, 670 B-11
Berkley, 15089 *H-5
BERRIEN CO., 162611 S-4
Berrien Sprs., 1951 T-4
Bertrand, 5500 T-4
Bessemer, 1957 B-10
Beverly Hills, 10086 *H-5
Big Rapids, 10704 M-6
Birch Run, 1719 O-11
Birmingham, 19081 Q-12
Blissfield, 3256 T-11
Bloomfield, 41651 *G-4
Bloomfield Hills, 3851 *G-5
Boyne City, 3292 H-7
BRANCH CO., 46460 T-7
Breckenridge, 1318 N-9
Bridgeport, 7849 O-10
Bridgman, 2449 T-4
Brighton, 7139 Q-11
Britton, 678 S-11
Bronson, 2346 T-7
Brooklyn, 1363 S-10
Brown City, 1310 O-13
Brownlee Park, 2588 R-7
Brownstown, 29147 *M-4
Buchanan, 4531 T-4
Bullock Creek, 750 N-9
Burr Oak, 771 T-7
Burton, 30 P-9
Burton, 30916 P-11
Byron, 582 P-10
Byron Cen., 3777 Q-6
Cadillac, 10167 L-7
Caledonia, 1278 Q-6
CALHOUN CO., 139191 S-8
Calumet, 812 A-13
Canton, 76366 *J-2
Capac, 2233 P-13
Carleton, 2874 S-12
Caro, 4193 N-12
Carrollton, 6602 N-10
Carson City, 1197 O-8
Carsonville, 493 N-13
Cascade, 2300 P-6
Caseville, 887 M-12
Caspian, 914 C-12
CASS CO., 51996 S-5
Cass City, 2606 N-12
Cassopolis, 1840 T-5
Cedar Sprs., 3234 O-6
Center Line, 8308 *H-7
Central Lake, 988 I-7
Centreville, 1555 T-6
CHARLEVOIX CO., 26722 H-7
Charlevoix, 2776 H-7
Charlotte, 9069 Q-8
Chassell, 710 A-13
CHEBOYGAN CO., 27463 H-9
Cheboygan, 5191 G-9
Chelsea, 4801 R-10
Chesaning, 2463 O-10
Chesterfield, 43838 *E-10
CHIPPEWA CO., 38780 E-9
CLARE CO., 31653 M-8
Clare, 3233 M-8
Clarkston, 932 Q-12
Clawson, 12337 *H-6
Climax, 748 S-7
CLINTON CO., 69329 P-9
Clinton, 95648 *G-8
Clinton, 2354 S-10
Clio, 2619 O-11
Cloverville, 1950 O-5
Coldwater, 10783 T-8
Coleman, 1266 M-9
Coloma, 1524 S-4
Colon, 1189 S-7
Columbiaville, 817 O-12
Commerce, 5000 Q-11
Comstock, 5600 P-3
Comstock Park, 10674 P-6
Concord, 1112 S-8
Constantine, 2161 T-6
Coopersville, 4222 P-5
Corunna, 3377 P-10
Covert, 640 R-4
CRAWFORD CO., 15074 J-8
Croswell, 2548 O-14
Crystal Falls, 1649 C-13
Cutlerville, 15114 P-6
Davison, 5372 P-11
Dearborn, 94090 R-12
Dearborn Hts., 56176 *J-4
Decatur, 1890 S-5
Deckerville, 928 N-13
Deerfield, 968 T-11
DELTA CO., 38347 F-3
Delton, 500 R-7
Detroit, 886671 R-13
De Witt, 4441 P-9
Dexter, 3198 R-10
DICKINSON CO., 28032 C-14
Dimondale, 1346 Q-8
Dollar Bay, 1050 A-13
Dorr, 1600 Q-6
Douglas, 1196 Q-5
Dowagiac, 5955 S-5
Drayton Plains Q-12
Dryden, 813 P-12
Dundee, 3892 S-11
Durand, 3868 P-10
Eagle Lake, 1160 T-5
E. Grand Rapids, 10384 *B-3
E. Jordan, 2338 H-7
Eastlake, 569 L-4
E. Lansing, 46419 Q-9
Eastpointe, 33180 R-13
E. Tawas, 2852 K-11
EATON CO., 107394 R-8
Eaton Rapids, 5266 R-8
Ecorse, 10757 *L-6
Edmore, 1258 N-7
Edwardsburg, 1114 T-5
Elk Rapids, 1710 I-6
Elkton, 806 M-12
Elsie, 1005 P-9
EMMET CO., 33580 G-7
Erie, 690 T-11
Escanaba, 12679 F-2
Essexville, 3590 N-10
Evart, 1734 M-7
Fairgrove, 619 N-11
Farmington, 10035 *H-3
Farmington Hills, 80223 R-12
Farwell, 850 M-8
Fennville, 1446 Q-5
Ferndale, 21460 R-12
Ferrysburg, 2993 P-4
Flat Rock, 9560 S-12
Flint, 118551 P-11
Flushing, 8110 P-10
Forest Hills, 20942 *B-3
Fowler, 1081 P-8
Fowlerville, 3132 Q-10
Frankenmuth, 4803 O-11
Frankfort, 1493 J-4
Franklin, 2958 *H-4
Fraser, 15095 *G-8
Freeland, 5147 N-10
Fremont, 4256 N-5
Fruitport, 1087 O-5
Galesburg, 1926 R-7
Galien, 578 T-4
Garden City, 28960 R-12
Gaylord, 3730 I-8
GENESEE CO., 443883 P-11
Genesee, 1500 O-11
Gibraltar, 5191 S-12
Gladstone, 5255 F-2
GLADWIN CO., 27209 L-9
Gladwin, 3018 L-9
Gobles, 807 R-5
GOGEBIC CO., 16861 C-11
Goodrich, 1567 P-11
Grand Blanc, 7898 P-11
Grand Haven, 10586 P-4
Grand Ledge, 7768 Q-8
Grand Rapids, 193780 P-6
GRAND TRAVERSE CO., 83971 J-6
Grandville, 16711 P-6
Grant, 885 O-5
Grass Lake, 1171 R-10
GRATIOT CO., 42345 O-8
Grayling, 1943 J-8
Greenville, 8306 O-7
Grosse Ile, 10894 *M-6
Grosse Pointe, 5426 *J-8
Grosse Pointe Farms, 9325 *I-9
Grosse Pointe Park, 11905 *J-8
Grosse Pointe Shores, 2708 *I-9
Grosse Pointe Woods, 16317 R-13
Gwinn, 1965 E-1
Hagar Shores, 1509 S-4
Hamilton, 1170 Q-5
Hamtramck, 21994 R-13
Hancock, 4223 A-13
Harbert, 600 T-3
Harbor Beach, 1719 M-13
Harbor Sprs., 1594 G-7
Harper Woods, 13621 *I-8
Harrison, 2083 L-8
Hart, 1996 M-4
Hartford, 2433 S-5
Harvey, 1321 D-2
Haslett, 11292 Q-9
Hastings, 7166 Q-7
Hazel Park, 18391 *I-7
Hemlock, 1585 N-9
Hesperia, 987 N-5
Highland, 800 Q-11
Highland Park, 15430 R-12
HILLSDALE CO., 47066 T-8
Hillsdale, 7904 T-9
Holland, 34429 Q-5
Holly, 6375 P-11
Holt, 11315 Q-9
Homer, 1819 S-8
Houghton, 7076 A-13
HOUGHTON CO., 35705 A-12
Houghton Lake, 3749 K-8
Howard City, 1617 O-6
Howell, 9757 Q-10
Hubbell, 1105 A-13
Hudson, 2415 T-9
Hudsonville, 7052 P-5
Huntington Woods, 5928 *H-6
HURON CO., 34640 M-13
Ida, 1020 T-11
Imlay City, 3850 P-12
Indian Lake, 640 S-5
INGHAM CO., 278592 Q-9
Inkster, 28870 *K-4
Ionia, 12336 P-7
IONIA CO., 64608 P-7
IOSCO CO., 26992 K-11
IRON CO., 12299 C-12
Iron Mtn., 8173 D-13
Iron River, 3112 C-12
Ironwood, 5728 B-10
ISABELLA CO., 65618 N-8
Ishpeming, 6507 D-1
Ithaca, 3101 O-9
JACKSON CO., 163629 R-9
Jackson, 34879 R-9
Jenison, 17211 P-6
Jonesville, 2293 S-8
KALAMAZOO CO., 240536 S-6
Kalamazoo, 72700 R-6
Kalkaska, 2205 J-7
KALKASKA CO., 17239 J-7
Keego Hbr., 2791 *F-4
KENT CO., 596666 O-6
Kent City, 1074 O-6
Kentwood, 46491 P-6
KEWEENAW CO., 2195 A-13
Kingsford, 5565 D-13
Kingsley, 1524 J-6
Laingsburg, 1270 P-9
LAKE CO., 12069 M-5
Lake City, 940 K-7
Lake Fenton, 4876 P-11
Lake Linden, 1044 A-13
Lake Odessa, 2288 Q-7
Lake Orion, 2756 P-12
Lakeside, 1100 T-3
Lakeview, 1122 N-7
Lakewood Club, 1319 O-4
Lambertville, 9299 T-11
L'Anse, 2011 B-13
Lansing, 115518 Q-9
Lapeer, 9370 P-12
LAPEER CO., 93361 O-12
Lathrup Vil., 4157 *H-5
Laurium, 2046 A-13
Lawrence, 1030 S-5
Lawton, 1852 S-5
LEELANAU CO., 22157 I-5
LENAWEE CO., 102033 T-10
Leslie, 2268 R-9
Level Park, 3490 R-7
Lewiston, 990 I-9
Lexington, 1096 O-14
Lincoln Park, 38237 R-12
Linden, 3452 P-11
Litchfield, 1429 S-8
Little Lake, 800 D-2
LIVINGSTON CO., 181517 Q-10
Livonia, 97977 R-12
Lowell, 4140 P-7
LUCE CO., 6789 D-6
Ludington, 8292 M-4
Luna Pier, 1523 T-12
Lyons, 738 P-8
MACKINAC CO., 11331 E-7
Mackinaw City, 862 F-8
MACOMB CO., 829453 Q-13
Madison Hts., 30251 Q-12
Mancelona, 1386 I-7
Manchester, 2240 S-10
MANISTEE CO., 25226 K-5
Manistee, 6656 L-4
Manistique, 3460 F-4
Manitou Beach, 1400 S-9
Manton, 1219 K-6
Maple Rapids, 614 O-8
Marcellus, 1111 S-6
Marenisco, 700 C-11
Marine City, 4475 Q-14
Marion, 837 L-7
Marlette, 2070 O-12
MARQUETTE CO., 64760 D-1
Marquette, 20581 D-2
Marshall, 7363 R-8
Marysville, 10042 P-14
Mason, 7985 Q-9
MASON CO., 28986 L-4
Mattawan, 2838 S-6
Mayville, 1034 O-12
MECOSTA CO., 42391 N-7
Melvindale, 10612 *K-5
Memphis, 1123 P-13
Mendon, 933 S-6
Menominee, 8753 I-1
MENOMINEE CO., 24996 G-1
Merrill, 758 N-9
Michigan Cen., 4641 S-9
Middleville, 2790 Q-6
Midland, 41760 N-9
MIDLAND CO., 84064 N-9
Milan, 5376 S-11
Milford, 6587 Q-11
Millett, 770 Q-9
Millington, 1115 O-11
Mio, 2016 J-10
MISSAUKEE CO., 15299 K-7
Moline, 750 Q-6
MONROE CO., 153935 S-11
Monroe, 21791 T-12
Montague, 2339 N-4
MONTCALM CO., 63893 O-7
MONTMORENCY CO., 10445 I-9
Montrose, 1552 O-10
Morenci, 2352 T-10
Morrice, 888 P-10
Mt. Clemens, 17053 Q-13
Mt. Morris, 3321 O-11
Mt. Pleasant, 26253 N-8
Muir, 644 P-8
Munising, 2386 D-3
Muskegon, 39919 O-4
MUSKEGON CO., 175554 O-5
Muskegon Heights, 11821 O-4
Napoleon, 1254 S-10
Nashville, 1705 Q-7
Negaunee, 4471 D-1
NEWAYGO CO., 50019 N-5
Newaygo, 1685 N-6
New Baltimore, 11165 Q-13
Newberry, 1598 D-6
New Boston, 1300 *M-3
New Buffalo, 2274 T-3
New Haven, 4708 Q-13
New Hudson, 110 Q-11
New Lothrop, 598 O-10
Newport, 1070 S-12
Niles, 11738 T-4
N. Branch, 1008 O-12
N. Muskegon, 4012 O-4
Northport, 651 I-6
Northville, 6311 R-11
Norton Shores, 23479 O-4
Norway, 2973 D-14
Novi, 53115 R-11
Oak Hill, 920 L-4
OAKLAND CO., 1214361 P-12
Oak Park, 31194 R-12
OCEANA CO., 28473 N-4
OGEMAW CO., 21905 K-10
Okemos, 22805 Q-9
Olivet, 1789 R-8
Onaway, 961 H-9
ONTONAGON CO., 7363 B-11
Ontonagon, 1637 B-11
Orchard Lake, 2225 Q-12
Ortonville, 1509 P-11
OSCEOLA CO., 23750 M-7
OSCODA CO., 9298 J-9
Oscoda, 992 K-12
Oshtemo, 2000 R-6
Otisville, 845 O-11
OTSEGO CO., 24665 I-9
Otsego, 3941 R-6
OTTAWA CO., 255406 P-5
Ovid, 1439 P-9
Owosso, 15422 P-10
Oxford, 3564 P-12
Painesdale, 450 A-12
Palmer, 449 D-1
Parchment, 1813 O-2
Parkdale, 550 K-4
Parma, 879 R-9
Paw Paw, 3328 S-5
Paw Paw Lake, 3944 S-4
Pearl Beach, 3224 Q-14
Peck, 587 O-13
Pellston, 798 G-8
Pentwater, 984 M-4
Perry, 2052 P-10
Petersburg, 1138 T-11
Petoskey, 6198 H-7
Pigeon, 1130 M-12
Pinckney, 2435 R-10
Pinconning, 1349 M-10
Plainwell, 3996 R-6
Pleasant Ridge, 2501 *H-6
Plymouth, 9100 R-12
Pontiac, 67331 Q-12
Portage, 45277 S-6
Port Austin, 692 L-12
Port Huron, 31501 P-14
Portland, 3822 P-8
Port Sanilac, 645 N-14
Potterville, 2205 Q-8
PRESQUE ISLE CO., 14330 H-10
Quincy, 1657 S-8
Quinnesec, 1187 D-13
Ramsay, 1080 B-10
Rapid River, 800 F-3
Ravenna, 1238 O-5
Reading, 1104 T-8
Redford, 51622 R-12
Reed City, 2418 M-6
Reese, 1365 N-11
Republic, 614 C-13
Richmond, 5607 P-13
River Rouge, 9202 *K-6
Riverview, 12744 S-12
Rochester, 11209 Q-12
Rochester Hills, 69995 Q-12
Rockford, 5062 O-6
Rockwood, 3411 S-12
Rogers City, 3201 G-10
Romeo, 3815 P-13
Romulus, 23853 R-12
Roosevelt Park, 3810 O-4
Roscommon, 1105 K-8
ROSCOMMON CO., 26079 L-8
Rose City, 715 K-10
Roseville, 47708 Q-13
Royal Oak, 58299 Q-12
Rudyard, 1100 E-8
Saginaw, 58361 N-10
SAGINAW CO., 208356 O-10
St. Charles, 2150 O-10
ST. CLAIR CO., 171426 P-13
St. Clair, 5933 P-14
St. Clair Shores, 61561 Q-13
St. Ignace, 2446 F-8
St. Johns, 7436 P-9
ST. JOSEPH CO., 62984 T-6
St. Joseph, 8675 S-4
St. Louis, 6513 N-9
Saline, 8826 S-11
Sandusky, 2694 N-13
Sanford, 930 N-9
SANILAC CO., 44752 N-13
Saranac, 1332 P-7
Saugatuck, 1040 Q-5
Sault Ste. Marie, 14318 D-9
SCHOOLCRAFT CO., 8819 E-4
Schoolcraft, 1504 S-6
Scottville, 1273 M-4
Sebewaing, 1861 M-11
Shelby, 1971 N-4
Shepherd, 1379 N-8
Sheridan, 713 O-7
SHIAWASSEE CO., 72945 P-10
Shields, 6590 N-10
Shoreham, 851 S-4
Southfield, 76818 R-12
Southgate, 29572 S-12
S. Haven, 5157 R-4
S. Lyon, 11040 R-11
S. Range, 701 A-12
S. Rockwood, 1590 S-12
Sparta, 4046 O-6
Spring Arbor, 2188 S-9
Springfield, 5203 R-7
Spring Lake, 2383 P-5
Springport, 682 R-8
Stambaugh C-12
Standish, 2036 L-10
Stanton, 1527 O-7
Stephenson, 835 H-1
Sterling Hts., 128034 Q-13
Stevensville, 1164 S-4
Stockbridge, 1279 R-10
Sturgis, 11134 T-7
Sunfield, 595 Q-8
Sunrise Heights, 1350 R-7
Swartz Creek, 5341 P-11
Sylvan Lake, 1676 Q-12
Tawas City, 1952 K-11
Taylor, 64962 *L-4
Tecumseh, 8863 S-10
Tekonsha, 706 S-8
Temperance, 7757 T-11
Three Oaks, 1768 T-3
Three Rivers, 7342 T-6
Traverse City, 14513 J-6
Trenton, 19311 S-12
Trowbridge Park, 2012 D-1
Troy, 81168 Q-12
TUSCOLA CO., 58428 N-11
Ubly, 819 M-13
Union City, 1776 S-7
Union Lake, 8500 *F-3
Union Pier, 1100 T-3
Unionville, 594 N-11
Utica, 4913 *F-7
VAN BUREN CO., 78812 R-5
Vandercook Lake, 4809 S-9
Vassar, 2776 N-11
Vermontville, 797 Q-8
Vernon, 823 P-10
Vicksburg, 2189 S-6
Wakefield, 1956 B-10
Waldron, 577 T-9
Walker, 23420 *B-1
Walled Lake, 6919 Q-11
Warren, 135311 Q-13
Washington, 1850 Q-13
WASHTENAW CO., 341847 R-10
Waterford, 71981 Q-12
Watervliet, 1801 S-4
Wayland, 3948 Q-6
WAYNE CO., 1998217 R-12
Wayne, 18589 *K-3
Webberville, 1497 Q-10
Wells, 1000 F-2
W. Bloomfield, 64996 *G-3
W. Branch, 1905 K-9
Westland, 85623 R-12
Westphalia, 835 P-8
WEXFORD CO., 31876 K-6
White Cloud, 1432 N-6
Whitehall, 2839 N-4
White Pigeon, 1599 T-6
White Pine, 910 B-11
Whitmore Lake, 6574 R-11
Williamston, 3790 Q-9
Wixom, 13384 Q-11
Wolf Lake, 4455 O-5
Woodhaven, 13354 *M-5
Wyandotte, 26940 S-12
Wyoming, 70122 P-6
Yale, 1993 O-13
Ypsilanti, 21832 R-11
Zeeland, 5532 Q-5
Zilwaukee, 1735 N-10

Minnesota

Map pp. 108-113

* City keyed to pp. 112-113

Ada, 1555 H-2
Adams, 782 T-11
Adrian, 1231 T-3
Afton, 2861 P-10
Aitkin, 1997 K-8
AITKIN CO., 16174 J-9
Albany, 2007 M-6
Albert Lea, 17915 T-9
Albertville, 5733 O-8
Alden, 634 T-9
Alexandria, 10603 M-5
Amboy, 534 S-7
Andover, 29745 O-9
Annandale, 2996 O-7
Anoka, 17608 O-9
ANOKA CO., 323996 O-9
Appleton, 2870 O-3
Apple Valley, 49856 P-9
Arden Hills, 9780 *D-6
Argyle, 630 E-2
Arlington, 2063 Q-8
Arnold, 3032 J-12
Atwater, 1047 O-6
Aurora, 1751 G-11
Austin, 23469 T-10
Avon, 1269 N-7
Babbitt, 1616 G-12
Bagley, 1205 G-5
Balaton, 625 R-3
Bald Eagle, 1800 *C-9
Barnesville, 2295 J-2
Battle Lake, 778 K-4
Baudette, 1029 D-6
Baxter, 7400 K-7
Bayport, 3249 O-10
BECKER CO., 31868 I-4
Becker, 3868 N-8
Belgrade, 718 N-5
Bellaire, 1900 *D-9
Belle Plaine, 4546 Q-8
BELTRAMI CO., 42871 E-6
Bemidji, 13296 H-6
Benson, 3189 N-4
BENTON CO., 38505 M-8
Bertha, 448 K-5
Big Lake, 8804 N-8
BIG STONE CO., 5481 N-2
Birchwood Vil., 935 *D-9
Bird Island, 1176 P-6
Biwabik, 945 G-11
Blackduck, 755 G-7
Blaine, 54084 O-9
Blooming Prairie, 1962 S-10
Bloomington, 81164 P-9
BLUE EARTH CO., 58030 S-7
Blue Earth, 3452 T-7
Bovey, 661 H-9
Braham, 1574 M-10
Brainerd, 13684 K-7
Breckenridge, 3373 K-2
Brewster, 492 T-4
Brooklyn Cen., 27551 *D-4
Brooklyn Park, 68550 *B-3
Brooten, 623 N-5
Browerville, 721 L-6
BROWN CO., 26534 R-6
Brownsdale, 713 S-10
Browns Valley, 631 M-1
Brownton, 792 P-7
Buffalo, 13290 O-8
Buffalo Lake, 762 P-6
Buhl, 988 H-10
Burnsville, 59159 *J-4
Butterfield, 526 S-6
Byron, 4509 R-11
Caledonia, 2939 T-13
Cambridge, 7198 N-9
Canby, 1784 P-3
Cannon Falls, 3914 Q-10
CARLTON CO., 34026 J-10
Carlton, 795 J-11
Carver, 2268 P-8
CARVER CO., 84864 P-8
CASS CO., 28910 J-7
Cass Lake, 867 H-6
Centerville, 3765 *B-8
Ceylon, 387 T-6
Champlin, 23302 *A-2
Chanhassen, 23229 P-9
Chaska, 22820 P-9
Chatfield, 2462 S-12
CHIPPEWA CO., 12802 O-4
CHISAGO CO., 49400 N-10
Chisago City, 3071 N-10
Chisholm, 4701 H-10
Chokio, 441 N-3
Circle Pines, 5356 *B-7
Clara City, 1353 P-5
Claremont, 609 R-10
Clarissa, 602 L-6
Clarkfield, 879 P-4
Clarks Gr., 721 S-9
CLAY CO., 53838 I-3
Clearbrook, 536 G-5
CLEARWATER CO., 8476 G-5
Cleveland, 707 R-8
Clinton, 415 N-2
Cloquet, 11476 J-11
Cohasset, 2508 H-8
Cokato, 2700 O-7
Cold Spr., 3646 N-7
Coleraine, 1041 H-9
Cologne, 1197 P-8
Columbia Hts., 18110 *D-5
COOK CO., 5367 A-11
Cook, 622 F-10
Coon Rapids, 62417 O-9
Corcoran, 5683 O-9
Cosmos, 574 P-6
Cottage Gr., 32553 P-10
Cottonwood, 1123 Q-4
COTTONWOOD CO., 11834 S-5
Crookston, 7929 G-2
Crosby, 2222 K-8
Crosslake, 2039 J-7
CROW WING CO., 59917 J-8
Crystal, 21645 *E-3
DAKOTA CO., 383592 P-9
Danube, 506 P-5
Dassel, 1268 O-7
Dawson, 1448 P-3
Dayton, 4622 O-9
Deephaven, 3721 *G-1
Deer River, 924 H-8
Delano, 4551 O-8
Dellwood, 1068 *C-9
Detroit Lakes, 7914 J-4
Dilworth, 3452 I-2
DODGE CO., 19595 S-10
Dodge Cen., 2524 R-10
DOUGLAS CO., 35138 L-4
Duluth, 84896 J-12
Eagan, 63665 *J-7
Eagle Bend, 590 L-5
Eagle Lake, 2028 R-8
E. Bethel, 12013 N-9
E. Grand Forks, 7734 F-1
Eden Prairie, 60649 *I-1
Eden Valley, 925 N-6
Edgerton, 976 S-3
Edina, 45567 *H-3
Elbow Lake, 1225 L-3
Elgin, 938 R-12
Elk River, 21329 O-9
Ellendale, 649 S-9
Ellsworth, 521 T-3
Elmore, 696 T-7
Ely, 3633 F-12
Esko, 550 J-11
Evansville, 554 L-4
Eveleth, 3661 H-11
Excelsior, 2294 P-9
Eyota, 1708 S-12
Fairfax, 1279 Q-6
Fairmont, 10505 T-7
Falcon Hts., 5469 *F-6
FARIBAULT CO., 15506 T-8
Faribault, 22047 R-9
Farmington, 17740 Q-10
Fergus Falls, 13722 K-3
Fertile, 866 G-3
FILLMORE CO., 21368 T-12
Floodwood, 503 I-10
Foley, 2373 M-8
Forest Lake, 17353 O-10
Fosston, 1515 G-4
Frazee, 1396 J-4
FREEBORN CO., 31946 S-9
Freeport, 469 M-6
Fridley, 26515 *D-5
Fulda, 1272 S-4
Gaylord, 2194 Q-7
Gibbon, 764 Q-6
Gilbert, 1772 H-11
Glencoe, 5553 P-7
Glenville, 701 T-9
Glenwood, 2564 M-5
Glyndon, 1168 I-2
Golden Valley, 20003 *E-3
Goodhue, 929 Q-11
GOODHUE CO., 45585 Q-10
Good Thunder, 570 S-8
Goodview, 3339 R-13
Graceville, 574 N-2
Grand Marais, 1426 B-12
Grand Meadow, 946 S-11
Grand Rapids, 8277 H-9
Granite Falls, 2988 P-4
GRANT CO., 6114 M-3
Greenbush, 770 D-3
Grove City, 600 O-6
Hallock, 1087 C-2
Halstad, 575 H-2
Hancock, 694 N-4
Hanley Falls, 300 P-4
Harmony, 1119 T-12
Harris, 1245 N-10
Hastings, 20910 P-10
Hawley, 1892 J-3
Hayfield, 1370 S-10
Hector, 1140 P-6
Henderson, 936 Q-8
Hendricks, 677 Q-2
HENNEPIN CO., 1119364 O-8
Henning, 812 K-5
Herman, 425 M-3
Hermantown, 8861 J-11
Heron Lake, 766 S-5
Hibbing, 16509 H-10
Hills, 595 T-2
Hilltop, 760 *D-5
Hinckley, 1440 L-10
Hoffman, 649 M-4
Hokah, 595 S-14
Holdingford, 710 M-7
Hopkins, 16825 *G-2
Houston, 1001 S-13
HOUSTON CO., 19941 S-13
Howard Lake, 1957 O-8
Hoyt Lakes, 1999 G-12
HUBBARD CO., 18861 I-5
Hugo, 9683 *B-9
Hutchinson, 13722 P-7
Independence, 3528 O-8
International Falls, 6332 D-9
Inver Grove Hts., 33182 *J-9
Ironton, 540 K-8
Isanti, 5167 N-9
ISANTI CO., 37664 N-9
Isle, 873 L-9
ITASCA CO., 44384 G-9
Ivanhoe, 621 Q-3
Jackson, 3454 T-5
JACKSON CO., 11182 T-5
Janesville, 2148 R-8
Jasper, 574 S-2
Jordan, 5120 P-9
KANABEC CO., 16215 M-9
KANDIYOHI CO., 41199 O-5
Karlstad, 722 D-2
Kasota, 689 R-8
Kasson, 5333 R-10
Keewatin, 1105 H-10
Kenyon, 1665 R-10
Kerkhoven, 711 O-5
Kiester, 510 T-8
Kimball, 687 N-7
KITTSON CO., 4792 C-2
KOOCHICHING CO., 13907 E-8
LAC QUI PARLE CO., 7604 O-3
La Crescent, 5095 S-14
Lafayette, 514 Q-7
LAKE CO., 11156 G-13
Lake Benton, 667 R-3
Lake City, 5282 Q-12
Lake Crystal, 2516 R-7
Lake Elmo, 7615 O-10
Lakefield, 1698 T-5
Lakeland, 1865 P-10
LAKE OF THE WOODS CO., 4421 D-5
Lake Park, 830 I-3
Lakeville, 51484 Q-9
Lamberton, 805 R-5
Landfall, 699 *G-9
Lanesboro, 767 S-12
Lauderdale, 2215 *F-6
Le Center, 2308 Q-8
Le Roy, 917 T-11
Lester Prairie, 1601 P-8
Le Sueur, 4257 Q-8
LE SUEUR CO., 27490 Q-8
Lewiston, 1485 S-12
Lexington, 2079 *B-6
LINCOLN CO., 6050 Q-2
Lindstrom, 3934 N-10
Lino Lakes, 19424 O-10
Litchfield, 6658 O-7
Little Canada, 9543 *E-8
Little Falls, 8139 L-7
Littlefork, 714 E-9
Long Lake, 1827 P-9
Long Prairie, 2944 L-6
Lonsdale, 2409 Q-9
Luverne, 4466 T-3
Lyle, 576 T-10
LYON CO., 24472 R-4
Mabel, 743 T-13
Madelia, 2218 R-7
Madison, 1654 O-3
Madison Lake, 906 R-8
MAHNOMEN CO., 5113 H-4
Mahnomen, 1176 H-3
Mahtomedi, 8017 *D-10
Mankato, 34976 R-8
Mantorville, 1180 R-10
Maple Gr., 59756 O-9
Maple Lake, 1878 O-8
Maple Plain, 2081 O-8
Mapleton, 1653 S-8
Maplewood, 35085 *E-8
Marble, 678 H-9
Marine On St. Croix, 621 O-10
MARSHALL CO., 9965 E-3
Marshall, 12291 Q-4
MARTIN CO., 21002 S-6
Mazeppa, 784 R-11
McIntosh, 623 G-4
MCLEOD CO., 36636 P-7
Medford, 1164 R-9
MEEKER CO., 23371 O-6
Melrose, 3145 M-6
Menahga, 1197 J-5
Mendota Hts., 11338 *H-7
Milaca, 2954 M-8
MILLE LACS CO., 25680 L-8
Minneapolis, 372811 O-9
Minneota, 1377 Q-3
Minnesota Lake, 659 S-8
Minnetonka, 50045 *G-1
Montevideo, 5365 P-4
Montgomery, 3076 Q-9
Monticello, 10882 N-8
Moorhead, 34081 I-2
Moose Lake, 2551 K-10
Mora, 3449 M-9
Morgan, 846 Q-6
Morris, 5091 N-3
MORRISON CO., 32788 M-8
Morristown, 1021 R-9
Mound, 9416 P-8
Mounds View, 12106 *C-6
Mtn. Iron, 2945 G-11
Mtn. Lake, 2008 S-6
MOWER CO., 38799 T-11
MURRAY CO., 8852 R-4
Nashwauk, 897 H-9
New Brighton, 20738 *D-6
New Hope, 20296 *D-3
New London, 1196 O-6
Newport, 3654 *I-9
New Prague, 6439 Q-9
New Richland, 1159 S-9
New Ulm, 13619 R-7
New York Mills, 1186 K-5
Nicollet, 991 R-7
NICOLLET CO., 30848 Q-7
Nisswa, 2068 K-7
NOBLES CO., 20508 T-3
NORMAN CO., 7003 H-2
N. Branch, 10234 N-10
Northfield, 18671 Q-10
N. Mankato, 12078 R-8
N. Oaks, 4141 *D-7
N. St. Paul, 11355 *E-9
Norwood Young America, 3317 P-8
Oakdale, 27389 *F-10
Ogilvie, 477 M-9
Olivia, 2504 P-5
OLMSTED CO., 135189 R-11
Onamia, 916 L-8
Oronoco, 937 R-11
Ortonville, 2011 N-2
Osakis, 1568 M-5
Osseo, 2551 *C-2
OTTER TAIL CO., 57658 K-3
Owatonna, 24133 R-9
Parkers Prairie, 998 L-5
Park Rapids, 3445 I-5
Paynesville, 2243 N-6
Pelican Rapids, 2357 J-3
Pengilly, 850 H-9
PENNINGTON CO., 13608 F-3
Pequot Lakes, 1874 J-7
Perham, 2711 J-4
Pierz, 1316 L-7
PINE CO., 28485 K-11
Pine City, 3323 M-10
Pine Island, 3170 R-11
Pine River, 958 J-7
PIPESTONE CO., 9421 R-2
Pipestone, 4161 S-2
Plainview, 3296 R-12
Plymouth, 69701 *E-1
POLK CO., 31133 F-2
POPE CO., 11252 N-4
Preston, 1377 T-12
Princeton, 4694 N-9
Prior Lake, 22168 P-9
Proctor, 2779 J-12
Ramsey, 22074 O-9
RAMSEY CO., 494920 O-10
Randall, 627 L-7
Raymond, 766 O-5
RED LAKE CO., 4317 F-3
Redlake, 1430 F-6
Red Lake Falls, 1590 F-3
Red Wing, 15799 Q-11
REDWOOD CO., 16022 Q-5
Redwood Falls, 5272 Q-5
RENVILLE CO., 16764 Q-6
Renville, 1282 P-5
RICE CO., 60949 Q-9
Rice, 1038 M-7
Richfield, 33497 *H-4
Richmond, 1255 N-7
Robbinsdale, 13331 *E-3
Rochester, 94950 S-11
ROCK CO., 9520 S-2
Rockford, 3808 O-8
Rogers, 6042 O-9
Rollingstone, 644 R-13
ROSEAU CO., 16495 D-4
Roseau, 2814 C-4
Rosemount, 19311 P-10
Roseville, 32079 *E-7
Round Lake, 409 T-4
Royalton, 919 M-7
Rush City, 2986 M-10
Rushford, 1786 S-13
Sacred Heart, 526 P-5
St. Anthony, 7560 *E-5
St. Bonifacius, 2320 P-8
St. Charles, 3526 S-12
St. Clair, 784 R-8
St. Cloud, 65792 N-7
St. Francis, 7101 N-9
St. James, 4437 S-6
St. Joseph, 5437 N-7
ST. LOUIS CO., 197179 H-10
St. Louis Park, 43296 *G-3
St. Michael, 14319 O-8
St. Paul, 275150 P-10
St. Paul Park, 5193 P-10
St. Peter, 10529 R-8
Sandstone, 2519 L-10
Sartell, 12668 M-7
Sauk Ctr., 3915 M-6
Sauk Rapids, 11523 N-7
Savage, 26581 P-9
Scanlon, 836 J-11
SCOTT CO., 119825 Q-9
Sebeka, 680 J-5
Shakopee, 31233 P-9
Sherburn, 1060 T-6
SHERBURNE CO., 81752 N-8
Shoreview, 26855 *D-7
Shorewood, 7452 P-9
SIBLEY CO., 15237 Q-7
Silver Bay, 1982 H-14
Silver Lake, 784 P-7
Slayton, 1953 S-4
Sleepy Eye, 3478 R-6
Soudan, 900 G-11
S. St. Paul, 19362 *H-8
Spicer, 1105 O-6
Springfield, 2135 R-5
Spr. Grove, 1281 T-13
Spr. Lake Park, 6699 *C-5
Spr. Valley, 2480 T-11
Staples, 3121 K-6
Starbuck, 1280 N-4
STEARNS CO., 142654 N-6
STEELE CO., 35755 S-9
Stephen, 672 D-2
STEVENS CO., 9826 N-3
Stewart, 547 P-7
Stewartville, 5494 S-11
Stillwater, 17378 O-10
SWIFT CO., 11324 O-4
Taylors Falls, 1011 N-11
Thief River Falls, 8377 F-3
TODD CO., 24603 L-6
Tower, 469 G-11
Tracy, 2089 R-4
TRAVERSE CO., 3810 M-2
Trimont, 712 S-6
Truman, 1201 S-7
Twin Valley, 822 H-3
Two Harbors, 3533 I-13
Tyler, 1118 R-3
Ulen, 561 I-3
Vadnais Hts., 12586 *D-8
Verndale, 554 K-6
Victoria, 5702 P-8
Virginia, 8666 G-11
WABASHA CO., 22200 Q-12
Wabasha, 2553 Q-12
Wabasso, 656 Q-5
Waconia, 8692 P-8
Wadena, 4107 K-5
WADENA CO., 13650 K-6
Waite Park, 6832 N-7
Walker, 1170 I-6
Walnut Gr., 561 R-4
Wanamingo, 1043 R-10
Warren, 1630 E-2
Warroad, 1699 C-5
Waseca, 9445 R-9
WASECA CO., 19330 S-8
WASHINGTON CO., 220426 O-10
Watertown, 3932 P-8
Waterville, 1881 R-9
Watkins, 935 N-7
WATONWAN CO., 11234 S-6
Waverly, 952 O-8
Wayzata, 3941 *F-1
Welcome, 681 T-6
Wells, 2485 S-8
Westbrook, 762 R-4
W. Concord, 826 R-10
W. St. Paul, 18955 *H-7
Wheaton, 1488 M-2
White Bear Lake, 23733 O-10
WILKIN CO., 6802 K-2
Willernie, 524 *D-10
Willmar, 18183 O-5
Windom, 4416 S-5
Winnebago, 1419 S-7
Winona, 26587 R-13
WINONA CO., 49276 S-12
Winsted, 2367 P-8
Winthrop, 1290 Q-7
Woodbury, 52479 *G-10
Woodland, 462 *G-1
Worthington, 11092 T-4
WRIGHT CO., 110730 O-7
Wykoff, 448 S-12
Wyoming, 3820 N-10
YELLOW MEDICINE CO., 10449 P-3
Zimmerman, 4724 N-9
Zumbrota, 2966 R-11

Mississippi

Map pp. 114-115

Abbeville, 427 C-7
Aberdeen, 6227 D-9
Ackerman, 1631 F-8
ADAMS CO., 32099 J-3
ALCORN CO., 35306 B-9
AMITE CO., 13435 K-4
Amory, 7415 D-9
Anguilla, 813 F-4
Arcola, 525 F-4
Artesia, 481 E-9
Ashland, 564 B-8
ATTALA CO., 19552 F-7
Baldwyn, 3352 B-9
Batesville, 7708 C-6
Bay St. Louis, 8317 M-8
Bay Sprs., 2194 I-8
Bear Town, 1300 K-5
Beaumont, 976 K-9
Belmont, 1965 C-10
Belzoni, 2541 F-5
Benoit, 584 E-4
BENTON CO., 7852 B-8
Bentonia, 501 G-5
Beulah, 446 D-4
Biloxi, 50209 M-9
Blue Mtn., 713 B-8
Bogue Chitto, 700 J-5
BOLIVAR CO., 38641 D-4
Bolton, 611 H-5
Bond, 500 L-8
Booneville, 8585 B-9
Boyle, 677 E-5
Brandon, 19390 H-6
Brookhaven, 9907 J-5
Brooklyn, 900 K-8
Brooksville, 1151 F-9
Bruce, 2032 D-8
Buckatunna, 600 J-9
Bude, 1030 J-4
Burnsville, 1040 B-10
Byhalia, 716 B-7
Caledonia, 974 E-10
CALHOUN CO., 14652 D-7
Calhoun City, 1815 D-8
Canton, 12507 G-6
Carriere, 880 L-7
CARROLL CO., 10397 E-6
Carson, 500 J-7
Carthage, 4771 G-7
Cary, 386 G-4
Centreville, 1591 K-4
Charleston, 2054 D-6
CHICKASAW CO., 19184 D-8
CHOCTAW CO., 9572 E-8
CLAIBORNE CO., 11492 I-4
CLARKE CO., 17670 I-9
Clarksdale, 19297 C-5
CLAY CO., 21223 E-9
Cleveland, 12818 D-5
Clinton, 26017 H-5
COAHOMA CO., 29002 C-5
Coffeeville, 947 D-7
Coldwater, 1649 B-6
Collins, 2761 J-7
Columbia, 6408 K-7
Columbus, 24425 E-9
Como, 1321 C-6
COPIAH CO., 29164 I-5
Corinth, 14256 A-9
Courtland, 478 C-6
COVINGTON CO., 20273 J-7
Crawford, 634 F-9
Crenshaw, 924 C-6
Crosby, 351 K-4
Crowder, 757 C-6
Cruger, 435 E-6
Crystal Sprs., 5913 I-5
Decatur, 1426 H-8
De Kalb, 923 G-9
De Lisle, 680 M-8
Derma, 1126 D-8
DESOTO CO., 137004 B-6
D'Iberville, 7900 M-9
D'Lo, 392 I-6
Drew, 2215 D-5
Duck Hill, 1451 E-7
Dumas, 458 B-9
Duncan, 558 D-5
Durant, 2845 F-7
Ecru, 1015 C-8
Edwards, 1305 H-5
Elliott, 1100 E-7
Ellisville, 3735 J-8
Enterprise, 454 H-9
Escatawpa, 3566 M-9
Ethel, 458 F-7
Eupora, 2265 E-8
Fayette, 2133 J-4
Fernwood, 400 K-5
Flora, 1478 G-6
Florence, 3063 H-6
Flowood, 6762 C-3
Forest, 6029 H-7
FORREST CO., 75095 K-8
Foxworth, 600 K-6
FRANKLIN CO., 8411 J-4
French Camp, 389 F-7
Friars Pt., 1405 C-5
Fulton, 4102 C-10
Gautier, 16846 M-9
GEORGE CO., 21259 L-9
Georgetown, 351 I-6
Glen Allan, 500 F-4
Glendale, 1300 J-8
Gloster, 1060 K-4
Goodman, 1220 F-6
GREENE CO., 13183 K-9
Greenville, 38724 E-4
Greenwood, 17344 E-6
Grenada, 14569 D-7
GRENADA CO., 22861 E-6
Gulfport, 72464 M-8
Gunnison, 605 D-4
Guntown, 1311 C-9
HANCOCK CO., 46711 M-7
HARRISON CO., 193810 L-8
Hatley, 473 D-10
Hattiesburg, 47176 K-8
Hazlehurst, 4372 I-5
Heidelberg, 810 I-8
Hernando, 9890 B-6
Hickory, 512 H-8
Hickory Flat, 542 B-8
HINDS CO., 249345 H-5
Hollandale, 3189 F-4
Holly Sprs., 8014 B-7
HOLMES CO., 21099 F-6
Horn Lake, 22151 A-6
Houlka, 705 D-8
Houston, 3980 D-8
HUMPHREYS CO., 10527 F-5
Hurley, 985 L-9
Indianola, 11321 E-5
Inverness, 1061 E-5
Isola, 717 F-5
ISSAQUENA CO., 1909 G-4
ITAWAMBA CO., 23359 C-9
Itta Bena, 2019 E-6
Iuka, 2987 B-10
JACKSON CO., 135940 L-9
Jackson, 177977 H-6
JASPER CO., 18162 I-8
JEFFERSON CO., 9432 I-4
JEFFERSON DAVIS CO., 13158 J-6
JONES CO., 66160 J-8
Jonestown, 1643 C-5
Jonestown, 350 G-5
Jumpertown, 406 B-9
KEMPER CO., 10246 G-9
Kilmichael, 735 E-7
Kiln, 2040 M-7
Kosciusko, 7334 F-7
LAFAYETTE CO., 40842 C-7
Lake, 404 H-8
LAMAR CO., 44616 K-7
Lamar Park, 570 F-1
Lambert, 1818 C-6
LAUDERDALE CO., 77218 H-9
Lauderdale, 650 G-9
Laurel, 18298 J-8
LAWRENCE CO., 13502 J-6
LEAKE CO., 22453 G-7
Leakesville, 1007 K-9
LEE CO., 78793 C-9
LEFLORE CO., 36431 E-5
Leland, 5157 E-4
Le Tourneau, 200 H-4
Lexington, 1941 F-6
Liberty, 686 K-4
LINCOLN CO., 33906 J-5
Long Beach, 17283 M-8
Lorman, 560 I-4
Louin, 336 I-8
Louise, 296 F-5
Louisville, 6797 F-8
LOWNDES CO., 59895 E-9
Lucedale, 2890 L-9
Lumberton, 2476 K-7
Lyon, 391 C-5
Macon, 2353 F-9
MADISON CO., 84286 G-6
Madison, 16737 H-6
Magee, 4294 I-7
Magnolia, 2079 K-5
Mantachie, 1134 C-9
Marion, 1389 H-9
MARION CO., 25235 K-6
Marks, 1893 C-6
MARSHALL CO., 35659 B-7
Mathiston, 716 E-8
Mayersville, 698 G-4
McComb, 13244 K-5
McLain, 583 K-9
McNeill, 1050 L-7
Meadville, 508 J-4
Mendenhall, 2544 I-6
Meridian, 38605 H-9
Merigold, 624 D-5
Metcalfe, 1236 E-4
Mississippi State, 15680 E-9
Mize, 283 I-7
MONROE CO., 37704 D-9
MONTGOMERY CO., 11829 E-7
Monticello, 1724 J-6
Moorhead, 2472 E-5
Morgantown, 2900 J-3
Morton, 3441 H-7
Moselle, 700 J-8
Moss Pt., 15125 M-9
Mound Bayou, 2018 D-5
Mt. Olive, 900 I-7
Myrtle, 558 B-8
Natchez, 16966 J-3
Nellieburg, 1354 G-1
NESHOBA CO., 29905 G-8
Nettleton, 2019 D-9
New Albany, 8009 C-8
New Augusta, 696 K-8
New Hebron, 446 I-6
Newton, 3700 H-8
NEWTON CO., 22366 H-8
N. Carrollton, 475 E-6
N. Gulfport M-1
N. Tunica, 1450 B-5
Noxapater, 415 F-8
NOXUBEE CO., 12202 F-9
Oakland, 597 D-6

2000 Census populations or latest available estimate.
Index to Canada and Mexico cities and towns, pages 274-275.

Ocean Sprs., 17783 M-9
Okolona, 2955 D-9
OKTIBBEHA CO., 41247 E-8
Olive Branch, 27964 A-7
Osyka, 496 K-5
Ovett, 630 J-8
Oxford, 13618 C-7
Pace, 370 D-4
Palmer, 2800 K-8
PANOLA CO., 35331 C-6
Pascagoula, 25173 M-9
Pass Christian, 6851 M-8
Pearl, 23111 H-6
Pearlington, 1684 M-7
PEARL RIVER CO., 52659 K-7
Pelahatchie, 1490 H-7
Perkinston, 100 L-8
PERRY CO., 12160 K-8
Petal, 10088 J-8
Philadelphia, 7618 G-8
Philipp, 350 D-6
Picayune, 10830 M-7
Pickens, 1243 G-6
PIKE CO., 39426 K-5
Piney Woods, 100 I-6
Plantersville, 1318 C-9
PONTOTOC CO., 28208 C-8
Pontotoc, 5784 C-8
Poplarville, 2663 L-7
Port Gibson, 1765 I-4
Potts Camp, 509 B-8
PRENTISS CO., 25593 B-9
Prentiss, 1061 J-6
Purvis, 2445 K-7
Quitman, 2388 I-9
QUITMAN CO., 9512 D-5
Raleigh, 1257 I-7
RANKIN CO., 131841 H-6
Raymond, 1681 H-5
Red Banks, 580 B-7
Richton, 1008 J-8
Ridgeland, 21236 H-6
Rienzi, 326 B-9
Ripley, 5633 B-8
Rolling Fk., 2237 F-4
Rosedale, 2421 D-4
Rose Hill, 250 I-8
Roxie, 564 J-4
Ruleville, 2935 D-5
Saltillo, 3789 C-9
Sandersville, 801 I-8
Sardis, 2033 C-6
Schlater, 371 E-5
Scooba, 597 G-9
SCOTT CO., 28739 H-7
Senatobia, 6869 B-6
Shannon, 1704 C-9
SHARKEY CO., 5967 G-4
Shaw, 2236 E-5
Shelby, 2701 D-5
Sherman, 606 C-9
Shubuta, 648 I-9
Shuqualak, 547 F-9
Sidon, 597 E-6
Silver City, 315 F-5
SIMPSON CO., 27944 I-6
Sledge, 489 C-6
SMITH CO., 16058 I-7
Smithville, 879 D-10
Soso, 384 I-8
Southaven, 38840 A-6
Star, 550 I-6
Starkville, 22131 E-9
State Line, 547 J-9
STONE CO., 14862 L-8
Stonewall, 1098 H-9
Stringer, 430 I-8
Summit, 1603 K-5
Sumner, 384 D-5
Sumrall, 1163 J-7
Sunflower, 642 E-5
SUNFLOWER CO., 32311 E-5
TALLAHATCHIE CO., 14191 D-6
TATE CO., 26548 B-6
Taylorsville, 1297 I-7
Tchula, 2254 F-6
Terry, 701 I-6
Thaxton, 585 C-8
Tie Plant, 300 D-7
TIPPAH CO., 21212 B-8
TISHOMINGO CO., 19202 B-10
Tishomingo, 317 B-10
Tremont, 396 C-10
TUNICA CO., 10321 B-5
Tunica, 1089 B-5
Tupelo, 35673 C-9
Tutwiler, 1336 D-5
Tylertown, 1898 K-6
UNION CO., 26784 B-8
Union, 2102 G-8
University C-7
Utica, 922 I-5
Vaiden, 856 E-7
Vancleave, 4910 L-9
Vardaman, 1019 D-8
Verona, 3379 C-9
Vicksburg, 25752 H-4
Walnut, 759 A-8
Walnut Gr., 1260 G-7
Waltersville, 350 H-4
WALTHALL CO., 15460 K-6
WARREN CO., 49131 H-5
WASHINGTON CO., 59220 E-4
Washington, 750 J-3
Water Valley, 3822 C-7
Waveland, 7227 M-8
WAYNE CO., 21291 I-9
Waynesboro, 5719 J-9
Webb, 540 D-6
WEBSTER CO., 10092 E-7
Weir, 530 F-8
Wesson, 1692 J-5
W. Point, 11582 E-9
Wheeler, 600 B-9
WILKINSON CO., 10269 K-3
Winona, 4934 E-7
WINSTON CO., 19870 F-8
Woodville, 1162 K-3
YALOBUSHA CO., 13417 D-7
YAZOO CO., 28195 G-6
Yazoo City, 11879 G-5

Missouri

Map pp. 116-121

* City keyed to pp. 120-121
‡ Independent city: Not included in any county.

ADAIR CO., 24509 C-13
Adrian, 1839 G-9
Advance, 1216 K-19
Affton, 20535 *G-5
Agency, 587 D-8
Albany, 1832 B-9
Alton, 648 L-16
Anderson, 1902 L-9
ANDREW CO., 16899 C-8
Appleton City, 1318 H-10
Arbyrd, 507 N-18
Arcadia, 532 J-17
Archie, 958 G-9
Arnold, 20413 G-18
Ash Gr., 1491 J-11
Ashland, 2175 F-14
ATCHISON CO., 6246 B-7
AUDRAIN CO., 25759 E-14
Aurora, 7307 K-10
Auxvasse, 996 F-15
Ava, 3078 K-13
Avondale, 529 H-4
Ballwin, 30481 G-17
Barnhart, 6108 G-18
BARRY CO., 35599 L-10
BARTON CO., 13057 J-9
BATES CO., 17027 H-9
Battlefield, 3612 K-11
Bella Villa, 655 *G-6
Belle, 1348 H-15
Bellefontaine Neighbors, 10616 *C-6
Bel-Nor, 1526 *D-5
Bel-Ridge, 2970 *D-5
Belton, 24140 F-9
Benton, 729 K-20
BENTON CO., 18854 G-11
Berkeley, 9631 *C-5
Bernie, 1801 L-19
Bertrand, 710 K-20
Bethany, 3060 B-10
Beverly Hills, 575 *D-6
Bevier, 729 D-13
Billings, 1142 K-11
Birch Tree, 619 K-15
Bismarck, 1558 I-17
Black Jack, 6920 *C-6
Bland, 571 H-15
Bloomfield, 1888 K-19
Blue Sprs., 53099 F-9
Blue Summit, 1200 I-5
Bolivar, 10179 I-11
BOLLINGER CO., 12325 J-18
Bonne Terre, 6520 I-17
BOONE CO., 143326 E-13
Boonville, 8669 F-13
Bourbon, 1408 H-16
Bowling Green, 5185 E-16
Branson, 7010 L-12
Braymer, 962 D-10
Breckenridge Hills, 4608 *D-5
Brentwood, 7365 *F-5
Bridgeton, 15259 *C-4
Brookfield, 4506 C-12
Brunswick, 895 D-12
BUCHANAN CO., 84904 D-8
Bucklin, 496 C-12
Buckner, 2724 E-10
Buffalo, 3006 I-12
Burlington Jct., 613 B-8
BUTLER CO., 41338 L-18
Butler, 4249 H-9
Cabool, 2140 K-14
CALDWELL CO., 9307 D-10
California, 4137 G-13
CALLAWAY CO., 42541 F-14
Calverton Park, 1303 *C-5
CAMDEN CO., 39432 I-13
Camdenton, 3061 H-13
Cameron, 9141 D-9
Campbell, 1872 L-19
Canton, 2502 B-15
CAPE GIRARDEAU CO., 71161 J-19
Cape Girardeau, 36204 J-20
Cardwell, 751 N-18
Carl Jct., 6483 K-9
CARROLL CO., 10193 D-11
Carrollton, 4012 E-11
Carsonville, 2000 *D-5
CARTER CO., 5910 K-17
Carterville, 1916 *L-3
Carthage, 13096 K-9
Caruthersville, 6450 M-20
CASS CO., 94232 F-9
Cassville, 3095 L-10
CEDAR CO., 14160 I-10
Cedar Hill, 1703 G-17
Center, 637 D-15
Centralia, 3657 E-14
Chaffee, 3006 K-19
CHARITON CO., 8124 D-12
Charlack, 1380 *D-5
Charleston, 5129 K-20
Chesterfield, 47020 G-17
Chillicothe, 8686 C-11
CHRISTIAN CO., 67266 K-12
Clarence, 906 D-14
CLARK CO., 7323 B-15
Clarkson Valley, 2602 *F-2
Clarkton, 1280 M-19
CLAY CO., 202078 E-9
Claycomo, 1280 G-4
Clayton, 16061 G-18
CLINTON CO., 20715 D-9
Clinton, 9414 G-10
COLE CO., 72757 G-13
Cole Camp, 1160 G-12
Columbia, 91814 F-14
Concord, 16689 *G-5
Concordia, 2413 F-11
Conway, 774 J-12
Cool Valley, 1033 *D-6
COOPER CO., 17294 F-12
Corder, 426 E-11
Country Club Hills, 1318 *D-6
Country Club Village, 1897 C-8
Crane, 1442 K-11
CRAWFORD CO., 23932 I-16
Crestwood, 11691 *F-5
Creve Coeur, 16975 F-18
Crocker, 1010 I-14
Crystal City, 4508 H-18
Cuba, 3447 H-16
DADE CO., 7830 J-10
DALLAS CO., 16437 I-12
DAVIESS CO., 8121 C-10
Dearborn, 531 D-8
DEKALB CO., 12342 C-9
Dellwood, 5027 *C-6
DENT CO., 15083 I-15
Desloge, 5143 I-17
De Soto, 6552 H-17
Des Peres, 8619 *F-4
Dexter, 7596 L-19
Diamond, 846 K-9
Dixon, 1548 H-14
Doe Run, 300 I-18
Doniphan, 1924 L-17
Doolittle, 670 I-14
DOUGLAS CO., 13594 K-13
Drexel, 1115 G-9
DUNKLIN CO., 32545 N-19
Duquesne, 1692 *M-3
E. Prairie, 3117 L-20
Edgerton, 546 D-9
Edina, 1162 B-14
Edmundson, 803 *D-5
Eldon, 4934 G-13
El Dorado Sprs., 3849 I-10
Ellington, 1013 J-17
Ellisville, 9353 *F-2
Elsberry, 2417 E-17
Eminence, 550 K-16
Essex, 530 L-19
Eureka, 8957 G-17
Excelsior Sprs., 11472 E-9
Fairfax, 622 B-7
Fair Grove, 1283 J-12
Farmington, 15176 I-18
Fayette, 2701 E-13
Fenton, 4376 *G-4
Ferguson, 21458 *D-5
Festus, 10905 H-18
Flordell Hills, 887 *D-6
Florissant, 51812 *C-5
Forsyth, 1706 L-12
FRANKLIN CO., 99090 G-16
Fredericktown, 4035 J-18
Frontenac, 3517 *E-4
Fulton, 12101 F-14
Gainesville, 607 L-13
Gallatin, 1776 C-10
Garden City, 1667 G-9
GASCONADE CO., 15745 G-15
GENTRY CO., 6555 B-9
Gerald, 1238 G-16
Gideon, 1019 M-19
Gladstone, 27306 E-9
Glasgow, 1205 E-12
Glenaire, 587 G-5
Glendale, 5595 *F-5
Golden City, 918 J-10
Goodman, 1233 L-9
Gower, 1433 D-9
Granby, 2230 K-9
Grandview, 24549 F-9
Grant City, 826 B-9
Grantwood Vil., 888 *G-5
Gray Summit, 2640 G-17
Green City, 650 B-12
GREENE CO., 250784 J-11
Greenfield, 1299 J-10
Greenwood, 4512 F-9
GRUNDY CO., 10327 B-11
Hale, 478 D-11
Hallsville, 955 E-14
Hamilton, 1811 D-10
Hanley Hills, 2079 *E-5
Hannibal, 17649 D-16
Hardin, 590 E-10
HARRISON CO., 8876 B-10
Harrisonville, 9790 G-9
Hartville, 603 J-13
Hayti, 3066 M-19
Hazelwood, 25535 *C-5
HENRY CO., 22577 G-11
Herculaneum, 3172 H-18
Hermann, 2735 F-15
HICKORY CO., 9271 H-12
Higbee, 652 E-13
Higginsville, 4660 E-11
High Ridge, 4236 G-17
Hillsboro, 1784 H-17
Hillsdale, 1421 *D-6
Holcomb, 697 M-19
Holden, 2543 F-10
Hollister, 3835 L-12
HOLT CO., 5081 B-7
Holts Summit, 3384 G-14
Hopkins, 561 A-8
Horine, 923 H-18
Hornersville, 681 N-19
House Springs, 300 G-17
Houston, 2005 J-14
HOWARD CO., 9957 E-13
HOWELL CO., 38400 L-14
Humansville, 986 I-11
Huntsville, 1625 D-13
Iberia, 673 H-14
Independence, 110208 E-9
IRON CO., 10273 I-16
Ironton, 1362 I-17
JACKSON CO., 662959 F-9
Jackson, 12982 J-19
Jamesport, 516 C-10
JASPER CO., 110624 J-9
Jasper, 1037 J-9
JEFFERSON CO., 213669 H-17
Jefferson City, 39062 G-14
Jennings, 14926 *D-6
JOHNSON CO., 50784 G-10
Jonesburg, 707 F-16
Joplin, 47183 K-9
Kahoka, 2193 B-15
Kansas City, 444965 E-9
Kearney, 7399 E-9
Kennett, 11028 M-19
Keytesville, 516 D-12
Kimberling City, 2520 L-11
King City, 944 C-9
Kirksville, 16986 B-13
Kirkwood, 27038 *F-4
Knob Noster, 2734 F-11
KNOX CO., 4171 C-14
La Belle, 666 C-14
LACLEDE CO., 34492 I-13
Laddonia, 600 E-15
Ladue, 8269 *E-5
LAFAYETTE CO., 33108 F-10
La Grange, 949 C-15
Lake Lotawana, 1921 F-9
Lake Ozark, 1915 H-13
Lakeshire, 1318 *G-5
Lake Tapawingo, 809 J-7
Lake Waukomis, 913 G-3
Lake Winnebago, 1065 M-6
Lamar, 4602 J-9
La Monte, 1062 F-11
Lancaster, 745 A-13
La Plata, 1442 C-13
Lathrop, 2328 D-9
LAWRENCE CO., 37127 K-10
Lawson, 2406 D-10
Leadwood, 1173 I-17
Lebanon, 13336 I-13
Lees Summit, 80338 L-6
Lemay, 17215 *G-6
LEWIS CO., 10186 B-15
Lexington, 4632 E-10
Liberal, 811 J-9
Liberty, 29042 E-9
Licking, 1500 J-15
Lilbourn, 1237 L-20
LINCOLN CO., 47727 F-16
Lincoln, 1103 G-11
LINN CO., 13133 C-12
Linn, 1424 G-15
LIVINGSTON CO., 14291 C-11
Lockwood, 962 J-10
Louisiana, 3881 D-16
Lowry City, 738 H-11
MACON CO., 15600 C-13
Macon, 5428 D-13
MADISON CO., 12151 J-18
Madison, 562 D-14
Malden, 4635 L-19
Manchester, 18970 *F-3
Mansfield, 1352 K-13
Maplewood, 8808 *F-5
Marble Hill, 1512 J-19
Marceline, 2405 D-12
MARIES CO., 8989 H-14
MARION CO., 28375 C-15
Marionville, 2161 K-11
Marlborough, 2191 *F-5
Marshall, 12403 E-12
Marshfield, 6763 J-12
Marston, 563 L-20
Maryland Hts., 26544 *D-4
Maryville, 10567 B-8
Mattese, 2500 *H-5
Matthews, 552 L-20
Maysville, 1165 C-9
MCDONALD CO., 22844 L-9
Mehlville, 28822 *G-5
Memphis, 2003 B-14
MERCER CO., 3595 B-11
Mexico, 11018 E-14
Milan, 1849 B-12
MILLER CO., 24712 H-13
Miller, 792 K-10
Miner, 1268 K-20
MISSISSIPPI CO., 13599 K-20
Moberly, 13921 D-13
Moline Acres, 2579 *C-6
Monett, 8349 K-10
MONITEAU CO., 15084 G-13
MONROE CO., 9379 D-14
Monroe City, 2556 D-15
MONTGOMERY CO., 12166 F-15
Montgomery City, 2513 F-15
Morehouse, 960 L-19
MORGAN CO., 20436 G-12
Morley, 815 K-20
Mound City, 1110 B-7
Mtn. Grove, 4594 K-14
Mtn. View, 2546 K-15
Mt. Vernon, 4402 K-10
Murphy, 9048 *H-3
Naylor, 614 L-17
Neosho, 11130 K-9
Nevada, 8457 I-9
Newburg, 479 I-14
New Florence, 777 F-15
New Franklin, 1113 F-13
New Haven, 1950 G-16
New London, 992 D-16
NEW MADRID CO., 18566 L-19
New Madrid, 3131 L-20
NEWTON CO., 55554 K-9
Nixa, 15925 K-11
NODAWAY CO., 21710 B-8
Noel, 1515 L-9
Norborne, 792 E-11
Normandy, 5032 *D-6
N. Kansas City, 5388 H-3
Northwoods, 4435 *D-6
Novinger, 524 B-13
Oak Grove, 6763 F-10
Oak Grove, 385 H-16
Oakland, 1579 *F-5
Oakville, 35309 *H-6
Odessa, 4841 F-10
O'Fallon, 69694 F-17
Olivette, 7455 *E-5
Olympian Vil., 677 H-18
Oran, 1259 K-19
OREGON CO., 10403 L-16
Oregon, 901 C-8
Orrick, 867 E-10
OSAGE CO., 13485 G-14
Osage Beach, 4259 H-13
Osceola, 818 H-11
Overland, 16082 *D-4
Owensville, 2544 G-15
OZARK CO., 9490 L-13
Ozark, 15265 K-12
Pacific, 7098 G-17
Pagedale, 3486 *E-5
Palmyra, 3443 C-15
Paris, 1468 D-14
Park Hills, 8525 I-17
Parkville, 5116 E-8
Parma, 805 L-19
Pasadena Hills, 1122 *D-6
Peculiar, 3832 F-9
PEMISCOT CO., 19412 M-19
PERRY CO., 18571 I-19
Perry, 657 D-15
Perryville, 7935 I-19
PETTIS CO., 40121 F-11
Pevely, 4208 H-18
PHELPS CO., 42125 I-15
Piedmont, 1975 K-17
Pierce City, 1442 K-10
PIKE CO., 18762 D-16
Pilot Gr., 739 F-12
Pilot Knob, 684 I-17
Pine Lawn, 4092 *D-6
Pineville, 868 L-9
PLATTE CO., 82085 D-8
Platte City, 4907 E-8
Plattsburg, 2442 D-9
Pleasant Hill, 6747 F-9
Pleasant Valley, 3445 G-5
Point Lookout, 1200 *J-9
POLK CO., 28892 I-11
Poplar Bluff, 16912 L-18
Portage Des Sioux, 351 *A-5
Portageville, 3071 M-19
Potosi, 2709 I-17
Princeton, 969 B-11
PULASKI CO., 44187 I-14
Purdy, 1146 L-10
PUTNAM CO., 5168 A-12
Puxico, 1150 K-18
Queen City, 646 B-13
RALLS CO., 9761 D-15
RANDOLPH CO., 25336 D-13
RAY CO., 24101 E-10
Raymore, 15530 F-9
Raytown, 28923 F-9
Republic, 10637 K-11
REYNOLDS CO., 6585 J-16
Rich Hill, 1500 H-9
Richland, 1776 I-13
Richmond, 6075 E-10
Richmond Hts., 9309 *E-5
RIPLEY CO., 13851 L-17
Riverside, 2964 G-3
Riverview, 2995 *C-7
Rock Hill, 4700 *F-5
Rock Port, 1343 B-7
Rogersville, 2239 K-12
Rolla, 17717 I-15
Russellville, 735 G-13
St. Ann, 13092 *D-5
ST. CHARLES CO., 329940 F-17
St. Charles, 62304 F-18
ST. CLAIR CO., 9686 H-10
St. Clair, 4405 G-16
Ste. Genevieve, 4454 H-19
STE. GENEVIEVE CO., 18198 I-18
ST. FRANCOIS CO., 61661 I-17
St. George, 1242 *G-5
St. James, 4041 H-15
St. John, 6558 *D-5
St. Joseph, 72661 D-8
ST. LOUIS CO., 1004666 G-17
St. Louis, 344362 ‡G-18
St. Peters, 54209 F-17
St. Robert, 3155 I-14
Salem, 4789 I-15
SALINE CO., 23075 E-12
Salisbury, 1635 D-13
Sappington, 7287 *G-5
Sarcoxie, 1340 K-10
Savannah, 4925 C-8
SCHUYLER CO., 4308 B-13
SCOTLAND CO., 4928 B-14
SCOTT CO., 41143 K-20
Scott City, 4584 J-20
Sedalia, 20430 F-12
Senath, 1641 M-18
Seneca, 2237 L-9
Seymour, 1960 K-13
SHANNON CO., 8367 K-15
Shelbina, 1886 D-14
SHELBY CO., 6744 C-14
Shelbyville, 686 C-14
Shrewsbury, 6393 *F-5
Sikeston, 17180 K-20
Slater, 1954 E-12
Smithton, 502 G-12
Smithville, 7118 E-9
S. West City, 919 L-8
Spanish Lake, 21337 *C-7
Sparta, 1226 K-12
Springfield, 150298 K-11
Stanberry, 1192 B-9
Steele, 2169 N-19
Steelville, 1454 H-16
Stewartsville, 746 D-9
Stockton, 2004 I-10
STODDARD CO., 29714 L-19
STONE CO., 30931 L-11
Stover, 1022 G-12
Strafford, 1909 J-12
Sturgeon, 913 E-14
Sugar Cr., 3598 I-5
SULLIVAN CO., 6907 B-12
Sullivan, 6613 H-16
Sunset Hills, 8374 *G-4
Sweet Sprs., 1551 F-11
Sycamore Hills, 705 *D-5
TANEY CO., 42985 L-12
Taos, 862 G-14
Tarkio, 1866 B-7
TEXAS CO., 24614 J-14
Thayer, 2171 L-15
Tipton, 3142 G-13
Trenton, 6121 C-11
Troy, 9862 F-16
Union, 8897 G-16
Unionville, 1981 B-12
University City, 37170 *E-5
Valley Park, 6405 *G-3
Van Buren, 817 K-16
Vandalia, 4067 E-15
Velda City, 1542 *D-6
Velda Vil. Hills, 1063 *D-6
VERNON CO., 20441 I-9
Verona, 720 K-10
Versailles, 2662 G-12
Viburnum, 811 I-16
Vienna, 635 H-14
Vinita Park, 1837 *D-5
Wardsville, 967 G-14
WARREN CO., 28764 F-16
Warrensburg, 17769 F-10
Warrenton, 6612 F-16
Warsaw, 2268 H-11
Warson Woods, 1906 *F-4
WASHINGTON CO., 24032 H-16
Washington, 14136 G-16
Waverly, 807 E-11
WAYNE CO., 13097 K-18
Waynesville, 3511 I-14
Weatherby Lake, 1870 G-2
Webb City, 10764 K-9
WEBSTER CO., 34745 J-12
Webster Groves, 22896 *F-5
Wellington, 783 E-10
Wellston, 2370 *E-6
Wellsville, 1398 E-15
Wentzville, 17988 F-17
Weston, 1644 D-8
W. Plains, 11348 L-15
Wilbur Park, 467 *F-6
Wildwood, 34831 *F-1
Willard, 3330 J-11
Willow Sprs., 2116 K-14
Winchester, 1585 *F-3
Windsor, 3265 G-11
Winfield, 850 F-17
Winona, 1317 K-16
Woods Heights, 776 E-10
Woodson Ter., 4111 *D-5
WORTH CO., 2174 B-9
WRIGHT CO., 18306 J-13
Wright City, 2440 F-16

Montana

Map pp. 122-125

Absarokee, 1234 I-11
Alberton, 422 F-3
Anaconda, 8948 H-6
Ashland, 464 I-16
Augusta, 284 E-6
Baker, 1628 G-20
BEAVERHEAD CO., 8773 K-6
Belfry, 219 J-12
Belgrade, 7033 I-8
Belt, 610 E-9
Bigfork, 1421 C-4
BIG HORN CO., 13149 J-13
Big Sandy, 643 C-10
Big Sky, 1221 J-8
Big Timber, 1725 I-10
Billings, 98721 I-13
Billings Heights, 6000 M-19
Black Eagle, 914 E-8
BLAINE CO., 6629 C-12
Boulder, 1436 H-7
Box Elder, 794 C-10
Bozeman, 33535 I-9
Bridger, 752 J-12
Broadus, 445 I-18
BROADWATER CO., 4517 G-8
Brockton, 243 C-18
Browning, 1078 B-6
Busby, 695 I-15
Butte, 32282 H-6
CARBON CO., 9902 J-12
CARTER CO., 1320 I-19
Cascade, 798 E-8
CASCADE CO., 79569 F-8
Charlo, 439 E-4
Chester, 811 B-9
Chinook, 1299 B-11
Choteau, 1738 D-7
CHOUTEAU CO., 5463 C-8
Circle, 584 E-17
Clyde Park, 348 I-9
Colstrip, 2331 H-16
Columbia Falls, 4440 C-4
Columbus, 1897 I-12
Conrad, 2600 C-7
Coram, 337 C-4
Corvallis, 443 G-4
Crow Agency, 1552 I-14
Culbertson, 714 C-19
CUSTER CO., 11267 H-17
Custer, 145 H-14
Cut Bank, 3167 B-7
DANIELS CO., 1836 A-17
Darby, 835 H-4
DAWSON CO., 8688 E-18
Deer Lodge, 3313 G-6
DEER LODGE CO., 8948 H-5
Denton, 288 E-10
Dillon, 3988 J-6
Drummond, 332 G-5
Dutton, 372 D-8
E. Glacier Park, 396 C-5
E. Helena, 1848 G-7
Ekalaka, 395 H-19
Ennis, 973 J-7
Eureka, 1028 A-2
Evergreen, 6215 C-4
Fairfield, 635 E-7
Fairview, 666 D-20
FALLON CO., 2717 H-19
Fallon, 138 F-18
FERGUS CO., 11551 E-12
FLATHEAD CO., 83172 D-5
Forest Park, 1000 F-19
Forsyth, 1888 H-16
Ft. Belknap Agency, 1262 C-12
Ft. Benton, 1475 D-9
Ft. Peck, 229 C-16
Frazer, 452 C-17
Fromberg, 492 J-12
GALLATIN CO., 78210 J-8
Gardiner, 851 K-9
GARFIELD CO., 1199 F-15
Geraldine, 258 E-10
Gildford, 185 B-10
GLACIER CO., 13552 A-6
Glasgow, 3018 C-16
Glendive, 4670 F-19
GOLDEN VALLEY CO., 1159 G-11
GRANITE CO., 2965 G-5
Great Falls, 56338 E-8
Hamilton, 4443 H-4
Hardin, 3510 I-14
Harlem, 806 B-12
Harlowton, 941 G-11
Havre, 9390 B-11
Havre North, 973 B-11
Hays, 702 D-12
Helena, 27383 G-7
HILL CO., 16304 C-10
Hobson, 231 F-11
Hot Sprs., 565 D-3
Hungry Horse, 934 C-4
Hysham, 262 H-15
JEFFERSON CO., 11170 H-7
Joliet, 601 J-12
Jordan, 339 E-15
JUDITH BASIN CO., 2198 F-9
Kalispell, 18480 C-4
LAKE CO., 28297 D-3
Lakeside, 1679 C-4
Lame Deer, 2018 I-16
Laurel, 6342 I-12
LEWIS AND CLARK CO., 58449 E-6
Lewistown, 6099 F-11
Libby, 2648 B-2
LIBERTY CO., 2003 B-9
Lima, 227 K-6
LINCOLN CO., 19193 B-2
Lincoln, 1100 F-6
Livingston, 7146 I-9
Lockwood, 4306 I-13
Lodge Grass, 522 J-15
Lolo, 3388 F-4
MADISON CO., 7274 J-7
Malta, 1922 C-14
Manhattan, 1465 I-8
Martin City, 331 C-4
MCCONE CO., 1805 D-17
MEAGHER CO., 1999 F-8
Medicine Lake, 228 B-19
Miles City, 8162 G-17
Milltown, 175 F-4
MINERAL CO., 4014 F-3
Missoula, 62923 F-4
MISSOULA CO., 100086 F-4
MUSSELSHELL CO., 4497 G-13
Nashua, 303 C-16
Noxon, 230 C-1
Orchard Homes, 5199 M-12
Paradise, 184 E-3
PARK CO., 15968 I-9
Park City, 870 I-12
PETROLEUM CO., 470 E-13
Philipsburg, 959 G-5
PHILLIPS CO., 4179 B-13
Pinesdale, 832 G-3
Plains, 1247 E-3
Plentywood, 1774 B-19
Polson, 4828 D-4
PONDERA CO., 6087 C-7
Poplar, 904 C-18
POWDER RIVER CO., 1705 J-17
POWELL CO., 6999 G-6
PRAIRIE CO., 1105 F-17
RAVALLI CO., 39940 H-4
Red Lodge, 2401 J-12
Richey, 179 D-18
RICHLAND CO., 9096 D-19
Roberts, 320 J-12
Ronan, 1968 E-4
ROOSEVELT CO., 10524 C-18
ROSEBUD CO., 9212 G-16
Roundup, 1916 G-13
Rudyard, 275 B-9
Ryegate, 304 H-12
Saco, 203 C-14
St. Ignatius, 823 E-4
St. Regis, 315 E-2
Sand Coulee, 250 E-8
SANDERS CO., 11057 D-2
Savage, 300 E-19
Scobey, 991 B-17
Seeley Lake, 1436 E-5
Shelby, 3304 B-7
Sheridan, 689 J-7
SHERIDAN CO., 3524 A-19
Sidney, 4470 D-20
SILVER BOW CO., 32982 I-6
Somers, 556 C-4
Stanford, 428 F-10
Stevensville, 1855 G-4
STILLWATER CO., 8493 H-12
Sunburst, 346 B-7
Superior, 910 E-3
SWEET GRASS CO., 3672 H-11
Terry, 563 F-18
TETON CO., 6240 D-6
Thompson Falls, 1392 D-2
Three Forks, 1845 I-8
TOOLE CO., 5031 B-8
Townsend, 1950 H-8
TREASURE CO., 689 H-15
Troy, 982 B-1
Twin Bridges, 418 I-6
Ulm, 750 E-8
Valier, 472 C-7
VALLEY CO., 7143 B-15
Vaughn, 701 E-8
Victor, 859 G-4
Walkerville, 700 H-6
Westby, 148 A-20
W. Glacier, 425 B-4
W. Yellowstone, 1223 K-8
WHEATLAND CO., 2037 H-11
Whitefish, 7067 C-4
Whitehall, 1156 I-7
White Sulphur Sprs., 1017 G-9
WIBAUX CO., 951 F-19
Wibaux, 505 F-20
Wolf Pt., 2623 C-17
Worden, 506 H-13
YELLOWSTONE CO., 136691 H-13

Nebraska

Map pp. 126-129

ADAMS CO., 33070 L-13
Ainsworth, 1717 F-10
Albion, 1672 H-14
Alda, 651 K-13
Alliance, 8331 G-3
Alma, 1110 M-11
Ansley, 493 J-11
ANTELOPE CO., 7004 G-14
Arapahoe, 954 M-10
Arlington, 1192 I-18
Arnold, 618 I-9
ARTHUR CO., 378 I-5
Ashland, 2493 J-18
Atkinson, 1151 F-12
Auburn, 3076 L-19
Aurora, 4282 K-14
Axtell, 708 L-12
BANNER CO., 733 I-1
Bassett, 660 F-11
Battle Cr., 1178 H-15
Bayard, 1155 H-2
Beatrice, 12890 M-17
Beaver City, 597 M-10
Beemer, 717 H-17
Bellevue, 47334 J-19
Benkelman, 914 M-6
Bennet, 681 K-18
Bennington, 913 I-18
Bertrand, 791 L-11
BLAINE CO., 484 H-9
Blair, 7765 I-18
Bloomfield, 1049 F-15
Blue Hill, 798 M-13
BOONE CO., 5772 H-14
BOX BUTTE CO., 11374 G-2
BOYD CO., 2261 E-12
Boys Town, 891 J-18
Bridgeport, 1493 H-3
Broken Bow, 3311 I-10
BROWN CO., 3328 F-10
BUFFALO CO., 43572 K-12
BURT CO., 7455 H-18
Burwell, 1063 H-12
BUTLER CO., 8720 J-16
Butte, 344 E-12
Cairo, 787 K-13
Callaway, 625 J-10
Cambridge, 971 M-9
CASS CO., 25734 K-18
CEDAR CO., 9066 F-16
Cedar Bluffs, 617 I-17
Central City, 2891 J-14
Ceresco, 899 J-17
Chadron, 5320 E-3
Chappell, 935 J-4
CHASE CO., 3866 L-5
CHERRY CO., 6098 F-7
CHEYENNE CO., 9993 J-2
Clarkson, 680 H-16
CLAY CO., 6733 L-14
Clay Cen., 813 L-14
Coleridge, 501 F-16
COLFAX CO., 10433 I-16
Columbus, 20909 I-16
Cozad, 4222 K-10
Crawford, 1035 E-2
Creighton, 1187 F-14
Crete, 6308 L-17
Crofton, 710 E-15
Culbertson, 559 M-8
CUMING CO., 9688 H-17
Curtis, 736 L-8
CUSTER CO., 11410 J-10
DAKOTA CO., 20349 F-17
Dakota City, 1880 F-18
David City, 2558 J-16
DAWES CO., 8636 E-3
DAWSON CO., 24617 K-10
Decatur, 583 G-18
Deshler, 790 M-15
DEUEL CO., 2004 J-5
De Witt, 577 L-17
DIXON CO., 6155 F-17
Dodge, 683 H-17
DODGE CO., 36078 I-17
Doniphan, 762 K-13
Dorchester, 630 L-16
DOUGLAS CO., 486929 J-18
DUNDY CO., 2133 M-6
Eagle, 1155 K-18
Edgar, 508 L-14
Elgin, 681 H-14
Elkhorn, 8192 J-18
Elm Cr., 867 K-11
Elmwood, 715 K-18
Elwood, 712 L-10
Emerson, 816 G-17
Exeter, 679 L-16
Fairbury, 4020 M-16
Fairmont, 659 L-15
Falls City, 4218 M-20
FILLMORE CO., 6385 L-15
Ft. Calhoun, 917 I-19
FRANKLIN CO., 3421 M-12
Franklin, 980 M-12
Fremont, 25314 I-18
Friend, 1204 L-16
FRONTIER CO., 2795 L-8
Fullerton, 1259 I-14
FURNAS CO., 5019 M-9
GAGE CO., 23306 L-17
GARDEN CO., 1997 I-5
GARFIELD CO., 1816 H-12
Geneva, 2149 L-15
Genoa, 883 I-15
Gering, 7767 H-1
Gibbon, 1753 K-12
Gordon, 1589 E-5
GOSPER CO., 2020 L-10
Gothenburg, 3692 K-9
Grand Island, 44546 K-13
Grant, 1145 K-6
GRANT CO., 670 H-5
GREELEY CO., 2512 I-13
Greeley, 477 I-13
Gretna, 4860 J-18
HALL CO., 55104 K-13
HAMILTON CO., 9568 K-14
HARLAN CO., 3462 M-11
Hartington, 1587 F-16
Harvard, 943 L-14
Hastings, 25437 L-13
HAYES CO., 1027 L-7
Hay Sprs., 585 E-4
Hebron, 1410 M-15
Hemingford, 916 G-3
Henderson, 999 K-15
Hershey, 568 J-7
Hickman, 1356 L-17
HITCHCOCK CO., 2970 M-7
Holdrege, 5349 L-11
HOLT CO., 10784 G-12
Homer, 603 F-18
HOOKER CO., 744 H-7
Hooper, 798 I-17
HOWARD CO., 6708 J-13
Howells, 635 H-16
Humboldt, 852 M-19
Humphrey, 768 H-15
Imperial, 1876 L-6
Indianola, 611 M-9
JEFFERSON CO., 7925 M-16
JOHNSON CO., 4695 L-18
Kearney, 28958 K-12
KEARNEY CO., 6774 L-12
KEITH CO., 8330 J-6
Kenesaw, 913 L-13
KEYA PAHA CO., 902 E-10
Kimball, 2341 J-1
KIMBALL CO., 3782 J-1
KNOX CO., 8916 F-15
LANCASTER CO., 264814 K-17
Laurel, 924 F-16
La Vista, 15692 D-17
Lexington, 10085 K-10
Lincoln, 239213 K-17
LINCOLN CO., 35636 K-7
LOGAN CO., 740 I-9
Louisville, 1073 J-18
LOUP CO., 686 H-11
Loup City, 924 J-12
Lyons, 912 H-18
Macy, 956 G-18
MADISON CO., 35488 H-15
Madison, 2309 H-15
McCook, 7680 M-8
MCPHERSON CO., 507 I-7
MERRICK CO., 8066 J-14
Milford, 2053 K-16
Minatare, 784 H-2
Minden, 2913 L-12
Mitchell, 1796 H-1
MORRILL CO., 5165 H-3
Morrill, 941 G-1
Mullen, 497 G-7
NANCE CO., 3666 I-14
Nebraska City, 7035 K-19
Neligh, 1542 G-14
Nelson, 539 M-14
NEMAHA CO., 6965 L-19
Newman Gr., 774 H-15
Norfolk, 23946 G-15
N. Bend, 1211 I-17
N. Platte, 24324 J-8
NUCKOLLS CO., 4739 M-14
Oakland, 1298 H-18
Ogallala, 4696 J-6
Omaha, 414521 J-19
O'Neill, 3483 F-13
Ord, 2129 I-12
Osceola, 902 J-15
Oshkosh, 766 I-4
Osmond, 746 F-15
OTOE CO., 15509 K-18
Overton, 655 K-11
Oxford, 806 M-10
Papillion, 20431 J-19
PAWNEE CO., 2878 N-18
Pawnee City, 946 M-19
Paxton, 548 J-7
Pender, 1165 G-17
PERKINS CO., 3057 K-6
Peru, 778 L-19
PHELPS CO., 9449 L-11
PIERCE CO., 7600 G-15
Pierce, 1730 G-15
Plainview, 1279 F-15
PLATTE CO., 31262 I-15
Plattsmouth, 7023 J-19
POLK CO., 5421 J-15
Ponca, 1042 F-17
Ralston, 6193 C-17
Randolph, 888 F-16
Ravenna, 1281 J-12
Red Cloud, 1029 M-13
RED WILLOW CO., 11060 M-8
RICHARDSON CO., 8732 M-19
ROCK CO., 1567 G-11
Rushville, 902 E-4
St. Edward, 733 I-14
St. Paul, 2268 J-13
SALINE CO., 14195 L-16
Sargent, 612 I-11
SARPY CO., 139371 J-18
SAUNDERS CO., 20458 J-17
Schuyler, 5327 I-16
Scottsbluff, 14814 H-1
SCOTTS BLUFF CO., 36752 H-1
SEWARD CO., 16739 K-16
Seward, 6776 K-16
Shelby, 648 J-15
Shelton, 1125 K-13
SHERIDAN CO., 5668 F-4
SHERMAN CO., 3112 J-12
Sidney, 6442 J-3
SIOUX CO., 1458 F-1
S. Sioux City, 11979 F-18
Spalding, 502 H-13
Spencer, 504 E-13
Springfield, 1497 J-18
STANTON CO., 6534 H-16
Stanton, 1629 H-16
Stromsburg, 1165 J-15
Stuart, 577 F-12
Superior, 1903 M-14
Sutherland, 1223 J-7
Sutton, 1394 L-15
Syracuse, 1835 K-18
Tecumseh, 1951 L-18
Tekamah, 1814 H-18
Terrytown, 650 H-1
THAYER CO., 5436 M-15
THOMAS CO., 623 H-8
THURSTON CO., 7365 G-17
Tilden, 1053 G-15
Trenton, 477 M-7
Utica, 825 K-16
Valentine, 2786 E-8
Valley, 1829 I-18
VALLEY CO., 4402 I-12
Verdigre, 486 F-14
Wahoo, 4063 J-17
Wakefield, 1340 G-17
Walthill, 917 G-18
WASHINGTON CO., 19772 I-18
Wauneta, 577 L-7
Waverly, 2693 K-18
WAYNE CO., 9211 G-16
Wayne, 5163 G-16
WEBSTER CO., 3762 M-13
Weeping Water, 1118 K-18
W. Point, 3476 H-17
WHEELER CO., 820 H-13
Wilber, 1799 L-17
Winnebago, 798 G-18
Wisner, 1200 H-17
Wood River, 1200 K-13
Wymore, 1615 M-17
York, 7888 K-15
YORK CO., 14397 K-15
Yutan, 1217 J-18

Nevada

Map pp. 130-131

* City keyed to p. 28
† City keyed to p. 133
‡ Independent city: Not included in any county.

Alamo, 400 J-8
Austin, 350 F-5
Battle Mtn., 2871 D-6
Beatty, 1154 K-6
Blue Diamond, 282 L-8
Boulder City, 15177 L-9
Caliente, 1148 I-9
Carlin, 2083 D-7
Carson City, 56062 ‡F-2
CHURCHILL CO., 24556 F-4
CLARK CO., 1710551 K-8
Crystal Bay, 1500 F-1
Dayton, 5907 F-2
DOUGLAS CO., 47017 G-2
East Las Vegas, 11087 L-4
ELKO CO., 45570 C-7
Elko, 16685 C-7
Ely, 3918 F-9
ESMERALDA CO., 787 I-5
Eureka, 600 F-7
EUREKA CO., 1428 E-6
Fallon, 8103 F-3
Fernley, 8543 F-2
Gabbs, 318 G-4
Gardnerville, 3357 G-2
Hawthorne, 3311 H-3
Henderson, 232146 L-9
HUMBOLDT CO., 17129 C-4
Incline Village, 5500 *A-2
Indian Sprs., 1302 K-8
Jackpot, 600 A-9
LANDER CO., 5114 E-6
Las Vegas, 545147 L-8
Laughlin, 7076 N-9
LINCOLN CO., 4391 I-9
Logandale, 1000 K-9
Lovelock, 1878 E-3
Lund, 200 G-8
LYON CO., 47515 F-2
Mason, 400 G-2
McGill, 1054 F-9
Mesquite, 13523 K-10
Mina, 350 H-4
Minden, 2836 G-2
MINERAL CO., 4910 H-3
N. Las Vegas, 176635 L-8
NYE CO., 40477 H-6
Overton, 1200 K-9
Owyhee, 1017 A-7
Pahrump, 24631 L-7
Panaca, 600 I-9
PERSHING CO., 6360 D-3
Pioche, 800 I-9
Reno, 203550 F-2
Ruth, 500 F-8
Schurz, 721 G-3
Silver Sprs., 4708 F-2
South Hills, 1100 †J-2
Sparks, 82051 F-2
Spring Creek, 10548 D-8
Spring Valley, 117390 L-2
Stateline, 1215 G-1
STOREY CO., 4074 F-2
Summit Village, 1000 *C-3
Sunrise Manor, 156120 K-4
Sun Valley, 19461 †G-2
Tonopah, 2627 H-5
Verdi, 1500 F-1
Virginia City, 930 F-2
Wadsworth, 881 F-2
Walker Lake, 400 G-3
WASHOE CO., 389872 D-2
Wells, 1295 C-8
West Wendover, 4966 D-10
WHITE PINE CO., 8994 F-8
Winnemucca, 7726 C-5
Yerington, 3486 G-3
Zephyr Cove, 1000 G-1

New Hampshire

Map pp. 132-133

Alstead, 500 L-4
Alton, 1000 J-8
Alton Bay, 900 J-8
Amherst, 900 M-7
Antrim, 1389 L-6
Ashland, 1500 I-7
Atkinson, 900 M-9
Bartlett, 900 G-8
Bedford, 1800 M-7
BELKNAP CO., 61547 J-8
Belmont, 1200 J-7
Bennington, 850 L-6
Berlin, 10097 E-8
Bethlehem, 800 F-7
Bow, 700 L-7
Bradford, 600 K-6
Bristol, 1670 I-7
Campton, 700 H-7
Canaan, 700 I-6
Canobie Lake, 700 M-8
CARROLL CO., 47439 G-9
Center Hbr., 650 I-8
Cen. Ossipee, 600 I-9
Charlestown, 1145 K-4
CHESHIRE CO., 77287 L-4
Chester, 600 M-8
Claremont, 13388 K-4
Colebrook, 1100 C-7
Concord, 42336 K-7
Contoocook, 1444 K-7
Conway, 1692 H-9
COOS CO., 33655 D-8
Danville, 700 M-9
Derry, 22661 M-8
Dover, 28486 K-10
Dublin, 650 M-5
Durham, 9024 L-9
E. Derry, 850 M-8
E. Hampstead, 1400 M-9
Enfield, 1698 I-5
Epping, 1673 L-9
Exeter, 9759 L-9
Farmington, 3468 J-9
Fitzwilliam, 650 M-5
Franconia, 600 F-7
Franklin, 8763 J-7
Fremont, 900 L-9
Gilmanton, 700 J-8
Gilsum, 400 L-5
Goffstown, 3200 L-7
Gorham, 1773 F-8
GRAFTON CO., 84708 H-6
Greenfield, 900 M-6
Greenland, 1400 L-10
Greenville, 1131 M-6
Groveton, 1197 E-7
Hampstead, 900 M-9
Hampton, 9126 M-10
Hampton Beach, 600 M-10
Hampton Falls, 550 M-10
Hanover, 8162 I-5
Henniker, 1627 K-6
HILLSBOROUGH CO., 401291 M-6
Hillsborough, 1842 L-6
Hinsdale, 1713 M-4
Hooksett, 3609 L-8
Hudson, 7814 M-8
Jaffrey, 2802 M-6
Keene, 22778 M-5
Kingston, 1400 M-9
Laconia, 17060 J-7
Lancaster, 1695 E-7
Lebanon, 12606 I-5
Lincoln, 900 G-7
Lisbon, 1070 G-6
Little Boars Head, 120 L-10
Littleton, 4431 F-6
Londonderry, 11417 M-8
Manchester, 109691 L-8
Marlborough, 1089 M-5
Meredith, 1739 I-7
Merrimack, 2400 M-7
MERRIMACK CO., 146881 K-6
Milford, 8293 M-7
Milton, 1100 J-9
Nashua, 87321 M-7
Newfields, 700 L-9
New Ipswich, 800 N-6
New London, 1400 J-6
Newmarket, 5124 L-9
Newport, 4008 K-5
Newton, 650 M-9
N. Branch, 150 L-6
N. Conway, 2069 G-9
Northfield, 1500 J-7
N. Hampton, 500 L-10
N. Salem, 300 M-8
N. Stratford, 400 D-7
N. Walpole, 800 L-4
N. Woodstock, 600 G-7
Peterborough, 2944 M-6
Pinardville, 5779 B-4
Pittsfield, 1669 K-8
Plaistow, 2200 M-9
Plymouth, 3528 I-7
Portsmouth, 20674 L-10
Raymond, 2839 L-8
Rochester, 30004 K-9
ROCKINGHAM CO., 295076 L-8
Rollinsford, 1500 K-10
Rye, 850 L-10
Rye Beach, 450 L-10
Salem, 12000 M-8
Sanbornville, 1200 J-9
Seabrook, 900 M-10
Somersworth, 11720 K-10
S. Hooksett, 5282 L-8
STRAFFORD CO., 119015 K-9
Stratham, 800 L-9
SULLIVAN CO., 43041 K-4
Sunapee, 1000 J-5
Suncook, 5362 L-8
Tamworth, 600 H-8
Tilton, 1300 J-7
Troy, 1200 M-5
Twin Mtn., 300 F-7
Walpole, 800 L-4
Warner, 750 K-6
Warren, 550 H-6
W. Chesterfield, 550 M-4
Westport, 500 M-4
W. Swanzey, 1118 M-4
Westville, 400 M-9
Whitefield, 1089 F-7
Wilton, 1236 M-7
Winchester, 1832 M-4
Winnisquam, 650 J-7
Wolfeboro, 2979 J-8
Wolfeboro Falls, 600 I-8
Woodsville, 1081 G-6

New Jersey

Map pp. 134-137

* City keyed to pp. 146-148
‡ City keyed to p. 182

Aberdeen, 18333 H-12
Absecon, 7989 P-10
Allendale, 6754 D-12
Allentown, 1858 J-10
Alpha, 2455 G-6
Alpine, 2368 D-14
Asbury Park, 16624 J-13
Atco, 3500 N-8
ATLANTIC CO., 271015 P-8
Atlantic City, 40368 Q-10
Atlantic Highlands, 4625 H-13
Audubon, 9047 M-7
Avalon, 2133 S-9
Avenel, 17552 G-11
Avon-By-The-Sea, 2188 J-13
Barrington, 7050 M-7
Basking Ridge, 4000 F-10

***, †, ‡, See explanation under state title in this index.**
County names are listed in capital letters and in boldface type.

Bayonne, 59987 F-12
Beachwood, 10738 L-12
Belford, 1340 H-13
Belleville, 35928 E-12
Bellmawr, 11159 M-6
Belmar, 5962 J-13
Belvidere, 2732 E-7
BERGEN CO., 902561 C-12
Bergenfield, 26056 D-13
Berkeley Hts., 13407 F-10
Berlin, 7844 M-7
Bernardsville, 7612 F-10
Beverly, 2670 K-7
Blackwood, 4692 M-7
Bloomfield, 47683 E-12
Bloomingdale, 7654 D-11
Bogota, 8150 A-5
Boonton, 8555 E-11
Bordentown, 3989 K-9
Bound Brook, 10168 G-10
Bradley Beach, 4782 J-13
Bridgeton, 23959 P-6
Bridgewater, 7000 G-9
Brielle, 4878 K-13
Brigantine, 12861 P-11
Brooklawn, 2315 ‡G-5
Brookwood, 4000 K-11
Browns Mills, 11257 L-10
Browntown, 2400 I-11
Budd Lake, 8100 E-9
Buena, 3848 P-7
BURLINGTON CO., 450743 M-9
Burlington, 9791 K-8
Butler, 8091 D-11
Caldwell, 7489 E-11
Camden, 80010 L-6
CAMDEN CO., 518249 N-8
Candlewood, 4000 K-12
Cape May, 3760 T-7
CAPE MAY CO., 99286 R-8
Cape May Court House, 4704 S-8
Carlstadt, 6018 B-4
Carneys Pt., 6914 N-4
Carteret, 21460 G-12
Cedar Gr., 12300 E-12
Centre City, 1800 M-6
Chatham, 8439 F-11
Cheesequake, 300 H-11
Cherry Hill, 69319 L-7
Chesilhurst, 1865 N-8
Cinnaminson, 14583 L-7
Clark, 14597 G-11
Clayton, 7447 N-6
Clementon, 4944 M-7
Cliffside Park, 23035 E-13
Cliffwood Beach, 3538 H-12
Clifton, 79922 E-12
Clinton, 2621 G-8
Closter, 8669 D-13
Collingswood, 14083 L-7
Colonia, 17811 G-11
Cranford, 22578 G-11
Cresskill, 8449 D-13
Crestwood Vil., 8392 L-11
CUMBERLAND CO., 153252 Q-6
Deal, 1043 J-13
Delanco, 3316 K-7
Delran, 13178 L-7
Denville, 13812 E-10
Dover, 18441 E-10
Dumont, 17474 D-13
Dunellen, 6994 G-10
E. Brunswick, 46756 H-11
E. Hanover, 9926 E-11
E. Newark, 2262 D-3
E. Orange, 68190 F-12
E. Rutherford, 8960 B-4
E. Windsor, 4000 J-10
Eatontown, 14088 I-13
Edgewater, 9646 B-6
Edgewater Park, 2000 K-8
Edison, 97597 H-11
Egg Hbr. City, 4497 O-9
Elizabeth, 125809 F-12
Elmer, 1379 O-6
Elmwood Park, 18905 A-3
Emerson, 7334 D-13
Englewood, 26207 E-13
Englewood Cliffs, 5738 E-13
Espanong, 3000 D-9
ESSEX CO., 791057 E-12
Ewing, 35707 J-8
Fairfield, 7063 E-11
Fair Haven, 5899 I-13
Fair Lawn, 31408 D-12
Fairview, 13565 C-6
Fairview M-6
Fairview, 125 M-8
Fanwood, 7228 G-11
Finderne, 3000 G-10
Flemington, 4171 H-8
Florence, 5500 K-8
Florham Park, 12626 F-11
Folsom, 1972 O-8
Fords, 15032 H-11
Forked River, 4914 M-12
Ft. Lee, 37175 E-13
Franklin, 5233 C-10
Franklin Lakes, 11302 D-12
Freehold, 11439 J-11
Frenchtown, 1503 H-7
Garfield, 29772 E-12
Gibbsboro, 2468 M-7
Gibbstown, 3758 M-5
Gilford Park, 8668 L-12
Glassboro, 19290 N-6
Glendola, 2400 J-13
Glen Gardner, 1999 F-7
Glen Ridge, 7020 C-2
Glen Rock, 11457 D-12
GLOUCESTER CO., 276910 O-7
Gloucester City, 11582 M-6
Green Brook, 2400 G-10
Groveville, 2500 J-9
Guttenberg, 10885 C-5
Hackensack, 43735 E-13
Hackettstown, 9375 E-8
Haddonfield, 11591 M-7
Haledon, 8398 D-12
Hamburg, 3567 C-10
Hamilton Square, 11000 J-9
Hammonton, 13585 O-8
Hampton, 1608 F-7
Harrison, 14060 F-12
Hasbrouck Hts., 11643 E-13
Hawthorne, 18268 D-12
Hazlet, 12000 H-12
High Bridge, 3770 F-8
Highland Park, 14268 H-11
Highlands, 4998 I-13
Hightstown, 5293 J-10
Hillsdale, 10089 D-13
Hillside, 21747 F-12
Hoboken, 39900 F-13
Hopatcong, 16001 D-9
Hopewell, 2036 I-8
HUDSON CO., 603521 F-13
HUNTERDON CO., 130404 G-7
Irvington, 60695 F-12
Iselin, 16698 G-11
Jamesburg, 6521 I-10
Jersey City, 239614 F-13
Keansburg, 10619 H-12
Kearny, 38771 F-12
Kendall Park, 9006 H-10
Kenvil, 2500 E-9
Keyport, 7505 H-12
Kinnelon, 9631 D-11
Lakehurst, 2683 L-11
Lakewood, 36065 K-12
Lambertville, 3840 I-7
Laurence Hbr., 6227 H-12
Lavallette, 2747 L-13
Lawrenceville, 4081 I-9
Leonardo, 3975 H-13
Leonia, 8853 B-6
Lincoln Park, 10899 D-11
Lincroft, 6255 I-12
Linden, 40014 G-12
Lindenwold, 17265 M-7
Linwood, 7398 Q-10
Little Falls, 11793 E-12
Little Ferry, 10775 B-5
Little Silver, 6137 I-13
Livingston, 27391 E-11
Lodi, 24310 E-13
Long Branch, 32091 I-13
Long Valley, 1818 F-8
Loveladies, 200 N-12
Lyndhurst, 19383 E-12
Madison, 15918 F-11
Magnolia, 4389 M-7
Mahwah, 12000 C-12
Manahawkin, 2004 N-12
Manasquan, 6201 K-13
Manville, 10404 G-10
Maple Shade, 18700 L-7
Margate City, 8666 Q-10
Marlton, 10260 M-8
Matawan, 8819 I-12
Mays Ldg., 2321 P-9
Maywood, 9442 A-4
Medford, 2400 L-8
Medford Lakes, 4185 M-8
Mendham, 5172 F-9
MERCER CO., 366256 I-8
Mercerville, 15000 J-9
Merchantville, 3820 L-7
Metuchen, 13383 G-11
Middlesex, 13938 G-10
MIDDLESEX CO., 789516 I-11
Middletown, 24000 I-12
Midland Park, 6952 D-12
Millburn, 19765 F-11
Millington, 2500 F-10
Milltown, 7130 H-10
Millville, 27886 P-7
Mine Hill, 2800 E-9
MONMOUTH CO., 635952 I-12
Monmouth Beach, 3593 I-13
Montclair, 38658 E-12
Montvale, 7306 D-13
Montville, 2600 D-11
Moonachie, 2812 B-5
Moorestown, 19000 L-7
MORRIS CO., 490593 E-10
Morris Plains, 5629 E-10
Morristown, 18851 E-10
Mtn. Lakes, 4336 E-11
Mountainside, 6635 F-11
Mt. Arlington, 5332 D-9
Mt. Ephraim, 4467 ‡G-6
Mt. Freedom, 1900 E-10
Mt. Holly, 10639 L-8
National Park, 3223 M-6
Neptune, 19000 J-13
Neptune City, 5176 J-13
Netcong, 3294 E-9
Newark, 280666 F-12
New Brunswick, 50156 H-10
New Egypt, 2519 K-10
Newfield, 1661 O-7
New Providence, 11905 F-11
Newton, 8416 C-9
N. Arlington, 15179 C-3
N. Bergen, 48414 E-13
N. Branch, 1300 G-9
N. Brunswick, 36287 H-10
N. Caldwell, 7284 E-12
N. Cape May, 3618 T-7
Northfield, 8025 Q-10
N. Haledon, 9073 D-12
N. Middletown, 3165 H-12
N. Plainfield, 21608 G-10
Northvale, 4564 D-13
N. Wildwood, 4778 T-8
Nutley, 27362 E-12
Oakland, 13645 D-12
Oaklyn, 4116 ‡F-6
OCEAN CO., 558341 L-11
Ocean City, 15330 Q-10
Oceanport, 5780 I-13
Ogdensburg, 2631 C-9
Old Bridge, 22833 H-11
Old Tappan, 5903 D-13
Oradell, 8005 D-13
Orange, 32868 F-12
Oxford, 2283 E-7
Palisades Park, 18857 E-13
Palmyra, 7641 L-7
Paramus, 26545 D-13
PASSAIC CO., 499060 C-11
Passaic, 68338 E-12
Paterson, 149843 D-12
Paulsboro, 6096 M-6
Pennington, 2696 I-8
Pennsauken, 35737 L-7
Penns Gr., 4824 N-4
Pennsville, 11657 N-4
Pequannock D-11
Perth Amboy, 48797 H-11
Phillipsburg, 14920 F-6
Pine Beach, 2025 L-12
Pine Hill, 11305 M-7
Piscataway, 50500 G-10
Pitman, 9251 N-6
Plainfield, 47642 G-11
Plainsboro, 2000 I-9
Pleasantville, 19032 Q-10
Pompton Lakes, 11313 D-11
Port Monmouth, 3742 H-12
Port Norris, 1507 R-7
Pt. Pleasant, 19861 K-13
Pt. Pleasant Beach, 5397 K-13
Port Reading, 3829 G-12
Princeton, 13495 I-9
Princeton Jct., 2382 I-9
Rahway, 27563 G-11
Ramblewood, 6003 L-7
Ramsey, 14558 C-12
Raritan, 6391 G-9
Red Bank, 1100 ‡G-4
Red Bank, 11876 I-13
Ridgefield, 11014 E-13
Ridgefield Park, 12746 B-5
Ridgewood, 24790 D-12
Ringwood, 12809 C-11
Rio Grande, 2444 T-8
Riverdale, 2635 D-11
River Edge, 10911 D-13
Riverside, 7974 K-7
Riverton, 2739 L-7
River Vale, 9449 D-13
Robertsville, 2500 I-11
Rochelle Park, 5528 A-4
Rockaway, 6419 E-10
Roebling, 3000 K-8
Roselle, 21265 G-11
Rumson, 7233 I-13
Runnemede, 8520 M-7
Rutherford, 17967 E-12
Saddle Brook, 13155 A-4
SALEM CO., 66346 O-5
Salem, 5812 O-4
Sayreville, 43017 H-11
Sayre Woods S., 10000 I-11
Scotch Plains, 22732 F-11
Sea Bright, 1790 I-13
Sea Girt, 2069 K-13
Sea Isle City, 2968 R-9
Seaside Hts., 3220 L-13
Seaside Park, 2301 L-13
Secaucus, 15623 E-13
Sewell, 2000 N-6
Shrewsbury, 3742 I-13
Silverton, 4800 L-12
Slackwoods, 6000 J-9
Somerdale, 5155 M-7
SOMERSET CO., 319900 H-9
Somerset, 23040 H-10
Somers Pt., 11701 Q-9
Somerville, 12478 G-9
S. Amboy, 7975 H-11
S. Bound Brook, 4505 G-10
S. Hackensack, 2106 A-5
S. Orange, 16964 F-12
S. Plainfield, 23064 G-11
S. River, 16060 H-11
S. Toms River, 3698 L-12
Sparta, 9755 D-9
Spotswood, 8237 I-11
Springfield, 14429 F-11
Spring Lake, 3506 J-13
Spring Lake Hts., 5135 J-13
Stanhope, 3701 D-9
Stirling, 1800 F-10
Stratford, 7184 M-7
Succasunna, 4000 E-9
Summit, 21200 F-11
SUSSEX CO., 153130 C-9
Sussex, 2189 B-9
Swedesboro, 2050 N-5
Teaneck, 39260 E-13
Tenafly, 14362 D-13
Thorofare, 1700 M-6
Tinton Falls, 17274 J-13
Toms River, 86327 L-12
Totowa, 10592 E-12
Trenton, 84639 J-8
Tuckerton, 3780 O-11
Twin Rivers, 7422 J-10
UNION CO., 531457 F-11
Union, 54405 F-11
Union Beach, 6659 H-12
Union City, 65128 F-13
Upper Saddle River, 8509 C-12
Ventnor City, 12737 Q-10
Verona, 13533 E-12
Villas, 9064 S-7
Vineland, 58164 P-7
Waldwick, 9650 D-12
Wallington, 11491 B-4
Wanaque, 10616 C-11
WARREN CO., 110376 F-7
Washington, 6876 F-7
Watchung, 6170 G-10
Wayne, 54069 D-12
Weehawken, 12385 D-5
Wenonah, 2332 M-6
W. Berlin, 3000 M-7
Westfield, 29918 G-11
W. Long Branch, 8286 I-13
W. Milford, 26410 C-11
W. New York, 46667 E-13
W. Orange, 44943 F-12
W. Paterson, 11245 A-2
Westville, 4466 M-6
Westville Gr., 1500 ‡G-5
Westwood, 10994 D-13
Wharton, 6222 E-10
White Horse, 9373 J-9
Whitman Square, 3500 N-7
Wildwood, 5291 T-8
Wildwood Crest, 3872 T-8
Williamstown, 11812 N-7
Willingboro, 36291 K-8
Woodbine, 2569 R-8
Woodbridge, 18309 G-11
Woodbury, 10435 M-6
Woodbury Hts., 3022 M-6
Woodlynne, 2745 ‡F-5
Wood-Ridge, 7634 B-4
Woodstown, 3312 N-5
Wrightstown, 746 K-9
Wyckoff, 16508 D-12
Yardville, 3500 J-9

New Mexico

Map pp. 138-139

Acomita, 800 E-3
Adobe Acres, 2500 N-7
Agua Fria, 2051 M-4
Alameda, 6000 E-5
Alamogordo, 36245 I-6
Albuquerque, 494236 E-5
Alcalde, 377 C-5
Alto, 800 H-6
Anthony, 7904 J-5
Arenas Valley, 500 I-2
Arroyo Seco, 500 B-6
Artesia, 10481 I-8
Aztec, 7084 B-3
Bayard, 2397 I-2
Belen, 7121 F-4
BERNALILLO CO., 603562 E-4
Bernalillo, 6938 D-5
Black Rock, 1252 E-1
Bloomfield, 7442 B-3
Bluewater, 500 E-3
Bosque Farms, 3969 E-5
Capitan, 1500 H-6
Carlsbad, 25300 J-8
Carrizozo, 1063 G-6
Casa Blanca, 669 E-3
CATRON CO., 3409 G-2
Cedar Crest, 1060 E-5
Chama, 1173 B-5
Chamisal, 301 C-6
Chaparral, 6117 J-5
CHAVES CO., 61860 H-9
Chimayo, 2924 C-6
CIBOLA CO., 27620 E-3
Cimarron, 877 B-7
Clayton, 2186 B-10
Cloudcroft, 764 I-6
Clovis, 33357 F-10
Cochiti Pueblo, 507 D-5
COLFAX CO., 13755 B-7
Columbus, 1841 K-3
Cordova, 700 C-6
Crownpoint, 2630 D-2
Cuba, 616 C-4
Cubero, 500 E-3
CURRY CO., 45846 F-10
Datil, 300 G-3
DE BACA CO., 2016 F-8
Deming, 14876 J-3
Dexter, 1230 H-8
Dixon, 850 C-6
DONA ANA CO., 189444 I-4
Dona Ana, 1379 J-4
Dulce, 2623 B-4
EDDY CO., 51437 J-8
Edgewood, 1791 E-5
Espanola, 9655 C-5
Estancia, 1552 E-5
Eunice, 2602 J-10
Farmington, 43161 B-2
Five Points, 4200 M-8
Flora Vista, 1383 B-2
Ft. Stanton, 100 H-6
Ft. Sumner, 1060 F-8
Fruitland, 800 B-2
Gallina, 430 C-4
Gallup, 19378 D-1
Gamerco, 400 D-1
Garfield, 200 I-4
Gila, 350 I-2
GRANT CO., 29747 I-1
Grants, 9043 E-3
GUADALUPE CO., 4369 F-7
Hacienda Acres, 600 J-4
Hagerman, 1162 H-8
Hanover, 450 I-2
HARDING CO., 740 C-9
Hatch, 1654 I-4
HIDALGO CO., 5139 K-1
High Rolls, 450 I-6
Hobbs, 29006 I-10
Hurley, 1378 I-2
Isleta, 1703 E-5
Jal, 2021 J-10
Jemez Pueblo, 1953 D-4
Jemez Sprs., 388 D-4
Kirtland, 6190 B-2
Laguna, 423 E-3
Lake Arthur, 432 I-8
Lake Valley, 300 C-2
La Luz, 1615 I-6
La Mesa, 1000 J-4
La Mesilla, 2205 J-4
Las Cruces, 82671 J-4
Las Vegas, 14020 D-7
La Union, 700 K-5
LEA CO., 56719 H-9
Lemitar, 450 G-4
LINCOLN CO., 21007 G-6
Logan, 986 D-9
Lordsburg, 2815 J-1
Los Alamos, 11909 C-5
LOS ALAMOS CO., 18822 C-5
Los Lunas, 11338 E-4
Los Padillas, 2500 E-4
Los Ranchos de Albuquerque, 5396 L-8
Loving, 1313 J-8
Lovington, 9603 I-10
LUNA CO., 26498 J-2
Magdalena, 877 G-4
McCartys, 300 E-3
MCKINLEY CO., 71918 D-3
Melrose, 728 F-9
Mescalero, 1233 H-6
Mesquite, 948 J-4
Milan, 2524 E-3
Mora, 1200 C-6
MORA CO., 5107 C-7
Moriarty, 1808 E-5
Mountainair, 1078 F-5
Nambe, 1246 C-6
Navajo, 2097 C-1
Ojo Caliente, 350 C-5
Organ, 500 J-5
OTERO CO., 63538 I-6
Paguate, 474 E-3
Pajarito, 1500 E-4
Pecos, 1407 D-6
Pena Blanca, 661 D-5
Penasco, 572 C-6
Peralta, 3750 E-5
Placitas, 3452 D-5
Playas, 700 J-2
Pojoaque, 1261 C-5
Portales, 11295 F-10
Prewitt, 460 D-3
Pueblo Pintado, 247 C-3
QUAY CO., 9259 E-9
Questa, 1913 B-6
Ramah, 407 E-2
Ranchos de Taos, 2390 C-6
Raton, 6944 B-8
Red River, 495 B-6
Reserve, 338 G-1
RIO ARRIBA CO., 40828 B-4
Rio Rancho, 66599 E-5
ROOSEVELT CO., 18238 G-9
Roswell, 45199 H-8
Roy, 239 C-8
Ruidoso, 8812 H-6
Ruidoso Downs, 1972 H-6
San Antonio, 450 G-4
Sandia Park, 700 E-5
SANDOVAL CO., 107460 D-4
San Felipe Pueblo, 2080 D-5
San Jon, 274 E-9
SAN JUAN CO., 126208 B-2
San Juan Pueblo, 800 C-5
SAN MIGUEL CO., 29530 D-7
San Rafael, 600 E-3
Santa Clara, 1842 I-2
Santa Cruz, 423 C-5
SANTA FE CO., 140855 E-5
Santa Fe, 70631 D-6
Santa Rosa, 2509 E-7
Santo Domingo Pueblo, 2550 D-5
Shiprock, 8156 B-2
SIERRA CO., 12815 I-4
Silver City, 9999 I-2
SOCORRO CO., 18148 G-5
Socorro, 8621 G-4
Springer, 1224 C-8
Sunland Park, 14089 K-5
Talpa, 450 C-6
TAOS CO., 31722 B-6
Taos, 5126 C-6
Taos Pueblo, 1264 B-6
Tatum, 693 H-10
Texico, 1060 F-10
Thoreau, 1863 D-2
Tierra Amarilla, 700 B-5
Tijeras, 499 E-5
Tohatchi, 1037 C-1
Tome, 600 F-4
TORRANCE CO., 17501 F-6
Truchas, 500 C-6
Truth or Consequences, 7071 H-4
Tucumcari, 5335 E-9
Tularosa, 2858 I-5
Tyrone, 950 I-2
UNION CO., 3850 B-9
University Park, 3460 J-4
Vado, 3003 J-4
VALENCIA CO., 69417 F-4
Vanderwagen, 300 E-1
Vaughn, 469 F-7
Velarde, 450 C-6
Villanueva, 280 E-6
Wagon Mound, 352 C-7
Waterflow, 320 B-2
Williamsburg, 496 H-4
Zuni, 6367 E-1

New York

Map pp. 140-149

Index keys SA to SJ refer to Southern NY, pp. 140-141, NA to NN refer to Northern NY, pp. 142-145
* City keyed to pp. 146-149

Adams, 1663 NF-12
Adams Center, 1500 NF-12
Addison, 1765 NM-8
Akron, 3067 NI-5
Albany, 93523 NK-19
ALBANY CO., 297414 NK-18
Albertson, 5200 SF-8
Albion, 5766 NH-6
Alden, 2613 NJ-5
Alexandria Bay, 1100 ND-12
Alfred, 5009 NL-7
ALLEGANY CO., 50602 NL-6
Allegany, 1831 NM-5
Altamont, 1720 NJ-18
Altona, 1056 NA-19
Amagansett, 1067 SE-13
Amawalk, 1390 SD-7
Amenia, 1115 NN-20
Amherst, 45800 NI-4
Amityville, 9477 SF-8
Amsterdam, 17749 NI-18
Andover, 1037 NM-7
Angelica, 877 NL-6
Angola, 2194 NK-3
Angola on the Lake, 1771 NK-3
Apalachin, 1126 NM-12
Arcade, 1951 NK-5
Arlington, 12481 SB-7
Armonk, 3461 SD-7
Armor, 1550 NJ-4
Athens, 1733 NL-19
Atlantic Beach, 1973 SG-7
Attica, 2496 NJ-5
Auburn, 27941 NJ-10
Au Sable Forks, 670 NC-19
Averill Park, 1517 NK-19
Avoca, 986 NL-8
Avon, 2972 NJ-7
Babylon, 12659 SF-9
Bainbridge, 1354 NL-14
Baldwin, 23455 SG-8
Baldwinsville, 7149 NI-11
Ballston Spa, 5574 NI-19
Balmville, 3339 SB-6
Batavia, 15661 NI-6
Bath, 5589 NL-8
Baxter Estates, 993 *E-16
Bayberry, 6200 ND-7
Bayport, 8662 SI-14
Bay Shore, 23852 SF-9
Bayville, 7123 SE-8
Beacon, 14836 SC-6
Bedford, 1724 SD-8
Bedford Hills, 3200 SD-7
Belfast, 1100 NL-6
Bellerose, 1153 *H-16
Bellerose Ter., 2157 *H-16
Bellport, 2359 SF-10
Belmont, 912 NL-6
Bergen, 1195 NI-6
Berlin, 1200 NJ-20
Bethpage, 16543 SF-8
Big Flats, 2482 NM-9
Big Tree, 1000 NJ-4
Binghamton, 45492 NM-12
Black River, 1327 NE-13
Blasdell, 2578 NJ-4
Blauvelt, 5200 SE-6
Blooming Gr., 500 SC-6
Bloomington, 800 NN-18
Blue Pt., 4407 SI-14
Boght Corners, 1150 SG-5
Bohemia, 9871 SI-13
Bolivar, 1139 NM-6
Bolton Ldg., 1600 NG-19
Boonville, 2095 NG-14
Brasher Falls, 750 NB-16
Brentwood, 53917 SF-9
Brewerton, 3453 NH-12
Brewster, 2158 SC-8
Briarcliff Manor, 7938 SD-7
Bridgehampton, 1381 SE-13
Brighton, 35584 NC-9
Brightwaters, 3251 SF-9
Broadacres, 1280 SA-11
Broadalbin, 1407 NI-18
Brockport, 8134 NH-6
Brocton, 1487 NL-2
BRONX CO., 1357589 *E-13
Bronxville, 6455 *B-13
Brookville, 3439 *F-19
BROOME CO., 196947 NM-14
Brownville, 1047 NE-12
Buchanan, 2249 SD-6
Buffalo, 279745 NJ-3
Bullville, 900 SB-5
Burnt Hills, 1620 NI-18
Cadyville, 900 NB-19
Cairo, 1390 NL-18
Caledonia, 2223 NI-7
Calverton, 5704 SE-11
Cambridge, 1875 NI-20
Camden, 2288 NH-13
Camillus, 1211 NI-11
Canajoharie, 2191 NJ-16
Canandaigua, 11391 NJ-8
Canastota, 4429 NI-13
Canisteo, 2281 NL-7
Canton, 6060 NC-15
Carmel, 5650 SC-7
Carthage, 3790 NE-13
Castile, 1012 NK-6
Castleton on Hudson, 1585 NK-19
Catskill, 4367 NL-19
CATTARAUGUS CO., 82502 NL-4
Cattaraugus, 1029 NL-3
CAYUGA CO., 81454 NJ-11
Cayuga Hts., 3699 NK-11
Cazenovia, 2698 NJ-13
Cedarhurst, 6082 *K-16
Celoron, 1232 NM-2
Centereach, 27285 SE-10
Cen. Moriches, 6655 SF-11
Centerport, 5446 SE-9
Central Islip, 31950 SF-9
Central Square, 1658 NH-12
Central Valley, 1857 SC-6
Chadwicks, 2100 NI-14
Champlain, 1159 NA-20
Champlain Park, 1200 NB-20
Chappaqua, 9468 SD-7
Chatham, 1761 NL-19
CHAUTAUQUA CO., 136409 NL-2
Chazy, 1000 NA-20
Cheektowaga, 79988 NE-5
CHEMUNG CO., 89512 NM-10
CHENANGO CO., 51755 NK-13
Chenango Bridge, 2890 NM-12
Chester, 3604 SC-5
Chili Cen., 4350 NI-7
Chittenango, 4901 NI-13
Churchville, 1901 NI-6
Cicero, 1100 NI-12
Circleville, 1350 SB-5
Clarence, 2100 NI-4
Clarence Cen., 1747 NI-4
Claverack, 1000 NL-19
Clayton, 1866 ND-12
Clifton Park, 1200 NJ-19
Clifton Sprs., 2195 NI-9
CLINTON CO., 82047 NB-18
Clinton, 1918 NI-14
Clintondale, 1424 SB-6
Clinton Park, 880 SJ-5
Clyde, 2181 NI-10
Cobleskill, 4706 NK-17
Coeymans, 835 NK-19
Cohoes, 15085 NJ-19
Coldenham, 330 SB-6
Cold Spr., 2009 SC-6
Cold Spring Hbr., 4975 SH-10
Colonie, 8236 NJ-19
COLUMBIA CO., 63622 NL-20
Commack, 36367 SF-9
Congers, 8303 SD-7
Conklin, 1800 NM-13
Constantia, 1107 NH-12
Coopers Plains, 750 NM-9
Cooperstown, 1938 NJ-15
Copake, 1200 NM-20
Coram, 34923 SE-10
Corinth, 2472 NH-19
Corning, 10551 NM-9
Cornwall On Hudson, 3110 SC-6
Cortland, 18522 NK-12
CORTLAND CO., 48622 NK-12
Coxsackie, 2853 NL-19
Cross River, 980 SD-8
Croton Falls, 970 SC-8
Croton-on-Hudson, 7803 SD-7
Crown Pt., 1000 NE-20
Crugers, 1752 SD-7
Cuba, 1586 NL-5
Cuddebackville, 1100 SC-4
Cutchogue, 2849 SE-12
Dannemora, 4108 NB-19
Dansville, 4640 NK-7
Deer Park, 28316 SF-9
Defreestville, 960 NK-19
DELAWARE CO., 47534 NL-15
Delevan, 1047 NK-5
Delhi, 2720 NL-15
Delmar, 8292 NK-19
Demarest, 5005 *B-11
Depew, 15798 NJ-4
Deposit, 1636 NM-14
Derby, 1200 NJ-3
De Witt, 8244 NI-12
Dexter, 1138 NE-12
Dix Hills, 26024 SH-11
Dobbs Ferry, 11070 SE-7
Dolgeville, 2095 NI-16
Dover Plains, 1996 SA-8
Downsville, 1100 NM-15
Dryden, 1833 NK-11
Dundee, 1645 NK-9
Dunkirk, 12493 NK-2
DUTCHESS CO., 294849 SA-8
Earlville, 777 NJ-13
E. Atlantic Beach, 2257 *L-16
E. Aurora, 6418 NJ-4
Eastchester, 18564 *B-14
E. Glenville, 6064 NJ-18
E. Greenbush, 4085 NK-19
E. Hampton, 1357 SE-13
E. Hills, 6745 SF-8
E. Islip, 14078 SI-12
E. Marion, 756 SD-12
E. Meadow, 37461 SF-8
E. Middletown, 6061 SC-5
E. Northport, 20845 SE-9
E. Norwich, 2675 *E-19
Eastport, 1486 SF-11
E. Rochester, 6366 NI-8
E. Rockaway, 10263 *J-17
E. Syracuse, 3076 NF-9
Eden, 3579 NK-3
Elbridge, 1074 NI-11
Elizabethtown, 950 ND-19
Ellenville, 3954 SA-5
Elma, 2491 NJ-4
Elmira, 29928 NM-10
Elmira Hts., 4011 NM-10
Elmont, 32657 SF-7
Elmsford, 4727 SH-7
Elsmere, 4200 NK-19
Endicott, 12639 NM-12
Endwell, 11706 NM-12
ERIE CO., 930703 NK-3
Escarpment, 1200 NA-2
ESSEX CO., 38676 NE-19
Fair Haven, 872 NH-10
Fairmount, 10795 NI-11
Fairport, 5576 NI-8
Fairview, 2887 SI-7
Falconer, 2419 NM-2
Falconwood, 1500 ND-2
Farmingdale, 8668 SJ-10
Farmingville, 16458 SF-10
Fayetteville, 4171 NI-12
Ferndale, 850 NN-16
Fishkill, 1749 SB-7
Flanders, 3643 SE-11
Floral Park, 15737 *H-16
Florida, 2781 SC-5
Flower Hill, 4485 *F-16
Fluvanna, 900 NM-2
Fonda, 779 NI-17
Forestport, 900 NG-14
Ft. Covington, 1200 NA-16
Ft. Edward, 3120 NH-19
Ft. Montgomery, 1418 SC-6
Ft. Plain, 2211 NJ-16
Ft. Salonga, 9634 SG-11
Frankfort, 2452 NI-15
FRANKLIN CO., 51033 NC-17
Franklin Park, 2600 NE-9
Franklin Square, 29342 *H-17
Franklinville, 1778 NL-5
Fredonia, 10735 NK-2
Freeport, 43519 SG-8
Frewsburg, 1965 NM-3
Friendship, 1176 NL-6
FULTON CO., 55625 NI-17
Fulton, 11525 NH-11
Galeville, 4476 NE-8
Gang Mills, 3304 NM-9
Garden City, 21697 *H-18
Gardiner, 856 SB-6
Gardnertown, 4533 SB-6
Garwood, 4145 *J-3
Gasport, 1248 NH-4
Gates, 29300 NI-7
GENESEE CO., 59257 NJ-6
Geneseo, 7809 NJ-7
Geneva, 13509 NJ-9
Germantown, 862 NM-19
Getzville, 2300 NI-4
Glasco, 1692 NM-18
Glen Cove, 26633 SF-8
Glenham, 2000 SB-7
Glenmont, 1200 NK-19
Glens Falls, 14108 NH-19
Glenwood Ldg., 3541 *E-17
Gloversville, 15283 NI-17
Goldens Bridge, 1578 SC-7
Gorham, 950 NJ-9
Goshen, 5437 SC-5
Gouverneur, 4127 ND-14
Gowanda, 2716 NK-3
Grand Gorge, 1000 NL-17
Grand Island, 800 NI-3
Granville, 2623 NG-20
Great Neck, 9605 SF-7
Great Neck Estates, 2738 *F-15
Greece, 65000 NH-7
Greene, 1690 NL-13
GREENE CO., 49682 NL-17
Green Island, 2572 NJ-19
Greenlawn, 13286 SH-11
Greenport, 2079 SD-12
Greenville, 493 NL-18
Greenville, 8648 SI-7
Greenwich, 1886 NI-20
Greenwood Lake, 3461 SD-5
Groton, 2432 NK-11
Guilderland, 1900 SI-2
Hagaman, 1317 NI-18
Halesite, 2582 SH-10
Half Hollow Hills, 4950 SI-11
Hamburg, 9637 NJ-4
HAMILTON CO., 5228 NF-16
Hamilton, 3550 NJ-13
Hammondsport, 707 NL-8
Hampton Bays, 12240 SE-12
Hancock, 1139 NN-14
Hbr. Hills, 563 *F-15
Harriman, 2284 SC-6
Harrington Park, 4906 *A-10
Harris Hill, 4881 NI-4
Harrison, 25827 SE-7
Hartsdale, 9830 SI-7
Hastings-on-Hudson, 7702 SE-7
Hauppauge, 20100 SH-12
Haverstraw, 10487 SD-6
Haworth, 3414 *B-10
Head of the Hbr., 1505 SG-13
Hempstead, 52829 SF-8
Henrietta, 1200 NI-7
Herkimer, 7264 NI-15
HERKIMER CO., 63780 NG-15
Hewlett, 7060 *J-16
Hicksville, 41260 SF-8
Highland, 5060 SA-6
Highland Falls, 3761 SC-6
Highland Mills, 3468 SC-6
Highland-on-the-Lake, 1800 NJ-3
Hillcrest, 7106 SD-6
Hilton, 5957 NH-7
Hinsdale, 900 NM-5
Holbrook, 27512 SH-13
Holland, 1261 NK-4
Holley, 1750 NH-6
Holtsville, 17006 SH-14
Homer, 3303 NK-12
Honeoye Falls, 2571 NI-7
Hoosick Falls, 3350 NJ-20
Hopewell Jct., 2610 SB-7
Hornell, 8762 NL-7
Horseheads, 6366 NM-10
Houghton, 1748 NL-6
Hudson, 7145 NL-19
Hudson Falls, 6864 NH-19
Hughsonville, 1400 SB-7
Huguenot, 800 SC-4
Huguenot *M-6
Huntington, 18403 SF-8
Huntington, 18403 SE-9
Huntington Bay, 1493 SG-10
Huntington Sta., 29910 SF-9
Hurley, 3561 NN-18
Hyde Park, 100 NK-15
Hyde Park, 2650 NN-18
Ilion, 8330 NI-15
Indian Vil., 700 NI-12
Inwood, 9325 SG-7
Irondequoit, 52354 NH-7
Islip, 20575 SF-9
Islip Ter., 5641 SI-12
Ithaca, 29766 NK-11
Jamesport, 1526 SE-12
Jamestown, 30381 NM-2
JEFFERSON CO., 116384 NE-13
Jefferson Valley, 6700 SC-7
Jericho, 100 NB-19
Jericho, 13045 SF-8
Johnson City, 14955 NM-12
Johnstown, 8572 NI-17
Jordan, 1346 NI-11
Katonah, 2400 SD-7
Keeseville, 1796 NC-19
Kenilworth, 7743 *I-4
Kenmore, 15555 NI-4
Kensington, 1195 *F-15
Kensington *J-11
Kerhonkson, 1732 NN-17
Keuka Park, 1200 NK-9
Kinderhook, 1320 NL-19
KINGS CO., 2486235 SG-7
Kings Park, 15976 SE-9
Kings Pt., 5257 SF-7
Kingston, 23067 NN-18
Lackawanna, 18175 NJ-4
Lake Carmel, 8663 SC-7
Lake Delta, 2020 NH-14
Lake Erie Beach, 4499 NK-3
Lake George, 991 NG-19
Lake Gr., 10670 SF-10
Lake Katrine, 2396 NM-18
Lakeland, 2852 NE-7
Lake Luzerne, 1150 NH-19
Lake Peekskill, 2150 SC-7
Lake Placid, 2757 ND-18
Lake Ronkonkoma, 19701 SH-13
Lake Success, 2824 *G-16
Lake View, 150 NJ-3
Lakeville, 1200 NJ-7
Lakewood, 3132 NM-2
Lancaster, 11490 NJ-4
Lansing, 3417 NK-11
Larchmont, 6487 SE-7
Lattingtown, 1862 SE-8
Lawrence, 6501 SG-7
Le Roy, 4290 NI-6
Levittown, 53067 SF-8
LEWIS CO., 26571 NF-13
Lewiston, 2687 NH-3
Liberty, 3923 NN-16
Lido Beach, 2825 SG-8
Lima, 2425 NJ-7
Lindenhurst, 28248 SF-9
Little Falls, 5026 NI-16
Little Valley, 1090 NL-4
Liverpool, 2415 NE-7
LIVINGSTON CO., 64205 NK-7
Livingston Manor, 1355 NN-16
Livonia, 1527 NJ-7
Lloyd Hbr., 3702 SE-8
Loch Sheldrake, 1050 NN-16
Lockport, 21271 NI-4
Locust Gr., 9700 *F-20
Locust Valley, 3521 SF-8
Long Beach, 35336 SG-8
Loudonville, 10822 SI-5
Lowville, 3250 NF-14
Lynbrook, 19640 SG-8
Lyndon, 4593 NI-12
Lyndonville, 847 NH-5
Lyon Mtn., 458 NB-18
Lyons, 3553 NI-9
Macedon, 1531 NI-8
MADISON CO., 70337 NJ-13
Mahopac, 8478 SC-7
Mahopac Falls, 1200 SC-7
Maine, 1110 NM-12
Malone, 5929 NB-17
Mamaroneck, 18350 SE-7
Manchester, 1457 NI-8
Manhasset, 8362 *F-16
Manlius, 4695 NI-12
Manorhaven, 6328 *E-16
Manorville, 11131 SE-11
Maplewood, 800 SH-5
Maplewood, 23868 *H-4
Marathon, 1034 NL-12
Marcellus, 1793 NI-11
Marion, 1100 NI-9
Marlboro, 2339 SB-6
Massapequa, 22652 SF-8
Massapequa Park, 17270 SJ-10
Massena, 10859 NA-15
Mastic, 15436 SF-11
Mastic Beach, 11543 SF-11
Mattituck, 4198 SE-12
Mattydale, 6367 NI-12
Maybrook, 4068 SC-5
Mayville, 1721 NL-1
Maywood, 3400 NJ-19
McGraw, 973 NK-12
McKownville, 4850 SI-3
Mechanicville, 4997 NJ-19
Medford, 21985 SF-10
Medina, 6235 NH-5
Menands, 3825 NJ-19
Mendon, 1000 NI-8
Merrick, 22764 SG-8
Mexico, 1560 NG-11
Middleburgh, 1554 NK-17
Middle Hope, 3000 SB-6
Middle Island, 9702 SE-10
Middleport, 1826 NH-5
Middletown, 26067 SC-5
Middleville, 539 NI-15
Middleville, 1400 SG-11
Millbrook, 1559 NN-19
Millerton, 931 NM-20
Millwood, 1000 SD-7
Milton, 1251 SB-6
Mineola, 18978 SF-8
Minetto, 1086 NH-11
Mineville, 950 NE-19
Minoa, 3255 NI-12
Modena, 900 SB-6
Mohawk, 2569 NI-15
Mohegan Lake, 3600 SC-7
Mongaup Valley, 750 SB-3
MONROE CO., 733366 NH-7
Monroe, 8127 SC-6
Monsey, 14504 SD-6
Montauk, 3851 SD-14
Montgomery, 4238 SB-5
MONTGOMERY CO., 48968 NJ-16
Monticello, 6649 SB-4
Montour Falls, 1781 NL-10
Montrose, 2250 SD-7
Moravia, 1326 NJ-11
Morrisonville, 1702 NB-19
Morrisville, 2304 NJ-13
Mountain Lodge, 1000 SC-6
Mt. Ivy, 6536 SD-6
Mt. Kisco, 10331 SD-7
Mt. Morris, 2978 NJ-6
Mt. Vernon, 67924 SE-7
Mt. Vernon, 2800 NJ-3
Munsey Park, 2594 *F-16
Muttontown, 3516 *E-19
Nanuet, 16707 SD-6
Napanoch, 1168 SA-5
Naples, 1050 NK-8
Nassau, 1132 NK-19
NASSAU CO., 1333137 SF-8
Nedrow, 2265 NI-12
Nesconset, 11992 SH-13
Newark, 9411 NI-9
Newark Valley, 1038 NL-12
New Baltimore, 960 NK-19
New Berlin, 1123 NK-14
Newburgh, 28548 SB-6
New City, 34038 SD-6
New Falconwood, 1200 ND-2
Newfane, 3129 NH-4
New Hamburg, 1080 SB-6
New Hampton, 1200 SC-5
New Hartford, 1843 NI-14
New Hyde Park, 9472 *H-16
New Lebanon, 950 NK-20
New Milford, 16318 *B-10
New Paltz, 6765 SA-6
New Rochelle, 72967 SE-7
New Suffolk, 337 SE-12
Newtonville, 2300 SH-4
New Windsor, 9077 SC-6
NEW YORK CO., 1593200 *G-10
New York, 8143197 SG-6
New York Mills, 3146 NI-14
NIAGARA CO., 217008 NH-4
Niagara Falls, 52866 NI-3
Nimmonsburg, 900 NM-12
Niskayuna, 4892 NJ-19
Nissequogue, 1571 SE-9
Niverville, 1737 NK-19
Norfolk, 1334 NB-15
N. Bellmore, 20079 *I-19
N. Bloomfield, 2260 NI-7
N. Boston, 2680 NJ-4
N. Chili, 2300 NI-7
N. Collins, 1033 NK-3
N. Creek, 700 NF-18
N. Hornell, 834 NL-7
N. New Hyde Park, 14542 *G-16
Northport, 7587 SE-9
N. Salem, 930 SC-8
N. Sea, 4493 SE-12
N. Syracuse, 6726 NI-12
N. Tonawanda, 32072 NI-3
N. Valley Stream, 15789 *I-16
Northville, 1159 NH-18
Norwich, 7233 NK-14
Norwood, 1627 NB-15
Norwood, 6249 *A-11
Noyack, 2696 SE-12
Nunda, 1280 NK-6
Nyack, 6676 SD-7
Oakdale, 8075 SI-13
Oakfield, 1721 NI-5
Oceanside, 32733 SG-8
Odessa, 608 NL-10
Ogdensburg, 11422 NB-14
Olcott, 1156 NH-4
Old Brookville, 2244 *E-18
Old Forge, 1450 NF-15
Olean, 14799 NM-5
ONEIDA CO., 234105 NH-13
Oneida, 10923 NI-13
Oneonta, 13206 NK-15
ONONDAGA CO., 458053 NI-12
Ontario, 1000 NH-8
ONTARIO CO., 104461 NJ-8
ORANGE CO., 372893 SD-5
Orange Lake, 6085 SB-6
Orchard Park, 3147 NJ-4
Orient, 709 SD-13
Oriskany, 1423 NI-14
ORLEANS CO., 43387 NH-6
Ossining, 23547 SD-7
OSWEGO CO., 123373 NG-12
Oswego, 17705 NG-11
Otego, 1007 NL-15
Otisville, 1060 SC-4
OTSEGO CO., 62746 NK-15
Owego, 3794 NM-11
Oxford, 250 SC-5
Oxford, 1571 NL-13
Oyster Bay, 6826 SF-8
Painted Post, 1805 NM-9
Palenville, 1120 NM-18
Palmyra, 3429 NI-8
Patchogue, 11901 SF-10
Patterson, 1200 SB-8
Pawling, 2313 SB-8
Pearl River, 15553 SE-6
Peconic, 1081 SD-12
Peekskill, 24044 SC-7
Pelham, 6364 *C-14
Pelham Manor, 5395 *C-14
Penfield, 6300 NI-8
Penn Yan, 5170 NK-9
Perry, 3792 NJ-6
Peru, 1514 NC-19
Phelps, 1950 NI-9
Philadelphia, 1560 ND-13
Philmont, 1427 NL-19
Phoenicia, 381 NM-17
Phoenix, 2198 NH-11
Pine Bush, 1539 SB-5
Pine Island, 1500 SD-5
Pine Plains, 1412 NM-19
Pitcher Hill, 5000 NE-8
Pittsford, 1352 NI-8
Plainview, 25637 SF-8
Plandome Hts., 955 *F-16
Plattekill, 1050 SB-6
Plattsburgh, 19181 NB-20
Plattsburgh West, 1289 NB-19
Pleasant Valley, 1839 SA-7
Pleasantville, 7130 SD-7
Poestenkill, 1024 NJ-19
Pomona, 2945 SD-6
Port Byron, 1268 NI-10
Port Chester, 27886 SE-8
Port Dickinson, 1626 NM-12
Port Ewen, 3650 NN-18
Port Henry, 1089 NE-20
Port Jefferson, 7935 SE-10
Port Jervis, 9202 SC-4
Portland, 950 NL-2
Portville, 994 NM-5
Port Washington, 15215 SF-8
Port Washington N., 3294 *E-16
Potsdam, 9705 NB-15
Poughkeepsie, 30355 SB-7
Pound Ridge, 1000 SD-8
Prattsburgh, 950 NK-8
Pulaski, 2345 NG-12
Purdys, 970 SC-8
PUTNAM CO., 100507 SC-8
Putnam Lake, 3855 SC-8
QUEENS CO., 2241600 SF-8
Quogue, 1116 SF-11
Randolph, 1266 NM-3
Ransomville, 1488 NH-3
Ravena, 3323 NK-19
Red Hook, 1825 NM-19
Red Oaks Mill, 4930 SB-7
Rensselaer, 7859 NK-19
RENSSELAER CO., 155251 NJ-20
Rhinebeck, 3126 NN-18
Richfield Sprs., 1194 NJ-15
RICHMOND CO., 464573 SG-6
Richmondville, 798 NK-16
Ridge, 13380 SE-10
Ripley, 1030 NL-1
Riverhead, 10513 SE-11
Rochester, 211091 NI-7
Rock City Falls, 700 NI-18
Rock Hill, 1056 SB-4
ROCKLAND CO., 292916 SD-6
Rockville Ctr., 24237 SG-8
Rocky Pt., 10185 SE-10
Roessleville, 10753 SI-4
Rome, 34344 NH-14
Ronkonkoma, 20029 SH-13
Roscoe, 597 NN-15
Roselle Park, 13189 *J-4
Rosendale, 1374 NN-18
Roslyn, 2879 *F-17
Rotterdam, 20536 NJ-18
Rotterdam Jct., 1000 NJ-18
Rouses Pt., 2400 NA-20
Russell Gardens, 1056 *G-16
Rye, 14992 SE-7
Rye Brook, 9471 SI-9
Sackets Hbr., 1418 NE-12
Sagaponack, 587 SE-13
Sag Hbr., 2368 SE-13
St. James, 13268 SG-13
St. Johnsville, 1620 NI-16
ST. LAWRENCE CO., 111380 ND-15
St. Regis Falls, 950 NB-16
Salamanca, 5851 NM-4
Salem, 911 NH-20
Sands Pt., 2838 SF-7
Sandy Beach, 2350 NI-3
San Remo, 8550 SH-12
Saranac Lake, 4923 ND-18
SARATOGA CO., 214859 NH-18
Saratoga Sprs., 28036 NI-19
Saugerties, 3930 NM-18
Sauquoit, 930 NI-14
Savona, 798 NL-8
Sayville, 16735 SF-10
Scarsdale, 17763 SE-7
Schenectady, 61280 NJ-18
SCHENECTADY CO., 149078 NJ-18
SCHOHARIE CO., 32277 NK-16
Schoharie, 988 NK-17
Schroon Lake, 1100 NF-19
SCHUYLER CO., 19342 NL-9
Schuylerville, 1389 NI-19
Scotia, 7958 NJ-18
Scottsville, 2071 NI-7
Sea Cliff, 4996 *E-17
Seaford, 15791 *I-20
Selden, 21861 SE-10
SENECA CO., 34855 NJ-10
Seneca Falls, 6837 NJ-10
Sewaren, 2780 *M-4
Shelter Island, 1234 SD-12
Shelter Island Hts., 981 SD-12
Sherburne, 1446 NK-14
Sherrill, 3164 NI-13
Shinnecock Hills, 1749 SE-12
Shortsville, 1298 NI-8
Shrub Oak, 1812 SC-7
Sidney, 3905 NL-14
Silver Cr., 2863 NK-3
Silver Sprs., 813 NK-6
Skaneateles, 2589 NI-11
Skaneateles Falls, 850 NI-11
Sleepy Hollow, 9977 SD-7
Slingerlands, 2100 SJ-3
Sloan, 3576 NE-4
Sloatsburg, 3092 SD-6
Smithtown, 26901 SH-12
Sodus, 1673 NH-9
Sodus Pt., 1147 NH-9
Solvay, 6606 NI-11
Sound Beach, 9807 SE-10
Southampton, 4109 SE-12
S. Cairo, 950 NL-18
S. Corning, 1202 NM-9
S. Fallsburg, 2061 SB-4
S. Floral Park, 1583 *H-16
S. Glens Falls, 3445 NH-19
S. Lockport, 8552 NI-4
Southold, 5465 SD-12
Southport, 7396 NM-10
S. Salem, 12300 SD-8
S. Valley Stream, 5638 *J-16
Southwood, 900 NG-9
Sparrow Bush, 1200 SC-4
Speigletown, 1200 NJ-19
Spencerport, 3519 NH-7
Springs, 4950 SE-13
Spr. Valley, 25355 SD-6
Springville, 4311 NK-4
Staatsburg, 911 NN-18
Stamford, 1269 NL-16
Stanford Hts., 1050 NJ-18
Stannards, 868 NM-6
Star Lake, 860 ND-15
Steamburg, 900 NM-3
STEUBEN CO., 98632 NL-8
Stillwater, 1706 NI-19
Stone Ridge, 1173 NN-18
Stony Brook, 13727 SE-10
Stony Pt., 11744 SD-6
Stottville, 1355 NL-19
Suffern, 10897 SD-6
SUFFOLK CO., 1474927 SE-11
SULLIVAN CO., 76539 SA-3
Swan Lake, 1200 SA-3
Sycaway, 1950 SH-6
Sylvan Beach, 1075 NH-13
Syosset, 18544 SF-8
Syracuse, 141683 NI-12
Tappan, 6757 SE-6
Tarrytown, 11346 SE-7
Taunton, 1050 NF-7
Terryville, 10589 SG-14
Theresa, 824 ND-13
Thomaston, 2580 *F-16
Ticonderoga, 2700 NF-20
Tillson, 1709 NN-18
TIOGA CO., 51475 NM-11
Tivoli, 1171 NM-18
TOMPKINS CO., 100018 NL-10
Tonawanda, 15335 NI-3
Town Line, 2521 NJ-4
Troy, 48310 NJ-19
Trumansburg, 1588 NK-10
Tuckahoe, 1741 SE-12
Tuckahoe, 6256 SE-12
Tully, 891 NJ-12
Tupper Lake, 3856 ND-17
Twin Orchards, 1600 SB-10
ULSTER CO., 182693 SA-6
Unadilla, 1070 NL-14
Union Cen., 1500 NM-12
Uniondale, 23011 *H-18
Union Sprs., 1069 NJ-10
University Gardens, 4138 *G-16
Utica, 59336 NI-14
Vails Gate, 3319 SC-6
Valatie, 1910 NL-19
Valhalla, 5379 SE-7
Valley Cottage, 9269 SD-7
Valley Stream, 35799 SG-7
Verdoy, 1000 SG-4
Vernon, 1171 NI-13
Verona, 600 NI-13
Verona Beach, 700 NH-13
Verplanck, 777 SD-6
Vestal, 5000 NM-12
Vestal Cen., 800 NM-12
Victor, 2547 NI-8
Vil. of the Branch, 2209 SH-12
Voorheesville, 2782 NK-18
Waddington, 939 NB-14
Walden, 6755 SB-6
Walker Valley, 758 SB-5
Wallkill, 2143 SB-6
Walton, 2951 NM-15
Wanakah, 1600 NJ-3

Wantagh, 18971 ... *I-20
Wappingers Falls, 5085 ... SB-7
WARREN CO., 65548 ... NG-18
Warrensburg, 3208 ... NG-19
Warsaw, 3701 ... NJ-6
Warwick, 6571 ... SD-5
WASHINGTON CO., 63024 ... NH-20
Washington Mills, 1700 ... SC-12
Washingtonville, 6236 ... SC-6
Waterloo, 5134 ... NJ-10
Water Mill, 1724 ... SE-12
Watertown, 27220 ... NE-12
Waterville, 1682 ... NJ-14
Watervliet, 9889 ... NJ-19
Watkins Glen, 2099 ... NL-9
Waverly, 4493 ... NM-11
Wawarsing, 800 ... SA-5
Wayland, 1842 ... NK-7
WAYNE CO., 93609 ... NI-9
Webster, 5089 ... NH-8
Weedsport, 1970 ... NI-10
Wellsville, 4773 ... NM-6
W. Babylon, 43452 ... SF-9
Westbury, 14691 ... SF-8
Westbury, 150 ... NH-10
W. Carthage, 2158 ... NE-13
WESTCHESTER CO., 940807 ... SD-8
W. Corners, 1800 ... NM-12
W. Elmira, 5136 ... NM-10
Westfield, 3464 ... NL-1
W. Glens Falls, 6721 ... NH-19
Westhampton, 2864 ... SF-11
Westhampton Beach, 1957 ... SF-11
W. Hurley, 2105 ... NM-18
Westmere, 7188 ... NJ-18
Westmoreland, 950 ... NI-14
Westons Mills, 1608 ... NM-5
W. Point, 7138 ... SC-6
W. Sand Lake, 2439 ... NK-19
W. Sayville, 5003 ... SJ-13
W. Seneca, 45943 ... NJ-4
Westvale, 5166 ... NI-11
W. Webster, 8700 ... NH-8
W. Winfield, 843 ... NJ-15
Whitehall, 2648 ... NG-20
White Plains, 56733 ... SE-7
Whitesboro, 3854 ... SA-12
Whitney Pt., 939 ... NL-12
Willard, 600 ... NK-10
Williamson, 1850 ... NH-9
Williamsville, 5315 ... ND-5
Williston Park, 7113 ... *G-17
Willow Pt., 1700 ... SB-10
Willsboro, 950 ... ND-20
Wilson, 1167 ... NH-4
Windsor, 872 ... NM-13
Witherbee, 750 ... NE-19
Wolcott, 1664 ... NH-10
Woodbourne, 1200 ... NN-16
Woodbury, 9010 ... SH-10
Woodlawn Beach, 1000 ... NG-4
Woodmere, 16447 ... *J-16
Woodsburgh, 822 ... *K-16
Woodstock, 2187 ... NM-18
Worcester, 900 ... NK-16
Wurtsboro, 1263 ... SB-4
Wyandanch, 10546 ... SI-11
Wynantskill, 3018 ... SI-6
WYOMING CO., 42693 ... NJ-5
Yaphank, 5025 ... SF-10
YATES CO., 24756 ... NK-8
Yonkers, 196425 ... SE-7
Yorkshire, 1403 ... NK-5
Yorktown Hts., 7972 ... SD-7
Yorkville, 2613 ... NI-14
Youngstown, 1901 ... NH-3
Youngsville, 850 ... NN-16

North Carolina

Map pp. 150-155

* City keyed to pp. 154-155

Aberdeen, 4794 ... G-9
Ahoskie, 4324 ... C-16
ALAMANCE CO., 140533 ... D-9
Albemarle, 15325 ... F-7
ALEXANDER CO., 35492 ... D-4
Alexander Mills ... F-2
ALLEGHANY CO., 10900 ... B-4
Andrews, 1703 ... M-2
Angier, 4107 ... F-11
ANSON CO., 25499 ... G-8
Ansonville, 618 ... G-7
Apex, 28551 ... E-11
Archdale, 9428 ... D-8
Arlington ... C-5
ASHE CO., 25347 ... B-4
Asheboro, 23639 ... E-8
Asheville, 72231 ... E-1
Atlantic, 1150 ... H-18
Atlantic Beach, 1803 ... H-17
Aulander, 893 ... C-16
Aurora, 581 ... F-17
AVERY CO., 17641 ... D-2
Ayden, 4798 ... F-15
Badin, 1250 ... F-7
Banner Elk, 958 ... C-2
Bannertown, 1000 ... B-6
Bayboro, 716 ... G-17
BEAUFORT CO., 46018 ... E-17
Beaufort, 4119 ... H-17
Belhaven, 1965 ... E-17
Belmont, 8779 ... F-5
Belwood, 1006 ... F-3
Benson, 3282 ... F-12
BERTIE CO., 19480 ... D-16
Bessemer City, 5319 ... F-4
Bethel, 1689 ... D-15
Bethesda, 30 ... *B-4
Beulaville, 1098 ... H-14
Biltmore Forest, 1497 ... E-1
Biscoe, 1715 ... F-8
Black Mtn., 7650 ... E-1
BLADEN CO., 32938 ... I-12
Bladenboro, 1713 ... I-11
Blowing Rock, 1424 ... C-3
Boger City, 554 ... F-4
Boiling Spr. Lakes, 4107 ... K-13
Boiling Sprs., 3883 ... F-3
Boone, 13192 ... C-3
Boonville, 1113 ... C-6
Brevard, 6643 ... M-5
Broadway, 1102 ... F-10
BRUNSWICK CO., 89162 ... J-13
Bryson City, 1361 ... L-3
Buies Cr., 2215 ... F-11
BUNCOMBE CO., 218876 ... E-1
Burgaw, 3756 ... I-14
BURKE CO., 89399 ... D-3
Burlington, 47592 ... D-9
Burnsville, 1628 ... D-1
Butner, 5792 ... C-11
Buxton, 1480 ... F-20
CABARRUS CO., 150244 ... F-6
CALDWELL CO., 79122 ... D-3
CAMDEN CO., 8967 ... B-18
Candor, 829 ... F-8
Canton, 4002 ... L-5
Cape Carteret, 1400 ... H-16
Carolina Beach, 5388 ... K-14
Carrboro, 16425 ... D-10
CARTERET CO., 62525 ... H-16
Carthage, 1935 ... F-9
Cary, 106439 ... E-11
Castle Hayne, 1116 ... J-14
CASWELL CO., 23608 ... C-9
CATAWBA CO., 151641 ... E-4
Cedar Point, 818 ... H-16
Chadbourn, 2105 ... J-11
Chapel Hill, 49543 ... D-10
Charlotte, 610949 ... F-5
CHATHAM CO., 58002 ... E-10
CHEROKEE CO., 25796 ... M-1
Cherryville, 5455 ... F-4
China Gr., 3714 ... E-6
Chocowinity, 731 ... E-16
CHOWAN CO., 14528 ... C-17
Claremont, 1104 ... E-4
Clarkton, 702 ... I-12
CLAY CO., 9765 ... M-2
Clayton, 12943 ... E-12
Clemmons, 16430 ... D-7
CLEVELAND CO., 98288 ... F-3
Cleveland, 823 ... E-6
Clinton, 8768 ... G-13
Clyde, 1357 ... L-4
Coats, 2028 ... F-11
Colfax, 1050 ... *G-11
Columbia, 784 ... D-18
COLUMBUS CO., 54746 ... I-11
Columbus, 994 ... F-1
Concord, 61092 ... F-6
Connelly Springs, 1885 ... E-4
Conover, 7093 ... E-4
Conway, 704 ... B-15
Cooleemee, 957 ... E-6
Cornelius, 18870 ... F-5
Cramerton, 3005 ... G-5
CRAVEN CO., 90795 ... F-16
Creedmoor, 3155 ... C-11
Crouse, 900 ... F-4
Cullowhee, 3579 ... L-4
Cumberland, 730 ... G-11
CUMBERLAND CO., 304520 ... H-11
CURRITUCK CO., 23112 ... B-19
Dallas, 3411 ... F-4
DARE CO., 33903 ... E-20
DAVIDSON CO., 154623 ... E-7
Davidson, 8581 ... F-5
DAVIE CO., 39136 ... D-6
Denton, 1472 ... E-7
Dobson, 1508 ... C-6
Drexel, 1894 ... E-3
Dunn, 9889 ... F-12
DUPLIN CO., 51985 ... G-14
DURHAM CO., 242582 ... D-11
Durham, 204845 ... D-11
E. Bend, 666 ... C-6
E. Flat Rock, 4122 ... F-1
Eastover, 1376 ... G-11
E. Spencer, 1764 ... E-7
Eden, 15679 ... B-8
Edenton, 5001 ... C-17
EDGECOMBE CO., 54129 ... D-14
Elizabeth City, 18456 ... C-18
Elizabethtown, 3844 ... I-12
Elkin, 4315 ... C-5
Ellerbe, 993 ... G-8
Elm City, 1381 ... D-14
Enfield, 2302 ... C-14
Enka, 5000 ... L-5
Erwin, 4792 ... F-11
Fair Bluff, 1165 ... J-10
Fairmont, 2618 ... I-10
Fairplains, 2051 ... C-4
Faison, 770 ... G-13
Farmville, 4546 ... E-15
Fayetteville, 129928 ... G-11
Fearrington Village, 903 ... *D-1
Fletcher, 4522 ... F-1
Forest City, 7273 ... F-2
FORSYTH CO., 325967 ... C-7
Four Oaks, 1765 ... F-12
FRANKLIN CO., 54429 ... C-12
Franklin, 3611 ... M-3
Franklinton, 1899 ... C-12
Fremont, 1441 ... E-13
Fuquay-Varina, 12200 ... E-11
Gamewell, 3866 ... D-3
Garland, 833 ... H-12
Garner, 22364 ... E-12
Garysburg, 1202 ... B-15
GASTON CO., 196137 ... F-4
Gaston, 936 ... B-14
Gastonia, 68964 ... F-4
GATES CO., 11224 ... B-17
Gibsonville, 4569 ... C-9
Glen Alpine, 1072 ... E-3
Goldsboro, 38670 ... F-13
Gorman, 1002 ... D-11
GRAHAM CO., 8085 ... M-2
Graham, 13952 ... D-9
Grandy, 950 ... C-19
Granite Falls, 4573 ... E-4
Granite Quarry, 2232 ... E-6
Granthams, 950 ... G-16
GRANVILLE CO., 53674 ... B-11
GREENE CO., 20026 ... E-14
Greensboro, 231962 ... D-8
Greenville, 69517 ... E-15
Grifton, 2066 ... F-15
GUILFORD CO., 443519 ... D-9
HALIFAX CO., 56023 ... C-15
Hamlet, 5824 ... H-9
Harkers Island, 1525 ... H-18
HARNETT CO., 103692 ... F-11
Harrisburg, 5145 ... F-6
Hatteras, 1150 ... F-20
Havelock, 21827 ... H-16
Haw River, 1981 ... D-10
Hays, 1731 ... C-5
HAYWOOD CO., 56482 ... K-4
Hazelwood ... L-4
HENDERSON CO., 97217 ... F-1
Henderson, 16213 ... C-12
Hendersonville, 11396 ... F-1
Henrietta, 1000 ... F-3
HERTFORD CO., 23574 ... C-16
Hertford, 2104 ... C-18
Hickory, 40232 ... E-4
Hiddenite, 880 ... D-5
Highlands, 941 ... M-4
High Pt., 95086 ... D-8
High Shoals, 749 ... F-4
Hildebran, 1840 ... E-4
Hillsborough, 5382 ... D-10
HOKE CO., 41016 ... G-10
Holly Sprs., 15228 ... E-11
Hope Mills, 12782 ... G-11
Hudson, 3061 ... D-3
Huntersville, 36377 ... F-5
HYDE CO., 5413 ... E-19
Indian Trail, 16473 ... G-6
IREDELL CO., 140924 ... D-5
Jackson, 672 ... B-15
JACKSON CO., 35368 ... M-4
Jacksonville, 62628 ... H-15
Jamestown, 2997 ... D-8
Jamesville, 478 ... D-16
Jefferson, 1366 ... B-4
JOHNSTON CO., 146437 ... F-12
JONES CO., 10311 ... G-15
Jonesville, 2276 ... C-5
Kannapolis, 39041 ... F-6
Kenansville, 881 ... G-14
Kenly, 1830 ... E-13
Kernersville, 21361 ... C-8
Kill Devil Hills, 6550 ... C-20
King, 6353 ... C-7
Kings Mtn., 10862 ... F-4
Kinston, 22851 ... F-15
Kitty Hawk, 3358 ... C-20
Kure Beach, 2171 ... K-14
La Grange, 2804 ... F-14
Lake Waccamaw, 1460 ... J-12
Landis, 3064 ... E-6
Laurel Hill, 2400 ... H-9
Laurinburg, 15810 ... H-9
LEE CO., 55704 ... E-10
LENOIR CO., 57961 ... G-14
Lenoir, 17912 ... D-3
Lewiston, 598 ... C-16
Lewisville, 9547 ... D-7
Lexington, 20398 ... D-7
Liberty, 2712 ... D-9
Lillington, 3162 ... F-11
LINCOLN CO., 69851 ... F-4
Lincolnton, 10393 ... F-4
Littleton, 662 ... B-14
Locust, 2526 ... F-6
Long View, 4840 ... E-4
Louisburg, 3356 ... C-13
Lowell, 2671 ... F-5
Lucama, 865 ... E-13
Lumberton, 21591 ... I-11
MACON CO., 32148 ... M-3
Madison, 2239 ... C-8
MADISON CO., 20256 ... K-5
Magnolia, 969 ... H-13
Maiden, 3264 ... E-4
Manteo, 1301 ... D-20
Marble, 830 ... M-2
Marion, 5013 ... E-2
Marshall, 837 ... K-5
Marshallberg, 700 ... H-18
Mars Hill, 1834 ... D-1
Marshville, 2820 ... G-7
MARTIN CO., 24643 ... D-16
Matthews, 25306 ... G-6
Maxton, 2629 ... H-10
Mayodan, 2497 ... B-8
Maysville, 990 ... H-16
McAdenville, 631 ... *B-8
MCDOWELL CO., 43201 ... E-2
Mebane, 8945 ... D-10
MECKLENBURG CO., 796372 ... G-5
Middlesex, 851 ... E-13
Midland, 2834 ... G-6
Mint Hill, 17871 ... G-6
MITCHELL CO., 15784 ... D-1
Mocksville, 4464 ... D-6
Monroe, 29987 ... G-6
MONTGOMERY CO., 27322 ... F-8
Montreat, 661 ... E-1
MOORE CO., 81685 ... F-9
Mooresville, 20488 ... E-5
Moravian Falls, 1440 ... D-4
Morehead City, 8847 ... H-17
Morganton, 17041 ... E-3
Morgantown, 2180 ... C-9
Morven, 563 ... H-8
Mt. Airy, 8454 ... B-6
Mt. Gilead, 1387 ... G-8
Mt. Holly, 9676 ... F-5
Mt. Olive, 4442 ... G-13
Mt. Pleasant, 1429 ... F-6
Mulberry, 2269 ... C-4
Murfreesboro, 2221 ... B-16
Murphy, 1565 ... M-1
Nags Head, 3076 ... D-20
NASH CO., 91378 ... D-13
Nashville, 4477 ... D-13
Nebo, 840 ... E-2
New Bern, 24106 ... G-16
Newell, 1050 ... *A-13
NEW HANOVER CO., 179553 ... J-14
Newland, 686 ... D-2
Newport, 3840 ... H-17
Newton, 13016 ... E-4
Norlina, 1060 ... B-13
NORTHAMPTON CO., 21483 ... B-15
N. Wilkesboro, 4204 ... C-4
Norwood, 2160 ... G-7
Oakboro, 1180 ... G-7
Oak Island, 7679 ... K-13
Oak Ridge, 4196 ... C-8
Ocracoke, 769 ... G-19
Old Ft., 968 ... E-2
ONSLOW CO., 152440 ... H-15
ORANGE CO., 118386 ... C-10
Oteen, 1650 ... E-1
Oxford, 8530 ... C-12
PAMLICO CO., 12735 ... G-17
PASQUOTANK CO., 38270 ... B-18
Pembroke, 2693 ... H-10
PENDER CO., 46429 ... I-13
PERQUIMANS CO., 12080 ... C-18
PERSON CO., 37217 ... C-11
Pfafftown, 1050 ... C-7
Pikeville, 709 ... F-13
Pilot Mtn., 1277 ... C-6
Pinebluff, 1220 ... G-9
Pinehurst, 11437 ... G-9
Pine Level, 1450 ... F-13
Pinetops, 1320 ... D-14
Pineville, 3650 ... G-5
Pisgah Forest, 2150 ... M-5
PITT CO., 142570 ... F-15
Pittsboro, 2452 ... E-10
Pleasant Garden, 4911 ... D-8
Plymouth, 3964 ... D-17
POLK CO., 19134 ... F-2
Polkton, 2514 ... G-7
Princeton, 1200 ... F-13
Princeville, 1670 ... D-15
Raeford, 3594 ... G-10
Raleigh, 341530 ... E-12
Ramseur, 1704 ... E-9
Randleman, 3653 ... E-8
RANDOLPH CO., 138367 ... E-8
Ranlo, 2197 ... F-4
Red Sprs., 3484 ... H-10
Reidsville, 14778 ... C-9
Richlands, 827 ... H-15
RICHMOND CO., 46781 ... G-8
Rich Square, 1025 ... C-15
Riegelwood, 1200 ... J-13
River Bend, 2755 ... G-16
Roanoke Rapids, 16458 ... B-14
Robbins, 1217 ... F-9
Robbinsville, 736 ... L-2
Robersonville, 1637 ... D-15
ROBESON CO., 127586 ... I-10
Rockingham, 9220 ... H-8
ROCKINGHAM CO., 92614 ... C-8
Rockwell, 1982 ... E-7
Rocky Mt., 56626 ... D-14
Roper, 588 ... D-17
Roseboro, 1297 ... G-12
Rose Hill, 1377 ... H-13
Rosewood, 4300 ... F-13
ROWAN CO., 135099 ... E-6
Rowland, 1148 ... I-10
Roxboro, 8755 ... C-11
Rural Hall, 2577 ... C-7
RUTHERFORD CO., 63771 ... F-2
Rutherford College, 1283 ... E-3
Rutherfordton, 4099 ... F-2
St. Pauls, 2264 ... H-11
Salisbury, 27563 ... E-6
SAMPSON CO., 63063 ... G-12
Sanford, 26710 ... F-10
Sawmills, 4931 ... D-3
SCOTLAND CO., 37180 ... H-9
Scotland Neck, 2240 ... C-15
Seaboard, 666 ... B-15
Seagate, 4590 ... M-20
Sedgefield, 1000 ... *H-13
Selma, 6646 ... E-13
Shallotte, 1588 ... K-12
Sharpsburg, 2460 ... D-14
Shelby, 21263 ... F-3
Siler City, 8079 ... E-9
Silver City, 1146 ... G-10
Skyland, 2000 ... F-1
Smithfield, 11970 ... F-12
Snow Hill, 1442 ... F-14
Southern Pines, 11881 ... G-9
South Gastonia, 5433 ... K-19
Southport, 2725 ... K-13
Sparta, 1797 ... B-5
Spencer, 3345 ... E-6
Spindale, 3921 ... F-2
Spr. Hope, 1272 ... D-13
Spr. Lake, 8197 ... G-11
Spruce Pine, 1998 ... D-2
Stallings, 3854 ... G-6
Stanley, 3094 ... F-5
Stanleyville, 4779 ... C-7
STANLY CO., 58964 ... F-7
Stantonsburg, 712 ... E-14
Star, 810 ... F-8
Statesville, 24875 ... E-5
Stedman, 651 ... G-11
STOKES CO., 45858 ... C-7
Stokesdale, 3524 ... C-8
Stoneville, 988 ... B-8
Stony Pt., 1380 ... D-5
Summerfield, 7228 ... C-8
Surf City, 1716 ... I-15
SURRY CO., 72601 ... B-6
SWAIN CO., 13167 ... L-3
Swannanoa, 4132 ... E-1
Swansboro, 1338 ... H-16
Swepsonville, 952 ... D-10
Sylva, 2398 ... L-4
Tabor City, 2629 ... J-11
Tarboro, 10600 ... D-15
Taylorsville, 1855 ... D-4
Thomasville, 25872 ... D-7
Toast, 1922 ... B-6
TRANSYLVANIA CO., 29626 ... M-5
Triangle, 850 ... F-5
Trinity, 6915 ... D-8
Troutman, 1706 ... E-5
Troy, 3269 ... F-8
Tryon, 1752 ... G-1
Tuxedo, 1100 ... F-1
TYRRELL CO., 4157 ... D-18
UNION CO., 162929 ... H-6
Valdese, 4530 ... E-3
VANCE CO., 43771 ... C-12
Vanceboro, 846 ... F-16
Vander, 1204 ... G-11
Vass, 770 ... F-10
Wadesboro, 5263 ... G-7
WAKE CO., 748815 ... D-12
Wake Forest, 20126 ... D-12
Walkertown, 4294 ... C-7
Wallace, 3531 ... H-13
Walnut Cove, 1571 ... C-7
Walnut Creek, 854 ... F-14
Wanchese, 1527 ... D-20
WARREN CO., 19729 ... C-13
Warrenton, 770 ... B-13
Warsaw, 3092 ... G-13
WASHINGTON CO., 13282 ... D-17
Washington, 9841 ... E-16
WATAUGA CO., 42472 ... C-3
Waxhaw, 3207 ... H-6
WAYNE CO., 114448 ... F-14
Waynesville, 9386 ... L-4
Weaverville, 2508 ... E-1
Weddington, 8465 ... G-6
Welcome, 3538 ... D-7
Weldon, 1315 ... B-14
Wendell, 4516 ... E-12
W. Jefferson, 1082 ... B-4
Whispering Pines, 2137 ... F-10
Whitakers, 773 ... C-14
Whiteville, 5212 ... J-11
WILKES CO., 67390 ... C-4
Wilkesboro, 3204 ... C-4
Williamston, 5650 ... D-16
Wilmington, 95476 ... J-14
WILSON CO., 76281 ... E-14
Wilson, 46967 ... E-14
Windsor, 2231 ... D-16
Wingate, 2866 ... G-6
Winston-Salem, 193755 ... D-7
Winterville, 4688 ... E-15
Winton, 920 ... B-16
Woodfin, 3277 ... K-5
Woodland, 797 ... C-16
Wrightsville, 750 ... M-20
Wrightsville Beach, 2567 ... J-14
YADKIN CO., 37668 ... C-6
Yadkinville, 2867 ... C-6
YANCEY CO., 18201 ... D-1
Yanceyville, 2147 ... B-10
Zebulon, 4218 ... D-12

North Dakota

Map pp. 156-157

Abercrombie, 290 ... G-13
Adams, 188 ... B-11
ADAMS CO., 2433 ... H-4
Anamoose, 264 ... D-8
Aneta, 261 ... D-11
Arthur, 377 ... E-12
Ashley, 783 ... H-9
BARNES CO., 11075 ... F-11
Beach, 1000 ... F-2
Belcourt, 2440 ... A-8
Belfield, 820 ... F-3
BENSON CO., 6999 ... C-9
Berthold, 442 ... C-5
Beulah, 3036 ... E-5
BILLINGS CO., 813 ... E-3
Binford, 178 ... D-11
Bismarck, 57377 ... F-7
Bottineau, 2157 ... A-7
BOTTINEAU CO., 6741 ... A-7
Bowbells, 361 ... A-5
BOWMAN CO., 3048 ... H-2
Bowman, 1513 ... G-3
BURKE CO., 2032 ... A-4
BURLEIGH CO., 73818 ... F-7
Burlington, 1016 ... C-6
Buxton, 348 ... D-12
Cando, 1172 ... B-9
Cannon Ball, 864 ... G-7
Carrington, 2148 ... E-9
Carson, 284 ... G-6
CASS CO., 131019 ... E-12
Casselton, 1920 ... F-12
CAVALIER CO., 4330 ... B-10
Cavalier, 1443 ... A-12
Center, 593 ... E-6
Cooperstown, 945 ... D-11
Crosby, 1017 ... A-3
Devils Lake, 6816 ... C-10
DICKEY CO., 5487 ... H-10
Dickinson, 15666 ... F-4
DIVIDE CO., 2149 ... A-3
Drake, 287 ... C-7
Drayton, 852 ... B-12
DUNN CO., 3442 ... E-4
Dunseith, 748 ... A-8
EDDY CO., 2626 ... D-9
Edgeley, 578 ... G-10
Edmore, 239 ... B-10
Elgin, 600 ... G-5
Ellendale, 1500 ... H-10
Emerado, 483 ... C-12
EMMONS CO., 3845 ... G-8
Enderlin, 1055 ... F-12
Fairmount, 386 ... H-13
Fargo, 90672 ... F-13
Fessenden, 547 ... D-9
Finley, 447 ... D-11
Flasher, 272 ... G-6
Fordville, 246 ... C-11
Forman, 476 ... H-12
Ft. Totten, 952 ... C-10
FOSTER CO., 3580 ... D-10
Gackle, 298 ... F-9
Garrison, 1216 ... D-6
Gilby, 232 ... C-12
Glenburn, 338 ... B-6
Glen Ullin, 829 ... F-5
GOLDEN VALLEY CO., 1739 ... E-2
Golden Valley, 174 ... E-5
Grafton, 4248 ... B-12
GRAND FORKS CO., 65940 ... D-12
Grand Forks, 49792 ... C-13
GRANT CO., 2615 ... G-5
Granville, 255 ... C-7
Grenora, 194 ... B-2
GRIGGS CO., 2497 ... D-11
Gwinner, 709 ... G-12
Halliday, 215 ... E-4
Hankinson, 1011 ... H-13
Harvey, 1759 ... D-8
Harwood, 638 ... F-13
Hatton, 684 ... D-12
Hazelton, 210 ... G-8
Hazen, 2356 ... E-5
Hebron, 754 ... F-5
Hettinger, 1231 ... H-4
HETTINGER CO., 2486 ... G-4
Hillsboro, 1529 ... E-13
Hoople, 270 ... B-12
Hope, 268 ... E-12
Horace, 1069 ... F-13
Hunter, 307 ... E-12
Jamestown, 14826 ... F-10
Kenmare, 1098 ... B-5
KIDDER CO., 2481 ... E-8
Killdeer, 683 ... E-4
Kindred, 574 ... F-13
Kulm, 391 ... G-10
Lakota, 754 ... C-11
LAMOURE CO., 4384 ... G-10
Lamoure, 885 ... G-11
Langdon, 1863 ... A-10
Lansford, 242 ... B-6
Larimore, 1325 ... C-12
Leeds, 452 ... C-9
Leonard, 241 ... F-12
Lidgerwood, 746 ... H-12
Lignite, 158 ... A-4
Lincoln, 2297 ... F-7
Linton, 1158 ... G-8
Lisbon, 2237 ... G-12
LOGAN CO., 2059 ... G-9
Maddock, 483 ... C-9
Mandan, 17225 ... F-7
Mandaree, 558 ... D-4
Manvel, 341 ... C-12
Mapleton, 611 ... F-13
Max, 262 ... D-6
Mayville, 1931 ... D-12
McClusky, 342 ... D-7
MCHENRY CO., 5511 ... C-7
MCINTOSH CO., 3013 ... H-9
MCKENZIE CO., 5594 ... D-2
MCLEAN CO., 8604 ... D-6
McVille, 433 ... D-11
Medina, 310 ... F-9
MERCER CO., 8364 ... E-5
Michigan, 311 ... C-11
Milnor, 676 ... G-12
Minnewaukan, 307 ... C-9
Minot, 34984 ... C-6
Minto, 626 ... C-12
Mohall, 754 ... A-6
MORTON CO., 25528 ... F-6
Mott, 718 ... G-4
MOUNTRAIL CO., 6513 ... C-4
Munich, 235 ... B-10
Napoleon, 750 ... G-8
Neche, 424 ... A-12
NELSON CO., 3424 ... C-11
New England, 543 ... G-3
New Leipzig, 247 ... G-5
New Rockford, 1372 ... D-9
New Salem, 890 ... F-6
New Town, 1415 ... C-4
Noonan, 150 ... A-3
Northwood, 884 ... D-12
Oakes, 1848 ... G-11
OLIVER CO., 1813 ... E-6
Page, 206 ... E-12
Park River, 1438 ... B-11
Parshall, 1027 ... C-5
Pembina, 599 ... A-12
PEMBINA CO., 8038 ... B-11
PIERCE CO., 4291 ... C-8
Portland, 578 ... D-12
Powers Lake, 273 ... B-4
RAMSEY CO., 11429 ... B-10
RANSOM CO., 5810 ... G-12
Ray, 525 ... B-3
Reeder, 167 ... H-3
Regent, 182 ... G-4
RENVILLE CO., 2422 ... A-5
Reynolds, 341 ... D-12
Richardton, 581 ... F-4
RICHLAND CO., 17340 ... G-12
Riverdale, 264 ... D-6
ROLETTE CO., 13864 ... B-8
Rolette, 540 ... B-8
Rolla, 1442 ... A-9
Rugby, 2688 ... B-8
St. John, 360 ... A-8
St. Thomas, 416 ... B-12
SARGENT CO., 4150 ... G-12
Sawyer, 348 ... C-6
Scranton, 286 ... G-3
Selfridge, 220 ... H-7
SHERIDAN CO., 1430 ... D-7
Sherwood, 230 ... A-6
Sheyenne, 308 ... D-9
SIOUX CO., 4182 ... H-6
SLOPE CO., 709 ... G-2
S. Heart, 296 ... F-3
Stanley, 1222 ... B-4
Stanton, 326 ... E-6
STARK CO., 22073 ... F-4
STEELE CO., 2007 ... D-11
Steele, 694 ... F-8
Strasburg, 491 ... H-8
STUTSMAN CO., 20835 ... E-9
Surrey, 870 ... C-6
Tappen, 188 ... F-9
Thompson, 962 ... D-12
Tioga, 1090 ... B-3
Tolna, 191 ... D-10
Tower City, 240 ... F-12
TOWNER CO., 2544 ... B-9
Towner, 516 ... B-7
TRAILL CO., 8321 ... D-12
Turtle Lake, 527 ... D-7
Underwood, 739 ... D-6
Valley City, 6439 ... F-11
Velva, 966 ... C-7
Wahpeton, 8220 ... G-13
Walhalla, 982 ... A-11
WALSH CO., 11607 ... C-11
WARD CO., 55767 ... C-6
Washburn, 1264 ... E-6
Watford City, 1357 ... D-3
WELLS CO., 4574 ... D-8
W. Fargo, 19487 ... F-13
Westhope, 492 ... A-6
WILLIAMS CO., 19282 ... B-3
Williston, 12193 ... C-2
Willow City, 211 ... B-8
Wilton, 745 ... E-7
Wimbledon, 216 ... E-10
Wishek, 1000 ... G-9
Wyndmere, 503 ... G-12
Zap, 218 ... E-5

Ohio

Map pp. 158-165

Index keys NA to NN refer to Northern OH, pp. 158-161, SA to SN refer to Southern OH, pp. 162-165

Aberdeen, 1670 ... SI-6
Ada, 5847 ... NJ-5
ADAMS CO., 28454 ... SH-8
Addyston, 955 ... SG-1
Adena, 776 ... NM-19
Akron, 210795 ... NH-16
Albany, 815 ... SF-13
Alger, 888 ... NJ-5
ALLEN CO., 106234 ... NJ-4
Alliance, 22801 ... NI-17
Amanda, 722 ... SC-10
Amberley, 3276 ... SK-4
Amberly, 900 ... SI-20
Amelia, 3481 ... SG-3
Amherst, 11872 ... NF-12
Amsterdam, 558 ... NL-18
Andover, 1247 ... NE-20
Anna, 1442 ... NL-3
Ansonia, 1115 ... NM-1
Antwerp, 1649 ... NG-1
Apple Cr., 983 ... NJ-14
Arcanum, 2032 ... SA-2
Archbold, 4505 ... NE-3
Arlington, 1293 ... NI-6
Arlington Hts., 821 ... SK-3
ASHLAND CO., 54123 ... NH-12
Ashland, 21550 ... NI-12
Ashley, 1285 ... NL-9
Ashtabula, 20321 ... NC-19
ASHTABULA CO., 103221 ... ND-19
Ashville, 3252 ... SC-9
ATHENS CO., 62062 ... SF-14
Athens, 20918 ... SE-13
Attica, 925 ... NH-9
Atwater, 850 ... NH-17
AUGLAIZE CO., 47242 ... NK-4
Aurora, 14353 ... NG-16
Austintown, 31627 ... NH-19
Avon, 15741 ... NF-13
Avondale ... SC-4
Avondale, 3050 ... NI-16
Avon Lake, 20608 ... NE-13
Bainbridge, 1048 ... SF-8
Ballville, 3255 ... NG-8
Baltimore, 2919 ... SB-11
Barberton, 27192 ... NH-15
Barnesville, 4149 ... SA-18
Barton, 465 ... NN-19
Batavia, 1669 ... SG-4
Bay View, 662 ... NF-10
Bay Vil., 15236 ... NF-14
Beach City, 1109 ... NK-15
Beachwood, 11535 ... NF-16
Beavercreek, 39655 ... SC-4
Bedford, 13571 ... NF-16
Bedford Hts., 10855 ... NF-16
Bellaire, 4738 ... NN-19
Bellbrook, 6960 ... SD-4
Belle Cen., 796 ... NK-5
Bellefontaine, 13009 ... NL-5
Bellevue, 8029 ... NG-10
Bellville, 1754 ... NK-11
BELMONT CO., 69228 ... NN-17
Beloit, 1016 ... NI-18
Belpre, 6560 ... SF-16
Berea, 18242 ... NF-14
Bergholz, 753 ... NK-19
Berlin, 1000 ... NK-14
Berlin Hts., 658 ... NG-11
Bethel, 2590 ... SH-4
Bethesda, 1379 ... SA-18
Bettsville, 761 ... NG-8
Beverly, 1272 ... SD-16
Bevis, 1100 ... SF-2
Bexley, 12322 ... SB-9
Black Horse, 500 ... NG-17
Blacklick Estates, 9518 ... SB-10
Blanchester, 4348 ... SF-5
Bloomdale, 709 ... NG-6
Bloomingburg, 850 ... SD-7
Bloomville, 1012 ... NH-9
Blue Ash, 11747 ... SF-3
Bluffton, 4013 ... NI-5
Boardman, 37215 ... NH-19
Bolivar, 900 ... NJ-16
Boston Hts., 1207 ... NG-16
Botkins, 1181 ... NL-3
Bowerston, 424 ... NL-17
Bowling Green, 29793 ... NF-6
Bradford, 1891 ... NN-2
Bradner, 1159 ... NF-7
Bratenahl, 1312 ... SK-18
Brecksville, 13250 ... NG-15
Bremen, 1251 ... SC-12
Brentwood, 5500 ... SF-2
Brentwood Lake, 650 ... NG-13
Brewster, 2318 ... NJ-15
Briarwood Beach ... NH-14
Bridgeport, 2107 ... NN-19
Bridgetown, 12569 ... SF-2
Brilliant, 1600 ... NM-20
Brimfield, 3248 ... NH-16
Broadview Hts., 17505 ... NG-15
Brookfield, 1288 ... NG-20
Brooklyn, 10901 ... NF-15
Brooklyn Hts., 1510 ... SM-17
Brook Park, 20059 ... NF-14
Brookside Estates, 670 ... SF-18
Brookville, 5317 ... SB-3
BROWN CO., 44398 ... SI-5
Brunswick, 35159 ... NG-14
Bryan, 8360 ... NF-2
Buckeye Lake, 3060 ... SB-12
Bucyrus, 12885 ... NJ-9
Buffalo, 200 ... SB-16
Burlington, 2794 ... SK-11
Burton, 1446 ... NF-17
BUTLER CO., 350412 ... SE-1
Butler, 908 ... NK-11
Byesville, 2597 ... SB-16
Cadiz, 3396 ... NM-18
Calcutta, 3491 ... NJ-20
Caldwell, 1911 ... SC-16
Caledonia, 556 ... NK-9
Cambridge, 11562 ... SA-16
Camden, 2264 ... SD-1
Campbell, 8888 ... NH-20
Camp Dennison, 600 ... SK-5
Canal Fulton, 5054 ... NI-15
Canal Winchester, 5652 ... SB-10
Canfield, 7153 ... NH-19
Canton, 79478 ... NJ-16
Cardington, 1992 ... NK-9
Carey, 3868 ... NI-7
Carlisle, 5688 ... SD-3
CARROLL CO., 29388 ... NJ-18
Carrollton, 3297 ... NK-18
Castalia, 906 ... NF-10
Cedarville, 4037 ... SC-5
Celina, 10348 ... NK-2
Centerburg, 1483 ... NM-10
Centerville, 23162 ... SD-4
Chagrin Falls, 3808 ... NF-16
CHAMPAIGN CO., 39698 ... NN-4
Champion, 4727 ... NG-19
Chardon, 5280 ... NE-17
Chauncey, 1105 ... SE-13
Cherry Gr., 4555 ... SG-3
Chesapeake, 879 ... SK-12
Chesterland, 2646 ... NE-16
Cheviot, 8235 ... SF-2
Chillicothe, 22081 ... SE-9
Churchill, 2601 ... NG-19
Cincinnati, 308728 ... SG-2
Circleville, 13559 ... SD-9
CLARK CO., 142376 ... SB-6
Clayton, 13194 ... SB-3
Clearview, 750 ... NF-13
CLERMONT CO., 190589 ... SH-3
Cleveland, 452208 ... NF-15
Cleveland Hts., 48029 ... NE-15
Cleves, 2574 ... SF-1
CLINTON CO., 42570 ... SD-6
Clinton, 1395 ... NI-15
Clyde, 6143 ... NG-9
Coal Gr., 2081 ... SJ-11
Coldwater, 4438 ... NL-1
Colerain Hts., 2600 ... SF-2
COLUMBIANA CO., 110928 ... NI-18
Columbiana, 5807 ... NI-19
Columbus, 730657 ... SB-9
Columbus Gr., 2178 ... NI-4
Conneaut, 12648 ... NC-20
Continental, 1188 ... NH-3
Convoy, 1065 ... NI-1
Coolville, 546 ... SF-15
Copley, 750 ... NH-15
Corning, 616 ... SD-13
Cortland, 6640 ... NF-19
COSHOCTON CO., 36945 ... NM-13
Coshocton, 11632 ... NM-14
Covedale, 6360 ... SM-1
Covington, 2575 ... NN-3
Craig Beach, 1209 ... NH-18
CRAWFORD CO., 45774 ... NI-9
Crestline, 4964 ... NJ-10
Creston, 2140 ... NI-14
Cridersville, 1796 ... NK-4
Crooksville, 2485 ... SC-13
Crystal Lakes, 1411 ... SB-4
Curtice, 800 ... NE-7
CUYAHOGA CO., 1335317 ... NG-15
Cuyahoga Falls, 50494 ... NH-16
Cuyahoga Hts., 559 ... SM-18
Dalton, 1582 ... NJ-15
Damascus, 950 ... NI-18
Danville, 1096 ... NL-12
Darbydale, 600 ... SB-8
DARKE CO., 52983 ... NM-1
Dayton, 158873 ... SC-4
Deer Park, 5615 ... SF-3
DEFIANCE CO., 39112 ... NF-1
Defiance, 16150 ... NG-3
DeForest, 1150 ... NB-12
De Graff, 1174 ... NM-5
DELAWARE CO., 150268 ... NM-10
Delaware, 31322 ... NM-8
Delhi Hills, 20000 ... SM-2
Delphos, 6820 ... NI-3
Delta, 2927 ... NE-4
Dennison, 2927 ... NL-17
Deshler, 1849 ... NG-5
Devola, 2771 ... SE-16
Dillonvale, 750 ... NM-19
Dover, 12516 ... NK-16
Doylestown, 2851 ... NI-15
Dresden, 1427 ... NN-13
Drexel, 2057 ... SC-3
Dry Run, 750 ... SI-9
Dublin, 34964 ... NN-8
Duncan Falls, 600 ... SB-14
Dunkirk, 961 ... NJ-6
E. Alliance, 1175 ... NI-18
E. Canton, 1619 ... NJ-17
E. Cleveland, 25708 ... NE-15
Eastlake, 19795 ... ND-16
E. Liverpool, 12396 ... NK-20
E. Palestine, 4805 ... NI-20
E. Sparta, 786 ... NJ-16
Eastview ... SL-9
Eaton, 8242 ... SC-2
Eaton Estates, 1409 ... NG-13
Eden Park, 430 ... SI-9
Edgerton, 2015 ... NF-1
Edon, 863 ... NE-1
Elida, 1894 ... NJ-3
Elmore, 1408 ... NF-8
Elmwood Place, 2439 ... SL-3
Elyria, 56061 ... NF-13
Englewood, 12727 ... SB-3
Enon, 2581 ... SB-5
ERIE CO., 78665 ... NF-10
Euclid, 49619 ... NE-16
Evendale, 2880 ... SK-4
Excello, 50 ... SD-3
Fairborn, 31650 ... SB-4
Fairfax, 1783 ... SL-4
Fairfield, 42294 ... SE-2
FAIRFIELD CO., 138423 ... SB-11
Fairhope, 1720 ... NJ-17
Fairlawn, 7202 ... NH-15
Fairport Hbr., 3223 ... ND-17
Fairview Park, 16528 ... NF-14
Farmersville, 964 ... SC-3
FAYETTE CO., 28199 ... SD-8
Fayette, 1326 ... ND-3
Felicity, 915 ... SH-4
Findlay, 39118 ... NH-6
Finneytown, 13492 ... SK-3
Flushing, 931 ... NN-18
Forest, 1455 ... NJ-7
Forest Hills, 200 ... NA-15
Forest Park, 18069 ... SF-2
Forestville, 10978 ... SG-3
Ft. Loramie, 1459 ... NL-3
Ft. Recovery, 1323 ... NL-1
Ft. Shawnee, 3790 ... NJ-4
Fostoria, 13395 ... NH-7
Frankfort, 1040 ... SE-8
FRANKLIN CO., 1090771 ... SB-8
Franklin, 12410 ... SD-3
Franklin Furnace, 1537 ... SJ-10
Frazeysburg, 1298 ... NN-13
Fredericktown, 2526 ... NL-11
Freeport, 409 ... NM-17
Fremont, 17049 ... NF-8
Fruit Hill, 3945 ... SG-3
FULTON CO., 42955 ... NE-4
Gahanna, 33077 ... SA-10
Galion, 11449 ... NJ-10
GALLIA CO., 31362 ... SH-13
Gallipolis, 4212 ... SI-13
Gambier, 2050 ... NL-12
Garfield Hts., 29042 ... NF-15
Garrettsville, 2222 ... NG-17
Gates Mills, 2370 ... NE-16
GEAUGA CO., 95218 ... NE-17
Geneva, 6478 ... ND-18
Geneva-on-the-Lake, 1537 ... NC-18
Genoa, 2351 ... NE-7
Georgetown, 3720 ... SH-5
Germantown, 5157 ... SD-3
Ghent, 1600 ... NG-15
Gibsonburg, 2460 ... NF-7
Girard, 10490 ... NG-19
Glandorf, 952 ... NH-4
Glendale, 2139 ... SJ-3
Glenmoor, 2192 ... NJ-20
Glouster, 2029 ... SD-13
Gnadenhutten, 1294 ... NL-16
Golf Manor, 3682 ... SL-3
Goshen, 730 ... SF-4
Grafton, 5855 ... NG-13
Grand Rapids, 998 ... NF-5
Grandview Hts., 6273 ... SB-9
Granville, 5281 ... NN-11
Gratis, 905 ... SC-2
Green, 23463 ... NI-16
GREENE CO., 151996 ... SC-4
Greenfield, 5146 ... SE-7
Greenhills, 3758 ... SJ-3
Greensburg ... NI-16
Green Sprs., 1235 ... NG-9
Greentown, 3154 ... NI-16
Greenview ... SK-7
Greenville, 13166 ... NN-1
Greenwich, 1549 ... NH-11
Groesbeck, 7202 ... SF-2
Grove City, 30892 ... SB-9
Groveport, 4753 ... SB-10
GUERNSEY CO., 41123 ... NM-16
Hamden, 940 ... SF-11
HAMILTON CO., 806652 ... SF-1
Hamilton, 61943 ... SE-2
Hamilton Meadows, 2100 ... SB-9
Hamler, 678 ... NG-4
HANCOCK CO., 73503 ... NI-5
Hanover, 956 ... NN-12
HARDIN CO., 32032 ... NJ-6
HARRISON CO., 15920 ... NM-18
Harrison, 7821 ... SF-1
Harrisville, 265 ... NM-19
Hartville, 2389 ... NI-16
Heath, 8888 ... SA-12
Hebron, 2149 ... SB-12
HENRY CO., 29453 ... NG-4
Hicksville, 3533 ... NG-1
HIGHLAND CO., 42818 ... SF-7
Highland Hts., 8621 ... SK-20
Highland Hills, 1421 ... SM-19
Highland Park, 700 ... NI-16
Hilliard, 26656 ... SA-8
Hillsboro, 6677 ... SF-6
Hiram, 1192 ... NG-17
HOCKING CO., 29009 ... SE-11
Holgate, 1165 ... NG-4
Holland, 1326 ... NE-6
HOLMES CO., 41567 ... NK-14
Hopedale, 994 ... NM-18
Hubbard, 8006 ... NG-20
Huber Hts., 38089 ... SB-4
Hudson, 23084 ... NG-16
HURON CO., 60385 ... NG-11
Huron, 7581 ... NF-11
Independence, 6869 ... NF-15
Ironton, 11417 ... SJ-11
Jackson, 6240 ... SG-11
JACKSON CO., 33526 ... SH-11
Jackson Cen., 1459 ... NL-4
Jamestown, 1854 ... SC-6
JEFFERSON CO., 70599 ... NK-19
Jefferson, 3514 ... ND-19
Jeffersonville, 1247 ... SD-7
Jewett, 795 ... NL-18
Johnstown, 3883 ... NN-10
Junction City, 858 ... SC-12
Kalida, 1124 ... NI-3
Kendall Hts., 850 ... NB-8
Kent, 28135 ... NH-16
Kenton, 8169 ... NK-6
Kenwood, 7423 ... SK-4
Kettering, 55481 ... SC-4
Killbuck, 899 ... NK-14
Kingston, 1037 ... SE-10
Kingsville, 650 ... NC-19
Kinsman, 600 ... NF-20
Kirtland, 7251 ... NE-16
KNOX CO., 58398 ... NM-12
Lagrange, 1920 ... NG-13
LAKE CO., 232466 ... ND-17
Lake Cable, 2500 ... NB-8
Lake Milton, 1100 ... NH-18
Lakemore, 2649 ... NH-16
Lakeside, 950 ... NE-10
Lakeview, 1097 ... NL-5
Lakewood, 53244 ... NF-14
Lancaster, 36063 ... SC-11
Lansing, 400 ... NN-19
La Rue, 735 ... NK-7
Laurel Ridge, 2350 ... NI-17
LAWRENCE CO., 63112 ... SK-11
Leavittsburg, 2200 ... NG-18
Lebanon, 19978 ... SE-4
Leesburg, 1341 ... SE-7
Leetonia, 2043 ... NI-19
Leipsic, 2232 ... NH-4
Lewisburg, 1784 ... SB-2
Lexington, 4224 ... NJ-11
Liberty Cen., 1117 ... NF-4
LICKING CO., 154806 ... NN-11
Lima, 38608 ... NJ-4
Lincoln Hts., 3817 ... SK-3
Lincoln Vil., 9482 ... SB-9
Lisbon, 3082 ... NJ-19
Little Farms ... SI-17
Lockland, 3393 ... SK-3
Lodi, 3287 ... NH-13
LOGAN CO., 46580 ... NL-5
Logan, 7090 ... SD-12
London, 9396 ... SB-7
Lorain, 67820 ... NF-13
LORAIN CO., 296307 ... NG-13
Lordstown, 3636 ... NG-19
Loudonville, 2982 ... NK-12
Louisville, 9367 ... NI-17
Loveland, 11219 ... SF-3
Loveland Park, 1799 ... SJ-6
Lowell, 602 ... SD-16
Lowellville, 1200 ... NH-20
Lucas, 608 ... NJ-12
LUCAS CO., 448229 ... NE-5
Lucasville, 1588 ... SH-9
Luckey, 988 ... NF-7
Lynchburg, 1432 ... SF-5
Lyndhurst, 14450 ... NE-16
Macedonia, 10314 ... NG-16
Mack, 2000 ... SL-1
Madeira, 8330 ... SF-3
MADISON CO., 41295 ... SC-7
Madison, 3070 ... ND-18
Magnolia, 935 ... NK-17
MAHONING CO., 254274 ... NH-19
Malta, 680 ... SC-14
Malvern, 1229 ... NJ-17
Manchester, 4000 ... NI-15
Manchester, 2082 ... SI-6
Mansfield, 50615 ... NJ-11
Mantua, 1026 ... NG-17
Maple Hts., 24739 ... NF-15
Marble Cliff, 610 ... SH-18
Marblehead, 857 ... NE-10
Mariemont, 3127 ... SG-3
Marietta, 14270 ... SE-16
MARION CO., 65932 ... NK-9
Marion, 36494 ... NK-8
Marshallville, 817 ... NI-15
Martins Ferry, 6860 ... NN-19
Marysville, 17483 ... NM-7
Mason, 28847 ... SE-3
Massillon, 32150 ... NJ-16
Masury, 2618 ... NG-20
Maumee, 14285 ... NE-6
Mayfield, 3242 ... SK-20
Mayfield Hts., 18380 ... NE-16
McArthur, 2037 ... SF-12
McClure, 746 ... NF-5
McComb, 1688 ... NH-5
McConnelsville, 1762 ... SC-15
McDonald, 3357 ... NB-13
McKinley Hts., 700 ... NG-19
Mechanicsburg, 1716 ... NN-6
Medina, 26461 ... NH-14
MEDINA CO., 167010 ... NH-14
Medway, 2000 ... SB-4
MEIGS CO., 23232 ... SG-14
Mendon, 703 ... NJ-2
Mentor, 51485 ... ND-16
Mentor-on-the-Lake, 8293 ... ND-16
MERCER CO., 41202 ... NK-1
MIAMI CO., 101619 ... NN-3
Miamisburg, 19796 ... SD-3
Miamitown, 730 ... SF-1
Middleburg Hts., 15437 ... NF-14
Middlefield, 2411 ... NF-18
Middle Pt., 579 ... NI-2
Middleport, 2517 ... SG-14
Middletown, 51472 ... SD-3
Milan, 1381 ... NG-11
Milford, 6325 ... SF-3
Milford Cen., 684 ... NM-7
Millbury, 1156 ... NE-7
Millersburg, 3582 ... NK-14
Millersport, 967 ... SB-11
Millville, 873 ... SE-1
Mineral City, 855 ... NK-16
Mineral Ridge, 3900 ... NH-19
Minerva, 3976 ... NJ-17
Minerva Park, 1275 ... NN-9
Mingo Jct., 3426 ... NL-20
Minster, 2820 ... NL-3
Mogadore, 3966 ... NH-16
Monroe, 10410 ... SE-3
MONROE CO., 14698 ... SB-17
Monroeville, 1396 ... NG-10
MONTGOMERY CO., 547435 ... SC-2
Montgomery, 10015 ... SF-3
Montpelier, 4135 ... NE-2
Moraine, 6702 ... SC-4
Moreland Hills, 3199 ... SM-20
MORGAN CO., 14958 ... SD-14
MORROW CO., 34322 ... NK-9
Morrow, 1500 ... SE-4
Mt. Carmel, 4308 ... SG-3
Mt. Carmel Hts., 1200 ... SM-5
Mt. Gilead, 3547 ... NK-10
Mt. Healthy, 6600 ... SF-2
Mt. Orab, 2909 ... SG-5
Mt. Repose, 4102 ... SF-3
Mt. Sterling, 1840 ... SC-8
Mt. Vernon, 16000 ... NL-11
Mulberry, 3139 ... SF-3
Munroe Falls, 5300 ... NA-6
MUSKINGUM CO., 85579 ... SB-15
Napoleon, 9169 ... NF-4
Navarre, 1431 ... NJ-16
Neffs, 1138 ... NN-19
Negley, 900 ... NJ-20
Nelsonville, 5444 ... SE-13
Nevada, 785 ... NJ-8
Newark, 47301 ... NN-12
New Athens, 352 ... NM-18
New Boston, 2189 ... SI-9
New Bremen, 2993 ... NL-3
Newburgh Hts., 2243 ... SM-18
New Carlisle, 5639 ... SB-4
Newcomerstown, 3952 ... NM-15
New Concord, 2660 ... SA-15
New Holland, 782 ... SD-8
New Knoxville, 915 ... NK-3
New Lebanon, 4208 ... SC-3
New Lexington, 4632 ... SC-13
New London, 2668 ... NH-12
New Madison, 780 ... SB-1
New Matamoras, 922 ... SD-18
New Miami, 2502 ... SE-2
New Middletown, 1620 ... NI-20
New Paris, 1546 ... SB-1
New Philadelphia, 17430 ... NL-16
Newport, 700 ... SE-17
New Richmond, 2463 ... SH-3
New Springfield, 600 ... NI-20
New Straitsville, 808 ... SD-13
Newton Falls, 4833 ... NG-18
Newtown, 3692 ... SG-3
New Vienna, 1380 ... SE-6
New Washington, 960 ... NI-10
New Waterford, 1391 ... NI-20
Niles, 20016 ... NG-19
NOBLE CO., 14156 ... SC-16
N. Baltimore, 3343 ... NG-6
Northbrook, 11076 ... SF-2
N. Canton, 16780 ... NI-16
N. College Hill, 9359 ... SF-2
Northfield, 3722 ... NF-16
Northfield Cen., 2570 ... NG-16
N. Industry, 2700 ... NJ-16
N. Jackson, 900 ... NH-19
N. Kingsville, 2638 ... NC-19
N. Lawrence, 800 ... NI-15
N. Lewisburg, 1590 ... NM-6
N. Lima, 900 ... NI-20
N. Olmsted, 32653 ... NF-14
N. Perry, 935 ... ND-17
N. Randall, 864 ... SM-19
Northridge, 8487 ... SB-4
Northridge, 6853 ... SA-6
N. Ridgeville, 26108 ... NF-13
N. Royalton, 29538 ... NG-15
Northwood, 5499 ... NE-7
Norton, 11563 ... NH-15
Norwalk, 16505 ... NG-11
Norwood, 19997 ... SF-2
Oak Hbr., 2816 ... NE-8
Oak Hill, 1656 ... SH-11
Oakwood, 3620 ... SN-20
Oakwood, 8749 ... SC-4
Oakwood, 571 ... NH-3
Oberlin, 8280 ... NG-12
Obetz, 4079 ... SB-9
Ohio City, 758 ... NJ-1
Olmsted Falls, 8437 ... SN-14
Oneida ... SE-3
Ontario, 5350 ... NJ-10
Orange, 3357 ... SM-20
Oregon, 19175 ... NE-7
Orrville, 8485 ... NI-14
Orwell, 1515 ... NE-18
OTTAWA CO., 41583 ... NE-7
Ottawa, 4479 ... NH-4
Ottawa Hills, 4608 ... ND-6
Ottoville, 864 ... NI-3
Overlook ... SL-9
Owensville, 830 ... SG-4
Oxford, 22123 ... SD-1
Page Manor ... SC-4
Painesville, 17789 ... ND-17
Painesville on the Lake, 850 ... ND-17
Pandora, 1214 ... NI-5
Parkman, 600 ... NF-18
Parma, 81469 ... NF-15
Parma Hts., 20657 ... NF-14
Pataskala, 12624 ... SA-11
PAULDING CO., 19537 ... NG-1
Paulding, 3430 ... NH-2
Payne, 1149 ... NH-1
Peebles, 1845 ... SH-7
Pemberville, 1351 ... NF-7
Pepper Pike, 5794 ... NF-16
Perry, 1267 ... ND-17
PERRY CO., 35246 ... SC-13
Perry Hts., 8900 ... NC-8
Perrysburg, 16980 ... NE-6
Perrysville, 822 ... NK-12
Petersburg, 950 ... NI-20
Pettisville, 500 ... NE-3
Phillipsburg, 607 ... SB-3
Philo, 769 ... SB-14
PICKAWAY CO., 52989 ... SD-9
Pickerington, 15878 ... SB-10
PIKE CO., 28146 ... SG-9
Piketon, 1973 ... SG-9
Pioneer, 1428 ... ND-2
Piqua, 20883 ... NN-3
Pisgah, 1000 ... SE-3
Plain City, 3462 ... NN-8
Pleasant Hill, 1140 ... NN-3
Pleasant Run Farms, 4731 ... SJ-2
Pleasant Valley, 500 ... SE-9
Pleasantville, 856 ... SC-11
Plymouth, 1860 ... NI-10
Poast Town, 150 ... SD-3
Poland, 2750 ... NH-20
Pomeroy, 1999 ... SG-14
PORTAGE CO., 155631 ... NG-17
Portage Lakes, 9870 ... NH-16
Port Clinton, 6336 ... NE-9
Portsmouth, 20101 ... SI-9
Powhatan Pt., 1703 ... SB-19
PREBLE CO., 42527 ... SC-1
Proctorville, 629 ... SK-12
Prospect, 1142 ... NL-8
PUTNAM CO., 34928 ... NI-4

Queen Acres, 650 SE-2
Quincy, 703 NM-4
Racine, 757 SH-14
Randolph, 750 NH-17
Ravenna, 11510 NG-17
Reading, 10320 SF-2
Reedurban, 4400 NJ-16
Reminderville, 2512 NF-16
Reno, 850 SE-17
Rensselaer Park, 850 SK-3
Republic, 595 NH-9
Reynoldsburg, 33059 SB-10
Richfield, 3553 NG-15
RICHLAND CO., 127949 NI-11
Richmond Dale, 700 SF-10
Richmond Hts., 10521 NE-16
Richville, 1600 NJ-16
Richwood, 2132 NL-7
Rio Grande, 875 SH-12
Ripley, 1813 SI-5
Risingsun, 607 NG-7
Rittman, 6311 NI-14
Riverside, 22733 SL-9
Rockford, 1118 NJ-1
Rocky River, 19681 NF-14
Rosemount, 2043 SI-9
Roseville, 1922 SC-13
ROSS CO., 75197 SE-8
Ross, 1971 SF-1
Rossford, 6387 NE-6
Russells Pt., 1557 NL-5
Sabina, 2831 SD-6
Sagamore Hills, 1930 NG-15
Sahara Sands, 650 NB-8
St. Bernard, 4528 SF-2
St. Clairsville, 5075 NN-19
St. Henry, 2347 NL-1
St. Marys, 8238 NK-2
St. Paris, 1983 NN-4
Salem, 12005 NI-19
Salineville, 1363 NK-19
Sandusky, 26666 NF-10
SANDUSKY CO., 61676 NF-8
Sardinia, 901 SG-5
Sawyerwood, 1730 NC-6
Schoenbrunn, 700 NL-16
Scio, 781 NL-18
SCIOTO CO., 76561 SI-8
Sciotodale, 982 SI-10
Seaman, 1084 SH-6
Sebring, 4706 NI-18
SENECA CO., 57483 NH-8
Seven Hills, 12041 NF-15
Seven Hills, 2000 SJ-2
Seven Mile, 727 SE-2
Seville, 2462 NH-14
Shadyside, 3562 SA-20
Shaker Hts., 27723 NF-15
Sharonville, 13079 SF-3
Shawnee, 657 SD-13
Sheffield, 3360 NF-13
Sheffield Lake, 9157 NF-13
Shelby, 9471 NI-10
SHELBY CO., 48736 NL-4
Sherwood, 807 NG-2
Shiloh, 710 NI-11
Shiloh, 11272 SB-3
Shreve, 1516 NJ-13
Sidney, 20188 NM-4
Silver Lake, 3159 NH-16
Silverton, 4734 SL-4
Singing Hills SD-4
Smithfield, 825 NM-19
Smithville, 1312 NI-14
Solon, 22335 NF-16
Somerset, 1577 SC-12
S. Amherst, 1800 NF-12
S. Bloomfield, 1540 SC-9
S. Charleston, 1821 SB-6
S. Euclid, 22210 NE-16
S. Lebanon, 3172 SE-4
S. Point, 3922 SK-11
S. Russell, 3992 NF-16
S. Webster, 751 SI-10
S. West Hubbard, 1200 NC-14
S. Zanesville, 1986 SB-14
Spencer, 809 NH-13
Spencerville, 2209 NJ-3
Springboro, 16403 SD-3
Springdale, 9809 SF-2
Springfield, 63302 SB-5
STARK CO., 380608 NI-17
Steubenville, 19314 NL-20
Stow, 34404 NH-16
Strasburg, 2607 NK-16
Streetsboro, 14210 NG-16
Strongsville, 43949 NG-14
Struthers, 11240 NH-20
Stryker, 1391 NE-2
Sugarcreek, 2159 NK-15
Summerside, 5523 SM-5
Summerside Estates, 1700 SM-5
Summit, 700 NC-13
SUMMIT CO., 546604 NH-15
Sunbury, 3225 NM-9
Sunnyland, 250 NB-15
Surrey Hill, 700 NB-12
Swanton, 3557 NE-5
Sycamore, 894 NI-8
Sylvania, 19069 ND-6
Syracuse, 877 SG-14
Tallmadge, 17408 NH-16
Terrace Pk., 2136 SL-5
The Plains, 2931 SE-13
The Vil. of Indian Hill, 5661 SK-5
Thornville, 1034 SB-12
Tiffin, 17438 NH-8
Tiltonsville, 1244 NM-19
Timberlake, 749 ND-16
Tipp City, 9357 SB-4
Toledo, 301285 NE-6
Toronto, 5402 NL-20
Trenton, 10488 SD-2
Trotwood, 26608 SC-3
Troy, 22343 NN-3
TRUMBULL CO., 219296 NF-19
Turpin Hills, 4960 SM-4
TUSCARAWAS CO., 91944 NM-16
Tuscarawas, 986 NL-16
Twinsburg, 17380 NG-16
Uhrichsville, 5647 NL-16
UNION CO., 45751 NM-7
Union, 5920 SB-3
Union City, 1701 NM-1
Uniontown, 2802 NI-16
University Hts., 13242 NF-16
Upper Arlington, 31550 SA-9
Upper Sandusky, 6455 NJ-8
Urbana, 11561 NN-5
Urbancrest, 873 SB-9
Utica, 2109 NM-11
Valleyview, 568 SH-17
Valley View, 2099 SN-18
Vandalia, 14298 SB-4
Van Wert, 10435 NI-2
VAN WERT CO., 29154 NJ-2
Venice Hts., 1300 NA-12
Vermilion, 11000 NF-12
Versailles, 2539 NM-2
Viking Vil., 1230 SM-5
Villa Nova, 800 NK-2
VINTON CO., 13429 SF-11
Wadsworth, 19951 NH-15
Wakeman, 964 NG-12
Walbridge, 3096 NE-7
Walton Hills, 2347 SN-19
Wapakoneta, 9602 NK-3
Warren, 45796 NG-19
WARREN CO., 196622 SE-4
Warrensville Hts., 14223 NF-15
Warsaw, 787 NL-13
WASHINGTON CO., 62210 SD-16
Washington Court House, 13466 SD-7
Washingtonville, 773 NI-19
Waterford, 600 SD-15
Waterville, 5189 NE-6
Wauseon, 7311 NE-4
Waverly, 4406 SG-9
Wayne, 847 NG-7
WAYNE CO., 113697 NI-14
Wayne Lakes, 666 SA-1
Waynesburg, 983 NJ-17
Waynesfield, 819 NK-4
Waynesville, 2980 SD-4
Wellington, 4648 NG-12
Wellston, 6025 SG-11
Wellsville, 4034 NK-20
W. Alexandria, 1343 SC-2
W. Carrollton, 13198 SC-3
W. Chester, 800 SE-3
Westerville, 34722 NN-9
Westfield Cen., 1151 NH-14
W. Jefferson, 4287 SB-8
W. Lafayette, 2535 NM-15
Westlake, 31331 NF-14
W. Liberty, 1760 NM-5
W. Mansfield, 697 NL-6
W. Milton, 4684 SB-3
Weston, 1655 NF-5
W. Portsmouth, 3458 SI-9
W. Salem, 1488 NI-13
W. Union, 3108 SI-7
W. Unity, 1803 NE-2
Westview, 530 NF-14
Wheelersburg, 6471 SI-10
Whitehall, 18052 SB-10
Whitehouse, 3303 NE-5
White Oak, 13277 SF-2
Wickliffe, 13205 NE-16
Wilberforce, 1579 SC-5
Wildbrook Acres, 1500 SK-3
Willard, 6818 NH-10
WILLIAMS CO., 38688 NE-1
Williamsburg, 2332 SG-4
Williamsdale, 600 SE-2
Williamsport, 1020 SD-9
Williston, 600 NE-7
Willoughby, 22336 NE-16
Willoughby Hills, 8459 NE-16
Willowick, 14004 NE-16
Wilmington, 12474 SE-5
Winchester, 1086 SH-6
Windham, 2749 NG-18
Wintersville, 3889 NL-19
Withamsville, 3145 SG-3
WOOD CO., 123929 NG-6
Woodlawn, 2584 SK-3
Woodmere, 782 SL-20
Woodsfield, 2501 SC-18
Woodville, 2003 NF-7
Woodworth, 700 NI-20
Wooster, 25668 NJ-14
Wooster Hts., 850 NJ-11
Worthington, 13202 NN-9
WYANDOT CO., 22813 NJ-7
Wyoming, 7719 SK-3
Xenia, 23600 SC-5
Yellow Sprs., 3665 SC-5
Yorkville, 1189 NM-19
Youngstown, 82837 NH-20
Zanesville, 25253 SB-14

Oklahoma

Map pp. 166-169

Ada, 15999 H-15
ADAIR CO., 21988 E-20
Adair, 708 C-18
Afton, 1106 C-19
Alex, 657 H-12
ALFALFA CO., 5725 C-11
Allen, 957 H-16
Altus, 19899 I-9
Alva, 4900 C-10
Anadarko, 6584 G-11
Antlers, 2508 J-18
Apache, 1597 H-11
Arapaho, 709 F-10
Ardmore, 24280 J-14
Arkoma, 2191 F-20
Arnett, 497 D-8
Asher, 434 H-14
ATOKA CO., 14456 J-16
Atoka, 3044 I-16
Barnsdall, 1280 C-16
Bartlesville, 34734 C-17
Beaver, 1414 B-6
BEAVER CO., 5379 C-7
BECKHAM CO., 18880 G-8
Beggs, 1375 E-16
Bethany, 19786 F-13
Bethel Acres, 2833 G-14
Billings, 562 C-13
Binger, 708 G-11
Bixby, 18600 E-17
Blackwell, 7297 B-14
BLAINE CO., 12859 E-11
Blair, 823 H-9
Blanchard, 3678 G-13
Boise City, 1322 B-2
Bokchito, 570 J-16
Bokoshe, 462 G-19
Boley, 1102 F-15
Boswell, 701 J-17
Bristow, 4397 E-16
Broken Arrow, 86228 E-17
Broken Bow, 4170 J-20
BRYAN CO., 37815 J-16
Buffalo, 1102 B-8
Burns Flat, 1731 G-9
Cache, 2406 I-10
CADDO CO., 30229 G-11
Caddo, 965 J-16
Calera, 1784 K-16
CANADIAN CO., 98701 F-12
Canton, 602 E-11
Canute, 528 F-9
Carmen, 373 C-11
Carnegie, 1603 G-11
CARTER CO., 47125 J-13
Catoosa, 6440 D-17
Cement, 530 H-12
Chandler, 2859 F-15
Checotah, 3533 F-18
Chelsea, 2262 C-18
Cherokee, 1485 C-11
CHEROKEE CO., 44671 E-19
Cheyenne, 733 F-8
Chickasha, 16849 G-12
Choctaw, 10529 F-14
CHOCTAW CO., 15297 J-17
Chouteau, 1992 D-18
CIMARRON CO., 2833 B-2
Claremore, 17161 D-17
Clayton, 724 I-18
CLEVELAND CO., 224898 G-13
Cleveland, 3247 D-15
Clinton, 8363 F-10
COAL CO., 5743 I-16
Coalgate, 1889 I-16
Colbert, 1094 K-15
Colcord, 851 D-19
Collinsville, 4325 D-17
COMANCHE CO., 112429 I-11
Comanche, 1516 I-12
Commerce, 2573 B-19
Copan, 809 B-17
Cordell, 2885 G-10
Corn, 578 G-10
COTTON CO., 6589 J-11
Countyline, 300 I-13
Covington, 542 D-13
Coweta, 8352 E-17
Cowlington, 137 G-19
CRAIG CO., 15078 C-18
CREEK CO., 68708 E-15
Crescent, 1336 E-13
Cushing, 8267 E-15
CUSTER CO., 25208 F-9
Cyril, 1169 H-11
Davenport, 886 F-15
Davidson, 345 J-9
Davis, 2648 I-14
DELAWARE CO., 39146 C-19
Delaware, 472 B-17
Del City, 21945 F-13
Depew, 569 E-15
Dewar, 908 F-17
DEWEY CO., 4568 E-9
Dewey, 3288 B-17
Dickson, 1203 J-14
Dill City, 529 G-9
Drumright, 2877 E-15
Duncan, 22306 I-12
Durant, 14795 J-16
Dustin, 445 G-16
Edmond, 74881 F-13
Eldorado, 498 I-8
Elgin, 1278 H-11
Elk City, 10743 F-9
ELLIS CO., 3963 D-8
Elmore City, 763 I-13
El Reno, 16097 F-12
Enid, 46416 D-12
Erick, 1045 G-8
Eufaula, 2789 G-18
Fairfax, 1505 C-15
Fairland, 1012 C-19
Fairview, 2629 D-11
Fletcher, 1038 H-11
Forest Park, 1171 K-5
Forgan, 493 B-6
Ft. Cobb, 651 G-11
Ft. Gibson, 4252 E-18
Ft. Towson, 611 J-18
Frederick, 4195 I-10
Garber, 802 D-13
GARFIELD CO., 56958 C-12
GARVIN CO., 27228 H-13
Geary, 1290 F-11
Geronimo, 950 I-11
Glencoe, 562 D-14
Glenpool, 8960 E-17
Goodwell, 1129 C-4
Gore, 907 F-19
GRADY CO., 49369 H-12
Grandfield, 1007 J-10
Granite, 1797 H-9
GRANT CO., 4779 B-12
GREER CO., 5901 H-8
Grove, 5752 C-19
Guthrie, 10800 E-13
Guymon, 10643 C-4
Haileyville, 899 H-18
Hammon, 454 F-9
HARMON CO., 3030 H-8
HARPER CO., 3313 C-8
Harrah, 4939 F-14
Hartshorne, 2073 H-18
HASKELL CO., 12183 G-19
Haskell, 1776 E-17
Healdton, 2777 J-13
Heavener, 3246 H-20
Helena, 1392 C-11
Hennessey, 2050 D-12
Henryetta, 6110 F-17
Hinton, 2183 F-11
Hobart, 3805 H-9
Holdenville, 5538 G-16
Hollis, 2087 H-7
Hominy, 3733 D-16
Hooker, 1721 B-5
Howe, 715 H-20
HUGHES CO., 13835 G-16
Hugo, 5521 J-18
Hulbert, 533 E-19
Hydro, 1045 F-11
Idabel, 6916 K-19
Inola, 1725 D-18
JACKSON CO., 26518 I-8
Jay, 2840 C-19
JEFFERSON CO., 6461 J-12
Jenks, 13095 E-17
JOHNSTON CO., 10259 I-15
Jones, 2611 J-7
KAY CO., 46480 B-14
Kellyville, 918 E-16
Keota, 530 G-19
Keyes, 367 B-2
Kiefer, 1313 E-16
KINGFISHER CO., 14302 E-12
Kingfisher, 4501 E-12
Kingston, 1526 J-15
KIOWA CO., 9848 H-10
Kiowa, 701 H-17
Konawa, 1434 H-15
Krebs, 2120 H-17
Lamont, 436 C-13
Langley, 683 C-19
Langston, 1688 E-14
LATIMER CO., 10635 H-18
Laverne, 1016 C-8
Lawton, 90234 I-11
Leedey, 333 E-9
LE FLORE CO., 49528 I-19
Lexington, 2079 H-13
LINCOLN CO., 32311 E-14
Lindsay, 2890 H-13
Locust Gr., 1576 D-18
LOGAN CO., 36894 E-13
Lone Gr., 5075 J-14
Lone Wolf, 474 H-9
LOVE CO., 9126 J-13
Luther, 1083 F-14
Madill, 3688 J-15
MAJOR CO., 7364 D-10
Mangum, 2745 H-8
Mannford, 2758 D-16
Marietta, 2526 K-14
Marlow, 4531 I-12
MARSHALL CO., 14461 J-15
Maud, 1159 G-15
MAYES CO., 39471 C-18
Maysville, 1296 H-13
McAlester, 18105 H-17
MCCLAIN CO., 30096 H-13
MCCURTAIN CO., 33992 I-19
McCurtain, 479 G-19
MCINTOSH CO., 19965 G-17
McLoud, 4050 F-14
Medford, 1072 B-13
Meeker, 989 F-14
Miami, 13565 B-19
Midwest City, 54890 F-13
Minco, 1767 G-12
Moore, 47697 G-13
Mooreland, 1221 C-9
Morris, 1326 F-17
Morrison, 625 D-14
Mounds, 1278 E-16
Mtn. Park, 382 H-10
Mtn. View, 830 G-10
Muldrow, 3168 F-20
MURRAY CO., 12880 I-14
Muskogee, 39766 E-18
MUSKOGEE CO., 70607 F-18
Mustang, 15887 F-13
Newcastle, 6303 G-13
Newkirk, 2162 B-14
Nichols Hills, 3997 J-4
Nicoma Park, 2388 K-7
Ninnekah, 1046 H-12
NOBLE CO., 11211 C-14
Noble, 5518 G-13
Norman, 101719 G-13
N. Enid, 833 D-12
Nowata, 4034 C-17
NOWATA CO., 10864 B-17
Oakhurst, 2731 D-16
Oilton, 1143 D-15
Okarche, 1158 F-12
Okay, 593 E-18
Okeene, 1210 D-11
Okemah, 2970 F-16
OKFUSKEE CO., 11434 F-15
OKLAHOMA CO., 684543 F-13
Oklahoma City, 531324 F-13
Okmulgee, 12854 F-17
OKMULGEE CO., 39732 E-17
Olustee, 645 I-9
Oologah, 1121 C-17
OSAGE CO., 45416 C-15
OTTAWA CO., 32866 B-19
Owasso, 23771 D-17
Paden, 430 F-15
Panama, 1396 G-20
Paoli, 654 H-14
Pauls Valley, 6178 H-14
Pawhuska, 3533 C-16
PAWNEE CO., 16860 D-14
Pawnee, 2204 D-15
PAYNE CO., 69151 E-14
Perkins, 2186 E-14
Perry, 5105 D-14
Picher, 1625 B-19
Piedmont, 4685 F-13
Pink, 1219 G-14
PITTSBURG CO., 44641 H-17
Pocola, 4373 G-20
Ponca City, 25070 C-14
Pond Cr., 824 C-12
PONTOTOC CO., 35346 I-15
Porter, 581 E-18
Porum, 733 F-18
Poteau, 8152 G-20
POTTAWATOMIE CO., 68272 G-14
Prague, 2124 F-15
Pryor, 9227 D-18
Purcell, 5858 H-13
PUSHMATAHA CO., 11693 I-18
Quapaw, 975 B-19
Quinton, 1081 G-18
Ralston, 360 C-15
Ramona, 574 C-17
Red Oak, 572 H-19
Ringling, 1082 J-13
Roff, 724 I-15
ROGER MILLS CO., 3311 E-8
ROGERS CO., 80757 D-17
Roland, 3110 F-20
Rush Sprs., 1324 H-12
Ryan, 854 J-12
Salina, 1454 D-18
Sallisaw, 8621 F-19
Sand Sprs., 17667 D-16
Sapulpa, 20619 E-16
Savanna, 744 H-17
Sayre, 2836 G-8
Seiling, 821 D-10
Seminole, 6913 G-15
SEMINOLE CO., 24770 G-15
Sentinel, 860 G-9
SEQUOYAH CO., 40868 F-20
Shattuck, 1235 D-8
Shawnee, 29824 G-14
Shidler, 520 C-15
Skiatook, 6290 D-17
Slaughterville, 3839 G-13
Snyder, 1452 I-10
S. Coffeyville, 801 B-17
Spavinaw, 574 D-19
Spencer, 3840 J-6
Sperry, 1017 D-17
Spiro, 2287 G-20
STEPHENS CO., 42946 I-13
Sterling, 748 H-12
Stigler, 2821 G-19
Stillwater, 40906 D-14
Stilwell, 3472 E-20
Stonewall, 471 I-15
Stratford, 1484 H-14
Stroud, 2755 E-15
Sulphur, 4877 I-14
Tahlequah, 16075 E-19
Talihina, 1234 H-19
Tecumseh, 6516 G-14
Temple, 1149 J-11
Terral, 359 K-12
TEXAS CO., 20112 B-4
Texhoma, 928 C-3
The Village, 9827 F-13
Thomas, 1150 E-10
TILLMAN CO., 8513 I-10
Tipton, 841 I-9
Tishomingo, 3136 J-15
Tonkawa, 3132 C-14
Tulsa, 382457 D-17
TULSA CO., 572059 E-17
Turley, 3231 D-17
Tuttle, 5365 G-12
Tyrone, 857 B-5
Valley Brook, 788 L-5
Valliant, 759 J-19
Velma, 693 I-13
Verden, 682 G-12
Vian, 1460 F-19
Vici, 647 D-9
Vinita, 6017 C-18
WAGONER CO., 64183 E-18
Wagoner, 7877 E-18
Wakita, 396 B-12
Walters, 2610 I-11
Wapanucka, 432 I-16
Warner, 1443 F-18
Warr Acres, 9475 K-3
WASHINGTON CO., 49149 C-17
WASHITA CO., 11471 G-9
Watonga, 5588 E-11
Waukomis, 1201 D-12
Waurika, 1857 J-12
Wayne, 727 H-14
Waynoka, 930 C-10
Weatherford, 9738 F-10
Webbers Falls, 724 F-19
Welch, 600 B-19
Weleetka, 954 G-16
Wellston, 826 F-14
Westville, 1652 E-20
Wetumka, 1420 G-16
Wewoka, 3437 G-15
Wilburton, 2934 H-18
Wilson, 1623 J-13
Wister, 1025 H-20
WOODS CO., 8546 C-10
Woodward, 11931 D-9
WOODWARD CO., 19088 C-9
Wright City, 814 J-19
Wynnewood, 2314 I-14
Wynona, 535 C-16
Yale, 1254 D-15
Yukon, 22032 F-13

Oregon

Map pp. 170-173

Albany, 44797 F-4
Aloha, 41741 C-4
Amity, 1463 D-4
Applegate, 100 M-3
Ashland, 20829 M-4
Astoria, 9784 A-2
Athena, 1218 B-13
Aumsville, 3202 E-4
Aurora, 879 D-5
BAKER CO., 16287 E-15
Baker City, 9703 E-15
Bandon, 2908 J-1
Barview, 1872 J-1
Bay City, 1162 C-2
Beaverton, 85775 C-4
Bend, 67152 H-8
BENTON CO., 78640 F-3
Bly, 700 L-8
Boardman, 3051 B-11
Brookings, 6297 M-1
Brownsville, 1517 G-4
Bunker Hill, 1462 J-1
Burns, 2755 I-12
Canby, 14989 D-5
Cannon Beach, 1700 B-2
Canyon City, 595 G-12
Canyonville, 1397 K-3
Carlton, 1501 D-4
Cascade Locks, 1109 C-6
Cave Jct., 1380 M-2
Central Pt., 15672 M-4
Charleston, 700 J-1
Chenoweth, 3412 C-8
Chiloquin, 723 L-6
CLACKAMAS CO., 368470 E-5
Clackamas, 5177 M-20
Clatskanie, 1631 B-4
CLATSOP CO., 36798 B-3
Coburg, 999 G-4
COLUMBIA CO., 48065 B-4
Columbia City, 1797 B-4
Condon, 708 D-10
COOS CO., 64711 J-2
Coos Bay, 15823 J-1
Coquille, 4254 J-1
Cornelius, 10820 C-4
Corvallis, 49553 F-3
Cottage Gr., 8724 H-4
Crater Lake K-6
Creswell, 4632 H-4
CROOK CO., 22067 G-9
Culver, 898 F-8
CURRY CO., 22427 L-1
Dallas, 14001 E-3
Dayton, 2206 D-4
Depoe Bay, 1363 E-2
DESCHUTES CO., 141382 H-7
Dillard, 350 J-3
DOUGLAS CO., 104202 J-3
Drain, 1039 I-3
Dufur, 582 D-8
Durham, 1427 M-18
Eagle Pt., 7496 L-4
Elgin, 1642 C-15
Enterprise, 1800 C-16
Estacada, 2435 D-5
Eugene, 144515 H-4
Fairview, 9327 C-5
Falcon Hts., 800 M-6
Falls City, 1014 E-3
Florence, 7841 H-2
Forest Gr., 19689 C-4
Four Corners, 13922 F-20
Garden Home, 4900 L-18
Gardiner, 540 H-2
Garibaldi, 927 C-2
Gearhart, 1077 B-2
Gervais, 2292 D-4
Gilchrist, 500 I-7
GILLIAM CO., 1794 D-10
Gladstone, 12117 D-5
Glendale, 897 K-3
Gleneden Beach, 900 E-2
Glenwood, 80 C-3
Glide, 1690 J-4
Gold Beach, 1930 L-1
Gold Hill, 1062 L-4
GRANT CO., 7297 F-12
Grants Pass, 28882 L-3
Green, 6174 J-3
Gresham, 96072 C-5
Halsey, 745 G-4
Happy Valley, 8282 M-20
Harbor, 2622 M-1
HARNEY CO., 6898 J-12
Harrisburg, 3265 G-4
Hayesville, 18222 E-20
Heppner, 1438 D-11
Hermiston, 14657 B-12
Hillsboro, 84533 C-4
Hines, 1493 I-12
HOOD RIVER CO., 21284 C-7
Hood River, 6480 C-7
Hubbard, 2545 D-4
Huntington, 481 G-16
Independence, 8193 E-4
JACKSON CO., 195322 L-4
Jacksonville, 2230 M-4
JEFFERSON CO., 20100 F-7
Jefferson, 2607 F-4
John Day, 1605 G-12
Joseph, 1005 D-16
JOSEPHINE CO., 80761 L-2
Junction City, 5369 G-3
Keizer, 34644 E-4
King City, 2058 M-17
KLAMATH CO., 66192 L-6
Klamath Falls, 19882 M-6
Lafayette, 2898 D-4
La Grande, 12440 D-14
LAKE CO., 7313 J-9
Lake Oswego, 36502 D-5
Lakeside, 1488 I-1
Lakeview, 2378 M-10
LANE CO., 335180 H-4
La Pine, 5799 I-7
Lebanon, 13834 F-4
LINCOLN CO., 45994 F-2
Lincoln Beach, 2078 E-2
Lincoln City, 7849 E-2
LINN CO., 108914 F-5
Lowell, 923 H-4
Lyons, 1083 E-5
Madras, 5300 F-8
MALHEUR CO., 31330 J-15
Mapleton, 900 H-2
MARION CO., 305265 E-5
Maywood Park, 748 K-20
McMinnville, 29646 D-4
Medford, 70147 M-4
Merrill, 897 N-7
Metzger, 3354 M-18
Mill City, 1593 F-5
Milton-Freewater, 6445 B-14
Milwaukie, 20810 M-19
Molalla, 6737 D-5
Monmouth, 8987 E-3
MORROW CO., 11666 D-11
Mt. Angel, 3355 E-4
MULTNOMAH CO., 672906 C-6
Myrtle Cr., 3528 K-3
Myrtle Pt., 2509 J-1
Newberg, 20681 D-4
Newport, 9833 F-2
N. Bend, 9843 I-1
N. Plains, 1775 C-4
Nyssa, 3068 H-17
Oak Grove, 12808 M-19
Oakland, 973 I-3
Oakridge, 3147 I-5
Ontario, 11125 H-17
Oregon City, 30221 D-5
Pendleton, 16636 C-13
Philomath, 4213 F-3
Phoenix, 4375 M-4
Pilot Rock, 1525 C-13
POLK CO., 70295 E-3
Portland, 533427 C-5
Port Orford, 1180 K-1
Powers, 754 K-2
Prairie City, 965 F-13
Prineville, 8908 G-8
Rainier, 1816 B-4
Raleigh Hills, 5865 L-18
Redmond, 19771 G-8
Reedsport, 4361 I-2
Riddle, 1023 K-3
Rockaway Beach, 1308 C-2
Rogue River, 1941 L-3
Roseburg, 20727 J-3
St. Helens, 11874 B-4
Salem, 148751 E-4
Sandy, 7871 D-6
Santa Clara, 12834 A-6
Scappoose, 5913 C-4
Scio, 704 F-4
Seaside, 6116 B-2
Shady Cove, 2301 L-4
Sheridan, 5570 D-3
SHERMAN CO., 1749 D-9
Sherwood, 15398 D-4
Siletz, 1132 F-2
Silverton, 8233 E-4
Sisters, 1212 G-7
Springfield, 55641 H-4
Stanfield, 1979 B-12
Stayton, 7184 E-4
Sublimity, 2374 E-4
Sunnyside, 6791 M-20
Sutherlin, 7281 J-3
Svensen, 550 A-3
Sweet Home, 8389 G-4
Talent, 6018 M-4
The Dalles, 11894 C-8
Tigard, 47968 D-4
TILLAMOOK CO., 25277 C-2
Tillamook, 4471 C-2
Toledo, 3434 F-2
Tri-City, 3519 K-3
Troutdale, 14898 C-5
Tualatin, 25881 D-4
Turner, 1571 E-4
UMATILLA CO., 73878 C-13
Umatilla, 6306 B-12
UNION CO., 24540 D-14
Union, 1945 D-15
Vale, 1926 H-16
Veneta, 3477 H-3
Vernonia, 2287 B-4
Waldport, 2094 F-2
Wallowa, 824 C-15
WALLOWA CO., 7014 C-16
Warren, 970 B-4
Warrenton, 4310 A-2
WASCO CO., 23593 E-8
WASHINGTON CO., 499794 C-3
W. Linn, 25094 D-5
Weston, 714 B-13
Westport, 280 A-3
W. Slope, 6442 L-18
WHEELER CO., 1455 E-10
White City, 6199 L-4
Willamina, 1874 E-3
Wilsonville, 16075 D-4
Winchester, 2700 J-3
Winchester Bay, 488 I-1
Winston, 4764 J-3
Woodburn, 21736 D-4
Yachats, 678 G-2
YAMHILL CO., 92196 D-3
Yamhill, 823 D-4
Yoncalla, 1059 I-3

Pennsylvania

Map pp. 174-183

Index keys WA to WT refer to Western PA, pp. 174-177, EA to ET refer to Eastern PA, pp. 178-181.
* City keyed to pp. 182-183

Abington, 10000 *A-5
Acmetonia, 1500 *H-9
ADAMS CO., 99749 EP-2
Adamstown, 1301 EN-8
Akron, 4009 EO-7
Albion, 1558 WE-2
Alburtis, 2203 EM-10
Aldan, 4294 *F-2
Aliquippa, 11105 WL-2
ALLEGHENY CO., 1235841 WM-4
Allentown, 106992 EL-11
Allison, 850 WP-4
Allison Park, 6000 WM-4
Almedia, 1056 EJ-6
Altoona, 47176 WM-11
Ambler, 6349 EO-12
Ambridge, 7329 WL-3
Ancient Oaks, 3161 EM-10
Andalusia, 3500 *B-8
Annville, 4518 EN-6
Apollo, 1672 WL-6
Archbald, 6290 EG-10
ARMSTRONG CO., 70586 WK-6
Arnold, 5401 WL-5
Ashland, 3159 EK-7
Ashley, 2726 EI-9
Ashtola, 150 WO-9
Aspinwall, 2789 *I-7
Atglen, 1350 EP-8
Athens, 3301 ED-6
Atlas, 1200 EK-6
Atlasburg, 500 WN-2
Auburn, 813 EL-8
Audubon, 6549 EO-11
Avalon, 4962 WM-3
Avella, 500 WN-1
Avis, 1472 EI-2
Avoca, 2712 EB-10
Avon, 2856 EN-7
Avondale, 1095 EQ-9
Avonia, 1331 WD-3
Avonmore, 789 WM-6
Baden, 4172 WL-3
Bainbridge, 900 EO-5
Bairdford, 800 WL-4
Bakerstown, 1000 WL-4
Baldwin, 18842 *L-6
Bally, 1102 EN-10
Bangor, 5305 EK-12
Baresville, 800 EQ-4
Bareville, 1250 EO-8
Bath, 2768 EL-11
Bausman, 300 ET-8
BEAVER CO., 177377 WL-2
Beaver, 4550 WL-2
Beaverdale, 800 WN-9
Beaver Falls, 9402 WK-2
Beaver Meadows, 963 EJ-9
Beaver Sprs., 634 EL-3
Beavertown, 882 EL-3
Bechtelsville, 975 EN-10
BEDFORD CO., 50091 WO-10
Bedford, 3051 WP-10
Beech Cr., 704 EJ-1
Belfast, 1301 EK-12
Bell Acres, 1384 WL-3
Bellefonte, 6161 WK-14
Belle Vernon, 1163 WO-4
Belleville, 1386 WL-14
Bellevue, 8231 WM-3
Bellwood, 1916 WL-11
Belmont, 2846 WT-2
Ben Avon, 1800 *I-4
Bensalem, 58745 *A-8
Bentleyville, 2448 WO-3
Benton, 923 EI-7
BERKS CO., 396314 EM-8
Berlin, 2130 WP-8
Bernville, 881 EM-8
Berwick, 10352 EJ-7
Berwyn, 3000 EP-11
Bessemer, 1126 WJ-1
Bethel Park, 32313 WN-3
Bethlehem, 72895 EL-11
Big Beaver, 2168 WK-2
Biglerville, 1152 EP-3
Birdsboro, 5191 EN-9
Bishop, 800 WN-3
Black Lick, 1438 WM-7
Blaine Hill, 1100 WN-4
BLAIR CO., 126795 WN-11
Blairsville, 3460 WM-7
Blakely, 6817 EG-10
Blanchard, 621 EJ-1
Blandburg, 550 WL-11
Blandon, 1200 EM-9
Blawnox, 1480 *I-8
Bloomingdale, 2100 ES-9
Bloomsburg, 12915 EJ-6
Blossburg, 1477 EF-3
Blue Ball, 800 EO-8
Blue Bell, 6395 EO-12
Blue Ridge Summit, 1500 ER-2
Boalsburg, 3578 WK-14
Bobtown, 1100 WQ-3
Boiling Sprs., 2769 EO-3
Bonneauville, 1457 EQ-3
Boston, 1300 *N-9
Boswell, 1290 WO-8
Bovard, 700 WN-6
Bowmanstown, 898 EK-10
Boyertown, 3946 EN-10
Brackenridge, 3322 WL-5
Braddock, 2744 *K-8
Braddock Hills, 1879 *K-8
Bradenville, 1300 WN-6
Bradford, 8651 WD-10
BRADFORD CO., 62537 EE-6
Branch Dale, 436 EL-7
Brentwood, 9811 WN-4
Bridgeport, 4402 EO-11
Bridgeville, 5022 WN-3
Bridgewater, 859 WL-2
Bristol, 9810 EO-13
Brockway, 2101 WI-9
Brodheadsville, 1637 EJ-11
Brookhaven, 7849 EQ-11
Brookside, 2200 WC-4
Brookville, 4077 WI-8
Broomall, 11046 EP-11
Broughton, 3000 *M-6
Brownstown, 1000 EO-7
Brownstown, 834 WN-8
Brownsville, 2690 WP-4
Browntown, 900 EB-9
Bryn Athyn, 1354 EO-13
Buck Hill Falls, 950 EI-11
Buckingham, 2000 EN-13
BUCKS CO., 621342 EM-12
Burgettstown, 1521 WN-2
Burnham, 2065 EL-1
Bushkill, 1200 EI-13
Butler, 14521 WK-4
BUTLER CO., 182087 WJ-4
Butztown, 1500 EA-5
Cairnbrook, 1000 WO-9
California, 5072 WO-4
Caln, 850 EP-9
CAMBRIA CO., 148073 WM-10
Cambridge Sprs., 2282 WE-3
CAMERON CO., 5639 WG-11
Campbelltown, 2415 EN-6
Camp Hill, 7424 EO-4
Canadensis, 1200 EI-12
Canadohta Lake, 572 WE-5
Canonsburg, 8810 WN-3
Canton, 1745 EF-4
CARBON CO., 61959 EJ-9
Carbondale, 9348 EG-10
Carlisle, 18108 EO-3
Carnegie, 8149 *K-4
Carnot, 4500 WM-3
Carrolltown, 996 WL-9
Carroll Valley, 3505 EQ-2
Castanea, 1189 EI-2
Castle Shannon, 8269 WN-3
Catasauqua, 6553 EL-11
Catawissa, 1557 EJ-6
Cecil, 900 WN-3
Cementon, 1100 EL-10
Cen. Square, 700 EO-12
Cen. Valley, 900 EM-11
Centerville, 1700 ES-7
Centerville, 3294 WP-4
Central City, 1195 WO-9
CENTRE CO., 140561 WJ-13
Centre Hall, 1080 WK-14
Cetronia, 1000 EB-2
Chadds Ford, 1200 EQ-10
Chalfant, 814 *K-8
Chalfont, 4198 EN-12
Chalkhill, 400 WQ-5
Chambersburg, 17961 WP-14
Charleroi, 4696 WO-4
Chatwood, 1000 EP-10
Cheltenham, 34923 *B-5
CHESTER CO., 474027 EP-9
Chester, 37058 EQ-11
Chester Hts., 2479 EQ-11
Chester Hill, 880 WK-12
Cheswick, 1790 *H-9
Chevy Chase Hts., 1511 WL-7
Chicora, 1004 WJ-5
Chinchilla, 1300 EA-13
Christiana, 1091 EP-8
Churchill, 3350 *J-8
Churchville, 4469 EO-13
Clairton, 8081 *N-8
Claridge, 1200 WN-5
CLARION CO., 40589 WI-6
Clarion, 5507 WI-6
Clarks Green, 1572 EA-13
Clarks Summit, 5010 EG-10
Claysburg, 1503 WN-10
Claysville, 695 WO-2
CLEARFIELD CO., 82783 WJ-11
Clearfield, 6339 WJ-11
Cleona, 2107 EN-6
Clifton Hts., 6626 *E-2
CLINTON CO., 37439 EI-1
Clymer, 1467 WL-8
Coaltown, 1200 WJ-2
Coatesville, 11495 EP-9
Cochranton, 1092 WG-3
Cokeburg, 679 WO-3
Collegeville, 5055 EO-11
Collingdale, 8501 *F-2
Colmar, 800 EN-12
Colonial Park, 13259 EN-5
COLUMBIA CO., 64939 EJ-6
Columbia, 10092 EP-6
Columbus, 1200 WD-6
Colver, 1035 WM-9
Colwyn, 2394 *F-3
Conewago Heights, 900 EO-5
Confluence, 793 WQ-6
Conneaut Lake, 676 WF-2
Conneautville, 807 WE-2
Connellsville, 8644 WP-5
Conshohocken, 7711 EO-11
Conway, 2191 WL-2
Conyngham, 1865 EJ-8
Coopersburg, 2570 EM-11
Coplay, 3371 EL-10
Coral, 400 WM-7
Coraopolis, 5754 WM-3
Cornwall, 3447 EN-6
Corry, 6548 WE-5
Coudersport, 2551 WE-12
Courtdale, 754 EA-8
Crabtree, 320 WN-6
Crafton, 6289 WM-3
CRAWFORD CO., 89442 WF-3
Creighton, 1500 WL-5
Cresson, 1538 WM-10
Cressona, 1563 EL-7
Crucible, 600 WP-4
Cuddy, 1200 WN-3
CUMBERLAND CO., 223089 EO-2
Curtisville, 1173 WL-4
Curwensville, 2540 WJ-10
Daisytown, 1100 WP-4
Dale, 1416 WN-8
Dallas, 2508 EH-8
Dallastown, 4080 EQ-5
Dalton, 1233 EG-9
Danboro, 500 EN-12
Danielsville, 750 EK-10
Danville, 4640 EJ-5
Darby, 10046 EP-12
DAUPHIN CO., 253995 EM-5
Dauphin, 725 EN-4
Davidsville, 1119 WO-8
Dawson Ridge, 1200 WL-2
Deemston, 791 WP-3
DELAWARE CO., 555648 EP-11
Delaware Water Gap, 822 EJ-12
Delmont, 2498 WM-5
Delta, 725 ER-7
Denver, 3646 EO-8
Derrick City, 1000 WD-10
Derry, 2869 WN-7
Devon, 2000 EP-11
Dickerson Run, 400 WP-5
Dickson City, 5967 EG-10
Dillsburg, 2321 EO-4
Dingmans Ferry, 1000 EI-13
Distant, 750 WJ-6
Dixonville, 600 WL-8
Donora, 5420 WO-4
Dormont, 8696 WN-3
Dorneyville, 1450 EC-2
Douglassville, 1200 EN-10
Dover, 1922 EP-4
Downingtown, 7858 EP-10
Doylestown, 8225 EN-12
Dravosburg, 1888 *M-7
Drifton, 800 EJ-9
Dry Tavern, 500 WP-3
Dublin, 2183 EN-12
Du Bois, 7838 WI-9
Duboistown, 1233 EI-4
Duke Cen., 850 WD-10
Dunbar, 1172 WP-5
Duncannon, 1496 EN-4
Duncansville, 1194 WM-11
Dunlo, 750 WN-9
Dunmore, 13968 EC-13
Dunnstown, 1365 EI-2
Dupont, 2626 EB-10
Duquesne, 6875 WN-4
Duryea, 4414 EH-9
Dushore, 613 EG-6
Eagleville, 4458 EO-11
E. Bangor, 995 EK-12
E. Berlin, 1430 EP-4
E. Berwick, 1998 EJ-7
E. Brady, 1007 WJ-5
E. Butler, 658 WK-4
E. Conemaugh, 1214 WN-9
E. Faxon, 3000 EI-4
E. Greenville, 3085 EM-11
E. Lansdowne, 2517 *E-2
E. McKeesport, 2204 *L-9
Easton, 26267 EL-12
E. Petersburg, 4346 EO-7
E. Pittsburgh, 1897 *L-8
E. Springfield, 400 WD-2
E. Stroudsburg, 10621 EJ-12
E. Uniontown, 2760 WP-5
E. Vandergrift, 706 WL-5
E. Washington, 1912 WO-2
E. York, 8782 WS-10
Ebensburg, 2938 WM-9
Economy, 9291 WL-3
Eddystone, 2381 EQ-11
Edgemont, 900 ES-3
Edgewood, 2619 EK-6
Edgewood, 3098 *K-8
Edgeworth, 1623 WM-3
Edinboro, 6737 WE-3
Edwardsville, 4741 EH-9
Effort, 1000 EJ-11
Egypt, 1300 EA-2
Eighty Four, 800 WO-3
Eldred, 824 WD-11
Elizabeth, 1505 WN-4
Elizabethtown, 11892 EO-6
Elizabethville, 1295 EM-5
ELK CO., 33577 WG-10
Elkland, 1722 ED-2
Ellport, 1132 WK-2
Ellsworth, 1039 WO-3
Ellwood City, 8262 WK-2
Elmhurst, 834 EH-10
Elrama, 600 WN-4
Elysburg, 2067 EK-6
Emigsville, 2467 EP-5
Emlenton, 756 WI-5
Emmaus, 11351 EM-11
Emporium, 2362 WG-11
Emsworth, 2442 WM-3
Enhaut, 950 ET-4
Enola, 5627 EN-4
Ephrata, 13092 EO-7
ERIE CO., 280446 WD-4
Erie, 102612 WC-3
Espy, 1428 EJ-6
Estherton, 1200 ES-3
Etna, 3671 WM-4
Evansburg, 1536 EO-11
Evans City, 1957 WK-3
Everett, 1888 WP-11
Everson, 806 WO-5
Exeter, 6007 EB-9
Export, 856 WM-5
Exton, 4267 EP-10
Factoryville, 1197 EG-9
Fairchance, 2097 WQ-5
Fairdale, 1955 WQ-4
Fairfield, 511 EQ-2
Fairfield, 1100 WC-4
Fairhope, 1800 WO-4
Fairview, 1988 WD-3
Falling Spring, 200 EQ-1
Falls Cr., 945 WI-9
Farmington, 250 WQ-5
Farmington, 800 EB-4
Farrell, 5999 WI-1
Faxon, 1500 EI-4
FAYETTE CO., 146142 WP-5
Fayette City, 684 WO-4
Fayetteville, 2774 EP-1
Fellsburg, 1000 WO-4
Ferndale, 1724 WN-8
Fernway, 12188 WL-3
Fleetwood, 4006 EM-9
Flemington, 1269 EI-2
Fogelsville, 950 EL-10
Folcroft, 6906 *F-2
Ford City, 3258 WK-6
FOREST CO., 5739 WG-7
Forest City, 1795 EF-11
Forest Gr., 2600 *I-3
Forest Hills, 6424 *K-8
Ft. Loudon, 1200 WP-13
Ft. Washington, 3680 EO-12
Forty Ft., 4331 EH-9
Foster Brook, 800 WD-10
Fountain Hill, 4595 EL-11
Fox Chapel, 5238 *I-8
Frackville, 4199 EK-7
Franklin, 6879 WH-4
FRANKLIN CO., 137409 WP-13
Franklin Park, 11765 WL-3
Frazer, 2000 EP-10
Fredericksburg, 1140 WF-3
Fredericksburg, 987 EM-6
Fredericktown, 200 WP-3
Freedom, 1665 WL-2
Freeland, 3455 EJ-9
Freeport, 1854 WL-5
Friedens, 1673 WP-8
Frisco, 850 WK-2
FULTON CO., 14673 WP-12
Gabby Hts., 1200 WO-2
Galeton, 1301 WF-14
Gallitzin, 1666 WM-10
Gap, 1611 EP-8
Garden View, 2679 EI-4
Gastonville, 3002 WN-4
Geistown, 2443 WN-9
Gettysburg, 8014 EQ-3
Ghennes Hts., 900 WO-4
Gibsonia, 3500 WL-4
Gilberton, 838 EK-7
Gilbertsville, 4242 EN-10
Girard, 3017 WD-2
Girardville, 1674 EK-7
Glassport, 4675 WN-4
Glenburn, 1212 EG-9
Glen Lyon, 1881 EI-8
Glen Moore, 1000 ES-9
Glenmoore, 900 EO-9
Glenolden, 7309 *F-2
Glen Rock, 1853 EQ-5
Glenwood, 3000 ES-3
Gordon, 753 EL-7
Grassflat, 700 WJ-12
Graterford, 900 EO-11
Great Bend, 686 ED-9
Greeley, 1000 EG-13
Greenawalds, 1200 EA-2
Greencastle, 3838 WQ-14
GREENE CO., 39808 WQ-2
Greenock, 2400 *N-9
Greensburg, 15569 WN-6
Greentown, 1000 EH-11
Green Tree, 1350 EP-11
Green Tree, 4453 *K-5
Greenville, 6355 WG-2
Greenwood, 1600 WM-11
Grill, 750 ET-12
Grindstone, 600 WP-4
Grove City, 7764 WI-3
Halifax, 844 EM-4
Hallam, 2513 EP-6
Hallstead, 1168 ED-9
Hamburg, 4183 EM-8
Hamilton Park, 3500 ET-8
Hamlin, 1100 EH-11
Hanover, 14990 EQ-4
Hanover, 800 EA-4
Harborcreek, 1500 WC-4
Harleysville, 8795 EN-11
Harmarville, 1100 *H-8
Harmony, 902 WK-3
Harrisburg, 47472 EN-4
Harrison City, 155 WN-5
Harrisville, 908 WI-4
Harveys Lake, 2868 EH-8
Harwick, 1100 *H-9
Hastings, 1336 WL-9
Hatboro, 7288 EO-12
Hatfield, 2872 EN-11
Hawk Run, 900 WJ-12
Hawley, 1292 EG-12
Hayti, 950 EP-9
Hazleton, 22125 EJ-8
Hecktown, 1200 EL-11
Hegins, 1200 EL-6
Heidelberg, 1174 WN-3
Heilwood, 786 WL-8
Hellertown, 5615 EL-11
Hereford, 850 EM-10
Herminie, 856 WN-5
Hermitage, 16571 WH-2
Hershey, 12771 EN-5
Hesston, 175 WM-12
Hibbs, 200 WP-4
Hickory, 850 WN-2
Highland Park, 1900 ET-2
Highland Park, 1446 EL-1
Highspire, 2625 EO-5
Hilldale, 600 EB-9
Hiller, 1234 WP-4
Hillsville, 600 WJ-1
Hilltown, 800 EN-12
Hokendauqua, 3411 EL-11
Holland, 5300 EO-13
Hollidaysburg, 5519 WM-11
Hollywood, 800 *B-5
Homer City, 1755 WM-7
Homestead, 3535 *K-7
Hometown, 1399 EK-8
Honesdale, 4849 EG-12
Honey Brook, 1388 EO-9
Hooversville, 732 WO-8
Hopwood, 2006 WQ-5
Horsham, 14779 EO-12
Hostetter, 460 WN-6
Houserville, 1809 WK-13
Houston, 1276 WN-3
Houtzdale, 902 WK-11
Howard, 665 WJ-14
Hudson, 1150 EB-8
Hughestown, 1469 EB-10
Hughesville, 2114 EI-5
Hulmeville, 874 EO-13
Hummelstown, 4402 EN-5
Hummels Wharf, 641 EK-4
HUNTINGDON CO., 45947 WN-12
Huntingdon, 6876 WM-12
Hyde, 1491 WJ-10
Hyde Park, 2200 ES-13
Hyndman, 978 WQ-9
Imperial, 2200 WM-2
INDIANA CO., 88703 WL-8
Indiana, 15016 WL-7
Indianola, 900 WM-4
Industry, 1845 WL-2
Ingram, 3478 *J-4
Inkerman, 735 EB-9
Intercourse, 1200 EP-8
Iona, 800 EN-7
Irwin, 4187 WN-5
Jacksonwald, 1100 ET-14
Jacobus, 1198 EQ-5
Jamestown, 604 WG-2
Jamison, 850 EN-12
Jeannette, 10196 WN-5
JEFFERSON CO., 45759 WH-8
Jefferson Hills, 9642 WN-4
Jenkintown, 4404 EO-12
Jenners, 250 WO-8
Jermyn, 2244 EG-10
Jerome, 1068 WO-8
Jersey Shore, 4426 EI-3
Jessup, 4579 EG-10
Jim Thorpe, 4892 EK-9
Johnsonburg, 2817 WG-10
Johnstown, 22539 WN-8
Jonestown, 1008 EN-6
JUNIATA CO., 23507 EM-2
Juniata Gap, 1100 WA-13
Kane, 3893 WF-9
Kelayres, 600 EK-8
Kenhorst, 2652 EN-9
Kenilworth, 1576 EO-10
Kennett Square, 5292 EQ-10
Kersey, 700 WH-10
King of Prussia, 18511 EO-11
Kingston, 13176 EH-9
Kissel Hill, 750 EO-7
Kittanning, 4454 WK-6
Knox, 1122 WI-6
Koppel, 808 WK-2
Korn Krest, 850 EA-6
Kulpmont, 2838 EK-6
Kulpsville, 8005 EN-11
Kutztown, 4926 EM-9
La Belle, 350 WP-4
Laboratory, 850 WO-3
LACKAWANNA CO., 209525 EG-9
Laflin, 1507 EB-9
Lake Ariel, 1250 EG-11
Lake City, 2981 WD-2
Lake Harmony, 850 EJ-10
Lamar, 900 EJ-1
Lampeter, 800 EP-7
Lancaster, 54757 EP-7
LANCASTER CO., 490562 EP-7
Landisville, 1400 EO-6
Langeloth, 1500 WN-2
Langhorne, 1974 EO-13
Lansdale, 15913 EN-12
Lansdowne, 10789 EP-12
Lansford, 4210 EK-9
Larimer, 750 WN-5

Larksville, 4519 EI-8
Latrobe, 8654 WN-6
Lattimer Mines, 600 EJ-8
Laughlintown, 950 WO-7
Laureldale, 3752 EN-9
Laurel Run, 701 EI-9
Laurys Sta., 1100 EL-10
Lavelle, 600 EK-7
LAWRENCE CO., 92809 WI-2
Lawrence, 1100 WN-3
Lawrence Park, 4048 WC-4
Leaders Hts., 1200 WT-10
LEBANON CO., 125578 EN-6
Lebanon, 23986 EN-6
Leechburg, 2269 WL-5
Lee Park, 3600 EI-9
Leesport, 1916 EM-8
Leetsdale, 1152 WL-3
LEHIGH CO., 330433 EL-10
Lehighton, 5523 EK-10
Leisenring, 600 WP-5
Leith, 900 WQ-5
Lemont, 2116 WK-13
Lemoyne, 3952 ET-3
Leola, 1100 EO-7
Level Green, 2500 WN-5
Levittown, 53966 EO-14
Lewisburg, 5562 EJ-4
Lewistown, 8649 EL-1
Liberty, 2509 *M-8
Library, 6000 WN-3
Light Street, 881 EJ-6
Ligonier, 1622 WN-7
Lilly, 895 WM-10
Limerick, 800 EO-10
Lime Ridge, 951 EJ-9
Lincoln, 1151 *N-8
Lincoln Hts., 300 WN-5
Lincoln Park, 1800 ET-11
Linesville, 1122 WF-2
Linglestown, 6414 EN-5
Linntown, 1542 EJ-4
Linwood, 3374 EQ-11
Listie, 700 WP-8
Lititz, 9008 EO-7
Littlestown, 4131 EQ-3
Liverpool, 884 EM-4
Llewellyn, 800 EL-7
Lock Haven, 8784 EI-2
Loganville, 1026 EQ-5
Long Pond, 900 EJ-11
Lorain, 705 WN-9
Lorane, 2994 EN-9
Loretto, 1166 WM-10
Lost Cr., 500 EK-7
Lower Burrell, 12444 WL-5
Lucernemines, 951 WM-7
Ludlow, 500 WF-8
Luxor, 750 WN-6
LUZERNE CO., 312861 EI-7
Luzerne, 2805 EH-9
LYCOMING CO., 118395 EH-3
Lykens, 1862 EM-5
Lyndon, 750 EP-7
Lyndora, 1300 WK-4
Lynnwood, 1300 EA-7
Lynnwood, 1200 WO-4
Macungie, 3111 EM-10
Madera, 1000 WK-11
Mahanoy City, 4462 EK-8
Mainland, 2000 EN-11
Malvern, 3100 EP-11
Manchester, 2436 EP-5
Manheim, 4659 EO-7
Manor, 2792 WN-5
Manor Ridge, 1000 ET-8
Mansfield, 3354 EE-3
Marcus Hook, 2266 EQ-11
Marienville, 1325 WG-8
Marietta, 2603 EP-6
Marion, 800 WQ-14
Marion Hts., 702 EK-6
Mars, 1707 WL-3
Marshallton, 1437 EK-6
Martinsburg, 2157 WN-11
Martins Cr., 1200 EK-12
Marysville, 2428 EN-4
Masontown, 3469 WQ-4
Matamoras, 2591 EH-14
Mather, 1000 WP-3
Mayfield, 1713 EG-10
Maytown, 2604 EO-6
McAdoo, 2140 EK-8
McAlisterville, 765 EL-3
McCandless, 29022 WL-3
McClure, 949 EL-2
McConnellsburg, 1044 WP-13
McDonald, 2181 WN-2
McGovern, 2538 WN-2
MCKEAN CO., 44370 WE-11
McKeesport, 22701 WN-4
McKees Rocks, 6201 WM-3
McMurray, 4726 WN-3
McSherrystown, 2804 EQ-4
Meadow Lands, 900 WO-2
Meadville, 13368 WF-3
Mechanicsburg, 8818 EO-4
Media, 5451 EP-11
MERCER CO., 119598 WH-2
Mercer, 2297 WI-3
Mercersburg, 1549 WQ-13
Meridian, 3794 WK-4
Merrittstown, 200 WP-4
Meyersdale, 2340 WQ-8
Middleburg, 1356 EK-4
Middletown, 8944 EO-5
Midland, 2969 WL-2
Midway, 946 WN-2
MIFFLIN CO., 46235 WM-14
Mifflinburg, 3578 EK-4
Mifflintown, 846 EM-2
Mifflinville, 1213 EJ-7
Milesburg, 1149 WJ-14
Milford, 1214 EH-14
Millcreek, 52666 WD-3
Millersburg, 2491 EM-4
Millersville, 7583 EP-7
Mill Hall, 1490 EI-2
Millheim, 736 EK-2
Mill Run, 400 WP-6
Millvale, 3772 WM-4
Millville, 957 EI-6
Milroy, 1386 EL-1
Milton, 6484 EJ-4
Minersville, 4337 EL-7
Mocanaqua, 1000 EI-8
Mohnton, 3071 EN-8
Mohrsville, 700 EM-8
Monaca, 5973 WL-2
Monessen, 8307 WO-4
Monongahela, 4562 WO-4
MONROE CO., 163234 EJ-11
Monroeville, 28175 WM-5
Mont Alto, 1760 EQ-1
Mont Clare, 1800 EO-11
MONTGOMERY CO., 775883 EN-11
Montgomery, 1619 EI-4
Montgomeryville, 12031 EN-12
MONTOUR CO., 18032 EJ-5
Montoursville, 4628 EI-4
Montrose, 1596 EE-9
Moon, 1000 WM-2
Moon Run, 400 WM-3
Moosic, 5738 EH-9
Morgan, 800 WN-3
Morgantown, 700 EO-9
Morrisdale, 600 WJ-12
Morrisville, 1443 WP-3
Morrisville, 9810 EO-14
Morton, 2665 *F-1
Moscow, 1916 EH-10
Mountainhome, 1169 EI-12
Mtn. Top, 15269 EI-9
Mt. Allen, 2000 EO-4
Mt. Carmel, 6053 EK-6
Mt. Cobb, 2140 EH-10
Mt. Holly Springs, 1911 EO-3
Mt. Jewett, 1026 WF-10
Mt. Joy, 6944 EO-6
Mt. Lebanon, 33017 *L-4
Mt. Morris, 1300 WQ-3
Mt. Oliver, 3772 *K-6
Mt. Penn, 2994 EN-9
Mt. Pleasant, 4531 WO-6
Mt. Pocono, 2997 EI-11
Mt. Union, 2392 WN-13
Mt. Vernon, 2200 *N-9
Mountville, 2746 EP-6
Mt. Wolf, 1345 EP-5
Muncy, 2533 EI-5
Munhall, 11513 WM-4
Murrysville, 19441 WM-5
Muse, 1000 WN-3
Myerstown, 3106 EN-7
Nanticoke, 10382 EI-8
Nanty-Glo, 2903 WM-9
Narberth, 4154 EP-12
Natrona Hts., 10934 WL-5
Nazareth, 6023 EL-11
Neffsville, 1000 EO-7
Nemacolin, 1034 WQ-4
Nescopeck, 1452 EJ-7
Nesquehoning, 3356 EK-9
New Beaver, 1637 WK-2
New Bedford, 800 WI-1
New Berlin, 830 EK-4
New Berlinville, 800 EN-10
New Bethlehem, 1007 WJ-7
New Bloomfield, 1091 EN-3
New Brighton, 6275 WK-2
New Britain, 2313 EN-12
New Castle, 25030 WJ-2
New Cumberland, 7127 EO-4
New Derry, 800 WN-7
New Eagle, 2276 WO-4
New Florence, 749 WN-8
New Freedom, 3889 ER-5
New Holland, 5140 EO-8
New Hope, 2276 EN-13
New Kensington, 14085 WM-5
Newmanstown, 1536 EN-7
New Milford, 845 EE-9
New Oxford, 1773 EQ-4
New Philadelphia, 1109 EL-8
Newport, 1467 EM-3
New Salem, 850 WP-4
New Sheffield, 2000 WL-2
New Stanton, 2055 WO-5
Newtown, 2256 EO-13
Newtown, 1400 EB-7
Newtown Square, 11300 EP-11
Newville, 1323 EO-2
New Wilmington, 2480 WI-2
Nicholson, 680 EF-9
Norristown, 30689 EO-11
NORTHAMPTON CO., 287767 EK-11
Northampton, 9699 EL-11
N. Apollo, 1355 WL-6
N. Belle Vernon, 2024 WO-4
N. Bend, 800 WH-14
N. Braddock, 5996 *K-8
N. Cambria, 4022 WL-9
N. Catasauqua, 2863 EA-3
N. Charleroi, 1354 WO-4
N. East, 4331 WC-5
NORTHUMBERLAND CO., 92610 EK-5
Northumberland, 3586 EK-5
N. Wales, 3229 EO-12
N. Warren, 2400 WE-7
N. Washington, 500 WM-5
N. Weissport, 900 EK-10
N. York, 1649 EP-5
Norvelt, 1100 WO-6
Norwood, 5852 *F-2
Nuangola, 651 EI-8
Nuremberg, 231 EJ-8
Oakdale, 1466 WM-3
Oakland, 1516 WM-2
Oakmont, 6587 WM-4
Oak Park, 700 EO-12
Oaks, 850 EO-11
Ohioville, 3686 WL-1
Oil City, 10942 WG-5
Oklahoma, 873 WL-5
Old Forge, 8558 EH-9
Oley, 900 EN-9
Oliver, 2925 WP-5
Olyphant, 4900 EG-10
Orchard Hills, 2152 WL-6
Orwigsburg, 2995 EL-8
Osceola Mills, 1188 WK-11
Oxford, 4682 EQ-9
Paint, 1060 WO-9
Palmer Hts., 3612 EL-12
Palmerton, 5279 EK-10
Palmyra, 6957 EN-6
Palo Alto, 1016 EL-7
Paoli, 5425 EP-11
Paradise, 1028 EP-8
Paris, 200 WM-1
Parker, 765 WI-5
Parker Ford, 800 EO-10
Parkesburg, 3445 EP-9
Parkhill, 300 WS-2
Parkside, 2212 EQ-11
Parkville, 6593 EQ-4
Patton, 1923 WL-10
Paxtang, 1505 EF-4
Paxtonia, 5254 EA-5
Pen Argyl, 3670 EK-12
Penbrook, 2926 ES-3
Penndel, 2397 EO-13
Penn Hills, 46809 WM-4
Pennsburg, 3371 EN-11
Penns Creek, 668 EK-4
Pennside, 3000 ET-13
Perkasie, 8736 EN-11
PERRY CO., 44728 EN-3
Perryopolis, 1748 WO-5
PHILADELPHIA CO., 1463281 EP-12
Philadelphia, 1463281 EP-12
Philipsburg, 2942 WK-12
Phoenixville, 15420 EO-10
PIKE CO., 56337 EH-13
Pilgrim Gardens, 1650 *E-1
Pine Gr., 2079 EM-7
Pine Gr. Mills, 1141 WL-13
Pineville, 950 EN-13
Pitcairn, 3449 *K-9
Pittsburgh, 316718 WM-4
Pittston, 7689 EB-10
Plains, 4694 EH-9
Pleasant Gap, 1611 WK-14
Pleasant Hills, 7940 WN-4
Pleasant Hills, 1650 ER-4
Pleasant Unity, 600 WN-6
Pleasantville, 1200 WR-10
Plum, 26452 WM-5
Plumsteadville, 1300 EN-12
Plymouth, 6161 EI-8
Plymouth Meeting, 6034 *A-2
Plymptonville, 1040 WJ-11
Pocono Pines, 1013 EI-11
Pocono Summit, 1500 EI-11
Polk, 1009 WH-4
Pomeroy, 750 EP-9
Portage, 2686 WN-10
Port Allegany, 2260 WE-11
Port Carbon, 1919 EL-8
Pt. Marion, 1276 WQ-4
Pt. Pleasant, 800 EM-12
Port Royal, 973 EM-2
Port Vue, 3965 WM-4
POTTER CO., 17834 WF-13
Pottstown, 21551 EN-10
Pottsville, 14764 EL-7
Primrose, 600 EL-7
Pringle, 947 EA-8
Progress, 9647 ES-3
Prospect, 1273 WJ-3
Prospect Park, 6449 EQ-11
Punxsutawney, 6036 WJ-8
Quakertown, 8823 EM-11
Quarryville, 2101 EQ-8
Rahns, 700 EO-11
Rankin, 2168 *K-8
Reading, 80855 EN-9
Reamstown, 3498 EO-8
Red Hill, 2357 EN-11
Red Lion, 6084 EQ-6
Reedsville, 858 EL-1
Rehrersburg, 600 EM-7
Reiffton, 2888 ET-13
Reightown, 350 WL-11
Renovo, 1243 WH-14
Republic, 1396 WP-4
Reynoldsville, 2609 WI-9
Rheems, 1557 EO-6
Richboro, 6678 EO-13
Richland, 1479 EN-7
Richlandtown, 1351 EM-11
Ridgeview, 800 ES-4
Ridgway, 4302 WH-9
Ridley Park, 7062 *G-1
Riegelsville, 847 EL-12
Rillton, 900 WN-5
Rimersburg, 1018 WJ-6
Ringtown, 783 EK-7
Riverside, 1820 EJ-5
Roaring Spr., 2309 WN-11
Robertsdale, 240 WO-12
Robesonia, 2059 EN-8
Robinson, 650 WN-7
Rochester, 3804 WL-2
Rockledge, 2537 *B-5
Rockwood, 933 WP-7
Rohrerstown, 1200 ES-8
Roscoe, 814 WO-4
Roseto, 1662 EK-12
Rose Valley, 928 EP-11
Rossiter, 790 WK-8
Rossmoyne, 1100 ET-2
Rothsville, 3017 EO-7
Roulette, 1000 WE-12
Rouzerville, 862 ER-1
Rowes Run, 400 WP-4
Royalton, 941 EO-5
Royersford, 4330 EO-10
Ruffs Dale, 800 WO-5
Rural Ridge, 1000 WL-4
Rural Valley, 874 WK-7
Russell, 1200 WD-8
Russellton, 1530 WL-4
Rutledge, 838 *F-1
Sadsburyville, 700 EP-9
Saegertown, 1057 WF-3
Sagamore, 450 WK-7
St. Clair, 3064 EL-7
St. Lawrence, 1800 EN-9
St. Marys, 13873 WG-10
St. Michael, 850 WN-9
St. Thomas, 900 WP-13
Salisbury, 829 WQ-8
Saltsburg, 907 WM-6
Salunga, 950 EO-6
Sanatoga, 7734 EN-10
Sand Hill, 2345 EN-6
Sandy, 1687 WI-9
Sandy Lake, 718 WH-3
Sankertown, 645 WM-10
Saxonburg, 1636 WK-4
Saxton, 772 WO-11
Saylorsburg, 500 EK-11
Sayre, 5606 ED-6
Scalp Level, 818 WN-9
Schaefferstown, 984 EN-7
Schnecksville, 1989 EL-10
School Lane Hills, 1840 ES-8
SCHUYLKILL CO., 147447 EL-7
Schuylkill Haven, 5283 EL-7
Schwenksville, 1360 EN-11
Sciota, 700 EJ-11
Scotland, 650 EP-1
Scotrun, 650 EJ-11
Scottdale, 4567 WO-5
Scranton, 73120 EH-10
Selinsgrove, 5417 EK-4
Sellersville, 4496 EN-11
Seneca, 966 WH-5
Sewickley, 3674 WM-3
Sewickley Heights, 940 *H-3
Shamokin, 7581 EK-6
Shamokin Dam, 1466 EK-5
Shanksville, 230 WP-8
Sharon, 15504 WH-1
Sharon Hill, 5357 *F-2
Sharpsburg, 3366 WM-4
Sharpsville, 4281 WH-2
Shavertown, 2000 EA-8
Sheffield, 1268 WF-8
Shenandoah, 5296 EK-7
Shenandoah Hts., 1298 EK-7
Shickshinny, 907 EI-8
Shillington, 5031 EN-8
Shiloh, 10192 EP-5
Shinglehouse, 1190 WD-12
Shippensburg, 5605 EP-1
Shiremanstown, 1480 EO-4
Shoemakersville, 2118 EM-8
Shrewsbury, 3525 EQ-5
Silverdale, 976 EN-12
Simpson, 1500 EF-10
Sinking Spr., 3443 EN-8
Skippack, 2889 EO-11
Slatedale, 600 EL-10
Slateford, 250 EJ-12
Slatington, 4413 EL-10
Slickville, 372 WM-6
Sligo, 701 WI-6
Slippery Rock, 3210 WJ-3
Slovan, 1100 WN-2
Smethport, 1617 WE-11
Smithfield, 822 WQ-4
Smithfield, 4181 WM-12
Smock, 600 WP-4
Snow Shoe, 778 WJ-13
SNYDER CO., 38207 EK-3
Somerset, 6500 WP-8
SOMERSET CO., 78907 WQ-7
Souderton, 6691 EN-11
S. Coatesville, 1062 EP-9
S. Connellsville, 2199 WP-5
S. Fork, 1070 WN-9
S. Greensburg, 2254 WN-6
S. Lakemont, 1100 WB-13
Southmont, 2146 WN-8
S. Mountain, 600 EQ-2
S. New Castle, 766 WJ-2
S. Pottstown, 2135 EO-10
S. Temple, 1400 ER-13
S. Uniontown, 3500 WQ-5
S. Waverly, 985 ED-6
Southwest Greensburg, 2284 WN-6
S. Williamsport, 6189 EI-4
Spears, 1199 WO-4
Spring City, 3284 EO-10
Springdale, 3597 WM-4
Springfield, 23677 *E-1
Spr. Garden, 11207 WT-10
Spr. Grove, 2212 EQ-4
Spr. House, 3290 EO-12
Springhouse Farms, 750 EB-2
Spr. Mount, 2205 EN-11
Springtown, 750 EM-12
Spry, 4903 WT-10
Stafore Estates, 1200 EA-4
Star Brick, 800 WE-7
Star Jct., 500 WO-5
State College, 38720 WK-13
State Line, 1100 WR-14
Steelton, 5667 EO-5
Stewartstown, 2009 EQ-6
Stewartsville, 700 *M-10
Stiles, 800 EA-2
Stoneboro, 1061 WH-3
Stonybrook, 1500 EP-5
Stony Cr. Mills, 2500 ET-13
Stowe, 3585 EN-10
Strabane, 1100 WN-3
Strafford, 4500 EP-11
Strasburg, 2745 EP-7
Strongstown, 400 WM-8
Stroudsburg, 6264 EJ-12
Sturgeon, 1000 WN-3
Sugarcreek, 5115 WG-4
Sugar Notch, 972 EI-9
SULLIVAN CO., 6391 EH-6
Summerdale, 800 ES-2
Summit Hill, 3010 EK-9
Sunbury, 10086 EK-5
Sunset Valley, 2700 *N-10
Susquehanna, 1628 EE-10
SUSQUEHANNA CO., 42124 EE-9
Sutersville, 607 WN-4
Swarthmore, 6146 *F-1
Swiftwater, 600 EJ-11
Swissvale, 9043 *K-8
Swoyersville, 4930 EH-9
Sykesville, 1199 WJ-9
Sylvan Hills, 1000 WB-13
Tamaqua, 6754 EK-8
Tannersville, 1200 EJ-11
Tarentum, 4677 WL-5
Tarrs, 600 WO-5
Tatamy, 1044 EL-12
Taylor, 6227 EH-9
Telford, 4633 EN-11
Temple, 1491 EN-9
Templeton, 400 WJ-6
Terre Hill, 1243 EO-8
Thorndale, 3561 EP-9
Throop, 3949 EB-13
Tidioute, 746 WF-6
TIOGA CO., 41649 EF-3
Tionesta, 592 WG-6
Tipton, 1225 WL-11
Tire Hill, 900 WN-8
Titusville, 5862 WF-5
Tobyhanna, 1200 EI-11
Topton, 1975 EM-10
Toughkenamon, 1375 EQ-9
Towanda, 3024 EF-6
Tower City, 1343 EM-6
Trafford, 3106 WN-5
Trainer, 1861 EQ-11
Trappe, 3422 EO-11
Tremont, 1725 EL-7
Tresckow, 964 EK-8
Trevorton, 2010 EK-5
Trexlertown, 1000 EM-10
Trooper, 6061 EO-11
Troy, 1485 EE-5
Trucksville, 1650 EA-8
Trumbauersville, 1071 EM-11
Tullytown, 2000 EO-14
Tunkhannock, 1825 EG-8
Turtle Cr., 5704 *K-9
Tuscarora, 939 EK-8
Tyrone, 5324 WL-11
UNION CO., 43131 EJ-3
Union City, 3364 WE-4
Union Deposit, 700 EN-5
Uniontown, 11935 WP-5
Unionville, 900 EQ-9
Upland, 2910 EQ-11
Upper Darby, 79620 EP-12
Upper St. Clair, 20053 WN-3
Valley Forge, 1500 EO-11
Valley View, 1677 EL-6
Vandergrift, 5190 WL-5
Vanport, 1375 WL-2
VENANGO CO., 55928 WG-4
Verona, 2931 WM-4
Versailles, 1615 WN-4
Vestaburg, 975 WP-4
Wall, 684 *K-9
Walmo, 900 WJ-2
Walnutport, 2136 EK-10
Warminster, 32980 EO-12
WARREN CO., 42033 WE-6
Warren, 9648 WE-7
Warrington, 7000 EN-12
WASHINGTON CO., 206406 WO-3
Washington, 15136 WO-2
Washington Crossing, 850 EN-13
Waterford, 1420 WD-4
Watsontown, 2148 EJ-4
Waverly, 1000 EG-10
Waymart, 1447 EG-11
WAYNE CO., 50113 EE-11
Wayne Hts., 1805 EQ-1
Waynesboro, 9700 EQ-1
Waynesburg, 4142 WP-3
Weatherly, 2621 EJ-9
Webster, 400 WO-4
Weedville, 950 WH-10
Weigelstown, 10117 WS-8
Wellsboro, 3342 EF-2
Wernersville, 2393 EN-8
Wescosville, 1250 EC-2
Wesleyville, 3443 WC-4
W. Brownsville, 1045 WP-4
W. Catasauqua, 700 EA-3
W. Chester, 18047 EP-10
W. Conshohocken, 1512 *B-1
W. Enola, 800 ES-2
W. Fairview, 1403 ES-2
Westfield, 1158 EE-1
Westgate Hills, 110 EL-11
W. Grove, 2640 EQ-9
W. Hazleton, 3375 EJ-8
W. Homestead, 2060 *K-7
W. Kittanning, 1580 WK-6
W. Lancaster, 800 ET-8
W. Lawn, 1578 EN-8
W. Leechburg, 1263 WL-5
W. Leisenring, 600 WP-5
W. Mayfield, 1153 WK-2
W. Middlesex, 884 WI-2
W. Mifflin, 21236 *L-8
W. Milton, 850 EJ-4
Westmont, 5234 WN-8
WESTMORELAND CO., 367635 WM-5
Westmoreland City, 1400 WN-5
W. Nanticoke, 1200 EI-8
W. Newton, 2948 WO-5
W. Pittsburg, 1100 WJ-2
W. Pittston, 4870 EH-9
W. Reading, 4005 ET-12
W. View, 6863 WM-3
W. Wyoming, 2722 EA-9
W. Wyomissing, 3016 ET-12
W. York, 4230 EP-5
Wexford, 1100 WL-3
Wheatland, 724 WI-1
Whitaker, 1255 *K-7
Whitehall, 14268 EL-11
Whitehall, 13744 *L-6
White Haven, 1153 EJ-9
White Oak, 8185 WN-4
Wiconisco, 1300 EM-5
Wilcox, 1000 WG-10
Wilkes-Barre, 41337 EI-9
Wilkinsburg, 18008 WM-4
Williamsburg, 1276 WM-12
Williamsport, 30112 EI-4
Williamstown, 1372 EM-5
Willow Grove, 16234 EO-12
Willow Street, 7258 EP-7
Wilmerding, 2011 *L-9
Wilson, 7753 EL-12
Winburne, 550 WJ-12
Windber, 4119 WO-9
Wind Gap, 2827 EK-11
Windsor, 1311 EP-6
Windsor Park, 1100 ET-1
Wolfdale, 2873 WO-2
Womelsdorf, 2766 EN-7
Woodland, 400 WJ-11
Woodland Park, 950 EH-14
Woodlawn, 1850 EL-10
Woodside, 100 EJ-9
Woolrich, 800 EI-2
Worcester, 900 EO-11
Wormleysburg, 2651 EN-4
Worthington, 741 WK-5
Wrightsville, 2255 EP-6
Wyalusing, 549 EF-7
Wyano, 750 WO-5
WYOMING CO., 28160 EG-7
Wyoming, 3053 EH-9
Wyomissing, 10434 EN-8
Yardley, 2542 EN-14
Yeadon, 11506 EP-12
Yeagertown, 1035 EL-1
Yoe, 1012 EP-5
York, 40418 EP-5
YORK CO., 408801 EP-5
York Haven, 797 EO-5
Yorkshire, 1700 WS-11
Youngsville, 1723 WE-7
Youngwood, 3171 WN-5
Yukon, 1200 WO-5
Zelienople, 4010 WK-3
Zieglerville, 900 EN-11
Zion, 2054 WK-14

Rhode Island

Map pp. 184-185

AAbbott Run Valley, 1800 B-7
Albion, 170 B-6
Allenton, 650 G-6
Anthony, 3400 E-5
Arnold Mills, 640 B-7
Ashaway, 1537 I-3
Ashton, 910 B-6
Barrington, 16819 E-7
Berkeley, 910 B-6
Block Island, 836 L-5
Bradford, 1497 I-3
Bristol, 22469 F-8
BRISTOL CO., 52743 E-8
Carolina, 880 H-4
Central Falls, 19159 C-7
Charlestown, 2000 I-4
Chepachet, 1100 C-4
Common Fence Pt., 900 F-8
Coventry, 8600 E-5
Cranston, 81614 D-6
Cumberland Hill, 7738 B-6
Davisville, 550 F-6
Diamond Hill, 910 B-6
E. Greenwich, 11865 F-6
E. Providence, 49515 D-7
Esmond, 5000 C-6
Forestdale, 550 B-5
Glendale, 860 B-4
Greenville, 8626 C-5
Harmony, 1050 C-5
Harris, 1250 E-5
Harrisville, 1561 B-4
Hope Valley, 1649 H-4
Island Park, 1550 F-8
Jamestown, 4999 H-7
Johnston, 29163 D-6
KENT CO., 171590 F-4
Kingston, 5446 H-5
Lonsdale, 4200 C-7
Manville, 3200 B-6
Mapleville, 1600 B-4
Matunuck, 580 I-5
Middletown, 3800 G-8
Mt.View, 700 F-6
Narragansett, 3671 I-6
NEWPORT CO., 83740 G-8
Newport, 25340 H-7
N. Kingstown, 3000 G-6
N. Providence, 32411 C-6
Oakland, 600 B-4
Pascoag, 4742 B-4
Pawtucket, 73742 C-7
Peacedale, 3400 H-6
Portsmouth, 4200 F-8
PROVIDENCE CO., 639653 C-4
Providence, 176862 D-7
Quidnessett, 2000 F-6
Quidnick, 2700 E-5
Quonochontaug, 2000 J-4
Saylesville, 3800 C-6
Shannock, 1100 H-4
Slatersville, 2400 A-5
S. Hopkinton, 500 I-3
Tiverton, 7282 F-8
Union Vil., 2300 B-5
Valley Falls, 11599 C-7
Wakefield, 300 H-6
Warren, 11385 E-8
Warwick, 87233 E-7
WASHINGTON CO., 128463 G-5
Watch Hill, 580 J-2
Westerly, 17682 I-3
W. Kingston, 1400 H-5
W. Warwick, 29581 E-5
Woonsocket, 44328 A-6
Wyoming, 1100 H-4

South Carolina

Map pp. 186-187

ABBEVILLE CO., 26133 D-4
Abbeville, 5732 D-4
Aiken, 27490 F-6
AIKEN CO., 150181 E-6
Alcolu, 600 E-9
Allendale, 3897 G-7
ALLENDALE CO., 10917 H-7
ANDERSON CO., 175514 C-3
Anderson, 25899 C-3
Andrews, 3110 F-11
Arcadia, 2000 G-1
Arcadia Lakes, 833 I-3
Arial, 2607 B-3
Arkwright, 680 G-2
Bamberg, 3552 F-7
BAMBERG CO., 15880 G-8
BARNWELL CO., 23345 G-6
Barnwell, 4874 G-7
Batesburg-Leesville, 5575 E-6
Beaufort, 12058 I-8
BEAUFORT CO., 137849 I-8
Beech Island, 1500 F-5
Belton, 4568 C-4
Bennettsville, 9351 C-11
Berea, 14158 I-4
BERKELEY CO., 151673 G-10
Bishopville, 3831 D-9
Blacksburg, 1898 A-6
Blackville, 2919 F-7
Bluffton, 2341 J-8
Boiling Springs, 4544 A-5
Bowling Green, 500 A-7
Bowman, 1179 F-8
Branchville, 1052 G-8
Brunson, 576 H-7
Bucksport, 1117 E-12
Buffalo, 1426 B-6
Burton, 7180 I-8
CALHOUN CO., 15100 E-8
Calhoun Falls, 2264 D-3
Camden, 7000 D-8
Capitol View, 4000 D-8
Cayce, 12432 J-2
Central, 4039 B-3
CHARLESTON CO., 330368 H-10
Charleston, 106712 H-10
Cheraw, 5474 B-10
CHEROKEE CO., 53844 A-6
Chesnee, 1022 A-5
Chester, 6199 B-7
CHESTER CO., 33228 C-7
Chesterfield, 1338 B-10
CHESTERFIELD CO., 43435 B-9
City View, 1254 I-4
CLARENDON CO., 33363 E-9
Clemson, 12364 B-3
Clinton, 9071 C-5
Clio, 752 C-11
Clover, 4251 A-7
COLLETON CO., 39605 H-9
Columbia, 117088 D-7
Conestee, 580 B-4
Converse, 1200 A-5
Conway, 13442 E-12
Cowpens, 2330 A-5
DARLINGTON CO., 67346 C-10
Darlington, 6525 C-10
Denmark, 3130 F-7
Denny Ter., 1750 D-7
Dentsville, 13049 H-3
DILLON CO., 30974 C-11
Dillon, 6366 C-11
DORCHESTER CO., 112858 G-9
Drayton, 1400 G-3
Due West, 1287 C-4
Duncan, 2977 B-5
Dunean, 4158 I-4
Easley, 18852 B-4
East Gaffney, 3349 A-6
Eastover, 779 E-8
EDGEFIELD CO., 25528 E-5
Edgefield, 4520 E-5
Elloree, 709 F-8
Enoree, 1100 B-5
Estill, 2394 H-7
Eureka Mill, 1737 B-7
Fairfax, 3178 G-7
FAIRFIELD CO., 24047 C-7
Fairforest, 800 G-1
Florence, 31269 D-10
FLORENCE CO., 131097 D-11
Folly Beach, 2263 H-10
Forest Acres, 9991 I-3
Forestbrook, 3391 J-12
Ft. Mill, 8257 A-8
Fountain Inn, 6729 B-5
Gaffney, 12934 A-6
Gantt, 13962 J-4
Gaston, 1389 E-7
GEORGETOWN CO., 60983 F-11
Georgetown, 8941 F-12
Glendale, 1000 B-5
Gloverville, 2805 F-6
Golden Grove, 2348 B-4
Goose Cr., 32516 G-10
Graniteville, 1100 F-5
Gray Court, 1005 C-5
Great Falls, 2095 C-8
Greenville, 56676 B-4
GREENVILLE CO., 407383 B-4
GREENWOOD CO., 67979 D-5
Greenwood, 22378 D-5
Greer, 21421 B-4
HAMPTON CO., 21329 H-7
Hampton, 2799 H-7
Hanahan, 13818 H-10
Hardeeville, 1843 I-7
Harleyville, 695 G-9
Hartsville, 7414 C-10
Heath Sprs., 860 C-8
Hemingway, 524 E-11
Hilton Head Island, 34497 J-8
Holly Hill, 1364 F-9
Hollywood, 4307 H-9
Honea Path, 3597 C-4
HORRY CO., 226992 D-12
Inman, 1918 A-5
Inman Mills, 1151 A-5
Irmo, 11223 D-7
Isle of Palms, 4579 H-10
Iva, 1180 C-3
Jackson, 1644 F-5
James Island, 4400 H-10
JASPER CO., 21398 I-7
Jefferson, 703 B-9
Joanna, 1609 C-5
Johnsonville, 1460 E-11
Johnston, 2352 E-5
Jonesville, 927 B-6
Judson, 2456 J-4
Kensington, 600 F-12
KERSHAW CO., 56486 C-9
Kershaw, 1631 C-8
Kingstree, 3363 E-10
Ladson, 13264 G-10
La France, 900 C-3
Lake City, 6690 E-10
Lake Forest, 1000 I-5
Lake View, 792 C-12
Lamar, 1003 D-10
LANCASTER CO., 63113 B-8
Lancaster, 8371 B-8
Lando, 300 B-7
Landrum, 2518 A-5
Lane, 544 F-10
Latta, 1462 C-11
Laurel Bay, 6625 I-8
LAURENS CO., 70293 C-5
Laurens, 9824 C-5
LEE CO., 20638 D-9
Lesslie, 2268 B-8
LEXINGTON CO., 235272 E-6
Lexington, 13586 D-7
Liberty, 3004 B-3
Livingston, 144 F-7
Loris, 2305 D-13
Lugoff, 6278 D-8
Lyman, 2765 B-5
Manning, 4025 E-9
Marietta, 1200 A-4
MARION CO., 34904 D-11
Marion, 6997 D-11
MARLBORO CO., 28021 C-10
Mauldin, 19343 B-4
Mayesville, 1042 D-9
McBee, 719 C-9
McColl, 2409 B-11
MCCORMICK CO., 10108 D-4
McCormick, 2657 E-4
Monarch Mills, 1930 B-6
Moncks Corner, 6525 G-10
Montmorenci, 900 F-6
Mt. Pleasant, 57932 H-10
Mullins, 4855 D-12
Murrells Inlet, 5519 F-12
Myrtle Beach, 26593 E-13
Newberry, 10659 D-6
NEWBERRY CO., 37250 D-5
New Ellenton, 2259 F-6
Nichols, 405 D-12
Ninety Six, 1922 D-5
Norris, 841 B-3
North, 788 F-7
N. Augusta, 19467 F-5
N. Charleston, 86313 H-10
N. Myrtle Beach, 14096 E-13
Oak Grove, 8183 E-7
OCONEE CO., 69577 B-2
Olanta, 628 E-10
Orangeburg, 14460 F-8
ORANGEBURG CO., 92167 F-8
Pacolet, 2727 B-6
Pacolet Mills B-6
Pageland, 2544 B-9
Pamplico, 1158 D-11
Paris, 1950 B-4
Park Place, 1500 I-4
Pendleton, 3050 B-3
PICKENS CO., 113575 B-3
Pickens, 2974 B-3
Piedmont, 4684 B-4
Pinewood, 501 E-9
Port Royal, 9347 I-8
Prosperity, 1098 D-6
Quinby, 867 D-11
Ravenel, 2306 H-9
Reidville, 502 B-5
RICHLAND CO., 340078 E-8
Ridgeland, 2618 I-7
Ridge Spr., 797 E-6
Ridgeville, 1960 G-9
Riverside, 2350 I-4
Rock Hill, 59554 B-7
Roebuck, 1725 B-5
St. Andrews, 10000 B-12
St. Andrews, 21814 H-1
St. George, 2119 G-8
St. Matthews, 2025 E-8
St. Stephen, 1740 F-10
Saluda, 2969 D-6
SALUDA CO., 18895 D-6
Sans Souci, 7836 I-4
Scranton, 999 E-11
Seneca, 7962 B-3
Shannontown, 1500 E-9
Simpsonville, 15135 B-4
Socastee, 14295 E-12
Society Hill, 697 C-10
S. Congaree, 2334 E-7
Spartanburg, 38379 B-5
SPARTANBURG CO., 266809 B-5
Springdale, 2918 E-7
Springfield, 490 F-7
Sullivans Island, 1897 H-10
Summerton, 1053 F-9
Summerville, 37714 G-9
SUMTER CO., 105517 E-9
Sumter, 39679 E-9
Surfside Beach, 4772 E-12
Swansea, 686 E-7
Taylors, 20125 B-4
Tega Cay, 4372 A-7
Timmonsville, 2385 D-10
Travelers Rest, 4237 A-4
Turbeville, 724 E-10
Union, 8321 B-6
UNION CO., 28539 B-6
Utica, 1322 B-3
Varnville, 2048 H-7
Wagener, 872 F-7
Walhalla, 3727 B-2
Walterboro, 5548 H-8
Ware Shoals, 2377 C-4
Warrenville, 1000 F-5
Watts Mills, 1479 C-5
Welcome, 6390 J-4
Wellford, 2282 B-5
W. Columbia, 13413 J-2
Westminster, 2669 B-2
W. Pelzer, 899 B-4
Westview, 2000 G-1
Westville, 2200 I-4
Whitehall, 3600 D-7
Whitmire, 1526 C-6
Whitney, 1500 F-2
WILLIAMSBURG CO., 35395 E-11
Williamston, 3878 C-4
Williston, 3260 F-6
Winnsboro, 3612 C-7
Winnsboro Mills, 2263 C-7
Woodruff, 4105 B-5
Yemassee, 839 H-8
York, 7233 A-7
YORK CO., 190097 B-7

South Dakota

Map pp. 188-189

Aberdeen, 24098 B-10
Alcester, 889 G-13
Alexandria, 676 F-11
Alpena, 247 E-10
Arlington, 952 D-12
Armour, 736 F-10
Aurora, 458 D-13
AURORA CO., 2901 F-10
Avon, 543 G-11
Baltic, 932 E-13
BEADLE CO., 15896 D-10
Belle Fourche, 4675 D-2
BENNETT CO., 3585 G-5
Beresford, 2027 G-13
Big Stone City, 570 B-13
Bison, 342 B-4
Black Hawk, 2432 E-3
Blunt, 360 D-8
Bonesteel, 270 G-9
BON HOMME CO., 7087 G-11
Bowdle, 523 B-8
Box Elder, 2992 E-3
Brandon, 7176 F-13
Bridgewater, 592 F-11
Bristol, 341 B-11
Britton, 1282 A-11
Brookings, 18715 D-12
BROOKINGS CO., 28121 D-13
BROWN CO., 34706 B-10
Bruce, 255 D-12
BRULE CO., 5187 F-9
Bryant, 392 D-11
Buffalo, 341 B-3
BUFFALO CO., 2100 E-9
Burke, 606 G-9
BUTTE CO., 9326 C-3
CAMPBELL CO., 1565 A-8
Canistota, 700 F-12
Canton, 3165 F-13
Castlewood, 681 C-12
Centerville, 864 G-12
Chamberlain, 2259 E-9
Chancellor, 315 F-12
CHARLES MIX CO., 9194 F-10
Cherry Cr., 300 D-5
Clark, 1186 C-11
CLARK CO., 3799 C-11
CLAY CO., 12995 G-12
Clear Lake, 1243 C-13
CODINGTON CO., 26010 C-12
Colman, 559 E-12
Colome, 312 G-8
Colton, 658 E-12
Corsica, 625 F-10
CORSON CO., 4366 A-6
Crooks, 1077 F-12
Custer, 1991 E-2
CUSTER CO., 7904 F-3
DAVISON CO., 18777 F-11
DAY CO., 5757 B-12
Deadwood, 1296 D-2
Dell Rapids, 3188 E-13
Delmont, 244 G-10
De Smet, 1089 D-11
DEUEL CO., 4296 C-13
DEWEY CO., 6161 C-6
Doland, 270 C-10
DOUGLAS CO., 3309 F-10
Dupree, 450 C-5
Eagle Butte, 1817 C-6
Edgemont, 823 F-2
EDMUNDS CO., 4112 B-9
Elk Pt., 1836 H-13
Elkton, 619 D-13
Emery, 526 F-11
Estelline, 687 D-12
Ethan, 318 F-11
Eureka, 988 A-8
Faith, 474 C-5
FALL RIVER CO., 7355 G-3
FAULK CO., 2386 C-9
Faulkton, 703 C-9
Flandreau, 2327 E-13
Ft. Pierre, 2069 D-7
Ft. Thompson, 1375 E-9
Frederick, 243 A-10
Freeman, 1223 F-12
Garretson, 1152 E-13
Gary, 212 C-13
Gayville, 393 G-12
Geddes, 245 G-10
Gettysburg, 1169 C-8
GRANT CO., 7384 C-12
GREGORY CO., 4290 F-9
Gregory, 1186 G-9
Groton, 1365 B-10
HAAKON CO., 1912 D-6
HAMLIN CO., 5707 C-12
HAND CO., 3307 D-9
HANSON CO., 3747 E-11
HARDING CO., 1218 B-3
Harrisburg, 1875 F-13
Hartford, 2065 F-12
Hayti, 362 D-12
Hecla, 299 A-10
Hermosa, 335 E-3
Herreid, 415 A-8
Highmore, 808 D-9
Hill City, 846 E-2
Hosmer, 261 B-8
Hot Sprs., 4102 F-2
Hoven, 436 B-8
Howard, 945 E-11
Hudson, 391 G-13
HUGHES CO., 16875 D-8
Humboldt, 549 F-12
Hurley, 399 F-12
Huron, 11086 D-10
HUTCHINSON CO., 7581 F-11
HYDE CO., 1614 D-9
Ipswich, 887 B-9
Irene, 410 G-12
Iroquois, 258 D-11
Isabel, 237 B-6
JACKSON CO., 2858 F-5
Jefferson, 590 H-13
JERAULD CO., 2136 E-10
JONES CO., 1033 E-7
Kadoka, 668 E-5
Kennebec, 284 E-8
Keystone, 319 E-3
Kimball, 693 F-9
KINGSBURY CO., 5532 D-11
LAKE CO., 11039 E-12
Lake Andes, 783 G-10
Lake Norden, 433 D-12
Lake Preston, 677 D-12
Langford, 283 B-11
LAWRENCE CO., 22395 D-2
Lead, 2891 D-2
Lemmon, 1229 A-5
Lennox, 2092 F-12
Leola, 411 A-9
LINCOLN CO., 33381 G-13
Little Eagle, 370 B-7
Lower Brule, 599 E-8
LYMAN CO., 3919 E-8
Madison, 6223 E-12
Marion, 833 F-12
MARSHALL CO., 4418 A-11
Martin, 1048 G-5
MCCOOK CO., 5930 E-12
McIntosh, 217 A-6
McLaughlin, 772 A-7
MCPHERSON CO., 2617 A-9
MEADE CO., 24623 D-4
MELLETTE CO., 2088 F-7
Menno, 697 G-11
Midland, 158 E-6
Milbank, 3357 B-13
Miller, 1364 D-9
MINER CO., 2584 E-11
MINNEHAHA CO., 160087 E-12
Mission, 949 F-7
Mitchell, 14696 F-11
Mobridge, 3279 B-7
Montrose, 476 F-12
MOODY CO., 6637 E-13
Mt. Vernon, 461 F-10
Murdo, 535 E-7
Newell, 621 C-3
New Underwood, 653 E-3
N. Sioux City, 2494 H-13
Oacoma, 408 E-9
Onida, 665 D-8
Parker, 1001 F-12
Parkston, 1560 F-11
Parmelee, 650 F-6
PENNINGTON CO., 93580 E-4
PERKINS CO., 3023 B-4
Philip, 756 E-5
Piedmont, 350 D-3
Pierre, 14052 D-7
Pine Ridge, 3171 G-4
Plankinton, 567 F-10
Platte, 1318 F-9
Pollock, 289 A-7
POTTER CO., 2351 C-8
Presho, 628 E-8
Pringle, 121 F-2
Pukwana, 281 E-9
Rapid City, 62167 E-3
Redfield, 2318 C-10
ROBERTS CO., 10044 B-12
Roscoe, 297 B-9
Rosebud, 1557 G-6
Rosholt, 439 A-12
Roslyn, 204 B-11
St. Francis, 736 G-6
St. Lawrence, 182 D-9
Salem, 1393 F-12
SANBORN CO., 2541 E-11
Scotland, 830 G-11
Selby, 690 B-8
SHANNON CO., 13657 F-4
Sioux Falls, 139517 F-13
Sisseton, 2540 A-12
S. Shore, 260 C-12
Spearfish, 9355 D-2
Spencer, 157 F-11
SPINK CO., 6899 C-10
Springfield, 1522 G-11
STANLEY CO., 2829 D-7
Stickney, 308 F-10
Sturgis, 6260 D-2
SULLY CO., 1430 C-8
Summit, 273 B-12
Tabor, 384 G-11
Tea, 2455 F-12
Timber Lake, 441 B-6
TODD CO., 9882 G-7
Tripp, 666 G-11
TRIPP CO., 6065 G-8
Tulare, 202 C-10
TURNER CO., 8520 F-12
Tyndall, 1155 G-11
UNION CO., 13462 G-13
Valley Sprs., 809 F-13
Veblen, 263 A-12
Vermillion, 9964 G-12
Viborg, 799 G-12
Volga, 1442 D-12
Wagner, 1601 G-10
Wakonda, 345 G-12
Wakpala, 200 B-7
Wall, 808 E-4
WALWORTH CO., 5494 B-8
Wanblee, 641 F-5
Warner, 430 B-10
Watertown, 20265 C-12
Waubay, 607 B-12
Webster, 1751 B-11
Wessington, 228 D-10
Wessington Sprs., 926 E-10
White, 499 D-13
White Lake, 389 F-10
White River, 586 F-7
Whitewood, 826 D-2
Willow Lake, 266 D-11
Wilmot, 531 B-12
Winner, 2917 F-8
Wolsey, 388 D-10
Woonsocket, 676 E-10
Worthing, 745 F-13
Yankton, 13716 G-12
YANKTON CO., 21718 G-12
ZIEBACH CO., 2631 C-6

Tennessee

Map pp. 190-193

* City keyed to p. 195

Adams, 588 B-10
Adamsville, 2062 F-6
Alamo, 2380 D-4
Alcoa, 8388 D-19
Alexandria, 860 C-13
Algood, 3188 C-15
Allardt, 657 B-16
Altamont, 1166 F-14
ANDERSON CO., 72430 C-18
Apison, 500 G-16
Ardmore, 1116 G-11
Arlington, 3534 F-2
Asbury, 300 *J-8
Ashland City, 4550 C-10
Ashwood, 500 E-10
Athens, 13878 F-17
Atoka, 5676 E-2
Atwood, 982 D-5
Bartlett, 43263 F-2
Baxter, 1333 C-14
Bean Sta., 2773 K-16
BEDFORD CO., 42204 E-12
Beersheba Sprs., 561 F-14
Belle Meade, 3100 C-7
Bells, 2307 E-4
BENTON CO., 16467 C-7
Benton, 1103 G-17
Berry Hill, 684 I-8
Berrys Chapel, 3000 D-11
Bethel Sprs., 771 F-6
Bethpage, 2266 B-12
Big Sandy, 518 C-7
Birchwood, 480 F-16
Blaine, 1717 C-20
BLEDSOE CO., 12928 E-15
Bloomingdale, 10350 J-18
BLOUNT CO., 115335 E-19
Blountville, 2959 J-18
Bluff City, 1602 J-18
Bolivar, 5652 F-4
Boones Creek, 2000 *M-3
Bradford, 1073 C-5
BRADLEY CO., 92092 G-17
Brentwood, 32426 D-11
Briarwood, 590 B-9
Briceville, 800 C-19
Brighton, 2441 E-2
Bristol, 24994 J-19
Brownsville, 10720 E-4
Bruceton, 1486 C-7
Bulls Gap, 716 K-16
Burlison, 443 E-2
Burns, 1402 C-9
Butler, 500 K-19
Byrdstown, 875 B-16
Calhoun, 513 F-17
Camden, 3736 C-7
Campaign, 500 D-14
CAMPBELL CO., 40686 B-19
CANNON CO., 13337 D-13
Capleville, 580 G-2
CARROLL CO., 29121 D-6
Carson Spr., 700 L-16
Carter, 500 J-19
CARTER CO., 58865 K-19
Carthage, 2268 C-13
Caryville, 2380 C-18
Celina, 1369 B-15
Centerville, 4002 D-9
Chapel Hill, 1019 E-11
Charleston, 644 F-17
Charlotte, 1155 C-9
Chattanooga, 154762 G-15
CHEATHAM CO., 38603 B-10
CHESTER CO., 15941 E-5
Church Hill, 6370 J-17
CLAIBORNE CO., 31033 B-20
Clarksville, 112878 B-9
CLAY CO., 7992 B-14
Cleveland, 38186 G-17
Clifton, 2679 F-7
Clinton, 9381 C-19
Coalmont, 971 F-14
COCKE CO., 34929 L-16
COFFEE CO., 50869 F-13
Collegedale, 7215 G-16
Collierville, 37564 G-2
Collinwood, 1045 G-8
Colonial Hts., 7067 *K-9
Columbia, 33777 E-10
Cookeville, 27743 C-15
Copperhill, 482 G-18
Cornersville, 937 F-11
Counce, 700 G-6
Covington, 9018 E-2
Cowan, 1756 G-13
Crab Orchard, 900 D-17
CROCKETT CO., 14595 D-4
Cross Plains, 1517 B-11
Crossville, 10424 D-16
CUMBERLAND CO., 51346 D-16
Cumberland Furnace, 300 C-9
Dandridge, 2347 C-20
DAVIDSON CO., 575261 C-11
Dayton, 6443 E-16
DECATUR CO., 11686 E-7
Decatur, 1450 E-17
Decaturville, 846 E-7
Decherd, 2190 F-13
DEKALB CO., 18254 D-14
DICKSON CO., 45894 C-9
Dickson, 12873 C-9
Dover, 1495 B-8
Dresden, 2703 B-5
Drummonds, 500 E-2
Ducktown, 409 G-18
Dunlap, 4681 F-15
DYER CO., 37829 C-3
Dyer, 2418 C-4
Dyersburg, 17466 C-3
Eagleville, 458 E-11
E. Ridge, 19821 G-16
Eastview, 629 G-6
Edgemont, 500 L-16
Elizabethton, 13944 K-19
Ellendale F-2
Englewood, 1666 F-18
Erin, 1442 B-8
Erwin, 5786 L-18
Estill Sprs., 2179 F-13
Ethridge, 555 F-9
Etowah, 3712 F-18
Fairview, 7190 D-10
Fall Branch, 1313 K-17
Farragut, 19054 D-19
FAYETTE CO., 34458 F-3
Fayetteville, 7034 G-12
FENTRESS CO., 17159 B-16
Finley, 1000 C-3
Forest Hills, 5168 L-7
Franklin, 53311 D-11

FRANKLIN CO., 41003 G-13
Friendship, 612 D-4
Friendsville, 921 D-19
Gadsden, 560 D-4
Gainesboro, 859 B-14
Gallatin, 26720 B-12
Gallaway, 712 F-3
Gates, 863 D-3
Gatlinburg, 4426 E-20
Germantown, 37480 G-2
GIBSON CO., 48148 C-4
GILES CO., 29297 F-10
Gilt Edge, 483 E-2
Gleason, 1426 C-6
Goodlettsville, 15320 B-11
Gordonsville, 1130 C-13
GRAINGER CO., 22283 C-20
Grand Jct., 316 G-4
Gray, 1273 K-18
Graysville, 1426 F-16
GREENE CO., 65318 K-17
Greeneville, 15383 L-17
Greenfield, 2084 C-5
Green Hill, 7068 C-12
Grimsley, 700 C-16
Gruetli-Laager, 1907 F-14
GRUNDY CO., 14608 F-14
Halls, 2236 D-3
Halls Crossroads, 1250 C-19
HAMBLEN CO., 59898 K-16
HAMILTON CO., 310935 F-16
Hampton, 2000 K-19
HANCOCK CO., 6704 J-16
HARDEMAN CO., 28170 G-4
HARDIN CO., 25930 G-7
Harriman, 6725 D-18
Harrison, 7630 I-14
Harrogate, 3985 B-20
Hartsville, 7677 B-13
HAWKINS CO., 56196 J-17
HAYWOOD CO., 19656 E-3
HENDERSON CO., 26425 E-6
Henderson, 6061 F-5
Hendersonville, 44876 C-11
Henning, 1282 E-3
HENRY CO., 31511 C-7
HICKMAN CO., 23793 E-9
Hohenwald, 3791 E-9
Hollow Rock, 946 C-7
Hornbeak, 424 B-4
HOUSTON CO., 7988 C-8
Humboldt, 9269 D-5
HUMPHREYS CO., 18212 C-8
Huntingdon, 4186 D-6
Huntland, 886 G-12
Huntsville, 1194 B-18
Iron City, 379 G-9
Jacksboro, 1992 B-19
Jackson, 62099 E-5
JACKSON CO., 11072 C-14
Jakestown, 500 D-12
Jamestown, 1865 B-16
Jasper, 3082 G-14
JEFFERSON CO., 48394 C-20
Jefferson City, 7931 C-20
Jellico, 2514 A-19
JOHNSON CO., 18116 K-20
Johnson City, 58718 K-18
Jonesborough, 4550 K-18
Karns, 1458 D-19
Kenton, 1301 C-4
Kimball, 1353 G-14
Kimberlin Hts., 680 D-20
Kingsport, 44130 J-18
Kingston, 5472 D-18
Kingston Sprs., 2870 C-10
KNOX CO., 404972 C-20
Knoxville, 180130 D-19
Lafayette, 4177 B-13
La Follette, 8166 B-19
LAKE CO., 7583 B-3
Lake City, 1844 C-19
Lakeland, 7388 F-2
Lake Tansi Vil., 2621 D-16
Lakewood, 2388 C-11
LAUDERDALE CO., 26795 D-2
La Vergne, 25885 D-12
LAWRENCE CO., 41101 F-9
Lawrenceburg, 10911 F-9
Lebanon, 23043 C-12
Leipers Fork, 510 D-10
Lenoir City, 7675 D-18
LEWIS CO., 11435 E-9
Lewisburg, 10790 F-11
Lexington, 7667 E-6
Limestone, 550 K-17
LINCOLN CO., 32392 G-11
Linden, 981 E-8
Livingston, 3489 B-15
Lobelville, 909 D-8
Lookout Mtn., 1898 K-11
Loretto, 1710 G-9
Loudon, 4745 E-18
LOUDON CO., 43387 E-18
Luttrell, 955 C-20
Lynchburg, 6024 F-12
Lynn Garden, 4000 *J-8
Lynnville, 339 F-10
MACON CO., 21549 A-13
MADISON CO., 94916 E-5
Madisonville, 4352 E-18
Manchester, 9497 F-13
Maple Hill, 410 *J-4
MARION CO., 27757 G-14
MARSHALL CO., 28372 F-11
Martin, 10151 B-5
Maryville, 25851 D-19
Mascot, 2119 C-20
MAURY CO., 76292 E-10
Maury City, 717 D-4
Maynardville, 1915 C-20
McEwen, 1668 C-8
McKenzie, 5434 C-6
MCMINN CO., 51327 F-17
McMinnville, 13242 E-14
MCNAIRY CO., 25285 F-6
Medina, 1290 D-5
MEIGS CO., 11657 E-17
Memphis, 672277 F-1
Michie, 663 G-6
Middleton, 622 G-5
Middle Valley, 11854 G-16
Midtown, 1306 D-18
Milan, 7823 D-5
Millersville, 6114 B-11
Millington, 10306 F-2
MONROE CO., 43185 E-18
Monteagle, 1220 F-14
Monterey, 2791 C-15
MONTGOMERY CO., 147202 B-9
MOORE CO., 6024 F-12
MORGAN CO., 20157 C-17
Morgantown, 600 E-16
Morrison, 700 E-13
Morrison City, 1900 *J-8
Morristown, 26187 K-16
Moscow, 541 G-3
Mosheim, 1775 K-17
Mtn. City, 2419 J-20
Mt. Carmel, 5270 J-17
Mt. Juliet, 18099 C-12
Mt. Pleasant, 4452 E-10
Munford, 5652 E-2
Murfreesboro, 86793 D-12
Nashville, 549110 C-11
Newbern, 3089 C-4
New Hope, 1025 G-14
New Johnsonville, 1964 D-7
New Market, 1318 C-20
Newport, 7299 L-16
New Tazewell, 2882 B-20
Niota, 796 E-18
Nolensville, 2571 D-11
Norris, 1439 C-19
Oak Hill, 4747 L-8
Oakland, 2469 F-3
Oak Ridge, 27297 D-18
Obion, 1109 C-4
OBION CO., 32213 B-4
Oliver Sprs., 3275 C-18
Oneida, 3677 B-18
Ooltewah, 5681 G-16
Orebank, 1300 *J-9
OVERTON CO., 20523 B-15
Palmer, 738 F-15
Paris, 9874 B-6
Parsons, 2445 E-7
Pegram, 2166 C-10
PERRY CO., 7574 E-8
Petersburg, 596 F-11
Petros, 1350 C-18
Philadelphia, 572 E-18
PICKETT CO., 4821 A-16
Pigeon Forge, 5784 D-20
Pikeville, 1863 E-16
Piperton, 950 G-3
POLK CO., 15944 G-19
Portland, 10342 B-12
Powell, 7534 C-19
Powells Crossroads, 1221 G-15
Prospect, 600 G-16
Pulaski, 7917 F-10
Puryear, 670 B-6
PUTNAM CO., 66580 C-15
Ramsey, 700 M-14
Red Bank, 11726 I-12
Red Boiling Sprs., 1059 B-14
RHEA CO., 29918 E-16
Riceville, 700 F-17
Rickman, 750 C-15
Ridgely, 1593 C-3
Ridgeside, 386 G-15
Ridgetop, 1680 B-11
Ripley, 7772 D-3
ROANE CO., 52889 D-17
Roan Mtn., 1160 K-19
Robbins, 500 B-17
ROBERTSON CO., 60379 B-11
Rockford, 813 D-19
Rockwood, 5426 D-17
Rogersville, 4283 K-16
Russellville, 1200 K-16
Rutherford, 1245 C-5
RUTHERFORD CO., 218292 D-12
Ruthton, 900 J-19
Rutledge, 1261 C-20
St. Joseph, 858 G-9
Sale Cr., 1200 F-16
Saltillo, 346 F-7
Samburg, 258 B-3
Savannah, 7200 F-7
SCOTT CO., 21868 B-18
Scotts Hill, 914 E-7
Selmer, 4618 G-6
Sequatchie, 600 G-14
SEQUATCHIE CO., 12691 F-15
SEVIER CO., 79282 D-20
Sevierville, 14788 D-20
Sewanee, 2361 G-13
Seymour, 8850 D-20
Sharon, 935 C-5
SHELBY CO., 909035 G-2
Shelbyville, 18648 F-12
Sherwood, 500 G-13
Signal Mtn., 7146 G-15
SMITH CO., 18647 B-13
Smithville, 4160 D-14
Smyrna, 33497 D-12
Sneedville, 1317 J-16
Soddy-Daisy, 11985 F-16
Somerville, 2907 F-3
S. Carthage, 1321 C-13
S. Fulton, 2452 B-5
S. Pittsburg, 3123 G-14
Sparta, 4766 D-15
Spencer, 1694 E-15
Spr. City, 2009 E-17
Springfield, 15916 B-11
Spr. Hill, 17148 E-10
Stanton, 604 E-3
STEWART CO., 12969 B-8
Strawberry Plains, 700 C-20
SULLIVAN CO., 152716 J-19
Sullivan Gardens, 100 J-18
Summertown, 900 F-9
Summitville, 450 E-13
SUMNER CO., 145009 B-12
Sunbright, 590 C-17
Surgoinsville, 1744 J-17
Sweetwater, 6117 E-18
Talbott, 550 C-20
Tazewell, 2150 B-20
Tellico Plains, 930 F-18
Tennessee Ridge, 1311 C-8
TIPTON CO., 55998 E-2
Tiptonville, 4099 B-3
Tracy City, 1698 F-14
Trenton, 4577 D-5
Trezevant, 893 C-6
Trimble, 726 C-4
TROUSDALE CO., 7677 B-13
Troy, 1249 B-4
Tullahoma, 18909 F-13
Tusculum, 2211 K-17
UNICOI CO., 17572 L-18
Unicoi, 3481 K-18
UNION CO., 19076 B-19
Union City, 10788 B-4
Valley Forge, 2200 *N-5
VAN BUREN CO., 5470 E-15
Vonore, 1383 E-18
Walden, 2005 G-15
Walland, 500 E-20
Walnut Hill, 2756 *J-4
WARREN CO., 39753 E-14
Wartburg, 913 C-17
Wartrace, 564 E-12
WASHINGTON CO., 112507 K-18
Watauga, 431 K-18
Watertown, 1392 C-13
Waverly, 4134 C-8
WAYNE CO., 16909 F-8
Waynesboro, 2175 F-8
WEAKLEY CO., 33732 B-5
Westmoreland, 2165 B-13
Westover, 600 E-5
Westwood E-10
WHITE CO., 24253 D-14
White Bluff, 2372 C-10
White House, 8723 B-11
White Pine, 2055 L-16
Whiteside, 600 G-15
Whiteville, 4489 F-4
Whitwell, 1604 F-15
Wildwood, 530 D-19
WILLIAMSON CO., 153595 D-10
WILSON CO., 100508 C-12
Winchester, 7752 G-13
Woodbury, 2524 D-13
Woodland Mills, 288 B-4
Wrigley, 450 D-9

Texas

Map pp. 194-205

Index keys WA to WT refer to Western TX, pp. 198-201, EA to ET refer to Eastern TX, pp. 202-205.
* City keyed to pp. 194-195
† City keyed to pp. 196-197

Abernathy, 2762 WG-10
Abilene, 114757 WJ-14
Addison, 13667 †E-10
Agua Dulce, 729 EO-6
Alamo, 15976 ES-5
Alamo Hts., 7113 EL-4
Alba, 479 ED-10
Albany, 1833 EE-3
Aldine, 13979 EK-10
Aledo, 2524 EE-6
Algoa, 400 EL-11
Alice, 19519 EP-5
Allen, 69222 ED-8
Alpine, 6065 WO-7
Alto, 1156 EG-11
Alton, 7057 WO-1
Alvarado, 3977 EE-7
Alvin, 22171 EL-11
Alvord, 1309 EC-6
Amarillo, 183021 WD-10
Ames, 1145 EJ-12
Amherst, 765 WG-9
Anahuac, 2083 EK-12
ANDERSON CO., 56408 EG-10
ANDREWS CO., 12748 WJ-8
Andrews, 9391 WJ-9
ANGELINA CO., 81557 EH-11
Angleton, 18761 EL-10
Anna, 1750 EC-8
Anson, 2332 WJ-14
Anthony, 4072 WK-1
Anton, 1172 WG-10
ARANSAS CO., 24640 EO-7
Aransas Pass, 8877 EO-7
ARCHER CO., 9095 EC-4
Archer City, 1859 EC-4
Arcola, 1217 EL-10
Argyle, 2969 ED-7
Arlington, 362805 EE-7
ARMSTRONG CO., 2173 WD-11
Arp, 932 EE-11
Asherton, 1331 WS-14
Aspermont, 831 WI-13
ATASCOSA CO., 43226 EM-4
Athens, 12559 EF-9
Atlanta, 5677 EC-12
Aubrey, 2210 EC-7
AUSTIN CO., 26123 EK-8
Austin, 690252 EJ-6
Avinger, 455 ED-12
Azle, 10350 ED-6
Bacliff, 6962 EK-11
BAILEY CO., 6726 WF-8
Baird, 1680 EE-3
Balch Sprs., 19475 EE-8
Balcones Hts., 2991 ER-11
Ballinger, 4019 WL-14
Balmorhea, 472 WM-7
BANDERA CO., 19988 EK-3
Bandera, 1123 EK-3
Bangs, 1623 EG-3
Banquete, 600 EO-6
Barrett, 2872 *C-8
Barstow, 384 WL-7
Bartlett, 1701 EI-6
Bartonville, 1369 ED-7
BASTROP CO., 69932 EK-6
Bastrop, 7297 EJ-7
Batesville, 1298 EM-2
Batson, 200 EJ-12
Bay City, 18323 EM-9
BAYLOR CO., 3843 EB-3
Bayou Vista, 1693 EL-11
Baytown, 68371 EK-11
Beach City, 1777 EK-11
Beasley, 673 EL-9
Beaumont, 111799 EJ-13
Beaumont Place, 8000 *C-7
Beckville, 760 EE-12
Bedford, 48390 †F-6
BEE CO., 32873 EN-6
Beeville, 13560 EN-6
BELL CO., 256057 EH-6
Bellaire, 17206 EK-10
Bellmead, 9555 EG-7
Bells, 1270 EC-8
Bellville, 4303 EK-9
Belton, 15530 EH-6
Benavides, 1591 EP-5
Benbrook, 21922 EE-6
Ben Wheeler, 500 EE-9
Bertram, 1304 EI-5
Beverly Hills, 2071 WF-6
Bevil Oaks, 1276 EJ-12
BEXAR CO., 1518370 EK-4
Big Lake, 2591 WM-11
Big Sandy, 1349 EE-10
Big Spr., 24253 WK-11
Big Wells, 750 EN-2
Bishop, 3204 EP-6
BLANCO CO., 9110 EI-4
Blanco, 1609 EJ-4
Blessing, 861 EM-9
Blooming Gr., 918 EF-8
Bloomington, 2562 EN-8
Blossom, 1486 EB-10
Blue Mound, 2358 †F-4
Blue Ridge, 939 EC-8
Boerne, 8054 EK-4
Bogata, 1314 EC-10
Boling, 1000 EL-9
Bonham, 10556 EC-8
Booker, 1330 WA-13
BORDEN CO., 648 WI-11
Borger, 13305 WC-11
BOSQUE CO., 18053 EF-6
Bosqueville WE-5
Bovina, 1804 WF-8
BOWIE CO., 90643 EB-11
Bowie, 5543 EC-5
Boyd, 1300 ED-6
Brackettville, 1830 WQ-13
Brady, 5345 EH-3
BRAZORIA CO., 278484 EL-10
Brazoria, 2897 EM-10
BRAZOS CO., 156305 EI-8
Breckenridge, 5649 EE-3
Bremond, 896 EH-8
Brenham, 14161 EJ-8
BREWSTER CO., 9079 WO-8
Bridge City, 8800 EJ-13
Bridgeport, 5659 EC-6
BRISCOE CO., 1644 WE-11
Bronte, 981 WK-13
BROOKS CO., 7687 EQ-5
Brookshire, 3601 EK-9
BROWN CO., 38664 EF-3
Brownfield, 9173 WI-9
Brownsboro, 856 EE-10
Brownsville, 167493 ET-7
Brownwood, 19566 EG-3
Bruceville-Eddy, 1534 EH-7
Bryan, 66306 EI-8
Bryson, 537 ED-4
Buchanan Dam, 1688 EI-4
Buda, 3948 EJ-6
Buffalo, 1910 EG-9
Buffalo Gap, 446 WK-14
Bullard, 1562 EF-10
Buna, 2269 EI-13
Bunker Hill Vil., 3710 *D-3
Burkburnett, 10378 EB-4
BURLESON CO., 17238 EI-8
Burleson, 29613 EE-6
BURNET CO., 41676 EI-5
Burnet, 5562 EI-5
Byers, 530 EB-5
Cactus, 2629 WB-10
Caddo Mills, 1211 ED-8
CALDWELL CO., 36523 EK-6
Caldwell, 3862 EI-8
CALHOUN CO., 20606 EN-8
CALLAHAN CO., 13516 EF-2
Calvert, 1403 EH-8
Camelot, 4000 ER-13
CAMERON CO., 378311 ES-7
Cameron, 5900 EI-7
CAMP CO., 12238 ED-11
Campbell, 779 EC-9
Camp Wood, 864 WP-14
Canadian, 2258 WC-13
Canton, 3591 EE-9
Canutillo, 5129 WK-1
Canyon, 13353 WE-10
Carrizo Sprs., 5681 WS-14
Carrollton, 118870 ED-7
CARSON CO., 6586 WC-11
Carthage, 6611 EF-12
CASS CO., 30155 EC-11
Castle Hills, 4172 ER-11
CASTRO CO., 7640 WE-9
Castroville, 2936 EL-4
Cedar Hill, 41582 †J-8
Cedar Park, 48139 EI-6
Celeste, 848 EC-8
Celina, 3716 EC-7
Center, 5781 EF-12
Center Pt., 750 EK-3
Centerville, 944 EH-9
CHAMBERS CO., 28411 EK-12
Chandler, 2470 EE-10
Channelview, 29685 *D-8
Charlotte, 1796 EM-4
CHEROKEE CO., 48464 EF-10
Chico, 1069 EC-5
CHILDRESS CO., 7676 WE-13
Childress, 6606 WF-13
Chillicothe, 736 EA-2
China, 1079 EJ-12
China Grove, 1283 ES-13
Christoval, 422 WM-13
Cibolo, 7804 EP-14
Cisco, 3833 EE-3
Clarendon, 2021 WE-12
Clarksville, 3611 EB-10
Claude, 1328 WD-11
CLAY CO., 11287 EC-5
Cleburne, 29184 EE-6
Cleveland, 8032 EJ-11
Clifton, 3642 EG-6
Clint, 985 WL-2
Cloverleaf, 23508 *D-7
Clute, 10731 EM-10
Clyde, 3673 EE-2
Coahoma, 915 WJ-11
COCHRAN CO., 3289 WG-8
Cockrell Hill, 4289 †H-9
COKE CO., 3612 WK-13
Coldspring, 763 EI-11
COLEMAN CO., 8665 EG-2
Coleman, 4829 EG-3
College Sta., 72388 EI-8
Colleyville, 22394 †F-6
COLLIN CO., 659457 EC-7
COLLINGSWORTH CO., 2968 WE-13
Collinsville, 1471 EC-7
Colmesneil, 631 EH-12
COLORADO CO., 20736 EK-8
Colorado City, 4018 WJ-12
Columbus, 3934 EK-8
COMAL CO., 96018 EK-5
COMANCHE CO., 13709 EF-4
Comanche, 4302 EF-4
Combes, 2840 ES-6
Comfort, 2358 EK-3
Commerce, 8971 EC-9
Como, 645 ED-10
CONCHO CO., 3735 EH-1
Conroe, 47042 EJ-10
Converse, 12650 EL-5
COOKE CO., 38847 EB-6
Coolidge, 882 EG-8
Cooper, 2185 EC-9
Coppell, 38704 †E-8
Copperas Cove, 30643 EH-5
Corinth, 17980 ED-7
Corpus Christi, 283474 EO-7
Corrigan, 1931 EH-11
Corsicana, 26052 EF-8
CORYELL CO., 75802 EH-5
COTTLE CO., 1746 WF-13
Cotulla, 3655 EN-3
Crandall, 3475 EE-8
CRANE CO., 3837 WL-9
Crane, 3044 WL-9
Crawford, 789 EG-6
CROCKETT CO., 3934 WM-11
Crockett, 7039 EH-10
CROSBY CO., 6686 WH-11
Crosby, 1714 EK-11
Crosbyton, 1749 WH-11
Cross Plains, 1118 EF-3
Crowell, 1062 WG-14
Crowley, 9691 EE-6
Crystal City, 7224 WR-14
Cuero, 6770 EM-7
CULBERSON CO., 2627 WK-5
Cumby, 637 EC-9
Cushing, 653 EF-11
Cut and Shoot, 1244 EJ-10
Daingerfield, 2470 ED-11
Daisetta, 1090 EJ-12
Dalhart, 7146 WB-9
DALLAM CO., 6174 WA-9
Dallas, 1213825 ED-7
DALLAS CO., 2305454 EE-8
Dalworthington Gardens, 2359 †H-6
Danbury, 1667 EL-10
DAWSON CO., 14256 WI-10
Dawson, 906 EF-8
Dayton, 6622 EJ-11
DEAF SMITH CO., 18538 WD-9
Decatur, 6031 EC-6
Deer Park, 28993 EK-11
De Kalb, 1790 EC-11
De Leon, 2386 EF-4
Dell City, 408 WK-4
Del Rio, 36020 WQ-12
DELTA CO., 5480 EC-9
Del Valle, 1300 EJ-6
Denison, 23648 EB-8
Denton, 104153 EC-7
DENTON CO., 554642 EC-7
Denver City, 3994 WI-8
Deport, 698 EC-10
De Soto, 44653 †J-10
Detroit, 743 EB-10
Devine, 4409 EM-4
Deweyville, 1190 EJ-13
DEWITT CO., 20507 EM-6
D'Hanis, 600 EL-3
Diboll, 5441 EH-11
DICKENS CO., 2646 WG-12
Dickinson, 17898 EL-11
Dilley, 4167 EN-3
DIMMIT CO., 10395 EN-2
Dimmitt, 3981 WF-9
DONLEY CO., 3889 WD-12
Donna, 15846 ES-5
Doucette, 250 EI-12
Dripping Springs, 1666 EJ-5
Driscoll, 822 EP-6
Dublin, 3662 EF-5
Dumas, 13887 WC-10
Duncanville, 35150 EE-7
DUVAL CO., 12578 EO-5
Eagle Lake, 3693 EK-9
Eagle Pass, 25571 WR-13
Early, 2774 EG-3
Earth, 1077 WF-9
E. Bernard, 1729 EL-9
EASTLAND CO., 18393 EE-4
Eastland, 3813 EE-4
E. Tawakoni, 966 ED-9
Ector, 632 EC-8
ECTOR CO., 125339 WK-9
Edcouch, 4426 ES-6
Eden, 2447 WM-14
Edgecliff, 2523 †I-4
Edgewood, 1451 EE-9
Edinburg, 62735 ES-5
Edna, 5870 EM-8
Edroy, 420 EO-6
EDWARDS CO., 1987 WO-13
El Campo, 10884 EL-9
Eldorado, 1809 WN-12
Electra, 2938 EB-3
Elgin, 8689 EJ-6
Elkhart, 1260 EG-10
El Lago, 2963 *G-9
ELLIS CO., 133474 EE-7
Elmendorf, 711 EL-5
Elm Mott, 950 EG-7
El Paso, 598590 WK-2
EL PASO CO., 721598 WK-2
Elsa, 6458 ES-5
Emory, 1332 ED-9
Encinal, 653 EO-3
Encino, 177 EQ-5
Ennis, 18735 EE-8
ERATH CO., 34076 EE-4
Escobares, 1954 ES-4
Euless, 51226 ED-7
Eustace, 874 EE-9
Evadale, 1430 EI-13
Everman, 5733 †I-4
Fabens, 8043 WL-2
Fairfield, 3508 EG-9
Falfurrias, 5050 EQ-5
FALLS CO., 17646 EH-7
Falls City, 606 EM-5
FANNIN CO., 33142 EB-9
Farmers Branch, 26487 ED-7
Farmersville, 3357 EC-8
Farwell, 1318 WF-8
FAYETTE CO., 22537 EK-7
Ferris, 2298 EE-8
FISHER CO., 4089 WI-13
Flatonia, 1421 EK-7
Flint, 700 EE-10
Florence, 1109 EI-6
Floresville, 7024 EL-5
Flower Mound, 63526 †D-7
FLOYD CO., 7174 WF-11
Floydada, 3294 WG-11
FOARD CO., 1518 EB-2
Forest Hill, 13227 †I-5
FORT BEND CO., 463650 EL-9
Ft. Davis, 1050 WN-6
Ft. Gates, 300 EG-6
Ft. Hancock, 1713 WL-3
Ft. Stockton, 7268 WN-8
Ft. Worth, 624067 EE-6
Franklin, 1489 EH-8
FRANKLIN CO., 10200 EC-10
Frankston, 1233 EF-10
Fredericksburg, 10432 EJ-4
Freeport, 12605 EM-10
Freer, 3081 EO-4
FREESTONE CO., 18800 EG-9
Fresno, 6603 EK-10
Friendswood, 33094 EK-11
FRIO CO., 16387 EM-4
Friona, 3735 WE-9
Frisco, 70793 ED-7
Fritch, 2089 WC-11
Frost, 709 EF-7
Fulshear, 936 EK-9
Fulton, 1663 EO-7
GAINES CO., 14712 WI-8
Gainesville, 16569 EC-7
Galena Park, 10221 *D-6
GALVESTON CO., 277563 EL-12
Galveston, 57466 EL-12
Ganado, 1871 EM-8
Gardendale, 1197 WK-9
Garden Ridge, 2538 EP-14
Garfield, 1660 EJ-6
Garland, 216346 ED-8
Garrison, 846 EF-12
Garwood, 850 EL-8
GARZA CO., 5002 WH-11
Gatesville, 15651 EG-6
Gause, 500 EI-8
Georgetown, 39015 EI-6
George W., 2342 EN-5
Gholson, 948 EG-7
Giddings, 5442 EJ-7
GILLESPIE CO., 23088 EJ-3
Gilmer, 5141 ED-11
GLASSCOCK CO., 1327 WK-11
Glenn Heights, 9324 †J-10
Glen Rose, 2567 EF-6
Godley, 992 EE-6
Goldthwaite, 1824 EG-4
Goliad, 2006 EN-7
GOLIAD CO., 7102 EM-7
GONZALES CO., 19587 EL-6
Gonzales, 7514 EL-6
Gordon, 465 EE-4
Gorman, 1258 EF-4
Graford, 602 ED-5
Graham, 8715 ED-4
Granbury, 7360 EE-6
Grandfalls, 371 WM-8
Grand Prairie, 144337 ED-7
Grand Saline, 3228 EE-9
Grandview, 1567 EF-7
Granger, 1331 EI-6
Grapeland, 1421 EG-10
Grapevine, 47460 ED-7
GRAY CO., 21479 WC-12
GRAYSON CO., 116834 EC-7
Greenville, 25637 ED-9
GREGG CO., 115649 EE-11
Gregory, 2264 EO-7
GRIMES CO., 25192 EI-9
Groesbeck, 4353 EG-8
Groom, 587 WD-12
Groves, 15006 EJ-13
Groveton, 1138 EH-11
Grulla, 1801 ES-4
Gruver, 1122 WB-11
GUADALUPE CO., 103032 EL-5
Gun Barrel City, 5962 EE-9
Gunter, 1561 EC-7
HALE CO., 36233 WF-10
Hale Cen., 2180 WG-10
HALL CO., 3700 WF-12
Hallettsville, 2497 EL-7
Hallsburg, 533 EG-7
Hallsville, 2897 EE-12
Haltom City, 39875 ED-6
HAMILTON CO., 8105 EG-5
Hamilton, 2920 EG-5
Hamlin, 2018 WI-13
Hamshire, 600 EK-12
Hankamer, 600 EK-12
HANSFORD CO., 5230 WA-11
Happy, 615 WE-10
HARDEMAN CO., 4291 EA-2
HARDIN CO., 50976 EI-13
Hardin, 797 EJ-12
Hargill, 950 ER-5
Harker Hts., 21337 EH-6
Harlingen, 62318 ES-6
HARRIS CO., 3693050 EK-10
HARRISON CO., 63459 ED-11
Hart, 1101 WF-10
HARTLEY CO., 5450 WB-9
HASKELL CO., 5541 EC-2
Haskell, 2782 WI-14
Haslet, 1449 ED-6
Hawkins, 1471 EE-10
Hawley, 603 WJ-14
HAYS CO., 124432 EJ-5
Hearne, 4710 EI-8
Hebbronville, 4498 EQ-4
Hebron, 159 ED-7
Hedwig Vil., 2295 *D-3
Helotes, 6187 EK-4
HEMPHILL CO., 3422 WB-13
Hemphill, 1069 EG-13
Hempstead, 6546 EJ-9
Henderson, 11496 EF-11
HENDERSON CO., 80017 EF-9
Henrietta, 3325 EB-5
Hereford, 14472 WE-9
Hewitt, 12987 EG-7
Hickory Creek, 3044 †B-7
Hico, 1337 EF-5
Hidalgo, 10889 ES-5
HIDALGO CO., 678275 ES-5
Higgins, 437 WB-14
Highland Park, 8793 †F-10
Highlands, 7089 EK-11
Highland Village, 15105 †C-7
HILL CO., 35424 EF-7
Hill Country Village, 1073 EQ-12
Hillister, 300 EI-12
Hillsboro, 9000 EF-7
Hilshire Vil., 720 *D-4
Hitchcock, 7193 EL-11
HOCKLEY CO., 22787 WG-9
Holland, 1090 EI-6
Holliday, 1681 EB-4
Hollywood Park, 3210 EQ-12
Hondo, 8779 EL-3
Honey Gr., 1836 EC-9
HOOD CO., 47930 EE-5
Hooks, 2924 EC-12
HOPKINS CO., 33381 EC-10
Horizon City, 8695 WK-2
Houmont Park, 2500 *C-7
HOUSTON CO., 23218 EG-10
Houston, 2016582 EK-10
HOWARD CO., 32522 WJ-11
Howe, 2709 EC-8
Hubbard, 1680 EF-7
Hudson, 4054 EH-11
HUDSPETH CO., 3295 WL-3
Huffman, 3000 EJ-11
Hughes Sprs., 1876 ED-11
Hull, 1400 EJ-12
Humble, 14803 EJ-11
Hungerford, 645 EL-9
HUNT CO., 82543 EC-9
Hunters Creek Vil., 4445 *D-3
Huntington, 2073 EH-12
Huntsville, 36699 EI-10
Hurst, 37967 ED-7
Hutchins, 2941 †I-11
HUTCHINSON CO., 22484 WB-11
Hutto, 7401 EI-6
Idalou, 2046 WG-11
Imperial, 428 WM-9
Inez, 1787 EM-8
Ingleside, 9531 EO-7
Ingram, 1838 EJ-3
Iowa Park, 6175 EB-4
Iraan, 1172 WM-10
IRION CO., 1756 WL-12
Irving, 193649 ED-7
Italy, 2091 EF-7
Itasca, 1618 EF-7
Jacinto City, 9945 *D-6
JACK CO., 9064 EC-5
Jacksboro, 4610 EC-5
JACKSON CO., 14339 EM-8
Jacksonville, 14395 EF-10
Jamaica Beach, 1115 EL-11
JASPER CO., 35587 EH-13
Jasper, 7531 EH-13
Jayton, 472 WH-13
JEFF DAVIS CO., 2306 WM-5
JEFFERSON CO., 247571 EK-13
Jefferson, 1992 ED-12
Jersey Vil., 7087 *C-3
Jewett, 922 EG-9
JIM HOGG CO., 5029 EQ-4
JIM WELLS CO., 40951 EO-5
Joaquin, 946 EF-13
JOHNSON CO., 146376 EF-6
Johnson City, 1469 EJ-4
JONES CO., 19736 EE-1
Jones Cr., 2130 EM-10
Jonestown, 1869 EJ-5
Joshua, 5500 EE-6
Jourdanton, 4235 EM-4
Junction, 2654 WN-14
Justin, 2938 ED-6
Karnack, 300 ED-12
KARNES CO., 15351 EM-5
Karnes City, 3430 EM-6
Katy, 13255 EK-9
KAUFMAN CO., 89129 EE-8
Kaufman, 7872 EE-8
Keene, 5952 EE-6
Keller, 35706 †E-5
Kemah, 2386 EK-11
Kemp, 1258 EE-8
KENDALL CO., 28607 EJ-4
Kendleton, 522 EL-9
KENEDY CO., 417 EQ-6
Kenedy, 3408 EM-6
Kennedale, 6547 †I-5
KENT CO., 782 WH-12
Kerens, 1803 EF-8
Kermit, 5281 WK-8
KERR CO., 46496 EK-2
Kerrville, 22010 EJ-3
Kilgore, 11858 EE-11
Killeen, 100233 EH-6
KIMBLE CO., 4591 EI-2
KING CO., 307 WG-13
Kingsland, 4584 EI-4
Kingsville, 24740 EP-6
Kingwood, 42000 EJ-11
KINNEY CO., 3327 WP-13
Kirby, 8612 EL-5
Kirbyville, 2029 EI-13
KLEBERG CO., 30757 EP-6
KNOX CO., 3781 EC-2
Knox City, 1083 WH-14
Kosse, 517 EH-8
Kountze, 2153 EI-12
Kress, 779 WF-10
Krum, 3368 EC-7
Kyle, 17770 EK-5
LaCoste, 1369 EL-4
Lacy-Lakeview, 5804 WD-6
Ladonia, 699 EC-9
La Feria, 6815 ES-6
Lago Vista, 5573 EI-5
La Grange, 4620 EK-7
Laguna Vista, 2600 ES-7
Laird Hill, 400 EE-11
La Joya, 4486 ES-4
Lake Brownwood, 1694 EG-3
Lake Dallas, 7000 ED-7
Lakehills, 4668 EL-3
Lake Jackson, 27386 EM-10
Lakeport, 910 EE-11
Lakeside, 1164 †G-2
Lakeside City, 1032 EB-4
Lake Tanglewood, 857 WD-10
Lakeway, 8852 EJ-5
Lake Worth, 4681 †G-3
LAMAR CO., 49644 EB-10
La Marque, 13860 EL-11
LAMB CO., 14467 WF-9
Lamesa, 9321 WI-10
LAMPASAS CO., 19669 EH-5
Lampasas, 7465 EH-5
Lancaster, 32233 †J-11
La Porte, 33136 EK-11
La Pryor, 1491 WR-14
Laredo, 208754 EP-2
LA SALLE CO., 6016 EN-3
LAVACA CO., 18925 EL-7
La Vernia, 1087 EL-5
La Villa, 1455 ES-6
League City, 61490 EK-11
Leander, 17851 EI-6
LEE CO., 16526 EJ-7
Lefors, 540 WD-12
Leming, 600 EM-4
LEON CO., 16344 EG-9
Leonard, 2071 EC-8
Leon Valley, 9650 ER-10
Levelland, 12777 WH-9
Lewisville, 90348 ED-7
Lexington, 1245 EJ-7
LIBERTY CO., 75141 EJ-11
Liberty, 8433 EJ-11
Liberty Hill, 1491 EI-5
LIMESTONE CO., 22763 EG-8
Lindale, 4030 EE-10
Linden, 2201 ED-12
Lindsay, 956 EC-7
LIPSCOMB CO., 3101 WB-13
Little Elm, 18012 †B-9
Littlefield, 6329 WG-9
Little River, 1591 EH-6
LIVE OAK CO., 11717 EO-5
Live Oak, 10942 EL-5
Livingston, 6401 EI-11
LLANO CO., 18236 EI-4
Llano, 3348 EI-4
Lockhart, 13567 EK-6
Lockney, 1878 WG-11
Loeb, 200 EJ-13
Lolita, 548 EM-8
Lometa, 853 EH-4
Lone Oak, 554 ED-9
Lone Star, 1589 ED-11
Longview, 75609 EE-11
Lopezville, 4476 WO-3
Loraine, 617 WJ-12
Lorena, 1595 EH-7
Lorenzo, 1288 WG-11
Los Fresnos, 5192 ES-7
Lott, 672 EH-7
Louise, 977 EL-8
LOVING CO., 62 WK-7
Lowry Crossing, 1722 ED-8
LUBBOCK CO., 252284 WG-10
Lubbock, 209737 WH-10
Lucas, 3971 ED-8
Lufkin, 33522 EG-11
Luling, 5386 EK-6
Lumberton, 9637 EJ-13
Lyford, 1986 ES-6
LYNN CO., 6237 WH-10
Lytle, 2646 EL-4
Mabank, 2622 EE-9
MADISON CO., 13167 EH-9
Madisonville, 4250 EH-9
Magnolia, 1187 EJ-10
Malakoff, 2370 EF-9
Manchaca, 1500 EJ-6
Manor, 1877 EJ-6
Mansfield, 37976 EE-7
Manvel, 3287 EL-10
Marathon, 455 WO-7
Marble Falls, 6745 EI-5
Marfa, 1978 WO-6
Marion, 1118 EL-5
MARION CO., 10952 ED-12
Markham, 1138 EM-9
Marlin, 6206 EH-7
Marshall, 24006 EE-12
Mart, 2531 EG-7
MARTIN CO., 4391 WJ-10
Martindale, 1060 EK-6
MASON CO., 3880 EI-3
Mason, 2211 EI-3
Matador, 673 WG-12
MATAGORDA CO., 37849 EM-10
Matagorda, 850 EM-9
Mathis, 5462 EO-6
Maud, 1015 EC-12
Mauriceville, 2743 EJ-13
MAVERICK CO., 51181 WQ-13
Maypearl, 876 EE-7
McAllen, 123622 ES-5
McCamey, 1598 WM-9
MCCULLOCH CO., 7956 EH-2
McGregor, 4847 EG-6
McKinney, 96581 EC-8
McLean, 792 WD-13
MCLENNAN CO., 224668 EG-7
MCMULLEN CO., 883 EN-4
McQueeney, 2527 EK-5
Meadow, 631 WH-10
Meadowood Acres, 500 ET-9
Meadows, 6442 EK-10
MEDINA CO., 43027 EL-3
Melissa, 2435 EC-8
Memphis, 2403 WE-13
Menard, 1538 WN-14
MENARD CO., 2201 EI-2
Mercedes, 14185 ES-6
Meridian, 1527 EF-6
Merkel, 2592 WJ-14
Mertzon, 833 WM-12
Mesquite, 129902 ED-8
Mexia, 6742 EG-8
Miami, 543 WC-12
MIDLAND CO., 121371 WK-10
Midland, 99227 WK-10
Midlothian, 13188 EE-7
MILAM CO., 25354 EI-7
Miles, 815 WL-13
Milford, 726 EF-7
MILLS CO., 5237 EG-4
Millsap, 390 EE-5
Mineola, 4994 EE-10
Mineral Wells, 16919 ED-5
Mission, 60146 ES-5
Mission Bend, 30831 *E-2
Missouri City, 69941 EK-10
MITCHELL CO., 9413 WJ-12
Monahans, 6325 WL-8
MONTAGUE CO., 19677 EB-5
Mont Belvieu, 2525 EK-11
Monte Alto, 1611 ES-5
MONTGOMERY CO., 378033 EJ-10
Moody, 1393 EH-6
MOORE CO., 20348 WB-10
MORRIS CO., 12936 EC-11
Morton, 1962 WG-9
MOTLEY CO., 1299 WF-12
Moulton, 930 EK-7
Mt. Pleasant, 14760 EC-11
Mt. Vernon, 2583 EC-10
Muenster, 1665 EC-6
Muleshoe, 4579 WF-9
Munday, 1349 EC-2
Murchison, 636 EE-9
Murphy, 11026 †D-13
NACOGDOCHES CO., 60468 EF-11
Nacogdoches, 30806 EG-11
Naples, 1405 EC-11
Nash, 2352 EC-12
Nassau Bay, 4056 EK-11
Natalia, 1794 EL-4
NAVARRO CO., 48687 EF-8
Navasota, 7253 EJ-9
Nederland, 16751 EJ-13
Needville, 3288 EL-9
Nevada, 621 ED-8
New Boston, 4624 EC-12
New Braunfels, 47168 EK-5
New Caney, 3000 EJ-11
Newcastle, 571 ED-4
Newgulf EL-9
New Hope, 699 †A-13
New London, 991 EE-11
NEWTON CO., 14309 EI-13
Newton, 2351 EH-13
New Waverly, 925 EI-10
Nixon, 2246 EL-6
Nocona, 3250 EB-6
NOLAN CO., 14878 WJ-13
Nolanville, 2257 EH-6
Nome, 503 EJ-12
Normangee, 763 EH-9
N. Houston, 2000 EK-10
N. Richland Hills, 61115 ED-7
N. Zulch, 550 EH-9
NUECES CO., 319704 EP-6
Oak Point, 2391 †A-8
Oak Ridge North, 3306 EJ-10
Oakwood, 497 EG-9
OCHILTREE CO., 9385 WA-12
Odem, 2484 EO-6
Odessa, 93546 WK-9
O'Donnell, 974 WI-10
Olden, 500 EE-4
OLDHAM CO., 2118 WC-9
Old Ocean, 950 EL-10
Old River-Winfree, 1747 EJ-11
Olmito, 1198 ES-6
Olmos Park, 2314 ER-11
Olney, 3340 EC-4
Olton, 2275 WF-10
Omaha, 970 EC-11
Orange, 18052 EJ-13
ORANGE CO., 84983 EJ-13
Orangefield, 900 EJ-13
Orange Gr., 1402 EO-6
Ore City, 1166 ED-11
Overton, 2321 EE-11
Oyster Cr., 1227 EM-11
Ozona, 3436 WN-11
Paducah, 1363 WG-13
Palacios, 5166 EM-9
Palestine, 17912 EG-10
Palmer, 2074 EE-8
PALO PINTO CO., 27478 EE-4
Palo Pinto, 425 ED-5
Pampa, 16744 WC-12
Panhandle, 2609 WD-11
PANOLA CO., 22997 EE-12
Pantego, 2330 †H-6
Paris, 26539 EB-10
PARKER CO., 102801 ED-5
Parker, 2513 †C-13
PARMER CO., 9754 WE-8
Pasadena, 143852 EK-11
Pearland, 56790 EK-11
Pearsall, 7772 EM-3
Pecos, 8251 WL-7
PECOS CO., 15859 WN-9
Pelican Bay, 1587 †E-2
Penitas, 1182 ES-5
Perryton, 8096 WB-12
Petersburg, 1255 WG-11
Petrolia, 806 EB-5
Pettus, 608 EN-6
Pflugerville, 27531 EJ-6
Pharr, 58986 ES-5
Phillips, 900 WC-11
Pilot Pt., 4042 EC-7
Pine Forest, 631 EJ-13
Pinehurst, 2230 EJ-13
Pineland, 916 EG-13
Piney Point Vil., 3421 *D-3
Pittsburg, 4553 ED-11
Placedo, 700 EM-8
Plains, 1457 WH-8
Plainview, 21991 WF-11
Plano, 250096 ED-8
Pleak, 1099 EL-10
Pleasanton, 9375 EM-4
POLK CO., 46640 EI-11
Port Aransas, 3667 EO-7
Port Arthur, 56684 EK-13
Port Bolivar, 1300 EL-12
Pt. Comfort, 736 EM-8
Porter, 7000 EJ-11
Port Isabel, 5373 ES-7
Portland, 16219 EO-7
Port Lavaca, 11696 EN-8
Port Neches, 13131 EJ-13
Port O'Connor, 1200 EN-8
Post, 3802 WI-11
Poteet, 3626 EM-4
Poth, 2145 EM-5
POTTER CO., 119852 WC-10
Pottsboro, 1992 EB-8
Prairie View, 4658 EJ-9
Premont, 2836 EP-5
PRESIDIO CO., 7722 WN-5
Presidio, 4775 WP-5
Preston, 450 EB-8
Price, 650 EF-11
Princeton, 4115 EC-8
Progreso, 5082 ES-6
Prosper, 4207 EC-7
Quanah, 2715 WF-14
Queen City, 1591 EC-12
Quinlan, 1457 ED-9
Quitaque, 396 WF-12
Quitman, 2198 ED-10
RAINS CO., 11305 ED-9
Ralls, 2122 WG-11
RANDALL CO., 110053 WE-10
Ranger, 2535 EE-4
Rankin, 725 WM-10
Raymondville, 9483 ER-6
REAGAN CO., 2995 WL-11
REAL CO., 3031 EK-2
Red Oak, 7171 EE-7
RED RIVER CO., 13575 EB-10
Redwater, 883 EC-12
Reese Vil., 42 WG-10
REEVES CO., 11638 WL-7
Refugio, 2797 EN-7
REFUGIO CO., 7639 EN-7
Rendon, 9022 †J-5
Reno, 2864 ED-6
Reno, 2954 EB-10
Richardson, 99187 ED-7
Richland Hills, 8047 †G-5
Richmond, 13262 EK-10
Riesel, 1004 EG-7
Rio Grande City, 13651 ES-4
Rio Hondo, 2082 ES-6
Rising Star, 842 EF-3
River Oaks, 6910 †G-3
Roanoke, 3518 ED-7
Robert Lee, 1070 WK-13
ROBERTS CO., 820 WC-12
ROBERTSON CO., 16192 EH-8
Robinson, 9062 EG-7
Robstown, 12484 EO-6
Roby, 638 WJ-13
Rochester, 347 WH-14
Rockdale, 6048 EI-7
Rockport, 9041 EO-7
Rocksprings, 1181 WP-13
ROCKWALL CO., 62944 ED-8
Rockwall, 29354 ED-8
Rogers, 1102 EH-7
Rollingwood, 1359 WS-9
Roma, 10900 ES-3
Ropesville, 524 WH-10
Roscoe, 1273 WJ-13
Rosebud, 1394 EH-7
Rose City, 519 EA-14
Rosenberg, 30322 EK-10
Rotan, 1486 WI-13
Round Rock, 86316 EI-6
Rowlett, 53664 †E-13
Roxton, 699 EC-9
Royse City, 5589 ED-8
Rule, 639 WI-14
Runaway Bay, 1329 ED-5
Runge, 1084 EM-6
RUNNELS CO., 10974 EF-1
Rusk, 5234 EF-11
RUSK CO., 47971 EF-11
Sabinal, 1656 EL-2
SABINE CO., 10416 EG-13
Sabine Pass EK-13
Sachse, 17009 †D-13
Saginaw, 17701 †F-3
St. Francis Vil., 500 †I-2
St. Jo, 988 EB-6
San Angelo, 88014 WL-13
San Antonio, 1256509 EL-4
San Augustine, 2465 EG-13
SAN AUGUSTINE CO., 8907 EG-12
San Benito, 24699 ES-6
Sanderson, 861 WO-9
San Diego, 4589 EP-5
Sand Sprs., 600 WJ-11
San Elizario, 11046 WL-2
Sanger, 6354 EC-7
San Isidro, 270 ER-5
SAN JACINTO CO., 24801 EI-10
San Juan, 30773 ES-5
San Leon, 4365 *H-10
San Marcos, 46111 EK-5
SAN PATRICIO CO., 69209 EO-7
San Saba, 2615 EH-4
SAN SABA CO., 6076 EH-3
Sansom Park, 4121 †G-3
Santa Anna, 1026 EG-3
Santa Fe, 10498 EL-11
Santa Rosa, 2946 ES-6
San Ygnacio, 1000 EQ-3
Saratoga, 1200 EJ-12
Savoy, 886 EC-8
Schertz, 26668 EL-5
SCHLEICHER CO., 2742 WM-12
Schulenburg, 2742 EK-7
SCURRY CO., 16217 WI-12
Seabrook, 10907 EK-11
Seadrift, 1390 EN-8
Seagoville, 11112 EE-8
Seagraves, 2321 WI-9
Sealy, 6038 EK-9
Sebastian, 1864 ES-6
Seguin, 24230 EL-5
Seminole, 5954 WJ-9
Seth Ward, 1926 WF-11
Seymour, 2704 EC-3
SHACKELFORD CO., 3167 ED-2
Shady Shores, 2108 †B-7
Shallowater, 2170 WG-10
Shamrock, 1841 WD-13
SHELBY CO., 26346 EF-12
Sheldon, 1831 EK-11
Shenandoah, 1715 EJ-10
Shepherd, 2282 EI-11
Sherman, 36790 EC-8
SHERMAN CO., 3002 WB-10
Shiner, 2019 EL-7
Shoreacres, 1588 EK-11
Sierra Blanca, 533 WM-4
Silsbee, 6722 EJ-13
Silverton, 706 WF-11
Sinton, 5509 EO-6
Skellytown, 610 WC-12
Skidmore, 1013 EN-6
Slaton, 5727 WH-11
Smiley, 482 EL-6
SMITH CO., 190594 EE-11
Smithville, 4370 EK-7
Snyder, 10580 WJ-12
Socorro, 29685 WK-2
Somerset, 1779 EL-4
SOMERVELL CO., 7578 EE-5
Somerville, 1753 EJ-8
Sonora, 3008 WN-12
Sour Lake, 1716 EJ-12
S. Houston, 16219 *F-7
Southlake, 24902 †E-6
S. Padre Island, 2588 ES-7
Southside Place, 1600 *E-4
Spearman, 2924 WB-12
Spring, 36385 EJ-10
Springtown, 2639 ED-6
Spr. Valley, 3599 *D-3
Spur, 1027 WH-12
Stafford, 19227 EK-10
Stamford, 3253 WI-14
Stanton, 2262 WK-10
STARR CO., 60941 ER-4
STEPHENS CO., 9561 ED-4
Stephenville, 15948 EF-5
STERLING CO., 1303 WK-12
Sterling City, 1013 WK-12
Stinnett, 1860 WC-11
Stockdale, 1579 EL-5
STONEWALL CO., 1372 WH-13
Stowell, 1572 EK-12
Stratford, 1923 WB-10
Strawn, 758 EE-4
Sudan, 1040 WG-9
Sugar Land, 75754 EK-10
Sullivan City, 4346 ES-4
Sulphur Sprs., 15228 EC-10
Sundown, 1540 WH-9
Sunnyvale, 3817 †G-13
Sunray, 1942 WB-10
Sunset, 365 EC-6
SUTTON CO., 4212 WN-13
Sweeny, 3622 EM-10
Sweetwater, 10694 WJ-13
SWISHER CO., 7828 WE-11
Taft, 3429 EO-7
Tahoka, 2730 WI-10
Talco, 582 EC-10
TARRANT CO., 1620479 ED-7
Tatum, 1188 EE-12
TAYLOR CO., 125039 EF-1
Taylor, 15014 EI-6
Taylor Lake Vil., 3547 *G-9
Teague, 4630 EG-8
Telferner, 700 EM-7
Temple, 55447 EH-6
Tenaha, 1100 EF-12
Terrell, 17665 ED-8
TERRELL CO., 996 WN-9
Terrell Hills, 5108 ER-12
TERRY CO., 12419 WH-10
Texarkana, 35746 EC-12
Texas City, 44274 EL-11
The Colony, 37972 ED-7
The Woodlands, 55649 EJ-10
Thorndale, 1330 EI-7
Thrall, 847 EI-7
Three Rivers, 1764 EN-5
Throckmorton, 789 ED-3
THROCKMORTON CO., 1618 ED-3
Tiki Island, 1177 *B-8
Tilden, 450 EN-4
Timpson, 1144 EF-12
Tioga, 878 EC-7
TITUS CO., 29445 EC-11
Tivoli, 700 EN-8
Tomball, 9938 EJ-10
Tom Bean, 995 EC-8
TOM GREEN CO., 103611 WL-13
Tornillo, 1609 WL-2
Town West, 6166 *F-2
TRAVIS CO., 888185 EJ-5
Trenton, 703 EC-8
Trinidad, 1147 EF-9
Trinity, 2780 EH-10
TRINITY CO., 14363 EH-11
Trophy Club, 7334 †D-5
Troup, 2052 EF-11
Troy, 1365 EH-7
Tulia, 4714 WF-10
Turkey, 492 WF-12
Tuscola, 714 WK-14
Tye, 1141 WJ-14
TYLER CO., 20617 EI-12
Tyler, 91936 EE-10
Universal City, 16653 EL-5

University Park, 23806 †F-11
UPSHUR CO., 37881 ED-11
UPTON CO., 3056 WL-10
Uvalde, 16441 WQ-14
UVALDE CO., 26955 EL-2
Valley Mills, 1145 EG-6
Valley View, 808 EC-7
VAL VERDE CO., 47596 WO-12
Van, 2574 EE-10
Van Alstyne, 2760 EC-8
Vanderbilt, 411 EM-8
Van Horn, 2157 WM-5
Van Vleck, 1411 EM-9
VAN ZANDT CO., 52491 EE-9
Vega, 898 WD-9
Vernon, 11077 EA-3
Victoria, 61790 EM-7
VICTORIA CO., 85648 EM-7
Vidor, 11290 EJ-13
Von Ormy, 800 EL-4
Waco, 120465 EG-7
Waelder, 1009 EK-7
Wake Vil., 5226 EC-12
WALKER CO., 62735 EH-10
WALLER CO., 34821 EK-9
Waller, 1998 EJ-9
Wallis, 1271 EK-9
Walnut Sprs., 805 EF-6
WARD CO., 10237 WL-7
WASHINGTON CO., 31521 EJ-8
Waskom, 2129 EE-13
Watauga, 23548 †F-5
Waxahachie, 25454 EE-7
Weatherford, 23315 ED-5
WEBB CO., 224695 EP-3
Webster, 8852 EK-11
Weimar, 2016 EK-8
Wellington, 2090 WE-13
Wells, 792 EG-11
Weslaco, 31442 ES-6
West, 2711 EG-7
W. Columbia, 4240 EL-10
Westfield, 800 EJ-10
W. Lake Hills, 3021 WS-9
W. Odessa, 17799 WH-1
W. Orange, 3993 EJ-13
Westover Hills, 680 †H-3
W. Tawakoni, 1655 ED-9
W. University Place, 14886 *E-4
Westworth, 2870 †G-3
Wharton, 9374 EL-9
WHARTON CO., 41554 EL-9
WHEELER CO., 4799 WC-13
Wheeler, 1217 WD-13
White Deer, 1071 WD-12
Whitehouse, 7122 EE-10
White Oak, 6130 EE-11
Whitesboro, 4001 EC-7
White Settlement, 15736 ED-6
Whitewright, 1780 EC-8
Whitney, 2049 EF-6
WICHITA CO., 125894 EB-4
Wichita Falls, 99846 EB-4
Wickett, 422 WL-8
WILBARGER CO., 13896 EB-3
WILLACY CO., 20382 ER-6
WILLIAMSON CO., 333457 EI-6
Willis, 4172 EI-10
Wills Pt., 3855 EE-9
Wilmer, 3571 †J-12
WILSON CO., 37529 EL-5
Wimberley, 3797 EK-5
Windcrest, 5090 ER-13
Wink, 883 WK-8
WINKLER CO., 6690 WK-8
Winnie, 2914 EK-12
Winnsboro, 3794 ED-10
Winters, 2728 WK-14
WISE CO., 56696 EC-6
Wolfe City, 1647 EC-9
Wolfforth, 2942 WH-10
WOOD CO., 40855 ED-10
Woodsboro, 1626 EN-7
Woodville, 2313 EI-12
Woodway, 8689 EG-7
Wortham, 1089 EG-8
Wylie, 29061 ED-8
YOAKUM CO., 7408 WH-9
Yoakum, 5720 EL-7
Yorktown, 2265 EM-6
YOUNG CO., 18000 ED-4
ZAPATA CO., 13373 EQ-3
Zapata, 4856 EQ-3
ZAVALA CO., 11796 EM-2
Zavalla, 656 EH-12

Utah

Map pp. 206-209

Alta, 365 E-9
American Fk., 21372 E-8
Aurora, 942 I-8
Ballard, 599 E-12
Bear River City, 800 B-8
Beaver, 2558 K-6
BEAVER CO., 6204 J-5
Bicknell, 335 J-9
Blanding, 3135 L-13
Bluffdale, 6569 E-8
Bountiful, 41085 D-8
BOX ELDER CO., 46440 C-4
Brigham City, 18355 B-8
CACHE CO., 98055 B-8
CARBON CO., 19437 G-11
Castle Dale, 1615 H-10
Cedar City, 23983 L-6
Centerfield, 1051 H-8
Centerville, 14898 D-8
Charleston, 424 E-9
Circleville, 476 K-7
Clarkston, 620 A-8
Clearfield, 27413 C-8
Cleveland, 510 H-10
Clinton, 17735 D-1
Coalville, 1451 D-9
Copperton, 800 E-8
Corinne, 648 B-8
Cottonwood, 5800 H-20
Cottonwood Hts., 27569 I-20
DAGGETT CO., 943 D-12
DAVIS CO., 268187 D-7
Delta, 3106 H-7
Draper, 35119 E-8
Duchesne, 1481 F-11
DUCHESNE CO., 15354 F-11
E. Carbon, 1281 G-11
Elsinore, 735 J-7
EMERY CO., 10711 I-10
Enoch, 4167 L-6
Enterprise, 1419 L-4
Ephraim, 4977 H-9
Erda, 2473 E-7
Escalante, 744 L-9
Eureka, 793 F-8
Fairview, 1163 G-9
Farmington, 14357 D-8
Ferron, 1571 I-9
Fillmore, 2178 I-7
Ft. Duchesne, 621 E-12
Fountain Green, 941 G-9
GARFIELD CO., 4470 L-9
Garland, 1982 B-8
Goshen, 775 F-8
GRAND CO., 8743 H-12
Granite, 1989 J-20
Grantsville, 7494 E-7
Green River, 952 I-11
Gunnison, 2700 H-8
Harrisville, 5020 A-2
Heber City, 9147 E-9
Helper, 1878 G-10
Henefer, 728 D-9
Herriman, 11226 K-17
Hildale, 1973 N-6
Hinckley, 732 H-6
Holden, 391 H-7
Holladay, 19319 D-8
Honeyville, 1300 B-8
Huntington, 2062 H-10
Huntsville, 655 C-8
Hurricane, 10989 M-5
Hyde Park, 2858 L-17
Hyrum, 6061 B-8
IRON CO., 38311 K-5
Ivins, 6738 M-4
JUAB CO., 9113 G-6
Kamas, 1502 E-9
Kanab, 3516 N-7
KANE CO., 6202 M-8
Kanosh, 478 I-7
Kaysville, 22510 C-8
Kearns, 33659 H-17
La Verkin, 4105 M-5
Layton, 61782 C-8
Lehi, 31730 E-8
Levan, 801 G-8
Lewiston, 1663 A-8
Lindon, 9679 F-1
Loa, 498 J-8
Logan, 47357 B-8
Maeser, 2855 E-13
Magna, 22770 G-16
Manti, 3185 H-8
Mantua, 782 B-8
Mapleton, 5972 F-9
Mendon, 936 B-8
Midvale, 27170 I-19
Midway, 2737 E-9
Milford, 1437 J-6
MILLARD CO., 12284 I-6
Minersville, 838 K-6
Moab, 4807 J-13
Mona, 1140 G-8
Monroe, 1831 J-7
Montezuma Cr., 507 M-13
Monticello, 1913 L-13
Morgan, 2932 D-8
MORGAN CO., 7906 C-8
Moroni, 1276 G-9
Mt. Pleasant, 2703 G-9
Murray, 44555 D-8
Myton, 559 F-12
Naples, 1459 E-13
Neola, 533 E-12
Nephi, 5045 G-8
Newton, 655 A-8
N. Logan, 6730 M-18
N. Ogden, 16542 C-8
N. Salt Lake, 10538 E-19
Ogden, 78309 C-8
Orangeville, 1353 H-10
Orderville, 586 M-6
Orem, 89713 E-8
Panguitch, 1477 L-7
Paradise, 683 B-8
Park City, 8066 D-9
Parowan, 2532 L-6
Payson, 16442 F-8
Perry, 3081 B-8
PIUTE CO., 1365 J-8
Plain City, 4320 C-8
Pleasant Gr., 29376 E-8
Price, 8081 G-10
Providence, 5516 B-8
Provo, 113459 F-8
Randolph, 472 B-9
Redmond, 790 I-8
RICH CO., 2051 B-9
Richfield, 7044 I-8
Richmond, 1849 A-8
Riverdale, 7934 C-2
River Heights, 1334 N-17
Riverton, 32089 E-8
Roosevelt, 4553 E-12
Roy, 35229 C-8
St. George, 64201 N-4
Salem, 4725 F-8
Salina, 2382 I-8
SALT LAKE CO., 948172 D-7
Salt Lake City, 178097 D-8
Sandy, 89664 E-8
SAN JUAN CO., 14104 L-12
SANPETE CO., 24044 H-9
Santa Clara, 5864 N-4
Santaquin, 6901 F-8
SEVIER CO., 19386 I-9
Smithfield, 7589 A-8
South Jordan, 40209 J-18
S. Ogden, 15195 C-8
S. Salt Lake, 21411 G-19
S. Weber, 5593 D-3
Spanish Fk., 26606 F-9
Spring City, 1003 H-9
Spring Glen, 900 G-10
Springville, 25309 F-9
Stansbury Park, 2385 D-7
Stockton, 573 E-7
SUMMIT CO., 35001 D-9
Sunnyside, 376 G-11
Sunset, 4947 C-8
Syracuse, 17938 C-8
Taylorsville, 58009 H-18
TOOELE CO., 51311 E-6
Tooele, 28369 E-7
Tremonton, 6286 B-7
Tropic, 463 L-8
UINTAH CO., 26995 F-12
Uintah, 1225 C-8
Union, 10500 I-19
UTAH CO., 443738 F-9
Vernal, 7960 E-13
WASATCH CO., 18974 E-10
Washington, 13669 N-5
WASHINGTON CO., 118885 M-5
Washington Ter., 8352 C-2
WAYNE CO., 2450 K-10
WEBER CO., 210749 C-8
Wellington, 1558 G-10
Wellsville, 2575 B-8
Wendover, 1620 D-4
W. Haven, 5558 B-1
W. Jordan, 91444 E-8
W. Point, 7650 D-1
W. Valley City, 113300 D-8
Willard, 1663 C-8
Woods Cross, 8019 D-8

Vermont

Map pp. 210-211

ADDISON CO., 36965 F-3
Alburg, 521 A-2
Arlington, 1199 K-3
Bakersfield, 370 B-4
Barre, 9128 E-5
Barton, 756 C-6
Beecher Falls, 350 A-9
Bellows Falls, 3019 K-5
BENNINGTON CO., 36999 K-3
Bennington, 9168 L-3
Berlin Corners, 360 E-5
Bethel, 970 G-5
Bomoseen, 250 H-3
Bradford, 815 F-7
Brandon, 1684 G-3
Brattleboro, 8289 L-5
Bridgewater, 300 H-5
Bristol, 1801 F-3
Burlington, 38531 D-3
CALEDONIA CO., 30440 D-6
Canaan, 360 A-9
Castleton, 650 H-3
Cen. Rutland, 500 H-3
Charlotte, 350 E-2
Chelsea, 500 F-5
Chester, 550 J-5
Chester Depot, 500 J-5
CHITTENDEN CO., 149613 D-3
Colchester, 450 D-3
Concord, 350 D-7
Danby, 350 J-3
Danville, 360 D-6
Derby, 695 B-7
Derby Line, 798 A-7
Dorset, 600 J-3
E. Arlington, 620 K-3
E. Barre, 700 F-5
E. Dorset, 350 J-3
E. Middlebury, 500 G-3
E. Montpelier, 600 E-5
E. Poultney, 500 I-3
Enosburg Falls, 1473 B-4
ESSEX CO., 6602 C-8
Essex Cen., 850 D-3
Essex Jct., 8841 D-3
Fairfax, 350 C-3
Fair Haven, 2435 H-2
Fairlee, 400 G-6
Forest Dale, 350 G-3
FRANKLIN CO., 47914 C-4
Gilman, 500 D-8
Grafton, 300 K-5
GRAND ISLE CO., 7703 B-2
Graniteville, 500 F-5
Groton, 400 E-6
Hardwick, 1400 D-6
Hartford, 500 H-6
Hartland, 500 I-5
Highgate Cen., 350 B-3
Hinesburg, 400 E-3
Hyde Park, 426 C-5
Hydeville, 450 H-2
Island Pond, 849 B-7
Jeffersonville, 569 C-4
Jericho, 1457 D-3
Johnson, 1410 C-5
Jonesville, 330 D-4
LAMOILLE CO., 24495 C-5
Lower Vil., 300 D-4
Ludlow, 1037 I-4
Lyndon, 450 D-7
Lyndon Cen., 300 D-7
Lyndonville, 1222 D-7
Manchester, 723 K-3
Manchester Cen., 2069 K-3
Middlebury, 6252 F-3
Milton, 1537 C-3
Montgomery Cen., 380 B-5
Montpelier, 8003 E-5
Morrisville, 2057 D-5
Moscow, 260 D-4
Newbury, 431 F-7
Newport, 5207 B-6
N. Bennington, 1368 L-2
N. Clarendon, 550 I-3
Northfield, 3157 F-5
N. Hyde Park, 380 C-5
N. Pownal, 350 L-2
N. Springfield, 750 J-5
N. Troy, 621 A-6
Norwich, 1000 H-6
ORANGE CO., 29287 F-6
ORLEANS CO., 27640 B-6
Orleans, 847 B-6
Pittsford, 650 H-3
Plainfield, 600 E-5
Poultney, 1556 I-2
Pownal, 320 M-2
Proctor, 1979 H-3
Proctorsville, 480 I-5
Putney, 1150 L-5
Quechee, 600 H-5
Randolph, 2200 G-5
Readsboro, 400 M-3
Richford, 1425 A-5
Richmond, 700 D-3
Rochester, 500 G-4
Roxbury, 300 F-4
Rutland, 17046 H-3
RUTLAND CO., 63743 I-3
St. Albans, 7476 B-3
St. Albans Bay, 500 B-3
St. Johnsbury, 6319 D-7
St. Johnsbury Cen., 450 D-7
Saxtons River, 496 K-5
Shaftsbury, 772 K-3
Shelburne, 400 D-3
S. Barre, 1242 E-5
S. Burlington, 16993 D-3
S. Hero, 350 C-2
S. Londonderry, 400 J-4
S. Royalton, 750 G-5
S. Ryegate, 450 E-6
Springfield, 3938 J-5
Stowe, 450 D-5
Swanton, 2573 B-3
Troy, 300 B-6
Underhill, 400 D-4
Vergennes, 2763 F-2
Waitsfield, 320 E-4
Wallingford, 948 I-3
Warren, 370 F-4
WASHINGTON CO., 59478 E-5
Washington, 320 F-5
Waterbury, 1683 E-4
Waterbury Cen., 500 D-4
Websterville, 450 F-5
Wells, 400 I-3
Wells River, 342 F-7
W. Branch, 250 D-4
W. Burke, 367 C-7
Westminster, 269 K-5
Weston, 300 J-4
W. Pawlet, 300 J-2
W. Rupert, 180 J-2
W. Rutland, 2263 H-3
White River Jct., 2569 H-6
Whitingham, 330 L-4
Wilder, 1636 H-6
Williamstown, 700 F-5
Williston, 450 D-3
Wilmington, 600 L-4
WINDHAM CO., 44143 K-4
WINDSOR CO., 58028 I-5
Windsor, 3714 I-6
Winooski, 6353 D-3
Winooski Park, 400 L-9
Woodstock, 961 H-5

Virginia

Map pp. 212-217

* City keyed to pp. 216-217
† City keyed to pp. 224-225
‡ Independent city: Not included in any county.

Abingdon, 7925 D-6
Accomac, 545 I-19
ACCOMACK CO., 39424 I-20
Achilles, 650 K-17
Adwolf, 1457 M-1
ALBEMARLE CO., 90717 G-10
Alexandria, 135337 ‡E-15
ALLEGHANY CO., 16715 I-6
Allison Gap, 700 D-7
Altavista, 3385 L-8
AMELIA CO., 12273 K-12
Amelia Court House, 900 K-12
Amherst, 2225 J-9
AMHERST CO., 32134 J-8
Amonate, 400 K-1
Annalee Hts., 1800 †G-4
Annandale, 54994 E-14
Appalachia, 1771 C-3
Appomattox, 1729 K-9
APPOMATTOX CO., 13967 J-9
ARLINGTON CO., 195965 D-14
Arlington, 195965 D-15
Arvonia, 750 I-11
Ashland, 6996 I-14
Atkins, 1138 L-1
AUGUSTA CO., 69725 G-8
Austinville, 850 M-3
Baileys Crossroads, 23166 †G-5
Banners Corner, 300 D-5
Bassett, 1338 M-6
Bastian, 420 K-2
BATH CO., 4937 H-7
Bay View, 180 K-19
Bedford, 6211 ‡K-7
BEDFORD CO., 65286 K-7
Bel Air, 1500 †G-4
Belle Haven, 6269 †I-6
Belle Haven, 478 I-19
Belle View, 2300 †E-3
Belvedere, 2200 †H-4
Bensley, 5435 *E-8
Berryville, 3157 C-12
Big Rock, 650 B-5
Big Stone Gap, 5854 D-3
Blacksburg, 39130 K-4
Blackstone, 3558 L-12
BLAND CO., 6943 K-2
Bland, 600 L-2
Bluefield, 4989 K-2
Blue Ridge, 3188 J-6
Boissevain, 900 K-1
Bon Air, 16213 *C-6
BOTETOURT CO., 32027 J-6
Bowling Green, 995 H-14
Boyce, 453 D-12
Boydton, 466 M-11
Boykins, 607 M-15
Bridgewater, 5413 F-9
Bristol, 17335 ‡E-5
Broadway, 2460 F-9
Brodnax, 300 M-12
Brookneal, 1259 L-9
Broyhill Park, 3700 †G-3
BRUNSWICK CO., 17920 M-13
Buchanan, 1236 J-7
BUCHANAN CO., 24755 C-6
BUCKINGHAM CO., 16058 I-10
Buckingham, 350 J-10
Bucknell Manor, 2350 †I-6
Buena Vista, 6437 ‡I-8
Burke, 57737 †I-2
Burkeville, 474 K-11
Callao, 550 H-16
CAMPBELL CO., 52339 K-9
Cape Charles, 1423 K-18
CAROLINE CO., 25563 H-14
CARROLL CO., 29438 M-3
Carrsbrook, 950 H-11
Carver Gardens, 500 *F-3
Castlewood, 2036 D-5
Cave Spr., 24941 H-1
Cedar Bluff, 1073 L-1
Cedarville, 450 D-11
Centreville, 48661 E-14
Chantilly, 41041 D-14
Chapel Acres, 1200 †J-3
CHARLES CITY CO., 7119 J-15
CHARLOTTE CO., 12404 L-10
Charlotte Court House, 446 L-10
Charlottesville, 40437 ‡H-10
Chase City, 2382 M-11
Chatham, 1298 M-8
Cheriton, 485 K-19
Chesapeake, 218968 ‡M-18
Chester, 17890 J-14
Chesterbrook, 1600 †F-4
CHESTERFIELD CO., 288876 K-13
Chesterfield, 3558 J-14
Chester Gap, 400 E-11
Chilhowie, 1787 M-1
Chincoteague, 4416 H-20
Christiansburg, 17926 K-4
Churchville, 400 G-8
Claremont, 338 K-15
CLARKE CO., 14205 D-12
Clarksville, 1289 M-10
Claypool Hill, 1719 L-1
Clear Brook, 190 C-12
Clearbrook, 550 K-6
Clifton Forge, 4077 I-6
Clinchco, 413 C-5
Clintwood, 1518 C-4
Cloverdale, 2986 J-6
Coeburn, 1982 C-4
Collinsville, 7777 M-6
Colonial Beach, 3515 G-15
Colonial Heights, 17567 ‡K-14
Concord, 500 K-9
Courtland, 1251 M-15
Covington, 6205 ‡I-6
CRAIG CO., 5154 J-5
Craigsville, 1016 H-8
Crewe, 2291 K-12
Crozet, 2820 H-10
Culmore, 5200 †G-4
CULPEPER CO., 42530 F-12
Culpeper, 12047 F-12
CUMBERLAND CO., 9378 J-11
Dahlgren, 997 G-15
Dale City, 55971 E-14
Daleville, 1454 J-6
Damascus, 1083 E-6
Dante, 700 C-5
Danville, 46143 ‡N-8
Dayton, 1345 F-9
Deltaville, 1000 J-17
DICKENSON CO., 16243 C-5
Dillwyn, 445 J-11
DINWIDDIE CO., 25391 L-14
Disputanta, 550 K-15
Dooms, 1282 H-9
Drakes Branch, 484 L-10
Dryden, 1253 D-3
Dublin, 2208 L-4
Dumfries, 4816 F-14
Dunn Loring, 7861 †F-3
E. Stone Gap, 500 D-3
Edinburg, 861 E-10
Elkton, 2606 F-10
Elliston, 950 K-5
Emory, 1300 D-6
Emporia, 5587 ‡M-14
Engleside, 28582 †J-5
Esserville, 300 C-4
ESSEX CO., 10492 H-15
Ettrick, 5627 K-14
Ewing, 436 D-1
Exmore, 1393 J-19
FAIRFAX CO., 1006529 E-14
Fairfax, 21963 ‡E-14
Fairlawn, 2211 K-4
Fair Port, 450 H-17
Falls Church, 10781 ‡D-14
Falmouth, 3624 G-14
Farmville, 6876 K-11
FAUQUIER CO., 64997 E-12
Ferrum, 1313 L-6
Ferry Farms, 4000 G-14
Fieldale, 929 M-6
Fishers Hill, 200 D-11
Fishersville, 4998 H-9
Five Mile Fk., 700 G-13
FLOYD CO., 14649 L-4
Floyd, 434 L-5
FLUVANNA CO., 24751 I-11
Fork Union, 400 I-11
Franconia, 31907 †I-4
FRANKLIN CO., 50345 L-5
Franklin, 8594 ‡M-16
FREDERICK CO., 69123 C-11
Fredericksburg, 20732 ‡G-14
Fries, 573 M-3
Front Royal, 14499 D-11
Gainesville, 4382 E-13
Galax, 6676 ‡M-3
Gate City, 2072 E-4
GILES CO., 17098 K-3
Glade Spr., 1537 M-1
Glasgow, 1019 I-8
Glen Allen, 12562 *A-7
Glenwood N-8
GLOUCESTER CO., 37787 J-16
Gloucester, 150 J-17
Gloucester Pt., 9429 K-17
GOOCHLAND CO., 19360 I-12
Goochland, 600 I-12
Gordonsville, 1617 G-11
Goshen, 399 H-7
Grafton, 1050 *H-4
GRAYSON CO., 16366 M-1
Great Falls, 8549 †D-2
GREENE CO., 17418 G-11
GREENSVILLE CO., 11088 M-13
Gretna, 1222 L-8
Grottoes, 2168 G-9
Grove, 680 *G-3
Groveton, 21296 †I-5
Grundy, 1004 B-5
HALIFAX CO., 36284 M-9
Halifax, 1293 M-9
Hamilton, 718 C-13
Hampden Sydney, 1264 K-11
Hampton, 145579 ‡L-17
HANOVER CO., 97426 I-13
Hanover, 500 I-14
Harman, 600 B-5
Harris Grove, 170 *G-5
Harrisonburg, 40438 ‡F-9
Hayes, 1000 *F-5
Hayfield, 2350 †J-4
Haymarket, 1083 E-13
HENRICO CO., 280581 J-14
HENRY CO., 56501 M-6
Herndon, 21965 D-14
HIGHLAND CO., 2475 G-7
Highland Sprs., 15137 *C-9
Hilander Park, 400 D-5
Hillsville, 2716 M-3
Hillwood, 1650 †G-4
Hollins, 14309 F-3
Holmes Run Acres, 1400 †G-3
Honaker, 921 C-6
Hopewell, 22690 ‡K-14
Horse Pasture, 2255 M-6
Hot Springs, 300 H-6
Hunterdale, 600 M-15
Huntington, 8325 †I-6
Hurley, 600 B-6
Hurt, 1245 L-8
Hybla Valley, 16721 †J-5
Independence, 921 M-2
Iron Gate, 386 I-6
Irvington, 658 I-17
ISLE OF WIGHT CO., 33417 L-16
Ivanhoe, 550 M-3
JAMES CITY CO., 57525 K-16
Jarratt, 562 M-14
Jefferson Vil., 2500 †G-4
Jewell Ridge, 350 B-6
Jolivue, 1037 H-9
Jonesville, 980 D-2
Keezletown, 400 F-10
Kenbridge, 1319 L-12
Keokee, 316 D-3
Keysville, 782 L-11
Kilmarnock, 1215 I-17
KING AND QUEEN CO., 6796 I-15
KING GEORGE CO., 20637 G-15
King George, 550 G-15
Kings Park, 6500 †H-3
Kings Park W., 6300 †H-2
Kings Point, 500 *F-2
KING WILLIAM CO., 14732 I-15
Lackey, 500 *G-4
La Crosse, 604 M-12
Ladd, 410 H-9
Lakeside, 11157 *B-7
LANCASTER CO., 11593 I-17
Langley, 1450 †E-4
Laurel, 14875 *A-7
Lawrenceville, 1157 M-13
Lebanon, 3225 D-5
LEE CO., 23686 D-2
Leesburg, 36269 D-13
Lexington, 6776 ‡I-7
Lightfoot, 400 J-16
Lincolnia, 15788 †H-4
Lincolnia Hts., 1800 †H-4
Lorton, 17786 E-14
LOUDOUN CO., 255518 D-13
LOUISA CO., 30020 H-12
Louisa, 1510 H-12
Lovettsville, 1160 C-13
Lovingston, 600 I-9
Lowmoor, 367 I-6
LUNENBURG CO., 13194 L-11
Luray, 4865 E-11
Lynchburg, 66973 ‡J-8
Lynch Sta., 500 K-8
MADISON CO., 13398 F-11
Madison Hts., 11584 J-8
Manassas, 37569 ‡E-14
Manassas Park, 11622 ‡E-14
Mappsville, 400 H-20
Marion, 6164 M-1
Marshall, 900 E-12
Martinsville, 14925 ‡M-6
MATHEWS CO., 9194 J-17
Mathews, 700 J-17
Matoaca, 2273 *H-7
Max Meadows, 512 L-3
McClure, 350 C-5
McGaheysville, 550 G-10
McKenney, 481 L-13
McLean, 38929 †F-4
Meadowview, 900 D-6
Mechanicsville, 30464 *B-9
MECKLENBURG CO., 32529 M-11
Melfa, 448 I-19
Merrifield, 11170 †G-3
Middleburg, 880 D-13
MIDDLESEX CO., 10493 I-17
Middletown, 1098 D-11
Midlothian, 450 J-13
Milford, 500 H-14
Mineral, 459 H-12
Monroe, 400 J-8
MONTGOMERY CO., 84303 L-4
Montross, 305 G-16
Montvale, 550 J-7
Mt. Jackson, 1766 E-10
Mt. Sidney, 500 G-9
Narrows, 2150 K-3
Nassawadox, 607 J-19
NELSON CO., 15101 I-9
New Alexandria, 950 †I-6
New Baltimore, 550 E-13
Newington, 19784 †J-4
NEW KENT CO., 16107 J-15
New Market, 1831 E-10
Newport News, 179899 ‡L-17
Nickelsville, 435 D-4
Norfolk, 231954 ‡L-18
Norge, 1000 J-16
NORTHAMPTON CO., 13548 J-19
N. Springfield, 9173 †H-3
NORTHUMBERLAND CO., 12874 H-17
Norton, 3677 ‡C-4
NOTTOWAY CO., 15560 K-12
Oakton, 29348 †G-2
Oakwood, 500 B-6
Occoquan, 757 E-14
Onancock, 1477 I-19
Onley, 496 I-19
Orange, 4429 G-12
ORANGE CO., 30246 G-12
PAGE CO., 23831 F-10
Parklawn, 2400 †H-4
Parksley, 833 I-19
Parrott, 590 K-4
PATRICK CO., 19209 M-4
Pearisburg, 2768 K-3
Pembroke, 1167 K-4
Pender, 500 †G-1
Pennington Gap, 1753 D-3
Petersburg, 32604 ‡K-14
Pimmit Hills, 6152 †F-3
PITTSYLVANIA CO., 61854 L-8
Plasterco, 300 D-6
Pocahontas, 432 K-2
Poquoson, 11811 ‡K-17
Portsmouth, 100169 ‡L-17
Pound, 1087 C-4
POWHATAN CO., 26598 J-12
PRINCE EDWARD CO., 20455 K-10
PRINCE GEORGE CO., 36725 K-15
PRINCE WILLIAM CO., 348588 E-14
PULASKI CO., 35081 L-3
Pulaski, 9088 L-3
Purcellville, 4680 C-13
Quantico, 622 F-14
Queens Lake, 1400 *E-3
Quinby, 350 I-19
Radford, 14575 ‡K-4
RAPPAHANNOCK CO., 7271 E-11
Raven, 2593 C-6
Ravensworth, 3000 †H-3
Ravenwood, 2550 †G-4
Remington, 676 F-13
Rescue, 400 L-17
Reston, 56407 D-14
Rich Cr., 680 J-3
Richlands, 4116 C-6
RICHMOND CO., 9114 H-16
Richmond, 193777 ‡J-14
Ridgeway, 798 N-6
Ripplemead, 550 K-4
Riverdale, 630 M-9
ROANOKE CO., 88172 K-5
Roanoke, 92631 ‡K-6
ROCKBRIDGE CO., 21242 H-7
ROCKINGHAM CO., 71251 E-9
Rocky Mt., 4568 L-6
Rose Hill, 15058 †I-5
Rose Hill, 714 D-1
Round Hill, 639 C-13
Roxbury J-15
Rural Retreat, 1354 L-2
RUSSELL CO., 28949 C-6
Rustburg, 1271 K-9
St. Paul, 964 D-5
Salem, 24654 ‡K-6
Saltville, 2267 L-1
Sandston, 4200 *C-10
Saxis, 337 H-19
SCOTT CO., 22962 D-4
Seaford, 2700 K-17
Sedley, 560 M-15
Selma, 485 I-6
Shawsville, 1029 K-5
Shenandoah, 1870 F-10
SHENANDOAH CO., 39184 E-10
Sleepy Hollow, 640 †G-4
Smithfield, 6840 L-16
SMYTH CO., 32640 L-1
SOUTHAMPTON CO., 17585 M-15
S. Boston, 8115 M-9
S. Hill, 4607 M-12
Spotsylvania, 600 G-13
SPOTSYLVANIA CO., 116549 H-13
Springfield, 30417 †I-4
STAFFORD CO., 117874 F-13
Stafford, 1600 F-14
Stanley, 1331 F-10
Stanleytown, 1515 M-6
Staunton, 23337 ‡G-9
Stephens City, 1247 D-11
Stephenson, 560 C-12
Sterling, 20512 D-14
Strasburg, 4269 D-11
Stuart, 925 M-5
Stuarts Draft, 8367 H-9
Suffolk, 78994 ‡M-17
Sugar Gr., 741 M-1
Sugar Loaf, 2500 H-1
SURRY CO., 7013 K-15
SUSSEX CO., 12071 L-14
Tabb, 950 K-17
Tangier, 694 H-18
Tappahannock, 2155 H-16
Tazewell, 4404 K-1
TAZEWELL CO., 44795 L-1
Temperanceville, 750 H-20
Timberlake, 10683 K-8
Timberville, 1703 E-10
Toano, 1200 J-16
Tookland, 500 B-5
Trammel, 400 C-5
Triangle, 5500 F-14
Troutville, 432 J-6
Tyler Park, 1250 †G-4
Tysons Corner, 18540 †F-3
Urbanna, 548 I-16
Vansant, 989 B-5
Varina, 3000 *E-9
Verona, 3638 G-9
Victoria, 1789 L-11
Vienna, 14842 D-14
Vinton, 7734 K-6
Virginia Beach, 438415 ‡L-18
Virginia Hills, 2840 †I-5
Wakefield, 971 L-15
WARREN CO., 35556 D-12
Warrenton, 8635 E-13
Warsaw, 1366 H-16
WASHINGTON CO., 52085 D-6
Waverly, 2176 L-15
Waynesboro, 21269 ‡H-9
Waynewood, 3450 †J-6
Weber City, 1283 E-4
Wellington, 1750 †J-6
WESTMORELAND CO., 17227 G-15
W. Point, 3013 J-16
W. Springfield, 28378 †I-3
Weyanoke, 1500 †H-4
White Stone, 349 I-17
Wicomico, 1350 K-17
Williamsburg, 11751 ‡K-16
Willis Wharf, 250 J-19
Wilton Woods, 1400 †I-5
Winchester, 25119 ‡C-11
Windsor, 2429 M-16
WISE CO., 41997 C-4
Wise, 3282 C-4
Woodbridge, 31941 E-14
Woodlawn, 2249 M-3
Woodstock, 4229 E-10
WYTHE CO., 28421 L-2
Wytheville, 8038 L-2
YORK CO., 61758 K-16
York Ter., 800 *F-2
Yorktown, 203 K-17

Washington

Map pp. 218-223

* City keyed to pp. 222-223

Aberdeen, 16358 H-3
ADAMS CO., 16803 H-17
Airway Hts., 4647 F-19
Alderwood Manor, 15329 E-7
Algona, 2644 *K-9
Allyn, 850 G-6
Anacortes, 16083 C-6
Arlington, 15277 D-8
ASOTIN CO., 21178 K-20
Asotin, 1124 J-20
Auburn, 47086 G-7
Bainbridge Island (Winslow), 21951 F-7
Battle Ground, 13237 L-7
Beaver, 600 D-2
Bellevue, 117137 F-7
Bellingham, 74547 B-7
BENTON CO., 157950 J-13
Benton City, 2971 K-14
Bingen, 689 M-9
Black Diamond, 3929 G-8
Blaine, 4330 A-6
Bonney Lake, 14611 *N-10
Bothell, 30916 F-7
Bremerton, 37828 F-6
Brewster, 2140 D-13
Bridgeport, 2043 E-13
Brier, 6344 *A-8
Browns Pt., 1950 *K-6
Bryn Mawr, 1500 *G-9
Buckley, 4473 H-8
Buena, 800 J-12
Burbank, 3303 K-15
Burien, 30737 G-7
Burlington, 8247 C-7
Camas, 16671 M-7
Carnation, 1828 F-8
Carson, 1000 M-8
Carthcart, 3015 E-8
Cashmere, 2985 F-12
Castle Rock, 2104 K-6
Centralia, 15404 I-6
Central Park, 2558 H-4
Chehalis, 7205 I-6
CHELAN CO., 69791 E-11
Chelan, 3684 E-13
Cheney, 10356 F-19
Chewelah, 2285 D-18
CLALLAM CO., 69689 E-4
Clallam Bay, 900 D-3
CLARK CO., 403766 M-7
Clarkston, 7304 J-20
Clearlake, 942 C-7
Cle Elum, 1796 H-11
Clinton, 868 E-7
Clyde Hill, 2943 *D-9
Colchester, 200 *F-5
Colfax, 2780 H-19
College Place, 8945 L-17
COLUMBIA CO., 4129 K-18
Colville, 5029 C-18
Concrete, 800 C-9
Connell, 2980 I-16
Cosmopolis, 1646 H-4
Coulee City, 637 F-14
Coulee Dam, 1080 E-15
Country Homes, 5203 *A-2
Coupeville, 1813 D-6
COWLITZ CO., 97325 K-6
Darrington, 1333 D-9
Davenport, 1726 F-17
Dayton, 2703 J-18
Deer Park, 3105 E-19
Desert Aire, 1124 I-13
Des Moines, 28767 G-7
Dishman, 10031 F-19
DOUGLAS CO., 34977 F-14
Duvall, 5710 F-8
Eagledale, 650 *D-5
Eastgate, 4558 *E-10
E. Wenatchee, 8819 G-12
Eatonville, 2328 I-7
Edgewood, 9718 *L-8
Edmonds, 39937 E-7
Electric City, 980 E-15
Ellensburg, 16914 H-11
Elma, 3164 H-4
Enumclaw, 10896 G-8
Ephrata, 7178 G-14
Everett, 96604 E-7
Everson, 2067 A-7
Fairwood, 2000 *H-10
Fall City, 1638 F-8
Federal Way, 83088 G-7
Ferndale, 9977 B-7
FERRY CO., 7542 C-16
Fife, 5567 *L-7
Fircrest, 6086 *L-5
Fords Prairie, 1961 I-5
Forks, 3192 E-2
FRANKLIN CO., 63011 J-15
Freeland, 1313 E-7
Friday Hbr., 2096 C-6
GARFIELD CO., 2344 J-19
Garfield, 632 H-20
Gig Hbr., 6620 G-7
Gold Bar, 2286 E-9
Goldendale, 3713 L-11
Grand Coulee, 925 E-15
Grandview, 8908 K-13
Granger, 2836 K-12
Granite Falls, 2863 D-8
GRANT CO., 81229 G-14
Grayland, 1002 I-3
GRAYS HARBOR CO., 70900 G-4
Greenacres, 5158 F-20
Hansville, 1700 E-7
Hazelwood, 700 *F-10
Hollywood, 800 *B-10
Hoquiam, 9030 H-3
Hunts Point, 461 *D-9
Ilwaco, 981 J-3
Inglewood, 6500 F-8
ISLAND CO., 79252 C-7
Issaquah, 17059 F-8
JEFFERSON CO., 28666 F-4
Kalama, 1938 L-6
Kelso, 11854 K-6
Kenmore, 19564 *A-9
Kennewick, 60997 K-15
Kent, 81800 G-7
Kettle Falls, 1588 B-17
KING CO., 1793583 F-9
Kirkland, 45814 F-7
KITSAP CO., 240661 F-6
Kittitas, 1133 H-12
KITTITAS CO., 36841 H-11
Klickitat, 417 L-10
KLICKITAT CO., 19839 L-11
Lacey, 33368 H-6
La Conner, 784 C-7
Lake Forest Park, 12476 *B-8
Lake Stevens, 7558 E-8
Lakewood, 57671 D-7
Langley, 1018 D-7
La Push, 500 E-2
Leavenworth, 2206 F-11
LEWIS CO., 72449 I-6
Lexington, 800 K-6
LINCOLN CO., 10381 F-16
Long Beach, 1386 J-3
Longview, 36137 K-6
Lynden, 10697 A-7
Lynnwood, 33504 E-7
Lynwood Cen., 700 *E-5
Mabton, 2038 K-13
Maltby, 8267 E-8
Manchester, 4958 *F-5
Maplewood Heights, 3300 G-8
Marysville, 29889 D-8
MASON CO., 54359 G-5
McCleary, 1475 H-5
Mead, 2150 E-19
Medical Lake, 4190 F-18
Medina, 3032 *D-9
Mercer Island, 22862 *E-9
Meridian Heights, 600 *I-10
Midland, 7414 *N-7
Mill Creek, 13501 E-7
Millwood, 1604 *B-4
Milton, 6468 *L-8
Monroe, 15653 E-8
Montesano, 3399 H-4
Morgan Acres, 1500 *B-3
Morton, 1083 J-7
Moses Lake, 16793 H-14
Mountlake Ter., 20251 E-7
Mt. Vernon, 29271 C-7
Moxee, 1411 J-12
Mukilteo, 19857 E-7
Naches, 681 I-11
Napavine, 1449 J-6
Neah Bay, 794 C-2
Newcastle, 9287 *F-10
Newport, 2157 D-20
Normandy Park, 6178 *H-8
N. Bend, 4589 F-8
N. Puyallup, 2886 *M-8
Oak Hbr., 22327 D-6
Ocean Park, 1459 J-3
Ocean Shores, 4467 H-3
Odessa, 942 G-16
Okanogan, 2398 C-14
OKANOGAN CO., 39782 B-13
Olalla, 600 *H-5
Olympia, 44114 H-6
Omak, 4755 C-14
Opportunity, 25065 F-19
Orchards, 17852 M-6
Oroville, 1599 A-14
Orting, 4789 H-7
Othello, 6221 I-15
Otis Orchards, 3200 F-20
PACIFIC CO., 21579 J-4
Pacific, 5722 *L-9
Pacific Beach, 1200 G-3
Packwood, 1050 J-9
Palouse, 945 H-20
Parkland, 24053 H-7
Parkwater *B-4
Pasadena Park, 1700 *B-4
Pasco, 46494 K-15
Pe Ell, 680 J-5
PEND OREILLE CO., 12673 B-19
Peshastin, 900 F-11
PIERCE CO., 753787 H-8
Pomeroy, 1480 J-19
Port Angeles, 18927 D-5
Port Hadlock, 3476 D-6
Port Orchard, 7986 F-6
Pt. Roberts, 800 A-5
Port Townsend, 9001 D-6
Poulsbo, 7593 F-6
Prosser, 5140 K-14
Pullman, 25262 I-20
Puyallup, 35861 H-7
Quilcene, 591 E-6
Quincy, 5568 G-13
Rainier, 1649 I-6
Raymond, 2995 I-4
Redmond, 47579 F-8
Renton, 55817 F-7
Republic, 988 B-16
Richland, 44317 K-15
Ridgefield, 2869 L-6
Ritzville, 1721 H-17
Riverton Hts., 11188 *G-8
Rosalia, 600 G-19
Roslyn, 994 G-10
Royal City, 1952 I-14
Ruston, 746 G-7
Salmon Cr., 16767 M-6
Sammamish, 34364 F-8
SAN JUAN CO., 15274 C-5
SeaTac, 25081 *H-8
Seattle, 573911 F-7
Sedro-Woolley, 10045 C-7
Selah, 6875 I-11
Sequim, 5162 D-5
Shelton, 9065 G-5
Sheridan Beach, 6518 *B-8
Shoreline, 52024 F-7
Silverdale, 15816 F-6
SKAGIT CO., 113171 C-8
SKAMANIA CO., 10664 L-8
Skyway, 8500 *G-9
Snohomish, 8720 E-8
SNOHOMISH CO., 655944 E-9
Snoqualmie, 6082 F-8
Soap Lake, 1844 G-14
S. Bend, 1831 I-3
S. Hill, 31623 *N-8
S. Wenatchee, 1991 G-12
Spanaway, 21588 H-7
SPOKANE CO., 440706 F-19
Spokane, 196818 F-19
Spokane Valley, 81380 F-19
Stanwood, 5068 D-7
Steilacoom, 6140 H-6
STEVENS CO., 42013 D-18
Stevenson, 1256 M-8
Sultan, 3943 E-8
Sumas, 1069 A-7
Summit, 8041 *N-7
Sumner, 9298 G-7
Sunnyside, 14426 K-13
Tacoma, 195898 G-7
Tekoa, 772 G-20
Tenino, 1584 I-6
THURSTON CO., 228867 I-7
Toledo, 676 J-6
Tonasket, 970 B-14
Toppenish, 9207 J-12
Trentwood, 4388 *B-5
Tukwila, 16969 *G-9
Tumwater, 13331 H-6
Twisp, 915 C-12
Union Gap, 5707 J-12
University Place, 30425 *L-5
Vancouver, 157493 M-6
Vashon, 10123 G-7
Vashon Hts., 700 *G-6
Veradale, 9387 *C-5
WAHKIAKUM CO., 3849 J-5
Waitsburg, 1224 K-17
WALLA WALLA CO., 57558 J-17
Walla Walla, 30989 K-17
Wapato, 4619 J-12
Warden, 2635 H-15
Washougal, 10732 M-7
Waterville, 1155 F-13
Wenatchee, 29374 G-12
Westport, 2402 H-3
W. Richland, 9907 K-14
WHATCOM CO., 183471 B-8
White Cen., 20975 *F-7
White Salmon, 2280 M-9
WHITMAN CO., 40170 H-18
Wilbur, 901 E-16
Winlock, 1209 J-6
Wishram, 324 M-10
Wollochet, 300 *L-4
Woodinville, 9889 *B-10
Woodland, 4336 L-6
Woodmont Beach, 3550 *J-8
Woodway, 1257 *A-7
Yakima, 81214 J-12
YAKIMA CO., 231586 J-11
Yarrow Pt., 1022 *D-9
Yelm, 4543 H-6
Zenith *I-8
Zillah, 2599 J-12

West Virginia

Map pp. 226-227

Alderson, 1092 I-6
Amherstdale, 1100 H-3
Ansted, 1604 G-5
Arthurdale, 1500 C-9
Athens, 1182 J-5
BARBOUR CO., 15689 D-8
Barboursville, 3185 F-2
Barrackville, 1290 B-8
Barrett, 200 H-4
Beaver, 1378 H-5
Beckley, 16936 H-5
Belington, 1814 D-8
Belle, 1187 G-4
Belmont, 1009 C-5
Benwood, 1496 A-6
BERKELEY CO., 93394 B-13
Berkeley Sprs., 703 B-13
Bethany, 985 B-2
Bethlehem, 2547 A-6
Big Chimney, 650 F-4
Blair, 500 H-3
Blennerhassett, 3225 C-4
Bluefield, 11119 J-5
Bolivar, 1080 C-14
Boomer, 600 G-5
BOONE CO., 25703 H-4
Bradley, 2371 H-5
Bramwell, 412 J-5
BRAXTON CO., 14851 E-6
Brenton, 700 I-4
Bridgeport, 7486 C-7
BROOKE CO., 24515 B-2
Buckhannon, 5687 D-7
Buffalo, 1204 E-3
CABELL CO., 94031 F-2
CALHOUN CO., 7387 E-5
Cameron, 1142 A-7
Caretta, 600 J-4
Cedar Gr., 823 G-4
Cedar Gr., 350 C-4
Ceredo, 1631 G-12
Chapmanville, 1145 H-3
Charleston, 51176 F-4
Charles Town, 3704 C-14
Charmco, 150 H-6
Chattaroy, 1136 I-2
Chesapeake, 1567 G-4
Chester, 2436 A-2
Clarksburg, 16439 C-7
CLAY CO., 10356 F-5
Clay, 580 F-5
Clearview, 563 C-2
Clendenin, 1056 F-4
Clothier, 270 H-3
Coalwood, 700 J-4
Colliers, 600 B-2
Cowen, 506 F-7
Crab Orchard, 2761 H-5
Craigsville, 2204 F-6
Cross Lanes, 10353 F-3
Culloden, 2940 F-3
Daniels, 1846 I-5
Danville, 540 G-3
Davis, 577 D-9
Delbarton, 442 I-2
Despard, 1039 C-7
DODDRIDGE CO., 7476 C-6
Dunbar, 7740 F-3
E. Bank, 896 G-4
Eccles, 900 H-5
Eleanor, 1491 F-3
Elizabeth, 972 D-4
Elk Forest, 600 I-14
Elkins, 7109 D-8
Elkview, 1182 F-4
Elm Gr. J-11
Enterprise, 939 C-7
Fairmont, 19049 C-8
Fairview, 436 B-7
FAYETTE CO., 46823 H-5
Fayetteville, 2657 G-5
Follansbee, 2971 B-2
Ft. Ashby, 1354 B-11
Ft. Gay, 818 G-1
Franklin, 824 E-10
Gary, 801 J-4
Gassaway, 884 E-6
Gauley Bridge, 706 G-5
GILMER CO., 6950 D-6
Glasgow, 743 G-4
Glen Dale, 1475 A-6
Glen Fk., 450 I-4
Glen Jean, 400 H-5
Glenville, 1482 D-6
Grafton, 5407 C-8
GRANT CO., 11673 D-10
Grantsville, 546 D-5
Grant Town, 641 B-8
GREENBRIER CO., 35027 G-7
Guthrie, 600 H-13
Hamlin, 1100 G-2
HAMPSHIRE CO., 22025 C-11
HANCOCK CO., 31350 A-2
HARDY CO., 13287 D-11
HARRISON CO., 68369 C-7
Harrisville, 1861 C-5
Henderson, 315 E-2
Henlawson, 500 H-3
Hico, 900 G-5
Hinton, 2696 I-6
Holden, 1105 H-3
Hometown, 350 F-3
Huntington, 49198 F-2
Hurricane, 5968 F-3
Iaeger, 314 I-3
Institute, 1800 F-3
Inwood, 2084 C-13
JACKSON CO., 28403 E-4
JEFFERSON CO., 49206 C-14
Jeffrey, 500 H-3
Jolo, 500 J-3
Julian, 200 G-3
Junior, 448 D-8
KANAWHA CO., 193559 F-4
Kenova, 3391 F-1
Keyser, 5410 C-11
Keystone, 395 J-4
Kimball, 360 J-4
Kimberly, 500 G-5
Kincaid, 450 G-5
Kingwood, 2926 C-9
Kistler, 700 H-3
Lavalette, 1100 F-2
Lesage, 250 F-2
LEWIS CO., 17199 E-7
Lewisburg, 3595 H-7
LINCOLN CO., 22374 G-2
LOGAN CO., 36237 H-2
Logan, 1547 H-3
Lubeck, 1303 C-4
Lumberport, 969 C-7
Mabscott, 1364 H-5
Madison, 2634 G-3
Malden, 850 G-4
Mallory, 1143 H-3
Man, 716 H-3
Mannington, 2080 B-7
MARION CO., 56509 B-7
Marlinton, 1247 G-8
Marlowe, 700 B-14
Marmet, 1626 G-4
MARSHALL CO., 34337 A-6
Martinsburg, 15996 C-13
MASON CO., 25761 E-3
Mason, 1052 D-3
Masontown, 649 B-9
Matewan, 501 I-2
Maybeury, 300 J-4
MCDOWELL CO., 24273 J-4
McMechen, 1831 A-6
MERCER CO., 61589 I-5

*, †, ‡, See explanation under state title in this index.
County names are listed in capital letters and in boldface type.

Middlebourne, 853 C-6
Mill Cr., 658 E-8
Milton, 2262 F-2
Minden, 1000 H-5
MINERAL CO., 27028 C-11
Mineral Wells, 200 C-4
MINGO CO., 27210 H-2
Monongah, 912 C-7
MONONGALIA CO., 84386 B-8
MONROE CO., 13507 I-6
Montcalm, 885 J-5
Montgomery, 2030 G-5
Moorefield, 2408 D-11
MORGAN CO., 16022 B-12
Morgantown, 28292 B-8
Moundsville, 9567 A-6
Mt. Gay, 700 H-3
Mt. Hope, 1411 H-5
Mullens, 1653 I-4
Nettie, 600 G-6
New Cumberland, 1043 A-2
Newell, 1602 A-2
New Haven, 1528 D-3
New Manchester, 700 A-2
New Martinsville, 5791 B-6
NICHOLAS CO., 26464 F-6
Nitro, 6750 F-3
Northfork, 454 J-4
Nutter Ft., 1649 C-7
Oak Hill, 7312 H-5
Oceana, 1478 I-4
Odd, 200 I-5
OHIO CO., 45112 B-2
Omar, 600 H-3
Paden City, 2737 B-6
Parkersburg, 32020 C-4
Parsons, 1400 D-9
Paw Paw, 507 B-12
PENDLETON CO., 7844 E-10
Pennsboro, 1196 C-6
Petersburg, 2634 D-10
Peterstown, 497 J-6
Philippi, 2826 D-8
Piedmont, 943 C-11
Pinch, 2811 F-4
Pine Grove, 543 B-6
Pineville, 676 I-4
PLEASANTS CO., 7376 C-5
Pleasant Valley, 3119 C-8
Poca, 1028 F-3
POCAHONTAS CO., 8851 F-8
Pocatalico, 1500 F-4
Pt. Pleasant, 4481 E-2
Powellton, 1796 G-5
Pratt, 535 G-4
PRESTON CO., 30115 B-9
Princeton, 6222 J-5
Prosperity, 1310 H-5
PUTNAM CO., 54443 F-3
Racine, 450 G-4
Rainelle, 1511 H-6
RALEIGH CO., 79167 H-5
Ramage, 200 H-3
Rand, 2200 G-4
RANDOLPH CO., 28571 E-8
Ranson, 3793 C-14
Ravenswood, 3991 D-3
Reader, 500 B-6
Red Jacket, 728 I-2
Richwood, 2369 G-7
Ridgeley, 709 B-11
Ripley, 3266 E-4
RITCHIE CO., 10540 D-5
ROANE CO., 15407 E-4
Rock Cr, 200 H-4
Roderfield, 1000 I-3
Romney, 1975 C-11
Ronceverte, 1544 H-7
Rowlesburg, 620 C-9
Rupert, 944 H-6
Ruth, 175 F-4
Ruthdale, 65 J-12
St. Albans, 11105 F-3
St. Marys, 1954 C-5
Salem, 1976 C-7
Seth, 750 G-4
Shady Spr., 2078 I-5
Shepherdstown, 1158 C-14
Shinnston, 2240 C-7
Sissonville, 4399 F-4
Sistersville, 1512 B-5
Smithers, 858 G-5
Sophia, 1260 I-5
S. Charleston, 12700 F-4
Spencer, 2258 E-4
Spring Valley, 900 G-12
Squire, 450 J-4
Star City, 1369 B-8
Stonewood, 1859 C-7
SUMMERS CO., 13740 I-6
Summersville, 3369 G-6
Sutton, 993 E-6
Switzer, 1138 H-3
TAYLOR CO., 16291 C-8
Terra Alta, 1496 C-9
Thomas, 411 D-9
Tornado, 1111 F-3
Triadelphia, 796 C-2
TUCKER CO., 6943 D-9
TYLER CO., 9340 C-6
Union, 550 I-7
UPSHUR CO., 23712 E-7
Valley Gr., 405 C-2
Verdunville, 500 H-3
Vienna, 10770 C-4
War, 692 J-4
WAYNE CO., 42091 G-2
Wayne, 1154 G-2
WEBSTER CO., 9804 F-7
Webster Sprs., 787 F-7
Weirton, 19544 B-2
Welch, 2371 J-4
Wellsburg, 2727 B-2
W. Liberty, 1203 B-2
W. Logan, 397 H-3
Weston, 4241 D-7
Westover, 3926 B-8
W. Pea Ridge, 2500 G-14
W. Union, 808 C-6
WETZEL CO., 17117 B-6
Wheeling, 29639 A-6
White Sulphur Sprs., 2352 H-7
Whitman, 450 H-3
Williamson, 3181 I-2
Williamstown, 2955 C-4
Winfield, 2011 F-3
WIRT CO., 5896 D-4
WOOD CO., 87047 D-4
WYOMING CO., 24479 I-4

Wisconsin

Map pp. 228-233

* City keyed to pp. 232-233

Abbotsford, 1901 H-7
Adams, 1781 K-8
ADAMS CO., 20828 L-9
Albany, 1133 P-9
Algoma, 3197 I-14
Allouez, 14875 S-3
Alma, 899 J-4
Altoona, 6448 I-5
Amery, 2868 G-2
Amherst, 973 J-10
Antigo, 8282 G-10
Appleton, 70217 J-12
Arcadia, 2348 J-4
Argyle, 784 P-8
Ashland, 8306 C-6
ASHLAND CO., 16627 D-6
Ashwaubenon, 16911 S-2
Athens, 1045 H-8
Augusta, 1370 I-5
Baldwin, 3509 H-2
Balsam Lake, 1026 F-2
Bangor, 1375 L-6
Baraboo, 10927 M-9
Barron, 3151 G-4
BARRON CO., 45834 F-4
BAYFIELD CO., 15145 C-5
Bayfield, 602 B-6
Bayside, 4215 *B-6
Beaver Dam, 15153 M-11
Belgium, 2008 M-13
Belleville, 2114 O-9
Bellevue, 200 J-13
Belmont, 894 O-7
Beloit, 35621 P-10
Benton, 979 P-7
Berlin, 5213 K-11
Big Bend, 1267 O-12
Birnamwood, 779 H-10
Biron, 851 J-9
Black Cr., 1224 J-12
Black Earth, 1283 N-9
Black River Falls, 3485 J-6
Blair, 1261 J-5
Blanchardville, 774 O-8
Bloomer, 3280 H-5
Bloomington, 688 O-6
Bonduel, 1390 I-12
Boscobel, 3373 N-6
Boyceville, 1034 H-3
Boyd, 641 H-6
Brandon, 888 L-11
Brillion, 2910 K-13
Brodhead, 3068 P-10
Brookfield, 39656 N-13
BROWN CO., 238987 J-13
Brown Deer, 11611 *B-5
Bruce, 731 F-5
BUFFALO CO., 13968 J-4
Buffalo, 1042 J-4
Burlington, 11148 P-12
BURNETT CO., 16528 E-2
Butler, 1822 *D-4
Caddy Vista, 900 *J-6
Cadott, 1313 H-5
CALUMET CO., 44137 K-12
Cambria, 789 M-10
Cambridge, 1227 O-10
Cameron, 1655 G-4
Campbellsport, 1930 M-12
Cascade, 696 L-13
Cashton, 1018 L-6
Cassville, 1045 P-6
Cedarburg, 11298 N-13
Cedar Gr., 2012 M-13
Centuria, 953 F-2
Chetek, 2150 G-4
Chilton, 3617 K-12
CHIPPEWA CO., 59950 H-5
Chippewa Falls, 13374 H-5
CLARK CO., 34098 I-7
Clear Lake, 1077 G-3
Cleveland, 1401 K-13
Clinton, 3124 P-11
Clintonville, 4399 I-11
Colby, 1664 H-7
Coleman, 706 H-13
Colfax, 1070 H-4
COLUMBIA CO., 55364 M-10
Columbus, 5101 M-10
Combined Locks, 3000 O-4
Coon Valley, 748 L-6
Cornell, 1392 G-5
Crandon, 1867 F-11
CRAWFORD CO., 17134 N-6
Crivitz, 1030 G-13
Cross Plains, 3418 N-9
Cuba City, 2104 P-7
Cudahy, 18316 O-13
Cumberland, 2242 F-3
DANE CO., 458106 N-9
Darien, 1635 P-11
Darlington, 2341 P-8
Deerfield, 2202 N-10
De Forest, 8438 N-10
Delafield, 6767 N-12
Delavan, 8370 P-11
Denmark, 1990 J-13
De Pere, 23375 J-13
Dickeyville, 1056 P-7
DODGE CO., 88103 M-11
Dodgeville, 4840 O-8
DOOR CO., 28349 I-14
DOUGLAS CO., 44208 C-3
Dousman, 1885 N-12
Dresser, 844 G-2
DUNN CO., 41708 H-4
Durand, 1898 I-3
Eagle, 1769 O-12
Eagle River, 1608 E-10
E. Troy, 4224 O-12
EAU CLAIRE CO., 94089 I-5
Eau Claire, 62570 I-4
Edgar, 1327 H-8
Edgerton, 5102 O-10
Elkhart Lake, 1068 L-13
Elkhorn, 9021 P-12
Ellsworth, 3060 I-2
Elm Gr., 6182 *E-3
Elmwood, 796 I-3
Elroy, 1527 L-7
Evansville, 4658 O-10
Fairchild, 516 I-6
Fall Cr., 1213 I-5
Fall River, 1280 M-10
Fennimore, 2357 O-6
Fitchburg, 22040 T-7
FLORENCE CO., 4974 E-12
Florence, 750 E-12
FOND DU LAC CO., 99337 L-12
Fond du Lac, 42435 L-12
Fontana, 1951 P-12
Footville, 757 P-10
FOREST CO., 9961 F-11
Ft. Atkinson, 11949 O-11
Fountain City, 1026 K-4
Fox Lake, 1458 M-11
Fox Pt., 6741 N-13
Franklin, 33263 O-13
Frederic, 1233 F-2
Fredonia, 2192 M-13
French Island, 4410 L-5
Friendship, 766 K-8
Galesville, 1462 K-5
Gays Mills, 618 M-6
Genoa City, 2742 P-12
Germantown, 19245 N-13
Gillett, 1188 H-12
Glendale, 12880 N-13
Glenwood City, 1225 H-3
Grafton, 11625 M-13
GRANT CO., 49671 O-6
Grantsburg, 1397 E-2
GREEN CO., 35165 P-9
Green Bay, 101203 J-13
Greendale, 13860 *G-5
Greenfield, 35753 O-13
GREEN LAKE CO., 19168 L-10
Green Lake, 1125 L-11
Greenwood, 1082 I-7
Hales Corners, 7535 O-13
Hammond, 1695 H-2
Hartford, 13017 M-12
Hartland, 8672 N-12
Hayward, 2293 E-5
Hazel Green, 1205 P-7
Highland, 817 N-7
Hilbert, 1087 K-12
Hillsboro, 1303 L-7
Holmen, 7446 K-5
Horicon, 3604 M-11
Hortonville, 2630 J-11
Howard, 15912 I-13
Howards Grove, 3034 L-13
Hudson, 11367 H-2
Hurley, 1678 C-8
Hustisford, 1106 M-11
Independence, 1246 J-5
Iola, 1232 J-10
IOWA CO., 23569 N-7
IRON CO., 6649 D-7
Iron Ridge, 987 M-12
Iron River, 900 C-5
Jackson, 6036 M-12
JACKSON CO., 19758 J-7
Janesville, 61962 P-10
JEFFERSON CO., 79328 N-11
Jefferson, 7592 O-11
Johnson Cr., 2024 N-11
JUNEAU CO., 26725 K-8
Juneau, 2587 M-11
Kaukauna, 14656 J-12
Kenosha, 95240 P-13
KENOSHA CO., 160544 P-14
Kewaskum, 3607 M-12
Kewaunee, 2877 J-14
KEWAUNEE CO., 20840 J-14
Kiel, 3507 K-13
Kimberly, 6230 J-12
King, 750 J-10
Kohler, 1991 L-13
Lac du Flambeau, 1646 E-8
LA CROSSE CO., 108958 L-5
La Crosse, 50287 L-5
Ladysmith, 3789 F-5
La Farge, 799 M-6
LAFAYETTE CO., 16310 P-8
Lake Delton, 3053 M-9
Lake Geneva, 8223 P-12
Lake Mills, 5241 N-11
Lake Nebagamon, 1089 C-4
Lancaster, 3977 O-6
LANGLADE CO., 20735 G-10
Lannon, 1006 *C-2
Laona, 750 F-11
Lena, 501 H-13
LINCOLN CO., 30319 G-8
Little Chute, 10870 J-12
Lodi, 3030 N-9
Lomira, 2410 M-12
Loyal, 1282 I-7
Luck, 1209 F-2
Luxemburg, 2211 I-13
Madison, 221551 N-10
Manawa, 1333 J-11
MANITOWOC CO., 81949 K-13
Manitowoc, 33917 K-14
Maple Bluff, 1297 R-8
MARATHON CO., 128941 H-8
Marathon, 1529 H-8
MARINETTE CO., 43406 G-12
Marinette, 11275 H-14
Marion, 1241 I-11
Markesan, 1349 L-10
MARQUETTE CO., 15237 L-9
Marshall, 3561 N-10
Marshfield, 18796 I-8
Mauston, 4291 L-8
Mayville, 5055 M-12
Mazomanie, 1528 N-8
McFarland, 7383 N-10
Medford, 4189 G-7
Mellen, 808 D-6
Menasha, 16306 K-12
MENOMINEE CO., 4580 H-11
Menomonee Falls, 34125 N-13
Menomonie, 15244 H-3
Mequon, 23820 N-13
Mercer, 1300 D-8
Merrill, 10145 G-9
Merrillan, 586 J-6
Merton, 2643 N-12
Middleton, 15816 N-9
Milltown, 905 F-2
Milton, 5464 O-11
MILWAUKEE CO., 921654 N-13
Milwaukee, 578887 N-13
Mineral Pt., 2495 O-8
Minocqua, 1280 E-9
Mishicot, 1413 J-14
Mondovi, 2618 I-4
Monona, 7716 N-10
Monroe, 10563 P-9
MONROE CO., 42644 L-7
Montello, 1483 L-10
Monticello, 1132 O-9
Montreal, 778 C-7
Mosinee, 3996 I-9
Mt. Calvary, 935 L-12
Mt. Horeb, 6188 O-9
Mukwonago, 6857 O-12
Muscoda, 1408 N-7
Muskego, 22872 O-13
Necedah, 878 K-8
Neenah, 24596 K-12
Neillsville, 2694 I-7
Nekoosa, 2585 J-8
Neopit, 839 H-11
New Berlin, 38547 *F-3
Newburg, 1206 M-13
New Glarus, 2058 O-9
New Holstein, 3200 K-13
New Lisbon, 2464 L-8
New London, 6926 J-11
New Richmond, 7726 G-2
Niagara, 1805 I-13
N. Fond du Lac, 5024 L-12
N. Freedom, 627 M-8
N. Hudson, 3747 H-2
N. Prairie, 1938 O-12
Oak Cr., 32312 O-13
Oakfield, 1021 L-12
Oconomowoc, 13711 N-12
OCONTO CO., 37666 H-12
Oconto, 4564 H-13
Oconto Falls, 2729 H-12
Okauchee, 1500 N-12
Omro, 3282 K-11
Onalaska, 15701 L-5
Oneida, 1070 J-12
ONEIDA CO., 36994 F-10
Oostburg, 2772 L-13
Oregon, 8493 O-9
Orfordville, 1336 P-10
Osceola, 2685 G-2
Oshkosh, 63485 K-11
Osseo, 1661 I-5
OUTAGAMIE CO., 171006 J-12
Owen, 914 H-7
OZAUKEE CO., 86072 M-13
Paddock Lake, 3150 P-13
Palmyra, 1763 O-11
Pardeeville, 2125 M-10
Park Falls, 2464 E-7
Pell Lake, 2988 P-12
PEPIN CO., 7380 I-3
Pepin, 925 J-3
Peshtigo, 3346 H-13
Pewaukee, 8918 N-12
Phillips, 1499 F-7
PIERCE CO., 39102 I-3
Pittsville, 847 J-8
Plain, 768 N-8
Plainfield, 899 K-9
Platteville, 9854 O-7
Pleasant Prairie, 18551 P-13
Plover, 11256 J-9
Plymouth, 8217 L-13
POLK CO., 44329 F-2
PORTAGE CO., 67585 J-9
Portage, 10035 M-9
Port Edwards, 1797 J-8
Port Washington, 10892 M-13
Potosi, 728 P-6
Poynette, 2563 M-9
Prairie du Chien, 5880 N-5
Prairie du Sac, 3547 N-9
Prentice, 563 F-7
Prescott, 4009 I-1
PRICE CO., 15220 F-7
Princeton, 1463 L-10
Pulaski, 3540 I-12
RACINE CO., 195708 O-13
Racine, 79392 O-13
Randolph, 1820 M-10
Random Lake, 1585 M-13
Redgranite, 2243 K-10
Reedsburg, 8497 M-8
Reedsville, 1162 K-13
Reeseville, 692 N-11
Rhinelander, 7889 F-9
Rib Lake, 858 G-8
Rice Lake, 8361 F-4
RICHLAND CO., 18403 M-7
Richland Cen., 5177 M-7
Rio, 998 M-10
Ripon, 7268 L-11
River Falls, 13254 H-2
River Hills, 1630 *B-5
Roberts, 1484 H-2
ROCK CO., 157538 O-10
Rothschild, 5096 H-9
RUSK CO., 15198 F-5
ST. CROIX CO., 77144 H-2
St. Croix Falls, 2132 F-2
St. Francis, 9382 O-13
St. Nazianz, 806 K-13
Salem, 1150 P-13
SAUK CO., 57746 M-8
Sauk City, 3006 N-9
Saukville, 4184 M-13
SAWYER CO., 16975 E-5
Schofield, 2160 H-9
Seymour, 3432 J-12
Sharon, 1570 P-11
Shawano, 8441 I-11
SHAWANO CO., 41335 I-11
SHEBOYGAN CO., 114610 L-13
Sheboygan, 48872 L-14
Sheboygan Falls, 7527 L-13
Shell Lake, 1372 E-4
Sherwood, 2290 K-12
Shiocton, 920 J-11
Shorewood, 13192 N-13
Shorewood Hills, 1671 S-6
Shullsburg, 1198 P-7
Silver Lake, 2513 P-12
Siren, 1015 E-2
Sister Bay, 879 A-13
Slinger, 4358 M-12
Solon Sprs., 577 C-4
Somerset, 2539 G-2
S. Milwaukee, 20849 O-13
Sparta, 8827 K-6
Spencer, 1833 I-7
Spooner, 2670 E-4
Spring Green, 1436 N-8
Spring Valley, 1283 H-3
Stanley, 3304 H-6
Stevens Pt., 24298 J-9
Stockbridge, 676 K-12
Stoddard, 817 L-5
Stoughton, 12646 O-10
Stratford, 1515 I-8
Strum, 971 I-5
Sturgeon Bay, 9180 H-14
Sturtevant, 6190 O-13
Sun Prairie, 25392 N-10
Superior, 26779 B-3
Sussex, 9812 N-12
TAYLOR CO., 19766 G-7
Theresa, 1265 M-12
Thiensville, 3123 N-13
Thorp, 1554 H-6
Tigerton, 744 I-10
Tomah, 8620 K-7
Tomahawk, 3829 F-9
TREMPEALEAU CO., 27812 J-5
Trempealeau, 1459 K-5
Turtle Lake, 1008 G-3
Twin Lakes, 5513 P-12
Two Rivers, 12144 K-14
Union Gr., 4614 P-13
Valders, 995 K-13
VERNON CO., 29055 M-6
Verona, 10166 O-9
VILAS CO., 22330 D-9
Viola, 659 M-6
Viroqua, 4424 M-6
Wabeno, 960 F-11
Wales, 2610 O-12
WALWORTH CO., 99844 O-11
Walworth, 2682 P-11
Washburn, 2281 B-6
WASHBURN CO., 16601 E-4
WASHINGTON CO., 126158 M-12
Waterford, 4828 O-12
Waterloo, 3282 N-10
Watertown, 22816 N-11
WAUKESHA CO., 378971 O-12
Waukesha, 67658 N-12
Waunakee, 10360 N-9
Waupaca, 5877 J-10
WAUPACA CO., 52563 J-10
Waupun, 10558 L-11
Wausau, 37292 H-9
Wausaukee, 551 G-13
WAUSHARA CO., 24789 K-10
Wautoma, 2103 K-10
Wauwatosa, 45014 *E-4
W. Allis, 58798 *F-4
W. Baraboo, 1373 M-9
W. Bend, 29549 M-12
Westby, 2142 L-6
Westfield, 1211 L-9
W. Milwaukee, 4012 *F-5
W. Salem, 4709 L-5
Weyauwega, 1772 J-11
Whitefish Bay, 13508 N-13
Whitehall, 1628 J-5
Whitelaw, 732 K-13
Whitewater, 14311 O-11
Whiting, 1691 J-9
Wild Rose, 756 K-10
Williams Bay, 2668 P-12
Wind Lake, 5202 O-13
Wind Pt., 1839 O-13
WINNEBAGO CO., 159482 K-11
Winneconne, 2445 K-11
Wisconsin Dells, 2559 M-9
Wisconsin Rapids, 17621 J-8
Wittenberg, 1123 I-10
Wonewoc, 802 L-7
WOOD CO., 75234 I-8
Woodruff, 1500 E-9
Woodville, 1276 H-3
Wrightstown, 2248 J-12
Wyocena, 754 M-10

Wyoming

Map pp. 234-235

Afton, 1831 E-4
ALBANY CO., 30890 G-11
Baggs, 354 H-9
Bairoil, 96 F-9
Bar Nunn, 1292 E-10
Basin, 1224 B-8
Big Horn, 198 B-10
BIG HORN CO., 11333 B-8
Big Piney, 455 F-5
Buffalo, 4290 B-10
Byron, 548 B-8
CAMPBELL CO., 37405 C-11
CARBON CO., 15331 G-9
Casper, 51738 E-10
Cheyenne, 55731 H-13
Cody, 9100 B-7
Cokeville, 492 F-4
CONVERSE CO., 12766 E-11
Cowley, 582 A-8
CROOK CO., 6182 B-12
Dayton, 717 A-9
Diamondville, 695 G-5
Douglas, 5581 E-12
Dubois, 991 D-6
E. Thermopolis, 258 D-8
Eden, 388 G-6
Edgerton, 173 D-11
Encampment, 442 H-10
Etna, 123 E-4
Evanston, 11459 H-4
Evansville, 2328 E-11
Ft. Laramie, 231 F-13
Ft. Washakie, 1477 E-7
FREMONT CO., 36491 E-8
Gillette, 22685 B-12
Glenrock, 2351 E-11
GOSHEN CO., 12243 G-13
Green River, 11787 H-6
Greybull, 1752 B-8
Guernsey, 1118 F-13
Hanna, 863 G-10
HOT SPRINGS CO., 4537 C-7
Hudson, 416 E-8
Hulett, 429 B-13
Jackson, 9038 D-5
Jeffrey City, 106 F-9
JOHNSON CO., 7721 C-10
Kaycee, 273 D-10
Kemmerer, 2560 G-5
La Barge, 421 F-5
Lander, 6898 E-7
LARAMIE CO., 85163 H-13
Laramie, 26050 H-12
LINCOLN CO., 15999 F-4
Lingle, 490 F-13
Lovell, 2277 B-8
Lusk, 1348 E-13
Lyman, 1937 H-5
Marbleton, 811 F-5
Medicine Bow, 265 G-11
Meeteetse, 347 C-7
Midwest, 431 D-11
Mills, 2898 G-2
Moorcroft, 845 C-12
Mtn. View, 103 G-1
Mtn. View, 1163 H-5
NATRONA CO., 69799 E-9
Newcastle, 3221 C-13
NIOBRARA CO., 2286 E-13
Orchard Valley, 1800 H-13
Osage, 215 C-13
PARK CO., 26664 C-7
Pine Bluffs, 1162 H-14
Pinedale, 1658 E-6
PLATTE CO., 8619 G-12
Powell, 5288 B-7
Ranchester, 717 A-9
Rawlins, 8658 G-9
Reliance, 665 G-7
Riverton, 9430 E-8
Rock Sprs., 18772 G-7
Rolling Hills, 467 E-11
Saratoga, 1714 H-10
SHERIDAN CO., 27389 A-10
Sheridan, 16333 B-10
Shoshoni, 659 D-8
Sinclair, 406 G-10
Story, 887 B-10
SUBLETTE CO., 6926 F-6
Sundance, 1184 B-13
Superior, 239 G-7
SWEETWATER CO., 37975 H-8
Ten Sleep, 315 C-9
TETON CO., 19032 C-5
Thermopolis, 2905 D-8
Torrington, 5533 F-13
UINTA CO., 19939 H-4
Upton, 857 C-13
Wamsutter, 265 G-8
WASHAKIE CO., 7933 C-8
WESTON CO., 6671 C-13
Wheatland, 3464 G-12
Wilson, 1294 D-5
Worland, 4967 C-8

CANADA Cities and Towns

Alberta

Map pp. 238-241

* City keyed to p. 236

Airdrie, 20382 H-16
Alix, 825 G-17
Athabasca, 2415 C-16
Banff, 7135 I-15
Barrhead, 4213 D-15
Bashaw, 825 F-17
Bassano, 1320 I-18
Beaverlodge, 2110 B-11
Bentley, 1035 G-16
Berwyn, 546 A-12
Black Diamond, 1866 I-16
Blackfalds, 3042 G-16
Bon Accord, 1532 D-16
Bonnyville, 5709 D-19
Bow Island, 1704 J-19
Bowden, 1174 G-16
Boyle, 836 C-17
Brooks, 11604 I-18
Bruderheim, 1202 D-17
Calgary, 878866 I-16
Calmar, 1902 E-16
Camrose, 14854 F-17
Canmore, 10792 I-15
Cardston, 3475 L-17
Carstairs, 2254 H-16
Castor, 935 G-18
Claresholm, 3622 J-17
Coaldale, 6008 K-18
Cochrane, 11798 I-16
Cold Lake, 11520 C-19
Consort, 634 G-19
Coronation, 902 G-19
Crossfield, 2389 H-16
Crowsnest Pass, 6262 K-16
Daysland, 779 F-18
Delburne, 719 G-17
Devon, 4969 E-16
Didsbury, 3932 H-16
Drayton Valley, 5801 E-15
Drumheller, 7785 H-17
Eckville, 1019 G-16
Edmonton, 666104 E-17
Edson, 7585 E-14
Elk Pt., 1440 D-19
Evansburg E-15
Fairview, 3150 A-12
Falher, 1109 B-13
Foremost, 531 K-19
Forestburg, 870 F-18
Ft. Macleod, 2990 K-17
Ft. McMurray *E-4
Ft. Saskatchewan, 13121 E-17
Ft. Vermilion *E-4
Fox Cr., 2337 D-13
Gibbons, 2654 D-17
Grand Centre C-19
Grande Cache, 3828 E-11
Grande Prairie, 36983 C-12
Grimshaw, 2435 A-13
Hanna, 2986 H-18
Hardisty, 743 F-19
High Level, 3444 *E-4
High Prairie, 2737 B-13
High River, 9345 J-16
Hinton, 9405 E-13
Hythe, 582 B-11
Innisfail, 6928 G-16
Jasper, 4180 F-12
Killam, 1004 F-18
Kitscoty, 671 E-19
Lac La Biche, 2776 C-18
Lacombe, 9384 G-16
Lake Louise H-14
Lamont, 1692 D-17
Leduc, 15032 E-16
Legal, 1058 D-16
Lethbridge, 67374 K-17
Lloydminster, 13148 E-20
Magrath, 1993 K-17
Manning, 1293 *E-4
Mannville, 722 E-19
Mayerthorpe, 1570 D-15
McLennan, 804 B-13
Medicine Hat, 51249 J-20
Milk River, 879 L-18
Millet, 2037 F-16
Morinville, 6540 E-21
Mundare, 653 E-17
Nanton, 1841 J-17
Okotoks, 11664 I-16
Olds, 6607 H-16
Onoway, 847 E-16
Oyen, 1020 H-20
Peace River, 6240 A-13
Penhold, 1729 G-16
Picture Butte, 1701 J-17
Pincher Cr., 3666 K-16
Ponoka, 6330 F-16
Provost, 1980 F-19
Raymond, 3200 K-18
Red Deer, 67707 G-16
Redcliff, 4372 J-19
Redwater, 2172 D-17
Rimbey, 2118 F-16
Rocky Mtn. House, 13121 E-17
Rycroft, 609 B-12
St. Albert, 53081 E-16
St. Paul, 5061 D-18
Sedgewick, 865 F-18
Sexsmith, 1653 B-11
Sherwood Park E-17
Slave Lake, 6600 B-15
Smoky Lake, 1011 D-17
Spirit River, 1100 B-11
Spruce Gr., 15983 E-16
Stettler, 5215 G-17
Stirling, 877 K-18
Stony Plain, 9589 E-16
Strathmore, 7621 I-17
Sundre, 2267 H-15
Swan Hills, 1807 C-15
Sylvan Lake, 7493 G-16
Taber, 7671 K-18
Thorsby, 799 E-16
Three Hills, 2902 H-17
Tofield, 1818 E-17
Trochu, 1033 H-17
Turner Valley, 1608 I-16
Two Hills, 1091 E-18
Valleyview, 1856 C-13
Vauxhall, 1112 J-18
Vegreville, 5376 E-18
Vermilion, 3948 E-19
Viking, 1052 E-18
Vulcan, 1762 J-17
Wabamun, 601 E-15
Wabasca-Desmarais A-16
Wainwright, 5117 F-19
Wembley, 1497 C-11
Westlock, 4819 D-16
Wetaskiwin, 11154 F-17
Whitecourt, 8334 D-14

British Columbia

Map pp. 238-241

* City keyed to p. 236

Abbotsford, 115463 L-8
Armstrong, 4256 J-11
Ashcroft, 1788 J-9
Barrière I-10
Black Cr. G-9
Burnaby, 193954 L-7
Burns Lake, 1942 D-5
Cache Cr., 1056 I-9
Campbell River, 28456 J-5
Castlegar, 7002 L-13
Chase, 2460 I-11
Chemainus L-6
Chetwynd, 2591 B-9
Chilliwack, 62927 L-8
Cl er H-10
Coldstream, 9106 J-11
Comox, 11172 K-5
Courtenay, 18304 K-5
Cranbrook, 18476 K-15
Creston, 4795 L-14
Crofton L-7
Cumberland, 2618 K-5
Dawson Cr., 10754 B-10
Delta, 96950 N-2
Duncan, 4699 L-6
Elkford, 2589 J-15
Enderby, 2818 J-11
Esquimalt, 16127 M-7
Fernie, 4611 K-15
Fort Nelson, 4188 *D-3
Fort St. James, 1927 D-6
Fort St. John, 16034 A-10
Fraser Lake, 1268 D-6
Fruitvale, 2025 L-13
Gold River, 1359 K-4
Golden, 4020 I-13
Grand Forks, 4054 L-12
Greenwood, 666 L-12
Hope, 6184 L-9
Houston, 3577 C-4
Hudson's Hope, 1039 A-9
Invermere, 2858 J-14
Kamloops, 77281 J-10
Kelowna, 96288 K-11
Kimberley, 6484 K-14
Kitimat, 10285 D-2
Ladysmith, 6587 L-6
Lake Cowichan, 2827 L-6
Langley, 23643 L-8
Lillooet, 2741 I-8
Lions Bay, 1379 K-7
Logan Lake, 2185 J-10
Lumby, 1618 J-11
Mackenzie, 5206 B-8
Maple Ridge, 63169 C-6
Merritt, 7088 J-9
Mission, 31272 L-8
Montrose, 1067 L-13
Nakusp, 1698 J-13
Nanaimo, 73000 L-6
Nelson, 9298 K-13
New Westminster, 54656 M-3
N. Vancouver, 44303 L-7
Oak Bay, 17798 M-7
Ocean Falls F-3
Okanagan Falls L-11
Oliver, 4224 L-11
One Hundred Mile House, 1739 H-9
Osoyoos, 4295 L-11
Oyama J-11
Parksville, 10323 L-6
Peachland, 4654 K-11
Penticton, 30985 K-11
Port Alberni, 17743 L-5
Port Alice, 1126 J-3
Port Coquitlam, 51257 L-7
Port Hardy, 4574 I-3
Port McNeill, 2821 I-3
Port Moody, 23816 L-7
Powell River, 12983 K-6
Prince George, 72406 D-8
Prince Rupert, 14643 C-1
Princeton, 2610 K-10
Qualicum Beach, 6921 K-6
Quesnel, 10044 F-8
Revelstoke, 7500 I-12
Richmond, 164345 L-7
Robson L-13
Rossland, 3646 L-12
Royston K-5
Salmo, 1120 L-13
Salmon Arm, 15210 J-11
Sechelt, 7775 K-7
Sicamous, 2720 I-11
Sidney, 10929 M-7
Smithers, 5414 C-4
Sparwood, 3812 K-15
Squamish, 14247 K-7
Summerland, 10713 K-11
Surrey, 347825 L-7
Tahsis, 600 J-4
Terrace C-3
Trail, 7575 L-13
Tumbler Ridge, 1851 C-10
Ucluelet, 1559 L-5
Valemount, 1195 F-11
Vancouver, 545671 L-7
Vanderhoof, 4390 D-7
Vernon, 33494 J-11
Victoria, 74125 M-7
Westbank K-11
Whistler, 8896 J-7
White Rock, 18250 L-7
Williams Lake, 11153 G-8
Youbou L-6

Manitoba

Map pp. 244-245

* City keyed to p. 236

Altona, 3434 M-17
Arborg, 959 J-17
Ashern I-15
Austin L-15
Baldur M-14
Beausejour, 2772 K-18
Benito, 415 H-12
Binscarth, 445 J-12
Birch River G-12
Birtle, 715 K-12
Boissevain, 1495 M-13
Bowsman, 320 G-12
Brandon, 39716 L-14
Camperville H-13
Carberry, 1513 L-14
Carman, 2831 L-16
Churchill, 963 *E-7
Cormorant C-13
Cranberry Portage C-12
Crystal City, 414 M-15
Cypress River L-15
Dauphin, 8085 I-13
Deloraine, 1026 M-13
Dominion City M-17
Duck Bay G-13
E. Selkirk K-17
Easterville E-14
Elkhorn, 470 L-12
Elm Creek L-16
Elphinstone J-13
Emerson, 655 M-17
Erickson, 448 K-14
Ethelbert, 335 I-13
Fisher Branch I-16
Flin Flon, 6000 B-11
Gilbert Plains, 757 I-13
Gimli, 1657 J-17
Gladstone, 848 K-15
Glenboro, 656 L-14
Grand Rapids, 355 E-14
Grandview, 814 I-13
Gretna, 563 M-17
Grunthal L-18
Hamiota, 858 K-13
Hartney, 446 M-13
Holland L-15
Killarney, 2221 M-14
La Broquerie, 2894 L-18
Lac du Bonnet, 1089 K-18
Lorette L-18
Lundar J-16
Lynn Lake, 699 *F-6
MacGregor, 882 L-15
Manitou, 775 M-15
McCreary, 522 J-14
Melita, 1111 M-12
Miami M-16
Minitonas, 538 G-12
Minnedosa, 2426 K-14
Moose Lake D-13
Morden, 6142 M-16
Morris, 1673 M-17
Neepawa, 3325 K-14
Niverville, 1921 L-17
Norway House D-16
Notre Dame de Lourdes, 619 L-15
Oak Lake, 359 L-13
Oakville L-16
Onanole J-14
Pilot Mound, 676 M-15
Pinawa, 1500 K-19
Pine Falls, 650 J-18
Plum Coulee, 725 M-16
Portage la Prairie, 12976 K-16
Powerview, 750 J-18
Rapid City, 424 K-13
Reston L-12
Rivers, 1119 K-13
Riverton, 594 I-17
Roblin, 1818 I-12
Rossburn, 568 J-12
Russell, 1587 J-12
St. Adolphe L-17
St. Claude, 558 L-16
St. Georges J-18
St. Jean Baptiste M-17
St. Laurent K-16
St. Malo M-17
Ste. Anne, 1513 L-18
Ste. Rose du Lac, 1047 I-14
Sandy Lake J-13
Selkirk, 9752 K-17
Shoal Lake, 801 K-13
Snow Lake, 1207 B-13
Somerset, 459 M-15
Souris, 1683 L-13
Steinbach, 9227 L-18
Stonewall, 4012 K-17
St-Pierre-Jolys, 893 L-17
Swan River, 4032 G-12
Teulon, 1058 K-17
The Pas, 5795 D-12
Thompson, 13256 *F-6
Treherne, 644 L-15
Tyndall K-18
Virden, 3109 L-12
Wabowden B-15
Warren K-17
Wawanesa, 516 L-14
Winkler, 7943 M-16
Winnipeg, 619544 L-17
Winnipeg Beach, 801 J-17
Winnipegosis, 621 H-14

New Brunswick

Map pp. 254-255

Alma, 290 I-8
Alma, 290 I-8
Aroostook, 380 F-3
Atholville, 1381 D-5
Balmoral, 1836 D-6
Bas-Caraquet, 1689 D-8
Bath, 592 G-4
Bathurst, 12924 E-7
Belledune, 1923 D-6
Beresford, 4414 D-7
Bertrand, 1269 D-8
Blacks Harbour, 1082 J-5
Blackville, 1015 G-6
Bouctouche, 2426 G-8
Campbellton, 7798 D-5
Canterbury, 399 H-4
Cap-Pele, 2266 H-9
Caraquet, 4442 D-8
Charlo, 1449 D-6
Chipman, 1432 H-6
Clair, 863 E-2
Dalhousie, 3975 D-6
Debec H-3
Dieppe, 14951 H-8
Doaktown, 955 G-6
Dorchester, 954 H-9
Edmundston, 17373 E-3
Eel River Crossing, 1335 D-6
Elgin I-8
Fairvale J-6
Florenceville, 762 G-4
Fredericton, 47560 H-5
Gagetown, 682 I-6
Geary I-5
Grand Bay J-6
Grand Falls/Grand Sault, 5858 F-3
Grande-Anse, 853 D-7
Hampton, 3997 I-6
Hartland, 902 G-4
Havelock H-7
Hillsborough, 1288 H-8
Juniper G-4
Kedgwick, 1184 D-4
Lac-Baker, 226 E-2
Lamèque, 1580 D-8
Lawrence Sta. I-4
Lorne D-6
Maugerville H-6
McAdam, 1513 I-4
Memramcook, 4719 H-8
Millville, 319 H-4
Minto, 2776 H-6
Miramichi, 18508 F-7
Moncton, 61046 H-8
Nackawic, 1042 H-4
Neguac, 1697 E-8
New Maryland, 4284 I-5
Nigadoo, 983 D-7
N. Head K-5
Norton, 1370 I-7
Oromocto, 8843 I-5
Penniac H-5
Perth-Andover, 1908 F-4
Petit Rocher, 1966 D-7
Petitcodiac, 1444 H-7
Plaster Rock, 1219 F-4
Pointe-Verte, 1041 D-7
Port Elgin, 436 H-9
Quispamsis, 13757 J-6
Renforth K-17
Rexton, 810 G-8
Richibucto, 1341 G-8
Riverview, 17010 H-8
Rivière-Verte, 856 E-3
Robertville D-7
Rogersville, 1248 G-7
Rothesay, 11505 J-6
Sackville, 5361 H-9
St. Andrews, 1869 J-4
St. George J-5
Saint John, 69661 J-6
St. Martins, 374 J-7
St. Stephen, 4667 J-4
Salisbury, 1954 H-8
Seal Cove K-5
Shediac, 4892 H-8
Shemogue H-9
Shippagan, 2872 D-8
St-Antoine, 1472 G-8
St-Basile E-3
Ste-Anne-de-Madawaska, 1168 E-3
St-Isidore, 877 E-8
St-Jacques E-2
St-Léonard E-3
St-Louis de Kent, 991 G-8
St-Quentin, 2280 E-4
Sussex, 4182 I-7
Sussex Corner, 1321 I-7
Taymouth H-5
Tide Head, 1149 D-5
Tracadie-Sheila, 4724 E-8
Tracy, 601 I-5
Upper Kent G-4
Welsford I-6
Westfield J-6
Wilsons Beach K-5
Woodstock, 5198 H-4

Newfoundland and Labrador

Map pp. 256-257

Arnold's Cove, 1024 E-19
Badger, 906 D-18
Baie Verte, 1492 C-18
Bay Roberts, 5237 E-20
Bishop's Falls, 3688 D-18
Bonavista, 4021 D-20
Botwood, 3221 D-18
Buchans, 877 D-17
Burgeo, 1782 E-17
Burin, 2470 F-19
Carbonear, 4759 E-20
Catalina, 995 D-20
Channel-Port aux Basques, 4637 E-16
Clarenville, 5104 E-19
Corner Brook, 20103 D-17
Deer Lake, 4769 D-17
Dunville F-19
Durrell C-19
Englee, 694 B-18
Fogo, 803 C-19
Fortune, 1615 F-18
Gambo, 2084 D-19
Gander, 9651 D-19
Glenwood, 845 D-19
Glovertown, 2163 D-19
Goulds E-20
Grand Bank, 2841 F-18
Grand Falls-Windsor, 13340 D-18
Happy Valley-Goose Bay, 7969 B-20
Harbour Breton, 2079 E-18
Harbour Grace, 3380 E-20
Hare Bay, 1065 D-19
Isle aux Morts, 813 E-16
Joe Batt's Arm C-19
La Scie, 1063 C-18
Labrador City, 7744 B-19
Lawn, 779 F-18
Lewisporte, 3312 D-19
Marystown, 5908 F-18
Mt. Pearl, 24964 E-20
Musgrave Harbour, 1294 D-19
Nain, 1159 A-20
Norris Pt., 786 C-17
Pasadena, 3133 D-17
Peterview, 811 D-18
Placentia, 4426 F-19
Pouch Cove, 1669 E-20
Rocky Harbour, 1002 C-17
Roddickton, 1003 B-18
St. Alban's, 1372 E-18
St. Anthony, 2730 B-18
St. George's, 1354 E-16
St. John's, 99182 E-20
St. Lawrence, 1558 F-18
Shoal Harbour E-19
Springdale, 3045 D-18
Stephenville, 7109 D-16
Stephenville Crossing, 1993 D-16
Torbay, 5474 E-20
Wabana, 2679 E-20
Wabush, 1894 B-19
Wesleyville D-19
Whitbourne, 930 F-20
Witless Bay, 1056 F-20

Northwest Territories

Map p. 236

Aklavik, 632 B-3
Ft. McPherson, 761 B-3
Ft. Providence, 753 D-4
Ft. Simpson, 1163 D-4
Ft. Smith, 2185 E-5
Hay River, 3510 E-4
Inuvik, 2894 B-3
Tuktoyaktuk, 930 A-4
Yellowknife, 16541 D-5

Nova Scotia

Map pp. 255-257

Advocate Harbour J-8
Amherst, 9470 I-9

Population figures from latest available census.

Annapolis Royal, 550 K-7
Antigonish, 4754 I-13
Arichat I-14
Aylesford J-8
Baddeck H-14
Barrington N-7
Barrington Passage N-7
Bear River K-7
Berwick, 2282 J-8
Bridgetown, 1035 K-7
Bridgewater, 7621 L-9
Brighton I-6
Brookfield J-10
Brooklyn M-8
Canning J-9
Canso, 992 J-14
Chester K-9
Chéticamp G-14
Cheverie J-9
Church Pt. L-6
Clark's Harbour, 944 N-7
Clementsport K-7
Clementsvale K-7
Dartmouth K-10
Debert I-10
Deep Brook K-7
Digby, 2111 K-6
Dingwall F-15
Dominion H-16
Elmsdale K-10
Enfield K-10
Falmouth J-9
Five Islands J-9
Freeport L-6
Glace Bay H-16
Grand-Étang G-14
Granville Ferry K-7
Great Vil. J-10
Guysborough I-13
Halifax, 359111 K-10
Hantsport, 1202 J-9
Havre Boucher I-13
Hebron M-6
Hilden J-10
Hopewell I-11
Hubbards K-9
Ingonish F-15
Ingonish Beach G-15
Inverness H-14
Joggins I-9
Kentville, 5610 J-9
Kingston K-8
L'Ardoise I-14
Larrys River J-14
Lawrencetown K-7
Little Brook L-6
Liverpool M-8
Lockeport, 701 M-8
Louisbourg H-16
Louisdale I-14
Lunenburg, 2568 L-9
Mabou H-13
Maccan I-9
Mahone Bay, 991 L-9
Maitland J-10
Meteghan L-6
Meteghan River L-6
Middle Musquodoboit J-11
Middleton, 1744 K-8
Milford Sta. J-10
Milton M-8
Mulgrave, 904 I-13
Musquodoboit Harbour K-11
New Germany L-8
New Glasgow, 9432 I-12
New Minas J-9
New Ross K-9
New Waterford G-15
N. Sydney H-15
Oxford, 1332 I-10
Parrsboro, 1529 J-9
Petite Rivière L-9
Pictou, 3875 I-11
Pleasant Bay F-14
Port Hastings I-13
Port Hawkesbury, 3701 I-14
Port Hood H-13
Port Maitland M-6
Port Medway L-8
Port Morien H-16
Pugwash I-10
River Hebert I-9
River John I-11
St. Peters I-14
Sheet Harbour K-12
Shelburne, 2013 M-7
Sherbrooke J-13
Ship Harbour K-11
Shubenacadie J-10
Springhill, 4091 I-9
Stellarton, 4809 I-11
Stewiacke, 1388 J-10
Sydney H-15
Sydney Mines G-15
Tatamagouche I-10
Three Mile Plains K-9
Tiverton L-6
Trenton, 2798 I-12
Truro, 11457 J-10
Tusket M-6
Upper Musquodoboit J-11
Valley J-11
Waterville J-8
Waverley K-10
Wedgeport M-6
W. Arichat I-14
Western Shore L-9
Westport L-6
Westville, 3879 I-11
Weymouth L-6
Whycocomagh H-14
Windsor, 3778 K-9
Wolfville, 3658 J-9
Yarmouth, 7561 M-6

Nunavut

Map pp. 236-237

Arviat, 1899 E-7
Ikaluktutiak C-6
Iqaluit, 5236 D-10
Kangiqsliniq D-7
Kugluktuk, 1212 C-5
Pangnirtung, 1276 C-10
Qamani'tuaq D-7

Ontario

Map pp. 246-249

Acton J-9
Ailsa Craig K-6
Ajax, 73753 I-11
Aldershot I-20
Alexandria E-19
Alfred D-18
Alliston H-9
Almonte E-16
Alvinston L-5
Amherstburg, 20339 M-3
Amherstview H-15
Angus H-9
Arnprior, 7192 E-16
Arthur I-8
Athens, 3053 G-17
Atikokan, 3632 L-14
Atwood I-7
Aurora, 40167 I-10
Aylmer, 7126 L-7
Ayr J-8
Bancroft, 4089 F-13
Barrie, 103710 H-10
Barriefield H-15
Barry's Bay E-13
Bath H-15
Bayfield J-6
Beachville D-15
Beamsville K-10
Beaverton H-11
Belle River M-4
Belleville, 45986 H-14
Belmont K-7
Blenheim M-5
Blind River, 3969 C-4
Bloomfield I-14
Blyth I-6
Bobcaygeon G-12
Bolton I-9
Bonfield, 2064 C-11
Bothwell L-5
Bourget E-18
Bowmanville I-11
Bracebridge, 13751 F-10
Bradford H-10
Brampton, 325428 I-9
Brantford, 86417 K-8
Bridgenorth H-12
Brighton, 9449 H-13
Brights Grove K-5
Brockville, 21375 G-17
Bruce Mines, 627 C-2
Brussels I-7
Burford K-8
Burk's Falls, 940 D-10
Burlington, 150836 J-9
Cache Bay C-9
Calabogie E-15
Caledon, 50595 I-9
Caledonia K-9
Callander C-10
Cambridge, 110372 J-8
Campbellford H-13
Cannington H-11
Capreol B-7
Cardinal F-17
Carleton Place, 9083 F-16
Casselman, 2910 E-18
Cayuga K-9
Chalk River C-14
Chapleau M-19
Chatham M-5
Chesley H-7
Chesterville F-18
Clifford I-7
Clinton J-6
Cobalt, 1229 M-20
Cobden D-15
Cobourg, 17172 I-12
Cochrane, 5690 L-20
Colborne I-13
Colchester N-3
Coldwater G-10
Collingwood, 16039 G-9
Collins Bay H-15
Cookstown H-10
Cornwall, 45640 F-19
Corunna K-4
Courtland L-8
Creemore H-9
Crystal Beach K-11
Deep River, 4135 C-13
Deseronto, 1796 H-14
Drayton I-8
Dresden L-5
Dryden, 8198 K-14
Dundalk H-8
Dunnville K-10
Durham H-7
Dutton L-6
Eganville E-14
Elliot Lake, 11956 B-4
Elmira J-8
Elmvale G-9
Elora I-8
Embrun E-17
Englehart, 1595 M-20
Erin, 11052 I-9
Espanola, 5449 C-6
Essex, 20085 M-4
Exeter J-6
Fenelon Falls G-11
Fergus I-8
Fonthill K-10
Forest K-5
Ft. Erie, 28143 K-11
Ft. Frances, 8315 L-13
Frankford H-13
Gananoque, 5167 H-16
Georgetown J-9
Geraldton K-17
Glencoe L-6
Gloucester E-17
Goderich, 7604 I-6
Gore Bay, 898 D-5
Grand Bend J-6
Grand Valley I-8
Gravenhurst, 10899 F-10
Grimsby, 21297 K-10
Guelph, 106170 J-9
Haileybury, 4543 M-20
Haliburton F-12
Hamilton, 490268 K-9
Hanover, 6869 H-7
Harriston I-7
Harrow N-4
Harrowsmith G-15
Hastings H-13
Havelock G-13
Hawkesbury, 10314 D-19
Hearst, 5825 K-18
Hensall J-6
Hillsburgh I-9
Hornepayne, 1362 L-18
Huntsville, 17338 E-10
Ingersoll, 10977 K-7
Ingleside F-18
Iroquois F-17
Iroquois Falls, 5217 L-20
Kanata E-16
Kapuskasing, 9238 L-19
Keewatin K-13
Kemptville F-17
Kenora, 15838 K-13
Keswick H-10
Kettle Pt. K-5
Killaloe E-14
Kincardine, 11029 H-6
Kingston, 114195 H-15
Kingsville, 19619 N-4
Kirkland Lake, 8616 L-20
Kitchener, 190399 J-8
L'Orignal D-18
Lakefield H-12
Lanark F-16
Lancaster E-19
Lansdowne G-16
LaSalle, 25285 M-3
Leamington, 27138 N-4
Limoges E-18
Lindsay H-11
Listowel I-7
Little Current D-6
London, 336539 K-7
Long Sault F-18
Longlac K-17
Lucan K-6
Lucknow I-6
Madoc, 2044 G-14
Malton G-1
Manitouwadge, 2949 L-17
Manotick E-17
Marathon, 4416 L-17
Markdale H-8
Markham, 208615 I-10
Marmora, 3985 G-13
Massey C-5
Mattawa, 2270 C-11
Maxville E-18
Meaford G-8
Merlin M-5
Merrickville F-17
Metcalfe E-17
Midland, 16214 G-9
Mildmay H-7
Millbrook H-12
Milton, 31471 J-9
Milverton J-7
Minden F-11
Mississauga, 612925 J-10
Mitchell J-7
Morrisburg F-18
Mt. Albert H-10
Mt. Brydges K-6
Mt. Forest I-8
Mt.Pleasant K-8
Nanticoke L-9
Napanee, 15132 H-15
Nepean E-17
New Hamburg J-8
New Liskeard, 4906 M-20
Newmarket, 65788 H-10
Niagara Falls, 78815 K-11
Niagara-on-the-Lake, 13839 K-11
Nipigon, 1964 L-16
Nobleton I-10
N. Bay, 52771 C-10
N. Gower F-17
Norwood H-13
Oakville, 144738 J-10
Odessa H-15
Oil Sprs., 758 L-5
Omemee H-12
Orangeville, 25248 I-9
Orillia, 29121 G-10
Oshawa, 139051 I-11
Ottawa, 774072 E-17
Owen Sound, 21431 G-7
Palmerston I-7
Paris K-8
Parry Sound, 6124 E-8
Pembroke, 13490 D-14
Penetanguishene, 8316 G-9
Perth, 6003 F-16
Petawawa, 14398 D-14
Peterborough, 71446 H-12
Petrolia, 4849 K-5
Pickering, 87139 I-11
Picton I-14
Plantagenet E-18
Port Burwell L-7
Port Colborne, 18450 K-10
Port Credit J-10
Port Elgin G-6
Port Hope I-12
Port McNicoll G-9
Port Perry H-11
Port Rowan L-8
Port Stanley L-7
Powassan, 3252 C-10
Prescott, 4228 G-17
Preston J-8
Rainy River, 981 L-13
Renfrew, 7942 E-15
Richmond E-17
Richmond Hill, 132030 I-10
Ridgetown M-5
Ripley H-6
Rockland E-17
Rockwood J-9
Rodney L-6
Russell, 12412 E-17
St. Catharines, 129170 K-10
St. Clements J-8
St. George K-9
St. Jacobs J-8
St. Mary's, 6293 J-7
St. Thomas, 33236 L-7
Sarnia, 70876 K-5
Sauble Beach G-7
Sault Ste. Marie, 74566 B-1
Schreiber, 1448 L-16
Seaforth J-6
Sharon H-10
Shelburne, 4122 H-9
Simcoe L-8
Smiths Falls, 9140 F-16
Smooth Rock Falls, 1830 L-19
South River, 1040 D-10
Southampton G-6
Spanish C-5
Stayner H-9
Stoney Cr. K-9
Stoney Pt. M-4
Stouffville, 22008 I-10
Stratford, 29676 J-7
Strathroy K-6
Streetsville J-9
Sturgeon Falls C-9
Sudbury, 155219 B-7
Sunderland H-11
Sundridge, 983 D-10
Sutton H-10
Sydenham G-15
Tara G-7
Tavistock J-7
Tecumseh, 25105 M-4
Teeswater I-7
Terrace Bay, 1950 L-17
Thamesford K-7
Thamesville L-5
Thedford K-5
Thessalon, 1386 C-3
Thornbury G-8
Thorold, 18048 K-10
Thunder Bay, 109016 L-15
Tilbury M-4
Tillsonburg, 14052 L-8
Timmins, 43686 L-20
Toronto, 2481494 I-10
Trenton H-13
Tweed, 5612 G-14
Uxbridge, 17377 H-10
Vankleek Hill D-19
Verner B-9
Walkerton H-7
Wallaceburg L-4
Wasaga Beach, 12419 G-9
Waterdown I-19
Waterloo, 86543 J-8
Watford K-5
Wawa M-18
Welland, 48402 K-10
Wellesley, 9365 J-8
Wellington I-14
W. Lorne L-6
Westport, 647 G-15
Wheatley M-4
Whitby, 87413 I-11
Whitney E-12
Wiarton G-7
Winchester F-17
Windsor, 208402 M-3
Wingham I-7
Woodstock, 33061 K-8
Woodville H-11
Wyoming K-5
Zurich J-6

Prince Edward Island

Map pp. 254-257

Alberton, 1115 F-9
Borden H-10
Charlottetown, 32245 H-11
Georgetown, 721 H-12
Kensington, 1385 G-10
Montague, 1945 H-11
Mt. Stewart, 312 G-11
Murray Harbour, 357 H-12
Murray River, 435 H-12
O'Leary, 860 G-9
Souris, 1248 G-12
Summerside, 14654 G-10
Tignish, 831 F-9

Québec

Map pp. 250-253

Acton Vale, 7299 L-9
Alma, 25918 G-11
Amos, 13044 F-2
Amqui, 6473 G-16
Asbestos, 6580 L-10
Ayer's Cliff, 1102 N-18
Baie-Comeau, 23079 F-15
Baie-St-Paul, 7290 I-12
Barraute, 2010 G-3
Beauceville, 6261 K-12
Beauharnois, 11464 M-14
Beaupré, 2761 J-12
Bécancour, 11051 K-10
Bedford, 2667 M-9
Bégin, 924 G-11
Berthierville, 3939 K-16
Bic G-15
Black Lake, 4109 L-11
Blainville, 36029 L-8
Bonaventure, 2756 H-19
Brome, 286 M-9
Bromptonville, 5571 M-18
Brownsburg L-13
Cabano, 3213 I-14
Cacouna H-14
Campbell's Bay, 766 L-4
Candiac, 12675 F-13
Cap-Chat, 2913 F-17
Cap-de-la-Madeleine J-17
Cap-St-Ignace, 3204 I-20
Carleton H-18
Causapscal, 2634 G-17
Chandler, 3004 G-20
Charlemagne, 5662 A-14
Charny I-19
Châteauguay, 41003 M-8
Château-Richer, 3442 I-20
Chicoutimi G-12
Chute-aux-Outardes, 1968 F-15
Clermont, 3078 I-13
Coaticook, 8988 N-10
Compton, 3047 M-18
Contrecoeur, 5222 L-9
Cookshire, 1543 M-11
Coteau-du-Lac, 5573 M-14
Cowansville, 12032 M-9
Danville, 4301 L-18
Delisle, 4208 G-11
Desbiens, 1128 G-10
Deschambault, 1263 J-18
Disraëli, 2635 L-11
Donnacona, 5479 J-11
Drummondville, 46599 L-10
Dunham, 3215 N-9
E. Angus, 3570 M-11
E. Broughton, 2367 K-12
Ferme-Neuve, 2947 J-6
Forestville, 3748 F-14
Fort-Coulonge, 1661 L-4
Gaspé, 14932 F-20
Gatineau, 226696 M-5
Girardville, 1285 F-10
Granby, 44121 M-9
Grand-Mère K-9
Grenville-sur-la-Rouge, 1315 L-7
Hébertville, 2425 G-11
Hudson, 4796 M-14
Huntingdon, 2666 M-7
Iberville, 9424 M-8
Joliette, 17837 L-8
Jonquière, 54842 G-11
Kingsey Falls, 2023 L-18
L'Assomption, 15615 L-8
L'Avenir, 1277 L-17
L'Épiphanie, 4208 L-15
L'Île-Perrot, 9375 M-14
L'Islet, 3866 J-12
L'Isle-Verte, 1519 H-14
La Baie, 19940 G-12
La Doré, 1553 F-9
La Guadeloupe, 1716 L-12
La Malbaie-Pointe-au-Pic I-13
La Pérade J-17
La Pocatière, 4518 I-13
La Prairie, 18896 F-14
La Sarre, 7728 F-1
La Tuque, 11298 I-9
Lac-à-la-Croix G-11
Lac-au-Saumon, 1539 G-16
Lac-Bouchette, 1370 G-10
Lac-Etchemin, 2276 K-12
Lachute, 11628 L-7
Lac-Mégantic, 5897 M-12
Lacolle, 1503 N-15
Lanoraie K-15
Laurier-Sta., 2376 J-19
Laurierville, 1528 K-18
Laval, 343005 C-12
Lavaltrie, 5967 L-15
Lebel-sur-Quévillon, 3236 E-4
Les Escoumins, 2106 G-14
Les Méchins, 1220 F-17
Lévis, 121999 J-11
Longueuil, 371934 D-14
Louiseville, 7622 K-9
Luceville, 1351 G-15
Lyster, 1685 K-11
Macamic, 1519 F-1
Magog, 14283 M-10
Malartic, 3704 G-2
Maniwaki, 3571 K-5
Mansonville N-17
Marieville, 7240 M-16
Mascouche, 29556 A-13
Maskinongé, 1087 K-16
Matagami, 1939 D-3
Matane, 11635 F-16
Métabetchouan-Lac-à-la-Croix G-11
Mistassini F-10
Montebello, 1039 L-6
Mont-Joli, 5886 G-15
Mont-Laurier, 7365 J-6
Montmagny, 11654 J-12
Mont-Rolland K-14
Montréal, 1812723 M-8
Mont-Tremblant K-7
Morin-Hts., 2575 L-7
Murdochville, 1171 F-19
N. Hatley, 746 M-18
Napierville, 3073 M-15
New Richmond, 3760 G-18
Nicolet, 7928 K-9
Normandin, 3524 F-10
Normétal, 1019 E-1
Notre-Dame-du-Lac, 2152 I-15
Oka, 3194 M-14
Ormstown, 3647 N-14
Outremont D-12
Papineauville, 2247 L-6
Pierrefonds M-14
Pierreville, 950 L-9
Plessisville, 6756 K-11
Pointe-du-Lac K-17
Pont-Rouge, 7146 I-18
Port-Cartier, 6412 D-17
Portneuf, 1436 J-10
Price, 1800 G-15
Princeville, 5703 K-10
Québec, 507986 J-11
Rawdon, 8648 K-15
Repentigny, 54550 L-8
Richmond, 3424 L-10
Rigaud, 6095 M-13
Rimouski, 41549 G-15
Rivière-Bleue, 1477 I-14
Rivière-du-Loup, 17772 H-14
Rivière-Rouge, 1984 K-6
Robertsonville, 1705 K-19
Roberval, 10906 G-10
Rock Island N-18
Rougemont, 2583 M-16
Rouyn-Noranda, 39611 G-1
Roxton Falls, 1300 L-17
Roxton Pond, 3527 M-17
Saguenay, 60008 G-12
Saint-Ambroise, 3463 G-11
Saint-Anselme, 3224 K-12
Saint-Apollinaire, 3930 J-19
Saint-Aubert, 1365 J-13
Saint-Basile [-Sud], 2575 I-18
Saint-Boniface-de Shawinigan, 3998 J-16
Saint-Bruno, 2384 G-11
Saint-Camille-de-Lellis, 907 K-13
Saint-Casimir, 1582 K-10
Saint-Charles-de-Bellechasse, 2237 I-20
Saint-Chrysostome, 2590 N-14
Saint-Constant, 22577 M-15
Saint-Damase, 1327 M-16
Saint-Denis-sur-Richelieu, L-16
Saint-Dominique, 2231 L-16
Sainte-Adèle, 9215 L-7
Sainte-Agathe-des-Monts, 7116 L-7
Sainte-Anne-de-Beaupré, 2752 J-12
Sainte-Anne-des-Monts, 6835 F-17
Sainte-Blandine G-15
Sainte-Croix, 1533 K-11
Sainte-Julie, 26580 L-15
Saint-Elzéar, 1769 J-20
Saint-Eustache, 40378 M-8
Saint-Félicien, 10622 G-10
Saint-Félix-de-Valois, 5465 K-15
Saint-Ferréol-les-Neiges, 2014 J-12
Saint-Flavien, 1492 J-19
Saint-François-du-Lac, 1976 K-16
Saint-Gabriel, 2775 G-15
Saint-Gédéon-de-Beauce, 1829 L-12
Saint-Georges J-17
Saint-Georges, 20787 L-12
Saint-Germaine-de-Grantham, 3661 L-17
Saint-Gervais, 1910 J-12
Saint-Gilles, 1803 J-19
Saint-Guillaume Nord J-7
Saint-Honoré-de-Shenley, L-20
Saint-Honoré-de-Témiscouata, 804 I-14
Saint-Hubert M-15
Saint-Hyacinthe, 38739 L-9
Saint-Jean-sur-Richelieu, 37386 M-8
Saint-Jérôme, 59614 L-7
Saint-Joseph-de-Beauce, 4487 K-12
Saint-Léonard-d'Aston, 2231 K-17
Saint-Lin-Laurentides L-14
Saint-Louis-du-Ha! Ha!, 1427 I-14
Saint-Michel-de-Bellechasse, 1633 I-20
Saint-Nicéphore L-10
Saint-Nicolas I-19
Saint-Pacôme, 1706 I-13
Saint-Pamphile, 2847 J-13
Saint-Pascal, 3643 I-13
Saint-Paul-de-Montminy, 853 J-12
Saint-Prime, 2702 G-10
Saint-Raphaël, 2231 J-12
Saint-Raymond, 8836 J-10
Saint-Rémi, 5736 M-8
Saint-Sauveur-des-Monts, 3316 L-14
Saint-Siméon, 984 H-13
Saint-Tite, 3845 J-10
Saint-Victor, 2460 L-12
Saint-Zacharie, 2100 K-20
Saint-Zotique, 4158 M-13
Sainte-Madeleine, 2011 L-16
Sainte-Marie, 11320 K-12
Sainte-Marthe, 1094 M-13
Sainte-Pétronille, 1038 B-3
Sainte-Thècle, 2513 I-17
Sainte-Thérèse, 24269 L-14
Sainte-Véronique, 1050 K-6
Salaberry-de-Valleyfield, 26170 M-7
Sawyerville, 836 M-11
Sayabec, 1999 G-16
Senneterre, 3275 G-4
Sept-Îles, 23791 D-17
Shawinigan, 52040 K-9
Shawinigan-Sud J-16
Shawville, 1582 L-4
Sherbrooke, 75916 M-10
Sorel-Tracy L-9
Squatec H-15
Stanstead, 2995 N-10
Sutton, 1631 N-17
Tadoussac, 870 H-13
Terrebonne, 43149 L-15
Thetford Mines, 16628 L-11
Thurso, 2436 L-6
Tracy L-9
Tring-Jonction, 1333 K-20
Trois-Pistoles, 3635 H-14
Trois-Rivières, 122395 K-9
Valcourt, 2411 M-17
Val-David, 3819 K-14
Val-d'Or, 31430 G-3
Vallée-Jonction, 1882 K-12
Varennes, 19653 L-8
Vaudreuil-Dorion, 19920 M-14
Verchéres, 4782 L-15
Victoriaville, 38841 L-10
Ville-Marie, 2770 H-1
Warwick, 4874 L-10
Waterloo, 3993 M-9
Waterville, 1824 M-18
Weedon, 2646 L-11
Windsor, 5321 M-10
Yamachiche, 2631 K-16

Saskatchewan

Map pp. 242-245

* City keyed to p. 236

Aberdeen, 534 G-6
Allan, 679 H-6
Alsask, 178 H-1
Arborfield, 411 E-9
Arcola, 532 L-10
Asquith, 574 G-5
Assiniboia, 2483 L-6
Avonlea, 412 K-7
Balcarres, 622 J-9
Balgonie, 1239 J-8
Battleford, 3820 F-4
Beauval, 843 A-5
Bengough, 401 M-7
Bienfait, 786 M-10
Big River, 741 D-5
Biggar, 2243 G-4
Birch Hills, 957 F-7
Blaine Lake, 508 F-5
Bredenbury, 354 J-11
Broadview, 669 K-10
Bruno, 571 G-7
Buffalo Narrows, 1137 *F-5
Burstall, 388 J-1
Cabri, 483 J-3
Canora, 2200 H-11
Carlyle, 1260 L-11
Carnduff, 1017 M-11
Carrot River, 1017 E-9
Central Butte, 439 J-5
Choiceland, 370 E-8
Churchbridge, 796 J-11
Coleville, 313 H-2
Colonsay, 426 H-6
Coronach, 822 M-6
Craik, 418 I-6
Creighton, 1556 B-11
Cudworth, 766 G-7
Cumberland House, 632 D-11
Cupar, 602 J-8
Cut Knife, 556 F-3
Dalmeny, 1610 G-5
Davidson, 1035 I-6
Delisle, 884 G-5
Denare Beach, 784 B-11
Duck Lake, 624 F-6
Dundurn, 596 H-6
Eastend, 576 L-2
Eatonia, 474 I-2
Edam, 429 E-3
Elrose, 517 I-4
Esterhazy, 2348 J-11
Estevan, 10242 M-10
Eston, 1048 I-3
Foam Lake, 1218 H-9
Ft. Qu'Appelle, 1940 J-9
Frontier, 302 M-3
Glaslyn, 375 E-4
Gravelbourg, 1187 L-5
Green Lake, 498 C-4
Grenfell, 1067 K-10
Gull Lake, 1016 K-3
Hafford, 401 F-5
Hague, 711 F-6
Hanley, 495 H-6
Hepburn, 475 F-5
Herbert, 812 J-5
Hudson Bay, 1783 F-11
Humboldt, 5161 G-7
Indian Head, 1758 J-9
Ituna, 709 I-9
Kamsack, 2009 H-11
Kelvington, 1007 G-9
Kerrobert, 1111 G-2
Kindersley, 4548 H-2
Kinistino, 702 F-8
Kipling, 1037 K-10
Kyle, 478 J-4
La Loche, 2136 *F-5
La Ronge, 2727 A-7
Lafleche, 446 L-5
Lampman, 650 M-10
Langenburg, 1107 J-11
Langham, 1145 G-5
Lanigan, 1289 H-7
Lashburn, 783 E-2
Leader, 914 I-2
Leask, 447 E-6
Lemberg, 306 J-10
Leroy, 413 H-8
Lloydminster, 7840 E-2
Lumsden, 1581 J-7
Luseland, 602 G-2
Macklin, 1330 F-2
Maidstone, 995 E-3
Maple Cr., 2270 K-2
Marshall, 633 E-2
Martensville, 4365 G-5
Meadow Lake, 4582 C-4
Melfort, 5559 F-8
Melville, 4453 J-10
Midale, 496 M-9
Milestone, 542 K-8
Montmartre, 465 K-9
Moose Jaw, 32131 K-7
Moosomin, 2361 K-11
Mossbank, 379 K-6
Naicam, 761 G-8
Nipawin, 4275 E-9
Nokomis, 436 H-7
Norquay, 485 H-11
N. Battleford, 13692 F-4
Osler, 823 G-6
Outlook, 2129 H-5
Oxbow, 1132 M-11
Paradise Hill, 486 D-3
Pelican Narrows, 690 A-10
Pense, 533 K-7
Pierceland, 449 B-2
Pilot Butte, 1850 J-8
Ponteix, 550 L-4
Porcupine Plain, 820 F-10
Preeceville, 1074 H-10
Prince Albert, 34291 E-7
Qu'Appelle, 648 J-9
Quill Lake, 439 G-8
Radisson, 401 F-5
Radville, 735 M-8
Raymore, 625 I-8
Redvers, 917 L-11
Regina, 178225 K-8
Regina Beach, 1039 J-7
Rocanville, 887 K-11
Rockglen, 450 M-6
Rose Valley, 395 G-9
Rosetown, 2471 H-4
Rosthern, 1504 F-6
Rouleau, 434 K-7
St. Louis, 474 F-7
St. Walburg, 672 D-3
Saltcoats, 494 I-11
Saskatoon, 196811 G-5
Shaunavon, 1775 L-3
Shellbrook, 1276 E-6
Southey, 693 J-8
Spiritwood, 907 E-5
Springside, 525 I-10
Star City, 482 F-8
Stoughton, 720 L-10
Strasbourg, 760 I-7
Sturgis, 627 H-10
Swift Current, 14821 K-4
Theodore, 381 I-10
Tisdale, 3063 F-9
Turtleford, 465 D-3
Unity, 2243 F-3
Wadena, 1412 H-9
Wakaw, 884 F-7
Waldheim, 889 F-6
Wapella, 354 K-11
Warman, 3481 G-6
Watrous, 1808 H-7
Watson, 794 G-8
Wawota, 538 L-11
Weyburn, 9534 L-9
White Fox, 436 E-9
Whitewood, 947 K-11
Wilkie, 1282 F-3
Willow Bunch, 395 M-6
Wolseley, 766 K-9
Wynyard, 1919 H-8
Yellow Grass, 422 L-8
Yorkton, 15107 I-10

Yukon Territory

Map p. 236

Beaver Creek, 88 B-2
Carcross, 152 C-2
Carmacks, 431 C-2
Dawson, 1251 B-2
Faro, 313 C-2
Haines Jct., 531 C-2
Mayo, 366 B-2
Ross River, 337 C-2
Teslin, 123 C-2
Watson Lake, 912 D-3
Whitehorse, 19058 C-2

MEXICO Cities and Towns

Mexico

Map pp. 258-259

Acámbaro, 55516 G-8
Acaponeta, 18145 F-5
Acapulco, 620656 I-8
Acatlán, 14976 H-9
Acayucan, 47826 H-10
Agua Prieta, 60420 B-4
Aguascalientes, 594092 G-7
Aguililla, 9179 H-7
Álamos, 8034 D-4
Aldama, 15481 C-5
Allende, 18679 D-7
Alvarado, 22608 H-10
Ameca, 34703 G-6
Amecameca, 29949 H-8
Apan, 25119 H-9
Apatzingán de la Constitución, 93756 H-7
Arandas, 39478 G-7
Arcelia, 16114 H-8
Ario de Rosales, 14209 H-7
Arriaga, 23154 I-11
Atlixco, 82838 H-9
Atoyac, 19514 I-8
Autlán de Navarro, 39310 H-6
Becal, 6401 G-12
Buenaventura, 5678 C-5
Cárdenas San Luis Potosí, 14738 F-8
Cárdenas Tabasco, 78637 H-11
Caborca, 49917 B-3
Cadereyta, 55468 E-8
Campeche, 190813 G-12
Cananea, 30515 B-4
Cancún, 397191 G-14
Castaños, 19794 D-7
Celaya, 277750 G-8
Cerralvo, 8173 E-8
Cerritos, 12932 F-8
Champotón, 23035 H-12
Chetumal, 121602 H-13
Chiapa de Corzo, 29341 I-11
Chihuahua, 657876 C-5
Chilapa de Alvarez, 22511 I-8
Chilpancingo de los Bravos, 142746 I-8
China, 8918 E-8
Cholula, 70715 H-9
Cihuatlán, 15697 H-6
Cintalapa, 32745 I-11
Ciudad Acuña, 108159 C-7
Ciudad Altamirano, 23336 H-8
Ciudad Anáhuac, 15976 D-8
Ciudad Camargo, 37456 D-6
Ciudad del Carmen, 126024 H-12
Ciudad de México, 8605239 H-8
Ciudad Guzmán, 85118 H-6
Ciudad Hidalgo, 54854 H-8
Ciudad Juárez, 1187275 B-5
Ciudad Lerdo, 58862 E-6
Ciudad Madero, 182325 F-9
Ciudad Mante, 80533 F-8
Ciudad Netzahualcóyotl, 1225083 I-3
Ciudad Obregón, 250790 D-4
Ciudad Valles, 105721 G-8
Ciudad Victoria, 249029 F-8
Coatzacoalcos, 225973 H-10
Cocula, 13715 G-6
Colima, 119639 H-6
Comitán de Domínguez, 70311 I-12
Compostela, 15797 G-6
Concepción del Oro, 6475 E-7
Córdoba, 133807 H-9
Cosamaloapan, 28496 H-10
Cozumel, 59225 G-14
Cuatrociénegas, 8907 D-7
Cuauhtémoc, 85387 C-5
Cuautla, 136932 H-8
Cuernavaca, 327162 H-8
Culiacán, 540823 E-5
Delicias, 98615 D-6
Durango, 427135 F-6
Ebano, 22133 F-9
Ejutla, 7699 I-9
El Dorado, 13575 E-5
El Fuerte, 10728 D-4
El Salto, 19210 F-6
Emiliano Zapata, 17246 H-12
Empalme, 38533 D-3
Ensenada, 223492 A-1
Escárcega, 25911 H-12
Escuinapa de Hidalgo, 27914 F-5
Felipe Carrillo Puerto, 18545 G-13
Fresnillo, 97023 F-7
Frontera, 20965 H-11
Gómez Palacio, 210113 E-6
Guadalajara, 1646183 G-6
Guadalupe, 78879 F-7
Guamúchil, 57547 E-4
Guanajuato, 74874 G-7
Guasave, 62801 E-4
Guaymas, 97593 D-3
Hecelchakán, 9427 G-12
Hermosillo, 545928 C-3
Hidalgo del Parral, 98876 D-5
Huajuapan de León, 43073 H-9
Huatabampo, 29789 D-4
Huauchinango, 46671 G-9
Huetamo, 21335 H-7
Huixtla, 26990 J-11
Iguala, 104759 H-8
Irapuato, 319148 G-7
Isla, 24036 H-10
Ixtlán del Río, 21157 G-6
Izúcar de Matamoros, 39693 H-9
Jalpa, 13586 G-7
Jerez, 37558 F-7
Jiménez, 31195 D-6
Juan Aldama, 14058 E-6
Juchitán, 64642 I-10
La Paz, 162954 E-3
La Piedad Cavadas, 70703 G-7
Lagos de Moreno, 79592 G-7
León, 1020818 G-7
Linares, 53681 E-8
Los Mochis, 200906 E-4
Los Reyes de Salgado, 36095 H-7
Madera, 14810 C-4
Magdalena, 22023 B-3
Manzanillo, 94893 H-6
Mapastepec, 14836 J-11
Martínez de la Torre, 49565 G-9
Matamoros Coahuila, 44053 E-6
Matamoros Tamaulípas, 376279 E-9
Matehuala, 64206 F-8
Matías Romero, 19979 I-10
Mazatlán, 327989 F-5
Melchor Muzquiz, 32094 D-7
Meoqui, 19498 D-5
Mérida, 662530 G-13
Mexicali, 549873 A-2
Mexico City, 8605239 H-8
Miahuatlán, 16724 I-9
Miguel Auza, 12592 E-6
Minatitlán, 109193 H-10
Mocorito, 5093 E-4
Monclova, 192554 D-7
Montemorelos, 37713 E-8
Monterrey, 1110909 E-8
Morelia, 549996 H-7
Moroleón, 40512 G-7
Motul, 19868 G-13
Nacozari de García, 11193 B-4
Nava, 17730 C-8
Navojoa, 98187 D-4
Navolato, 26095 E-4
Nogales, 156854 B-3
Nueva Rosita, 36974 D-7
Nuevo Casas Grandes, 50378 B-5
Nuevo Laredo, 308828 D-8
Oaxaca, 251846 I-9
Ocotlán Jalisco, 75942 G-7
Ocotlán Oaxaca, 12583 I-9
Ojinaga, 20371 C-6
Ometepec, 16933 I-9
Orizaba, 118552 H-9
Pachuca, 231602 G-8
Papantla de Olarte, 48804 G-9
Paraíso, 22085 H-11
Parras, 31032 E-7
Pátzcuaro, 47993 H-7
Pénjamo, 32035 G-7
Perote, 30848 H-9
Petatlán, 20012 I-7
Peto, 16572 G-13
Piedras Negras, 126386 C-8
Pijijiapan, 13931 I-11
Poza Rica, 151441 G-9
Progreso, 44354 G-13
Puebla, 1271673 H-9
Puerto Peñasco, 30466 B-2
Puerto Vallarta, 151432 G-6
Querétaro, 536463 G-8
Reynosa, 403718 E-9
Rincón de Romos, 22570 F-7
Ríoverde, 46691 G-8
Río Grande, 29214 F-7
Rosario, 13998 F-5
Sabinas, 47578 D-7
Sabinas Hidalgo, 30910 D-8
Sahuayo de Morelos, 57827 G-7
Salamanca, 137000 G-7
Salina Cruz, 72218 I-10
Saltillo, 562587 E-7
Salvatierra, 34066 G-7
San Andrés Tuxtla, 54853 H-10
San Blas, 8812 G-5
San Buenaventura, 17904 D-7
San Cristóbal, 112442 I-11
San Felipe, 24935 G-7
San Fernando, 27053 E-9
San Francisco del Oro, 5175 D-5
San Juan del Río, 99483 G-8
San Luis Potosí, 629208 F-7
San Luis Río Colorado, 126645 A-2
San Pedro Pochutla, 12404 I-10
Santa Ana, 9689 B-3
Santa Bárbara, 9943 D-5
Santa Rosalía, 10609 D-3
Santiago Ixcuintla, 17950 G-6
Santiago Papasquiaro, 22571 E-5
Santiago Pinotepa Nacional, 24347 I-9
Santo Domingo Tehuantepec, 37068 I-10
Saucillo, 9754 D-6
Sayula, 24051 H-6
Silao, 61661 G-7
Sombrerete, 18668 F-6
Tacámbaro, 20517 H-7
Tamazunchale, 20699 G-9
Tamiahua, 5153 G-9
Tampico, 295442 F-9
Tantoyuca, 25492 G-9
Tapachula, 179839 J-11
Taxco, 50488 H-8
Tecalitlán, 12828 H-6
Tecate, 52394 A-1
Tecolotlán, 8174 G-6
Tecomán, 74106 H-6
Tecpan de Galeana, 13924 I-8
Tecuala, 14584 F-5
Tehuacán, 204598 H-9
Tempoal, 12291 G-9
Teocaltiche, 21518 G-7
Tepatitlán, 74262 G-7
Tepic, 265817 G-6
Tequila, 24024 G-6
Teziutlán, 56029 H-9
Tiacolula de Matamoros, 11087 I-10
Ticul, 28502 G-13
Tierra Blanca, 44565 H-10
Tihuatlán, 11791 G-9
Tijuana, 1148681 A-1
Tizimín, 39525 G-13
Tlalnepantla, 714735 G-2
Toluca, 435125 H-8
Tonalá, 31212 I-11
Torreón, 502964 E-6
Tulancingo, 94637 G-9
Tuxpan Nayarit, 22248 G-5
Tuxpan Veracruz, 74527 G-9
Tuxtepec, 84199 H-10
Tuxtla Gutiérrez, 424579 I-11
Uruapan del Progreso, 225816 H-7
Valladolid, 37332 G-13
Valle Hermoso, 43018 E-9
Valparaíso, 10468 F-6
Venustiano Carranza, 13906 I-11
Veracruz, 411582 H-10
Villa Unión, 13140 F-5
Villahermosa, 330846 H-11
Villanueva, 11057 F-7
Xalapa, 373076 H-9
Zacapu, 49086 H-7
Zacatecas, 113947 F-7
Zacoalco, 15648 G-6
Zacualtipán, 16216 G-8
Zamora, 122881 H-7
Zihuatanejo, 56853 I-7

	Acapulco, GR	Albany, NY	Albuquerque, NM	Amarillo, TX	Anchorage, AK	Atlanta, GA	Baltimore, MD	Bangor, ME	Billings, MT	Birmingham, AL	Bismarck, ND	Boise, ID	Boston, MA	Brownsville, TX	Buffalo, NY	Cabo San Lucas, BS	Cairo, IL	Calgary, AB	Cancún, QR	Casper, WY	Charleston, SC	Charleston, WV	Charlotte, NC	Cheyenne, WY	Chicago, IL	Chihuahua, CI	Cincinnati, OH	Cleveland, OH	Columbus, OH	Concord, NH	Dallas, TX	Davenport, IA	Daytona Beach, FL	Denver, CO	Des Moines, IA
Acapulco, GR		2944	1589	1500	5192	1980	2636	3299	2470	1854	2520	2529	3036	828	2740	2926	1967	3021	1254	2195	2296	2415	2224	2015	2297	1083	2302	2554	2413	3114	1364	2238	2146	1930	2047
Albany, NY	2944		2081	1796	4492	1006	337	399	2075	1091	1662	2507	164	2116	295	3862	1088	2460	3592	1910	896	664	768	1773	820	2391	727	478	617	149	1674	969	1162	1816	1138
Albuquerque, NM	1589	2081		285	3716	1404	1926	2480	994	1256	1140	944	2245	993	1792	1781	1098	1545	2405	719	1725	1555	1630	539	1343	506	1399	1606	1465	2225	647	1146	1736	439	977
Amarillo, TX	1500	1796	285		3692	1119	1641	2195	970	971	948	1245	1960	790	1507	2066	813	1521	2244	695	1440	1270	1345	515	1058	621	1114	1321	1180	1940	362	967	1451	430	798
Anchorage, AK	5192	4492	3716	3692		4389	4377	4545	2722	4337	2834	2805	4656	4482	4203	4599	4021	2171	5936	2997	4581	4156	4441	3177	3663	4222	3963	4013	4020	4497	4150	3614	4823	3277	3499
Atlanta, GA	1980	1006	1404	1119	4389		674	1361	1831	149	1559	2179	1098	1152	896	3122	418	2357	2628	1582	321	503	244	1445	713	1513	464	716	575	1176	794	786	434	1419	899
Baltimore, MD	2636	337	1926	1641	4377	674		639	1960	783	1547	2392	404	1808	378	3707	843	2345	3284	1795	563	369	436	1658	705	2083	523	380	416	454	1366	854	829	1696	1023
Bangor, ME	3299	399	2480	2195	4545	1361	639		2474	1446	2061	2906	249	2471	694	4261	1493	2565	3947	2309	1198	1019	1071	2172	1219	2746	1126	877	1016	228	2029	1368	1464	2215	1537
Billings, MT	2470	2075	994	970	2722	1831	1960	2474		1779	417	620	2239	1760	1786	2315	1426	551	3214	275	2136	1739	1996	455	1246	1500	1546	1596	1603	2219	1428	1112	2265	555	943
Birmingham, AL	1854	1091	1256	971	4337	149	783	1446	1779		1507	2127	1183	1026	905	2977	366	2305	2502	1530	470	570	393	1393	661	1368	467	719	578	1261	649	734	556	1339	847
Bismarck, ND	2520	1662	1140	948	2834	1559	1547	2061	417	1507		1039	1826	1703	1373	2734	1191	802	3157	522	1751	1326	1611	601	833	1646	1133	1183	1190	1806	1168	784	1993	701	669
Boise, ID	2529	2507	944	1245	2805	2179	2392	2906	620	2127	1039		2671	2035	2218	1980	1774	755	3345	703	2484	2134	2344	735	1702	1446	1958	2028	2024	2651	1703	1536	2613	830	1367
Boston, MA	3036	164	2245	1960	4656	1098	404	249	2239	1183	1826	2671		2208	459	4026	1230	2624	3684	2074	963	756	836	1937	984	2483	891	642	781	73	1766	1133	1229	1980	1302
Brownsville, TX	828	2116	993	790	4482	1152	1808	2471	1760	1026	1703	2035	2208		1849	2529	1076	2311	1476	1485	1468	1524	1396	1305	1480	681	1411	1663	1522	2286	547	1421	1318	1220	1230
Buffalo, NY	2740	295	1792	1507	4203	896	378	694	1786	905	1373	2218	459	1849		3573	799	2171	3325	1621	864	439	658	1484	531	2093	438	189	328	439	1376	680	1130	1527	849
Cabo San Lucas, BS	2926	3862	1781	2066	4599	3122	3707	4261	2315	2977	2734	1980	4026	2529	3573		2879	2632	3726	2145	3443	3336	3366	2177	3106	1859	3180	3387	3246	4006	2326	2940	3405	2097	2771
Cairo, IL	1967	1088	1098	813	4021	418	843	1493	1426	366	1191	1774	1230	1076	799	2879		1977	2552	1177	723	474	583	1040	375	1320	361	613	472	1308	603	407	852	1014	494
Calgary, AB	3021	2460	1545	1521	2171	2357	2345	2565	551	2305	802	755	2624	2311	2171	2632	1977		3765	826	2549	2124	2409	1006	1631	2051	1931	1981	1988	2517	1979	1582	2791	1106	1467
Cancún, QR	1254	3592	2405	2244	5936	2628	3284	3947	3214	2502	3157	3345	3684	1476	3325	3726	2552	3765		2939	2944	3000	2872	2759	2934	1899	2887	3139	2998	3762	2001	2875	2794	2674	2684
Casper, WY	2195	1910	719	695	2997	1582	1795	2309	275	1530	522	703	2074	1485	1621	2145	1177	826	2939		1887	1537	1747	180	1105	1225	1361	1431	1427	2054	1153	939	2016	280	770
Charleston, SC	2296	896	1725	1440	4581	321	563	1198	2136	470	1751	2484	963	1468	864	3443	723	2549	2944	1887		471	208	1750	911	1834	619	721	638	1013	1115	1038	329	1724	1207
Charleston, WV	2415	664	1555	1270	4156	503	369	1019	1739	570	1326	2134	756	1524	439	3336	474	2124	3000	1537	471		265	1400	486	1768	193	250	167	834	1051	613	737	1374	782
Charlotte, NC	2224	768	1630	1345	4441	244	436	1071	1996	393	1611	2344	836	1396	658	3366	583	2409	2872	1747	208	265		1610	771	1757	479	515	432	886	1038	898	474	1584	1067
Cheyenne, WY	2015	1773	539	515	3177	1445	1658	2172	455	1393	601	735	1937	1305	1484	2177	1040	1006	2759	180	1750	1400	1610		968	1045	1224	1294	1290	1917	973	802	1879	100	633
Chicago, IL	2297	820	1343	1058	3663	713	705	1219	1246	661	833	1702	984	1480	531	3106	375	1631	2934	1105	911	486	771	968		1594	293	341	350	964	933	175	1147	1011	333
Chihuahua, CI	1083	2391	506	621	4222	1513	2083	2746	1500	1368	1646	1446	2483	681	2093	1859	1320	2051	1899	1225	1834	1768	1757	1045	1594		1655	1907	1766	2561	717	1503	1763	945	1334
Cincinnati, OH	2302	727	1399	1114	3963	464	523	1126	1546	467	1133	1958	891	1411	438	3180	361	1931	2887	1361	619	193	479	1224	293	1655		252	111	871	938	420	885	1211	589
Cleveland, OH	2554	478	1606	1321	4013	716	380	877	1596	719	1183	2028	642	1663	189	3387	613	1981	3139	1431	721	250	515	1294	341	1907	252		142	622	1190	490	987	1337	659
Columbus, OH	2413	617	1465	1180	4020	575	416	1016	1603	578	1190	2024	781	1522	328	3246	472	1988	2998	1427	638	167	432	1290	350	1766	111	142		761	1049	486	904	1277	655
Concord, NH	3114	149	2225	1940	4497	1176	454	228	2219	1261	1806	2651	73	2286	439	4006	1308	2517	3762	2054	1013	834	886	1917	964	2561	871	622	761		1844	1113	1279	1960	1282
Dallas, TX	1364	1674	647	362	4150	794	1366	2029	1428	649	1168	1703	1766	547	1376	2326	603	1979	2001	1153	1115	1051	1038	973	933	717	938	1190	1049	1844		852	1089	882	683
Davenport, IA	2238	969	1146	967	3614	786	854	1368	1112	734	784	1536	1133	1421	680	2940	407	1582	2875	939	1038	613	898	802	175	1503	420	490	486	1113	852		1220	845	167
Daytona Beach, FL	2146	1162	1736	1451	4823	434	829	1464	2265	556	1993	2613	1229	1318	1130	3405	852	2791	2794	2016	329	737	474	1879	1147	1763	885	987	904	1279	1089	1220		1853	1333
Denver, CO	1930	1816	439	430	3277	1419	1696	2215	555	1339	701	830	1980	1220	1527	2097	1014	1106	2674	280	1724	1374	1584	100	1011	945	1211	1337	1277	1960	882	845	1853		676
Des Moines, IA	2047	1138	977	798	3499	899	1023	1537	943	847	669	1367	1302	1230	849	2771	494	1467	2684	770	1207	782	1067	633	333	1334	589	659	655	1282	683	167	1333	676	
Detroit, MI	2564	648	1586	1301	3950	726	533	1047	1533	729	1120	1965	812	1673	359	3369	623	1918	3149	1368	839	368	633	1231	278	1837	262	169	202	792	1200	427	1105	1274	596
Dodge City, KS	1685	1629	463	246	3654	1120	1432	2028	932	972	752	1207	1793	997	1340	2244	677	1483	2451	657	1441	1110	1258	477	873	867	947	1154	1013	1773	462	707	1526	386	538
Duluth, MN	2446	1293	1376	1197	3201	1190	1178	1692	861	1138	448	1483	1457	1629	1004	3170	811	1169	3083	1002	1382	957	1242	1032	464	1733	764	814	821	1437	1082	420	1624	1075	397
Durango, CO	1801	2194	212	497	3434	1616	1989	2593	828	1468	1080	734	2358	1205	1905	1812	1310	1263	2617	553	1937	1667	1842	479	1389	718	1504	1715	1570	2338	859	1223	1948	379	1054
Edmonton, AB	3194	2495	1718	1694	1998	2392	2380	2548	724	2340	837	928	2659	2484	2206	2805	2024	173	3938	999	2584	2159	2444	1179	1666	2224	1966	2016	2023	2500	2152	1617	2826	1279	1502
El Paso, TX	1322	2307	267	432	3983	1429	1999	2662	1261	1284	1407	1207	2399	836	1939	1693	1236	1812	2138	986	1750	1684	1673	806	1490	239	1571	1753	1612	2477	633	1293	1712	706	1124
Ely, NV	2181	2450	821	1106	3186	2122	2335	2849	758	2017	1177	386	2614	1807	2161	1593	1717	1075	2997	646	2427	2077	2287	678	1645	1098	1901	1971	1967	2594	1468	1479	2556	678	1310
Eureka, CA	2670	3079	1370	1655	2904	2751	2964	3478	1305	2626	1724	677	3243	2296	2790	1796	2346	1209	3486	1275	3056	2706	2916	1307	2274	1587	2530	2600	2596	3223	2017	2108	3106	1402	1939
Fargo, ND	2437	1472	1314	1011	3024	1369	1357	1871	607	1317	194	1229	1636	1620	1183	2924	1003	992	3074	712	1561	1136	1421	791	643	1673	943	993	1000	1616	1085	594	1803	876	479
Flagstaff, AZ	1782	2408	327	612	3559	1731	2253	2807	1071	1583	1467	859	2572	1320	2119	1454	1425	1388	2598	822	2052	1882	1957	866	1670	699	1726	1933	1792	2552	974	1473	2063	766	1304
Fresno, CA	2231	2959	922	1207	3238	2326	2848	3358	1258	2178	1677	723	3123	1857	2670	1357	2020	1575	3047	1193	2647	2477	2552	1225	2154	1148	2321	2480	2387	3103	1569	1988	2658	1145	1819
Gallup, NM	1703	2220	139	424	3526	1543	2065	2619	1133	1395	1279	826	2384	1132	1931	1642	1237	1355	2519	858	1864	1694	1769	678	1482	620	1538	1745	1604	2364	786	1285	1875	578	1116
Gaspé, QC	3696	783	2718	2433	4810	1789	1119	514	2666	1874	2253	3098	761	2805	969	4502	1755	2830	4281	2501	1678	1402	1551	2364	1411	2969	1394	1152	1291	739	2332	1560	1944	2407	1729
Grand Junction, CO	1971	2060	382	674	3325	1665	1942	2459	664	1585	945	625	2224	1375	1771	1853	1260	1154	2787	389	1970	1620	1830	344	1255	888	1457	1581	1523	2204	1128	1089	2099	246	920
Grants Pass, OR	2738	2976	1352	1637	2736	2648	2861	3375	1137	2608	1556	509	3140	2364	2687	1864	2243	1041	3554	1172	2953	2603	2813	1204	2171	1655	2427	2497	2493	3120	1999	2005	3082	1299	1836
Great Falls, MT	2692	2207	1216	1192	2499	2053	2092	2606	222	2001	549	581	2371	1982	1918	2337	1648	328	3436	497	2296	1871	2156	677	1378	1722	1678	1728	1735	2351	1650	1329	2487	777	1165
Green Bay, WI	2497	1038	1448	1258	3544	929	923	1437	1127	877	714	1749	1202	1680	749	3242	582	1512	3134	1074	1127	702	987	1104	209	1794	509	559	566	1182	1133	331	1363	1147	469
Guadalajara, JA	518	2710	1197	1167	4913	1746	2402	3065	2191	1620	2187	2137	2802	628	2407	2366	1634	2742	1358	1916	2062	2082	1990	1736	1964	691	1969	2221	2080	2880	1031	1883	1912	1636	1714
Halifax, NS	3763	863	2944	2659	5023	1825	1103	466	2879	1910	2466	3311	713	2935	1158	4725	1957	3043	4411	2714	1662	1483	1535	2577	1624	3210	1590	1341	1480	692	2493	1773	1928	2620	1942
Houston, TX	1183	1761	890	605	4397	797	1453	2116	1675	671	1415	1950	1853	355	1495	2446	722	2226	1831	1400	1113	1170	1041	1220	1089	804	1057	1309	1168	1931	247	1117	963	1035	948
Idaho Falls, ID	2403	2290	818	1028	2826	1962	2175	2689	338	1910	757	282	2454	1818	2001	1977	1557	655	3219	377	2267	1917	2127	518	1485	1320	1741	1811	1807	2434	1486	1319	2396	613	1150
Indianapolis, IN	2246	789	1292	1007	3851	528	592	1188	1434	476	1021	1851	953	1379	500	3073	311	1819	2883	1254	728	303	588	1117	181	1543	110	314	173	933	882	313	962	1104	482
International Falls, MN	2588	1457	1518	1339	3075	1354	1342	1856	863	1302	450	1485	1621	1771	1168	3180	975	1095	3225	968	1546	1121	1406	1047	628	1875	928	978	985	1601	1224	654	1788	1132	539
Jackson, MS	1625	1331	1055	770	4283	386	1023	1686	1688	241	1453	2047	1423	797	1130	2736	380	2239	2273	1497	707	810	630	1317	747	1127	692	944	803	1501	408	760	681	1226	828
Jacksonville, FL	2058	1072	1648	1363	4735	346	739	1374	2177	468	1905	2525	1139	1230	1040	3317	764	2703	2706	1928	239	647	384	1791	1059	1675	795	897	814	1189	1001	1132	90	1765	1245
Juneau, AK	4614	3914	3138	3114	865	3811	3799	3967	2144	3759	2256	2227	4078	3904	3625	4021	3443	1593	5358	2419	4003	3578	3863	2599	3085	3644	3385	3435	3442	3919	3572	3036	4245	2699	2921
Kansas City, MO	1853	1285	783	604	3619	811	1088	1684	1024	759	789	1372	1449	1036	996	2564	406	1575	2490	775	1116	766	976	638	529	1140	603	810	669	1429	489	363	1245	608	194
Knoxville, TN	2110	834	1400	1115	4212	216	526	1189	1766	257	1382	2114	926	1282	706	3181	353	2180	2758	1517	370	313	230	1380	542	1557	250	502	361	1004	840	669	636	1354	838
La Crosse, WI	2342	1107	1250	1071	3422	1004	992	1506	954	952	592	1576	1271	1525	818	3044	625	1390	2979	876	1196	771	1056	906	278	1607	578	628	635	1251	956	196	1438	949	271
Laredo, TX	937	2106	776	660	4352	1142	1798	2461	1630	1016	1583	1720	2198	203	1803	2295	1030	2181	1640	1355	1458	1478	1386	1175	1360	608	1365	1617	1476	2276	427	1279	1308	1090	1110
Las Vegas, NV	1936	2563	576	861	3455	1980	2445	2962	967	1832	1386	632	2727	1562	2274	1350	1674	1284	2752	797	2301	2123	2206	829	1758	853	1960	2084	2026	2707	1223	1592	2312	749	1423
Lexington, KY	2238	807	1378	1093	4042	387	546	1196	1609	403	1212	1957	933	1347	518	3159	297	2010	2823	1360	542	177	402	1223	372	1591	80	332	191	1011	874	496	808	1197	665
Lincoln, NE	1993	1332	814	597	3494	1002	1217	1731	856	950	664	1178	1496	1176	1043	2582	597	1407	2630	581	1307	957	1167	444	527	1229	783	853	849	1476	641	361	1436	487	192
Little Rock, AR	1679	1359	881	596	4002	529	1051	1714	1407	381	1172	1785	1451	788	1061	2641	288	1958	2264	1235	850	736	755	1055	655	1032	623	875	734	1529	315	611	935	964	576
Los Angeles, CA	2016	2836	799	1084	3457	2203	2725	3235	1240	2055	1659	846	3000	1642	2547	1142	1897	1557	2832	1070	2524	2354	2429	1102	2031	933	2198	2357	2264	2980	1439	1865	2518	1022	1696

	Detroit, MI	Dodge City, KS	Duluth, MN	Durango, CO	Edmonton, AB	El Paso, TX	Ely, NV	Eureka, CA	Fargo, ND	Flagstaff, AZ	Fresno, CA	Gallup, NM	Gaspé, QC	Grand Junction, CO	Grants Pass, OR	Great Falls, MT	Green Bay, WI	Guadalajara, JA	Halifax, NS	Houston, TX	Idaho Falls, ID	Indianapolis, IN	International Falls, MN	Jackson, MS	Jacksonville, FL	Juneau, AK	Kansas City, MO	Knoxville, TN	La Crosse, WI	Laredo, TX	Las Vegas, NV	Lexington, KY	Lincoln, NE	Little Rock, AR	Los Angeles, CA
Acapulco, GR	2564	1685	2446	1801	3194	1322	2181	2670	2437	1782	2231	1703	3696	1971	2738	2692	2497	518	3763	1183	2403	2246	2588	1625	2058	4614	1853	2110	2342	937	1936	2238	1993	1679	2016
Albany, NY	648	1629	1293	2194	2495	2307	2450	3079	1472	2408	2959	2220	783	2060	2976	2207	1038	2710	863	1761	2290	789	1457	1331	1072	3914	1285	834	1107	2106	2563	807	1332	1359	2836
Albuquerque, NM	1586	463	1376	212	1718	267	821	1370	1314	327	922	139	2718	382	1352	1216	1448	1197	2944	890	818	1292	1518	1055	1648	3138	783	1400	1250	776	576	1378	814	881	799
Amarillo, TX	1301	246	1197	497	1694	432	1106	1655	1011	612	1207	424	2433	674	1637	1192	1258	1167	2659	605	1028	1007	1339	770	1363	3114	604	1115	1071	660	861	1093	597	596	1084
Anchorage, AK	3950	3654	3201	3434	1998	3983	3186	2904	3024	3559	3238	3526	4810	3325	2736	2499	3544	4913	5023	4397	2826	3851	3075	4283	4735	865	3619	4212	3422	4352	3455	4042	3494	4002	3457
Atlanta, GA	726	1120	1190	1616	2392	1429	2122	2751	1369	1731	2326	1543	1789	1665	2648	2053	929	1746	1825	797	1962	528	1354	386	346	3811	811	216	1004	1142	1980	387	1002	529	2203
Baltimore, MD	533	1432	1178	1989	2380	1999	2335	2964	1357	2253	2848	2065	1119	1942	2861	2092	923	2402	1103	1453	2175	592	1342	1023	739	3799	1088	526	992	1798	2445	546	1217	1051	2725
Bangor, ME	1047	2028	1692	2593	2548	2662	2849	3478	1871	2807	3358	2619	514	2459	3375	2606	1437	3065	466	2116	2689	1188	1856	1686	1374	3967	1684	1189	1506	2461	2962	1196	1731	1714	3235
Billings, MT	1533	932	861	828	724	1261	758	1305	607	1071	1258	1133	2666	664	1137	222	1127	2191	2879	1675	338	1434	863	1688	2177	2144	1024	1766	954	1630	967	1609	856	1407	1240
Birmingham, AL	729	972	1138	1468	2340	1284	2017	2626	1317	1583	2178	1395	1874	1585	2608	2001	877	1620	1910	671	1910	476	1302	241	468	3759	759	257	952	1016	1832	403	950	381	2055
Bismarck, ND	1120	752	448	1080	837	1407	1177	1724	194	1467	1677	1279	2253	945	1556	549	714	2187	2466	1415	757	1021	450	1453	1905	2256	789	1382	592	1583	1386	1212	664	1172	1659
Boise, ID	1965	1207	1483	734	928	1207	386	677	1229	859	723	826	3098	625	509	581	1749	2137	3311	1950	282	1851	1485	2047	2525	2227	1372	2114	1576	1720	632	1957	1178	1785	846
Boston, MA	812	1793	1457	2358	2659	2399	2614	3243	1636	2572	3123	2384	761	2224	3140	2371	1202	2802	713	1853	2454	953	1621	1423	1139	4078	1449	926	1271	2198	2727	933	1496	1451	3000
Brownsville, TX	1673	997	1629	1205	2484	836	1807	2296	1620	1320	1857	1132	2805	1375	2364	1982	1680	628	2935	355	1818	1379	1771	797	1230	3904	1036	1282	1525	203	1562	1347	1176	788	1642
Buffalo, NY	359	1340	1004	1905	2206	1939	2161	2790	1183	2119	2670	1931	969	1771	2687	1918	749	2407	1158	1495	2001	500	1168	1130	1040	3625	996	706	818	1803	2274	518	1043	1061	2547
Cabo San Lucas, BS	3369	2244	3170	1812	2805	1693	1593	1796	2924	1454	1357	1642	4502	1853	1864	2337	3242	2366	4725	2446	1977	3073	3180	2736	3317	4021	2564	3181	3044	2295	1350	3159	2582	2641	1142
Cairo, IL	623	677	811	1310	2024	1236	1717	2346	1003	1425	2020	1237	1755	1260	2243	1648	582	1634	1957	722	1557	311	975	380	764	3443	406	353	625	1030	1674	297	597	288	1897
Calgary, AB	1918	1483	1169	1263	173	1812	1075	1209	992	1388	1575	1355	2830	1154	1041	328	1512	2742	3043	2226	655	1819	1095	2239	2703	1593	1575	2180	1390	2181	1284	2010	1407	1958	1557
Cancún, QR	3149	2451	3083	2617	3938	2138	2997	3486	3074	2598	3047	2519	4281	2787	3554	3436	3134	1358	4411	1831	3219	2883	3225	2273	2706	5358	2490	2758	2979	1640	2752	2823	2630	2264	2832
Casper, WY	1368	657	1002	553	999	986	646	1275	712	822	1193	858	2501	389	1172	497	1074	1916	2714	1400	377	1254	968	1497	1928	2419	775	1517	876	1355	797	1360	581	1235	1070
Charleston, SC	839	1441	1382	1937	2584	1750	2427	3056	1561	2052	2647	1864	1678	1970	2953	2296	1127	2062	1662	1113	2267	728	1546	707	239	4003	1116	370	1196	1458	2301	542	1307	850	2524
Charleston, WV	368	1110	957	1667	2159	1684	2077	2706	1136	1882	2477	1694	1402	1620	2603	1871	702	2082	1483	1170	1917	303	1121	810	647	3578	766	313	771	1478	2123	177	957	736	2354
Charlotte, NC	633	1258	1242	1842	2444	1673	2287	2916	1421	1957	2552	1769	1551	1830	2813	2156	987	1990	1535	1041	2127	588	1406	630	384	3863	976	230	1056	1386	2206	402	1167	755	2429
Cheyenne, WY	1231	477	1032	479	1179	806	678	1307	791	866	1225	678	2364	344	1204	677	1104	1736	2577	1220	518	1117	1047	1317	1791	2599	638	1380	906	1175	829	1223	444	1055	1102
Chicago, IL	278	873	464	1389	1666	1490	1645	2274	643	1670	2154	1482	1411	1255	2171	1378	209	1964	1624	1089	1485	181	628	747	1059	3085	529	542	278	1360	1758	372	527	655	2031
Chihuahua, CI	1837	867	1733	718	2224	239	1098	1587	1673	699	1148	620	2969	888	1655	1722	1794	691	3210	804	1320	1543	1875	1127	1675	3644	1140	1557	1607	608	853	1591	1229	1032	933
Cincinnati, OH	262	947	764	1504	1966	1571	1901	2530	943	1726	2321	1538	1394	1457	2427	1678	509	1969	1590	1057	1741	110	928	692	795	3385	603	250	578	1365	1960	80	783	623	2198
Cleveland, OH	169	1154	814	1715	2016	1753	1971	2600	993	1933	2480	1745	1152	1581	2497	1728	559	2221	1341	1309	1811	314	978	944	897	3435	810	502	628	1617	2084	332	853	875	2357
Columbus, OH	202	1013	821	1570	2023	1612	1967	2596	1000	1792	2387	1604	1291	1523	2493	1735	566	2080	1480	1168	1807	173	985	803	814	3442	669	361	635	1476	2026	191	849	734	2264
Concord, NH	792	1773	1437	2338	2500	2477	2594	3223	1616	2552	3103	2364	739	2204	3120	2351	1182	2880	692	1931	2434	933	1601	1501	1189	3919	1429	1004	1251	2276	2707	1011	1476	1529	2980
Dallas, TX	1200	462	1082	859	2152	633	1468	2017	1085	974	1569	786	2332	1128	1999	1650	1133	1031	2493	247	1486	882	1224	408	1001	3572	489	840	956	427	1223	874	641	315	1439
Davenport, IA	427	707	420	1223	1617	1293	1479	2108	594	1473	1988	1285	1560	1089	2005	1329	331	1883	1773	1117	1319	313	654	760	1132	3036	363	669	196	1279	1592	496	361	611	1865
Daytona Beach, FL	1105	1526	1624	1948	2826	1712	2556	3106	1803	2063	2658	1875	1944	2099	3082	2487	1363	1912	1928	963	2396	962	1788	681	90	4245	1245	636	1438	1308	2312	808	1436	935	2518
Denver, CO	1274	386	1075	379	1279	706	678	1402	876	766	1145	578	2407	246	1299	777	1147	1636	2620	1035	613	1104	1132	1226	1765	2699	608	1354	949	1090	749	1197	487	964	1022
Des Moines, IA	596	538	397	1054	1502	1124	1310	1939	479	1304	1819	1116	1729	920	1836	1165	469	1714	1942	948	1150	482	539	828	1245	2921	194	838	271	1110	1423	665	192	576	1696
Detroit, MI		1109	751	1652	1953	1733	1908	2537	930	1913	2417	1725	1136	1518	2434	1665	496	2231	1349	1319	1748	294	915	954	1015	3372	765	512	565	1627	2021	342	790	885	2294
Dodge City, KS	1109		937	505	1656	610	1064	1779	761	790	1385	602	2242	632	1676	1154	1009	1352	2492	709	990	840	1079	869	1438	3076	344	1028	811	821	1039	933	350	597	1262
Duluth, MN	751	937		1453	1204	1523	1709	2168	258	1703	2218	1515	1614	1319	2000	993	329	2113	1827	1347	1201	652	164	1176	1536	2623	593	1013	239	1509	1822	843	591	975	2095
Durango, CO	1652	505	1453		1436	479	543	1262	1254	358	953	170	2785	170	1159	968	1525	1409	2998	1102	608	1397	1510	1267	1860	2856	901	1612	1327	988	614	1490	865	1093	830
Edmonton, AB	1953	1656	1204	1436		1985	1248	1382	1027	1561	1748	1528	2813	1327	1214	501	1547	2915	3026	2399	828	1854	1078	2286	2738	1420	1622	2215	1425	2354	1457	2045	1497	2005	1730
El Paso, TX	1733	610	1523	479	1985		971	1460	1375	572	1021	381	2865	649	1528	1483	1595	930	3126	753	1081	1439	1665	1043	1624	3405	930	1473	1397	602	726	1507	961	948	806
Ely, NV	1908	1064	1709	543	1248	971		667	1367	494	457	682	3041	434	648	780	1781	1744	3254	1711	420	1794	1623	1876	2468	2608	1315	2057	1583	1573	245	1900	1121	1642	518
Eureka, CA	2537	1779	2168	1262	1382	1460	667		1914	1043	456	1231	3670	1153	168	1132	2410	2233	3883	2213	971	2423	2170	2425	3018	2326	1944	2686	2212	2062	795	2529	1750	2251	654
Fargo, ND	930	761	258	1254	1027	1375	1367	1914		1641	1867	1453	2063	1120	1746	739	524	2104	2276	1332	947	831	260	1265	1715	2446	601	1192	402	1500	1576	1022	476	984	1849
Flagstaff, AZ	1913	790	1703	358	1561	572	494	1043	1641		595	188	3045	435	1025	1093	1775	1345	3271	1217	733	1619	1845	1382	1975	2981	1110	1727	1577	1174	249	1705	1141	1208	472
Fresno, CA	2417	1385	2218	953	1748	1021	457	456	1867	595		783	3550	901	503	1280	2290	1794	3763	1774	920	2214	2123	1977	2570	2660	1753	2322	2092	1623	398	2300	1630	1803	215
Gallup, NM	1725	602	1515	170	1528	381	682	1231	1453	188	783		2857	361	1213	1060	1587	1311	3083	1029	700	1431	1657	1194	1787	2948	922	1539	1389	915	437	1517	953	1020	660
Gaspé, QC	1136	2242	1614	2785	2813	2865	3041	3670	2063	3045	3550	2857		2651	3567	2798	1477	3363	592	2451	2881	1426	1787	2114	1854	4232	1898	1617	1698	2759	3154	1474	1923	2017	3427
Grand Junction, CO	1518	632	1319	170	1327	649	434	1153	1120	435	901	361	2651		1050	859	1391	1579	2864	1279	499	1350	1376	1472	2011	2747	854	1600	1193	1158	505	1443	731	1210	778
Grants Pass, OR	2434	1676	2000	1159	1214	1528	648	168	1746	1025	503	1213	3567	1050		964	2266	2301	3780	2242	786	2320	2002	2407	2994	2158	1841	2583	2093	2130	776	2426	1647	2233	722
Great Falls, MT	1665	1154	993	968	501	1483	780	1132	739	1093	1280	1060	2798	859	964		1259	2413	3011	1897	360	1566	995	1910	2399	1921	1246	1927	1137	1852	989	1757	1078	1629	1262
Green Bay, WI	496	1009	329	1525	1547	1595	1781	2410	524	1775	2290	1587	1477	1391	2266	1259		2164	1690	1280	1467	397	493	954	1275	2966	665	758	204	1560	1894	588	663	846	2167
Guadalajara, JA	2231	1352	2113	1409	2915	930	1746	2235	2104	1345	1794	1311	3363	1579	2303	2413	2164		3529	953	2011	1913	2255	1391	1824	4335	1520	1876	1987	604	1501	1905	1660	1346	1579
Halifax, NS	1349	2492	1827	2998	3026	3126	3254	3883	2276	3271	3763	3083	592	2864	3780	3011	1690	3529		2580	3094	1652	2000	2150	1838	4445	2148	1653	1911	2925	3367	1660	2136	2178	3640
Houston, TX	1319	709	1347	1102	2399	753	1711	2213	1332	1217	1774	1029	2451	1279	2242	1897	1280	953	2580		1733	1025	1489	442	875	3819	732	927	1221	349	1466	993	888	434	1559
Idaho Falls, ID	1748	990	1201	608	828	1081	420	971	947	733	920	700	2881	499	786	360	1467	2011	3094	1733		1634	1203	1830	2308	2248	1155	1897	1294	1688	629	1740	961	1568	902
Indianapolis, IN	294	840	652	1397	1854	1439	1794	2423	831	1619	2214	1431	1426	1350	2320	1566	397	1913	1652	1025	1634		816	683	874	3273	496	359	466	1309	1853	186	676	591	2091
International Falls, MN	915	1079	164	1510	1078	1665	1623	2170	260	1845	2123	1657	1787	1376	2002	995	493	2255	2000	1489	1203	816		1340	1700	2497	735	1177	403	1651	1832	1007	733	1117	2105
Jackson, MS	954	869	1176	1267	2286	1043	1876	2425	1265	1382	1977	1194	2114	1472	2407	1910	954	1391	2150	442	1830	683	1340		593	3705	664	497	990	787	1631	628	859	262	1849
Jacksonville, FL	1015	1438	1536	1860	2738	1624	2468	3018	1715	1975	2570	1787	1854	2011	2994	2399	1275	1824	1838	875	2308	874	1700	593		4157	1157	546	1350	1220	2224	718	1348	847	2430
Juneau, AK	3372	3076	2623	2856	1420	3405	2608	2326	2446	2981	2660	2948	4232	2747	2158	1921	2966	4335	4445	3819	2248	3273	2497	3705	4157		3041	3634	2844	3774	2877	3464	2916	3424	2879
Kansas City, MO	765	344	593	901	1622	930	1315	1944	601	1110	1753	922	1898	854	1841	1246	665	1520	2148	732	1155	496	735	664	1157	3041		746	467	916	1357	589	195	383	1630
Knoxville, TN	512	1028	1013	1612	2215	1473	2057	2686	1192	1727	2322	1539	1617	1600	2583	1927	758	1876	1653	927	1897	359	1177	497	546	3634	746		827	1272	1976	173	937	525	2199
La Crosse, WI	565	811	239	1327	1425	1397	1583	2212	402	1577	2092	1389	1698	1193	2093	1137	204	1987	1911	1221	1294	466	403	990	1350	2844	467	827		1383	1696	657	465	849	1969
Laredo, TX	1627	821	1509	988	2354	602	1573	2062	1500	1174	1623	915	2759	1158	2130	1852	1560	604	2925	349	1688	1309	1651	787	1220	3774	916	1272	1383		1328	1301	1056	742	1408
Las Vegas, NV	2021	1039	1822	614	1457	726	245	795	1576	249	398	437	3154	505	776	989	1894	1499	3367	1466	629	1853	1832	1631	2224	2877	1357	1976	1696	1328		1946	1234	1457	275
Lexington, KY	342	933	843	1490	2045	1507	1900	2529	1022	1705	2300	1517	1474	1443	2426	1757	588	1905	1660	993	1740	186	1007	628	718	3464	589	173	657	1301	1946		780	559	2177
Lincoln, NE	790	350	591	865	1497	961	1121	1750	476	1141	1630	953	1923	731	1647	1078	663	1660	2136	888	961	676	733	859	1348	2916	195	937	465	1056	1234	780		578	1507
Little Rock, AR	885	597	975	1093	2005	948	1642	2251	984	1208	1803	1020	2017	1210	2233	1629	846	1346	2178	434	1568	591	1117	262	847	3424	383	525	849	742	1457	559	578		1680
Los Angeles, CA	2294	1262	2095	830	1730	806	518	654	1849	472	215	660	3427	778	722	1262	2167	1579	3640	1559	902	2091	2105	1849	2430	2879	1630	2199	1969	1408	275	2177	1507	1680	

	Louisville, KY	Mackinaw City, MI	Memphis, TN	Mexico City, DF	Miami, FL	Milwaukee, WI	Minneapolis, MN	Minot, ND	Missoula, MT	Mobile, AL	Monterrey, NL	Montgomery, AL	Montréal, QC	Nashville, TN	Needles, CA	New Orleans, LA	New York, NY	Norfolk, VA	North Platte, NE	Odessa, TX	Oklahoma City, OK	Omaha, NE	Ottawa, ON	Page, AZ	Pendleton, OR	Philadelphia, PA	Phoenix, AZ	Pierre, SD	Pittsburgh, PA	Portland, ME	Portland, OR	Pueblo, CO	Québec, QC	Raleigh, NC	Redding, CA
Acapulco, GR	2201	2680	1818	219	2373	2380	2292	2627	2713	1655	791	1820	3129	2027	1872	1534	2835	2538	1937	1304	1560	2024	3041	1919	2742	2738	1646	2309	2592	3167	2949	1821	3286	2387	2564
Albany, NY	830	926	1222	2725	1415	921	1235	1769	2417	1335	2252	1166	226	1012	2616	1432	159	509	1556	2028	1536	1278	310	2439	2720	243	2544	1615	474	267	2927	1924	373	628	2925
Albuquerque, NM	1306	1726	1014	1376	1963	1351	1222	1224	1128	1245	961	1302	2151	1223	535	1173	2022	1910	702	399	544	869	2063	452	1157	1941	463	966	1651	2348	1364	330	2308	1759	1217
Amarillo, TX	1021	1441	729	1287	1678	1141	1043	1055	1312	960	806	1017	1866	938	820	888	1737	1625	473	258	259	652	1778	737	1458	1656	748	737	1366	2063	1665	321	2023	1474	1502
Anchorage, AK	3969	3741	4072	4979	5050	3592	3260	2725	2554	4469	4498	4427	4244	4148	3567	4463	4483	4564	3355	3950	3942	3436	4160	3422	2587	4434	3695	3041	4133	4507	2490	3386	4398	4481	2911
Atlanta, GA	418	992	391	1761	661	812	1132	1666	2173	329	1288	160	1222	243	1939	468	873	558	1228	1150	860	995	1161	1856	2392	772	1867	1391	686	1229	2599	1442	1379	407	2597
Baltimore, MD	618	811	914	2417	1082	806	1120	1654	2302	1003	1944	834	562	704	2461	1124	203	234	1441	1720	1382	1163	531	2378	2605	102	2389	1500	251	507	2812	1719	709	295	2810
Bangor, ME	1229	1325	1577	3080	1717	1320	1634	2168	2816	1690	2607	1521	300	1367	3015	1787	443	811	1955	2383	1935	1677	425	2838	3119	545	2943	2014	821	132	3326	2323	229	930	3324
Billings, MT	1537	1361	1477	2257	2492	1175	843	444	340	1874	1776	1869	2099	1590	1079	1868	2066	2147	633	1228	1220	841	1777	934	744	2017	1207	491	1716	2342	891	664	2256	2064	1155
Birmingham, AL	366	952	243	1635	783	760	1080	1614	2121	261	1162	92	1307	189	1791	342	982	707	1176	1005	712	943	1246	1708	2340	885	1719	1339	753	1314	2547	1270	1464	556	2473
Bismarck, ND	1139	948	1242	2307	2220	762	430	111	759	1639	1729	1597	1686	1318	1498	1633	1653	1734	475	1206	960	606	1364	1353	1163	1604	1603	211	1303	1929	1310	810	1843	1651	1574
Boise, ID	1885	1983	1825	2316	2840	1741	1465	1066	370	2237	1901	2217	2531	1938	744	2228	2498	2544	955	1343	1495	1233	2443	722	218	2449	922	1113	2148	2774	425	939	2688	2473	525
Boston, MA	994	1090	1314	2817	1482	1085	1399	1933	2581	1427	2344	1258	324	1104	2780	1524	208	576	1720	2120	1700	1442	449	2603	2884	310	2708	1779	586	117	3091	2088	403	695	3089
Brownsville, TX	1310	1863	927	609	1545	1563	1475	1810	2102	827	186	992	2238	1136	1498	706	2007	1710	1203	632	743	1207	2150	1445	2248	1910	1272	1492	1701	2339	2455	1111	2395	1559	2190
Buffalo, NY	541	637	924	2527	1383	632	946	1480	2128	1164	1949	995	402	716	2327	1243	399	576	1267	1730	1247	989	341	2150	2431	388	2255	1326	216	562	2638	1635	559	637	2636
Cabo San Lucas, BS	3087	3502	2795	2697	3632	3145	3016	2761	2287	2914	2354	2983	3935	3004	1339	2793	3803	3691	2359	1974	2325	2637	3847	1591	2117	3722	1318	2623	3432	4129	2109	2111	4092	3540	1690
Cairo, IL	260	755	169	1754	1079	465	753	1298	1768	566	1176	456	1188	177	1633	560	1029	863	823	957	553	590	1100	1550	1987	950	1561	986	651	1361	2194	1037	1345	712	2192
Calgary, AB	1937	1589	2028	2808	3018	1560	1228	693	388	2425	2327	2395	2264	2116	1396	2419	2451	2532	1184	1779	1771	1392	2180	1251	648	2402	1524	1009	2101	2527	795	1215	2418	2449	1113
Cancún, QR	2786	3317	2403	1029	3021	3017	2929	3264	3556	2303	1496	2468	3714	2612	2688	2182	3483	3186	2657	2086	2197	2661	3626	2735	3558	3386	2462	2946	3177	3815	3765	2565	3871	3035	3380
Casper, WY	1288	1330	1228	1982	2243	1077	848	591	617	1687	1501	1620	1934	1341	909	1678	1901	1947	358	953	945	636	1846	764	916	1852	958	413	1551	2177	1123	389	2091	1876	1121
Charleston, SC	614	1105	712	2077	582	1010	1324	1858	2478	645	1604	476	1121	548	2260	784	762	431	1533	1471	1181	1300	1092	2177	2697	661	2188	1696	654	1066	2904	1747	1268	280	2902
Charleston, WV	249	634	599	2202	990	585	899	1433	2081	826	1624	657	835	391	2090	911	555	410	1183	1405	1010	950	774	2007	2347	476	2018	1287	229	887	2554	1397	992	325	2552
Charlotte, NC	474	899	618	2005	727	870	1184	1718	2338	573	1532	404	984	408	2165	712	635	320	1393	1394	1086	1160	923	2082	2557	534	2093	1556	448	939	2764	1607	1141	169	2762
Cheyenne, WY	1151	1364	1091	1802	2106	1007	878	685	797	1507	1321	1483	1797	1204	941	1498	1764	1810	221	773	765	499	1709	723	948	1715	1002	436	1414	2040	1155	209	1954	1739	1153
Chicago, IL	299	411	536	2084	1374	92	406	940	1588	920	1506	751	844	472	1870	927	811	892	751	1231	798	473	756	1634	1915	762	1806	786	461	1087	2122	1119	1001	811	2120
Chihuahua, CI	1554	1977	1171	870	1990	1677	1579	1730	1630	1272	495	1374	2402	1380	789	1151	2282	2067	1208	365	795	1260	2314	836	1659	2185	563	1472	1945	2614	1866	836	2559	1916	1481
Cincinnati, OH	103	528	486	2089	1125	392	706	1240	1888	726	1511	557	827	278	1934	805	661	603	1007	1292	854	729	739	1851	2171	580	1862	1094	290	994	2378	1234	984	518	2376
Cleveland, OH	355	447	738	2341	1240	442	756	1290	1938	978	1763	809	585	530	2141	1057	486	567	1077	1544	1061	799	524	1960	2241	437	2069	1136	136	745	2448	1445	742	575	2446
Columbus, OH	214	468	597	2200	1157	449	763	1297	1945	837	1622	668	724	389	2000	916	554	577	1073	1403	920	795	663	1917	2237	473	1928	1143	183	884	2444	1300	881	492	2442
Concord, NH	974	1070	1392	2895	1532	1065	1379	1913	2561	1505	2422	1336	252	1182	2760	1602	258	626	1700	2198	1680	1422	377	2583	2864	360	2688	1759	636	96	3071	2068	329	745	3069
Dallas, TX	837	1316	454	1151	1316	1016	928	1275	1770	598	573	655	1765	663	1182	526	1565	1350	756	354	208	672	1677	1099	1916	1468	1069	957	1228	1897	2123	683	1922	1199	1864
Davenport, IA	424	560	549	2025	1447	214	358	891	1454	946	1425	824	993	545	1704	940	960	1023	585	1140	707	307	905	1468	1749	911	1609	672	610	1236	1956	953	1150	938	1954
Daytona Beach, FL	852	1371	797	1927	255	1246	1566	2100	2607	491	1454	464	1387	677	2271	634	1028	697	1662	1445	1266	1429	1358	2188	2826	927	2148	1825	920	1332	3033	1772	1534	546	3031
Denver, CO	1125	1407	1097	1717	2080	1050	921	785	897	1416	1236	1429	1840	1178	861	1407	1807	1784	264	689	674	542	1752	625	1043	1753	902	528	1457	2083	1250	109	1997	1713	1248
Des Moines, IA	593	729	617	1834	1560	372	243	776	1285	1014	1256	937	1162	658	1535	1008	1129	1192	416	971	538	138	1074	1299	1580	1080	1440	503	779	1405	1787	784	1319	1107	1785
Detroit, MI	365	292	748	2351	1387	379	693	1227	1875	988	1773	819	569	540	2121	1067	639	720	1014	1474	1041	736	481	1897	2178	590	2049	1073	289	915	2385	1382	726	693	2383
Dodge City, KS	861	1242	730	1472	1753	912	783	859	1274	1059	967	1062	1675	852	998	987	1570	1520	277	504	254	405	1587	915	1420	1489	926	541	1199	1896	1627	274	1832	1387	1625
Duluth, MN	770	423	965	2233	1851	393	157	474	1203	1362	1655	1228	1047	949	1934	1356	1284	1365	815	1370	937	537	919	1698	1607	1235	1839	640	934	1560	1754	1183	1204	1282	2018
Durango, CO	1418	1785	1226	1588	2175	1428	1299	1164	918	1457	1173	1514	2218	1435	566	1385	2127	2122	642	611	756	920	2130	262	947	2046	494	906	1756	2461	1154	270	2375	1971	1108
Edmonton, AB	1972	1744	2075	2981	3053	1595	1263	728	561	2472	2500	2430	2247	2151	1569	2466	2486	2567	1357	1952	1944	1439	2163	1424	821	2437	1697	1044	2136	2510	968	1388	2401	2484	1286
El Paso, TX	1470	1873	1087	1109	1939	1498	1369	1491	1391	1221	694	1290	2298	1296	662	1100	2198	1983	969	281	691	1016	2210	694	1420	2101	436	1233	1861	2530	1627	597	2455	1832	1354
Ely, NV	1828	2041	1775	1968	2783	1684	1555	1204	645	2066	1593	2107	2474	1881	357	1994	2441	2487	898	1252	1352	1176	2386	368	599	2392	535	1059	2091	2717	806	785	2631	2416	513
Eureka, CA	2457	2670	2384	2457	3333	2313	2150	1680	965	2615	2082	2672	3103	2510	835	2543	3070	3116	1527	1741	1914	1805	3015	1069	621	3021	1024	1688	2720	3346	414	1511	3260	3045	154
Fargo, ND	949	758	1054	2224	2030	572	240	284	949	1451	1646	1407	1496	1128	1688	1445	1463	1544	612	1310	877	418	1174	1543	1353	1414	1777	333	1113	1739	1500	984	1653	1461	1764
Flagstaff, AZ	1633	2053	1341	1569	2290	1678	1549	1517	1043	1572	1194	1629	2478	1550	208	1500	2349	2237	1029	726	871	1196	2390	137	1072	2268	136	1293	1978	2675	1279	657	2635	2086	890
Fresno, CA	2228	2550	1936	2018	2885	2193	2064	1704	1068	2167	1643	2224	2983	2145	387	2095	2950	2832	1407	1302	1466	1685	2895	672	887	2863	585	1671	2573	3226	748	1252	3140	2681	329
Gallup, NM	1445	1865	1153	1490	2102	1490	1361	1363	1010	1384	1075	1441	2290	1362	396	1312	2161	2049	841	538	683	1008	2202	313	1039	2080	324	1105	1790	2487	1246	469	2447	1898	1078
Gaspé, QC	1497	1248	1880	3483	2197	1512	1826	2085	3008	2118	2905	1949	568	1672	3253	2215	941	1291	2147	2606	2173	1869	695	3030	3311	1025	3181	2206	1179	644	3518	2515	430	1410	3516
Grand Junction, CO	1371	1651	1343	1758	2326	1294	1165	1029	809	1662	1343	1675	2084	1424	617	1653	2051	2030	508	781	920	786	1996	381	838	1999	571	772	1701	2327	1045	353	2241	1959	999
Grants Pass, OR	2354	2500	2366	2525	3309	2314	1982	1512	797	2597	2150	2654	3000	2407	890	2525	2967	3013	1424	1809	1896	1702	2912	1050	453	2918	1092	1630	2617	3243	246	1408	3157	2942	176
Great Falls, MT	1684	1493	1699	2479	2714	1307	975	548	167	2096	1998	2091	2231	1812	1101	2090	2198	2279	855	1450	1442	1063	1909	956	571	2149	1229	713	1848	2474	718	886	2388	2196	1036
Green Bay, WI	515	258	743	2284	1590	117	287	821	1469	1136	1706	967	910	688	2006	1134	1029	1110	887	1431	998	609	782	1770	1873	980	1911	712	679	1305	2020	1255	1067	1027	2256
Guadalajara, JA	1868	2347	1485	329	2139	2047	1959	2294	2321	1421	458	1586	2796	1694	1435	1300	2601	2304	1604	971	1227	1691	2708	1484	2350	2504	1209	1976	2259	2933	2548	1527	2953	2153	2129
Halifax, NS	1693	1461	2041	3544	2181	1725	2039	2298	3221	2154	3071	1985	781	1831	3479	2251	907	1275	2360	2847	2399	2082	908	3243	3524	1009	3407	2419	1285	596	3731	2728	643	1394	3729
Houston, TX	956	1469	573	964	1190	1163	1171	1522	2017	472	495	637	1884	782	1425	351	1652	1355	1003	549	455	919	1796	1342	2163	1555	1189	1204	1347	1984	2370	926	2041	1204	2107
Idaho Falls, ID	1668	1701	1608	2190	2623	1515	1183	784	310	2020	1834	2000	2314	1721	741	2011	2281	2327	738	1286	1278	1016	2226	596	495	2232	869	831	1931	2557	702	722	2471	2256	817
Indianapolis, IN	114	480	472	2033	1189	280	594	1128	1776	735	1455	566	859	287	1827	814	730	713	900	1180	747	622	771	1744	2064	649	1755	987	359	1056	2271	1127	1016	628	2269
International Falls, MN	934	587	1129	2375	2015	557	299	433	1205	1526	1797	1392	1221	1113	1944	1520	1448	1529	868	1512	1079	679	1137	1799	1609	1399	1981	589	1098	1724	1756	1240	1375	1446	2020
Jackson, MS	591	1127	212	1406	908	837	1062	1560	2030	190	933	247	1547	417	1590	180	1222	944	1085	764	615	852	1486	1507	2260	1125	1479	1248	993	1554	2467	1091	1704	793	2272
Jacksonville, FL	764	1281	709	1839	343	1158	1478	2012	2519	403	1366	376	1297	589	2183	546	938	607	1574	1357	1178	1341	1268	2100	2738	837	2060	1737	830	1242	2945	1684	1444	456	2943
Juneau, AK	3391	3163	3494	4401	4472	3014	2682	2147	1976	3891	3920	3849	3666	3570	2989	3885	3905	3986	2777	3372	3364	2858	3582	2844	2009	3856	3117	2463	3555	3929	1912	2808	3820	3903	2333
Kansas City, MO	517	898	453	1640	1472	568	439	896	1366	850	1062	849	1331	570	1318	844	1226	1176	421	777	344	188	1243	1233	1585	1145	1246	584	855	1552	1792	631	1488	1105	1790
Knoxville, TN	245	778	388	1891	877	641	955	1489	2108	513	1418	344	1050	178	1935	598	725	510	1163	1194	856	930	989	1852	2327	628	1863	1326	496	1057	2534	1377	1207	359	2532
La Crosse, WI	584	460	779	2129	1665	207	163	699	1296	1176	1529	1042	1131	763	1808	1170	1098	1179	689	1244	811	411	1043	1572	1700	1049	1713	514	748	1374	1847	1057	1288	1096	2058
Laredo, TX	1264	1743	881	724	1535	1443	1355	1690	1972	817	146	982	2192	1090	1264	696	1997	1700	1073	431	623	1087	2104	1228	1933	1900	1038	1372	1655	2329	2140	981	2349	1549	1956
Las Vegas, NV	1874	2154	1590	1723	2539	1797	1668	1413	939	1821	1348	1878	2587	1799	112	1749	2554	2486	1011	1007	1120	1289	2499	276	845	2502	290	1275	2204	2830	1021	856	2744	2335	641
Lexington, KY	72	608	422	2025	1048	471	785	1319	1951	662	1447	493	907	214	1913	741	732	587	1006	1228	833	773	819	1830	2170	653	1841	1169	406	1064	2377	1220	1064	502	2375
Lincoln, NE	708	923	648	1780	1663	566	437	771	1198	1045	1202	1040	1356	761	1346	1039	1323	1367	227	866	433	58	1268	1110	1391	1274	1277	459	973	1599	1598	595	1513	1296	1596
Little Rock, AR	522	1035	139	1466	1162	729	821	1279	1749	452	888	471	1450	348	1416	423	1250	1035	838	669	337	571	1362	1333	1998	1153	1344	967	913	1582	2205	895	1607	884	2098
Los Angeles, CA	2105	2427	1813	1803	2745	2070	1941	1686	1212	2027	1428	2096	2860	2022	264	1906	2827	2709	1284	1087	1343	1562	2772	549	1010	2740	370	1548	2450	3103	967	1129	3017	2558	548

	Regina, SK	Reno, NV	Roanoke, VA	Robbinsville, NC	Roswell, NM	Saginaw, MI	St. George, UT	St. Louis, MO	Salt Lake City, UT	San Antonio, TX	San Diego, CA	San Francisco, CA	Sault Ste. Marie, ON	Savannah, GA	Seattle, WA	Shreveport, LA	Sioux City, IA	Sioux Falls, SD	Spokane, WA	Springfield, MO	Sturgis, SD	Sudbury, ON	Tallahassee, FL	Tampa, FL	Thunder Bay, ON	Toronto, ON	Tulsa, OK	Twin Falls, ID	Vancouver, BC	Washington, DC	Whitehorse, YT	Wichita, KS	Winnemucca, NV	Winnipeg, MB	Yuma, AZ
Acapulco, GR	2758	2381	2368	2126	1445	2572	2057	1997	2190	1087	1938	2397	2738	2155	3019	1421	2114	2199	2912	1787	2249	2922	1895	2170	2634	2796	1626	2411	3157	2596	4469	1717	2402	2656	1766
Albany, NY	2014	2729	584	897	2010	735	2443	1038	2206	1956	2896	2953	809	938	2897	1553	1337	1398	2616	1250	1762	631	1231	1270	1189	400	1433	2389	3035	371	3769	1475	2565	1693	2725
Albuquerque, NM	1282	1021	1658	1463	198	1618	608	1043	605	715	816	1097	1784	1656	1434	833	964	1096	1327	833	840	1968	1485	1760	1564	1818	650	826	1572	1886	2993	593	958	1533	644
Amarillo, TX	1258	1306	1373	1178	214	1333	893	758	944	512	1101	1382	1499	1371	1735	548	747	794	1511	548	749	1683	1200	1475	1385	1533	365	1127	1873	1601	2969	417	1303	1230	929
Anchorage, AK	2482	3068	4335	4286	3774	3975	3335	3871	3040	4204	3581	3126	3683	4641	2315	4162	3341	3259	2413	3787	3015	3865	4640	4847	3242	4104	3868	2930	2241	4378	723	3785	3011	2806	3751
Atlanta, GA	1911	2401	430	149	1296	801	2048	557	1878	992	2157	2501	1050	252	2653	608	1085	1170	2372	685	1538	1188	265	458	1378	958	796	2061	2791	636	3666	970	2237	1590	1985
Baltimore, MD	1899	2614	276	589	1855	620	2325	841	2091	1648	2742	2838	869	605	2782	1245	1222	1283	2501	1053	1647	721	898	937	1310	490	1236	2274	2920	38	3654	1278	2450	1578	2570
Bangor, ME	2096	3128	939	1252	2409	1134	2842	1437	2605	2311	3295	3352	920	1240	3296	1908	1736	1797	3015	1649	2161	733	1533	1572	1303	630	1832	2788	3434	673	3822	1874	2964	1739	3124
Billings, MT	475	959	1918	1829	1052	1558	847	1276	552	1482	1300	1183	1282	2083	820	1613	746	664	539	1192	293	1466	2082	2289	1049	1766	1237	502	958	1961	1999	1063	795	723	1263
Birmingham, AL	1859	2277	515	270	1151	804	1864	505	1826	866	2012	2353	1010	401	2601	463	1033	1118	2320	527	1486	1191	305	580	1326	961	648	2009	2739	743	3614	822	2185	1538	1840
Bismarck, ND	356	1378	1505	1456	1198	1145	1266	1041	971	1433	1719	1602	869	1811	1239	1332	511	429	958	957	278	1053	1810	2017	636	1353	1038	921	1377	1548	2111	803	1214	413	1682
Boise, ID	1097	424	2313	2177	1142	1990	635	1624	340	1757	965	648	1904	2431	495	1888	1328	1286	423	1540	915	2088	2430	2637	1671	2198	1512	130	633	2393	2082	1338	260	1345	928
Boston, MA	2178	2893	676	989	2174	899	2607	1202	2370	2048	3060	3117	944	1005	3061	1645	1501	1562	2780	1414	1926	757	1298	1337	1327	564	1597	2553	3199	438	3933	1639	2729	1763	2889
Brownsville, TX	2055	2007	1540	1298	813	1755	1683	1180	1598	278	1564	2023	1921	1327	2525	593	1297	1382	2301	970	1628	2105	1067	1342	1817	1905	809	1917	2663	1768	3759	900	2028	1839	1392
Buffalo, NY	1725	2440	502	769	1721	446	2154	749	1917	1653	2607	2664	519	906	2608	1257	1048	1109	2327	961	1473	341	1122	1238	958	110	1144	2100	2746	389	3480	1186	2276	1404	2436
Cabo San Lucas, BS	2792	1580	3439	3244	1836	3394	1469	2824	1764	2251	1059	1523	3560	3318	2284	2514	2732	2753	2486	2614	2385	3744	3154	3429	3358	3602	2431	1850	2427	3667	3876	2374	1693	3040	1177
Cairo, IL	1543	1996	611	416	1027	647	1643	161	1473	880	1914	2220	813	670	2248	484	680	765	1967	269	1133	997	669	876	999	855	450	1656	2386	839	3298	523	1832	1222	1742
Calgary, AB	471	1276	2303	2254	1603	1943	1164	1827	869	2033	1617	1500	1703	2609	675	2164	1297	1215	443	1743	844	1885	2608	2815	1262	2124	1788	819	601	2346	1448	1614	1112	826	1580
Cancún, QR	3509	3197	3016	2774	2267	3209	2873	2634	3006	1732	2754	3213	3375	2803	3835	2069	2751	2836	3755	2424	3082	3559	2543	2818	3271	3381	2263	3227	3973	3244	5213	2354	3218	3293	2582
Casper, WY	622	925	1716	1580	777	1393	677	1027	402	1207	1130	1149	1359	1834	1097	1338	558	586	816	943	240	1543	1833	2040	1190	1601	962	585	1235	1796	2274	788	761	931	1093
Charleston, SC	2103	2706	398	348	1617	914	2353	862	2183	1308	2478	2822	1163	105	2958	929	1390	1475	2677	990	1843	1205	398	437	1570	974	1117	2366	3096	525	3858	1291	2542	1782	2306
Charleston, WV	1678	2356	179	376	1484	443	2003	512	1833	1328	2371	2580	692	513	2561	932	981	1066	2280	724	1434	780	729	845	1133	549	907	2016	2699	366	3433	956	2192	1357	2199
Charlotte, NC	1963	2566	192	208	1559	708	2213	722	2043	1236	2401	2727	957	250	2818	852	1250	1335	2537	850	1703	999	466	582	1398	768	1022	2226	2956	398	3718	1104	2402	1642	2229
Cheyenne, WY	743	957	1579	1443	597	1256	709	890	434	1027	1162	1181	1422	1697	1225	1158	594	615	996	806	301	1606	1696	1903	1220	1464	782	617	1363	1659	2454	608	793	1010	1183
Chicago, IL	1185	1924	665	616	1272	303	1638	300	1401	1210	2091	2148	469	953	2068	851	532	569	1787	512	933	653	964	1171	652	511	695	1584	2206	706	2940	719	1760	864	1987
Chihuahua, CI	1788	1298	1815	1620	442	1869	974	1294	1107	609	855	1314	2035	1709	1936	905	1350	1435	1829	1084	1346	2219	1512	1787	1921	2069	901	1328	2074	2043	3499	953	1319	1892	683
Cincinnati, OH	1485	2180	372	324	1328	337	1840	356	1657	1215	2215	2404	586	661	2368	819	788	873	2087	568	1241	724	729	922	952	494	751	1840	2506	524	3240	793	2016	1164	2043
Cleveland, OH	1535	2250	429	576	1535	256	1964	563	1727	1467	2417	2474	505	763	2418	1071	858	919	2137	775	1283	530	981	1095	946	299	958	1910	2556	381	3290	1000	2086	1214	2250
Columbus, OH	1542	2246	346	435	1394	277	1906	422	1723	1326	2281	2470	526	680	2425	930	854	926	2144	634	1290	669	840	1033	967	438	817	1906	2563	417	3297	859	2082	1221	2109
Concord, NH	2048	2873	754	1067	2154	879	2587	1182	2350	2126	3040	3097	872	1055	3041	1723	1481	1542	2760	1394	1906	685	1348	1387	1255	582	1577	2533	3179	488	3774	1619	2709	1691	2869
Dallas, TX	1520	1668	1098	903	500	1208	1255	633	1402	277	1361	1744	1374	990	2193	186	762	847	1969	423	1093	1558	838	1113	1270	1432	262	1585	2331	1326	3427	365	1761	1304	1189
Davenport, IA	1136	1758	792	743	1181	452	1472	265	1235	1129	1925	1982	618	1038	1934	807	366	451	1653	402	819	802	1037	1244	608	660	614	1418	2072	855	2891	553	1594	815	1790
Daytona Beach, FL	2345	2835	664	583	1591	1180	2344	991	2312	1158	2440	2833	1429	230	3087	903	1519	1604	2806	1119	1972	1471	251	139	1812	1240	1202	2495	3225	791	4100	1376	2671	2024	2268
Denver, CO	843	1052	1553	1417	497	1299	629	864	529	942	1082	1276	1465	1671	1320	1067	637	658	1096	761	401	1649	1642	1877	1263	1507	691	712	1458	1697	2554	517	888	1095	1083
Des Moines, IA	1021	1589	961	912	1012	621	1303	344	1066	960	1756	1813	787	1151	1765	736	197	282	1484	361	650	971	1150	1357	585	829	445	1249	1903	1024	2776	384	1425	700	1621
Detroit, MI	1472	2187	547	586	1515	101	1901	543	1664	1477	2354	2411	350	881	2355	1081	795	856	2074	755	1220	466	991	1184	791	236	938	1847	2493	534	3227	955	2023	1151	2230
Dodge City, KS	1104	1429	1289	1091	471	1134	1015	600	906	727	1279	1560	1300	1372	1697	647	500	544	1473	412	648	1484	1275	1550	1125	1342	324	1089	1835	1433	2931	154	1265	980	1107
Duluth, MN	723	1822	1136	1087	1411	615	1702	681	1465	1359	2155	2046	424	1442	1683	1135	454	423	1402	760	787	608	1441	1648	188	847	844	1365	1821	1179	2478	783	1658	380	2020
Durango, CO	1222	912	1870	1675	410	1677	494	1157	395	927	847	1136	1843	1868	1224	1045	1015	1036	1117	1045	780	2027	1697	1972	1641	1885	862	616	1362	2098	2711	659	748	1473	675
Edmonton, AB	485	1449	2338	2289	1776	1978	1337	1874	1042	2206	1790	1673	1686	2644	807	2165	1344	1262	616	1790	1017	1868	2643	2850	1245	2107	1871	992	733	2381	1275	1787	1285	809	1753
El Paso, TX	1549	1171	1731	1536	203	1765	847	1190	868	558	728	1187	1931	1625	1697	821	1111	1158	1590	980	1107	2115	1461	1736	1711	1965	797	1089	1835	1959	3260	740	1192	1594	556
Ely, NV	1235	317	2256	2120	1019	1933	213	1567	244	1529	578	541	2099	2374	876	1654	1271	1232	804	1439	886	2283	2320	2580	1897	2141	1369	256	1014	2336	2463	1195	271	1483	541
Eureka, CA	1547	352	2885	2749	1568	2562	914	2196	873	2018	778	281	2728	3003	589	2203	1900	1861	766	2112	1515	2912	2855	3130	2356	2770	2020	807	732	2965	2181	1910	514	1902	945
Fargo, ND	546	1568	1315	1266	1236	955	1456	853	1161	1350	1909	1792	679	1621	1429	1144	323	241	1148	769	470	863	1620	1827	446	1163	850	1111	1567	1358	2301	687	1404	221	1872
Flagstaff, AZ	1548	694	1985	1790	525	1945	293	1370	520	1042	489	770	2111	1983	1349	1160	1291	1423	1242	1160	1167	2295	1812	2087	1891	2145	977	741	1487	2213	2836	920	715	1860	317
Fresno, CA	1735	299	2580	2385	1120	2442	517	1965	812	1579	339	183	2608	2578	923	1755	1780	1801	997	1755	1433	2792	2407	2682	2406	2650	1572	756	1066	2808	2515	1515	463	1983	506
Gallup, NM	1421	882	1797	1602	337	1757	469	1182	487	854	677	958	1923	1795	1316	972	1103	1235	1209	972	979	2107	1624	1899	1703	1957	789	708	1454	2025	2803	732	840	1672	505
Gaspé, QC	2361	3320	1367	1680	2647	1192	3034	1675	2797	2609	3487	3544	1190	1720	3488	2213	1928	1989	3207	1887	2353	1003	2013	2052	1568	900	2070	2980	3431	1153	4087	2088	3156	2004	3362
Grand Junction, CO	1087	803	1799	1663	580	1543	385	1110	286	1097	838	1027	1709	1917	1115	1313	881	902	1008	1007	645	1893	1888	2123	1507	1751	937	507	1253	1943	2602	763	639	1339	752
Grants Pass, OR	1379	333	2782	2646	1550	2459	895	2093	770	2086	846	391	2421	2900	421	2185	1797	1803	598	2009	1432	2605	2837	3106	2188	2667	1981	634	564	2862	2013	1807	411	1734	1013
Great Falls, MT	473	981	2050	2001	1274	1690	869	1498	574	1704	1322	1205	1414	2305	647	1835	968	886	366	1414	515	1598	2304	2511	1181	1898	1459	524	785	2093	1776	1285	817	820	1285
Green Bay, WI	1066	2060	881	832	1472	241	1774	500	1537	1410	2227	2284	287	1169	1949	1042	526	495	1668	712	859	471	1180	1387	517	532	895	1631	2087	924	2821	855	1896	745	2092
Guadalajara, JA	2479	1946	2134	1892	1112	2239	1622	1664	1798	754	1413	1960	2405	1921	2627	1163	1781	1866	2520	1454	2037	2589	1661	1936	2301	2463	1293	2003	2765	2362	4190	1384	1967	2323	1268
Halifax, NS	2574	3533	1403	1716	2873	1405	3247	1901	3010	2775	3700	3757	1403	1704	3701	2372	2141	2202	3420	2113	2566	1216	1997	2036	1781	1113	2296	3193	3644	1137	4300	2338	3369	2217	3588
Houston, TX	1767	1911	1185	943	730	1361	1498	780	1649	199	1481	1940	1527	972	2440	239	1009	1094	2216	666	1340	1711	712	987	1513	1551	505	1832	2578	1413	3674	612	2008	1551	1309
Idaho Falls, ID	815	621	2096	1960	1016	1773	509	1407	214	1540	962	845	1622	2214	790	1671	1086	1004	509	1323	633	1806	2213	2420	1389	1981	1295	164	928	2176	2103	1121	457	1063	925
Indianapolis, IN	1373	2073	482	433	1221	345	1733	249	1550	1159	2108	2297	538	770	2256	787	681	766	1975	461	1134	722	779	986	840	526	644	1733	2394	593	3128	686	1909	1052	1936
International Falls, MN	626	1824	1300	1251	1553	779	1712	845	1417	1501	2165	2048	660	1606	1685	1277	579	497	1404	902	726	842	1605	1812	219	1081	986	1367	1696	1343	2352	925	1660	269	2162
Jackson, MS	1805	2076	755	510	910	1029	1663	495	1746	637	1771	2152	1185	582	2537	222	942	1027	2229	496	1395	1416	430	705	1364	1186	535	1929	2675	983	3560	709	2105	1484	1599
Jacksonville, FL	2257	2747	574	495	1503	1090	2256	903	2224	1070	2352	2745	1339	140	2999	815	1431	1516	2718	1031	1884	1381	163	202	1724	1150	1114	2407	3137	701	4012	1288	2583	1936	2180
Juneau, AK	1904	2490	3757	3708	3196	3397	2757	3293	2462	3626	3003	2548	3105	4063	1737	3584	2763	2681	1835	3209	2437	3287	4062	4269	2664	3526	3290	2352	1663	3800	211	3207	2433	2228	3173
Kansas City, MO	1141	1594	945	809	818	790	1237	256	1071	766	1599	1818	956	1063	1846	543	278	363	1565	168	731	1140	1062	1269	781	998	251	1254	1984	1089	2896	190	1430	820	1427
Knoxville, TN	1734	2336	258	74	1329	587	1983	492	1813	1122	2216	2497	836	412	2588	719	1020	1105	2307	620	1473	974	481	674	1201	744	792	1996	2726	486	3489	874	2172	1413	2044
La Crosse, WI	944	1862	950	901	1285	590	1576	495	1339	1233	2029	2086	489	1256	1776	1009	328	297	1495	634	661	673	1255	1462	427	798	718	1458	1914	993	2699	657	1698	623	1894
Laredo, TX	1935	1773	1530	1288	579	1635	1449	1060	1381	150	1330	1789	1801	1317	2210	559	1177	1262	2171	850	1508	1985	1057	1332	1697	1859	689	1602	2348	1758	3629	780	1794	1719	1158
Las Vegas, NV	1444	445	2234	2039	774	2046	121	1613	416	1284	335	573	2212	2232	1122	1409	1384	1405	1138	1409	1037	2396	2061	2336	2010	2254	1226	502	1260	2462	2732	1169	466	1692	296
Lexington, KY	1564	2179	356	247	1307	417	1826	335	1656	1151	2194	2403	666	584	2431	755	863	948	2150	547	1316	804	652	845	1031	574	730	1839	2569	543	3319	779	2015	1243	2022
Lincoln, NE	1016	1400	1136	1000	822	815	1114	447	877	906	1567	1624	981	1254	1668	738	153	238	1397	363	546	1165	1253	1460	779	1023	450	1060	1806	1218	2771	276	1236	695	1458
Little Rock, AR	1524	1902	783	588	810	927	1489	346	1484	592	1676	1978	1093	781	2275	196	661	746	1948	215	1114	1277	684	959	1163	1117	273	1667	2413	1011	3279	447	1843	1203	1504
Los Angeles, CA	1717	473	2457	2262	949	2319	394	1842	689	1364	124	381	2485	2455	1142	1627	1657	1678	1215	1632	1310	2669	2267	2542	2283	2527	1449	775	1285	2685	2734	1392	586	1965	291

	Acapulco, GR	Albany, NY	Albuquerque, NM	Amarillo, TX	Anchorage, AK	Atlanta, GA	Baltimore, MD	Bangor, ME	Billings, MT	Birmingham, AL	Bismarck, ND	Boise, ID	Boston, MA	Brownsville, TX	Buffalo, NY	Cabo San Lucas, BS	Cairo, IL	Calgary, AB	Cancún, QR	Casper, WY	Charleston, SC	Charleston, WV	Charlotte, NC	Cheyenne, WY	Chicago, IL	Chihuahua, CI	Cincinnati, OH	Cleveland, OH	Columbus, OH	Concord, NH	Dallas, TX	Davenport, IA	Daytona Beach, FL	Denver, CO	Des Moines, IA
Louisville, KY	2201	830	1306	1021	3969	418	618	1229	1537	366	1139	1885	994	1310	541	3087	260	1937	2786	1288	614	249	474	1151	299	1554	103	355	214	974	837	424	852	1125	593
Mackinaw City, MI	2680	926	1726	1441	3741	992	811	1325	1361	952	948	1983	1090	1863	637	3502	755	1589	3317	1330	1105	634	899	1364	411	1977	528	447	468	1070	1316	560	1371	1407	729
Memphis, TN	1818	1222	1014	729	4072	391	914	1577	1477	243	1242	1825	1314	927	924	2795	169	2028	2403	1228	712	599	618	1091	536	1171	486	738	597	1392	454	549	797	1097	617
Mexico City, DF	219	2725	1376	1287	4979	1761	2417	3080	2257	1635	2307	2316	2817	609	2527	2697	1754	2808	1029	1982	2077	2202	2005	1802	2084	870	2089	2341	2200	2895	1151	2025	1927	1717	1834
Miami, FL	2373	1415	1963	1678	5050	661	1082	1717	2492	783	2220	2840	1482	1545	1383	3632	1079	3018	3021	2243	582	990	727	2106	1374	1990	1125	1240	1157	1532	1316	1447	255	2080	1560
Milwaukee, WI	2380	921	1351	1141	3592	812	806	1320	1175	760	762	1741	1085	1563	632	3145	465	1560	3017	1077	1010	585	870	1007	92	1677	392	442	449	1065	1016	214	1246	1050	372
Minneapolis, MN	2292	1235	1222	1043	3260	1132	1120	1634	843	1080	430	1465	1399	1475	946	3016	753	1228	2929	848	1324	899	1184	878	406	1579	706	756	763	1379	928	358	1566	921	243
Minot, ND	2627	1769	1224	1055	2725	1666	1654	2168	444	1614	111	1066	1933	1810	1480	2761	1298	693	3264	591	1858	1433	1718	685	940	1730	1240	1290	1297	1913	1275	891	2100	785	776
Missoula, MT	2713	2417	1128	1312	2554	2173	2302	2816	340	2121	759	370	2581	2102	2128	2287	1768	388	3556	617	2478	2081	2338	797	1588	1630	1888	1938	1945	2561	1770	1454	2607	897	1285
Mobile, AL	1655	1335	1245	960	4469	329	1003	1690	1874	261	1639	2237	1427	827	1164	2914	566	2425	2303	1687	645	826	573	1507	920	1272	726	978	837	1505	598	946	491	1416	1014
Monterrey, NL	791	2252	961	806	4498	1288	1944	2607	1776	1162	1729	1901	2344	186	1949	2354	1176	2327	1496	1501	1604	1624	1532	1321	1506	495	1511	1763	1622	2422	573	1425	1454	1236	1256
Montgomery, AL	1820	1166	1302	1017	4427	160	834	1521	1869	92	1597	2217	1258	992	995	2983	456	2395	2468	1620	476	657	404	1483	751	1374	557	809	668	1336	655	824	464	1429	937
Montréal, QC	3129	226	2151	1866	4244	1222	562	300	2099	1307	1686	2531	324	2238	402	3935	1188	2264	3714	1934	1121	835	984	1797	844	2402	827	585	724	252	1765	993	1387	1840	1162
Nashville, TN	2027	1012	1223	938	4148	243	704	1367	1590	189	1318	1938	1104	1136	716	3004	177	2116	2612	1341	548	391	408	1204	472	1380	278	530	389	1182	663	545	677	1178	658
Needles, CA	1872	2616	535	820	3567	1939	2461	3015	1079	1791	1498	744	2780	1498	2327	1339	1633	1396	2688	909	2260	2090	2165	941	1870	789	1934	2141	2000	2760	1182	1704	2271	861	1535
New Orleans, LA	1534	1432	1173	888	4463	468	1124	1787	1868	342	1633	2228	1524	706	1243	2793	560	2419	2182	1678	784	911	712	1498	927	1151	805	1057	916	1602	526	940	634	1407	1008
New York, NY	2835	159	2022	1737	4483	873	203	443	2066	982	1653	2498	208	2007	399	3803	1029	2451	3483	1901	762	555	635	1764	811	2282	661	486	554	258	1565	960	1028	1807	1129
Norfolk, VA	2538	509	1910	1625	4564	558	234	811	2147	707	1734	2544	576	1710	575	3691	863	2532	3186	1947	431	410	320	1810	892	2067	603	567	577	626	1350	1023	697	1784	1192
North Platte, NE	1937	1556	702	473	3355	1228	1441	1955	633	1176	475	955	1720	1203	1267	2359	823	1184	2657	358	1533	1183	1393	221	751	1208	1007	1077	1073	1700	756	585	1662	264	416
Odessa, TX	1304	2028	399	258	3950	1150	1720	2383	1228	1005	1206	1343	2120	632	1730	1974	957	1779	2086	953	1471	1405	1394	773	1231	365	1292	1544	1403	2198	354	1140	1445	689	971
Oklahoma City, OK	1560	1536	544	259	3942	860	1382	1935	1220	712	960	1495	1700	743	1247	2325	553	1771	2197	945	1181	1010	1086	765	798	795	854	1061	920	1680	208	707	1266	674	538
Omaha, NE	2024	1278	869	652	3436	995	1163	1677	841	943	606	1233	1442	1207	989	2637	590	1392	2661	636	1300	950	1160	499	473	1260	729	799	795	1422	672	307	1429	542	138
Ottawa, ON	3041	310	2063	1778	4160	1161	531	425	1777	1246	1364	2443	449	2150	341	3847	1100	2180	3626	1846	1092	774	923	1709	756	2314	739	524	663	377	1677	905	1358	1752	1074
Page, AZ	1919	2439	452	737	3422	1856	2378	2838	934	1708	1353	722	2603	1445	2150	1591	1550	1251	2735	764	2177	2007	2082	723	1634	836	1851	1960	1917	2583	1099	1468	2188	625	1299
Pendleton, OR	2742	2720	1157	1458	2587	2392	2605	3119	744	2340	1163	218	2884	2248	2431	2117	1987	648	3558	916	2697	2347	2557	948	1915	1659	2171	2241	2237	2864	1916	1749	2826	1043	1580
Philadelphia, PA	2738	243	1941	1656	4434	772	102	545	2017	885	1604	2449	310	1910	388	3722	950	2402	3386	1852	661	476	534	1715	762	2185	580	437	473	360	1468	911	927	1753	1080
Phoenix, AZ	1646	2544	463	748	3695	1867	2389	2943	1207	1719	1603	922	2708	1272	2255	1318	1561	1524	2462	958	2188	2018	2093	1002	1806	563	1862	2069	1928	2688	1069	1609	2148	902	1440
Pierre, SD	2309	1615	966	737	3041	1391	1500	2014	491	1339	211	1113	1779	1492	1326	2623	986	1009	2946	413	1696	1287	1556	436	786	1472	1094	1136	1143	1759	957	672	1825	528	503
Pittsburgh, PA	2592	474	1651	1366	4133	686	251	821	1716	753	1303	2148	586	1701	216	3432	651	2101	3177	1551	654	229	448	1414	461	1945	290	136	183	636	1228	610	920	1457	779
Portland, ME	3167	267	2348	2063	4507	1229	507	132	2342	1314	1929	2774	117	2339	562	4129	1361	2527	3815	2177	1066	887	939	2040	1087	2614	994	745	884	96	1897	1236	1332	2083	1405
Portland, OR	2949	2927	1364	1665	2490	2599	2812	3326	891	2547	1310	425	3091	2455	2638	2109	2194	795	3765	1123	2904	2554	2764	1155	2122	1866	2378	2448	2444	3071	2123	1956	3033	1250	1787
Pueblo, CO	1821	1924	330	321	3386	1442	1719	2323	664	1270	810	939	2088	1111	1635	2111	1037	1215	2565	389	1747	1397	1607	209	1119	836	1234	1445	1300	2068	683	953	1772	109	784
Québec, QC	3286	373	2308	2023	4398	1379	709	229	2256	1464	1843	2688	403	2395	559	4092	1345	2418	3871	2091	1268	992	1141	1954	1001	2559	984	742	881	329	1922	1150	1534	1997	1319
Raleigh, NC	2387	628	1759	1474	4481	407	295	930	2064	556	1651	2473	695	1559	637	3540	712	2449	3035	1876	280	325	169	1739	811	1916	518	575	492	745	1199	938	546	1713	1107
Redding, CA	2564	2925	1217	1502	2911	2597	2810	3324	1155	2473	1574	525	3089	2190	2636	1690	2192	1113	3380	1121	2902	2552	2762	1153	2120	1481	2376	2446	2442	3069	1864	1954	3031	1248	1785
Regina, SK	2758	2014	1282	1258	2482	1911	1899	2096	475	1859	356	1097	2178	2055	1725	2792	1543	471	3509	622	2103	1678	1963	743	1185	1788	1485	1535	1542	2048	1520	1136	2345	843	1021
Reno, NV	2381	2729	1021	1306	3068	2401	2614	3128	959	2277	1378	424	2893	2007	2440	1580	1996	1276	3197	925	2706	2356	2566	957	1924	1298	2180	2250	2246	2873	1668	1758	2835	1052	1589
Roanoke, VA	2368	584	1658	1373	4335	430	276	939	1918	515	1505	2313	676	1540	502	3439	611	2303	3016	1716	398	179	192	1579	665	1815	372	429	346	754	1098	792	664	1553	961
Robbinsville, NC	2126	897	1463	1178	4286	149	589	1252	1829	270	1456	2177	989	1298	769	3244	416	2254	2774	1580	348	376	208	1443	616	1620	324	576	435	1067	903	743	583	1417	912
Roswell, NM	1445	2010	198	214	3774	1296	1855	2409	1052	1151	1198	1142	2174	813	1721	1836	1027	1603	2267	777	1617	1484	1559	597	1272	442	1328	1535	1394	2154	500	1181	1591	497	1012
Saginaw, MI	2572	735	1618	1333	3975	801	620	1134	1558	804	1145	1990	899	1755	446	3394	647	1943	3209	1393	914	443	708	1256	303	1869	337	256	277	879	1208	452	1180	1299	621
St. George, UT	2057	2443	608	893	3335	2048	2325	2842	847	1864	1266	635	2607	1683	2154	1469	1643	1164	2873	677	2353	2003	2213	709	1638	974	1840	1964	1906	2587	1255	1472	2344	629	1303
St. Louis, MO	1997	1038	1043	758	3871	557	841	1437	1276	505	1041	1624	1202	1180	749	2824	161	1827	2634	1027	862	512	722	890	300	1294	356	563	422	1182	633	265	991	864	344
Salt Lake City, UT	2190	2206	605	944	3040	1878	2091	2605	552	1826	971	340	2370	1598	1917	1764	1473	869	3006	402	2183	1833	2043	434	1401	1107	1657	1727	1723	2350	1402	1235	2312	529	1066
San Antonio, TX	1087	1956	715	512	4204	992	1648	2311	1482	866	1433	1757	2048	278	1653	2251	880	2033	1732	1207	1308	1328	1236	1027	1210	609	1215	1467	1326	2126	277	1129	1158	942	960
San Diego, CA	1938	2896	816	1101	3581	2157	2742	3295	1300	2012	1719	965	3060	1564	2607	1059	1914	1617	2754	1130	2478	2371	2401	1162	2091	855	2215	2417	2281	3040	1361	1925	2440	1082	1756
San Francisco, CA	2397	2953	1097	1382	3126	2501	2838	3352	1183	2353	1602	648	3117	2023	2664	1523	2220	1500	3213	1149	2822	2580	2727	1181	2148	1314	2404	2474	2470	3097	1744	1982	2833	1276	1813
Sault Ste. Marie, ON	2738	809	1784	1499	3683	1050	869	920	1282	1010	869	1904	944	1921	519	3560	813	1703	3375	1359	1163	692	957	1422	469	2035	586	505	526	872	1374	618	1429	1465	787
Savannah, GA	2155	938	1656	1371	4641	252	605	1240	2083	401	1811	2431	1005	1327	906	3318	670	2609	2803	1834	105	513	250	1697	953	1709	661	763	680	1055	990	1038	230	1671	1151
Seattle, WA	3019	2897	1434	1735	2315	2653	2782	3296	820	2601	1239	495	3061	2525	2608	2284	2248	675	3835	1097	2958	2561	2818	1225	2068	1936	2368	2418	2425	3041	2193	1934	3087	1320	1765
Shreveport, LA	1421	1553	833	548	4162	608	1245	1908	1613	463	1332	1888	1645	593	1257	2514	484	2164	2069	1338	929	932	852	1158	851	905	819	1071	930	1723	186	807	903	1067	736
Sioux City, IA	2114	1337	964	747	3341	1085	1222	1736	746	1033	511	1328	1501	1297	1048	2732	680	1297	2751	558	1390	981	1250	594	532	1350	788	858	854	1481	762	366	1519	637	197
Sioux Falls, SD	2199	1398	1096	794	3259	1170	1283	1797	664	1118	429	1286	1562	1382	1109	2753	765	1215	2836	586	1475	1066	1335	615	569	1435	873	919	926	1542	847	451	1604	658	282
Spokane, WA	2912	2616	1327	1511	2413	2372	2501	3015	539	2320	958	423	2780	2301	2327	2486	1967	443	3755	816	2677	2280	2537	996	1787	1829	2087	2137	2144	2760	1969	1653	2806	1096	1484
Springfield, MO	1787	1250	833	548	3787	685	1053	1649	1192	527	957	1540	1414	970	961	2614	269	1743	2424	943	990	724	850	806	512	1084	568	775	634	1394	423	402	1119	761	361
Sturgis, SD	2249	1762	840	749	3015	1538	1647	2161	293	1486	278	915	1926	1628	1473	2385	1133	844	3082	240	1843	1434	1703	301	933	1346	1241	1283	1290	1906	1093	819	1972	401	650
Sudbury, ON	2922	631	1968	1683	3865	1188	721	733	1466	1191	1053	2088	757	2105	341	3744	997	1885	3559	1543	1205	780	999	1606	653	2219	724	530	669	685	1558	802	1471	1649	971
Tallahassee, FL	1895	1231	1485	1200	4640	265	898	1533	2082	305	1810	2430	1298	1067	1122	3154	669	2608	2543	1833	398	729	466	1696	964	1512	729	981	840	1348	838	1037	251	1642	1150
Tampa, FL	2170	1270	1760	1475	4847	458	937	1572	2289	580	2017	2637	1337	1342	1238	3429	876	2815	2818	2040	437	845	582	1903	1171	1787	922	1095	1033	1387	1113	1244	139	1877	1357
Thunder Bay, ON	2634	1189	1564	1385	3242	1378	1310	1303	1049	1326	636	1671	1327	1817	958	3358	999	1262	3271	1190	1570	1133	1398	1220	652	1921	952	946	967	1255	1270	608	1812	1263	585
Toronto, ON	2796	400	1818	1533	4104	958	490	630	1766	961	1353	2198	564	1905	110	3602	855	2124	3381	1601	974	549	768	1464	511	2069	494	299	438	582	1432	660	1240	1507	829
Tulsa, OK	1626	1433	650	365	3868	796	1236	1832	1237	648	1038	1512	1597	809	1144	2431	450	1788	2263	962	1117	907	1022	782	695	901	751	958	817	1577	262	614	1202	691	445
Twin Falls, ID	2411	2389	826	1127	2930	2061	2274	2788	502	2009	921	130	2553	1917	2100	1850	1656	819	3227	585	2366	2016	2226	617	1584	1328	1840	1910	1906	2533	1585	1418	2495	712	1249
Vancouver, BC	3157	3035	1572	1873	2241	2791	2920	3434	958	2739	1377	633	3199	2663	2746	2427	2386	601	3973	1235	3096	2699	2956	1363	2206	2074	2506	2556	2563	3179	2331	2072	3225	1458	1903
Washington, DC	2596	371	1886	1601	4378	636	38	673	1961	743	1548	2393	438	1768	389	3667	839	2346	3244	1796	525	366	398	1659	706	2043	524	381	417	488	1326	855	791	1697	1024
Whitehorse, YT	4469	3769	2993	2969	723	3666	3654	3822	1999	3614	2111	2082	3933	3759	3480	3876	3298	1448	5213	2274	3858	3433	3718	2454	2940	3499	3240	3290	3297	3774	3427	2891	4100	2554	2776
Wichita, KS	1717	1475	593	417	3785	970	1278	1874	1063	822	803	1338	1639	900	1186	2374	523	1614	2354	788	1291	956	1104	608	719	953	793	1000	859	1619	365	553	1376	517	384
Winnemucca, NV	2402	2565	958	1303	3011	2237	2450	2964	795	2185	1214	260	2729	2028	2276	1693	1832	1112	3218	761	2542	2192	2402	793	1760	1319	2016	2086	2082	2709	1761	1594	2671	888	1425
Winnipeg, MB	2656	1693	1533	1230	2806	1590	1578	1739	723	1538	413	1345	1763	1839	1404	3040	1222	826	3293	931	1782	1357	1642	1010	864	1892	1164	1214	1221	1691	1304	815	2024	1095	700
Yuma, AZ	1766	2725	644	929	3751	1985	2570	3124	1263	1840	1682	928	2889	1392	2436	1177	1742	1580	2582	1093	2306	2199	2229	1183	1987	683	2043	2250	2109	2869	1189	1790	2268	1083	1621

	Detroit, MI	Dodge City, KS	Duluth, MN	Durango, CO	Edmonton, AB	El Paso, TX	Ely, NV	Eureka, CA	Fargo, ND	Flagstaff, AZ	Fresno, CA	Gallup, NM	Gaspé, QC	Grand Junction, CO	Grants Pass, OR	Great Falls, MT	Green Bay, WI	Guadalajara, JA	Halifax, NS	Houston, TX	Idaho Falls, ID	Indianapolis, IN	International Falls, MN	Jackson, MS	Jacksonville, FL	Juneau, AK	Kansas City, MO	Knoxville, TN	La Crosse, WI	Laredo, TX	Las Vegas, NV	Lexington, KY	Lincoln, NE	Little Rock, AR	Los Angeles, CA
Louisville, KY	365	861	770	1418	1972	1470	1828	2457	949	1633	2228	1445	1497	1371	2354	1684	515	1868	1693	956	1668	114	934	591	764	3391	517	245	584	1264	1874	72	708	522	2105
Mackinaw City, MI	292	1242	423	1785	1744	1873	2041	2670	758	2053	2550	1865	1248	1651	2500	1493	258	2347	1461	1469	1701	480	587	1127	1281	3163	898	778	460	1743	2154	608	923	1035	2427
Memphis, TN	748	730	965	1226	2075	1087	1775	2384	1054	1341	1936	1153	1880	1343	2366	1699	743	1485	2041	573	1608	472	1129	212	709	3494	453	388	779	881	1590	422	648	139	1813
Mexico City, DF	2351	1472	2233	1588	2981	1109	1968	2457	2224	1569	2018	1490	3483	1758	2525	2479	2284	329	3544	964	2190	2033	2375	1406	1839	4401	1640	1891	2129	724	1723	2025	1780	1466	1803
Miami, FL	1387	1753	1851	2175	3053	1939	2783	3333	2030	2290	2885	2102	2197	2326	3309	2714	1590	2139	2181	1190	2623	1189	2015	908	343	4472	1472	877	1665	1535	2539	1048	1663	1162	2745
Milwaukee, WI	379	912	393	1428	1595	1498	1684	2313	572	1678	2193	1490	1512	1294	2314	1307	117	2047	1725	1163	1515	280	557	837	1158	3014	568	641	207	1443	1797	471	566	729	2070
Minneapolis, MN	693	783	157	1299	1263	1369	1555	2150	240	1549	2064	1361	1826	1165	1982	975	287	1959	2039	1171	1183	594	299	1062	1478	2682	439	955	163	1355	1668	785	437	821	1941
Minot, ND	1227	859	474	1164	728	1491	1204	1680	284	1517	1704	1363	2085	1029	1512	548	821	2294	2298	1522	784	1128	433	1560	2012	2147	896	1489	699	1690	1413	1319	771	1279	1686
Missoula, MT	1875	1274	1203	918	561	1391	645	965	949	1043	1068	1010	3008	809	797	167	1469	2321	3221	2017	310	1776	1205	2030	2519	1976	1366	2108	1296	1972	939	1951	1198	1749	1212
Mobile, AL	988	1059	1362	1457	2472	1221	2066	2615	1451	1572	2167	1384	2118	1662	2597	2096	1136	1421	2154	472	2020	735	1526	190	403	3891	850	513	1176	817	1821	662	1045	452	2027
Monterrey, NL	1773	967	1655	1173	2500	694	1593	2082	1646	1194	1643	1075	2905	1343	2150	1998	1706	458	3071	495	1834	1455	1797	933	1366	3920	1062	1418	1529	146	1348	1447	1202	888	1428
Montgomery, AL	819	1062	1228	1514	2430	1290	2107	2672	1407	1629	2224	1441	1949	1675	2654	2091	967	1586	1985	637	2000	566	1392	247	376	3849	849	344	1042	982	1878	493	1040	471	2096
Montréal, QC	569	1675	1047	2218	2247	2298	2474	3103	1496	2478	2983	2290	568	2084	3000	2231	910	2796	781	1884	2314	859	1221	1547	1297	3666	1331	1050	1131	2192	2587	907	1356	1450	2860
Nashville, TN	540	852	949	1435	2151	1296	1881	2510	1128	1550	2145	1362	1672	1424	2407	1812	688	1694	1831	782	1721	287	1113	417	589	3570	570	178	763	1090	1799	214	761	348	2022
Needles, CA	2121	998	1934	566	1569	662	357	835	1688	208	387	396	3253	617	890	1101	2006	1435	3479	1425	741	1827	1944	1590	2183	2989	1318	1935	1808	1264	112	1913	1346	1416	264
New Orleans, LA	1067	987	1356	1385	2466	1100	1994	2543	1445	1500	2095	1312	2215	1653	2525	2090	1134	1300	2251	351	2011	814	1520	180	546	3885	844	598	1170	696	1749	741	1039	423	1906
New York, NY	639	1570	1284	2127	2486	2198	2441	3070	1463	2349	2950	2161	941	2051	2967	2198	1029	2601	907	1652	2281	730	1448	1222	938	3905	1226	725	1098	1997	2554	732	1323	1250	2827
Norfolk, VA	720	1520	1365	2122	2567	1983	2487	3116	1544	2237	2832	2049	1291	2030	3013	2279	1110	2304	1275	1355	2327	713	1529	944	607	3986	1176	510	1179	1700	2486	587	1367	1035	2709
North Platte, NE	1014	277	815	642	1357	969	898	1527	612	1029	1407	841	2147	508	1424	855	887	1604	2360	1003	738	900	868	1085	1574	2777	421	1163	689	1073	1011	1006	227	838	1284
Odessa, TX	1474	504	1370	611	1952	281	1252	1741	1310	726	1302	538	2606	781	1809	1450	1431	971	2847	549	1286	1180	1512	764	1357	3372	777	1194	1244	431	1007	1228	866	669	1087
Oklahoma City, OK	1041	254	937	756	1944	691	1352	1914	877	871	1466	683	2173	920	1896	1442	998	1227	2399	455	1278	747	1079	615	1178	3364	344	856	811	623	1120	833	433	337	1343
Omaha, NE	736	405	537	920	1439	1016	1176	1805	418	1196	1685	1008	1869	786	1702	1063	609	1691	2082	919	1016	622	679	852	1341	2858	188	930	411	1087	1289	773	58	571	1562
Ottawa, ON	481	1587	919	2130	2163	2210	2386	3015	1174	2390	2895	2202	695	1996	2912	1909	782	2708	908	1796	2226	771	1137	1486	1268	3582	1243	989	1043	2104	2499	819	1268	1362	2772
Page, AZ	1897	915	1698	262	1424	694	368	1069	1543	137	672	313	3030	381	1050	956	1770	1482	3243	1342	596	1744	1799	1507	2100	2844	1233	1852	1572	1228	276	1830	1110	1333	549
Pendleton, OR	2178	1420	1607	947	821	1420	599	621	1353	1072	887	1039	3311	838	453	571	1873	2350	3524	2163	495	2064	1609	2260	2738	2009	1585	2327	1700	1933	845	2170	1391	1998	1010
Philadelphia, PA	590	1489	1235	2046	2437	2101	2392	3021	1414	2268	2863	2080	1025	1999	2918	2149	980	2504	1009	1555	2232	649	1399	1125	837	3856	1145	628	1049	1900	2502	653	1274	1153	2740
Phoenix, AZ	2049	926	1839	494	1697	436	535	1024	1777	136	585	324	3181	571	1092	1229	1911	1209	3407	1189	869	1755	1981	1479	2060	3117	1246	1863	1713	1038	290	1841	1277	1344	370
Pierre, SD	1073	541	640	906	1044	1233	1059	1688	333	1293	1671	1105	2206	772	1630	713	712	1976	2419	1204	831	987	589	1248	1737	2463	584	1326	514	1372	1275	1169	459	967	1548
Pittsburgh, PA	289	1199	934	1756	2136	1861	2091	2720	1113	1978	2573	1790	1179	1701	2617	1848	679	2259	1285	1347	1931	359	1098	993	830	3555	855	496	748	1655	2204	406	973	913	2450
Portland, ME	915	1896	1560	2461	2510	2530	2717	3346	1739	2675	3226	2487	644	2327	3243	2474	1305	2933	596	1984	2557	1056	1724	1554	1242	3929	1552	1057	1374	2329	2830	1064	1599	1582	3103
Portland, OR	2385	1627	1754	1154	968	1627	806	414	1500	1279	748	1246	3518	1045	246	718	2020	2546	3731	2370	702	2271	1756	2467	2945	1912	1792	2534	1847	2140	1021	2377	1598	2205	967
Pueblo, CO	1382	274	1183	270	1388	597	785	1511	984	657	1252	469	2515	353	1408	886	1255	1527	2728	926	722	1127	1240	1091	1684	2808	631	1377	1057	981	856	1220	595	895	1129
Québec, QC	726	1832	1204	2375	2401	2455	2631	3260	1653	2635	3140	2447	430	2241	3157	2388	1067	2953	643	2041	2471	1016	1375	1704	1444	3820	1488	1207	1288	2349	2744	1064	1513	1607	3017
Raleigh, NC	693	1387	1282	1971	2484	1832	2416	3045	1461	2086	2681	1898	1410	1959	2942	2196	1027	2153	1394	1204	2256	628	1446	793	456	3903	1105	359	1096	1549	2335	502	1296	884	2558
Redding, CA	2383	1625	2018	1108	1286	1354	513	154	1764	890	329	1078	3516	999	176	1036	2256	2127	3729	2107	817	2269	2020	2272	2943	2333	1790	2532	2058	1956	641	2375	1596	2098	548
Regina, SK	1472	1104	723	1222	485	1549	1235	1547	546	1548	1735	1421	2361	1087	1379	473	1066	2479	2574	1767	815	1373	626	1805	2257	1904	1141	1734	944	1935	1444	1564	1016	1524	1717
Reno, NV	2187	1429	1822	912	1449	1171	317	352	1568	694	299	882	3320	803	333	981	2060	1944	3533	1911	621	2073	1824	2076	2747	2490	1594	2336	1862	1773	445	2179	1400	1902	473
Roanoke, VA	547	1289	1136	1870	2338	1731	2256	2885	1315	1985	2580	1797	1367	1799	2782	2050	881	2134	1403	1185	2096	482	1300	755	574	3757	945	258	950	1530	2234	356	1136	783	2457
Robbinsville, NC	586	1091	1087	1675	2289	1536	2120	2749	1266	1790	2385	1602	1680	1663	2646	2001	832	1892	1716	943	1960	433	1251	510	495	3708	809	74	901	1288	2039	247	1000	588	2262
Roswell, NM	1515	471	1411	410	1776	203	1019	1568	1236	525	1120	337	2647	580	1550	1274	1472	1112	2873	730	1016	1221	1553	910	1503	3196	818	1329	1285	579	774	1307	822	810	949
Saginaw, MI	101	1134	615	1677	1978	1765	1933	2562	955	1945	2442	1757	1192	1543	2459	1690	241	2239	1405	1361	1773	345	779	1029	1090	3397	790	587	590	1635	2046	417	815	927	2319
St. George, UT	1901	1015	1702	494	1337	847	213	914	1456	293	517	469	3034	385	895	869	1774	1620	3247	1498	509	1733	1712	1663	2256	2757	1237	1983	1576	1449	121	1826	1114	1489	394
St. Louis, MO	543	600	681	1157	1874	1190	1567	2196	853	1370	1965	1182	1675	1110	2093	1498	500	1664	1901	780	1407	249	845	495	903	3293	256	492	495	1060	1613	335	447	346	1842
Salt Lake City, UT	1664	906	1465	395	1042	868	244	873	1161	520	812	487	2797	286	770	574	1537	1798	3010	1649	214	1550	1417	1746	2224	2462	1071	1813	1339	1381	416	1656	877	1484	689
San Antonio, TX	1477	727	1359	927	2206	558	1529	2018	1350	1042	1579	854	2609	1097	2086	1704	1410	754	2775	199	1540	1159	1501	637	1070	3626	766	1122	1233	150	1284	1151	906	592	1364
San Diego, CA	2354	1279	2155	847	1790	728	578	778	1909	489	339	677	3487	838	846	1322	2227	1413	3700	1481	962	2108	2165	1771	2352	3003	1599	2216	2029	1330	335	2194	1567	1676	124
San Francisco, CA	2411	1560	2046	1136	1673	1187	541	281	1792	770	183	958	3544	1027	391	1205	2284	1960	3757	1940	845	2297	2048	2152	2745	2548	1818	2497	2086	1789	573	2403	1624	1978	381
Sault Ste. Marie, ON	350	1300	424	1843	1686	1931	2099	2728	679	2111	2608	1923	1190	1709	2421	1414	287	2405	1403	1527	1622	538	660	1185	1339	3105	956	836	489	1801	2212	666	981	1093	2485
Savannah, GA	881	1372	1442	1868	2644	1625	2374	3003	1621	1983	2578	1795	1720	1917	2900	2305	1169	1921	1704	972	2214	770	1606	582	140	4063	1063	412	1256	1317	2232	584	1254	781	2455
Seattle, WA	2355	1697	1683	1224	807	1697	876	589	1429	1349	923	1316	3488	1115	421	647	1949	2627	3701	2440	790	2256	1685	2537	2999	1737	1846	2588	1776	2210	1122	2431	1668	2275	1142
Shreveport, LA	1081	647	1135	1045	2165	821	1654	2203	1144	1160	1755	972	2213	1313	2185	1835	1042	1163	2372	239	1671	787	1277	222	815	3584	543	719	1009	559	1409	755	738	196	1627
Sioux City, IA	795	500	454	1015	1344	1111	1271	1900	323	1291	1780	1103	1928	881	1797	968	526	1781	2141	1009	1086	681	579	942	1431	2763	278	1020	328	1177	1384	863	153	661	1657
Sioux Falls, SD	856	544	423	1036	1262	1158	1232	1861	241	1423	1801	1235	1989	902	1803	886	495	1866	2202	1094	1004	766	497	1027	1516	2681	363	1105	297	1262	1405	948	238	746	1678
Spokane, WA	2074	1473	1402	1117	616	1590	804	766	1148	1242	997	1209	3207	1008	598	366	1668	2520	3420	2216	509	1975	1404	2229	2718	1835	1565	2307	1495	2171	1138	2150	1397	1948	1215
Springfield, MO	755	412	760	1045	1790	980	1439	2112	769	1160	1755	972	1887	1007	2009	1414	712	1454	2113	666	1323	461	902	496	1031	3209	168	620	634	850	1409	547	363	215	1632
Sturgis, SD	1220	648	787	780	1017	1107	886	1515	470	1167	1433	979	2353	645	1432	515	859	2037	2566	1340	633	1134	726	1395	1884	2437	731	1473	661	1508	1037	1316	546	1114	1310
Sudbury, ON	466	1484	608	2027	1868	2115	2283	2912	863	2295	2792	2107	1003	1893	2605	1598	471	2589	1216	1711	1806	722	842	1416	1381	3287	1140	974	673	1985	2396	804	1165	1277	2669
Tallahassee, FL	991	1275	1441	1697	2643	1461	2320	2855	1620	1812	2407	1624	2013	1888	2837	2304	1180	1661	1997	712	2213	779	1605	430	163	4062	1062	481	1255	1057	2061	652	1253	684	2267
Tampa, FL	1184	1550	1648	1972	2850	1736	2580	3130	1827	2087	2682	1899	2052	2123	3106	2511	1387	1936	2036	987	2420	986	1812	705	202	4269	1269	674	1462	1332	2336	845	1460	959	2542
Thunder Bay, ON	791	1125	188	1641	1245	1711	1897	2356	446	1891	2406	1703	1568	1507	2188	1181	517	2301	1781	1513	1389	840	219	1364	1724	2664	781	1201	427	1697	2010	1031	779	1163	2283
Toronto, ON	236	1342	847	1885	2107	1965	2141	2770	1163	2145	2650	1957	900	1751	2667	1898	532	2463	1113	1551	1981	526	1081	1186	1150	3526	998	744	798	1859	2254	574	1023	1117	2527
Tulsa, OK	938	324	844	862	1871	797	1369	2020	850	977	1572	789	2070	937	1981	1459	895	1293	2296	505	1295	644	986	535	1114	3290	251	792	718	689	1226	730	450	273	1449
Twin Falls, ID	1847	1089	1365	616	992	1089	256	807	1111	741	756	708	2980	507	634	524	1631	2001	3193	1832	164	1733	1367	1929	2407	2352	1254	1996	1458	1602	502	1839	1060	1667	775
Vancouver, BC	2493	1835	1821	1362	733	1835	1014	732	1567	1487	1066	1454	3431	1253	564	785	2087	2765	3644	2578	928	2394	1696	2675	3137	1663	1984	2726	1914	2348	1260	2569	1806	2413	1285
Washington, DC	534	1433	1179	2098	2381	1959	2336	2965	1358	2213	2808	2025	1153	1943	2862	2093	924	2362	1137	1413	2176	593	1343	983	701	3800	1089	486	993	1758	2462	543	1218	1011	2685
Whitehorse, YT	3227	2931	2478	2711	1275	3260	2463	2181	2301	2836	2515	2803	4087	2602	2013	1776	2821	4190	4300	3674	2103	3128	2352	3560	4012	211	2896	3489	2699	3629	2732	3319	2771	3279	2734
Wichita, KS	955	154	783	659	1787	740	1195	1910	687	920	1515	732	2088	763	1807	1285	855	1384	2338	612	1121	686	925	709	1288	3207	190	874	657	780	1169	779	276	447	1392
Winnemucca, NV	2023	1265	1658	748	1285	1192	271	514	1404	715	463	840	3156	639	411	817	1896	1965	3369	2008	457	1909	1660	2105	2583	2433	1430	2172	1698	1794	466	2015	1236	1843	586
Winnipeg, MB	1151	980	380	1473	809	1594	1483	1902	221	1860	1983	1672	2004	1339	1734	820	745	2323	2217	1551	1063	1052	269	1484	1936	2228	820	1413	623	1719	1692	1243	695	1203	1965
Yuma, AZ	2230	1107	2020	675	1753	556	541	945	1872	317	506	505	3362	752	1013	1285	2092	1268	3588	1309	925	1936	2162	1599	2180	3173	1427	2044	1894	1158	296	2022	1458	1504	291

	Louisville, KY	Mackinaw City, MI	Memphis, TN	Mexico City, DF	Miami, FL	Milwaukee, WI	Minneapolis, MN	Minot, ND	Missoula, MT	Mobile, AL	Monterrey, NL	Montgomery, AL	Montréal, QC	Nashville, TN	Needles, CA	New Orleans, LA	New York, NY	Norfolk, VA	North Platte, NE	Odessa, TX	Oklahoma City, OK	Omaha, NE	Ottawa, ON	Page, AZ	Pendleton, OR	Philadelphia, PA	Phoenix, AZ	Pierre, SD	Pittsburgh, PA	Portland, ME	Portland, OR	Pueblo, CO	Québec, QC	Raleigh, NC	Redding, CA
Louisville, KY		590	385	1988	1079	398	712	1246	1879	625	1410	456	930	177	1841	704	764	659	934	1191	761	701	842	1758	2098	683	1769	1097	393	1097	2305	1148	1087	574	2303
Mackinaw City, MI	590		916	2467	1653	375	521	894	1703	1211	1889	1042	681	763	2261	1290	917	998	1147	1614	1181	869	553	2030	2107	868	2189	968	567	1193	2254	1515	838	959	2516
Memphis, TN	385	916		1605	1024	626	851	1349	1819	398	1027	333	1313	211	1549	392	1113	898	874	808	470	641	1225	1466	2038	1016	1477	1037	776	1445	2245	1028	1470	747	2231
Mexico City, DF	1988	2467	1605		2154	2167	2079	2414	2500	1436	578	1601	2916	1814	1659	1315	2616	2319	1724	1091	1347	1811	2828	1706	2529	2519	1433	2096	2379	2948	2736	1608	3073	2168	2351
Miami, FL	1079	1653	1024	2154		1473	1793	2327	2834	718	1681	691	1640	904	2498	861	1281	950	1889	1672	1493	1656	1611	2415	3053	1180	2375	2052	1173	1585	3260	1999	1787	799	3258
Milwaukee, WI	398	375	626	2167	1473		335	869	1517	1019	1589	850	945	571	1909	1017	912	993	790	1314	881	512	857	1673	1921	863	1814	715	562	1188	2068	1158	1102	910	2159
Minneapolis, MN	712	521	851	2079	1793	335		537	1185	1248	1501	1170	1259	891	1780	1242	1226	1307	661	1216	783	383	1045	1544	1589	1177	1685	486	876	1502	1736	1029	1416	1224	2030
Minot, ND	1246	894	1349	2414	2327	869	537		715	1746	1836	1704	1518	1425	1525	1740	1760	1841	582	1313	1067	713	1390	1380	1119	1711	1653	318	1410	2036	1266	894	1675	1758	1601
Missoula, MT	1879	1703	1819	2500	2834	1517	1185	715		2216	2118	2211	2441	1932	1051	2210	2408	2489	975	1570	1562	1183	2119	906	404	2359	1179	833	2058	2684	551	1006	2598	2406	869
Mobile, AL	625	1211	398	1436	718	1019	1248	1746	2216		963	169	1551	448	1780	143	1202	887	1271	954	805	1038	1490	1697	2450	1101	1657	1434	1009	1558	2657	1281	1708	736	2462
Monterrey, NL	1410	1889	1027	578	1681	1589	1501	1836	2118	963		1128	2338	1236	1284	842	2143	1846	1219	568	769	1233	2250	1331	2114	2046	1058	1518	1801	2475	2321	1127	2495	1695	1976
Montgomery, AL	456	1042	333	1601	691	850	1170	1704	2211	169	1128		1382	279	1837	308	1033	718	1266	1011	802	1033	1321	1754	2430	932	1726	1429	840	1389	2637	1360	1539	567	2519
Montréal, QC	930	681	1313	2916	1640	945	1259	1518	2441	1551	2338	1382		1105	2686	1648	384	734	1580	2039	1606	1302	128	2463	2744	468	2614	1639	612	262	2951	1948	158	853	2949
Nashville, TN	177	763	211	1814	904	571	891	1425	1932	448	1236	279	1105		1758	527	903	688	987	1017	679	754	1017	1675	2151	806	1686	1150	568	1235	2358	1201	1262	537	2356
Needles, CA	1841	2261	1549	1659	2498	1909	1780	1525	1051	1780	1284	1837	2686	1758		1708	2557	2445	1123	943	1079	1401	2598	343	957	2476	226	1387	2186	2883	1135	865	2843	2294	716
New Orleans, LA	704	1290	392	1315	861	1017	1242	1740	2210	143	842	308	1648	527	1708		1323	1026	1281	882	733	1032	1587	1625	2441	1226	1536	1428	1094	1655	2648	1209	1805	875	2390
New York, NY	764	917	1113	2616	1281	912	1226	1760	2408	1202	2143	1033	384	903	2557	1323		375	1547	1919	1477	1269	464	2430	2711	109	2485	1606	389	311	2918	1857	531	494	2916
Norfolk, VA	659	998	898	2319	950	993	1307	1841	2489	887	1846	718	734	688	2445	1026	375		1593	1704	1366	1360	713	2362	2757	278	2373	1687	438	679	2964	1807	881	177	2962
North Platte, NE	934	1147	874	1724	1889	790	661	582	975	1271	1219	1266	1580	987	1123	1281	1547	1593		731	548	282	1492	887	1168	1498	1165	264	1197	1823	1375	372	1737	1522	1373
Odessa, TX	1191	1614	808	1091	1672	1314	1216	1313	1570	954	568	1011	2039	1017	943	882	1919	1704	731		432	897	1951	851	1556	1822	717	995	1582	2251	1763	580	2196	1553	1635
Oklahoma City, OK	761	1181	470	1347	1493	881	783	1067	1562	805	769	802	1606	679	1079	733	1477	1366	548	432		464	1518	996	1708	1396	1007	749	1106	1803	1915	558	1763	1215	1761
Omaha, NE	701	869	641	1811	1656	512	383	713	1183	1038	1233	1033	1302	754	1401	1032	1269	1360	282	897	464		1214	1165	1446	1220	1332	401	919	1545	1653	650	1459	1289	1651
Ottawa, ON	842	553	1225	2828	1611	857	1045	1390	2119	1490	2250	1321	128	1017	2598	1587	464	713	1492	1951	1518	1214		2375	2656	453	2526	1551	551	387	2670	1860	285	824	2861
Page, AZ	1758	2030	1466	1706	2415	1673	1544	1380	906	1697	1331	1754	2463	1675	343	1625	2430	2362	887	851	996	1165	2375		935	2393	273	1151	2103	2706	1142	531	2620	2211	915
Pendleton, OR	2098	2107	2038	2529	3053	1921	1589	1119	404	2450	2114	2430	2744	2151	957	2441	2711	2757	1168	1556	1708	1446	2656	935		2662	1135	1237	2361	2987	207	1152	2901	2686	525
Philadelphia, PA	683	868	1016	2519	1180	863	1177	1711	2359	1101	2046	932	468	806	2476	1226	109	278	1498	1822	1396	1220	453	2393	2662		2404	1557	308	413	2869	1776	615	393	2867
Phoenix, AZ	1769	2189	1477	1433	2375	1814	1685	1653	1179	1657	1058	1726	2614	1686	226	1536	2485	2373	1165	717	1007	1332	2526	273	1135	2404		1429	2114	2811	1337	793	2771	2222	918
Pierre, SD	1097	968	1037	2096	2052	715	486	318	833	1434	1518	1429	1639	1150	1387	1428	1606	1687	264	995	749	401	1551	1151	1237	1557	1429		1256	1882	1384	636	1796	1612	1534
Pittsburgh, PA	393	567	776	2379	1173	562	876	1410	2058	1009	1801	840	612	568	2186	1094	389	438	1197	1582	1106	919	551	2103	2361	308	2114	1256		689	2568	1486	769	499	2566
Portland, ME	1097	1193	1445	2948	1585	1188	1502	2036	2684	1558	2475	1389	262	1235	2883	1655	311	679	1823	2251	1803	1545	387	2706	2987	413	2811	1882	689		3194	2191	276	798	3192
Portland, OR	2305	2254	2245	2736	3260	2068	1736	1266	551	2657	2321	2637	2951	2358	1135	2648	2918	2964	1375	1763	1915	1653	2670	1142	207	2869	1337	1384	2568	3194		1359	3108	2893	421
Pueblo, CO	1148	1515	1028	1608	1999	1158	1029	894	1006	1281	1127	1360	1948	1201	865	1209	1857	1807	372	580	558	650	1860	531	1152	1776	793	636	1486	2191	1359		2105	1736	1357
Québec, QC	1087	838	1470	3073	1787	1102	1416	1675	2598	1708	2495	1539	158	1262	2843	1805	531	881	1737	2196	1763	1459	285	2620	2901	615	2771	1796	769	276	3108	2105		1000	3106
Raleigh, NC	574	959	747	2168	799	910	1224	1758	2406	736	1695	567	853	537	2294	875	494	177	1522	1553	1215	1289	824	2211	2686	393	2222	1612	499	798	2893	1736	1000		2891
Redding, CA	2303	2516	2231	2351	3258	2159	2030	1601	869	2462	1976	2519	2949	2356	716	2390	2916	2962	1373	1635	1761	1651	2861	915	525	2867	918	1534	2566	3192	421	1357	3106	2891	
Regina, SK	1491	1292	1594	2545	2572	1114	782	247	640	1991	2081	1949	1795	1670	1556	1985	2005	2086	827	1516	1312	958	1711	1411	986	1956	1684	563	1655	2058	1133	952	1949	2003	1451
Reno, NV	2107	2320	2035	2168	3062	1963	1834	1405	769	2266	1793	2323	2753	2160	557	2194	2720	2766	1177	1452	1565	1455	2665	719	588	2671	735	1338	2370	2996	578	1161	2910	2695	198
Roanoke, VA	428	813	646	2149	917	764	1078	1612	2260	759	1676	590	800	436	2193	856	475	280	1362	1452	1114	1129	739	2110	2526	378	2121	1466	365	807	2733	1576	957	169	2731
Robbinsville, NC	319	852	451	1907	810	715	1029	1563	2171	475	1434	306	1113	241	1998	614	788	488	1226	1257	919	993	1052	1915	2390	691	1926	1389	559	1120	2597	1440	1270	337	2595
Roswell, NM	1235	1655	943	1232	1818	1355	1257	1282	1394	1100	712	1157	2080	1152	733	1028	1951	1839	698	201	473	877	1992	650	1355	1870	579	962	1580	2277	1562	388	2237	1688	1415
Saginaw, MI	440	192	823	2359	1462	404	718	1252	1900	1063	1781	894	625	615	2153	1142	726	807	1039	1506	1073	761	537	1922	2203	677	2081	1098	376	1002	2410	1407	782	768	2408
St. George, UT	1754	2034	1622	1844	2571	1677	1548	1293	819	1853	1469	1910	2467	1807	233	1781	2434	2413	891	1007	1152	1169	2379	156	848	2382	411	1155	2084	2710	1055	736	2624	2342	760
St. Louis, MO	263	683	284	1784	1218	383	578	1148	1618	681	1206	595	1108	316	1578	675	979	922	673	931	498	440	1020	1495	1837	898	1506	836	608	1305	2044	887	1265	851	2042
Salt Lake City, UT	1584	1797	1524	1977	2539	1440	1311	998	524	1936	1562	1916	2230	1637	528	1927	2197	2243	654	1004	1194	932	2142	383	553	2148	656	815	1847	2473	760	638	2387	2172	719
San Antonio, TX	1114	1593	731	874	1385	1293	1205	1540	1824	667	296	832	2042	940	1220	546	1847	1550	925	354	473	937	1954	1167	1970	1750	994	1222	1505	2179	2177	833	2199	1399	1912
San Diego, CA	2122	2487	1830	1725	2667	2130	2001	1746	1272	1949	1350	2018	2920	2039	324	1828	2838	2726	1344	1009	1360	1622	2832	609	1102	2757	353	1608	2467	3163	1091	1146	3077	2575	672
San Francisco, CA	2331	2544	2111	2184	3060	2187	2058	1629	993	2342	1809	2399	2977	2320	562	2270	2944	2990	1401	1468	1641	1679	2889	847	812	2895	751	1562	2594	3220	636	1385	3134	2856	217
Sault Ste. Marie, ON	648	58	974	2525	1711	404	550	895	1624	1269	1947	1100	623	821	2319	1348	937	1056	1205	1672	1239	927	495	2088	2028	926	2247	997	625	882	2175	1573	780	1017	2574
Savannah, GA	656	1147	643	1936	483	1052	1384	1918	2425	539	1463	335	1163	495	2191	643	804	473	1480	1346	1112	1247	1134	2108	2644	703	2119	1643	696	1108	2851	1694	1310	322	2849
Seattle, WA	2359	2183	2299	2806	3314	1997	1665	1195	480	2727	2391	2691	2921	2412	1234	2718	2888	2969	1445	1833	1985	1663	2599	1212	277	2839	1412	1313	2538	3164	175	1429	3078	2886	596
Shreveport, LA	718	1231	335	1202	1130	925	981	1439	1955	412	705	469	1646	544	1368	344	1444	1166	941	542	393	731	1558	1285	2101	1347	1257	1127	1109	1776	2308	869	1803	1015	2050
Sioux City, IA	791	782	731	1901	1746	529	300	618	1088	1128	1323	1123	1361	844	1496	1122	1328	1391	377	987	554	95	1273	1260	1492	1279	1427	306	978	1604	1639	745	1518	1306	1746
Sioux Falls, SD	876	751	816	1986	1831	498	269	536	1006	1213	1408	1208	1422	929	1517	1207	1389	1470	398	1072	639	180	1334	1281	1410	1340	1559	224	1039	1665	1557	766	1579	1391	1707
Spokane, WA	2078	1902	2018	2699	3033	1716	1384	914	199	2415	2317	2410	2640	2131	1250	2409	2607	2688	1174	1769	1761	1382	2318	1105	205	2558	1378	1032	2257	2883	352	1205	2797	2605	670
Springfield, MO	475	895	285	1574	1346	595	606	1064	1534	682	996	617	1320	444	1368	676	1191	1134	589	721	288	356	1232	1285	1753	1110	1296	752	820	1517	1960	784	1477	979	1958
Sturgis, SD	1244	1115	1184	2036	2199	862	633	381	635	1581	1654	1576	1786	1297	1149	1575	1753	1834	371	1007	885	548	1698	1004	1039	1704	1303	176	1403	2029	1186	510	1943	1759	1361
Sudbury, ON	827	242	1158	2709	1724	588	734	1079	1808	1450	2131	1281	436	1002	2503	1529	759	917	1389	1856	1423	1111	308	2272	2212	748	2431	1181	557	695	2359	1757	593	978	2758
Tallahassee, FL	669	1255	546	1676	478	1063	1383	1917	2424	240	1203	213	1456	492	2020	383	1097	766	1479	1194	1015	1246	1427	1937	2643	996	1897	1642	912	1401	2850	1521	1603	615	2702
Tampa, FL	876	1450	821	1951	254	1270	1590	2124	2631	515	1478	488	1495	701	2295	658	1136	805	1686	1469	1290	1453	1466	2212	2850	1035	2172	1849	1028	1440	3057	1796	1642	654	3055
Thunder Bay, ON	958	499	1153	2421	2039	581	345	652	1391	1550	1843	1416	1002	1137	2122	1544	1343	1497	1003	1558	1125	725	918	1886	1795	1332	2027	828	1066	1265	1942	1371	1156	1458	2206
Toronto, ON	597	483	980	2583	1493	612	926	1460	2108	1220	2005	1051	333	772	2353	1299	528	685	1247	1706	1273	969	245	2130	2411	517	2281	1306	326	592	2618	1615	490	747	2616
Tulsa, OK	658	1078	406	1413	1429	778	690	1145	1579	725	835	738	1503	615	1185	692	1374	1302	565	538	105	437	1415	1102	1725	1293	1113	766	1003	1700	1932	622	1660	1151	1930
Twin Falls, ID	1767	1865	1707	2198	2722	1623	1347	948	389	2119	1783	2099	2413	1820	614	2110	2380	2426	837	1225	1377	1115	2325	604	343	2331	792	995	2030	2656	550	821	2570	2355	653
Vancouver, BC	2497	2321	2437	2944	3452	2135	1803	1294	618	2865	2529	2829	2865	2550	1372	2856	3026	3107	1583	1971	2123	1801	2781	1350	415	2977	1550	1451	2676	3302	318	1567	3019	3024	739
Washington, DC	615	812	874	2377	1044	807	1121	1655	2303	965	1904	796	596	664	2421	1084	237	196	1442	1680	1342	1164	569	2338	2606	136	2349	1501	252	541	2813	1720	743	257	2811
Whitehorse, YT	3246	3018	3349	4256	4327	2869	2537	2002	1831	3746	3775	3704	3521	3425	2844	3740	3760	3841	2632	3227	3219	2713	3437	2699	1864	3711	2972	2318	3410	3784	1767	2663	3675	3758	2188
Wichita, KS	707	1088	580	1504	1603	758	629	910	1405	899	926	912	1521	698	1128	890	1416	1366	391	590	157	310	1433	1045	1551	1335	1056	592	1045	1742	1758	428	1678	1233	1756
Winnemucca, NV	1943	2156	1883	2189	2898	1799	1670	1241	605	2295	1814	2275	2589	1996	578	2286	2556	2602	1013	1357	1553	1291	2501	639	424	2507	756	1174	2206	2832	512	997	2746	2531	360
Winnipeg, MB	1170	935	1273	2443	2251	793	461	297	987	1670	1865	1628	1438	1349	1804	1664	1684	1765	831	1529	1096	637	1354	1659	1341	1635	1996	552	1334	1701	1488	1203	1592	1682	1880
Yuma, AZ	1950	2370	1658	1553	2495	1995	1866	1709	1235	1777	1178	1846	2795	1867	184	1656	2666	2554	1346	837	1188	1513	2707	454	1141	2585	181	1610	2295	2992	1258	974	2952	2403	839

Regina, SK	Reno, NV	Roanoke, VA	Robbinsville, NC	Roswell, NM	Saginaw, MI	St. George, UT	St. Louis, MO	Salt Lake City, UT	San Antonio, TX	San Diego, CA	San Francisco, CA	Sault Ste. Marie, ON	Savannah, GA	Seattle, WA	Shreveport, LA	Sioux City, IA	Sioux Falls, SD	Spokane, WA	Springfield, MO	Sturgis, SD	Sudbury, ON	Tallahassee, FL	Tampa, FL	Thunder Bay, ON	Toronto, ON	Tulsa, OK	Twin Falls, ID	Vancouver, BC	Washington, DC	Whitehorse, YT	Wichita, KS	Winnemucca, NV	Winnipeg, MB	Yuma, AZ	
1491	2107	428	319	1235	440	1754	263	1584	1114	2122	2331	648	656	2359	718	791	876	2078	475	1244	827	669	876	958	597	658	1767	2497	615	3246	707	1943	1170	1950	Louisville, KY
1292	2320	813	852	1655	192	2034	683	1797	1593	2487	2544	58	1147	2183	1231	782	751	1902	895	1115	242	1255	1450	499	483	1078	1865	2321	812	3018	1088	2156	935	2370	Mackinaw City, MI
1594	2035	646	451	943	823	1622	284	1524	731	1830	2111	974	643	2299	335	731	816	2018	285	1184	1158	546	821	1153	980	406	1707	2437	874	3349	580	1883	1273	1658	Memphis, TN
2545	2168	2149	1907	1232	2359	1844	1784	1977	874	1725	2184	2525	1936	2806	1202	1901	1986	2699	1574	2036	2709	1676	1951	2421	2583	1413	2198	2944	2377	4256	1504	2189	2443	1553	Mexico City, DF
2572	3062	917	810	1818	1462	2571	1218	2539	1385	2667	3060	1711	483	3314	1130	1746	1831	3033	1346	2199	1724	478	254	2039	1493	1429	2722	3452	1044	4327	1603	2898	2251	2495	Miami, FL
1114	1963	764	715	1355	404	1677	383	1440	1293	2130	2187	404	1052	1997	925	529	498	1716	595	862	588	1063	1270	581	612	778	1623	2135	807	2869	758	1799	793	1995	Milwaukee, WI
782	1834	1078	1029	1257	718	1548	578	1311	1205	2001	2058	550	1384	1665	981	300	269	1384	606	633	734	1383	1590	345	926	690	1347	1803	1121	2537	629	1670	461	1866	Minneapolis, MN
247	1405	1612	1563	1282	1252	1293	1148	998	1540	1746	1629	895	1918	1195	1439	618	536	914	1064	381	1079	1917	2124	652	1460	1145	948	1294	1655	2002	910	1241	297	1709	Minot, ND
640	769	2260	2171	1394	1900	819	1618	524	1824	1272	993	1624	2425	480	1955	1088	1006	199	1534	635	1808	2424	2631	1391	2108	1579	389	618	2303	1831	1405	605	987	1235	Missoula, MT
1991	2266	759	475	1100	1063	1853	681	1936	667	1949	2342	1269	539	2727	412	1128	1213	2415	682	1581	1450	240	515	1550	1220	725	2119	2865	965	3746	899	2295	1670	1777	Mobile, AL
2081	1793	1676	1434	712	1781	1469	1206	1562	296	1350	1809	1947	1463	2391	705	1323	1408	2317	996	1654	2131	1203	1478	1843	2005	835	1783	2529	1904	3775	926	1814	1865	1178	Monterrey, NL
1949	2323	590	306	1157	894	1910	595	1916	832	2018	2399	1100	335	2691	469	1123	1208	2410	617	1576	1281	213	488	1416	1051	738	2099	2829	796	3704	912	2275	1628	1846	Montgomery, AL
1795	2753	800	1113	2080	625	2467	1108	2230	2042	2920	2977	623	1163	2921	1646	1361	1422	2640	1320	1786	436	1456	1495	1002	333	1503	2413	2865	596	3521	1521	2589	1438	2795	Montréal, QC
1670	2160	436	241	1152	615	1807	316	1637	940	2039	2320	821	495	2412	544	844	929	2131	444	1297	1002	492	701	1137	772	615	1820	2550	664	3425	698	1996	1349	1867	Nashville, TN
1556	557	2193	1998	733	2153	233	1578	528	1220	324	562	2319	2191	1234	1368	1496	1517	1250	1368	1149	2503	2020	2295	2122	2353	1185	614	1372	2421	2844	1128	578	1804	184	Needles, CA
1985	2194	856	614	1028	1142	1781	675	1927	546	1828	2270	1348	643	2718	344	1122	1207	2409	676	1575	1529	383	658	1544	1299	692	2110	2856	1084	3740	890	2286	1664	1656	New Orleans, LA
2005	2720	475	788	1951	726	2434	979	2197	1847	2838	2944	937	804	2888	1444	1328	1389	2607	1191	1753	759	1097	1136	1343	528	1374	2380	3026	237	3760	1416	2556	1684	2666	New York, NY
2086	2766	280	488	1839	807	2413	922	2243	1550	2726	2990	1056	473	2969	1166	1391	1470	2688	1134	1834	917	766	805	1497	685	1302	2426	3107	196	3841	1366	2602	1765	2554	Norfolk, VA
827	1177	1362	1226	698	1039	891	673	654	925	1344	1401	1205	1480	1445	941	377	398	1174	589	371	1389	1479	1686	1003	1247	565	837	1583	1442	2632	391	1013	831	1346	North Platte, NE
1516	1452	1452	1257	201	1506	1007	931	1004	354	1009	1468	1672	1346	1833	542	987	1072	1769	721	1007	1856	1194	1469	1558	1706	538	1225	1971	1680	3227	590	1357	1529	837	Odessa, TX
1312	1565	1114	919	473	1073	1152	498	1194	473	1360	1641	1239	1112	1985	393	554	639	1761	288	885	1423	1015	1290	1125	1273	105	1377	2123	1342	3219	157	1553	1096	1188	Oklahoma City, OK
958	1455	1129	993	877	761	1169	440	932	937	1622	1679	927	1247	1663	731	95	180	1382	356	548	1111	1246	1453	725	969	437	1115	1801	1164	2713	310	1291	637	1513	Omaha, NE
1711	2665	739	1052	1992	537	2379	1020	2142	1954	2832	2889	495	1134	2599	1558	1273	1334	2318	1232	1698	308	1427	1466	918	245	1415	2325	2781	569	3437	1433	2501	1354	2707	Ottawa, ON
1411	719	2110	1915	650	1922	156	1495	383	1167	609	847	2088	2108	1212	1285	1260	1281	1105	1285	1004	2272	1937	2212	1886	2130	1102	604	1350	2338	2699	1045	639	1659	454	Page, AZ
986	588	2526	2390	1355	2203	848	1837	553	1970	1102	812	2028	2644	277	2101	1492	1410	205	1753	1039	2212	2643	2850	1795	2411	1725	343	415	2606	1864	1551	424	1341	1141	Pendleton, OR
1956	2671	378	691	1870	677	2382	898	2148	1750	2757	2895	926	703	2839	1347	1279	1340	2558	1110	1704	748	996	1035	1332	517	1293	2331	2977	136	3711	1335	2507	1635	2585	Philadelphia, PA
1684	735	2121	1926	579	2081	411	1506	656	994	353	751	2247	2119	1412	1257	1427	1559	1378	1296	1303	2431	1897	2172	2027	2281	1113	792	1550	2349	2972	1056	756	1996	181	Phoenix, AZ
563	1338	1466	1389	962	1098	1155	836	815	1222	1608	1562	997	1643	1313	1127	306	224	1032	752	176	1181	1642	1849	828	1306	766	995	1451	1501	2318	592	1174	552	1610	Pierre, SD
1655	2370	365	559	1580	376	2084	608	1847	1505	2467	2594	625	696	2538	1109	978	1039	2257	820	1403	557	912	1028	1066	326	1003	2030	2676	252	3410	1045	2206	1334	2295	Pittsburgh, PA
2058	2996	807	1120	2277	1002	2710	1305	2473	2179	3163	3220	882	1108	3164	1776	1604	1665	2883	1517	2029	695	1401	1440	1265	592	1700	2656	3302	541	3784	1742	2832	1701	2992	Portland, ME
1133	578	2733	2597	1562	2410	1055	2044	760	2177	1091	636	2175	2851	175	2308	1639	1557	352	1960	1186	2359	2850	3057	1942	2618	1932	550	318	2813	1767	1758	512	1488	1258	Portland, OR
952	1161	1576	1440	388	1407	736	887	638	833	1146	1385	1573	1694	1429	869	745	766	1205	784	510	1757	1521	1796	1371	1615	622	821	1567	1720	2663	428	997	1203	974	Pueblo, CO
1949	2910	957	1270	2237	782	2624	1265	2387	2199	3077	3134	780	1310	3078	1803	1518	1579	2797	1477	1943	593	1603	1642	1156	490	1660	2570	3019	743	3675	1678	2746	1592	2952	Québec, QC
2003	2695	169	337	1688	768	2342	851	2172	1399	2575	2856	1017	322	2886	1015	1306	1391	2605	979	1759	978	615	654	1458	747	1151	2355	3024	257	3758	1233	2531	1682	2403	Raleigh, NC
1451	198	2731	2595	1415	2408	760	2042	719	1912	672	217	2574	2849	596	2050	1746	1707	670	1958	1361	2758	2702	3055	2206	2616	1930	653	739	2811	2188	1756	360	1880	839	Redding, CA
	1436	1857	1808	1340	1497	1324	1393	1029	1785	1777	1660	1234	2163	1062	1684	863	781	781	1309	508	1416	2162	2369	793	1655	1390	979	1072	1900	1759	1155	1272	357	1740	Regina, SK
1436		2535	2399	1219	2212	564	1846	523	1729	565	224	2378	2653	753	1854	1550	1511	793	1762	1165	2562	2506	2859	2010	2420	1734	457	896	2615	2345	1560	164	1684	684	Reno, NV
1857	2535		321	1587	622	2182	691	2012	1380	2474	2755	871	440	2740	977	1160	1245	2459	878	1613	844	656	772	1312	612	1050	2195	2878	236	3612	1135	2371	1536	2302	Roanoke, VA
1808	2399	321		1392	661	2046	555	1876	1138	2279	2560	910	390	2651	732	1083	1168	2370	683	1536	1048	414	607	1275	818	855	2059	2789	549	3563	937	2235	1487	2107	Robbinsville, NC
1340	1219	1587	1392		1547	806	972	803	535	871	1295	1713	1492	1632	688	972	1019	1593	762	898	1897	1340	1615	1599	1747	579	1024	1770	1815	3051	631	1156	1455	699	Roswell, NM
1497	2212	622	661	1547		1926	575	1689	1485	2379	2436	250	956	2380	1123	820	881	2099	787	1245	434	1066	1259	691	292	970	1872	2518	621	3252	980	2048	1127	2262	Saginaw, MI
1324	564	2182	2046	806	1926		1493	296	1405	454	692	2092	2300	1125	1441	1264	1285	1018	1390	917	2276	2093	2368	1890	2134	1320	517	1263	2326	2612	1146	484	1572	417	St. George, UT
1393	1846	691	555	972	575	1493		1323	910	1859	2070	741	809	2098	542	530	615	1817	212	983	925	808	1015	869	775	395	1506	2236	878	3148	446	1682	1072	1687	St. Louis, MO
1029	523	2012	1876	803	1689	296	1323		1320	749	747	1855	2130	830	1587	1027	988	723	1239	642	2039	2129	2336	1653	1897	1211	222	968	2092	2317	1037	359	1277	712	Salt Lake City, UT
1785	1729	1380	1138	535	1485	1405	910	1320		1286	1745	1651	1167	2247	409	1027	1112	2023	700	1358	1835	907	1182	1547	1709	539	1639	2385	1608	3481	630	1750	1569	1114	San Antonio, TX
1777	565	2474	2279	871	2379	454	1859	749	1286		505	2545	2353	1266	1549	1717	1738	1471	1649	1370	2729	2189	2464	2343	2587	1466	835	1409	2702	2858	1409	678	2025	172	San Diego, CA
1660	224	2755	2560	1295	2436	692	2070	747	1745	505		2602	2753	811	1930	1774	1735	885	1930	1389	2786	2582	2857	2234	2644	1747	681	954	2839	2403	1784	388	1908	672	San Francisco, CA
1234	2378	871	910	1713	250	2092	741	1855	1651	2545	2602		1205	2104	1289	811	780	1823	953	1144	184	1313	1508	441	423	1136	1786	2304	870	2960	1146	2214	877	2428	Sault Ste. Marie, ON
2163	2653	440	390	1492	956	2300	809	2130	1167	2353	2753	1205		2905	804	1337	1422	2624	937	1790	1247	299	338	1630	1016	1048	2313	3043	567	3918	1222	2489	1842	2181	Savannah, GA
1062	753	2740	2651	1632	2380	1125	2098	830	2247	1266	811	2104	2905		2378	1568	1486	281	2014	1115	2288	2904	3111	1871	2588	2002	620	143	2783	1592	1828	701	1417	1433	Seattle, WA
1684	1854	977	732	688	1123	1441	542	1587	409	1549	1930	1289	804	2378		821	906	2154	405	1274	1473	652	927	1323	1313	352	1770	2516	1205	3439	550	1946	1363	1377	Shreveport, LA
863	1550	1160	1083	972	820	1264	530	1027	1027	1717	1774	811	1337	1568	821		85	1287	446	453	995	1336	1543	642	1028	527	1210	1706	1223	2618	400	1386	542	1608	Sioux City, IA
781	1511	1245	1168	1019	881	1285	615	988	1112	1738	1735	780	1422	1486	906	85		1205	531	371	964	1421	1628	611	1089	612	1168	1624	1284	2536	485	1347	460	1740	Sioux Falls, SD
781	793	2459	2370	1593	2099	1018	1817	723	2023	1471	885	1823	2624	281	2154	1287	1205		1733	834	2007	2623	2830	1590	2307	1778	548	419	2502	1690	1604	629	1136	1434	Spokane, WA
1309	1762	878	683	762	787	1390	212	1239	700	1649	1930	953	937	2014	405	446	531	1733		899	1137	830	1143	948	987	185	1422	2152	1090	3064	258	1598	988	1477	Springfield, MO
508	1165	1613	1536	898	1245	917	983	642	1358	1370	1389	1144	1790	1115	1274	453	371	834	899		1328	1789	1996	975	1453	902	797	1253	1648	2292	728	1001	689	1333	Sturgis, SD
1416	2562	844	1048	1897	434	2276	925	2039	1835	2729	2786	184	1247	2288	1473	995	964	2007	1137	1328		1453	1579	623	245	1320	1970	2486	731	3142	1330	2398	1059	2612	Sudbury, ON
2162	2506	656	414	1340	1066	2093	808	2129	907	2189	2582	1313	299	2904	652	1336	1421	2623	830	1789	1453		275	1629	1223	951	2312	3042	860	3917	1125	2488	1841	2017	Tallahassee, FL
2369	2859	772	607	1615	1259	2368	1015	2336	1182	2464	2857	1508	338	3111	927	1543	1628	2830	1143	1996	1579	275		1836	1348	1226	2519	3249	899	4124	1400	2695	2048	2292	Tampa, FL
793	2010	1312	1275	1599	691	1890	869	1653	1547	2343	2234	441	1630	1871	1323	642	611	1590	948	975	623	1629	1836		862	1032	1553	1863	1311	2519	971	1846	436	2208	Thunder Bay, ON
1655	2420	612	818	1747	292	2134	775	1897	1709	2587	2644	423	1016	2588	1313	1028	1089	2307	987	1453	245	1223	1348	862		1170	2080	2725	499	3381	1188	2256	1298	2462	Toronto, ON
1390	1734	1050	855	579	970	1320	395	1211	539	1466	1747	1136	1048	2002	352	527	612	1778	185	902	1320	951	1226	1032	1170		1394	2140	1278	3145	174	1570	1069	1294	Tulsa, OK
979	457	2195	2059	1024	1872	517	1506	222	1639	835	681	1786	2313	620	1770	1210	1168	548	1422	797	1970	2312	2519	1553	2080	1394		758	2275	2207	1220	293	1227	798	Twin Falls, ID
1072	896	2878	2789	1770	2518	1263	2236	968	2385	1409	954	2304	3043	143	2516	1706	1624	419	2152	1253	2486	3042	3249	1863	2725	2140	758		2921	1518	1966	839	1427	1576	Vancouver, BC
1900	2615	236	549	1815	621	2326	878	2092	1608	2702	2839	870	567	2783	1205	1223	1284	2502	1090	1648	731	860	899	1311	499	1278	2275	2921		3655	1279	2451	1579	2530	Washington, DC
1759	2345	3612	3563	3051	3252	2612	3148	2317	3481	2858	2403	2960	3918	1592	3439	2618	2536	1690	3064	2292	3142	3917	4124	2519	3381	3145	2207	1518	3655		3062	2288	2083	3028	Whitehorse, YT
1155	1560	1135	937	631	980	1146	446	1037	630	1409	1784	1146	1222	1828	550	400	485	1604	258	728	1330	1125	1400	971	1188	174	1220	1966	1279	3062		1396	906	1237	Wichita, KS
1272	164	2371	2235	1156	2048	484	1682	359	1750	678	388	2214	2489	701	1946	1386	1347	629	1598	1001	2398	2488	2695	1846	2256	1570	293	839	2451	2288	1396		1520	762	Winnemucca, NV
357	1684	1536	1487	1455	1127	1572	1072	1277	1569	2025	1908	877	1842	1417	1363	542	460	1136	988	689	1059	1841	2048	436	1298	1069	1227	1427	1579	2083	906	1520		1988	Winnipeg, MB
1740	684	2302	2107	699	2262	417	1687	712	1114	172	672	2428	2181	1433	1377	1608	1740	1434	1477	1333	2612	2017	2292	2208	2462	1294	798	1576	2530	3028	1237	762	1988		Yuma, AZ

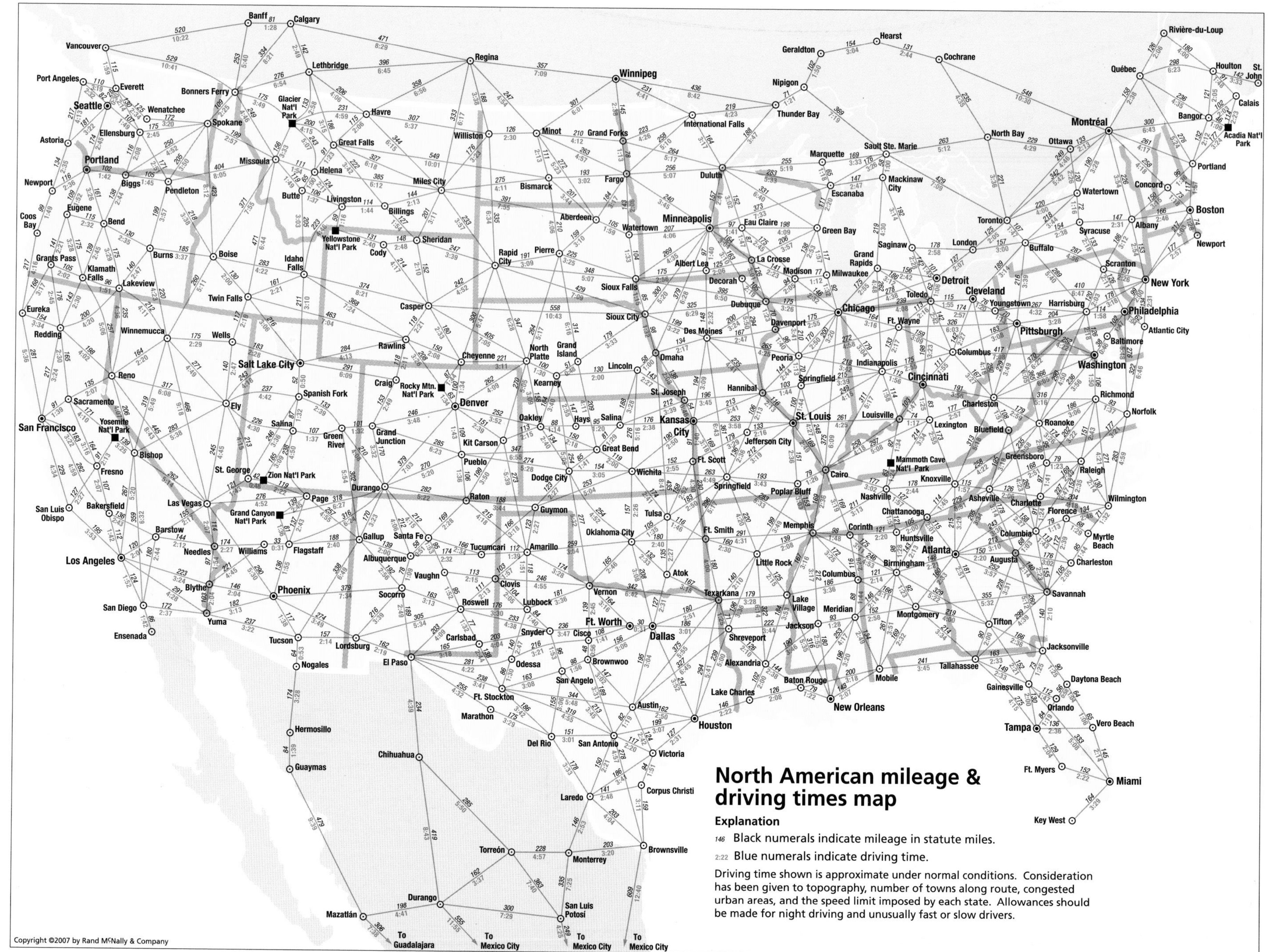
North American mileage & driving times map
Explanation
146 Black numerals indicate mileage in statute miles.
2:22 Blue numerals indicate driving time.
Driving time shown is approximate under normal conditions. Consideration has been given to topography, number of towns along route, congested urban areas, and the speed limit imposed by each state. Allowances should be made for night driving and unusually fast or slow drivers.

RAND McNALLY

Thank you for purchasing the Harley-Davidson® *Ride Atlas of North America*™ 2nd Edition from Rand McNally.

Please complete the information below so we will be able to serve you better. You can also e-mail your comments to: consumeraffairs@randmcnally.com. Please refer to the *Ride Atlas of North America* in your correspondence. (This information is for internal use ONLY and will NOT be distributed or sold to any external third party).

City/State/ZIP________________________ E-mail address ________________________

Where did you purchase the Ride Atlas of North America? (store & location) ________________________

How often do you use the Ride Atlas? ☐ Weekly ☐ Twice a month ☐ Monthly ☐ Every few months ☐ Never

For what do you use the Ride Atlas? ☐ Planning ☐ On-the-road navigation ☐ Both ☐ Coordinate group rides

☐ Other (Please explain) ________________________

On a scale of 1 to 7, with 7 being extremely helpful and 1 being extremely unhelpful, how helpful were the 25 suggested rides?
(Please circle.) 1 2 3 4 5 6 7

On a scale of 1 to 7, with 7 being extremely clear and 1 being extremely unclear, how clear was the map page information?
(Please circle.) 1 2 3 4 5 6 7

What do you look for when planning a ride? ________________________

What information would you add/change in the Ride Atlas to better meet your needs? ________________________

Where else do you look for ride information? ________________________

What motorcycle publications do you read? ☐ American Rider ☐ Cycle World ☐ Hog Tales ☐ Hot Bike ☐ Motorcyclists ☐ Other ________________________

What is the average length of your rides? ☐ Day trip ☐ 1 night ☐ 2 nights ☐ 3+ nights

Are you likely to buy updated versions of the Ride Atlas? ☐ Yes ☐ No ☐ Unsure

Would you recommend the Ride Atlas to someone else? ☐ Yes ☐ No ☐ Unsure

Please provide any additional comments and suggestions you have. ________________________

Age group ☐ 18-27 ☐ 28-37 ☐ 38-47 ☐ 48-57 ☐ 58+

Sex: ☐ Female ☐ Male

Total Household Income: ☐ $40,000 & below ☐ $41,000 to $65,000 ☐ $66,000 to $80,000 ☐ $80,000 to $100,000 ☐ $100,000 and above

Occupation: ☐ Full-Time ☐ Part-Time ☐ Retired ☐ Unemployed

Would you like to receive information about updated editions and special offers from Rand McNally? ☐ Yes ☐ No

Would you be interested in participating in future Ride Atlas opinion surveys? ☐ Yes ☐ No

THANK YOU FOR YOUR INPUT.

CUT ALONG DOTTED LINE

CUT ALONG DOTTED LINE

SG.06

TAPE SHUT

TAPE SHUT

HARLEY-DAVIDSON® RIDE ATLAS OF NORTH AMERICA™ SECOND EDITION

CUT ALONG DOTTED LINE

2ND FOLD LINE

NO POSTAGE
NECESSARY
IF MAILED
IN THE
UNITED STATES

BUSINESS REPLY MAIL

FIRST-CLASS MAIL PERMIT NO. 388 CHICAGO IL

POSTAGE WILL BE PAID BY ADDRESSEE

RAND MCNALLY
CONSUMER AFFAIRS
PO BOX 7600
CHICAGO IL 60680-9915

RAND McNALLY

The most trusted name on the map.

CUT ALONG DOTTED LINE

SGTG.06